UNDERSTANDING CONSTITUTIONAL LAW

Fourth Edition

UNDERSTANDING CONSTITUTIONAL LAW

Fourth Edition

John B. Attanasio
Judge James Noel Dean and Professor of Law &
Judge William Hawley Atwell Chair of Constitutional Law
Southern Methodist University
Dedman School of Law

Joel K. Goldstein
Vincent C. Immel Professor of Law
Saint Louis University School of Law

 LexisNexis

ISBN: 978-0-7698-4734-4
ISBN: 978-1-4224-8660-3 (eBook)

Library of Congress Cataloging-in-Publication Data

Attanasio, John.
Understanding constitutional law / John B. Attanasio, Joel K. Goldstein. — 4th ed.
p. cm.
    Rev. ed. of: Understanding constitutional law / Norman Redlich, John Attanasio, Joel K. Goldstein. 3rd ed. 2005.
    Includes index.
    ISBN 978-0-7698-4734-4
    1. Constitutional law—United States—Cases. I. Goldstein, Joel K. (Joel Kramer), 1953- II. Redlich, Norman.
Understanding constitutional law. III. Title.
KF4550.Z9R43 2012
342.73—dc23

2012015336

This publication is designed to provide authoritative information in regard to the subject matter covered. It is sold with the understanding that the publisher is not engaged in rendering legal, accounting, or other professional services. If legal advice or other expert assistance is required, the services of a competent professional should be sought.

NOTE TO USERS

To ensure that you are using the latest materials available in this area, please be sure to periodically check the LexisNexis Law School web site for downloadable updates and supplements at www.lexisnexis.com/lawschool.

Editorial Offices
121 Chanlon Rd., New Providence, NJ 07974 (908) 464-6800
201 Mission St., San Francisco, CA 94105-1831 (415) 908-3200
www.lexisnexis.com

MATTHEW◆BENDER

Acknowledgments

We mourn the death on June 10, 2011, of our co-author and friend, Norman Redlich. Norman was a giant in the law who made enormous contributions as a lawyer, scholar, academic administrator, public servant and citizen. In all respects he modeled professional excellence and human decency. Although a man of strong convictions and principles, he invariably gave those with different views a fair and courteous hearing and addressed their positions in a rational and intellectually honest manner. Notwithstanding his impressive accomplishments, Norman displayed constant humility. We are grateful for the inspiration he provided and the opportunity to have been associated with him. His passing is a great loss and we miss him.

Norman did not play a part in preparing this Fourth Edition although his thought influences much of it. We also pay tribute to Bernard Schwartz who co-authored, with Norman, the first edition of this book. He died on December 23, 1997. He was a leading scholar of the Constitution and the work of the Supreme Court. We are grateful to him for his contributions to shaping this book in its original form. His influence continues in these pages.

A number of people over the years helped us produce this Fourth Edition. We would like to thank Kathleen Spartana for her administrative and editing work. Since the Third Edition was published, we have benefited from the work of research assistants Jennifer Allen, Jessica Benoit, Rachel Berland, Heather S. Bethancourt, Kristen Brown, Lacey Smith Cesarz, Henry Childs, John T. Davis, Kate Douglas, Christine Falgout, Jessie Gasch, Anthony Gilbreth, John J. Greffet, Matthew Guyman, Ryan Hardy, Meredith Head, Eric Hoffmann, Maxwell Huber, Sarah Jackson, Ausra Laurusaite-Kromelis, Sarah Lopano, Michael Lyons, Nathan McArthur, Leslie Mattingly, Mandi Montgomery, John Moore, Stacy Osmond, Heather J. Panko, Daniel Pearson, David Poell, Tina Potter, Molly Quinn, Bennett J. Rawicki, Justin Reinus, Joshua R. Reznick, Lacey Searfoss, Jonathan Skrabacz, Niel Smith, Paul Stohr, Kevin Sullivan, Phong Tran, Elizabeth Mills Viney, Elise Voges, and Ryan Yager for their contributions, and Brenda Aylesworth, Tina Brosseau, Mary Dougherty, and Stephanie Haley for their help over the years in typing (and retyping) the book. As always, we appreciate the institutional support of the Dedman School of Law at Southern Methodist University and of Saint Louis University School of Law including through the latter's summer research program. Finally, we are grateful to Pali Parekh of LexisNexis Mathew Bender for her skillful editing.

Joel Goldstein is primarily responsible for the first seven chapters which Bernard Schwartz had prepared in the first edition. John Attanasio prepared chapters 8 to 17; he and Norman Redlich had worked on those portions of the book previously.

John B. Attanasio
Joel K. Goldstein
April, 2012

TABLE OF CONTENTS

TABLE OF CONTENTS

TABLE OF CONTENTS

TABLE OF CONTENTS

TABLE OF CONTENTS

TABLE OF CONTENTS

TABLE OF CONTENTS

xi

TABLE OF CONTENTS

TABLE OF CONTENTS

Chapter 1

THE CONSTITUTION AND CONSTITUTIONAL ARGUMENT

INTRODUCTION

Understanding constitutional law is an ambitious undertaking. The subject is complex and can be viewed from different angles. An effort to understand constitutional law may profitably consider the Constitution, the events leading to it, its operation in practice, the interaction of the various institutions it created, and the rules, principles and doctrines which are known as constitutional law.

This chapter introduces the notion of a Constitution and describes in broad terms the historical events leading to the ratification of our Constitution. It then discusses structural arrangements used to control government. Section 1.04 addresses the need for constitutional interpretation and some theories regarding it. Section 1.05 explores different types of constitutional arguments commonly employed.

§ 1.01 CONSTITUTIONS

The word "constitution" is used in several different senses. At times it describes the basic rules, written and unwritten, which create and control government. Alternatively, "Constitution" may denote a document which contains those rules which provide the framework for government. Both senses of the word apply to the American system. Unlike the British constitution, our Constitution is a written document which delegates and defines governmental power.

The Constitution's primary purpose is to create a national government, distribute powers between national and state government, and limit government to protect individual liberty.[1] As such, constitutional government signifies an arrangement in which institutions of state are subject to, not superior to, law. Under American constitutional assumptions, "We the People of the United States"[2] delegated power to the Constitution which allocated it among the governing institutions it created. A singular feature of our Constitution is that its text can be formally changed only with great difficulty. Formal amendment requires a) a proposal by either two-thirds of the House of Representatives and Senate or by a convention called by request of two-thirds of the state legislatures and b) ratification by three-fourths of the states.[3] Only 27 constitutional amendments have been ratified, and ten of those came in a package shortly after the Constitution itself was adopted. In essence, the Consti-

---

[1] *See, e.g.*, Marbury v. Madison, 5 U.S. (1 Cranch) 137, 176 (1803).

[2] U.S. CONST. pmbl.

[3] U.S. CONST. art. V.

1

tution's terms are placed outside the reach of normal political action.

The English scholar, Sir Kenneth C. Wheare, observed that "[i]f we investigate the origins of modern Constitutions, we find that, practically without exception, they were drawn up and adopted because people wished to make a fresh start, so far as the statement of their system of government was concerned."[4] The experience in the United States was no exception.

§ 1.02 RATIFYING THE CONSTITUTION

The Constitution represented a "fresh start" after the initial period under the Articles of Confederation. The thirteen colonies had ratified the Articles after the Revolutionary War concluded in 1781. The Articles created a weak national government. States retained their sovereignty and all powers not "expressly delegated" to the United States.[5] The national government consisted of Congress; there was no executive or judiciary. Congress had limited power. It could not tax or regulate interstate commerce.

In hindsight, it is not difficult to understand the problems the new nation experienced. Without an executive and judiciary, the national government lacked means to enforce federal law. "Congress simply could not make anyone, except soldiers, do anything," wrote historian Leonard Levy. "It acted on the states, not on people."[6] Some States adopted protectionist laws which predictably spawned retaliatory measures. These measures eroded any semblance of national unity. Shays' Rebellion in the fall-winter of 1786-87 raised the spectre of anarchy and persuaded many of the need for a stronger national government.[7]

The Constitutional Convention convened in Philadelphia on May 25, 1787, specifically to consider changes to the Articles of Confederation. The Convention consisted of representatives of 12 of the states, all but Rhode Island. Under the terms of the Articles, any change required unanimous consent. Five days later, the Convention voted to create a national government comprised of legislative, executive, and judicial branches. Thus, within a few days of gathering, the delegates decided to abandon, rather than salvage, the Articles.[8] The vote was not unanimous; Connecticut opposed the motion and New York was divided.[9] Under the terms of the Articles, the motion failed. But those who met in Philadelphia were no longer proceeding under the prior arrangement. Edwin M. Yoder, Jr., an astute constitutional historian, observed, "The fifty-five framers performed radical surgery with a clearer notion of need than mandate from the constituents they represented, who in any case were not a mass electorate. They worked in the name of 'the people of the

---

[4] K. C. WHEARE, MODERN CONSTITUTIONS 6 (1966).

[5] Articles of Confederation, 1777 art. II, in U.S.C. at XLVII (2000).

[6] Leonard W. Levy, *Introduction: American Constitutional History, 1776–1789, in* THE FRAMING AND RATIFICATION OF THE CONSTITUTION 6 (Leonard W. Levy & Dennis S. Mahoney eds., 1987).

[7] Stanley Elkins and Eric McKitrick, *The Founding Fathers: Young Men of the Revolution*, 76 POL. SCI. Q. 181 (1961).

[8] Levy, *supra* note 6, at 11.

[9] CLINTON L. ROSSITER, 1787: THE GRAND CONVENTION 172 (1987).

United States,' but could afford to deliberate in secret and in indifference to 'public opinion' in the modern sense."[10]

Delegates approached the Convention with different visions of the shape government should take. Virginia offered a plan for a strong national government which could regulate individuals. New Jersey, however, proposed a plan more hospitable to smaller states. It asked for a unicameral Congress in which each state would have an equal voice and for a Supreme Court which would be the only national court. Small states typically wanted equal representation in the legislature, whereas large states thought seats should be allocated based on population.

During the next four months, behind closed doors, the delegates reached compromises regarding their competing ideals and interests. A bicameral Congress was proposed with a House of Representatives based on population and a Senate based on equal representation. Under the Madisonian Compromise, named for James Madison, the delegates agreed to create a Supreme Court but to give Congress discretion to "ordain and establish" lower federal courts.[11] The method of selecting the executive proved controversial. Some thought the President should be elected by the people; others would have assigned Congress that task. One group doubted the people had sufficient information to make the choice; the other, feared legislative selection would make the President too weak and dependent. Repeated votes failed to resolve the issue. Ultimately, the delegates compromised. Electors chosen in each state would meet solely to choose a President and Vice President. Each state would have the number of electors equal to its representatives in Congress.

The Convention adjourned on September 17, 1787 after nearly four months of deliberation which produced a proposed new constitution signed by 39 of the delegates including George Washington, Benjamin Franklin, James Madison and Alexander Hamilton. Attention then turned towards securing ratification by at least nine states as Article VII of the Constitution required. In some states the issue was hotly contested.

Some 85 essays advocating ratification of the Constitution were initially published separately from October 27, 1787 to August 16, 1788 in New York City newspapers under the pseudonym, Publius, to address strong anti-federalist sentiment in New York. In fact, the essays were written by Alexander Hamilton, James Madison, and John Jay, the first two of whom had served as delegates to the Convention. Subsequently assembled and published as The Federalist Papers, the collection has a threefold significance. It provides insight into the subjective understanding of at least two delegates to the Convention, Madison and Hamilton, regarding constitutional meaning and content. It provides some inkling of how the Constitution was understood by at least some people in New York who may have read the essays before ratifying the Constitution. Finally, it is a classic American work in political theory.[12]

---

[10] EDWIN M. YODER, JR., THE HISTORICAL PRESENT: USES AND ABUSES OF THE PAST 60 (1997).

[11] U.S. CONST. art. III, § 1.

[12] *See* THE FEDERALIST. In *Cohens v. Virginia*, 19 U.S. (6 Wheat.) 264, 418–19 (1821), Chief Justice John Marshall wrote: "The opinion of the *Federalist* has always been considered as of great authority.

Ratification came easily in some small states — Delaware, New Jersey, Georgia, Connecticut, Maryland — and by a 2 to 1 margin in Pennsylvania after some sharp tactics by James Wilson and others. But Massachusetts agreed by only a 187 to 168 vote after some who initially opposed the Constitution were persuaded. Massachusetts also expressed its opinion that certain amendments, one of which was an early draft of the Tenth Amendment, would comfort concerns. South Carolina agreed by a 2 to 1 margin but with four recommendations, including an early version of the Tenth Amendment. New Hampshire became the ninth state to ratify on June 21, 1788 by a 57 to 47 vote with twelve proposed amendments. The debates in Virginia and New York, both critical states, were contentious, and ratification prevailed by narrow margins, 89-79 and 30-27 respectively.[13] North Carolina did not approve the Constitution until late 1789; Rhode Island waited until May, 1790.

The founders appreciated the fact that they had undertaken a momentous task. Alexander Hamilton wrote in the Federalist #1:[14]

> It has been frequently remarked that it seems to have been reserved to the people of this country, by their conduct and example, to decide the important question, whether societies of men are really capable or not of establishing good government from reflection and choice, or whether they are forever destined to depend for their political constitutions on accident and force. If there be any truth in the remark, the crisis at which we are arrived may with propriety be regarded as the era in which that decision is to be made; and a wrong election of the part we shall act may, in this view, deserve to be considered as the general misfortune of mankind.

§ 1.03 THE STRUCTURAL CONSTITUTION

The Constitution sought both to protect individual liberty from governmental tyranny and to provide a government able to respond well to public needs. The framers were well aware of the delicacy of their task. Wrote James Madison:[15]

> If men were angels, no government would be necessary. If angels were to govern men, neither external nor internal controls on government would be necessary. In framing a government which is to be administered by men over men, the great difficulty lies in this: You must first enable the government to control the governed; and in the next place oblige it to control itself.

But how to oblige government to control itself?

It is a complete commentary on our constitution; and is appealed to by all parties in the questions to which that instrument has given birth. Its intrinsic merit entitles it to this high rank; and the part two of its authors performed in framing the constitution, put it very much in their power to explain the views with which it was framed. These essays having been published while the constitution was before the nation for adoption or rejection, and having been written in answer to objections founded entirely on the extent of its powers, and on its diminution of State sovereignty, are entitled to the more consideration where they frankly avow that the power objects to is given, and defend it."

[13] See generally Rossiter, supra note 9, at 285–98.

[14] THE FEDERALIST No. 1 (Alexander Hamilton).

[15] THE FEDERALIST No. 51 (James Madison).

Constitutions typically employ two different strategies to restrain government from invading individual freedom. At times constitutions design their architecture to restrain government. They arrange institutions in such a manner as to divide power and introduce obstacles to governmental action. Alternatively, constitutions often contain a Bill of Rights which place certain rights beyond the reach of government.

The American Constitution initially relied on the first strategy. "Ambition must be made to counteract ambition,"[16] prescribed Madison. Government must be designed in a way which would allow it to respond to the people's needs yet divide power to prevent tyranny. Although the original Constitution contained some specific safeguards of individual liberties,[17] the Bill of Rights was not added until 1791. In fact, at Philadelphia a proposal to add a Bill of Rights was unanimously defeated.[18]

Some Anti-Federalists insisted that a Bill of Rights would assuage their concern about the Constitution. Hamilton argued that a Bill of Rights was "unnecessary," given limitations already included in Article I, and even "dangerous." He feared that inclusion of a Bill of Rights would expand governmental powers in unanticipated directions by encouraging the argument that any powers not explicitly limited were implicitly conferred. "They would contain various exceptions to powers which are not granted; and, on this very account, would afford a colorable pretext to claim more than were granted. For why declare that things shall not be done which there is no power to do?"[19] Madison thought a Bill of Rights could not effectively control a majority intent on acting.[20] Others, including Madison, thought adding a Bill of Rights might induce states like North Carolina and Rhode Island to join the Union.[21] The first Congress proposed 12 amendments; ten were ratified by three-fourths of the state legislatures in 1791.[22] To be sure, many of those amendments, as well as others adopted later, have proved the source of important rights of individuals against national or state government. Chapters 8 and on explore those issues.

Yet the Constitution relied primarily on various structural devices to limit governmental power.[23] "In the compound republic of America," wrote Madison, "the power surrendered by the people is first divided between two distinct governments, and then the portion allotted to each subdivided among distinct and separate departments."[24] Power was divided between Nation and State, the concept of

---

[16] Id.

[17] See, e.g., Const. art. I, §§ 9, 10.

[18] JACK N. RAKOVE, ORIGINAL MEANINGS: POLITICS AND IDEAS IN THE MAKING OF THE CONSTITUTION, 288 (1996).

[19] THE FEDERALIST No. 84 (Alexander Hamilton).

[20] RAKOVE supra note 18, at 332.

[21] See DAVID P. CURRIE, THE CONSTITUTION IN CONGRESS: THE FEDERALIST PERIOD, 1789–1801, at 110 (1997).

[22] AKHIL REED AMAR, THE BILL OF RIGHTS: CREATION AND RECONSTRUCTION 8 (1998).

[23] See JOHN HART ELY, DEMOCRACY AND DISTRUST: A THEORY OF JUDICIAL REVIEW 92–93 (1980).

[24] THE FEDERALIST No. 51.

Federalism. Congress' power was limited to that "herein granted,"[25] with the remainder residing with the States or the People.[26] On the other hand, the Supremacy Clause declared federal law supreme over state law and bound state officials to respect and enforce federal law even when it conflicted with state law.[27] The States were given influence in constituting the national government. State legislatures chose each State's senators and electors chosen in each State chose the President and Vice President.

The Constitution also divided power between the three branches of the federal government, the concept known as Separation of Powers. Indeed, the vesting clause of each of the first three articles implied this division. Article I vested legislative power in a Congress, Article II vested executive power in the President, and Article III vested judicial power in a Supreme Court and such other courts Congress might choose to create. Moreover, the Constitution created various checks and balances between governmental institutions. The President could propose legislation,[28] but a bill could not become law unless both the House and the Senate passed it and the President signed it.[29] If the President chose to veto legislation, a two-thirds majority of each house was required to pass it.[30] Ultimately, the Court's power to review legislation to ascertain its constitutionality, which was implicit in the structure of the Constitution,[31] was recognized.[32]

§ 1.04 CONSTITUTIONAL INTERPRETATION

The Constitution is the basic source from which government derives its authority, but it provides only an outline of the governmental system. A Constitution is a unique document, a truth implicit in Chief Justice John Marshall's admonition that "we must never forget that it is a *Constitution* we are expounding."[33] "A constitution, to contain an accurate detail of all the subdivisions of which its great powers will admit, and of all the means by which they may be carried into execution, would partake of a prolixity of a legal code, and could scarcely be embraced by the human mind,"[34] wrote Chief Justice Marshall. A Constitution which attempted to anticipate all contingencies would "never be understood by the public"[35] and would prove insufficiently flexible to adapt to changing circumstances. Instead, the Constitution provided a framework many details of which were left unsaid. "We do not expect to find in a constitution minute details," wrote Justice Strong in 1870. "It

---

[25] U.S. Const. art. I, § 1.

[26] U.S. Const. amend. X.

[27] U.S. Const. art. VI.

[28] U.S. Const. art. II, § 3.

[29] U.S. Const. art. I, § 7.

[30] U.S. Const. art. I, § 7.

[31] The Federalist No. 78 (Alexander Hamilton).

[32] Marbury v. Madison, 5 U.S. (1 Cranch) 137 (1803).

[33] McCulloch v. Maryland, 17 U.S. (4 Wheat.) 316, 407 (1819).

[34] *Id.* at 407.

[35] *Id.*

is necessarily brief and comprehensive."[36] The "nature" of a Constitution "requires that only its great outlines should be marked, its important objects designated"[37] and the rest left to be deduced.

Professor Laurence H. Tribe has referred to the constitutional document as the "visible" Constitution to distinguish it from its "invisible" partner. The "visible" Constitution does not address many critical issues such as why we accept it as law, how we know what it consists of, how we determine what it means, and what it does, in fact, mean in many instances.[38]

Thus, the Constitution requires interpretation. To be sure, some clauses direct clear outcomes. For instance, the Constitution provides that no one is eligible to be President until they have reached age 35,[39] that each state gets two senators[40] and that conviction for treason must be based "on the testimony of two witnesses to the same overt act, or on confession in open court."[41] These provisions give relatively clear direction regarding the subjects they address. But the meaning of other constitutional provisions is less clear. The Fifth and Fourteenth Amendments protect against deprivations of "life, liberty or property without due process of law." Concepts like life, liberty and property are contestable and mean different things to different people. And what is due process of law? The Eighth Amendment proscribes "cruel and unusual punishments"; does capital punishment come within that prohibition? Does the guarantee of the Equal Protection Clause in the Fourteenth Amendment pertain to equal opportunity, equal outcome, or something else? And what is an "establishment of religion" about which Congress cannot legislate?[42]

Much of the Bill of Rights is notoriously "open textured," but the ambiguous areas do not reside simply in those amendments. The Constitution's structural clauses raise numerous question, too. What does it mean to empower Congress "[t]o regulate commerce . . . among the several states?"[43] A substantial amount of litigation has addressed that question during the twentieth century. The President can appoint officers of the United States with the advice and consent of the Senate;[44] but suppose the President wants to remove an officer? The Constitution does not speak specifically to that contingency. The Constitution provides that the Chief Justice presides when the President is tried on impeachment.[45] Who presides if the Vice President is impeached? Can the Vice President, as President of the

---

[36] Legal Tender Cases, 79 U.S. (12 Wall.) 457, 532 (1871).

[37] *McCulloch*, 17 U.S. at 407. *See also Legal Tender Cases*, 79 U.S. at 532. ("It prescribes outlines, leaving the filling up to be deduced from the outlines.").

[38] LAURENCE H. TRIBE, THE INVISIBLE CONSTITUTION 6–8 (2008).

[39] U.S. CONST. art. II, § 1, cl. 5.

[40] U.S. CONST. art. I, § 3, cl. 1.

[41] U.S. CONST. art. III, § 3, cl. 1.

[42] U.S. CONST. amend. I.

[43] U.S. CONST. art. I, § 8, cl. 3.

[44] U.S. CONST. art. II, § 2, cl. 2.

[45] U.S. CONST. art. I, § 3, cl. 6.

Senate,[46] preside?[47] Suppose there is no Chief Justice; can someone else preside over the President's impeachment trial? If so, who? Congress can support an army[48] and provide for a navy[49] but the Constitution says nothing about an air force. Is it unconstitutional?

These examples are illustrative, not exhaustive. One can easily multiply questions to which the Constitution does not speak directly or clearly. The U.S. Reports, and constitutional law casebooks, are filled with cases addressing contested language in the Constitution. Constitutional interpretation thus becomes a necessary task of those charged with acting in accordance with the Constitution.

This raises the question regarding how one interprets and argues about the Constitution. The appropriate method of constitutional analysis is controversial. Various judges and scholars adopt different orientations concerning constitutional interpretation.[50] Some believe constitutional interpretation should focus on the text. Many text based theories call for constitutional language to be construed consistently with the original understanding.[51] Originalists typically contend that original intent or understanding provides the most natural meaning of a document, or furnishes the best way to limit judicial discretion, or gives appropriate respect to the work of the founding generation. Alternatively, others advocate a "living constitution." They take their inspiration in part from John Marshall's observation that the "Constitution [is] intended to endure for ages to come, and, consequently, to be adapted to the various *crises* of human affairs."[52] They advocate reading the text in accordance with contemporary, rather than original, understandings.[53] Some advocates of a "living constitution" believe legal precedent and/or ongoing practice are more important in constitutional interpretation.[54] Thus, Professor David Strauss endorses a common law approach to constitutional interpretation. He argues:[55]

> The common law tradition rejects the notion that law must be derived from some authoritative source and finds it instead in understandings that evolve over time. And it is the common law approach, not the approach that

---

[46] U.S. Const. art. I, § 3, cl. 4.

[47] For different views, *see* Joel K. Goldstein, *Can the Vice President Preside at His Own Impeachment Trial? A Critique of Bare Textualism*, 44 St. Louis U. L.J. 849 (2000) (no); Michael Stokes Paulsen, *Someone Should Have Told Spiro Agnew*, 14 Const. Comment. 245 (1997) (yes).

[48] U.S. Const. art. I, § 8, cl. 12.

[49] U.S. Const. art. I, § 8, cl. 13.

[50] *See* Richard H. Fallon, Jr., *How to Choose a Constitutional Theory*, 87 Cal. L. Rev. 535, 541–45 (1999).

[51] *See, e.g.*, Robert H. Bork, The Tempting of America: The Political Seduction of the Law (1990).

[52] McCulloch v. Maryland, 17 U.S. (4 Wheat.) 316, 415 (1819). *See also* Cohens v. Virginia, 19 U.S. (6 Wheat.) 264, 387 (1821) ("But a constitution is framed for ages to come, and designed to approach immortality as nearly as human institutions can approach it.").

[53] *See, e.g.*, Paul Brest, *The Misconceived Quest for the Original Understanding*, 60 B.U. L. Rev. 204, 209–17 (1980).

[54] *See, e.g.*, David A. Strauss, The Living Constitution (2010); David A. Strauss, *Common Law Constitutional Interpretation*, 63 U. Chi. L. Rev. 877 (1996).

[55] Strauss, *Common Law*, at 879.

connects law to an authoritative text, or an authoritative decision by the Framers or by 'we the people,' that best explains, and best justifies, American constitutional law today.

Some theories are process-oriented. For instance, Professor John Hart Ely argued that the Constitution was primarily focused on assuring fair processes, not certain outcomes. Taking his cues from Justice Stone's famous footnote four in *United States v. Carolene Products Co.*,[56] he argued that other than the Constitution's clear commands, constitutional interpretation should properly focus on making sure that political processes are open to participation by all on a fair basis. Protecting fair and democratic decision-making processes, not producing certain substantive outcomes, was the "paramount mission of constitutional interpretation," he argued. Accordingly, courts should most carefully review government actions which impaired the democratic process or which disadvantaged minority groups which had historically be disadvantaged.[57] Others characterize a commitment to process-based theories as "puzzling."[58] Professor Laurence Tribe argued, for instance, that such theories elevate one substantive value, democratic participation, beyond others, and ignore the many constitutional provisions which reflect commitments to other values. Professor Christopher Eisgruber argued that constitutional interpretation involves "principled argument about moral and political issues," particularly as it focuses on certain clauses.[59]

This synopsis neither provides an exhaustive catalogue of constitutional theories nor does it offer more than a few sound bites from those it includes. The literature includes numerous possible approaches and those mentioned here lend themselves to discussion (and scrutiny) in book length treatments.

§ 1.05 CONSTITUTIONAL ARGUMENT

If it is difficult to agree on a prescriptive theory, it is easier to describe the types of constitutional arguments which governmental officials and lawyers typically make. These modes of constitutional arguments can be divided into several categories.

[1] Textual Argument

The text of the Constitution is a starting point for constitutional interpretation. Virtually all students of constitutional law agree that clear textual commands merit substantial deference and that even contestable provisions must be engaged rather than ignored. "Liberty" may be subject to different meanings but we must at least acknowledge that concept is under discussion. Textualism comports with a sense of law as a positive system of rules.[60] Moreover, textualism has a democratic

---

[56] 304 U.S. 144, 152–53 n.4 (1938).

[57] ELY, *supra* note 23.

[58] Laurence H. Tribe, *The Puzzling Persistence of Process-Based Constitutional Theories*, 59 YALE L.J. 1063 (1980).

[59] CHRISTOPHER L. EISGRUBER, CONSTITUTIONAL SELF-GOVERNMENT 6 (2001).

[60] *See, e.g.*, ELY, *supra* note 23, at 3 (explaining basis behind textualism).

character to it. The text is available to all. Citizens can interpret it in some fashion without recourse to the original records or philosopher's tomes more accessible to law professors and academics. Although some see the text in originalist terms, meaning forever what it meant at ratification,[61] others believe textualism allows constitutional meaning to evolve to comport with the way in which language is understood today.[62] As Professor Philip Bobbitt put it, "one power of textual argument is that it provides a valve through which contemporary values can be intermingled with the Constitution."[63] Finally, some defend textualism as a way to restrain judicial choice, to keep judges from introducing their own political and moral sensibilities into constitutional argument.

Textualism has limits, too. The Constitution often fails to resolve difficult questions, either because it does not speak directly or clearly to a problem that arises. The examples mentioned earlier are illustrative. Can the President abrogate a treaty by his own action?[64] The Constitution does not contain an explicit answer. Under the Commerce Clause Congress can regulate commerce among the States. Suppose Congress had not regulated a particular area of commercial life. Can the States regulate that matter or is the constitutional grant of power to Congress exclusive? The Constitution's text does not contain specific language to answer those questions either. Yet as Professor Bobbitt points out, "in a Constitution of limited powers what is *not* expressed must also be interpreted."[65] Constitutional analysis must construe interpret textual silence, a challenge which often leaves us wondering and reaching disputed interpretations.

At times, the Constitution uses language which is in John Hart Ely's phrase, "open-textured";[66] formulations so general and abstract that they invite interpretation. Does the Eighth Amendment's ban on "cruel and unusual punishments" preclude the death penalty? What is the meaning of "liberty" in the Due Process Clause of the Fifth and Fourteenth Amendments? Even if we engage the text, its open-textured language may not point in only one direction. And the Ninth Amendment[67] might be viewed as a textual invitation to go beyond the constitution in searching for protected rights.

Finally, if we examine constitutional practice we find that the text often does not play a crucial role. On some occasions, courts decide cases based on concepts not stated in the Constitution. The Constitution's text does not explicitly confer a general right of privacy, yet decisions prohibiting states from outlawing use of contraceptives or acknowledging a woman's right to terminate a pregnancy rest on that concept. Even if the Equal Protection Clause provided a basis to outlaw State

---

[61] *See, e.g.*, South Carolina v. United States, 199 U.S. 437, 448 (1905) ("The Constitution is a written instrument. As such its meaning does not alter. That which it meant when adopted, it means now.").

[62] PHILIP BOBBITT, CONSTITUTIONAL FATE 33 (1982).

[63] *Id.* at 36.

[64] *See* Goldwater v. Carter, 444 U.S. 996 (1979).

[65] BOBBIT, *supra* note 62, at 38.

[66] *See generally* ELY, *supra* note 23, at 13–14.

[67] U.S. CONST. amend. IX ("The enumeration in the Constitution, of certain rights, shall not be construed to deny or disparage others retained by the people.").

sponsored school segregation, as the Court held in *Brown v. Board of Education*[68] in 1954, that clause only limits action of the States. There is no such clause in the text vis a vis the Federal Government. Does that mean that the Federal Government could operate segregated schools even though the States could not? Such an outcome would seem inconceivable. The Court avoided that result by finding an equal protection component in the Due Process Clause of the Fifth Amendment.[69] But that approach created other textual anomalies. "In the important cases, reference to and analysis of the constitutional text plays a minor role,"[70] wrote Professor Thomas C. Grey in 1976.

These criticisms do not sideline textual analysis from constitutional interpretation. The text certainly does decide some issues, e.g. the age of eligibility to be President, Senator or Representative. Even when it may not be decisive, it may at least limit the terms of discussion; the Eighth Amendment applies to "punishments," the Commerce Clause allows Congress to regulate "commerce," and so forth.[71] If the text restrains judges by focusing their attention on the Constitution's language, it also empowers them by suggesting they are free to reject decades of doctrine if it is inconsistent with the text.

An application of textual argument is the technique which Professor Akhil Reed Amar has labeled "intratextualism."[72] It involves using the Constitution as a dictionary to help define its recurring words and phrases by reference to their meaning elsewhere in the document. As will be seen later, John Marshall used this technique in *McCulloch v. Maryland*[73] and other cases also use it to interpret constitutional language. Yet some critique intratextualism contending that it mistakenly attributes greater coherence to the document than appropriate and it assumes judges have greater capacity to reach correct interpretations then they do.[74]

Because the text is often not conclusive, the judiciary has developed other modes of analysis to help give meaning to general constitutional language in specific cases. In addition to the text, several other modes of argument command widespread support.[75]

---

[68] 347 U.S. 483 (1954).

[69] Bolling v. Sharpe, 347 U.S. 497 (1954).

[70] Thomas C. Grey, *Do We Have an Unwritten Constitution?*, 27 STAN. L. REV. 703, 707–08 (1975).

[71] *See* Richard H. Fallon, Jr., *A Constructivist Coherence Theory of Constitutional Interpretation*, 100 HARV. L. REV. 1189, 1196 (1987).

[72] Akhil Reed Amar, *Intratextualism*, 112 HARV. L. REV. 747 (1999).

[73] 17 U.S. (4 Wheat) 316 (1819).

[74] Adrian Vermeule & Ernest A. Young, *Hercules, Herbert, and Amar: The Trouble with Intratextualism*, 113 HARV. L. REV. 730 (2000).

[75] *See generally* BOBBITT, *supra* note 62; CHARLES A. MILLER, THE SUPREME COURT AND THE USES OF HISTORY 14–38 (1969); Fallon, *supra* note 71.

[2] Intent of the Framers

At least three types of historical arguments find their way into legal and judicial utterances. First, some view constitutional interpretation as a quest to capture and apply the intent of the framers. These originalist arguments generally seek to discover and enforce either the intent of the drafters or ratifiers of the original Constitution or the understanding of the generation alive at that time. (Of course, for amendments, originalists emphasize the intent or understandings related to the amendments). Proponents of originalism often advance one or more of four justifications for giving it strong weight. First, ratification of the Constitution was the positive act which elevated it from paper to law. It was ratified by a democratic act which required supermajoritarian support. Those who ratified it presumably understood its language to achieve certain purposes. Accordingly, those understandings are what became law.[76] Second, the founding generation was a unique collection of individuals acting in a time of heightened political consciousness. Their intent deserves deference because of their heroic and enlightened character. Further, originalism represents a strategy to confine the discretion allowed unelected judges. A jurist bound to apply original meaning is limited in a way that one licensed to interpret an ever-evolving Constitution is not. Finally, originalism gives the Constitution some rigor. If the Constitution is viewed as being elastic enough to accommodate changing conditions it will stretch until it loses all ability to restrain.[77]

Originalism, too, poses some problems. First, can the intent of the framers or ratifiers or the understanding of their generation really be fathomed? No official minutes were kept at the Constitutional Convention. Records there and at the various ratifying conventions are fragmentary. Only a fraction of what was said was preserved and some portions are cryptic.[78] The comments of a speaker may, or may not, have reflected the views or rationales of the greater number who were silent or whose thoughts were not preserved. Sources like The Federalist Papers may tell us how Hamilton, Madison, and Jay defended constitutional provisions, but their explanations may not have reflected the sentiments of other framers or those of ratifiers, most of whom were not familiar with these essays. The framers and ratifiers may not have anticipated or addressed some issues in a form that is preserved. Technological advance and historical developments introduce new problems and contexts beyond the imagination of earlier generations. Even when the founding generation did anticipate issues, it may be treacherous to ascribe to a group the articulated views of the few who may have spoken.[79] And it is difficult to determine with any certainty how the founding generation understood much constitutional language. In *Brown v. Board of Education*, the Court rescheduled arguments ostensibly so the parties could brief what the original understanding of

---

[76] *See generally* KEITH E. WHITTINGTON, CONSTITUTIONAL INTERPRETATION: TEXTUAL MEANING, ORIGINAL INTENT, AND JUDICIAL REVIEW (1999); ANTONIN SCALIA, A MATTER OF INTERPRETATION: FEDERAL COURTS AND THE LAW (1997); *See also* ELY, *supra* note 23, at 15–18 (discussing originalism).

[77] *See, e.g.*, SCALIA, *supra* note 76, at 47.

[78] *See, e.g.*, YODER, *supra* note 10, at 79–80.

[79] *See, e.g.*, Brest, *supra* note 53, at 229; Daniel A. Farber, *The Originalism Debate: A Guide for the Perplexed*, 49 OHIO ST. L.J. 1085 (1989).

the Fourteenth Amendment was regarding school desegregation. But after many of the nation's ablest lawyers and historians labored for months to elucidate the subject, the Court concluded that the historical argument was "at best . . . inconclusive."[80]

Capturing original intent may be particularly problematic when those doing the recovery are lawyers and judges rather than historians. As Professor Charles A. Miller wrote, "historians as scholars can generally state the matter more objectively than can advocates as historians."[81] The work of a historian rests on certain assumptions which may prove controversial. Often accounts of the past reflect more the view of historians than history itself. Yet historians, even with their limitations, are likely to be more trained in the historical craft than are lawyers and judges, and better able to transport themselves back into the world view of earlier times to recreate what prior generations thought or to understand the public meaning of their work. Moreover, they presumably do not approach an historical issue as advocates in the same way lawyers do.

Even if we can recapture original intent, we may ask how relevant it should be. The framers lived in different times with different problems. Moreover, as a group of white men, many of whom owned slaves, they hardly reflect the demographic reality of our times. Transformative events — westward expansion, the Civil War, immigration, two World Wars, the Great Depression, the change from an agrarian to industrial society, the civil rights movement, and many more — left quite a different world from the one Madison, Hamilton, and Jay knew. Should the Constitution bind contemporary people to the specific choices of those who lived two centuries ago?[82]

Finally, originalism cannot account for numerous decisions of the Supreme Court. The First Amendment has been interpreted to protect a broad "market place of ideas" which seems to extend far beyond the view of the founders. The Equal Protection Clause outlaws racial segregation of schools and much gender discrimination which was not within the aim of those who ratified it. And it has been made applicable against the federal government, an interpretive move hard to defend on originalist grounds.[83]

[3] Ongoing Practice

A second type of historical argument involves ongoing history, or what might be termed an adverse possession theory of constitutional interpretation. These arguments rest on the premise that constitutional meaning evolves to embrace changing reality. In part, the Constitution changes in response to the accepted interpretations of government officials (such as Presidents, legislators, etc.) over a

---

[80] Brown v. Board of Educ., 347 U.S. 483, 489 (1954).

[81] MILLER, *supra* note 75, at 157.

[82] *See generally* STEPHEN BREYER, MAKING OUR DEMOCRACY WORK: A JUDGE'S VIEW 76–80 (2010); RICHARD H. FALLON, JR., IMPLEMENTING THE CONSTITUTION 13–14 (2001).

[83] *See* FALLON, *supra* note 82, at 15–16.

period of time.[84] It also responds to accommodate changes in social practice, technology and morality. Whereas original intent history seeks to confine judges to constitutional meaning at the time a constitutional text was generated, ongoing history "allows the Constitution to move with the prevailing temper of the country and may therefore be considered forward-looking."[85] In part, ongoing history reflects judicial deference to the ability of members of the legislative and executive branches to interpret the constitution. It assumes that these figures would act in accordance with the constitution and accords their behavior over time significance in understanding constitutional meaning.

Ongoing history may allow the Constitution to change to accommodate new circumstances or to recognize traditional practice. But how does one decide which practices are significant in changing constitutional meaning and which are not? American society oppressed African-Americans and excluded women from certain preferred roles for centuries. The longevity of these practices would not seem a basis to accord them constitutional sanction. Indeed, it has not. One escape from this quandary is to admit ongoing practice to shape the meaning of provisions respecting institutional practice and behavior, but not regarding those directly impacting individual liberty. Chief Justice Marshall used this approach in *McCulloch v. Maryland*.[86] There he suggested that past practice might be appropriate in certain cases in which "the great principles of liberty are not concerned."[87] Yet, at times, justices do look to tradition to determine whether practices like homosexuality,[88] abortion[89] and assisted suicide[90] are constitutionally protected. Moreover, accepting Chief Justice Marshall's formulation does not eliminate the difficulty but simply limits it to cases dealing with institutions. At times the Court has found past practice suggestive of constitutional meaning; at other times, not. In *Stuart v. Laird*, Justice William Patterson used ongoing practice to respond to the argument that the Constitution precluded Supreme Court justices from sitting on circuit courts. He wrote:[91]

> To this objection, which is of recent date, it is sufficient to observe, that practice and acquiescence under it for a period of several years, commencing with the organization of the judicial system, affords an irresistible answer, and has indeed fixed the construction.

Less than two decades later, Chief Justice Marshall thought the earlier decisions of the executive and legislative branches, in favor of a national bank, suggestive of its constitutionality.[92] But 164 years later, in *Immigration and Naturalization Service*

---

[84]   *See, e.g.*, McCulloch v. Maryland, 17 U.S. (4 Wheat.) 316, 401–02 (1819).

[85]   *See* MILLER, *supra* note 75, at 25.

[86]   *McCulloch*, 17 U.S. at 401–02.

[87]   *Id.* at 401.

[88]   *See, e.g.*, Bowers v. Hardwick, 478 U.S. 186 (1986), *overruled by* Lawrence v. Texas, 539 U.S. 558 (2003).

[89]   *See, e.g.*, Roe v. Wade, 410 U.S. 113 (1973).

[90]   *See, e.g.*, Washington v. Glucksberg, 521 U.S. 702 (1997).

[91]   Stuart v. Laird, 5 U.S. (1 Cranch) 299, 309 (1803).

[92]   *McCulloch*, 17 U.S. at 401.

v. Chadha,[93] Chief Justice Burger suggested that the increased frequency of legislative veto provisions in federal statutes "sharpened rather than blunted"[94] the judicial scrutiny.

[4] Judicial Doctrine; Precedent

A third type of historical argument relates to judicial doctrine or precedent. These distinct, yet closely related, types of constitutional arguments use judicial formulations of the past to decide new constitutional cases. According to Professor Charles A. Miller, "[c]onstitutional doctrines are formulas extracted from a combination of the constitutional text and a series of related cases. Typically stated in shorthand fashion, they may be used almost as an emendation on the constitutional text."[95] Or as Professor Charles Fried put it, "[d]octrine is the work of judges and of those who comment on and rationalize their decisions."[96] Doctrine would include the early twentieth century ideas that government could not interfere with liberty of contract,[97] that equal protection was satisfied by separate but equal facilities,[98] that government could regulate commerce directly but not indirectly,[99] as well as contemporary pronouncements in favor of applying strict scrutiny to classifications based on race[100] or against commandeering state government.[101] Precedent involves the use of previously decided cases to resolve later cases, and may be used by way of analogy or as binding authority. Most doctrine is identified with some precedent.

Judicial decisions add gloss to the Constitution's text. The holdings and concepts embodied in judicial opinions often assume a life of their own and become the stuff of constitutional law.[102] Constitutional law includes judge-made rules which are developed in case-law, especially the decisions of the Supreme Court that affect the distribution or the exercise of governmental authority.

Doctrine and precedent both reflect a common law approach to constitutional law. They assign high status to judicial decisions and the principles they articulate. To be sure, as Justice Oliver Wendell Holmes observed, "[g]eneral propositions do not decide concrete cases";[103] although this admonition most clearly states a limitation on doctrine, precedent, too, does not always cover precisely the diverse situations new cases present.

---

[93] 462 U.S. 919 (1983).

[94] *Id.* at 944.

[95] MILLER, *supra* note 75, at 15.

[96] Charles Fried, *Constitutional Doctrine*, 107 HARV. L. REV. 1140 (1994).

[97] Lochner v. New York, 198 U.S. 45 (1905).

[98] Plessy v. Ferguson, 163 U.S. 537 (1896).

[99] United States v. E. C. Knight, 156 U.S. 1 (1895).

[100] Grutter v. Bollinger, 539 U.S. 306 (2003).

[101] New York v. United States, 505 U.S. 144 (1992).

[102] *See, e.g.*, Strauss, *Common Law*, *supra* note 54, at 899–900.

[103] Lochner v. New York, 198 U.S. 45, 75 (1905) (Holmes, J. dissenting).

Reliance on precedent has some clear advantages. It preserves judicial resources, adds some certainty and stability to constitutional law, links current decisions to those of the past, and limits judicial discretion.[104]

Yet some question why doctrine and precedent should receive such deference. As Professor Fried posed the problem, "our allegiance and that of the judges is ultimately owed to the Constitution itself. Because only the Constitution has the authority of a founding document, the question arises: is it not wrong to substitute the course of judgments in the Supreme Court for that authority authentically discerned?"[105] The legal realists pointed out that judges have policy preferences and accordingly their decisions may mask as law their political predispositions. Why should later generations honor and perpetuate the work of earlier jurists? Critics complain that constitutional meaning turns on the text and original intent, not on subsequent interpretations.[106] As Justice William O. Douglas put it,

> a judge looking at a constitutional decision may have compulsions to revere past history and accept what was once written. But he remembers above all else that it is the Constitution which he swore to support and defend, not the gloss which his predecessors may have put on it. So he comes to formulate his own views, rejecting some earlier ones as false and embracing others. He cannot do otherwise unless he lets men long dead and unaware of the problems of the age in which he lives do his thinking for him.[107]

Moreover, doctrine often takes on a life of its own quite independent of text and original intent. Terms like "separate but equal," "clear and present danger," "direct or indirect effects," and "strict scrutiny" become vehicles to resolve cases even though they do not appear in the text itself.

Stare decisis, the practice of following precedent, is practiced in constitutional adjudication although not with the same rigor as in statutory cases. Justice Louis Brandeis explained:

> *Stare decisis* is usually the wise policy, because in most matters it is more important that the applicable rule of law be settled than that it be settled right . . . . But in cases involving the Federal Constitution, where corrections through legislative action is practically impossible, this Court has often overruled its earlier decisions. The Court bows to the lessons of experience and the force of better reasoning, recognizing that the process of trial and error, so fruitful in the physical sciences, is appropriate also in the judicial function.[108]

Thus, at times the Court explicitly or implicitly abandons or overrules pernicious or anachronistic precedents or doctrine, as it did in *Brown* when it rejected the notion

---

[104] *See generally* Geoffrey R. Stone, *Precedent, the Amendment Process, and Evolution in Constitutional Doctrine*, 11 HARV. J.L. & PUB. POL'Y 67, 70 (1988).

[105] Fried, *supra* note 96, at 1140.

[106] *See, e.g.*, Gary Lawson, *An Interpretivist Agenda*, 15 HARV. J.L. & PUB. POL'Y 157, 161 (1992).

[107] William O. Douglas, *Stare Decisis*, *in* 1 BENJAMIN N. CARDOZO MEMORIAL LECTURES 285.

[108] Burnet v. Coronado Oil & Gas Co., 285 U.S. 393, 406–08 (1932) (Brandeis, J., dissenting).

from *Plessy v. Ferguson*[109] that "separate but equal" was consistent with the Fourteenth Amendment; or as it did when it stopped using "freedom of contract" from *Lochner* to proscribe governmental regulations. Professor Michael Gerhardt reports that the Supreme Court expressly overruled 208 precedents in 133 cases between 1789 and June, 2005.[110]

Yet the Court has also applied doctrine or precedent even though some justices with votes critical to establishing a majority indicated that they thought the earlier decision may have been wrong. Thus, in *Planned Parenthood v. Casey*[111] the Court affirmed the central holding of *Roe v. Wade*,[112] which recognized a woman's constitutional right to terminate a pregnancy, even though three justices repeatedly suggested that they (or some of them) may have had misgivings about *Roe* as an original matter. In *Casey*, Justices O'Connor, Kennedy and Souter suggested whether *stare decisis* should apply should turn upon several criteria: Was the earlier rule workable? Had it engendered substantial reliance? Had "related principles of law . . . so far developed as to have left the old rule no more than a remnant of abandoned doctrine?" Had facts changed so much "to have robbed the old rule of significant application or justification?"[113] Similarly, the Court applied judicial doctrine in an interesting manner in deciding that the warnings to criminal suspects it required in *Miranda v. Arizona*[114] were constitutionally required. In *Dickerson v. United States*,[115] the Court considered the constitutionality of 18 U.S.C. § 3501 which conflicted with *Miranda*. Although several members of the Court's majority apparently had misgivings about "*Miranda*'s reasoning and its resulting rule"[116] that the warnings *Miranda* prescribed were constitutionally compelled, the Court declined, on *stare decisis* grounds, to overrule that famous decision. The Court that decided *Miranda* and subsequent Courts had treated *Miranda* as stating a constitutional rule. Its "doctrinal underpinnings" had not suffered sufficient deterioration to overrule the decision even though several members of the Court's seven justice majority would have interpreted the Constitution differently as an original matter.

In dissent, Justice Scalia, joined by Justice Thomas, pointed out that Chief Justice Rehnquist and Justices O'Connor and Kennedy were "on record as believing that a violation of *Miranda* is *not* a violation of the Constitution."[117] He accused the majority of adopting "a significant *new*, if not entirely comprehensible, principle of constitutional law" that the Court could strike down a congressional statute "not only when what they prescribe violates the Constitution, but when what they

---

[109] 163 U.S. 537 (1896).

[110] MICHAEL J. GERHARDT, THE POWER OF PRECEDENT 9 (2008).

[111] 505 U.S. 833 (1992).

[112] 410 U.S. 113 (1973).

[113] *Casey*, 505 U.S. at 855.

[114] 384 U.S. 436 (1966).

[115] 530 U.S. 428 (2000).

[116] *Id.* at 443.

[117] *Id.* at 445.

prescribe contradicts a decision of [the] Court that 'announced a constitutional rule?' "[118]

Yet the Court has not always applied these tests since *Casey* in determining whether to apply or abandon an earlier doctrine. Thus, in *Lawrence v. Texas*,[119] for instance, the Court overruled *Bowers v. Hardwick*[120] without assessing the earlier case against all of the *Casey* principles.

[5] Structural Arguments

In addition to historical arguments, constitutional interpretation often relies on structural argument, inferences from the structures and relationships of the Constitution.[121] Such arguments identify concepts implicit in the Constitution's architecture to interpret the document. Thus, constitutional concepts of federalism, separation of powers, checks and balances, rule of law, democratic accountability and so forth emerge from constitutional structures although those terms do not themselves appear in the Constitution. Structural reasoning is linked to the text because it draws general conclusions based upon the document. It differs from textual argument because it draws meaning not from a particular clause but from the relationship between, and the principles that emerge from, various clauses. Structural reasoning features prominently in some of Chief Justice John Marshall's seminal opinions, such as *Marbury v. Madison*[122] and *McCulloch v. Maryland*.[123] Thus, in *Marbury* he concluded that the Constitution is paramount law, that Congress' powers are limited, and that citizens with rights must have remedies from basic concepts relating to constitutionalism and rule of law. In *McCulloch*, he cited the structural idea that constitutions are created to succeed and accordingly Congress can exercise means necessary to accomplish its enumerated ends. Moreover, he used the structural independence of the federal government and its democratic character as a basis to preclude a state from taxing its agencies. Structural reasoning is by no means a relic of earlier times. Professors Brannon P. Denning and Glenn Reynolds point out its prevalence in many recent decisions of the Rehnquist Court.[124] Proponents, like Charles Black, Jr., argued that "the method of reasoning from structure and relation" is more likely "to make sense — current, practical sense" than some other forms of legal reasoning.[125]

Yet critics find structural argument elusive and malleable. To identify federalism or separation of powers as constitutional concepts does not provide very precise guidance in resolving specific cases. Thus, structural reasoning may not restrain judges but rather give them license to reach results they wish to reach. Moreover,

---

[118] *Id.*

[119] 539 U.S. 558 (2003).

[120] 478 U.S. 186 (1986).

[121] *See generally* CHARLES L. BLACK, JR., STRUCTURE AND RELATIONSHIP IN CONSTITUTIONAL LAW (1969).

[122] 5 U.S. (1 Cranch) 137 (1803).

[123] 17 U.S. (4 Wheat.) 316 (1819).

[124] *See* Brannon P. Denning & Glenn Harlan Reynolds, *Comfortably Penumbral*, 77 B.U. L. REV. 1089 (1997).

[125] BLACK, *supra* note 121, at 22.

structural argument generally seems better suited for questions involving the relationship of different institutions of government; they are less useful "to the task of protecting human rights,"[126] although occasionally it occurs in those cases.[127]

[6] Consequential Arguments

Prudential or consequentialist arguments proceed from the assumption that constitutional interpretation should consider likely outcomes. This approach seeks to lend rationality to constitutional interpretation. It often balances competing constitutional principles. Thus, in *McCulloch v. Maryland*, Chief Justice Marshall justified the Court's conclusion that Congress had power to create a national bank by considering the difficulties that would exist if Congress lacked such a power. The Constitution was to succeed, not fail, and accordingly it needed to be interpreted in a fashion which "the exigencies of the nation may require."[128] Prudential arguments may, at times, lead the Court to duck deciding a case to avoid institutional harm.[129] It may lead a Court to hold that the federal government cannot operate segregated schools, as the Court held in *Bolling v. Sharpe*,[130] the companion case to *Brown v. Board of Education*. In *Bolling*, Chief Justice Warren wrote that "[i]n view of our decision that the Constitution prohibits the states from maintaining racially segregated public schools, it would be unthinkable that the same Constitution would impose a lesser duty on the Federal Government."[131] Consequential arguments may lead the Court to uphold a presidential foreign policy initiative to avoid adverse international impact.[132]

Consequential arguments, however, may involve the Court in speculation regarding political reactions. Considering outcomes strikes some as policy-oriented, not law-oriented, and involving courts in legislating, not adjudicating. Is this an appropriate role for judges? Such judicial activity might also lead to "intellectual laziness" if it becomes a substitute for engaging other legal materials.[133]

[7] Ethical Argument

At times, courts and lawyers invoke ethical or value arguments. These assertions seek to vindicate what is deemed moral, just, or desirable. Sometimes the open-ended language of the Constitution seems to invite moral arguments as when the Court must define "liberty" or "equal protection." On other occasions,

---

[126] Bobbitt, *supra* note 62, at 89.

[127] *See, e.g.*, Griswold v. Connecticut, 381 U.S. 479 (1965) (majority opinion using structural reasoning to find constitutional right of privacy).

[128] *McCulloch*, 17 U.S. at 408–09. *See also* Breyer, *supra* note 82, at 80–87.

[129] *See, e.g.*, Alexander Bickel, The Least Dangerous Branch (1962).

[130] 347 U.S. 497 (1954).

[131] *Id.* at 500.

[132] *See, e.g.*, Dames & Moore v. Regan, 453 U.S. 654 (1981).

[133] Richard Posner, *Pragmatic Adjudication*, 18 Cardozo L. Rev. 1, 16 (1996).

they are invoked when other arguments seem inconclusive. As Professor Ronald Dworkin writes, "[t]he moral reading proposes that we all — judges, lawyers, citizens — interpret and apply these abstract clauses on the understanding that they invoke moral principles about political decency and justice."[134] Moral argument has its critics, however.

It is sometimes criticized as contestable since different people will reach different results in moral reasoning. As such, some view moral argument as representing an effort to incorporate personal sentiments into constitutional law. Moreover, introducing moral argument into constitutional interpretation may diminish the role of elected decisionmakers. Some argue that elected officials, not unelected judges, can best reflect the people's moral convictions.[135]

[8] Sociological Evidence

Courts sometimes use social facts as a basis for deciding constitutional cases.[136] The Brandeis brief, offered in *Muller v. Oregon*,[137] pioneered this approach.[138] Rather than devote his brief to a discussion of legal precedents, then attorney Louis D. Brandeis submitted a brief which focused almost entirely on presenting sociological data to show the reasonableness of the conclusions the Oregon legislature had reached. Attorneys challenging school desegregation in the 1950s employed extensive psychological and sociological evidence to support their ultimately successful claim that separate but equal violated equal protection because of its impact on African-American children.[139] More recently, in a Michigan affirmative action case, the Court relied on evidence regarding the beneficial effects of affirmative action programs in college admissions.[140]

Sociological argument raises some problems. When presented in briefs, rather than offered in evidence, there may not be effective opportunity to impeach the evidence and offer rebuttal.[141] Moreover, its use may make legal principles turn on sociological data and accordingly be vulnerable to a change in circumstance. Would racial segregation be constitutional if findings showed it to be beneficial?[142]

---

[134] RONALD DWORKIN, FREEDOM'S LAW: THE MORAL READING OF THE AMERICAN CONSTITUTION 2 (1996).

[135] *See generally* Michael W. McConnell, *The Importance of Humility in Judicial Review: A Comment on Ronald Dworkin's "Moral Reading" of the Constitution*, 65 FORDHAM L. REV. 1269 (1997).

[136] *See generally* MILLER, *supra* note 75, at 17–20.

[137] 208 U.S. 412 (1908).

[138] ALPHEUS T. MASON, BRANDEIS: A FREE MAN'S LIFE (1946).

[139] *See generally* RICHARD KLUGER, SIMPLE JUSTICE (1977).

[140] *See* Grutter v. Bollinger, 539 U.S. 306 (2003).

[141] PAUL A. FREUND, THE SUPREME COURT OF THE UNITED STATES 151 (1961).

[142] *See* MILLER, *supra* note 75, at 19.

[9]   Comparative Constitutional Argument

Finally, some justices have recently argued that the practices and experiences of other countries furnish a basis for reaching decisions in American constitutional law. In cases dealing with assisted suicide,[143] homosexuality,[144] and affirmative action,[145] some justices have cited the way other countries handle these issues in resolving American constitutional principles. Although this type of argument appears most often in cases involving constitutional rights, it has also appeared in cases dealing with constitutional structure too.[146] Not all embrace the use of comparative constitutional law in interpreting our Constitution. In fact, its use has become very controversial with originalists. Thus, Justice Scalia has suggested that the American Constitution should be interpreted without reference to the experience abroad.

§ 1.06   CONCLUSION

Some of the previous discussion has implicitly assumed that courts and lawyers have a special role in constitutional argument. Indeed, much constitutional argument is addressed to, or used by, the judiciary. The following chapter will introduce and explore the institution of judicial review, which recognizes the important judicial role in interpreting the Constitution. The judiciary is the primary source of constitutional law, but it is by no means the only institution that shapes constitutional meaning. The President[147] and members of the executive and legislative branches[148] also take oaths to enforce the Constitution, an obligation which arguably allows them to interpret it. Indeed, Presidents Thomas Jefferson,[149] Andrew Jackson,[150] Abraham Lincoln[151] and Franklin D. Roosevelt[152] among others at times suggested that they had some independent authority to interpret the Constitution. Officials in the executive and legislative branches interpret the Constitution in the regular course of their duties.[153] When, for instance, the House of Representatives considered impeaching Presidents Richard M. Nixon and William Jefferson Clinton it had to interpret the Impeachment Clause to determine whether the acts alleged constituted "other high crimes and misdemeanor."[154]

---

[143] *See* Washington v. Glucksberg, 521 U.S. 702, 718 n.16 (1997).

[144] *See* Lawrence v. Texas, 539 U.S. 558, 572–73 (2003).

[145] *See Grutter*, 539 U.S. at 344. (Ginsburg, J., concurring).

[146] *See, e.g.*, Printz v. United States, 521 U.S. 898, 976–78 (1997) (Breyer, J., dissenting).

[147] U.S. CONST. art. II, § 1, cl. 8.

[148] U.S. CONST. art. VI, cl. 3.

[149] THE WRITINGS OF THOMAS JEFFERSON 311 (Paul L. Ford ed., 1898) (Letter to John B. Colvin, Sept. 20, 1810).

[150] 3 MESSAGES AND PAPERS OF THE PRESIDENTS 1145 (James Richardson ed., 1897).

[151] *Abraham Lincoln, Special Session Message, in* 7 MESSAGES AND PAPERS OF THE PRESIDENTS 3210 (James Richardson ed., 1897).

[152] GERALD GUNTHER, CASES AND MATERIALS ON CONSTITUTIONAL LAW 24 (12th ed. 1991).

[153] *See generally* LOUIS FISHER, CONSTITUTIONAL DIALOGUES: INTERPRETATION AS POLITICAL PROCESS (1988).

[154] U.S. CONST. art. II, § 4.

Congress sometimes considers constitutional arguments in legislating. For instance, Senator Thomas F. Eagleton argued and voted against the War Powers Resolution in 1973 because he concluded that the measure unconstitutionally gave the President some of Congress' power to declare war.[155] When the bill passed nonetheless, President Nixon vetoed it because he thought it unconstitutionally encroached on the President's power.[156] In each case, their interpretation was based on their reading of the Constitution and their assessment of other constitutional materials. Neither Senator Eagleton's nor President Nixon's actions were unprecedented. On the contrary, members of the executive and legislative branches often consider constitutional arguments for or against proposed actions. At times the judiciary recognizes that one of the political branches has a superior right or competence to interpret a particular part of the Constitution. On other occasions, the Court adopts, or is influenced by, the constitutional views of the executive or legislative branches.

Moreover, the interpretation of constitutional terms and the operation of constitutional institutions changes due to the behavior of non-judicial actors. Professor Cass Sunstein has argued that often "changes in constitutional arrangements and understandings have been a product of ordinary democratic processes, producing adjustments in constitutional understandings over time."[157]

---

[155] Thomas F. Eagleton, War and Presidential Power 163 (1974).

[156] Richard M. Nixon, Veto of the War Powers Resolution (Oct. 24, 1973), *in* Public Papers of the Presidents: Richard Nixon 1973, at 311 (1975).

[157] Cass Sunstein, A Constitution of Many Minds: Why the Founding Document Doesn't Mean What It Meant Before 3 (2009).

Chapter 2

THE COURTS AND JUDICIAL REVIEW

INTRODUCTION

Any effort to understand American Constitutional law must quickly encounter the institution of judicial review. It is, of course, as Chief Justice John Marshall suggested, a Constitution being expounded, and accordingly the Constitution itself is the touchstone of constitutional law. But it is hard to discuss constitutional law without coming to grips with judicial review, the power of the federal courts to review legislation to determine whether it is consistent with the Constitution.

The very concept invites questions. What authorizes courts to exercise this power? What is its scope? How can one reconcile judicial review with principles of democratic accountability so basic to our system? Do courts alone interpret the Constitution or is that task shared with other branches? What, if any, restraints exist on the federal judiciary?

This chapter addresses these subjects. It begins by discussing *Marbury v. Madison*, the foundational case for many principles of American constitutional law. Sections which follow focus on judicial review in cases affirming the Supreme Court's power to examine acts of Congress as well as state action. It then discusses the establishment of the federal courts that exercise judicial review and their jurisdiction. The chapter addresses congressional authority to establish and abolish courts and to control the jurisdiction of the federal courts, including the Supreme Court.

The chapter then turns to judicial review in operation, stressing the constitutional requirement of a "case" or "controversy" before federal judicial power may be exercised. Different aspects of the "case" or "controversy" requirement are presented: advisory opinions, standing, mootness, ripeness and, last of all, political questions. Unless the "case" or "controversy" requirement is met, the federal courts may not exercise their review power — no matter how compelling the argument to adjudicate a specific constitutional issue.

§ 2.01 MARBURY v. MADISON

Marbury v. Madison[1] represents the foundational case in American constitutional law. It articulated or suggested many central principles of that enterprise. Four, perhaps, are most critical. First, *Marbury* enunciated the basic structural idea that our government is based upon the rule of law. Second, *Marbury* pronounced that the Constitution is paramount law such that any inconsistent

---

[1] Marbury v. Madison, 5 U.S. (1 Cranch) 137 (1803).

statute is invalid. Third, *Marbury* held that ours is a system of limited government. Finally, *Marbury* held that the judiciary has the power of judicial review.

[1] Historical Context

Marbury arose in historic times. Its context is important in understanding the case. The 1800 presidential election produced a victory for the Democrat-Republicans and Vice President Thomas Jefferson and a defeat for the Federalists and President John Adams. The Federalists loss of the White House and Congress brought history's first democratic transition. During the closing months of Federalist control,[2] the party sought to establish a bastion of power in the third branch of government, the judiciary. The Circuit Judge Act, passed on February 13, 1801, reduced the Supreme Court from six justices to five, eliminated the duty of its justices to ride circuit to hear cases around the country, and created sixteen new circuit judges. The political benefits of the reforms to the Federalists were clear. Reducing the size of the Court would deny Jefferson an appointment; the new circuit judgeships provided patronage for a party about to leave office. Yet the changes also had certain salutary purposes. If the Supreme Court justices no longer had to ride circuit, they could function as a national court of stature to balance the work of the other branches. Creating circuit judges relieved the justices of this burdensome duty and, along with the additional judges, made the judiciary more efficient.

Two weeks later, and only one week before Adams' term ended, Congress passed the Organic Act of the District of Columbia which allowed the President to appoint 42 justices of the peace for the District. In the closing days of his administration, President Adams appointed various Federalist loyalists, including William Marbury, to these newly-created judicial positions.

Secretary of State John Marshall had been appointed Chief Justice of the Supreme Court after John Jay had declined the post which he had previously held; Jay thought the high court "so defective it would not obtain the energy, weight, and dignity which was essential to its affording due support to the national government."[3] Marshall continued to serve as Secretary of State even after taking office as Chief Justice. Marshall was given signed commissions of Marbury and others to deliver in the closing hours of Adams' administration. The commissions of some, like Marbury, were not tendered before Adams' term ended. Upon taking office, Jefferson directed that the remaining commissions, including Marbury's, not be delivered. Marbury sought a writ of mandamus directing Jefferson's Secretary of State, James Madison, to deliver the commission.

The case came to the Supreme Court in 1803. Marbury had filed suit in December, 1801 but the new Congress had abolished the June and December, 1802 terms of the Court. It had also repealed the Judiciary Act of 1801 which had created the circuit judgeships and returned the justices to the arduous task of circuit riding. These actions undermined the independence and authority of the

---

[2] Prior to the adoption of the Twentieth Amendment in 1933, presidential terms began and ended on March 4.

[3] *Quoted in* LEONARD BAKER, JOHN MARSHALL: A LIFE IN LAW 352 (1974).

Court, yet the Court was ill-equipped to resist them. Indeed, the Court felt compelled to affirm Congress' ability to repeal the 1801 Act in *Stuart v. Laird*.[4]

[2] The Opinion

Against this background, *Marbury* came to the Court. The case presented Marshall with a clear problem. Marbury's petition asked the Court to order Madison to deliver the commission, thereby reversing President Jefferson's contrary direction. If the Court granted Marbury's claim and ordered Jefferson to deliver the commissions, it would risk a potentially humiliating (or worse) confrontation with the executive branch. How could the new judiciary, with the low prestige Jay described, force the executive to take action it did not wish to take? On the other hand, if the Court denied Marbury's petition as beyond its power, it would appear to have acquiesced to the reality of its impotence.

Marshall extricated the Court from this Hobson's choice through an ingenious opinion which avoided that confrontation with Jefferson which the Court could not afford while nonetheless establishing important principles that strengthened its hand. Ultimately, Marshall ruled that the Court lacked jurisdiction over Marbury's case because the statute under which Marbury proceeded was unconstitutional. As Professor Robert G. McCloskey concluded, "The decision is a masterwork of indirection, a brilliant example of Marshall's capacity to sidestep danger while seeming to court it, to advance in one direction while his opponents are looking in another."[5]

Marshall began his opinion by concluding that Marbury was entitled to the commission.[6] Marbury's appointment was complete once signed and sealed. The nonoccurring delivery was merely a formality. By law Marbury was entitled to a four year term. If Marbury were removable at will, determining when his appointment was complete would be irrelevant since it would be revocable. Since he was appointed for a fixed term, however, his appointment was irrevocable and conferred a vested property right on him. By withholding the commission, Madison was violating the law.

Marshall then turned to a second question, whether law gave Marbury a legal remedy for the violation of his legal rights. Marshall's response articulated the basic American principle of the rule of law.

> The very essence of civil liberty certainly consists in the right of every individual to claim the protection of the laws, whenever he receives an injury. One of the first duties of government is to afford that protection . . . . The government of the United States has been emphatically termed a government of laws, and not of men. It will certainly cease to deserve this

---

[4] 5 U.S. (1 Cranch) 299 (1803), a capitulation which signaled the Court's weakness.

[5] Robert G. McCloskey, The American Supreme Court 40 (1960).

[6] Much useful scholarship has been written about *Marbury. See*, for instance, William E. Nelson, *Marbury v. Madison*: The Origins and Legacy of Judicial Review (2000), William W. Van Alstyne, *A Critical Guide to* Marbury v. Madison, 1969 Duke L.J. 1.

high appellation, if the laws furnish no remedy for the violation of a vested legal right.[7]

But did this grand principle mean that the "supreme executive" was answerable in court for the conduct of his job? Sometimes he is and sometimes he is not, concluded Marshall, the answer turning on "the nature of that act."[8] In the exercise of "political powers," the President and his subordinates had "discretion" for which the President was "accountable only to his country in his political character, and to his own conscience."[9] For these acts, the President and administration were not answerable judicially, only politically. But where executive officials were assigned duties in which they are "directed peremptorily to perform certain acts" on which "the rights of individuals are dependent" they are "amenable to the laws" and cannot disregard such "vested rights of others."[10]

Accordingly, Marshall articulated a framework for determining whether executive acts are judicially reviewable. Where an executive official acts in an area where the President has "constitutional or legal discretion" the acts are political and not subject to judicial scrutiny; where law assigns the executive a duty on which "individual rights depend" an individual who suffers injury from the breach of duty has a legal remedy in court. In concluding that the executive branch was answerable in court for violations of legal rights, Marshall articulated, though in dicta, an important component of the rule of law.

Since Marbury was appointed for a term of years, he had a vested right, not one over which the executive had political discretion. Thus, Marbury's claim was one courts could consider. And the Secretary of State was an officer to whom a court could issue a mandamus under the terms of § 13 of the Judiciary Act of 1789, the provision under which Marbury was proceeding.

These two conclusions outlined in the first parts of the opinion — Marbury was entitled to his commission and the executive was amenable to suit in such circumstances — would suggest that the Court was headed for the fateful collision with the executive branch. But the Court escaped the confrontation with Jefferson and Madison by veering off on a surprising, yet historic, detour.

Having disposed of the merits of the case, Marshall turned to the question of the Court's jurisdiction, a somewhat anomalous order of analysis. Marbury had initiated his case in the Supreme Court under the authority of § 13. That section, as Marshall construed it, empowered the Court to issue a writ of mandamus to an officer of the United States.[11] The interpretation of § 13 Marshall adopted, however, raised the

---

[7] *Marbury*, 5 U.S. at 163.

[8] *Id.* at 165.

[9] *Id.* at 165–66.

[10] *Id.* at 166.

[11] Marshall's interpretation was contestable. The statute may have simply conferred power on the Supreme Court to issue a writ of mandamus in appellate cases or to have that power in cases otherwise within its jurisdiction. *See* DAVID P. CURRIE, THE CONSTITUTION IN THE SUPREME COURT 67–68 & n.22 (1985). If so, § 13 would not have conferred original jurisdiction on the Court and Marbury's claim would have been dismissed. Under either reading, § 13 would not have been inconsistent with the Constitution and accordingly *Marbury* would not have established judicial review.

question whether such an exercise of original jurisdiction by the Supreme Court was consistent with the Constitution? Marshall reasoned that Article III granted the Court original jurisdiction in only two types of cases — those "affecting ambassadors, other public ministers and counsuls, and those in which a state shall be a party."[12] In all other cases identified in Article III, the Court's jurisdiction was appellate. Marbury's claim fell in neither category of original jurisdiction. Even so, if Congress could expand the Court's original jurisdiction, the Court might still have power to consider Marbury's petition. (And since Marshall had already addressed the merits and ruled in Marbury's favor, the outcome in that event was clear). Yet Marshall rejected this possibility. The fact that the Constitution divided the Court's jurisdiction between original and appellate suggested that it did not mean to empower the legislature to expand original jurisdiction.[13]

In retrospect, other points might have been made regarding this issue. The Constitution might simply have stated an initial allocation between the Court's original and appellate jurisdiction but one subject to change. Instead of Marshall's inference that the Constitution would not have allocated cases to these categories if redistribution were permitted, an alternative conclusion would suggest that the Constitution allowed a different division, but unless one was made, the initial position stood as stated. In other words, the two types of cases in the Court's original jurisdiction were simply a starting point subject to change.

The Appellate Jurisdiction or Exceptions Clause conferred appellate jurisdiction over other cases "with such Exceptions, and under such Regulations as the Congress shall make."[14] This clause might support the inference that when the Constitution wanted to allow a change in the initial allocation it specifically authorized one. The lack of an "exceptions" clause in connection with the Original Jurisdiction Clause might support Marshall's view that no expansion of that type of jurisdiction was allowed. Alternatively, the Exceptions Clause permits *reductions* of the Court's appellate jurisdiction, not expansions. Perhaps that clause should therefore be read as a limitation. Under this approach, Congress could reallocate the Court's jurisdiction except to the extent the Exceptions Clause limited that authority. Finally, the Exceptions Clause might allow Congress to move "excepted" forms of appellate jurisdiction from the Court's appellate, to original, jurisdiction.

Marshall's interpretation was contestable but it certainly was not frivolous. Indeed, in *Stuart v. Laird*, Charles Lee had argued in a different context that the Constitution limited the Court's original jurisdiction to two types of cases and that "[n]o act of Congress can extend the original jurisdiction of the Supreme Court beyond the bounds limited by the Constitution."[15] Similarly, in the Federalist Papers, Alexander Hamilton had argued that the Court's original jurisdiction "would be confined to two classes of causes," suggesting that at least one important framer in 1788 agreed with and publicized the interpretation Marshall ultimately

---

[12] U.S. Const. art. III, § 2, cl. 2.

[13] *Marbury*, 5 U.S. at 174.

[14] U.S. Const. art. III, § 2, cl. 2.

[15] Stuart v. Laird, 5 U.S. (1 Cranch) 299, 305 (1803).

adopted 15 years later.[16]

In any event, Marshall concluded that the Constitution imposed a ceiling, not a floor, on the Court's original jurisdiction. To the extent § 13 sought to expand the Court's original jurisdiction it violated the Constitution. The Court could only issue a mandamus in Marbury's case incident to its appellate jurisdiction. But Marbury's case did not implicate the Court's appellate jurisdiction since it asked the Court to direct the writ to the executive branch rather than to review a lower court proceeding.

Marshall's conclusion that § 13 conflicted with Article III raised a central issue in the case: whether a statute "repugnant to the Constitution" was nonetheless the law of the land. In creating the Constitution, the people exercised their "original right" and set forth "fundamental" principles. The Constitution was designed in part to limit government. If Congress could legislate beyond the bounds the Constitution set, Congress would not be limited.[17] The Constitution was paramount law which trumped any inconsistent statute. Section 13 was invalid because it violated the Constitution. That Congress had duly enacted § 13 was not dispositive.

Marshall's conclusion that § 13 was unconstitutional suggested Marshall's willingness to depart from original intent. Section 13 was passed by a Congress which included numerous members who had attended the Constitutional Convention in Philadelphia or one of the state ratifying conventions and signed by President George Washington. Presumably, these men who adopted the Constitution knew what it meant. Surely they must have crafted § 13 so it would be consistent with their understanding of the limits of federal judicial power in the document they created. Yet Marshall held § 13 unconstitutional even though its adoption by founders must have suggested their intent regarding constitutional meaning.

Not only was Marshall not guided by this arguable original intent, he did not rely on that form of argument in deciding the case. The founders probably did not enjoy the same special stature among their contemporaries that history assigned them. Moreover, in 1803 the constitution did not itself command the credibility it subsequently claimed. Marshall assumed the responsibility to educate his contemporaries regarding its merit. Marshall may not have relied on the framers' intent in part because he did not believe that style of argument would persuade his contemporaries that the Constitution would lead to good government.[18] Marshall's willingness to overturn § 13 went further and implicitly rejected originalism as a dispositive mode of constitutional argument. Marshall relied primarily on structural argument in arguing that the Constitution was paramount. He inferred that principle from the Constitution's design and the principles underlying it. However, toward the end of the opinion, Marshall invoked the Supremacy Clause to bolster this conclusion. He pointed out that it listed the Constitution before mentioning laws and treaties, and only gave effect to laws made in pursuance of the Constitution.[19] This point confirmed the preeminent status of the Constitution,

---

[16] THE FEDERALIST No. 81 (Alexander Hamilton).

[17] *Marbury*, 5 U.S. at 176–77.

[18] *See* Christopher Eisgruber, *John Marshall's Judicial Rhetoric*, 1996 SUP. CT. REV. 439.

[19] *Marbury*, 5 U.S. at 180.

according to Marshall.

Marshall's reliance on the Supremacy Clause to demonstrate the primacy of the Constitution was not entirely convincing. The statement that the Constitution and all federal statutes made "in pursuance thereof" are supreme law is subject to at least two readings. "In pursuance thereof" could mean "consistent with" as Marshall argued, thereby suggesting that the only valid statutes were those in accord with the Constitution. Alternatively, it could have a chronological meaning, separating those statutes passed before the Constitution (which were not supreme laws) from those passed later (which were). Under that interpretation, the Supremacy Clause would not seem to elevate the Constitution above federal statutes.

But Marshall's conclusion was supported by the structural principle that the Constitution was adopted in part to limit government. Without a principle of constitutional preeminence, the only checks on government would be those the democratic process imposed. Moreover, the disparity between the onerous requirements for amending the Constitution (a super majority in each house of Congress and super majority state action) and the more modest requirements of passing a simple law suggested the superior authority of the Constitution. Further, the Exceptions Clause itself implies that the Constitution trumps statutory law. If Congress could override the Constitution by passing statutes, there would be no need to authorize Congress to change the Court's appellate jurisdiction in that manner.[20] Finally, Hamilton had written in the Federalist Papers "that the Constitution ought to be the standard of construction for the laws, and that wherever there is an evident opposition, the laws ought to give place to the Constitution" a principle he, too, deduced from "the general theory of a limited Constitution."[21]

Having established that the Constitution is supreme, Marshall had one more major concept to establish, the power of judicial review. The concept that the Constitution was supreme did not compel the conclusion that the Court had the power to decide when a statute clashed with the Constitution. Marshall argued that courts were not bound to enforce legislative acts like § 13 "repugnant to the Constitution." The survival of limited government required that the Court review the constitutionality of statutes in the course of deciding cases. "It is emphatically the province and duty of the judicial department to say what the law is," wrote Marshall in *Marbury*'s most quoted passage.[22] The traditional function of the judge was to decide cases, a task that required interpreting the law. That function, in American theory, necessarily involves the power to determine whether a law offends the Constitution. If repugnancy exists, the judge must give effect to that of superior obligation, the Constitution.

Marshall invoked several specific clauses of the Constitution to support his point. He defended the power of judicial review by pointing out that Article III extended

---

[20] *See* John Harrison, *The Constitutional Origins and Implications of Judicial Review*, 84 Va. L. Rev. 333, 347 (1998).

[21] The Federalist No. 81 (Alexander Hamilton).

[22] *Marbury*, 5 U.S. at 177.

the "judicial power" to "all cases arising under the Constitution."[23] The jurisdictional grant implied that the Court should consider the Constitution in deciding a case. Chief Justice Marshall also pointed out that judges take an oath to support the Constitution which implied that they may interpret it.[24]

These arguments may not be as conclusive as Marshall suggested. The jurisdictional grant could be just that — a grant of power to decide a certain species of cases without suggesting that the Court had power to declare that the legislature had acted unlawfully. Moreover, the judicial oath begged the question. Legislators and Presidents also take an oath to support the Constitution. If the judges' oath empowered them to interpret the Constitution, does not the legislators' and Presidents' oaths give them the same license? Moreover, the Oath Clause at most directs officials to enforce the Constitution. That duty would include enforcing whatever guidance the Constitution contained or implied regarding who interprets the Constitution. But the direction to enforce the Constitution does not necessarily suggest that the enforcer is the authoritative interpreter.

The final portion of Marshall's opinion asserted three fundamental principles of American constitutional law — ours is a government of limited power, the Constitution is paramount law, and the Court has a power of judicial review in cases before it, i.e., to examine whether or not a legislative act is consistent with the Constitution. At times, Marshall skipped from point to point, blurring the distinctions between the three concepts.[25] He no doubt sought to emphasize the relationship between the various ideas and to strengthen each argument by associating them with the others.

Marbury established foundational principles regarding our system of government. Marshall's arguments articulated the basic commitment to the rule of law which subjected government to limits. *Marbury* illustrated that principle through Marshall's criticism of the executive's refusal to give Marbury his commission and through his statement of the ideal. Yet he also signalled that concept by his refusal to allow Congress to expand the Court's original jurisdiction. To be sure, this decision was strategic. Presumably, Marshall preferred not to have jurisdiction so he could avoid a confrontation with Jefferson and Madison. Yet it also signalled the Court's unwillingness to assume a power which it did not believe the Constitution gave it. This posture was rich in symbolism for it communicated the judiciary's adherence to the rule of law even when that commitment ostensibly cost it jurisdiction. In so doing, it solidified its claim to a more significant power, that of judicial review.

---

[23] *Id.* at 178.

[24] *Id.* at 180.

[25] *See, e.g.*, Van Alstyne, *supra* note 6, at 17.

§ 2.02   JUDICIAL REVIEW

[1]   Constitutional Arguments

The doctrine of judicial review is a central feature of the constitutional system. It empowers courts, in cases before them, to examine legislation to assess its compliance with the Constitution. The doctrine is a central tenet from Chief Justice Marshall's landmark opinion in *Marbury v. Madison*.[26]

The Constitution does not expressly authorize judicial review. Nor do the textual reeds Marshall relied on compel the conclusion that the Constitution gave the judiciary that power. Article III provides that "[t]he judicial power shall extend to all cases . . . arising under this Constitution."[27] But that clause might simply confer jurisdiction rather than license courts to interpret the Constitution. Judges do, as Marshall pointed out, take an oath to support the Constitution. But that does not necessarily anoint them as interpreters. Others, including the legislators who enacted the statutes, also take oaths. Moreover, the question remains: Who does the Constitution empower to interpret?

Yet judicial review, too, might be inferred from the Constitution's history, text and structure. Although the text does not compel judicial review it is at least hospitable to the institution. Considerable evidence suggested the framers intended to lodge such a power in the federal courts.[28] Many delegates to the Constitutional Convention seem to have assumed federal courts would have such a power.[29] Judicial review was part of the legal tradition of the time. Written constitutions had developed from the colonial commitment to limited government. Those documents could succeed only if treated as fundamental law, a concept which suggested judicial enforcement of their provisions.

The principles Marshall articulated resonated with contemporary thought. Alexander Hamilton had foreshadowed much of Marshall's argument in Federalist No. 78. "The interpretation of the laws is the proper and peculiar province of the courts. A Constitution is . . . a fundamental law," wrote Hamilton, making the case for ratification of the Constitution. The courts were duty-bound to interpret the Constitution and the statutes and give effect to the former in case of "an irreconcilable variance between the two."[30] Between the Revolution and *Marbury v. Madison*, state courts asserted or exercised review power in at least 20 cases.[31]

---

[26] 5 U.S. (1 Cranch) 137 (1803).

[27] U.S. Const. art. III, cl. 1.

[28] *See generally* Bernard Schwartz, A History of the Supreme Court 22–24, 41–43 (1993); Alexander M. Bickel, The Least Dangerous Branch: The Supreme Court at the Bar of Politics 15–16 (1962).

[29] Richard H. Fallon, Jr. et al., Hart and Wechsler's the Federal Courts and the Federal System 11–12 (5th ed. 2003).

[30] The Federalist No. 78 (Alexander Hamilton).

[31] *See, e.g.*, Bernard Schwartz, The Great Rights of Mankind: A History of the American Bill of Rights 95–100 (1992).

Indeed, in *Stuart v. Laird*[32] the Court also considered, and upheld, the constitutionality of Congress' repeal of the Judiciary Act of 1801,. In so doing, implicitly, the Court exercised a power to review the constitutionality of acts of Congress. If the Court lacked the power of judicial review, it had no right to consider the validity of the law at issue in *Stuart v. Laird*. Marshall himself affirmed, in *Marbury*, not that the Constitution established judicial review, but that it "confirms and strengthens the principle."[33]

Judicial review helps make constitutional provisions legally enforceable rules rather than just hortatory expressions of maxims of political morality. The people enacted a written Constitution to restrain government. Absent legal machinery to enforce the Constitution, its limitations would depend entirely on the democratic process.

Yet relying on democratic institutions alone to enforce the Constitution runs substantial risk. A Constitution exists in part to limit the powers of political majorities by removing certain options from the people's representatives. Vesting the political branches with the sole authority to interpret the Constitution may not be quite like hiring the fox to guard the chicken coop, but it does invite the legislature to aggrandize its power and leave minorities at risk.

Of course, giving that role to the federal judiciary also runs a risk. It, too, may abuse its power. As Alexander Bickel pointed out, "the Constitution does not limit the power of the legislature alone. It limits that of the courts as well, and it may be equally absurd, therefore, to allow courts to set the limits."[34] On the other hand, the Constitution gives federal judges life tenure and salary protection to insulate them from majoritarian pressures. They would seem to have greater incentive to enforce constitutional boundaries. Of course, the judiciary may be inclined, consciously or unconsciously, to favor its own institutional interests. But possessed of neither the purse nor the sword, it is the "least dangerous" branch and thus is least likely to encroach on the turf of other branches or suppress individual freedoms.[35]

Moreover, judicial review has come to be, in some fashion, an accepted institution of American government. Countless cases apply it. Regardless of its textual and historical basis, the doctrine is a firmly established practice of American government too entrenched to consider displacing.

[2] Later Formulations of Judicial Review

Marshall reiterated the power of judicial review on other occasions. Thus, in *McCulloch v. Maryland*,[36] he began by noting that the case involved a challenge to the validity of an act of Congress. "On the Supreme Court of the United States has the Constitution of our country devolved this important duty," he said reasserting

---

[32] 5 U.S. (1 Cranch) 299 (1803).

[33] *Marbury*, 5 U.S. at 180.

[34] BICKEL, *supra* note 28, at 3–4.

[35] *See* THE FEDERALIST No. 78 (Alexander Hamilton).

[36] 17 U.S. (4 Wheat.) 316 (1819).

the power of judicial review.[37] Later, in the same opinion, he suggested that if Congress "adopt[ed] measures which are prohibited by the Constitution . . . it would become the painful duty of this tribunal, should a case requiring such a decision come before it, to say that such an act was not the law of the land."[38] Two years later, in *Cohens v. Virginia* he wrote:

> If such be the constitution, it is the duty of the Court to bow with respectful submission to its provisions. If such be not the constitution, it is equally the duty of this Court to say so; and to perform that task which the American people have assigned to the judicial department.[39]

Since *Marbury*, the Court has frequently invoked its role as constitutional interpreter. Although the Court did not declare another federal law unconstitutional until 1857, at different stages of our history it has deployed that power more frequently. Particularly when its authority has been challenged, the Court has asserted its power in strong language.

Thus, in *Cooper v. Aaron*, the Court responded to southern resistence to judicial school desegregation orders by invoking *Marbury*. "This decision declared the basic principle that the federal judiciary is supreme in the exposition of the law of the Constitution, and that principle has ever since been respected by this Court and the Country as a permanent and indispensable feature of our constitutional system."[40]

Cooper v. Aaron involved a challenge to federal judicial authority by state officials but the Court has issued similar statements vis a vis Congress[41] and the Executive.[42] The Rehnquist Court deployed the *Marbury* principle more frequently, often invoking *Marbury* as support when it held unconstitutional some act of a coordinate branch.[43]

In *Marbury*, Marshall's use of judicial review allowed him to sidestep a confrontation with the Executive. By 1974, when the Court decided *United States v. Nixon* the concept was sufficiently robust for the Court to deploy it to order President Richard M. Nixon to disclose communications which revealed his criminal complicity in the Watergate coverup. The Court unanimously rejected Nixon's claim that he, not it, had power to interpret the Constitution regarding access to presidential documents. It relied on *Marbury* to support its claim. To be sure, Nixon's political weakness limited his ability to contest the Court's claim. Yet his ultimate compliance with the Court's order spoke volumes regarding the status of judicial review.

---

[37] *Id.* at 401.

[38] *Id.* at 423.

[39] 19 U.S. (6 Wheat.) 264, 377 (1821).

[40] 358 U.S. 1, 18 (1958).

[41] *See, e.g.*, Powell v. McCormack, 395 U.S. 486 (1969).

[42] *See, e.g.*, United States v. Nixon, 418 U.S. 683 (1974).

[43] *See, e.g.*, United States v. Morrison, 529 U.S. 598, 616 n.7 (2000); City of Boerne v. Flores, 521 U.S. 507, 516 (1997); Clinton v. Jones, 520 U.S. 681, 703 (1997); Miller v. Johnson, 515 U.S. 900, 922 (1995); United States v. Lopez, 514 U.S. 549, 566 (1995); Plaut v. Spendthrift Farm, Inc., 514 U.S. 211, 218 (1995).

Although the Court did not mention *Marbury* by name in *Bush v. Gore*,[44] the *per curiam* opinion reflected the *Marbury* metaphor of the Court as constitutional interpreter. It concluded:

> None are more conscious of the vital limits on judicial authority than are the Members of this Court, and none stand more in admiration of the Constitution's design to leave the selection of the President to the people, through their legislatures, and to the political sphere. When contending parties invoke the process of the courts, however, it becomes our unsought responsibility to resolve the federal and constitutional issues the judicial system has been forced to confront.[45]

Indeed, the passage was reminiscent of Chief Justice Marshall's prose in *McCulloch v. Maryland* quoted earlier.[46]

The Court's action in *Bush v. Gore*, regardless of one's view of the merits, was historic in its implications regarding judicial review. On two occasions, it granted certiorari in response to petitions from Governor George W. Bush to review decisions of the Florida Supreme Court regarding the manual recount of Florida's vote.[47] The Court issued three decisions in two cases over a span of only eight days.[48] Its decision in *Bush v. Gore* effectively ended Vice President Al Gore's effort to recount Florida's vote and established Governor Bush as the next President.

Scholars differ on the merits of the decision and of its underlying rationale and the propriety of the Court accepting Governor Bush's invitation to involve itself. Regardless of one's view of these issues or of the wisdom of the Court's course, the fact that the Court took and decided the case is telling.

The case illustrates the robust role the Court has assumed in interpreting the Constitution. Whereas Chief Justice Marshall exercised judicial review to decline jurisdiction being bestowed on the Court, the *per curiam* opinion in *Bush v. Gore* interpreted the Constitution to resolve a Presidential election.

Moreover, two centuries of historical development made the five justices who joined the *Bush v. Gore* majority far more confident than Chief Justice Marshall felt. Whereas realities may have imposed circumspection on Chief Justice Marshall in dodging a confrontation with the executive branch, those joining the *per curiam* demonstrated little caution in exercising their "unsought responsibility."

Marbury, of course, identified the rule of law with the requirement that a judicial remedy be available to enforce every right. This norm is not always realized; the legal system compromises this principle by granting immunities from legal recourse or by occasionally imposing procedural or other barriers which leave rights

---

[44] 531 U.S. 98 (2000).

[45] *Id.* at 111.

[46] See Text accompanying footnotes 36 to 38 in this chapter. *McCulloch*, 17 U.S. at 423. *See also McCulloch*, 17 U.S. at 400–401.

[47] *See* Bush v. Gore, 531 U.S. 98 (2000); Bush v. Palm Beach County Canvassing Bd., 531 U.S. 70 (2000).

[48] In addition to the two decisions cited above, the Court granted Governor Bush's application for a stay of the recount in a 5-4 decision. Bush v. Gore, 531 U.S. 1046 (2000).

unvindicated. *Bush v. Gore* provided a rather prominent instance in which the Court sacrificed the principle from *Marbury*. The *per curiam* opinion did not upset the decision of the Florida Supreme Court that Vice President Gore had a right to a recount. It found, however, that no remedy could be afforded to vindicate Vice President Gore's right given the exigencies of the electoral calendar.

Marshall took occasion to reassert the Court's power of judicial review during his tenure on the Court. Yet it is important to keep perspective on the value of that institution to his work. On Marshall's watch, the Court did not wield the power to strike down numerous acts of Congress. On the contrary, it was not until 1857 in *Dred Scott v. Sandford*[49] that the Court held another act of Congress unconstitutional. Marshall suggested that the power of judicial review should rarely be used to invalidate a law.

> The question, whether a law be void for its repugnancy to the constitution, is, at all times, a question of much delicacy, which ought seldom, if ever, to be decided in the affirmative, in a doubtful case . . . . The opposition between the constitution and the law should be such that the judge feels a clear and strong conviction of their incompatibility with each other.[50]

On the other hand, the Marshall Court reviewed federal statutes which it found constitutional, thereby adding legitimacy to Congress' work.

§ 2.03   SOLE OR ULTIMATE INTERPRETER?

To be sure, other officials also have responsibilities to interpret the Constitution and at times various presidents, members of Congress and state officials have asserted such a prerogative. In vetoing a law the Court had previously upheld, President Andrew Jackson said:

> It is as much the duty of the House of Representatives, of the Senate, and of the President to decide upon the constitutionality of any bill or resolution which may be presented to them for passage or approval as it is of the supreme judges when it may be brought before them for judicial decision . . . . The authority of the Supreme Court must not, therefore be permitted to control the Congress or Executive when acting in their legislative capacities, but to have only such influence as the force of their reasoning may deserve,[51]

Other Presidents have sounded similar themes.[52] These claims are controversial. Still, a growing body of scholarship suggests that in addition to the judiciary other

---

[49] 60 U.S. (19 How.) 393 (1857).

[50] Fletcher v. Peck, 10 U.S. (6 Cranch) 87, 128 (1810).

[51] Andrew Jackson Veto Message (July 10, 1832), *in* MESSAGES AND PAPERS OF THE PRESIDENTS 1145 (1897).

[52] *See, e.g.*, Abraham Lincoln's First Inaugural Address (Mar. 4, 1861), *in* MESSAGES AND PAPERS OF THE PRESIDENTS.

branches must also interpret the Constitution. Some question the idea that the Court is the ultimate interpreter.[53]

Although not totally free of ambiguity, much of *Marbury* is consistent with a robust interpretive role for other institutions. *Marbury* can be read as claiming simply the power to review statutes as they arise in cases before the Court, not as making the Court the exclusive or ultimate constitutional voice. The strongest statement — "It is emphatically the province and duty of the judicial department to say what the law is" — comes in a paragraph discussing the Court's power to decide *cases*. The fact that the Court can interpret law in deciding cases need not mean that its interpretation thereafter binds all future governmental action. Elsewhere, *Marbury* seems to recognize that other branches also interpret law. "*[C]ourts*, as well as other departments, are bound by [the Constitution]."[54] The Constitution provides "a rule for the government of *courts*, as well as of the legislature."[55] If courts must interpret the Constitution to keep within its limits, presumably other branches also have some power to interpret based on the fact that it binds them, too. If *Marbury* is understood as establishing simply a power of judicial review of statutes that arise in cases before courts but not claiming for the Court the status of the sole or final arbitrator of all constitutional questions, the necessary conflict between *Marbury* and declarations of Andrew Jackson, et al. is less severe.

Alternatively, *Marbury* might stand for the proposition that the Court is the final constitutional interpreter regarding some, but not all, constitutional questions. Constitutional issues which arise in some contexts are left to other branches to interpret. Thus during the Nixon and Clinton impeachment proceedings, members of Congress had to interpret "other high crimes and misdemeanors" to determine whether the acts charged were impeachable. Similarly, a president might decide to issue a veto or pardon based on constitutional grounds.

Yet there is some sense in which many believe that the Court occupies a special role as constitutional interpreter. During the twentieth century, the Court has invoked *Marbury* as articulating "the basic principle that the federal judiciary is supreme in the exposition of the law of the Constitution."[56] *Cooper* and some of the Court's other pronouncements assert this doctrine of judicial supremacy. The implication of this position is that other branches of government must generally defer to the Court's constitutional interpretations. One function of law is to resolve certain disputes. It arguably cannot discharge this role if decisions are not accorded deference.

---

[53] *See, e.g.,* MARK TUSHNET, TAKING THE CONSTITUTION AWAY FROM THE COURTS (1999); LOUIS FISHER, CONSTITUTIONAL DIALOGUES: INTERPRETATION AS POLITICAL PROCESS (1988); Neal Devins & Louis Fisher, *Judicial Exclusivity and Political Instability*, 84 VA. L. REV. 83 (1998); Michael Stokes Paulsen, *The Most Dangerous Branch: Executive Power to Say What the Law Is*, 83 GEO. L.J. 217 (1994).

[54] *Marbury,* 5 U.S. at 180 (emphasis in original).

[55] *Id.* (emphasis in original).

[56] Cooper v. Aaron, 358 U.S. 1, 18 (1958). *See also* Clinton v. Jones, 520 U.S. 681 (1997); United States v. Nixon, 418 U.S. 683 (1974). *But see* STEPHEN BREYER, MAKING OUR DEMOCRACY WORK: A JUDGE'S VIEW 62–63 (2010) (pointing out that the Court in *Cooper* extended *Marbury* in order "to make clear its power to issue highly unpopular constitutional decisions").

Constitutional law helps coordinate disparate views of multiple actors, something that cannot occur if each can perpetually resist decisions he does not like.[57] Some institution must perform this function and the Court is deemed best suited for this role. Lacking the purse and sword and a democratic mandate, it is perhaps least likely to abuse such a power. Life tenure and salary protection insulate the judiciary from public pressure and allow its members to consider the claims of unrepresented parties, too. Nor can the Court itself initiate judicial review; some third party must invite its involvement. Finally, the judicial process, which features argument, elaborated decisions, and the judges' training, equips them for this role.[58] In practice, the Court's constitutional decisions receive substantial, though not complete, deference as the final word.

§ 2.04 JUSTIFICATIONS OF JUDICIAL REVIEW

Since *Marbury*, judges and scholars have focused much attention on the justifications behind judicial review. The central dilemma arises from the challenge that judicial view is undemocratic since it vests in unelected judges the power to override on constitutional grounds the work of the people's representatives. The great historian, Henry Steele Commager, argued that judicial review was an anomaly in a democratic system since it allowed an unelected and unremovable branch to reject the work of the elected and accountable branches.[59] Moreover, judges, like other officials, may exceed constitutional limits and abuse their power. To canvass suggested possibilities would fill a book in itself. The following paragraphs suggest some theories without making any claim to providing a comprehensive account.

In one prominent early article,[60] James B. Thayer sought to justify judicial review by limiting it to a "clear mistake" rule. Judges should only "disregard" a statute when the coordinate legislature "have not merely made a mistake, but have made a very clear one — so clear that it is not open to rational question."[61] This show of judicial humility would help reconcile judicial review with the democratic basis of our system. Moreover, under any circumstances, the judiciary can do relatively little to prevent abuse. "Under no system can the power of courts go far to save a people from ruin; our chief protection lies elsewhere."[62] That being so, judicial modesty might encourage the people to assume a more active role in keeping their representatives in check.

---

[57] Larry Alexander & Frederick Schauer, *On Extrajudicial Constitutional Interpretation*, 110 HARV. L. REV. 1359 (1997).

[58] *See, e.g.*, BICKEL, *supra* note 28.

[59] Henry Steele Commager, *Judicial Review and Democracy*, 19 VA. Q. 417 (1943). *See also* BICKEL, *supra* note 28, at 16 ("The root difficulty is that judicial review is a counter-majoritarian force in our system.").

[60] James B. Thayer, *The Origin and Scope of the American Doctrine of Constitutional Law*, 7 HARV. L. REV. 129 (1893).

[61] *Id.* at 144.

[62] *Id.* at 156.

Seventy years later, Professor Alexander Bickel[63] argued that the Court was well-equipped to interpret the Constitution to articulate "certain enduring values"[64] because it was the least dangerous branch. Life tenure freed the justices from paralyzing anxieties regarding job security and allowed them to interpret the Constitution impartially. The justices' legal training prepared them well for that enterprise.[65] Judges have unique "capacities for dealing with matters of principle." Moreover, "[j]udges have, or should have, the leisure, the training, and the insulation to follow the ways of the scholar in pursuing the ends of government."[66] Although judicial review was a "deviant institution in the American democracy" it could achieve "a tolerable accommodation with the theory and practice of democracy."[67]

Bickel's contemporary, Professor Charles L. Black, Jr., justified judicial review on a different basis.[68] Its main role was to provide legitimacy to governmental conduct. The power to invalidate carried with it the more important power to validate. "What a government of limited power needs . . . is some means of satisfying the people that it has taken all steps humanly possible to stay within its powers."[69] The Court's power to strike down actions as unconstitutional allows it to validate those actions it approves.

Professor, later Judge, Robert H. Bork[70] argued that judicial review was justified to the extent it remained true to the original understanding of the Constitution. Like Chief Justice Marshall, he linked judicial review to the existence of a written Constitution and its status as law.[71] The Constitution placed certain issues "off-limits for judges."[72] He wrote:[73]

> In both its vindication of principle against democratic majorities and its vindication of democracy against unprincipled judicial activism, the philosophy of original understanding does better by far than any other theory of constitutional adjudication can. If that is not good enough, judicial review under the Constitution cannot be legitimate. I think it is good enough.

Professor John Hart Ely[74] advocated a representation reinforcing theory of judicial review. He took his inspiration from Justice Stone's famous footnote in *United States v. Carolene Products Co.*,[75] which suggested that courts should most strictly

---

[63] BICKEL, *supra* note 28.

[64] *Id.* at 24.

[65] *See id.* at 25.

[66] *Id.* at 25–26.

[67] *Id.* at 28.

[68] CHARLES L. BLACK, JR., THE PEOPLE AND THE COURT (1960).

[69] *Id.* at 52.

[70] ROBERT H. BORK, THE TEMPTING OF AMERICA: THE POLITICAL SEDUCTION OF THE LAW (1990).

[71] *Id.* at 28.

[72] *Id.* at 163.

[73] *Id.* at 163–64.

[74] *See* JOHN HART ELY, DEMOCRACY AND DISTRUST: A THEORY OF JUDICIAL REVIEW (1980).

[75] 304 U.S. 144, 152–53 n.4 (1938).

scrutinize legislation which violated a specific provision of the Constitution, which restricted the political process which might otherwise remedy undesirable legislation, or which was directed at racial or religious minorities. Focusing on the latter two clauses, Professor Ely reasoned that the Constitution placed a high value on decisions democratically made. Where political processes were impeded or insular minorities were oppressed, it is fair to assume that either the democratic process cannot work or has failed to work. The Court's role is to act as a backstop, to review governmental acts where one can conclude that the political process is undermined.

Professor Christopher L. Eisgruber[76] finds a different justification of, and role for, judicial review. He sees the Constitution "as a practical device that launches and maintains a sophisticated set of institutions which, in combination, are well-suited to implement self-government."[77] Judicial review is not an exception to democratic rule in part because democracy is not synonymous with majority rule. Rather, the Court is "a kind of representative institution well-shaped to speak on behalf of the people about questions of moral and political principle."[78]

Finally, another contemporary scholar, Richard H. Fallon, Jr.[79] sees the Court as engaged not in a philosopher's search for "one right answer." Rather, Professor Fallon describes the Court as serving "a more multifaceted [role] of 'implementing' constitutional norms" by seeking collaborative solutions to constitutional questions as they arise in cases.[80] He regards the question regarding the propriety of judicial review as a "serious one."[81] He points out, however, that courts often examine decisions by relatively invisible and unaccountable officials, that legislatures rarely act based on careful consideration of "ultimate constitutional principles,"[82] and that other political actors, in practice, often operate on the assumption of judicial review. Thus, the Court acts "as an institution of, rather than as an impediment to, constitutional democracy."[83] He predicts that, on balance, "the exercise of independent judicial judgment is likely, over time, to lead to better specification and implementation of constitutional values than would an alternative regime."[84]

§ 2.05 REVIEW OF STATE ACTION

In *Marbury*, the Court reviewed, and held unconstitutional, an act of Congress. Critical as the power to review Congress' acts has been, it represents only part, and not the most important part, of the doctrine of judicial review. The Court did not strike down another act of Congress during the remainder of Marshall's tenure as Chief Justice. It did, however, in a number of notable cases, address the constitu

---

[76] Christopher L. Eisgruber, Constitutional Self-Government (2001).

[77] *Id.* at 3.

[78] *Id.*

[79] Richard H. Fallon, Jr., Implementing the Constitution (2001).

[80] *Id.* at 5.

[81] *Id.* at 9.

[82] *Id.*

[83] *Id.*

[84] *Id.* at 10.

tionality of state legislative acts. The power to review the validity of *state* action is probably more important if the Constitution is to survive as supreme law throughout the land. As Justice Oliver Wendell Holmes later put it, "I do not think the United States would come to an end if we lost our power to declare an Act of Congress void. I do think the Union would be imperiled if we could not make that declaration as to the law of the several States."[85]

[1] Fletcher v. Peck

In *Fletcher v. Peck*,[86] the Supreme Court held a Georgia law unconstitutional. Georgia's legislature had been bribed in 1795 to pass a law directing the sale of Alabama and Mississippi for a pittance. The following year it repealed the grant. The Court, after ducking questions of legislative motive,[87] found the repeal violated the Contract Clause.[88] In so ruling, Marshall rejected the notion that a state was an isolated sovereign free of restrictions except those in its own constitution. On the contrary, the Federal Constitution circumscribes state legislatures.[89] The Supreme Court must have the authority to review the constitutionality of state laws to enforce those limitations.

Fletcher laid a second cornerstone in the foundation of our constitutional law-judicial review over state legislatures. This doctrine was insufficient alone to preserve the Constitution as supreme law. The federal judiciary also required power to review state court decisions to maintain the supremacy of federal law over conflicting state law or action.

[2] Martin v. Hunter's Lessee

The first Judiciary Act, which the first Congress adopted in 1789, recognized the Supreme Court's vital function of upholding national supremacy through its power to review state-court decisions. Section 25 of the 1789 Act empowered the Supreme Court to review the decisions of state courts that (a) invalidated a statute or treaty of the United States or an act of a federal official; (b) upheld a state statute or act of a state official against a claim that it was contrary to the Constitution, treaties, or laws of the United States; or (c) denied a "title, right, privilege or exemption specially set up or claimed by either party" under the Constitution, or any treaty or statute of, or commission held under, the United States. The fact that Congress authorized Supreme Court review over state decisions adverse to federal law suggested that it wanted some check on state court decisions which might erode federal law due to state hostility to or underevaluation of federal interests. Subsequent versions have expanded the Supreme Court's jurisdiction to hear state court appeals.[90]

---

[85] Oliver Wendell Holmes, Collected Legal Papers 295–96 (1920).

[86] 10 U.S. (6 Cranch) 87 (1810).

[87] *Id.* at 130.

[88] U.S. Const. art. I, § 10, cl. 1 (No State shall . . . pass any Law impairing the Obligation of Contracts.).

[89] *See, e.g.*, U.S. Const. art. I, § 10; amend. XIV.

[90] The present provision is in 28 U.S.C. § 1257.

Throughout our history, § 25 and its more recent versions have been subject to both legislative and judicial attacks. Early assaults gave rise to landmark decisions in *Martin v. Hunter's Lessee*[91] and *Cohens v. Virginia*.[92]

Martin arose after the highest court of Virginia refused to follow the Supreme Court's mandate in an earlier case. The Supreme Court had reversed a decision of the Virginia Court of Appeals in the earlier case as contrary to a treaty. The Supreme Court then issued its mandate to the Virginia court "commanding" entry of judgment in accordance with the Supreme Court decision. After lengthy argument and consideration, the Virginia court declined to obey the mandate, declaring that § 25 of the Judiciary Act "is not in pursuance of the constitution of the United States." The Virginia Court did not deny that it was bound by the United States' Constitution. It contended rather that in cases initiated in state courts, it was the final voice.

The Supreme Court rejected Virginia's position. The Constitution extended judicial power and the Supreme Court's appellate jurisdiction to "all cases . . . arising under . . . the laws of the United States and treaties," not just to those commenced in federal court, Justice Story wrote for the Court. "It is the *case*, then, and not the *Court*, that gives the jurisdiction,"[93] he asserted. This formulation proved too much; surely the Court did not claim jurisdiction to hear appeals from foreign courts which interpreted American law. Moreover, Justice Story's reliance on the argument that the "letter of the Constitution" disclosed no "qualification" regarding the tribunal from where the law arose was not conclusive proof for his position. After all, the Constitution is silent regarding a number of central principles, e.g., judicial review.

But some of his other arguments fortified his textual conclusions. The framers expected some cases involving federal law to be filed in state court with appeal to the Supreme Court. If Congress did not create lower federal courts, Supreme Court appellate review would be necessary to extend federal judicial power to the extent Article III required.[94] Moreover, the Virginia court's refusal to comply with the mandate was an insult to the constitutional structure. Supreme Court review of state court decisions, as described in § 25, was a prerequisite to the survival of an effective written constitution in a federation. Absent such review, state court decisions might infringe critical national interests[95] and jeopardize the supremacy of federal law. Moreover, a central revising authority must exist to control the discordant judgments of the state judiciaries and harmonize them with the laws, treaties, and Constitution of the United States.[96] Justice Story echoed Alexander Hamilton's view in The Federalist Papers #80 that "the mere necessity of

---

[91] 14 U.S. (1 Wheat.) 304 (1816).

[92] 19 U.S. (6 Wheat.) 264 (1821).

[93] 14 U.S. at 338 (emphasis in original).

[94] *Id.* at 341–42.

[95] *Id.* at 347.

[96] *Id.* Marshall recused himself due to a personal interest. Nonetheless, some suspect he played a role in the opinion Justice Joseph Story wrote for the Court. *See* BERNARD SCHWARTZ, A HISTORY OF THE SUPREME COURT 44 (1993).

uniformity in the interpretation of the national laws" argued for federal courts.[97]

[3]   Cohens v. Virginia

Despite the unqualified nature of Justice Story's assertion of the Supreme Court's review power over state-court decisions, the question emerged again, in slightly different form, five years later, in *Cohens v. Virginia*.[98] A Virginia court had convicted two brothers of violating that state's prohibition on the sale of lottery tickets. Defendants had claimed an Act of Congress authorized the District of Columbia lottery. After their state court conviction, defendants brought the case to the Supreme Court. They claimed that any state law prohibiting sale of lottery tickets conflicted with federal law and was void. Virginia again contested the Supreme Court appellate jurisdiction as an infringement on state courts.

No personal interest sidelined Marshall who wrote the opinion upholding appellate jurisdiction over state courts. Virginia's argument against jurisdiction, Marshall declared, violated the Constitution. The states were members of a nation with a government competent to attain all national objects; they were not independent sovereigns. The Supreme Court must have power to revise the decisions of local tribunals on national questions. It would be unnatural to suppose that the Constitution would entrust the survival of its laws to state, rather than federal courts.[99] State judges often were dependent on the state legislature and thus could not be relied upon to protect federal rights.[100]

[4]   Cooper v. Aaron

Marshall's opinion upheld the constitutionality of § 25 of the Judiciary Act and the competence of the Supreme Court to review state court decisions. Yet some have continued to resist the jurisdiction of the federal courts as contrary to federalism. For instance, in *Cooper v. Aaron*,[101] the Court was compelled to reassert the authority of the federal judiciary and the obligation of state officials to support the Constitution. Arkansas officials contested the authority of federal courts to order school desegregation to enforce the mandate of *Brown v. Board of Education*.[102] The Court acknowledged the significance of the case not only by issuing an opinion which all nine justices signed as co-authors but also by specific language. "As this case reaches us it raises questions of the highest importance to the maintenance of our federal system of government,"[103] the opinion began. The Court rejected Arkansas' argument and reaffirmed the supremacy of the Constitution and the role of the federal judiciary in interpreting it.[104]

---

[97] The Federalist No. 80 (Alexander Hamilton).

[98] 19 U.S. (6 Wheat.) 264 (1821).

[99] *Id.* at 387–88.

[100] *Id.* at 386–87.

[101] 358 U.S. 1 (1958).

[102] 347 U.S. 483 (1954).

[103] 358 U.S. at 4.

[104] *Cooper*, 358 U.S. at 18.

[5] Bush v. Gore

The Supreme Court's power to review decisions of state courts received its most prominent recent illustration in *Bush v. Gore*.[105] There the Supreme Court reviewed and reversed a decision of the Florida Supreme Court ordering a statewide manual recount of certain ballots during the 2000 presidential election. The majority thought the case raised a substantial question of federal law-whether the Florida court's order violated the Equal Protection Clause of the Fourteenth Amendment-and concluded that it did. That analysis, if accepted, provided clear basis for the Court's jurisdiction.

Chief Justice Rehnquist's concurring opinion (which Justices Scalia and Thomas joined), added a further wrinkle regarding the Court's powers to review state court decisions. In addition to the Equal Protection Clause, the Rehnquist concurrence argued that the Florida Supreme Court's order violated Article II of the Constitution which authorizes states to appoint electors "in such manner as the *Legislature* thereof may direct."[106] The Court had foreshadowed this issue in *Bush v. Palm Beach County Canvassing Board*,[107] its initial foray into the 2000 election. There the Court unanimously vacated and remanded the Florida Supreme Court's initial decision regarding the Florida protest and contest statutes because the Court was "unclear" regarding whether the Florida Supreme Court had relied on the Florida Constitution to circumscribe the Florida legislature's authority under Article II, § 1, cl. 2.[108] A reasonable implication of the Court's order is that the Florida court could not rely on the Florida Constitution. Even so, *Bush v. Palm Beach County Canvassing Board* seemed to leave open the possibility that state judicial review of presidential elections could occur if it took "as its cue state legislative enactments rather than state constitution or common law authority."[109]

In *Bush v. Gore*, Chief Justice Rehnquist argued that in order to determine whether the Florida Supreme Court, in ordering the recount, had "infringed upon the legislature's authority" the Court had to examine Florida State law as it existed prior to the Florida Supreme Court's decision.[110] In certain instances, the Constitution "requires this Court to undertake an independent, if still deferential, analysis of state law," the Chief Justice wrote.[111] He argued:

> This inquiry does not imply a disrespect for state *courts* but rather a respect for the constitutionally prescribed role of state *legislatures*. To attach definitive weight to the pronouncement of a state court, when the very question at issue is whether the court has actually departed from the statutory meaning, would be to abdicate our responsibility to enforce the

---

[105] 531 U.S. 98 (2000).

[106] U.S. Const. art. II, § 1, cl. 2 (emphasis added).

[107] 531 U.S. 70 (2000).

[108] *Id.* at 78.

[109] Samuel Issacharoff, *Political Judgments*, 68 U. Chi. L. Rev. 637, 643 (2001).

[110] 531 U.S. at 114.

[111] *Id.*

explicit requirements of Article II.[112]

In reviewing state court decisions, the Court generally accepts state court interpretations of that state's law. Chief Justice Rehnquist's concurrence departed from this usual deference. Four dissenting justices acknowledged that "this Court must sometimes examine state law in order to protect federal rights,"[113] but argued that far greater deference was owed the decision of the highest state court regarding its interpretation of state law.[114] They suggested that instances in which the Court had rejected such a state court decision were aberrations based on extraordinary circumstances. In one early case which the Chief Justice cited,[115] the Court held that Virginia's highest court had misinterpreted its property laws to deny a British subject's right to land as guaranteed by federal treaty. The case "occurred amidst vociferous States' rights attacks" on the Court.[116] In two other cases upon which the Chief Justice relied,[117] the Court reviewed state court decisions interpreting state law in unsupported ways to deny rights to African-Americans. "The [Florida Supreme Court] surely should not be bracketed with state high courts of the Jim Crow South,"[118] wrote Justice Ginsberg.

Some defend the Rehnquist concurrence as a proper departure from the general rule that federal courts defer to state courts regarding state law. In essence, the federal interest in presidential elections combined with the specification, in Article II, § 1, cl. 2, of the state legislature are deemed to justify federal judicial review of state court interpretations of state law.

Judge (then Professor) Michael McConnell argued that "in this unique context, there is a constitutionally-based federal interest in ensuring that state executive and judicial branches adhere to the rules for selecting electors established by the Legislature, and do not use their interpretive and enforcement powers to change the rules after the fact."[119]

Chief Justice Rehnquist's citation of the three cases may suggest that he questioned the motives and character of the action of the Florida Supreme Court. After all, in the cases cited, federal review of state law may have been justified in part by the suspicion that the state courts were manipulating state law to deny someone a federal right. Professor David Strauss, for instance, argued that the majority's conduct in *Bush v. Gore* generally rested on a conviction that "the Florida Supreme Court would try to give the election to Vice President Gore and would act

---

[112] *Id.* at 115 (emphasis in original).

[113] *Id.* at 137.

[114] *Id.* at 123, 133, 137.

[115] Fairfax's Devisee v. Hunter's Lessee, 11 U.S. (7 Cranch) 603 (1813).

[116] *Bush*, 531 U.S. at 140.

[117] NAACP v. Alabama *ex rel.* Patterson, 357 U.S. 449 (1958); Bouie v. City of Columbia, 378 U.S. 347 (1964).

[118] *Bush*, 531 U.S. at 141.

[119] Michael W. McConnell, *Two-and-a-Half-Cheers for* Bush v. Gore, 68 U. Chi. L. Rev. 657, 663 (2001). *See also* Richard A. Epstein, *In such Manner as the Legislature Thereof May Direct: The Outcome in* Bush v. Gore *Defended*, 68 U. Chi. L. Rev. 613 (2001).

improperly if necessary to accomplish that objective."[120] However, Professor Strauss discounted that conclusion, based on his assessment of the substantive merits of the Florida Supreme Court's opinion and based on the fact that the Florida Supreme Court ruled against Vice President Gore on various other issues.

§ 2.06 JUDICIAL INDEPENDENCE

In order to insulate federal courts from majoritarian control, the framers attached two attributes to federal judges. They provided that Article III judges would enjoy lifetime tenure during "good behavior" and that their salary could not be reduced.[121] The framers thought these protections necessary to secure an independent judiciary that could enforce individual rights in the face of majoritarian pressure.[122] Thus Hamilton thought life tenure during good behavior was an "excellent barrier to the encroachments and oppressions of the representative body." It was "the best expedient which can be devised in any government to secure a steady, upright, and impartial administration of the laws."[123] Judicial independence would "guard the Constitution and the rights of individuals."[124]

Similarly, the framers thought salary protection a sound way of safeguarding judicial independence. As Hamilton put it, *"a power over a man's subsistence amounts to a power over his will."*[125] By denying the Congress the power to reduce judicial pay, the framers sought to insulate the judiciary from political control. These features distinguish federal judges from judges in many state courts, a point Chief Justice Marshall made in *Cohens v. Virginia*. More recently, the Court has suggested the Compensation Clause may also provide an incentive for able lawyers to accept appointment to the federal bench.[126]

The Compensation Clause does not exempt federal judges from all exposure. For instance, Congress can repeal planned judicial raises before they take effect (though not once they vest).[127] The nondiscriminatory nature of a freeze, i.e. the fact it applied to other government officials, did not justify repealing a judicial increase. Other officials simply did not enjoy the same constitutional protection as did the judiciary. The Constitution did not except nondiscriminatory reductions from the protection the Compensation Clause affords federal judges.[128]

---

[120] *See, e.g.*, David A. Strauss, Bush v. Gore: *What Were They Thinking?*, 68 U. Chi. L. Rev. 737 (2001); Jack Balkin, Bush v. Gore *and the Boundary Between Law and Politics*, 110 Yale L.J. 1407, 1434–35 (2001) (arguing Florida Supreme Court's rulings against Gore rebut criticisms of it as partisan).

[121] U.S. Const. art. III, § 1.

[122] *See, e.g.*, The Federalist Nos. 78, 79 (Alexander Hamilton).

[123] *Id.* No. 78.

[124] *Id.*

[125] *Id.* No. 79 (emphasis in original).

[126] United States v. Will, 449 U.S. 200, 221 (1980).

[127] *Id.* at 226–29.

[128] *Id.* at 226.

Although the Court initially held that the Clause freed federal judges of the obligation to pay income taxes,[129] it subsequently concluded that federal judges were subject to nondiscriminatory taxes enacted prior to their appointment.[130] The Court held that appointment to the federal bench did not relieve federal judges of normal burdens of citizenship, including the duty to pay general taxes.[131]

In *United States v. Hatter*,[132] the Court held that Congress could impose on judges the same nondiscriminatory tax generally applied but could not subject judges to "specially unfavorable treatment." Thus Congress could extend the Medicare tax (and benefits) to all federal employees, including federal judges, who previously had been exempt.[133] But a law extending a Social Security tax to federal employees violated the Compensation Clause because it, in effect, allowed all but federal judges to avoid the tax.[134]

§ 2.07 JUDICIAL DEPENDENCE

Although life tenure and compensation protection insulate federal judges from some political pressures, they are not wholly independent. The Constitution provides that federal judges are nominated by the President and appointed only with the advice and consent of the Senate.[135] The political nature of the selection and confirmation process guaranty that political considerations influence the composition of the federal judiciary including the Supreme Court where the stakes are greatest.[136] Judges are also subject to impeachment, trial and removal for treason, bribery and other high crimes and misdemeanors although this remedy is rarely invoked.

Courts depend in part on executive enforcement to give effect to their judgments. John Marshall presumably worried over how Jefferson and Madison would respond if served a mandamus. Nearly three decades later, President Andrew Jackson supposedly reacted to the Court's decision in *Worcester v. Georgia*,[137] with the remark: "John Marshall has made his decision; now let him enforce it!" The story may be apocryphal but it illustrates the extent to which the judiciary relies on the executive to enforce its orders.

Yet, the federal executive branch has rarely refused to enforce judicial decisions. President John F. Kennedy expressed a typical attitude when he sent federal troops to enforce a court order. "My obligation under the Constitution and the statutes of

---

[129] Evans v. Gore, 253 U.S. 245 (1920); Miles v. Graham, 268 U.S. 501, 509 (1925).

[130] O'Malley v. Woodrough, 307 U.S. 277, 282 (1939).

[131] *Id.*

[132] 532 U.S. 557, 561 (2001).

[133] *Id.* at 571–72.

[134] *Id.* at 572.

[135] U.S. Const. art. II, § 2, cl. 2.

[136] *See generally* Henry J. Abraham, Justices, Presidents, Senators: A History of U.S. Supreme Court Appointments from Washington to Bush Ii (5th ed. 2005); Joel K. Goldstein, *Choosing Justices: How Presidents Decide*, 26 J.L. & Pol. 425 (2011).

[137] 31 U.S. (6 Pet.) 515 (1832).

the United States was and is to implement the orders of the court with whatever means are necessary . . . ."[138] The judiciary has exercised power largely due to the overriding sense that the Constitution itself depends on respect for the courts and the law they dispense. Indeed, even Richard M. Nixon obeyed a Court order that he produce tapes of incriminatory conversations which traced his participation in the Watergate coverup to an early date. Publication of these conversations hastened the end of his presidency.

The judiciary is also dependent on the legislative branch. The extent of the dependence becomes clear from the language of Article III: "The judicial Power of the United States shall be vested in one supreme Court, and in such inferior Courts as the Congress may from time to time ordain and establish . . . ." This provision mandates a Supreme Court but seems to give Congress discretion regarding whether to "ordain and establish" lower federal courts. This approach reflected the Madisonian Compromise which James Madison brokered between those framers who wanted the Constitution to create lower federal courts and those who preferred to entrust state courts with the duty to handle virtually all litigation. As such, lower federal courts owe their existence to Congress which established them by statute.

Similarly, the jurisdiction of the federal courts, with the exception of the original jurisdiction of the Supreme Court, is largely dependent on Congress subject to the outer limits the Constitution allows. Congress also can control the Supreme Court's appellate jurisdiction based on the Exceptions Clause which confers appellate jurisdiction on the Court over specified cases "with such Exceptions, and under such Regulations as the Congress shall make."[139] Finally, the Necessary and Proper Clause[140] allows Congress to pass other laws regarding jurisdiction in federal and state courts over various types of cases.

Congressional control over federal courts raises a fundamental question in constitutional theory. To what extent can Congress eliminate the federal judiciary or abolish its jurisdiction (other than the Supreme Court's original jurisdiction)? From time to time, critics of controversial Supreme Court decisions — banning organized prayer in public schools or allowing abortions — propose stripping the federal courts of their jurisdiction over those subjects. The following sections discuss separately issues pertinent to the Supreme Court and lower federal courts respectively. But certain general issues are worth considering at the outset. *Marbury* asserted the structural principle fundamental to the rule of law that the laws must furnish a remedy to redress violations of right. Marshall wrote: "The government of the United States has been emphatically termed a government of laws, and not of men. It will certainly cease to deserve this high appellation, if the laws furnish no remedy for the violation of a vested legal right."[141] This structural principle of our Constitution would be jeopardized if Congress could deny access to all courts.

---

[138] John F. Kennedy's Radio and Television Report to the Nation on the Situation at the University of Mississippi (Sept. 30, 1962), *in* PUBLIC PAPERS OF THE PRESIDENTS: JOHN F. KENNEDY 1962, at 727 (1963).

[139] U.S. CONST. art. III, § 2, cl. 2.

[140] *Id.* art. I, § 8, cl. 18.

[141] Marbury v. Madison, 5 U.S. (1 Cranch) 137, 163 (1803).

Moreover, the Constitution presupposes three-part government, with each branch imposing checks on the others. Obviously, if Congress can abolish the Court's constitutional prerogative of judicial review, the constitutional architecture will undergo a failure at the foundation.

Finally, proposals to strip federal courts of all jurisdiction encounter a further problem. Generally they rest on the tacit premise that absent federal review, state courts and legislatures or Congress would act contrary to the disliked Supreme Court decisions. These decisions are entitled however, to be considered part of the supreme law of the land until they are overruled.

Defiance of them would raise constitutional issues under the Supremacy Clause. On the other hand, if Congress or the states agreed to follow prevailing, yet unpopular, precedent, the jurisdiction stripping strategy would backfire; it would, ironically, freeze into constitutional law the disliked decisions because, absent the possibility of Supreme Court review, only constitutional amendment could provide redress.

§ 2.08 COURT ORGANIZATION: THE SUPREME COURT

The Constitution itself established the Supreme Court.[142] But it says nothing about the size of that Court, a subject Congress has addressed by statute. The size of the Court has ranged from six initially to five, to seven, to nine, to ten, to seven again, and finally in 1869 to the present size of nine. Congress can also control the Court's organization and functioning. Indeed in 1801 Congress changed the Court's terms so that it did not sit for fourteen months (between December, 1801 and February, 1803). Congress also can prescribe procedural and other rules for the Court.[143] Thus, initially Congress assigned the Justices to the various circuits it created, an assignment that required them to preside over trials. Still, the constitutional basis of the Supreme Court limits congressional authority. The Supreme Court has functioned as a continuing governmental institution since February 2, 1790 and its existence is constitutionally guaranteed.

The Constitution does not impose any age, residency, citizenship or occupational requirements for Supreme Court Justices. Every Justice to date has been a lawyer, but that reflects practice, not legal requirement.[144]

§ 2.09 SUPREME COURT JURISDICTION

The Constitution treats differently the Supreme Court's original and appellate jurisdiction. Article III expressly specifies original jurisdiction and Congress is given no power of revision. The Court's original jurisdiction is conferred by the

---

[142] U.S. CONST. art. III, § 1 ("The judicial Power of the United States, shall be vested in one supreme Court.").

[143] *See* Wayman v. Southard, 23 U.S. (10 Wheat.) 1 (1825).

[144] *See* EDWIN M. YODER, JR., VACANCY: A JUDICIAL MISADVENTURE (2010) (novel discussing appointment of non-lawyer to Court).

Constitution and can be exercised without legislative action.[145] In practice, it accounts for a tiny portion of the Court's work.

Congress cannot add to the two categories the Constitution placed in the Court's original jurisdiction.[146] Professor Akhil Reed Amar suggests that geographic considerations helped explain the placement of these two categories. Foreign envoys would likely reside in the nation's capital so their countries should be sued there. States could be represented there, too, by their senators.[147]

Congress has, however, made the Court's original jurisdiction concurrent with jurisdiction in lower federal courts or state courts with respect to most cases within it. Thus, the Court's original jurisdiction is exclusive regarding "all controversies between two or more states"[148] but not regarding cases to which ambassadors and other foreign envoys are parties, controversies between the United States and a state, and actions by a state against citizens of another state or aliens.[149]

The Constitution treats the Supreme Court's appellate jurisdiction differently. Article III makes the Court's appellate jurisdiction subject to such exceptions and regulations as Congress may prescribe.[150] Under the Exceptions Clause appellate power of the Supreme Court extends to specified cases within its appellate power subject to Congress' power to divest it of that jurisdiction.[151]

The Supreme Court's appellate jurisdiction is "strictly speaking, conferred by the Constitution."[152] Thus, the Judiciary Act of 1789 did not actually confer appellate jurisdiction on the Court. Rather, according to Chief Justice Marshall, the first Congress intended to make exceptions to the appellate jurisdiction of the Supreme Court[153] in giving effect to Article III when it enacted the Judiciary Act of 1789. The grant of appellate jurisdiction implicitly denied jurisdiction in cases not mentioned. Marshall's approach has won acceptance.[154]

The crucial question relates to the extent of congressional control over the Supreme Court's appellate jurisdiction. How far may Congress go under the Exceptions Clause? Could it except from the Court's appellate jurisdiction all cases other than, say, admiralty cases? Some argue that the Exceptions Clause gives Congress such plenary power. "Congress need not give this court any appellate power; it may withdraw appellate jurisdiction once conferred and it may do so even

---

[145] *See* California v. Arizona, 440 U.S. 59, 65 (1979); Kentucky v. Dennison, 65 U.S. (24 How.) 66, 98 (1861).

[146] Marbury v. Madison, 5 U.S. (1 Cranch) 137, 174–76 (1803).

[147] Akhil Reed Amar, *Marbury, Section 13, and the Original Jurisdiction of the Supreme Court*, 56 U. Chi. L. Rev. 443, 463–78 (1989).

[148] 28 U.S.C. § 1251(a).

[149] 28 U.S.C. § 1251(b).

[150] *See* U.S. Const. art. III, § 2, cl. 2.

[151] The Francis Wright, 105 U.S. 381, 385 (1882); Durousseau v. United States, 10 U.S. (6 Cranch) 307, 314 (1810).

[152] *Ex parte* McCardle, 74 U.S. 506, 512–13 (1869).

[153] *See Durousseau*, 10 U.S. at 314.

[154] *See Ex parte McCardle*, 74 U.S. at 513.

while a case is *sub judice*," wrote Justice Frankfurter.[155] Yet the text of Article III seems to impeach any claim that Congress possesses plenary control over the Court's appellate competence. An "exception" is just that; the term presupposes some substantial core that remains. It seems inconceivable that the Constitution intended to vest in Congress authority to nullify the practical exercise of the judicial power. More likely, the purpose was to authorize exceptions and regulations consistent with the essential function of the Supreme Court in the constitutional system.[156] The framers created a three-part government with a system of checks and balances to safeguard liberty. Congress could undermine that structure if it could dispense with the judiciary. Indeed, such a possibility seems at war with basic structural principles in *Marbury* — the concepts of limited government, rule of law and judicial review. If Congress has broad power to limit lower courts, a subject discussed below, the role of the Supreme Court, especially in its appellate role, becomes all the more critical. If Congress could abolish lower federal courts under the Ordain and Establish Clause[157] and slash the Court's appellate jurisdiction under the Exceptions Clause Congress could reduce a coordinate department to servility and erode the judicial check on unconstitutional governmental action.

Moreover, some suggest that the Exceptions Clause found its way into the Constitution largely to give Congress flexibility regarding the Supreme Court's review of lower court *factual* determinations. Under this view, Congress could not reduce the Court's appellate jurisdiction regarding particular issues of *law*.[158]

Those who argue for broad congressional power over the Court's appellate jurisdiction cite *Ex parte McCardle*[159] for support. A Mississippi newspaper editor who had been arrested under the Reconstruction Acts and held for trial by military commission petitioned for habeas corpus. A lower court denied the writ and McCardle appealed to the Supreme Court under an 1867 statute which authorized appeals to the Court from circuit court decisions in such cases.

The Court unanimously decided that it had subject matter jurisdiction,[160] heard arguments on the merits, and took the matter under advisement. Many feared the Court would invalidate the military governments of Reconstruction in part because of its earlier decision against the wartime trial of civilians by military commission in *Ex parte Milligan*.[161] To avoid such a result, Congress repealed the 1867 statute to the extent it authorized appeal to the Supreme Court from circuit court judgments in habeas corpus cases and prohibited the Court from acting on appeals that had been or might be taken. The Court then heard argument regarding

---

[155] National Mut. Ins. Co. v. Tidewater Transfer Co., 337 U.S. 582, 655 (1949) (Frankfurter, J., dissenting).

[156] *See* FALLON ET. AL., *supra* note 29, at 1364–65.

[157] U.S. CONST. art. III, § 1 ("The judicial Power of the United States, shall be vested in one Supreme Court, and in such inferior courts as the Congress may from time to time ordain and establish.").

[158] *See generally* LINDA S. MULLENIX ET AL., UNDERSTANDING FEDERAL COURTS AND JURISDICTION 34–35 (1998).

[159] 74 U.S. (7 Wall.) 506 (1869).

[160] *See Ex parte* McCardle, 73 U.S. (6 Wall.) 318 (1868).

[161] 71 U.S. (4 Wall.) 2 (1866).

Congress' authority to remove its jurisdiction over a case already submitted on the merits.

"The first question necessarily is that of jurisdiction," wrote the Court, for if jurisdiction had been removed, "it is useless, if not improper, to enter into any discussion of other questions."[162] *McCardle* unanimously acknowledged congressional power over its appellate jurisdiction based upon the Exceptions Clause. The repealing act plainly withdrew jurisdiction over the appeal. The Court decreed itself precluded from questioning legislative intent. The appeal, therefore, was dismissed even though the repealing Act was designed simply to prevent a decision on the constitutionality of the Reconstruction Acts.

To be sure, *McCardle* was far-reaching. The Court upheld a law Congress passed to prevent the Court from reviewing the constitutionality of a statute.[163] Still, the Court did not hold that Congress could validly oust it of all appellate jurisdiction in habeas corpus cases. The repealing act at issue lacked that extreme effect. At the end of its opinion, the Court went out of its way to assert that the 1868 jurisdiction stripping act only removed jurisdiction over appeals under the 1867 Act; "jurisdiction which was previously exercised" (i.e. under the Judiciary Act of 1789) was not affected. Prior to the 1868 statute at issue in *McCardle*, the Supreme Court could review denials of habeas corpus by lower courts either on appeal[164] or on petition to it for habeas corpus.[165] The *McCardle* statute eliminated the first avenue but left unimpaired the other method of invoking the Court's review in habeas corpus cases. A few months later, *Ex parte Yerger*[166] held that after *Ex parte McCardle* the Supreme Court could still review lower court habeas denials by petitions in the Supreme Court under the 1789 Act.

The Court more recently explained this result in *Felker v. Turpin*,[167] which involved Title I of the Antiterrorism and Effective Death Penalty Act of 1996. The statute required dismissal of a claim presented in a state prisoner's second or successive federal habeas application if the claim was already presented, unless a court of appeals panel granted leave to file a second or successive habeas application in the district court; the statute declared that a panel's grant or denial of authorization to file such an application shall not be appealable or subject of a petition for writ of certiorari. In upholding Title I, the Court explained that *Ex parte Yerger* decided that the *McCardle* statute barring review by appeal of a circuit court judgment in a habeas corpus case did not deprive the Supreme Court of power

---

[162] *Ex parte McCardle*, 74 U.S. (7 Wall.) at 512. Compare the Court's approach to that in *Marbury* where jurisdiction issues were addressed last.

[163] *See* BERNARD SCHWARTZ, FROM CONFEDERATION TO NATION: THE AMERICAN CONSTITUTION, 1835–1877, at 187 (1973).

[164] Under the 1867 statute already mentioned.

[165] Under § 14 of the first Judiciary Act, Ch. 20 Stat. 73, 81 (1789), a person confined under color of federal authority and denied release by the circuit court could petition the Supreme Court for habeas corpus, as well as for the common-law writ of certiorari to bring up the record below. The Supreme Court, in issuing habeas corpus in such a case, after its denial by the circuit court, has been held to be acting in the exercise of its appellate jurisdiction. *Ex parte* Yerger, 75 U.S. (8 Wall.) 85, 102 (1869).

[166] *See id.* at 104–06.

[167] 518 U.S. 651 (1996).

to entertain a habeas petition under the Judiciary Act of 1789.[168]

Based on *Yerger, Felker* concluded that Title I of the Antiterrorism Act did not repeal the Court's authority to entertain original habeas petitions. Though the 1996 Act precluded the Court from reviewing, by appeal or petition for certiorari, a judgment on an application for leave to file a second habeas petition in district court, it did not mention the Court's authority to hear habeas petitions filed as original matters. Repeal by implication was not favored. The Court in *Felker*, as in *Yerger*, declined to find a repeal of the 1789 Judiciary Act habeas corpus provision by implication.[169]

This conclusion answered the habeas constitutional challenge against the Antiterrorism Act:

> The Act does remove our authority to entertain an appeal or a petition for a writ of certiorari to review a decision of a court of appeals exercising its 'gatekeeping function' over a second petition. But since it does not repeal our authority to entertain a petition for habeas corpus there can be no plausible argument that the Act has deprived this Court of appellate jurisdiction in violation of Article III, § 2.[170]

If the *McCardle* statute had tried to deny the Supreme Court all jurisdiction in habeas corpus cases it would have encountered another problem. The Habeas Corpus Clause provides that "[t]he Privilege of the Writ of Habeas Corpus shall not be suspended, unless when in cases of Rebellion or Invasion the public safety may require it."[171] The Clause seems to contemplate some habeas corpus writ from some court. More recent decisions of the Court seem to recognize some constitutional right to the writ[172] subject to suspension in dire circumstances. To the extent there is a constitutional right to habeas review, Congress' ability to restrict it, absent circumstances the Suspension Clause addresses, would be limited.

In *United States v. Klein*,[173] the Supreme Court recognized that congressional power over jurisdiction is limited.[174] Klein sought to recover compensation for confiscated property under a federal statute that permitted such claims provided the claimant was loyal to the United States. The Court had previously held a presidential pardon for war-time activities constituted proof the person had not

---

[168] *Id.* at 660.

[169] *Id.* But does *Felker* overrule *Marbury* with respect to Congress' ability to add to the Court's original jurisdiction? After all, a habeas petition is not one of the two categories of cases described in Article III. In fact, in *Ex parte Bollman*, 8 U.S. (4 Cranch) 75, 100–01 (1807) Chief Justice Marshall held that a habeas petition filed initially in the Supreme Court fell within the Court's appellate, not original, jurisdiction since typically some court had previously considered the matter. Justice Johnson dissented based on *Marbury*. *Id.* at 101.

[170] *Felker*, 518 U.S. at 661–62.

[171] U.S.C. art. I, § 9, cl. 2.

[172] *See, e.g.*, Immigration and Naturalization Service v. St. Cyr, 533 U.S. 289, 301 (2001); *Felker*, 518 U.S. at 663.

[173] 80 U.S. (13 Wall.) 128 (1872).

[174] *Id.* at 146.

aided the South.[175] While *Klein* was pending, Congress passed legislation to the effect that a pardon could not be used to prove loyalty, and in fact demonstrated the opposite, and deprived the Court of jurisdiction in any such case predicated on a pardon. The statute was phrased in jurisdictional terms, making the decision relevant to the present discussion. It provided that, in the cases specified, neither the Court of Claims nor the Supreme Court had jurisdiction and must dismiss any cases involved. The statute was not a proper exercise of the Exceptions Clause because Congress did not "intend to withhold appellate jurisdiction except as a means to an end," to deny to presidential pardons the effect the Court said they had.[176]

Klein is a confusing case and its meaning is controversial. It may hold that despite congressional authority to make exceptions and regulations, Congress cannot manipulate jurisdiction to dictate to the Supreme Court the result in a particular case. Alternatively, it may mean simply that Congress cannot make exceptions to the Court's appellate jurisdiction which violate some other constitutional limitation. In any event, *Klein* suggests that the Constitution imposes some limits on Congress' ability to control the Court's appellate jurisdiction although the case has not been used to strike down other laws restricting federal courts.[177]

Article III presumably does not give Congress unlimited power over the Supreme Court's appellate jurisdiction. Congress lacks power to make exceptions that eliminate the appellate jurisdiction altogether or leave little of it. Congress can modify, not eviscerate, judicial review.

§ 2.10   LEGISLATIVE CONTROL OVER LOWER COURTS' JURISDICTION

The lower federal courts lack clear constitutional foundation. Article III refers to them only in general terms, when it states that judicial power shall also be vested "in such inferior Courts as the Congress may from time to time ordain and establish." The Ordain and Establish clause suggests that the Constitution left Congress free to establish inferior courts or not, as it thought appropriate.[178] Quite clearly, the Constitution contemplated that "cases within the judicial cognizance of the United States not only might but would arise in the state courts in the exercise of their ordinary jurisdiction."[179] Moreover, the Supremacy Clause bound state judges to recognize federal law as supreme, a requirement which would have been unnecessary if they were not expected to decide some cases involving federal law.

Of course, the fact that some federal cases could originate in state court does not prove that federal courts were optional. To be sure, some have questioned whether Congress has unlimited discretion regarding the existence of lower federal courts.

---

[175] United States v. Padelford, 76 U.S. (9 Wall.) 531 (1870).

[176] *Klein*, 80 U.S. at 145.

[177] Howard M. Wasserman, *The Irrepressible Myth of Klein*, 79 U. Cin. L. Rev. 53 (2011).

[178] *See* Lockerty v. Phillips, 319 U.S. 182, 187 (1943). *See also* Palmore v. United States, 411 U.S. 389, 401 (1973) ("was not constitutionally required to create inferior Art. III courts").

[179] Martin v. Hunter's Lessee, 14 U.S. (1 Wheat.) 304, 340 (1816). *See also id.* at 342.

In *Martin v. Hunter's Lessee*, Justice Story, for instance, argued that the language of Article III "is manifestly designed to be mandatory upon the legislature."[180] He relied on language in Article III that the judicial power "shall be vested" to conclude that the Constitution obligated Congress to vest all judicial power set out in Article III. Accordingly, Congress was obliged to create at least some inferior federal courts.

Justice Story's view has not prevailed. On the contrary, the law has recognized that Congress has large discretion to create or abolish inferior federal courts.[181] In *Palmore v. United States*, Justice Byron White expressed the conventional view. "The decision with respect to inferior federal courts, as well as the task of defining their jurisdiction, was left to the discretion of Congress. That body was not constitutionally required to create inferior Art. III courts to hear and decide cases within the judicial power of the United States . . . ."[182] Others make more modest claims, suggesting, for instance, that lower federal courts must exist to hear at least those matters not within the jurisdiction of the state courts or the original jurisdiction of the Supreme Court. Absent lower federal courts with at least that jurisdiction some rights would lack judicial remedies, a violation of the principle stated in *Marbury*.

It may seem inefficient for a federal judicial system to operate alongside the state courts. Yet, the existence of the federal courts with competence over matters specified in Article III serves some basic objects of the Constitution. Justice Story articulated these basic principles in *Martin v. Hunter's Lessee*. Federal courts play a critical role in preserving the supremacy of federal law. A federal judiciary is needed to interpret and apply the laws of the Union and to compel obedience to them. Also, Justice Story suggested that federal courts might be necessary to vindicate national interests. State courts might on occasion favor, or be perceived to favor, local interests.[183] In some instances, federal courts were needed to provide an impartial tribunal. Other cases might raise issues "touching the safety, peace, and sovereignty of the nation" which would justify federal jurisdiction.[184] Moreover, federal courts are needed to assure that federal law is interpreted uniformly.[185]

Congress has assumed that it has discretion regarding federal court jurisdiction. Congress has never given lower federal courts the full range of jurisdiction Article III would allow. The first Congress did not give federal courts all the jurisdiction Article III authorized it to bestow.[186] The bulk of business of the lower federal courts under the 1789 statute concerned admiralty matters, civil and criminal cases involving federal offenses, and miscellaneous litigation depending on the citizenship of litigants. Although a federal court system was created in large part to vindicate federal rights, Congress did not give the lower federal courts federal question

---

[180] *Id.* at 328.

[181] *See* Palmore v. United States, 411 U.S. 389 (1973); Glidden Co. v. Zdanok, 370 U.S. 530 (1962).

[182] 411 U.S. at 400–01.

[183] *Martin*, 14 U.S. at 347.

[184] *Id.*

[185] *Id.* at 347–48.

[186] DAVID P. CURRIE, THE CONSTITUTION IN CONGRESS 48 (1997).

jurisdiction until 1875.[187] The Constitution authorized jurisdiction over controversies between citizens of different states, but the 1789 Judiciary Act restricted diversity jurisdiction to suits where the amount in controversy exceeded $500. Subsequent judicial codes have imposed such a jurisdictional-amount requirement (with the necessary amount raised at different times).[188] Making access to the federal courts dependent on the value of the amount in dispute is controversial, but the power of Congress to impose jurisdictional-amount requirements has never seriously been doubted. In conferring less than full federal judicial power, the First Congress signalled that it did not believe all Article III power must be conferred on a federal court.

Congress exercised legislative authority to alter lower federal court jurisdiction as early as 1802 when it repealed the Judiciary Act of 1801 (creating a whole new system of circuit and district courts).[189] In *Stuart v. Laird*,[190] perhaps feeling some pressure from the assertive Jeffersonian Congress, the Court upheld the act on the grounds that Congress could establish such inferior tribunals as it deemed proper and could transfer a cause from one such tribunal to another. *Stuart* established the authority of Congress to create and abolish inferior courts. It rejected the argument that Supreme Court justices could not ride circuit in part based on past practice. "[P]ractice and acquiescence under it for a period of several years, commencing with the organization of the judicial system, affords an irresistible answer, and has indeed fixed the construction."[191]

The Supreme Court has upheld congressional discretion over the jurisdiction of the federal courts. *Sheldon v. Sill*[192] involved Section 11 of the first Judiciary Act, which barred an action by an assignee of a chose in action where the assignment created diversity which had not existed. The assignee claimed that Section 11 was invalid because Article III confirmed the right of a citizen of any state to sue a citizen of another. Put differently, he claimed that Section 11 resulted in some part of the Article III jurisdiction not being conferred. The Court categorically rejected this argument. Congress "having a right to prescribe . . . may withhold from any court of its creation jurisdiction of any of the enumerated controversies."[193] The Court's holding pivoted largely on its reasoning that the greater power to decide whether to establish lower federal courts implied the lesser power to establish such courts, but without the full jurisdiction Article III would allow. Professor Larry Yackle has questioned the reasoning, if not the result, in *Sheldon*. He argued that the power to prescribe is not a lesser included power of the power to create, but a different power. The Court might have logically concluded that Congress had to either create lower federal courts with full Article III power or not create them.[194]

---

[187] 1 Stat. 73, 77 (1789); *Palmore*, 411 U.S. at 401.

[188] It is now $75,000. *See* 28 U.S.C. § 1332.

[189] 2 Stat. 132 (1802), repealing 2 Stat. 89 (1801).

[190] 5 U.S. (1 Cranch) 299 (1803).

[191] *Id.* at 309.

[192] 49 U.S. (8 How.) 441 (1850).

[193] *Id.* at 449.

[194] LARRY W. YACKLE, FEDERAL COURTS 61 (1999).

Nonetheless, *Sheldon* confirmed congressional authority to confer on the inferior federal courts less than the full jurisdiction the Constitution allows.

Some statutes which the Court has upheld illustrate ways in which Congress might restrict jurisdiction. In 1922, the Court upheld the federal Anti-Injunction Act which prevented federal courts from enjoining pending state court contract suits. The Court reasoned that Congress controlled the jurisdiction of lower courts under the Constitution.[195] Thereafter, in *Lauf v. E. G. Shinner & Co.*,[196] the Court upheld the Norris-La Guardia Act[197] which limited the power of federal courts to issue injunctions in cases involving labor disputes. "There can be no question of the power of Congress thus to define and limit the jurisdiction of the inferior courts of the United States,"[198] said the Court in upholding that restriction.

A few years later, the Court upheld the Emergency Price Control Act of 1942[199] which in part provided that those aggrieved by price and rent control orders could only raise judicial challenges to their validity in a special Emergency Court of Appeals. In *Lockerty v. Phillips*,[200] a district court suit to enjoin enforcement of a price order on the ground that it violated the Constitution, petitioners argued that Congress could not deprive the federal courts of authority to review the constitutionality of a statute. The Court rejected the argument. "The Congressional power to ordain and establish inferior courts includes the power 'of investing them with jurisdiction either limited, concurrent, or exclusive, and of withholding jurisdiction from them in the exact degrees and character which to Congress may seem proper for the public good.' "[201] The Supreme Court expressly upheld congressional authority to create the Emergency Court with specialized jurisdiction in its particular field.[202]

The Emergency Price Control Act confined the criminal competence of the district courts since they could enforce price and rent orders in criminal proceedings but could not consider the validity of the orders the violation of which gave rise to the prosecution. *Yakus v. United States*[203] upheld Congress' power to restrict the federal courts' criminal jurisdiction. The Court thought these provisions presented "no novel constitutional issue."[204] Congress could allocate jurisdiction so that only the Emergency Court of Appeals could determine the validity of the orders while other federal courts could consider whether the accused had violated an order. A dissent argued that the arrangement offended *Marbury* in denying a federal court the right to examine the constitutionality of a statute or regulation.[205] The majority

---

[195] *See* Kline v. Burke Constr. Co., 260 U.S. 226, 234 (1922).

[196] 303 U.S. 323 (1938).

[197] 47 Stat. 70 (1932).

[198] *Lauf*, 303 U.S. at 330.

[199] 56 Stat. 23 (1942).

[200] 319 U.S. 182 (1943).

[201] *Lockerty v. Phillips*, 319 U.S. at 187. *See also Kline*, 260 U.S. at 234.

[202] *See* Yakus v. United States, 321 U.S. 414 (1944); Lockerty v. Phillips, 319 U.S. 182 (1943).

[203] 321 U.S. 414 (1944).

[204] *Id.* at 444.

[205] *Id.* at 468 (Rutledge, J., dissenting).

was not persuaded, perhaps because a different court could address that issue.

Nonetheless, these cases might be given a more limited reading. *Lauf* might be seen as a case which approved removing one particular remedy while leaving federal jurisdiction in place. *Lockerty* and *Yakus* approved an arrangement which left a court to weigh constitutional arguments.

None of these cases reach the situation which occasionally is proposed, depriving the federal courts of jurisdiction over a type of case, e.g., abortion, school prayer or busing, that has engendered controversial judicial rulings. No decision specifically addresses that question in part because Congress to date has not passed such legislation.

Thus, it is not at all clear that Congress could restrict federal court jurisdiction to eliminate all opportunity to enforce constitutional rights. To do so would contravene the *Marbury* principle that the rule of law requires judicial remedies for violations of rights.[206] The Due Process Clause of the Fifth Amendment provides an additional restriction on Congress' power to remove jurisdiction. Congressional authority to prescribe judicial jurisdiction must preserve the essential function of the courts in vindicating the rights the Constitution guarantees.

The Due Process Clause may not necessarily require that every litigant be entitled to bring her federal claim initially in a lower federal court. The Madison compromise suggests the Constitution was open to the possibility that state courts might serve that function. Professor Henry Hart, in his famous "dialogue" argued that a state court forum would suffice as the initial arbiter of a federal claim.[207]

Yet suppose no state forum was available. Cases hold that state courts lack jurisdiction to direct to federal officials a writ of habeas corpus[208] or a writ of mandamus.[209] If Congress removed federal jurisdiction to issue those writs, a litigant might have no recourse to enforce federal rights.

The Portal-to-Portal Act[210] provides an instructive case. Congress enacted it to redress incorrect judicial interpretations of the Fair Labor Standards Act of 1938 (FLSA)[211] which subjected many employers to unanticipated, and potentially ruinous, liabilities. The Portal-to-Portal Act eliminated the liabilities and provided that no federal or state court would have jurisdiction to enforce liability under the FLSA. In *Battaglia v. General Motors Corp.*,[212] the Court of Appeals for the Second Circuit held that Congress' effort to withdraw jurisdiction was subject to the Fifth Amendment. Although Congress had power to restrict the jurisdiction of the lower federal courts, it could not do so in a way that would deprive a litigant of due

---

[206] *See* Marbury v. Madison, 5 U.S. (1 Cranch) 137, 163 (1803). *Cf.* Guam v. Olsen, 431 U.S. 195, 204 (1977) (statute that denied litigants access to Article III courts "might present constitutional questions").

[207] Henry M. Hart, Jr., *The Power of Congress to Limit the Jurisdiction of Federal Courts: An Exercise in Dialectic*, 66 Harv. L. Rev. 1362 (1953).

[208] Tarble's Case, 80 U.S. (13 Wall.) 397 (1871); Ableman v. Booth, 62 U.S. (21 How.) 506 (1859).

[209] M'Clung v. Silliman, 19 U.S. (6 Wheat.) 598 (1821).

[210] 29 U.S.C. § 252(d).

[211] 29 U.S.C. §§ 201–19.

[212] 169 F.2d 254, 257 (2d Cir. 1948).

process. Similarly, Congress cannot structure jurisdiction in a manner which offends separation of powers principles. Thus a statute which empowered the executive branch to review and revise judicial decisions was invalid[213] as was one under which Congress reinstated cases the courts had dismissed.[214] The power to decide a case was the power to resolve it; Congress could not require federal courts to reopen final judgments.

§ 2.11 NON-ARTICLE III ADJUDICATION

Congress may affect judicial conduct not only by restricting the jurisdiction of Article III courts but also by assigning some work within their competence to tribunals that do not have the Article III safeguards of life tenure and salary protection. Congress might do so for a variety of reasons. In some instances, it might prefer to avoid establishing additional life tenured judgeships to preserve flexibility. Alternatively, administrative agencies might provide a more efficient means of adjudicating certain disputes.

Still, this power poses some danger. Unless regulated, this legislative power could subvert the basic constitutional separation of powers and checks and balances.

Congress' power to create non-Article III courts comes from enumerated powers in Article I combined with the Necessary and Proper Clause. Chief Justice Marshall recognized the legitimacy of "legislative courts" which rested on certain legislative powers granted to Congress.[215] Various legislative powers, coupled with the Necessary and Proper Clause,[216] are deemed to authorize Congress to create Article I courts. Thus, the Necessary and Proper Clause, a) combined with Congress' power over land and naval forces[217] confers power to establish non-Article III military tribunals; b) combined with Congress' power to govern territories[218] allows it to establish territorial courts;[219] c) combined with Congress' power to tax enables it to create the Tax Court;[220] d) combined with Congress' power to make laws for the District of Columbia,[221] allows Congress to set up a system of courts, with judges lacking Article III protections. Such courts could try criminal, as well as civil cases, if the criminal laws involved applied only in the District of Columbia. In *Palmore v. United States*[222] the Court held that trials by judges in the District of Columbia who lacked life tenure did not deprive defendants

---

[213] Hayburn's Case, 2 U.S. (2 Dall.) 409 (1792).

[214] Plaut v. Spendthrift Farm, Inc., 514 U.S. 211 (1995).

[215] American Insurance Co. v. Canter, 26 U.S. (1 Pet.) 511 (1828).

[216] U.S. Const. art. I, § 8, cl. 18 ("To make all Laws which shall be necessary and proper for carrying into Execution the foregoing Powers, and all other Powers vested by this Constitution in the Government of the United States, or in any Department or Officer thereof.").

[217] *See* U.S. Const. art. I, § 8, cl. 14.

[218] U.S. Const. art. IV, § 3, cl. 2.

[219] *See* American Insurance Co. v. Canter, 26 U.S. (1 Pet.) 511 (1828).

[220] *See generally* Northern Pipeline Constr. Co. v. Marathon Pipe Line Co., 458 U.S. 50, 64–66 (1982).

[221] *See* U.S. Const. art. I, § 8, cl. 17.

[222] 411 U.S. 389 (1973).

of due process any more than do trials by state judges without Article III protection.[223]

Finally, the Court has recognized Congress' authority to create Article I courts to adjudicate civil disputes between citizens and the federal government. The Court first articulated this doctrine in *Murray's Lessee v. Hoboken Land & Improvement Co.* where it said:[224]

> there are matters, involving public rights, which may be presented in such form that the judicial power is capable of acting on them, and which are susceptible of judicial determination, but which Congress may or may not bring within the cognizance of the Courts of the United States, as it may deem proper.

Public rights encompass a range of categories. The paradigmatic public rights are "claims against the United States" for "money, land or other things."[225] Presumably the doctrine of sovereign immunity insulated the United States from liability on such claims absent congressional consent.[226] Congress could condition that consent on trial of such claims in a legislative court. Initially, the Court of Claims was constituted as a legislative court.[227] Claims involving social security benefits, tax deductions, or government licenses are susceptible to trial in legislative courts. Finally, immigration cases have been viewed as involving public rights.[228] Congress had delegated adjudicatory authority to a host of administrative agencies. For instance, the Federal Trade Commission enforces "public rights" against violations of antitrust policy; Congress may commit the determination of cases involving such rights to agencies.[229]

In *Northern Pipeline Construction Co. v. Marathon Pipe Line Co.*,[230] the Court addressed the question of what adjudicatory authority Congress could delegate to non-Article III tribunals. In the Bankruptcy Reform Act of 1978 Congress had given bankruptcy judges, who did not enjoy life tenure, some Article III power. *Northern Pipeline* raised the question whether such Article I courts could decide questions based on state created common law rights of the bankrupt. The Court struck down the grant of Article III power. The *Northern Pipeline* plurality opinion interpreted Article III literally subject to some exceptions based on historical practice. It invoked the public rights-private rights dichotomy as the hinge on which delegation of adjudicatory authority to non-Article III tribunals turned. The opinion conceded that Congress could create agencies to adjudicate "public rights," i.e. disputes between the government and others, but not disputes between individuals that involve only "private rights." "Our precedents clearly establish that *only*

---

[223] *See id.*

[224] 59 U.S. (18 How.) 272, 284 (1856).

[225] *Ex parte* Bakelite Corp., 279 U.S. 438, 452 (1929).

[226] *Id. See also* Northern Pipeline Co. v. Marathon Pipe Line Co., 458 U.S. 50, 67 (1982).

[227] *Id.* at 67–68. Williams v. United States, 289 U.S 553 (1933).

[228] *See* Richard Fallon, Jr., *Of Legislative Courts, Administrative Agencies, and Article III*, 101 HARV. L. REV. 915, 967 (1988).

[229] *Northern Pipeline*, 458 U.S. at 67.

[230] 458 U.S. 50 (1982).

controversies in the former category may be removed from Art. III courts and delegated to . . . administrative agencies for their determination."[231] This issue has more than semantic consequence. If non-Article III tribunals may adjudicate only matters of public right, the practice of administrative agencies adjudicating a range of cases between private parties, (e.g. worker's compensation) is constitutionally suspect. Moreover, the dichotomy is somewhat anomalous. The private rights cases which *Northern Pipeline* forbade to Article I courts are, in one sense, at the periphery of Article III. The suits involving state-created common law rights come into federal courts essentially through diversity jurisdiction. Yet *Northern Pipeline* viewed these as paradigmatic Article III cases while allowing Article I tribunals to adjudicate cases based on statutory created claims of federal right.[232]

The Court addressed the issue of whether Article I courts could decide private law disputes in *Thomas v. Union Carbide Agricultural Products Co.*[233] There it reviewed a statute requiring binding arbitration of private claims for compensation from the Environmental Protection Agency owing to its use of data submitted for pesticide registration. The provision was attacked on the ground that it involved adjudication of "private rights" that, under *Northern Pipeline*, must be committed to an Article III court. The Court rejected the challenge. According to Justice O'Connor's opinion, the public rights-private rights dichotomy did not provide "a bright line test for determining the requirements of Article III."[234] Justice O'Connor wrote that Congress could, for a valid legislative purpose, create a private right "so closely integrated into a public regulatory scheme as to be a matter appropriate for agency resolution."[235] The Court rejected *Northern Pipeline*'s suggestion that legislative courts were confined to a limited number of situations, adopting a balancing test instead.

The following year, the Court considered whether the Commodity Futures Trading Commission, an Article I tribunal, could decide state law counterclaims related to matters within its jurisdiction.[236] In an opinion by Justice O'Connor, the Court again rejected a formalistic approach and articulated a balancing test in which no single factor was decisive, "with an eye to the practical effect that the congressional action will have on the constitutionally assigned role of the federal judiciary."

> Among the factors upon which we have focused are the extent to which the 'essential attributes of judicial power' are reserved to Article III courts, and, conversely, the extent to which the non-Article III forum exercises the range of jurisdiction and powers normally vested only in Article III courts, the origins and importance of the right to be adjudicated, and the concerns that drove Congress to depart from the requirements of Article III.[237]

---

[231] *Id.* at 70.

[232] . MULLENIX ET AL., *supra* note 158, at 38.

[233] 473 U.S. 568 (1985).

[234] *Id.* at 586.

[235] *Id.* at 593–94.

[236] Commodity Futures Trading Comm'n v. Schor, 478 U.S. 833 (1986).

[237] *Id.* at 851.

Although *Thomas* and *Schor* suggested an erosion of the public rights doctrine, the Court may have added some vitality to it in a later case involving whether a private litigant was entitled to a jury trial in a case brought against him by a bankruptcy trustee to recover for alleged fraud.[238] The Court recognized that the public rights doctrine "limits" Congress' latitude to deny a jury trial to cases that could properly be brought before an Article I court. The Court did not follow the balancing approach of *Thomas* and *Schor*, perhaps because the case involved the Seventh Amendment right to a jury trial. The Court said that the public rights exception could include a case in which the Federal Government was not a party provided Congress, for a valid purpose, created "a seemingly 'private' right that is so closely integrated into a public regulatory scheme as to be a matter appropriate for agency resolution with limited involvement by the Article III judiciary."[239]

More recently, the Court manifested its concern to establish some more definite parameters in the public rights doctrine. In *Stern v. Marshall* it held that Congress could not confer power on a Bankruptcy Court to enter a final judgment on a state law counterclaim that was not resolved in ruling on a creditor's proof of claim. Allowing Congress to take such claims from federal courts would transform Article III "from the guardian of individual liberty and separation of powers we have long recognized into mere wishful thinking."[240]

The use of one type of non-Article III court, military tribunals, assumed greater significance since President George W. Bush issued his November, 2001 Executive Order authorizing such tribunals to try noncitizens for terrorism related offenses. Military courts have limited jurisdiction. Thus, *Ex parte Milligan*[241] held that a military court could not try an American civilian for an alleged federal offense while civilian courts were operating. Similarly, family of military personnel cannot be tried for felonies by military courts.[242] On the other hand, in *Ex parte Quirin* the Court upheld the authority of Congress and the President to provide for use of military courts to try eight German saboteurs who landed in the United States during World War II for hostile purposes. The Court upheld the use of a military tribunal to try them, although one was an American citizen, because they were unlawful combatants not entitled to the protections of the laws of war.

In *Hamdi v. Rumsfeld*,[243] the Court held that the Government could not detain an American citizen on American soil as an enemy combatant without affording some opportunity at least to challenge that classification in a meaningful manner. The Court left open, however, the possibility that such a determination could be made "by an appropriately authorized and properly constituted military tribunal." Absent such a meaningful process, a court receiving a petition for a writ of habeas corpus from an alleged enemy combatant must ensure that "the minimum requirements of due process arc achieved."

---

[238] Granfinanciera, S. A. v. Nordberg, 492 U.S. 33 (1989).

[239] *Id.* at 54.

[240] Stern v. Marshall, 131 S. Ct. 2594 (2011).

[241] 71 U.S. (4 Wall.) 2 (1866).

[242] Reid v. Covert, 354 U.S. 1 (1957).

[243] 542 U.S. 507, 537 (2004).

§ 2.12 CASES AND CONTROVERSIES

[1] Doctrines of Justiciability: An Overview

The justiciability doctrines address, in general terms, criteria for the sort of disputes federal courts can adjudicate. Federal courts must confine their power of review to cases warranting the judicial function. The Constitution delegated to federal courts "the judicial Power" which, under Article III, extends only to "Cases" and "Controversies." Article III both confers the federal judicial power and limits it to nine categories of cases and controversies between the parties in federal courts.[244] The federal courts may only entertain complaints which meet the Article III requirement of alleging an actual case or controversy.[245]

The various justiciability doctrines generally respond to three separate concerns. "Standing" addresses the "who" question-is the litigant before the Court the right party to invoke its jurisdiction? The "when" question — is the question ripe for judicial attention? — is addressed by the doctrines of ripeness and mootness. The political question doctrine discriminates on "what" grounds; certain topics are beyond judicial competence regardless of who raises them or when they are brought to court. The Advisory Opinion doctrine, in a sense, cuts across all three grounds.

To some extent the justiciability doctrines are derived from the Constitution, either from the "case or controversy" requirement with respect to the "who" and "when" doctrines or from particular constitutional commitments of subjects to other branches of government in case of the political question doctrine. Structural principles of separation of power and checks and balances also provide further justification. The justiciability doctrines reflect the allocation to courts of the duty to decide cases or controversies but not to intrude on the domain of the other branches. In other instances, prudential concerns provide the rationale; although the Court has constitutional power to hear a matter, it deems it prudent not to exercise that power.

Many of the justiciability doctrines are implicit in *Marbury*. Marshall repeatedly tied judicial intervention to protection of rights[246] and related the power of judicial review to the need to decide controversies.[247] These doctrines implicate doctrines of standing, ripeness/mootness, and political questions.[248]

The justiciability doctrines provide some comfort against fears of a judiciary eager to expand its own space and enhance its own power. The Constitution does not explicitly require that a litigant have standing and that her case be ripe, not moot. Instead, these restraints on the federal courts were judicially recognized.

---

[244] *See* Singleton v. Wulff, 428 U.S. 106, 123 (1976) (Powell, J.).

[245] *See* O'Shea v. Littleton, 414 U.S. 488, 493 (1974).

[246] *Marbury*, 5 U.S. at 162–64, 167, 177.

[247] *Id.* at 177–78.

[248] *See* Henry P. Monaghan, *Constitutional Adjudication: The Who and When*, 82 YALE L.J. 1363, 1365 (1973).

Even when rooted in particular textual clauses, they have depended on judicial interpretation for their life and impact.

To be sure, the doctrines are sometimes invoked in part to serve particular instrumental purposes of the judiciary. They reflect the belief that courts should confine themselves to deciding matters presented in an adversary context which enhance judicial resolution and "furnish . . . a safeguard against premature or ill-advised decisions in the constitutional field."[249] At times, justiciability doctrines facilitate efficient and effective judicial decisions by making sure courts are presented with a full record of factual and legal materials on which to rule. They also serve as a filter to protect the courts' dockets from being overburdened by too many cases and those of particular types. They respond to fairness concerns by limiting judicial intervention to instances of real disputes between aggrieved parties.

The justiciability doctrines are constitutional and prudential requirements applicable in federal courts only. This fact may create problems when a state court adjudicates a case on the merits in a situation where a federal court would dismiss the action as nonjusticiable. Thus in *Doremus v. Board of Education*[250] taxpayers challenged under the Establishment Clause a New Jersey statute providing for reading of the Old Testament in public schools. The highest state court upheld the statute on the merits. Taxpayers appealed to the Supreme Court only to have their appeal dismissed for lack of federal standing. The dismissal on justiciability grounds of the federal appeal left the statute and the state court opinion in place.

[2] Advisory Opinions

The Supreme Court has construed the "Case" or "Controversy" requirement to preclude federal courts from giving advice to other departments outside of formal cases or controversies. Indeed, when George Washington sought an advisory opinion on questions of international law in 1793, the first Court politely declined. Chief Justice Jay replied by letter that the advice sought was beyond the Court's competence.[251] The Court invoked the structural principle of checks and balances and its status as a court of last resort as "considerations" mitigating against an extrajudicial reply. Moreover, it pointed out that Article II gave the President power only to require opinions from heads of executive departments, not from the federal courts.[252]

Later, in *Chicago & Southern Air Lines, Inc. v. Waterman S.S. Corp. Civil Aeronautics Bd.*,[253] the Court dismissed a petition which asked it to review an

---

[249] Paul A. Freund, The Supreme Court of the United States: Its Business, Purposes, and Performance 17 (1961).

[250] 342 U.S. 429 (1952).

[251] Letter from Chief Justice Jay (Aug. 8, 1793), *in* Bernard Schwartz, A Basic History of the U.S. Supreme Court 97–98 (1968).

[252] U.S. Const. art. II, § 2, cl. 1 ("The President . . . may require the Opinion, in writing, of the Principal officer in each of the executive Departments, upon any subject relating to the Duties of their respective offices.").

[253] 333 U.S. 103 (1948).

order of the Civil Aeronautics Board subject to later review by the President. The statutory scheme improperly put the federal courts in the business of rendering advisory opinions. Justice Jackson explained:

> To revise or review an administrative decision which, has only the force of a recommendation to the President, would be to render an advisory opinion in its most obnoxious form — advice that the President has not asked, tendered at the demand of a private litigant, on a subject concededly within the President's exclusive, ultimate control. This Court early and wisely determined that it would not give advisory opinions even when asked by the Chief Executive. It has also been the firm and unvarying practice of Constitutional Courts to render no judgments not binding and conclusive on the parties and none that are subject to later review or alteration by administrative action.[254]

The need for an actual "Case or Controversy" and the refusal to permit advisory opinions made the declaratory judgment procedure controversial at its inception. When the matter first came before the Supreme Court, some expressed doubt that constitutional limitations on federal judicial power would permit any federal declaratory judgments.[255] The Court, in indicating that the declaratory judgment technique was inconsistent with Article III, viewed the declaratory judgment as an advisory opinion.

The Supreme Court soon abandoned this equation. In *Nashville, Chattanooga & St. Louis Ry. Co. v. Wallace*,[256] it reviewed a state court declaratory judgment and held a controversy could be justiciable in an Article III court in a suit for an injunction even though the relief sought was declaratory rather than coercive. Congress subsequently enacted the Federal Declaratory Judgment Act, which provided that "in cases of actual controversy," the federal courts may "declare the rights and other legal relations" of any party "whether or not further relief is or could be sought."[257]

The Federal Declaratory Judgment Act was held constitutional in a case in which an insurance company sought a declaration that the assured's coverage had lapsed.[258] Chief Justice Hughes found that the lawsuit involved a genuine dispute between adverse parties regarding contractual rights. The controversy was "definite and concrete, not hypothetical or abstract."[259] The Act did not grant federal judges power to render advisory opinions on hypothetical facts, but to declare present rights on established facts[260] arising out of a substantial controversy "of

---

[254] *Id.* at 113–14.

[255] *See* Willing v. Chicago Auditorium Ass'n, 277 U.S. 274, 289 (1928); Liberty Warehouse Co. v. Grannis, 273 U.S. 70, 74 (1927).

[256] 288 U.S. 249 (1933).

[257] Now 28 U.S.C. § 2201 (1994).

[258] Aetna Life Ins. Co. v. Haworth, 300 U.S. 227 (1937).

[259] *Id.* at 242.

[260] *Id.*

sufficient immediacy and reality."[261]

Few criticize the Court's refusal to render advisory opinions. Decisions without a true case suffer from being divorced from the reality of actual facts. Advisory opinions are consequently bound to move in an unreal atmosphere and to be based on sterilized issues. The absence of concrete facts may also deprive the Court of opportunities to avoid constitutional decisions or to render narrow decisions. The absence of a genuine controversy may encourage collusive suits. Finally, the prohibition against advisory opinions responds to judicial efficiency concerns by preserving judicial resources for actual cases and controversies. The ban against advisory opinions, like other justiciability doctrines, rests on constitutional and prudential concerns.

Although Article III does not allow advisory opinions, they are not totally foreign to American experience. State courts, of course, are not governed by Article III and a number of state courts are authorized to give them.

[3] Feigned and Hypothetical Cases

Federal courts cannot adjudicate a friendly suit, collusively arranged between non-adverse parties to obtain the judicial resolution of some constitutional issue.[262] The reasons are not difficult to fathom; one egregious case illustrates the problem.

A tenant sued to recover treble damages against a landlord under the Emergency Price Control Act.[263] The landlord asserted the unconstitutionality of the Act. The district court accepted that argument and dismissed the case on its merits, based on the unconstitutionality of the statute. On appeal, the Supreme Court dismissed, but for different reasons. The underlying action had been collusive. Plaintiff brought the case under a fictitious name as a "friendly suit" at defendant's request. Plaintiff did not hire, or even meet, "his" attorney. Plaintiff was to incur no expense and did not even know the relief he sought until he read about it in a newspaper. In fact, defendant was the real party on both sides of the case, an arrangement he hoped would improve his prospects for success.[264] The suit was collusive because it was not "in any real sense adversary."[265]

The Court similarly declines to decide abstract, hypothetical or contingent questions.[266] These problems might be intellectually interesting but the Court does not exist to resolve hypotheticals.[267] *Muskrat v. United States*[268] illustrated the

---

[261] Maryland Casualty Co. v. Pacific Coal & Oil Co., 312 U.S. 270, 273 (1941). *See also* Lake Carriers Ass'n v. MacMullan, 406 U.S. 498, 506 (1972).

[262] *See* Ashwander v. Tennessee Valley Auth., 297 U.S. 288, 346 (1936) (Brandeis, J., concurring).

[263] United States v. Johnson, 319 U.S. 302 (1943).

[264] *Id.* at 303–04. A party may bring a test case if real adverse interests exist between the parties. *See, e.g.*, Buchanan v. Warley, 245 U.S. 60, 73–73 (1917). And a plaintiff may violate a law for the purpose of instituting a case if plaintiff is actually affected by the law. Evers v. Dwyer, 358 U.S. 202, 203–04 (1958).

[265] *Johnson*, 319 U.S. at 305.

[266] Alabama Fed'n of Labor v. McAdory, 325 U.S. 450, 461 (1945).

[267] *See, e.g.*, Rizzo v. Goode, 423 U.S. 362, 372 (1976).

[268] 219 U.S. 346 (1911).

refusal to determine a constitutional issue absent an actual case. Congress authorized several Native Americans to sue the United States to test the validity of certain statutes regarding the transfer of certain Indian lands and distribution of the proceeds. Plaintiffs sued under this statute, but did not allege that the laws involved affected them and did not assert a real danger the laws would be enforced to deprive them of rights. The Court ruled invalid Congress' attempt to secure a constitutional interpretation in the abstract. No true "Case" or "Controversy" was presented since the United States had no interest adverse to the claimants[269] but had essentially arranged the suit to determine the constitutionality of certain legislation. The power of judicial review, "the most important and delicate duty of this Court, is not given to it as a body with revisory power over the action of Congress, but because the rights of the litigants in justiciable controversies require the Court to choose between the fundamental law and a law purporting to be connected within constitutional authority but in fact beyond the power delegated to the Legislative branch of the Government."[270]

[4] Standing

[a] Constitutional Requirements

To have standing to sue, an individual bringing a lawsuit in federal court must have a direct personal interest in the governmental act she challenges. A plaintiff raising only a general grievance claiming only harm common to other citizens based on misapplication of laws does not state a "Case" or "Controversy"[271] and does not have "standing."[272] Rather, plaintiff must allege some personal injury that distinguishes her from others; unless she is hurt personally, she is seeking only an abstract judgment on the validity of the act.

Standing often is obvious. Statutes normally affect those directed to do, or not to do, specified things. Those with standing include landowners whose property is restricted by zoning law,[273] parents required to send children to public instead of religious schools,[274] a railroad company whose rates are fixed by statute,[275] teachers whose freedom is limited by a law proscribing certain activities,[276] and a couple denied the right to use contraceptive devices by a state statute.[277] The existence of standing should not be confused with the merits of the underlying dispute. A party may have standing to assert a claim on which she is not entitled to prevail. Standing

---

[269] *Id.* at 361.

[270] *Id.*

[271] *See* Lujan v. Defenders of Wildlife, 504 U.S. 555, 573–74 (1992).

[272] *See* Valley Forge Christian College v. Americans United, 454 U.S. 464, 475 (1982). "Of one thing we may be sure: Those who do not possess Art. III standing may not litigate as suitors in the courts of the United States." *Id.* at 475–76.

[273] Euclid v. Ambler Realty Co., 272 U.S. 365 (1926).

[274] Pierce v. Society of The Sisters, 268 U.S. 510 (1925).

[275] *Ex parte* Young, 209 U.S. 123 (1908).

[276] Adler v. Bd. of Educ., 342 U.S. 485 (1952).

[277] Poe v. Ullman, 367 U.S. 497 (1961).

simply means that the party has the right to assert the claim in federal court, not that her claim has merit.

. The persons described above had standing because the statutes they challenged were addressed to a class which included them. The statutes directly affected their personal or property rights. Persons who are the subject, or more accurately, the objects, of statutory provisions can normally establish harm from the governmental action or inaction in question.[278] The Supreme Court has articulated three standing requirements as the "irreducible constitutional minimum."[279] First, plaintiff must allege past or imminent injury in fact to her, i.e., harm. Second, defendant's conduct must have caused the harm, i.e. causation. Finally, a favorable court ruling must be able to redress the injury.[280]

A litigant's interest in having the government act in accordance with law, taken alone, does not confer standing. Put differently, such a case is not "judicially cognizable."[281] Thus, a plaintiff lacked standing to challenge the practice of some members of Congress serving in military reserve units[282] as violating the Incompatibility Clause.[283] The interest the litigant had was no different than that of any other citizen. Such a "generalized grievance" was too "abstract" to constitute a "concrete" harm. Similarly, in *Allen v. Wright*,[284] parents of African American children lacked standing to challenge the failure of the Internal Revenue Service to deny tax exempt status to racially discriminatory schools.[285] On the other hand, a different claimed injury, their children's diminished ability to be educated in an integrated school, was a judicially cognizable harm in part because it impacted the parents in a way distinct from its effect on the community generally.[286]

At times, standing turns upon a plaintiff's ability to allege facts sufficiently specific to demonstrate personal *harm* or *injury in fact*. Thus, in *Sierra Club v. Morton*[287], the Court found plaintiff Sierra Club did not have standing to seek to enjoin construction of a ski resort in Mineral King Valley since it failed to allege that any members had used the area. It lacked standing absent some claim the ski resort would significantly affect its members Similarly, in *Lujan v. Defenders of Wildlife*[288] the Court found another environmental group lacked standing because its members alleged only vague intentions to visit an area "some day" to view endangered species

---

[278] Lujan v. Defenders of Wildlife, 504 U.S. 555, 561–62 (1992).

[279] *Id.* at 560.

[280] *Id.* at 560–61.

[281] Allen v. Wright, 468 U.S. 737, 754 (1984).

[282] Schlesinger v. Reservists Committee to Stop the War, 418 U.S. 208 (1974).

[283] U.S. Const. art. I, § 6, cl. 2 ("No Person holding any Office under the United States, shall be a member of either House during his continuance in office.").

[284] 468 U.S. 737, 754–55 (1984).

[285] *Id.* at 754–55.

[286] *Id.* at 756.

[287] 405 U.S. 727 (1972). Justice Byron White reportedly suggested that had a single Sierra Club member strolled through the park it would have had standing. *See* Bob Woodward & Scott Armstrong, The Brethren: Inside the Supreme Court 164 (1974).

[288] 504 U.S. 555 (1992).

rather than describing a concrete plan.[289]

The Court has exhibited some reluctance to recognize standing in cases which are not brought "to enforce specific legal obligations whose violation works a direct harm" but rather are brought "to seek a restructuring of the apparatus established by the Executive Branch to fulfill its legal duties."[290] Basic separation of powers ideas explain this reticence; the Executive Branch, not the judiciary, bears the duty to "take care that the laws be faithfully executed,"[291] the Court has explained.[292]

Plaintiff must establish *causation* in addition to harm. Thus, in *Allen v. Wright*, the parents established a cognizable injury in their child's diminished ability to be educated in a racially integrated school, but could not show that the injury was caused by the IRS's failure to deny tax exemptions to certain segregated schools. The number of such schools was uncertain and the impact of the IRS action on plaintiffs' children was speculative.[293] Similarly, indigent plaintiffs failed to establish standing to challenge an IRS ruling that relaxed requirements that non-profit hospitals provide free care. The plaintiffs had been harmed by the lack of medical care but they could not trace the harm to the IRS action.[294]

Finally, plaintiff must prove *redressability* in order to establish standing. Thus, an unwed mother lacked standing to seek to require Texas to prosecute her child's father for non-support. Even if plaintiff succeeded in her suit and Texas convicted the offender, that result would not redress her grievance (i.e., lack of support) but only result in jailing the deadbeat dad.[295] Similarly, in *Warth v. Seldin*,[296] Rochester residents with low and moderate incomes challenged a suburb's zoning ordinance for effectively excluding persons of their economic circumstances from living in the town. Petitioners lacked standing, the Court said, because they did not allege specific, concrete facts demonstrating that the practices harmed *them*, and that they would benefit from the Court's intervention. They could not show that the relief sought would redress any injury they had suffered.

Standing of a plaintiff who is the object of a regulation is usually clear. The standing hurdle is highest when plaintiff alleges injury from the government's regulation of, or failure to regulate, someone else.[297] In *Lujan v. Defenders of Wildlife*, the Court suggested that plaintiff had a heavy burden to establish standing to challenge a regulation (or lack of regulation) of third parties since the causation and redressability elements would turn on conduct of others.[298]

---

[289] *Id.* at 564. *See also* Summers v. Earth Island Institute, 555 U.S. 488 (2009).

[290] *Allen v. Wright*, 468 U.S. at 761.

[291] U.S. Const. art. II, § 3.

[292] *See, e.g., Lujan*, 504 U.S. at 577; *Allen*, 468 U.S. at 761.

[293] *Allen*, 468 U.S. at 758–59.

[294] Simon v. E. Ky. Welfare Rights Org., 426 U.S. 26 (1976).

[295] Linda R. S. v. Richard D., 410 U.S. 614 (1973).

[296] 422 U.S. 490 (1975).

[297] *Lujan*, 504 U.S. at 561–62.

[298] *Id.* at 562.

Friends of the Earth, Inc. v. Laidlaw Environmental Services (TOC), Inc.[299] tested the standing principles articulated in *Lujan v. Defenders of Wildlife* and other recent cases. There the Court addressed "an important question concerning the operation of the citizen-suit provisions of the Clean Water Act."[300] A provision of the act empowered "any citizen" to bring suit to enforce limitations in a National Pollutant Discharge Elimination System (NPDES) permit by seeking civil penalties payable to the United States and an injunction. Laidlaw contended that Friends of the Earth (FOE) lacked standing; since Laidlaw's mercury discharge violations had not harmed the environment, plaintiff could claim no injury. But the Court held the relevant inquiry was "not injury to the environment but injury to the plaintiff,"[301] a test which could be satisfied by averments that aesthetic and recreational value of the area was compromised for actual users. Plaintiffs claimed they had used the area recreationally in the past but were deterred from using it now due to their concerns regarding Laidlaw's activities. The Court distinguished *Lujan*, where the allegations of use were less concrete, from here, where the affiants' "reasonable concerns about the effects of [Laidlaw's] discharges directly affected those affiants' recreational, aesthetic and economic interests."[302] Justice Scalia filed a vigorous dissent (in which Justice Thomas joined). Justice Scalia disparaged the weight of the affiants' "concerns" in view of the absence of environmental harm. The Court's opinion, he said, rendered the injury-in-fact requirement "a sham."[303] "If there are permit violations, and a member of a plaintiff environmental organization lives near the offending plant, it would be difficult not to satisfy today's lenient standard,"[304] he wrote, a conclusion that will no doubt please environmental groups.

Environmental cases continue to generate many of the Court's standing decisions. In *Massachusetts v. Environmental Protection Agency*,[305] the Court held that Massachusetts had standing to challenge the EPA's refusal to regulate greenhouse gas emissions. Following Justice Kennedy's *Lujan* concurrence, the Court recognized that where Congress has conferred "a procedural right to protect . . . concrete interests" a party may exercise that right "without meeting all the normal standards for redressability and immediacy" that the Court had laid out in *Lujan v. Defenders of Wildlife*. Instead of requiring such a petitioner to show a likelihood that a favorable decision would redress the alleged injury, the Court explained that a litigant vested with a procedural right satisfies standing requirements "if there is some possibility that the requested relief will prompt the injury-causing party to reconsider the decision that allegedly harmed the litigant." Moreover, the Court emphasized the "special position and interest" of Massachusetts as a state, not simply a private individual as in *Lujan*. Massachusetts' ownership of a great deal of the allegedly affected territory confirmed its concrete stake in the outcome of the case. The Court was untroubled by the vast number of

---

[299] 528 U.S. 167 (2000).

[300] *Id.* at 173.

[301] *Id.* at 181.

[302] *Id.* at 183–84.

[303] *Id.* at 201 (Scalia, J., dissenting).

[304] *Id.*

[305] 549 U.S. 497 (2007).

sources of pollution which contribute to the proliferation of greenhouse gases and global warming; federal courts did not forfeit jurisdiction simply because a remedial change might have a small and incremental impact.

Two years later, in *Summers v. Earth Island Institute*,[306] the Court (5-4) held that an environmental group lacked standing to challenge a governmental regulation after settling a portion of the lawsuit in which it had alleged a concrete injury against it. Writing for the majority, Justice Scalia stated that to allow standing to persist in those circumstances "would fly in the face of Article III's injury-in-fact requirement." Justice Scalia's majority opinion also rejected claims that petitioners had suffered procedural injury in being denied the right to file comments on certain governmental actions since they had no concrete interest at stake. The four dissenters reasoned that where "a plaintiff has *already* been subject to the injury it wishes to challenge" the plaintiff must only show a "realistic likelihood" that the challenged conduct will recur and harm them in to establish an injury-in-fact.

[b] Prudential Requirements

In addition to the constitutional standards derived from the "Case" or "Controversy" language, the Court has imposed various prudential standing requirements. The prudential principles, like the constitutional requirements, reflect a concern regarding the appropriate role of the judiciary in a democracy. Unlike the constitutional requirements, Congress can modify or override prudential considerations.[307] The prudential standing requirements include the limitations on third party standing, the zone of interests test, and, according to some authority, the rule against standing based on a generalized grievance.

[i] Rights of Others

Even when a plaintiff meets the Article III standing requirements so the controversy is within their constitutional power to resolve, federal courts hesitate to reach the merits of disputes involving the rights of absent third parties. A litigant may normally assert "his own legal rights and interests, and cannot rest his claim to relief on the legal rights or interests of third parties."[308] Several considerations account for the judicial reticence to allow litigants to assert the rights of others. The right-holder may prefer not to litigate her rights in court or in the forum chosen. In such circumstances, is it fair to allow a third party to raise issues that impact others? Moreover, the Court might not have to address the issues if it does not allow third parties to raise them. Finally, the Court may believe the issues will be more rigorously presented or benefit from a factual context if litigated by actual stake-holders. The courts will sometimes consider rights of absent third parties if (1) the litigant has a close relationship with the person whose right he seeks to assert; and (2) "some genuine obstacle" impedes the third person's assertion of his rights.[309]

---

[306] 555 U.S. 488 (2009).

[307] Bennett v. Spear, 520 U.S. 154, 162 (1997).

[308] Warth v. Seldin, 422 U.S. 490, 499 (1975). *See also* Singleton v. Wulff, 428 U.S. 106, 114 (1976).

[309] *Singleton*, 428 U.S. at 115–16.

For instance, a court allowed the National Association for the Advancement of Colored People, in resisting a court order that it disclose its membership, to assert the First and Fourteenth Amendment rights of those members to allow them to remain anonymous; to require the members themselves to appear would nullify the right claimed.[310] Similarly a covenantor who breached a racially restrictive covenant by selling a house to black buyers could raise the buyers' right to equal protection in a damage suit another covenantor brought. Since it would be difficult for buyers to assert their own rights,[311] the seller could assert those rights. The Court held that Missouri doctors could challenge a State statute that excluded from Medicaid benefits abortions not "medically indicated." The doctors had standing since if they prevailed, they would benefit by receiving payment for abortions. As a prudential matter, they could also assert the constitutional rights of their patients with whom they had a close relationship particularly since the patients faced formidable obstacles to asserting their own rights.[312]

The Court has also held that a white criminal defendant had standing to challenge discrimination against blacks in the selection of his grand jury. In *Campbell v. Louisiana*,[313] the Court, speaking through Justice Kennedy, reasoned that someone accused of a crime suffers a significant injury in fact when discriminatory selection procedures taint the integrity of the grand jury selection process. Such a defendant, the Court argued, shares an interest in eradicating discrimination with excluded grand jurors who may be dissuaded from asserting their own rights due to economic disincentives.

In *Elk Grove v. Newdow*,[314] the Court invoked prudential standing doctrine to hold that a noncustodial parent lacked standing to challenge, on his daughter's behalf, a California law which required every public school to begin each day by reciting the Pledge of Allegiance. Newdow, an atheist, claimed that the law violated the First Amendment's guarantees under the Establishment and Free Exercise Clauses. Sandra Banning, the mother and legal custodian of Newdow's daughter, contended that her daughter believed in God, was not bothered by reciting "under God" in the Pledge, and would be harmed by inclusion in the lawsuit.

The Court noted that third party standing generally fell within "the prudential dimensions of the standing doctrine."[315] Consistent with the federal judiciary's general reluctance to intervene in cases which turn on domestic relations issues, the Court concluded that it was "improper" for federal courts "to entertain a claim by a plaintiff whose standing to sue is founded on family law rights that are in dispute when prosecution of the lawsuit may have an adverse effect on the person who is the source of the plaintiff's claimed standing."[316] Since California had deprived Newdow of the right to sue as next friend, he lacked prudential standing.

---

[310] *See* NAACP v. Alabama, 357 U.S. 449 (1958).

[311] *See* Barrows v. Jackson, 346 U.S. 249 (1953).

[312] *Singleton*, 428 U.S. at 115–16.

[313] 523 U.S. 392 (1998).

[314] 542 U.S. 1 (2004).

[315] *Id.* at 12.

[316] *Id.* at 17.

[ii]   Zones of Interests

The zone of interests test requires a plaintiff's grievance be within the zone of interests of the statute or constitutional provision invoked.[317] Litigants are only within the zone of interests of a statute if they are part of the class it was designed to protect. Thus, in *Bennett v. Spear*,[318] the Court held that certain ranchers challenging government action were within the zone of interests of the Endangered Species Act (ESA). The ranchers objected to action that withheld water from their irrigation district to preserve certain endangered species. By providing that "any person may commence a civil suit" Congress negated or expanded the zone of interests to include not only environmentalists but also those injured by preservation.[319] Similarly, in *Federal Election Commission v. Akins*,[320] the Court interpreted the Federal Election Commission Act to allow a suit by voters to compel the Federal Election Commission to require an organization to disclose certain information. The Court detected no congressional intent to limit the statute's protection to candidates, political parties, or political committees.[321]

[iii]   Generalized Grievance

Although the generalized grievance principle initially was described as "prudential"[322] the Court more recently has treated it as constitutional.[323] *Akins* suggests that the generalized grievance disqualification only applies when the harm is not only "widely shared" but is also "abstract and indefinite." Both criteria must be met. No impediment arises when a harm common to many or all is specific and concrete.[324] Thus, a law denying all the freedom to criticize the government would not be a generalized grievance simply because it applied across the board since the harm would be concrete. On the other hand, a generally held interest in having the government follow the Constitution or some part of it is too abstract to ground standing.

[c]   Citizen Standing

Instances where a litigant asserts standing as a citizen present the classic case of a generalized grievance. The Court has rejected the idea that citizenship confers standing to require the government to follow or enforce the law. Thus, in *Schlesinger v. Reservists Committee to Stop the War*,[325] citizens lacked standing to sue to prevent members of Congress from serving in the military reserves under

---

[317] 520 U.S. 154, 163 (1997).

[318] *Id.*

[319] *Id.* at 163–64.

[320] 524 U.S. 11 (1998).

[321] *Id.* at 20.

[322] Warth v. Seldin, 422 U.S. 490, 498–500 (1975).

[323] *See* Lujan v. Defenders of Wildlife, 504 U.S. 555, 576 (1992). *See also Akins*, 524 U.S. at 23 ("Whether styled as a constitutional or prudential limit.").

[324] *Akins*, 524 U.S. at 24.

[325] 418 U.S. 208 (1974).

the Incompatibility Clause.[326] Plaintiffs' grievance was generalized and common to all; allowing a citizen to sue on that basis alone would violate basic principles of separation of powers. Similarly, in *United States v. Richardson*[327] a citizen could not sue to protest the secrecy of Central Intelligence Agency expenditures as violating the Statement and Accounts Clause of Article I, § 9. cl. 7.[328]

These cases illustrate a central dilemma. The refusal to recognize citizen standing may create some cases in which no private citizen can sue to enforce a constitutional provision. Indeed, the Court recognized this possibility in both cases. On the other hand, if the Court permitted citizens to bring such suits, little would remain of the standing requirement. The resolution may reside in a realization that some constitutional issues may be left to the political process. The Executive or Legislative branches, or the electorate, not the courts, may have the final word regarding such issues.

[d] Taxpayers

Suppose, however, a taxpayer believes government funds are being spent in execution of invalid laws. Does her status as taxpayer confer standing to challenge the law? In *Frothingham v. Mellon*,[329] the Court said no. Plaintiff, as a taxpayer, sued to enjoin, on constitutional grounds, a federal statute that provided for appropriations to be apportioned among the states. Plaintiff argued that the appropriations would increase future taxation. The Supreme Court dismissed, holding that plaintiff, as a federal taxpayer, did not have standing to challenge a congressional enactment.

Frothingham stated that a federal taxpayer's interest was too minute and remote to justify standing. Moreover, a federal taxpayer has no personal interest in the challenged statute. Consequently, the federal taxpayer failed to allege the type of direct injury required for standing.[330]

No doubt in *Frothingham* the Court feared that allowing any taxpayer to raise constitutional issues even if she lacked a unique personal interest would open the floodgates of constitutional-law litigation. The spectre may be more theoretical than real. Constitutional cases are often expensive and time-consuming; they are rarely filed as a lark.

Strictly applied, *Frothingham* would render some invalid legislation immune from constitutional attack. Absent taxpayer standing, congressional appropriations could never be subjected to judicial challenge. Thus, if Congress made grants to

---

[326] U.S. Const. art. 1 § 6, cl. 2 ("No Senator or Representative shall, during the time for which he was elected, be appointed to any civil office under the Authority of the United States, which shall have been created, or the emoluments whereof shall have been increased during such time; and no person holding any office under the United States, shall be a member of either House during his continuance in office.").

[327] 418 U.S. 166 (1974).

[328] The Statement and Accounts Clause provides that "a regular Statement and Account of the Receipts and Expenditures of all public money shall be published from time to time."

[329] 262 U.S. 447 (1923).

[330] *Id.* at 487. On the other hand, a municipal taxpayer had a "direct and immediate" interest in the expenditure of local dollars. *Id.* at 486.

church-related schools in violation of the First Amendment, *Frothingham* would preclude judicial review. To avoid that result, the Court modified the *Frothingham* doctrine in *Flast v. Cohen*[331] where it upheld the standing of a federal taxpayer to challenge congressional expenditures for violating the Establishment Clause of the First Amendment.

For standing to exist under *Flast*, (1) the taxpayer must attack an expenditure under the Taxing and Spending Clause (it is not enough "to allege an incidental expenditure of tax funds in the administration of an essentially regulatory statute");[332] and (2) the taxpayer must demonstrate that the challenged expenditure exceeds a "specific constitutional limitation (e.g., the Establishment Clause) on that power.[333]

Flast has been applied strictly. *Valley Forge Christian College v. Americans United*[334] showed that taxpayers will not have standing to challenge all actions which may violate the Establishment Clause. The government conveyed a military hospital to a church-related college under a federal statute authorizing the Secretary of Health, Education and Welfare to transfer surplus governmental property to educational institutions. Taxpayers claimed the conveyance violated the Establishment Clause. The Court never reached that issue because it ruled they failed the first prong of the *Flast* test. The action they challenged was not an exercise of power under the Taxing and Spending Clause, but of power to dispose of federal property under the Property Clause of Article IV.[335]

In *Schlesinger v. Reservists to Stop the War*,[336] the Court found no standing in a challenge that the membership of certain congressmen in the military reserves violated the Incompatibility Clause.[337] To the extent plaintiff alleged taxpayer standing, the Court found it failed to satisfy the first *Flast* criteria since plaintiff challenged Executive Branch action in allowing congressmen to serve in the military reserves, not legislative action under the Taxing and Spending Clause. Again, the Court saw no concrete injury and only a generalized grievance. On the same day it decided *Schlesinger*, the Court in *United States v. Richardson*,[338] held that a taxpayer lacked standing to challenge a statute that allowed the Central Intelligence Agency to maintain the secrecy of its accounting. The taxpayer had claimed the practice violated the Accounts Clause[339] of the Constitution and undermined his ability to vote intelligently. But the Court held that the taxpayer failed to allege that funds were being spent contrary to a "specific constitutional

---

[331] 392 U.S. 83 (1968).

[332] *Id.* at 102.

[333] *Id.* at 102–03.

[334] 454 U.S. 464 (1982).

[335] *Id.* at 479–80 (Art. IV, § 3, cl. 2 provides, in pertinent part: "The Congress shall have Power to dispose of . . . Property belonging to the United States").

[336] 418 U.S. 208 (1974).

[337] *See* U.S. Const. art. I, § 6, cl. 2.

[338] 418 U.S. 166 (1974).

[339] *See* U.S. Const. art. I, § 9, cl. 7 ("a regular Statement and Account of the Receipts and Expenditures of all public Money shall be published from time to time").

limitation" on Congress' power to tax and spend.[340] Moreover, it discounted his complaint as a generalized grievance.

More recently, the Court has reaffirmed the very limited nature of the *Flast* exception. In *DaimlerChrysler Corp. v. Cuno*, the Court held that state and local taxpayers lacked standing to challenge a franchise tax credit and property tax exemption under the Commerce Clause.[341] The Court reasoned that the rights protected under the Commerce Clause differ fundamentally from those the Establishment Clause safeguards.[342] Further, applying *Flast* to the Commerce Clause would "leave no principled way of distinguishing those other constitutional provisions that we have recognized constrain governments' taxing and spending decisions"[343] and would "be quite at odds with . . . [the] narrow application [of the *Flast* test] in our precedent and *Flast's* own promise that it would not transform federal courts into forums for taxpayers' 'generalized grievances.' "[344]

In *Hein v. Freedom From Religion Foundation, Inc.*,[345] the Court, in a plurality opinion by Justice Alito, concluded that the *Flast* exception did not apply unless a party challenges a specific congressional action or appropriation or asks the Court to invalidate an enactment or legislatively created program. Respondents challenged a 2001 executive order which created the White House Office of Faith-Based and Community Initiatives on the grounds that it violated the Establishment Clause. Justice Alito, joined by Chief Justice Roberts and Justice Kennedy, concluded that the *Flast* two-part test was not satisfied because the challenge was not directed at an exercise of congressional power. Justices Scalia and Thomas agreed that respondent lacked standing but reached that conclusion because they viewed *Flast* as "irreconcilable" with Article III. They would overrule, not distinguish, *Flast*. The four dissenters thought the *Flast* exception should apply when a taxpayer challenges the expenditure by an executive agency of identifiable sums of tax dollars for religious purposes.

The Court further narrowed the *Flast* taxpayer standing exception in a 5-4 decision in *Arizona Christian School Tuition Organization v. Winn*,[346] where the Court held that the *Flast* exception to the normal rule against general taxpayer standing did not apply where a taxpayer challenged as unconstitutional under the First Amendment an Arizona tax credit (as opposed to a tax expenditure) given to support religious study. Although the Court acknowledged that tax credits could have similar effects as tax expenditures, it reasoned that the *Flast* exception did not apply to tax credits since they did not involve an extraction and expenditure of some portion of the objecting taxpayer's funds.

---

[340] *Richardson*, 418 U.S. at 175.

[341] DaimlerChrysler Corp. v. Cuno, 547 U.S. 332, 346 (2006).

[342] *Id.* at 347.

[343] *Id.* at 348.

[344] *Id.*

[345] 551 U.S. 587 (2007).

[346] 131 S. Ct. 1436 (2011).

[e] Voter Standing

The Court held in *Federal Election Commission v. Akins*[347] that litigants had standing as voters to sue to compel a government agency to require a third party to disclose information allegedly helpful in voting. In *Akins*, a group of voters sued to compel the Federal Election Commission (FEC) to require the American Israel Public Affairs Committee (AIPAC) to disclose information concerning membership, contributions, and expenditures. The voters claimed the information would help them assess candidates. In a 6-3 decision, the Court held that the voters had standing to pursue the action.

The Court found that Congress used broad language in the Federal Election Campaign Act (FECA) that reflected its intent "to cast the standing net broadly" and to include voters within those interests protected.[348]

Accordingly, FECA satisfied any prudential standing requirements.[349] Moreover, the Court held the *Flast* test inapplicable and that the voters met the three constitutional standing requirements-injury in fact, causation, and redressability. Lack of access to information that might prove helpful in voting constituted harm that was concrete and particular.[350] As such, *Akins* did not involve the sort of "generalized grievance" the Court had refused to entertain on other occasions. Writing for the majority, Justice Breyer suggested that courts had invoked the "generalized grievance" language to dismiss cases for lack of standing when the harm asserted was both "widely shared" and "of an abstract and indefinite nature."[351] Here, however, the fact that many shared the alleged informational injury did not preclude Congress from allowing voter suits because the injury was "sufficiently concrete and specific." The Court implied that the relationship between the alleged injury and "voting, the most basic of political rights," may have influenced its decision.[352] The dissenters, led by Justice Scalia, were not assuaged. They complained that the voters' harm, if any, was not "particularized" and not "differentiated" and that the lawsuit unconstitutionally gave the judiciary the Chief Executive's function to assure the proper execution of the laws.[353]

The Court has not always found that litigants had standing to complain that the government was not disclosing pertinent information. Indeed, the dissenters found *Akins* indistinguishable from *United States v. Richardson*[354] where the Court held that a taxpayer asserted only a "generalized grievance" by challenging the

---

[347] 524 U.S. 11 (1998).

[348] *Id.* at 19.

[349] *Id.* at 20. Congress provided that "Any person who believes a violation of [FECA] . . . has occurred, may file a complaint with the [FEC]" and that "[a]ny party aggrieved by an [FEC order] dismissing a complaint filed by such party . . . may file a petition" in federal district court to review that dismissal. *Id.* at 19.

[350] *Id.* at 24–25.

[351] *Id.* at 23.

[352] *Akins*, 524 U.S. at 25. The Court found the harm fairly traceable to the FEC's decision not to require the disclosure and concluded that the courts could redress the voters' injury. *Id.* at 25.

[353] *Id.* at 36 (Scalia, J., dissenting).

[354] 418 U.S. 166 (1974).

government's failure to disclose Central Intelligence Agency expenditures as violative of the Accounts Clause.[355] The majority, however, distinguished *Richardson* from *Akins* on three grounds: (1) the *Flast* logical nexus test was applied in *Richardson* (where it was not met) but not in *Akins*; (2) *Richardson* focused on taxpayer, not voter, standing; (3) *Richardson*, but not *Akins*, involved a claim under the Accounts clause that the Court implied might not be subject to enforcement by a citizen; *Akins* raised a claim regarding information useful in voting for which Congress had conferred standing.[356]

[f] Congressional Standing

Individual legislators lack standing to challenge in court legislative actions that simply diminish their collective political power without affecting their private interests. In *Raines v. Byrd*,[357] six members of Congress alleged that the Line Item Veto Act (LIVA) diluted their voting power and diminished congressional power in violation of the Constitution. Although LIVA authorized "[a]ny Member of Congress or any individual adversely affected . . . [to] bring an action,"[358] the Court found that legislators did not meet the Article III standing requirements. Specifically, the Court, speaking through Chief Justice Rehnquist, concluded that the legislators "have alleged no injury to themselves as individuals" and that "the institutional injury they allege is wholly abstract and widely dispersed."[359]

Byrd does not, of course, mean that legislators never have standing to challenge official actions. Thus in *Powell v. McCormack*,[360] Representative Adam Clayton Powell had standing to contest his exclusion from the House of Representatives and loss of salary. In *Powell*, unlike *Byrd*, the legislator had suffered a private loss, not simply a diminution of political power that he shared with colleagues.

In *Coleman v. Miller*,[361] the Court had previously held in a 5-4 decision that state legislators had standing to litigate an institutional injury. The *Coleman* plaintiffs included 20 Kansas state senators who voted against the Child Labor Amendment to the Constitution. They sought a writ of mandamus to compel state officials to recognize that the Kansas state legislature had not ratified the proposed amendment that carried only if the lieutenant governor's tie-breaking vote was counted.

The Court, in *Byrd*, limited *Coleman* at most to the proposition that legislators whose votes would have been sufficient to defeat (or enact) a specific legislative act have standing to sue if that legislative action goes into effect (or does not go into effect) on the grounds that their votes have been completely nullified.[362]

---

[355] The Accounts Clause provides that "a regular Statement and Account of the Receipts and Expenditures of all public Money shall be published from time to time." U.S. Const. art. I, § 9, cl. 7.

[356] *See Akins*, 524 U.S. at 22–25.

[357] 521 U.S. 811 (1997).

[358] *Id.* at 815.

[359] *Id.* at 829.

[360] 395 U.S. 486 (1969).

[361] 307 U.S. 433 (1939).

[362] *See Byrd*, 521 U.S. at 825–26.

The legislators in *Byrd* had opposed LIVA but could not claim that their votes against it had been nullified. The *Byrd* majority identified three factors that may have influenced its decision: (1) plaintiffs had not been authorized by their respective Houses of Congress to bring the action; (2) Congress had adequate legislative remedies available including repeal of LIVA; (3) other plaintiffs would have standing to challenge LIVA.[363]

Although the Court reserved decision as to whether the result would have differed absent any of these factors, its listing of them arguably limited its holding and may suggest some open issues.

[5] Ripeness

As its name implies, ripeness deals with the timing of a lawsuit. Courts cannot consider constitutional issues prematurely. Whereas standing doctrine seeks to restrict judicial cases to those where the "right" plaintiff brings the action, ripeness endeavors to limit judicial review to cases brought at the "right" time. A constitutional question is ripe for judicial review only when the governmental act being challenged has a direct adverse effect on the individual making the challenge.

Ripeness, accordingly, responds to a separation of powers concern by postponing judicial intervention until it is clear a dispute exists. As such, it minimizes the instances of judicial review of the actions of other branches. It also serves needs of the adversary system by deferring litigation until a dispute has developed sufficiently.

Ripeness involves the question of whether the issue is fit for review.[364] Put differently, fitness for review pivots in part on whether the claim turns on contingent events or whether the facts have sufficiently developed to make harm definite. Courts consider, too, the hardship on the parties of deferring review.[365]

To some extent ripeness and standing are interrelated and indeed may describe similar circumstances. Thus, the absence of an injury might cause a court to conclude that plaintiff lacks standing since she has not been harmed or that the case was not yet ripe.

O'Shea v. Littleton[366] illustrated the shared space. There, the Court dismissed as nonjusticiable an action against officials for allegedly discriminating against blacks in certain judicial matters. Since none of the plaintiffs had been identified as having been defendants in the offending courtrooms the Court held the case nonjusticiable. One might argue that plaintiffs lacked standing (since they had not been harmed) or that the dispute was not yet ripe (to the extent their harm had not yet occurred).

Ripeness turns primarily on two factors: What would be the hardship to the parties of withholding judicial consideration? How fit are the issues for judicial

---

[363] *Id.* at 829.

[364] Abbott Laboratories v. Gardner, 387 U.S. 136, 149 (1967).

[365] *Id.*

[366] 414 U.S. 488 (1974).

determination?[367]

Sometimes ripeness depends on whether the act involves provisions that are self-executing or those that are not. A law is self-executing if its mere existence adversely affects private rights and obligations, if it requires those subject to do or not do specified acts and subjects them to specified legal consequences for noncompliance. Such statutes may be ripe for challenge before they are applied to any individual.

Euclid v. Ambler Realty Co.[368] and *Pierce v. Society of Sisters*[369] illustrate how self-executing laws are often subject to judicial review even before enforcement. *Euclid* involved a suit to enjoin a zoning ordinance that restricted the use of plaintiff's property to residential purposes. The government had not threatened enforcement. Still, the Court rejected the argument that the suit was premature. The landowner complained that the existence of the ordinance significantly impaired the land's value. This allegation made the case ripe for pre-enforcement challenge.[370]

In *Pierce*, private schools sued to enjoin enforcement of a state statute that required parents to send children to public schools. Although the statute had not yet become effective, the Court regarded its existence as an immediate threat to the private schools. Parents would be reticent to disobey the law and face criminal penalty. They would also not delay removing their children from the private schools until the statute took effect.

Absent immediate judicial review, statutes like that at issue in *Pierce* present an affected person with a Hobson's Choice. Either she must comply (in which case she will lose her right to raise her constitutional argument) or violate the law and set up its invalidity as a criminal defense.[371] But the latter course risks incurring the criminal penalty provided in the statute.

Ex parte Young[372] made clear that a federal court may review a criminal sanction prior to any prosecutions. The Court there heard an injunction suit challenging the constitutionality of a state criminal statute prior to its enforcement. Courts often follow this approach.

These decisions rest on the premise that it is often a mistake to require a law to be violated and consequences imposed before determining its validity. *United Public Workers v. Mitchell*[373] reflected a contrary view. Federal employees sued to restrain enforcement of the Hatch Act which precluded federal employees from participating in political management or campaigns. Plaintiffs claimed the statute violated their constitutional right to engage in political activities, but the Court

---

[367] *Abbott Laboratories*, 387 U.S. at 149; Poe v. Ullman, 367 U.S. 497, 508–09 (1961).

[368] 272 U.S. 365 (1926).

[369] 268 U.S. 510 (1925).

[370] 272 U.S. at 386.

[371] *See Abbott Laboratories*, 387 U.S. at 152–53 (allowing preenforcement review of new labeling regulations for drugs).

[372] 209 U.S. 123, 163–65 (1908).

[373] 330 U.S. 75 (1947).

deemed it unripe since prior to violation only a "hypothetical threat" to plaintiffs' rights existed.[374] Yet the existence of the challenged statute restricted the right of federal employees to engage in political activities prior to enforcement.

Subsequently, the Supreme Court treated as ripe for review situations where the challenged statute had self-executing impact. In *Adler v. Board of Education*,[375] teachers challenged a state statute that provided for the removal of teachers who had engaged in specified "subversive" activities. Although plaintiffs had not engaged in any of the proscribed activities, the Court held that the suit could be maintained. Like statutes discussed above, this provision presented teachers with the dilemma of complying with its prescriptions or incurring the risk of substantial penalties to exercise constitutional rights.

After *Mitchell*, the Court again addressed a pre-enforcement challenge to the Hatch Act. Some federal employees, who had not violated the law, alleged that the Civil Service Commission was threatening to enforce the Hatch Act's prohibition regarding certain political activity in which they desired to engage. The Court decided the case on the merits, though without distinguishing the case from *Mitchell* on the ripeness issue.[376]

Fitness for review turns in large part on the extent to which resolution of an issue hinges on its facts. For example, in *Socialist Labor Party v. Gilligan*,[377] the Court dismissed on ripeness grounds an action challenging an Ohio law which limited ballot access by requiring a party file an affidavit confirming its loyalty to the United States. The Court observed that the record disclosed little about the Ohio requirement. There was no evidence of injury and "the law's future effect remains wholly speculative,"[378] wrote the Court.

Poe v. Ullman[379] raised another aspect of ripeness, whether a party can bring a pre-enforcement challenge to a statute that remains on the books yet is never enforced. *Poe* involved a declaratory judgment action that a state statute prohibiting use of contraceptives was unconstitutional. The highest state court upheld the statute on the merits. The Supreme Court affirmed, on the grounds that the statute was not ripe for review. Although the statute contained a criminal penalty, a sharply divided Court ruled that "the mere existence of a state penal statute would constitute insufficient grounds to support a federal court's adjudication of its constitutionality in proceedings brought against the State's prosecuting officials if real threat of enforcement is wanting."[380] The Court noted that only one violation (a "test case") had been prosecuted in more than 80 years.[381] The Court inferred that Connecticut had effectively nullified its law.[382]

---

[374] *Id.* at 89–90.

[375] 342 U.S. 485 (1952).

[376] United States Civil Serv. Comm'n v. National Ass'n of Letter Carriers, 413 U.S. 548 (1973).

[377] 406 U.S. 583 (1972).

[378] *Id.* at 589.

[379] 367 U.S. 497 (1961).

[380] *Id.* at 507.

[381] *Id.* at 501.

Fear of enforcement under these circumstances was "chimerical."[383]

By contrast, in *Epperson v. Arkansas*,[384] the Court disposed of the justiciability issue without even recognizing it as a serious issue in a challenge to a state law prohibiting the teaching of evolution. The statute was "presently more of a curiosity than a vital fact of life," but the Court pronounced itself dutibound to decide the constitutional issues.[385]

Epperson's resolution of the ripeness issue has one advantage over the treatment in *Poe*. So long as a criminal law remains on the books it may be enforced even if prosecutors have long ignored it. Otherwise, the criminal penalty may inhibit certain conduct even though prosecutions have not been brought.

[6] Mootness

Like ripeness, mootness addresses a timing question: When is a suit appropriate for adjudication? Whereas ripeness asks whether the suit is ready for review, mootness considers whether the case or controversy has disappeared. "[W]e have no power . . . to adjudicate a case that no longer presents an actual, ongoing dispute between the named parties."[386] The mootness doctrine filters out cases which no longer present real controversies. Moreover, it spares courts from investing resources in cases which present no live issue. A court may dismiss a case as moot on its own motion.[387]

For instance, in one case a plaintiff claimed a state university law school had not admitted him due to his race. The trial court granted an injunction ordering the plaintiff's admission. By the time the Supreme Court heard argument plaintiff was in his final quarter of law school and the university said it would allow him to graduate regardless of the outcome of the litigation. Accordingly, the Court deemed the case moot.[388]

The Court has recognized an exception to the mootnesss doctrine when the underlying dispute is "capable of repetition, yet evading review."[389] This exception requires that (1) the challenged action be too short in duration to be fully litigated before its cessation or expiration, and (2) "there was a reasonable expectation that the *same complaining party* would be subjected to the same action again."[390] In *Roe v. Wade*[391] a single pregnant woman challenged the constitutionality of a state abortion law. The case was challenged as moot because plaintiff, though pregnant

---

[382] *Id.* at 502.

[383] *Id.* at 508.

[384] 393 U.S. 97 (1968).

[385] *Id.* at 102.

[386] Honig v. Doe, 484 U.S. 305, 332–33 (1988) (Scalia, J., dissenting).

[387] North Carolina v. Rice, 404 U.S. 244, 246 (1971).

[388] *See* De Funis v. Odegaard, 416 U.S. 312, 319–20 (1974).

[389] Kremens v. Bartley, 431 U.S. 119, 133 (1977).

[390] SEC v. Sloan, 436 U.S. 103, 109 (1978) (emphasis in original).

[391] 410 U.S. 113 (1973).

when suit was filed, was not when the case reached the Court almost three years later. Although an actual controversy generally must exist at all stages of litigation, the Court rejected the mootness argument. Pregnancy comes to term before the usual appellate process is complete. Judicial review would be effectively denied absent some modification of mootness doctrine. "Our laws should not be that rigid."[392] Pregnancy thus provides a classic occasion for a conclusion of non-mootness; a rigid concept of mootness would mean that it would always evade review.[393]

Courts also do not apply the mootness doctrine when a party voluntarily stops a challenged conduct during litigation without creating the reasonable likelihood that it will not later resume that activity. The courts suspect strategic conduct designed to improve litigation prospects while leaving the defendant "free to return to his old ways."[394] The case will be dismissed as moot only if defendant can shoulder the heavy burden of showing the lack of a "reasonable expectation" of the wrong recurring.[395]

In *Friends of the Earth, Inc. v. Laidlaw*,[396] a defendant in an environmental case sought to have a case against it dismissed as moot on the grounds that it had rectified all permit violations. The Court rejected its argument. Voluntary cessation cases were measured against a "stringent" standard. Such a case becomes moot only if defendant bears the "formidable burden of showing that it is absolutely clear the allegedly wrongful behavior could not reasonably be expected to recur."[397]

Later the same term. in *City of Erie v. Pap's A.M.*,[398] the Court rejected a mootness challenge to a case involving the constitutionality of Erie's antinudity statute even though the alleged violator (Kandyland) had closed its doors before the case reached the Court. Closing the facility did not moot the case since Kandyland was still incorporated and could resume operations. The Court noted a characteristic of the case that separated it from "run of the mill voluntary cessation" cases.[399] Pap's had prevailed in the Pennsylvania Supreme Court in its challenge to the law's constitutionality. If a mootness objection precluded review by an Article III court, the state court decision would stand, thereby precluding Erie from enforcing its ordinance. The Court was troubled by the prospect of a party who prevails below moving to dismiss a case on mootness grounds based on its voluntary cessation and thereby preserving its favorable judgment without allowing its adversary to appeal.

---

[392] *Id.* at 125.

[393] *See also* First Nat'l Bank of Boston v. Bellotti, 435 U.S. 765 (1978).

[394] United States v. W. T. Grant Co., 345 U.S. 629, 632 (1953).

[395] *Id.* at 633.

[396] 528 U.S. 167 (2000).

[397] *Id.* at 190.

[398] 529 U.S. 277 (2000).

[399] *Id.* at 288.

A case may, however, be moot where the party who ceases operation was the state court loser. In *City News and Novelty, Inc. v. City of Waukesha*,[400] the Court, on similar facts, dismissed as moot an appeal from a state court judgment which upheld the municipality's action against an entity that thereafter ceased operations. The party that ceased operations in *City News* "left the fray as a loser, not a winner." Accordingly, the municipality in *City News* was not left "under the weight of an adverse judgment."[401] Nor could the party manipulate the Court's jurisdiction as the Court implied Kandyland may have done.[402]

The Court has, from time to time, described mootness as "the doctrine of standing set in a time frame: The requisite personal interest that must exist at the commencement of the litigation (standing) must continue throughout its existence (mootness)."[403] In *Laidlaw*,[404] the Court qualified that depiction in large part based on exceptions. Whereas the plaintiff bears the burden of proving standing by showing that the challenged behavior is likely to occur or continue and that injury is "impending," the "defendant claiming that its voluntary compliance moots a case bears the formidable burden of showing that it is absolutely clear" the challenged behavior "could not reasonably be expected to recur."[405] Thus, in some instances "the prospect that a defendant will engage in (or resume) harmful conduct may be too speculative to support standing, but not too speculative to overcome mootness."[406] Moreover, whereas mootness allows a "capable of repetition, yet evading review" exception, standing does not. In *Laidlaw*, defendant argued that its subsequent compliance with its permit and closure of its facility mooted plaintiff's lawsuit. The Court viewed these as facts the lower court could consider in deciding whether it was "absolutely clear" *Laidlaw*'s permit violations "could not reasonably be expected to recur."[407]

[7] Political Question

The political question doctrine is the final justiciability doctrine. It puts certain questions outside the bounds of judicial decision based on the subject matter involved. The title may stem from *Marbury v. Madison*, where Chief Justice Marshall spoke of certain "[q]uestions, in their nature political."[408] Marshall introduced the concept to distinguish issues where the President or executive officers had unlimited discretion from those involving rights. The former might be termed political questions; the latter, judicial matters. The political question doctrine as now practiced extends beyond that narrow boundary.

---

[400] 531 U.S. 278 (2001).

[401] *Id.* at 284.

[402] *Id.* at 283–84.

[403] Arizonans for Official English v. Arizona, 520 U.S. 43, 68 n.22 (1997).

[404] 528 U.S. 167 (2000).

[405] *Id.* at 190.

[406] *Id.*

[407] *Id.* at 193.

[408] 5 U.S. (1 Cranch) 137, 170 (1803).

At the outset, it is helpful to clear up a misconception the term may create. The political question doctrine does not withdraw from judicial review all matters with political overtones. On the contrary, courts frequently decide such matters. The political fortunes of Richard M. Nixon, William Clinton, George W. Bush and Al Gore were strongly influenced by judicial decisions.[409] Yet the political consequences alone did not make the cases political questions (although some argued that some of the cases should have been so regarded for other reasons). Rather, political questions are those which are committed to, or more appropriately decided by, a political branch, not the judiciary.

It is also worth noting that the political question doctrine relates to separation of powers concerns, not federalism issues. Thus, it involves the relationship between the federal judiciary and the other branches of the national government, not that between the federal courts and state government.[410]

In *Baker v. Carr*,[411] the Court articulated six strands of the political question doctrine: (1) "A textually demonstrable constitutional commitment of [an] issue to a coordinate political department"; (2) "a lack of judicially discoverable and manageable standards for resolving it"; (3) "the impossibility of deciding without an initial policy determination of a kind clearly for nonjudicial discretion"; (4) a court's inability to resolve an issue without expressing disrespect for a coordinate branch; (5) "an unusual need" to defer to a prior political decision; (6) a situation where government must speak in one voice.[412] In *Vieth v. Jubelirer*,[413] Justice Scalia, for himself and three others, observed that the six *Baker v. Carr* tests "are probably listed in descending order of both importance and certainty."[414]

All strands need not be present for the court to find a political question. They rarely, if ever, are. On the other hand, some strands may, on occasion reinforce each other. Thus, Chief Justice Rehnquist observed that "the lack of judicially manageable standards may strengthen the conclusion that there is a textually demonstrable commitment to a coordinate branch."[415] Although the Court often invokes one or more of these criteria in political question cases, they provide principles to consult rather than rules.

In *Luther v. Borden*,[416] a classic early political question case, a dispute broke out regarding the identity of the lawful government of Rhode Island. The incumbent government had declared participation in certain elections to be unlawful. Thereafter, Sheriff Luther Borden entered the home of election commissioner Martin Luther to seek evidence of who had voted in the proscribed election. Luther sued for trespass. Borden claimed that his behavior was protected governmental

---

[409] *See, e.g.,* Bush v. Gore, 531 U.S. 98 (2000); Clinton v. Jones, 520 U.S. 681 (1997); United States v. Nixon, 418 U.S. 683 (1974).

[410] Baker v. Carr, 369 U.S. 186, 210 (1962).

[411] 369 U.S. 186 (1962).

[412] *Id.* at 217.

[413] 541 U.S. 267 (2004).

[414] *Id.* at 278.

[415] Nixon v. United States, 506 U.S. 224, 228–29 (1993).

[416] 48 U.S. (7 How.) 1 (1849).

action. Luther, however, argued that the government Borden served violated the Constitution's Guarantee Clause.[417] The Court ducked. It claimed that the case raised a political question because "[u]nder this article of the Constitution it rests with Congress to decide what government is the established one in a State."[418] The Guarantee Clause does not, of course, textually commit the power to Congress. Rather, it provides that the "United States shall guarantee to every State in this Union a Republican Form of Government."[419] Needless to say, the "United States" is not Congress. But Chief Justice Taney reasoned that Congress implicitly made that decision when its houses determined whether to seat the representatives and senators a state sent to Washington, D.C.

In *Nixon v. United States*,[420] Judge Walter Nixon sought judicial review of the Senate's action in convicting and removing him from office after he was impeached by the House of Representatives. He challenged Senate Rule XI under which he was tried because it allowed a committee of the Senate, not the whole body, to hear witnesses. The Court held that Nixon's challenge raised a nonjusticiable political question. In part, it argued that the Constitution committed that issue to the Senate by providing it "shall have the sole Power to try all Impeachments."[421] The use of "sole" was intended, the Court said, to preclude judicial review. Perhaps, but an alternative explanation of the Constitution's use of "sole" sees it as emphasizing the separate roles of the House and Senate in impeachment proceedings especially since the only other time the Constitution uses "sole" is in the House Impeachment Clause.[422] The Court also concluded that "try" was ambiguous and accordingly gave the Court no judicially manageable standards.

Although the Court invoked these strands from the classic *Baker* statement, the more convincing justification for the Court's result were three structural arguments it advanced. First, because judges might later preside over criminal proceedings of previously impeached officials, judicial review of impeachment might create a real or perceived conflict of interest. Second, impeachment is an important check on judicial conduct that would be avoided if the Court could review and control the handling of that check. Finally, judicial review would interfere with the need to resolve with finality the right of an individual to hold office. The insult could be more egregious following presidential impeachment and removal.

The political-question doctrine has had its greatest scope regarding foreign affairs. Thus, in *Chicago & Southern Air Lines*, Justice Jackson argued that once the President approved orders of the Civil Aeronautics Board regarding foreign air transportation "the final orders embody Presidential discretion as to political

---

[417] U.S. Const. art. IV, § 4 ("The United States shall guarantee to every State in this Union a Republican Form of Government, and shall protect each of them against Invasion; and on Application of the Legislature, or of the Executive (when the Legislature cannot be convened) against domestic Violence.").

[418] *Luther*, 48 U.S. at 42.

[419] U.S. Const. art. IV, § 4.

[420] 506 U.S. 224 (1993).

[421] U.S. Const. art. I, § 3, cl. 6.

[422] U.S. Const. art. I, § 2, cl. 5.

matters beyond the competence of the courts to adjudicate."[423]

In *Goldwater v. Carter*,[424] Justice Rehnquist, speaking for four justices, wrote,

> I am of the view that the basic question presented by the petitioners in this case is 'political' and therefore nonjusticiable because it involves the authority of the President in the conduct of our country's foreign relations and the extent to which the Senate or the Congress is authorized to negate the action of the President.[425]

The case involved the question whether President Jimmy Carter could unilaterally abrogate the United States' treaty with Taiwan incident to his recognition of the People's Republic of China. Justice Rehnquist's view reflected a frequent inclination in cases dealing with foreign affairs but was controversial. Justice Powell denied that the case presented a political question. The Constitution made no textual commitment of the issue to the President; the text was silent regarding who could abrogate treaties. The text did address the making of treaties — it required the President get the advice and consent of two-thirds of the Senate — and the status of treaties — they are supreme law of the land. These provisions implied the President lacked unilateral authority. Deciding the extent of the President's power raised questions regarding separation of powers, not foreign affairs, and was susceptible to judicial resolution. Similarly, Justice Brennan argued that the political question doctrine precluded courts from reviewing the foreign policy decisions of branches authorized to make them but did not apply to "the *antecedent* question whether a particular branch has been constitutionally designated as the repository of political decisionmaking power."[426]

The political question doctrine has been applied to questions involving recognition of foreign governments,[427] relating to sovereignty over a given area,[428] involving the diplomatic status of foreign representatives,[429] and regarding the existence of a state of war or belligerency[430] and the relation of the United States to any conflict.[431] The doctrine has also applied to issues involving military force including questions involving employment of the armed forces abroad.[432] and relating to the commencement and duration of a war in which the United States is

---

[423] Chicago & Southern Air Lines v. Waterman S.S. Corp., 333 U.S. 103, 114 (1948).

[424] 444 U.S. 996 (1979).

[425] *Id.* at 1002 (Rehnquist, J., concurring).

[426] *Id.* at 1007 (Brennan, J., dissenting).

[427] United States v. Belmont, 301 U.S. 324, 330 (1937).

[428] *See* Williams v. Suffolk Ins. Co., 38 U.S. (13 Pet.) 415, 422 (1839); Foster v. Neilson, 27 U.S. (2 Pet.) 253, 306–07 (1829).

[429] *See In re Baiz*, 135 U.S. 403 (1890).

[430] *See* The Three Friends, 166 U.S. 1, 63 (1897); The Divina Pastora, 17 U.S. (4 Wheat.) 52, 63–64 (1819).

[431] *See* United States v. Palmer, 16 U.S. (3 Wheat.) 610, 634–35 (1818).

[432] *See* Johnson v. Eisentrager, 339 U.S. 763, 789 (1950); Durand v. Hollins, 8 F. Cas. 111 (4 Blatchf. 451) (C.C.S.D.N.Y. 1860). *But compare* Holtzman v. Schlesinger, 414 U.S. 1304, 1311 (1973) (growing body of lower court opinion that such question is justiciable).

engaged.[433]

The political question doctrine is most compelling in many foreign affairs issues. Courts often lack information to make such decisions. Moreover, it would often be undesirable to have the government speak with more than one voice,[434] especially if they took different stances.[435] Nonetheless, the Court has often decided on the merits cases with foreign policy or national security implications.[436]

The political question doctrine also applies to some cases dealing with internal affairs. These include questions relating to the constitutional guaranty of a republican form of government,[437] involving the constitutional guaranty against domestic violence,[438] concerning the organization and procedure of the legislative department[439] and the deliberative processes of a national political convention,[440] relating to whether laws have been validly enacted,[441] and concerning the procedure followed in impeachment proceedings.[442]

The matters which relate to internal affairs typically either relate to domestic use of the armed forces to fulfill the guaranties of Article IV, or involve the internal autonomy of the legislative department and political conventions. The judicial refusal to decide questions concerning legislative organization and procedure or the enactment of a legislative act involve the internal functioning of a coordinate department. Separation of powers considerations lead judges to respect the internal autonomy of the legislature.

The Supreme Court has removed some such issues from the political question category. In *Powell v. McCormack*[443] the Court held that the judiciary could review whether a member of Congress who met the requirements for membership the Constitution prescribed could be excluded. In *Bond v. Floyd*,[444] the Court ruled it could review exclusion of a legislator on grounds that infringe a specific constitutional limitation, e.g., when a member is excluded on racial grounds.

---

[433] *See* Ludecke v. Watkins, 335 U.S. 160, 168–70 (1948); The Protector, 79 U.S. (12 Wall.) 700 (1871).

[434] *See* Baker v. Carr, 369 U.S. 186, 211 (1962).

[435] *See* Williams v. Suffolk Ins. Co., 38 U.S. (13 Pet.) 415, 420 (1839).

[436] *See, e.g.*, Hamdi v. Rumsfeld, 542 U.S. 507 (2004); Dames & Moore v. Regan, 453 U.S. 654 (1981).

[437] *See* Ohio *ex rel.* Bryant v. Akron Park Dist., 281 U.S. 74 (1930); Pacific States Tel. & Tel. Co. v. Oregon, 223 U.S. 118 (1912); Minor v. Happersett, 88 U.S. (21 Wall.) 162 (1875); Luther v. Borden, 48 U.S. (7 How.) 1 (1849).

[438] *See* Luther v. Borden, 48 U.S. (7 How.) 1 (1849); Martin v. Mott, 25 U.S. (12 Wheat.) 19 (1827).

[439] *See* Barry v. United States *ex rel.* Cunningham, 279 U.S. 597 (1929); United States v. Ballin, 144 U.S. 1 (1892).

[440] *See* O'Brien v. Brown, 409 U.S. 1 (1972). *Compare* Cousins v. Wigoda, 419 U.S. 477 (1975) (state courts may not interfere with selection of delegates to national convention).

[441] *See* Field v. Clark, 143 U.S. 649 (1892). The same is true of a constitutional amendment. *See* Coleman v. Miller, 307 U.S. 433 (1939).

[442] *See* Nixon v. United States, 506 U.S. 224 (1993).

[443] 395 U.S. 486 (1969).

[444] 385 U.S. 116 (1966).

Prior to 1962, the Court had included legislative apportionment within the political question doctrine. *Baker v. Carr*[445] repudiated that rule. Voters had challenged a Tennessee apportionment statute as contrary to equal protection. Tennessee's legislature had not been reapportioned for more than 50 years although state demography had changed. The population ratio for the most and the least populous districts was more than nineteen to one. The Supreme Court held that a justiciable controversy was presented.

Some argue that the Court should have deemed *Bush v. Gore*[446] a political question and avoided addressing it on that ground.[447] Neither the *per curiam* nor Chief Justice Rehnquist's concurrence discussed the doctrine. The closest reference was the Court's insistence of its "unsought responsibility"[448] to resolve issues before the judiciary, a tacit rejection of the doctrine.

Several dissenting justices suggested the Court should have avoided the case. Justice Breyer, for instance, noted that the importance of a presidential election "is political, not legal." The Court "should resist the temptation unnecessarily to resolve tangential legal disputes, where doing so threatens to determine the outcome of the election."[449] Moreover, the Twelfth Amendment gives Congress "the authority and responsibility to count electoral votes,"[450] a suggestion that the Constitution committed the issue to Congress. Congress, as a politically account-able body, was arguably best suited to decide the dispute.[451]

The Court had rejected the argument that a challenge to a Michigan law regulating selection of electors was a political question in *McPherson v. Blacker*.[452] The state statute called for selection of electors in districts and directed them to vote on a different day than did federal law. Unlike *Bush v. Gore*, the challenge and decision occurred prior to the election. The issues involved and timing in *McPherson* no doubt mitigated the risks that the Court's action would be perceived as being politically motivated.[453] Moreover, as Professor Friedman points out, judicial intervention was more appropriate in *McPherson* to consider the state's electoral system before the election took place since Congress could not do so at that time. If Congress subsequently found Michigan's scheme improper, Michigan's electoral votes might have been excluded. In *McPherson*, early judicial action avoided that problem. In *Bush v. Gore*, however, the election had already occurred. Congress would have decided the question if the Court had passed.[454]

---

[445] 369 U.S. 186 (1962).

[446] 531 U.S. 98 (2000).

[447] *See, e.g.*, Richard D. Friedman, *Trying to Make Peace with* Bush v. Gore, 29 FLA. ST. U. L. REV. 811 (2001).

[448] 531 U.S. at 111.

[449] *Id.* at 153.

[450] *Id.*

[451] *See also* Breyer, *supra* note 56, at 69–70. Jack M. Balkin, Bush v. Gore *and the Boundary Between Law and Politics*, 110 YALE L.J. 1407, 1432 (2001).

[452] 146 U.S. 1 (1892).

[453] *See* Friedman, *supra* note 447.

[454] *Id.*

Although some suggest restricting the political question doctrine to foreign affairs where the argument for judicial self-limitation is strongest the doctrine continues to have wider application. In one sense, the doctrine constitutes something of an exception or affront to a principle of *Marbury*. The political-question doctrine is something of an anomaly in a system in which governmental acts may ordinarily be judicially weighed to determine their constitutional compliance. It represents something of a challenge to those who see the judiciary as the ultimate arbiter on constitutional questions. On the other hand, *Marbury* may be seen as suggesting a variation of the doctrine since it recognized some instances where the Court could not review executive action.

Chapter 3

CONGRESSIONAL POWER

INTRODUCTION

The Constitution assigns importance to legislative power. The very first Article establishes Congress. It is longer than those creating the Executive and Judiciary combined. Article I begins by providing that "All legislative Powers herein granted shall be vested in a Congress." This Vesting Clause is significant in at least two respects. First, it purports to grant *all* legislative powers it bestows on Congress. The language would suggest that no other branch possesses any legislative power — a false impression. The President participates in the Treaty Power[1] and his duty to give Congress information about the state of the union and make legislative recommendations[2] and his veto power[3] also involve him in legislation. The Vesting Clause also signals the relatively limited nature of legislative power. Not "all legislative powers" are vested but simply those "herein granted," a limitation that appears in Article I's grant of legislative powers but not in the parallel clauses in Articles II and III. Moreover, the Clause is followed by an enumeration in Article I of eighteen types of legislative powers.[4] Other legislative power is given Congress elsewhere.[5] Congressional authority is thus limited to those powers granted, consistent with a limited Federal government,[6] yet practice has allowed some expansion beyond formal constraints.

This chapter addresses some of Congress' most significant powers. It begins by discussing the structure of Congress. The doctrine of implied powers, which *McCulloch v. Maryland* recognized, was confirmed by the Necessary and Proper Clause. We then discuss the General Welfare Clause and the Taxing and Spending powers it modifies, and Congress' fiscal powers. The chapter then considers, in turn, Congress' power over citizenship and the Senate's power to advise and consent to treaties. The final three sections address issues relating to Congress' ability to enforce the Civil War Amendments to the Constitution. The chapter does not discuss the crucial Commerce Clause, which is the topic of Chapters 4 and 6.

---

[1] U.S. Const. art. II, § 2, cl. 2.

[2] *Id.*; § 3.

[3] *Id.* art. I, § 7.

[4] *Id.*; art. I, § 8.

[5] *See, e.g., id.* amend. XIV, § 2; amend. XIV, § 5; amend. XV, § 2; amend. XVI; amend. XIX; amend. XX, § 4; amend. XXIII, § 2; amend. XXIV, § 2; amend. XXVI, § 2.

[6] *See* McCulloch v. Maryland, 17 U.S. (4 Wheat.) 316 (1819); Marbury v. Madison, 5 U.S. (1 Cranch) 137 (1803).

§ 3.01   STRUCTURE OF CONGRESS

[1]   Composition and Election

Congress consists of two houses, the Senate and House of Representatives, in which together are vested "[a]ll legislative powers herein granted."[7] Article I further defines the terms of each—members of the House are chosen for two year terms, Senators are chosen for six-year terms,[8] with one-third chosen every two years.[9] Each state has two Senators. Representatives are chosen in districts in each state based on population.[10] The bicameral legislature represented one of the critical compromises between the large and small states. The large states wanted representation based on population, the small states insisted on equal state representation. The bicameral compromise with one house following each approach resolved that impasse. Representatives and Senators are elected "by the People."[11] The Constitution confers a right of qualified voters "to cast their ballots and have them counted at congressional elections."[12] The words "by the People" mean that, to the extent practicable, "one [person's] vote in a congressional election is to be worth as much as another's."[13] Thus, States must draw congressional districts so all voters in a State have substantially the same voice in electing their representatives.[14]

Initially, state legislatures elected Senators.[15] Popular election of Senators became constitutionally mandated after ratification of the Seventeenth Amendment in 1913. That Amendment also provides for special elections to fill Senate vacancies and allows the state legislature to empower the Governor to fill vacancies pending special elections. States have so authorized the Governor with special elections to follow at the next two-year interval.

---

[7] U.S. Const. art. I, § 1.

[8] *Id.* art. I, § 2, cl. 1; § 3, cl. 1; amend. XVII.

[9] *Id.* art. I, § 3, cl. 1.

[10] *Id.* art. I, § 2, cl. 1, 3; § 3, cl. 1.

[11] *Id.* art. I, § 2, cl. 1; amend. XVII.

[12] United States v. Classic, 313 U.S. 299, 315 (1941).

[13] Wesberry v. Sanders, 376 U.S. 1, 7–8 (1964).

[14] *Id.*; Kirkpatrick v. Preisler, 394 U.S. 526, 531 (1969).

[15] U.S. Const. art. I, § 3, cl. 1.

[2] Qualifications

The Constitution sets the qualifications for representatives and Senators, as summarized below.[16]

	Senator	Representative
Age (minimum)	30	25
Citizen of U.S.	9 years	7 years
Inhabitant of State Chosen From When Elected	X	X

These qualifications are exclusive. In *United States Term Limits v. Thornton*,[17] the Court held that the States may not add additional qualifications; thus, a State's effort to impose term limits on federal legislators violated the Constitution. The Court reached that conclusion partly based on a textual argument. The respective Qualifications Clauses do not state that the qualifications listed are, or are not, exclusive. But just as the Court concluded in *Marbury* that the enumeration of two categories of cases in the Court's original jurisdiction signalled exclusivity, the Court implicitly invoked the *expressio unius* maxim to conclude that the Qualifications Clauses set a ceiling not a floor. The Court also deployed structural arguments. A basic principle of democracy suggests citizens should be accorded substantial latitude in choosing their representatives. Moreover, members of the House and Senate are representatives and servants of the Nation, not of the constituency that sends them. To allow States to impose additional qualifications on national representatives would allow them to obstruct the operation of the Federal Government.

Justice Thomas' dissent, which three others joined, viewed the Qualifications Clauses as setting constitutional minimums. They might impose the exclusive set of national qualifications, but did not restrict the States from adding others. Such a power was reserved to the States by the Tenth Amendment, Justice Thomas argued. The latter claim was resisted by the majority which countered that the States could only reserve powers they initially possessed; prior to the creation of the National Government they had no power to add qualifications for its officers.

The House or Senate may not exclude someone who meets the specified qualifications.[18] In *Powell v. McCormack*, the Court reviewed action by the House in refusing to seat Representative Adam Clayton Powell in 1967 based on financial improprieties. Although the Constitution makes each house "the judge of the Elections, Returns and Qualifications of its members,"[19] the "Qualifications" are limited to the three set out above.[20] Each house may, however, punish its members

---

[16] *Id.* art. I, § 2, cl. 2; § 3, cl. 2.

[17] 514 U.S. 779, 783 (1995). *See generally* Kathleen M. Sullivan, *Dueling Sovereignties*: U.S. Term Limits, Inc. v. Thornton, 109 HARV. L. REV. 78 (1995).

[18] Powell v. McCormack, 395 U.S. 486 (1969).

[19] U.S. CONST. art. 1, § 5, cl. 1.

[20] *Powell*, 395 U.S. at 548.

"for disorderly behavior" and expel them by a two-thirds vote.[21] The grant of power to each house to police the conduct of its members does not imply that Congress is disabled from enacting laws governing certain behavior of Congressmen. Thus, a federal statute could constitutionally bar members from being compensated for representing a person in which the United States had an interest.[22] In furtherance of these and other powers, each house has some power to punish contempts against their process and institution even when committed by a non-member.[23] The Article I Elections Clause gives States power to regulate the "times, places and manner of holding elections for Senators and Representatives" subject to Congress' authority to "make or alter such regulations except as to the places of choosing Senators."[24] This provision confers on the States "broad power" regarding *procedural* matters relating to congressional elections; it does not, however, license them to dictate electoral outcomes or favor a class of candidates.[25] Thus in *Cook v. Gralike*, the Court struck down a Missouri law which would require identifying on the ballot any candidate who failed to act in certain specified ways to advance a term limits amendment.[26] Congress is not limited to regulating general elections; its power "includes the authority to regulate primary elections when . . . they are a step in the exercise by the people of their choice of representatives in Congress."[27] The State's power includes providing for a recount under specified circumstances; a recount does not usurp the Senate's power to judge elections and returns.[28]

The 2000 elections raised the issue whether a dead person could be elected to the Senate. Missouri Governor Mel Carnahan was killed in a plane crash several weeks before the November election. Under state law, his death came after the deadline for removing a candidate from the ballot. His supporters waged a campaign to elect him nonetheless; the state's new Governor announced that if Governor Carnahan was elected posthumously, he would appoint Governor Carnahan's widow, Jean, to fill the vacancy.[29] Missouri voters chose Carnahan over the incumbent senator, John Ashcroft. Some suggested[30] that Carnahan could not properly be elected. They argued that a Senator must be a "person," a "citizen of the United States" and "when elected, . . . an inhabitant of that state for which . . . chosen."[31] When elected, the deceased Governor Carnahan was not an "inhabitant" of Missouri. Alternatively, a textual rebuttal might argue that the Qualifications Clause addresses qualifications to *be* a Senator, not to be elected as

---

[21] U.S. Const. art. I, § 5, cl. 2.

[22] Burton v. United States, 202 U.S. 344 (1906).

[23] *See, e.g.*, Barry v. United States *ex rel.* Cunningham, 279 U.S. 597 (1929); Marshall v. Gordon, 243 U.S. 521 (1917); Anderson v. Dunn, 19 U.S. 204 (1821).

[24] U.S. Const. art. I, § 4, cl. 1.

[25] Cook v. Gralike, 531 U.S. 510, 523–26 (2001).

[26] *Id.* at 524–26.

[27] *Classic*, 313 U.S. at 317.

[28] Roudebush v. Hartke, 405 U.S. 15, 25–26 (1972).

[29] U.S. Const. amend. XVII, cl. 2.

[30] *See, e.g.*, Viet D. Dinh, *Dead Men Can't Win*, WALL ST. J., Nov. 9, 2000, at A26.

[31] U.S. Const. art. I, § 3, cl. 3.

such. Although, a person cannot *be* a Senator unless she meets the age and citizenship requirements and inhabited her state when elected she arguably need not meet these requirements to be elected. Accordingly, the fact that Governor Carnahan was not an inhabitant when elected would not prevent his election; Mrs. Carnahan presumably met all three qualifications when appointed by the Missouri Governor under authority of the Seventeenth Amendment. Senator Ashcroft conceded defeat and accordingly the Senate did not address the issue.

[3] Delegation of Legislative Power

The Constitution confers on Congress "all legislative powers herein granted."[32] To what extent might Congress delegate legislative powers to a coordinate branch or to administrative agencies? The nondelegation doctrine precluded Congress from delegating legislative power to administrative agencies. The doctrine enjoyed a brief reign during the mid 1930s when declared in *Panama Refining Co. v. Ryan*[33] and *Schechter Poultry Corp. v. United States*.[34] The Court has more recently reiterated that the constitutional "text permits no delegation of those [legislative] powers,"[35] but this statement is not nearly so draconian as it might seem. For the Court has routinely found the non-delegation principle satisfied in cases since the mid 1930s provided Congress articulates some "intelligible principle" to which the delegatee must conform.[36] In that event, such legislative action is not "a forbidden delegation of legislative power."[37] The Court has found the "intelligible principle" absent only twice[38] in cases which the Court recently characterized as involving delegations providing effectively no guidance.[39] In *Whitman v. American Trucking Assn's, Inc.*, the Court reversed a lower court decision[40] which had found the Clean Air Act (CAA) violated the non-delegation principle. The discretion CAA allowed was "well within the outer limits of our nondelegation precedents," Justice Scalia wrote for himself and six others.[41]

[4] Legislating Procedures

The Constitution prescribes certain procedures Congress must follow when legislating. In order for a bill to become "a law," it must pass the House and Senate in identical form (bicameralism) and be "presented" to the President for signature or veto (presentment).[42] The Constitution does not use the word "veto," referring

---

[32] U.S. CONST. art. 1, § 1.

[33] 293 U.S. 388 (1935).

[34] 295 U.S. 495 (1935).

[35] Whitman v. American Trucking Assn's, Inc., 531 U.S. 457, 472 (2001).

[36] J. W. Hampton, Jr., & Co. v. United States, 276 U.S. 394, 409 (1928).

[37] *Id.*

[38] *See* Panama Refining Co. v. Ryan, 293 U.S. 388 (1935); A. L. A. Schechter Poultry Corp. v. United States, 295 U.S. 495 (1935).

[39] *Whitman*, 531 U.S. at 474.

[40] American Trucking Assn's, Inc. v. EPA, 175 F.3d 1027, 1034 (1999).

[41] *Whitman*, 531 U.S. at 474.

[42] U.S. CONST. art. I. § 7, cl. 2.

instead to the President's prerogative to "return a bill" to the originating House with "his objections."[43] Congress could then pass the bill only with a two-thirds majority in each house.

Although the Court has upheld delegations of legislative power to administrative agencies, it has not allowed Congress to deviate from bicameralism and presentment. For instance, during the last two-thirds of the twentieth century, Congress began to attach legislative veto provisions to measures empowering the Executive branch or administrative agencies to take some action. These veto provisions took different forms but generally allowed Congress, one house, or one committee, to reverse executive or administrative action. For instance, the Immigration and Naturalization Act[44] allowed either house, by resolution, to overturn the Attorney General's decision to allow a deportable alien to remain in the United States. When one Chadha overstayed his student visa, the Attorney General made just such a decision to suspend deportation only to have the House of Representatives exercise its one house veto by passing a resolution opposing that decision. Chadha challenged the constitutionality of the legislative veto.[45]

In an opinion for the Court, Chief Justice Burger held the legislative veto unconstitutional. The Court rejected the ongoing history argument that the "increasing frequency" of legislative vetoes testified to the constitutionality of the practice.[46] Instead, that fact "sharpened rather than blunted" the Court's scrutiny.[47] The Court concluded that the formal requirements of bicameralism and presentment applied to any legislation. The legislative veto was legislation because its effect was to alter "the legal rights, duties, and relations of persons, including the Attorney General, Executive Branch officials and Chadha, all outside the legislative branch."[48]

Justice White dissented. In contrast to Chief Justice Burger's formalistic opinion which emphasized text and bright line rules, Justice White urged a more flexible approach which focused on the way in which the legislative veto really operated. He viewed the Court's decision as "of surpassing importance" because it struck down more than 200 statutory provisions.[49] Far from being a device by which Congress aggrandized its power, the legislative veto allowed Congress to delegate power to the executive while retaining a modicum of review authority. The innovation enabled government to adapt to demands of a changing world without imperiling basic distribution of government power.

On occasions, the Constitution assigns different duties to the two houses of Congress. Thus, only the Senate has a role in giving advice and consenting to treaties and to appointment of officers the President nominates. The House has the sole power to impeach whereas the Senate has the sole power to try impeachments.

---

[43] *Id.*

[44] 8 U.S.C. § 1254(c)(2).

[45] INS v. Chadha, 462 U.S. 919 (1983).

[46] *Id.* at 944.

[47] *Id.* at 943.

[48] *Id.* at 952.

[49] *Id.* at 967 (White, J., dissenting).

If the Electoral College fails to produce a President and Vice President, the House is the contingent elector of the President, the Senate, of the Vice President. Both the House and Senate must approve revenue bills like other legislation. Yet all bills for the raising of revenue must "originate" in the House although the Senate may "propose or concur with amendments."[50]

[5] Legislative Immunity

The Speech or Debate Clause[51] assures Congress wide freedom of speech, debate, and deliberation in the legislative process.[52] It protects the independence of the legislature against "prosecution by an unfriendly executive and conviction by a hostile judiciary."[53] The main purpose of the Clause is to allow Congress to legislate without fear of criminal prosecution. The Clause is "read broadly, to include not only 'words spoken in debate,' but anything 'generally done in a session of [Congress] by one of its members in relation to the business before it.' "[54] Thus, the Speech or Debate Clause confers legislative immunity for, among other activities, written reports and votes in Congress,[55] the investigative work of congressional committees,[56] and placing classified documents in the official public record.[57] It protects against executive inquiry into acts that occur in the regular course of the legislative process and the motivation for those acts. Thus, the Clause precluded a prosecution based upon inquiries into the motivations and language of a Congressman's speech on the House floor.[58] It does not insulate a member of Congress from scrutiny by the house in which they serve or by their electorate.

The Clause does not generally immunize members of Congress from criminal prosecution relating to all acts they regularly perform. In *United States v. Brewster*,[59] the Supreme Court overturned a District Court dismissal of the Government's indictment of a former Senator for bribery. The Court distinguished between "purely legislative activities" protected by the Speech or Debate Clause and "political" activities not afforded the Clause's protection.[60] The Clause's

---

[50] U.S. Const. art. I, § 7; *see* Flint v. Stone Tracy Co., 220 U.S. 107, 142–43 (1911).

[51] U.S. Const. art. I, § 6, cl. 1. ("[The Senators and Representatives] shall in all Cases, except Treason, Felony and Breach of the Peace, be privileged from Arrest during their Attendance at the Session of their respective Houses, and in going to and returning from the same; and for any Speech or Debate in either House, they shall not be questioned in any other Place.").

[52] Gravel v. United States, 408 U.S. 606, 616 (1972).

[53] United States v. Johnson, 383 U.S. 169, 179 (1966).

[54] *Id.* at 179 (quoting Kilbourn v. Thompson, 103 U.S. 168, 204 (1881)).

[55] *Kilbourn v. Thompson*, 103 U.S. at 204.

[56] Eastland v. U.S. Servicemen's Fund, 421 U.S. 491, 504 (1975); Tenney v. Brandhove, 341 U.S. 367, 377 (1951).

[57] *Gravel*, 408 U.S. at 615–16.

[58] *Johnson*, 383 U.S. at 184–85.

[59] 408 U.S. 501 (1972).

[60] *Id.* at 512. "Political" activities include a "wide range of legitimate 'errands' performed for constituents, the making of appointments with Government agencies, assistance in securing Government contracts, preparing . . . 'news letters' to constituents, news releases, and speeches delivered outside the Congress." *Id.*

privilege extends only to what is necessary to preserve the integrity of the legislative process. Because the Government's bribery indictment did not involve an inquiry into legislative acts or motivations, the Speech or Debate Clause provided no protection to Senator Brewster.[61]

Gravel v. United States[62] implicated not only the Speech or Debate Clause at the end of Article I, Section 6, clause 1 but the Privilege from Arrest Clause which precedes it. Congressman Gravel read from the classified "Pentagon Papers" during a subcommittee meeting, placed the 47 volume study in the public record and arranged for its private republication. The Government subpoenaed Gravel's congressional aide to testify before a grand jury investigating the private republication. Gravel intervened, claiming that the Speech or Debate Clause privilege applied to the private republication of the Pentagon Papers and protected his aide as well as himself.

The Court held that the Privilege from Arrest Clause exempts members of Congress from arrest in civil cases only.[63] The narrow scope of that privilege reflects the judgment that "legislators ought not stand above the law they create but ought generally be bound by it as ordinary persons."[64] Even in civil suits, the privilege from arrest applies only "during their Attendance at the Session of their respective Houses, and in going to and returning from the same" so as not obstruct the legislative process. Members are not exempt from service,[65] the obligations of subpoena,[66] or "from testifying at trials or grand jury proceedings involving third-party crimes where questions do not require testimony about or impugn a legislative act."[67] The Speech or Debate Clause protected Senator Gravel from "question[ing] in any other Place for any speech or debate in either House."[68] It did not protect him from prosecution for the private republication of the Pentagon Papers, activity "in no way essential to the deliberations of the Senate."[69]

In *Gravel*, the Court also held that congressional aides and their members are to be "treated as one" under the Speech or Debate Clause.[70] The Court viewed this extension as "an expression of policy designed to aid in the effective functioning of government" given the "complexities and magnitude of governmental activity."[71] However, because the private republication of the Pentagon Papers was not privileged, the Court held that Gravel's aide could not invoke the testimonial privilege.

---

[61] *Id.* at 528–29.

[62] 408 U.S. 606 (1972).

[63] *Id.* at 614.

[64] *Id.* at 615.

[65] *Id.*

[66] *Id.*

[67] *Id.* at 622.

[68] *Gravel*, 408 U.S. at 615.

[69] *Id.*

[70] *Id.* at 616.

[71] *Id.* at 617.

The private republication of libelous material likewise falls outside of the Clause's protection.[72] Actions which are not "purely legislative," but are official or "political" acts, are not privileged,[73] and members of Congress are bound by the law as ordinary persons.[74]

§ 3.02 IMPLIED POWERS

Article I confers not only the powers specifically enumerated but also those reasonably implied. Accordingly, the legislative power vested in Congress exceeds the express grants Article I lists.

The doctrine of implied powers is implicit in the structure of the Constitution, an issue *McCulloch v. Maryland*[75] settled. Congress had incorporated the Bank of the United States as a depository for federal funds and a source of bank notes. The Constitution did not expressly authorize the federal government to establish a national bank, but hinted in that direction by conferring power to impose and collect taxes, to borrow money, to regulate commerce, to declare war, and to support armies and navies, powers a national bank would facilitate. Moreover, the first Congress had created a bank. Its charter had not been renewed to the nation's embarrassment during the War of 1812.

Marshall might have avoided the question of implied powers entirely. He began his opinion by arguing that the historical experience with, and the acquiescence to, the Bank after long debate created a constitutional presumption in its favor. In essence, Marshall argued that historical practice can shape constitutional meaning. Practice is particularly significant in this regard if it involved adjustments of the power of institutions as opposed to "great principles of liberty," was based on deliberation, and had generated reliance. The argument was certainly a respectable one that has been mirrored elsewhere.[76] Marshall thought the arguments based on ongoing practice were relevant and persuasive but not essential; they were not advanced "under the impression, that, were the question entirely new, the law would be found irreconcilable with the Constitution."[77]

Marshall preferred to rely on a more ambitious, and more persuasive, theory of implied powers. Marshall used some textual arguments to bolster his argument that the Constitution gave Congress implied, as well as enumerated, powers. Unlike the Articles of Confederation, the Constitution did not limit Congress to powers "expressly" granted. Moreover, Article I § 9 contained some limitations on powers not expressly granted Congress. Why include such limitations on Congress if

---

[72] Doe v. McMillan, 412 U.S. 306, 316–17 (1973).

[73] *Brewster*, 408 U.S. at 512.

[74] *Gravel*, 408 U.S. at 615.

[75] 17 U.S. (4 Wheat.) 316 (1819). On *McCulloch* generally, see MARK. R. KILLENBECK, M'CULLOCH v. MARYLAND: SECURING A NATION (2006).

[76] *See, e.g.*, Dames & Moore v. Regan, 453 U.S. 654, 686 (1981); Youngstown Sheet & Tube Co. v. Sawyer, 343 U.S. 579, 610–11 (1952) (Frankfurter, J., concurring); United States v. Midwest Oil Co., 236 U.S. 459, 474 (1915).

[77] *McCulloch*, 17 U.S. (Wheat.) at 402.

Congress did not have implied powers? But Marshall's primary argument came from the Constitution's structure. No one could expect a Constitution to specify all powers and all means it conferred, reasoned Marshall. To do so, it "would partake of the prolixity of a legal code."[78] The people would not understand such a document, Marshall argued, an implicit expression of his view of its democratic character. "[W]e must never forget that it is a constitution we are expounding." The Constitution should be construed in a way to allow the government it created to succeed, not to create obstacles destined to frustrate it at each turn.

In *McCulloch*, John Marshall argued that the enumeration of the major powers, set forth in Article I, § 8, implied the existence of those needed to carry them out:

> But it may with great reason be contended, that a government, entrusted with such ample powers, on the due execution of which the happiness and prosperity of the nation so vitally depends, must also be entrusted with ample means for their execution. The power being given, it is the interest of the nation to facilitate its execution.[79]

This was not some thin argument pulled from thin air. It was a compelling structural argument with a logical plausibility. Moreover, it seemed consistent with the framers' likely intent. Just as Hamilton's Federalist No. 78 supported Marshall's conclusions regarding judicial review in *Marbury*, so, too did Madison's Federalist No. 44 provide originalist support for Marshall's doctrine of implied powers in *McCulloch*. Even had the Constitution not contained the Necessary and Proper clause, wrote Madison, "there can be no doubt that all the particular powers requisite as means of executing the general powers would have resulted to the government by unavoidable implication." For Madison thought it basic that "wherever the end is required, the means are authorized; wherever a general power to do a thing is given, every particular power necessary for doing it is included."[80]

The doctrine of implied powers, which Madison and Marshall inferred from the structure of the Constitution, was confirmed by the text in the last clause of Article I, § 8. The prior 17 clauses of that section enumerate specific powers conferred on Congress. Clause 18 authorizes Congress "To make all Laws which shall be necessary and proper for carrying into Execution the foregoing Powers, and all other Powers vested by this Constitution in the Government of the United States, or in any Department or Officer thereof."

After articulating his theory as an implication of the Constitution's structure,[81] Marshall proceeded to connect it to the Necessary and Proper Clause. *McCulloch* rejected the view that the Necessary and Proper Clause conferred power on Congress only to pass laws that were "absolutely necessary." By authorizing it to make "necessary" laws, the Constitution could not have meant to confine Congress to those laws that were indispensable. Elsewhere the Constitution used the phrase "absolutely necessary." So "necessary" must impose a less exacting standard which

---

[78] *Id.* at 407.

[79] *McCulloch*, 17 U.S. at 408. *See also* THE FEDERALIST No. 44 (James Madison).

[80] THE FEDERALIST No. 44 (James Madison). *See also* THE FEDERALIST No. 33 (Alexander Hamilton).

[81] *See* CHARLES L. BLACK, JR., STRUCTURE AND RELATIONSHIP IN CONSTITUTIONAL LAW, 22–33 (1969).

must be broadly construed. Nor was "necessary" a limitation on Congress' power, as Maryland argued, especially because the clause was listed with the grants of powers in § 8, not the limits of § 9. "Let the end be legitimate, let it be within the scope of the Constitution, and all means which are appropriate, which are plainly adapted to that end, which are not prohibited, but consist with the letter and spirit of the Constitution are constitutional."[82] Marshall's construction enabled the Necessary and Proper Clause to become a source of federal legislative authority. His formulation has been reiterated by subsequent courts. Thus in *The Legal Tender Cases*,[83] Justice Strong argued that "in the judgment of those who adopted the Constitution, there were powers created by it, neither expressly specified nor deducible from any one specified power, or ancillary to it alone, but which grew out of the aggregate of powers conferred upon the government, or out of the sovereignty instituted." Similarly, in *Ex parte Yarborough*,[84] Justice Miller explained that constitutional interpretation must embrace the doctrine "universally applied" to written instruments, "that what is implied is as much a part of the instrument as what is expressed." This principle is necessarily applied to constitutional interpretation, Justice Miller wrote, "by reason of the inherent inability to put into words all derivative powers," a difficulty the Constitution recognized by including the Necessary and Proper Clause.

The clause has stretched many powers of the federal government. It, of course, does not authorize Congress to do anything which is "necessary and proper." Rather, the license to legislate relates to laws necessary and proper "for carrying into execution" other powers set out in the Constitution. Thus, legislation under the clause must also relate to some other constitutional provision. Moreover, the Necessary and Proper Clause does not simply expand other Article I powers. Instead, it relates to "the foregoing powers" (i.e., Article I powers) as well as to "all other powers vested by this Constitution in the Government of the United States, or in any Department or officer thereof." In other words, the Clause does not simply confer additional congressional power with respect to other grants of power to Congress. It confers power on Congress to legislate to give effect to every other power in the Constitution. Thus, the authority of Congress under the clause includes power to pass laws to carry out treaties,[85] to organize a department of government,[86] to collect revenue,[87] to acquire property by eminent domain,[88] to make treasury notes legal tender,[89] to create corporations,[90] to exclude and deport aliens,[91] to pass banking laws,[92] to determine marine law,[93] to regulate the civil

---

[82] *McCulloch*, 17 U.S. (4 Wheat.) at 421.

[83] 79 U.S. (12 Wall.) 457, 535 (1871).

[84] 110 U.S. 651, 658 (1884).

[85] *See* Neely v. Henkel, 180 U.S. 109, 121 (1901).

[86] Boske v. Comingore, 177 U.S. 459 (1900).

[87] *See* Murray v. Hoboken Land & Improvement Co., 59 U.S. (13 How.) 272, 281 (1856).

[88] *See* Kohl v. United States, 91 U.S. (1 Otto) 367 (1876).

[89] *See* Legal Tender Cases, 79 U.S. (12 Wall.) 457 (1871).

[90] *McCulloch*, 17 U.S. (4 Wheat.) 316.

[91] *See* Fong Yue Ting v. United States, 149 U.S. 698 (1893).

[92] Franklin Nat. Bank of Franklin Square v. People of New York, 347 U.S. 373 (1954).

service,[94] to address foreign affairs,[95] to build the Capitol and White House,[96] to protect voters from intimidation,[97] and to enact the Federal Criminal Code.[98]

Marshall used the postal power to demonstrate the operation of the clause in *McCulloch* and that example well illustrates its utility. Article I, § 8 authorizes Congress "[t]o establish Post Offices and post Roads" but contains no express power to move and deliver the mail or to punish those who commit postal crimes. The Necessary and Proper Clause expands the Postal Clause to furnish those necessary and proper powers.[99]

The Supreme Court demonstrated the breadth of the Necessary and Proper Clause in *United States v. Comstock*[100] when it upheld Congress's power to pass a federal statute authorizing civil commitment of mentally ill, sexually dangerous federal prisoners after their criminal sentence ended. The Court rejected Justice Thomas's argument that the Necessary and Proper Clause only allows Congress to pursue means which directly execute an enumerated power. It rested its conclusion on "five considerations, taken together."

The Court reasoned that the Necessary and Proper Clause conferred a broad power which allowed Congress to pursue means which were connected by a chain of reasoning to any enumerated power. The Constitution grants few enumerated powers to create federal crimes (counterfeiting, treason, piracies and felonies on the high seas) yet Congress has criminalized much conduct as a means to enforce various enumerated powers (e.g., mail theft or fraud). Having done so, it may also use the Necessary and Proper Clause to establish a federal prison system, regulate its administration and adopt other criminal laws to protect against threats to it as means reasonably related to those ends.

The Court pointed out that a long history of governmental conduct offered precedents for the civil commitment statute at issue and this ongoing history was suggestive, though not conclusive, of its constitutionality. Moreover, Congress was acting in an area where the federal government had a responsibility as custodian of prisoners. The statute also accounted for state interests by requiring that the justice department contact the state which would have jurisdiction over the prisoner and surrender him or her to it if it prefers to accept responsibility. Finally, the statute was not too remote from an enumerated power nor was it too sweeping. The combination of these factors established the constitutionality of the statute. *Comstock* left many questions regarding how broadly it will apply and regarding the application of the five considerations in future cases.

---

[93] *See* Swanson v. Marra Bros., 328 U.S. 1 (1946).

[94] White v. Berry, 171 U.S. 366 (1898).

[95] Kennedy v. Mendoza-Martinez, 372 U.S. 144 (1963).

[96] The Legal Tender Cases, 79 U.S. (12 Wall.) 457, 535 (1871).

[97] *Ex parte* Yarbrough, 110 U.S. 651 (1884).

[98] *See* Logan v. United States, 144 U.S. 263, 283–84 (1892); United States v. Hall, 98 U.S. 343 (1879); United States v. Fox, 95 U.S. 670 (1878).

[99] *See McCulloch*, 17 U.S. at 417.

[100] 130 S. Ct. 1949 (2010).

The expansive uses of the Necessary and Proper Clause does have its critics. Justice Scalia dismissed the Clause as the "best hope of those who defend ultra vires congressional action."[101] He reasoned that a law executing the Commerce Clause which infringed on state sovereignty was not a *"proper"* law.[102] Nonetheless, the Necessary and Proper Clause has proven a powerful source of national power when appended to the Commerce Clause, a topic discussed in the next chapter, or when coupled with other Clauses.

§ 3.03 GENERAL WELFARE

Although the Constitution expressly uses the term *"general welfare"* in the Tax and Spend Clause, the Constitution accords the Federal Government no blanket police power to promote public welfare. Article I, Section 8 begins by providing that: "[t]he Congress shall have Power to lay and collect Taxes, Duties, Imposts and Excises, to pay the Debts and provide for the common Defence and general Welfare of the United States." Despite some contrary contentions, this clause does not delegate blanket authority to the Federal Government to promote the general welfare, a position which would render the rest of Section 8 superfluous. The General Welfare Clause is not an independent grant of power, but a qualification of the taxing and spending powers.

The founders did not agree on how it qualified those powers. James Madison thought the taxing and spending power was confined to the enumerated fields the Constitution committed to Congress,[103] whereas Alexander Hamilton thought the General Welfare Clause provided additional power not limited by the scope of other enumerated powers. He thought Congress could tax and spend as appropriate to advance the general welfare.[104] In *United States v. Butler*,[105] the Supreme Court endorsed Hamilton's view. Madison's approach, rendered the "general welfare" phrase "mere tautology."[106] "While, therefore, the power to tax is not unlimited, its confines are set in the clause which confers it, and not in those of section 8 which bestow and define the legislative powers of the Congress. It results that the power of Congress to authorize expenditure of public moneys for public purposes is not limited by the direct grants of legislative power found in the Constitution."[107]

Congress can tax and spend for the general welfare of the United States.[108] When taken with the Necessary and Proper Clause,[109] the General Welfare Clause, though only a qualification of the taxing and spending power, confers generous authority.

---

[101] Printz v. United States, 521 U.S. 898, 923 (1997).

[102] *Id.* at 923–24 (emphasis in original).

[103] *See* THE FEDERALIST No. 41 (James Madison).

[104] *See* THE FEDERALIST No. 34 (Alexander Hamilton).

[105] 297 U.S. 1 (1936).

[106] *Id.* at 65.

[107] *Id.* at 66.

[108] *See* Buckley v. Valeo, 424 U.S. 1, 90 (1976).

[109] *See id.*

§ 3.04　TAXING POWER

[1]　Broad Power of Taxation For National Purposes

The Constitution gives the Federal Government a broad power to tax for all national purposes. Indeed, the founders appreciated that allowing government to tax many objects would have several advantages. It would distribute the burden across industries and across states.[110]

To be sure, Congress may exercise this authority only to "provide for the common Defense and general Welfare," but, as suggested above, these purposes impose slight limitation. They, especially "general welfare," are sufficiently capacious to comprehend a broad exercise of taxing power. Congress, not the courts, determines whether a given exercise of the tax power will promote the general welfare.[111] Courts will upset Congress' conclusion only in an extreme case.[112] The Court has consistently refused to pass on the "reasonableness" of a tax otherwise within the power of Congress.[113] "General welfare" is not a static concept but one which changes to accommodate historical events.[114]

Although the Constitution provides that "direct taxes shall be apportioned among the several states . . . according to their respective numbers"[115] this provision has imposed little restraint on Congress' power.[116] The Court essentially limited direct taxes to those on real property and Capitation[117] and accordingly left Congress broad latitude to impose "indirect taxes."[118] Although the Court, in a 5-4 decision, declared a federal income tax unconstitutional in *Pollock v. Farmers' Loan & Trust Co.*,[119] the decision seemed based in part on the conclusion that the income tax impacted real property and thus was a direct tax which needed to be apportioned. In any event, the Sixteenth Amendment overturned *Pollock* in 1913.[120] The direct tax prohibition seems to have theoretical significance at most,[121]

---

[110] *See* The Federalist No. 35 (Alexander Hamilton).

[111] *See* Helvering v. Davis, 301 U.S. 619, 640 (1937).

[112] *See* Cincinnati Soap Co. v. United States, 301 U.S. 308, 313 (1937); *see also Helvering*, 301 U.S. at 640 ("The discretion belongs to Congress, unless the choice is clearly wrong, a display of arbitrary power, not an exercise of judgment.").

[113] *See* Pittsburgh v. Alco Parking Corp., 417 U.S. 369, 373 (1974).

[114] *Helvering*, 301 U.S. at 641.

[115] U.S. Const. art. I., § 2.

[116] *See also* U.S. Const. art. I, § 9 ("No capitation or other direct, tax shall be laid unless in proportion to the census.").

[117] *See* Veazie Bank v. Fenno, 75 U.S. (8 Wall.) 533, 544 (1869).

[118] *See, e.g., id.* (Tax on state bank notes was indirect); Springer v. United States, 102 U.S. 586 (1881) (Civil War Income Tax imposed indirect tax); Hylton v. United States, 3 U.S. (3 Dall.) 171 (1796) (Tax on carriages was indirect).

[119] 157 U.S. 429 (1895).

[120] It provides "The Congress shall have power to lay and collect taxes on incomes, from whatever source derived, without apportionment among the several States, and without regard to any census or enumeration."

[121] *See* Flint v. Stone Tracy Co., 220 U.S. 107 (1911).

unless perhaps Congress imposed a national tax on real property.

[2] Purpose of Taxation

Governments tax primarily to obtain revenue to fund government spending. Yet taxation, and its specific applications, inevitably have economic and regulatory consequences. Significantly, the text does not restrict the tax power to revenue generation only. Rather, Congress may tax to promote the general welfare. "[T]he power to tax," John Marshall famously observed, "involves the power to destroy."[122] But it may produce other results, too. "It is not only the power to destroy, but it is also the power to keep alive."[123]

Taxation to preserve has been relatively uncontroversial. Congress initially used the tax power to impose tariffs to protect American industry from foreign competition.[124] Taxation also provides a means to regulate. A tax might suppress an undesirable activity. The Court followed a meandering path to this conclusion. In *Veazie Bank v. Fenno*,[125] the Court considered a 10% federal tax on state bank notes used as currency to eliminate the state notes.[126] Nonetheless, the tax was upheld. Congress could have accomplished its purposes by using an enumerated power, i.e. passing a law under its power to provide for a national currency[127] to prohibit the local notes. Accordingly, it was irrelevant that Congress taxed to destroy, not to raise revenue. The Court implicitly seemed to acknowledge that Congress could tax to regulate.[128]

In *McCray v. United States*,[129] the Court rejected the proposition that it might strike down a tax within Congress' formal power based on legislative motive. Congress had imposed a steeper tax on margarine colored to resemble butter than on uncolored margarine. The tax was challenged as an impermissible attempt to control the manufacture of margarine, a matter beyond the commerce power as then construed. The Court dismissed the argument. Congress' power depended on what the Constitution conferred, not on "the consequence arising from the exercise of lawful authority."[130] The tax raised revenue and accordingly it was within Congress' power. Neither Congress' purpose nor the measure's effect changed that fact. The Court left open the possibility that it might intervene in case of an extreme abuse of the taxing power "where it was plain to the judicial mind that the power had been called into play not for revenue but solely for the purpose of

---

[122] *McCulloch*, 17 U.S. (4 Wheat.) at 431.

[123] Nicol v. Ames, 173 U.S. 509, 515 (1899).

[124] *See* J. W. Hampton, Jr. & Co. v. United States, 276 U.S. 394 (1928).

[125] 75 U.S. (8 Wall.) 533 (1869).

[126] The tax did actually drive the state bank notes then circulating out of existence in short order. *See* Cities' Savings & Loan Ass'n v. Topeka, 87 U.S. 655, 663–64 (1875).

[127] U.S. Const. art. I, § 8, cl. 5.

[128] *See also* United States v. Doremus, 249 U.S. 86, 93 (1919) (Narcotics Drug Act of 1914 upheld despite regulatory purpose and effect); McCray v. United States, 195 U.S. 27 (1904) (Federal tax on colored oleomargarine upheld despite regulatory purpose and effect.).

[129] 195 U.S. 27 (1904).

[130] *Id.* at 59.

destroying rights which could not be rightfully destroyed consistently with the principles of freedom and justice upon which the Constitution rests."[131] The *Child Labor Tax Case*[132] posed the problem whether its tax power allowed Congress to reach an activity beyond its power otherwise. The Court had invalidated as beyond the Commerce Clause a federal law barring from interstate commerce products made by child labor.[133] Congress then taxed profits of employers of children. The legislative intent was no mystery. Congress sought to use its taxing power to accomplish what it could not achieve under the Commerce Clause. The Court found the tax invalid. The regulatory motive was apparent on the very face of the statute, Chief Justice Taft reasoned. It was not left to supposition. Moreover, unlike *Veazie Bank* Congress had no independent regulatory power in this instance.

United States v. Butler[134] applied the *Child Labor Tax* approach. The Agricultural Adjustment Act of 1933 used incentives to restrict farm production. It taxed agricultural commodities and distributed the proceeds to farmers who decreased production. This exercise was intended to regulate agricultural production, a matter then deemed within the reserved power of the states. The Court held the law unconstitutional. Congress could not, under then prevailing Commerce Clause decisions, directly regulate agricultural production; therefore it could not regulate such production under the guise of exercising taxing power. The tax was void, not because it was not a tax for the general welfare, but because an improper motive inspired it.

The Court has since repudiated the limitation *Butler* imposed on the taxing power. Instead it has embraced the *McCray* approach which defers to Congress. Many post-*Butler* decisions have upheld taxes whose animating purpose was regulation. In *Sonzinsky v. United States*,[135] the Court upheld excise taxes imposed on dealers, manufacturers and importers of firearms. On its face, the law was "only a taxing measure" and the fact that it might deter some trade of firearms did not invalidate that feature. "Every tax is in some measure regulatory," wrote Justice Stone. "To some extent it interposes an economic impediment to the activity taxed as compared with others not taxed. But a tax is not any the less a tax because it has a regulatory effect."[136]

Thirteen years later, the Court articulated the principle more expansively in *United States v. Sanchez*.[137] A tax is not invalid "merely because it regulates, discourages, or even definitely deters the activities taxed,"[138] even though it generates little revenue[139] and treats raising revenue as a secondary purpose at

---

[131] *Id.* at 64.

[132] Bailey v. Drexel Furniture Co., 259 U.S. 20 (1922).

[133] Hammer v. Dagenhart, 247 U.S. 251 (1918).

[134] 297 U.S. 1 (1936).

[135] 300 U.S. 506 (1937).

[136] *Id.* at 513.

[137] 340 U.S. 42 (1950).

[138] *See Sanchez*, 340 U.S. at 44.

[139] *Id.*

best.[140]

Moreover, the Court has rejected *Butler's* limitation of taxing power to those regulatory ends within Congress' direct authority. In *Sanchez* the Court upheld a heavy federal tax imposed on dealers in marijuana even though it touched activities otherwise beyond congressional regulatory power.[141] Similarly *United States v. Kahriger*[142] considered a law that levied a tax of fifty dollars per year on bookies and required them to register with the federal Collector of Internal Revenue. The law's primary purpose was to suppress gambling, a regulatory object which did not render the law invalid.

Though broad, the tax power may not be exercised in violation of constitutional rights. Thus, Congress may not impose a tax on newspapers alone in violation of the First Amendment[143] or use the taxing power to compel self-incrimination barred by the Fifth Amendment.[144]

§ 3.05 SPENDING POWER

The same clause that confers the power to tax also conveys the power to spend. It provides that "[t]he Congress shall have power . . . to pay the debts and provide for the common defense and general welfare of the United States . . . ." Congress is accorded broad discretion to decide which expenditures will promote the general welfare.[145]

Butler construed the Spending Clause, as well as the Taxing Clause. In *Butler*, the Court held that the spending power was not limited to the purposes set out in Article I's specific grants of legislative power but rather extended beyond those grants so long as exercised to provide for the general welfare.[146] In so doing, the Court adopted the Hamilton approach over that Madison advocated. But the Court concluded that Congress must pursue "matters of national as distinguished from local, welfare."[147] In *Butler*, a federal expenditure for a "local" end Congress could not directly attain was held invalid. The spending scheme was unconstitutional because its purpose was to regulate agricultural production, a "local" end prohibited to Congress under the then-prevailing interpretation of the Tenth Amendment.

The Court has subsequently rejected *Butler's* limitation on the spending power as well as its interpretation of the taxing power. If the courts will not examine a tax law to ferret out an improper purpose, the same should be true of spending

---

[140] Hampton & Co. v. United States, 276 U.S. 394 (1928).

[141] *See Sanchez*, 340 U.S. at 44.

[142] 345 U.S. 22 (1953).

[143] *See* Grosjean v. American Press Co., 297 U.S. 233 (1936).

[144] *See* Leary v. United States, 395 U.S. 6 (1969); Marchetti v. United States, 390 U.S. 39 (1968).

[145] Buckley v. Valeo, 424 U.S. 1, 90 (1976); South Dakota v. Dole, 483 U.S. 203, 207 (1987) ("In considering whether a particular expenditure is intended to serve general public purposes, courts should defer substantially to the judgment of Congress."); Helvering v. Davis, 301 U.S. 619, 640 (1937).

[146] 297 U.S. at 65–66.

[147] *Id.* at 67.

measures.[148] Funds disbursed to advance Congress' vision of the general welfare are not suspect because they bring action in an area Congress cannot regulate directly. Congress may condition expenditures on terms it sets.[149] It may use the power of the purse to pursue regulatory objectives by conditioning disbursements.

The Social Security Act gave States benefits if they enacted unemployment compensation laws according to federal standards. The Court rejected the contention that the Social Security Act attempted to coerce the States in an unconstitutional manner.[150] The Constitution allowed Congress to disburse federal funds on condition to achieve its social goals. "When money is spent to promote the general welfare, the concept of welfare or the opposite is shaped by Congress, not the States."[151]

In *Buckley v. Valeo*, the Court employed similar reasoning to uphold public financing of presidential election campaigns under the Federal Election Campaign Act. The Court rejected attacks on the statute as contrary to the general welfare. The wisdom of the means Congress chose was irrelevant; the Court deferred to Congress' belief that they were "necessary and proper" to promote the general welfare.[152] In fact, as the Court later stated, "The level of deference to the congressional decision is such that [it may be] questioned whether 'general welfare' is a judicially enforceable restriction at all."[153]

South Dakota v. Dole[154] upheld a federal law that reduced the amount of federal highway funds distributed to States that allowed the purchase of alcoholic beverages by persons under 21. In articulating a flexible spending power, the Court reiterated some general restrictions. The spending must be for "the general welfare," an area where Congress' judgments receive substantial deference. Congress must impose any conditions on the States' receipt of funds unambiguously so the States' consent is knowing, i.e., a clear statement rule. The conditions must relate to the federal interest in the particular national program. Finally, the spending power may not be used to induce the States to engage in unconstitutional activities. Thus, a grant of federal funds conditioned on racially discriminatory state action would be an illegitimate exercise of the spending power.

The condition on distribution of federal highway funds was closely related to one of the program's purposes, promoting safe travel on interstate arteries. The Court observed that "in some circumstances the financial inducement" Congress offered "might be so coercive as to pass the point" where pressure becomes compulsion.[155] The small percentage of federal highway funds at stake (5%) did not cross that line.

---

[148] *Cf.* South Dakota v. Dole, 483 U.S. 203, 207 (1987) (Court should defer to Congress regarding propriety of expenditure).

[149] *See* Lau v. Nichols, 414 U.S. 563, 569 (1974).

[150] *Steward Machine*, 301 U.S. at 589. *See also* Helvering v. Davis, 301 U.S. 619 (1937).

[151] *Id.* at 645.

[152] Buckley v. Valeo, 424 U.S. 1, 91 (1976).

[153] *Dole*, 483 U.S. at 207 n.2.

[154] *Id.*

[155] *Id.* at 211.

Rust v. Sullivan[156] tested the rule of deference to exercises of the spending power. It addressed regulations forbidding doctors in federally funded facilities from abortion counseling. The Court rejected the claim that the regulation intruded on doctors' First Amendment rights. Government can selectively fund a program to encourage certain activities. The regulations do not force doctors to relinquish First Amendment rights but merely to keep those activities separate from funded facilities.

In *Sabri v. United States*,[157] the Court held that under Article I of the Constitution, Congress could criminalize bribery of state and local officials of entities receiving federal funds even absent any connection between the forbidden conduct and the federal funds. Sabri was indicted for violating 18 U.S.C. 666(a)(2) which proscribed attempting to bribe a state, local, or tribal official with an entity that received more than $10,000 in federal benefits. Sabri challenged the law as facially invalid because it failed to require a connection between the bribe and federal funds. In a unanimous decision, the Court rejected Sabri's argument. Under the Spending Clause, Congress could appropriate money to promote the general welfare and under the Necessary and Proper Clause it could take action to make certain that federal funds were not diverted from the general welfare to corrupt applications. Congress was not limited to legislating with respect to bribes traceable to federal programs since the federal interest encompassed having any untrustworthy officials in possession of federal funds.

§ 3.06   FISCAL POWERS

Congress' other fiscal powers rest on its power to borrow[158] and to coin money.[159] These grants, taken with the implied powers from the Necessary and Proper Clause,[160] give Congress the fiscal powers generally associated with sovereignty.[161]

McCulloch held that the fiscal powers of Congress included authority to charter banks with the right to issue circulating notes. *McCulloch*'s logic gave Congress sweeping authority over currency. The Court relied on *McCulloch* in approving other measures relating to the banking system.[162]

Controversy arose, however, over the federal government's power to make its bills legal tender, a question the Supreme Court addressed in connection with the "greenbacks" issued during the Civil War. The relevant statute made those

---

[156] 500 U.S. 173 (1991).

[157] 541 U.S. 600 (2004).

[158] U.S. CONST. art. I, § 8, cl. 2. "The Congress shall have power . . . to borrow money on the credit of the United States."

[159] *Id.*; U.S. CONST. art. I, § 8, cl. 5. "The Congress shall have power . . . to coin money, regulate the value thereof, and of foreign coin."

[160] *See* Norman v. Baltimore & O.R. Co., 294 U.S. 240, 303 (1935).

[161] *See* The Legal Tender Cases, 110 U.S. 421, 447 (1884).

[162] *See, e.g.,* Farmers' & Mechanics' Nat'l Bank v. Dearing, 91 U.S. 29, 33 (1875); First Nat'l Bank v. Fellows, 244 U.S. 416 (1917); Smith v. Kansas City Title & Trust Co., 255 U.S. 180 (1921).

Treasury notes legal tender at face value. The *Legal Tender Cases*[163] held that the nation's fiscal powers included authority to issue paper money as legal tender. The power to coin money included authority to make Treasury notes legal tender to carry into execution the government's powers. In so ruling, the Court overturned a divided decision of the prior year, in part due to changes in court personnel.[164]

The Constitution gives Congress authority to "regulate the Value" of currency.[165] Congress can do more than set the face value of money. It can also regulate the value of the monetary unit by varying its gold content. *Norman v. Baltimore & O. R. Co.*[166] arose from congressional and executive action reducing the gold content of the dollar. The Treasury suspended its gold payments and required all persons to exchange their gold and certificates for other currency. A Joint Resolution abrogated "gold clauses" (which gave obligees a right to require payment in gold) in all contracts and government bonds and required that all contracts and bonds be "discharged upon payment, dollar for dollar, in any coin or currency "which" at the time of payment is legal tender for public and private debts."[167] The holder of a bond with an interest coupon payable in gold, issued before the gold content of the dollar was lowered, sued for payment in gold or for its equivalent in legal tender. The Court held the payee must accept the devalued dollars. Congress may determine what constitutes valid money and fix its value. Congress could alter rights from private contracts, such as the gold clauses. Pursuant to its power to regulate currency, Congress cannot, however, use this power to vary the terms of its own obligations. In *Perry v. United States*[168] the Court held that Congress could not abrogate gold clauses in federal government contracts.

§ 3.07   CITIZENSHIP

[1]   Becoming and Remaining a Citizen

Congress possesses significant powers relating to citizenship. The Fourteenth Amendment makes citizenship depend solely on place of birth or the fact of naturalization.[169] Such persons are citizens of the nation and of the states in which they live.[170] Congress cannot alter the constitutional effect of birth within the United States.[171]

---

[163] 79 U.S. 457 (1871), *overruling* Hepburn v. Griswold, 75 U.S. (8 Wall.) 603 (1870).

[164] *See generally* ERIC J. SEGALL, SUPREME MYTHS: WHY THE SUPREME COURT IS NOT A COURT AND ITS JUSTICES ARE NOT JUDGES (2012); Charles Fairman, MR. JUSTICE MILLER AND THE SUPREME COURT, 1862–1895, at 149–78 (1939).

[165] U.S. CONST. art. I, § 8, cl. 5.

[166] 294 U.S. 240 (1935).

[167] *Id.* at 292.

[168] 294 U.S. 330 (1935).

[169] *See* U.S. CONST. amend. XIV, § 1. ("All persons born or naturalized in the United States, and subject to the jurisdiction thereof, are citizens of the United States and of the state wherein they reside.").

[170] *See id.*

[171] *See* United States v. Wong Kim Ark, 169 U.S. 649, 703 (1898).

The Naturalization Power is quite broad, however. The Constitution itself does not confer citizenship on children of American citizens born abroad. Congress, under its naturalization power[172] has, nevertheless, provided for the citizenship of such children.[173]

The cases emphasize the broad congressional discretion to fix the conditions on which naturalization is to be granted or withheld.[174] The Naturalization Clause empowers Congress to prescribe the rules under which aliens may secure citizenship.[175] In addition to setting general rules governing naturalization, Congress may grant citizenship to named individuals by special act or provide for collective naturalization.[176] Congress may adopt such methods for naturalizing aliens as it chooses. Under the Constitution, a naturalized citizen enjoys the same privilege of citizenship as the native except regarding eligibility to high office.[177] "Citizenship obtained through naturalization is not a second-class citizenship"[178] although a naturalized citizen is not eligible to be President,[179] a limitation which may make little sense but has little impact.

The Constitution, however, limits Congress' ability to remove citizenship from naturalized citizens. In *Schneider v. Rusk*,[180] the Court struck down a statute providing that a naturalized citizen forfeited citizenship if she resided for three years in her country of origin. The discriminatory statute curtailed naturalized citizens' rights to live abroad in a way permitted to other citizens.[181] *Schneider* does not apply to those outside the Fourteenth Amendment's definition of citizens i.e., "persons born or naturalized in the United States." Congress may provide that a person, who acquires American citizenship by virtue of having been born abroad to parents one of whom is a citizen, shall lose citizenship unless he resides in the United States continuously for five years between ages 14 and 28.[182]

Absent expatriation by voluntary renunciation, Congress lacks power to remove citizenship.[183] In *Afroyim v. Rusk*,[184] an American citizen was refused a passport

---

[172] *See* U.S. CONST. art. I, § 8, cl. 4 ("The Congress shall have Power . . . [t]o establish a uniform Rule of Naturalization.").

[173] *See* 8 U.S.C. § 1401(c), (d), (g) (1994).

[174] *See* Mathews v. Diaz, 426 U.S. 67, 79–80 (1976); Schneiderman v. United States, 320 U.S. 118, 131 (1943).

[175] *See* Fiallo v. Bell, 430 U.S. 787, 792 (1977).

[176] Thus, Congress provided for the collective citizenship of citizens of Hawaii when that territory was annexed. Collective naturalization can also be exercised with regard to particular classes. Indians were not considered citizens until Congress provided by statute that native born Indians should be citizens at birth. *See* Boyd v. Nebraska, 143 U.S. 135, 162 (1892); *see also* Contzen v. United States, 179 U.S. 191 (1900) (Texas). Collective naturalization may also be provided for by treaty providing for cession of territory to this country. *See Boyd*, 143 U.S. at 164.

[177] *See* Knauer v. United States, 328 U.S. 654, 658 (1946).

[178] *Id.*

[179] U.S. CONST. art. II, § 1, cl. 5.

[180] 377 U.S. 163 (1964).

[181] " 'It creates indeed a second-class citizenship.' " *Id.* at 169.

[182] Rogers v. Bellei, 401 U.S. 815 (1971).

[183] *Compare Schneider*, 377 U.S. at 166.

on the ground that he had lost his citizenship by voting in a foreign election. The Court ruled that Congress lacked authority to expatriate someone who voted in a foreign election because such voting may not be a voluntary relinquishment of citizenship.

[2] Freedom of Movement

Freedom of movement is an essential attribute of citizenship which is protected by due process, and, accordingly beyond Congress' power to limit.[185] Although the Constitution does not expressly protect a right to travel such a right is implicit in the constitutional structure. John Hart Ely explained that the right allowed people access to government services as well as escape from a hostile majority.[186]

The right of free movement includes the right to travel abroad which is a component of "liberty" which the Due Process Clauses guarantee.[187] As such, governmental action restricting the right to a passport abroad is subject to narrow construction.[188] Congress has greater power over travel abroad than over domestic movement. The constitutional right of interstate travel is virtually unqualified; international travel can be regulated subject to due process.[189] The potential foreign policy impact of international travel allows Congress to authorize restrictions of some foreign travel.[190]

§ 3.08 TREATY POWER

The power to make treaties is a significant, though unique, aspect of legislative authority. The Constitution assigns the treaty power to the President and Senate and places it in Article II, not Article I. The President has "power, by and with the advice and consent of the Senate, to make treaties, provided two thirds of the Senators present concur."[191] Although the normal legislative requirements of bicameralism and presentment do not apply, the treaty power is a legislative power because the Supremacy Clause expressly makes treaties (along with the Constitution and federal laws) "the supreme Law of the Land." Unless a treaty makes clear that it is not self-executing,[192] it becomes part of our law equal in status to a federal statute. A court will resort to a treaty for a rule of decision as it would to a statute.

---

[184] 387 U.S. 253 (1967). *See* Trop v. Dulles, 356 U.S. 86 (1958) (loss of citizenship may not be imposed for desertion from armed forces).

[185] It is also beyond state restrictive power. *See* Edwards v. California, 314 U.S. 160 (1941). *See also* Shapiro v. Thompson, 394 U.S. 618 (1969) (freedom of movement restricted by residence requirements in welfare laws).

[186] JOHN HART ELY, DEMOCRACY AND DISTRUST: A THEORY OF JUDICIAL REVIEW 178–79 (1980).

[187] *See* Aptheker v. Secretary of State, 378 U.S. 500, 505 (1964); Kent v. Dulles, 357 U.S. 116, 129 (1958).

[188] *Id.*

[189] *See* Califano v. Gautier Torres, 435 U.S. 1, 4 n.6 (1978).

[190] *See* Zemel v. Rusk, 381 U.S. 1, 15 (1965).

[191] U.S. CONST. art. II, § 2, cl. 2.

[192] Such a treaty is one that calls for legislation to make it effective.

As part of "the supreme Law of the Land," a treaty overrides conflicting state laws. For example, in *Ware v. Hylton*,[193] the Court held that the Treaty of Peace with Britain prevailed over state law regarding debts Americans owed British subjects. A treaty does not necessarily override a conflicting federal statute. Article VI assigns "Laws of the United States," and treaties equal status as part of "the supreme Law of the Land."[194] The Court will attempt to construe a treaty and federal statute on the same subject to give effect to both when it may do so "without violating the language of either."[195] Where such construction proves impossible, the one with the later date controls.[196]

The treaty power is conferred without any explicit limitations.[197] Although no treaty has been held unconstitutional, a treaty is subject to basic constitutional limitations[198] notwithstanding the contrary implication in *Missouri v. Holland*.[199] There a federal statute regulating shooting of migratory birds had been held unconstitutional.[200] A subsequent treaty with Great Britain regulated shooting seasons in the United States and Canada, and provided that the countries would ask their legislatures to implement the treaty. Subsequently, Congress did so. This law was challenged as violating the Tenth Amendment, the same grounds that proved fatal to the earlier regulatory law. The Court upheld the statute. The earlier decisions holding the regulatory law unconstitutional did not govern the treaty power. The Court gave several reasons for its decision. Statutes are the supreme law only when made in pursuance of the Constitution while treaties have that status when made under the authority of the United States.[201] The Constitution imposed no textual limit on the treaty power. No "invisible radiation from the general terms of the Tenth Amendment"[202] could apply where "a national interest of very nearly the first magnitude"[203] was involved. The birds were only briefly in Missouri, mitigating its interest. The measure, which was beyond Congress' power, was valid when passed to give effect to a treaty. This implies the treaty power may accomplish what Congress could not achieve alone. The inapplicability of the Tenth Amendment may have been due to the fact that the Treaty Power was given to the Federal Government and thus neither it nor laws implementing treaties were powers reserved to the States. The Court might have thought the States' interest protected by the fact that a super majority of the Senate was needed to ratify the treaty.

---

[193] 3 U.S. (3 Dall.) 199 (1796).

[194] Whitney v. Robertson, 124 U.S. 190, 194 (1888).

[195] *Id.*

[196] *See* Cook v. United States, 288 U.S. 102, 118–20 (1933); The Cherokee Tobacco, 78 U.S. (11 Wall.) 616, 621 (1871).

[197] *See* Asakura v. Seattle, 265 U.S. 332, 341 (1924).

[198] *Id. See Cherokee Tobacco*, 78 U.S. at 616, 620–21.

[199] 252 U.S. 416 (1920).

[200] *See* United States v. McCullagh, 221 F. 288 (D. Kan. 1915); United States v. Shauver, 214 F.154 (E.D. Ark. 1914).

[201] *See Holland*, 252 U.S. at 433.

[202] *Id.* at 434.

[203] *Id.* at 435.

Missouri v. Holland raised the spectre of regulating by treaty subjects beyond congressional authority. Such fears seem largely unjustified. *Holland* relied on Article VI under which laws "made in Pursuance" of the Constitution are the supreme law of the land, while treaties "made, or which shall be made, under the Authority of the United States" are placed in the same position. It is doubtful that this language was meant to place treaties, and laws under them, beyond the limits of the Constitution. The language rather probably sought to grandfather treaties made before the Constitution was ratified.

The Supreme Court recognized that the Constitution limits treaties in *Reid v. Covert*.[204] Under a federal statute, an American civilian residing on a military base in England with her husband, a soldier in the United States Air Force, was tried by court-martial for murder. American military courts exercised jurisdiction over servicemen or their dependents under an agreement with Britain. The Court rejected the Government's defense of the statute under the Necessary and Proper Clause. According to Justice Black, however, "no agreement with a foreign nation can confer power on the Congress . . . free from the restraints of the Constitution."[205]

Reid v. Covert suggested that the treaty power is subject to the Constitution's substantive limitations. It would be anomalous if the Federal Government could circumvent constitutional restrictions by concluding treaties with a foreign country and thereby assume powers the Constitution otherwise withheld.

Although two-thirds of the Senate must advise and consent to a treaty for it to become law, it is not clear that rescission of the treaty needs Senate participation. In *Goldwater v. Carter*,[206] Senator Barry Goldwater challenged President Jimmy Carter's action in abrogating the United States' treaty with Taiwan. He argued that rescission required two-thirds support in the Senate. The Court deemed the issue nonjusticiable, either as a political question,[207] or as unripe.[208]

In *Medellin v. Texas*,[209] the Court, in a 6-3 decision, limited the binding force of treaties on state law. *Medellin* held that although a treaty constitutes an international commitment, it is not binding domestic law unless: (1) Congress has enacted statutes implementing it, or (2) the treaty itself conveys the intention that it shall be "self-executing" and is ratified on that basis. The issue arose as a result of a ruling by the International Court of Justice (ICJ) requiring the United States to provide new review of criminal cases involving Mexican foreign nationals who had not been advised of their rights under the Vienna Convention on Consular Relations (which gives foreign nationals accused of a crime the right to meet with diplomats from their home country). Since the treaty was not self-executing a decision by ICJ interpreting it was not binding domestic law. The Court further held that such international obligations do not become binding merely because the President of

---

[204] 354 U.S. 1 (1957).

[205] *Id.* at 16. *See also* De Geofroy v. Riggs, 133 U.S. 258 (1890) (same).

[206] 444 U.S. 996 (1979).

[207] Justice Rehnquist, Chief Justice Burger, Justice Stewart, and Justice Stevens.

[208] Justice Powell.

[209] 552 U.S. 491 (2008).

the United States declared that states would abide by the ICJ decision.

§ 3.09   CIVIL RIGHTS ENFORCEMENT AND STATE ACTION

Congress possesses important powers to enforce the Thirteenth,[210] Fourteenth[211] and Fifteenth[212] Amendments, the three Reconstruction era amendments ratified after the Civil War. Each amendment specifically empowers Congress to enforce its provisions with appropriate legislation. Congress passed legislation to enforce these amendments, including the Civil Rights Acts of 1866 (giving all citizens the same right "as is enjoyed by white citizens" in various areas) and of 1875 (which contained a provision outlawing racial discrimination in various places of public accommodations).[213] The Court construed these statutes narrowly or in some cases held them unconstitutional.[214] In particular, in the *Civil Rights Cases*[215] the Court, in an 8-1 decision, struck down the 1875 Civil Rights Act and restricted Congress' power to regulate private conduct. Congress, under the Thirteenth Amendment, could address slavery but not try to end private discrimination. The Fourteenth Amendment did not license Congress to regulate private behavior. Congress subsequently largely abandoned the area for the better part of a century before again legislating to protect civil rights in the 1960s. Before addressing that subject, it is helpful to discuss the "state action" concept, which limits the reach of the Fourteenth and Fifteenth Amendments unaided by enforcement legislation. That leads to a discussion whether congressional power includes authority to extend the amendments to cases where state action is absent.

State Action

The *Civil Rights Cases*[216] invalidated the public accommodations section of the Civil Rights Act of 1875 which prohibited racial discrimination in inns, public conveyances, and places of amusement. The Court acted based on the ground that the Act addressed wholly private discriminatory action beyond enforcement power the Fourteenth Amendment delegated to Congress. Congress was limited to remedying state action.[217]

---

[210] The Thirteenth Amendment (1865) bans slavery and involuntary servitude except as a criminal punishment.

[211] The Fourteenth Amendment (1868) confers citizenship on all persons born or naturalized in the United States, precludes a state from denying a citizen the privileges and immunities of United States' citizens or denying any person life, liberty, or property without due process of laws, or of denying any person the equal protection of the laws.

[212] The Fifteenth Amendment (1870) provides that neither the federal nor state government may deny any American citizen the right to vote based on race, color, or prior servitude.

[213] *See generally* BERNARD SCHWARTZ, A HISTORY OF THE SUPREME COURT 165–68 (1993).

[214] *See, e.g.*, Civil Rights Cases, 109 U.S. 3 (1883).

[215] *Id.*

[216] 109 U.S. 3 (1883).

[217] *Id.* at 11.

Some thought the limitation from the *Civil Rights Cases* was overruled in *United States v. Guest*,[218] when six members of the Court joined two opinions claiming that Section 5 of the Fourteenth Amendment empowered Congress to reach some private discrimination. "A majority of the members of the Court expresses the view today that [§] 5 empowers Congress to enact laws punishing *all* conspiracies to interfere with the exercise of Fourteenth Amendment rights, whether or not state officers or others acting under the color of state law are implicated in the conspiracy."[219]

On one argument, *Guest* rejected the *Civil Rights Cases'* interpretation of congressional power to enforce the Fourteenth Amendment. Although the Amendment speaks only to state action some thought § 5 authorized Congress to make laws necessary to protect rights under the Amendment; Congress might determine that prohibiting certain private action interfering with exercise of a Fourteenth Amendment right is necessary to vindicate the Amendment's promise.

In *United States v. Morrison*,[220] the Court reaffirmed the *Civil Rights Cases* and *United States v. Harris*[221] both of which limited Congress' ability to reach private conduct under § 5 of the Fourteenth Amendment. In so doing, it declared that contrary indications in *Guest* were dicta and did not establish any different doctrine.

Most "state action" cases have involved the Equal Protection Clause of the Fourteenth Amendment. Its text prohibits state action that denies equal protection of the laws.[222] It therefore draws an "essential dichotomy" between public and private activity.[223] The Equal Protection Clause erects no bar against private discriminatory conduct;[224] it does not preclude a private party from discriminating on racial grounds in conducting her personal affairs.[225] Only state racial discrimination violates the Constitution.[226]

"State action" exists most clearly when a person or agency formally identified as a state instrumentality takes action. State action includes legislative measures, whether a statute, ordinance, or administrative rule or regulation,[227] and executive action. Seemingly fair legislation is vulnerable if applied in discriminatory fashion.[228]

---

[218] 383 U.S. 745 (1966).

[219] *Id.* at 782 (Brennan, J., concurring in part and dissenting in part) (emphasis added).

[220] 529 U.S. 598 (2000).

[221] 106 U.S. 629 (1883).

[222] *See* U.S. Const. amend. XIV ("nor shall any state . . . ").

[223] Edmonson v. Leesville Concrete Co., Inc., 500 U.S. 614, 620 (1991).

[224] *See* Jackson v. Metropolitan Edison Co., 419 U.S. 345, 349 (1974).

[225] *See* Adickes v. S. H. Kress & Co., 398 U.S. 144, 169 (1970).

[226] *See* Georgia v. McCollum, 505 U.S. 42, 50 (1992); *Jackson*, 419 U.S. at 349.

[227] *See* Moose Lodge No. 107 v. Irvis, 407 U.S. 163, 179 (1972).

[228] *See, e.g.*, Yick Wo v. Hopkins, 118 U.S. 356 (1886); Arlington Heights v. Metropolitan Housing Dev. Corp., 429 U.S. 252, 266 (1977).

The doctrine is difficult to cabin. In *Shelley v. Kramer*,[229] a private party sought to enforce a covenant in an agreement restricting future sales of the real estate to whites. The party seeking enforcement denied the Fourteenth Amendment was implicated in the private dispute. The Court held, however, that judicial enforcement of the racially restrictive covenant constituted state action under the Fourteenth Amendment.

Yet if judicial enforcement constitutes state action, as it clearly does, the public-private distinction experiences considerable erosion. Yet presumably state trespass laws could be used to aid a home owner in keeping others off his property even if excluded based on race or religion. The state action requirement retains importance even though the rationale connecting different applications may sometimes be difficult to discern.

State action may occur when public officers and agencies act in an official capacity even if outside their authority[230] or contrary to state law.[231] Nor is state action limited to formal acts; when the police chief and the mayor of New Orleans announced blacks could not stage demonstrations to seek desegregated service in restaurants, their statements were tantamount to a local ordinance prohibiting such conduct.[232] State action is not, however, limited to action by state employees. It may exist if a private business or institution acts under state authority. *Pennsylvania v. Board of Trusts*[233] involved an equal-protection challenge to exclusion of blacks from a school established under a testamentary trust limiting enrollment to "poor white male orphans." The City of Philadelphia was the trustee and, by state statute, the trust was administered, and the school was operated, by the "Board of Directors of City Trusts of the City of Philadelphia." The school was private, but the Court found state action since a state agency was trustee.

The Court has recognized an exception to the state action doctrine when a private party discharges a public or governmental function. Calling this doctrine an "exception" may be a misnomer; put differently, the private conduct is attributed to the state under the circumstances. State action exists when a private person performs a governmental function[234] by exercising powers the state traditionally performed.[235] *Smith v. Allwright*,[236] the white primary case, illustrates this approach. The Court had previously struck down Texas statutes precluding blacks from voting.[237] Texas then delegated power to the State's political parties, which were non-state entities, to establish rules for their primary elections. The Court held that a primary election involved state action because a political party, though not a state entity, performed the public function of conducting the election. The

---

[229] 334 U.S. 1 (1948).

[230] *See* Iowa-Des Moines Nat'l Bank v. Bennett, 284 U.S. 239, 246 (1931).

[231] *See Raines*, 362 U.S. at 25; United States v. Classic, 313 U.S. 299, 326 (1941).

[232] *See* Lombard v. Louisiana, 373 U.S. 267, 270–72 (1963).

[233] 353 U.S. 230 (1957).

[234] *See McCollum*, 505 U.S. at 51.

[235] *See* Jackson v. Metropolitan Edison Co., 419 U.S. 345, 351 (1974).

[236] 321 U.S. 649 (1944).

[237] *See* Nixon v. Herndon, 273 U.S. 536 (1927); Nixon v. Condon, 286 U.S. 73 (1932).

State could not circumvent its constitutional responsibility by delegating control over an election to a private actor. Later, in *Evans v. Newton*,[238] the Court held that Macon, Georgia, could not avoid desegregating a park by transferring control to a private party. Running a park was a public function which the city could not escape in this manner.

Similarly the state action concept has been applied to a company-owned town where the town owner sought to prevent the Jehovah's Witnesses from distributing literature. The owner could not deny the exercise of constitutionally protected rights on the public streets.[239] These cases share the feature of exclusivity: the Democratic Party conducted the only meaningful elections in Texas and the company owned the only streets in its town.[240]

The Court expanded the company town theory in *Logan Valley*, where it held a private shopping center could not preclude striking workers from picketing because the Fourteenth Amendment applied to action by the shopping center infringing constitutional rights.[241] The *Logan Valley* doctrine was reconsidered in *Lloyd Corp. v. Tanner*,[242] where behavior of security guards in stopping distribution of anti-war material at a shopping center was ruled not state action. Although *Lloyd* distinguished, rather than overruled *Logan Valley*, the Court later suggested *Lloyd* could not be reconciled with *Logan Valley* and overruled the latter.[243] Accordingly, a shopping center, even a large self-contained one, is not the functional equivalent of a municipality and its action can no longer be considered "state action" for Fourteenth Amendment purposes.

State action is also found where government is sufficiently entangled with private conduct to attribute that behavior to the State. Is there a "sufficiently close nexus between the State and the challenged action?" The mere recitation of the test suggests that the entanglement exception turns largely on the facts of each case.

In *Burton v. Wilmington Parking Authority*,[244] the Court found state action by virtue of the government's entanglement with a racially discriminatory restaurant that rented space from a public parking authority. The restaurant was located on the State's land and paid the State rent. Its customers used the public parking lot. The State could have avoided the problem had its laws prohibited the discrimination.

Burton suggested a potentially sweeping expansion of the state action concept. The Court substantially narrowed the entanglement exception, however, in *Moose Lodge No. 107 v. Irvis*.[245] A private club had refused to serve Irvis, an African American. He argued the refusal constituted state action since the Pennsylvania

---

[238] 382 U.S. 296 (1966).

[239] *See March v. Alabama*, 326 U.S. 501 (1946).

[240] *See* Flagg Bros., Inc. v. Brooks, 436 U.S. 149, 158–59 (1978).

[241] *See* Amalgamated Food Employees Union v. Logan Valley Plaza, Inc., 391 U.S. 308 (1968).

[242] 407 U.S. 551 (1972).

[243] *See* Hudgens v. NLRB, 424 U.S. 507, 518 (1976).

[244] 365 U.S. 715 (1961).

[245] 407 U.S. 163 (1972).

liquor board had granted the liquor license. The Court adopted a fact intensive approach in finding state action absent. "[W]here the impetus for the discrimination is private, the State must have 'significantly involved itself with invidious discrimination' " to constitute state action.[246] Moose Lodge's building was located on private property and it portrayed itself as a private, rather than public, establishment. The surroundings did not imply a state operation.

Not all governmental aid to private persons makes their conduct state action for purposes of equal protection. *Moose Lodge* made clear that discrimination by a private party does not violate the Equal Protection Clause simply because it receives some state benefit.[247] To allow provision of common necessities such as water, sewage and garbage disposal, and police and fire protection to convert a recipient into a state actor would collapse the distinction between private and state conduct.[248]

Justice Douglas had argued that state action embraced discriminatory behavior of any business[249] subject to governmental regulation, particularly one operating under a state granted license.[250] The business "is thus an instrumentality of the State since the State charges it with duties to the public and supervises its performance."[251] His view has not prevailed. It was not followed, for instance, in *Jackson v. Metropolitan Edison Co.*[252] The Court refused to view behavior of a privately owned electric utility corporation as "state action." State regulation even if a monopoly does not alone attribute a business' action to the State for Fourteenth Amendment purposes.

The entanglement exception has been invoked in cases considering conduct which occurs in court. *Shelley v. Kraemer*[253] provides one example. Other cases deal with the discriminatory use of peremptory challenges in jury selection. In *Edmonson v. Leesville Concrete Co.*[254] the Court found that the behavior of a private litigant in a civil suit in striking persons from jury service based on race was state action. The courtroom setting entangled the government in the conduct.

In *Georgia v. McCollum*[255] the Court extended the state action concept to the case of a criminal defendant's use of those jury strikes. To state the outcome indicates its anomalous nature. Who is more adverse to the State than a criminal defendant? Yet the Court found the State sufficiently entangled to attribute to it the

---

[246] *Id.* at 173.

[247] *See, e.g.*, Columbia Broadcasting System v. Democratic Nat'l Comm., 412 U.S. 94 (1973) (broadcaster's receipt of FCC licenses held not to make their refusal of political advertising governmental action subject to constitutional free speech requirements).

[248] *Moose Lodge*, 407 U.S. at 173.

[249] As contrasted with a private club. *See Moose Lodge*, 407 U.S. at 180 (Douglas, J., dissenting).

[250] *See Lombard*, 373 U.S. at 282 (1963) (Douglas, J., concurring); Garner v. Louisiana, 368 U.S. 157, 184–85 (1961) (Douglas, J., concurring).

[251] *Id.* at 282–83 (Douglas, J., concurring).

[252] 419 U.S. 345 (1974).

[253] 334 U.S. 1 (1948).

[254] 500 U.S. 614 (1991).

[255] 505 U.S. 42 (1992).

harm to those excluded. The harm came from the exercise of a right or privilege which the States originated. Moreover, the defendant relied on state help to cause the harm. Jury selection is a unique governmental function and the courtroom setting conveyed the impression of judicial complicity in the conduct.[256]

In *American Manufacturers Mutual Insurance Co. v. Sullivan*,[257] the Court again considered the circumstances under which private parties may be deemed state actors under the Fourteenth Amendment. Pennsylvania's workers compensation system provided that a private insurer could seek a review of an employee's medical data prior to paying a bill. The Court of Appeals for the Third Circuit had held that the insurer's suspension of payment was state action. It reasoned that private insurers acting under the state workers' compensation system provide benefits and accordingly are state actors.

The Court disagreed. State action must be measured under a two part test. First, the alleged constitutional deprivation must be caused by the exercise of a state-created right or privilege of a state-imposed rule or by "a person for whom the State is responsible." Second, the party charged with the conduct must be someone "who may fairly be said to be a state actor."[258] Although the Court found the first requirement satisfied since the insurers acted pursuant to state statute the Court regarded a private insurer's decision to withhold payment as not fairly attributable to the State. The State had neither coerced nor significantly encouraged the insurers to so act. The State's "mere approval or acquiescence" was legally insufficient to transform the insurer's decisions into state action.[259]

State action is not, however, limited to those situations where a private organization exercises a governmental function or is coerced to act by the State. Instead, a private organization's regulatory conduct may be state action based upon "the pervasive entwinement" of state officials in its structure.[260] No single fact is "a necessary condition across the board for finding state action" nor is "any set of circumstances absolutely sufficient" since countervailing reasons might counsel against "attributing activity to the government."[261] Such a "pervasive entwinement" doctrine, in which no single factor alone is necessary or sufficient, commits courts to a fact intensive inquiry in determining whether private activity is state action.[262] Courts have found state action when the government subsidizes a public school which discriminates against minorities.[263]

---

[256] *Id.* at 54.

[257] 526 U.S. 40 (1999).

[258] *Id.* at 50.

[259] *Id.* at 52.

[260] Brentwood Academy v. Tennessee Secondary School Athletic Ass'n, 531 U.S. 288, 289 (2001).

[261] 531 U.S. at 295–96.

[262] *Id.* at 298–99.

[263] *See, e.g.*, Norwood v. Harrison, 413 U.S. 455 (1973) (textbook subsidy was state action); Gilmore v. City of Montgomery, 417 U.S. 556 (1974) (grant of exclusive use of recreational facilities was state action).

§ 3.10 CONGRESSIONAL ENFORCEMENT

The substantive provisions of the Fourteenth Amendment (i.e., Equal Protection Clause, Due Process Clause) are self-executing; they state constitutional norms which courts enforce. But the Amendment also provides, in its fifth section, that "Congress shall have power to enforce, by appropriate legislation, the provisions of this article." Although the Court interpreted this provision broadly during the 1960s to authorize Congress "to exercise its discretion in determining whether and what legislation is needed to secure the guarantees of the Fourteenth Amendment,"[264] the Court has more recently constricted its ambit in a series of cases.

In *Katzenbach v. Morgan*,[265] the Court interpreted Congress' § 5 power broadly. Section 4(e) of the Voting Rights Act of 1965 provided that a literacy test could not be used to preclude from voting anyone who had completed sixth grade in a school where the predominant language was not English. The provision overrode a New York law which required English literacy in order to vote. In so doing, Congress contradicted an earlier Supreme Court decision[266] that held a literacy test consistent with the Equal Protection Clause.

The Court upheld 4(e) in part on the grounds that Congress could find a literary test contradicted the Constitution. Congress was not confined under § 5 to outlawing those practices which the judiciary deemed inconsistent with Equal Protection. Instead, § 5 conferred on Congress the "same broad powers" as did the Necessary and Proper Clause. "Correctly viewed, § 5 is a positive grant of legislative power authorizing Congress to exercise its discretion in determining whether and what legislation is needed to secure the guarantees of the Fourteenth Amendment."[267] Congress might conclude that 4(e) was plainly adapted to enforce the Equal Protection Clause.

Alternatively, the legislation might be upheld on the grounds that Congress might reasonably have concluded that New York's literacy requirement invidiously discriminated. The Court could perceive a basis under which Congress may have thought the state measure reflected racial prejudice, thereby satisfying the deferential review suggested.

In dissent, Justice Harlan thought the decision an affront to *Marbury* to the extent it held that Congress, not the Court, could interpret the Constitution. It was for the Court, not Congress, to define the substantive reach of the Equal Protection Clause, he urged. If Congress could define the constitutional norm, it could dilute, as well as expand, it.[268]

The Court retreated from the idea that Congress could define the substantive scope of the Fourteenth Amendment in *City of Boerne v. Flores*[269] where it held that

---

[264] Katzenbach v. Morgan, 384 U.S. 641, 651 (1966).

[265] 384 U.S. 641 (1966).

[266] *See* Lassiter v. Northampton County Bd. of Elections, 360 U.S. 45 (1959).

[267] 384 U.S. at 651.

[268] *Id.* at 668.

[269] 521 U.S. 507 (1997).

congressional power to enforce the Fourteenth Amendment does not include authority to expand the substantive sweep of the Amendment. In *Employment Division v. Smith*,[270] the Court had upheld a neutral law banning use of peyote without recognizing any constitutional exception for religious use based on the Free Exercise Clause. Congress had subsequently passed the Religious Freedom Restoration Act (RFRA)[271] to require application of the "compelling interest" test in Free Exercise cases, the test *Smith* said was not required. *Boerne* held RFRA beyond the power conferred by the Fourteenth Amendment's Enforcement Clause. The Court stated that congressional enforcement power was remedial and preventive, not substantive. Congress lacked the power "to determine what constitutes a constitutional violation."[272] RFRA, in effect, changed the substantive scope of the Fourteenth Amendment by overriding the Supreme Court's interpretation of the Free Exercise Clause. State action valid under *Smith* would violate the RFRA. Section 5 did not allow Congress to change the Constitution.

"There must be a congruence and proportionality between the injury to be prevented or remedied and the means adopted to that end," wrote Justice Kennedy for the Court.[273] In essence, *City of Boerne* limited Congress' power under § 5 to addressing; (1) "conduct transgressing the Fourteenth Amendment's substantive provisions," and required that; (2) Congress "must tailor its legislative scheme to remedying or preventing such conduct."[274]

The Court further restrained Congress' power under § 5 in two companion cases it decided on June 23, 1999 by identical 5-4 divisions.[275] In one case the federal legislation failed to fall within the Amendment's "substantive" reach; in the other, Congress failed to show that its legislative scheme was commensurate with the conduct addressed.

In *College Savings Bank v. Florida Prepaid Postsecondary Education Expense Board*,[276] the Court held that § 5 did not empower Congress to abrogate a State's Eleventh Amendment immunity by enacting the Trademark Remedy Clarification Act (TRCA) to subject states to suit for false and misleading advertising under the Lanham Act. TRCA allegedly protected against state deprivations of two types of rights-freedom from a competitor's false advertising about its products and "a more generalized right to be secure in one's business interests."[277] The majority held that neither was a property right under the Due Process Clause of the Fourteenth Amendment; accordingly, Congress could enforce neither under § 5. Although the four dissenters thought Congress had power to subject States to suit, only Justice Stevens argued that the statute did protect property so that § 5 applied.

---

[270] 494 U.S. 872 (1990).

[271] 42 U.S.C. § 2000bb (2000).

[272] *City of Boerne*, 521 U.S. at 519.

[273] *Id.* at 520.

[274] Florida Prepaid Postsecondary Educ. Expense Bd. v. College Sav. Bank, 527 U.S. 627, 639 (1999).

[275] The majority consisted of Chief Justice Rehnquist and Justices O'Connor, Scalia, Kennedy, and Thomas; Justices Stevens, Souter, Ginsburg, and Breyer dissented.

[276] 527 U.S. 666 (1999).

[277] *Id.* at 672.

In *Florida Prepaid Postsecondary Education Expense Board v. College Savings Bank*,[278] the Court held that § 5 did not allow Congress to enact the Patent Remedy Act subjecting States to suit in federal court for patent infringement. Although patents are "property," the infringement of which Congress could protect against under § 5, the Court found insufficient evidence that Congress sought to remedy a Fourteenth Amendment violation through the Patent Remedy Act. The Court found the legislative record inadequate to document "widespread and persisting constitutional rights" to justify legislation under § 5. The four dissenters criticized the Court's scrutiny of the state of the legislative record as inappropriate and novel. The Court had not previously required a showing of "widespread and persisting" constitutional deprivations as a prerequisite for § 5 legislation. Unlike the RFRA, the Patent Remedy Act did not impact substantive law but instead sought to prevent States from asserting sovereign immunity to deny patentees property rights without any recourse. That legislative approach, the dissenters argued, was both congruent and proportional as *City of Boerne* required.

In *Kimel v. Florida Board of Regents*[279] the Court held that the Age Discrimination in Employment Act (ADEA) failed to satisfy the *City of Boerne* test. The substantive requirements ADEA imposed on States regarding age discrimination were "disproportionate to any unconstitutional conduct that conceivably could be targeted" by the law.[280] Congress' extension of ADEA to States "was an unwarranted response to a perhaps inconsequential problem."[281]

In *Board of Trustees v. Garrett*,[282] the Court again limited Congress' ability to subject States to private suits for money damages under § 5 of the Fourteenth Amendment. In a 5-4 decision, the Court held state governments immune from such damage suits for employment discrimination in violation of Title 1 of the Americans With Disabilities Act (ADA). The legislative record included extensive documentation of state discrimination against the disabled, but the majority found the record insufficient to show "the pattern of unconstitutional discrimination on which § 5 legislation must be based"[283] Since the ADA went beyond constitutional requirements, it could be justified under § 5 only if "proportionate" and "congruent" to remedy constitutional violations.[284]

Dean Larry Kramer suggested that *Kimel* and *Garrett* implicitly limited Congress' power under § 5 to situations where the States lacked any rational basis to discriminate based on age or disability. As such, they substantially limit Congress' § 5 power to cases of race or gender discrimination.[285]

---

[278] 527 U.S. 627 (1999).

[279] 528 U.S. 62 (2000).

[280] *Id.* at 83.

[281] *Id.* at 89.

[282] 531 U.S. 356 (2001).

[283] *Id.* at 368–72.

[284] *Id.* at 365.

[285] Larry Kramer, *The Supreme Court 2000 Term: Forward: We the Court*, 115 Harv. L. Rev. 4, 147–48 (2001).

Shortly thereafter, the Court deviated from the path of its decisions contracting Congress' § 5 power. In *Nevada Dept. of Human Resources v. Hibbs*,[286] the Court held that § 5 empowered Congress to abrogate state sovereign immunity under the Family and Medical Leave Act of 1993 (FMLA). The Court found that FMLA's family care leave provision was "congruent and proportional to the targeted violation." In the FMLA Congress sought to remedy gender discrimination. Since state action which draws distinctions based on gender is scrutinized with a degree of suspicion, it was relatively easy for Congress to demonstrate "a pattern of state constitutional violations" to justify its action. By contrast, the laws in *Kimel* and *Garrett* addressed discrimination based on age and disability respectively. State action discriminating in those respects is scrutinized according to the more relaxed rational basis review. Accordingly, Congress had to demonstrate a "widespread pattern" of state abuse to ground those laws, but it had failed to do.

The heightened standard of review for gender discrimination was clearly one determinant in the Court's decision in *Hibbs*. Moreover, the Court's opinion suggested that it was also more impressed with the evidence of state discrimination than it was with the showing in cases like *Kimel*, *Garrett* and *Morrison*.

Finally, the Court thought FMLA proportional to the problem since it was "narrowly targeted at the fault line between work and family — precisely where sex-based overgeneralization has been and remains strongest — and affects only one aspect of the employment relationship."

The majority rejected Justice Scalia's argument that, before FMLA could apply to a particular State, Congress needed to demonstrate that State had discriminated, not simply that States generally had done so. The Court also made clear that § 5 did not confine Congress to proscribing practices which violated the Fourteenth Amendment. Rather, it could "prohibit 'a somewhat broader swath of conduct, including that which is not itself forbidden by the Amendment's text' " in remedying discrimination.

During the following Court term, the Court, in a 5-4 decision in *Tennessee v. Lane*,[287] held Congress properly exercised its power under § 5 of the Fourteenth Amendment to abrogate the States' Eleventh Amendment immunity under Title II of the Americans with Disabilities Act of 1990. The case arose from a complaint by two paraplegics that the Tennessee state courthouses denied them access to the state judicial system. Tennessee moved to dismiss based on the Eleventh Amendment. Congress had clearly expressed its intent to abrogate the State's immunity ("A State shall not be immune under the eleventh amendment to the Constitution of the United States from an action in Federal or State court of competent jurisdiction for a violation of this chapter." 42 U.S.C. 12202) and the Court had power under § 5 since the legislation in question satisfied the congruence and proportionality test.

---

[286] 538 U.S. 721 (2003).

[287] 541 U.S. 509 (2004).

§ 3.11 INVOLUNTARY SERVITUDE

The Thirteenth Amendment guaranty against involuntary servitude is closely connected with the right to equal protection. Its purpose was to end slavery and to maintain a system of completely voluntary labor.[288]

In addition to outlawing slavery and forced labor, the Thirteenth Amendment allows Congress to pass laws to abolish all incidents of slavery. Although the Court had long construed Congress' powers under the Thirteenth Amendment restrictively,[289] it drastically revised its approach in 1968 in *Jones v. Alfred H. Mayer Co.*[290] where it allowed Congress to prohibit racial discrimination in the sale or rental of real property. Private sellers had refused to sell real estate to an African-American couple. The prospective purchasers sued, challenging the private racial discrimination. The Court upheld § 1982 of the Civil Rights Act of 1866 and found that it applied to private acts of racial discrimination. "Congress has the power . . . rationally to determine what are the badges and the incidents of slavery, and the authority to translate that determination into effective legislation."[291]

Congressional power to enforce the Thirteenth Amendment extends far beyond cases involving the actual imposition of slavery or involuntary servitude. Congress may create a statutory cause of action for black victims of a conspiratorial, racially motivated assault to deprive them of the basic rights the law secures to free men.[292] Congress may reach private conspiracies, as well as those under color of state law,[293] because the Thirteenth Amendment is not limited to "state action."

Under the Thirteenth Amendment, Congress may reach other private acts of racial discrimination,[294] comparable to the refusal in *Jones* to sell property to an African-American. It may prohibit racial discrimination in private contracts.[295] Thus in *Runyon v. McCrary* the Court held that 42 U.S.C. § 1981 prohibited a private school from excluding qualified students based on race and that the statute was within Congress' power under § 2 of the Thirteenth Amendment. The statute involved in *Jones* provided that "[a]ll persons within the jurisdiction of the United States shall have the same right in every State and Territory to make and enforce contracts . . . as is enjoyed by white citizens."[296] This language prohibits refusing to contract with another person based on race.[297] It affords private sector employees a right of action based on racial discrimination in employment.[298]

---

[288] *See* Pollock v. Williams, 322 U.S. 4, 17 (1944).

[289] *See, e.g.,* The Civil Rights Cases, 109 U.S. 3 (1883).

[290] 392 U.S. 409 (1968).

[291] *Id.* at 440.

[292] *See* Griffin v. Breckenridge, 403 U.S. 88 (1971).

[293] *See id.* at 98–99.

[294] *See* Runyon v. McCrary, 427 U.S. 160, 175 (1976).

[295] *See id.* at 168.

[296] 42 U.S.C. § 1981 (1994) (derived from the Civil Rights Act of 1866).

[297] *See Runyon,* 427 U.S. at 179.

[298] *See* McDonald v. Santa Fe Trail Transp. Co., 427 U.S. 273 (1976).

Congressional power under the Thirteenth Amendment is not limited to protection of any particular race. The civil rights statute that bars racial discrimination in contracts protects whites as well as non-whites.[299] Lack of ability to enter into contracts equally is an incident of slavery that may be reached under the Thirteenth Amendment even when the enforcement power is used to benefit a race that had not been enslaved.

---

[299] *See McDonald,* 427 U.S. at 289.

Chapter 4

COMMERCE CLAUSE

INTRODUCTION

The Commerce Clause[1] confers one of the most important powers of the Federal Government. It is the source of many regulatory laws Congress enacts, regarding trade, to be sure, but also addressing a range of other concerns — racial discrimination, environment, crime, safety, and many more.

This chapter traces the historical development of the Commerce Clause from John Marshall's day. It then examines the broader conception of commerce that developed during the twentieth century under which the Federal Government can regulate virtually all economic activities in the nation no matter how "local" they might be. A comparable development is discussed in connection with the scope of the power to "regulate" granted by the Commerce Clause. Although, in *United States v. Lopez*,[2] the Court retreated somewhat from its most permissive attitude toward congressional regulation, it has still left the Federal Government extensive room to legislate. Determining the extent and merit of that retreat represents one of the open questions in contemporary constitutional law.

§ 4.01 MARSHALL'S CONCEPTION

The Commerce Clause was added to the Constitution to remedy a defect of the Articles of Confederation.[3] Under the Articles, Congress lacked power to regulate commerce. Thus, when Britain closed its ports to American shipping in the 1780s America was powerless to retaliate in a uniform way.[4] Not only did the nation need the power to regulate foreign commerce, it also needed a means to prevent the States from imposing burdens on each other which would undermine unity.[5]

The Commerce Clause provided the fix. Its language is deceptively simple. Congress, it reads, shall have power "[t]o regulate Commerce with foreign Nations, and among the several States, and with the Indian Tribes."[6] The first clause is often known as the Foreign Commerce Clause and the last, the Indian Commerce Clause. The intermediate provision is generally referred to as the Commerce Clause and it

---

[1] U.S. Const. art. I, § 8, cl. 3.

[2] 514 U.S. 549 (1995).

[3] The Federalist No. 42 (James Madison).

[4] *See* Jack N. Rakove, Original Meanings: Politics and Ideas in the Making of the Constitution 26–27 (1996).

[5] The Federalist No. 42.

[6] U.S. Const. art. I, § 8, cl. 3.

has provided Congress authority for much regulation, and has been the source of substantial judicial controversy.

Gibbons v. Ogden[7] was the first case in which the Court had occasion to expound on the Commerce Clause. It arose from Robert Fulton's invention of the steamboat. New York had granted Fulton the exclusive right to navigate steam-propelled vessels. Ogden had secured a license from Fulton to operate steamboats on the Hudson River between New York and New Jersey. Gibbons, however, started to run his own steamboat line between the two states in defiance of the New York-granted monopoly; an act of Congress licensed his boats to engage in the coasting trade. Ogden secured an injunction in a New York court to restrain Gibbons from operating within New York waters. Gibbons appealed to the Supreme Court.

The argument turned in large part on the scope of the federal commerce power. Chief Justice John Marshall used the occasion for a full-scale discussion of the commerce power.

The Commerce Clause, on its face, vests in Congress the power "[t]o regulate Commerce." Marshall defined both the noun "commerce" and the verb "regulate" broadly in *Gibbons* to expand the scope and nature of Congress' authority.

Marshall rejected Ogden's argument that commerce equated to mere traffic (i.e. buying and selling) in commodities. The term instead covered all commercial intercourse — a conception extensive enough to include all business dealings, including navigation. In one compact paragraph, Marshall deployed an array of constitutional arguments to support his interpretation. The text compelled that conclusion since the plain meaning of "commerce" as understood by "[a]ll America" included navigation. The framers so understood the word. Indeed, "one of the primary objects" of the Constitution was to allow the federal government to regulate commerce, including navigation. To accept Ogden's interpretation would defeat a central purpose implicit in the structure of the Constitution.[8]

Marshall embraced an expansive interpretation of *regulate*, too. "What is this power?" he asked. "It is the power to regulate; that is, to prescribe the rule by which commerce is to be governed."[9]

Marshall saw the power to regulate as the plenary power to control. It included both the power to prescribe limits and the power to determine what shall remain unrestrained. "This power," wrote Marshall, "is complete in itself, may be exercised to its utmost extent, and acknowledges no limitations, other than are prescribed in the constitution."[10]

Marshall also construed the meaning of "among the several States" — i.e., the scope of the commerce subject to Congress' regulatory power. Marshall appreciated that the Commerce Clause did not state that "Congress shall have power to regulate commerce." The enumeration of three types (foreign, Indian and interstate) of

---

[7] 22 U.S. (9 Wheat.) 1 (1824).

[8] *Id.* at 190.

[9] *Id.* at 196.

[10] *Id.*

commerce which Congress could regulate suggested some class of commerce which was withheld from Congress.[11] Moreover, even within the center portion, Congress was not authorized to regulate commerce but commerce "among the several states." Marshall reasoned that the Constitution withheld "the exclusively internal commerce of a State."[12] Yet the commerce power did not stop at the state line. For "among" meant "intermingled with." As such, "commerce among the several states" included commerce in the interior of States. Marshall did not construe the clause as reaching "that commerce, which is completely internal, which is carried on between man and man in a State, or between different parts of the same State, and which does not extend to or affect other States."[13] In case the reader missed the point, Marshall repeated it a few sentences later.

> The genius and character of the whole government seem to be, that its action is to be applied to all the external concerns of the nation, and to those internal concerns which affect the States generally; but not to those which are completely within a particular State, which do not affect other States, and with which it is not necessary to interfere, for the purpose of executing some of the general powers of the government.[14]

Marshall drew no rigid line between the commerce over which Congress has authority and the "internal" commerce of the states. Marshall's approach was more flexible. As he saw it, the word *among* in the Commerce Clause "may very properly be restricted to that commerce which concerns more States than one."[15]

Marshall suggested a broad view of commerce. His test was not contingent on movement across state lines. Rather, he suggested the clause applied to particular commerce which affected more than one State. He excluded from the reach of the Commerce Clause only the "completely internal commerce of a state."[16] It is easy to underestimate the novelty of Marshall's approach, accustomed as we are to the Federal Government legislating over a wide domain. Yet Marshall's conception of the Commerce Clause as conferring more than simply the power to remove state imposed tariffs at interstate boundaries was controversial in his day.[17]

Of course, much of Marshall's discussion was dicta. The facts of the case clearly involved transportation from one state to another. No esoteric consideration of what it meant to "affect" or "concern" another state was needed since the case addressed federal and state power over an interstate commercial movement. Gibbons' coastwise license was conferred pursuant to the Commerce Clause and authorized him to operate interstate. Ogden's state conferred monopoly accordingly conflicted with Gibbons' federal license. Under the Supremacy Clause, Gibbons' federal right clearly prevailed.

---

[11] *Id.* at 195.

[12] *Id.*

[13] *Id.* at 194.

[14] *Id.* at 195.

[15] *Id.* at 194.

[16] *Id.* at 195.

[17] *See* ARCHIBALD COX, THE COURT AND THE CONSTITUTION 85–89 (1987); BERNARD SCHWARTZ, A HISTORY OF THE SUPREME COURT 47–49 (1993).

As is evident below, Marshall's recognition of "completely internal" commerce of a State was later exploited to support a rigid dichotomy between interstate and intrastate commerce under which only commerce that moved across state boundaries was subject to federal regulation. The State never relinquished exclusive power until its boundaries were passed.

To Marshall, however, the Commerce Clause arguably extended to all commerce that affected more States than one. "At the beginning Chief Justice Marshall described the Federal commerce power with a breadth never yet exceeded," wrote Justice Robert Jackson for the Court 118 years later.[18] Although much of Marshall's discussion was dicta unrestrained by reference to particular facts, Marshall seemingly recognized little constitutional restraint on Congress' powers under the Commerce Clause. He seemed to envision a relatively modest judicial role in policing limits on Congress' power. He emphasized instead political factors as "the sole restraints" on Congress to protect the people from abuse.[19]

> The wisdom and the discretion of Congress, their identity with the people, and the influence which their constituents possess at elections, are, in this, as in many other instances, . . . the sole restraints on which they have relied, to secure them from its abuse. They are the restraints on which the people must often rely solely, in all representative governments.

§ 4.02 PRODUCTIVE INDUSTRIES

[1] The E. C. Knight Formal Approach

Congress was relatively inactive during the nineteenth century. Accordingly, cases defining the Commerce Clause generally involved review of state, rather than federal, legislation, and the question of whether state legislation affecting interstate commerce intruded on a federal enclave. The post-Marshall approach became clear in *Kidd v. Pearson*.[20] It involved a state statute that prohibited the manufacture of liquor made for sale outside the State. The law was upheld on the ground that it involved the regulation of manufacturing, not of commerce. The Court reasoned that the power to regulate commerce did not confer federal authority over manufacturing of products intended for commercial transactions. Control over production was reserved to the States.

Although *Kidd* involved power of a State, its doctrine influenced the decision in *United States v. E. C. Knight Co.*,[21] the first important prosecution under the Sherman Anti-Trust Act. Defendant had obtained a virtual monopoly over the manufacture of refined sugar. The government alleged that the defendant had violated the Sherman Act by acquiring its principal competitors. The Supreme Court, however, held that Congress could not reach such acquisition of manufacturing power under the Commerce Clause.

---

[18] Wickard v. Filburn, 317 U.S. 111, 120 (1942) (citing *Gibbons*).

[19] *Gibbons*, 22 U.S. at 197.

[20] 128 U.S. 1 (1888).

[21] 156 U.S. 1 (1895).

E. C. Knight invoked three formal distinctions to confine the Commerce power more narrowly than the language in *Gibbons* would suggest. First, it distinguished between production (which Congress could not regulate) and commerce (which it could). "Commerce," stated the *E. C. Knight* Court, "succeeds to manufacture, and is not a part of it."[22] The same could be, and was, said of other productive industries.[23] These activities, though central to the nation's economy, were deemed beyond congressional power.

Second, *E. C. Knight* hinted at a distinction between direct and indirect effects. The Court did not deny that "the power to control the manufacture of a given thing" *affected* commerce, the criteria suggested in John Marshall's *Gibbons* dicta. But it discounted that effect as "secondary" rather than "primary," and as incidental and indirect. Congress could regulate activity that affected commerce directly, but not that which impacted it only indirectly. Federal power turned not on the magnitude of the impact on commerce but on the logical relationship between the regulation and commerce.

Finally, the Court recognized a third, and perhaps central, distinction — that between national and local activity. Congress could regulate national, but not local activity. The Court gave away its concern near the opinion's end. "Slight reflection will show that, if the national power extends to all contracts and combinations in . . . productive industries, whose ultimate result may affect external commerce, comparatively little of business operations and affairs would be left for state control."[24] This passage endorsed the doctrine of dual federalism, the idea that the Federal and State Governments operated in mutually exclusive spheres. The Court thought bright lines needed to be drawn to prevent federal power from obliterating all state regulatory authority.

E. C. Knight is often viewed as a triumph of "laissez-faire conservatism."[25] This characterization may be overstated. The formalistic distinctions the Court drew do not mean it sought to protect vast economic power from regulation. Indeed, the States possessed an array of legal devices to police economic behavior.[26]

E. C. Knight, like *Kidd*, adopted a much different approach than that hinted at in *Gibbons*. Its formal approach linked categories of activity, manufacturing or commerce, with authorized regulators, State or Federal Government respectively. It emphasized the logical connection between a regulation and activity (i.e., direct or indirect effect) rather than the magnitude of the impact on commerce. The *E. C. Knight* formal approach relied on these bright line rules to define activities Congress could and could not regulate under the Commerce Clause. The result was

---

[22] *Id.* at 12.

[23] *See* Coe v. Errol, 116 U.S. 517 (1886) (lumbering). *See* United States v. Butler, 297 U.S. 1 (1936) (agriculture); Oliver Iron Co. v. Lord, 262 U.S. 172 (1923) (mining); Champlin Refining Co. v. Corporation Comm'n, 286 U.S. 210 (1932) (oil production); Utah Power & Light Co. v. Pfost, 286 U.S. 165 (1932) (generation of electric power).

[24] *E. C. Knight Co.*, 156 U.S. at 16.

[25] *See* ARNOLD M. PAUL, CONSERVATIVE CRISIS AND THE RULE OF LAW: ATTITUDES OF BAR AND BENCH, 1887–1895, at 181 (1976).

[26] *See* Charles W. McCurdy, *The Knight Sugar Decision of 1895 and the Modernization of American Corporation Law*, 1869–1903, 53 BUS. HIST. REV. 304, 305–06 (1979).

the mechanical separation of "manufacturing" from "commerce," without regard to their economic continuity or interdependence. Manufacture was "purely local" activity beyond the reach of the Commerce Clause.

[2] Other Doctrinal Streams

Two other strands of Commerce Clause jurisprudence developed contemporaneously with *E. C. Knight*. In the *Shreveport Rate Case*,[27] the Court upheld congressional authority to regulate intrastate rail rates that discriminated against interstate rail carriers. The Court reasoned that Congress could regulate intrastate rail activity that had a close and substantial relationship to interstate rail traffic.[28] Although some have portrayed the *Shreveport* doctrine as an alternative doctrinal approach to *E. C. Knight*, these claims seem overstated. The doctrine "was always limited to the paradigmatic business affected with a public interest: rail carriage."[29] The *Shreveport* doctrine accordingly posed little threat to the prevailing jurisprudence.

In *Swift & Co. v. United States*,[30] the Court adopted a different approach. The government had brought a Sherman Act suit against price fixing by meat dealers. Defendants described their activity as local and beyond Congress' power. In upholding the action, Justice Holmes articulated the stream of commerce doctrine.

> When cattle are sent for sale from a place in one State, with the expectation that they will end their transit, after purchase, in another, and when in effect they do so, with only the interruption necessary to find a purchaser at the stock yards, and when this is a typical, constantly recurring course, the current thus existing is a current of commerce among the States, and the purchase of the cattle is a part and incident of such commerce.[31]

The stream or current of commerce doctrine, too, was limited to businesses affected with a public interest. During its first quarter century, the doctrine was only applied to stockyards and grain exchanges, both local businesses affected with a public interest.[32] But the stream of commerce doctrine was potentially subversive of the dual federalism that governed commerce clause jurisprudence. The prospect that the federal government could regulate all within the commerce flow threatened to wash away conceptual dams like direct-indirect and production-commerce. Ultimately, its imagery figured prominently in the demise of the dual federalism *E. C. Knight* represented.[33]

---

[27] Houston, E. & W. Tex. Ry. Co. v. United States, 234 U.S. 342 (1914).

[28] *Id.* at 355.

[29] Barry Cushman, Rethinking the New Deal Court: The Structure of a Constitutional Revolution 193 (1998).

[30] 196 U.S. 375 (1905).

[31] *Id.* at 398–99.

[32] *See* Barry Cushman, *Continuity and Change in Commerce Clause Jurisprudence*, 55 Ark. L. Rev. 1009, 1023 (2003).

[33] *See* Cushman, *supra* note 29, at 174–75.

[3] Early New Deal Cases

The consequence of the restricted conception of commerce became apparent when the Court reviewed legislation enacted to remedy the economic crisis of the early 1930s. In *Schechter Poultry Corp. v. United States*,[34] the Court considered the constitutionality of minimum wage and maximum hour provisions promulgated pursuant to the National Internal Recovery Act (NIRA) which a Brooklyn slaughterhouse operation had allegedly violated. Schechter purchased poultry that had moved interstate, slaughtered it, and sold it locally. The Court unanimously held that Congress had exceeded its power. Schechter was engaged in distribution, not commerce. Its activity had at most an indirect, not direct, effect on commerce. Nor could current of commerce doctrine save the statute because the interstate flow permanently stopped at the Brooklyn stockyard. Accordingly, the regulated activity was local, not national.[35] *Schechter* was a hard case for the government, involving as it did a small enterprise at the end of the interstate flow. But in *Carter v. Carter Coal Co.*,[36] the Supreme Court reviewed a federal law regulating prices in the coal industry and prescribing minimum wage and maximum hour conditions. In declaring this law, especially its labor provisions, invalid, the Court relied on the formalistic categories from *E. C. Knight* consistent with a narrow view of commerce.[37]

Mining, like manufacturing, was not commerce. The labor provisions of the law affected production, not commerce. It was irrelevant that labor practices in the coal industry affected interstate commerce, for the effect was not sufficiently "direct." "The distinction between a direct and an indirect effect turn[ed], not upon the magnitude of either the cause of the effect, but entirely upon the manner in which the effect has been brought about."[38] The test turned on logical relation, not on an empirical measure.

The regulations' direct effects were on production; certainly the regulations affected production which affected commerce but the law's effect on commerce was indirect. Stream of commerce theory could not rescue the measure regulating employment practices at the mines because the flow had not yet started at the point of regulation. Employer-employee relations in production "is a purely local activity"[39] for the States, not Nation, to regulate.

The Court's interpretation of commerce rendered Congress powerless to address the nation's depressed economy. Elimination of manufacturing, mining, agriculture, and other productive industries from the Commerce Clause substantially narrowed the economic sectors Congress could remedy. The grim economic background made lack of federal power conspicuous. With the economy

---

[34] 295 U.S. 495 (1935). For an account, *see* PETER H. IRONS, THE NEW DEAL LAWYERS 86–107 (1982).

[35] Similarly, in holding the Agricultural Adjustment Act unconstitutional, the Court noted that agriculture, like manufacturing or mining, is not commerce. *U.S. v. Butler*, 297 U.S. 1, 63–64 (1936).

[36] 298 U.S. 238 (1936).

[37] The Court invalidated the price fixing provisions on the grounds that they were not severable from the labor conditions. *Id.* at 315–16.

[38] *Id.* at 308.

[39] *Id.* at 304.

failing after the 1929 collapse, the call for national action was clear.

Carter Coal made this irrelevant. There was no federal power to regulate production, regardless of the size of the industry or the magnitude of the problems involved. Degree had no bearing on the existence of federal power; so far as the effect on commerce was concerned, there was no difference between the mining of one ton or ten million tons of coal. Production was purely local. Congress could not address the production crisis crippling the country.

In dissent, Justice Cardozo recognized this dilemma regarding the Act's regulation of prices. Although mining and agriculture "are not interstate commerce considered by themselves," he recognized that their relationship to commerce "may be such that for the protection of the one there is need to regulate the other."[40] The direct/indirect distinction was inadequate ("But a great principle of constitutional law is not susceptible of comprehensive statement in an adjective.")[41] Degree mattered. Instead of the logical, but unworkable, direct/indirect dichotomy, Cardozo suggested asking whether the relevant connection was "so close and intimate and obvious," as to support federal power. Cardozo sought to transform the old logical categories into an empirical approach.[42] Cardozo also hinted at moving away from the rulebound approach to an ad hoc, case by case adjudication. "Always the setting of the facts is to be viewed if one would know the closeness of the tie."[43]

[4] Jones & Laughlin

Within a year, the Court's ostensible attitude changed. In *NLRB v. Jones & Laughlin Steel Corp.*,[44] the Court considered the constitutionality of the National Labor Relations Act of 1935 (NLRA). That comprehensive regulation of labor relations guaranteed the right of employees to organize collectively and prohibited employers from interfering with that right or from refusing to bargain with employees' unions.

The NLRA applied to economic activities throughout the nation, including production and manufacture. Accordingly, the statute conflicted with the Court's prevailing jurisprudence. Under the Court's interpretation of the Commerce Clause, manufacturing, here of iron and steel, was not commerce subject to Congress' control. The company was an industrial giant whose activities clearly affected interstate commerce, but under the prevailing approach magnitude of effect did not create national authority over local production.

---

[40] *Id.* at 327 (Cardozo, J., dissenting). Justices Brandeis and Stone joined the dissent; Chief Justice Hughes concurred in the majority opinion but also thought the price regulation provisions were within Congress' power. Justice Cardozo did not reach the wage and hour regulations because he viewed the challenge as premature.

[41] *Id.*

[42] *Carter Coal*, 298 U.S. at 328.

[43] *Id.*

[44] 301 U.S. 1 (1937).

Yet after extensive argument[45] the Court departed from the restrictive approach to the meaning of commerce. Chief Justice Hughes regarded the fact that the employees were engaged in production as not determinative because the production plainly affected interstate commerce. Given the company's activities, it departed from reality to dismiss the substantial effect as only indirect. Instead, the Court moved away from the direct/ indirect nomenclature, suggesting that the pertinent question was whether the effect was sufficiently "close and intimate" or "close and substantial." Wrote Chief Justice Hughes for the five-justice majority:

> Although activities may be intrastate in character when separately considered, if they have such a close and substantial relation to interstate commerce that their control is essential or appropriate to protect that commerce from burdens and obstructions, Congress cannot be denied the power to exercise that control.[46]

In essence, Cardozo's *Carter Coal* approach of the prior year now commanded a majority. Indeed, *Jones & Laughlin* went beyond Cardozo's dissent, which had applied the "close and intimate" approach to price regulations, not to employee relations. Although the Court did not specifically rest its decision on the current of commerce, the metaphor clearly influenced its thinking; many saw it as dispositive.[47] As Professor Cushman points out, the availability of the current of commerce argument made it easier for the Court to "concede the persuasiveness of Cardozo's position."[48] Perhaps reference to it was necessary to secure Justice Robert's vote. It is interesting to note that although the majority opinion disclaimed direct reliance on the stream of commerce doctrine, Justice McReynolds' dissent assumed that concept was the basis of the decision.[49] Perhaps discussion he had heard at the Court's conference to decide the case gave him that impression.

Jones & Laughlin challenged the approach to Commerce Clause cases that animated decisions like *Carter Coal* which had declared that production was not commerce. *Jones & Laughlin* held production could be subject to congressional regulation. *Carter Coal* had found immaterial the evils that had induced Congress to act and their effect on interstate commerce, discounting extensive effects as indirect. *Jones & Laughlin* was fully cognizant of the toll that industrial strife would impose on interstate commerce, and refused to dismiss this effect as only indirect. Moreover, *Jones & Laughlin* suggested a new judicial approach to Commerce Clause cases. The Court, in *E. C. Knight*, *Schechter*, and *Carter Coal* had resorted to formal rules — production vs. commerce, direct vs. indirect, local vs. national — to assess Congress' legislative output. In *Jones & Laughlin*, the Court suggested it would henceforth proceed on a case by case basis. The judicial role, as before, would be substantial. But it would turn on ad hoc balancing rather than on wielding specific bright-line rules.

---

[45] For a discussion of the litigation strategy, *see* IRONS, *supra* note 34, at 254–71, 280–89; CUSHMAN, *supra* note 29, at 164–68.

[46] *Jones & Laughlin*, 301 U.S. at 37.

[47] *See* CUSHMAN, *supra* note 29, at 177–86.

[48] *Id.* at 171.

[49] *Jones & Laughlin*, 301 U.S. at 97–98, 100.

Jones & Laughlin thus signaled a departure from the restricted view that deemed productive industries beyond the commerce power. *Jones & Laughlin* held that manufacturing was not automatically beyond congressional authority.[50]

Jones & Laughlin involved an industrial giant whose activities had substantial impact on interstate commerce. But the Court also employed the *Jones & Laughlin* reasoning in cases involving much smaller companies with no serious economic effect. On the day it decided *Jones & Laughlin*, the Court applied its holding to a small manufacturing concern that produced less than one half of one percent of the clothing made in the country and employed only 800 workers.[51] The interruption of such a business would hardly imperil much commerce. Despite this reality, the Court ruled that *Jones & Laughlin* justified federal regulation. An employer's resistance to allowing workers to join unions and engage in collective bargaining tended "to lead to strikes and other labor disputes that burden and obstruct commerce."[52] Presumably, *Harry-Marks* made clear that interruption of the business involved did not have to cripple the economy for it to be reached under the Commerce Clause.

In *NLRB v. Fainblatt*,[53] the Court held that application of the Commerce Clause did not depend on the volume of commerce affected.[54] Congress' power under the Commerce Clause was "plenary and extends to all such commerce be it great or small."[55] Fainblatt, though only a small clothing manufacturer, was within Congress' reach because the commerce power required only that the activity regulated affect interstate commerce, not that it affect a relatively large proportion of such commerce. Moreover, because Fainblatt was a link in an interstate chain, the current of commerce imagery also lent support.[56]

The conventional view attributes the decision in *Jones & Laughlin* as influenced by President Franklin D. Roosevelt's court packing plan. Frustrated by the Court's action in holding New Deal legislation unconstitutional, Roosevelt proposed increasing the Court's membership by one justice for each incumbent over the age of 70, a formula which would have allowed FDR to add six justices to the Court. Roosevelt claimed the measure was needed to allow the Court to operate efficiently. Ultimately, the plan failed but in the interim the Court upheld some New Deal measures with Justice Roberts allegedly switching his frequent opposition to FDR measures to uphold them. This "switch in time" allegedly saved the nine justices.

---

[50] *Jones & Laughlin* did not overrule *Carter*.

[51] NLRB v. Friedman-Harry Marks Clothing Co., 301 U.S. 58 (1937). Professor Cushman points out that in *Jones & Laughlin* and *Friedman-Harry Marks* and their companion, *NLRB v. Fruehauf Trailer Co.*, 301 U.S. 49 (1937), the Court "located the enterprise in a current of interstate commerce and then proceeded to characterize the enterprise or the industry of which it was a part in the broad language of a business affected with a public interest." CUSHMAN, *supra* note 29, at 173.

[52] *Harry-Marks*, 301 U.S. at 75.

[53] 306 U.S. 601 (1939).

[54] *Id.* at 606.

[55] *Id.*

[56] *Id.* at 605.

More recent scholarship debunks this conventional account. Some of Justice Roberts "switches" occurred in votes the Court took before FDR's plan was announced. The plan never had majority support much less the two-thirds support then necessary to stop a Senate filibuster. Since the plan angered two conservative justices into deferring retirement it might have caused others to fight rather than switch.[57]

[5]　Darby and Wickard

Jones & Laughlin worked a significant change from *E. C. Knight* and *Carter Coal*. Yet the Court there approached the Commerce Clause quite differently than it would only a few years later. Although *Jones & Laughlin* made some inroads into the production/commerce distinction, it did not concede to Congress *carte blanche* to regulate production as the Court did a few years later. Nor did it abandon all deference to dual federalism.[58] The Court took those further steps in 1941 and 1942. First, in *United States v. Darby*,[59] the Court held that Congress could regulate productive activity that had a substantial effect on commerce. Unlike *Jones & Laughlin*, *Darby* was not influenced by the need to remove obstructions from the flow of commerce. Rather, Congress was empowered to regulate intrastate activity to prevent demoralization of the interstate market. Significantly, *Jones & Laughlin* received but passing mention.

Two 1942 decisions reflected further concessions of power to Congress to regulate local activities under an effect-on-commerce test. *United States v. Wrightwood Dairy Co.*[60] upheld application of federal regulation of the price of milk produced and sold intrastate. The intrastate milk competed with milk transported interstate. Failure to regulate the intrastate milk would affect the price of, and commerce in, interstate milk. Accordingly, the Commerce Clause included authority regarding local milk.

Wickard v. Filburn[61] endorsed far greater regulation of local activities. The Agricultural Adjustment Act of 1938 extended federal regulation of agricultural production to produce intended wholly for consumption on a farmer's farm. Appellee Filburn was, under the Act, penalized for producing more wheat than his allotted quota. He claimed Congress could not regulate his crop which never left his farm. The Court disagreed.

Wickard consolidated or contributed several important strands to Commerce Clause doctrine. First, it specifically rejected the old formal distinctions of *E. C. Knight* and *Carter Coal* — production vs. commerce, indirect vs. direct, local-national. Even if Filburn's activity was "local" and "though it may not be regarded as commerce,"[62] Congress was empowered to regulate such activity which exerts "a

---

[57] *See* CUSHMAN, *supra* note 29, at 11–32.

[58] *See* 301 U.S. at 30.

[59] 312 U.S. 100 (1941).

[60] 315 U.S. 110 (1942).

[61] 317 U.S. 111 (1942).

[62] *Id.* at 125.

substantial economic effect on interstate commerce."[63]

Second, *Wickard* made clear that the regulated intrastate activity need not itself impact commerce. Rather, Congress could reach local activities with trivial effects on commerce if the cumulative effect of such activities when aggregated was weighty enough. As Chief Justice Rehnquist explained four decades later:

> [I]n *Wickard v. Filburn* . . . the Court expanded the scope of the Commerce Clause to include the regulation of acts which taken alone might not have a substantial economic effect on interstate commerce, such as a wheat farmer's own production, but which might reasonably be deemed nationally significant in their cumulative effect, such as altering the supply-and-demand relationships in the interstate commodity market.[64]

Since home-grown, home-consumed product may affect the price and market conditions for wheat, Congress could regulate it. This wheat met the producer's need that would otherwise be purchased at the market. "Home-grown wheat in this sense competes with wheat in commerce."[65] Alternatively, if the price of wheat rose, possessors of home-grown wheat might decide to market it, which would reduce the market price.

Wickard left little, if any, activity totally immune from federal authority. If a trivial effect on interstate commerce capable of aggregation justifies federal regulation, the commerce power may reach practically every aspect of the economic system. A child's neighborhood lemonade stand could come within Congress' reach because the transactions, when aggregated with similar enterprises elsewhere, could impact commerce.

Finally, *Wickard* signaled a radical change in the Court's definition of its role in Commerce Clause cases. In *E. C. Knight* and *Carter Coal*, the Court had actively measured Commerce Clause legislation against formal tests. In *Jones & Laughlin*, it had announced its intent to engage in ad hoc balancing. Although the approaches differed, they both committed the Court to an active role in review of Commerce Clause legislation. In *Wickard*, however, the Court abdicated the field to Congress. It essentially retreated, treating the Commerce Clause as akin to a political question. Accordingly, *Wickard* marked a departure from *Jones & Laughlin*, not a continuation of its approach. It is telling that *Wickard* did not cite *Jones & Laughlin*.

---

[63] *Id.*

[64] Hodel v. Virginia Surface Mining Ass'n, 452 U.S. 264, 308 (1981) (Rehnquist, J., concurring).

[65] *Wickard*, 317 U.S. at 128.

§ 4.03 REGULATION VERSUS PROHIBITION

[1] Lottery Case

In *Gibbons*, Marshall had written that the power to regulate was the power to set the rules to govern commerce. That definition would seem to offer Congress a range of options. In the *Lottery Case*,[66] the Supreme Court confronted the question whether the power to regulate includes the power to prohibit. An Act of Congress prohibited the interstate transportation of lottery tickets. In upholding the law, the Court rejected a distinction between regulation and prohibition. Prohibition was included within the concept of regulation, at least when congressional power was used to protect commerce from harmful articles.

In his dissent in *E. C. Knight*, Justice Harlan had argued for a certain symmetry between the powers of the Federal and State governments in addressing evils. If a State could suppress a monopoly which harmed local trade, Congress should be able to attack a similar evil on a national level. In the *Lottery Case*, Justice Harlan applied that symmetry, this time for the Court. If a State, when considering legislation for the suppression of lotteries within its own limits, may properly consider the evils that inhere in the raising of money in that mode, why may not Congress, invested with the power to regulate commerce among the several States, provide that such commerce shall not be polluted by the carrying of lottery tickets from one State to another?

The Court followed the *Lottery Case* holding in later cases regarding federal laws closing the channels of commerce to commodities that themselves were dangerous or harmful or had an adverse effect. In some cases, the anticipated evil came from a defect in the commodity, such as diseased livestock,[67] adulterated and misbranded articles,[68] intoxicating liquors,[69] and diseased plants.[70] Alternatively, the purpose of the transportation was sometimes the vice to be avoided, e.g., lottery tickets,[71] women transported for immoral purposes,[72] stolen motor vehicles,[73] and kidnapped persons.[74]

In these cases, the commerce power was employed to prevent harm to the public even though the harm did not affect commerce. The commerce power was used to bar the shipment in commerce of articles to prevent a social, economic, or moral result Congress disapproved. The commerce power became, in effect, a national police power[75] through which Congress could reach any commerce it reasonably

---

[66] Champion v. Ames, 188 U.S. 321 (1903).

[67] *See also* Reid v. Colorado, 187 U.S. 137 (1902).

[68] *See* Hipolite Egg Co. v. United States, 220 U.S. 45 (1911).

[69] *See* Clark Distilling Co. v. Western Md. Ry. Co., 242 U.S. 311 (1917).

[70] *See* Oregon-Wash. R.R. & Nav. Co. v. Washington, 270 U.S. 87 (1926).

[71] *See* Champion v. Ames, 188 U.S. 321 (1903).

[72] *See* Hoke v. United States, 227 U.S. 308 (1913).

[73] *See* Brooks v. United States, 267 U.S. 432 (1925).

[74] *See* Gooch v. United States, 297 U.S. 124 (1936).

[75] *Brooks*, 267 U.S. at 436–37.

deemed injurious to public health, safety, morals, or welfare.

These cases established that Congress's power "to regulate" commerce included the power to prohibit certain movement in interstate commerce. Just as the power to regulate includes the power to prohibit, it also encompasses the power to promote. In *Wickard*, the Court made clear that the Commerce Clause licensed Congress to legislate to affect prices and markets. "The stimulation of commerce is a use of the regulatory function quite as definitely as prohibitions or restrictions thereon,"[76] wrote Justice Jackson for the Court. Together, these cases underscored and developed the capacious definition Marshall provided in *Gibbons*.

[2]   Child Labor Case

The law at issue in the *Lottery Case*, of course, involved transporting lottery tickets from one state to another. This interstate feature distinguished the *Lottery Case* from *E. C. Knight*. Yet the Court during the early 20th century was unwilling to give Congress *carte blanche* to regulate interstate moves.

In the *Child Labor Case*,[77] the Supreme Court limited Congress' prohibitory authority. Congress had prohibited interstate transportation of goods made in factories that employed children. On its face, this law, like that in *Champion*, merely banned interstate transportation. Yet the Court understood that Congress' aim was to suppress child labor in mining and production, intrastate activities (like gambling in lotteries). In 1918, the Court held, 5-4, that the congressional purpose to regulate production, a purely local event, rendered the law invalid. Congress could not use its interstate commerce power to regulate matters like manufacturing that were not then considered commerce.

The Court distinguished the decisions cited above upholding congressional power to close the channels of commerce to specified commodities. The articles involved in the prior cases were said to be harmful in and of themselves; transportation of them produced the evil that Congress could combat. In other words, Congress could prohibit their shipment to prevent an evil from occurring in the receiving State. By contrast, the goods at issue in the *Child Labor Case* were innocuous. Interstate transportation of the child-produced goods accomplished no evil since the harm involved in child labor in production had all occurred before the goods were sent into commerce.

This distinction is specious.[78] Some of the earlier decisions invoked transportation of people or things harmless in themselves. The Court had justified congressional prohibitions based on the evils involved in the purpose of the transportation. If Congress can prevent harm from innocent goods which occur after the interstate move, why can it not address evils which depend on subsequent access to interstate commerce?

Moreover, the Court was too quick to assume that the evil in *Hammer* did not occur in the receiving State. Employing child labor confers a competitive economic

---

[76] *Wickard*, 317 U.S. at 128.

[77] Hammer v. Dagenhart, 247 U.S. 251 (1918).

[78] *See* United States v. Darby, 312 U.S. 100, 116 (1941).

advantage over industries in States that limit their work force to adults. The resulting market demoralization could induce other States to imitate their practices by joining in a race to the bottom. The evil would not therefore be limited to State A but would spread to State B, too. Of course, the Court, in its pre-1937 analysis, could regard this effect as indirect and accordingly, irrelevant. But it seemed disingenuous to contend that the evil was confined to the State where production occurred.

The *Child Labor Case* ultimately rested on the motives behind the prohibitory law. Congress had used the commerce power to prohibit an activity it could not regulate directly under the *E. C. Knight* concept of commerce. Congress' ostensible regulation of interstate commerce was condemned because its underlying motive, to address production, was beyond Congress' direct powers. To permit Congress to address production "would sanction an invasion by the federal power of the control of a matter purely local in its character."[79]

The Court rendered its decision over a powerful dissent by Justice Holmes. Under his formalistic approach, Congress had power to regulate (and prohibit) goods crossing the state line which was all it had done. Legislative motive was not a subject of proper judicial inquiry.

[3] Darby and Bootstrapping

The Court essentially adopted Justice Holmes' dissent, and repudiated the *Child Labor Case* approach, in 1941 in *United States v. Darby*.[80] The Fair Labor Standards Act provided for setting federal standards for minimum wages and maximum hours and prohibited the interstate shipment of goods manufactured by employees whose wages or hours did not meet those standards. The Act was attacked in *Darby* on the predictable ground its motive was to regulate production, not commerce. The Court conceded this point. But a new generation of jurists were now on the Court and they no longer accepted the tests of years past. They regarded as irrelevant the end toward which a congressional exercise of power over commerce was aimed. "The motive and purpose of a regulation of interstate commerce are matters for the legislative judgment upon the exercise of which the Constitution places no restriction and over which the courts are given no control." *Darby* expressly rejected and overruled the *Child Labor Case* approach[81] that the motive of the prohibition or its effect to control production within the States could render a regulation invalid.

Darby embraced Chief Justice Marshall's capacious view of the power to regulate under the Commerce Clause. The Court adopted Marshall's definition of the power to regulate commerce as the power "to prescribe the rule by which commerce is to be governed."[82] The sole question was whether the law prescribed

---

[79] *Hammer*, 247 U.S. at 276.

[80] 312 U.S. 100 (1941).

[81] *Id.* at 115, 116–17.

[82] *Id.* at 113.

a rule to govern commerce. If so, the law was valid, regardless of its animating purpose.

Darby signalled the development of the Commerce Clause as a national police power, a process that the *Lottery Case* began. Under *Darby*, Congress could deploy the commerce power to vindicate a broad conception of public interest by outlawing any commerce inconsistent with that vision. Congress could regulate commerce to pursue a range of social, economic, or moral ends.

Darby gave Congress a vehicle to extend its commerce authority in other ways, too. The first part of *Darby* upheld the Fair Labor Standards Act's prohibition on interstate shipment of goods produced by employees who were paid too little or worked too long. The provision was a valid regulation of commerce since it prohibited movement of goods from one State to another. In the second part of its opinion, the Court upheld the statute's additional requirement that employees engaged in production conform to the federal wages and hours standards. The Court did so on two grounds — by reliance on the "affecting commerce" rationale discussed above and as a means to achieve the end of regulating commerce.

The second, or bootstrap approach, used the statute's prohibition on interstate shipment as an end to justify other means of regulation.

> Congress, having by the present Act adopted the policy of excluding from interstate commerce all goods produced for the commerce which do not conform to the specified labor standards, it may choose the means reasonably adapted to the attainment of the permitted end, even though they involve control of intrastate activities.[83]

The direct wage and hour regulation of production may be sustained as a "Necessary and Proper Clause" means, i.e., one "reasonably adapted to the attainment of the permitted end . . . of excluding from interstate commerce all goods produced . . . which do not conform to the specified labor standards."[84]

This bootstrap technique has broad potential. It would seem to permit Congress to "regulate any intrastate activity through a two-step bootstrap device . . . (1) prohibit interstate movement of goods or persons connected with the activity . . . and (2) directly regulate the intrastate activity itself, as a 'means reasonably adapted to the attainment of the permitted end' of interstate prohibition."[85]

[4]   Perez v. United States

The Court used the *Darby* bootstrap 30 years later in *Perez v. United States*.[86] A federal statute making "loan sharking" a crime was applied to a New York City "loan shark" who had threatened violence to collect money lent a local butcher. The Court held that Congress could make criminal petitioner's local activity because

---

[83] *Id.* at 121.

[84] *Id.*

[85] Gerald Gunther, Cases and Materials on Constitutional Law 136 (12th ed. 1991).

[86] 402 U.S. 146 (1971).

there was "a tie-in between local loan sharks and interstate crime."[87] Congressional hearings and reports demonstrated that loan sharking furnished organized crime with much of its revenue: "loan sharking in its national setting is one way organized interstate crime . . . syphons funds from numerous localities to finance its national operations."[88] In dissent, Justice Stewart argued that no rational basis showed "that loan sharking is an activity with interstate attributes that distinguish it in some substantial respect from other local crime."[89] On the other hand, one scholar suggested that *Perez* might be justified based on "the difficulty of proving in each individual case that the loan shark had an interstate connection even when it existed."[90] Thus Congress may reach even local loan sharking as a "means reasonably adapted to the attainment of the permitted end" of outlawing loan sharking with interstate connections.

§ 4.04   1964 CIVIL RIGHTS ACT

The Civil Rights Act of 1964 confirmed the broad scope of the modern commerce power. A key provision (Title II) entitled all persons to equal access to any public accommodation without racial or religious discrimination. The Act covered inns, hotels, motels, restaurants, and cafeterias if their "operations affect commerce," by, for instance, providing lodging to transient guests serving interstate travelers, or if a substantial proportion of the food they sell has "moved in commerce."

The fundamental object of the 1964 Civil Rights Act was to address "the deprivation of personal dignity that surely accompanies denials of equal access to public establishments." Nonetheless, Congress passed the law based on its commerce power since that objective could be readily achieved "by congressional action based on the commerce power."[91]

Congress' reliance on the commerce power made it unnecessary for the Court to look elsewhere to uphold the statute in *Heart of Atlanta Motel v. United States*.[92] Thus the Court did not need to ask whether the Jim Crow practices could be tied to state action or whether Congress could go beyond "state action" in enforcing the Fourteenth Amendment.

Heart of Atlanta and a companion case[93] considered the application of the Civil Rights Act to a motel that served transient guests, most of whom came from out of State, and a restaurant that imported from other States much of the food served. Justice Black made explicit the scope of the commerce power when he observed that "[i]t requires no novel or strained interpretation of the Commerce Clause to sustain

---

[87] *Id.* at 155.

[88] *Id.* at 157.

[89] *Id.*

[90] *See* Robert L. Stern, *The Commerce Clause Revisited — The Federalization of Intrastate Crime*, 15 ARIZ. L. REV. 271, 278 (1973).

[91] Heart of Atlanta Motel v. United States, 379 U.S. 241, 250 (1964) (quoting S. Rep. No. 872, at 16–17).

[92] 379 U.S. 241 (1964).

[93] Katzenbach v. McClung, 379 U.S. 294 (1964).

Title II as applied in either of these cases."[94]

The 1964 statute marked the further development of the commerce power. Almost any economic activity, including the motels and restaurants the 1964 Civil Rights Act covered, may affect commerce. That the actual impact of the particular motel involved in *Heart of Atlanta* was quantitatively slight was immaterial: "[i]f it is interstate commerce that feels the pinch, it does not matter how local the operation which applies the squeeze."[95]

§ 4.05 OUTER LIMITS

For nearly 60 years following *Jones & Laughlin*, the Commerce Clause expanded to stretch congressional power to new applications. During this period, Congress regulated under the Commerce Clause with increasing frequency; yet not once did the Court conclude Congress had exceeded its commerce authority. The Supreme Court had adopted Marshall's sweeping language and then some. At the beginning, said the Court in *Wickard*, "Marshall described the Federal commerce power with a breadth never yet exceeded."[96] Yet, in *Wickard*, the Court construed the power more broadly than Marshall had done and adopted a very deferential standard of review. A Court could invalidate Commerce Clause legislation, "only if it is clear that there is no rational basis for a congressional finding that the regulated activity affects interstate commerce, or that there is no reasonable connection between the regulatory means selected and the asserted ends."[97] The Commerce Clause was tantamount to a political question.

The expanded reach of the Commerce Clause was not greeted with universal enthusiasm. Justice Rehnquist asserted that it is not "sufficient that the person or activity reached have *some* nexus with interstate commerce. . . . [T]he regulated activity must have a *substantial* effect on interstate commerce."[98] Yet, in the very case in which he spoke, the opinion of the Court declared, "The court must defer to a congressional finding that a regulated activity affects interstate commerce, if there is any rational basis for such a finding."[99]

§ 4.06 LOPEZ: ANOTHER TURNING POINT?

The expansion of the Commerce Clause was interrupted in *United States v. Lopez*,[100] where the Court declared specifically, "congressional power under the Commerce Clause . . . is subject to outer limits."[101] In *Lopez*, for the first time in

---

[94] *Heart of Atlanta*, 379 U.S. at 270–71.

[95] *Id.* at 258.

[96] Wickard v. Filburn, 317 U.S. 111, 120 (1942).

[97] Hodel v. Indiana, 452 U.S. 314, 323–24 (1981).

[98] Hodel v. Virginia Surface Mining Ass'n, 452 U.S. 264, 310–11 (1981) (Rehnquist, J., concurring) (emphasis in original).

[99] *Id.* at 276.

[100] 514 U.S. 549 (1995).

[101] *Id.* at 556–57.

nearly 60 years, the Court ruled that a federal statute trespassed those limits. At issue was a law that made it a federal offense to possess a gun in or near a school. A student carrying a concealed handgun at school was found guilty of violating this statute. The conviction was reversed, in a 5-4 decision, on the ground that the law exceeded the commerce power.

Chief Justice Rehnquist's majority opinion identified three broad categories of activity that Congress may regulate under the commerce power: (1) the use of the channels of interstate commerce; (2) the instrumentalities of interstate commerce or persons or things in interstate commerce; (3) certain intrastate activities having a substantial relation to interstate commerce. The statute in *Lopez* could only be upheld under the third category as a regulation of an activity that substantially affects interstate commerce.

But the Court suggested a statute only comes within this third category if it regulates an economic or *commercial* activity.[102] The law at issue in *Lopez* was "a criminal statute that by its terms has nothing to do with 'commerce' or any sort of economic enterprise, however broadly one might define those terms."[103] *Lopez* thus limits congressional power under the third category to "regulations of activities that arise out of or are connected with a *commercial* transaction, which viewed in the aggregate, *substantially* affects interstate commerce."[104]

Lopez appeared to work three changes in prior practice. First, it seemed to limit intrastate activities that Congress could reach to economic or commercial activities. The opinion suggested that only for such economic activity could the trivial effects of isolated instances be aggregated to produce the requisite substantial effect.[105] Second, these activities must have a substantial effect on commerce, not simply an effect. The Court acknowledged that prior cases were ambiguous on this point and clarified it by adopting the "substantial effect" standard.[106] Finally, *Lopez* signaled some change in the wholly acquiescent judicial review of Commerce Clause laws the Court had practiced, suggesting the Court would give Commerce Clause cases closer scrutiny than had been the case.

Lopez did not foreclose all regulations under the Commerce Clause of intrastate non-economic activities like possession of a gun. The opinion suggested that the statute might have been upheld had it required that the gun possession was "connected in any way to interstate commerce" i.e., presumably by either the movement interstate of the weapon or possessor.[107] Similarly, had the regulation against simple possession been "an essential part of a larger regulation of economic

---

[102] *But see* Wickard v. Filburn, 317 U.S. 111 (1942) (Congress can regulate local activity which, though not "commerce," "exerts a substantial . . . effect on interstate commerce."); United States v. South-Eastern Underwriters Ass'n, 322 U.S. 533, 549 (1944) ("transactions [may] be commerce though non-commercial").

[103] *Lopez*, 514 U.S. at 561.

[104] *Id.* (emphasis added).

[105] *Id.* at 561, 567.

[106] *Id.* at 559. *See also id.* at 559, 560, 561, 565–66, 567.

[107] *Id.* at 551, 561–62.

activity" it might have passed muster.[108] This language appeared to contemplate the *Darby* bootstrap. In other words, in a statute regulating, say, sale of guns a prohibition against possession might be a sufficiently related means to achieve the end. Finally, it may be that *Lopez* still allowed Congress to regulate certain non-economic intrastate activities that alone would have such an impact on commerce that no aggregation would be required.

Although the *Lopez* approach appeared quite hostile to some recent Commerce Clause jurisprudence, no precedents of the post 1937 period were overturned and indeed some of the most permissive were explicitly endorsed. This treatment appears likely to have been a concession to secure the needed support of Justice Kennedy and Justice O'Connor. In their concurrence, they inferred from the history of Commerce Clause jurisprudence the lesson "that the Court as an institution and the legal system as a whole have an immense stake in the stability of our Commerce Clause jurisprudence as it has evolved to this point."[109] Since the Civil Rights Act of 1964 rested on the Commerce Clause, any change which could jeopardize that landmark would be ominous indeed. This commitment to *stare decisis* presumably protected some of the precedents that others in the majority may have found unappealing. Similarly, Justices Kennedy and O'Connor were unwilling to return to the formalistic distinctions that decided *E. C. Knight* and *Carter Coal*; they specifically criticized "the imprecision of content-based boundaries used without more to define the limits of the Commerce Clause."[110] *Lopez* left much ambiguity. The reliance on "economic" or commercial activity seemed in some respects to risk problems similar to those that doomed its content-based ancestor, production-commerce. On the other hand, if, home-grown, home-consumed wheat (*Wickard*) and loan-sharking (*Perez*) remained within Congress' reach, *Lopez* imposed only modest restraint. *Jones & Laughlin*, more than either *Carter Coal* or *Wickard*, seemed to have regained standing. Both the majority opinion and Kennedy concurrence invoked it favorably and it seemed to exemplify the "practical conception of the commerce power" that Justice Kennedy endorsed.[111] Justices Kennedy and O'Connor seemed prepared to engage in a greater level of scrutiny of Commerce Clause legislation than the Court had pursued since the 1930s.

Justices Kennedy and O'Connor also seemed anxious to apply the structural principle of federalism to strike a new balance. They suggested greater scrutiny for federal statutes that intrude on areas of "traditional state concern"[112] like education and street crime.

The ultimate significance of *Lopez* was subject to some doubt. Did it just reflect the Court's frustration with the federalization of street crime and the burden this imposed on federal judicial dockets? Was it simply a shot across the bow, designed to warn Congress to proceed cautiously, and with findings? The survival of *Wickard*, the exceptions the court mentioned, and the Kennedy-O'Connor concurrence left

---

[108] *Id.* at 561.

[109] *Id.* at 574 (Kennedy, J., concurring).

[110] *Lopez*, 514 U.S. at 574.

[111] *Id.* at 572–73.

[112] *Id.* at 580, 583.

questions regarding the extent to which *Lopez* worked a significant change.

§ 4.07   UNITED STATES v. MORRISON

Five years after *Lopez* the Court again held unconstitutional federal legislation based in part on the Commerce Clause in *United States v. Morrison*.[113] In *Morrison*, the Court struck down a portion of the Violence Against Women Act, 42 U.S.C. § 13981, in a 5-4 decision reflecting the exact division of justices as in *Lopez* and in other federalism decisions of recent years. Although *Morrison* essentially applied *Lopez*, it left open a number of questions regarding Commerce Clause doctrine. In *Morrison*, a female college student sued Morrison and another defendant for damages under the federal civil remedy the VAWA afforded. Defendants attacked the constitutionality of the act, a challenge which caused the United States to intervene to defend the federal statute. The Supreme Court granted certiorari to review the case after the United States Court of Appeals for the Fourth Circuit held § 13981's civil remedy unconstitutional.

In affirming that decision, Chief Justice Rehnquist began by interpreting his *Lopez* opinion, identifying "[s]everal significant considerations" which contributed to it. First, the Gun Free School Zone statute had nothing to do with commerce or economic activity. Second, it lacked an "express jurisdictional element which might limit its reach to a discrete set of firearm possessions" with an explicit connection to or effect on commerce. Third, neither the statute nor its legislative history made "express congressional findings" documenting the effects on commerce of gun possession in a school zone. Finally, "the link between gun possession and a substantial effect on interstate commerce was attenuated."[114]

Three of the four *Lopez* factors also supported the Court's conclusion that VAWA was unconstitutional. The gender motivated violence § 13981 addressed was not "economic activity" and it contained "no jurisdictional element." Although § 13981, unlike the statute at issue on *Lopez*, was supported by specific findings documenting the impact of the regulated activity on commerce, a congressional determination that a specific activity substantially affects commerce was insufficient to decide a question the Court claimed as a judicial, rather than legislative, issue. Finally, VAWA rested on an impermissible mode of reasoning that weighed attenuated effects from "the but-for causal chain from the initial occurrence of violent crime."[115]

The Court's reasoning raised several interesting issues. One might have thought that *Lopez* articulated a rule that the Commerce Clause only allowed Congress to address intrastate activities that were economic or commercial or alternatively, that trivial effects could only be aggregated if they involved economic activity. In *Morrison*, the Court went out of its way to state that it had not "adopt[ed] a categorical rule against aggregating the effects of any noneconomic activity" to

---

[113] 529 U.S. 598 (2000).

[114] *Id.* at 609–12.

[115] *Id.* at 615.

decide the case.[116] Does the absence of a categorical prohibition suggest that Congress could regulate some intrastate noneconomic activity? If so, how does one identify what noneconomic intrastate activity Congress can reach? Moreover, the Court's formulation mixed two ideas. The portion just quoted disclaimed creating a categorical rule against "aggregating the effects of any noneconomic activity"; the language that followed observed that prior decisions upheld regulation under the Commerce Clause "of intrastate activity only where that activity is economic in nature."[117] This is something of a nonsequitur.

It is conceptually possible that Congress might wish to regulate noneconomic activity which substantially affected commerce without aggregation, e.g., taking a bomb into the Stock Exchange. Was the Court backing away from a categorical rule about regulating noneconomic intrastate activities or only about aggregating such activities?

Morrison dispelled any thoughts that the Gun Free School Zones Act fell in *Lopez* due to lack of legislative findings. Congress made extensive findings regarding the VAWA but they were insufficient to save it. *Morrison* also makes clear that *Lopez* did not simply reflect the Court's effort to limit the federal judiciary's criminal docket as some speculated, since VAWA imposed a civil remedy (although directed against criminal activity).

The Court went out of its way to emphasize the much more active role it asserted in analyzing Commerce Clause challenges. Its discussion of the nondispositive nature of legislative findings regarding VAWA followed from this conclusion. Congress' findings were subject to judicial review. The Court specifically regarded whether regulated activity has a substantial effect on commerce as a judicial, not legislative, question. It abandoned the deference to Congress which *Darby*[118] and *Wickard*[119] inaugurated and which had characterized Commerce Clause jurisprudence until *Lopez*. Moreover, the Court's decision to invoke *Marbury*[120] to legitimize its role as the "ultimate expositor of the constitutional text" underscored its desire to make a point about separation of powers as well as federalism.[121] The Court was not simply recognizing a less robust federal role but was claiming for itself the role of chief enforcer of the boundaries. Finally, the Court's repeated references to *Jones & Laughlin*[122] suggested an active judicial role. Whereas *Wickard*'s near total deference to Congress was itself a form of a categorical rule, the new approach, like *Jones & Laughlin*, seemed designed to give the Court greater flexibility.

The discussion of the "attenuated effects" upon commerce of regulation of certain types of activities was reminiscent of the direct-indirect effects analysis of

---

[116] *Id.* at 613.

[117] *Id.*

[118] United States v. Darby, 312 U.S. 100 (1941).

[119] Wickard v. Filburn, 317 U.S. 111 (1942).

[120] Marbury v. Madison, 5 U.S. (1 Cranch) 137 (1803).

[121] *Morrison*, 529 U.S. at 616 n.7.

[122] NLRB v. Jones & Laughlin Steel Corp., 301 U.S. 1 (1937).

E. C. Knight[123] and *Carter Coal.*[124]

The Court's discussion in *Morrison* seemed something of a throwback to the "logical" approach of many of the pre-1937 cases, not the empirical or realistic approach that replaced it.

The majority seemed more intent on striking some distinctions between matters which Congress could reach and those reserved for the States, an enterprise the dissenters viewed as essentially for the political process. These restraints seemed designed to service a further distinction important to the majority; that between national and local spheres of influence. The majority saw some areas as being within the traditional ambit of State government. These included "noneconomic violent criminal conduct" not directed against interstate commerce as well as family law and unspecified "other areas of traditional state regulation."[125]

The majority essentially relied on doctrinal argument to sustain its conclusion. The doctrine came from the 1995 decision in *Lopez*. Although Justice Thomas, concurring, would have liked the Court to replace "its existing Commerce Clause jurisprudence with a standard more consistent with the original understanding,"[126] the majority seemed disinclined to follow his invitation or to deploy originalist argument.

Any requirement that Congress only regulate economic intrastate activity would be difficult to administer, Justice Breyer argued in dissent. Is a street mugging economic if the thug takes money? Would VAWA be constitutional if limited to restaurants, hotels, airports, train stations and other places of public accommodation?

§ 4.08   GONZALES v. RAICH

The Court's 2005 decision in *Gonzales v. Raich*[127] suggested that *Lopez* and *Morrison* represented relatively modest restrictions on Congress's Commerce Clause power. In *Raich*, the Court held, 6-3, that Congress had power to prohibit the local cultivation and use of marijuana for medical purposes. In *Raich*, the Court distinguished *Lopez* and *Morrison* and upheld challenged federal legislation based, in large part on *Wickard*. The core of the majority consisted of the four *Lopez-Morrison* dissenters (Justices Stevens, Souter, Ginsburg and Breyer). Justice Kennedy joined their opinion and Justice Scalia concurred with the result reached.

In accordance with California's Compassionate Use Act of 1996, Angel Raich and Diane Monson used marijuana for medical purposes pursuant to their physicians' direction and prescriptions. In each case, a physician had concluded that marijuana was the only available drug which provided effective treatment for the patient. Monson grew her own marijuana; Raich relied on her care givers.

---

[123]   United States v. E. C. Knight, 156 U.S. 1 (1895).

[124]   Carter v. Carter Coal Co., 298 U.S. 238 (1936).

[125]   *Morrison*, 529 U.S. at 615–17.

[126]   *Id.* at 627.

[127]   545 U.S. 1 (2005).

Acting pursuant to the federal Controlled Substances Act (CSA), federal drug enforcement agents confiscated and destroyed Monson's cannabis plants. Raich and Monson therefore sought declaratory and injunctive relief against the United States Attorney General and the head of the Drug Enforcement Agency. Although the District Court denied respondent's motion for a preliminary injunction on the ground that they could not demonstrate likelihood of success on the merits, the Court of Appeals for the Ninth Circuit reversed and directed the District Court to issue the preliminary injunction against the federal officials. The Supreme Court granted certiorari, vacated the Ninth Circuit judgment and remanded the case. Before the Court, Raich and Monson did not challenge the constitutionality generally of the CSA. Rather, they made the more limited challenge that "CSA's categorical prohibition of the manufacture and possession of marijuana as applied to the intrastate manufacture and possession of marijuana for medical purposes pursuant to California law exceeds Congress' authority under the Commerce Clause."[128]

The Court had little trouble concluding the CSA was "a valid exercise of federal power, even as applied to the troubling facts of this case."[129] It did so, ostensibly, within the boundaries earlier cases had set. *Raich* differed from *Lopez* and *Morrison*. Those cases raised challenges to the constitutionality of a statute *per se*. In *Raich*, Congress clearly had power to enact the statutory scheme but challenge was made instead to individual applications. This distinction was "pivotal" since where federal power extended to a regulated class of activities, courts could not exempt individual applications as trivial.[130] Moreover, unlike the Gun Free School Zones Act struck down in *Lopez*, CSA was an integral part of a larger economic regulation, the Comprehensive Drug Abuse Prevention and Control Act.[131] Whereas neither the Gun Free School Zones Act nor § 13981 of the Violence Against Women Act of 1994 struck down in *Morrison* regulated economic activity, CSA did since it regulated the production, distribution and use of a good. Moreover, "[p]rohibiting intrastate possession or manufacture" of marijuana was "a rational (and commonly utilized) means of regulating commerce"[132] in a product.

Whereas *Lopez* suggested that *Wickard* rubbed the boundary of the Commerce Clause, the Court in *Raich* found *Wickard* to be "of particular relevance."[133] *Wickard* had established that Congress could regulate noncommercial activity (i.e., production of items not for sale) "if it concludes that failure to regulate that class of activity would undercut the regulation of the interstate market in that commodity."[134] The Court viewed *Raich* as virtually a reprise of its 1942 precedent.[135]

---

[128] 545 U.S. at 15.

[129] *Id.* at 9.

[130] *Id.* at 23.

[131] *Id.*

[132] *Id.* at 26.

[133] *Id.* at 17.

[134] *Id.* at 18.

[135] *Id.* ("the similarities between this case and *Wickard* are striking").

To be sure, *Raich* fit within an exception *Lopez* acknowledged. *Lopez* implicitly held that Congress had power to pass laws regulating intrastate activity which were "an essential part of a larger regulation of economic activity, in which the regulatory scheme could be undercut under the intrastate activity were regulated."[136] This exception relied upon the Necessary and Proper Clause to expand Congress' normal Commerce Clause power. So long as Congress had power to regulate economic activity under the Commerce Clause it could also use means necessary to make the regulatory scheme effective.

It was not entirely clear whether the Commerce Clause alone was sufficient to support the result in *Raich* or whether the Commerce Clause needed the support of the Necessary and Proper Clause to do so. Justice Stevens framed the question presented as whether Congress' power under Art. I, § 8 "to make all laws which shall be necessary and proper for carrying into Execution"[137] its Commerce Clause power extends to prohibiting local cultivation and use of marijuana. Later the Court concluded that "Congress was acting well within its authority 'to make laws which shall be necessary and proper' to 'regulate Commerce . . . among the several States.' "[138] Other portions of the opinion suggested the Commerce Clause alone was sufficient. Justice Stevens discussed the Commerce Clause at length in broad form and concluded that the regulations at issue in *Wickard* and in *Raich* were "squarely within Congress' commerce power because production of the commodity meant for home consumption, be it wheat or marijuana, has a substantial effect on supply and demand in the national market for that commodity."[139]

In this respect, *Raich* was reminiscent of *United States v. Darby*.[140] There the Court invoked both theories to uphold the wage and hour provisions regarding employees engaged in production for interstate commerce. Those provisions were constitutional under the Commerce power because of their relationship to, and effect on, commerce. Alternatively, they were deemed constitutional under the Necessary and Proper Clause since reasonably adapted to an end which Congress could reach under the Commerce Clause, regulating shipment of goods in interstate commerce of goods made using improper labor.

The Court has generally relied on the Commerce Clause alone in upholding congressional regulation of intrastate activities. Indeed, even in *Lopez*, the Court viewed the Commerce Clause as authorizing Congress to regulate intrastate economic activities which substantially affect commerce. In *Raich* the Court seemed to hedge its bets — sometimes attributing federal power to the Commerce Clause while at other times leaning on the Necessary and Proper Clause, too.

Justice Scalia concurred with the Court's holding but only based on the Necessary and Proper Clause ground.[141] Justice Scalia articulated a narrower conception of the commerce power than did the other justices in the majority.

---

[136] 514 U.S. at 561.

[137] 545 U.S. at 5.

[138] *Id.* at 22.

[139] *Id.* at 19.

[140] 312 U.S. 100 (1941).

[141] 545 U.S. at 34.

Whereas the commerce power clearly extends to federal laws regulating instrumentalities and channels of commerce, he argued that it does not authorize regulation of intrastate activities which substantially affect, but are not part of, interstate commerce.[142] Congress can reach these activities only through the Necessary and Proper Clause (appended to the Commerce Clause), he wrote.[143]

Justice Scalia accordingly saw the Commerce Clause as cutting a narrower swath than did the others in the *Raich* majority. Standing alone, it does not allow Congress to reach intrastate transactions, even presumably intrastate economic transactions of the sort dicta in *Lopez* and *Morrison* blessed. It is only the Necessary and Proper Clause, when properly used, which provided federal power to reach these sorts of activities. That Clause does, however, allow Congress to reach not only economic activities that substantially affect commerce but also local activity that is "a necessary part of a more general regulation of intrastate commerce" even if it does not substantially affect commerce.

Justice O'Connor agreed with Justice Scalia that the power to regulate activities with a substantial connection to intrastate commerce stems from a combination of the Commerce and Necessary and Proper Clauses.[144] She contended, however, that Congress cannot immunize from judicial scrutiny federal regulation of local activity by packaging that regulation in a comprehensive statute. The majority's approach, Justice O'Connor wrote in her impassioned dissent, reduced *Lopez* to a case requiring Congress to follow certain procedures when it regulates local activity but one which afforded no meaningful substantive protection to state power. Justice O'Connor complained that the majority ignored the extent to which "the principle of state sovereignty embodied in the Tenth Amendment"[145] limits the Necessary and Proper Clause.

Justice Thomas, though joining Justice O'Connor's dissent, would go further in limiting federal power in this context. Under the "traditional" meaning of commerce which he attributed to the framers, the Commerce Clause could not justify regulating the intrastate, noncommercial activity at issue in *Raich*. Although the Necessary and Proper Clause presented a closer case, Justice Thomas concluded that the CSA, to the extent it imposed an intrastate ban, was not "necessary" since it was not "plainly adapted" to regulating interstate marijuana trade[146] nor was it proper since "Congress has encroached on States' traditional police powers to define the criminal law and to protect the health, safety, and welfare of their citizens."[147] Unlike the rest of the Court, Justice Thomas rejected the "substantial effects" test as "malleable" and unrooted in the Constitution.[148]

Raich seems to reclaim for the commerce power at least some of the ground which *Lopez* and *Morrison* seized. *Lopez* signaled a higher degree of judicial

---

[142] *Id.*

[143] *Id.*

[144] *Id.* at 43 (O'Connor, J., dissenting).

[145] *Id.* at 52.

[146] *Id.* at 61 (Thomas, J., dissenting).

[147] *Id.* at 66.

[148] *Id.* at 67.

scrutiny for Commerce Clause regulation of intrastate activity. Justice Stevens' majority opinion assigned the Court a much more "modest" role in Commence Clause cases.[149] He repeatedly applied a "rational basis" test. The Court's charge is not to determine whether the regulated intrastate activity substantially affected commerce but whether Congress had a rational basis to so conclude.[150] He embraced the test which Justice Breyer advanced in his *Lopez* dissent but which the Court there seemed to abandon.

The Court also interpreted "economic activity" to include "production, distribution and consumption of commodities."[151] Presumably, the majority would also include "provision of services" within its definition. In any event, Justice O'Connor viewed the Court's definition as expansive and as rendering all activity within Congress' reach and creating "a federal police power."[152]

Raich does seem to signal a significant setback for the Rehnquist Court's federalism revolution. *Wickard* seems more deeply rooted now than it did after *Lopez* gave it a somewhat reserved vote of confidence. The death of Chief Justice Rehnquist and retirement of Justice O'Connor deprived the Court of two of those most committed to the Rehnquist Court's federalism doctrines. It is probably too early to predict the shape of future Commerce Clause doctrine, particularly with four new justices joining the Court since *Raich*. Yet it seems likely that future doctrine will follow the more expansive *Raich* doctrine rather than take cues from *Lopez* and *Morrison*.

§ 4.09   SOME CONCLUDING OBSERVATIONS ABOUT THE COMMERCE CLAUSE

During the latter two-thirds of the twentieth century, and especially since *Darby* and *Wickard*, the Court recognized a broad congressional power to regulate pursuant to the Commerce Clause. Although *Lopez* and *Morrison* evidenced some disposition by a bare majority of the Court to narrow that power, *Raich* suggested that those cases may not impose serious limitations on Congress's power.

The Commerce Clause sometimes benefits from its association with the Necessary and Proper Clause. Dicta in *Lopez* recognized that Congress could reach non-economic activities as means reasonably adapted to implement comprehensive economic regulatory schemes and *Darby* (before) and *Raich* (since) among other cases illustrate instances in which the Court has upheld legislation which rested on the Commerce and Necessary and Proper Clauses working in tandem. Indeed, in his concurrence in *Raich*, Justice Scalia recognized that the latter clause allowed Congress to regulate non-economic local activities as a necessary part of a general regulation of interstate commerce.[153]

---

[149] *Id.* at 22 (majority opinion).

[150] *Id.* at 21, 22.

[151] *Id.* at 25–26.

[152] *Id.* at 49–50 (O'Connor, J., dissenting).

[153] *Raich*, 545 U.S. at 37 (Scalia, J., concurring in judgment).

In an important recent article, Professor Jack Balkin has argued that Justice Thomas and some originalist scholars have misportrayed the Commerce Clause as having been expanded beyond its original meaning. On the contrary, he argues that the original meaning of the Commerce Clause, when both its text and structural purpose are considered, was to allow the national government to regulate a broad array of intercourse where a national approach was needed because individual States could not regulate a problem or address the spillover effects between States or collective action problems that concerned multiple States.[154] Accordingly, he finds the Commerce Clause comfortably authorized Congress to regulate in a variety of areas. Professor Balkin's claim, which is developed in detail in his article, is controversial, and some other scholars writing before[155] and since[156] have reached quite different conclusions. This issue will no doubt be a topic of continuing discussion.

The debate over the constitutionality of the Patient Protection and Affordable Care Act will presumably provide an important test of the scope of Congress' commerce power and the first such test since Chief Justice Roberts, and Justices Alito, Sotomayor and Kagan joined the Court. Professor Balkin argues that Congress easily had power to pass the legislation under the Commerce Clause as well as other enumerated powers[157] whereas Professor Barnett is among those who believe the act transcended Congress's powers.[158]

As this book goes to press, the Court has under submission the cases addressing the constitutionality of the health care legislation. Please check the LexisNexis Law School web site for updated material regarding this decision as well as download-able supplements at www.lexisnexis.com/lawschool.

---

[154] Jack M. Balkin, *Commerce*, 109 MICH. L. REV. 1 (2010).

[155] *See, e.g.*, Randy E. Barnett, *New Evidence of the Original Meaning of the Commerce Clause*, 55 ARK. L. REV. 847 (2003); Randy E. Barnett, *The Original Meaning of the Commerce Clause*, 68 U. CHI. L. REV. 101 (2001).

[156] *See, e.g.*, Robert G. Natelson & David Kopel, *Commerce in the Commerce Clause: A Response to Jack Balkin*, 109 MICH. L. REV. FIRST IMPRESSIONS 55 (2010), http://www.michiganlawreview.org/assets/fi/109/natelsonkopel.pdf.

[157] Balkin, *supra* note 154, at 44–47.

[158] Randy E. Barnett, *Is Health-Care Reform Constitutional?*, WASH. POST, Mar. 21, 2010.

Chapter 5

THE FEDERAL SYSTEM

INTRODUCTION

The Federal system allocates power between the National and State Governments. Although the Constitution does not use the word "federalism," the concept represents one of the important structural ideas implicit in the document. The title of this chapter may indicate that what this book has to say about federalism is confined to the pages of this immediate discussion. Such a suggestion is misleading. Much in the preceding, and following, chapters relates to federalism. Judicial review of state legislation and state court decisions allows the federal judiciary to police state action. When federal legislative power grows to occupy a larger sphere, it displaces state power. Accordingly, discussions of the Commerce power and other powers of Congress impact federalism. The Dormant Commerce Clause and Privileges and Immunities Clause, topics of the next chapter, concern federalism, too, because they allow the federal judiciary to police the way in which States treat citizens of other States. Nor is the material on federalism limited to the chapters dealing with government institutions and structure. Some portions of the book which address rights implicate federalism issues in important ways. The Civil War Amendments conferred rights as against the States which Congress and the federal courts were empowered to enforce. They significantly redrew the balance between Nation and State in a manner which expanded national power.

"Federalism was our Nation's own discovery,"[1] Justice Anthony Kennedy observed. Yet defining that discovery has not been easy. Indeed, the character of our federalism has been a continuing source of controversy. Nonetheless, as Professor Ernest Young argues, "fidelity to the Constitution requires us to *have* federalism doctrine."[2]

§ 5.01 MAIN FEATURES

[1] Components of Federalism

More than a half century ago, Professor Edward Corwin identified the following features as intrinsic to American federalism: (1) a union of autonomous States; (2) the division of powers between the Federal Government and the States; (3) the direct operation of each government, within its assigned sphere, on all within its

---

[1] United States Term Limits, Inc. v. Thornton, 514 U.S. 779, 838 (1995) (Kennedy, J., concurring).

[2] Ernest A. Young, *Making Federalism Doctrine: Fidelity, Institutional Competence, and Compensating Adjustments*, 46 Wm. & Mary L. Rev. 1733, 1736 (2005).

territorial limits; (4) the provision of each government with the complete apparatus of law enforcement; and (5) federal supremacy over any conflicting assertion of state power.[3] The intervening years have witnessed a further shift of power from State to Nation and have added some gloss to Professor Corwin's formulation. Nonetheless, it continues to state some basic features of American federalism.

[2] Union of Previously Autonomous States

The Constitution brought previously autonomous States together into one union. The Constitution was formed, Chief Justice Marshall argued in *McCulloch v. Maryland*,[4] by action by the people, not by the state governments. To be sure, the delegates to the constitutional convention were chosen by the state legislatures and the proposal it produced was ultimately submitted to delegates meeting in the States — "where else should they have assembled?"[5] Marshall asked rhetorically. But the fact that the people met to act in States did not make their action any less that of the people, he asserted.

"We the people of the United States" the Constitution's preamble begins, language which provides some support for Marshall's conclusion. Even though the Constitution and government it created were of, by and for the people, it brought together into voluntary union autonomous governments, previously linked only by the loose bonds of the Confederation. Professor Mark Killenbeck has argued that many contemporary discussions of state sovereignty overlook or underemphasize the fact that the Constitution was established, and the Articles of Confederation jettisoned, to escape a regime in which state sovereignty and a weak central government produced a dysfunctional arrangement.[6] *McCulloch's* answer is not uniformly accepted. In 1995, the Court reaffirmed Marshall's conclusion that the Constitution emanates from the people, not the States, but only in a 5-4 decision with opinions analyzing this issue in sharply divergent ways.[7] The majority viewed the founding as "a 'revolutionary' act that replaced a confederation of sovereign states with a 'National Government' in which the 'representatives owe primary allegiance not to the people of a state, but to the people of the nation.' "[8] Under this "big bang" theory the Constitution emanated from the whole people (meeting for reasons of convenience in the various States), not from the States. Justice Thomas' dissent argued that the Constitution came from "the state people, not the federal people"[9] as an act of state sovereignty. The States retained all powers not specifically surrendered.

---

[3] *See* EDWARD S. CORWIN, THE CONSTITUTION OF THE UNITED STATES OF AMERICA: ANALYSIS AND INTERPRETATION xi–xii (1953).

[4] 17 U.S. (4 Wheat.) 316 (1819).

[5] *Id.* at 403.

[6] Mark R. Killenbeck, *The Physics of Federalism*, 51 KAN. L. REV. 1, 27, 33 (2002).

[7] United States Term Limits, Inc. v. Thornton, 514 U.S. 779 (1995).

[8] Kathleen Sullivan, *Dueling Sovereignties*: U.S. Term Limits, Inc. v. Thornton, 109 HARV. L. REV. 78, 88 (1995).

[9] *Id.* at 90.

Even under the prevailing *McCulloch* view, the States are not "mere political subdivisions of the United States."[10] They occupy a special position in our constitutional system and may exercise powers the Constitution does not vest in Congress or deny them.[11]

The Constitution did not produce "[a]n entire consolidation of the States into one complete national sovereignty."[12] States retained a degree of sovereignty. They were represented as states in the Senate, their senators were initially chosen by the state legislature, and no state could lose its equal representation in the Senate without its consent. At the same time, the States lost many attributes of sovereignty with adoption of the Constitution. The limitations on state power set forth in Article I, § 10 coupled with the Supremacy Clause suggest some limits which union placed on state sovereignty. The Civil War Amendments later imposed further restraints.

"[S]tate sovereignty is, [however,] a ghost that refused to remain in repose."[13] The Civil War defeated claims that States had a right of secession, but some have asserted lesser claims of state sovereignty to preclude enforcement of federal legislation or judicial orders. This doctrine of interposition, if honored, would exonerate the States from complying with federal commands to which they object. If accepted, it would allow the States to disrupt the Federal Government from functioning. The Constitution expressly refutes such claims of state power in the plain language of the Supremacy Clause.

Some Southern States used the interposition doctrine to resist federal enforcement of the Equal Protection Clause in the 1950s. After the Supreme Court held public school segregation unconstitutional,[14] the governments of several Southern States resisted judicial orders calling for an end to segregated schools. *Cooper v. Aaron*[15] rejected the claim that the Court's decisions invalidating school segregation did not bind the Governor and legislature of Arkansas. It reiterated the established principle that the Court's constitutional interpretations bind the States. If States would nullify federal action as claimed, the Constitution itself "becomes a solemn mockery."[16]

[3] Division of Powers Between Nation and States

The federal system divides power between Nation and States. "The Framers split the atom of sovereignty,"[17] Justice Kennedy wrote. Professor Killenbeck points out that Justice Kennedy's metaphor is misleading since the framers did not

---

[10] New York v. United States, 505 U.S. 144, 187 (1992).

[11] *See* Garcia v. San Antonio Metro. Transit Auth., 469 U.S. 528, 547 (1985).

[12] THE FEDERALIST No. 32 (Alexander Hamilton).

[13] Bernard Schwartz, National League of Cities v. Usery — *The Commerce Power and State Sovereignty Redivivus*, 46 FORDHAM L. REV. 1115 (1978).

[14] *See* Brown v. Board of Educ., 347 U.S. 483 (1954), 349 U.S. 294 (1955).

[15] 358 U.S. 1 (1958).

[16] *Id.* at 18 (quoting United States v. Peters, 9 U.S. (5 Cranch) 115, 136 (1809)).

[17] *U.S. Term Limits*, 514 U.S. at 838 (Kennedy, J., concurring).

create multiple sovereigns but "a national nucleus surrounded by state electrons."[18] The Federal Government possesses those powers the Constitution delegates to it either explicitly or implicitly. The States retain authority not granted the nation or retained by the people. The Constitution's text discloses this division. Congress is given only the legislative powers "herein granted,"[19] not all legislative power. Moreover, the enumeration of eighteen categories of legislative power in Article I suggests other authority not conferred. Finally, the Tenth Amendment reminds that some power is not given to the Federal Government.

To a great extent, the boundaries of the division were left to future generations to mark. Although the Articles of Confederation had limited the Federal Government to those powers "expressly delegated" to it[20] the framers had repeatedly declined to include such a limitation in the Constitution,[21] a point Chief Justice Marshall thought significant in *McCulloch*.[22] The Constitution clearly contemplated that the Federal Government would have some body of implied powers which might impact the States. Nonetheless, the States retained a separate basis of power. As Alexander Hamilton wrote in The Federalist:[23]

> An entire consolidation of the States into one complete national sover-
> eignty would imply an entire subordination of the parts; and whatever
> powers might remain in them would be altogether dependent on the
> general will. But as the plan of the convention aims only at a partial union
> or consolidation, the State governments would clearly retain all the rights
> of sovereignty which they before had, and which were not, by that act,
> *exclusively* delegated to the United States.

[4]   Direct Operation of States and Nation

The federal system featured the direct operation of both State and Federal Governments, within their assigned spheres, on all persons and property within their respective territorial limits. This attribute enhanced the status of the Nation compared to prior federations. The Federal Government received authority, not only over the member States, but also over their citizens. Accordingly, National Government could enforce its commands without dependence on State Government. And the Citizenship Clause of the Fourteenth Amendment subsequently established a direct and primary link between individual citizens and the nation.[24]

---

[18] Killenbeck, *supra* note 6, at 55. *See generally id.* at 55–57.

[19] U.S. Const. art. I, § 1.

[20] Articles of Confederation, 1777, art. II.

[21] 5 The Founders Constitution 403–04 (Philip Kurland & Ralph Lerner eds., 1988).

[22] 17 U.S. at 406 ("But there is no phrase in the [Constitution] which, like the articles of confederation, excludes incidental or implied powers; and which requires that everything granted shall be expressly and minutely described.").

[23] The Federalist No. 32 (Alexander Hamilton).

[24] U.S. Const. amend. XIV, § 1.

[5] Possession of Law-Enforcement Apparatus

Both State and Federal Governments can operate directly on those in their territorial jurisdiction because each government has its law enforcement apparatus. Because each can enforce its laws and decrees, each enjoys an independence neither could attain if it depended on the other to enforce its mandates.

Both Federal and State Government play crucial roles. Notwithstanding the expansion of federal authority during the twentieth century, the States still perform many essential governmental functions. States provide public education, fire and police protection, sanitation, public health, and parks and recreation, among other services. States may regulate their local economies through laws addressing banking, insurance, public utilities, local transportation, various occupations and professions. Finally, much law enforcement is performed locally.

[6] Federal Supremacy

Separate levels of government make contests inevitable. The action of each government often impinges on the other. The Supremacy Clause of Article VI resolves such conflicts in favor of the Federal Government. Federal law, within its allotted sphere, is supreme throughout the Nation. States cannot impede or control those laws.[25]

Marshall interpreted the Supremacy Clause to carry essentially two meanings: (1) the States may not interfere with the Federal Government; and (2) constitutional federal action prevails over inconsistent state action.

McCulloch v. Maryland expressed the first idea.[26] Maryland taxed the national bank, action which interfered with the functioning of the Federal Government. The national government was not designed to be "dependent on the States."[27] State taxation of the national bank or other federal instrumentalities would interfere with their independent operation.

"It is of the very essence of supremacy to remove all obstacles to its action within its own sphere, and so to modify every power vested in subordinate governments, as to exempt its own operations from their own influence."[28] *U. S. Term Limits* articulated a variation of that principle. It held that States could not add additional *qualifications* for Congress because to do so would interfere with the proper functioning of the national government.

Gibbons v. Ogden[29] represented the second idea. The Court held the New York statute invalid so far as it applied to coastwise vessels Congress licensed. The

---

[25] *See McCulloch*, 17 U.S. at 436; U.S. Const. art. VI ("This constitution, and the laws of the United States which shall be made in pursuance thereof, and all treaties made, or which shall be made, under the authority of the United States, shall be the supreme law of the land.").

[26] *See id.*

[27] *McCulloch*, 17 U.S. at 432.

[28] *Id.* at 427.

[29] 22 U.S. (9 Wheat.) 1 (1824).

Supremacy Clause dictated state law must yield to a federal law with which it conflicted.

In essence, the Supremacy Clause renders valid federal law supreme over State law even when the State acts within an area within its purview.[30] "If any one proposition could command the universal assent of mankind, we might expect it to be this — that the government of the Union, though limited in its power, is supreme within its sphere of action,"[31] Marshall wrote.

Article VI underscores federal supremacy in two other ways. The remaining part of the Supremacy Clause requires that state judges are bound by federal law even when that federal law conflicts with their state constitution or state laws.[32] Moreover, the Oath Clause commits officers of the state executive and judicial branches and members of state legislatures to support the Constitution.[33]

The characteristics which Professor Corwin identified suggest some of the advantages commonly associated with federalism. The vertical division between governing units helps prevent concentration of power. As such, federalism is seen as a means to prevent government tyranny and to promote individual liberty. Federalism also helps government operate more efficiently by allocating functions to the unit best equipped to discharge them. National government is empowered to handle matters which require a uniform approach whereas State government polices matters where proximity or diversity are valued.

Three other potential advantages of federalism perhaps receive less emphasis but are worth noting. The presence of multiple governments presents opportunities for experimentation with little risk to the whole. As Justice Brandeis observed: "It is one of the happy incidents of the federal system that a single courageous state may, if its citizens choose, serve as a laboratory; and try novel social and economic experiments without risk to the rest of the country."[34] Presumably successful experiments may be tried elsewhere whereas failed approaches may be avoided. Justice Brandeis's "laboratories of democracy" concept has become one of the enduring metaphors in constitutional discourse.

Federalism also allows for diverse arrangements which may be attractive to different groups. Minorities may exit one community to find sanctuary in a more hospitable one.

Federalism also affords more opportunities for individuals to join in civic life. As such, it may facilitate political and civic participation with a range of democratic benefits. Federalism may provide occasions for minorities to find a voice in governing matters which may impact national as well as local politics.[35]

---

[30] *See* License Cases, 46 U.S. (5 How.) 504, 574 (1847).

[31] *McCulloch*, 17 U.S. at 405.

[32] U.S. Const. art. VI, cl. 2.

[33] U.S. Const. art. VI, cl. 3.

[34] New State Ice Co. v. Liebmann, 285 U.S. 262, 311 (1932) (Brandeis, J., dissenting).

[35] *See generally* Heather K. Gerken, *Foreword: Federalism All the Way Down*, 124 Harv. L. Rev. 4, 6 (2010).

§ 5.02 RESERVED POWERS

[1] Tenth Amendment as Source of State Power

The Supremacy Clause, combined with the Article I powers, enables the Nation to limit and override much state activity. Defenders of a more expansive view of states' autonomy often invoke the Tenth Amendment as a source of countervailing state power. It provides: "The powers not delegated to the United States by the Constitution, nor prohibited by it to the States, are reserved to the States respectively, or to the people."[36] The text of the Tenth Amendment offers little help in solving concrete constitutional issues. It does confirm that all power is not given to the Federal Government. Yet the Tenth Amendment seems to contemplate a three-part division of governmental power — among the National Government, State Government, and the people. Although it makes clear that the Federal Government cannot exercise all power it provides no criteria to filter the non-federal part between the States and the people. Perceptions of the Tenth Amendment have fluctuated between competing views. Some see it as reinforcing, but not adding to, the proposition that the Federal Government has simply those powers the Constitution delegates to it. The Tenth Amendment was added to the Constitution to allay fears that the new government might seek to exercise powers not granted. As John Hart Ely explained, it provides "that the addition of the Bill of Rights is not to be taken to have changed the fact that powers not delegated are not delegated."[37] Under this view the Tenth Amendment does not curtail federal authority: "The amendment states but a truism that all is retained which has not been surrendered."[38] In this sense, the Amendment is redundant.

Alternatively, others see the Tenth Amendment as a significant restraint on federal activity. In *New York v. United States*,[39] for instance, Justice O'Connor wrote that "the Tenth Amendment confirms that the power of the federal government is subject to limits that may, in a given instance, reserve power to the States."[40]

[2] The Rise and Fall and Rise of the Tenth Amendment

During the early twentieth century, the Tenth Amendment was occasionally used to preclude the federal government from some forms of regulation.[41] Thus, in *The Child Labor Case*,[42] the Court found the regulation "in a twofold sense . . . repugnant to the Constitution. It not only transcends the authority delegated to Congress over commerce but also exerts a power as to a purely local matter to

---

[36] U.S. Const. amend. X.

[37] John H. Ely, Democracy and Distrust: A Theory of Judicial Review 35 (1980).

[38] United States v. Darby, 312 U.S. 100, 124 (1941). *See also New York v. United States*, 505 U.S. at 157 (text of Tenth Amendment is "tantology").

[39] 505 U.S. 144 (1992).

[40] Bernard Schwartz, National League of Cities v. Usery — *The Commerce Power and State Sovereignty Redivivus*, 46 Fordham L. Rev. 1115 (1978).

[41] *See generally* The Tenth Amendment and State Sovereignty (Mark R. Killenbeck ed., 2002).

[42] Hammer v. Dagenhart, 247 U.S. 251 (1918).

which the federal authority does not extend."[43] Similarly, the Court found Congress' efforts to use the taxing power to regulate production offensive to the Tenth Amendment.[44] Indeed, some viewed the Tenth Amendment as insuring a prominent role for States. As Justice McReynolds complained in his dissent in *National Labor Relations Board v. Jones & Laughlin Steel Corp.*:[45] "[t]he Constitution still recognizes the existence of states with indestructible powers; the Tenth Amendment was supposed to put them beyond controversy."[46]

Justice McReynolds may have seen the writing on the wall. Four years after his angry dissent, the Court reduced the Tenth Amendment to "a truism" in *United States v. Darby*.[47] For the next half-century, the Tenth Amendment displayed little muscle in constitutional adjudication.

Occasionally, some claim rested on the Amendment. In *Fry v. United States*,[48] the Court rejected a claim that applying a federal law to state employees intruded on state sovereignty. Towards the end of his opinion, however, Justice Thurgood Marshall dropped a footnote to respond to petitioners' claims based on the Tenth Amendment. In summarily rejecting their case, the Court acknowledged in dicta that the Tenth Amendment was "not without significance." It "expressly declares the constitutional policy that Congress may not exercise power in a fashion that impairs the States' integrity or their ability to function effectively in a federal system."[49]

The following year, however, the Court in a 5-4 decision recognized the Tenth Amendment as "an express declaration" of limitations on the power of Congress to regulate the States as States in *National League of Cities v. Usery*.[50] Although the Court invoked the Tenth Amendment, it did not develop it in much detail. It cited the *Fry* footnote dicta in support of the proposition that "our federal system of government imposes definite limits upon the authority of Congress to regulate the activities of the States as States by means of the commerce power."[51] The Court did not otherwise mention the Amendment and Justice Rehnquist stated the Court's holding as placing the challenged provisions outside the authority the Commerce Clause conferred.[52]

This treatment was consistent with Justice Rehnquist's view, as stated in his *Fry* dissent, that the Tenth Amendment did not "by its terms" prohibit the regulation of state employees. Rather, it represented "the understanding of those who drafted

---

[43] *Id.* at 276.

[44] *See, e.g.*, United States v. Butler, 297 U.S. 1 (1936); Bailey v. Drexel Furniture Co., 259 U.S. 20 (1922); *see also* Collector v. Day, 78 U.S. (11 Wall.) 113, 124–26 (1871) (using Tenth Amendment to curtail Congress' power to tax) *overruled by* Graves v. New York, 306 U.S. 466, 486 (1939).

[45] 301 U.S. 1 (1937).

[46] *Id.* at 97.

[47] 312 U.S. 100, 124 (1941).

[48] 421 U.S. 542 (1975).

[49] *Id.* at 547 n.7.

[50] 426 U.S. 833, 842 (1976).

[51] *Id.*

[52] *Id.* at 852.

and ratified the Constitution that the states were sovereign in many respects" and that Congress could not treat States like a private entrepreneur.[53] In subsequent years, the Court rejected numerous challenges to federal legislation based on the Tenth Amendment.[54]

Ultimately, in 1985, less than a decade after *National League of Cities* had breathed some life into the Tenth Amendment, the Court rejected the notion that the Amendment could give rise to judicial standards to protect the States. In *Garcia v. San Antonio Metropolitan Transit Authority*,[55] the Court overruled *National League of Cities*. The majority spilt little ink on dismissing the Tenth Amendment — indeed Justice Powell, in dissent, complained that the Court made "only a single passing reference"[56] to it. By ignoring it, however, the Court spoke volumes. Justice Powell thought the Tenth Amendment "was adopted specifically to ensure that the important role promised the States by the proponents of the Constitution was realized."[57] In dissent, Justice O'Connor foreshadowed the more robust role she saw for the Tenth Amendment. She complained that the Court had violated "[t]he *spirit* of the Tenth Amendment" which promised "that the States will retain their integrity in a system in which the laws of the United States are nevertheless supreme."[58]

Since the early 1990s, the Tenth Amendment has experienced something of a rebirth as the Court has taken pains to give it content. A narrow majority of the Rehnquist Court viewed the Amendment as expressing a structural limit on federal power.

In *Gregory v. Ashcroft*[59] Justice O'Connor invoked the Tenth Amendment as a structural support for state sovereignty. The authority to determine qualifications of a State's high officials was "a power reserved to the States under the Tenth Amendment."[60] The following year, she invoked the Tenth Amendment repeatedly in *New York v. United States*[61] en route to holding that federal legislation in question intruded on state sovereignty which the Tenth Amendment protected. Unlike prior opinions, she repeatedly invoked the Tenth Amendment and attributed to it a greater significance not displayed in other recent cases. She repeatedly described the Tenth Amendment as reserving sovereignty to States[62] and measured the legislation under discussion as to whether it violated the Tenth

---

[53] *Fry*, 421 U.S. at 557 (Rehnquist, J., dissenting).

[54] *See, e.g.*, Hodel v. Virginia Surface Mining & Reclamation Association, 452 U.S. 264 (1981); United Transportation Union v. Long Island R. R. Co., 455 U.S. 678 (1982); Federal Energy Regulatory Commission v. Mississippi, 456 U.S. 742 (1982); Equal Employment Opportunity Commission v. Wyoming, 460 U.S. 226 (1983).

[55] 469 U.S. 528 (1985).

[56] *Id.* at 560.

[57] *Id.* at 568.

[58] *Id.* at 585 (O'Connor, J., dissenting) (emphasis in original).

[59] 501 U.S. 452 (1991).

[60] *Id.* at 463.

[61] 505 U.S. 144 (1992).

[62] *Id.* at 156, 174, 177.

Amendment.[63] The text of the Tenth Amendment might be "essentially a tautology" but "the Tenth Amendment confirms that the power of the Federal Government is subject to limits that may, in a given instance, reserve power to the States. The Tenth Amendment thus directs us to determine, as in this case, whether an incident of state sovereignty is protected by a limitation on an Article I power . . . ."[64] In *U.S. Term Limits v. Thornton*,[65] the justices devoted much of their discussion to the Tenth Amendment. As is suggested below,[66] the Tenth Amendment need not have featured so prominently in the discussion which ostensibly turned upon whether a State could enact qualifications for the Senators and Representatives it sent to Congress in addition to those the Constitution sets out. Yet the dissent endorsed petitioners' claim that the Tenth Amendment reserved such a right to the States[67] and accordingly the majority discussed the Amendment at some length in adopting a more limited view of its impact. Justice Thomas and those who joined his dissent found "enshrined in the Tenth Amendment" the "basic principles" that constitutional silence about "the exercise of a particular power" means "the Federal Government lacks that power and the States enjoy it."[68]

It is not clear that Justice Scalia shares Justice O'Connor's enthusiasm for the Tenth Amendment.[69] Although he silently joined her opinion in *New York v. United States*, his subsequent majority opinion in *Printz v. United States*[70] made only passing reference to the Tenth Amendment, simply as making "express" the idea that some "[r]esidual state sovereignty" was implicit in Congress' enumeration of only specified powers in the national government.[71] His rather half-hearted reliance on the Tenth Amendment contrasted with that of Justice O'Connor's and Justice Thomas' separate concurrences.[72]

The Court has deployed the Tenth Amendment to support claims of sovereign immunity in state court. Thus, in *Alden v. Maine*[73] the Court suggested that the

---

[63] *Id.* at 173, 174, 177.

[64] *Id.* at 157. *See also id.* at 156 ("attribute of state sovereignty reserved by the Tenth Amendment"); *id.* at 159 ("the core of sovereignty retained by the States under the Tenth Amendment"); *id.* at 174 ("the sovereignty reserved to the States by the Tenth Amendment"); *id.* at 177 ("the core of state sovereignty reserved by the Tenth Amendment").

[65] 514 U.S. 779 (1995).

[66] See Text accompanying footnotes 78 to 83 in this chapter.

[67] 514 U.S. at 848–57.

[68] *Id.* at 848 (Thomas, J., dissenting).

[69] *See* Thomas W. Merrill, *The Making of the Second Rehnquist Court: A Preliminary Analysis*, 47 St. Louis U. L.J. 569, 614–15 (2003) (pointing out contrast between treatment of Tenth Amendment of Justices O'Connor and Scalia).

[70] 521 U.S. 898 (1997).

[71] *Id.* at 919.

[72] *Id.* at 935–36 (O'Connor, J., concurring) ("The Brady Act violates the Tenth Amendment."); *id.* at 936 (Thomas, J., concurring) (Court properly holds that "the Brady Act violates the Tenth Amendment.").

[73] 527 U.S. 706 (1999).

Tenth Amendment should "allay lingering concerns"[74] about state sovereignty. The dissent ridiculed this reliance on the Tenth Amendment. If it represented a constitutional commitment to sovereign immunity, the Court had erred in relying on the Eleventh Amendment in prior cases and indeed the Eleventh Amendment itself was superfluous. Justice Souter[75] found "no evidence that the Tenth Amendment constitutionalized a concept of sovereign immunity as inherent in the notion of statehood . . . ."[76]

The Court rejected a Tenth Amendment claim in *Reno v. Condon.*[77] A lower court had held that the Drivers Privacy Protection Act violated the Tenth Amendment because it required the States not disclose certain information from drivers' licenses. The Court reversed. The law, which applied to private conduct, too, prohibited conduct rather than requiring the States take any affirmative steps. The Court seemed to distinguish between Congress prohibiting conduct, which the Tenth Amendment did not preclude, and imposing affirmative duties on State Government, which the Amendment presumably proscribes. The fact that complying with the DPPA would require time and effort by the States did not violate the Tenth Amendment.

[3] What's A "Reserved Power"?

The Tenth Amendment states that powers the Constitution does not delegate to the United States nor prohibit to the States "are reserved to the States respectively, or to the people."[78] The Constitution apparently contemplates some body of powers "reserved" to the States or people but it does not identify with much precision what powers are "reserved."

The Court considered that question in *U.S. Term Limits, Inc. v. Thornton.*[79] The issue before the Court was whether Arkansas could impose term limits on those its voters sent to the United States Senate and House of Representatives. The Court held that the States lack any reserved powers to add qualifications for congressional membership to those the Constitution states. In a 5-4 decision, the Court held unconstitutional, a state law imposing term limits for the state's Senators and Representatives. The Court might have decided the case, Bernard Schwartz pointed out, "relatively easily under the Qualification Clauses of Article I,"[80] which specify the age, citizenship and residency requirements for Senators and Representatives.[81] It could have simply stated that these requirements were exclusive, the majority's position.

---

[74] *Id.* at 713.

[75] *Id.* at 761 (Souter, J., dissenting).

[76] *Id.*

[77] 528 U.S. 141 (2000).

[78] U.S. Const. amend. X.

[79] 514 U.S. 779 (1995).

[80] Bernard Schwartz, *Term Limits, Commerce, and the Rehnquist Court*, 31 Tulsa L.J. 521, 522 (1996).

[81] *See* U.S. Const. art. I, § 2, cl. 3, § 3, cl. 3.

Instead, both opinions contained lengthy discussions of the nature of the reserved power of the States, a subject that split the Court sharply. The majority argued that under the Tenth Amendment, the powers reserved to the States were limited to those they possessed prior to ratification. The States' pre-Tenth-Amendment "original powers," did not include adding qualifications; because congressional membership arose from the Constitution itself no such power was reserved. The Constitution provides the exclusive source of qualifications for members of Congress, and it "divested" States of any power to add qualifications. The Elections Clause[82] gave States authority to protect the integrity and regularity of the election process by regulating "Times, Places and Manner of holding Elections," but did not confer license to add qualifications.

The four dissenters disagreed. Speaking for them, Justice Thomas denied that the Tenth Amendment reserved powers were limited to those the States possessed before the Constitution was adopted. He argued that the States retained all authority not denied them. The States need not rely on any affirmative grant of power to prescribe qualifications for their representatives; because the Constitution did not deny the States the power, it was reserved by the Tenth Amendment. Justice Thomas took further exception to the majority's limitation of "reserved" powers to those the States previously enjoyed. "If someone says that the power to use a particular facility is reserved to some group, he is not saying anything about whether that group has previously used that facility. He is merely saying that the people who control the facility have designated that group as the entity with authority to use it."[83]

[4] The Tenth Amendment Summarized

The recent reinvigoration of the Tenth Amendment represented one of the important constitutional developments during what Professor Thomas Merrill termed "the Second Rehnquist Court."[84] Chief Justice Rehnquist and Justices O'Connor and Thomas displayed particular fondness for the Amendment and their jurisprudence fueled its growth. A few points in summary may be useful.

First, the development of the Tenth Amendment did not rest primarily on its text. Justice Thomas' discussion in *Term Limits* is an exception; other opinions, even by the Amendment's modern champions, often disclaim reliance on its language.[85] Indeed, the text of the Amendment presents three problems for those who would rely on it. First, it is, as Justice O'Connor concedes, "essentially a tautology."[86] Second, although the Amendment suggests some limit on the power of the Federal Government it does not state that powers withheld from Washington

---

[82] U.S. Const. art. I, § 4.

[83] *Term Limits*, 514 U.S. at 851–52.

[84] *See* Merrill, *supra* note 69.

[85] *See, e.g., Fry v. United States*, 421 U.S. at 557 (Rehnquist, J., dissenting) ("Disclaiming reliance on text of Tenth Amendment); *New York v. United States*, 505 U.S. at 156–57 ("Limits Tenth Amendment imposes" are not derived from the text of the Tenth Amendment itself, which . . . is essentially a tautology.); *Printz v. United States*, 521 U.S. at 2370 ("no constitutional text" speaking to question).

[86] *New York v. United States*, 505 U.S. at 157.

inevitably belong to the States. Rather, it divides such "reserved" power in some unspecified fashion between the States and the people. That problem is mitigated if one adopts Justice Thomas' view that "the people" are the people of the States.[87] Others suggest a different resolution. The Tenth Amendment, as James Madison proposed it, did not include "or to the people."[88] Those words were subsequently added without debate. Professor Jack Rakove suggests that "there is a sense in which the identification of the people as an entity distinct from both state and national governments illuminates the political underpinnings of federalism."[89] The Tenth Amendment says more clearly that there are limits to the powers of the Federal Government than it suggests that the States receive whatever is reserved.

Finally, the Tenth Amendment reserves *powers*. It does not, on its fact, reserve rights or immunities. Thus, to the extent some decisions use the Amendment as reserving something other than "powers" they would appear inconsistent with the text.

Although its text has offered little support, the Amendment has been seen as supporting a structural idea regarding federalism. Those who advance a strong version of the Tenth Amendment typically have this structural concept in mind.[90]

Moreover, the Court has used its recent precedents to support further holdings which protect States from federal regulation. This phenomenon was perhaps best illustrated in *Printz*. Although Justice Scalia said little about the Tenth Amendment, he rested the Court's opinion largely on its earlier decision in *New York v. United States*.[91]

The Court's reliance on the Tenth Amendment represents an effort to find judicially enforceable limitations on federal power. To this extent, it diverges from a competing impulse which suggests that the primary protections of States come from the political process.

[5] Police Power

The police power, the primary reserved power of the States, dates to early Supreme Court decisions. Chief Justice John Marshall first used the phrase in *Brown v. Maryland*.[92] Chief Justice Taney defined State police power as "nothing more or less than the powers of government inherent in every sovereignty to the

---

[87] *U.S. Term Limits*, 514 U.S. at 846, 848–49.

[88] Kurland & Lerner, *supra* note 21, at 26.

[89] Jack Rakove, *American Federalism: Was There an Original Understanding?*, *in* Killenbeck ed., *supra* note 41, at 127.

[90] *See, e.g., Fry*, 421 U.S. at 557 (Rehnquist, J., dissenting) (Tenth Amendment represents understanding of founders of state sovereignty); *Garcia*, 469 U.S. at 585 (O'Connor, J., dissenting) (spirit of Tenth Amendment protects state integrity).

[91] 521 U.S. at 925–28.

[92] 25 U.S. (12 Wheat.) 419, 443 (1827). *See* Gibbons v. Ogden, 22 U.S. (9 Wheat.) 1, 208 (1824) ("The acknowledged power of a State to regulate its police, its domestic trade, and to govern its own citizens, may enable it to legislate.").

extent of its dominions."[93] The police power operated over a relatively narrow scope during the nineteenth century, allowing private interests substantial leeway.

"Police power" is a vague concept which embraces a range of subjects.[94] The police power includes "[w]hatever affects the peace, good order, morals and health of the community."[95] Each person is subject to restraints on his own rights to "secure the general comfort, health and prosperity of the State."[96] As such, the police power justifies "the adoption of precautionary measures against social evils."[97]

The police power has expanded over time. Even in the Nineteenth Century, courts approached the police power with a touch of "we know it when we see it" attitude. The consensus included in its scope "the protection of the lives, health, and property of the citizens, and to the preservation of good order and public morals."[98] Later formulations include the education of the people and a state's industry, resources and wealth.[99] Laws addressing dilapidated housing may come within the police power[100] as may legislation to protect the right to vote free from an employer's coercion.[101]

§ 5.03 POLITICAL PROCESS AND FEDERALISM

The Court's jurisprudence has often looked to the political process to address issues of federalism. At times, the Court has found that such arguments counsel for, or against, claims of national or state right. Alternatively, sometimes such arguments are used to suggest that federalism must look to political, not jurisprudential, protection.

Chief Justice John Marshall invoked political process arguments in *McCulloch* in support of his conclusion that Maryland could not tax the national bank. The only security against an abuse of the power to tax, Marshall argued, was "found in the structure of the government itself," the fact that a legislature taxes its constituents who retain the power to turn them out of office.[102] This legitimating check did not exist, however, when a State sought to tax an instrumentality of the Federal Government. Just as the people of one State would not trust those of another State with a power to control even the most insignificant function of State Government, so, too, the people of the United States would never trust those of a State with this power over it. "In the legislature of the Union alone, are all represented. The

---

[93] License Cases, 46 U.S. (5 How.) 504, 583 (1847).

[94] *See* Universal Interpretive Shuttle Corp. v. Washington Metropolitan Area Transit Comm'n, 393 U.S. 186, 192 n.5 (1968); Munn v. Illinois, 94 U.S. (4 Otto) 113, 145 (1877).

[95] *Id.*

[96] Railroad Co. v. Husen, 95 U.S. (5 Otto) 465, 471 (1878).

[97] *Id.*

[98] Beer Co. v. Massachusetts, 97 U.S. (7 Otto) 25, 33 (1878).

[99] *See* Barbier v. Connolly, 113 U.S. 27, 31 (1885).

[100] Berman v. Parker, 348 U.S. 26, 32–33 (1954).

[101] Day-Brite Lighting v. Missouri, 342 U.S. 421, 424 (1952).

[102] *McCulloch*, 17 U.S. at 428.

legislature of the Union alone, therefore, can be trusted by the people with the power of controlling measures which concern all, in the confidence that it will not be abused."[103]

In an influential article, Professor Herbert Wechsler argued in 1954 that "the national political process in the United States — and especially the role of the states in the composition and selection of the central government — is intrinsically well adapted to retarding or restraining new intrusions by the center on the domain of the states."[104] Professor Wechsler noted that electors chosen by each State elect the President and that each State sent to Congress two Senators and a number of Representatives. Congress, not the Court, has "ultimate authority for managing our federalism"[105] argued Professor Wechsler. The main role the Framers saw for judicial review in federalism disputes "was the maintenance of national supremacy against nullification or usurpation by the individual states, the national government having no part in their composition or councils."[106] Professor Weschler thought the Court was "on weakest ground when it opposes its interpretation of the Constitution to that of Congress in the interest of the states . . . ."[107]

A quarter century later, Professor Jesse Choper advanced a "Federalism Proposal" which shared a common impulse with Wechsler's argument. He wrote:[108]

> The federal judiciary should not decide constitutional questions respecting the ultimate power of the national government vis-a-vis the states; rather, the constitutional issue of whether federal action is beyond the authority of the central government and thus violates "states' rights" should be treated as nonjusticiable, final resolution being relegated to the political branches — i.e., Congress and the President.

In *Garcia v. San Antonio Metropolitan Transit Authority*, the Court essentially adopted Professor Wechsler's analysis and Professor Choper's proposal. It found that "the principal means chosen by the Framers to ensure the role of the States in the federal system lies in the structure of the Federal Government itself."[109] In *Garcia*, the Court rejected the idea that the Tenth Amendment provided any judicially enforceable standards to protect States from generally applicable laws. In so doing, it argued that absent judicial enforcement of federalism norms the States would not be left vulnerable. The political system would afford them substantial protection consisting as it did of the States' representatives.[110] Justice Blackmun concluded:[111]

---

[103] *Id.* at 431.

[104] Herbert Wechsler, *The Political Safeguards of Federalism: The Role of the States in the Composition and Selection of the National Government*," 54 Colum. L. Rev. 543, 558 (1954).

[105] *Id.* at 560.

[106] *Id.* at 559.

[107] *Id.*

[108] Jesse H. Choper, Judicial Review and the National Political Process 175 (1980).

[109] *Garcia*, 469 U.S. at 550.

[110] *Garcia*, 469 U.S. at 550–54.

[111] *Id.* at 552.

In short, the Framers chose to rely on a federal system in which special restraints on federal power over the States inhered principally in the workings of the National Government itself, rather than in discrete limitations on the objects of federal authority. State sovereign interests, then, are more properly protected by procedural safeguards inherent in the structure of the federal system than by judicially created limitations on federal power.

Justice Blackmun's claim was, to be sure, controversial. In dissent, Justice Powell argued that the political process afforded insufficient protection for the States. Congressmen are "Members of the Federal Government" who are pulled to Washington and evidence a tendency to exceed the power given their institution.[112] Federal bureaucrats with no allegiance to the States draft and administer much federal legislation.[113] The role of the Electoral College in choosing the President does not make him the States' representative.[114] Even if the political process provided some safeguard, Justice Powell did not see it as reason to dispense with judicial protection as well.[115]

Political process arguments are not deployed exclusively to allow federal power at the expense of the States. In *New York v. United States*,[116] Justice O'Connor used political process arguments to support the Court's holding that the Federal Government could not compel States to regulate. When Washington forced States to regulate "the accountability of both state and federal officials is diminished."[117] Citizens may become confused regarding the source of unpopular regulation and blame local, instead of federal, officials.[118] "The Constitution . . . contemplates that a State's government will represent and remain accountable to its own citizens,"[119] observed Justice Scalia in *Printz v. United States*.

At times, political process arguments may push justices into seemingly inconsistent positions. In *Term Limits*, Justice Stevens argued for the majority that States could not impose additional qualifications on Senators and Congressmen because these officials were chosen by the people, not by the States,[120] and represent the people, not the States.[121] In the federal government, "representatives owe primary allegiance not to the people of a State, but to the people of the Nation."[122] Members of Congress were officers of the Union, not of their States. Their national character is underscored by the fact that their paycheck comes from

---

[112] *Id.* at 565 (Powell, J., dissenting).

[113] *Id.* at 576–77.

[114] *Id.* at 565.

[115] *Id.* at 565 n.8, 570.

[116] 505 U.S. 144 (1992).

[117] *Id.* at 168.

[118] *Id.* at 168–69.

[119] 521 U.S. 898, 921 (1997).

[120] *Term Limits*, 514 U.S. at 820–22.

[121] *Id.*

[122] *Id.* at 803.

the United States Treasury, not from the State in which they were chosen.[123] Yet Justice Stevens had joined Justice Blackmun's *Garcia* opinion which characterized Senators and Congressmen as representatives of the States that sent them, not of the nation. By the same token, the *Term Limits* dissenters viewed members of Congress as representatives of the States which selected them.[124] Chief Justice Rehnquist and Justice O'Connor joined this dissent although a decade earlier they joined Justice Powell's dissent in *Garcia* which argued that Congressmen acted as members of the National Government rather than as representatives of the States that elected them.

§ 5.04   SUPREMACY AND STATE TAXATION

[1]   Federal Immunity From State Taxation: An Overview

McCulloch v. Maryland[125] made clear that the Constitution precluded States from directly taxing the Federal Government. Maryland had sought to tax notes a branch of the Bank of the United States issued. Yet, as Marshall saw it, the power to tax involved the power to destroy. If a State could tax a federal agency it could essentially destroy it and thereby impair the operation of the Federal Government. The Bank of the United States must be immune from state taxation.

"The one constant here is, of course, is simple enough to express: a State may not, consistent with the Supremacy Clause, . . . lay a tax 'directly upon the United States.' "[126] *McCulloch* justified this principle not simply on the text of the Supremacy Clause. Rather, Chief Justice Marshall relied heavily on structural ideas about democracy to support his conclusion. In a democracy, a State would not over tax its residents since constituents could respond to any such abuse by replacing their government. But no such protection existed to prevent a State from oppressively taxing outsiders. A State could not be trusted to tax the Nation for it would have every incentive to impose the burden on nonresidents who would have no power to register their displeasure at the polls. The national government, where all were represented, could tax state institutions since these institutions enjoyed political representation in Congress. A State could not tax the whole, however, for some of those burdened had no avenue to gain political redress.

State power to tax federal functions and instrumentalities would be difficult to cabin. "If the States may tax one instrument, employed by the government in the execution of its powers, they may tax any and every other instrument,"[127] reasoned Chief Justice Marshall. He recited a parade of horribles ("They may tax the mail; they may tax the mint; . . .").[128] The simplest alternative is a bright line rule denying all such power. The Supreme Court "has never questioned the propriety of

---

[123] *Id.* at 809–10, 822.

[124] *Id.* at 857 (Thomas, J., dissenting).

[125] 17 U.S. (4 Wheat.) 316 (1819).

[126] United States v. New Mexico, 455 U.S. 720, 733 (1982).

[127] *McCulloch*, 17 U.S. at 432.

[128] *Id.*

absolute federal immunity from state taxation."[129]

Yet the bright line rule itself was difficult to restrain. Professor Paul A. Freund later observed that Marshall's power to tax/power to destroy formulation went "beyond the necessities of the case or the problem" and accordingly presented later generations with the need to devise more nuanced doctrine.[130]

Tax immunity exists only "when the levy falls on the United States itself, or on an agency or instrumentality so closely connected to the Government that the two cannot realistically be viewed as separate entities, at least insofar as the activity being taxed is concerned."[131] Federal tax immunity only applies if the tax falls on a body that is part of, or owned by, the Federal Government.

Thus, in *United States v. New Mexico*,[132] the Court held that private contractors who were managing government atomic laboratories were not immune from New Mexico's nondiscriminatory tax on gross receipts, sales, and use. Tax immunity did not exist simply because the Federal Government was affected by the tax on contractors or bore its burden. Nor were the contractors immune because they bought property for the Federal Government or because the tax fell on its earnings.[133] Tax immunity did not follow from simple agency status. Instead a private taxpayer must be incorporated into the government structure.[134] Here the contractors were not "constituent parts" of the Government but had a relationship with the Government "for limited and carefully defined purposes."[135] Accordingly the contractors were not immune from the gross receipts and use taxes. The sales tax posed a closer question since a purchasing agent might be so associated with the Government as to lack any independent role. The Court had so concluded in an earlier case[136] but the Court found that case distinguishable. There the purchase orders identified the Government as the purchaser, the contractor was not liable for the price and had no independent authority to order. Here the contractors bought items in their own name. The Court recently reaffirmed the doctrine from the case.[137]

McCulloch long supported a broad doctrine of tax immunity, which prevented a State from taxing the salary paid a federal officer.[138] No more. Federal officials have no immunity from nondiscriminatory state taxes imposed on all members of the community.[139] The Government is not burdened if its employees, like other

---

[129] *United States v. New Mexico*, 455 U.S. at 733.

[130] PAUL A. FREUND, ON LAW AND JUSTICE 13 (1968).

[131] *Id.* at 735. *See also* Arizona Dep't of Revenue v. Blaze Construction Co., 526 U.S. 32 (1999).

[132] 455 U.S. 720 (1982).

[133] *Id.* at 734–35.

[134] *Id.* at 737.

[135] *Id.* at 740–41.

[136] Kern-Limerick, Inc. v. Scurlock, 347 U.S. 110 (1954).

[137] *See* Arizona Dep't. of Revenue v. Blaze Const. Co., 526 U.S. 32 (1999).

[138] *See* Dobbins v. Commissioners of Erie County, 41 U.S. (16 Pet.) 435 (1842).

[139] *See* Graves v. New York *ex rel.* O'Keefe, 306 U.S. 466 (1939).

citizens, must pay taxes to state governments.[140]

Congress may, however, accord immunity beyond that implied from the Constitution. It may, for instance, exempt government contractors from state taxation.[141]

§ 5.05 SUPREMACY AND POLICE POWER

The Supremacy Clause also immunizes activities of the Federal Government from state regulation.[142] It has recognized "the fundamental importance of the principles shielding federal installations and activities from regulation by the States."[143] *Ohio v. Thomas*[144] established the principle in 1899. Ohio had convicted a federal officer for serving oleomargarine at a federal facility in violation of state law. Congress had, however, appropriated funds for purchase of the item and under these circumstances the federal official was exempt from state liability while discharging federal duties in accordance with law. More recently, the Court refused to allow a State to require federal installations to obtain state permits to discharge air or water pollutants.[145]

A State may not condition construction of a federal dam on the Federal Government getting approval of the state engineer.[146] If Congress has power to authorize the dam it need not get state permission to build it.

Johnson v. Maryland[147] illustrates the criteria for immunity. It reversed the state conviction of a Federal Government-mail truck driver for operating without a state driver's license. Justice Holmes thought Johnson not entitled to "a general immunity" from all state law which might incidentally affect his work, like rules regarding traffic signals or state negligence laws. Yet he concluded that a State could not require a federal employee to desist from performing his duties until he satisfied a state official.[148] The Court distinguished general rules that affect the federal employment incidentally, (in which the federal employee is subject to local law,[149] e.g., regulating turning at street corners), from situations like *Johnson* when the State tries to prescribe directly how a federal agency operates.

---

[140] *See* New York v. United States, 326 U.S. 572, 578 (1946).

[141] *United States v. New Mexico*, 455 U.S. at 744; *see also* Arizona Dep't. of Revenue v. Blaze Constr. Co., 526 U.S. 32 (1999).

[142] *See* Hancock v. Train, 426 U.S. 167, 178–79 (1976).

[143] *Id.* at 179.

[144] 173 U.S. 276 (1899).

[145] *See* Hancock v. Train, 426 U.S. 167 (1976); EPA v. California, 426 U.S. 200 (1976).

[146] Arizona v. California, 283 U.S. 423, 451–52 (1931).

[147] 254 U.S. 51 (1920).

[148] *Id.* at 57.

[149] United States v. Hart, 26 F. Cas. 193 (C.C.D. Pa. 1817).

§ 5.06 STATE TAX IMMUNITIES

McCulloch v. Maryland[150] may have suggested implicitly a reciprocal doctrine of intergovernmental immunity protecting both State and Federal Government.[151] Just as federal agencies could be destroyed by state taxation, state agencies would be vulnerable to federal taxation. *Collector v. Day*[152] held the salary of a state officer not subject to federal taxation. Because the Court then viewed a tax on income as a tax on its source, this holding reflected a symmetrical treatment of state and federal tax immunity. The Court also recognized private tax immunities comparable to those for federal government contractors.[153]

After the Court abandoned the theory that a tax on income is a tax on its source, *Day* and its progeny were overruled.[154] State employees and private persons who deal with the States no longer enjoy federal tax immunity, even though the taxation may burden the States concerned. An economic burden alone cannot support a claim of state immunity.[155] Even the holding that state bond interest was immune from a nondiscriminatory federal tax was overruled in *South Carolina v. Baker*.[156]

§ 5.07 STATE REGULATORY IMMUNITIES

A different problem arises regarding federal efforts to subject the States to the same regulatory laws applicable to individuals. The problem may be simply posed. Congress passes a law regulating, say minimum wages to be paid employees. The law is made applicable to States as well as private employers. Conceding that Congress has power to pass the law under the Commerce Clause, do the States merit some exemption by virtue of the fact that they are States?

Until 1976, the state autonomy argument won little support from the Court. In 1936, the Court held a state-owned railroad subject to the Federal Safety Appliance Act.[157] The Court rejected California's claims of certain state immunity from federal regulation. Similarly, in 1968, the Court upheld application of the Fair Labor Standards Act to state schools and hospitals.[158] Significantly, however, Justice Douglas' dissent criticized the measure as a violation of "state sovereignty protected by the Tenth Amendment."[159]

---

[150] 17 U.S. 316 (1819).

[151] *See New York v. United States*, 326 U.S. at 576.

[152] 78 U.S. (11 Wall.) 113 (1871).

[153] *See, e.g.*, Burnet v. Coronado Oil & Gas Co., 285 U.S. 393 (1932); Indian Motorcycle Co. v. United States, 283 U.S. 570 (1931).

[154] *See* Graves v. New York *ex rel.* O'Keefe, 306 U.S. 466 (1939) and Helvering v. Gerhardt, 304 U.S. 405 (1938), overruling *Day*; Helvering v. Mountain Producers Corp., 303 U.S. 376 (1938), overruling *Burnet*.

[155] *See Massachusetts v. United States*, 435 U.S. 444, 461 (1978).

[156] 485 U.S. 505 (1988).

[157] *See* United States v. California, 297 U.S. 175 (1936).

[158] *See* Maryland v. Wirtz, 392 U.S. 183 (1968).

[159] *Id.* at 201.

Since then, as the Court has conceded, its "jurisprudence in this area has traveled an unsteady path."[160] It gave sharply opposed answers in *National League of Cities v. Usery*,[161] and *Garcia v. San Antonio Metropolitan Transit Authority*,[162] decided only nine years apart. In *National League of Cities*, the Court ruled in a 5-4 decision that Congress could not subject the States to wage and hour requirements previously imposed on private employers. In so doing, it overruled in part *Wirtz*, which was decided only eight years earlier. The Court separated federal regulation of private, from public, employment and distinguished decisions establishing broad congressional authority under the Commerce Clause as involving laws regulating private entrepreneurs. A different situation arises, said the Court, when Congress exercises the commerce power in a manner infringing the states' role as essential elements of the federal system.

National League of Cities held that the Commerce Clause does not authorize regulation "directed . . . to the States as States."[163] States were immune from federal control infringing on their "freedom to structure integral operations in areas of traditional governmental functions."[164] The challenged provision violated this immunity by displacing states' choices in employment policies. Congress could not wield its commerce power to impair the states' "separate and independent existence"[165] — a concept implicit in the federal system. Justice Blackmun, who provided the majority's fifth vote, viewed its opinion as creating a balancing test that considered the weight of the federal interest involved.[166]

Garcia reached a diametrically opposed result only nine years later in another 5-4 decision. The Court might have held simply that operation of a mass-transit system was not a "traditional governmental function" and thus not exempt under *National League of Cities* from a federal regulatory law.[167] Such an analysis would have reached the same result (upheld the federal statute as applied) but preserved *National League of Cities*. Instead Justice Blackmun now changed course and wrote the Court's opinion overruling *National League of Cities* itself.

The Court furnished two principal reasons for overruling *National League of Cities*: (1) "the attempt to draw the boundaries of state regulatory immunity in terms of 'traditional governmental function' is . . . unworkable," and (2) such an attempt is "inconsistent with established principles of federalism."[168]

The Court concluded that the "traditional function" test was unworkable based on an analysis of cases applying it. A historical test could not accommodate change and failed to produce the promised certainty. Justice Blackmun found it "difficult,

---

[160] New York v. United States, 505 U.S. 144, 160 (1992).

[161] 426 U.S. 833 (1976).

[162] 469 U.S. 528 (1985).

[163] 426 U.S. at 845.

[164] *Id.* at 852.

[165] *Id.* at 845.

[166] *See id.* at 856.

[167] *See* Transportation Union v. Long Island R. R. Co., 455 U.S. 678 (1982).

[168] *Garcia*, 469 U.S. at 531, 546–47.

if not impossible, to identify an organizing principle" to separate state functions protected under *National League of Cities* from those subject to federal regulation. A historical standard could not truly provide the promised objectivity; various nonhistorical approaches also held little potential.[169] Trying to identify "uniquely" or "necessary" governmental services was futile and would dispatch courts on an exercise beyond their competence.

Garcia also rejected the underlying premise of *National League of Cities* — that federalism imposed judicially enforceable restrictions on the Commerce Clause and on congressional regulatory authority over the States. *National League of Cities* had declared that the Constitution prohibits federal regulation interfering with "traditional aspects of state sovereignty" which led to the "traditional governmental functions" test *Garcia* found problematic. *Garcia* rejected the view that the courts could rely on different attributes of state sovereignty to identify "principled constitutional limitations" on the commerce power. Indeed, according to Justice Blackmun, "the Constitution does not carve out express elements of state sovereignty that Congress may not employ its delegated powers to displace."[170] It is not for the courts "to employ freestanding conceptions of state sovereignty when measuring congressional authority under the Commerce Clause."[171]

How does this impact the States' relationship to federal regulatory authority? Obviously, State independence and autonomy are inconsistent with complete subjection to federal regulatory power. *Garcia* does not disagree with this; it acknowledges the Framers' interest "to ensure the role of the States in the federal system." But *Garcia* concludes that protecting the States from improper exertions of federal authority is not a judicial function. Instead, "the principal means . . . to ensure the role of the States in the federal system lies in the structure of the Federal Government itself."[172] The States' representation in Congress and role in selecting the executive and legislative branches of the Federal Government will protect them from undue federal invasion. Ultimately, the States must rely on the federal political process, not judicially enforceable constitutional limitations, to protect them from undue congressional encroachment. As such, the *Garcia* Court embraced the concept of political safeguards of federalism which Professor Wechsler had advanced in the 1950s and which echoed some of the ideas from Chief Justice Marshall's *Gibbons* opinion. Under *Garcia*, the scope of Congress' authority over the States under the Commerce Clause does not present a judicial question.

Garcia provoked three dissents reflecting the views of four members. Justice Powell criticized the Court's failure to defer to *stare decisis*, an argument whose force was somewhat limited by the fact that the overruled case, *National League of Cities*, had itself shown no deference to the precedent it displaced. Justice Powell reasoned that the Court's duty was to say what the law is and the balancing test the Court abandoned was an appropriate judicial intervention. The political process would provide little protection for the States. Members of the National Government

---

[169] *See id.* at 539.

[170] *Id.* at 550.

[171] *Id.*

[172] *Id.*

were federalized. They could not be expected to protect the States because their outlook was distinctly biased in favor of national interests by their beltway orientation. In any event, States were entitled to constitutional, not simply political, protection. Justice Rehnquist and Justice O'Connor each predicted that the Court would eventually police this area again. This pronouncement raised doubts about the stability of *Garcia* as a precedent.[173] Yet *Garcia* has remained on the books for more than 25 years, notwithstanding the addition of Justice Thomas to create a majority in many other federalism cases. Its survival may reflect a sense that the Court would be subjected to criticism if, having revised *Wirtz* and *National League of Cities*, it again shifted course by overturning *Garcia*. Alternatively, some justices necessary to form a majority against *Garcia* may be unwilling to return to a balancing test to immunize states from some generally applicable federal laws.

§ 5.08   COOPERATIVE FEDERALISM

[1]   The Federal Government and the States

The existence of two governments, Federal and State, can create friction as they each pursue their particular goals. In practice, they have tended to work well together. The Federal Government has frequently used state officers to implement its programs.

In recent years, congressional statutes have sought to enlist various state agencies in implementing federal programs. Must States lend their officials to execution of federal statutes? Absent State consent, can the National Government assign state officials duties under federal law?

The Supremacy Clause, of course, makes federal law the supreme law of the land. State officials must obey federal laws within Congress' powers.

Testa v. Katt[174] illustrates congressional power to bind state courts. In the Emergency Price Control Act, Congress authorized a person charged excessive prices to sue for treble damages in "any court of competent jurisdiction" — federal, state, or territorial. After suit was brought, the highest state court held the federal statute a "penal statute" that its state courts could not be required to enforce. The Supreme Court reversed, holding that the state court decision ignored the Supremacy Clause. Congress could constitutionally require state courts to adjudicate cases involving, and to decide cases according to, federal laws, including those contrary to local laws and policies.[175] Clearly, the Constitution contemplated that State courts would adjudicate some matters under federal law. The Supremacy Clause itself reflected that expectation as did the Madisonian Compromise which left creation of lower Federal Courts to Congress' discretion.

---

[173] *See id.* at 580 (Rehnquist), 589 (O'Connor).

[174] 330 U.S. 386 (1947).

[175] *See* Palmore v. United States, 411 U.S. 389, 402 (1973).

Federal power encounters limits, however, when it seeks to require States to regulate in accordance with Federal wishes. In *New York v. United States*,[176] the Court struck down a federal law that required a State that failed to plan for disposal of radioactive waste by a particular date to assume ownership and possession of the waste and to become liable for damages suffered by failure to do so. Clearly Congress had power under the Commerce Clause to address the problem of radioactive waste by "requiring or prohibiting certain acts." It lacked power, however, "to compel the States to require or prohibit those acts."[177] The Court concluded that the "take title" provision gave the States a "choice" between two unconstitutionally coercive alternatives — either accept ownership of private waste within its borders or regulate according to Congress' instructions. Congress could not compel the States to take either course so the choice between the two options was really no choice at all. As such, the provision invalidly attempted to "commandeer" States into federal service. "The Federal Government may not compel the States to enact or administer a federal regulatory program."[178] Relying on structural notions of federalism suggested by the Tenth Amendment, the Court concluded that State Governments are not regional offices or agencies of the Federal Government. Justice O'Connor also invoked a political process rationale in support of the majority's conclusion. She raised the spectre that when the Federal Government forced the State to act in a particular way, voters might misperceive the action as reflecting the preferences of the state officials and hold them accountable.

The Court was careful to distinguish, and bless, other regulatory techniques which Congress used in other parts of the statute. Congress could authorize States with disposal sites to tax radioactive waste from other States and then use a portion of the revenue to reward States complying with the federal program. The Commerce, Taxing and Spending powers authorized such an approach.[179] Congress also could authorize States with disposal sites to increase the cost of access to the sites. Since Congress could regulate the subject itself, it could give the States the option of regulating instead according to federal standards.[180]

Justice White wrote a vigorous dissent in which he castigated the Court's formalistic approach. He suggested a more flexible approach to federalism issues similar in some respects to the doctrine he had urged regarding separation of powers. Although he did not reject the Court's anticommandeering principle, he argued that in reality the facts at issue did not suggest coercion as the Court claimed. Rather, he said, Congress had simply responded to requests from state officials who helped tailor the federal statute. But Justice O'Connor replied that the involvement of state officials was irrelevant. "State officials cannot consent to the enlargement of" federal powers beyond constitutional bounds[181] because those

---

[176] 505 U.S. 144 (1992).

[177] *Id.* at 166.

[178] *Id.* at 188.

[179] *Id.* at 171–72.

[180] *Id.* at 173–74.

[181] *Id.* at 182.

limits are to protect individuals from concentrated power.[182] *Printz v. United States*[183] applied *New York v. United States* to strike down the Brady Act, a law Congress passed commanding local law enforcement officers to investigate prospective handgun purchasers and to perform certain related tasks. The Brady Act, in effect, compelled state officers to help administer a federal regulatory scheme. The Court ruled unconstitutional such congressional action compelling state officers to execute federal laws. The Constitution rejects the concept of a central government that may conscript state officers. Whereas *New York* precluded Congress from telling a state legislature what law to pass, *Printz* inhibited Congress from mandating that state executive officials administrater a federal program.

Printz was decided over vigorous dissents reflecting views of four justices. They found the Commerce Clause and Necessary and Proper Clause conferred the requisite federal power with no textual protection for the States. Historical materials, the dissenters argued, suggested the framers intended the Federal Government often to act though local officials.

New York v. United States and *Printz* clearly limit the ability of the Federal Government to require state legislators or state administration offices to run a federal program. They do not, however, preclude the Federal Government from influencing state conduct. Congress may itself regulate within areas within its power; it simply cannot direct state executive or legislative personnel to do its work for it. This is not to say that the Federal Government can impose no burden on State Government. The *Printz* majority distinguished the "precise issue" it addressed — "the forced participation of the states' executive in the actual administration of a federal program" — from federal statutes that simply require state officials to provide information to the Federal Government.[184] To be sure, the Court did not sanction such provisions but Justice O'Connor's concurrence at least hints that she thinks such measures pass constitutional muster.[185] Congress can clearly obtain state participation in federal programs by attaching conditions to appropriations. Thus, Congress can use the Spending Power, consistent with the criteria set out in *South Dakota v. Dole*[186] to persuade States to help implement a Federal program. Moreover, *Testa v. Katt* remains valid in its conclusion that Congress may require state courts to decide federal issues according to federal law. The specific constitutional recognition of this expectation for state courts which is contained in the Supremacy Clause caused the Court to view this situation differently.

Finally, in *Reno v. Condon*[187] the Court made clear that the principle of these cases does not obliterate all federal power to burden State officials. The Drivers Privacy Protection Act of 1994 (DPPA) regulated the disclosure and resale of

---

[182] *Id.* at 181.

[183] 521 U.S. 898 (1997).

[184] *Id.* at 918.

[185] *See id.* at 936.

[186] 483 U.S. 203 (1987).

[187] 528 U.S. 141 (2000).

personal information from State driver's licenses, an activity in which many States were engaged. To be sure, DPPA would require time and effort of State officials but this burden did not bring it within the proscription of *New York v. United States* and *Printz*.[188] Moreover, DPPA addressed State activities rather than the State's regulation of private activities.[189]

[2] Litigating Against a State

The doctrine of sovereign immunity limits the ability of courts to entertain lawsuits against States. The doctrine does not apply when the United States sues a State or when one State sues another. In either instance, the States are deemed to have waived any immunity by approving the Constitution. The question arises, however, regarding the extent to which a State can be sued in federal or state court by a private party. In recent years, the Court has issued a number of opinions which recognize a broader immunity of States from litigation. The Constitution speaks most directly to this subject in the Eleventh Amendment which provides: "The Judicial power of the United States shall not be construed to extend to any suit in law or equity, commenced or prosecuted against one of the United States by Citizens of another State, or by Citizens or Subjects of any Foreign State." The text of the Eleventh Amendment, of course, speaks to diversity cases, prohibiting in federal court a citizen of State A from suing State B. Its text does not address cases which raise federal questions although judicial doctrine makes clear that State sovereign immunity generally exists there, too.

The Eleventh Amendment responded to *Chisholm v. Georgia*[190] in which the Court held it had jurisdiction to decide a case between citizens of South Carolina seeking to recover a debt from Georgia. The justices had all helped form the Constitution and they upheld their jurisdiction in a 4-1 decision. Article III conferred federal jurisdiction over "controversies — between a State and citizens of another State," which would seem to cover the matter unless it applied only when the State was a plaintiff. But the Court's original jurisdiction applied to cases "in which a State shall be party," a broader formulation that arguably suggested a State could sue or be sued in federal court, though not itself dispositive of the issue raised in *Chisholm*. Nonetheless, some evidence suggests at least some framers did not intend to subject States to suit without their consent.[191]

In any event, *Chisholm* produced an outcry of opposition that culminated in the Eleventh Amendment. Although the text of the Amendment simply addressed the diversity situation of *Chisholm*, it was later construed to have broader meaning. In *Hans v. Louisiana*[192] the Court held that some principle of sovereign immunity precluded suit in federal court against a State even by its own citizen based on a federal claim.

---

[188] *Id.* at 150.

[189] *Id.*

[190] 2 U.S. (2 Dall.) 419 (1793).

[191] *See* THE FEDERALIST No. 81 (Alexander Hamilton).

[192] 134 U.S. 1 (1890).

Seminole Tribe v. Florida[193] broadened the state immunity from suit. The case was significant for the specific issue it decided as well as for its place as a key marker in the federalism work of the Rehnquist Court, decided as it was a year after *Lopez* by the same court division. A federal statute provided that an Indian tribe could conduct certain gaming activities only under a compact between the tribe and the pertinent State. The law, passed under the Indian Commerce Clause,[194] obligated the States to negotiate in good faith with an Indian tribe toward the formation of a compact and authorized a tribe to sue a State in federal court to compel performance of that duty. Two previous cases had upheld Congress in abrogating State sovereign immunity.[195] The Court in a 5-4 decision circumscribed Congress' ability to abrogate a State's sovereign immunity in federal court. Chief Justice Rehnquist's majority opinion reasoned that the Eleventh Amendment expresses a constitutional principle that State sovereign immunity limits the federal courts' Article III jurisdiction. The Court held that the Indian Commerce Clause does not grant Congress power to remove the States' sovereign immunity; consequently the statute cannot grant jurisdiction over a State absent its consent. In essence, the Court held that Congress' Article I powers (e.g., Commerce Clause) did not allow it to subject a State to suit in federal court for an alleged breach of a federal right. The Seminole Tribe's suit against Florida had to be dismissed.

Seminole Tribe limited Congress' ability to abrogate a State's Eleventh Amendment immunity from suit. *Union Gas*[196] had held in 1989 that the Commerce Clause empowered Congress to abrogate State immunity from suit. *Seminole Tribe* expressly overruled *Union Gas* and confined Congress' power to abrogate State Eleventh Amendment immunity to legislation under its enforcement power pursuant to the Fourteenth Amendment[197] which was adopted well after the Eleventh Amendment and which altered the pre-existing balance between State and Federal power under both Article III and the Eleventh Amendment. Eleventh Amendment immunity from suit does not otherwise yield when the suit involves an area, like regulation of Indian commerce, that is under exclusive federal control pursuant to power confirmed in Article I. "The Eleventh Amendment restricts the judicial power under Article III, and Article I cannot be used to circumvent the constitutional limitations placed upon federal jurisdiction."[198]

Although this language seems to apply to *any* Article I power, the Court subsequently recognized one instance in which Congress could make a State amenable to certain judicial proceedings pursuant to an Article I power. In *Central Community College v. Katz*, the Court rejected the sovereign immunity defense

---

[193] 517 U.S. 44 (1996).

[194] "The Congress shall have Power . . . To regulate Commerce . . . with the Indian Tribes." Article I, § 8.

[195] Pennsylvania v. Union Gas Co., 491 U.S. 1 (1989); Fitzpatrick v. Bitzer, 427 U.S. 445 (1976).

[196] Pennsylvania v. Union Gas Co., 491 U.S. 1 (1989). *Union Gas* was decided by a 5-4 vote; Justice White provided the fifth vote but disagreed with the analysis of his four colleagues.

[197] *See* Fitzpatrick v. Bitzer, 427 U.S. 445 (1976).

[198] *Seminole Tribe*, 517 U.S. at 72–73.

advanced by state agencies in the context of bankruptcy proceedings.[199] In a 5-4 decision, with the four justices who dissented in *Seminole Tribe* and *Alden v. Maine* joined by Justice O'Connor in the majority, the Court held that Congress' determination that the States should be amenable to proceedings to recover preferential transfers paid by a debtor was within Congress' power under the Bankruptcy Clause.[200] The majority reasoned that the assumption in *Seminole Tribe* that its holding would apply to the Bankruptcy Clause was erroneous and not fully debated, and therefore, the Court was not bound to follow the dicta quoted above.[201]

Based largely on its interpretation of the origins and early history of the Bankruptcy Clause, the Court concluded that in the Constitution the States waived any sovereign immunity defense in bankruptcy proceedings.[202] The dissent, written by Justice Thomas and joined by Chief Justice Roberts, Justice Scalia, and Justice Kennedy, argued that "[n]othing in the text, structure, or history of the Constitution indicates that the Bankruptcy Clause, in contrast to all of the other provisions of Article I, manifests the States' consent to be sued by private citizens.

Although the Court's decision in *Central Virginia Community College* seems to retreat from the protections afforded to State sovereign immunity in *Seminole Tribe* and its progeny, the fact that the Court grounded its holding in the unique nature of bankruptcy proceedings and the Bankruptcy Clause itself, and not in Congress' recent statutory attempt to abrogate state immunity in bankruptcy proceedings, distinguishes *Central Virginia Community College* from cases involving other Article I powers and suggests that the Court's reasoning in *Seminole Tribe* will continue to prevent Congress from abrogating sovereign immunity under these other Article I powers.

Seminole Tribe contracted the ability of the Federal Government to regulate state economic activities. Still, it did not strip the Federal Government of all ability to allow private citizens to sue States. In appropriate cases, Congress could still override the State's sovereign immunity under its § 5 enforcement powers under the Fourteenth Amendment. Moreover, since *Seminole Tribe* involved suit in federal court, it left open the possibility that Congress could subject States to suit by private citizens in state court.

In three decisions rendered on June 23, 1999 at the close of its 1998–99 term, the Court narrowed or closed those possibilities. Most significantly, in *Alden v. Maine*,[203] the Court held that Congress cannot, under Article I, subject a State against its will to suit by a private party for damages in state court. It thus held that the protection *Seminole Tribe* recognized, applied in State, as well as federal court. In two other cases decided the same day, the Court narrowed Congress' ability to abrogate State sovereign immunity under § 5 of the Fourteenth Amendment. All three cases rested on the same 5-4 split indicating how divided the

---

[199] 546 U.S. 356, 359 (2006).

[200] U.S. Const. art. I, § 8, cl. 4.

[201] *Central Community College,* 546 U.S. at 363.

[202] *Id.* at 368–79.

[203] 527 U.S. 706 (1999).

Rehnquist Court was on these federalism issues.

Not only did *Alden v. Maine* extend the Court's Eleventh Amendment jurisprudence, but it also reflected distinctive attitudes on several fundamental issues in constitutional law. In *Alden*, the Court further defined its attitude on federalism in a manner which reflected expanding deference to the notion of State sovereignty against claims by individuals based on federal law, while leaving less room in which federal law could operate. The decision also had implications for separation of powers; *Alden* and its companion cases accorded Congress less room to legislate and reflected a willingness of the federal judiciary to police more vigorously the boundaries which limit Congress' authority. Finally, *Alden* in particular reflected a willingness to engage in multiple forms of constitutional argument to circumvent arguably relevant textual language.

In *Alden*, Maine employees sued their employer, Maine, for compensatory damages for alleged violations of the Fair Labor Standards Act overtime provision. Their initial law suit in federal court was dismissed based on *Seminole Tribe* prompting plaintiffs to refile in Maine state courts. After the Maine courts dismissed the action based on sovereign immunity, the case came to the Supreme Court on certiorari.

In an opinion by Justice Kennedy, the majority[204] acknowledged that the Eleventh Amendment is neither the source, nor a limitation, of the State's sovereign immunity. That doctrine, the majority contended, "is a fundamental aspect of the sovereignty which the States enjoyed before ratification of the Constitution and which they retain today" except to the extent altered by the Constitution.[205]

The majority recognized that the text of the Eleventh Amendment afforded no support. Indeed, to a strict textualist it might be thought to embarrass the majority's position. Since the Eleventh Amendment by its language limits only "the Judicial power of the United States" from extending to suits "commenced or prosecuted against one of the United States by Citizens of another State,"[206] one might invoke the maxim *expressio unius* to argue that the Amendment accordingly leaves open suits in federal courts against the States by their own citizens and suits against States generally in non-federal fora. Moreover, one might argue that absent any textual limit preventing Congress from allowing employees to sue their State in state court, the Commerce and Necessary and Proper Clauses furnished such power.

The majority parried that suggestion by arguing that the Eleventh Amendment was intended simply to overrule *Chisholm v. Georgia*[207] which had allowed suit against Georgia by a citizen of another State. In the Eleventh Amendment, the Court said, Congress "chose not to enact language codifying the traditional

---

[204] Consisting of Chief Justice Rehnquist and Justices O'Connor, Scalia, Kennedy, and Thomas.

[205] *Alden*, 527 U.S. at 713.

[206] U.S. CONST. amend. XI.

[207] 2 U.S. (2 Dall.) 419 (1793).

understanding of sovereign immunity" but to overturn *Chisholm*.[208] Since "[t]he Eleventh Amendment confirmed rather than, established sovereign immunity as a constitutional principle," it did not define the scope of the constitutional protection.[209] The majority instead relied on three other types of constitutional arguments — structural, original intent, and judicial doctrine — to reach its result.

The majority devoted much of its opinion to establishing that those who drafted and ratified the original Constitution and the Eleventh Amendment were committed to the principle of States' sovereign immunity. This discussion provoked a lengthy response by Justice Souter, which Justices Stevens, Ginsburg and Breyer joined. Justice Souter deemed "insupportable" the majority's suggestion that any notion of sovereign immunity shielded States from suit under federal law "on a subject committed to national jurisdiction by Article I.[210] Sovereign immunity was, at best, a common law protection which lacked constitutional status. Accordingly, he argued, Congress could override the states' immunity in the exercise of its legislative power.

The majority also rested its decision on "the structure of the Constitution" namely "the essential principles of federalism and. the special role of the state courts in the constitutional design.[211] The *Alden* majority again found refuge in the Tenth Amendment as "confirm[ing] the promise implicit in the original document" regarding the states' role as sovereign entities.[212] The Tenth Amendment had once been dismissed as a "tautology" but some members of the Court have more recently inferred from it structural principles to fortify their notions of State sovereignty, a position the dissent derided.

The Court repeatedly invoked a notion of State "dignity" which it regarded as offended by suit in federal or state court. If the Constitution does not protect States from private suits for money, the Federal Government would be able to impair the financial integrity of the States, posing "a severe and notorious danger to the States and their resources."[213] The majority reasoned that the ability of the States to govern according to their wishes would be imperilled, reflecting a variant of the vice of federal commandeering the Court condemned in *New York v. United States*[214] and *Printz v. United States*.[215]

The dissenters were not persuaded. Justice Souter invoked John Marshall's proposition from *McCulloch v. Maryland*:

> In America, the powers of sovereignty are divided between the govern-
> ment of the Union, and those of the States. They are each sovereign, with
> respect to the objects committed to it, and neither sovereign with respect

---

[208] *Alden*, 527 U.S. at 723.

[209] *Id.* at 728–29.

[210] *Id.* at 762.

[211] *Id.* at 748.

[212] *Id.* at 714.

[213] *Id.* at 750.

[214] 505 U.S. 144 (1992).

[215] 521 U.S. 898 (1997).

to the objects committed to the other.[216]

Justice Souter argued that the Nation, not the States, is sovereign regarding the "national objective of the FLSA."[217] Notwithstanding the merits of any claims the States might have regarding areas where sovereignty was assigned to them, the States could claim no sovereign immunity in an area delegated to the Federal Government. Moreover, the Court's reliance on State dignity ran counter to the basic republican idea that government is of, by and for the people, not above them — that government is subject to law.

The Court further extended the doctrine of State sovereign immunity in *Federal Maritime Commission v. South Carolina State Ports Authority*.[218] In another 5-4 decision, the Court held that State sovereign immunity prohibits executive administrative agencies from adjudicating the claims of private parties against unconsenting States. After its requests to berth a ship were denied by South Carolina State Ports Authority (SCSPA), South Carolina Maritime Services, Inc. (Maritime Services) filed a complaint with the Federal Maritime Commission (FMC) seeking compensatory and injunctive relief. Justice Thomas, for the Court, reaffirmed that "the sovereign immunity enjoyed by the States extends beyond the literal text of the Eleventh Amendment."[219] The Framers did not intend the States to be subject to proceedings which were " 'anomalous and unheard of when the Constitution was adopted."[220] Observing the "strong similarities between FMC proceedings and civil litigation," the Court concluded that "[t]he affront to a State's dignity does not lessen when an adjudication takes place in an administrative tribunal as opposed to an Article III court."[221]

Justice Breyer wrote a dissent which Justices Stevens, Souter and Ginsburg joined. Though reasserting that *Seminole Tribe* and *Alden* were wrongly decided the dissenters argued that the Court's decision could not even stand on those precedents. Administrative proceedings typically involve Executive Branch agencies exercising Executive Branch powers to determine whether a state agency violated federal law. Such a paradigm stands outside the language or concerns of the Eleventh and Tenth Amendments. The decision "threatens to deny the Executive and Legislative Branches of Government the structural flexibility that the Constitution permits and which modern government demands."[222] It "set loose an interpretative principle that restricts far too severely the authority of the Federal Government to regulate innumerable relationships between State and citizen."[223]

---

[216] 17 U.S. (4 Wheat.) 316, 410 (1819).

[217] *Alden*, 527 U.S. at 800.

[218] 535 U.S. 743 (2002).

[219] *Id.* at 754.

[220] *Id.* at 755.

[221] *Id.* at 760.

[222] *Id.* at 786.

[223] *Id.* at 788.

These sovereign immunity decisions tested the notion that remedies should be available to vindicate violations of rights. In his *Alden* dissent, Justice Souter reminded that *Garcia v. San Antonio Metropolitan Transit Authority*,[224] established Congress' power to extend FLSA to state employees. *Garcia*, he argued, was not at issue and remained law. One might wonder, however, how much potency *Garcia* retains. It was decided over four dissenting voices, two of whom, then Justices Rehnquist and O'Connor, suggested it would one day be overruled. Although *Garcia* allows Congress to extend FLSA to state employees, *Seminole Tribe* and *Alden* prevent those same employees from vindicating any rights to money damages against an offending State in either federal or state court. *Garcia*, of course, overruled *National League of Cities v. Usery*,[225] which had held that Congress could not regulate traditional state activities. The *Garcia* majority regarded that standard as unworkable and ill-considered. Ironically, *Alden*, to some extent, goes beyond *Usery* since it largely immunizes State Governments not only when they engage in traditional state activity but when they act as entrepreneurs or in a manner the framers could not anticipate. *Garcia* has clearly suffered some significant erosion and may now offer little solace to state employees whose rights may be violated, but it is not *totally* compromised by *Seminole Tribe* and *Alden*. The sovereign immunity the Court recognized in this line of cases precludes lawsuits against States but not against lesser entities — cities, counties, officers. *Garcia's* survival juxtaposed with *Seminole Tribe* and *Alden*, introduces the anomalous situation of a private right to damages for violation of FLSA without a private remedy to vindicate that right against a State since *Seminole Tribe* and *Alden* precluded private citizens from suing States to recover money damages. Accordingly, several million state employees cannot seek monetary relief for violations by their employers. Certainly, the availability of remedies to enforce rights is a basic tenet of the Rule of Law. As John Marshall put it in *Marbury v. Madison*, the "very essence of civil liberty" is "the right of every individual to claim the protection of the laws, whenever he receives an injury."[226] The United State government will forfeit the "high appellation" of "a government of laws, and not of men," he said, "if the laws furnish no remedy for the violation of a vested legal right.[227]

Of course, the States are not immune from all remedies. The Department of Labor may sue to seek damages.[228] Prospective injunctive and declaratory relief may also be available against the responsible state official. Injured parties may also sue a state official personally for his/her wrongful or unconstitutional activity.

The question remains how efficacious these remaining remedies will be. The Department of Labor will not have the same personal interest or perhaps resolve that private parties might have. Moreover, it is somewhat ironic that a decision intended in part to protect the States from federal overreaching would prevent private citizens from seeking to vindicate harm they have suffered but would allow federal bureaucrats to litigate. Such a result creates an incentive to expand the

---

[224] 469 U.S. 528 (1985).

[225] 426 U.S. 833 (1976).

[226] 5 U.S. (1 Cranch) 137, 163 (1803).

[227] *Id.* at 163.

[228] 29 U.S.C. § 216(c).

Federal Government's litigation forces. Unless Congress grows the federal bureau-cracy with legions of new lawyers, an unlikely prospect these days, the government is unlikely to have the personnel to press these issues. This raises the specter of States violating federal law with impunity.

Sovereign immunity does not bar lawsuits a State consents to defend. States may and do waive sovereign immunity in some types of cases in response to political pressure. In this sense, the doctrine is not jurisdictional since the State may waive its defense. But in a companion case to *Alden*, the Court limited the situations in which it will find a State consented to be sued. In *College Savings Bank v. Florida Prepaid Postsecondary Education Expense Board*,[229] plaintiff sought to sue a State under the Lanham Act for allegedly making false claims regarding its product. Plaintiff claimed in part that Florida had constructively waived any sovereign immunity by engaging in activity Congress made clear would subject it to suit. The Court rejected the constructive waiver doctrine of *Parden v. Terminal Railway of the Alabama State Docks Department*,[230] a precedent of 35 years standing. In *Parden*, the Court had held that a State waived its Eleventh Amendment immunity by operating a railroad in interstate commerce. Congress had "conditioned the right to operate a railroad in interstate commerce upon amenability to suit in federal court."[231] By operating a railroad Alabama had constructively consented to suit. Although the four *Parden* dissenters thought waiver should not be inferred absent a clearer congressional statement of intent, all nine members of the *Parden* Court thought Congress had power "to condition a state's permit to engage in [federally regulated commercial conduct] on a waiver of the State's sovereign immunity from suits arising out of such business."[232] The doctrine had been eroded over the years by a series of decisions that essentially embraced the *Parden* dissenters' position in favor of a clear statement rule. Although the application of such a rule had signaled that constructive waiver was disfavored, the Court had not contradicted *Parden's* unanimous determination that the Court had power to condition certain state activity on waiver of Eleventh Amendment immunity.[233] In *College Savings Bank*, the Court declined "to salvage any remnant" of the constructive waiver doctrine.[234]

A State could waive its sovereign immunity only by its clear statement to that effect or by invoking the court's jurisdiction. Consent could not be inferred where a State voluntarily elects to participate in discretionary conduct the Federal Government regulates even when Congress had clearly specified that such conduct would subject it to suit. The Court, in its aversion to constructive waiver of sovereign immunity, relied on doctrine disfavoring constructive waiver when other constitu-tionally protected rights were at stake. "State sovereign immunity, no less than the right to trial by jury in criminal cases, is constitutionally protected," wrote Justice

---

[229] 527 U.S. 666 (1999).

[230] 377 U.S. 184 (1964).

[231] *Id.* at 192.

[232] *Id.* at 198.

[233] *See generally* Linda Mullinex et al., Understanding Federal Courts and Jurisdiction 517 (1998).

[234] 527 U.S. at 680.

Scalia for the Court.[235] The Court's equation of the protection afforded sovereign immunity to the most basic individual rights is striking, to say the least.

Moreover, the Court argued that "[t]here is a fundamental difference between a State's expressing unequivocally that it waives its immunity, and Congress's expressing unequivocally its intention that if the State takes certain action it shall be deemed to have waived that immunity."[236] The distinction appears more subtle and less fundamental than the Court suggests, however, and the dissent argued that a State's consent should properly be inferred when it engages in particular commercial activity which Congress has clearly provided indicates submission to suit. States have access to competent counsel and can be deemed to know of Congress' clear expressions. Moreover, Justice Breyer argued in dissent, where a State acts as an entrepreneur it is not clear why it should not be treated in a manner similar to its private competitors. Indeed, the market participant exception exempts States from Dormant Commerce Clause scrutiny when the State participates in, rather than regulates, a market. This is in part based on the premise that when a State engages in an activity like a private party it should enjoy the same entrepreneurial freedoms. It is not clear why the commercially inclined State should not also experience the same inconveniences as do its private competitors, including the prospect of being sued for allegedly breaking the law, at least where Congress has made this a consequence. The Court rejected this argument, concluding that neither text nor tradition favored allowing constructive waiver of sovereign immunity when a State engages in commercial activity but not when it exercises nondiscretionary police power. A State does, however, waive its Eleventh Amendment immunity when, after having consented to be sued on state law claims in state court, it removes such a claim to federal court. Having "voluntarily agreed to remove the case to federal court" it could not invoke the Eleventh Amendment immunity.[237]

Congress can presumably condition grants of federal funds to a State on obtaining its consent to be sued regarding related incidents. Justice Kennedy's majority opinion in *Alden* seemed to reaffirm this possibility ("Nor, subject to constitutional limitations, does the Federal Government lack the authority or means to seek the States' voluntary consent to private suits. *Cf. South Dakota v. Dole*, 483 U.S. 203 (1987)");[238] although Justice Scalia did not, in *College Savings Bank* explicitly so state, his opinion is also consistent with that conclusion. Justice Scalia drew, however, a distinction between a State accepting a conditional grant (from which apparently a waiver of sovereign immunity can be construed) and a State deciding to engage in a regulated activity (from which consent to be sued cannot be implied). The distinction between such a "gift" and a "sanction" is subtle to say the least.

Although *Seminole Tribe* and *Alden* precluded Congress from abrogating State sovereign immunity in federal and state court under Article I, they left open the

---

[235] *Id.* at 682.

[236] *Id.* at 680–81.

[237] Lapides v. Board of Regents of the University System of Georgia, 535 U.S. 613, 620 (2002).

[238] *Alden*, 527 U.S. at 755.

possibility that it could do so under § 5 of the Fourteenth Amendment. *Alden's* two companion cases narrowed that possibility. In *College Savings Bank*, the Court held that the Trademark Remedy Clarification Act could not abrogate State sovereign immunity under § 5 because the Due Process Clause of the Fourteenth Amendment did not protect the alleged property rights asserted. In *Florida Prepaid Postsecondary Education Expense Board v. College Savings Bank*,[239] the Court held Congress' attempted abrogation of State sovereign immunity regarding claims of patent infringement was invalid because the legislation did not seek to remedy a history of "widespread and persisting deprivation of constitutional rights."[240] In its 1997 decision, *City of Boerne v. Flores*,[241] the Court had held that legislation under § 5 must satisfy a two-part test: Congress must identify conduct violating substantive rights the Fourteenth Amendment protects and must tailor its legislation to remedying or preventing such conduct. Here the Court found "scant support" for Congress' conclusion that States deprived patent owners of property without due process. In order to do so, of course, it needed to subject Congress' legislative process to a relatively high degree of scrutiny.

In subsequent cases, the Rehnquist Court continued to narrow the extent to which Congress could abrogate state sovereign immunity under § 5 of the Fourteenthe Amendment. During its October 1999 term, the Court found § 5 did not empower Congress to abrogate State sovereign immunity in the Age Discrimination in Employment Act of 1967 (ADEA). ADEA made it unlawful for an employer, including a State, to discriminate in employment based on age.[242] In *Kimel v. Florida Board of Regents*,[243] the Court held that ADEA did not satisfy the "congruence and proportionality" test of *City of Boerne*.[244] ADEA imposed substantive requirements on States "disproportionate to any unconstitutional conduct that conceivably could be targeted" by it.[245] Congress' extension of ADEA to States "was an unwarranted response to a perhaps inconsequential problem."[246] The four dissenters from the Court's earlier sovereign immunity cases would have upheld the application of ADEA to the States on the grounds that *Seminole Tribe* was wrongly decided.

In *Board of Trustees v. Garrett*,[247] the Court continued the pattern of recent terms of restricting Congress' ability under § 5 of the Fourteenth Amendment to subject States to suit by private parties for money damages. In a 5-4 decision, the Court held State Governments immune from private damage suits for employment discrimination in violation of Title I of the Americans With Disabilities Act (ADA).[248]

---

[239] 527 U.S. 627 (1999).

[240] *Id.* at 645.

[241] 521 U.S. 507 (1997).

[242] 29 U.S.C. § 623(a)(1).

[243] 528 U.S. 62 (2000).

[244] *Id.* at 82, 83.

[245] *Id.* at 83.

[246] *Id.* at 89.

[247] 531 U.S. 356 (2001).

[248] *Id.* at 360.

Since the ADA went beyond constitutional requirements, it could be justified under § 5 only if "proportionate" and "congruent" to remedy constitutional violations.[249] The legislative record included extensive documentation of state discrimination against the disabled, but the majority found the record insufficient.[250]

During the 2002 term, however, the Court held Congress does have power under § 5 to create a private right of action for monetary relief against States for violating the Family and Medical Leave Act of 1993.[251] In his majority opinion, Chief Justice Rehnquist found the remedy congruent and proportional to the injury and concluded that Congress had ample evidence of state discrimination regarding family leave, often based on gender stereotypes.

The Court followed its decision in *Hibbs* the following term by holding in *Tennessee v. Lane*,[252] that Congress had properly abrogated the States' Eleventh Amendment immunity under Title II of the Americans with Disabilities Act of 1990 (ADA), which precluded denying a "qualified individual with a disability" "benefits of the services, programs or activities of a public entity."[253] The question resolved in *Lane* had been left open in *Garrett*,[254] in which the Court had held that the Eleventh Amendment barred suits under Title I of the ADA. *Lane* arose when two paraplegics complained that they were effectively denied access to Tennessee's state courthouses.

Congress had clearly stated its intent to abrogate the States' immunity.[255] The Court concluded that Title II was "prophylactic legislation" within the § 5 power because it proscribed practices which were "discriminatory in effect, if not in intent, to carry out the basic objectives of the Equal Protection Clause."[256] Title II sought to include a range of basic constitutional rights including, but not limited to, those involving access to the courts which the Due Process Clause of the Fourteenth Amendment protected. Congressional proceedings had disclosed that many individuals were denied access to courts due to disabilities. The basic rights at issue called for "a standard of judicial review at least as searching, and in some cases more searching, than the standard that applies to sex-based classifications" at issue in *Hibbs*.[257] The Court need not consider whether Title II was "appropriately tailored to serve its objectives" in all of its potential applications (e.g., seating at state-owned hockey arenas) but need ask only whether it met the congruence and proportionality test with respect to the issue in question relating to access to the

---

[249] *Id.*

[250] *Id.* at 368–72.

[251] Nevada Department of Human Resources v. Hibbs, 538 U.S. 721 (2003).

[252] 541 U.S. 509 (2004).

[253] 42 U.S.C. § 12132.

[254] Board of Trustees v. Garett, 531 U.S. 356, 360 n.1 (2001).

[255] "A State shall not be immune under the eleventh amendment to the Constitution of the United States from an action in Federal or State court of competent jurisdiction for a violation of this chapter." 42 U.S.C. § 12202.

[256] 541 U.S. at 520.

[257] *Id.* at 529.

judicial system.[258] To that application, Title II "unquestionably is valid" § 5 legislation. The "considerable evidence of the shortcomings of previous legislative responses" justified Congress in concluding that additional prophylactic legislation was needed and that when adopted, was a limited remedy appropriate in its scope.[259]

In dissent, Chief Justice Rehnquist (joined by Justices Kennedy and Thomas) argued that the Court had misapplied the congruence and proportionality test by considering evidence unrelated to access to courts issues and which involved "discrimination by nonstate governments."[260] Moreover, the dissent criticized the majority's "as applied" approach, arguing instead that the Court should have measured the full breadth of the statute . . . that Congress enacted against the scope of the constitutional right it purported to enforce."[261]

Justice Scalia also dissented, but in doing so suggested a new doctrinal approach. He had joined the congruence and proportionality test in the past with misgivings. He now "yield[ed] to the lessons of experience" and concluded that it, "like all such flabby tests, is a standing invitation to judicial arbitrariness and policy-driven decisionmaking."[262] Moreover, the test made the Court Congress' "taskmaster" and required it to "regularly check Congress's homework." The Court should not perform judicial review of congressional acts based only on a test "that has no demonstrable basis in the text of the Constitution and cannot objectively be shown to have been met or failed."[263] Justice Scalia would require that § 5 legislation "enforce, by appropriate legislation" the provisions of the Fourteenth Amendment; it should not serve as the basis for prophylactic measures "prohibiting primary conduct that is itself not forbidden by the Fourteenth Amendment."[264] Justice Scalia distinguished the cases authorizing a broader approach (except *Hibbs*) as involving racial discrimination which, he pointed out, was the Fourteenth Amendment's principal target.[265]

As is often the case, the Court's vindication of one structural principle, here a federalism which includes a robust notion of sovereign immunity, came at the expense of other structural principles. The consequence for the Rule of Law has already been mentioned — certain private rights are left without a private remedy for money damages against the state. The decisions also have ramifications for separation of powers. The Rehnquist Court showed Congress relatively little deference when some legislation impacted States. "Congress has vast power but not all power," wrote Justice Kennedy in *Alden*,[266] a refrain he also sounded in *City of Boerne*. This truism reflected the Rehnquist Court's belief that it must, and could,

---

[258] *Id.* at 531.

[259] *Id.*

[260] *Id.* at 541–42.

[261] *Id.* at 551–52.

[262] *Id.* at 557–58.

[263] *Id.* at 558.

[264] *Id.* at 558, 560.

[265] *Id.* at 561–63.

[266] *Alden*, 527 U.S. at 758.

actively umpire federalism disputes to restrict federal legislative intrusions into the domain of the States. Whereas *Garcia* rested on the premise that Congress would protect States, the Court in many of the sovereign immunity cases rejected any faith in the national political process as an enforcer of federalism. The Court's lack of confidence in the national political process as a safeguard of federalism mirrored the misgivings of the *Garcia* dissents. Instead, the Court fashioned bright-line rules to limit Congress' ability to exert its regulatory will over the States.

The Eleventh Amendment does not preclude a State from suing another State for money damages in federal court.[267] Although a State may not invoke the Supreme Court's original jurisdiction when it acts merely as trustee or agent or nominal party for its citizens who are the real parties in interest, it may so proceed when it shows a direct interest of its own is at stake.[268]

The Seminole Tribe also sought an injunction not only against Florida, but against its governor, too. *Ex parte Young*[269] had held that a suit against a state employee to enjoin official actions violating federal law was not a suit against the State the Eleventh Amendment barred. Under *Young*, the State may be "free to carry out its functions without judicial interference directed at the sovereign or its agents, but this immunity from federal jurisdiction does not extend to individuals who act as officers" in violation of law.[270] *Seminole Tribe*, however, held that *Young* did not allow suit against the governor because the statute imposing the duty to negotiate included a "carefully crafted and intricate remedial scheme."[271] "[W]here Congress has prescribed a detailed remedial scheme for the enforcement against a State of a statutorily created right, a court should hesitate before casting aside those limitations and permitting an action against a state officer based on *Ex parte Young*."[272]

The Court's resolution is somewhat anomalous. The Seminole Tribe sought, through its action against the governor, to benefit from the "carefully crafted and intricate remedial scheme" Congress provided. The Court, in effect, inferred that Congress would prefer Seminole Tribe have no remedy rather than to exercise an *Ex parte Young* action.[273]

---

[267] Kansas v. Colorado, 533 U.S. 1 (2001); Texas v. New Mexico, 482 U.S. 124 (1987).

[268] *Kansas v. Colorado*, 533 U.S. at 7–9 (2001) (Kansas' interest in preventing diversion from Arkansas River constituted direct interest.).

[269] 209 U.S. 123 (1908).

[270] Georgia R.R. v. Redwine, 342 U.S. 299, 305 (1952).

[271] *Seminole Tribe*, 517 U.S. at 73–74. The statute provided that the court could order the state and tribe to conclude a compact within 60 days if it found that the state had failed to negotiate in good faith. If the parties still failed to conclude a compact a mediator would select one to be enforced by regulations of the Secretary of the Interior from submissions by the parties.

[272] 517 U.S. at 74.

[273] *See generally* Vicki Jackson, *Seminole Tribe, the Eleventh Amendment, and the Political Evisceration of* Ex Parte Young, 72 N.Y.U. L. Rev. 495, 540 (1997); David Currie, Ex Parte Young *After* Seminole Tribe, 72 N.Y.U. L. Rev. 547 (1997).

In *Idaho v. Coeur d'Alene Tribe*,[274] the Court further limited *Ex parte Young* although in confusing fashion. It held that the Eleventh Amendment barred an action by the Tribe for a declaratory judgment establishing entitlement to certain submerged lands in Idaho. The bar applied to the suit against the State and to a *Young* action against state officials to prohibit them from acting in violation of the Tribe's rights in the lands.

The Court affirmed "the continuing validity of the *Young* doctrine"[275] but noted questions regarding "its proper scope and application."[276] Justice Kennedy and Chief Justice Rehnquist thought *Young* generally applies in two instances: 1) "where there is no state forum available to vindicate federal interests";[277] 2) "when the case calls for the interpretation of federal law."[278] Even in those cases the Court must engage in a case-by-case "careful balancing and accommodation of state interests when determining whether the *Young* exception applies in a given case."[279] *Coeur d'Alene* involved "the functional equivalent of a quiet title action which implicates special sovereignty interests."[280] The Tribe could not bring a quiet title action against the State; therefore it could not achieve "the functional equivalent" by a suit against state officers.

Writing for herself and two colleagues, Justice O'Connor concurred in the result but rejected Justice Kennedy's approach. The case she wrote, was:

> unlike a typical *Young* action . . . The *Young* doctrine rests on the premise that a suit against a state official to enjoin an ongoing violation of federal law is not a suit against the State. Where a plaintiff seeks to divest the State of all regulatory power over submerged lands — in effect, to invoke a federal court's jurisdiction to quiet title to sovereign lands — it simply cannot be said that the suit is not a suit against the State. I would not narrow our *Young* doctrine, but I would not extend it to reach this case.[281]

Young continues to provide a vehicle for relief against an "ongoing violation of federal law" when plaintiff seeks "prospective rather than retrospective" relief.[282]

The Court subsequently clarified the status of the *Ex Parte Young* doctrine by adopting Justice O'Connor's approach. Citing her concurrence in *Coeur d'Alene*, Justice Scalia, for the Court wrote:

> In determining whether the doctrine of *Ex Parte Young* avoids an Eleventh Amendment bar to suit, a court need only conduct a straightforward inquiry into whether [the] complaint alleges an ongoing violation of

---

[274] 521 U.S. 261 (1997).

[275] *Id.* at 269.

[276] *Id.*

[277] *Id.* at 270.

[278] *Id.* at 274.

[279] *Id.* at 278.

[280] *Id.* at 281.

[281] *Id.* at 296.

[282] *Id.* at 294.

federal law and seeks relief properly characterized as prospective.[283]

The Rehnquist Court was narrowly divided on many of these issues and several members held intense views about federalism issues. Although four new justices have joined the Court since 2005, it seems likely that federalism issues will continue to represent an area of doctrinal controversy for the Court.

---

[283] Verizon Maryland Inv. v. Public Service Commission of Maryland, 535 U.S. 635, 645 (2002).

Chapter 6

COMMERCE AND THE STATES: THE DORMANT COMMERCE CLAUSE

INTRODUCTION

Under their police power, the States regulate a substantial part of everyday life. As the Commerce Clause has been interpreted more expansively the potential for conflict between federal and state regulation increases. Within the parameters of the commerce power, Congress can, of course, displace state regulation. Suppose, however, Congress has left an area unregulated yet state legislation impacts commerce. Does the Constitution inhibit such state regulation on the grounds that Congress, not the States, has power to regulate interstate commerce? The Court has concluded that the Commerce Clause has a negative, as well as a positive, aspect. It not only confers authority on Congress to legislate over a wide area; it also restricts state power by its negative implication. It may invalidate state laws regulating subject matter of national importance even when Congress has been silent. Put differently, even when Congress has not acted, the Dormant Commerce Clause sometimes subjects state legislation to review. State legislation may be held invalid if it discriminates against or unduly burdens interstate commerce.

This chapter focuses primarily on the Dormant Commerce Clause. After discussing the purposes and constitutional arguments regarding the Dormant Commerce Clause in Section 6.01, the chapter discusses the historical evolution of the concept, beginning with classic cases of the Marshall Court, continuing with a discussion of *Cooley v. Board of Wardens*[1] of the Taney Court, the railroad cases of the late 19th and early 20th centuries, and the move towards a balancing approach. The chapter then outlines the modern approach in Section 6.03 and discusses separately the two primary tests now used in Sections 6.04 and 6.05. The chapter discusses the political process rationale in Section 6.06, which occasionally surfaces in Dormant Commerce Clauses cases, before discussing doctrine regarding state prohibitory laws in Section 6.07. The chapter presents various exceptions to the Dormant Commerce Clause, primarily the market participant exception and ability of Congress to consent to measures that would otherwise raise concerns. The chapter also discusses Congress' ability to preempt state regulation in Section 6.09. The chapter concludes by discussing the related Privileges and Immunities Clause of Article IV in Section 6.10.

---

[1] 53 U.S. (12 How.) 299 (1852).

§ 6.01 THE PURPOSE OF THE DORMANT COMMERCE CLAUSE

Absent the Commerce Clause, each State could ban the products of other States or inhibit their admission. Such practices, Madison thought, would "nourish unceasing animosities, and not improbably terminate in serious interruptions of the public tranquility."[2] The Constitution sought to end such economic isolation. The Commerce Clause advances two fundamental national purposes implicit in the Constitution. First, it helps maintain a national economic union unfettered by state-imposed barriers to interstate commerce. Justice Robert H. Jackson articulated this economic rationale in *H. P. Hood & Sons, Inc. v. Du Mond*[3] where he wrote:

> This principle that our economic unit is the Nation, which alone has the gamut of powers necessary to control of the economy, including the vital power of erecting customs barriers against foreign competition, has as its corollary that the states are not separable economic units . . . . Our system, fostered by the Commerce Clause, is that every farmer and every craftsman shall be encouraged to produce by the certainty that he will have free access to every market in the Nation . . . .

The Commerce Clause thus creates a "national 'common market' "[4] which the States cannot destroy by advancing their own economic interests at the expense of the nation.

The Commerce Clause also has a political rationale. It helps foster national political cohesion by inhibiting States from imposing reciprocal barriers that would divide rather than unite. As such, it reflects a commitment to the proposition that the States must, in Justice Cardozo's formulation, "sink or swim together" since "in the long run prosperity and salvation are in union and not division."[5]

The Commerce Clause empowers Congress to legislate to achieve these objects. But what if Congress remains silent or dormant? Are the States free to regulate in areas that may impact interstate commerce if Congress has, by its silence, left certain space within its domain empty?

The Constitution is silent on the question. It neither authorizes the States to act nor does it enjoin them from doing so.[6] The Commerce Clause provides that "Congress shall have power . . . to regulate Commerce . . . among the several states."[7] The grant of that power to Congress might be read as implicitly denying it to the States. On the other hand, in other instances the Constitution does not treat its grants to Congress as precluding state action. For instance, Article I, Section 8

---

[2] THE FEDERALIST No. 42 (James Madison).

[3] 336 U.S. 525, 538–39 (1949).

[4] Hunt v. Washington State Apple Adver. Comm'n, 432 U.S. 333, 350 (1977).

[5] Baldwin v. G. A. F. Seelig, Inc., 294 U.S. 511, 523 (1935).

[6] *See Hood & Sons*, 336 U.S. at 535 ("it does not say what the states may or may not do in the absence of congressional action").

[7] U.S. CONST. art. I, § 8, cl. 3.

empowers Congress to coin money and grant letters of marque, but these provisions alone apparently do not implicitly restrict the States from taking the same action. If they did, Article I, Section 10 would not need to expressly prohibit States from coining money and granting letters of marque. The framers included express prohibitions against state action in these areas but did not specifically forbid state regulations of commerce.[8] Thus, arguably, the States may regulate commerce without restriction.

Neither textual argument has prevailed. The Court has recognized that absent conflicting federal law the States retain "a residuum of power . . . to make laws governing matters of local concern which nevertheless in some measure affect interstate commerce or even, to some extent, regulate it."[9] Yet this state power is subject to constitutional limits imposed by the Commerce Clause even in its dormant state. The Court has long relied on the Commerce Clause, fortified by the Supremacy Clause, to infer this policing power of the Negative or Dormant Commerce Clause. For most of our history, the Commerce Clause has been deemed to include both an affirmative grant of power to Congress to regulate commerce and a negative aspect limiting States' intrusions into that sphere. "Perhaps even more than by interpretation of its written word, this Court has advanced the solidarity and prosperity of this Nation by the meaning it has given to these great silences of the Constitution,"[10] observed Justice Jackson.

Although the constitutional text does not compel a negative commerce power, other constitutional arguments do lend some support. First, some argue that the framers intended to preclude States from obstructing commerce to and from other States. The Articles of Confederation failed due largely to the government's impotence to remedy the States' divisive and parochial trade policies. A negative commerce power was needed in case Congress failed to reach a subject.[11] (Of course, it may be that the framers intended simply to give *Congress* power to override state regulation in which case congressional inaction might reflect a willingness to tolerate the state measure). Second, the Dormant Commerce Clause is defended as a means of fostering national unity. Division would ensue if States created trade barriers. The Dormant Commerce Clause is consistent with the Constitution's commitment to unity implicit in its structure. Third, an economic argument supports the concept; a national free market promotes efficiency. Finally, a political process argument supports the Negative Commerce Clause. There is something undemocratic about a State burdening outsiders who have not been represented in the State's legislative processes. Indeed, Chief Justice John Marshall made this argument in *McCulloch*.[12]

The affirmative and negative commerce clauses differ in two other significant ways. The extent of the restraints the Commerce Clause imposes on the States "appear nowhere in the words of the Commerce Clause, but have emerged

---

[8] *See* The License Cases, 46 U.S. (5 How.) 504, 579 (1847).

[9] Southern Pacific Co. v. Arizona, 325 U.S. 761, 767 (1945).

[10] *H. P. Hood*, 336 U.S. at 535.

[11] *See id.* at 533–35.

[12] 17 U.S. (4 Wheat.) 316 (1819).

gradually in the decisions of [the Supreme] Court giving effect to its basic purpose."[13] The Commerce Clause is essentially a delegation of power to Congress; for approximately six decades, the courts have largely abdicated the field to Congress. During this time courts have exercised deferential judicial review of federal laws under the Commerce Clause. The Dormant Commerce Clause, by contrast, empowers the federal judiciary in the first instance. What occasions analysis under it is congressional silence followed by state regulation, topped off by litigation.

Second, the consequences of judicial intervention in the two situations are quite different. When a court finds that a federal statute transcends Congress' power under the Commerce Clause, it rules the measure unconstitutional, essentially foreclosing legislative solution under it. When the Court finds a state statute offends the Dormant Commerce Clause, the Court strikes down the offending state measure. But judicial action under the Dormant Commerce Clause is subject to correction by Congress. Put differently, the durability of judicial work under the Dormant Commerce Clause is contingent on legislative approval or acquiescence. Congress can act, under the Commerce Clause, to endorse or override the Court's work under its dormant version.

At the outset, it is important to focus on the circumstances when Dormant or Negative Commerce Clause analysis becomes relevant. There are two crucial preconditions. First, the area the state has regulated must fall within the domain of the federal commerce power, something almost inevitable since *Wickard*, even after *Lopez* contracted its turf. If, however, the state regulation does not intrude on the space the Commerce Clause covers, the Dormant Commerce Clause does not restrain the State and it may act free from Commerce Clause inhibitions. Second, if the state regulation falls within the federal commerce power, the question then arises whether the state measure conflicts with any statute Congress has enacted. If so, the state statute fails under the Supremacy Clause and dormant commerce analysis becomes irrelevant. Dormant Commerce Clause scrutiny arises only when the state statute affects commerce and the federal government has not acted.

§ 6.02 HISTORICAL EVOLUTION

[1] Chief Justice Marshall's Views

Defining the limit on state power imposed by the clause has been the continuing task of the Court. John Marshall considered the possibility of some negative commerce clause in *Gibbons v. Ogden*.[14] The case was argued largely on the theory that the New York monopoly impermissibly intruded on Congress' commerce power. Marshall saw merit to the argument that the Commerce Clause precluded the States from regulating commerce. "There is great force in this argument, and the Court is not satisfied that it has been refuted,"[15] he wrote. But in *Gibbons* he

---

[13] Philadelphia v. New Jersey, 437 U.S. 617, 623 (1978).

[14] 22 U.S. (9 Wheat.) 1 (1824).

[15] *Id.* at 209.

did not reach that issue, deciding the case as he did on Supremacy Clause grounds. Although Marshall did not think a State could regulate interstate commerce since that was the power given Congress, he did not think the fact of some peripheral impact on commerce barred a State from acting under its police power. He distinguished between the *power* being exercised and the *subject matter* of the power. Marshall thought states could not seek to regulate commerce, but could act under their police power even though their laws affected commerce. Thus, in *Willson v. Black Bird Creek Marsh Co.*,[16] he upheld a State's power to construct a dam across a navigable creek as a proper exercise of state police power although Congress presumably could have regulated the creek under the Commerce Clause. Delaware's statute, under the circumstances, was not "repugnant" to Congress' commerce power "in its dormant state."[17]

Although Marshall flirted with the idea that the Commerce Clause represented an exclusive grant of power to Congress which precluded state legislation, his successor, Chief Justice Roger B. Taney, advanced the opposite view. He argued that "the State may nevertheless, for the safety or convenience of trade, or for the protection of the health of its citizens, make regulations of commerce for its own ports and harbours, and for its own territory; and such regulations are valid unless they come in conflict with a law of Congress."[18] Two years later, however, the Court, in an opinion by Justice McLean, seemed to endorse the view that Congress had the exclusive power to regulate commerce among the States. As such, the Court struck down state laws taxing passengers on vessels from foreign ports.[19] Yet the Court did not think the exclusivity of Congress' commerce power precluded the States from passing police power legislation to protect the health or safety of their citizens.[20]

[2] Local Pilot Case

The Supreme Court addressed the scope of state authority in *Cooley v. Board of Wardens*.[21] Pennsylvania law required vessels to use a local pilot in the port of Philadelphia or pay a fine. No federal statute governed the subject.[22] Accordingly, the case posed the question of the extent of state power over commerce in the face of congressional silence.

The Pennsylvania pilotage law was challenged on the grounds the Commerce Clause gave Congress exclusive authority to regulate commerce. Although the Court might have treated the Pennsylvania law as an exercise of its police power, not a commercial regulation, and dodged the issue as had earlier cases, it chose not to take that course. The Court had no problem finding that the Commerce Clause

---

[16] 27 U.S. (2 Pet.) 245 (1829).

[17] *Id.* at 252.

[18] The License Cases, 46 U.S. (5 How.) 504, 579 (1847).

[19] The Passenger Cases, 48 U.S. (7 How.) 283 (1849).

[20] *Id.* at 400.

[21] 53 U.S. (12 How.) 299 (1852).

[22] A federal statute existed, but did not affect the result. Accordingly, the Court treated the case as one in which the Congress had been silent.

covered navigation[23] and that the Pennsylvania statute regulated commerce within the scope of Congress' power.[24] But the Court rejected the contention that Congress' power was always exclusive. Instead, *Cooley* adopted an intermediate approach, concluding that whether congressional power was exclusive varied with the circumstances. The decisive criteria was the nature of the "subjects" being regulated. Some subjects required a uniform national rule; others needed diversity to accommodate local conditions. The States' freedom to act turned on whether the matter being regulated needed to be governed by a uniform national system: "Whatever subjects of this power are in their nature national, or admit only of one uniform system, or plan of regulation, may justly be said to be of such a nature as to require exclusive legislation by Congress."[25] State law could reach subjects where national uniformity was unnecessary. The pilotage requirement needed no uniform rule.

The *Cooley* approach was problematic. It did not suggest criteria to separate the national and local spheres. Thus, those labels were often used to state conclusions for judgments the basis of which was not always clear. The approach seemed to tolerate protectionist state measures within the local domain. It did not use legislative motive as a factor to guide its assessment.

Cooley's intermediate course rejected the polar options — that the States could regulate without limitation if Congress was silent and conversely that they were prohibited from regulating at all in a way that affected commerce. Whether a state regulation survived depended on whether its subject required a national or local approach.[26] *Cooley* recognized that even when Congress did not act, the Commerce Clause limited, but did not preclude, the State's ability to impact commerce. The *Cooley* national/local dichotomy survived into the twentieth century.

[3] Railroad Regulation

The *Cooley* test was applied to assess a variety of state regulations. *Munn v. Illinois*[27] upheld state authority to set rates of warehouses used in interstate commerce. The Court noted that the warehouses were located and did their business in Illinois.[28] "Their regulation is a thing of domestic concern,"[29] concluded the Court, confirming its local, rather than national character. A companion case[30] held that States could also regulate railroad rates. The road in question, like the warehouse in *Munn*, was "situated within the limits of a single State" and

---

[23] 53 U.S. at 315–16.

[24] *Id.* at 317.

[25] *Cooley*, 53 U.S. at 319.

[26] More recently, the *Cooley* approach has been applied to a Washington State law requiring tug escorts for oil tanker navigation in Puget Sound. Similar to a local pilotage requirement, a requirement that a tanker take on a tug escort when entering a particular body of water was deemed not the type of regulation that demanded a uniform national rule. *See* Ray v. Atlantic Richfield Co., 435 U.S. 151 (1978).

[27] 94 U.S. (4 Otto) 113 (1877).

[28] *Id.* at 135.

[29] *Id.*

[30] Chicago, B. & Q. R. Co. v. Iowa, 94 U.S. (4 Otto) 155 (1877).

accordingly "its regulation is a matter of domestic concern."[31] A decade later, however, in *Wabash, St. Louis & Pacific Railway v. Illinois*,[32] the Court invoked the national/local distinction to hold invalid a state statute regulating rates for interstate rail transportation. Interstate rate regulation was a subject of "general and national character" which required uniformity.[33] Such a subject could not be "safely and wisely remitted to local rules and local regulations."[34] Only the National Government could regulate interstate railroad rates uniformly.

The Court tolerated greater diversity regarding railroad safety. Believing that safety requirements should address local conditions, the Supreme Court upheld state statutes applicable to interstate trains that prohibited the use of stoves or furnaces to heat passenger cars,[35] ordered the elimination of dangerous grade crossings,[36] governed train speed,[37] and prescribed the manner in which interstate trains must approach various structures and intersections.[38] Such regulations were "eminently local in their character."[39] They were not "directed against interstate commerce"[40] but protected personal safety.[41]

In a series[42] of cases culminating in *DiSanto v. Pennsylvania*,[43] the Court articulated an alternative to *Cooley*, a distinction based on whether a State regulated interstate commerce directly or indirectly. In *DiSanto*, a State justified its law requiring a state license to sell tickets to travel abroad as necessary to preclude fraud. The Court rejected this rationale because the measure directly regulated interstate commerce. *DiSanto* distinguished between state laws that directly regulated commerce (so were invalid) and those whose effect was indirect (which were allowed). This mechanical test was short-lived; it was uncertain in application and ignored the often-critical matters of degree. Justice Stone criticized the test in dissent on these grounds.[44] *Cooley* and *DiSanto* both sought to define rigid categories of federal and state competence. Ultimately, the Court

---

[31] *Id.* at 163.

[32] 118 U.S. 557 (1886).

[33] *Id.* at 577.

[34] *Id.*

[35] *See* New York, N. H. & H. R. Co. v. New York, 165 U.S. 628 (1897).

[36] *See* Erie R.R. Co. v. Board of Public Util. Comm'rs, 254 U.S. 394 (1921).

[37] *See* Erb v. Morasch, 177 U.S. 584 (1900).

[38] *See* Crutcher v. Kentucky, 141 U.S. 47, 61 (1891). *But see* Seaboard Air Line Ry. Co. v. Blackwell, 244 U.S. 310 (1917) (striking down state law requiring trains to slow at crossings with effect of causing 124 stops in 123 miles).

[39] *Crutcher*, 141 U.S. at 61.

[40] *New York*, 165 U.S. at 632.

[41] *Erie*, 254 U.S. at 410.

[42] *See, e.g.*, Smith v. Alabama, 124 U.S. 465, 482 (1888) (upholding state law which affects interstate commerce "only indirectly, incidentally, and remotely"); Southern Ry. Co. v. King, 217 U.S. 524, 531 (1910); Silz v. Hesterberg, 211 U.S. 31, 40–41 (1908). *See generally* James W. Ely, Jr., *"The Railroad System Has Burst Through State Limits": Railroads and Interstate Commerce, 1830–1920*, 55 Ark. L. Rev. 933 (2003).

[43] 273 U.S. 34 (1927).

[44] *See id.* at 44 (Stone, J., dissenting).

distanced itself from such an approach, adopting instead a balancing test.

[4]   Towards a Balancing Test

In *Southern Pacific Co. v. Arizona*,[45] the Court used a balancing test to conclude that safety regulation demanded national uniformity. Arizona prohibited operation of a train longer than 14 passenger of 70 freight cars. The law was defended as a safety measure to reduce accidents. The Court doubted the merit of that claim.[46] Even so, the statute placed too heavy a burden on interstate train operation to survive. The Court must consider "the nature and extent of the burden which the state regulation of interstate trains, adopted as a safety measure, imposes on interstate commerce, and whether the relative weights of the state and national interests involved" justify the state law.[47] Any safety advantage could not outweigh the cost to interstate commerce. The efficiency of rail operations would be compromised if Arizona could enforce its law while train lengths were unregulated or subject to varying standards in other States.

In *Southern Pacific*, the Court distinguished its earlier decision in *South Carolina Highway Department v. Barnwell Bros.*[48] where the Court had upheld a state law prohibiting the use of trucks wider than ninety inches and heavier than 20,000 pounds.

To some extent, Chief Justice Stone may have felt stuck with *Barnwell*. He had written that opinion, too, perhaps at a different stage of his thought. In *Barnwell* he had suggested a level of judicial deference to legislative choice[49] that was not apparent in his later opinion. The Court suggested the two cases differed in the type of transportation involved. Few subjects of state regulation affecting commerce were "so peculiarly of local concern" as highways.[50] The *Barnwell* law aimed at both safety and highway conservation. The latter element justified the exertion of state power. In *Southern Pacific*, however, the Court thought the impact of the state law on commerce outweighed any local safety benefit. At the time, the states' role may have been more dominant in state highway systems than it now is.

More recent cases suggest that the Dormant Commerce Clause applies to highways, too. Thus, in one case the Court struck down an Illinois law requiring trucks use a particular type of rear fender mudguard and making illegal a different mudflap which was used in forty-five States. The Illinois law unreasonably burdened commerce while producing little safety benefit.[51] The Court also held invalid an Iowa prohibition against trucks longer than fifty-five feet on its highways

---

[45]   325 U.S. 761 (1945).

[46]   *Id.* at 779. The trial court had found the train-length restriction increased accidents because it resulted in a greater number of trains in operation.

[47]   325 U.S. at 770.

[48]   303 U.S. 177 (1938).

[49]   *Id.* at 185–86, 190, 191.

[50]   *Southern Pacific*, 325 U.S. at 783.

[51]   Bibb v. Navajo Freight Lines, Inc., 359 U.S. 520 (1959).

as applied to an interstate carrier. The challenged regulation placed a substantial burden on interstate commerce and made a dubious contribution to highway safety.[52]

§ 6.03 THE MODERN APPROACH

In recent decades, the Court has adopted an approach to Dormant Commerce Clause cases that incorporates a variation of the *Southern Pacific* balancing test. Although the discussion below does not account for all decisions in this area, it summarizes much of the Court's most significant jurisprudence in this area.

In essence, the Court begins by asking whether a state statute discriminates on its face or in its purpose or effect against out-of-staters or interstate commerce. If it does, the state law is subjected to strict scrutiny and is likely to be found unconstitutional.[53] On the other hand, if the law does not discriminate but pursues legitimate objectives with only an incidental impact on commerce, it is assessed under a more lenient balancing test that weighs the State's interest against the burden the law imposes on interstate commerce.[54] Whereas a discriminatory statute is presumptively invalid, a non-discriminatory law is likely to be upheld unless the burden on commerce greatly outweighs some legitimate state benefit.

§ 6.04 DISCRIMINATORY LAWS

The Dormant Commerce Clause seeks to prohibit States from regulating in a way which discriminates against out-of-state competition. This principle is simple to apply when a state law discloses its discriminatory character on its face. State laws that seek to accomplish such simple economic protectionism are per se invalid.[55] State measures designed to horde a State's natural resources are suspect. Thus, a New Jersey statute that forbade importation of out-of-state waste to preserve its landfill space for New Jersey citizens was unconstitutional; the State could not "isolate itself from a problem common to many by erecting a barrier against the movement of interstate trade."[56] The Court did not need to decide that an improper purpose animated the statute since the Court discriminated on its face and in its effect.[57]

Justice Jackson's opinion in *Hood & Sons v. Du Mond*[58] illustrates the Court's scrutiny when a State protects home industry against out-of-state competition. New York refused to license a Massachusetts milk distributor to open a facility from which it would ship milk to the Boston market. New York feared loss of needed

---

[52] *See* Kassel v. Consolidated Freightways Corp., 450 U.S. 662 (1981); *see also* Raymond Motor Transp., Inc. v. Rice, 434 U.S. 429 (1978).

[53] *See* Philadelphia v. New Jersey, 437 U.S. 617 (1978).

[54] *See* Pike v. Bruce Church, Inc., 397 U.S. 137, 142 (1970).

[55] *See* C & A Carbone, Inc. v. Clarkstown, 511 U.S. 383 (1994); City of Philadelphia v. New Jersey, 437 U.S. 617 (1978).

[56] *City of Philadelphia v. New Jersey*, 437 U.S. at 628.

[57] *Id.* at 626–29.

[58] 336 U.S. 525 (1949).

supply to the local market. New York could not protect its local market by excluding those who would export its products.

Cases involving blatant protectionism are easy. In *Philadelphia v. New Jersey*, for instance, Justice Stewart pointed out more than once that New Jersey's law discriminated on its face against out-of-state parties wishing to send waste into New Jersey.[59] But when a State employs regulatory power to discriminate against interstate commerce, it generally does not confess its sinister objective. Instead, it hides the true motive behind some pretext (e.g., that its action is based on the need for highway safety or to protect its inhabitants against infected products). The Supreme Court must then detect and expose the subterfuge.

Minnesota v. Barber[60] was illustrative. It involved a state statute which prohibited the sale of any meat unless an inspector within the State had inspected the animal within twenty-four hours before slaughter. The Court held that the law discriminated against interstate commerce because it excluded from the State's market all meat from animals slaughtered in other States. Seemingly, the State had acted to protect its citizens' health but its true purpose was to advantage local slaughterers.

In order to expose the subterfuge, the Court typically employs a "least restrictive alternative" approach. In essence, a state law that seems discriminatory in its purpose or means can survive only if the State can show it had a legitimate purpose and no alternative means that was less burdensome on interstate commerce to achieve the purpose. If the statute lacks this close fit between purpose and means, it raises the suspicion that the true motivation was less noble than the one the State advances in defense of the measure. This test imposes a heavy burden on the State to justify its legislature's conduct. As such, it gives state legislators incentive to explore ways of solving local problems which do not seek to burden outsiders.

In *Dean Milk Co. v. Madison*,[61] the Court found an impermissible economic motive inspired a local inspection requirement. A Madison, Wisconsin ordinance made it unlawful to sell milk unless pasteurized and bottled within five miles from the town center. This law excluded milk from plaintiff's pasteurization plants in Illinois less than 100 miles away. The Court found that the ordinance discriminated against interstate commerce. The claim that the ordinance was a health measure did not insulate it from scrutiny when the city deployed it to shield a local industry from outside competition. Less burdensome alternatives, such as inspection of plaintiff's plants by city officials or reliance on ratings obtained by officials where the plants were located, could have served local health interests. The State has the burden to justify its measure both in terms of local benefits flowing from it and the unavailability of nondiscriminatory alternatives adequate to protect the local interests at stake.[62]

---

[59] 437 U.S. at 628 ("On its face, it imposes on out-of-state commercial interests the full burden of conserving the State's remaining landfill space.").

[60] 136 U.S. 313 (1890).

[61] 340 U.S. 349 (1951).

[62] *See* Hunt v. Washington State Apple Adver. Comm'n, 432 U.S. 333, 353 (1977).

In *Dean Milk*, the Madison, Wisconsin ordinance failed to pass Dormant Commerce Clause muster even though it also adversely impacted milk pasteurized in Wisconsin at a distance from Madison.[63] "[O]ur prior cases teach that a State (or one of its political subdivisions) may not avoid the strictures of the Commerce Clause by curtailing the movement of articles of commerce through subdivisions of the State, rather than through the State itself."[64]

State statutes also may be found discriminatory if they prevent outsiders from access to a state market. In *Hughes v. Oklahoma*,[65] the Court struck down a state law that forbade transporting minnows out of State. Since the law discriminated on its face Oklahoma had to justify it based on the legitimate purpose/least restrictive alternative test. Although its stated purpose, conserving minnows, was legitimate, its means discriminated against out-of-staters rather than adopting alternatives (e.g., limiting in-staters' use of minnows) which would have distributed the burden impartially. The discrepancy between ends and means made Oklahoma's purpose suspect.

More recently, in *Granholm v. Heald*[66] the Court, in a 5-4 decision held unconstitutional state laws which regulated sale of wine from out-of-state wineries while permitting in-state sales. The laws violated the Dormant Commerce Clause and were not saved by the Twenty-First Amendment. The Court applied familiar Dormant Commerce Clause principles to these discriminatory laws and concluded that the Twenty-First Amendment did not authorize states "to pass nonuniform laws in order to discriminate against out-of-state goods[.] . . ." In dissent, Justice Thomas argued that the Twenty-First Amendment relieved the states from Dormant Commerce Clause restraints which would otherwise apply.

State statutes that discriminate against out-of-staters almost invariably fail to survive the legitimate state purpose/least restrictive alternative analysis. The exception was a Maine statute prohibiting importation of the golden shiners, a minnow used as live bait fish. One Robert Taylor was indicted for allegedly importing into Maine 158,000 live golden shiners in violation of a Maine law that proscribed introducing into Maine live bait fish from other states. Taylor challenged the law under the Dormant Commerce Clause. The facial discrimination occasioned the Court's strict scrutiny. But the Court found Maine did have a legitimate state purpose — protecting Maine's fragile fish ecology from the nasty parasites out-of-state bait fish carried — and had no nondiscriminatory alternative to save its minnows.[67] In dissent, Justice Stevens detected "something fishy about this case"[68] since other States did not ban out-of-state bait fish. Yet the Court found that Maine

---

[63] *See also* Fort Gratiot Sanitary Landfill, Inc. v. Michigan Dep't of Natural Resources, 504 U.S. 353 (1992) (forbidding discrimination against out-of-staters by also disadvantaging other communities in the state).

[64] *Fort Gratiot*, 504 U.S. at 361.

[65] 441 U.S. 322 (1979).

[66] 544 U.S. 460 (2005).

[67] *See* Maine v. Taylor, 477 U.S. 131 (1986).

[68] *Id.* at 152.

was not required "to develop new and unproven means of protection at an uncertain cost."[69]

Strict scrutiny does not apply simply to state measures that discriminate on their face. In fact, the most challenging applications come from statutes that are facially neutral. *Hunt v. Washington State Apple Advertising Commission*[70] provides a classic example. A North Carolina statute required that apples sold in closed container into the State could only display United States grades. State inspection certificates were banned. Washington, the nation's largest apple producer, challenged the statute that precluded Washington from attaching its own certificate attesting to its more rigorous exam which benefitted its apple growers in marketing their produce. The North Carolina law did not discriminate on its face since it applied to North Carolina apples, too. It did, however, discriminate in its effect since it would strip Washington apples of the competitive advantage they otherwise would enjoy by virtue of their rigorous inspection system.

The record contained evidence that North Carolina enacted the statute for a discriminatory motive. But the Court found it unnecessary to rely on that proof. Instead, based on the discriminatory effect, "the burden falls on the State to justify [the discrimination] both in terms of the local benefits flowing from the statute and the unavailability of nondiscriminatory alternatives adequate to preserve the local interests at stake."[71] The Court found little relationship between the restriction and its avowed purpose. Nondiscriminatory alternatives existed. Accordingly, the statute failed to survive this strict Dormant Commerce Clause scrutiny.

So, too, a Clarkstown, New York ordinance that required all solid waste be processed at a designated facility received the Dormant Commerce Clause's strict scrutiny. Although the statute was neutral on its face — it applied to all solid waste — and although it excluded not only out-of-state processors but other New York entrepreneurs — it had the impact of denying all out-of-state processors access to the Clarkstown supply of solid waste. The availability of nondiscriminatory alternatives doomed the measure.[72]

Yet not every facially neutral state law that disadvantages some out of state interest is invalid. In *Exxon Corp. v. Governor of Maryland*,[73] the Court upheld a Maryland statute that precluded petroleum producers or refiners from operating a retail gas station in Maryland and required them to extend all "voluntary allowances" uniformly to all customers. The producers and refiners adversely affected were out-of-staters. In a 7-1 decision, the Court found no Dormant Commerce Clause violation. Although some interstate companies were excluded, other interstate marketers (who neither produced nor refined petroleum) were not. The Act did not exclude interstate dealers or burden their conduct of business nor did it treat instate and out-of-state retailers differently.[74] The Dormant Commerce

---

[69] *Id.* at 147.

[70] 432 U.S. 333 (1977).

[71] *Id.* at 353.

[72] *See* C & A Carbone, Inc. v. Clarkstown, 511 U.S. 383 (1994).

[73] 437 U.S. 117 (1978).

[74] *See id.* at 126.

Clause "protects the interstate market, not particular interstate firms, from prohibitive or burdensome regulations."[75] The absence of in-state losers did not doom the state statute under these circumstances.

Interestingly, *Hunt* and *Exxon* were decided within a year of each other by the same Court. Yet only Justice Blackmun thought both laws were invalid. The two cases may suggest that the Court is most sensitive to state measures which threaten national unity. Maryland's law was directed at no one State; North Carolina's targeted Washington. Accordingly, the North Carolina law threatened the political "sink or swim" rationale whereas the Maryland law did not. Alternatively, the Court may have seen a legitimate purpose in Maryland's measure — better distribution of petroleum amidst the long fuel lines during the gas shortage in the late 1970s — whereas no redeeming virtue explained North Carolina's law.

Minnesota v. Clover Leaf Creamery Co.,[76] presented another leading case involving a facially neutral state law. There the Court upheld a Minnesota statute that banned sale of milk in plastic disposable containers but allowed it in paper containers. Minnesota's plywood industry stood to benefit while the plastics industry that suffered was outside the State. The Court was not troubled by these facts. The fact that some in-staters benefitted was not sufficient to establish a discriminatory effect since some out-of-staters also benefitted. In-state losers served as political surrogates for the out-of-state plastic container manufacturers. At times, the Court cites the existence of in-state losers as an argument for upholding laws which hurt some out-of-staters. The argument is that the insiders provide surrogate representation for the outside losers. Yet the presence of in-state losers does not assure that a law will survive the Court's scrutiny.[77] If it did, a crafty state legislature could insulate discriminatory legislation from dormant commerce clause scrutiny by designing its laws to hurt some minor in-state interests while protecting more significant constituents.

§ 6.05   *PIKE* BALANCING TEST

When the Court fails to find discriminatory impact, it employs a balancing test that compares benefits to legitimate state purpose against burdens on commerce. The Court stated the test in *Pike v. Bruce Church, Inc.:*[78] "Where the statute regulates even-handedly to effectuate a legitimate local public interest, and its effects on interstate commerce are only incidental, it will be upheld unless the burden imposed on such commerce is clearly excessive in relation to the putative local benefits."

State statutes that do not discriminate in purpose or effect typically are assessed against the forgiving *Pike* balancing test. Here, the presumption operates in favor of upholding the state statute. Thus, the statute in *Clover Leaf* easily passed muster

---

[75] *Id.* at 127–28.

[76] 449 U.S. 456 (1981).

[77] *See, e.g.,* Philadelphia v. New Jersey, 437 U.S. 617 (1978) (law invalid even though New Jersey loser).

[78] 397 U.S. 137, 142 (1970).

because the burdens on commerce were trivial compared to the State's interests in conservation and curing solid waste disposal problems.[79] Similarly, Maryland's restriction on petroleum producers imposed little pressure on commerce and addressed Maryland's interest in assuring an even distribution of gasoline products in time of energy shortage.

The *Pike* test has its critics. Justice Scalia, for instance, has argued that the Constitution, properly construed, mandates no Dormant Commerce Clause scrutiny. On *stare decisis* grounds, however, he has accepted "a self-executing, 'negative' Commerce Clause" against state laws that discriminate facially against interstate commerce or that are indistinguishable from the Court's earlier decisions.[80] Justice Scalia would not, however, then strike down facially neutral state statutes that discriminate in purpose or effect or that heavily burdened commerce.

The Court's decision in *United Haulers Assn., Inc. v. Oneida-Herkimer Solid Waste Management Authority*,[81] revealed a divergence among Justices Scalia and Thomas who had previously spoken with one voice regarding the negative Commerce Clause. In *United Haulers*, Justice Scalia maintained the position described above. Citing the lack of a textual basis for a Dormant Commerce Clause as well as the unworkability of the doctrine in practice, Justice Thomas argued that the Court's entire Dormant Commerce Clause jurisprudence should be discarded. The divergence provides an instance in which Justice Scalia seems willing to accept some precedent in the interest of continuity and predictability while Justice Thomas appears more willing to abandon judgments of previous Courts which he deems as inconsistent with the Constitution's text and the framers' intent.

The balancing test also suggests that some scale exists that can weigh safety benefits against commerce costs. Yet these values are not easily balanced.

§ 6.06   THE POLITICAL PROCESS RATIONALE

The concern about state regulations of commerce relates in part to the tendency of groups to favor their own interests at the expense of others. If unchecked by some restraining umpire, a state legislature may benefit its constituents and burden non-citizens.

When state legislation distributes benefits and burdens impartially within and without the State, the Court may conclude that the State's political process has functioned fairly, that out-of-state interests have been represented by in-state surrogates. When state legislation distributes the gains from a program to in-staters and externalizes the costs, the State's political process may not have considered fairly the interests of nonresidents. Accordingly, judicial scrutiny is invited.

---

[79] 449 U.S. 456 (1981).

[80] West Lynn Creamery, Inc. v. Healy, 512 U.S. 186, 210 (1994) (Scalia, J., concurring); Itel Containers Int'l Corp. v. Huddleston, 507 U.S. 60, 78–79 (1993) (Scalia, J., concurring).

[81] 550 U.S. 330 (2007).

Courts have been sensitive to this aspect of the Dormant Commerce Clause. Thus, in *Barnwell Bros.*, the Court upheld the state highway measure in part because it concluded that the similar effect on "shippers in interstate and intrastate commerce in large number within as well as without the state is a safeguard against their abuse."[82] Similarly, in *Clover Leaf*, the Court took comfort in the fact that the out-of-state plastic container interests were represented by some Minnesota losers. Conversely, when the, state's democratic process is compromised, the Court is less likely to be sympathetic to state legislation. In *West Lynn Creamery, Inc. v. Healy*[83] the Court struck down a Massachusetts regulation that assessed all fluid milk sold to Massachusetts retailers (two-thirds of which was produced out of State) and then distributed the proceeds to Massachusetts dairy farms. The combination of the evenhanded tax and in-state subsidy had a pernicious effect.

> [W]hen a nondiscriminatory tax is coupled with a subsidy to one of the groups hurt by the tax, a State's political processes can no longer be relied upon to prevent legislative abuse, because one of the in-state interests which would otherwise lobby against the tax has been mollified by the subsidy.[84]

§ 6.07 PROHIBITORY LAWS

[1] Quarantine and Inspection

The States retain some power to enact reasonable quarantine laws, applicable to interstate and local commerce although recent cases suggest that power is eroding. They may prevent introduction or spread of disease even though the state regulation may affect interstate commerce. Thus, to safeguard health, the Court upheld a New York statute forbidding the importation of cattle unless certified to be free of a certain infectious disease.[85] More recently, *Maine v. Taylor* upheld barriers on bringing live bait fish into Maine to protect against parasites that would jeopardize the state's marine ecology.[86] Such laws which regulate noxious articles, whatever their origin, are not impermissible protectionist measures.[87] Similarly, the State may protect its citizens from "confusion and deception in the marketing"[88] of products.

Limits, of course, exist. The Court struck down a state law that prohibited landfill operators from accepting solid waste that originated outside the county in which their facilities were located[89] and one that imposed a higher fee for the

---

[82] 303 U.S. at 187.

[83] 512 U.S. 186 (1994).

[84] *Id.* at 200.

[85] *See* Mintz v. Baldwin, 289 U.S. 346 (1933).

[86] *See* Maine v. Taylor, 477 U.S. 131 (1986).

[87] *See* Philadelphia v. New Jersey, 437 U.S. 617, 628 (1978).

[88] *Hunt*, 432 U.S. at 353.

[89] *See* Fort Gratiot Landfill, Inc. v. Michigan Dep't of Natural Resources, 504 U.S. 353 (1992).

disposal of out-of-state waste in landfills within the State.[90] The State may not discriminate against articles of commerce from outside the State absent some reason, other than their origin, to treat them differently. In *Philadelphia v. New Jersey*[91] the Court struck down a New Jersey law that banned importation of out-of-state waste. Justice Rehnquist argued in dissent that the "fact of life that New Jersey must somehow dispose of its own noxious items does not mean that it must serve as a depository for those of every other State."[92] The Court rejected this argument. Such a quarantine law was permitted only if the "very movement" of the banned good "risked contagion and other evils."[93] Similarly, an Alabama law taxing out-of-state hazardous waste was struck down as not a legitimate quarantine measure since Alabama allowed internal production of such waste.[94] Finally, in *Kassel v. Consolidated Freightways Corp.*[95] the Court struck down an Iowa law banning use of 65 foot double tractor trailers on its highways. Although the justices divided on what rationale was decisive, Professor Laurence H. Tribe suggested that *Kassel* stands for the principle that "under the commerce clause a state may not reduce the risks posed to its own citizens by the stream of commerce by diverting that stream out-of-state."[96] If he is right, this principle would seem to cut a hole in the quarantine principle.

[2] Embargo Measures

Embargo measures forbidding exports raise similar issues. Protectionist purposes may not justify a State in banning exports. In *Pike v. Bruce Church*,[97] the Court ruled invalid a prohibition against shipping uncrated cantaloupes to the grower's out-of-state crating plant. The prohibition served no health purpose. More recently, the Court invalidated an ordinance that required all nonhazardous solid waste to be processed at a local transfer facility before leaving town.[98] In effect, the ordinance hoarded solid waste to benefit the local facility that treated it.

Embargo measures must be based on a legitimate purpose which cannot otherwise be achieved. In *Sligh v. Kirkwood*,[99] the Court upheld a Florida law making it unlawful to ship out-of-state immature or unfit citrus fruits. The Court implied that Florida could bar shipment of green oranges to preserve the good name of Florida fruit. To the extent the Court's reasoning implies a State may use its embargo power to protect local economic interests, it is contrary to other precedent. Yet *Sligh* may be spun as a case upholding a Florida law directed

---

[90] *See* Oregon Waste Sys., Inc. v. Department of Envtl. Quality, 511 U.S. 93 (1994).

[91] 437 U.S. 617 (1978).

[92] *Id.* at 632.

[93] *Id.* at 629.

[94] Chemical Waste Management, Inc. v. Hunt, 504 U.S. 334 (1992).

[95] 450 U.S. 662 (1981).

[96] LAURENCE H. TRIBE, AMERICAN CONSTITUTIONAL LAW 422 (2d ed. 1988).

[97] 397 U.S. 137 (1970).

[98] *See* C & A Carbone, Inc. v. Clarkstown, 511 U.S. 383 (1994).

[99] 237 U.S. 52 (1915).

against deceptive practices, an interest endorsed in other contexts.[100] A State may use the embargo power to prevent fraud of which selling unripened fruit arguably is a type. Moreover, when a State acts against the economic interests of in-staters to protect out-of-staters, the concerns animating the Dormant Commerce Clause are not implicated.

It is generally difficult to justify such measures excluding outsiders from a local market. Thus, a State could not deny outsiders access to its limited landfill space.[101] In *Hughes v. Oklahoma*,[102] the Court struck down a law prohibiting the shipment out-of-state of minnows procured in Oklahoma. The statute clearly sought to hoard resources for local use.

The Dormant Commerce Clause addresses laws that impose discriminatory fees on outsiders as well as those that flatly deny access to the market. Thus, the Court struck down an Oregon law that taxed disposal of out-of-state waste almost three times as much as in-state waste ($2.25/ton U.S.85/ton) absent evidence of a cost differential to the State.[103]

The Court has upheld some restrictions on transfer of ground water out-of-state.[104] The restrictions — that a state official find the transfers reasonable, not contrary to conservation, or inimical to public welfare — were reasonable. Nebraska had also restricted intrastate transfers, so the measures were not discriminatory. Water, too, was deemed special and the Court thought Nebraska's conservation efforts should be rewarded. In essence, the burden on commerce did not greatly outweigh the state's benefit. But the Court struck down a further condition that water could not be exported to a State that did not grant reciprocal rights to its own water. The reciprocity requirement failed to satisfy the exacting scrutiny of the legitimate purpose/least restrictive alternative test.

§ 6.08   EXCEPTIONS TO THE DORMANT COMMERCE CLAUSE

[1] Market Participant Exception

Courts have recognized certain exceptions to the Dormant Commerce Clause where States are allowed to favor in-state interests or burden commerce. Some are judge-crafted exceptions that require no action by any other branch of government. First, if the State acts as a market participant, not as a regulator, the Dormant Commerce Clause does not apply and the State may favor its own

---

[100] *Cf. Hunt*, 432 U.S. at 353 (state has interest in protecting own citizens from deception).

[101] Philadelphia v. New Jersey, 437 U.S. 617 (1978); *see also* Fort Gratiot Sanitary Landfill v. Michigan Dep't of Natural Resources, 504 U.S. 353 (1992) (local government cannot exclude out-of-state garbage).

[102] 441 U.S. 322 (1979).

[103] Oregon Waste System, Inc. v. Department of Environmental Quality of the State of Oregon, 511 U.S. 93 (1994).

[104] Sporhase v. Nebraska, 458 U.S. 941 (1982).

citizens.[105] The market participant exception applies where the State operates a business or purchases or sells goods or services or otherwise acts in a proprietary capacity. The exception rests in part on the word "regulate" in the Commerce Clause. This language is deemed to impose restraints on state regulation of commerce, not participation in it.

The exception originated in *Hughes v. Alexandria Scrap Corp.*[106] In order to dispose of abandoned automobiles, Maryland imposed a program whereby the State would buy such vehicles. Although the State required more extensive documentation from out-of-state sellers, the Court upheld the discrimination against an argument that it violated the Dormant Commerce Clause. The State was acting as a market participant, not regulator, and in that role was free to favor its own.

Reeves, Inc. v. Stake,[107] is illustrative. South Dakota owned and operated a cement plant. The State decided to supply South Dakota customers before furnishing cement to others during a shortage. A Wyoming concrete distributor challenged the preference as violating the Dormant Commerce Clause. The Court rejected the contention, distinguishing between the States as market participants and regulators. Dormant Commerce Clause restrictions affect the States only as regulators. The limitations on state prohibitory and embargo power apply to state restrictions on commerce in a free market, not commerce that owes its existence to the State itself. Here the commerce the State restricted would not exist if South Dakota had not entered the cement producing business.

Although the paradigmatic situation for the market participant exception occurs when the State operates a business, it also may apply when the State sponsors a program that brings it into the market. Thus, in *White v. Massachusetts Council of Construction Employers,*[108] Boston was able to require that fifty percent of the work force on city sponsored jobs be city residents.

The market participant exception protects a State only from Dormant Commerce Clause scrutiny. It affords no defense to the Privileges and Immunities Clause. Nor does it insulate the State when it seeks to regulate as well as participate in the market. Thus in *South-Central Timber Development, Inc. v. Wunnicke,*[109] the Court struck down an Alaska law that required those who bought Alaska timber to process it in State. Alaska could favor its own in selling the timber, but could not seek to regulate the later conduct of its customers.

The Court rejected Maine's attempt to use the market participant exception to confer a tax benefit on certain in-state charitable organizations in *Camps Newfound/Owatonna, Inc. v. Town of Harrison.*[110] Maine exempted from a real estate tax in-state charities principally serving Maine residents while substantially

---

[105] *See* Hughes v. Alexandria Scrap Corp., 426 U.S. 794 (1976).

[106] *Id.*

[107] 447 U.S. 429 (1980).

[108] 460 U.S. 204 (1983).

[109] 467 U.S. 82 (1984) (plurality).

[110] 520 U.S. 564 (1997).

limiting the exemption available to local charities principally serving out-of-state residents.[111] Maine sought to justify the discriminatory tax treatment as a purchase of services from instate vendors to benefit its residents.[112] The Court, however, rejected the claim, because the tax exemption "cannot be characterized as a proprietary activity falling within the market-participant exception."[113] The Court suggested that market participant status required "direct state involvement in the market,"[114] whereas Maine was acting in a sovereign capacity, not as a market participant.[115] In contrast to the relatively narrow activities previously protected from Dormant Commerce Clause scrutiny under the market participant exception, Maine's exemption claimed so broad an area, charitable institutions, as to threaten federal regulation of states' discriminatory tax schemes.[116]

In addition to the somewhat strained textual argument, the market participant exception rests on other justifications.[117] Historically, the Commerce Clause grew out of concerns relating to the effect of states' discrimination on transactions between private parties, not when the State was a buyer or seller of goods or services.[118] Further, if States engage in the market they should be able to act like other entrepreneurs who may, if they wish, favor some customers over others.[119] (Of course, a State is not like other market participants since it may tax and claim immunity from suit). Moreover, if the State wishes to limit its profits by restricting its market why should it not be able to do so? Finally, spending programs seem less coercive than regulations or taxes and "seem less hostile to other states and less inconsistent with the concept of union than discriminatory regulation or taxation."[120]

[2] Additional Exceptions

In recent years, the Court has recognized additional exceptions to the Dormant Commerce Clause. In *General Motors Corp. v. Tracy*,[121] the Court arguably created a "public utilities" exception relieving certain state actions from scrutiny under Dormant Commerce Clause jurisprudence.[122] The Court, speaking through Justice Souter, determined that Ohio's exemption of sales and use taxes for "natural gas compan[ies]" (which were essentially in-state companies selling to

---

[111] *See id.* at 567–68.

[112] *See id.* at 566.

[113] *Id.* at 572.

[114] *Id.* at 593.

[115] *Camps Newfound/Owatonna, Inc.*, 520 U.S. at 593–94.

[116] *See id.*

[117] *See generally* Dan T. Coenen, *Untangling the Market-Participant Exemption to the Dormant Commerce Clause*, 88 Mich. L. Rev. 395 (1989).

[118] *Reeves*, 447 U.S. at 437.

[119] *Id.* at 438–39.

[120] Donald Regan, *The Supreme Court and State Protectionism: Making Sense of the Dormant Commerce Clause*, 84 Mich. L. Rev. 1091, 1194 (1986).

[121] 519 U.S. 278 (1997).

[122] *See id. See also Camps Newfound/Owatonna*, 520 U.S. at 607 (Scalia, J., dissenting).

residential consumers) did not unfairly discriminate against marketers of natural gas (which were mainly out-of-state entities selling to corporations like General Motors Corporation (GMC)).

In examining GMC's claim that the exemption disfavored out-of-state entities and discriminated against interstate commerce, the Court invoked the familiar principle that "any notion of discrimination assumes a comparison of substantially similar entities."[123] If the favored and disfavored products differ, they may appeal to separate markets and, as such, may not compete even if the regulatory preferences were removed.

The Court concluded that the in-state natural gas companies served residential consumers, a different market than the out-of-state entities addressed.[124] The Court determined that removing the disparity in tax treatment would not benefit interstate commerce.[125] Ohio's tax exemption for natural gas companies created a distinctive product that so differentiated the regulated natural gas companies from the independent interstate entities that the two types of organizations were not comparable under the Dormant Commerce Clause.[126]

Similarly, the Court has recognized that in some instances, at least, laws favoring local government do not run afoul of the Dormant Commerce Clause. In *United Haulers Assn., Inc. v. Oneida-Herkimer Solid Waste Management Authority*,[127] the Court upheld a flow control ordinance requiring that trash haulers deliver solid waste to a publicly owned processing plant. New York was discharging a traditional governmental function and accordingly was not subject to normal dormant Commerce Clause analysis. Writing for the Court, in an opinion joined by Justices Scalia, Souter, Ginsburg and Breyer, Chief Justice Roberts explained:

> Laws favoring local government . . . may be directed toward any number of legitimate goals unrelated to protectionism. Here the flow control ordinances enable the Counties to pursue particular policies with respect to the handling and treatment of waste generated in the Counties, while allocating the costs of those policies on citizens and businesses according to the volume of waste they generate.

> The contrary approach of treating public and private entities the same under the dormant Commerce Clause would lead to unprecedented and unbounded interference by the courts with state and local government. The dormant Commerce Clause is not a roving license for federal courts to decide what activities are appropriate for state and local government to undertake, and what activities must be the province of private market competition.

---

[123] *Id.* at 298.

[124] *See id.* at 302.

[125] *See id.*

[126] *See id.* at 310.

[127] 550 U.S. 330 (2007).

Dissenting, Justices Alito, Stevens and Kennedy found the case indistinguishable from *C & A Carbone, Inc.* v. *Clarkstown.*[128] They did not share the majority's conclusion that the public nature of the facility in question distinguished it in a meaningful way from that in the earlier case which, according to the dissenters, was only nominally private.

The following term, in *Department of Revenue v. Davis,*[129] the Court extended that analysis to a Kentucky income tax statute which exempted from state tax municipal bond interest from municipal bonds which Kentucky, but not other states, issued. Justice Souter explained that the *United Haulers* rationale, that "a government function is not susceptible to standard dormant Commerce Clause scrutiny owing to its likely motivation by legitimate objectives distinct from the simple economic protectionism the Clause abhors" applied "with even greater force to laws favoring a State's municipal bonds, given that the issuance of debt securities to pay for public projects is a quintessentially public function" deeply rooted in historical practice.[130]

Four members of the Court have suggested that the Court create a "domestic charities" exception to the Dormant Commerce Clause.[131] Joined by Chief Justice Rehnquist and Justices Thomas and Ginsburg, Justice Scalia posited that the existing exceptions are not expansive enough to cover the realm of state activities that should be free from Dormant Commerce Clause scrutiny.[132] Rather, on other occasions States should be able to provide social benefits directly or indirectly to its own residents without Dormant Commerce Clause scrutiny.[133]

[3] Congressional Consent

The Dormant Commerce Clause also does not apply when Congress authorizes state action that would otherwise be invalid under the Commerce Clause. In other words, Congress can consent to state measures that restrict commerce. Once Congress empowers the State to regulate or endorses existing state measures, Congress is no longer dormant. Congress first used this power to sanction state laws prohibiting sale of liquor. In *Leisy v. Hardin,*[134] the Court had held that the States may not prohibit the sale of liquor in its original package shipped from another State "in the absence of congressional permission."[135] The implication was that congressional assent might legitimate the state law. Following the *Leisy* dictum Congress permitted state prohibition laws to apply to sales of imported liquors in their original packages as if the liquor had been produced in the State.

---

[128] 511 U.S. 383 (1994).

[129] 553 U.S. 328 (2008).

[130] *Id.* at 342.

[131] *Camps Newfound/Owatonna,* 520 U.S. at 608 (Scalia, J., dissenting).

[132] *See id.* at 607.

[133] *See id.* at 607–08.

[134] 135 U.S. 100 (1890).

[135] *Id.* at 124.

The Court upheld the statute in *In re Rahrer*.[136] The Court saw no reason why Congress could not permit imported articles to fall at once within local jurisdiction. Congress then passed the Webb-Kenyon Law which prohibited the importation of liquor into any State in violation of that State's laws. The Court upheld this federal law as a proper regulation.[137]

These cases create a seemingly anomalous situation. If the Constitution forbids certain state action, how can Congress by consenting give that action validity?

The Supreme Court addressed that issue in *Prudential Insurance Co. v. Benjamin*.[138] Two years earlier, the Court had held that insurance was commerce which Congress could regulate.[139] In response, Congress passed a statute pursuant to its commerce power which authorized States to regulate insurance. This law was challenged as an improper extension of state power over interstate commerce. The Court disagreed. It held that congressional consent could validate a state law which absent such consent would violate the Dormant Commerce Clause.[140]

These cases serve to remind of the nature of the Dormant Commerce Clause. It does not absolutely prohibit state power over interstate commerce, but remains subject to Congressional override. The Commerce Clause is primarily a grant of power to Congress to regulate interstate commerce. The power to regulate includes the right to prescribe that commerce shall be subject to relevant state regulations. Accordingly, Congress may consent to state laws governing commerce. Put differently, the Dormant Commerce Clause might be seen as reflecting a constitutional presumption that absent federal legislation the Constitution inhibits state legislation affecting commerce. It polices that legislation with the strict scrutiny and *Pike* balancing tests. Once Congress acts to authorize state regulation, the constitutional presumption is rebutted. "When Congress so chooses, state actions that it plainly authorizes are invulnerable to constitutional attack under the Commerce Clause."[141] However, such state actions are still subject to attack on other grounds, such as for violating the Equal Protection Clause.[142]

§ 6.09 CONGRESSIONAL CONFLICT: PREEMPTION

Congress may also exclude state regulation in a particular area. A valid congressional provision is the supreme law of the land that, under the Supremacy Clause, supersedes any incompatible state law. Identifying incompatibility involves

---

[136] 140 U.S. 545 (1891).

[137] *See* James Clark Distilling Co. v. Western Maryland. R. Co., 242 U.S. 311, 325–31 (1917).

[138] 328 U.S. 408 (1946).

[139] *See* United States v. South-Eastern Underwriters Ass'n, 322 U.S. 533 (1944).

[140] *See also* Western and Southern Life Ins. Co. v. State Bd. of Equalization of California, 451 U.S. 648 (1981) (upholding state discriminatory tax on out-of-state insurance companies because McCarran-Ferguson Act removes Commerce Clause restriction); Northeast Bancorp, Inc. v. Board of Governors, 472 U.S. 159 (1985) (upholding state laws discriminating against some out-of-state holding companies based on federal legislative consent).

[141] Northeast Bancorp., Inc. v. Board of Governors, 472 U.S. 159, 174 (1985). *See* Metropolitan Life Ins. Co. v. Ward, 470 U.S. 869 (1985).

[142] *See* Metropolitan Life Ins. Co. v. Ward, 470 U.S. 869 (1985).

statutory interpretation, generally dependent on congressional intent which is the foundation of premption analysis.

Cases involving congressional action in an area where state regulation also exists fall into three categories: (1) when there is a conflict between the federal and the state legislation; (2) when Congress has preempted the entire field of regulation; and (3) when the federal and state laws are compatible. In the latter case, the two regulatory regimes may both operate, subject, of course, to any constitutional limits.

Express preemption follows from a clear congressional statement prohibiting regulation except by the federal government. The Court has identified two varieties of preemption: express preemption and implied preemption. Implied preemption occurs when the federal regulatory scheme is so pervasive to support a reasonable inference that Congress meant to exclude state regulation from the field (field preemption) or when a conflict between federal and state laws makes compliance with both impossible (conflict preemption).[143]

Direct conflict between a federal and state law presents a relatively easy situation. Even if Congress has not completely foreclosed state legislation in a particular area, a state statute is void if it conflicts with a valid federal law.[144] National supremacy requires the state statute yield.

Even when the Constitution does not commit exclusive power over a particular field to Congress, state regulation must fail if Congress has acted with an intent to preempt an entire field of regulation — when "the scheme of federal regulation is sufficiently comprehensive to make reasonable the inference that Congress 'left no room' for supplementary state regulation."[145] When Congress includes an express preemption provision, the outcome is relatively uncontroversial although questions may still remain regarding the extent of the intended preemption.[146] Implied preemption cases present closer questions.

Congress demonstrates the requisite intent most clearly when it includes an explicit preemption statement in a federal statute. That does not, however, eliminate the need for judicial interpretation since questions often remain regarding the scope of the preemption. In *Cipollone*, for instance, Congress had included two preemption provisions in federal court regarding warnings on cigarette packs. The issue was whether the language in them preempted a state common law action for damages. The Court held that one of the federal laws did not preempt state common law actions but the other, which outlawed requirements based on smoking "under state law" did preempt common law actions.[147] At times, the Court finds Congress intended to preempt state regulation in a field.

When Congress has enacted a comprehensive regulation of aircraft noise, a city ordinance restricting jet flights to curtail airport noise is invalid; the pervasive

---

[143] *See* Gade v. National Solid Waste Management Ass'n, 505 U.S. 88, 108 (1992).

[144] *See* Ray v. Atlantic Richfield Co., 435 U.S. 151, 158 (1978).

[145] California Sav. & Loan Ass'n v. Guerra, 479 U.S. 272, 281 (1987).

[146] *See, e.g.*, Cipollone v. Liggett Group, Inc., 505 U.S. 504 (1992).

[147] *Cipollone*, 505 U.S. 504 (1992).

nature of the federal scheme suggests congressional preemption.[148] Similarly, when Congress establishes a uniform federal regime controlling the design and size of oil tankers, a State may not impose its own design and size requirements, or bar super-tankers permitted by the federal law from its waters.[149]

The preemption issue raises questions of the proper distribution of federal and state power. If courts apply the preemption doctrine inflexibly, they risk ousting state power in areas where the State has a substantial interest in regulation of the conduct at issue.[150] When the field is one States traditionally occupy, the historic police powers of the States should not be lightly superseded.[151] Indeed, the Court has articulated a presumption of non-preemption in areas where States have traditionally regulated. In *Rice v. Santa Fe Elevator Corp.*,[152] the Court stated that when Congress legislates in an area of traditional state occupation "we start with the assumption that the historic police powers of the state were not to be superseded by the Federal Act unless that was the clear and manifest purpose of Congress."[153]

The clear purpose rule offers some, but not total, protection to state law. It only applies in areas States traditionally occupied, not in marine transport[154] or other areas where federal rules have been dominant. In *United States v. Locke*,[155] the Court held that a comprehensive federal regulatory scheme governing oil tankers preempted Washington's regulations addressing various navigation matters. The Court essentially confirmed the continuing vitality of the "basic analytic struc-ture"[156] of *Ray v. Atlantic Richfield Co.*[157] The state legislation benefitted from no presumption against preemption since it intruded on national and international maritime commerce, an area where the federal interest is paramount and uniform regulations are desirable. Some provisions of Washington law were invalid based on the concept of conflict preemption — compliance with both federal and state law was impossible or state law would complicate accomplishment of Congress' objectives.[158] Thus, Washington's reporting requirements ran afoul of Coast Guard regulations which were to be the exclusive law on the subject. Other Washington laws — dealing with training requirements, English language proficiency, navigation watch — failed under field preemption.[159]

---

[148] *See* Burbank v. Lockheed Air Terminal, Inc., 411 U.S. 624, 633 (1973).

[149] *See* Ray v. Atlantic Richfield Co., 435 U.S. 151 (1978).

[150] *See* Farmer v. United Bhd. of Carpenters, 430 U.S. 290, 302 (1977).

[151] *See* Jones v. Rath Packing Co., 430 U.S. 519, 525 (1977).

[152] 331 U.S. 218 (1947).

[153] *Id.* at 230.

[154] United States v. Locke, 529 U.S. 89, 108 (2000).

[155] 529 U.S. 89 (2000).

[156] *Id.* at 104.

[157] 435 U.S. 151 (1978).

[158] *Locke*, 529 U.S. at 115–16 (regarding Washington's casualty reporting requirement).

[159] *Id.* at 112–15.

Moreover, state law may be overcome with a clear statement of federal preemption. In *Crosby v. National Foreign Trade Council*,[160] the Court unanimously held that a Massachusetts law restricting state entities from doing business with Burma conflicted with a subsequent federal statute and accordingly was invalid. The state law undermined "the intended purpose and 'natural effect' of at least three provisions of the federal Act," those being "its delegation of effective discretion to the President to control economic sanctions against Burma, its limitation of sanctions solely to United States persons and new investment, and its directive to the President to proceed diplomatically in developing a comprehensive, multilateral strategy towards Burma."[161] The conflicts were not constitutionally irrelevant even though the statutes shared common goals and compliance with both was possible since "the inconsistency of sanctions here undermines the congressional calibration of force."[162]

Congress' failure to expressly preempt state statutes was not tantamount to implied consent. Justice Souter wrote that Congress' failure to provide for preemption expressly may reflect nothing more than the settled character of implied preemption doctrine that courts will dependably apply, and in any event, the existence of conflict cognizable under the Supremacy Clause does not depend on express congressional recognition that federal and state law may conflict."[163]

In contrast to other areas where the Rehnquist Court invoked federalism concerns to protect state interests against action by the federal government, that Court frequently held that federal law preempted state law even though the state law in question sometimes addressed areas of classic state concern.

For instance, in *Geier v. American Honda Motor Co.*,[164] the Court in a 5-4 decision, held that although by virtue of a savings provision, a state common law tort suit fell outside the area expressly preempted by a federal regulation promulgated pursuant to federal law, ordinary preemption principles applied nonetheless to preempt the state tort action. Congress could have nullified those ordinary preemption principles but must do so expressly. The express preemption and savings clauses do not impose any "special burden" on a party claiming conflict preemption.[165] A tort action in this case, for not having air bags in a 1987 car, would stand as an obstacle to the federal objective of giving manufacturers "a range of choices among different passive restraint devices."[166]

---

[160] 530 U.S. 363 (2000).

[161] *Id.* at 374.

[162] *Id.* at 380.

[163] *Id.* at 387–88.

[164] 529 U.S. 861 (2000).

[165] *Id.* at 870.

[166] *Id.* at 875.

§ 6.10 PRIVILEGES AND IMMUNITIES

It may seem odd to conclude a chapter on the Dormant Commerce Clause with a section on the Privileges and Immunities Clause of Article IV. Any inconsistencies between chapter title and the subject matter that follows will hopefully be excused based on the similarities between the Privileges and Immunities and Dormant Commerce Clauses. The Privileges and Immunities Clause of Article IV states that "[t]he citizens of each state shall be entitled to all Privileges and Immunities of citizens in the several states."

Article IV's Privileges and Immunities Clause comes from the longer version in the Articles of Confederation. The Clause does not create the rights it calls privileges and immunities; nor does it control the power of the States over their own citizens' rights. Instead, its purpose was "to help fuse into one Nation a collection of independent, sovereign States."[167] It declares "to the several States, that whatever those rights, as you grant or establish them to your own citizens, or as you limit or qualify, or impose restrictions on their exercise, the same, neither more nor less, shall be the measure of the rights of citizens of other States within your jurisdiction."[168] It seeks to guarantee "to a citizen of State A who ventures into State B the same privileges which the citizens of State B enjoy".[169] As Justice Kennedy wrote, "our Founders, in their wisdom, thought it important to our sense of nationhood that each State be required to make a genuine effort to treat nonresidents on an equal basis with residents."[170] The Court recently reaffirmed that the Article IV Privileges and Immunities Clause protects the right of an out-of-state citizen "to be treated as a welcome visitor rather than an unfriendly alien when temporarily present" in another state.[171]

The preceding should suggest that the Dormant Commerce Clause and Privileges and Immunities Clause share some common ground. Important differences exist in their reach.[172] First, unlike the Dormant Commerce Clause, the Privileges and Immunities Clause extends only to individual "citizens." It does not protect aliens or corporations. Second, whereas the Dormant Commerce Clause addresses both state statutes that discriminate against out-of-staters and neutral laws that burden commerce unduly, the Privileges and Immunities Clause only shares the former target — discriminatory measures. Third, the Privileges and Immunities Clause only protects what its name suggests — privileges and immunities. Finally, the various exceptions to the Dormant Commerce Clause, such as congressional consent and market participant, do not apply to the Privileges and Immunities Clause. Congress cannot consent to a State violating what Article IV protects. Nor can a State protect its action on the grounds that it was acting as a market participant, not regulator.

---

[167] Toomer v. Witsell, 334 U.S. 385, 395 (1948).

[168] Slaughter-House Cases, 83 U.S. (16 Wall.) 36, 77 (1873).

[169] *See Toomer*, 334 U.S. at 395.

[170] Barnard v. Thorstenn, 489 U.S. 546, 559 (1989).

[171] Saenz v. Roe, 526 U.S. 489, 500 (1999).

[172] *See generally* Brannon P. Denning, *Why the Privileges and Immunities Clause of Article IV Cannot Replace the Dormant Commerce Clause Doctrine*, 88 MINN. L. REV. 384 (2003).

The threshold question under Article IV, Section 2 then is whether the state action jeopardizes some privilege or immunity. The Court has confined the clause to activity "sufficiently basic to the livelihood of the Nation"[173] and to matters "bearing on the vitality of the Nation as a single entity."[174] These phrases hardly provide clear tests. In *Corfield v. Coryell*[175] Justice Bushrod Washington defined the term as referring to those rights "which are, in their nature, fundamental; which belong, of right, to the citizens of all free governments; and which have, at all times, been enjoyed by the citizens of the several states." He continued:

> What these fundamental principles are, it would perhaps be more tedious than difficult to enumerate. They may, however, be all comprehended under the following general heads: Protection by the government; the enjoyment of life and liberty, with the right to acquire and possess property of every kind, and to pursue and obtain happiness and safety; subject nevertheless to such restraints as the government may justly prescribe for the general good of the whole. The right of a citizen of one state to pass through, or to reside in any other state, for purposes of trade, agriculture, professional pursuits, or otherwise; to claim the benefit of the writ of habeas corpus; to institute and maintain actions of any kind in the courts of the state; to take, hold and dispose of property, either real or personal; and an exemption from higher taxes or impositions than are paid by the other citizens of the state; may be mentioned as some of the particular privileges and immunities of citizens, which are clearly embraced by the general description of privileges deemed to be fundamental: to which may be added, the elective franchise, as regulated and established by the laws or constitution of the state in which it is to be exercised. These, and many others which might be mentioned, are strictly speaking, privileges and immunities. . . .[176]

Clearly, privileges and immunities include basic constitutional rights. Thus, a State could not forbid out-of-staters from worshipping or engaging in political speech. The clause also protects the right of out-of-state women to obtain an abortion.[177] *Doe v. Bolton* goes further, however, to include as a privilege or immunity the right to obtain medical services out-of-state.[178] Thus, a State could not prohibit nonresidents from receiving medical care. Similarly, the right to protection of the laws and to police and fire department services must count among what the clause protects. Most cases under the clause deal with the right to engage in important economic pursuits. Clearly the right to pursue a trade is a "privilege." Thus, a State may not bar an otherwise qualified nonresident from admission to law practice.[179] The nonresident's interest in practicing law on equal terms with residents is a privilege

---

[173] Supreme Court of Virginia v. Friedman, 487 U.S. 59, 64 (1988) (quoting other cases).

[174] *Id.* at 64–65 (quoting other cases).

[175] 6 F. Cas. 546, 551 (C.C.E.D. Pa. 1823).

[176] *Id.* at 551–52.

[177] *See* Doe v. Bolton, 410 U.S. 179, 200 (1973).

[178] *See id.*

[179] *See Friedman*, 487 U.S. 59.

protected by the Clause.[180] Similarly, a state law regulating commercial shrimp fishing may not impose a license fee of $2,500 for each shrimp boat owned by a nonresident while charging a resident only $25.[181] On the other hand, recreational activity does not rank as a privilege or immunity.[182]

Determining that a State discriminates against out-of-staters with respect to a privilege or immunity, does not end the inquiry. A restriction that discriminates against citizens of other States is invalid unless "(i) there is a substantial reason for the difference in treatment; and (ii) the discrimination practiced against nonresidents bears a substantial relationship to the State's objective."[183] The test against which denials of privilege and immunities are measured accordingly resembles the strict scrutiny test under the Dormant Commerce Clause. State statutes implicating the clause fail if the State cannot meet its burden of justification. A complete bar of nonresidents from pursuing a calling lacks a substantial relationship to legitimate state objectives.[184]

In *Lunding v. New York Tax Appeals Tribunal*,[185] the Court struck down, under the Privileges and Immunities Clause of Article IV, a New York law that eliminated a pro rata deduction for nonresidents' alimony payments while preserving the benefit for residents. The statute failed because the State did not adequately justify the discriminatory treatment.

The privilege or immunity that triggered the Court's scrutiny was the right of a United States citizen to conduct business in States other than one's domicile without being subject to more onerous taxation than local residents. The Court applied the familiar requirement that to defend a law challenged under the Privilege and Immunities Clause, a State must demonstrate that " '(i) there is a substantial reason for the difference in treatment; and (ii) the discrimination practiced against nonresidents bears a substantial relationship to the State's objective.' "[186]

New York attempted to justify the differential treatment on the ground that because it could not tax income earned outside the State, it need not grant deductions connected to that income. The Court found the State's claim at odds with its history of granting deductions to nonresidents for both alimony and other nonbusiness expenses. The Court explained that it would be acceptable for a nonresident to pay higher taxes than a resident if the disparity was due to the former's higher profits in the state. Here, New York failed adequately to justify its facially discriminatory law.

---

[180] *See id.* at 70. In *Barnard v. Thorstenn*, 489 U.S. 546 (1989), the Virgin Islands bar admission residency requirement was similarly held to violate the Privileges and Immunities Clause.

[181] *See* Toomer v. Witsell, 334 U.S. 385 (1948).

[182] *See* Baldwin v. Fish & Game Comm'n, 436 U.S. 371 (1978) (Montana may charge higher fees for hunting licenses for non-residents).

[183] Supreme Court of New Hampshire v. Piper, 470 U.S. 274, 284 (1985).

[184] *See, e.g.*, United Bldg. & Constr. Trades Council v. Mayor of Camden, 465 U.S. 208 (1984); Hicklin v. Orbeck, 437 U.S. 518, 524–526 (1978).

[185] 522 U.S. 287 (1998).

[186] *Id.* at 298.

In *United Building & Construction Trades Council of Camden v. Mayor and Council of the City of Camden*,[187] the Court held that a city ordinance which required at least 40% of employees of contractors on city projects be residents implicated a Privilege and Immunity. "[T]he pursuit of a common calling is one of the most fundamental of those privileges" the clause protects.[188] Although "there is no fundamental right to government employment" the Court declined to view employees of city contractors as city employees. The market participant exception might insulate a law from attack under the Dormant Commerce Clause[189] but it did not apply to the Privileges and Immunities Clause.

---

[187] 465 U.S. 208 (1984).

[188] *Id.* at 219.

[189] *See* White v. Massachusetts Council of Constr. Employers, Inc., 460 U.S. 204 (1983).

Chapter 7

EXECUTIVE POWER

INTRODUCTION

The provisions of Article II regarding the Executive branch are, in several respects, unique. Whereas Article I creates and empowers a bicameral legislature consisting of hundreds of equal players, and Article III authorizes a multi-member Supreme Court and potentially a large number of inferior courts, Article II lodges all executive power in a single leader.

Moreover, some provisions of Article II are the most general in the Constitution. The powers vested in the President are stated in such a vague manner as to leave the precise authority granted somewhat obscure: "The executive Power shall be vested in a President. . . . The President shall be Commander-in-Chief of the Army and Navy . . . he shall take Care that the Laws be faithfully executed." The generality may have traced to difficulties the framers encountered in creating the executive. "There is hardly any part of the system which could have been attended with greater difficulty in the arrangement of it than [the executive branch],"[1] wrote Alexander Hamilton. In any event, the language of Article II is indefinite even compared to the articles defining the authority of the other branches.

These two features, a single executive leader and open-ended grants of power, have enabled the Presidency to grow in power during the 20th century. To be sure, other developments have set the context encouraging this evolution — the expanded international role of the United States, the rise of the welfare state, technological change that has transformed international relations, travel, and communication. Against this backdrop, the Presidency has emerged as a focal point of American political life.

The framers were committed to a concept of an energetic executive.[2] But they also believed it imperative to harness that energy so it would serve, not imperil, the ends of good government.[3] The effort to preserve the accountability of a powerful executive has posed a critical challenge for much of the last half of the 20th century.

This chapter addresses those subjects. Section 7.01 discusses the election of the President, both as the Constitution prescribes and in practice. Section 7.02 presents summaries of some different theories of presidential power as reflected in leading cases. The chapter then considers five different roles where the President exercises

---

[1] THE FEDERALIST No. 67 (Alexander Hamilton).

[2] See, e.g., THE FEDERALIST No. 70 (Alexander Hamilton) ("Taking it for granted, therefore, that all men of sense will agree in the necessity of an energetic executive.").

[3] Id.

executive power — the legislative role (Section 7.03), the administrative role (Section 7.04), the law-enforcement role (Section 7.05), the foreign affairs role (Section 7.06), and the role as Commander-in-Chief (Section 7.07). Section 7.08 addresses problems of presidential accountability — presidential privileges, immunities and impeachment. Presidential succession and disability are treated in Section 7.09. Section 7.10 addresses the Separation of Powers doctrine and recent decisions of the Supreme Court interpreting it.

§ 7.01 ELECTION

In contrast to the general treatment it accords presidential powers and duties, Article II, as superceded in part by the Twelfth Amendment, describes in some detail the mechanism for electing the President. Under it, the President is chosen by presidential electors the states "appoint" for this purpose. This method was one of the final compromises the founders reached; it made agreement to the Constitution possible.

The question of how to choose the President vexed and divided the framers. Some proposed direct election by the people; others, deeming the people uninformed, advocated some form of legislative election.[4] Yet such a plan, James Madison and others pointed out, might lead to legislative domination of the executive, thereby eroding the separation of powers doctrine intended to help guard against government tyranny. Ultimately, the framers struck a compromise. Electors chosen in each State would elect the President and Vice President. Each State would have a number of electoral votes equal to its representation in the house and senate, yet the electors would not be, indeed could not be, members of Congress.

Notwithstanding the controversy over the Electoral College, the founders considered it a proud achievement. "The mode of appointment of the Chief Magistrate of the United States is almost the only part of the system, of any consequence, which has escaped without severe censure or which has received the slightest mark of approbation from its opponents," wrote Alexander Hamilton. "[I]f the manner of it be not perfect, it is at least excellent."[5]

In retrospect, Hamilton's assessment was generous. By the fourth election, the system had shown flaws. As originally designed, each elector cast two votes for President with the winner, provided he won a majority, being President and the runner up, Vice President. The framers did not, however, anticipate the formation of national political parties.[6] In 1800, Thomas Jefferson and Aaron Burr ran as a ticket with the former intended for the Presidency. Since all of their party's electors voted for each, however, they ended in an electoral vote deadlock which threw the decision into the House of Representatives under the contingent election plan. Although Jefferson was ultimately elected, the episode led to the Twelfth Amendment which was ratified in 1804. It preserved the Electoral College system but

---

[4] Debates in the Federal Convention of 1787 Reported by James Madison, 40–42, 267–69 (Galliard Hunt & James B. Scott eds., 1920).

[5] THE FEDERALIST No. 68.

[6] *See* RICHARD HOFSTADTER, THE IDEA OF A PARTY SYSTEM (1969).

abandoned the single election, creating instead separate elections for President and Vice President.

The Electoral College system not only provides for election of the President and Vice President by electors rather than by the people, but it also gives States broad discretion in deciding how to choose electors. "The individual citizen has no federal constitutional right to vote for electors for the President of the United States unless and until the state legislature chooses a statewide election as the mean to implement its power to appoint members of the Electoral College."[7]

The 2000 Presidential election raised questions regarding the appropriate interpretation of constitutional provisions governing Presidential elections. These questions provided yet another reminder that the existence of relatively detailed constitutional provisions neither obviates constitutional ambiguity nor eliminates the need to interpret. The election presented one of the few instances in which the electoral vote winner lost the popular vote. Moreover, for the first time in our history, a Supreme Court decision essentially identified the presidential winner.

In *Bush v. Gore*, seven justices concluded that the Florida Supreme Court's order of manual recounts violated the Equal Protection Clause.[8] Florida law required counting legal votes upon determining the "intent of the voter."[9] Although this standard was "unobjectionable as an abstract proposition and a starting principle" the Court concluded that "the absence of specific standards to ensure its equal application" violated the Equal Protection Clause.[10] The *per curiam* opinion was limited "to the present circumstances."[11] Thus, its applicability to other presidential elections is subject to question. Justices Souter and Breyer did not join the *per curiam* but agreed that the Florida court's order violated Equal Protection. They thought the Supreme Court should remand the case to the Florida court to fashion substandards under which the recount could proceed.[12] The five justices who joined the *per curiam* ruled that insufficient time remained to allow the Florida court to order a recount consistent with the Equal Protection Clause.[13]

In *Bush v. Gore*, the Court considered the meaning of the provision that "[e]ach state shall appoint, in such Manner as the *Legislature* thereof may direct,"[14] Presidential electors. Governor George W. Bush argued that this language delegated the method of appointment to the Florida legislature. Accordingly, he contended, the Florida Supreme Court, in interpreting the Florida election law, invaded the authority the Constitution delegated to the Florida legislature.

Although the Court did not accept this argument, ruling for Governor Bush on other grounds, Chief Justice Rehnquist, joined by Justices Scalia and Thomas,

---

[7] Bush v. Gore, 531 U.S. 98, 104 (2000).

[8] *Id.* at 111, 134, 145–46.

[9] Fla. Stat. § 101.5614(5) (Supp. 2001).

[10] *Bush*, 531 U.S. at 106.

[11] *Id.* at 109.

[12] *Id.* at 134–35, 146.

[13] *Id.* at 110.

[14] U.S. Const. art. II, § 1, cl. 2.

essentially endorsed the Bush conclusion. Relying on dicta from *McPherson v. Blacker*,[15] the concurring justices viewed the constitutional provisions as one of the "few exceptional cases in which the Constitution imposes a duty or confers a power on a particular branch of the State's government."[16] They would have held "that the Florida Supreme Court's interpretation of the Florida election laws impermissibly distorted them beyond what a fair reading required, in violation of Article II."[17]

Significantly, six justices did not accept this position and four explicitly rejected it. Justice Stevens argued that the Constitution takes state legislatures "as they come — as creatures born of, and constrained by, their state constitutions."[18] Accordingly, the Florida legislature was subject to state judicial review.[19] Far from changing Florida's electoral law, Justice Stevens thought the Florida Supreme Court exercised normal judicial review consistent with Florida precedent and the election statute.[20] Justice Souter thought the Florida Supreme Court decision "within the bounds of reasonable interpretation."[21]

Although the Court's ruling did not turn on the Article II issue, a majority of the Court appears to have rejected the position that the Article II grant of power to the state legislature prohibits *all* state judicial review. The concurring justices did not rule out all state judicial review of the state legislature's scheme for choosing electors. Instead, they argued that the Florida Supreme Court went "beyond what a fair reading required";[22] elsewhere they criticized the Florida Supreme Court's holding as unreasonable.[23] Justice Souter's dissent, which three of his colleagues joined, reached a different conclusion yet applied a similar test — whether the Florida Court's decision was "within the bounds of reasonable interpretation."[24]

The Constitution uses *appoint* to suggest that the States have discretion regarding selection of electors. Early elections featured a variety of techniques for choosing electors, perhaps reflecting the contemporary sense of original intent.[25] State legislatures appointed electors themselves, or provided for popular vote in districts, or statewide. The fact that States have long chosen electors by popular vote may not entirely erode all constitutional power of States to use alternative methods.

Indeed, in 2000, Republican members of the Florida legislature contended that they had the power to appoint a slate of electors pledged to Governor Bush *after* the election and appeared ready to do so had the Court not decided *Bush v. Gore* in the

---

[15] 146 U.S. 1 (1892).

[16] *Bush*, 531 U.S. at 112.

[17] *Id.* at 115.

[18] *Id.* at 123.

[19] *Id.* at 123–24.

[20] *Id.* at 124.

[21] *Id.* at 131.

[22] *Id.* at 115.

[23] *Id.* at 119–20.

[24] *Id.* at 131.

[25] McPherson v. Blacker, 146 U.S. 1, 28–29 (1892).

manner it did. It is not at all clear that a state legislature's authority would extend this far. Professor Richard D. Friedman argues that the Constitution does not allow a state legislature "after the election to devise a new plan for selecting electors, or to select them itself."[26] Congress had exercised its power[27] to set a uniform date to select electors.[28] Congress might allow a State to hold a subsequent run-off if a State fails "to make a choice"[29] because, for instance, the State requires a majority vote which no candidate achieves. But a state legislature cannot subsequently choose a different slate of electors because the election is too close to call immediately or because the state lawmakers do not like the electoral result.[30]

The process Article II articulates has, in some respect, been reshaped by events.[31] Article II contemplated independent electors, able persons who would exercise their discretion. As national parties developed, virtually all electors cast their ballots for the nominees of the party on whose ticket they were elected.

Practice and selection criteria tend to produce electors who support their party's nominees. Suppose an elector votes for someone else? Since 1948, a few electors have refused to vote for the nominees on whose tickets they were chosen.

This recent experience has stimulated remedial efforts. The Democratic Committee of Alabama required candidates for elector to pledge to support the party's nominees in 1952. Party officials refused to certify in the Democratic primary a candidate for elector who declined to do so. The Court held that the Constitution does not bar an elector from pledging his choice publicly in advance. A party may condition running in its primary on making a loyalty pledge.[32]

A State apparently may not directly interfere with an elector casting her ballot, as by a law that electors "shall cast their ballots for the nominee of the national convention of the party by which they were elected."[33] Electors may vote their party's line, or be required to take an unenforceable pledge to do so, but may not be bound by statute to vote a certain way. The framers' idea of electoral independence continues as a matter of constitutional law even though rarely asserted and contrary to pervasive practice. The Constitution does not convert into a legal obligation a voluntary general practice.[34]

The election of 2000 raised, but did not answer, several other issues. The Twelfth Amendment provides that after the electors meet in their States to cast their votes for President and Vice President, the States shall compile lists of those receiving electoral votes, sign and certify such lists and transmit them sealed to the seat of government of the United States, directed to the President of the Senate; "the

---

[26] Richard D. Friedman, *Trying to Make Peace with* Bush v. Gore, 29 FLA. ST. U. L. REV. 811 (2001).

[27] *See* U.S. CONST. art. II, § 1, cl. 4 ("The congress may determine the time of choosing the electors.").

[28] 3 U.S.C. § 1.

[29] 3 U.S.C. § 2.

[30] *See* Friedman, *supra* note 26.

[31] In fact, much of Article II, § 1, cl. 3 was superceded by the Twelfth Amendment in 1804.

[32] Ray v. Blair, 343 U.S. 214, 225, 231 (1952).

[33] Opinion of the Justices, 34 So. 2d 598, 599 (Ala. 1948).

[34] *See Ray*, 343 U.S. at 233 (Jackson, J., dissenting).

President of the Senate shall, in the presence of the Senate and House of Representatives, open all the certificates, all the votes shall then be counted." The Constitution does not specify who does the counting, but Congress, by statute,[35] has delegated that role to itself, a choice which the text seems implicitly to support. The Constitution does not say that Congress has power to reject electoral votes certified by a State, but this conclusion, too, seems a natural inference from the Constitution's delegation to Congress of the duty to count the electoral votes. Congress' role has been the subject of some controversy.[36]

The Twelfth Amendment also provides that "The person having the greatest number of votes for President, shall be the President, if such number be a majority of the whole number of electors appointed." Assuming 538 electors, 270 are required for election of President and Vice President.

Suppose some State fails to appoint electors so that fewer than 538 electors are appointed. Would that lower the required majority to 50% plus one of the reduced number?

The Twentieth Amendment made January 20th the beginning and ending date for presidential and vice-presidential terms. Whereas the Constitution conditioned eligibility to be President on age (35), residency of the United States (14 years), and citizenship ("natural born citizen"), the Twenty- Second Amendment added an additional factor in 1951 — no person could be elected more than twice or, having served more than two years of someone else's term, more than once. Could someone who was barred from seeking another term as President run for Vice President? The Twenty- Second Amendment does not bar such a candidacy but the Twelfth Amendment seems to make eligibility to be Vice President turn on the same factors as President.

§ 7.02　THEORIES OF PRESIDENTIAL POWER

[1]　Historical Background

For over 200 years, constitutional scholars have debated the bounds of presidential power. The vesting clause that begins Article II provides that "[t]he executive power shall be vested in a President of the United States." If, as James Madison contended, the clause was designed simply to name the executive and establish its unitary character, it does not confer additional powers. Others have seen the Vesting Clause as a source of broader, inherent executive powers.

Alexander Hamilton, for instance, urged a broad theory of Presidential power. In defending President Washington's Proclamation of Neutrality, in 1793, he noted the difference between the language of Article I conferring "[a]ll legislative Powers herein granted" on Congress and that of Article II vesting "[t]he executive Power" in the President. He argued that the different modes of expression suggest that the

---

[35] 3 U.S.C. § 15.

[36] *See, e.g.*, DAVID P. CURRIE, THE CONSTITUTION IN CONGRESS, 1789–1801, at 288–91 (1997).

authority vested in the President is not limited to the specific enumerations in Article II.[37]

The scope of the Executive Vesting Clause has remained a topic of judicial and scholarly debate. Justice Robert H. Jackson rejected the Hamiltonian position. He regarded it as simply "an allocation to the presidential office of the generic powers thereafter stated."[38] If the Vesting Clause conferred broad powers on the Chief Executive, the subsequent specific grants — the Commander-in-Chief Clause, Take Care Clause, Pardon Power — would have been superfluous, he reasoned. Thus, under Justice Jackson's view, the Vesting Clause essentially identifies the officer who holds the powers and duties set out in Article II.

Not all agree. "The Executive Power Clause actually does what it says it does, i.e., it vests (or grants) a power over law execution in the President, and it vests that power in him alone,"[39] wrote Professors Steven G. Calabresi and Saikrishna B. Prakash. Their elaborate argument draws heavily from inferences from the constitutional text. The Judicial Vesting Clause in Article III is a "general grant of power to the federal judiciary."[40] Thus, "it makes sense to read the analogously worded Vesting Clause of Article II" as a "*general* grant of power."[41] Their reading does not render the rest of Article II superfluous, as Justice Jackson suggested. Redundancy may have virtue, they suggest.[42] Moreover, the specific clauses in Article II might be read as limitations on presidential power more expansively conferred in the Article II Vesting Clause.[43] Yet at least some of these clauses are worded as grants of power, not restrictions.

Theodore Roosevelt embraced the broad Hamiltonian view in his "Stewardship Theory." Roosevelt conceived of the President as "a steward of the people," who could "do anything that the needs of the Nation demanded unless such action was forbidden by the Constitution or by the laws."[44] His conception of the Presidency has influenced many later Presidents, but not his successor, William Howard Taft. Taft asserted that the President was confined to expressly delegated powers rather than possessing any "undefined residuum of power."[45]

The Theodore Roosevelt and Taft views illustrate conflicting constitutional attitudes towards executive power throughout American history. From a constitutional point of view, this competition has produced no clear and constant winner. In 1952, Justice Robert H. Jackson noted "the poverty of really useful and

---

[37] 15 THE PAPERS OF ALEXANDER HAMILTON 396 (Harold C. Syrett ed., 1969).

[38] Youngstown Sheet & Tube Co. v. Sawyer, 343 U.S. 579, 641 (1952) (Jackson, J., concurring).

[39] Steven G. Calabresi & Saikrishna B. Prakash, *The President's Power to Execute the Laws*, 104 YALE L.J. 541, 549 (1994).

[40] *Id.* at 571.

[41] *Id.* (emphasis added).

[42] *Id.* at 577.

[43] *See* Steven G. Calabresi & Kevin H. Rhodes, *The Structural Constitution: Unitary Executive, Plural Judiciary*, 105 HARV. L. REV. 1153, 1195, 1196 n.216 (1992); Calabresi & Prakash, *supra* note 39, at 577–79.

[44] THEODORE ROOSEVELT, AN AUTOBIOGRAPHY 388 (1913).

[45] WILLIAM HOWARD TAFT, OUR CHIEF MAGISTRATE AND HIS POWERS 140 (1925).

unambiguous authority applicable to concrete problems of executive power as they actually present themselves." He continued. "A century and a half of partisan debate and scholarly speculation yields no net result but only supplies more or less apt quotations from respected sources on each side of any question. They largely cancel each other."[46]

[2] Neagle Case

Little meaningful judicial authority addresses the inherent power of the President — i.e., the extent of his power to act even absent a specific delegation supporting the particular act. The scant authority that exists suggests the President possesses some inherent powers.

In re Neagle[47] involved an extraordinary fact pattern. One Terry (a former Chief Justice of California) had threatened the life of Supreme Court Justice Field. The Attorney General assigned a federal marshal, Neagle, to guard Justice Field. Terry attacked Justice Field and was shot and killed by Neagle. Local officials arrested and charged Neagle with murder. Neagle took the case to the Supreme Court on his application for habeas corpus.

Neagle argued that he had acted to protect Justice Field. But the State claimed that the Attorney General's order was invalid since no express federal law authorized it. The Court recognized the absence of statutory support but concluded that the Government had inherent power to protect its officials.

Neagle places this power to protect in the executive department. It alone has the necessary force and personnel which the President can deploy to fulfill the constitutional charge to "take Care that the Laws be faithfully executed."

This duty is not limited to enforcing acts of Congress or treaties of the United States "according to their *express terms*."[48] The President's duty includes the rights and obligations from the Constitution, federal statutes, and international agreements, as well as all protection the nature of our Government implies. It clearly included the authority to assign a guard for Supreme Court Justice Field.

Under *Neagle*, the President's duty under the Take Care Clause includes enforcing any obligation fairly inferred from the Constitution. The President, by virtue of the Take Care Clause, may act to enforce the laws or to protect federal rights even without statutory authorization. The President's Oath, which commits him to "preserve, protect and defend the Constitution of the United States"[49] may lend further textual support.

---

[46] *Youngstown Steel & Tube Co. v. Sawyer*, 343 U.S. at 634–35 (Jackson, J., concurring).

[47] 135 U.S. 1 (1890).

[48] *Id.* at 64.

[49] U.S. Const. art. II, § 1, cl. 8.

[3] Peace of the United States

In *Neagle*, the Court reasoned that the assault upon a federal judge violated the peace of the United States.[50] The Constitution vests the executive branch with means necessary to keep the peace. The Pullman Strike of 1894 also violated the "peace of the United States." A labor stoppage, accompanied by violence, paralyzed railroad traffic from Chicago. A federal court ordered union leaders not to obstruct the mails or interstate commerce. The injunction failed to control the violence. President Grover Cleveland dispatched troops to Chicago to restore order and railroad operation.

In re Debs[51] upheld the President's power to act against breaches of the "peace of the United States." In an emergency, the President may use the Nation's power, including its armed forces, to enforce the rights of the public and preserve the peace.

Similarly, President Eisenhower, in 1957, and President Kennedy, in 1962, sent troops to control violence in Little Rock, Arkansas, and Oxford, Mississippi respectively and enforce admission of black students to previously all-white schools. The Presidents acted, pursuant to statute, to remove the willful obstruction by state officials of federal court orders. *Neagle* and *Debs* suggest that Presidents Eisenhower and Kennedy could have acted without any statutory authorization under "the executive Power," to maintain the "peace of the United States" and to enforce its laws. Professor Henry P. Monaghan has argued that the Constitution implies an executive protective power, "a general authority to protect and defend the personnel, property, and instrumentalistics of the United States from harm."[52]

[4] United States v. Midwest Oil Co.

Law enforcement and security do not furnish the only context in which claims arise to exercise unenumerated presidential power. *United States v. Midwest Oil*[53] considered the propriety of President Taft's order withdrawing from private oil exploration certain public lands notwithstanding a statute declaring such land "free and open" to exploration. The Court held that the President's power, though not conferred by statute, had been established by a long practice of such orders acquiesced in by Congress.

[5] Steel Seizure Case

The *Steel Seizure* case presented the occasion for the judiciary's most extensive consideration of inherent presidential power.[54] President Truman had ordered Secretary of Commerce Charles Sawyer to seize the Nation's steel mills to avert a

---

[50] 135 U.S. at 69.

[51] 158 U.S. 564 (1895).

[52] Henry P. Monaghan, *The Protective Power of the Presidency*, 93 COLUM. L. REV. 1, 11 (1993).

[53] 236 U.S. 459 (1915).

[54] Youngstown Sheet & Tube Co. v. Sawyer, 343 U.S. 579 (1952).

strike. Truman thought the seizure necessary to avoid harm to national defense and the economy from a steel stoppage. Lacking statutory authorization, Truman relied on inherent constitutional power to seize a critical industry to prevent a stoppage during the Korean War caused by a labor dispute. The Supreme Court rejected Truman's position, 6-3.[55]

In the majority opinion, Justice Black reasoned that since no act of Congress authorized the President to seize the steel operations, his power, if any, must come from the Constitution. The Constitution did not expressly delegate to the President the power exercised and Justice Black did not find such a power "implied from the aggregate" of the President's constitutional powers. The Commander-in-Chief Clause authorized the President to direct the military forces but did not license him to invade private property in the domestic economy. The Take Care and Vesting Clauses at most made the President a law-enforcer, not a "lawmaker." In acting as he had, President Truman had arrogated to himself the powers of the legislative branch. Congress could have authorized the seizure but had not done so. Although the Constitution gave Congress power to make laws necessary and proper to carry into execution constitutional powers, it gave no such authority to the President. Because Congress had not permitted seizure of private property for public use, the President lacked power to seize the steel mills. Prior practice did not empower the President. Nor did it deprive Congress of the power the Constitution confers. Justice Black's rather formalistic opinion divided governmental power into distinct spheres (i.e., legislative, executive) based on a textual analysis of Article II. Neither practice nor exigencies could alter the constitutional scheme to confer the power President Truman exercised.

Justice Black's majority opinion lost some of its significance since each other Justice who joined it also filed a separate opinion which diverged somewhat from the Court's opinion. Justice Black saw the *Steel Seizure* case as a clear case of whether the President had inherent authority to act. The other majority Justices thought the issue not so starkly presented. In their view, the presidential seizure contradicted the expressed will of Congress.

The Taft-Hartley Act of 1947 contained provisions to deal with nationwide strikes. Congress established a procedure whereby the President could seek relief by injunction for an 80-day period against a threatened work stoppage. Four Justices[56] thought Congress had opposed the exercise of executive seizure authority by rejecting proposals to give the President power to take property to avert labor disputes.[57] The President must follow any specific procedures Congress has laid down to deal with the emergency.

Justice Frankfurter shared Justice Black's conclusion that the seizure was unconstitutional but reached that result through an altogether different path of

---

[55] All nine Justices had been appointed by Truman or his Democratic predecessor, Franklin D. Roosevelt. Although Truman's former Treasury Secretary, Chief Justice Fred Vinson, had advised Truman that his action was constitutional, only two of Vinson's colleagues agreed with him. Truman's former Attorney General, Justice Tom Clark, was one of those who regarded the President's action as unlawful. *See* David McCulloch, Truman 896–902 (1992).

[56] Justices Frankfurter, Jackson, Burton, and Clark.

[57] 343 U.S. at 586 (Black, J.); *id.* at 602–03 (Frankfurter, J., concurring).

reasoning. The issue did not turn, as Justice Black suggested, on a comprehensive survey of the President's constitutional powers. Rather, Justice Frankfurter found the legislative action decisive. Congress had implicitly declined to give the President the authority he had exercised. "Congress could not more clearly and emphatically have withheld authority . . . ."[58] Congress' deliberate decision not to extend to the President power to resolve labor strife by seizing industries was tantamount to an action denying him that power.

Hazards exist in Justice Frankfurter's approach of treating congressional silence as the functional equivalent of legislative action. Legislation typically involves uniform action by each house of Congress and presentment of the product to the President. But Presidents cannot veto legislative inaction. Moreover, legislators are less likely to be held accountable for laws they do not pass than for those they do.[59] Two majority Justices[60] appeared to assume that, absent congressional restrictions such as those Taft-Hartley imposed, the President did possess some inherent power to deal with national emergencies, a view they shared with the three dissenters. Justice Douglas thought the President could act without constitutional or congressional delegation of authority provided that power had not been given elsewhere. Since the Constitution gave Congress power to take property upon payment of just compensation, Justice Douglas thought Truman's action usurped legislative powers.[61]

Three Justices[62] clearly rejected any inherent presidential authority to seize the steel industry absent congressional authorization. Yet a majority of the *Steel Seizure* Justices did not deny inherent power in the President to meet emergencies. The three dissenting Justices articulated a broad view of presidential authority and at least two of the remaining Justices probably would have upheld the presidential action absent a contrary congressional policy. Justice Douglas thought the Takings Clause authorized Congress, not the President, to take the action in question.[63]

As mentioned, Justice Black rejected past presidential practice as a mode of shaping constitutional meaning. Justice Frankfurter disagreed. He wrote:

> It is an inadmissibly narrow conception of American constitutional law to confine it to the words of the Constitution and to disregard the gloss which life has written upon them. In short, a systematic, unbroken, executive practice, long pursued to the knowledge of the Congress and never before questioned, engaged in by Presidents who have also sworn to uphold the Constitution, making as it were such exercise of power part of the structure of our government, may be treated as a gloss on 'executive Power' vested in

---

[58] *Id.* at 602.

[59] *See* Laurence H. Tribe, American Constitutional Law 240 (2d ed. 1988).

[60] Justices Clark and Jackson.

[61] *Youngstown*, 343 U.S. at 629–34.

[62] Justices Black, Burton, and Douglas.

[63] 343 U.S. at 631–32 (Douglas, J., concurring).

the President . . . .[64]

[6]   Jackson's Categories and Inherent Power Limitations

Justice Jackson's concurring opinion in the *Steel Seizure* case has proven the most significant opinion in the case. Justice Jackson had wrestled with many problems dealing with the scope of presidential power as a close adviser to President Franklin D. Roosevelt and as Attorney General in his administration.[65] His opinion provides an often cited analysis of situations involving exercises of presidential power. Justice Jackson identified three separate categories of presidential action with different legal consequences:

1. Presidential action pursuant to congressional authority — "When the President acts pursuant to an express or implied authorization of Congress, his authority is at its maximum, for it includes all that he possesses in his own right plus all that Congress can delegate."[66] Presidential action, in these circumstances, is presumptively valid. Any challenger bears the heavy burden of demonstrating that the Federal Government lacks the power to do what its political branches have authorized.

2. Presidential action where Congress is silent — "[W]hen the President acts in absence of either a congressional grant or denial of authority he can only rely upon his own independent powers, but there is a zone of twilight in which he and Congress may have concurrent authority, or in which its distribution is uncertain." This situation resembles, in some respects the Dormant Commerce Clause. Where Congress leaves the field to the President, the efficacy of executive action will "depend on the imperatives of events and contemporary imponderables rather than on abstract theories of law."[67]

3. Presidential action contrary to congressional directions — "[W]hen the President takes measures incompatible with the expressed or implied will of Congress, his power is at its lowest ebb, for then he can rely only upon his own constitutional powers minus any constitutional powers of Congress over the matter."[68] Here the President's claim depends on the relative merits of his claim vs. Congress' authority to act.

The second category in which both executive and legislature may act, assumes some inherent presidential power exists. Yet such a power must be subject to two important limitations. First, like all governmental powers under the Constitution, presidential power may not be exercised in violation of other constitutional provisions. Thus, the President cannot infringe individual rights guaranteed by the Bill of Rights.

---

[64] *Id.* at 610–11 (Frankfurter, J., concurring).

[65] *See* ROBERT H. JACKSON, THAT MAN: AN INSIDER'S PORTRAIT OF FRANKLIN D. ROOSEVELT 75–110 (John Q. Barrett ed., 2003).

[66] *Youngstown*, 343 U.S. at 635 (Jackson, J., concurring).

[67] *Id.* at 637.

[68] *Id.*

Second, in this twilight zone presidential inherent power is subject to statute. Congress may, by statute, regulate the exercise of presidential power in this area. A President who acts contrary to statutory provisions falls under Justice Jackson's third category, where presidential authority is at its weakest.

Justice Jackson thought Truman's action presented a category three situation. Congress had "not left seizure of private property an open field but ha[d] covered it by . . . statutory policies inconsistent with this seizure . . . ."[69] Thus, Truman's action was subject to "the severe tests" of the third category "where it can be supported only by any remainder of executive power after subtraction of such powers as Congress may have over the subject."[70]

Justice Jackson's opinion has been the most enduring legacy of the case.[71] For instance, Justice Rehnquist used it as the touchstone in his majority opinion in *Dames & Moore v. Regan*,[72] which addressed the legality of presidential orders in connection with resolving the Iran hostage crisis. Justice Rehnquist, who served as law clerk to Justice Jackson during the term *Youngstown* was decided, modified his mentor's framework by observing "that executive action in any particular instance falls, not neatly in one of three pigeonholes, but rather at some point along a spectrum running from explicit congressional authorization to explicit congressional prohibition."[73]

More recently, in *Medellin v. Texas*,[74] the Court applied Justice Jackson's framework. President George W. Bush had directed that state courts give effect to a ruling by the International Court of Justice (ICJ) requiring the United States to provide new review of criminal cases involving Mexican foreign nationals who had not been advised of their rights under the Vienna Convention on Consular Relations (which gives foreign nationals accused of a crime the right to meet with diplomats from their home country). Since the treaty was not self-executing a decision by ICJ interpreting it was not binding domestic law. The Court further held that such international obligations do not become binding merely because the President of the United States declared that states would abide by the ICJ decision. Chief Justice Roberts wrote that "Justice Jackson's familiar tripartite scheme provides the accepted framework for evaluating executive action in this area."[75] The President lacked power unilaterally to convert a non-self-executing treaty into a self-executing treaty, a power reserved to Congress. President George W. Bush's effort to enforce a non-self-executing treaty conflicted with the implicit understanding of the Senate in ratifying the treaty and accordingly presented a category 3 situation where the President's power was low. There was no evidence

---

[69] *Id.* at 639.

[70] *Id.* at 640.

[71] *See* Christopher Bryant & Carl Tobias, *Youngstown Revisited*, 29 Hastings Const. L.Q. 373, 420–21 (2002).

[72] 453 U.S. 654 (1981).

[73] *Id.* at 669.

[74] 552 U.S. 491 (2008).

[75] 552 U.S. at 524.

that Congress had acquiesced in President Bush's effort to establish federal law to override applicable state law.

§ 7.03 PRESIDENT AS LEGISLATIVE LEADER

[1] Constitutional Basis for Legislative Role

Modern presidents have assumed a leadership role in legislation. Although this legislative authority is often attributed to political changes, it is work the Constitution suggests. The Constitution requires the President occasionally to report to Congress on the State of the Union and to "recommend to their Consideration such Measures as he shall judge necessary and expedient."[76] The State of the Union and Recommendation Clauses "envision the President as an active participant in the embryonic stages of law making."[77] In certain extraordinary situations, the President may continue or adjourn Congress.[78] And as the vice president has become associated with the executive branch,[79] the vice president's privilege of casting a tie-breaking vote in the Senate as a practical matter gives the President a little more power in the upper body on rare occasions. But the most significant legislative role the Constitution vests in the President is contained in Article I, not Article II.

[2] Veto Power

The veto power is essentially a legislative power since it implicates the President in the law-making process.[80] Although the framers probably conceived the veto as a means to protect against legislative encroachments of the executive and perhaps against unconstitutional measures generally,[81] it has long been recognized that the President may veto a bill for any reason. The veto allows the President to interpose a formidable obstacle to legislation and provides the President with substantial leverage in the legislative process.[82]

The Constitution does not use the word "veto." Instead, the power evolved from the Presentment Clause and the Objections Clause in Article I, § 7, cl. 2 of the Constitution. The former provides that "[e]very Bill" which passes the House and Senate "shall, before it become a law, be presented to the President of the United States." The latter gives the President two options. "If he approves he shall sign it, but if not he shall return it, with his Objections to the House in which it shall have originated, who shall enter the Objections at large in their Journal and proceed to

---

[76] U.S. Const. art. II, § 3.

[77] Vasan Kesavan & J. Gregory Sidak, *The Legislator-in-Chief*, 44 Wm. & Mary L. Rev. 1, 63 (2002).

[78] *Id.*

[79] *See* Joel K. Goldstein, *The New Constitutional Vice Presidency*, 30 Wake Forest L. Rev. 505 (1995).

[80] Buckley v. Valeo, 424 U.S. 1, 285 (1976) (White, J.).

[81] The Federalist No. 73 (Alexander Hamilton).

[82] Charles L. Black, Jr., *Some Thoughts on the Veto*, 40 Law & Contemp. Probs. 87 (1976).

reconsider it." In fact, several sentences later the Constitution discloses a third option available to the President.[83]

The President may elect to neither sign nor veto the bill in which case the inaction is treated as a failure to object, and the bill becomes law. The President has ten days from presentation of bills to approve or veto. The President may sign a bill when Congress is in recess[84] or after adjournment.[85] The two-thirds vote of each House required to override a presidential veto is two-thirds of a quorum, not two thirds of all the members.[86]

Congress cannot shorten the President's time to respond by adjourning nor can it use that tactic to deny the President the right to return a bill with objections. If "Congress by their adjournment prevent . . . [r]eturn" of legislation with presidential objections, the legislation does not become law unless the President signs it.[87] In other words, the normal default rule (a Bill passed by both houses becomes law unless vetoed) is inverted, creating the pocket veto rule.

In *The Pocket Veto Case*,[88] the Court held that congressional adjournment at the end of the first or second annual session creates a pocket veto opportunity. The originating house, to which the bill is to be returned, must be in session so it can receive the President's objections to the legislation and "proceed to reconsider it"[89] as the Constitution requires.[90] It was not sufficient that congressional officers or agents were available to receive the President's objections since the Constitution contemplated prompt consideration so the public would not be kept in suspense regarding the fate of the vetoed measure.[91] A pocket veto bill cannot be overridden by a two-thirds vote of each house.

A different rule applies when only one house recesses for a few days during a session. In *Wright v. United States*[92] President Roosevelt's return of a vetoed bill to the Senate during its three day recess triggered reconsideration of the bill. Congress was not adjourned since the House remained in session and the Senate's secretary was available to receive the President's objections. The considerations which drove *The Pocket Veto Case* did not apply.[93]

Chief Justice Hughes pointed out that the "two fundamental purposes" of the relevant clauses are to allow "suitable opportunity" a) for the President to consider

---

[83] U.S. CONST. art. I, § 7, cl. 2 ("If any Bill shall not be returned by the President within ten Days (Sundays excepted) after it shall have been presented to him, the Same shall be a Law, in like Manner as if he had signed it.").

[84] La Abra Silver Mining Co. v. United States, 175 U.S. 423, 451 (1899).

[85] Edwards v. United States, 286 U.S. 482 (1932).

[86] Missouri P. R. Co. v. Kansas, 248 U.S. 276, 280 (1919).

[87] U.S. CONST. art. I, § 7, cl. 2.

[88] 279 U.S. 655 (1929).

[89] U.S. CONST. art. I, § 7, cl. 2.

[90] 279 U.S. at 682.

[91] *Id.* at 684–85.

[92] 302 U.S. 583 (1938).

[93] *Id.* at 587–89.

legislation presented to him and b) for Congress to consider presidential objections. The Court should interpret the clauses to honor these purposes.[94]

The President may not veto only part of an enacted bill. The Supreme Court applied the Presentment Clause in rather formalistic fashion to strike down the Line Item Veto Act (LIVA) in *Clinton v. City of New York*.[95] LIVA, which Congress had passed in 1996, authorized the President, following specified procedures, to cancel three particular types of provisions that had been signed into law.[96] Under LIVA, Congress could pass a disapproval bill to nullify any such cancellation subject, of course, to the President's constitutional veto power. Although President Clinton properly followed LIVA's procedures in cancelling an item of new spending and a limited tax benefit, the Court, in a 6-3 decision, ruled that those actions went beyond the Chief Executive's constitutional power.

The Court, speaking through Justice Stevens, reasoned that the Constitution gave the President a role in enacting statutes but was "silent on the subject of unilateral Presidential action that either repeals or amends parts of duly enacted statutes."[97] Justice Stevens' reading of the historical materials suggested that the founders intended that the President accept or reject a bill in its entirety, a conclusion that caused him to construe the Constitution's silence as an "express prohibition" of LIVA. As such, short of a formal constitutional amendment, the LIVA procedure was unconstitutional.

The dissenters implicitly accepted the majority's conclusion that the Constitution's silence precluded Congress from authorizing the President to amend or repeal a statute. As they saw it, LIVA conferred no such thing. In effect, it simply gave the President power to refrain from spending certain authorized amounts, a power that judicial doctrine and historical practice made clear were constitutional.[98] Accordingly, the President had "simply executed a power" properly conferred by Congress.[99]

[3] Legislative Veto

The "legislative veto" represented Congress' effort to delegate certain powers to the executive while retaining some control over its decisions. In essence, legislative veto provisions would generally delay the effect of an executive action for a period of time, say sixty or ninety days, during which time a "legislative veto" by one house, both houses, or some subset (e.g., a committee) could disapprove the action. The feature began to be used sporadically in the 1930s. Its use multiplied in the

---

[94] *Id.* at 596.

[95] 524 U.S. 417 (1998).

[96] LIVA allowed the president to cancel "(1) any dollar amount of discretionary budget authority; (2) any item of new direct spending; or (3) any limited tax benefit." 524 U.S. at 436.

[97] *Id.* at 439.

[98] *Id.* at 465–69 (Scalia, J., dissenting).

[99] *Id.* at 475 (Breyer, J., dissenting).

1970s.[100] During that decade Congress created over fifty statutes with "legislative veto" provisions that allowed either or both Houses of Congress to annul by resolution executive and administrative action. By 1983, some 200 statutes provided for annulment by congressional resolution.[101]

In *Immigration & Naturalization Service v. Chadha*,[102] however, the Court struck down the legislative veto. The case arose from a challenge to the one-House veto of an INS determination to suspend deportation of an alien. Chief Justice Burger's majority opinion declared that allowing Congress to annul executive or administrative action by resolution of one or both Houses violated the separation of powers doctrine. The Constitution, he said, requires "that the legislative power of the Federal government be exercised in accord with a single, finely wrought and exhaustively considered procedure," namely by "bicameral passage followed by presentment to the President" for signature or veto. "It is beyond doubt that lawmaking was a power to be shared by both Houses and the President."[103] The legislative veto violated the Bicameralism and Presentment Clauses of the Constitution and impermissibly permitted Congress to exercise veto-proof lawmaking power.

The *Chadha* opinion illustrates a formalistic approach to the separation of powers that would have prevented the rise of modern administrative law. As Justice White's dissent points out, the Court's decision that all "lawmaking" must be shared by Congress and the President "ignores that legislative authority is routinely delegated to the Executive branch, to the independent regulatory agencies."[104] Justice White suggested that if Congress could delegate rule-making authority to agencies, it ought to be able to reserve for itself a modicum of oversight through a one house veto. If congressional action under the legislative veto is "lawmaking" that Congress and the President must share precisely as Article I states, why must not the administrative rule-making, which the technique attempts to control, conform to the constitutional formalities?

Chief Justice Burger displayed an antipathy to a functional approach to constitutional interpretations in other respects, too. That the one house veto might be "efficient, convenient and useful in facilitating functions of government" would not matter it if it violated the Constitution. Moreover, the frequency with which Congress inserted one house vetoes "sharpened rather than blunted" judicial scrutiny; ongoing practice was not persuasive.[105]

Notwithstanding *Chada*, Congress continues to find ways to place legislative veto provisions in new statutes. Constitutional scholar Louis Fisher reported that by 1999, more than 400 new legislative vetoes had been enacted, many vesting

---

[100] *See generally* LOUIS FISHER, THE POLITICS OF SHARED POWER: CONGRESS AND THE EXECUTIVE 73 (3d ed. 1993).

[101] INS v. Chadha, 462 U.S. 919, 967 (1983) (White, J., dissenting).

[102] 462 U.S. 919 (1983).

[103] *Id.* at 947.

[104] *Id.* at 984 (White, J., dissenting).

[105] *Id.* at 946.

control in various congressional committees.[106]

§ 7.04 ADMINISTRATIVE ROLE

[1] Appointing Power

As with many other constitutional arrangements, the appointing power divides functions between different institutions. The Constitution separates the power to create offices from the right to appoint to them. The Constitution empowers Congress to create "offices," an easy implication of the Necessary and Proper Clause.[107] Yet as will be seen below, Congress lacks power to appoint persons to fill the offices it creates. The denial of this power to Congress is consistent with the framers' rejection of parliamentary government and their commitment to separate institutions checking and balancing each other.

The Constitution subdivides officers in two classes: "officers" (or superior officers) and inferior officers. With respect to this division, it provides:

> . . . [H]e shall nominate, and by and with the Advice and Consent of the
> Senate, shall appoint Ambassadors, other public Ministers and Consuls,
> Judges of the supreme Court, and all other Officers of the United States,
> whose Appointments are not herein otherwise provided for, and which shall
> be established by Law: but the Congress may by Law vest the Appointment
> of such inferior Officers, as they think proper, in the President alone, in the
> Courts of Law, or in the Heads of Departments.[108]

As such the President nominates and, with the advice and consent of the Senate, appoints officers of the United States. The same clause applies to appointment of those officers who will serve as the President's principal associates in the Executive Branch and those who will constitute the judiciary. Traditionally, the Senate defers to the President to a much greater degree with respect to cabinet appointments than it does regarding judicial nominees, especially those to the Supreme Court or appellate courts.

Article II also expressly states that Congress may vest the appointment of "such inferior Officers as they think proper" in either the President, the courts, or "the Heads of Departments." Under the Constitution, all federal officers are either (1) officers who must be appointed by the President and confirmed by the Senate or (2) "inferior Officers" whose appointments may be vested by law (a) in the President, (b) the courts, or (c) department heads.

Article II specifies certain offices who must be appointed by the President with Senatorial consent. Yet "[t]he line between 'inferior' and 'principal' officers is . . . far from clear," the Court concluded in *Morrison v. Olson*.[109]

---

[106] *See* Louis Fisher, American Constitutional Law 248–50 (3d ed. 1999).

[107] U. S. Const. art. I, § 8, cl. 18.

[108] U.S. Const. art. II, § 2, cl. 2.

[109] 487 U.S. 654, 671 (1988).

Morrison v. Olson considered the constitutionality of the independent counsel provisions of the Ethics in Government Act of 1978. The law provided, in part, for the appointment of an independent counsel to investigate and perhaps prosecute certain high officials of the Executive Branch.

The independent counsel would be appointed by a special division of the federal judiciary based upon applications of the Attorney General. The constitutionality of that arrangement turned in part on whether an independent counsel was a principal officer who could only be appointed by the President with the Senate's advice and consent or an inferior officer who could be named in other ways.

In *Morrison v. Olson*, the Court identified no bright line test to decide the question but held that the independent counsel was an inferior officer based on the following factors: 1) he was subject to removal by a higher executive official, here the Attorney General, for sufficient cause; 2) he was empowered to perform only certain limited duties; 3) the officer had limited jurisdiction and 4) it had limited tenure.[110]

Yet the Court subsequently recognized that *Morrison* does not set forth the exclusive or definitive criteria for separating superior from inferior officers.[111] Moreover, the definition the Court later advanced seemed subversive of *Morrison*'s conclusion that the independent counsel was an inferior officer. In *Edmond*, Justice Scalia (who dissented in *Morrison*) wrote for the majority that

> [g]enerally speaking, the term 'inferior officer' connotes a relationship with some higher ranking officer or officers below the President: Whether one is an 'inferior' officer depends on whether he has a superior . . . [I]n the context of a Clause designed to preserve political accountability relative to important Government assignments, we think it evident that 'inferior officers' are officers whose work is directed and supervised at some level by others who were appointed by Presidential nomination with the advice and consent of the Senate.[112]

By definition, the work of an independent counsel is not "directed and supervised" by a presidential appointee and accordingly the independent counsel would seem to fall outside the *Edmond* test.

The "inferior officers" provision allows Congress to delegate the power to appoint officers who are not department heads or specified in Article II. Still, Article II confines the appointing power to the President, the courts, or department heads. If Congress divested the President of authority to appoint inferior officers, it would normally delegate that power to department heads who are themselves subject to the President's control.

Congress may also give "the Courts of Law" appointing power., and that power may, in appropriate cases, extend to interbranch appointment. That would, however, be improper if the interbranch appointment would impact the functioning of

---

[110] *Id.* at 671–72.

[111] Edmond v. United States, 520 U.S. 651, 661 (1997).

[112] *Id.* at 662–63.

another branch or "if there was some 'incongruity' between the functions normally performed by the courts and performance of their duty to appoint."[113] In *Morrison*, the Court allowed Congress to vest in a special court the appointment of an independent counsel to investigate and prosecute violations by high ranking officials because the counsel's functions were closely related to the work of the courts.[114] In so doing, it rejected the argument that inter-branch appointments violated principles of separation of powers. The same would presumably not be true of the judicial appointment of officers in an area where courts lack special knowledge or expertise, e.g., a law authorizing the courts to appoint officials in the Department of Agriculture.[115] One might also question the constitutional propriety of judges choosing prosecutors.[116]

Article I courts, too, may appoint inferior officers. Thus, in *Freytag v. Commissioner of Internal Revenue*, the Court held Congress could allow the Chief Judge of the United States Tax Court to appoint special trial judges without violating the Appointments Clause. "Court of law" was not limited to Article III courts.[117] Four justices who concurred viewed the Tax Court as a department, not a court of law.

Congress, however, cannot empower itself to designate the persons to fill the offices it creates. In *Buckley v. Valeo*,[118] the Court struck down the method Congress had provided to choose members of the Federal Election Commission whereby certain members were to be appointed by legislative leaders (in addition to those the President would name), subject to confirmation by a majority vote of both Houses. This provision violated the Appointments Clause of Article II, which made no provision for legislative appointment of such an officer. Any appointee exercising significant authority pursuant to the laws of the United States is an officer of the United States and must be appointed as prescribed by Article II, i.e., by the President subject to Senatorial confirmation, not by legislative leaders.

In addition to the two types of federal officers the Constitution contemplates — those appointed by the President with Senatorial consent, and "inferior officers," whose appointment may be delegated practice has created a third category, "employees" of the United States, who are subject to officers of the United States.[119] Such federal subordinates may be appointed in any manner specified by law.

---

[113] *Morrison*, 487 U.S. at 676.

[114] *Id.*

[115] *Id.* at 676 n.13.

[116] *See, e.g.*, Akhil Amar, *Intratextualism*, 112 HARV. L. REV. 747, 748, 809 (1999). *See also Ex parte Hennen*, 38 U.S. (13 Pet.) 230, 257–58 (1839) (questioning interbranch appointment).

[117] Freytag v. Commissioner of Internal Revenue, 501 U.S. 868 (1991).

[118] 424 U.S. 1 (1976).

[119] *Id.* at 126 n.162.

[2] Removal Power

The removal power is crucial to preserving presidential control over the executive branch. Although Presidents rarely use it, the very existence of the power helps make executive branch officials responsive to the President. The power of the Chief Executive to dismiss an officer at pleasure makes it costly for office holders to resist the President's will and helps make the President fairly accountable for activities of the executive branch.

To be sure, the Constitution does not explicitly confer any such removal power. This silence, coupled with the impeachment power, might indicate that only legislative removal was contemplated. But this conclusion is problematic. Some early evidence suggested that such a power was implicit. In an early vote, Congress provided that the President could remove the head of the newly created Department of Foreign Affairs.[120] This decision provided legislative recognition of presidential authority to remove department heads and accordingly provided an important constitutional gloss.[121]

Moreover, in *Marbury v. Madison*, Chief Justice Marshall assumed the existence of such a power. He thought it significant that Marbury was appointed for a term of years for otherwise he would be removable at will. This discussion suggested that the existence of presidential removal power was presumed. Of course, the Tenure of Office Act of 1867 forbade the removal of department heads without consent of the Senate. Its passage precipitated a constitutional crisis when President Andrew Johnson resisted it and was impeached (but not removed). That statute was an invalid infringement upon the President's power.[122] Clearly, the President has power to remove department heads at his discretion.[123]

Moreover, important structural principles support giving the President removal power. If the President is to lead and be held accountable for the executive branch, the President must control its principal agents. Accordingly, some removal power is inferred from the Vesting Clause and the President's duty to "take Care that the Laws be faithfully executed."[124]

In *Myers v. United States*,[125] the Court considered whether the same rule applied to other federal officers. A statute provided that postmasters "may be removed by the President with the advice and consent of the Senate." Otherwise, they served a four year term. After President Woodrow Wilson unilaterally removed Myers, he sued and the case came before the Court which ruled the statute invalid. The removal power is "an incident of the power to appoint them, and is in its nature an executive power,"[126] wrote Chief Justice (and former

---

[120] *See* David Currie, The Constitution in Congress, 1789–1801, at 37–41 (1997).

[121] Myers v. United States, 272 U.S. 52, 114 (1926); *Ex parte Hennen*, 38 U.S. at 258–59.

[122] *Myers*, 272 U.S. at 167–68, 176.

[123] *Ex parte Hennen*, 38 U.S. at 259.

[124] U.S. Const. art. II, § 3.

[125] 272 U.S. 52 (1926).

[126] *Id.* at 161. *See also Ex parte Hennen*, 38 U.S. at 259 (power of removal is incident to appointment power).

President) William Howard Taft. The Constitution's silence regarding removal, coupled with the Take Care Clause, suggested the President had power to remove.

Three justices dissented. Justice McReynolds, who had been Wilson's Attorney General, thought no removal power could be inferred absent clear constitutional language.[127] Justice Brandeis thought Senatorial approval of removals established a past practice which shaped constitutional meaning.

Justice Holmes thought Congress could restrict the President's power to remove incident to its power to create offices.[128] Justice Brandeis saw the case as raising the "narrow question of whether a President, who appoints under a statute creating an inferior office can ignore, while the Senate is in session, the very statute's prescription that removal of that inferior officer requires the Senate's advice and consent.[129] Justice Brandeis cited extensive legislative practice which allowed some Senate participation in discussions to remove inferior officers.[130]

Myers considered whether the President could remove a postmaster performing executive functions. It held that such an officer, appointed by the President with Senatorial consent, may be removed by the President alone, regardless of how Congress may seek to limit the President's authority.

But the majority opinion in *Myers* spoke beyond the immediate issue. It announced the broad doctrine that the Constitution gives the President unlimited power to remove all officers, other than judges, whom the President has appointed. Yet, as Justice Brandeis pointed out, Chief Justice Taft's sweeping declaration went well beyond the question the case presented. Moreover, many such officers do not perform purely executive functions which the President must control. In vesting various independent agencies with quasijudicial duties, Congress has often protected its officials from presidential removal to guaranty their independence from executive interference.

The Supreme Court, in *Humphrey's Executor v. United States*,[131] upheld this practice nine years later. President Franklin D. Roosevelt had removed a member of the Federal Trade Commission (FTC), who his predecessor had appointed. He claimed "that the aims and purposes of the Administration with respect to the work of the Commission can be carried out most effectively with personnel of my own selection." Yet the statute accorded members of the FTC a seven year term and limited presidential removal power to "inefficiency, neglect of duty, or malfeasance in office."[132]

In *Humphrey*, the Court held that the President lacked unlimited removal power over FTC members. Instead, the President's power to remove FTC members was limited to the causes the statute specified. The agency was entrusted with the adjudicatory powers to be exercised free from executive control.

---

[127] *Myers*, 272 U.S. at 178, 182.

[128] *Myers*, 272 U.S. at 177 (Holmes, J., dissenting).

[129] *Myer*, 272 U.S. at 240, 241.

[130] *Id.* at 250–64, 283–91.

[131] 295 U.S. 602 (1935).

[132] *Id.* at 619.

Humphrey rejected *Myers'* suggestion of an unlimited power to remove officials. *Myers* applied to "purely executive officers," who carried out the President's duty to execute the laws. But the President's constitutional removal power was limited regarding members of quasi-judicial or quasi-legislative agencies.

The Court further developed the distinction in *Wiener v. United States*.[133] President Eisenhower had dismissed his predecessor's appointment to the War Claims Commission. Although Congress had not restricted the President's power to remove, the Court held Eisenhower had gone too far. It distinguished between those who are part of the Executive branch and those who must operate independent of such interferences.[134]

Other recent cases have further articulated the principles governing those exercising some part of the executive power. In *Bowsher v. Synar*,[135] the Comptroller General, an officer subject to removal by Congress, had been given certain executive functions incident to reducing the federal budget deficit. The Court held that Congress could not reserve for itself power to remove an official charged with executing the laws (except by impeachment).

Morrison v. Olson narrowed the President's removal power. Congress had provided that the Attorney General could only remove an independent counsel for cause, a limitation inspired by Richard Nixon's order that Archibald Cox be fired to prevent him from pursuing tapes which showed Nixon's complicity in criminal activity. Unlike the statutes at issue in *Myers* and *Bowsher*, Congress did not reserve for itself any role in removal. Nor did it eliminate all presidential removal power; it simply limited it to "good cause." The Court abandoned language in *Humphrey's Executor* and *Wiener* which focused on whether the officer subject to removal was exercising quasi-legislative or quasi-judicial as opposed to purely executive functions. The Court held that Congress may limit the president's freedom to dismiss certain executive officials so long as such restrictions do not compromise the President's ability to fulfill the constitutional duties of the office. As such, the Court seemed to suggest a balancing test based on the circumstances.[136]

In a sharply divided decision, the Supreme Court held unconstitutional a statutory restriction on the president's ability to remove a principal officer who was restricted in his ability to remove an inferior officer.[137] In the opinion for a five person majority, Chief Justice Roberts wrote that the multilevel protection violated the Article II Vesting and Take Care Clauses. Although the Court had upheld "limited restrictions" on the president's removal power, the Chief Justice's opinion said that the multilevel protection "transforms" that power and deprives the President of the ability to discharge duties for which he is accountable. Justice Breyer's dissent argued that the Court had typically examined such restrictions by looking at how they would function and the likely impact on presidential and

---

[133] 357 U.S. 349 (1958).

[134] *Id.* at 353.

[135] 478 U.S. 714 (1986).

[136] Morrison v. Olson, 487 U.S. 654 (1988).

[137] Free Enterprise Fund v. Public Company Accounting Oversight Board, 130 S. Ct. 3138 (2010).

congressional and by being deferential to the judgments of political branches.[138]

§ 7.05 LAW ENFORCEMENT

[1] Constitutional Duty to Execute Laws

The Constitution imposes on the President the duty to "take care that the laws be faithfully executed."[139] The Take Care Clause confers perhaps the President's most basic responsibility, one that informs the President's other activities. Yet the Clause raises as many questions as it resolves. Must the President simply enforce congressional statutes? May the President choose not to enforce an act the President deems unconstitutional? To what extent may other branches participate in law execution?[140]

Although the Constitution often uses "Laws" to mean statutes, it is clear that the President must enforce the Constitution as well. Judicial doctrine, *In re Neagle*[141] for instance, suggests such an obligation. The President's Oath Clause reinforces this responsibility, committing the President not only to "faithfully execute" the presidential office but also to "preserve, protect, and defend the Constitution of the United States."[142]

The President's duty to enforce the Constitution as well as laws should not be controversial so long as no conflict appears between them. The more difficult question involves the extent of the President's power or duty to interpret the Constitution to determine whether any such conflict exists.

A traditional view compels the President to give effect to judicial or legislative judgments of constitutionality. Under this view, the President enforces measures deemed constitutional by the judicial and legislative branches, regardless of personal misgivings. In other respects, the veto and pardon power, for instance, the President is generally understood to be free to act on personal constitutional views. The traditional view had been questioned, however, and some commentators have argued that the Constitution's grant of executive powers would allow a President to decline to enforce a law that the President personally believes is unconstitutional.[143]

In practice, Presidents almost invariably enforce court orders and statutes. They sometimes enforce statutes in accordance with their own, rather than Congress', interpretation.

---

[138] *Free Enterprise Fund*, 130 S. Ct. 3138.

[139] U.S. Const. art. II, § 3.

[140] *See* Richard M. Pious, The American Presidency 49–50 (1979).

[141] 135 U.S. 1 (1890).

[142] U.S. Const. art. II, § 1, cl. 8.

[143] *See, e.g.*, Michael Stokes Paulsen, *The Most Dangerous Branch: Executive Power to Say What the Law Is*, 83 Geo. L.J. 217 (1994); Michael Stokes Paulsen, *The Merryman Power and the Dilemma of Autonomous Executive Branch Interpretation*, 15 Cardozo L. Rev. 81 (1993); Edwin Meese III, *The Law of the Constitution*, 61 Tul. L. Rev. 979 (1987).

[2]   Power to Pardon

The power "to grant Reprieves and Pardons" allows the President to mitigate the effect of enforcement of some laws. The framers apparently thought assigning the President, rather than a group, the power to pardon would encourage responsibility.[144]

The pardon power is broad. It extends to "Offenses against the United States, except in Cases of Impeachment."[145] This description does impose some limits. It only applies to offenses against federal, not state law. As such, it even extends to treason since "in seasons of insurrection or rebellion, there are often critical moments when a well-timed offer of pardon to the insurgents or rebels may restore the tranquility of the commonwealth . . . ."[146] It also does not apply to impeachments. Finally, it applies to criminal, but not civil, matters.[147]

The President need not wait until after conviction and sentence to exercise the power. A pardon may be granted at any time after an offense has been committed, either before legal proceedings commence, during their pendency, or after conviction and judgment.[148] Under Article II, the pardon power is general and unqualified, reaching "all offenses against the United States, except in cases of impeachment."[149]

Chief Justice Marshall followed the English common-law rule that a pardon was the private act of grace of the grantor, analogous to the transfer of property or a commercial transaction.[150] He viewed delivery and acceptance as essential components.

Marshall's conception would exclude using the pardoning power to grant group amnesty. History has taken a different view. Both Presidents Lincoln and Andrew Jackson proclaimed amnesties. Although Johnson's extensive use of this power was attacked as illegal in Congress, the Supreme Court held that "[p]ardon includes amnesty."[151] In 1977, President Jimmy Carter granted amnesty to those who violated the federal draft laws during the Vietnam era.

---

[144] THE FEDERALIST No. 74 (Alexander Hamilton) ("As the sense of responsibility is always strongest in proportion as it is undivided, it may be inferred that a single man would be most ready to attend to the force of those motives which might plead for a mitigation of the rigor of the law, and least apt to yield to considerations which were calculated to shelter a fit object of its vengeance.").

[145] U.S. CONST. art. II, § 2.

[146] THE FEDERALIST No. 74 (Alexander Hamilton).

[147] *See Ex parte* Grossman, 267 U.S. 87, 121–22 (1925) (President can pardon criminal but not civil contempt.).

[148] *Ex parte* Garland, 71 U.S. (4 Wall.) 333, 380 (1867).

[149] United States v. Thomasson, 28 F. Cas. 82, 85 (D. Ind. 1869). The extent of the power is illustrated by *Ex parte Grossman*, 267 U.S. 87 (1925) (criminal contempt sentence subject to pardon power).

[150] United States v. Wilson, 32 U.S. (7 Pet.) 150, 160–61 (1833).

[151] United States v. Klein, 80 U.S. (13 Wall.) 128, 147 (1872). *See* Armstrong v. United States, 80 U.S. (13 Wall.) 154 (1872) (upholding Johnson's unconditional general amnesty).

Marshall's analogy of a pardon to a private deed proved problematic, too, in *Burdick v. United States*.[152] Defendant invoked his right against self-incrimination to refuse to answer questions before a federal grand jury.

Defendant refused to accept the proffered "full and unconditional pardon for all offenses against the United States." He was convicted for contempt for not answering on the theory that the pardon removed all danger of incrimination. The Supreme Court reversed, adopting the Marshall reasoning that the unaccepted pardon had no force.

Burdick survives, but the Court has eliminated its practical restriction upon presidential authority. In *Biddle v. Perovich*,[153] the President commuted a death sentence to life imprisonment. Defendant attacked the commutation order and his incarceration on the ground that he had never accepted it. The Court held the *Burdick* reasoning inapplicable to commutation. The President can avoid the effect of *Burdick* by commuting or reducing the sentence imposed. Such action takes effect, under *Biddle*, even if the recipient claims to refuse consent.

The power to pardon includes the lesser power to commute sentences and the authority to remit fines, penalties, and forfeitures.[154] The President may grant a conditional pardon on terms consistent with the Constitution,[155] that an oath be taken,[156] parole never be granted,[157] and even that the grantee should not claim certain property.[158] The President cannot, however, compensate an individual he pardons; he "cannot touch moneys in the treasury of the United States, except expressly authorized by Act of Congress."[159]

Ex parte Garland[160] addressed the effect of a pardon. An 1865 statute required that any person who wanted to practice law in a federal court swear that he had never fought against the United States or aided its enemies. Garland, a former Confederate official, sought to appear before the Supreme Court without taking the oath. He argued that President Andrew Johnson had given him a "full pardon for all offenses committed by his participation, direct or implied, in the Rebellion." The Court ruled that the pardon relieved him from the duty to take the oath. The pardon restored his civil rights and made him as innocent as if the offense had never been committed. "[It] makes him as it were, a new man, and gives him a new credit and capacity."[161]

---

[152] 236 U.S. 79 (1915).

[153] 274 U.S. 480 (1927).

[154] Osborn v. United States, 91 U.S. 474, 477 (1876).

[155] Schick v. Reed, 419 U.S. 256, 264 (1974).

[156] *United States v. Klein*, 80 U.S. at 140–42.

[157] *Schick*, 419 U.S. at 267.

[158] Semmes v. United States, 91 U.S. 21, 27 (1875).

[159] Knote v. United States, 95 U.S. (5 Otto) 149, 154 (1877).

[160] 71 U.S. (4 Wall.) 333 (1867).

[161] *Id.* at 380–81. *But see* Carlesi v. New York, 233 U.S. 51 (1914) (Carlesi convicted in state court as second offender although prior federal crime was pardoned).

Congress' power to legislate regarding pardons is limited. An 1870 statute making proof of loyalty necessary to recover property abandoned and sold by the government during the Civil War, notwithstanding any presidential pardon or amnesty, was held invalid. Congress cannot change the effect of a pardon any more than the President can change a law.[162] But the pardoning power is not wholly beyond legislative reach. Congress may, under the Necessary and Property Clause, legislate regarding pardons in a manner which does not infringe upon presidential authority.[163] Moreover, Congress may pass acts of general amnesty,[164] which is a legitimate exercise of legislative power because it prescribes a general rule to govern future cases.

Although the President's power to pardon is broad, it presumably is not without limit. It is doubtful, for instance, that the Constitution would tolerate a self-pardon.[165] Such an action would offend the structural principle against judging one's own case.

§ 7.06 FOREIGN AFFAIRS

[1] Leading Role of President

The basic rule limiting the Federal Government to enumerated and "necessary and proper" implied powers applies most clearly to domestic affairs in practice, and, some believe, by design.[166] The Constitution divides the foreign affairs power between the President and the Congress. The Constitution suggests that the two political branches were to share this power and responsibility. To be sure, the Constitution gave the President certain powers. He was Commander-in-Chief of the Army and Navy[167] and "empowered" to receive Ambassadors and other public Ministers,[168] a duty which has broader implications, in addition to any power the Vesting Clause might confer. The Senate's advice and consent was required to confirm ambassadors and ratify treaties.[169] Congress was given power to regulate foreign commerce,[170] and define and punish international maritime crimes,[171] in

---

[162] *U.S. v. Klein*, 80 U.S. at 148.

[163] Congress may give the Secretary of the Treasury power to remit penalties and forfeitures, which does not in any way abridge the President's power to remit. *See, e.g.*, The Laura, 114 U.S. 411, 416–17 (1885). *Ex parte* United Sates, 242 U.S. 27, 52 (1916) (Congress may empower federal judges to suspend original sentences). United States v. Benz, 282 U.S. 304 (1931) (Congress can empower judges to reduce sentences to time served).

[164] *See, e.g.*, Brown v. Walker, 161 U.S. 591 (1896) (upholding a statute providing immunity from prosecution for persons testifying before federal agencies).

[165] *See* Brian C. Kalt, *Pardon Me?: The Constitutional Case Against Presidential Self-Pardons*, 106 YALE L.J. 779 (1996).

[166] *See* United States v. Curtiss-Wright Export Corp., 299 U.S. 304 (1936).

[167] U.S. CONST. art. II, § 2, cl. 1.

[168] U.S. CONST. art. II, § 3.

[169] U.S. CONST. art. II, § 2, cl. 2.

[170] U.S. CONST. art. I, § 8, cl. 3.

[171] U.S. CONST. art. I, § 8, cl. 10.

addition to its defense responsibilities,[172] most significantly the power to declare war.[173] In practice, however, the President has assumed the paramount role, particularly in recent times. This development occurred due to executive action and congressional abdication.[174] To be sure, early on Representative John Marshall declared "[t]he President is the sole representative with foreign nations."[175] Marshall's statement was accepted, not because of any sense that the executive performed solo in foreign affairs, but because of a consensus that he was the sole organ of communications.[176]

[2] Curtiss-Wright

Ambitious claims of presidential dominance in foreign policy trace to the Court's 1936 decision in *United States v. Curtiss-Wright Export Corporation*.[177] Defendant was indicted for selling 15 machine guns to Bolivia in violation of a Joint Resolution of Congress empowering the president to prohibit certain arms sales and a related presidential proclamation. The issue before the Court was the propriety of the delegation to the Chief Executive. Although the Court had recently struck down delegations of domestic power, it concluded that Congress had more latitude to extend authority to the executive in foreign affairs. The Court articulated a sweeping theory of presidential dominance in foreign matters. Justice Sutherland's argument for a more expansive presidential foreign affairs power began with the premise that the Constitution does not limit the Nation's foreign affairs as it did its domestic powers. Before the Constitution, the Union existed and exercised powers of "external sovereignty" — the powers of war and peace, to form diplomatic relations, and so forth — and these powers were independent of the Constitution. "Not only . . . is the federal power over external affairs in origin and essential character different from that over internal affairs, but participation in the exercise of the power is significantly limited,"[178] he wrote. Moreover:

> It is important to bear in mind that we are here dealing not alone with an authority vested in the President by an exertion of legislative power, but with such an authority plus the very delicate, plenary and exclusive power of the President as the sole organ of the federal government in the field of international relations — a power which does not require as a basis for its exercise an act of Congress, but which, of course, like every other governmental power, must be exercised in subordination to the applicable provision of the Constitution.[179]

---

[172] U.S. Const. art. I, § 8, cl. 11–15.

[173] U.S. Const. art. I, § 8, cl. 11.

[174] *See* Louis Fisher, *Congressional Abdication: War and Spending Power*, 43 St. Louis U. L.J. 931 (1999).

[175] 10 Annals of Cong. 606, 613–14 (Mar. 7, 1800).

[176] *See* Harold Hongju Koh, The National Security Constitution 81 (1990).

[177] 299 U.S. 304 (1936).

[178] *Id.* at 319.

[179] *Curtiss-Wright*, 299 U.S. at 319–20.

In addition to the various textual provisions, the Court advanced two justifications for constitutional deference to the President in foreign affairs. The President needed considerable discretion in foreign affairs to avoid "embarrassment." Moreover, the President had knowledge and expertise which would probably not be shared by others.

Curtiss-Wright holds simply that Congress may delegate broad foreign affairs authority to the President. It is important to recall that the President had acted pursuant to congressional resolution. The Court's expansive dicta has, however, been invoked to support presidential claims of foreign powers autonomy even absent any delegation from Congress. Scholars have criticized this reliance on *Curtiss-Wright*. Its enabling language is dicta, its history is suspect and it contains words of limitation that often are overlooked.[180] Still, the decision's influence continues.

[3] Power of Recognition

In the aftermath of *Curtiss-Wright* some broad lines of responsibility emerged. The President has constitutional power to conduct external relations and guide diplomacy. The President represents the Nation in dealing with foreign nations, a status implied from the President's position as head of the Executive Branch, which alone can implement foreign policy, and from the constitutional provisions. The President has the power to "appoint Ambassadors, other public Ministers and Consuls"[181] and "he shall receive Ambassadors and other public Ministers."[182] These provisions empower the President to conduct diplomatic relations with foreign nations.

Hamilton described the power to "receive Ambassadors" as "more a matter of dignity than of authority."[183] Yet it endows the President with exclusive authority to determine what governments to recognize. In receiving foreign ambassadors (and sending our own), the President identifies a country's lawful government. Some such decisions have significantly impacted external relations and domestic politics.

Whether to recognize a foreign government is a political question beyond judicial cognizance.[184] A different rule might lead to embarrassing consequences. A government recognized by the courts could, for instance, recover property in this country that might contravene the President's foreign policy.

---

[180] *See* LOUIS FISHER, PRESIDENTIAL WAR POWER 57–61 (1995); Koh, *supra* note 176, at 94.

[181] U.S. CONST. art. II, § 2, cl. 2.

[182] U.S. CONST. art. II, § 3.

[183] THE FEDERALIST No. 69 (Alexander Hamilton).

[184] United States v. Belmont, 301 U.S. 324, 330 (1937); Jones v. United States, 137 U.S. 202, 212 (1890). For more recent statements, *see* Baker v. Carr, 369 U.S. 186, 211–12 (1962); Guaranty Trust Co. v. United States, 304 U.S. 126, 137 (1938).

[4] Steel Seizure Case

Justice Jackson's opinion in the *Steel Seizure* case, addressed at Section 7.02[5], [6], offers a different model for allocating foreign affairs powers. It suggests that presidential power is greatest when Congress authorizes action (Category 1) and least when Congress withholds power (Category 3); in the latter instance, the President is disabled from acting, unless the Constitution accords the President exclusive control.[185]

Although Justice Jackson's formulation offers a consultative model of foreign affairs decision-making, it is subject to manipulation especially given the residual instinct to defer to the Executive. This tendency was evident in *Dames & Moore v. Regan*,[186] a 1981 opinion authored by Justice Jackson's former law clerk, Justice Rehnquist, regarding executive actions taken to settle the Iran hostage crisis. As part of the settlement, President Carter nullified various attachments awarded creditors against Iranian assets and suspended various claims against Iran pending in American courts. Pursuant to Justice Jackson's approach, the Court found the nullification had express statutory sanction but the suspension did not. Nonetheless, the Court managed to elevate the suspension to Category 1 based on Congress' failure to repudiate it and on past practice.

[5] Executive Agreements

Presidents have long made executive agreements with other countries which, though not treaties in the constitutional sense, are binding obligations of the United States. Indeed, the United States has entered into executive agreements with increasing frequency this century so that they far outnumber treaties to which it is a party.

Executive agreements can be divided into three main kinds: those concluded (1) pursuant to treaty, (2) pursuant to statute, and (3) by the executive alone, without any legislative authorization.[187] Executive agreements pursuant to treaty enjoy the force of the authorizing treaty provided they are within its scope. Congress has frequently authorized the President to negotiate executive agreements regarding postal matters, foreign commerce, and navigation. For instance, the Trade Agreements Act of 1934 authorized the President to enter into trade pacts with foreign government and to modify duties and import restrictions. Although the Constitution does not expressly authorize congressional executive agreements, they have been accepted in practice and constitute part of the law of the land. As such, they supersede inconsistent prior federal law and state law. They do not improperly delegate legislative power to the President.[188]

---

[185] *See* Youngstown Sheet & Tube Co. v. Sawyer, 343 U.S. 579, 635–38 (1952); *See* Koh, *supra* note 176, at 105–13.

[186] 453 U.S. 654 (1981).

[187] *See* PETER M. SHANE & HAROLD H. BRUFF, SEPARATION OF POWERS LAW: CASES AND MATERIALS 633 (1996).

[188] J. W. Hampton, Jr., & Co. v. United States, 276 U.S. 394, 411 (1928); Field v. Clark 143 U.S. 649, 693 (1892).

Executive agreements based upon statutes are not uncommon. Although they involve the conventional pattern of bicameral approval and presentment, rather than Senate advice and consent, they have been accorded the status of treaty.[189] Such presidential executive agreements may be authorized in advance or subsequently confirmed, by legislative action.

Executive agreements made without legislative authorization depend upon the President possessing constitutional authority to act without congressional sanction. Presidents typically identify four sources of constitutional authority: (1) the Vesting Clause, (2) the power to receive foreign emissaries, which makes the President the Nation's foreign representative, (3) the Commander-in-Chief Clause, and (4) the Take Care Clause.[190] According to *Curtiss-Wright*, the Constitution contemplates that the United States may enter into any agreement known in international law. As the Nation's foreign relations representative, the President must be able to negotiate executive agreements.[191] As Commander-in-Chief, the President may make armistice agreements.

Whether made with or without legislative authority, executive agreements are binding international obligations. They differ in their impact upon domestic law. Congressional-Executive agreements, like the Reciprocal Trade Agreements, alter duties provided by earlier federal law. But the President, solely on presidential authority, could not alter a federal statute by agreement with another power.

In *United States v. Pink*,[192] the Court upheld the Litvinov Agreement which President Franklin D. Roosevelt concluded with the Soviet Union without congressional sanction. Under the Agreement, the United States recognized the Soviet Union, which assigned to our government its interests in a Russian insurance company in New York, New York and was bound to enforce this agreement and to give priority to our government's rights over those of creditors.

Did *Pink* authorize an unconstitutional taking of property without due compensation in violation of the Fifth Amendment? Apparently not. Claims of American creditors and those related to the New York branch of the Russian insurer had been satisfied. New York was administering a fund for the benefit of other creditors. *Pink* did not suggest that compensation was unavailable or that the President could make commitments without regard to constitutional rights of American citizens. The United States could accord American claims priority by treaty so the same result should obtain by virtue of the executive agreement incident to the President's recognition power, wrote Justice William O. Douglas.

Still, the cases demonstrate that an executive agreement without statutory authorization may have domestic effect. In 1981, President Jimmy Carter signed a series of executive orders incident to an agreement with Iran to release Americans

---

[189] *See, e.g.*, B. Altman & Co. v. United States, 224 U.S. 583 (1912); Von Cotzhausen v. Nazro, 107 U.S. 215 (1883).

[190] Louis Fisher, Constitutional Conflicts Between Congress and the President 249 (4th ed. 1997).

[191] U.S. v. Belmont, 301 U.S. 324, 330 (1937).

[192] 315 U.S. 203 (1942).

held hostage. *Dames & Moore v. Regan*[193] considered the constitutionality of those executive agreements. President Carter had frozen all Iranian government assets in response to Iran's seizure of American hostages. Ultimately, the United States and Iran agreed that in return for the hostage release the United States would terminate American legal proceedings against Iran and would "nullify all attachments and judgments obtained therein, [and] prohibit all further litigation based on such claims."[194] The United States would also transfer such claims to a new Iran-United States Claims Tribunal for binding arbitration. Presidents Carter and Reagan issued executive orders implementing the agreement, including one that " 'suspended' all 'claims which may be presented to the . . . Tribunal.' "[195]

Petitioner had sued Iran in federal court prior to the agreement, claiming more than $3 million from the Iran Atomic Energy Organization. The court had ordered attachment of Iranian property to secure any judgment petitioner won. After the settlement, the court granted petitioner summary judgment but, due to the agreements and orders, stayed execution of its judgment, vacated all prejudgment attachments and stayed further proceedings. Petitioner then sued to prevent implementation of the settlement with Iran. It argued that the government's actions "were unconstitutional to the extent they adversely affect petitioner's final judgment . . . its execution of that judgment . . . its prejudgment attachments, and its ability to continue to litigate."

The Court, speaking through Justice Rehnquist, rejected petitioner's contentions and reaffirmed the President's power to enter into executive agreements settling such claims even though they essentially nullified a court judgment and its enforcement. No federal statute explicitly authorized the President to suspend private claims pending in American courts. The Court found, however, that Congress had in the past implicitly accepted the Chief Executive's right to engage in such activity. This past practice raised a presumption of congressional consent. Thus, the Court believed it was confronted with a situation in Justice Jackson's first category i.e., the President acts with congressional consent. Still, the Court took pains to "re-emphasize the narrowness of [its] decision."[196] It did not decide the "President possesses plenary power to settle claims, even as against foreign governmental entities."[197] Yet the Court was not prepared to deny him that power where the claim settlement was "a necessary incident to the resolution of a major foreign policy dispute between our country and another" and where Congress had acquiesced.

An executive agreement overrides state law. *United States v. Belmont*[198] arose from the Litvinov Assignment, part of an exchange of diplomatic correspondence whereby the United States recognized the Soviet Union. In the Litvinov Assignment the Soviet government transferred certain claims due it by American

---

[193] 453 U.S. 654 (1981).

[194] *Id.* at 665.

[195] *Id.* at 666.

[196] *Id.* at 667.

[197] *Id.* at 688.

[198] 301 U.S. 324 (1937).

nationals to our government. The United States sued a New York bank to recover funds a Russian corporation deposited before the Russian Revolution. The Soviet government had dissolved the corporation and nationalized its assets, including the deposit in question. Our government asserted that the Litvinov Assignment made the deposit United States property. Defendant contended that the Soviet decree was not competent to affect property in this country and that it violated the public policy of New York against giving enforcing confiscatory acts.

The Court rejected this argument, President Roosevelt and Commissar Litvinov had entered into a valid international agreement. Though not a treaty, it prevailed over New York's public policy because it was negotiated under authority of the President. A treaty clearly supersedes contrary state law or policy; *Belmont* gave an executive agreement the same effect.[199]

Under the Supremacy Clause, executive agreements, like treaties, trump state laws and policies. Executive agreements on presidential authority alone do not take precedence over federal statutes or treaties[200] because that would give the President the legislative power which the Constitution delegates to Congress.

In *American Insurance Association v. Garamendi*,[201] the Court held, in a 5-4 decision, that California's Holocaust Victim Insurance Relief Act of 1999 (HIVRA) conflicted with an executive agreement which President Clinton entered into with Germany whereby Germany would create a fund and apparatus to pay some compensation to Holocaust survivors for the atrocities of the Nazi period. President Clinton had agreed to take steps to dissuade American courts from entertaining suits against Germany and German companies to recover for Holocaust offenses. HIVRA, however, required insurance companies doing business in California to disclose information regarding life insurance policies sold in Europe between 1920 and 1945. Past practice and precedents confirmed the President's power to enter into executive agreements which preempted inconsistent state law, Justice Souter wrote for the Court.

§ 7.07 COMMANDER-IN-CHIEF

[1] Constitutional Duty of President

Although the text of the Constitution seems to give Congress the upper hand in defense matters — at least seven clauses of Article I give it defense responsibilities — the President has emerged as the dominant figure in military and defense matters. The President's solitary constitutional duty in this respect is to serve as "Commander-in-Chief of the Army and Navy of the United States" and state militias.[202] This textual reed has sufficed to support broad authority. Yet some scholars suggest that Congress has abdicated too much of its constitutional

---

[199] *See also* United States v. Pink, 315 U.S. 203 (1942).

[200] United States v. Guy W. Capps, Inc., 204 F.2d 655 (4th Cir. 1953), *aff'd on other grounds*, 348 U.S. 296 (1955).

[201] 539 U.S. 396 (2003).

[202] U.S. Const. art. II, § 2, cl. 1.

authority in military and defense matters.[203]

Article II, in declaring the President Commander-in-Chief of the armed forces, makes the President the highest officer in the military, as well as the civil, establishment. The President is not simply a ceremonial chief; the Constitution puts the armed forces directly under presidential command[204] to preserve civilian control of the military. Yet the Commander-in-Chief Clause also implied some limits. Alexander Hamilton stressed the respect in which the President's authority was "much inferior" to that of the King of England. The President's authority would "amount to nothing more than the supreme command and direction of the military and naval forces, as first general and admiral of the Confederacy."[205] The King, by contrast, could also raise and regulate his own forces and declare his own wars.[206] Hamilton's distinction suggests that at least some body of originalist thought was sensitive to the importance of dividing responsibility for military matters. Even if Hamilton's argument may have reflected strategic concerns, the fact that he made it suggests he anticipated a body of readers would be wary of presidential power.

As Commander-in-Chief, the President may appoint military officers.[207] The President also possesses some power to dismiss officers. Although Congress has authority under Article I, section 8, to "make Rules for the Government and Regulation of the land and naval Forces," absent congressional regulation, the President may make rules for their government, safety, and welfare.

The President, as Commander-in-Chief, has authority to play a role in military movements and strategy. He is supreme commander.[208] The President may, as did Abraham Lincoln, intrude directly in command matters. Like Franklin Roosevelt, the President may map the strategy of global conflict. The President may even, as did Woodrow Wilson, place American forces under foreign command. The President normally delegates actual command to military officers, but is not required to do so. The President may assume personal command in the field, as George Washington did in accompanying troops to suppress the Whisky Rebellion. President Truman himself decided in 1945 to drop the atomic bomb on Japan.

The President's power is clearest when he acts to repel attack. Indeed, at the Constitutional Convention an earlier draft of the Constitution gave Congress power "to make war"; the verb was changed to "declare" to remove any inhibitions against presidential action to defend against attack. The issues arose after President Lincoln blockaded Southern ports after the South attacked Fort Sumter in 1861. The Court agreed that the President "is not only authorized but bound to

---

[203] *See, e.g.*, LOUIS FISHER, PRESIDENTIAL WAR POWER (1995); Koh, *supra* note 176.

[204] Youngstown Sheet & Tube Co. v. Sawyer, 343 U.S. 579, 614 (1952) (Jackson, J., concurring).

[205] THE FEDERALIST No. 69 (Alexander Hamilton).

[206] *Id.*

[207] The President's authority is, however, limited by statutes determining the grades to which appointments may be made and specifying the qualifications of appointees.

[208] Fleming v. Page, 50 U.S. (9 How.) 603, 615 (1850).

resist force by force" without awaiting legislative approval.[209]

The Commander-in-Chief's use of the armed forces has largely escaped judicial control. Cases have held the President not legally accountable for using troops to address an emergency. For instance, *Martin v. Mott*[210] upheld a presidential order calling the militia into service during the War of 1812. President James Madison proceeded under an Act of 1795 authorizing him to engage the militia whenever the country "shall be invaded or be in imminent danger of invasion." A private in the New York militia was convicted for refusing to obey. The Court concluded that only the President could decide whether and when to call the militia. "The authority to decide whether the exigency has arisen," declared the Court, "belongs exclusively to the President and . . . his decision is conclusive upon all other persons."[211]

Executive military action has received greater deference from the other branches this century, especially since World War II. The concept of "repelling sudden attacks," which had furnished latitude in the past, expanded to encompass actions abroad to protect American property, personnel, or interests. During the Vietnam War, some questioned whether the judiciary should deem cases regarding presidential use of armed forces as political questions. Despite "a respectable and growing body of lower court opinion[s]" that cases challenging Presidential war-making in Vietnam presented justiciable controversies,[212] the Supreme Court continued to treat the issue as a political question,[213] although over vigorous dissents. At least one federal court ruled continued United States air operations over Cambodia. illegal[214] Justice Thurgood Marshall stated that "it seems likely that the President may not wage war without some form of congressional approval — except, perhaps, in the case of a pressing emergency or when the President is in the process of extricating himself from a war which Congress once authorized."[215] Justice Douglas, too, questioned treating such issues as political questions and urged that only Congress could declare war.[216]

[2] War Powers Resolution

The War Powers Resolution of 1973, which passed over President Nixon's veto, regulated presidential power to employ the armed forces abroad. It provides that, absent a declaration of war, the President shall report to Congress within 48 hours of introducing armed forces into hostilities or foreign territory. The operation must end within 60 days of the required report unless Congress declares war or specifically authorizes the use. The 60-day period may be extended no more than 30 days if the President certifies to Congress that unavoidable military necessity

---

[209] The Prize Cases, 67 U.S. (2 Black) 635, 668 (1863) (upholding President Lincoln's blockade of South after attack on Fort Sumter).

[210] 25 U.S. (12 Wheat.) 19, 30–31 (1827).

[211] *Id.* at 30.

[212] Holtzman v. Schlesinger, 414 U.S. 1304, 1311 (1973) (Marshall, J.).

[213] Orlando v. Laird, 404 U.S. 869 (1971); Mora v. McNamara, 389 U.S. 934 (1967).

[214] Holtzman v. Schlesinger, 361 F. Supp. 553 (E.D.N.Y. 1973).

[215] *Holtzman,* 414 U.S. at 1311–12 (Marshall, J.).

[216] *Id.* at 1317.

respecting the safety of the armed forces requires their continued use in connection with their prompt removal. Congress may refuse to support the President during the initial 60 to 90-day period or may thereafter terminate the action by concurrent resolution. Presidents generally fail to report under the requisite section, thereby delaying the 60-day clock.

President Nixon denounced the War Powers Resolution as an unconstitutional infringement upon the powers Article II vests in the Commander-in- Chief. Such a claim encounters the argument that the President exercises inherent power subject to statute. The Constitution, in requiring the President faithfully to execute the laws, does not except laws governing use of the armed forces abroad.

The Supreme Court expressed this view in an early pronouncement on presidential power. The President had ordered the seizure of a ship bound *from* a French port though a statute authorized seizure only of vessels sailing *to* French ports. In holding the seizure invalid, the Court refused to draw any distinction "between acts of civil and those of military officers; and between proceedings within the body of the country and those on the high seas."[217] The basic principle of subordination of presidential power to statute must be followed even though the case concerns military, not civil, action, taken beyond our borders.

Although Nixon and his successors have deemed the War Powers Act an intrusion on presidential powers, others identify other constitutional problems. One might question whether Congress can delegate power to make war for 60 days without a congressional declaration. Might the War Powers Act violate Congress', not the President's, power? Moreover, the concurrent resolution procedure would seem to run afoul of the Court's decision in *Chadha* invalidating the legislative veto.[218]

[3] September 11, 2001

The events of September 11, 2001, refocused attention on the constitutional processes by which the United States goes to war. Although the Constitution empowers Congress to declare war, the United States has often deployed military forces without a formal declaration. Indeed, on only five occasions has Congress declared war, most recently in World War II.

This is not to say that, as a matter of constitutional law or practice, the President can unilaterally commit the Nation to war. Oftentimes, Congress has passed a resolution authorizing use of military force, as it did in connection with the War in Vietnam and the 1991 war against Iraq. A more recent example of such a resolution is S. J. Res. 23 which the 107th Congress passed and President Bush signed on September 18, 2001. It authorized the President to use "all necessary and appropriate force" against those "nations, organizations, or persons he determines planned, authorized, committed, or ordered the terrorist attacks that occurred on September 11, 2001 or harbored such organizations or persons

---

[217] Little v. Barreme, 6 U.S. (2 Cranch) 170, 179 (1804).

[218] INS v. Chadha, 462 U.S. 919 (1983).

. . . ."[219]

The resolution avoided a debate that would have occurred in its absence. Scholars disagree regarding the scope of the President's authority to commit troops to battle unilaterally. The Constitution clearly allows the President to repel attacks and the War Powers Act authorizes use of force in event of "national emergency created by attack upon the United States, its territories or possessions, or its armed forces."[220] Although there is consensus that the President has power to respond unilaterally to defend the nation, Professor Phillip Trimble points out the "difficult issue is drawing the line beyond which the response requires additional legal justification."[221] Whereas some argue that the President's constitutional authority allows him to act unilaterally simply to repel attack, retaliate in necessary and appropriate fashion, and forestall direct imminent threats,[222] other contend his authority extends to broad preemptive action.[223]

S. J. Res. 23 clearly authorized President Bush to use force against those responsible for the September 11 attacks. It did not empower him to use force against those not connected to the September 11 attacks.

[4] Military Justice

Presidential power generally swells in war-time as military exigency is often used to justify unusual domestic measures. The Civil War tested the resiliency of the Constitution and provided the occasion for the exercise of broad presidential emergency powers.

President Lincoln took a number of actions which normally would have required legislation. He blockaded Southern ports, extended the term of enlistment, increased the size of the military, and disbursed public moneys to private citizens to purchase arms and supplies. Lincoln, historian David Donald wrote, "considered the prosecution of the war primarily a function of the Chief Executive, to be carried out with minimal interference from the other branches of the government and without excessive respect to constitutional niceties protecting individual rights."[224]

Lincoln, however, sought and received congressional approval of his actions. He defended his actions "whether strictly legal or not" based on four criteria: They (a) responded to "a popular demand" and (b) "a public necessity" (c) were within Congress' power and (d) would be confirmed.[225]

---

[219] S.J. Res. 23, 107th Cong. (2001) (enacted).

[220] *Id.*

[221] PHILLIP R. TRIMBLE, INTERNATIONAL LAW: UNITED STATES FOREIGN RELATIONS LAW 263 (2002).

[222] *Applying the War Powers Resolution to the War on Terrorism: Hearing Before the Subcommittee on the Constitution of the Senate Committee on the Judiciary*, 107th Cong. 55 (2002) (statement of Michael Glennon). *See generally id.* at 13–23 (statement of Louis Fisher 2002).

[223] *See, e.g.,* Robert J. Delahunty & John C. Yoo, *The President's Constitutional Authority to Conduct Military Operations Against Terrorist Organizations and the Nations that Harbor or Support Them*, 25 HARV. J.L. & PUB. POL'Y 487, 517 (2002) (arguing for broad presidential authority).

[224] DAVID HERBERT DONALD, LINCOLN 303 (1995).

[225] Abraham Lincoln, Special Session Message (July 4, 1861), *in* 7 MESSAGES AND PAPERS OF THE

President Lincoln suspended the writ of habeas corpus in 1861. Quite clearly, the privilege of the writ of habeas corpus can be suspended only under certain dire circumstances. The constitutional text,[226] which forbids suspension save in such occasions, implies that when those conditions arise, the privilege may temporarily give way. The more difficult issue relates to who has the power of suspension. The placement of the clause in Art. I § 9 as a limitation on the powers of Congress would seem to imply that the Constitution vests that power, in its restricted form, with Congress.

Congress was not in session, however, and President Lincoln decreed the suspension and asked Congress to approve his act. "Are all the laws, *but one*, to go unexecuted, and the Government itself go to pieces lest that one be violated?"[227] he asked rhetorically. When Chief Justice Roger Taney, acting as a presiding judge of a circuit court, issued a writ of habeas corpus to the general who had arrested one secessionist, the general disregarded it and denied entry to a marshal who sought to serve him with a contempt citation. "I have exercised all the power which the Constitution and Laws confer upon me, but that power has been resisted by a force too strong for me to overcome,"[228] wrote Taney. Not until 1863 did Congress act in support of suspension. In the meantime, Lincoln prevailed. "Whatever the respective merits of Taney's and Lincoln's positions, Taney commanded no troops and could not enforce his opinion, while Lincoln did and could,"[229] wrote historian James M. McPherson.

Military commissions have a long pedigree in American practice. They were used during the Mexican-American War, Civil War, and World War II under a variety of circumstances. Supreme Court decisions authorize their use to try alleged war criminals[230] as well as civilians alleged to have committed criminal offenses in occupied areas.[231] Some decisions authorize their use on enemy territory where American civil courts do not operate.[232]

The more difficult question involves the propriety of military tribunals within the United States. The two leading decisions, *Ex Parte Milligan*[233] and *Ex Parte Quirin*,[234] seem to point in different directions.

In *Ex Parte Milligan*,[235] the Court held that a military tribunal could not try an American citizen charged with conspiracy to aid the confederacy while civil courts

---

PRESIDENTS 3221, 3225 (James Richardson ed., 1897).

[226] U.S. CONST. art. I, § 9, cl. 2 ("The Privilege of the Writ of Habeas Corpus shall not be suspended, unless when in Cases of Rebellion or Invasion the public Safety may require it.").

[227] Abraham Lincoln, Special Session Message (July 4, 1861), *in* 7 MESSAGES AND PAPERS OF THE PRESIDENTS 3221, 3226 (James Richardson ed., 1897).

[228] *Ex parte* Merryman, 17 F. Cas. 144, 153 (C.C.D. Md. 1861).

[229] JAMES M. MCPHERSON, BATTLE CRY OF FREEDOM: THE CIVIL WAR ERA 289 (1988).

[230] *See, e.g.*, Application of Yamashita, 327 U.S. 1 (1946).

[231] *See, e.g.*, Madsen v. Kinsella, 343 U.S. 341 (1952).

[232] *See, e.g., id.*

[233] 71 U.S. (4 Wall.) 2 (1866).

[234] 317 U.S. 1 (1942).

[235] 71 U.S. (4 Wall.) 2 (1866).

were open and functioning. Milligan, a leading Copperhead, was arrested, convicted, and sentenced to be hanged during the Civil War by a military commission in Indiana. During the "late wicked Rebellion," Justice Davis wrote for the Court., "the temper of the times did not allow that calmness in deliberation and discussion so necessary to a correct conclusion of a purely judicial question."[236] With the "public safety" assured, the issue could be addressed dispassionately. Congress had authorized the President to suspend habeas corpus except that the writ should issue if a federal grand jury met but failed to indict a prisoner held by authority of the President.[237] Congress's Act of March 3, 1863, had authorized suspension of the writ but not indefinitely without common law judicial proceedings. Milligan, a civilian, had been improperly tried before a military tribunal rather than the Article III courts then operating in the jurisdiction of his alleged offense. Although the Constitution allowed suspension of the writ of habeas corpus under the circumstances specified, it did not authorize denying civilians trial in a common law court and accordingly neither the President nor Congress could authorize trial of an American civilian by military tribunal where the civil courts were open. Under *Milligan*, the military tribunals cannot supplant operating civil courts.

During World War II, however, the Court, in *Ex Parte Quirin*, upheld the power of a military tribunal to try eight German saboteurs captured in the United States, one of whom was an American citizen. The eight saboteurs had discarded their military uniforms upon disembarking from a German submarine. The indictment charged them with violating "the law of war." The Court found that Congress had authorized use of military commissions to try offenses against the law of war. Thus, *Ex Parte Quirin* did not require the Court to reach the question of whether the President had unilateral power to convene military tribunals. Military tribunals could be used to try "unlawful combatants," e.g., enemy combatants without uniforms, including the American citizen. The Court distinguished *Ex Parte Milligan* — Milligan was not an unlawful belligerent — and limited the older case to its facts.

In *Ex Parte Quirin*, the determination that defendants were unlawful belligerents may not have involved disputed facts. In other instances, it may. The distinction the Court drew in *Ex Parte Quirin* regarding unlawful combatants, while accurate, is problematic since it makes jurisdiction turn on the substantive outcome of the proceeding. The Court, of course, decided *Ex Parte Milligan* after the Civil War ended and *Ex Parte Quirin* while World War II was underway but it is difficult to extract a legal principle from this factual difference.

It is therefore difficult to harmonize the two cases on doctrinal grounds. In *Ex Parte Milligan* military tribunals on American soil lacked jurisdiction over Milligan while civilian courts were operating; in *Ex Parte Quirin* they possessed jurisdiction over the German saboteurs even though civilian courts were available.

The circumstances surrounding *Ex Parte Quirin* also might counsel reading it narrowly. The case arose during World War II. The Court convened during its

---

[236] *Id.* at 109.

[237] 12 Stat. 755 (1863).

summer recess to hear the case and announced its decision within a few days. The opinion articulating its reasons was not forthcoming for several months. In the interim, six of the saboteurs were executed. While believing the result correct, Chief Justice Stone had difficulty arriving at the rationale and the Court was divided among competing justifications.[238]

These cases gained new prominence in the aftermath of 9/11. Professor Richard Fallon has pointed out that the terrorist attack gave President George W. Bush "an opportunity for reconstructive presidential leadership" to advance a vision of expansive presidential leadership as constitutionally sanctioned and necessary. Yet the Court's disposition of various cases relating to the War on Terror constituted a rejection of the ambitious theories President Bush advanced about presidential power.[239] President Bush's Military Order of November 13, 2001, authorized establishment of military commissions to prosecute any non-citizen who the President determines "is or was" a member of al Qaida or had engaged in terrorism against the United States. The President's Order gave the military tribunals "exclusive jurisdiction" regarding such individuals and denied such individuals "any remedy" in "any court of the United States or any State thereof."[240]

The Supreme Court addressed questions raised by President Bush's order during the October 2003 term in *Hamdi v. Rumsfeld*.[241] The Court divided among four opinions, with none commanding a majority, although at least five justices agreed on some important points and ultimately eight justices rejected the claims for sweeping presidential power which the Bush administration urged.

The case involved claims brought on behalf of an American citizen who had been captured in Afghanistan, allegedly on the battlefield, and was being held in the United States as an enemy combatant. Hamdi brought a writ of habeas corpus to challenge his detention as unlawful.

Writing for four justices,[242] Justice O'Connor concluded that Congress had authorized the detention in its Authorization for Use of Military Force (AUMF). The authorization for the President to use "all necessary and appropriate force" was sufficiently capacious to include detention of enemy combatants. Thus, the President was not relying simply on the constitutional powers of his office. Moreover, *Ex parte Milligan* was inapposite since it involved not an enemy at war, but a citizen seized at home. Nonetheless, the plurality concluded that "a citizen held in the United States as an enemy combatant" must "be given a meaningful opportunity to contest the factual basis for [the] detention before a neutral decisionmaker."[243] The plurality concluded that someone in Hamdi's position was

---

[238] *See* ALPHEUS T. MASON, HARLAN FISKE STONE: PILLAR OF THE LAW 653–666 (1956).

[239] Richard H. Fallon, Jr., *The Supreme Court, Habeas Corpus, and the War on Terror: An Essay on Law and Political Science*, 110 COLUM. L. REV. 352, 372 (2010).

[240] Military Order, Detention, Treatment, and Trial of Certain Non-Citizens in the War Against Terrorism, § 7(b)(2)-(i), 66 Fed. Reg. 57, 833, 57, 835–36 (Nov. 13, 2001).

[241] 542 U.S. 507 (2004).

[242] Chief Justice Rehnquist, Justices O'Connor, Kennedy, and Breyer.

[243] 542 U.S. at 509.

entitled to notice of the charges against him and "a fair opportunity to rebut the Government's factual assertions before a neutral decisionmaker."[244] This requirement was not tantamount to a full-blown trial before an Article III court. On the contrary, "the exigencies of the circumstances" might require tailoring the proceedings to avoid burdening the Executive too greatly during wartime. The plurality entertained the possibility that the requisite due process could be satisfied by "an appropriately authorized and properly constituted military tribunal." Yet the plurality also rejected the Government's claim that the judiciary's role must be "heavily circumscribed."[245]

Justices Souter and Ginsburg agreed with the plurality in denying the Executive's claim that Hamdi was entitled to little or no judicial review and they agreed that Hamdi was entitled to challenge the claim that he was an enemy combatant (although they would have afforded greater opportunity than did the plurality). They disagreed with the plurality's conclusion that the AUMF encompassed detention of an enemy combatant.

Justices Scalia and Stevens dissented from the plurality's approach. They concluded that the Government had two options, neither of which was what the plurality prescribed. It must either prosecute persons like Hamdi in federal court for treason or other offense or, if wartime circumstances made that course unpalatable, Congress might temporarily relax usual protections by temporarily suspending the writ of habeas corpus. Since the Government had taken neither course, its action was unlawful. Justices Scalia and Stevens thought Hamdi's case closer to *Milligan*, since civilian courts were open, than to *Quirin*, a problematic decision but one in which the petitioners were admittedly enemy forces.

All eight justices joining the three opinions described above rejected the claims the Bush administration advanced for broad presidential power. Justice Thomas, however, argued that the detention of Hamdi was well within the war powers of the Federal Government and the judiciary lacked "the expertise and capacity to second guess that decision."[246] In essence, Justice Thomas saw the case as a political question. He agreed, however, with the plurality in finding the detention authorized by the AUMF.

After deciding some high profile cases on non-constitutional grounds in which detainees challenged their custody through habeas petitions,[247] the Court shed further light on constitutional limitations on executive power in war time in *Boumediene v. Bush*.[248] Aliens who were detained at Guantanamo sought to challenge their custody through a habeas petition. The Military Commissions Act of 2006 (MCA), the Court held, stripped federal courts of jurisdiction to hear habeas petitions of detainees which were pending when it was enacted. That statutory interpretation adverse to the petitioners presented the question

---

[244] *Id.* at 533.

[245] *Id.* at 535.

[246] *Id.* at 579. He articulated a theory of broad presidential powers regarding foreign affairs and national security.

[247] *See, e.g.*, Hamdan v. Rumsfeld, 548 U.S. 557 (2006); Rasul v. Bush, 542 U.S. 466 (2004).

[248] 553 U.S. 723 (2008).

regarding the constitutionality of the statute and the Court, in a 5-4 decision by Justice Kennedy, held that it was. The habeas privilege applied to those held in Guantanamo Bay and neither of the prerequisites for suspension (rebellion or invasion) were present. Both Justice Kennedy's majority opinion and Justice Scalia's dissent looked to the original intent behind the Suspension Clause and found no case where a noncitizen held outside the Crown's sovereignty had invoked habeas relief. Whereas Justice Scalia thought that finding dispositive, Justice Kennedy did not, in part because he questioned the assumptions that the historical record was complete or that it answered the questions before it since 18th century courts may not have faced situations similar to that before the Court. Justice Kennedy's opinion rested on the premise that questions over extraterritoriality and the scope of the Constitution's due process protections should turn on objective factors and practical concerns, not formalism.

Although Justice Scalia argued that *Johnson v. Eisentrager*,[249] held that the writ of habeas corpus did not apply to a noncitizen held outside the United States, the Court rejected that reading of *Eisentrager*. Instead, the Court used *Eisentrager* to develop a functional, three-factor test regarding the reach of the Suspension Clause: "(1) the citizenship and status of the detainee and the adequacy of the process through which that status determination was made; (2) the nature of the sites where apprehension and then detention took place; and (3) the practical obstacles inherent in resolving the prisoner's entitlement to the writ." Applying this functionalist test, Court held that the Suspension Clause applied fully at Guantanamo Bay.

To allow Congress and the President "to switch the Constitution on or off at will . . . would permit a striking anomaly in our tripartite system of government, leading to a regime in which Congress and the President, not this Court, say 'what the law is' " contrary to *Marbury*,[250] the Court reasoned. Justice Kennedy rebutted any suggestion that the Court's decision eroded presidential power.

> Our opinion does not undermine the Executive's powers as Commander in Chief. On the contrary, the exercise of those powers is vindicated, not eroded, when confirmed by the Judicial Branch. Within the Constitution's separation-of-powers structure, few exercises of judicial power are as legitimate or as necessary as the responsibility to hear challenges to the authority of the Executive to imprison a person.[251]

Chief Justice Roberts, joined by Justices Scalia, Thomas and Alito, dissented. They argued that the alternative procedures set forth in the MCA were sufficient to afford petitioners procedural protections against improper executive detention.

Justice Scalia's dissent argued, in forceful language, that the Court had exceeded its competence in second guessing the executive on national security matters. The majority opinion played a "game of bait-and-switch" on the president which would

---

[249] 339 U.S. 763 (1950).

[250] *Boumediene*, 553 U.S. at 765.

[251] *Id.* at 797.

jeopardize American lives in service of "an inflated notion of judicial supremacy."[252]

Military tribunals are sometimes referred to as Article II courts because they typically rest on an exertion of the President's power as Commander-in-Chief.[253] In *Ex Parte Milligan*, the Court said, in dicta, that even Congress lacked power to authorize military commissions in areas served by functioning civilian courts. Four members of the Court disagreed. The argument was academic because Congress had not authorized the tribunals. Yet the entire Court agreed that congressional authorization was "at least a necessary requirement for such tribunals."[254] In *Ex Parte Quirin*, the Court observed that it need not decide whether the Commander-in-Chief clause alone authorized the President to create military commissions since Congress had authorized them under the circumstances there. Later in *Madsen v. Kinsella*, the Court implied that Congress might limit the President's power to create military tribunals.[255]

§ 7.08   PRESIDENTIAL ACCOUNTABILITY

[1]   The President as Defendant

In *Marbury v. Madison*,[256] the Court suggested that at times the executive branch could be held accountable in court for its conduct but on other occasions it enjoyed immunity. In essence, if executive conduct allegedly violated an individual's rights, a court could assert jurisdiction over even the Secretary of State; if the executive enjoyed discretion the Constitution gave him, the Court could not consider the matter. *Marbury*, of course, involved James Madison as the defendant, not President Thomas Jefferson. It therefore did not reach the question of whether the President could be sued.

Mississippi v. Johnson[257] involved an action against President Andrew Johnson to enjoin him from enforcing the Reconstruction Acts on the ground that they were unconstitutional. Based on the separation of powers doctrine, the Court decided such an action could not be maintained. "The Congress is the legislative department of the government; the President is the executive department. Neither can be restrained in its action by the judicial department."[258] Although the Court clearly held that it lacked power to enjoin the President from executing a law alleged to be unconstitutional it did not go so far as to say that the President could never be sued. More recently, the Court indicated that "in general" a federal court

---

[252] *Id.* at 827, 842.

[253] David J. Bederman, *Article II Courts*, 44 MERCER L. REV. 825, 831 (1993).

[254] Neal K. Katyal & Laurence H. Tribe, *Waging War, Deciding Guilt: Trying the Military Tribunals*, 111 YALE L.J. 1259, 1279 (2002).

[255] 343 U.S. 341, 348–49 (1952) (President may create wartime military tribunals absent congressional action.).

[256] 5 U.S. (1 Cranch) 137 (1803).

[257] 71 U.S. (4 Wall.) 475 (1867).

[258] *Id.* at 500.

lacks jurisdiction to enjoin the President regarding performance of official duties.[259]

Justice Scalia has argued that "[t]he apparently unbroken historical tradition supports the view . . . implicit in the separation of powers established by the Constitution, that the . . . President . . . may not be ordered to perform particular executive . . . acts at the behest of the Judiciary."[260] Similarly, Justice Scalia thought the courts could not issue a declaratory judgment against the President. The lack of judicial power to enjoin the President does not mean that presidential action is unreviewable because the legality of Presidential action can ordinarily be examined in a suit to enjoin those charged with enforcing the President's order.[261] Thus in the *Steel Seizure Case*,[262] the steel companies tested the validity of President Truman's order in an action against the Secretary of Commerce, the instrument for the execution of the President's order. In the extraordinary case where only an order directed against the President will prove effective, *United States v. Nixon*[263] holds that the President may be sued in a federal court and ordered to produce presidential documents under certain circumstances.

[2] Executive Privileges and Immunities

In recent years, the question of executive privilege has generated increased interest. The President has claimed the power to withhold information when he deems disclosure contrary to the public interest. President Nixon asserted the right to withhold from courts evidence crucial to a pending criminal prosecution.

The Court considered, and rejected, Nixon's bold assertion in *United States v. Nixon*.[264] The Court refused to quash a subpoena to the President issued on motion of the Watergate Special Prosecutor. The subpoena directed the President to produce certain tape recordings and documents relating to his conversations with aides, which were needed as evidence in criminal prosecutions. The Court recognized a presumptive privilege for presidential communications based on the President's expectation of confidentiality of personal conversations and correspondence. The presumptive privilege is, however, only a qualified one.[265] A claim of privilege based only on the generalized interest in confidentiality cannot prevail over the demonstrated specific need for evidence in a pending criminal trial. Hence Nixon was subject to the subpoena to produce information relevant to an ongoing criminal prosecution since the Court's need for evidence in a criminal case outweighed his generalized interest in preserving the confidentiality of his conversations.[266] The Court indicated that a different result might be reached

---

[259] Franklin v. Massachusetts, 505 U.S. 788, 802–03 (1992). Only four members of the Court jointed that part of the opinion but Justice Scalia made clear his agreement with this view.

[260] *Id.* at 827 (Scalia, J., concurring).

[261] *Id.* at 828.

[262] 343 U.S. 579 (1952).

[263] 418 U.S. 683 (1974).

[264] The Court's decision was unanimous with Justice Rehnquist not participating.

[265] *Nixon*, 418 U.S. at 706.

[266] *Id.* at 713.

given a need to protect military, diplomatic, or national security secrets. Here, no such claim was made. Similarly, the Court suggested that the President's claims would have greater weight against disclosure in a civil case in a or congressional proceeding.[267]

The *Nixon* case rejects the claim of an absolute immunity in the President from judicial process based on the separation of powers. The Court insisted that it had the right "to say what the law is" in any case involving the legality of claims relating to exercises of power by the executive and legislative branches.[268]

Thereafter, in *Nixon v. Administrator of General Services*,[269] the Court held that the executive privilege survived a particular President's term.[270] Nonetheless, Nixon was not entitled to an absolute barrier to outside disclosure of his papers and effects. A practice of making presidential papers available in libraries had existed. Review by archivists and later public disclosure of Nixon's papers would not interfere with a President's interest in receiving confidential advice.

In *Cheney v. United States District Court for the District of Columbia*,[271] the Court concluded that executive privilege need not be asserted for the Government to object to production of certain sensitive documents in civil litigation based on separation of powers concerns.

The dispute arose when various public interest groups brought actions alleging that the National Energy Policy Development Group (NEPDG) which President George W. Bush created under the Chairmanship of Vice President Richard B. Cheney, violated the Federal Advisory Committee Act (FACA). More specifically, the litigants claimed that NEPDG regularly met with certain nongovernmental employees, including lobbyists, who accordingly were *de facto* members thereby subjecting the body to disclosure and open-meeting requirements of FACA. Litigants sued Vice President Cheney and other governmental and nongovernmental defendants and sought an injunction requiring them to produce materials subject to FACA. The United States District Court allowed plaintiffs to direct discovery to Vice President Cheney et al. regarding NEPDG's structure and membership. The Vice President filed an interlocutory appeal and sought a writ of mandamus from the Court of Appeals to vacate the lower court's discovery orders. The Court of Appeals dismissed the Vice President's appeal and declined to issue the writ, in part on the grounds that other remedies were available. In particular, under *United States v. Nixon*,[272] the court said the Government must assert executive privilege with particularity to protect the President's prerogatives.

The Supreme Court did not agree. The presence, as a party subject to discovery orders, of the Vice President and those "in closest operational proximity to the President" with respect to the process of advising the President removed the case

---

[267] *Id.* at 712 n.19.

[268] *Id.* at 705.

[269] 433 U.S. 425 (1977).

[270] *Id.* at 449.

[271] 542 U.S. 367 (2004).

[272] 418 U.S. 683 (1974).

from normal rules governing interlocutory appeals of discovery orders. The Executive should not have to claim executive privilege to respond to discovery but could avail itself of general separation of powers arguments. Executive privilege should be invoked in extraordinary circumstances, not as a matter of routine. Although the President was not above the law, other branches of government should recognize "the paramount necessity of protecting the Executive Branch from vexatious litigation that might distract it from the energetic performance of its constitutional duties."[273] The appellate court's reliance on *United States v. Nixon* was misplaced. Whereas *United States v. Nixon* was a criminal case, this case was a civil proceeding in which information sought from the Executive had less weight. Whereas the criminal justice system afforded certain protections against prosecutorial overreaching, including the accountability of prosecutors, civil litigants were not subject to such restraints.

What about civil liability? Under *Nixon v. Fitzgerald*,[274] the President is immune from civil suits for damages caused by official acts. Fitzgerald, a Pentagon employee, had sued President Nixon and various White House aides for allegedly eliminating his job to retaliate against him for his whistle blowing activities. Although the Court held that other executive officials had only a qualified immunity from civil liability for official acts,[275] it held in a 5-4 decision that the President enjoys absolute immunity from damage actions based on official acts. The Court reasoned that litigation would distract the President from Presidential duties and the spectre of personal liability might interfere with decision-making.

However, *Clinton v. Jones*[276] held that this immunity does not extend to suits for damages arising out of events that occurred before the President took office. The same would be true, the Court suggests, of damage suits based on "Presidential action not taken in an official capacity" — i.e., "acts outside official duties." There is, the opinion declared, no "immunity from suit for unofficial acts."

To be sure, President Clinton did not claim absolute immunity for prior personal conduct. He simply asked that the case be deferred until he left office. The Court expressed confidence in the judiciary's ability to manage litigation without interfering with the President's conduct of his office. Given the national preoccupation with the case as it developed, one might question the Court's assessment of the practical impact of such litigation on the office and the judiciary's ability to manage it.

The long-term effect of *Jones* is more difficult to assess. The President may now be subject to suit for personal actions. But that scarcely affects the broad Presidential immunity for official acts. The course of the litigation against President Clinton may raise questions about the judiciary's ability to avoid disruption of executive functions, an issue Justice Scalia prophesied in his dissent

---

[273] *Id.* at 369.

[274] 457 U.S. 731 (1982).

[275] Harlow v. Fitzgerald, 457 U.S. 800, 818 (1982) (officials immune from civil liability if conduct "does not violate clearly established statutory or constitutional rights of which a reasonable person would have known").

[276] 520 U.S. 681 (1997).

in *Morrison v. Olson*. Presumably, suits against the President relating to unofficial transactions will occur infrequently and will involve less spectacular claims than those asserted in *Clinton v. Jones*.

In *Cheney v. United States District Court*,[277] the Court sounded more deferential to the Executive than it had in *Clinton v. Jones*. As mentioned, the Court spoke of the need for the judiciary to "give recognition to the paramount necessity of protecting the Executive Branch from vexatious litigation that might distract it from the energetic performance of its constitutional duties."[278] The Court left open the possibility, however, that the lower courts could shape appropriate discovery orders which would allow the case to proceed against the Vice President and other close presidential advisors without unduly impairing the Executive Branch's performance.

[3] Impeachment

Generally, presidential impeachment has been a theoretical possibility, not a realistic prospect. For the first 185 years of our history, only one president, Andrew Johnson, was impeached. The impeachment proceedings against President Nixon in 1974 and against President Clinton in 1998–99 have changed that perception. They focused attention on the constitutional provision governing removal of federal officers. That brief provision raises several legal issues. First, who may be impeached? Article II limits impeachment to the President, Vice President, and "all Civil Officers of the United States."[279] Congressmen are not officers of the United States within the meaning of the Impeachment Clause and accordingly are not included.[280] Other federal civil officers are subject to impeachment. Most impeachment proceedings have targeted federal judges. Resignation does not immunize an officer from impeachment as a constitutional matter although practically speaking it may take much of the momentum out of the effort. An impeachment proceeding may result in removal from office and disqualification from holding further office.[281]

A second important question is what offenses are impeachable. The Impeachment Clause authorizes impeachment for "Treason, Bribery, or other high Crimes and Misdemeanors."[282] "So what does the term mean? It is ambiguous, capable of expansive and restrictive interpretations, and it is up to the members of the House and Senate to decipher its meaning," wrote Richard M. Pious, a leading student of the presidency.[283] Is this language limited to criminal offenses?

---

[277] 542 U.S. 367 (2004).

[278] *Id.* at 369.

[279] U.S. Const. art. II, § 4.

[280] For a different view, *see* Raoul Berger, Impeachment: The Constitutional Problems 214–23 (1973).

[281] U.S. Const. art. I, § 3, cl. 7.

[282] U.S. Const. art. II, § 4.

[283] Richard M. Pious, *Impeaching the President: The Intersection of Constitutional and Popular Law*, 43 St. Louis U. L.J. 859, 867 (1999).

The impeachment of President Andrew Johnson in 1868 proceeded upon the theory that impeachment need not depend on an indictable offense. The articles against Johnson alleged no indictable offense, but were based on his failure to execute certain laws and his public utterances attacking Congress. Johnson's defense insisted an indictable offense was the prerequisite for impeachment. Johnson escaped removal by a single vote in the Senate.

Diverse factors may have influenced votes, and accordingly it is difficult to view the Johnson proceeding as precedent for either view.

Historically, most impeachments have been against federal judges. A broad conception of impeachable offenses has prevailed with respect to federal judges. Some federal judges have been impeached for behavior inconsistent with their office. For instance, Judge John Pickering in 1803 and Judge Mark Delahay were impeached for intoxication on the bench. Justice Samuel Chase was impeached in 1804 for allegedly letting his political views color his conduct of trials as a circuit judge. Other judges have been impeached for using their office for an improper purpose. Of course, federal judges hold office during "good behavior"[284] which may account for the broader interpretation of "other high Crimes and Misdemeanors." Hence a federal judge may be impeached for misconduct short of an indictable offense.[285] The Constitution does state a uniform standard for impeachable conduct for Presidents, Vice Presidents, executive and judicial officers, a fact which might suggest that the same standard does apply to all. On the other hand, the Constitution empowers the Senate to advise and consent to presidential nominations for the same two branches yet traditionally the Senate exercises more intense scrutiny over some judicial, than executive, nominations

The impeachment proceeding against President Nixon reflected the view that criminal conduct was not a prerequisite for impeachment of an executive officer. The House Judiciary Committee adopted three articles of impeachment which charged both indictable offenses and abuses of executive power. Congress and the country debated whether a President could be removed for misconduct short of criminality. Nixon resigned to avoid certain impeachment after revelation of a tape recording of a conversation that revealed Nixon had obstructed investigation of criminal conduct, itself an indictable offense. In fact, Nixon's impeachment proceeding would have had direct evidence of criminal conduct on which to base removal of the President which was at odds with his duty to enforce the laws. The impeachment proceedings against President Clinton raised a different issue. He was charged with perjury and obstruction of justice relating to his relationship with a former White House intern. His defense denied the charges and argued that even if true, they did not rise to the level of "other high crimes and misdemeanors" the Constitution requires. Although the alleged offenses were indictable, Clinton argued that not every such offense justified impeachment or removal. The use of the phrase "other high crimes and misdemeanors" after "treason" and "bribery" implies that it refers to similar serious public offenses. Clinton was impeached in the House on essentially a straight party line vote and acquitted by the Senate.

---

[284] U.S. Const. art. III, § 1.

[285] Edward S. Corwin, The Constitution of the United States: Analysis and Interpretation 504 (1953).

It seems likely that impeachment is not limited to indictable crimes. Presumably a President who was derelict in Presidential duties, perhaps by refusing to show up for work or to discharge official duties, could be impeached.[286] Impeachment is, after all, a remedy to help preserve constitutional government. The paradigmatic case of impeachment relates to abuse of power.[287] Moreover, the argument seems sound that certain criminal conduct in private matters should not give rise to impeachment.[288] On the other hand, it is possible to conjure up activity outside the President's official conduct — murder[289] or rape, for instance — that would make it intolerable for the President to continue. Ultimately, the concept of an impeachable offense must adapt to embrace those activities that so violate public sensibilities as to make it unacceptable that a President continue.

On the other hand, the impeachment standard was not intended to license Congress to remove the President based on whim or simply based on political disagreement. The founders rejected proposals to allow impeachment at the pleasure of Congress[290] or for maladministration.[291]

The Constitution, of course, provides that the Chief Justice presides when the President is tried for impeachment. His participation adds an air of solemnity to the proceedings and removes the vice president from presiding, a clear conflict of interest for one who is both, in modern practice, the President's chosen successor but also the person next in line. The Constitution does not provide for an alternate chair when the Vice President is tried, a scenario that almost occurred as recently as 1973 when Spiro T. Agnew considered insisting that he be impeached rather than resign. This omission leads some scholars to conclude that the Vice President could preside over her own impeachment trial.[292] On the other hand, structural ideas regarding checks and balances and conflict of interest might dictate a contrary conclusion.[293]

§ 7.09 SUCCESSION AND DISABILITY

Presidential succession and inability has presented one of the vexing problems in American history. When President William Henry Harrison died in 1841 barely one month into his term, Vice President John Tyler took the presidential oath and insisted he was President, not simply Vice President acting as President as many thought. The controversy traced to a textual ambiguity. Article II, Section 1, Clause

---

[286] See CHARLES L. BLACK, JR., IMPEACHMENT 33–36 (1974).

[287] Michael J. Gerhardt, *Putting the Law of Impeachment in Perspective*, 43 ST. LOUIS U. L.J. 905, 921 (1999).

[288] Black, *supra* note 286, at 36.

[289] *Id.* at 39. *See also* Gerhardt, *supra* note 287, at 925.

[290] 2 RECORDS OF THE CONSTITUTIONAL CONVENTION OF 1787, at 550 (Max Farrand ed., 1966).

[291] *Id.* at 550–55.

[292] Michael Stokes Paulsen, *Someone Should Have Told Spiro Agnew*, 14 CONST. COMMENT. 245 (1997); Stephen L. Carter, *The Political Aspects of Judicial Power: Some Notes on the Presidential Immunity Decision*, 131 U. PA. L. REV. 1341, 1357 & n.72 (1983).

[293] Joel K. Goldstein, *Can the Vice President Preside at His Own Impeachment Trial?: A Critique of Bare Textualism*, 44 ST. LOUIS U. L.J. 849 (2000).

6 provided that in case of removal, death, resignation, or inability of the President "to discharge the powers and duties of the said office, the same shall devolve on the Vice President . . . ." If "the same" was the "said office" Tyler was right; if it referred simply to "the powers and duties" of the office, Tyler assumed the authority and responsibility but not the position itself. In any event, the Tyler precedent was followed on each of the seven other occasions when a President died in office.[294] The Twenty-fifth Amendment, ratified in 1967, expressly provides that on the removal, death, or resignation of the President, "the Vice President shall become President," thereby distinguishing those contingencies from presidential inability.

The Twenty-fifth Amendment also recognized the transformation of the American Vice Presidency into an executive position of importance.[295] Section two provides a mechanism to fill a vice-presidential vacancy by presidential nomination subject to confirmation by each House of Congress. This provision enabled the Federal Government to avoid problems that might have arisen with the resignation in 1973 and 1974 of both the Vice President and the President. On the resignation of Vice President Agnew in October 1973, President Nixon nominated Gerald R. Ford as Vice President and, in accordance with the Amendment, Ford took office once confirmed by a majority vote of both Houses of Congress. When Nixon resigned as President in August 1974, Ford succeeded to the Presidency and nominated Nelson A. Rockefeller as Vice President. He, too, was confirmed by the vote of the two Houses. Ford and Rockefeller were accepted as legitimate leaders since they had secured their positions under the Twenty-fifth Amendment's express provisions.[296]

The Twenty-fifth Amendment recognizes that the President may be disabled from performing presidential functions by causes short of death. It provides a method for determining when Presidential disability exists, thereby addressing one of the principal gaps in the Constitution. The Amendment makes clear that, in the event of a disability that renders the President unable to discharge the powers and duties of the office, the Vice President becomes Acting President until the disability is removed. For the first time in our history, the Constitution provides for administration of the executive power when the President becomes incapacitated.

In July 1985, President Reagan transferred power to Vice President George Bush for several hours while the Chief Executive underwent surgery under anesthesia. Although Reagan claimed he was not using Section Three of the Amendment, he followed its procedures exactly and it afforded the only basis to make the transfer. In 2002, President George W. Bush briefly transferred power to

---

[294] *See generally* John D. Feerick, From Falling Hands (1965).

[295] *See generally* Joel K. Goldstein, *The New Constitutional Vice Presidency*, 30 Wake Forest L. Rev. 505 (1995).

[296] *See* John D. Feerick, The Twenty-Fifth Amendment: Its Complete History and Applications 117–90 (1992); Joel K. Goldstein, The Modern American Vice Presidency: The Transformation of a Political Institution 228–48 (1982); John D. Feerick, *Presidential Succession and Inability: Before and After the Twenty-Fifth Amendment*, 79 Fordham L. Rev. 907 (2010); Joel K. Goldstein, *Taking from the Twenty-Fifth Amendment: Lessons in Ensuring Presidential Continuity*, 79 Fordham L. Rev. 959 (2010).

Vice President Richard Cheney while the President underwent a medical procedure. He did so again in 2007 under similar circumstances.

The Twenty-fifth Amendment addresses who decides the existence of presidential disability. The Amendment recognizes that the President personally possesses the power to declare disability. It also empowers the Vice President and a majority of the Cabinet or of such other body as Congress may by law provide to declare that the President is unable to fulfill the powers and duties of the office. Congress is empowered to decide the issue only in case of dispute between the President and the officers designated.

§ 7.10   SEPARATION OF POWERS

It is perhaps useful to close this survey of constitutional issues relating to executive power with some comments regarding the structural concept of separation of powers. Tucking this topic into a chapter on executive power is somewhat misleading. Separation of powers issues do not revolve solely around the executive. Indeed, much of the preceding chapters address division of power between the branches of the national government. For instance, the propriety of judicial review, the justiciability doctrines and legislative oversight of the federal courts all involve separation of powers concerns. Yet there is some method in discussing separation of powers here. Many of the difficult separation of powers cases the Court has addressed during the past several decades do involve the executive branch.

Like federalism, the separation of powers doctrine is not expressly provided for in the Constitution. It is, however, a fundamental structural concept implicit in it as a conclusion logically following from the creation of the three branches. "It may be stated then, as a general rule inherent in the American constitutional system, that . . . the Legislature cannot exercise either executive or judicial power; the executive cannot exercise either legislative or judicial power; the judiciary cannot exercise either executive or legislative power."[297] The "general rule" must accommodate exceptions. In a sense, separation of powers is a misnomer. As the perceptive political scientist Richard Neustadt pointed out, "The Constitutional Convention of 1787 is supposed to have created a government of 'separate powers.' It did nothing of the sort. Rather, it created a government of separated institutions *sharing* powers."[298] As Justice Brandeis pointed out in his *Myers* dissent, "The separation of the powers of government did not make each branch completely autonomous. It left each in some measure dependent upon the others, as it left to each power to exercise, in some respects, functions in their nature executive, legislative and judicial."[299] Some of the interdependence flowed from the related doctrine of checks and balances, the metaphor which captures the extent to which the various governmental institutions exercise power over each other. Yet the interdependence also reflects a degree of accommodation and compromise which is necessary for government to operate. As Chief Justice Burger later explained in *United States v.*

---

[297] Springer v. Philippine Islands, 277 U.S. 189, 201 (1928).

[298] RICHARD E. NEUSTADT, PRESIDENTIAL POWER AND THE MODERN PRESIDENTS: THE POLITICS OF LEADERSHIP FROM ROOSEVELT TO REAGAN 29 (1990) (emphasis in original).

[299] *Myers*, 272 U.S. at 291.

Nixon, "[i]n designing the structure of our Government and dividing and allocating the sovereign power among three co-equal branches, the Framers of the Constitution sought to provide a comprehensive system, but the separate powers were not intended to operate with absolute independence."[300]

The Court has said that the separation of powers between three branches is "essential to the preservation of liberty."[301] As Justice Brandeis put it: "The doctrine of the separation of powers was adopted by the convention of 1787 not to promote efficiency, but to preclude the exercise of arbitrary power. The purpose was not to avoid friction but, by means of the inevitable friction incident to the distribution of the governmental powers among three departments, to save the people from autocracy."[302]

The separation of powers is violated when Congress exercises responsibilities of other branches.[303] Congress cannot exercise executive functions or control an officer who discharges such duties. *Metropolitan Washington Airports Authority v. Citizens for Abatement of Noise*[304] illustrates the first type of case. Congress authorized transfer of two Washington, D.C. airports to an agency created by a compact between Virginia and the District of Columbia. A Board of Review composed of nine members of Congress was given authority to veto decisions of the agency. The Court held that the statute violated the separation of powers. If the power given to the review board was executive, separation of powers precluded an agency of Congress, such as the board composed of its members, from exercising such power.

Nor may Congress vest executive power in an office it controls. *Bowsher v. Synar*[305] held that the assignment to the Comptroller General of certain functions under the Gramm-Rudman Act was invalid. The Comptroller General was appointed by the President, but could be removed from office by a joint resolution of Congress. Gramm-Rudman gave the Comptroller General power to order program-by-program reductions in federal spending to reach targeted deficit levels. The Court ruled that this arrangement violated the separation of powers. By placing the responsibility for execution of the statute in an officer subject to its removal power, "Congress in effect has retained control over the execution of the Act and has intruded into the executive function. The Constitution does not permit such intrusion."[306]

Bowsher found the Comptroller General directly subject to congressional control based on the legislature's removal power. Congress reserved that power to make the Comptroller General a legislative officer; Comptrollers General have so viewed themselves. Accordingly, wrote Chief Justice Burger, "[w]e see no escape from the conclusion that, because Congress has retained removal authority over the Comp

---

[300] 418 U.S. 683, 707 (1974).

[301] Mistretta v. United States, 488 U.S. 361, 380 (1989).

[302] *Myers,* 272 U.S. at 293.

[303] *Mistretta,* 488 U.S. at 382.

[304] 501 U.S. 252 (1991).

[305] 478 U.S. 714 (1986).

[306] *Id.* at 734.

troller General, he may not be entrusted with executive powers."[307]

The Court deemed the powers assigned the Comptroller General "executive powers." The Comptroller General must exercise judgment and interpret the act in exercising the powers assigned by Congress, and "[i]nterpreting a law enacted by Congress to implement the legislative mandate is the very essence of 'execution' of the law." Gramm-Rudman "gives the Comptroller General the ultimate authority to determine the budget cuts to be made,"[308] and that is the type of decision typically made by officers charged with executing a statute.

Bowsher allows Congress to determine the nature of the executive duty it imposes. But Congress' role ends once it passes a law. Congress can thereafter control execution of its law only by legislating. Because the responsibility for execution of the statute was placed in an officer subject to its removal power, Congress violated the constitutional command that it play no direct role in the execution of the laws.

In *Bowsher* the Court adopted a simple (perhaps, simplistic) and "distressingly formalistic view of separation,"[309] and struck down a power that did not fit into the Justices' rigid classification. The Court invalidated a congressional scheme that was not intended to make the Comptroller General subservient to Congress, but to insulate a vital office from political pressures. The alternative the Court left, subjecting the Comptroller General to White House control, threatened the independence of such an office.

Bowsher contrasts with *Morrison v. Olson*,[310] a seminal separation of powers case in the Rehnquist Court. *Morrison* upheld the law that provided for appointment of an "independent counsel" to investigate and prosecute high-ranking government officials for criminal violations. Under the statute, an independent counsel "may be removed from office . . . by the personal action of the Attorney General and only for good cause."

The Court held that the "good cause" restriction for removal of the independent counsel did not impermissibly interfere with the President's constitutionally appointed functions. Unlike *Bowsher*, the Act gave the executive branch some removal power. Even though counsel was "independent" of executive branch supervision to a greater extent than other federal prosecutors, the Court concluded the executive branch retained sufficient control to ensure that the President could perform all constitutionally assigned duties.

In *Chadha, Bowsher*, and *Metropolitan Washington Airports Authority*, the Court adopted a formalistic approach to separation of powers. In those cases, the Court relied upon a rigid separation of powers theory which viewed the vesting clause of each of the first three articles of the Constitution as stating a boundary which could not be crossed. These cases shared an outlook with Justice Black's *Youngstown* opinion. In addition to literal interpretation of the text and reliance on

---

[307] *Id.* at 732.

[308] *Id.* at 732–33.

[309] *Id.* at 759 (White, J., dissenting).

[310] 487 U.S. 654 (1988).

original intent as stating the limits of a branch's competence, formalistic approaches tend, too, to emphasize logical connections rather than focusing on motivations and consequences and tend to enforce limits between the branches with bright line rules rather than balancing tests.

Morrison v. Olson departed from that formalistic approach and adopted a more flexible, functional attitude. Rather than strike down the statute as conferring executive power on someone independent of the President, the Court asked whether features of the law — appointment by a panel of judges or limitation on removal — would "impair the constitutional functions"[311] assigned the President.

The Court concluded that the President's "need to control" the Independent Counsel was not "so central to the functioning of the Executive Branch" to allow the President to terminate him at will.[312] This functional approach perceived overlapping areas of competence rather than strict boundaries, an evolutionary rather than textual and historical approach, and use of balancing tests to determine whether new arrangements could be accommodated. Accordingly, the Court balanced the impact of a practice on a branch against the purpose served. By contrast, Justice Scalia' dissent reflected a formalistic approach akin to *Bowsher, Chadha*, and *Metropolitan Washington Airports Authority.*

If *Morrison* signalled a shift to a functional approach,[313] it is not at all clear it has carried the day. In *Metropolitan Washington Airports Authority*,[314] discussed above, the Court reverted to a formal approach reminiscent of *Chadha* and *Bowsher.*

It is difficult to discover a principle to harmonize these divergent approaches. It may be that the Court's antennae become most sensitive when Congress seems to be giving itself some new power, as arguably occurred in *Chadha, Bowsher*, and *Washington Airports.* This spectre of legislative aggrandizement may cause the Court to wield formal constitutional provisions aggressively to preserve traditional ways of proceeding. On the other hand, when Congress limits the executive without enhancing its own power, e.g., independent counsel, the Court may be more receptive to functional analysis as in *Morrison.* This type of analysis does not, however, explain the Court's decision in *Clinton v. City of New York*,[315] which employed formalistic reasoning to invalidate the line item veto act that enhanced the President's power.

Nor does it speak to the Court's receptivity to innovations that involve the judiciary in new ways. Thus in *Mistretta v. United States*[316] the Court was confident that federal judges serving on a Sentencing Committee posed no incongruous

---

[311] *Id.* at 675–76.

[312] *Id.* at 691–92.

[313] The Court also employed a functional approach to uphold involvement of Article III judges on a sentencing commission. *Mistretta*, 488 U.S. 361.

[314] 501 U.S. 252 (1991).

[315] 524 U.S. 417 (1998).

[316] 488 U.S. 361 (1989).

situation. Nor did a three judge panel appointing an independent counsel compromise judicial independence.[317]

Ultimately, the framers sought to protect liberty not simply by separating governmental power but also by relying on each branch to resist intrusions on its domain. "Ambition must be made to counteract ambition,"[318] wrote James Madison in one of his most profound insights. In the Court's more recent words, "the greatest security against tyranny — the accumulation of excessive authority in a single Branch — lies not in a hermetic division among the Branches, but in a carefully crafted system of checked and balanced power within each Branch."[319]

---

[317] *See* Morrison v. Olson, 487 U.S. 654 (1988).

[318] THE FEDERALIST No. 51 (James Madison).

[319] *Mistretta*, 488 U.S. at 381.

Chapter 8

LIBERTY, PROPERTY, AND DUE PROCESS, TAKING AND CONTRACT CLAUSES

INTRODUCTION

While this Chapter comprehends a number of provisions of the Constitution, the focus rests on the multi-faceted concept of due process. The Due Process Clauses of the Fifth and Fourteenth Amendments have been invoked in a number of distinct contexts to protect various classes or categories of rights. Although it has limits, one classification occasionally used would describe some due process rights as property rights and others as personal rights. Another classifying principle for rights guaranteed by the Due Process Clause involves the distinction between substantive and procedural rights. As some cases in the last section of this chapter indicate, this distinction may also have limits. Nevertheless, using these Due Process Clauses to guarantee overtly substantive rights has caused considerable scholarly debate and controversy.

The Chapter begins with some introductory materials focusing on whether the Due Process Clause of the Fourteenth Amendment incorporates provisions of the Bill of Rights and makes particular amendments applicable against the states. The doctrinally rich *Slaughter-House Cases* go beyond the question of incorporation to discuss the extent to which rights provided by the Federal Constitution limit the power of state governments. Section 8.02 treats the selective incorporation of the guarantees of the Bill of Rights as applied against the states, focusing on the rights of the accused. While the *Slaughter-House* Court broadly rejected incorporating provisions of the Bill of Rights against the states, the Court has now applied the overwhelming majority of the guarantees to the states.

Section 8.03 considers a spectrum of property rights protected by the Constitution. The first subsection reviews the Court's unsuccessful and controversial efforts to guarantee property rights using the doctrine of substantive due process. The second and third subsections turn to consider the modern Court's efforts to guarantee property rights using the Contracts Clause of Article I, § 10, and the Takings Clause of the Fifth Amendment. The principal tool for the modern Court's protection of property rights has been the Takings Clause. Unlike substantive due process, the Takings Clause does not invalidate a regulation, but only requires government compensation for the property taken. At times, however, the required compensation renders the regulation economically impractical. The most clear cut way to find a taking is physical invasion of property. Unlike its earlier forays into substantive due process jurisprudence, the Court's takings jurisprudence has shied away from invalidating economic regulations although the line between economic regulations and physical takings has proven difficult to etch.

Section 8.04 combines some of the themes discussed in the preceding two sections, focusing on rights that are both personal and substantive. Specifically, the section treats the use of the Due Process Clause — and, less frequently, the Ninth Amendment — to guarantee substantive rights of a personal nature. The focus is on procreative liberty and the abortion issue. Various subsections examine the Court's responses to claims for other substantive personal rights involving such areas as birth control, family, homosexual relationships, and the right to die.

Finally, the cases included in § 8.05 blur the two unifying themes of this Chapter. Entitled "Personal Property Rights: New Forms of Protection for New Property Interests," the section treats property rights that involve such areas as employment and subsistence. The cases considered contrast with the decidedly commercial thrust of the cases dealt with in § 8.03. Moreover, the cases combine procedural and substantive elements.

§ 8.01   INTRODUCTION TO THE INCORPORATION CONTROVERSY AND THE BILL OF RIGHTS

The Incorporation Controversy addresses the issue of whether the Fourteenth Amendment incorporates the protections of the Bill of Rights to make them applicable against the states. Before the adoption of the Fourteenth Amendment in 1868, the Supreme Court held in *Barron v. Mayor of Baltimore*[1] that the protections found in the Bill of Rights were not applicable against the states. The Fourteenth Amendment, which explicitly applied the guarantees of due process, equal protection, and privileges and immunities of United States citizenship against abridgement by the states, reopened the door for the argument that the Bill of Rights should also be applied against the states. The Supreme Court first addressed this argument in the *Slaughter-House Cases*.[2]

Slaughter-House is important for several reasons. *Slaughter-House* was the Supreme Court's first interpretation of the Civil War Amendments, which applied against the states.[3] The Court refused the invitation to redistribute power away from the states and toward the federal government. In particular, the opinion narrowly construed the Due Process, Equal Protection, and Privileges and Immunities Clauses of the Fourteenth Amendment. Most of the decision has since been reversed, and the Court has much more liberally construed the Fourteenth Amendment; however, the Court's interpretation of the Privileges and Immunities Clause of the Fourteenth Amendment still stands. The Supreme Court essentially wrote the Privileges and Immunities Clause of the Fourteenth Amendment out of

---

[1] In *Barron v. Mayor of Baltimore*, 32 U.S. (7 Pet.) 243 (1833), the plaintiff brought a Fifth Amendment action claiming that he should receive just compensation because the City had redirected streams, consequently destroying the value of his wharf. The Supreme Court rejected the plaintiff's claim and held that "the provision in the fifth amendment to the constitution, declaring that private property shall not be taken for public use, without just compensation, is intended solely as a limitation on the exercise of power by the government of the United States, and is not applicable to the legislation of the states." *Id.* at 250–51.

[2] 83 U.S. 36 (1873).

[3] The Thirteenth, Fourteenth, and Fifteenth Amendments were adopted in 1865, 1868, and 1870, respectively.

the Constitution. Lastly, the Supreme Court rejected a substantive due process claim.

The controversy in *Slaughter-House* arose out of a law passed in New Orleans that granted exclusive monopoly rights to slaughter animals in the New Orleans area to the Slaughter-House Company. The plaintiffs in the *Slaughter-House Cases* were butchers in the New Orleans area whom the monopoly law prevented from practicing their trade. The butchers raised four constitutional challenges to the monopoly law: (1) that it created involuntary servitude prohibited by the Thirteenth Amendment; (2) that it abridged the privileges and immunities of citizens of the United States in violation of § 1 of the Fourteenth Amendment; (3) that it denied the butchers the equal protection of the laws in violation of § 1 of the Fourteenth Amendment; and (4) that it deprived the butchers of their property without due process of law in violation of § 1 of the Fourteenth Amendment. The Court rejected all four constitutional challenges, relying heavily on its interpretation of the history and purpose of the post-Civil War Amendments.

Justice Miller, writing for a 5-4 majority, began his discussion of the post-Civil War Amendments by indicating that the amendments share a strong "unity of purpose,"[4] which must be construed in the context of the "history of the times."[5] In this connection, the Court discussed the history of African slavery, the Civil War, and the Emancipation Proclamation of President Abraham Lincoln that first freed the slaves. This history, and the injustices surrounding it, prompted the adoption of the post-Civil War Amendments. The Court believed that the "prevailing purpose" of the Amendments was to free the slaves, and that fact had to be taken into account "in any fair and just construction" of them.[6] This interpretation of the Amendments acknowledged the Civil War's purpose of freeing and guaranteeing individual rights for the slaves. The Court, however, either rejected or ignored the War's other purpose of asserting the power of the national government over the states in matters of individual rights.

The *Slaughter-House* majority quickly disposed of three of the four constitutional challenges made by the butchers. The prohibition of the Thirteenth Amendment was limited to slavery and similar forms of involuntary servitude. The Court also rejected equal protection challenges. Again relying on the history and purpose of the Amendments, the Court held that the Equal Protection Clause was only intended to apply to discrimination against the ex-slaves, although it might eventually be extended to prohibit other forms of racial discrimination. In dismissing the due process challenge, the Court refused to construe the Clause to extend substantive due process protection for the butchers. The butchers claimed that the law's restraint on the free exercise of their trade deprived them of both a property right to lawful employment and a liberty right to choose their own occupation in violation of the Due Process Clause of the Fourteenth Amendment.[7] The Court

---

[4] *Slaughter-House*, 83 U.S. at 67.

[5] *Id.*

[6] *Id.* at 72.

[7] This is similar to the substantive due process argument that was adopted by the Court in *Lochner v. New York. See infra* § 8.05.

reasoned that no previous interpretation of the Due Process Clause of the Fifth Amendment ever held that a restraint on the exercise of a person's trade was a deprivation of property. Thus, the Due Process Clause of the Fourteenth Amendment should not either.

Perhaps the most important part of the opinion was its rejection of the butchers' challenge that the law violated the Privileges and Immunities Clause of the Fourteenth Amendment.[8] The butchers argued that gainful employment was a privilege of citizenship of the United States and the law abridged that privilege. In rejecting the butchers' privileges and immunities challenge, the Court relied on the distinction between the definition of a citizen of the United States and a citizen of a state.

The Court cited the first sentence of § 1 of the Fourteenth Amendment[9] to support this distinction. Such differentiation was highly relevant to the Court's construction of the Privileges and Immunities Clause of the Fourteenth Amendment, because it spoke only of the privileges and immunities of citizens of the United States, and not of privileges and immunities of citizens of the states. Thus, the Court concluded that the Fourteenth Amendment only protected the privileges and immunities of citizens of the United States. Consequently, the Clause only prohibited state interference with certain privileges of national citizenship. Protection of "fundamental" property and civil rights[10] was within the jurisdiction of the several states, and not the federal government.

Federal privileges and immunities were limited to those rights "which owe their existence to the Federal government, its National character, its Constitution, or its laws."[11] The Court listed these rights as including: the right to " 'come to the seat of government to assert any claim he may have upon that government, to transact any business he may have with it, to seek its protection, to share its offices, to engage in administering its functions.' "[12] They also included: the right of " 'free access to its seaports, through which all operations of foreign commerce are conducted, to the subtreasuries, land offices, and courts of justice in the several States.' "[13] Also recognized were: the right to "demand the care and protection of

---

[8] This part of the opinion addresses the Privileges and Immunities Clause of the Fourteenth Amendment, and not that of Article Four of the Constitution which prohibits a state from discriminating against nonresidents of that state in certain respects to favor residents. *See supra* § 6.11.

[9] "All persons born or naturalized in the United States, and subject to the jurisdiction thereof, are citizens of the United States and of the State wherein they reside." U.S. Const. amend. XIV. This Citizenship Clause fundamentally altered the legal source of citizenship, making citizenship primarily federal, not derivative of state citizenship. The Citizenship Clause effectively overruled *Dred Scott v. Sanford*, 60 U.S. 393 (1857), which had refused to recognize a slave as a U.S. citizen because the state of Missouri did not consider him a citizen.

[10] These fundamental civil rights are those "privileges and immunities . . . which belong of right to the citizens of all free governments, and which have at all times been enjoyed by citizens of the several States which compose this Union." Such rights include: "protection by the government, with the right to acquire and possess property of every kind, and to pursue and obtain happiness and safety." *Slaughter-House*, 83 U.S. at 76.

[11] *Id.* at 79.

[12] *Id.*

[13] *Id.*

the Federal Government over his life, liberty, and property when on the high seas or within the jurisdiction of a foreign government . . . . The right to peaceably assemble and petition for redress of grievances, the privilege of the writ of habeas corpus . . . . The right to use the navigable waterways of the United States, however they may penetrate the territory of the several States," and "all rights secured to our citizens by treaties with foreign nations."[14] The Privileges and Immunities Clause of the Fourteenth Amendment protected these "national rights" against infringement by the states.

This construction of the Privileges and Immunities Clause basically rendered the clause meaningless. The privileges and immunities of national citizenship that the majority addressed were already protected against state infringement by the Supremacy Clause. Thus, the majority's construction of the Privileges and Immunities Clause essentially wrote it out of the Constitution.

The Court's construction of the Privileges and Immunities Clause, and all three post-Civil War amendments, was really motivated by a fear of the tremendous flow of power from state governments to the federal courts or to Congress that could have occurred under a broader construction of the Fourteenth Amendment. The Court exhibited its concern over such a shift in power from the states to the national government throughout the opinion. Stressing a belief in the federal system of checks and balances and a national government of limited powers, the Court stated that a broad construction of the Fourteenth Amendment and a finding for the butchers would have constituted the Court as a permanent "censor upon all legislation of the states, on the civil rights of their own citizens, with authority to nullify such as it did not approve as consistent with those rights."[15] Obviously the Court was motivated, at least to some degree, by a desire to prevent such a radical change in the structure of the government as it had existed during the eighty years prior to adoption of the Fourteenth Amendment.

Justice Field's dissent challenged the majority's interpretation of the Fourteenth Amendment's Privileges and Immunities Clause. He argued that the Fourteenth Amendment made everyone a citizen of the United States first, and state citizenship reflected only a person's residence. As a result, the national government, rather than the states, protected a person's fundamental rights, privileges, and immunities. Also dissenting, Justice Bradley would have struck down the law because it deprived the butchers of their liberty to choose lawful employment without due process of law. Justice Bradley's view was significant because it marked acceptance of substantive due process[16] which later became prominent for a time in economic rights cases.[17] Substantive due process now underpins the right to choose an abortion and other personal rights not specifically enumerated in the Bill of

---

[14] *Id.*

[15] *Id.* at 78.

[16] The butchers did not claim that they lacked their day in court or that their procedural rights had otherwise been violated. Instead, they claimed that the law violated their liberty interest protected by the Due Process Clause. *See infra* §§ 8.05, 8.06 for detailed discussions of substantive due process.

[17] *See* Lochner v. New York, 198 U.S. 45 (1905).

Rights.[18]

The majority's decision in *Slaughter-House* is still good law. The Privileges or Immunities Clause of the Fourteenth Amendment remains essentially written out of the Constitution.[19] The Clause has rarely made an impact since *Slaughter-House*, with the exception of *Saenz v. Roe*[20] and Justice Thomas' concurring opinion in *McDonald v. City of Chicago*.[21]

In *Saenz v. Roe*, the Court employed the Privileges or Immunities Clause to invalidate a California law which offered less welfare benefits to new residents than to residents who had lived in California for more than 12 months. The Court held that the Privileges or Immunities Clause protects — as an aspect of the broader "right to travel" — "the right of the newly arrived citizen to the same privileges and immunities enjoyed by other citizens of the same State."[22] California's discriminatory classification of new residents infringed upon the right to travel by punishing newcomers to California. Citing *Slaughter-House*, the Court explained that the right to claim " 'the same rights as other citizens of that state' " is a privilege of citizens of the United States, and thus protected under the Fourteenth Amendment from abridgement by the states.[23]

Justice Thomas dissented, joined by Chief Justice Rehnquist. Justice Thomas disagreed that the Privileges or Immunities Clause guarantees "equal access to public benefits," because the Clause, as understood at the time of ratification, protects "fundamental rights, rather than every public benefit established by positive law."[24] The terms "privileges" and "immunities" contain a rich history, and "were understood to refer to those fundamental rights and liberties specifically enjoyed by English citizens, and more broadly, by all persons."[25] The Members of Congress who enacted the Fourteenth Amendment repeatedly cited the landmark case *Corfield v. Coryell*[26] to explain the meaning of the Privileges or Immunities Clause. *Corfield* provided a list of fundamental rights encompassed under the terms "privileges" and "immunities," such as "the enjoyment of life and liberty, with the right to acquire and possess property . . . . The right of a citizen of one state to pass through, or to reside in any other state, for purposes of trade . . . to claim the

---

[18] *See* Roe v. Wade, 410 U.S. 113 (1973).

[19] *Twining v. New Jersey*, 211 U.S. 78 (1908), afforded a slightly different formulation of the rights guaranteed by the Clause: "Thus, among the rights and privileges of national citizenship recognized by this court are the right to pass freely from state to state, . . . the right to petition Congress for a redress of grievances, . . . the right to vote for national officers, . . . the right to enter the public lands, . . . the right to be protected against violence while in the lawful custody of a United States marshal, . . . and the right to inform the United States authorities of violations of its laws." *Id.* at 97. As with rights discussed in *Slaughter-House*, the Supremacy Clause also guarantees these against interference by the states. *See also* Hague v. CIO, 307 U.S. 496 (1939).

[20] 526 U.S. 489 (1999).

[21] 130 S. Ct. 3020 (2010) (Thomas, J., concurring in the judgment); *see infra* § 8.03.

[22] *Saenz*, 526 U.S. at 502.

[23] *Id.* at 503.

[24] *Id.* at 527 (Thomas, J., dissenting).

[25] *Id.* at 524.

[26] 6 F. Cas. 546 (C.C.E.D. Pa. 1823).

benefit of the writ of habeas corpus; to institute and maintain actions of any kind in the courts of the state; to take, hold and dispose of property."[27] Despite this historical evidence behind the Privileges or Immunities Clause, the *"Slaughter-House Cases* sapped the Clause of any meaning."[28]

Although the Privileges and Immunities Clause remains a possible source of constitutional protections, some of its role has been filled by other constitutional provisions.

Thus, in the 120 years since *Slaughter-House*, the Court has expanded its protections of "fundamental" rights and applied many of the Bill of Rights protections against the states by means other than the Privileges and Immunities Clause. Many of these developments involve the Equal Protection and Due Process Clauses discussed in *Slaughter-House*. Using the Due Process Clause of the Fourteenth Amendment, the Court has incorporated most of the Bill of Rights against the states. By expanding the meaning of "liberty" in the Due Process Clauses of the Fifth and Fourteenth Amendments, the Court has fashioned procedural and substantive due process protections against both national and state governments. The Court has also expanded the Equal Protection Clause to apply to discrimination based on ethnicity, gender, and certain other impermissible classifications.

§ 8.02 THE "INCORPORATION CONTROVERSY" AND THE RIGHTS OF THE ACCUSED

The "Incorporation Controversy" refers to the debate about whether the Due Process Clause of the Fourteenth Amendment incorporates the protections of the Bill of Rights to make them applicable against the states. In *Barron v. Baltimore*,[29] decided before the Civil War, the Court held that the protections of the Bill of Rights were not applicable against the states. The holding in *Barron* settled the incorporation controversy until the enactment of the Fourteenth Amendment.

As the different opinions in *Slaughter-House* illustrate, the incorporation controversy involves important questions of federalism. Did the Fourteenth Amendment rearrange the powers of the states in relation to the federal government? More specifically, did it reverse the holding in *Barron* and make the Bill of Rights applicable against the states?

The incorporation controversy reached a climax in the rights of the criminally accused, highlighted by two radically different views on incorporation: the "total incorporation" idea espoused by Justice Black,[30] and the competing vision advanced by Justice Cardozo, Justice Harlan, and Professor Charles Fairman.[31] The latter

---

[27] *Id.* at 551–52.

[28] *Saenz*, 526 U.S. at 527 (Thomas, J., dissenting).

[29] 32 U.S. 243 (1833).

[30] *See* Adamson v. California, 332 U.S. 46 (1947) (Black, J., dissenting).

[31] *See* Palko v. Connecticut, 302 U.S. 319 (1937) (Cardoza, J.); Duncan v. Louisiana, 391 U.S. 145 (1968) (Black, J., concurring); C. Fairman, *Does the Fourteenth Amendment Incorporate the Bill of Rights?*, 2 STAN. L. REV. 5 (1949).

school of thought highlighted the fact that the Fourteenth Amendment imposed on the states certain notions of "fundamental fairness" that were "implicit in the concept of ordered liberty."[32]

Justice Black's total incorporation approach was simple: he felt that the Fourteenth Amendment incorporated all of the protections of the Bill of Rights against the states. Furthermore, Justice Black believed that the Bill of Rights protections were the only protections guaranteed to the citizens of the states by the Federal Constitution. Justice Black argued that the Fourteenth Amendment clearly outlined the relationship between the federal government and the states: the Federal Constitution prohibited the states from denying its citizens full protection under the Bill of Rights and also prevented federal judges from requiring the states to provide their citizens with more than those guarantees.

In contrast, the "due process/fundamental fairness" notion advanced by Justice Harlan was not tied to any specific language in the Constitution beyond the Due Process Clause. Justice Harlan argued that the Fourteenth Amendment did not incorporate any of the Bill of Rights protections against the states *per se*. Instead, Justice Harlan felt that "due process is an evolving concept,"[33] and that "the Due Process Clause of the Fourteenth Amendment requires that [a state's judicial] procedures be fundamentally fair in all respects."[34] Therefore, Justice Harlan would only apply those Bill of Rights protections to the states that were "essential to basic fairness."[35]

Before the Harlan/Black incorporation debate, the Supreme Court had rejected the notion of incorporation in *Palko v. Connecticut*.[36] The defendant in *Palko* was charged with first degree murder. The jury found the defendant guilty of second degree murder. The state appealed the conviction to the Superior Court of Errors under a Connecticut Statute that allowed the state to appeal in criminal cases. The Court of Errors ordered a new trial, in which the defendant was found guilty of first degree murder and sentenced to death. The defendant challenged the statute allowing the state to appeal in criminal cases, arguing that it violated the Fifth Amendment guarantee against double jeopardy. The defendant claimed that the Fourteenth Amendment incorporated all of the Bill of Rights protections against the states, or, at least, that it incorporated the Fifth Amendment's protection against double jeopardy.

Writing for the Court, Justice Cardozo specifically rejected the defendant's total incorporation argument:

> in the appellant's view the Fourteenth Amendment is to be taken as embodying the prohibitions of the Fifth. His thesis is even broader. Whatever would be a violation of the original bill of rights [sic] (Amend

---

[32] *Palko*, 302 U.S. at 325.

[33] *Duncan*, 391 U.S. at 183.

[34] *Id.* at 172.

[35] *Id.*

[36] 302 U.S. 319 (1937).

ments I to VIII) if done by the federal government is now equally unlawful by force of the Fourteenth Amendment if done by a state. There is no such general rule.[37]

Justice Cardozo explained that only those Bill of Rights protections that were "implicit in the concept of ordered liberty"[38] had been applied against the states. A specific Bill of Rights protection would be applicable against the states only if it was a " 'principle of justice so rooted in the traditions and conscience of our people as to be ranked as fundamental.' "[39] Some protections, such as those in the First Amendment, and the protection against the taking of property without just compensation, had already been applied against the states. Justice Cardozo concluded that the Fifth Amendment right to be free from double jeopardy was not such a principle, so that the Fourteenth Amendment did not incorporate it against the states.

In *Adamson v. California*,[40] the Supreme Court applied the reasoning from *Palko* to hold that the Fifth Amendment's protection against self-incrimination did not apply to the states. In *Adamson*, the criminal defendant admitted, during trial, to committing previous crimes. A California statute prevented the prosecution from commenting further on the previous crimes at trial. The statute did allow the state to expand on the defendant's failure to explain away other evidence, or if the defendant testified, to use the prior convictions to impeach the defendant's testimony.

The defendant in *Adamson* challenged the statute on Fifth and Fourteenth Amendment grounds, claiming that the privilege against self-incrimination was a fundamental right applicable against the states through the Fourteenth Amendment. Reaffirming the holding in *Palko*, the Court rejected the defendant's argument that the protection against self-incrimination was fundamental. Using the *Palko* analysis, the Court held that the privilege against self-incrimination was not "implicit in the concept of ordered liberty." Consequently, the California statute did not violate the defendant's due process rights.

Adamson is no longer good law,[41] and the case is important not for its holding but for Justice Black's famous dissent in support of total incorporation of the Bill of Rights. Justice Black's argument was based essentially on federalism concerns and on the legislative history of the Fourteenth Amendment. In an appendix attached to the dissenting opinion, he outlined his extensive research on the legislative history of the Fourteenth Amendment.

Justice Black then strongly criticized the majority's "ordered liberty" approach, saying that it gave far too much discretion and limitless power to the individual Justices:

---

[37] *Id.* at 323.

[38] *Id.* at 325.

[39] *Id.*

[40] 332 U.S. 46 (1947).

[41] *See supra* note 31.

> This decision reasserts a constitutional theory . . . that this Court is endowed by the Constitution with boundless power under 'natural law' periodically to expand and contract constitutional standards to conform to the Court's conception of what at a particular time constitutes 'civilized decency' and 'fundamental principles of liberty and justice.'[42]

For Justice Black, the problem with the Court substituting its own "concepts of decency and fundamental justice for the language of the Bill of Rights,"[43] was that this boundless discretion frustrated the "great design" of the Constitution (referring to Federalism concerns), and would inevitably lead to undesirable consequences. The Court would be allowed to "roam at large in the broad expanses of policy and morals and to trespass, all too freely, on the legislative domain of the states as well as the Federal Government."[44]

The result of the incorporation controversy is that the Court has adopted a process of incorporation known as selective incorporation. Selective incorporation is a process in which the Supreme Court has used the "liberty" clause of the Fourteenth Amendment to apply most of the protections of the Bill of Rights against the states. The test to determine whether a specific provision of the Bill of Rights should be made applicable to the states was "whether given this kind of system a particular procedure is fundamental — whether, that is, a procedure is necessary to an Anglo-American regime of ordered liberty."[45]

The process of selective incorporation was highlighted in *Duncan v. Louisiana*.[46] In *Duncan*, the defendant was convicted of a misdemeanor punishable by a maximum of two years in prison. The defendant requested a jury trial, but was refused because the Louisiana Constitution granted jury trials only in cases where the sentence involved capital punishment or imprisonment at hard labor. The defendant claimed that the Sixth and Fourteenth Amendments guaranteed his right to a jury trial in a state criminal prosecution in which a sentence of two years could be imposed.

Applying the selective incorporation test discussed above, the Supreme Court accepted the defendant's argument and struck down the Louisiana Constitution's jury trial requirements. The Court reasoned that "trial by jury in criminal cases is fundamental to the American scheme of justice, [and therefore] we hold that the Fourteenth Amendment guarantees a right of jury trial in all criminal cases which — were they to be tried in a federal court — would come within the Sixth Amendment's guarantee."[47]

Duncan was also famous for yet another round of the Black versus Harlan debate, and it illustrated the strengths and weaknesses of both arguments. Justice Black filed a concurring opinion that cited his dissent in *Adamson*, opining that

---

[42] 332 U.S. at 69.

[43] *Id.* at 89.

[44] *Id.* at 90.

[45] *Duncan*, 391 U.S. at 149 n.14.

[46] 391 U.S. 145 (1968).

[47] *Id.* at 149.

selective incorporation was preferable to not applying any of the Bill of Rights protections at all. Justice Black stated that although he believed that the Fourteenth Amendment made all of the Bill of Rights protections applicable against the states, he would support the Court's selective incorporation plan as long as it continued on the course of applying "most of the specific Bill of Rights' protections applicable to the states."[48] Justice Black argued, however, that selective incorporation was less historically supportable.

Justice Black then advanced his argument for total incorporation, and criticized Justice Harlan's "theory."[49] He reemphasized his belief that the legislative history of the Fourteenth Amendment clearly indicated that both the Amendment's supporters and opponents believed that it would make the Bill of Rights applicable against the states.

Justice Black highlighted his basic criticisms of Justice Harlan's "ordered liberty" approach. He rejected Justice Harlan's evolving concept of due process as giving federal judges too much discretion. Justice Black found it "impossible" to believe that a Constitution carefully written to limit governmental power would give such limitless power and discretion to federal judges. Justice Black then attacked Justice Harlan's position that due process required only "fundamental fairness." Consistent with his criticism of "ordered liberty," Justice Black felt that fundamental fairness "depends entirely on the particular judge's idea of ethics and morals instead of requiring him to depend on the boundaries fixed by the written words of the Constitution."[50] Justice Black also maintained that no historical evidence supported Justice Harlan's claim that due process only required an arbitrary sense of fundamental fairness.

Lastly, Justice Black addressed Justice Harlan's argument that total incorporation prevented states from experimenting with progressive social or criminal reforms. Justice Black responded by stating that concerns of federalism should not allow the states to experiment with the constitutional protections required by the Bill of Rights.

Justice Harlan wrote a vigorous dissent, attacking both the majority's selective incorporation and Justice Black's total incorporation approaches. Justice Harlan's opinion was based heavily on a famous article by Professor Charles Fairman entitled *Does the Fourteenth Amendment Incorporate the Bill of Rights? The Original Understanding.*[51] Justice Harlan first declared his essential position that the Due Process Clause of the Fourteenth Amendment "was meant neither to incorporate, nor to be limited to, the specific guarantees of the first eight Amendments."[52] He referred to what he called "the overwhelming historical evidence" compiled by Professor Fairman which demonstrated that the authors and supporters of the Fourteenth Amendment had not intended the Amendment to incorporate the Bill of Rights against the states.

---

[48] *Id.* at 164.

[49] *Id.* at 171.

[50] *Id.* at 169.

[51] *See* Fairman, *supra* note 31.

[52] *Duncan*, 391 U.S. at 174.

Justice Harlan then stated that the broad language of the Fourteenth Amendment demonstrated that its authors did not want the nation limited to 19th century ideas of due process of law. Instead, he argued that "due process is an evolving concept and that old principles are subject to re-evaluation in light of later experience."[53]

In Justice Harlan's view, the words "liberty" and "due process of law" in the Due Process Clause should be defined with reference to American traditions and our governmental system. This approach was used by the Court throughout its history until the recent adoption of selective incorporation. The Court had defined liberty by "isolating freedoms that Americans of the past and of the present considered more important than any countervailing public objective."[54] Applying this "ordered liberty" analysis, Justice Harlan examined the history of trial by jury and concluded that the defendant's trial was fundamentally fair and therefore passed scrutiny under the Due Process Clause of the Fourteenth Amendment.

Justice Harlan concluded by explaining that the unfortunate result of total, and even selective, incorporation would prevent societal progress by restricting criminal or social reforms. If any such reforms were fundamentally unfair, the Supreme Court, state courts, and the political process would correct them.

Duncan demonstrated the end result of selective incorporation. Most of the Bill of Rights have been applied or incorporated by the Court against the states including: the right to compensation for property taken by the state;[55] the rights of speech, press and religion covered by the First Amendment;[56] the Second Amendment right to keep and bear arms;[57] the Fourth Amendment rights to be free from unreasonable searches and seizures and to have excluded from criminal trials any evidence illegally seized;[58] the right guaranteed by the Fifth Amendment to be free of compelled self-incrimination;[59] and the Sixth Amendment rights to counsel;[60] to a speedy[61] and public trial;[62] to confrontation of opposing witnesses;[63] and to compulsory process for obtaining witnesses.[64] The Supreme Court's use of selective incorporation has come very close to Justice Black's ideal of total incorporation. In fact, the Court has incorporated all of the procedural protections of the Bill of Rights, namely the Fourth, Fifth, Sixth, and Eighth Amendments, except the Sixth Amendment right to indictment by a grand jury, the Seventh Amendment right to civil jury trial, and the Eighth Amendment protection against excessive bail. It also

---

[53] *Id.* at 183.

[54] *Id.* at 177.

[55] *See* Chicago, Burlington & Quincy R.R. Co. v. Chicago, 166 U.S. 226 (1897).

[56] *See, e.g.*, Fiske v. Kansas, 274 U.S. 380 (1927).

[57] *See* McDonald v. City of Chicago, 130 S. Ct. 3020 (2010).

[58] *See* Mapp v. Ohio, 367 U.S. 643 (1961).

[59] *See* Malloy v. Hogan, 378 U.S. 1 (1964).

[60] *See* Gideon v. Wainwright, 372 U.S. 335 (1963).

[61] *See* Klopfer v. North Carolina, 386 U.S. 213 (1967).

[62] *See* In re Oliver, 333 U.S. 257 (1948).

[63] *See* Pointer v. Texas, 380 U.S. 400 (1965).

[64] *See* Washington v. Texas, 388 U.S. 14 (1967).

has not applied the Third Amendment right not to have soldiers quartered in one's home.

Although the Supreme Court has applied most of the specific provisions of the Bill of Rights against the states, a related issue arises as to whether the states will be held to the same standards as those imposed by the federal requirements. In many instances, a majority of the Court has applied the Bill of Rights to the states with the same rules required of the federal government. For example, in *Mapp v. Ohio*,[65] the Court applied against the state government the exclusionary rule remedy that it had previously applied against the federal government. However, in cases involving jury size[66] and unanimous verdicts, the Court has not constitutionally imposed on the states federal statutory requirements, such as unanimous verdicts. A related controversy amplified in a jury decision involves whether federal standards for applying the exclusionary rule[67] should be lowered to make the state standards equivalent.[68]

The incorporation controversy was not limited to whether the specific protections of the Bill of Rights were applicable to the states; it also involved whether the Due Process Clause made federal criminal procedures not found in the Bill of Rights applicable against the states. For example, the *In re Winship*[69] Court held that the Due Process Clause required proof of guilt beyond a reasonable doubt in a state juvenile proceeding. Consistent with *Winship*, the Court has used procedural due process to strike down various state procedures as unconstitutional,[70] but has recognized that states do have more discretion when the procedure is not covered by a more specific guarantee of the Bill of Rights.[71] In *Cooper v. Oklahoma*,[72] a unanimous Court held that an Oklahoma procedural rule requiring a criminal defendant to prove his incompetence by clear and convincing evidence violated due process. The well-settled test for incompetence is whether the defendant is presently able to rationally communicate with his lawyer, and rationally and

---

[65] 367 U.S. 643 (1961).

[66] *See, e.g.*, Williams v. Florida, 399 U.S. 78 (1970) (upholding the use of six-member juries in state trials).

[67] *See* Pennsylvania Bd. of Probation & Parole v. Scott, 524 U.S. 357 (1998) (exclusionary rule does not apply to illegal seizures of evidence to be admitted at parole revocation hearings); United States v. Leon, 468 U.S. 897 (1984) (created the "good-faith" exception to the exclusionary rule and held that it applied equally to the federal government and the states).

[68] *See* Apodaca v. Oregon, 406 U.S. 404 (1972) (upholding a state's requirement of a 10-of-12 juror majority for a conviction). *Cf.* Burch v. Louisiana, 441 U.S. 130 (1979) (overturned state non-petty conviction by a non-unanimous six-person jury).

[69] 397 U.S. 358 (1970).

[70] *See* Pacific Mutual Life Ins. Co. v. Haslip, 499 U.S. 1 (1991).

[71] *See* Hudson v. Palmer, 468 U.S. 517 (1984) (holding that prisoners do not have a constitutional expectation of privacy in their jail cells because the Fourth Amendment did not apply within a prison cell); Block v. Rutherford, 468 U.S. 576 (1984) (upholding the search of a cell of a pretrial detainee conducted while the prisoner was absent); *and* Schall v. Martin, 467 U.S. 253 (1984) (In upholding a New York statute regarding pretrial detention of juveniles, the Court recognized that different standards in determining pretrial detention for adults and juveniles were permissible.).

[72] 517 U.S. 348 (1996).

factually able to understand the proceedings against him. *Medina v. California*[73] held that a State may presume a defendant competent to stand trial and require the defendant to prove his incompetence by a preponderance of the evidence.

However, if required to prove his incompetence by clear and convincing evidence, an incompetent defendant could erroneously be found competent, which can result in dire consequences, as a defendant who could not effectively communicate with his attorney could also "be unable to exercise other 'rights deemed essential to a fair trial.' "[74] On the other hand, the consequences of an erroneous finding of incompetence were slight because the State may detain an incompetent defendant for a reasonable time to decide if he would foreseeably become competent to stand trial. "A heightened standard does not decrease the risk of error, but simply reallocates that risk between the parties."[75]

In *Bennis v. Michigan*,[76] the Court denied a due process challenge to a court-ordered forfeiture of an innocent owner's interest in property. Defendant was the joint owner of an automobile that her husband had used in order to engage in sexual activity with a prostitute. The state court declared defendant's vehicle a public nuisance and ordered the car's forfeiture and sale. Defendant claimed that she was deprived of due process, arguing that she was entitled to contest the forfeiture by showing that she had no knowledge of her husband's intended illegal use of the car. Writing for a 5-4 majority, Chief Justice Rehnquist found it has long been established that an innocent owner's interest in property used in a crime may be forfeited even though the owner did not know the property was to be put to illegal use. Chief Justice Rehnquist distinguished this case from *Austin v. United States*[77] on the grounds that this nuisance abatement was not a punitive action, but an equitable one in which the trial court judge had remedial discretion to consider alternatives to forfeiting the entire interest in the automobile. Distinct from any punitive purpose, forfeiture deterred further criminal use of the property. The trial judge exercised this discretion when he declined to divide the proceeds from the sale of the car (purchased for $600) as defendants owned another car and little would remain from the sale after costs were assessed.

In a dissent joined by Justices Souter and Breyer, Justice Stevens maintained that the car should not have been forfeited because it did not constitute an instrumentality of the crime. Second, the Court had "consistently recognized an exception for truly blameless individuals."[78] Finally, the majority's holding was inconsistent with *Austin* as the forfeiture at issue was excessive punishment.

In *Caperton v. A.T. Massey Coal Co.*,[79] the Court required the recusal of a state supreme court justice under the Due Process Clause. A jury found defendant Massey Coal Co. liable and awarded $50 million to plaintiff Caperton. While the

---

[73] 505 U.S. 437 (1992).

[74] 517 U.S. at 364.

[75] *Id.* at 366.

[76] 516 U.S. 442 (1996).

[77] 509 U.S. 602 (1993).

[78] 516 U.S. at 466.

[79] 129 S. Ct. 2252 (2009).

appeal of Massey's case was pending, Blankenship, Massey's CEO, donated almost $2.5 million to a political organization that opposed an incumbent state supreme court justice, and supported his opponent, Benjamin. Blankenship also made over $500,000 of independent expenditures to support Benjamin's campaign.

Following Benjamin's election, Caperton unsuccessfully moved to recuse him. The West Virginia Supreme Court of Appeals (3-2) set aside Caperton's jury verdict.

Justice Kennedy stated that judicial recusals rarely involve constitutional issues as prejudice or personal bias alone is insufficient unless the " 'probability of actual bias' " rose to the level of a due process violation.[80] Notably, when a judge has a financial interest in the outcome of a case or when a judge participated in an earlier proceeding, judicial disqualification was required. For example, a judge could not try the cases of parties before him whom he had charged with perjury and criminal contempt. Not every attack on a judge should result in recusal. For example, a judge may try a lawyer whom he has charged with " 'disruptive, recalcitrant and disagreeable commentary,' " as the lawyer did not attack " 'the integrity of the judge carrying such potential for bias as to require disqualification.' "[81] The Court inquired "whether the average judge in his position is 'likely' to be neutral, or whether there is an unconstitutional 'potential for bias.' "[82]

While actual bias would require recusal, the Court could not easily review Justice Benjamin's finding lack of actual bias. Instead, Justice Kennedy applied an objective standard, asking "whether, 'under a realistic appraisal of psychological tendencies and human weakness,' the interest 'poses such a risk of actual bias or prejudgment that the practice must be forbidden.' "[83]

Thus, "not every campaign contribution by a litigant or attorney creates a probability of bias" requiring recusal.[84] Instead, the Court analyzes "the contribution's relative size in comparison to the total amount of money contributed to the campaign, the total amount spent in the election, and the apparent effect such contribution had on the outcome of the election."[85]

The Court focused on Blankenship's $3 million contribution to the campaign against the incumbent, which "eclipsed the total amount spent by all other Benjamin supporters and exceeded by 300% the amount spent by Benjamin's campaign committee."[86] In mandating recusal, the Court did not require that a contribution be a "necessary and sufficient cause"[87] of victory. Instead, Justice Kennedy ruled "that Blankenship's significant and disproportionate influence — coupled with the temporal relationship between the election and the pending case

---

[80] *Id.* at 2257.

[81] *Id.* at 2262 (quoting *Mayberry v. Pennsylvania*, 400 U.S. 455, 465–66 (1971) (quoting *Ungar v. Sarafite*, 376 U.S. 575, 584 (1964))).

[82] *Id.* at 2262.

[83] *Id.* at 2263 (quoting *Withrow v. Larkin*, 421 U.S. 35, 47 (1975)).

[84] *Id.* at 2263.

[85] *Id.* at 2264.

[86] *Id.*

[87] *Id.*

— " 'offer a possible temptation to the average man as a judge to forget the burden of proof required to convict the defendant, or which might lead him not to hold the balance nice, clear and true.' " "[88] The Court reiterated that these facts are extreme, making a flood of recusal motions unlikely. Legislated codes of judicial conduct, more vigorous than due process requirements, would lead most disqualification disputes to be resolved without invoking the Constitution.[89]

Chief Justice Roberts dissented, joined by Justices Scalia, Thomas, and Alito. Historically, the Due Process Clause required a judge's disqualification only "when the judge has a financial interest in the outcome of the case, and when the judge is presiding over certain types of criminal contempt proceedings."[90] Bias or the appearance of bias never merited disqualification, at common law or under the Constitution. The majority's " 'probability of bias' "[91] standard will increase allegations of judicial bias and erode public confidence in judicial impartiality more than a failure to recuse.

Chief Justice Roberts noted a number of factors that could create the appearance or probability of bias, including "friendship with a party or lawyer, prior employment experience, membership in clubs or associations, prior speeches and writings, religious affiliation, and countless other considerations."[92] These reasons, he said, never before mandated recusal under the Due Process Clause. It was also "unclear whether the new probability of bias standard is somehow limited to financial support in judicial elections, or applies to judicial recusal questions more generally."[93]

The case was not so extreme as the majority believed. Beyond Blankenship's direct $1,000 contribution, Benjamin and his campaign had no control over Blankenship's other expenditures. Moreover, another independent group received $2 million from the plaintiffs' bar. Moreover, Blankenship spent heavily during many prior state elections.

Justice Scalia also dissented, concerned with the ambiguity that the decision introduced in recusal standards in all litigated cases in states that elect judges.

---

[88] *Id.* at 2265 (quoting *Aetna Life Ins. Co. v. Lavoie*, 475 U.S. 813, 825 (1986) (quoting *Ward v. Vill. of Monroeville*, 409 U.S. 57, 60 (1972) (quoting *Tumey v. Ohio*, 273 U.S. 510, 532 (1927)))).

[89] "The ABA Model Code's test for appearance of impropriety is 'whether the conduct would create in reasonable minds a perception that the judge's ability to carry out judicial responsibilities with integrity, impartiality and competence is impaired.'" *Id.* at 2266 (quoting MODEL CODE OF JUDICIAL CONDUCT Canon 2 (2004)).

[90] *Id.* at 2267.

[91] *Id.*

[92] *Id.* at 2268.

[93] *Id.* at 2269.

§ 8.03 THE SECOND AMENDMENT

The Supreme Court has interpreted the Second Amendment "right to bear arms" as securing an individual right to possess firearms, unrelated to service in a militia.[94] The Court then incorporated the Second Amendment against the states in *McDonald v. City of Chicago*.[95]

In *District of Columbia v. Heller*,[96] the Court held that the District of Columbia's law banning the possession of handguns in private homes and the requirement that lawful firearms be kept inoperable violated the Second Amendment. The District of Columbia prohibited the registration of handguns and made it a crime to carry an unregistered firearm. No one could carry a handgun without a license, and only the chief of police could issue a license for one year. Further, residents were required to keep even their lawful firearms, such as registered long guns, "unloaded and dissembled or bound by a trigger lock." There were exceptions for guns located in a place of business that were being used for lawful recreational activities.

Justice Scalia began the majority opinion by reciting the Second Amendment: "A well regulated Militia, being necessary to the security of a free State, the right of the people to keep and bear Arms, shall not be infringed." The Court interpreted the Constitution using the ordinary everyday meaning of its words and phrases that voters at the time of the Framing could understand. While the Court would not utilize "secret or technical" meanings unknown to the ordinary citizens of the time, it would utilize idiomatic meanings.

The Second Amendment had two parts: the prefatory clause and the operative clause. The prefatory clause described the purpose of the operative clause but did not limit it. The operative clause codified the "right of the people." The Constitution used this term two other times, once in the First Amendment's Assembly-and-Petition Clause and another time in the Fourth Amendment's Search-and-Seizure Clause. The Ninth Amendment also used very similar terminology. In contrast, the militia was a "subset of 'the people' — those who were male, able bodied, and within a certain age range." Therefore, interpreting "militia" as an organized militia "fits poorly with the operative clause's description of the holder of that right as 'the people.' "

The Second Amendment protected all bearable arms and not just those that existed at the formation of the United States. Moreover, to "keep Arms," protected individuals regardless of service in a militia. The term "bear" implied carrying a weapon for "offensive or defensive action," but did not connote "participation in a structured military organization." Moreover, at the time of the founding, "bear Arms" had an "idiomatic meaning that was significantly different from its natural meaning: 'to serve as a soldier [or] do military service.' " The connection to the military or war was only clear when one bore arms "against" someone. In his dissent, Justice Stevens placed great weight on the original draft of the Second Amendment in which James Madison included a conscientious-objector clause.

---

[94] District of Columbia v. Heller, 554 U.S. 570 (2008).

[95] 130 S. Ct. 3020 (2010).

[96] 554 U.S. 570 (2008).

Justice Scalia retorted that the clause was not intended to exempt people who objected to going to war but, instead, was intended for those who objected to the use of weapons.

Justice Scalia turned to a historical analysis of the Second Amendment. The English Bill of Rights contains a provision stating that Protestants could never be disarmed. This predecessor to the Second Amendment was an individual right that had nothing to do with military service and applied only to the Crown, not Parliament. Moreover, Blackstone described the English right as, "the right of having and using arms for self-preservation and defence." As the Stuarts had tried to disarm their enemies, George III tried to disarm the most rebellious American colonists.

While the Second Amendment "conferred an individual right to keep and bear arms," it was limited just as the First Amendment's right of free speech was limited.

The prefatory clause read, "A well regulated Militia, being necessary to the security of a free State . . . ." The Petitioners defined militias by the Militia Clauses (Article I, § 8, clauses 15–16). However, the Clause empowered Congress to organize rather than create "the" militia, not "a" militia. This terminology connoted a body already in existence. The phrase "security of a free state" connoted the "security of a free polity," and not the security of each state as argued by the dissent.

In addressing the relationship between the prefatory and operative Clauses, it was understood that the right to bear arms allowed for a citizen militia that could be used to oppose an oppressive military force. The threat of disarmament by the new Federal government prompted this right to be codified in a written Constitution, unlike some English rights.

Justice Scalia noted the Second Amendment could not have ensured the creation of a citizen's militia to protect against tyranny if it simply had guaranteed a right to keep and use weapons as part of an organized militia. If Congress alone had retained the ability to organize the militia, it could have controlled who could participate in the militia and who could keep and use weapons just as the Stuart Kings had.

Four pre-Second Amendment provisions in state constitutions and seven analogous provisions in state constitutions adopted between 1789-1820 confirm that the founding generation conceived the Second Amendment as "an individual right to bear arms for defensive purposes."

Justice Scalia next rejected Justice Stevens' reliance on the unaccepted proposals for the Second Amendment as well as the debates leading up to the Amendment's passage. "It is dubious to rely on such history to interpret a text that was widely understood to codify a pre-existing right, rather than to fashion a new one."

The Court buttressed its position by analyzing how the Second Amendment was interpreted from its ratification through the end of the 19th century. Justice Stevens equated these interpretive sources with post-enactment legislative history. Post-enactment legislative history referred to statements made, after a law has been enacted, by people who drafted or voted for the law making these statements irrelevant to congressional decision-making. Instead, Justice Scalia relied on the *"public understanding"* of a law after its enactment.

Three important founding-era legal scholars, including Joseph Story, understood the Second Amendment "to protect an individual right unconnected with militia service" and abolitionists regularly invoked the Second Amendment to justify having weapons for self-defense purposes. Prior to the Civil War, 19th century case law universally interpreted the Second Amendment to support an individual right not related to militia service. After the Civil War, congressional debate observed that the founding generation "were for every man bearing his arms about him and keeping them in his house, his castle, and for his own defense." Similarly, all legal scholars after the Civil War whom the Court had read determined that the Second Amendment secured an individual right unrelated to militia service.

Justice Stevens' dissent heavily relied on *United States v. Miller.*[97] That case upheld convictions for carrying an unregistered short-barreled shotgun across state lines against Second Amendment claims. "Read in isolation, *Miller's* phrase 'part of ordinary military equipment' could mean that only those weapons useful in warfare are protected." Such an interpretation could have meant that the National Firearms Act that placed restrictions on machine guns could have been unconstitutional because machine guns had been used in warfare. Consequently, the majority interpreted the Second Amendment not to afford protection to "weapons not typically possessed by law-abiding citizens for lawful purposes, such as short-barreled shotguns."

Justice Scalia concluded that the Court's prior decisions did not preclude "our adoption of the original understanding of the Second Amendment." That the Court had not interpreted the Second Amendment for so long was not surprising as the federal government did not regulate the possession of the weapons "by law-abiding citizens," and for much of American history the Bill of Rights had not been incorporated against the states. Indeed, the Court did not find a law to violate the First Amendment until 1931.

The Court was careful to note that the Second Amendment right to bear arms was not unlimited. Nothing in the opinion should be "taken to cast doubt on longstanding prohibitions on the possession of firearms by felons and the mentally ill, or laws forbidding the carrying of firearms in sensitive places such as schools and government buildings, or laws imposing conditions and qualifications on the commercial sale of arms." Moreover, the Court recognized the limitation in *Miller* that the Second Amendment protected weapons "in common use at the time." The Court noted the historical practice going back to Blackstone of prohibiting "dangerous or unusual weapons."

A militia at the time of the Second Amendment's ratification was all the able-bodied men who brought weapons from home. Today for a militia to be as effective as one in the 18th century, it would require very sophisticated weapons that ordinary citizens do not have. However, technological advancements in weaponry should not alter the Court's interpretation of the right.

---

[97] 307 U.S. 174 (1939).

Pivotal to the Second Amendment right has been the inherent right of self-defense. As the handgun is the most popular weapon to protect the home and family, banning it is unconstitutional under any standard of scrutiny. And it is not enough to permit other firearms, like long guns. The District of Columbia's requirement that all firearms in the home be kept inoperable at all times was also unconstitutional because it impeded the core lawful purpose of self-defense.

The Court did not address the licensing requirement because respondent conceded at oral argument that he did not contest it if it was "not enforced in an arbitrary and capricious manner." The Court also made clear that its decision did not suggest that "laws regulating the storage of firearms to prevent accidents" were invalid. In response to Justice Breyer's criticism that the majority did not "establish a level of scrutiny for evaluating Second Amendment restrictions," Justice Scalia criticized Justice Breyer's balancing approach. He knew "of no other enumerated constitutional right whose core protection has been subjected to a freestanding 'interest-balancing' approach." Such an approach which rested on "future judges' assessments of its usefulness is no constitutional guarantee at all."

The Court also responded to Justice Breyer's other criticisms that the Court has left in doubt many of the specific applications of the Second Amendment right and that the Court has not provided historical justifications of the regulations that it has indicated were permissible. As this was the Court's extensive analysis of the Second Amendment, the decision could not cover the entire area.

The Court held that the District's handgun ban and its requirement that handguns be kept inoperable both violated the Second Amendment. However, the Second Amendment still allowed a variety of permissible tools to combat crime, including some handgun regulations.

Justice Stevens dissented, joined by Justices Souter, Ginsburg, and Breyer. Justice Stevens thought that the Second Amendment and its Framers evidenced no intention to restrict regulation of personal firearms outside of military use by state militias. *United States v. Miller*[98] held that the Second Amendment protected the right to have arms service in state militias but not for "nonmilitary use and ownership of weapons." The Court affirmed this holding in *Lewis v. United States*[99] and hundreds of lower courts have followed it.

Justice Stevens' textual analysis began with the prefatory clause: "A well regulated Militia, being necessary to the security of a free State." While this language resembled that found in several contemporaneous state Declarations of Rights, the Framers of the Second Amendment did not include any additional language protecting the use of weapons for hunting or self defense, as did the state declarations of Pennsylvania and Vermont. As with the First and Fourth Amendments, the words "the people" included all individuals. Contradicting its own interpretation, the majority later confined Second Amendment protection to "law-abiding, responsible citizens," which consequently only extended to a "subset" of the individuals protected by the First and Fourteenth Amendments. Not only is

---

[98]   307 U.S. 174 (1939).

[99]   445 U.S. 55 (1980).

"bear arms" commonly read to mean military service, but both contemporaneous texts and the Oxford dictionary point to a strictly military application. The phrase "to keep" appeared in several state militia laws when the Constitution was framed; it required militia members to store weaponry at their homes, ready for use in military service.

Taken together, the Second Amendment articulated "a right to use and possess arms in conjunction with service in a well-regulated militia." Even if alternate meanings could be read into the Amendment, the Court should not lightly stray from precedent and the ends articulated by the Amendment's preamble.

The Militia Clauses of Article I and the Second Amendment are paradigmatic examples of the "Framers' 'splitting the atom of sovereignty.' " Specifically, the Framers allowed Congress to call up, "organize, arm, and discipline the militia" and to govern that part of the militia employed by the national government. In turn, the states could commission officers and train the militia following the discipline outlined by Congress. In drafting the Second Amendment, James Madison considered and rejected several state proposals which specifically mentioned a right to possess firearms for personal use. Also, an exemption for religious objectors was removed from the original text amid concerns that Congress could claim that the faithful could not bear arms. Such drafting choices illustrated the purpose of prohibiting Congress from disarming state militias.

The historical sources cited by the Court were vaguely instructive, if at all. The English Bill of Rights, enabling only certain Protestants to bear arms was created to address different concerns and lacked militia-specific phrasing. Moreover, the right applied only to a certain societal class and to the extent allowed by Parliament. Justice Story saw the Second Amendment as a necessary safeguard for democratic governance because it checked on centralized federal power. The post-Civil War legislative history invoked by the majority could not explain the Framers' intent, as the legislators' comments were made well after the amendment was written, during heated partisan debate.

Turning finally to precedent, minor Second Amendment objections did not affect the passage of the first Federal laws expressly limiting ownership of firearms for personal use. Moreover, the *Miller* Court was presented with much of the same evidence presented here: *Miller* turned not on whether a gun is likely to be used for self-defense, but whether it was better suited for military or civilian use. The Court tried to discount *Miller* by noting the failure of those attacking the gun control law to file briefs or present oral argument to the Court. However, *Marbury v. Madison*[100] suffered a similar defect as only one party argued before the Court. More importantly, *Miller* was a unanimous decision which has been relied upon for almost 70 years.

As "most citizens are law-abiding" and the need to self-defense frequently arises outside the home, the Court may strike down many other gun control laws in the future.

---

[100] 5 U.S. 137 (1803).

Justice Breyer filed a separate dissenting opinion, joined by Justices Stevens, Souter, and Ginsburg. Justice Breyer argued that the majority erred for two reasons: first, the Second Amendment was designed to protect militia-related interests rather than self-defense. Second, the Amendment was not intended to provide absolute protection from government regulation of fire arms. Justice Breyer joined Justice Stevens' dissent regarding the first error and he focused on the government's latitude to respond to "serious, indeed life-threatening problem[s]."

During colonial times, the three largest cities Boston, Philadelphia, and New York all had some type of regulation on discharging weapons within city limits. Moreover, several municipalities — including the above three — regulated the storage of gunpowder, an important part of an operational weapon, in order to prevent fires. It is unclear whether all of these laws prohibited the storage of gunpowder within a gun, such as the law in Boston did, but either way it increased the time to reload weapons to fire a second shot.

The Court correctly rejected the respondent's proffered strict scrutiny test, by broadly endorsing prohibitions on concealed weapons and on criminals carrying weapons — which strict scrutiny good well invalidate. The Court had previously held "compelling" protecting the safety of citizens and preventing crime. When a law impacted complex competing constitutional interests, Justice Breyer suggested a proportionality test which considered a statute's effect upon individuals and the government together with the existence of a clearly better, less restrictive, alternative. When applying the proportionality standard, the Court generally deferred to the legislature when the legislature probably had greater expertise and fact finding capacity.

The basic issue in this case was whether the statute's burdens were disproportionate to the City's legitimate objectives. When the District of Columbia had adopted the ban in 1974, a national report revealed that over the past few years handguns had been used in approximately 54% of all murders, 87% of murders of law enforcement officers, 60% of robberies, and 26% of assaults nationwide. Moreover, the presence of a firearm made a crime seven times more likely to be deadly than one perpetrated with another weapon.

The respondent argued that European statistical studies showed that stricter guns laws were related to more murders, not fewer. The respondent also pointed to a study which showed that armed homeowners deterred 98.8% of robbers. Justice Breyer noted the District's crime rate did increase after the handgun ban took effect. Nevertheless, it did not necessarily follow that these phenomena occurred "*because of [the ban]*." It is impossible to predict what the crime rate in the District would have been if the handgun ban had not passed.

The District presented statistical studies that showed handgun regulations reduced crime. Specifically, one study indicated that firearm restrictions reduced homicide, suicide, and accidents at home. When the Court applied intermediate scrutiny in First Amendment cases, its only obligation was to ensure that the legislature's conclusions were based on reasonable inferences and substantial evidence. The District's decision met this test.

The District's handgun ban did not interfere with military training. Citizens of the District could register and keep weapons such as rifles and shotguns in their homes and were also allowed to use these weapons for recreational purposes. In sum, the ban's burden on the Second Amendment's primary objective or any sports-related or hunting-related objectives was small or nonexistent. The ban did, however, prevent a resident from having a loaded gun in his home and, consequently, made it more difficult for a homeowner to use a handgun in self-defense.

In this case, there was no clearly better, less burdensome alternative to the District's handgun ban. The ban allowed law enforcement officials to assume that any handgun they saw was illegal and take the appropriate actions against the armed person.

The handgun ban did not disproportionately burden Second Amendment-protected interests. First, the law addressed a serious problem in the District — handgun fatalities — while allowing residents to own rifles and shotguns. Secondly, the Second Amendment mentions militias, not self-defense. Finally, the majority's stand that the Second Amendment afforded a right to possess weapons "typically possessed by law-abiding citizens for lawful purposes" was unclear.

McDonald v. City of Chicago[101] held that the Second Amendment right established in *District of Columbia v. Heller* was "fully applicable to the States" through incorporation by the Fourteenth Amendment. A plurality opinion written by Justice Alito — and joined by the Chief Justice, Justice Scalia and Justice Kennedy — incorporated the Second Amendment through the Due Process Clause, while Justice Thomas' decisive fifth vote effected incorporation through the Privileges or Immunities Clause. By applying the Second Amendment to the States, the Court invalidated Chicago laws that banned possession of handguns.

The plurality used the Due Process Clause to apply the Second Amendment to the states, as for many decades incorporation has occurred through that avenue rather than the Privileges or Immunities Clause. There was no reason to "disturb" the approach of the *Slaughter-House Cases* toward the Privileges or Immunities Clause.[102] The plurality declined to adopt Justice Black's theory of "total incorporation," but noted that very few provisions of the Bill of Rights remained unincorporated. Incorporated protections applied in the same way against the States as they did against federal encroachment.

To incorporate through the Due Process Clause, the plurality required that the right was "fundamental to *our* scheme of ordered liberty," or the right was " 'deeply rooted in this Nation's history and tradition.' "[103] The plurality, joined by Justice Thomas, found that the debates of the 39th Congress about the Fourteenth Amendment referred to this right as fundamental. "Evidence from the period immediately following the ratification of the Fourteenth Amendment" confirmed this.[104] Moreover, the legal commentators and state constitutions of the time

---

[101]   130 S. Ct. 3020, 3026 (2010).

[102]   *Id.* at 3031.

[103]   *Id.* at 3036.

[104]   *Id.*

treated the right to keep and bear arms as fundamental.

The plurality thought that due process should not be interpreted using the practices of other nations. Such reasoning was "of course, inconsistent with the long-established standard we apply in incorporation cases."[105] The fact that countries such as "England, Canada, Australia, Japan, Denmark, Finland, Luxembourg, and New Zealand either ban or severely limit handgun ownership," did not entail a lack of Fourteenth Amendment protection.[106] Many of the Bill of Rights protecting criminal defendants "are virtually unique to this country."[107] While the United States incorporated the Establishment Clause against the states, several countries listed above "that municipal respondents recognize as civilized have established state churches."[108]

This ruling, as made clear in *Heller*, did not cast "doubt on such longstanding regulatory measures as 'prohibitions on the possession of firearms by felons and the mentally ill,' 'laws forbidding the carrying of firearms in sensitive places such as schools and government buildings, or laws imposing conditions and qualifications on the commercial sale of arms.' "[109] *Heller* rejected the argument that the right to bear arms only protected militias, instead finding self-defense " 'the *central component* of the right.' "[110] The number of homicide victims in Chicago this year equaled that of American soldiers killed in Afghanistan and Iraq, and "80% of the Chicago victims were black."[111]

The plurality disagreed with Justice Stevens that incorporated provisions of the Bill of Rights "need not be identical in shape or scope to the rights protected against Federal Government infringement," explaining that "the Court, for the past half-century, has moved away from the two-track approach."[112] Instead, determining which guarantees of the Bill of Rights apply against "the States must be governed by a single, neutral principle."[113]

Concurring, Justice Scalia acquiesced in incorporation through the Due Process Clause because that avenue is " 'both long established and narrowly limited.' "[114] Defending historical interpretation, he conceded that analyzing history "requires resolving threshold questions, and making nuanced judgments about which evidence to consult and how to interpret it." Nevertheless, the issue "is not whether the historically focused method is a *perfect means* of restraining aristocratic judicial Constitution-writing; but whether it is the *best means available* in an imperfect

---

[105] *Id.* at 3044.

[106] *Id.*

[107] *Id.* For example, "the United States affords criminal jury trials far more broadly than other countries. Similarly, our rules governing pretrial interrogation differ from those in countries sharing a similar legal heritage. And the 'Court-pronounced exclusionary rule . . . is distinctively American.' "

[108] *Id.* at 3045.

[109] *Id.* at 3047.

[110] *Id.* at 3048.

[111] *Id.* at 3049.

[112] *Id.* at 3048.

[113] *Id.*

[114] *Id.* at 3050 (Scalia, J., concurring).

world."[115] It is "less subjective" than "a variety of vague ethico-political First Principles whose combined conclusion can be found to point in any direction the judges favor."[116] The historical method limits judicial discretion. In this connection, "*any* historical methodology, under *any* plausible standard of proof," would produce the same result on the constitutionality of the death penalty, "prohibiting abortion, assisted suicide, or homosexual sodomy."[117] Even Justice Stevens' approach "would not *replace* history with moral philosophy, but would have courts consider *both*."[118]

Justice Thomas concurred in part and in the judgment. He disagreed that the Second Amendment "is enforceable against the States through a clause that speaks only to 'process,'" and instead would incorporate it through the Privileges or Immunities Clause of the Fourteenth Amendment.[119] From the time of Blackstone to the Amendment's ratification, the terms "privileges" and "immunities," whether they stand by themselves or bar "paired together, were used interchangeably with the words 'rights,' 'liberties,' and 'freedoms.'"[120] The goal of interpreting constitutional text "is to discern the most likely public understanding of a particular provision" upon adoption.[121] Comments by legislators could help to establish how people used or understood a word or phrase. The "right to keep and bear arms was understood to be a privilege of American citizenship guaranteed by the Privileges or Immunities Clause."[122]

The *Cruikshank*[123] decision deserved no respect as precedent. *Cruikshank* held that "the right to keep and bear arms was not a privilege of American citizenship, thereby overturning the convictions of militia members responsible for the brutal Colfax Massacre."[124] That holding meant blacks could only look to state governments for protection of their right to keep and bear arms, and it "enabled" private forces, "often with the assistance of local governments, to subjugate the newly freed slaves."[125] Justice Thomas expressed no view on regulating firearm possession for noncitizens. The issue arose because the Privileges or Immunities Clause applies only to citizens, whereas the Due Process Clause "covers all 'person[s].'" The claimant here was a citizen.

Justice Stevens dissented. "The so-called incorporation question" was already "correctly resolved in the late 19th century" by *Cruikshank*.[126] The Due Process Clause involves more than *process*. By the Civil War or "much earlier, the phrase

---

[115] *Id.* at 3057–58.

[116] *Id.* at 3058.

[117] *Id.*

[118] *Id.*

[119] *Id.* at 3059 (Thomas, J., concurring in part and in the judgment).

[120] *Id.* at 3063.

[121] *Id.* at 3072.

[122] *Id.* at 3077.

[123] United States v. Cruikshank, 92 U.S. 542 (1876).

[124] *McDonald*, 130 S. Ct. at 3086.

[125] *Id.* at 3087.

[126] *Id.* at 3088 (Stevens, J., dissenting).

'due process of law' had acquired substantive content."[127] Against incorporation, Justice Stevens argued that the Bill of Rights was drafted only to directly constrain the Federal Government, and although the Fourteenth Amendment "profoundly altered our legal order, it 'did not unstitch the basic federalist pattern woven into our constitutional fabric.' "[128] The plurality's statement that the Court has " 'abandoned', a 'two-track approach to incorporation,' " was exaggerated — although it has moved away from a two-track approach to incorporating the criminal procedure guarantees.[129]

This ruling applied a uniform national standard to an area where the "relevant regulatory interests vary significantly across localities."[130] It also prevented States' "beneficent 'experimentation,' " and "implicates the States' core police powers."[131]

Undercutting any notion that the right to bear arms was "fundamental to a life of liberty," America's oldest allies almost uniformly regulate firearms extensively. "While the 'American perspective' must always be our focus, it is silly — indeed, arrogant — to think we have nothing to learn about liberty from the billions of people beyond our borders."[132]

The preamble to the Second Amendment demonstrated its structural function to protect the states from the federal government, even though the *Heller* Court tries to write that preamble out of the Constitution. As many different firearm regulations were now implicated, "today's decision invites an avalanche of litigation."[133] Justice Stevens also criticized historical analysis as casting federal judges as "amateur historians."[134]

Justice Breyer also dissented, joined by Justices Ginsburg and Sotomayor. The British Declaration of Right allowed private persons to "possess guns only 'as allowed by law,' " and " 'Parliament had the power' to arm the citizenry."[135] *Heller's* historical account "would lose a poll taken among professional historians of this period, say, by a vote of 8 to 1."[136] Where history was so opaque, the Court "should consider the basic values that underlie a constitutional provision and their contemporary significance," and a provision's "relevant consequences and practical justifications."[137]

Legislatures were better able to find answers to the "complex empirically based questions" surrounding firearm regulations: "Does the right to possess weapons for self-defense extend outside the home? To the car? To work? What sort of guns are

---

[127] *Id.* at 3090.

[128] *Id.* at 3093.

[129] *Id.* at 3094.

[130] *Id.* at 3095.

[131] *Id.*

[132] *Id.* at 3111.

[133] *Id.* at 3115.

[134] *Id.* at 3119.

[135] *Id.* at 3122 (Breyer, J., dissenting).

[136] *Id.*

[137] *Id.*

necessary for self-defense? Handguns? Rifles? Semiautomatic weapons? When is a gun semi-automatic?"[138] Other questions include: "Does the presence of a convicted felon in the house matter? When do registration requirements become severe to the point that they amount to an unconstitutional ban? Who can possess guns and of what kind? Aliens? Prior drug offenders?"[139]

Incorporation stifles federalism, which empowers "States to reflect local preferences and conditions."[140] Gun ownership differ significantly across the Nation. In the relatively sparsely populated Western States of Alaska, Montana, and Wyoming 60% of households kept a gun, while fewer than 15% of households did in the densely populated Eastern States of Rhode Island, New Jersey, and Massachusetts. Factors that weighed against incorporation include: "the police power, the superiority of legislative decisionmaking, the need for local decisionmaking, the comparative desirability of democratic decisionmaking, the lack of a manageable judicial standard, and the life-threatening harm that may flow from striking down regulations."[141]

The right to bear arms was not considered fundamental when the Fourteenth Amendment was ratified. The Second Freedman's Bureau Act recognized a "constitutional right to bear arms . . . without *respect to race or color, or previous condition of slavery,*" which is "an *antidiscrimination* provision."[142] Moreover, "why would those who wrote the *Fourteenth Amendment* have wanted to give such a right to Southerners who had so recently waged war against the North?"[143] Also, "in every State and many local communities, highly detailed and complicated regulatory schemes governed (and continue to govern) nearly every aspect of firearm ownership."[144] This "breadth of existing regulations" demonstrated that "States and local governments maintain substantial flexibility to regulate firearms — much as they seemingly have throughout the Nation's history — even in those States with an arms right in their constitutions."[145] Nothing in American history showed that *Heller's* right to private armed self-defense was " 'deeply rooted in this Nation's history or tradition' or is otherwise 'fundamental.' Indeed, incorporating the right recognized in *Heller* could change the law in many of the 50 States."[146]

---

[138] *Id.* at 3126.

[139] *Id.* at 3126–27.

[140] *Id.* at 3128.

[141] *Id.* at 3129.

[142] *Id.* at 3133.

[143] *Id.*

[144] *Id.* at 3135.

[145] *Id.* at 3135–36.

[146] *Id.* at 3136.

§ 8.04 VAGUENESS

In *City of Chicago v. Morales*,[147] the Court invalidated Chicago's Gang Congregation Ordinance as unconstitutionally vague on its face. Justice Stevens, joined by Justices Souter and Ginsburg, agreed that an ordinance would be constitutional if it directly prohibited conduct that threatened safety and security, property values, and the overall stability of a neighborhood — three of the reasons behind the Chicago ordinance. However, the law's scope was uncertain because it "broadly covers a significant amount of additional activity." The plurality stated that the "freedom to loiter for innocent purposes is part of the 'liberty' protected by the Due Process Clause of the Fourteenth Amendment."

A majority of six Justices held that the broad ordinance failed to "establish minimal guidelines to govern law enforcement." In particular, the Court criticized the uncertainty of the " 'no apparent purpose' standard" to be used by officers in enforcing it. The majority did find that a reasonable belief requirement "would no doubt be sufficient if the ordinance only applied to loitering that had an apparently harmful purpose or effect, or possible if it only applied to loitering by persons reasonably believed to be criminal gang members." While this definition included harmless conduct, it excluded apparently harmful conduct. The Court accepted as definitive the Illinois Supreme Court's construction of the ordinance as not applying to those whose purposes were apparent. The majority "refused to accept the general order issued by the police department as a sufficient limitation on the 'vast amount of discretion' granted to the police in its enforcement."

Justice O'Connor, joined by Justice Breyer, concurred in part with Justice Stevens' opinion and concurred in the judgment. She stated that "reasonable alternatives" could still combat gangs. Examples included loitering laws that limit the area and method of enforcement or required a harmful purpose or gang membership.

Justice O'Connor found that a more narrow construction of the term "loiter" would have cured the ordinance's vagueness problems. She suggested that loiter could mean " 'to remain in any one place with no apparent purpose other than to establish control over identifiable areas, to intimidate others from entering those areas, or to conceal illegal activities.' "

Dissenting, Justice Scalia criticized the majority for "ignoring our rules governing facial challenges." Except in free speech cases subject to the doctrine of overbreadth, the Court has required litigants to "establish that the statute was unconstitutional in all its applications" before "declaring a statute to be void in all its applications." The problem with the existing laws "is that the intimidation and lawlessness do not occur when the police are in sight."

Justice Thomas filed a separate dissent joined by Chief Justice Rehnquist and Justice Scalia. The ordinance is not vague. "Any fool would know that a particular category of conduct would be within [its] reach." Prohibitions on loitering date back to the Norman Conquest. The decision protected gang members at the expense of law-abiding citizens.

---

[147] 527 U.S. 41 (1999).

§ 8.05   REGULATION OF BUSINESS AND OTHER PROPERTY INTERESTS

[1]   Liberty of Contract Under the Due Process Clauses

This Section highlights the Court's use of the Fourteenth Amendment to strike down state economic regulations during the first half of the twentieth century. Although *Slaughter-House* rejected the use of the Fourteenth Amendment to scrutinize state economic regulations, the Court's Due Process Clause jurisprudence shifted toward the close of the 1800s.

The Court took the step that it had been unwilling to take in *Slaughter-House*. Slowly rejecting the limitations outlined in *Slaughter-House*, it invaded the powers of the states by subjecting them to the restrictions of the Federal Constitution. The Court's new interpretation of the Fourteenth Amendment limited state powers by applying certain individual rights guaranteed by the Constitution and the Bill of Rights against the states. This resulted in a shift in power from state legislatures to the federal courts — exactly what the majority in *Slaughter-House* had feared. At the core of the shift in the Court's Fourteenth Amendment jurisprudence was its use of the doctrine of substantive due process to scrutinize and strike down state economic regulation.

Substantive due process is the concept that there are certain rights so fundamental to our traditions of justice that, no matter what procedural guarantees government affords, government cannot abridge those rights. The basis of substantive due process has generally been the "liberty" clause of the Fourteenth Amendment (*i.e.*, government would be violating a person's liberty despite the procedural guarantees afforded). Substantive due process requires a broad reading of the word "liberty" in the Due Process Clauses of the Fifth and Fourteenth Amendment. This is the same substantive due process analysis that the Court uses today in such areas as privacy, birth control, and childbearing.[148]

The Court adopted substantive due process in *Allgeyer v. Louisiana*.[149] The line between "substantive" and "procedural" due process is not always clear. For example, in 1897 the Court applied to the states the Fifth Amendment right to compensation for property taken for public use,[150] a decision not generally categorized as involving "substantive" due process.

In *Allgeyer*, the Court invalidated, as a violation of the freedom of contract, a statute requiring owners of property in Louisiana to obtain property insurance only from insurance companies licensed in the state. The Court gave an expansive reading to the concept of "liberty" that became prevalent in later decisions.

Perhaps, the most famous case using this doctrine during this era was *Lochner v. New York*.[151] In *Lochner*, the owner of a bakery challenged a New York statute

---

[148]   *See supra* § 8.04.

[149]   165 U.S. 578 (1897).

[150]   Chicago, Burlington & Quincy R.R. Co. v. Chicago, 166 U.S. 226 (1897).

[151]   198 U.S. 45 (1905).

that prohibited the employment of bakery employees for more than 10 hours a day or 60 hours a week. Although the statute restricted liberty of contract *between* the employees and the employers, the bakery owner claimed that the statute violated the employer's and employee's liberty of contract to purchase and sell labor. Instead of balancing the interests of the employees against the employers, the Court balanced the contract interests of employers and employees against the interest of New York in regulating public welfare.

The liberty of contract right being asserted in *Lochner* was a substantive due process right based on the Liberty Clause of the Fourteenth Amendment,[152] not the Contract Clause of Article I, § 10 of the Constitution.[153]

New York claimed that the statute was a valid exercise of its police power; that is, its right to regulate the safety, health, morals, and general welfare of the citizens of New York. The state had to exercise its police power, however, within the boundaries of the Fourteenth Amendment. When a state enacts a statute under its police power, the Fourteenth Amendment required that the statute have "a more direct relation, as a means to an end, and the end itself must be appropriate and legitimate."[154] Applying this test, the Court ruled that the New York statute was unconstitutional because it did not have an "appropriate and legitimate" end.

The Court identified two possible ends for the statute: enforcement of the labor law and protecting the health of the bakers. The Court quickly dismissed the labor law justification: "There is no reasonable ground for interfering with the liberty of person or the right of free contract, by determining the hours of labor, in the occupation of a baker."[155] The only legitimate police power end was the protection of the safety, morals, or general welfare of the public. Since the healthiness of bread was not affected by the number of hours worked by the bakers, the health of the bakers themselves was the only end that the Court was willing to explore.

The Court then rejected protecting the health of the bakers as a legitimate end. The health of the bakers did not need protection because baking was not an unhealthy trade, a fact supported by statistics, the common understanding of the baking trade, and the idea that all occupations were unhealthy in some way. "If this statute be valid . . . there would seem to be no length to which legislation of this nature might not go."[156] The majority feared that sustaining the regulation would lead down a slippery slope, eventually allowing the state to regulate the hours of other professions. Would the legislature be able to regulate the work week of professionals such as doctors, lawyers, and scientists? The majority feared that this road would subject all citizens to the mercy of legislative majorities. Fearing legislative invasion into all aspects of private life, the Court used substantive due process to prevent legislatures from enacting laws that drew lines, with respect to an individual's freedom, that the Court considered arbitrary.

---

[152] "The right to purchase or to sell labor is part of the liberty protected by [the Fourteenth Amendment], unless there are circumstances which exclude this right." 198 U.S. at 53.

[153] "No state shall . . . pass any . . . Law impairing the Obligation of Contracts."

[154] 198 U.S. at 57.

[155] *Id.*

[156] *Id.* at 58.

Dissenting, Justice Holmes criticized the majority's holding that labor laws were not a legitimate legislative end. He emphasized that the bakery employees were not equal to the owners in bargaining power. Consequently, labor laws were a legitimate and appropriate legislative end. Justice Holmes also argued that the majority was constitutionalizing theories of laissez-faire capitalism and Herbert Spencer's Social Darwinism. To avoid infusing the Constitution with the Court's personal predilections, Justice Holmes would apply a reasonableness test to the means and ends of the statute. He would utilize a stricter standard only when "a rational and fair man necessarily would admit that the statute proposed would infringe fundamental principles as they have been understood by the traditions of our people and our law."[157] This approach was an early expression of the "two-tiered" methodology of rationality and strict scrutiny that later became the basis for much of the modern Court's constitutional jurisprudence.

Justice Harlan also dissented. Driven by concerns of separation of powers and federalism, Justice Harlan argued that the courts should not inquire into the wisdom of legislation. He viewed such decisions as policy judgments best left to the legislature. Instead, the Court's scrutiny should be limited to whether there is a "real or substantial relation between the means employed by the state and the end sought to be accomplished by its legislation."[158]

Applying that analysis to the facts in *Lochner*, Justice Harlan concluded that the statute was a valid exercise of New York's police power. The means used by New York had a substantial relation to the legislative end of protecting the health of the bakers. Justice Harlan also noted the bakers' position of unequal bargaining power.

Between the turn of the century and the late 1930s, the Court used substantive due process and other theories, including the Commerce Clause,[159] to invalidate various types of economic regulations. The Court did not strike down all economic regulations. In *Muller v. Oregon*[160] and *Bunting v. Oregon*,[161] the Court upheld statutes establishing maximum ten hour days for female and male factory workers, respectively. In these decisions the Court emphasized that liberty of contract was not an absolute, and that states could pass regulations to protect the public interest. However, in *Adkins v. Children's Hospital*,[162] the Court struck down a minimum wage law for women. Dissenting, Justice Holmes argued that upholding maximum hour laws and overturning minimum wage laws was inconsistent.

The programs of President Franklin Delano Roosevelt's New Deal during the 1930s increased the controversy regarding the use of substantive due process to invalidate economic regulation. In its 1934 decision, *Nebbia v. New York*,[163] the Court indicated a possible retreat from its substantive due process jurisprudence. Nebbia, a grocery store owner, was convicted of selling milk below the price

---

[157] *Id.* at 76.

[158] *Id.* at 69.

[159] *See supra* § 4.02.

[160] 208 U.S. 412 (1908).

[161] 243 U.S. 426 (1917).

[162] 261 U.S. 525 (1923).

[163] 291 U.S. 502 (1934).

established by the New York Milk Control Board. New York had created the Board in an attempt to save its failing dairy industry by regulating prices. *Nebbia* brought a Fourteenth Amendment challenge to the New York Milk Control Law, claiming that it violated both the Due Process and Equal Protection Clauses.

The Court upheld the law as a valid exercise of the state's police power to protect public welfare. The language of the opinion seemed to signal increased legislative discretion with a narrow and more deferential standard of review: when a state passed laws which were "seen to have a reasonable relation to a proper legislative purpose, and are neither arbitrary nor discriminatory, the requirements of due process are satisfied."[164] Justice Roberts concluded that the New York Milk Control Law satisfied this requirement.

Comparing the *Nebbia* Court's reasonableness standard with the much stricter scrutiny test in *Lochner*, it is easy to see why many observers felt that *Nebbia* marked a shift to a more deferential review of economic legislation. During the next two years, however, the Supreme Court used federalism and substantive due process rationales to strike down many key provisions of the New Deal. The victims included the National Industrial Recovery Act,[165] the Agricultural Adjustment Act,[166] and the Bituminous Coal Conservation Act.[167] These invalidated statutes were central components of the New Deal legislative program, designed to combat the Great Depression. The standoff between Roosevelt and the Supreme Court (described by the President as the "Nine Old Men") resulted in the New Deal constitutional crisis of the mid 1930s. Determined to continue with his legislative program, President Roosevelt, following his overwhelming re-election in 1936, proposed a "Court packing plan" that would have allowed the President to appoint a new Supreme Court Justice for each incumbent who was 70 years old and had served ten years on the Supreme Court. The plan would have provided the President six new appointments. The plan generated enormous controversy and was criticized by many of the President's supporters.

Disaster was avoided when the Supreme Court made the famous "switch-in-time-that-saved-nine" compromise in the spring of 1937. The shifting votes of Chief Justice Hughes and Justice Roberts enabled the Court to uphold several key New Deal provisions including the National Labor Relations Act[168] and the Social Security Act.[169]

By virtue of this crucial shift,[170] the Court relinquished its authority in the economic regulation arena in part by abandoning its strict substantive due process

---

[164] *Id.* at 537.

[165] *See* Schechter Poultry Corp. v. United States, 295 U.S. 495 (1935).

[166] *See* United States v. Butler, 297 U.S. 1 (1936).

[167] *See* Carter v. Carter Coal Co., 298 U.S. 238 (1936).

[168] *See* NLRB v. Jones & Laughlin Steel Corp., 301 U.S. 1 (1937).

[169] *See* Steward Machine Co. v. Davis, 301 U.S. 548 (1937); Helvering v. Davis, 301 U.S. 619 (1937).

[170] For further reading on the court-packing controversy, *see, e.g.*, Leuchtenburg, *The Origins of Franklin D. Roosevelt's "Court-Packing" Plan*, 1966 SUP. CT. REV. 347; R. JACKSON, THE STRUGGLE FOR JUDICIAL SUPREMACY (1941); Currie, *The Constitution in the Supreme Court: The New Deal, 1931–1940*, 54 U. CHI. L. REV. 504 (1987); Barry Cushman, *Rethinking the New Deal Court*, 80 VA. L. REV. 201 (1994)

scrutiny in favor of a policy of tremendous judicial deference to economic legislation. The Court outlined its new deference in *United States v. Carolene Products Co.*[171] At issue was Congress' 1923 "Filled Milk Act" that prohibited the shipment into interstate commerce of skimmed milk that had been combined with any fat or oil (other than milk fat) to resemble real milk. The defendant, indicted for violating the Act, claimed that the "Filled Milk Act" violated due process and was outside the realm of Congress' Commerce Clause power.

Writing for the majority, Justice Stone quickly dismissed the Commerce Clause challenge. Justice Stone held that the "Filled Milk Act" was a valid exercise of Congress' Commerce Clause power to protect the health and welfare of the public. Dismissing the due process challenges, Justice Stone announced the Court's deferential review of economic regulations:

> [R]egulatory legislation affecting ordinary commercial transactions is not to be pronounced unconstitutional unless in the light of the facts made known or generally assumed it is of such character as to preclude the assumption that it rests upon some rational basis within the knowledge and experience of the legislators.[172]

Justice Stone emphasized that the Court would no longer scrutinize the ends sought to be achieved by legislation, because that was "a matter for the legislative judgment and not that of courts."[173] Applying this analysis to the facts in *Carolene Products*, Justice Stone concluded that Congress had a rational basis to believe that the "Filled Milk Act" would protect the public from skimmed milk thought to be injurious to health.

In *Williamson v. Lee Optical of Oklahoma*,[174] the Supreme Court established what is now generally agreed to be the current standard of judicial review for economic regulation. The Court stated that "the law need not be in every respect logically consistent with its aims to be constitutional. It is enough that there is an evil at hand for correction, and that it *might be thought* that the particular legislative measure was a rational way to correct it."[175] Thus, the Court need not consider the actual legislative purpose when evaluating economic legislation. The Court could, and has demonstrated a willingness to, create a hypothetical legislative purpose to validate a statute. This rational basis scrutiny was applicable to due process and equal protection challenges to economic or social regulation.

Far more important than the holding in *Carolene Products* was the famous footnote four in the opinion, where the Court listed areas in which this extremely deferential standard of review would not apply. The footnote explained the Court's decision to expand its protection of personal rights:

(disputing that political pressure caused the apparent switch in the Court's philosophy).

[171] 304 U.S. 144 (1938).

[172] *Id.* at 152.

[173] *Id.* at 151.

[174] 348 U.S. 483 (1955).

[175] *Id.* at 487–88 (emphasis added).

There may be narrower scope for operation of the presumption of constitutionality when legislation appears on its face to be within a specific prohibition of the Constitution, such as those of the first ten amendments, which are deemed equally specific when held to be embraced within the Fourteenth.

It is unnecessary to consider now whether legislation which restricts those political processes which can ordinarily be expected to bring about repeal of undesirable legislation, is to be subjected to more exacting judicial scrutiny under the general prohibitions of the Fourteenth Amendment than are most other types of legislation. On restrictions upon the right to vote, see . . . ; on restraints upon the dissemination of information, see . . . ; on interferences with political organizations, see . . . ; as to prohibition of peaceable assembly, see . . . .

Nor need we enquire whether similar considerations enter into the review of statutes directed at particular religious or national, or racial minorities; whether prejudice against discrete and insular minorities may be a special condition, which tends seriously to curtail the operation of those political processes ordinarily to be relied upon to protect minorities, and which may call for a correspondingly more searching judicial inquiry.[176]

This footnote embodied the political settlement reached as a result of the New Deal Constitutional Crisis; the Supreme Court would curtail its scrutiny of economic rights and expand its scrutiny of more "personal" rights. In effect, footnote four was a blueprint for the modern Supreme Court's jurisprudence.

There are three basic sets of personal rights at the heart of footnote four: the rights of the accused (amendments four through eight), restrictions on the political process (the rights of voting, association, and free speech), and the rights of "discrete and insular minorities." Why did the Court retain scrutiny over these areas? Does something make the Court superior to the Legislature in protecting these three types of "personal rights," but not economic rights?

By definition, "discrete and insular minorities" are groups that have historically been unsuccessful at protecting their interests in the majoritarian democratic political process. The same was true for those accused of committing crimes, who are relatively weak when pitted against the prosecutorial power of the state. Moreover, it was necessary to closely scrutinize restrictions on the political process because that process could not police itself. Most obviously, political groups in power could attempt to exclude political groups out of power to solidify their power. When this occurred, the political process needed a neutral referee: "the referee is to intervene only when one team is gaining unfair advantage, not because the 'wrong' team has scored. Our government cannot be said to be 'malfunctioning' simply because it sometimes generates outcomes with which we disagree, however strongly."[177] All three of these interests require the protection of a counter-

---

[176] *Carolene Products*, 304 U.S. at 152 n.4.

[177] JOHN H. ELY, DEMOCRACY AND DISTRUST 103 (1980).

majoritarian institution that could check the interests of the majority.

The legislature is elected by a majority of the people, which makes it well-suited to protect majoritarian and utilitarian interests. Because the long-run distribution of societal wealth is a utilitarian issue, it is the proper realm of the legislature that was structured to reflect the greatest good for the greatest number. Federal judges are noticeably removed from the majoritarian political process; they are appointed for life. This makes the courts functionally superior to the legislature in protecting the interests of "discrete and insular minorities," and the political process itself. Therefore, courts were deemed better suited to protect counter-majoritarian "personal" rights.

The modern Court has not abandoned safeguarding property rights.[178] Most notable is the guarantee of just compensation when government takes private property. The modern Court also affords very limited protection to liberty of contract.

[2]   Economic Regulation and the Contract Clause of Article I, Section 10

The Contract Clause of Article I, § 10, prohibits a state, but not the Federal government, from passing a "law impairing the obligation of contracts." Although the modern Court exerts some scrutiny over economic regulation under the Contract Clause, it currently does so only in limited circumstances.

As part of its withdrawal of scrutiny of economic regulation toward the end of the New Deal, the Court adopted a very deferential approach to Contract Clause scrutiny.[179] Until the 1970s, the Court continued this deferential approach. Several cases then indicated a shift toward considerably greater scrutiny. At least with respect to the Contract Clause, however, the pendulum has swung back as the Court has reinstated its more deferential approach.

The Court's contradictory jurisprudence under the Contract Clause began with *United States Trust Co. v. New Jersey*[180] in which a 4-3 plurality invalidated a law rearranging a state's financial obligations to bondholders. New York and New Jersey repealed a covenant promising private investors in the Port Authority that their money would not be invested in mass transit. Writing for the plurality, Justice Blackmun held that legislative authorization to invest in the unprofitable field of mass transit violated the Contract Clause.

Unlike state interference with private contracts, which deserved legislative deference, a *public* contract in which the government was a party, required

---

[178]   For further reading on footnote four, *see* J. Ely, *supra* note 177; L. Lusky, By What Right? (1975); B. Ackerman, *Beyond Carolene Products*, 98 Harv. L. Rev. 713 (1985); J. Attanasio, *Everyman's Constitutional Law: A Theory of the Power of Judicial Review*, 72 Geo. L.J. 1665 (1984); L. Lusky, *Footnote Redux: A Carolene Products Reminiscence*, 82 Colum. L. Rev. 1093 (1982); L. Powell, *Carolene Products Revisited*, 82 Colum. L. Rev. 1087 (1982).

[179]   *See, e.g.*, Home Bldg. & Loan Ass'n v. Blaisdell, 290 U.S. 398 (1934) (upholding a law that extended the time to redeem property from foreclosure sale).

[180]   431 U.S. 1 (1977).

scrutiny because "the state's self-interest is at stake."[181] Without such scrutiny, the state could reduce, at will, its own financial obligations under the contract. Consequently, the Court would accept a law impairing public contracts involving the Port Authority only if it was "both reasonable and necessary to serve the admittedly important purposes"[182] of reducing automobile use and promoting mass transit. The means of totally repealing the covenant were neither necessary to achieve those goals nor reasonable under the circumstances. Indeed, the states could have pursued such goals with means that did not affect the states' covenant with the Port Authority's bondholders at all. For example, the states could have taxed parking or tunnel use and utilized the revenues to subsidize mass transit.

In a dissent joined by Justices White and Marshall, Justice Brennan objected to the Court's use of the Contract Clause to control legislative policy decisions. He criticized the "reasonable and necessary" standard, as the word "reasonable" generally indicated *de minimis* scrutiny, while the word "necessary" normally suggested strict scrutiny.

In 1978, the Court increased scrutiny for *private* contracts under Contract Clause in *Allied Structural Steel Co. v. Spannaus*.[183] In that case, the Court invalidated a Minnesota law modifying existing pension plans by imposing a surcharge on inadequate plans. Writing for the majority, Justice Stewart declared that the Contract Clause "must be understood to impose some limits upon the power of a state to abridge existing contractual relationships, even in the exercise of its otherwise legitimate police power."[184]

Justice Stewart found that the Court's normal deference to state legislation concerning broad social and economic issues did not apply in this case. The law did not even purportedly deal with a broad, generalized economic or social problem. It did not operate in an area already subject to state regulation at the time the company's contractual obligations were originally undertaken, but invaded an area never before subject to regulation by the State. The legislation did not temporarily alter the contractual relationships of those within its coverage, but worked a severe, permanent, and immediate change in those relationships-irrevocably and retroactively. Its narrow aim was leveled, not at every Minnesota employer, not even at every Minnesota employer who left the State, but only at those who had in the past been sufficiently enlightened as voluntarily to agree to establish pension plans for their employees.[185] Many of these criteria were vague and amorphous. They left open the possibility for greatly expanded scrutiny under the Contract Clause.

In a dissent joined by Justices White and Marshall, Justice Brennan asserted that the Contract Clause applied only when existing contractual obligations were diminished or nullified. Justice Brennan argued that the Court improperly

---

[181] *Id.* at 26.

[182] *Id.* at 29.

[183] 438 U.S. 234 (1978).

[184] *Id.* at 242.

[185] *See id.* at 250 (citations omitted).

expanded the scope of the Contract Clause to prohibit the creation of new legislatively-imposed duties.

Although *United States Trust* and *Spannaus* seemed to indicate the Court's willingness to use the Contract Clause to invalidate state regulation of both public and private contracts, subsequent cases have demonstrated a renewal of deference to state legislative decisions in both areas. The Court announced the prevailing standard for Contract Clause challenges in *Energy Reserves Group, Inc. v. Kansas Power & Light Co.*[186] The statute at issue interfered with a price escalation clause in a private natural gas contract.

Under the current three-prong test, the threshold inquiry for scrutiny was the requirement that state law must substantially impair the contractual relationship. This requirement has proven fairly difficult to satisfy. In making this determination, prior regulation of the affected industry has been an important consideration.

If a court determined that the challenged law substantially impaired the contractual relationship, the state must justify its action by having "a significant and legitimate public purpose behind the regulation, such as the remedying of a broad and general social or economic problem."[187] After concluding that a legitimate purpose justified the regulation, the court must decide "whether the adjustment of 'the rights and responsibilities of contracting parties' "[188] was "reasonable" and "appropriate."

Applying the test to the facts of the case, the Court questioned whether the price controls were even a substantial impairment of the price escalator contractual provisions. Whether a substantial impairment existed hinged on the reasonable expectations of the contracting parties. As natural gas was a heavily regulated industry, the imposition of price controls could have been reasonably expected.

Even if a substantial impairment had existed, the price controls advanced the legitimate interest of protecting consumers against higher prices in the context of natural gas deregulation. Finally, the means chosen were reasonable. Absent circumstances such as special interest or the involvement of the government as a contracting party,[189] the Court afforded great deference to economic and social legislation. The temporary nature of the price regulation at issue reinforced its reasonableness.

In *Exxon Corp. v. Eagerton*,[190] the Court rejected a Contract Clause challenge to an act prohibiting oil companies from passing on several taxes to consumers, even though pre-existing contracts required consumer absorption of such tax increases. The Court held that substantial impairment did not exist when a

---

[186] 459 U.S. 400 (1983).

[187] *Id.* at 411–12 (citations omitted).

[188] *Id.* at 412.

[189] The Court found that such circumstances existed in *United States Trust* and *Spannaus*, and distinguished the cases on these grounds.

[190] 462 U.S. 176 (1983).

"generally applicable rule of conduct"[191] had an incidental effect on contracts: the restriction at issue in *Eagerton* applied regardless of whether a particular contract contained a pass-through provision. The Court's unwillingness to find a substantial impairment in this context accentuated its renewed deference in the Contract Clause area.

The Contract Clause does not apply to the federal government, which is restricted by the Due Process Clause of the Fifth Amendment from impairing its own contractual obligations or those of others. However, the Due Process Clause affords little protection against impairments of contractual obligations wrought by the federal government. In *National Railroad Passenger Corp. v. Atchison, Topeka & Santa Fe Railway Co.*,[192] the Court unanimously upheld a Congressional statute altering the reimbursement scheme compelling the railroads to indemnify Amtrak for the cost of providing pass privileges to the railroads' employees. The railroads argued that Congress violated the agreements by which the railroads had turned their passenger service over to Amtrak. Although these agreements had been entered into pursuant to a federal statute, the Court held that they did not constitute a contractual agreement between the United States and the railroads. Nor was there any contractual right created either by the 1970 statute establishing Amtrak or by a 1972 act creating the reimbursement formula that was altered again in 1979. The Court would not lightly assume a Congressional intent to bind itself; and in any case, Congress had explicitly reserved a broad power to alter the statute. Congress had not bargained away its Commerce Clause power to alter the reimbursement formula.

The Court also rejected the claim that Congress had violated the Due Process Clause by impairing a private contractual right. Congress remained free to " 'adjus[t] the burdens and benefits of economic life.' "[193] To meet the due process standard, Congress need only show that it acted rationally in spreading the costs of employee passenger travel among the various parties.

[3] Government Takings of Property Requiring Just Compensation

[a] The Public Use Requirement

The Fifth Amendment's guarantee against taking without just compensation was one of the earliest constitutional protections of economic rights incorporated into the Fourteenth Amendment.[194] The power of "eminent domain" allows federal, state, or local governments to take private property for public use, so long as government pays the owner just compensation, which is the fair market value of the property.

---

[191] *Id.* at 191.

[192] 470 U.S. 451 (1985).

[193] *Id.* at 476.

[194] *See* Chicago, Burlington & Quincy R. Co. v. Chicago, 166 U.S. 226 (1897).

The Fifth Amendment does not prohibit government takings of property, but only requires just compensation. The explicit language of the amendment only permits government to take property for public use. In *Hawaii Housing Authority v. Midkiff,*[195] the Court interpreted the "public use" requirement broadly. A Hawaii statute sought to redistribute the state's heavily concentrated land ownership by transferring fee simple title to tenants occupying privately-owned property. The Land Reform Act of 1967 allowed the state to condemn the property, compensate the landowner, and sell title to the tenant.

Writing for a unanimous Court, Justice O'Connor upheld the statute. Although the Act transferred title from one private owner to another, Justice O'Connor found the attempt to distribute ownership more evenly among the community to be a valid public purpose.[196] Showing deference to legislative judgment, the Court stated that the exercise of eminent domain need only be rationally related to its objective.

Following *Midkiff, Kelo v. City of New London*[197] held that a city's taking property for economic development did not violate the public use requirement of the Takings Clause. The City targeted for economic revitalization an area near a new private $300 million research facility. The targeted area would contain research and development office space and support the nearby state park or marina with visitor parking or retail.

Writing for the majority, Justice Stevens said "it has long been accepted that the sovereign may not take the property of A for the sole purpose of transferring it to another private party B, even though A is paid just compensation." However, government "may transfer property from one private party to another" for future public use. The takings at issue were not intended to help any "private entity, but instead, to revitalize the local economy." Although a private developer would be involved, the identities of the private parties to whom it would lease the space were unknown when the plan was adopted.

Public purposes "will often benefit individual private parties." The Court deferred to the legislature regarding the plan's effectiveness and the lands necessary to carry it out. States may "impose 'public use' requirements that are stricter than the federal baseline."

Justice Kennedy concurred. *Hawaii Housing Authority v. Midkiff*[198] permitted a taking "as long as it is 'rationally related to a conceivable public purpose.' " Still, the public use requirement may forbid transfers favoring particular private entities, "with only incidental or pretextual public benefits." However, this taking was part "of a comprehensive development plan meant to address a serious city-wide depression" when "the identity of most of the private beneficiaries [was] unknown."

Justice O'Connor dissented, joined by Chief Justice Rehnquist, and Justices Scalia and Thomas. "The Court effectively eliminates the 'for public use' require- ment. Consequently, private property can be "transferred to another private owner,

---

[195]   467 U.S. 229 (1984).

[196]   *Id.* at 244.

[197]   545 U.S. 469 (2005).

[198]   467 U.S. 229 (1984).

so long as it might be upgraded," even when the only advantage was increased tax revenues or increasing the prosperity of an already prosperous city. The likely beneficiaries of this rule would be "citizens with disproportionate influence and power in the political process, including large corporations and development firms."

In a separate dissent, Justice Thomas would reconsider *Hawaii Housing Authority v. Midkiff*: Urban renewal projects frequently displaced blacks.

[b] Physical versus Regulatory Takings

The scope of the Takings Clause remains critical. While finding a taking does not preclude regulation, it determines which government actions require compensation. The easiest way to find a taking is through government occupation or expropriation of property for itself. Physical invasions can comprise takings even if government does not expropriate the property for itself. In *Loretto v. Teleprompter Manhattan CATV Corp.*,[199] the Court found that cable television companies' permanent encroachments on rental property were takings, even though the physical invasion of the apartment house only consisted of cables less than 1/2 inch in diameter and had a minimal economic impact on the owner. The Court held that a permanent physical occupation caused by the government is basically a *per se* taking.

A taking need not be a complete physical occupation of the property to be compensable, although government appropriation of property for its own use is more likely to result in a taking. To the extent that regulations diminish the value of property, they could be deemed takings requiring just compensation. Widespread use of regulatory takings would increase the cost of government regulation and thereby severely impair government's ability to regulate. It could also revisit *Lochner*-type problems of severely circumscribing government regulations. Perhaps, for this reason, the Court has been reluctant to find regulatory takings.

The early defining case balancing property rights and police power was *Pennsylvania Coal Co. v. Mahon*.[200] In *Pennsylvania Coal*, a state statute prohibited mining in areas where a building might be caused to sink as a result of the quarry. The Kohler Act took part of the coal company's property by prohibiting it from mining certain coal.

Writing for the majority, Justice Holmes delineated the test that would dominate the Court's takings jurisprudence for years to come. He balanced the extent of the property right's diminution with the public interest served by the regulation. Regulation to a certain extent was permissible, but regulation that "goes too far"[201] was considered a taking.

Justice Holmes found that the Kohler Act served a limited public interest and was not justified by public safety concerns. He invalidated the Act because he found the extent of the taking to be too great. Commenting on the general validity of the

---

[199] 458 U.S. 419 (1982).

[200] 260 U.S. 393 (1922).

[201] *Id.* at 415.

Act, Justice Holmes noted that the Kohler Act was not a valid exercise of the police power because it served only the private interests of the landowners and coal companies affected. Health and safety concerns would have been adequately addressed by giving notice of the mining to the affected homes' occupants. Secondly, the Kohler Act lacked validity because it diminished the value of the affected land and made coal mining in the affected areas "commercially impracticable."[202]

In *Pennsylvania Coal*, Justice Holmes also established his "reciprocity of advantage"[203] theory by which property owners were expected to endure certain regulations restricting property rights if there was greater societal benefit. For example, in *Miller v. Schoene*[204] the Court held that the Takings Clause did not require Virginia to compensate the owners of cedar trees that the state had destroyed to prevent the spread of disease. Regardless of whether the trees constituted a nuisance under common law or statute, Virginia could destroy them to avert an impending danger.

Pennsylvania Coal was seriously called into question in *Keystone Bituminous Coal Ass'n v. DeBenedictis*.[205] The Court refused a takings challenge in a factual situation very similar to that of *Pennsylvania Coal*. In *Keystone*, a coal mining association and various corporations challenged the Pennsylvania Subsidence Act, which required vast quantities of coal to be left unmined as surface support for structures on top of coal mines. Although *Keystone* did not expressly overrule *Pennsylvania Coal*, the Court dramatically narrowed that case (particularly those parts that Justice Stevens considered an advisory opinion).

Writing for a 5-4 majority, Justice Stevens distinguished *Pennsylvania Coal* on two grounds. First, the Subsidence Act at issue in *Keystone*, in contrast to the Kohler Act in *Pennsylvania Coal*, exhibited a real interest in safety. Unlike the Kohler Act, the Subsidence Act did not provide a blanket exemption that allowed mining wherever the coal company also owned the surface estate.[206] Second, in contrast to the interests of private property in the Kohler Act, the Subsidence Act articulated broader public interests in conservation and in the environment.

One theory that Justice Stevens used to uphold the Subsidence Act was the nuisance exception to a taking. Under this exception, individuals have no right to use their property to create a public nuisance; therefore, the state's prohibition of that activity did not deprive the owner of any lawful use of his property. In *Keystone*, Pennsylvania's prohibition of coal mine subsidence did not deprive the companies of any lawful uses of the affected property. Therefore, the Court refused to find a regulatory taking.

This concept related to Justice Holmes' "reciprocity of advantage" theory from *Pennsylvania Coal*. In *Keystone*, the coal companies' mineral rights affected the

---

[202] *Id.* at 414.

[203] *Id.* at 415.

[204] 276 U.S. 272 (1928).

[205] 480 U.S. 470 (1987).

[206] The Subsidence Act did, however, empower the state to permit such exemption.

surface owner's property rights. In an economically integrated society, government had the power to regulate the distribution of these advantages without owing compensation to either party.

Another theory supporting the finding of no regulatory taking was that the companies failed to make a sufficient showing of diminution of investments or investment-backed expectations. The majority viewed the regulation as only affecting one *strand* of the total mineral estate. This characterization of what was being taken was the central point of conflict between the majority and the dissent. The dissent focused on the fact that 27 million tons of coal were "taken" by the regulation, whereas the majority stressed that the coal taken represented only 2 percent of the company's coal located in the mines at issue.

From the majority's perspective, the regulation's operation on a very small percentage of the total amount of coal in place did not affect the coal company's reasonable, investment-backed expectations. In short, the regulation did not render profitable mining "commercially impracticable," as the Kohler Act did in *Pennsylvania Coal.*

Justice Stevens also rejected the coal companies' argument that the regulation had the effect of taking their support estate, which according to the regulation had to be left in place in the affected areas. The Court refused to predicate constitutional jurisprudence on state-law distinctions between support estates, mineral estates and surface estates. Instead, it preferred to consider the regulation's effect on the property rights as a whole. Even if the Court had been willing to consider the support estate separately, the record lacked evidence of the affected percentage of the support estate, which would have been necessary to sustain the heavy burden of a facial challenge.

The Court's view of a regulation's effect on the total "bundle" of property rights figures prominently in modern Takings Clause analysis. In *Penn Central Transportation Co. v. New York,*[207] the Court rejected a takings challenge to a New York City landmarks preservation statute that was applied so as to restrict a developer's right to build a skyscraper over Grand Central Station, one of many historic buildings that had been designated as a landmark. The Court found that the restrictions imposed were substantially related to the promotion of the general welfare. They not only permitted reasonable beneficial use of the landmark site, but also allowed the owner to transfer development rights from the landmark site to other property of the owner, thereby permitting development of such other property beyond applicable zoning restrictions.

Writing for the majority, Justice Brennan listed several factors, similar to the ones in *Keystone*, that helped to determine whether a taking had occurred: "The economic impact of the regulation on the claimant and, particularly, the extent to which the regulation has interfered with distinct investment-backed expectations are, of course, relevant considerations. So, too, is the character of the governmental action."[208] Moreover, a " 'taking' may more readily be found when the interference

---

[207] 438 U.S. 104 (1978).

[208] *Id.* at 124.

with the property can be characterized as a physical invasion . . . than when interference arises from some public program adjusting the benefits and burdens of economic life to promote the common good."[209]

The Court relied on the "bundle of sticks" theory of property ownership to find that the regulation did not interfere with property rights as a whole. Justice Brennan analogized the statute to a zoning ordinance. The dissent found no reciprocity of advantage in the regulation, and said it did not evenly distribute burdens like zoning, but concentrated the burden on landmark owners.

In *Babbitt v. Youpee*[210] the Court struck down as an unconstitutional taking a law requiring certain fractional interests of devised Indian land to escheat to the tribe. Youpee's will devised to his children and potential heirs his several undivided interests in his land. These lands, worth $1,239, escheated to the tribal government. The Court held that this escheating provision completely abrogated one of the sticks in the bundle of property rights: the statute unconstitutionally restricted the rights of a testator to direct the descent of property. The land's value, unlike the value of its yearly production, could not be said to be minimal.

[i]   Regulatory Takings

Consistent with *Keystone* and *Penn Central*, the Court generally has continued to demonstrate reluctance in finding regulatory takings. In *Connolly v. Pension Benefit Guaranty Corp.*,[211] the Court rejected a Takings Clause challenge to a statute that required employers who withdrew from certain government insured multi-member pension plans to pay a proportionate share of vested benefits. The government imposed the requirement to avoid having to pay benefits to plans that terminated with insufficient assets. The employers claimed that the congressionally-mandated liability comprised a taking because it exceeded the amount for which employers would have been liable under their collective bargaining agreements. Creating a financial burden and interfering with an existing agreement did not constitute a taking, particularly when the amount was not out of proportion to the employers' experience with the plan and consequently was within reasonable, investment-backed expectations.

In *First English Evangelical Lutheran Church v. County of Los Angeles*,[212] the Court stated that the Takings Clause required government compensation for temporary takings. An interim ordinance, enacted after fire and flooding destroyed a church retreat, temporarily prohibited the church from rebuilding. Writing for the majority, Chief Justice Rehnquist found that temporary takings, depriving a landowner of all use of his land, were indistinguishable from permanent takings. The Court held that a constitutionally sufficient remedy required just compensation for the use of property during the time the invalidated ordinance was in effect.

---

[209] *Id.*

[210] 519 U.S. 234 (1997).

[211] 475 U.S. 211 (1986).

[212] 482 U.S. 304 (1987).

The dissent in *First English* expressed concern that the majority's holding would chill government regulation in the land use area. If government was required to compensate landowners for regulations later found by the courts to be takings, government might fear enacting many land use laws.

The Court in *Lucas v. South Carolina Coastal Council* held that regulations which "prohibit all economically beneficial use of land" constitute a taking.[213] The South Carolina legislature passed a law prohibiting construction in certain coastal zones, which barred Lucas from building homes on island land he had recently purchased. Justice Scalia, writing for the Court, explained that compensation must accompany a regulation which "declares 'off-limits' all economically productive or beneficial uses of land."[214] The government's only defense to a "total taking" is if a court would have prohibited use of the land anyway under property-law principles such as nuisance.[215]

In *Tahoe-Sierra Preservation Council, Inc. v. Tahoe Regional Planning Agency*,[216] the Court held that a government order, stopping all development while "devising a comprehensive land-use plan," did not constitute a "*per se* taking of property requiring compensation." While studying the "impact of development on Lake Tahoe and designing a strategy for environmentally sound growth," the Tahoe Regional Planning Agency (TRPA) ordered two moratoria, which, in combination, prohibited construction on certain land for 32 months, and on certain other land for 8 months.

Applying the *Penn Central* framework, Justice Stevens concluded that no *per se* taking had occurred. Condemnations and physical takings involve a "straightforward" *per se* takings analysis; however, the Court's regulatory takings jurisprudence, as in this case, "is characterized by 'essentially ad hoc, factual inquires,'" carefully weighing all the circumstances. *Penn Central's* framework "focuses both on the character of the action and on the nature and extent of the interference with rights in the parcel as a whole." As land use regulations were "ubiquitous" and generally affected property values in "tangential" and "unanticipated" ways, treating them all as *per se* takings would deter governments from regulating at all.

In *First English Evangelical Lutheran Church v. County of Los Angeles*,[217] the California courts decided that a taking had occurred, and the Supreme Court only decided the question of remedy. Indeed, *First English* stated that the county's authority to enact safety regulations might preclude a temporary, total denial of property use from being considered a taking. Moreover, the *First English* Court recognized "'the quite different questions that would arise in the case of normal delays in obtaining building permits, changes in zoning ordinances, variances, and the like which [were] not before us.'" A taking occurs when government permits

---

[213] 505 U.S. 1003, 1029 (1992).

[214] *Id.* at 1030.

[215] *Id.*

[216] 535 U.S. 302 (2002).

[217] 482 U.S. 304 (1987).

" '*no* productive or economically beneficial use of land.' "[218] If there is not a total taking of the entire parcel, then *Penn Central* applies.

Justice Stevens considered whether the burden of regulation was more fairly placed on the property owner or on the entire public. Justice Stevens rejected a *per se* rule because it would apply to many exercises of police power, including " 'normal delays in obtaining building permits, changes in zoning ordinances, variances, and the like,' as well as to orders temporarily prohibiting access to crime scenes, businesses that violate health codes, [and] fire-damaged buildings." Planners must have adequate time to make "well-reasoned decisions." Government's interest in well-reasoned decisions becomes "even stronger" when regional planning occurs. In any event, assuring Lake Tahoe's "pristine state" will only help property values.

Chief Justice Rehnquist dissented, joined by Justices Scalia and Thomas. For Chief Justice Rehnquist, "the 'temporary' denial of all viable use of land for six years is a taking." Certain categories of public and private nuisances, such as fast-food restaurants, can still be abated without effecting a taking. Similarly, short-term building delays caused by "zoning and permit regimes are a longstanding feature of state property law and part of a landowner's reasonable investment-backed expectations." Justice Thomas dissented, joined by Justice Scalia. He said that *First English* treated all total deprivations as takings, regardless of whether they are temporary or permanent. Justice Thomas also maintained that "potential future value bears on the amount of compensation" rather than on whether a taking had occurred.

[ii] Takings as a Government Condition for Granting a Permit

In *Nollan v. California Coastal Commission*,[219] the Court held that conditioning a building permit on a landowner's grant of a public easement across his land constituted a taking. When the plaintiff wanted to rebuild on his property, the state conditioned the granting of the building permit on the landowner giving the state a 10-foot easement running parallel to the beach. The state contended that if it was not required to permit development at all, it could require such an easement to further legitimate public purposes. The Court held that the access condition violated the Takings Clause.

Writing for the Court, Justice Scalia found that the government had not established a nexus between a legitimate governmental objective of nondevelopment and the means of exacting the easement. In the majority's opinion, the permit condition did nothing to aid the public already using the community beaches to view or enjoy the waterfront. It did not reduce obstacles to viewing the beach caused by the construction of the new home, alleviate psychological barriers to using the beach, or remedy beach congestion also caused by the construction of the new home.

---

[218] *See* Lucas v. South Carolina Coastal Council, 505 U.S. 1003 (1992). As Chief Justice Rehnquist noted in his dissent, while the taking in *Lucas* lasted only two years, the one here lasted almost six.

[219] 483 U.S. 825 (1987).

Dissenting, Justice Brennan, joined by Justice Marshall, criticized the majority's introduction of this new nexus requirement. Particularly when combined with the *First English* requirement of just compensation for a temporary taking, the nexus requirement would only serve to increase the chilling effect on land use regulation. The vagueness of the *Nollan* nexus requirement only exacerbated this chilling effect on potential regulation.

The Court more extensively defined this nexus requirement in *Dolan v. City of Tigard*.[220] In *Dolan*, a 5-4 majority of the Court invalidated a zoning commission's conditioning a building permit on the dedication of some property for public use, because "rough proportionality" did not exist between the conditions and the improvement's impact.

Plaintiff Florence Dolan challenged the City of Tigard's permit condition requiring her to dedicate part of her property for flood control and traffic alleviation. These conditions would exact 7,000 square feet, or 10 percent of Dolan's property, and were adopted pursuant to the city's Master Drainage Plan and the Community Development Code. Writing for the Court, Chief Justice Rehnquist invalidated both of these conditions. The city's action would surely have been a taking had the city simply required Dolan to dedicate her land to public use, rather than making the dedication a condition of zoning approval. On the other hand, "land use regulation does not effect a taking if it 'substantially advance[s] legitimate state interests' and does not 'den[y] an owner economically viable use of his land.' "[221] The Chief Justice explained that what set this case apart from zoning and other land use regulations was (1) the specific, adjudicative nature of the conditions, and (2) the fact that the conditions did not simply regulate Dolan's use of her property, but required her to surrender part of her property to public access. As such, the case involved the unconstitutional conditions doctrine. Specifically, "the government may not require a person to give up a constitutional right — here the right to receive just compensation when property is taken for a public use — in exchange for a discretionary benefit conferred by the government where the property sought has little or no relationship to the benefit."[222]

To evaluate the constitutionality of the permit conditions, the Court employed a two-pronged approach: (1) does the "essential nexus," required by *Nollan*, exist between the conditions and the legitimate state interests that the city seeks to advance by them; and (2) does a sufficient connection exist between the conditions and the impact of the new development? The dedication of land for a public drainage system theoretically could advance the city's interest in flood control, and the pathway provision could reduce traffic congestion. Thus both conditions satisfied the "essential nexus" prong.

Turning to the second prong, the Court outlined a "rough proportionality" test: "the city must make some sort of individualized determination that the required dedication is related both in nature and extent to the impact of the proposed

---

[220] 512 U.S. 374 (1994).

[221] *Dolan*, 512 U.S. at 385 (quoting *Agins v. Tiburon*, 447 U.S. 255, 260 (1980)).

[222] *Id.*

development."[223] In applying the second prong to the public drainage system, the Court emphasized that the "city has never said why a public greenway, as opposed to a private one, was required in the interest of flood control."[224] A public greenway deprived Dolan of her right to exclude others, one of the most essential property rights. Depriving Dolan of her right to decide when and where the public would enter her property was not proportional to her development's potential impact on drainage into the creek. The bicycle pathway dedication condition likewise encroached on Dolan's right to exclude. While the Court did not require a "precise mathematical calculation," the city had to "make some effort to quantify its findings in support of the dedication for the pedestrian/bicycle pathway beyond the conclusory statement that it could offset some of the traffic demand generated."[225] The city did not find that the bicycle pathway " '*will*, or is *likely to*, offset some of the traffic demand.' "[226]

Justice Stevens dissented, joined by Justices Blackmun and Ginsburg. Justice Stevens first asserted the absence of any doubt that the impact of Dolan's development would justify the city in denying her permit outright. He then agreed with the majority that this fact did not give the city carte blanche to impose arbitrary conditions in lieu of a permit denial. Nevertheless, he criticized the Court's new "rough proportionality" test. Justice Stevens emphasized the inherent uncertainty in predicting the effects of urban development.

In a separate dissent, Justice Souter argued that the city had established the *Nollan* nexus by calculating the increased traffic flow of 435 trips and submitting studies correlating decreased traffic congestion with alternative means of transportation. He also argued that the majority, through its expansion of "regulatory takings" doctrine, was resurrecting the kind of substantive due process approach exemplified by the discredited *Lochner* case.

[iii] Takings Clause in Other Contexts

As discussed in *Keystone* and *Penn Central*, land use regulation other than condemnation can prompt takings claims. Zoning is a common government regulation of property that can result in Takings Clause challenges. As illustrated in *Penn Central*, the Court generally affords zoning measures substantial deference. *Goldblatt v. Hempstead*,[227] for example, denied a takings challenge to a zoning ordinance that forced the plaintiff out of the sand and gravel business by prohibiting, for safety reasons, excavations below the water table.

Several of the Court's land use opinions involve rent control regulations. In *Pennell v. City of San Jose*,[228] the Court rejected a challenge to a San Jose rent control statute. The takings claim was based on a provision of the statute that

---

[223] *Id.* at 391.

[224] *Id.* at 393.

[225] *Id.* at 395–96.

[226] *Id.* at 395.

[227] 369 U.S. 590 (1962).

[228] 485 U.S. 1 (1988).

allowed tenant hardship to be considered as an objective factor by hearing officers in determining whether to approve a rent increase proposed by a landlord. The landlords argued that the provision was invalid because it forced them to subsidize housing for impoverished tenants. Chief Justice Rehnquist concluded that the takings claim was premature because tenant hardship was but one of the totality of factors relied upon by the hearing officers, who could approve requested increases even if hardship would result.

In *Yee v. City of Escondido*,[229] the Court rejected the claim made by mobile home park owners that a municipal rent control ordinance, when considered along with California's Mobilehome Residency Law, violated the Takings Clause. The regulations limited the bases of terminating tenancy and imposed rent ceilings. These laws did not effectuate a physical invasion of the property; whether these laws effected a regulatory taking was an issue not before the Court. While Justice O'Connor listed the "right to exclude" as one of the most important sticks in the bundle of property rights, she refused to sustain a facial challenge on the grounds of physical impairment, preferring instead to characterize the regulations as use regulations. Had the State not permitted termination of a tenancy, a facial or as-applied challenge may have been appropriate. However, California did provide a means for raising rent and for termination of the tenancy for nonpayment of rent, or for applying it to other uses.

The Takings Clause can also apply to property interests beyond real property. *Ruckelshaus v. Monsanto Co.*,[230] addressed trade secrets, and shed light on what comprises a reasonable, investment-backed expectation. The Federal Insecticide, Fungicide, and Rodenticide Act (FIFRA) required pesticide companies to submit information about certain products monitored by the Environmental Protection Agency (EPA). In 1972, Congress modified the law to permit companies to designate certain information as trade secrets that could not be publicly disclosed. In 1978, Congress amended the law to allow public disclosure of health, safety, and environmental data submitted to the EPA even if the information constituted a trade secret. In response to Monsanto's challenge that revealing their trade secrets was a taking, the Court held that disclosure of post-1978 information did not comprise a taking. Since Monsanto was aware of the disclosure condition, and the condition was rationally related to a legitimate government interest, disclosure was simply an exchange of information for the economic benefit of registration. Nor was there any investment-backed expectation in disclosure of pre-1972 information: in such a heavily regulated industry as pesticides, the company could have had no reasonable, investment-backed expectation of confidentiality. For the 1972-1978 period, however, Congress itself had created such an expectation by its explicit promise of confidentiality. Consequently, EPA disclosure of trade secrets submitted during that time period would comprise a taking.

In *Andrus v. Allard*,[231] the Court upheld a law that prohibited the sale of property because the law only deprived the owner of one strand of his whole

---

[229] 503 U.S. 519 (1992).

[230] 467 U.S. 986 (1984).

[231] 444 U.S. 51 (1979).

property interest. The statutes at issue prohibited commercial dealing in parts of birds that had been legally killed before the laws became effective. The challenge to the statutes resulted from appellees' prosecution for selling Indian artifacts containing such bird parts.

The statutes did not however, prohibit possession, transportation, donation, or exhibition of the property for a profit. The Court considered the entire property to determine whether the regulation deprived owners of their reasonable investment-backed expectations. It examined whether the owner could still have made a profit from the property, taken as a whole, after the regulation. The modern Court also has focused on this factor in its Contract Clause jurisprudence.[232]

In *Phillips v. Washington Legal Foundation*,[233] the Texas law at issue required Texas attorneys entrusted with nominal or short term funds to deposit those funds into an Interest on Lawyers Trust Account (IOLTA). The interest proceeds from IOLTA accounts were to fund low-income legal assistance programs. The Court determined that the interest earned on the IOLTA accounts was "private property" of the client whose funds comprised the principal deposited into the account. Writing for the Court, Chief Justice Rehnquist rejected the argument that the interest lacked the character of private property because the funds could not " 'reasonably be expected to generate interest income on their own.' "[234] Texas followed the English common law rule established in the mid-1700s that " 'interest follows principal.' "[235] A state could not salvage confiscatory regulations by changing its longstanding rule. A characterization as property derives not only from an item's economic value but also from prerogatives of use, possession, and disposition. The Court remanded to the lower court the issues of whether a taking existed or compensation was required.

Justice Souter dissented, joined by Justices Stevens, Ginsburg, and Breyer. No taking existed as the accounts do not resemble an investment, and the client could not earn interest, with or without IOLTA. Justice Breyer, joined by Justices Souter and Ginsburg, filed a separate dissent, arguing that no one could have expected to receive interest without IOLTA.

While *Phillips* held that interest generated by IOLTA accounts was the property of the clients who owned the principal, the Court did not address whether the State had "taken" the income nor did it address the amount of just compensation that the clients were due. *Brown v. Legal Foundation of Washington*[236] held that a law requiring that funds that cannot earn interest for a client be deposited in an IOLTA account was not a regulatory taking. The IOLTA program only regulated funds that could not earn net interest for the client. An attorney acts in an ethical and legal way when he deposited multiple clients' funds into a single bank account. A *per se* taking could have occurred had the law required the interest earned on funds deposited into an IOLTA account to be

---

[232] *See supra* § 8.05[2].

[233] 524 U.S. 156 (1998).

[234] *Id.* at 169.

[235] *Id.* at 174.

[236] 538 U.S. 216 (2003).

transferred to a third party for a legitimate public use. In *Brown*, however, no taking occurred as the owner's pecuniary loss was zero. This net interest was determined after transaction costs, administrative costs, and bank fees had been deducted. In *Penn Central Transportation Co. v. New York City*, the Court denied a taking because the transaction did not have an "adverse economic impact" on the petitioners and it "did not interfere with any investment-backed expectation."[237] Just compensation is not measured by the government's gain, but rather by the property owner's loss. If the owner's net loss is zero, the compensation due is also zero.

As computer technology advances, net interest could be able to accumulate with smaller amounts of money held for shorter periods of time. As this occurs, *Washington* required that more trust money be invested for the clients' benefit. Moreover, a law that required this interest to be transferred to another for a legitimate public use could be construed as a *per se* taking, which would require just compensation to the client.

Justice Scalia dissented, joined by Chief Justice Rehnquist and Justices Kennedy and Thomas. Commonly, the state owes owners of confiscated property just compensation measured by its fair market value. Whether the clients could have earned interest without IOLTA's pooling arrangement was irrelevant. Justice Kennedy filed a separate dissent.

In the criminal forfeiture context, the Court in *Bennis v. Michigan*[238] held that the Takings Clause does not apply when the government lawfully acquires property by an equitable forfeiture action under a public nuisance statute.

The Court has also considered whether the Takings Clause can apply to action by the judicial branch. In *Stop the Beach Renourishment, Inc. v. Florida Department of Environmental Protection* the Court unanimously found no Fifth Amendment taking.[239] Under Florida law, as interpreted by the Florida Supreme Court, the beachfront owners had suffered no property right infringement from the state filling in submerged coastline as public land. The disagreement among the Justices arose over the plurality's assertion that the Takings Clause applies to the judicial branch, which the other Justices found was unnecessary to reach the result as no taking had occurred.

The Florida Supreme Court had concluded that the doctrine of avulsion permitted the State to reclaim the restored beach as public land. The property owners appealed on the grounds that "the Florida Supreme Court's decision itself effected a taking of the Members' littoral rights contrary to the *Fifth* and *Fourteenth Amendments*."[240]

Justice Scalia wrote for a unanimous Court in holding that no taking occurred under Florida law as interpreted by the Florida Supreme Court's assertion that the Takings Clause applies to the judicial branch. However, Justice Scalia, who

---

[237] *Id.* at 234.

[238] 516 U.S. 442 (1996). For additional discussion of this case, *see supra* § 8.02.

[239] 130 S. Ct. 2592 (2010).

[240] *Id.* at 2600.

maintained that "the particular state *actor* is irrelevant," was only joined by the Chief Justice and Justices Thomas and Alito.[241] A state cannot "do by judicial decree what the *Takings Clause* forbids it to do by legislative fiat."[242] Had the Supreme Court found "that the Florida Supreme Court had effected an uncompensated taking" it would not have ordered Florida to pay compensation. Instead, the Court would simply have reversed "the judgment that the Beach and Shore Preservation Act can be applied" to the property, leaving the "power to effect a *compensated* taking" with the Florida Legislature.[243]

Justice Kennedy, joined by Justice Sotomayor, concurred in part and in the judgment. Justice Kennedy agreed with Justice Breyer that "this case does not require the Court to determine whether, or when, a judicial decision determining the rights of property owners can violate the *Takings Clause of the Fifth Amendment*."[244] Instead of the Takings Clause, the Due Process Clause offers a "strong footing" for overruling as "arbitrary or irrational" a judicial taking.[245] Judicial takings raise difficult questions, such as a temporary taking that would occur if a state court rescinded its decision that changed the law. Such issues should caution the Court not to "reach beyond the necessities of the case to recognize a judicial takings doctrine."

Justice Breyer also concurred in part and in the judgment, joined by Justice Ginsburg. As state courts decide so many property rights cases each year, the plurality's approach may result in "constitutional review of many, perhaps large numbers of, state-law cases in an area of law familiar to state, but not federal, judges."[246] Justice Stevens took no part in the case.

[4]   Economic Penalties

A final area of the Court's economic rights jurisprudence involves excessive penalties. In recent years, the Court has examined general challenges to large punitive awards first under the Excessive Fines Clause of the Eighth Amendment and then under the Due Process Clause. In *Browning-Ferris Industries, Inc. v. Kelco Disposal, Inc.*,[247] the Court refused to apply the Excessive Fines Clause to punitive damages awards in cases between private parties. Plaintiff Kelco was awarded $51,146 in compensatory damages and $6 million in punitive damages. Defendant appealed claiming that the punitive damages award, 117 times larger than the actual compensatory damages, violated the Eighth Amendment's proscription against excessive fines.

Writing for the majority, Justice Blackmun emphasized that the Framers had not intended the Excessive Fines Clause to apply "when the government neither

---

[241] *Id.* at 2602.

[242] *Id.* at 2601.

[243] *Id.* at 2607.

[244] *Id.* at 2613 (Kennedy, J., concurring).

[245] *Id.* at 2615.

[246] *Id.* at 2619 (Breyer, J., concurring).

[247] 492 U.S. 257 (1989).

has prosecuted the action nor has any right to receive a share of the damages awarded."[248] The Excessive Fines Clause did not apply between private parties. The Court noted, however, that its ruling did not foreclose the possibility of a due process challenge for disproportionate punitive awards.

In *United States v. Bajakajian*,[249] the Court invalidated, under the Excessive Fines Clause, the forfeiture of $357,144 as a penalty for the crime of transporting more than $10,000 in currency. Federal law specifically provided that those violating the law would forfeit the unreported property. Writing for the Court, Justice Thomas struck down the forfeiture because forfeiture of all the currency was "grossly disproportional to the gravity of his offense."[250]

Generally, forfeiture in an *in rem* or *in personam* action constitutes a fine if it is meant, even to a small degree, to be punishment. The statute at issue dealt with criminal, *in personam* forfeitures, which generally are regarded as punitive. The Court rejected the government's argument that the currency was an instrumentality of the crime because the government proceeded against Bajakajian *in personam* rather than against the currency *in rem*. In any event, the cash did not "facilitate the commission of the crime" in the way that a automobile conceals and transports goods to facilitate the crime of tax avoidance.

Having established that the forfeiture was punitive, the Court then assessed whether it was grossly disproportional by measuring the forfeiture against the seriousness of the crime. The maximum criminal sentence for failing to report was six months and a fine of $5,000. The forfeiture was significantly larger than the District Court's $5,000 fine and was not comparable to or measurable by any governmental loss in which the purpose of monetary forfeiture was to reimburse some loss of the Government. Moreover, the procedure was civil, not criminal.

Justice Kennedy's dissenting opinion argued that the cash was an instrumentality of the crime because the cash was the object of the crime of cash smuggling. Furthermore, not reporting the transportation of currency often indicated other crimes, like drug smuggling and tax evasion. Without the forfeiture, the fine was a modest cost of conducting the illegal business.

Pacific Mutual Life Insurance Co. v. Haslip[251] rejected a due process challenge to punitive damages that were more than four times compensatory damages and 200 times the amount of plaintiff's out-of-pocket expenses. The case involved an Alabama woman who was denied a medical insurance payment after one of Pacific Mutual's agents absconded with her premiums.

Justice Blackmun, writing for the majority, declared that the common law method of assessing punitive damages was not *per se* unconstitutional, as state and federal courts have consistently allowed punitive awards. Justice Blackmun acknowledged that unlimited jury discretion could invite extreme, unwarranted results. Therefore, he reviewed the acceptability of the damage award based on the

---

[248] *Id.* at 264.

[249] 524 U.S. 321 (1998).

[250] *Id.* at 324.

[251] 499 U.S. 1 (1991).

facts of the case. Although the Court refused to "draw a mathematical bright line,"[252] it did say that "general concerns of reasonableness and adequate guidance from the court when the case is tried to a jury properly enter into the constitutional calculus."[253]

On the procedural side, the Court emphasized the thoroughness of jury instructions and Alabama's post-trial procedures for examining punitive damages awards. It also noted that as long as the state court had made an inquiry into the rational relation between the size of the punitive verdict and the magnitude of the offense and had reviewed the relationship between punitive and compensatory damages, then the award would pass constitutional muster. The Court also recognized the state's valid justification of the award as serving the interests of both deterrence and retribution.

In *TXO Production Corp. v. Alliance Resources*,[254] the Court rejected both substantive and procedural due process challenges attempting to set aside a punitive damages award that was 526 times greater than actual damages. TXO had agreed to purchase oil and gas rights from Alliance in exchange for cash and royalties. Subsequently, TXO attempted to subvert Alliance's title to mineral rights by producing a 1958 quitclaim deed in an effort to renegotiate the price. TXO brought a lawsuit challenging Alliance's legal title; Alliance counterclaimed for slander of title. The jury awarded Alliance $19,000 in actual damages and $10 million in punitive damages.

Writing for a plurality of four, Justice Stevens stated that the Fourteenth Amendment placed substantive limits on punitive damages awards. Safeguards in the judicial process were essential to combat arbitrariness. In this case, jury members were subject to pretrial questioning as a method of assessing their impartiality. Furthermore, the jury's proffered verdict was a result of deliberation based on evidence presented by both sides. Finally, the award was reviewed and upheld by both the trial court and the court of appeals. "Assuming that fair procedures were followed, a judgment that is a product of that process is entitled to a strong presumption of validity."[255]

Intra-jurisdictional and inter-jurisdictional comparisons were not dispositive in analyzing jury-awarded punitive damages. This analysis, however, could be a useful factor in considering whether, for instance, a jury rendered its verdict based on biases against an out-of-state business. A punitive damages award must be tested, as it was in *Haslip*, according to its overall reasonableness. The Court concluded that "the disparity between the punitive award and the potential harm[256] does not, in our view, 'jar one's constitutional sensibilities.'"[257]

---

[252] *Id.* at 18.

[253] *Id.*

[254] 509 U.S. 443 (1993).

[255] *Id.* at 457.

[256] Estimates of the potential money at stake to Alliance ranged from $5 million to $8.3 million.

[257] *TXO Prod.*, 509 U.S. at 462.

The Court refused solely to focus attention on the magnitude of the award, a point repeatedly emphasized by TXO. "The punitive damages award in this case is certainly large, but in light of the amount of money potentially at stake, the bad faith of petitioner, the fact that the scheme employed in this case was part of a larger pattern of fraud, trickery, and deceit, and petitioner's wealth, we are not persuaded that the award was so 'grossly excessive' as to be beyond the power of the state to allow."[258]

Justice Scalia, joined by Justice Thomas, concurred in the judgment. He rejected a substantive due process right to review punitive damages. Justice O'Connor, joined by Justice White, dissented. Intra-jurisdictional and inter-jurisdictional comparisons indicated that the award in this case was excessive. Moreover numerical and historical comparisons supported the same conclusion.

In *BMW of North America v. Gore*,[259] the Court held that a $2 million punitive damages award against BMW violated the Due Process Clause because it was "grossly excessive"[260] in light of the $4,000 compensatory damages award. BMW had adopted a nationwide non-disclosure policy for repairs that cost less than 3 percent of the price of its new cars. While the policy was consistent with the disclosure laws of approximately 25 other states, and had never been "adjudicated unlawful," an Alabama jury found that BMW had fraudulently failed to disclose that plaintiff's car had been repainted, which cost $601.37, or less than 1.5 percent of its price. The $4,000 compensatory damages awarded was the difference in value between the plaintiff's refinished BMW and a new one. The jury awarded $4 million in punitive damages based on the number of repainted cars that BMW sold nationwide; however the Alabama Supreme Court reduced the punitive award to $2 million, holding that it could only be based on Alabama conduct.

Writing for a 5-4 majority, Justice Stevens opined that Alabama's legitimate interests in punishing and deterring unlawful conduct afforded it considerable flexibility in determining punitive awards. However, Alabama could not punish the company for behavior that was legal in other states and did not impact Alabama or its residents. BMW was entitled to fair notice of the potential magnitude of the penalty that Alabama might impose. "Three guideposts"[261] indicated that BMW did not receive such notice, and consequently that the $2 million punitive damages award was grossly excessive.

First, and perhaps most importantly, BMW's conduct was not particularly reprehensible. The harm was purely economic, as repainting did not diminish the car's safety, performance, or appearance. Moreover, the record did not establish "indifference to or reckless disregard for the health and safety of others."[262] The record disclosed no deliberate falsities, misconduct, or concealment of bad motives. BMW could have reasonably assumed that other states' disclosure laws provided "a

---

[258] *Id.*

[259] 517 U.S. 559 (1996).

[260] *Id.* at 562.

[261] *Id.* at 574.

[262] *Id.* at 576.

safe harbor for non-disclosure of minor repairs"[263] making it difficult to anticipate that Alabama would find its non-disclosure policy fraudulent.

Second, the ratio of the punitive award "to the actual harm inflicted on the plaintiff"[264] suggested excessiveness. While the Court had previously allowed a 4 to 1 ratio in *Pacific Mutual Life Insurance Co. v. Haslip*, and a 10 to 1 ratio in *TXO Production Corp. v. Alliance Resources Corp.*, the $2 million punitive award at issue was 500 times the amount of compensatory damages. However, the Court did not base reversal simply on a " 'mathematical bright line,' "[265] as in some instances small compensatory awards may justify a higher ratio than large ones.

Third, the punitive award far exceeded civil or criminal sanctions for similar misconduct. The maximum penalty under Alabama's Deceptive Trade Practices Act was $2,000, and no state's penalty exceeded $10,000. Neither these statutes nor any judicial decisions anywhere afforded BMW fair notice that its non-disclosure policy might subject it to a multimillion dollar penalty.

In any event, as the record disclosed no pattern of failure to comply with known statutory requirements, a lesser award would presumably have sufficed to induce compliance with Alabama law. As a large corporation, BMW's active involvement "in the national economy implicates the Federal interest in preventing individual states from imposing undue burdens on interstate commerce."[266]

Justice Breyer, joined by Justices O'Connor and Souter, concurred in the judgment. While punitive awards generally were strongly presumed valid, Alabama's vague standards did not sufficiently constrain the jury's discretion. Moreover, the $2 million dollar award grossly exceeded Alabama's "legitimate punitive damages objectives."[267]

Justice Scalia dissented, joined by Justice Thomas. Justice Scalia believed the Due Process Clause did not provide substantive protection against unreasonable punitive awards, but only protected the opportunity to challenge the award in state court. Moreover, the majority's discussion of BMW's punishment for its lawful actions in other states was dicta because the Alabama Supreme Court had recalculated the jury's punitive award without relying on BMW's actions in other states.

Justice Ginsburg also dissented, joined by Chief Justice Rehnquist. Justice Ginsburg maintained that the Court was unnecessarily addressing an issue traditionally left to states. She also criticized the lack of standards that the Court provided to the states. The Court would oversee this area unaided by the lower Federal courts.

---

[263] *Id.* at 577.

[264] *Id.* at 580.

[265] *Id.* at 583.

[266] *Id.* at 585.

[267] *Id.* at 595.

Cooper Industries, Inc. v. Leatherman Tool Group, Inc.[268] held that appeals courts should review punitive damages awards de novo, rather than with an abuse-of-discretion standard. Analogizing to *United States v. Bajakajian*,[269] Justice Stevens characterized punitive damages as "private fines"[270] that serve to punish and deter; as such, they are "quasi-criminal"[271] in nature. The majority gave three reasons for favoring de novo review. First, independent review was necessary, as it was difficult to articulate the exact meaning of certain legal concepts. Second, those legal concepts took on meaning only through actual application. Third, " 'de novo review tends to unify precedent' and 'stabilize the law,' "[272] which facilitated " 'the uniform treatment' "[273] of individuals.

BMW of North America v. Gore[274] used three criteria to evaluate the constitutionality of punitive awards: "(1) the degree or reprehensibility of the defendant's misconduct, (2) the disparity between the harm (or potential harm) suffered by the plaintiff and the punitive damages award, and (3) the difference between the punitive damages awarded by the jury and the civil penalties authorized or imposed in comparable cases."[275] Appellate courts were better suited to evaluate "the third *Gore* criterion, which calls for a broad legal comparison."[276] While trial courts could be more suited to analyze the first factor, both courts were "equally capable of analyzing the second factor."[277]

Concurring, Justice Thomas continued to assert that *Gore* should be overruled. In dissent, Justice Ginsburg argued that appellate courts should review punitive damages awards using an abuse-of-discretion standard.

In *State Farm Mutual Automobile Insurance Co. v. Campbell*,[278] the Court held that an award for punitive damages that totaled 145 times the amount of compensatory damages was disproportionate and violated the Due Process Clause. While trying to pass 6 vans on a two-lane highway, Campbell crossed into the lane of oncoming traffic and caused an accident which killed one driver and left another permanently disabled. After declining settlement offers for the policy limit of $25,000 per claimant, State Farm assured that the Campbell's were free from liability. State Farm also told the Campbell's that they would not need to obtain counsel as the insurance company would represent their interests.

At trial a jury awarded the claimants $185,849. Counsel for State Farm suggested to the Campbell's that they might consider selling their house in order

---

[268] 532 U.S. 424 (2001).

[269] 524 U.S. 321 (1998).

[270] 532 U.S. at 432.

[271] *Id.*

[272] *Id.* at 436.

[273] *Id.*

[274] 517 U.S. at 559 (1996).

[275] 532 U.S. at 440.

[276] *Id.*

[277] *Id.*

[278] 538 U.S. 408 (2003).

to pay the judgment. The insurance company refused to appeal. Although State Farm eventually paid the entire judgment, the Campbell's sued them for bad faith, fraud, and intentional infliction of emotional distress. The jury awarded the Campbell's $2.6 million in compensatory damages and $145 million in punitive damages. The trial court reduced this award to $1 million in compensatory damages and $25 million in punitive damages. The Utah Supreme Court, however, reinstated the $145 million punitive award.

BMW of North America, Inc. v. Gore[279] imposed three guideposts that are used to determine whether an award is grossly excessive. The first was established in *State Farm* when the Utah Supreme Court condemned the insurance company not for its actions directed at the Campbell's, but for its nationwide policies. A state may not assess punitive damages for unlawful conduct that occurred outside its jurisdiction.[280] While punishment should be limited to the conduct at issue, the Court's prior holdings permitted harsher consequences for a repeat offender than for a first time offender. Repeated misconduct was more deserving of punishment than a one-time offense. However, in order to punish a defendant as a recidivist, courts must ensure that the current and prior offenses were the same. This guidepost did not allow a court to punish a defendant for "any malfeasance," which the lower court in *State Farm* had extended to encompass over a 20-year period.

The second *Gore* guidepost indicated that an award of more than four times the amount of compensatory damages moved close to the limit that was constitutionally allowable. The *Gore* Court referred to a legislative history that spanned the past 700 years permitting awards designed to deter and punish, which were worth two to four times the amount of compensatory damages. Although this history was not a strict guideline, it was instructive. When the compensatory award was substantial, however, due process might restrict punitive damages to an amount equal to actual damages. The limit had to be determined individually for each case based on the facts and circumstances surrounding the defendant's behavior and on the harm that the plaintiff endured. Punitive awards had to be reasonable and proportionate to this harm and the actual damages awarded. In *State Farm*, the Campbell's received $1 million for a year and a half of emotional distress. This amounted to a substantial compensatory award.

The third guidepost discussed in *Gore* allowed a court to look to penalties in similar cases. This Court had previously considered criminal penalties that would be allowed. In Utah, a $10,000 fine could be imposed for fraud. The punitive award of $145 million was neither reasonable nor proportionate to the insurance company's misconduct. The sanction was "an irrational and arbitrary deprivation of the property of the defendant."[281]

---

[279] 517 U.S. 559 (1996).

[280] When certain behavior was lawful in one jurisdiction and unlawful in another, the lawful out-of-state conduct may be used to show the "deliberateness and culpability" of the unlawful in-state action. However, in this situation a jury must be instructed that this demonstration could not be used to punish a defendant for conduct that was "lawful in the jurisdiction where it occurred."

[281] 538 U.S. at 429.

In dissent, Justice Scalia expressed his opinion that scrutiny of punitive awards was "insusceptible of principled application."[282] In a separate dissent, Justice Ginsburg concluded that the "numerical controls" that this decision established were inappropriate. *Gore* used "flexible guides."

In *Philip Morris USA v. Williams*,[283] the Court held that the Due Process Clause prohibited juries from considering harm to third parties when awarding punitive damages. As a result of a jury trial and subsequent appeals, the plaintiff was awarded $821,000 in compensatory damages and $79.5 million in punitive damages.

The Due Process Clause allowed individuals the right to present every available defense; however defendants could not do this against allegedly injured nonparties who were not before the court. While juries could consider the harm that the defendant could have caused, this consideration was limited to harm caused to the plaintiff. Justice Breyer did allow the jury to consider in assessing punitive damages the overall harm caused by the defendant in determining the reprehensibility of the defendant's act, one of the three guideposts in *BMW of North America, Inc. v. Gore*.[284] The Court did not reach the issue of whether the punitive damages award at issue violated *State Farm* by being more than three to four times the size of the compensatory damages award.

Dissenting, Justice Stevens warned about the dangers of expanding the "unchartered area" of substantive due process where guideposts were "scarce and open-ended."[285] Also dissenting, Justice Thomas found no basis in the Constitution for limiting the size of punitive damage awards. Finally, in her dissent, Justice Ginsburg emphasized the confusing task the jury faces in not considering harm to third parties to assess punitive damages, but considering it to determine the reprehensibility of the defendant's actions.

In *Exxon Shipping Co. v. Baker*,[286] the Court reduced over $5 billion in punitive damages stemming from the Exxon Valdez oil spill to a one-to-one ratio with compensatory damages. At the time of the accident, the ship's Captain, Hazelwood, had a blood alcohol level "three times the legal limit for driving in most states." While working for Exxon, and with the knowledge of his employers, Hazelwood completed an alcohol treatment program. Hazelwood's employers were unaware that he later stopped attending follow-up treatment and Alcoholics Anonymous meetings. Contested testimony was offered at trial, however, that "Hazelwood drank with Exxon officials and members of Exxon management knew of his relapse." There also was no evidence that Exxon monitored Hazelwood after he returned from the alcohol treatment program.

Following the spill, Exxon spent approximately $2.1 billion on cleanup efforts and settled both state and federal environmental damage claims for over $1 billion.

---

[282] *Id.*

[283] 549 U.S. 346 (2007).

[284] 517 U.S. 559 (1996).

[285] 549 U.S. at 360–61.

[286] 554 U.S. 471 (2008).

In this case, the jury awarded plaintiffs $287 million in compensatory damages and $5 billion in punitive damages, which the Ninth Circuit later remitted to $2.5 billion.

The Court first considered whether maritime law allowed corporate liability for punitive damages based on acts of managerial agents. The Court was evenly split (Justice Alito did not participate). Consequently, the Court left undisturbed the decision of the Ninth Circuit ruling that Exxon was liable for Hazelwood's acts. However, the Supreme Court's decision on this issue had no precedential effect.

The Court next addressed punitive damages, which had to conform to Federal maritime law, rather than under its constitutional due process analysis. The Court quoted a recent study comparing punitive and compensatory jury awards in "state civil trials" that reported a median ratio "of just 0.62:1, but a mean ratio of 2.90:1, and a standard deviation of 13.81." Justice Souter compared the need to reduce "unjustified disparities" in punitive damages with the need for consistency in criminal sentencing. The Court also drew from *State Farm v. Campbell*,[287] which held that "a single digit maximum" of punitive to compensatory damage awards "is appropriate in all but the most exceptional of cases." The Court concluded that "constitutional upper limits confirm that the 1:1 ratio is not too low."

Justice Stevens concurred in part and dissented in part, noting that legislatures rather than courts generally promulgate "caps and ratios." Justice Ginsburg also concurred in part and dissented in part. She asked whether the Court would later "rule, definitively, that 1:1 is the ceiling due process requires." Concurring in part and dissenting in part, Justice Breyer noted that Exxon's "egregious" conduct "justifie[d] a considerably higher ratio" than the 1:1 the Court had used in its most recent due process decision.

§ 8.06   LIBERTY IN PROCREATION AND OTHER PERSONAL MATTERS

[1]   The Childbearing Decision: Contraception and Abortion

During the *Lochner* era, the Court occasionally extended substantive due process rights in cases not involving economic interests. For example, in *Meyer v. Nebraska*,[288] the Court reversed the conviction of a teacher who had violated a state law that prohibited foreign language instruction. The Court gave content to the Due Process Clause of the Fourteenth Amendment by saying:

> Without doubt, [the Due Process Clause] denotes not merely freedom from bodily restraint but also the right of the individual to contract, to engage in any of the common occupations of life, to acquire useful knowledge, to marry, establish a home and bring up children, to worship God according to the dictates of its own conscience, and generally to enjoy those privileges

---

[287] 543 U.S. 874 (2004).

[288] 262 U.S. 390 (1923).

long recognized at common law as essential to the orderly pursuit of happiness by free men.[289]

Another early example of substantive due process analysis in the personal rights area was *Pierce v. Society of Sisters*.[290] In this 1925 case, a law requiring public school attendance was invalidated based on the parents' right to direct the upbringing and education of their children. Today, the laws struck down in *Meyer* and *Pierce* would probably have been set aside by current First Amendment doctrines of freedom of speech and religion.

For many years after what appeared to be the demise of substantive due process in 1937, *Skinner v. Oklahoma*[291] was the only case that could be called a substantive due process decision. The *Skinner* Court invalidated an Oklahoma statute that allowed the state to sterilize habitual criminals guilty of crimes reflecting "moral turpitude." The Court relied on a conglomeration of due process and equal protection doctrines, the latter often referred to as the "fundamental rights" strand of equal protection analysis. The Court invalidated the statute on equal protection grounds, holding that the law required unequal treatment of similarly-situated criminals. For example, it mandated sterilization for those thrice-convicted of robbery but not for bailors thrice-convicted of embezzlement. Even though those who were sterilized were not a protected class for equal protection purposes,[292] Justice Douglas held that the statute discriminated with respect to a fundamental right. The right was derived from a substantive due process analysis: "Marriage and procreation are fundamental to the very existence and survival of the race."[293] The *Skinner* Court might have derived the fundamental right from the Eighth Amendment prohibition against cruel and unusual punishment, but it did not.

Griswold v. Connecticut[294] was significant because many scholars viewed the decision as a return to the substantive due process analysis disavowed by the Court in the post-*Lochner* era. In *Griswold*, administrators of the Planned Parenthood League of Connecticut were arrested and charged under state statutes prohibiting the use or provision of contraceptives. The League prescribed contraceptive devices to married persons and counseled them on their use, typically for a fee.

Writing for the majority, Justice Douglas refused to rely explicitly on substantive due process analysis, asserting that the Court does not sit as a "super-legislature" to review legislation on social and economic matters. Instead, Justice Douglas argued that "specific guarantees in the Bill of Rights have penumbras, formed by emanations from those guarantees that help give them life and substance."[295] Specifically, the First Amendment Right of Association, the Fourth Amendment protection against unreasonable searches, the Fifth Amendment protection against

---

[289] *Id.* at 399.

[290] 268 U.S. 510 (1925).

[291] 316 U.S. 535 (1942).

[292] *See infra* Chapter 12.

[293] *Skinner*, 316 U.S. at 541.

[294] 381 U.S. 479 (1965).

[295] *Id.* at 484.

self-incrimination, and the Ninth Amendment[296] combined to create a "zone of privacy" impenetrable by government. Based on this "penumbras" analysis, Justice Douglas held that the statutes in *Griswold* were overbroad in infringing on the privacy of the marital relationship. In prohibiting the use of contraceptives (as opposed to their manufacture or sale), the law appeared to allow police to search the marital bedroom for evidence of contraceptives.

In their separate concurrences, Justices Goldberg and White agreed with Justice Douglas' conclusion that the *Griswold* statutes were unconstitutional, but their analyses differed. Justice Goldberg, joined by Chief Justice Warren and Justice Brennan, used the Ninth Amendment to support his position that the Fourteenth Amendment Due Process Clause protected a fundamental right to "marital privacy." Justice Goldberg found substantial historical problems with using the Fourteenth Amendment to incorporate the Ninth Amendment against the states, as the Framers had intended the Ninth Amendment to limit the power of the Federal government, not the states. Instead, he construed the Amendment as expressing the Framers' belief that the first eight amendments were not to be considered an exhaustive list of fundamental rights. In finding a right of marital privacy, Justice Goldberg looked to " 'the traditions and [collective] conscience of our people' " to determine whether the principle was " 'so rooted [there] . . . as to be ranked as fundamental.' "[297] Justice Goldberg also stated that the "entire fabric of the Constitution"[298] suggested a right of marital privacy. He disputed the position of the dissenters that marital privacy should not be recognized as a right simply because it was not explicitly recognized in the Constitution-without such an implicit right to privacy, the state could, for example, pass a law requiring sterilization after two children.

As the statute at issue infringed this fundamental right to marital privacy, Justice Goldberg required that the statute be necessary to achieve a compelling state interest. In applying this highest level of scrutiny, Justice Goldberg found the *Griswold* statutes were not necessary to advance Connecticut's proffered interest in protecting the marital relationship against extra-marital affairs. Less restrictive alternatives were available whose constitutionality were "beyond doubt." Justice Goldberg carefully confined his opinion to protecting the marital relationship against state infringements, for example, laws against adultery and fornication.

Justice Harlan concurred in the judgment. Consistent with his earlier opinions,[299] Justice Harlan found that the statute violated due process by infringing on "basic values 'implicit in the concept of ordered liberty.' "[300] Justice Harlan denied that his theory hinged constitutional interpretation on the personal predilections of individual judges. He listed as restraints on judicial power reliance on history in

---

[296] "The enumeration in the Constitution, of certain rights, shall not be construed to deny or disparage others retained by the people." U.S. CONST. amend. IX.

[297] *Griswold*, 381 U.S. at 487 (quoting *Snyder v. Commonwealth of Massachusetts*, 291 U.S. 97, 105 (1934)).

[298] *Id.* at 495.

[299] *See* Adamson v. California, 332 U.S. 46 (1947) (Harlan, J., dissenting), *supra* § 8.02.

[300] *Griswold*, 381 U.S. at 500.

identifying fundamental rights and the continued vitality of federalism and separation of powers.

Justice White also concurred in the judgment. He imposed a less exacting standard than Justices Goldberg and Harlan, requiring the statute to be "reasonably necessary for the effectuation of a legitimate and substantial state interest." According to Justice White, both the means and the end asserted by the state were invalid. The *Griswold* statutes swept broadly into an impermissible end of deterring *all* illicit sexual relationships. Such laws could not be enforced against married couples and it was unnecessary to do so if the goal was to prevent extra-marital promiscuity.

Justices Black and Stewart each wrote separate dissents. Neither could find support for a "right of privacy" in a specific constitutional provision. Although both dissenting Justices personally disagreed with the Connecticut statutes, they were concerned with judicial legislation. In this connection, Justice Black accused the Court of acting like a "super-legislature."

Although the marital relationship was the central tenet in *Griswold*, a series of subsequent cases expanded the decision's scope. In *Eisenstadt v. Baird*,[301] the Court invalidated a Massachusetts statute banning distribution of contraceptives to unmarried individuals. Somewhat like *Skinner v. Oklahoma*,[302] the *Eisenstadt* Court employed a combination of equal protection and substantive due process analyses.[303]

The Court further broadened access to contraceptives in *Carey v. Population Services International*.[304] The statute at issue prohibited distribution of contraceptives to persons under 16 (except by licensed physician to married females between 14 and 16), required a licensed pharmacist to distribute contraceptives, and prohibited their advertisement. Writing for the Court, Justice Brennan invalidated the requirement that a licensed pharmacist distribute contraceptives because it significantly burdened an individual's right to make childbearing decisions without serving a compelling state interest. The Court held that the ban on advertisements infringed on the First Amendment protection of commercial speech without any legitimate justification.

Denying access to minors presented a much closer question. The statute even prohibited parents from distributing contraceptives to their own children. A plurality opinion by Justice Brennan held that the restriction could be upheld only if it served " 'any significant state interest . . . that is not present in the case of an adult.' "[305] Reflecting the diminished decision-making capacity of minors, this test imposed less scrutiny than on laws prohibiting contraceptive use by adults.

---

[301] 405 U.S. 438 (1972).

[302] 316 U.S. 535 (1942).

[303] Although the Court ostensibly subjected the statute to a rationality test, it actually applied a standard that approached strict scrutiny.

[304] 431 U.S. 678 (1977).

[305] *Id.* at 693 (quoting *Planned Parenthood v. Danforth*, 428 U.S. 52, 75 (1976)).

The plurality found that the blanket prohibition on contraceptives for minors was foreclosed by decisions like *Planned Parenthood v. Danforth*[306] which had invalidated similar restraints on a minor's access to abortion. The plurality also doubted that limiting access to contraceptives would discourage sexual activity among the young.

Justices White, Powell, and Stevens each wrote separate opinions concurring only in the judgment of the plurality in striking down that part of the statute that prohibited distribution of contraceptives to minors. All three Justices appeared to apply a more relaxed standard of scrutiny than the plurality for regulating the distribution of contraceptives to minors as long as there was no prohibition of distribution by parents. Chief Justice Burger and Justice Rehnquist each dissented. With their votes, it would appear that a majority of five Justices would have allowed substantial regulation of the distribution of contraceptives to minors so long as parents could give contraceptives to their children.

Critical to the Court's modern substantive due process jurisprudence are the cases involving a woman's right to choose an abortion. The first case to guarantee that right was *Roe v. Wade*.[307] The Texas statute invalidated in *Roe* made it a crime to procure or attempt an abortion except to save the life of the mother.

In *Roe*, Justice Blackmun premised the right to choose an abortion on the constitutional right of privacy which derived from the concept of personal liberty in the Due Process Clause.[308] In describing the scope of modern substantive due process, the Court relied on the *Palko v. Connecticut*[309] formulation of rights that are "fundamental" or "implicit in the concept of ordered liberty."[310] The ambit of these rights extended to marriage, procreation, contraception, family relationships, child rearing, and education.

Against this due process privacy or liberty right of the woman to choose to have an abortion, the state asserted an interest in protecting the rights of the fetus. Justice Blackmun rejected the argument that the fetus was a person for purposes of Fourteenth Amendment protection. Relying on various provisions including the definition of citizens in the Fourteenth Amendment, the census provisions, and the qualifications for various elected officials, Justice Blackmun concluded that the Constitution only protected those who were already born. By focusing on legal personhood, the Court avoided the question of when life begins, a question on which medicine, philosophy, and theology differ.

The *Roe* Court did not reject the state's interest in preserving fetal life altogether, however. At the point of viability, the Court found the state's interest grew sufficiently compelling to outweigh the mother's interest in choosing an abortion so long as the mother's life or health was not endangered. Justice

---

[306]   428 U.S. 52 (1976).

[307]   410 U.S. 113 (1973).

[308]   He also relied in some degree on the Ninth Amendment and on the "penumbras" analysis advanced by Justice Douglas in *Griswold*.

[309]   *See supra* § 8.02.

[310]   *Palko*, 302 U.S. at 324.

Blackmun chose this point of viability because it was the point at which the fetus could exist independent of the mother outside the womb, even if only with artificial aid. Justice Blackmun posited a "trimester" approach to state regulation of abortion. During approximately the first trimester, the abortion decision must be left strictly to the mother and her attending physician without state interference. During approximately the second trimester, the state could regulate only to protect the health of the mother. At the point of viability, which occurs at approximately the start of the third trimester, the state could regulate or even forbid abortion except to protect the mother's life or health.

The trimester system of *Roe* represented the Court's attempt to balance the woman's interests in choosing an abortion and in controlling her body, against the state's interests in protecting maternal health and the potential life of the fetus. In dissent, Justice Rehnquist criticized the trimester approach as "judicial legislation."[311]

Justice Douglas concurred, but he found it more difficult to justify the result in *Roe* with the "penumbras" analysis he employed in *Griswold*. Instead, Justice Douglas relied more heavily on tradition, the Ninth Amendment, and the Due Process Clause. Although he had dissented in *Griswold*, Justice Stewart concurred based on the doctrine of *stare decisis*.

In separate dissents, Justices White and Rehnquist criticized the Court for engaging in a brand of social policy analysis reminiscent of *Lochner*.[312] Both would impose a rationality standard of review.

Justice Rehnquist's dissent noted that the majority of states had restricted abortions for over a century. Consequently, "the asserted right to an abortion was not 'so rooted in the traditions and conscience of our people as to be ranked as fundamental.'"[313] In contrast, Justice Blackmun asserted, based on his examination of history, that at the time of the adoption of the Fourteenth Amendment, "prevailing legal abortion practices were far freer than they are today."[314]

The reasoning of *Roe* applied to a much broader range of abortion restrictions than those in this fairly restrictive statute. In *Doe v. Bolton*,[315] a companion case to *Roe* decided the same day, the Court invalidated a Georgia law based on the new Model Penal Code's provisions regarding abortion, which was far less restrictive on abortion than the statute in *Roe*. The Georgia law restricted abortion to protect the life or health of the mother, to prevent the birth of a fetus with a serious birth defect, or to end a pregnancy resulting from rape. The Court also invalidated various procedural requirements imposed by the *Bolton* statute. It did uphold a requirement that a physician exercise medical judgment "in light of all factors — physical, emotional, psychological, familial, and the woman's age — relevant to the

---

[311] *Roe*, 410 U.S. at 174.

[312] *See supra* § 8.04.

[313] *Roe*, 410 U.S. at 174.

[314] *Id.* at 158.

[315] 410 U.S. 179 (1973).

well-being of the patient."[316]

Following *Roe*, state legislatures attempted to restrict abortion in many ways. Supreme Court decisions reacting to state legislation fall into four principal categories: spousal notification and consent requirements which have generally been denied, parental notification and consent requirements which have been upheld with a judicial bypass option, withdrawal of public funding for abortion which has been upheld, and direct restrictions on abortion which were generally invalidated prior to *Webster v. Reproductive Health Services*[317] and *Planned Parenthood v. Casey*.[318]

Planned Parenthood v. Danforth[319] reflects an early treatment of many of these issues. In *Danforth*, the Court invalidated most of the restrictions in a Missouri statute that limited a woman's access to abortion. In an opinion written by Justice Blackmun, the Court found that a provision requiring any single woman under age 18 to receive parental consent to obtain an abortion unduly burdened the woman's privacy right recognized in *Roe*. The *Danforth* Court also struck down provisions requiring a married woman to obtain her husband's written consent in order to receive an abortion. The woman's interest outweighed her husband's interest in the pregnancy as she was more directly and immediately affected by the pregnancy.

In a similar manner, the Court's 1992 decision in *Planned Parenthood v. Casey*[320] struck down a spousal notification requirement. The Court held that such a notification requirement generally would only be necessary in dysfunctional, including violent, marriages and could be a substantial deterrent to abortion in the context of such relationships. In a normal marriage, the abortion decision would be discussed.

The *Danforth* Court also invalidated a prohibition on saline amniocentesis abortions, the method that was used most often in abortions performed after the first trimester. The Court concluded that the prohibition was unreasonably designed to inhibit, and actually did inhibit, second trimester abortions.

The Court re-examined the issue of parental consent for minors three years later in *Bellotti v. Baird*.[321] Eight members of the Court held unconstitutional a Massachusetts provision requiring an unmarried minor to obtain the consent of both parents or the authorization of a state judge if parental consent was denied. The *Bellotti* Court was split 4-4, however, with four Justices suggesting that some limited parental role may exist, particularly in light of the somewhat different constitutional status of minors.[322]

---

[316] *Bolton*, 410 U.S at 192.

[317] 492 U.S. 490 (1989).

[318] 505 U.S. 833 (1992).

[319] 428 U.S. 52 (1976).

[320] 505 U.S. 833 (1992).

[321] 443 U.S. 622 (1979).

[322] Justice Powell's plurality opinion provided the critical fifth vote necessary to strike down the statute. Justice Powell's opinion emphasized that the statute imposed an undue burden by requiring a judge to withhold consent from even a minor found fully competent to make the decision independently

In *H.L. v. Matheson*,[323] the Court did recognize a limited parental interest in some abortion decisions of minors. Specifically, *Matheson* rejected a facial challenge by a minor — living with and dependent on her parents — to a Utah statute requiring parental notification, "if possible," for minors seeking an abortion. The Court reasoned that the parental notice provision did not amount to an invalid veto power over the minor's abortion decision and was narrowly drawn to serve important state interests, at least as applied to non-mature and non-emancipated minors.

The Court again confronted parental notice in *Hodgson v. Minnesota*.[324] The *Hodgson* Court struck down a Minnesota statute requiring that both parents of an unemancipated minor be notified 48 hours before the minor had an abortion. However, a different majority of Justices upheld the same notification requirement with the addition of a judicial bypass option. This judicial bypass allowed a judge to order an abortion without parental consent if the judge determined that the minor was mature and capable of making the decision herself or if the judge determined that the abortion would be in the best interest of the child.

In *Ohio v. Akron Center for Reproductive Health*,[325] the Court upheld a judicial bypass procedure allowing an abortion without notifying parents. To obtain the judicial bypass, the minor had to prove that "she has sufficient maturity and information to make an intelligent decision," or that a parent has subjected her to "a pattern of physical, sexual, or emotional abuse," or that "notice is not in her best interests."[326] As the proceeding was ex parte, the minor must establish one of these by "clear and convincing evidence." The trial procedure could take up to 22 days and the appeal was required to be decided within five days after it had been docketed.[327] Government could require one or both parents to consent to the minor's choice of abortion if it included a judicial bypass option.

Planned Parenthood v. Casey[328] allowed government to require that parental consent be informed. The minor's parents had to be provided with certain information about the abortion 24 hours before the abortion was to be performed. If consent was not provided, a judicial bypass procedure was available.

The Court has allowed government extensive discretion in deciding whether to provide public funding for abortion. Three companion cases decided in 1977 concluded that neither the Constitution nor any federal legislation required states to fund non-therapeutic abortions for indigent women. *Beal v. Doe*[329] upheld Pennsylvania's Medicaid Plan that limited public assistance to abortions certified as medically necessary by two physicians in addition to the mother's attending

---

and by requiring parental notification in every instance.

[323] 450 U.S. 398 (1981).

[324] 497 U.S. 417 (1990).

[325] 497 U.S. 502 (1990).

[326] *Id.* at 507.

[327] The Court refused to entertain a challenge to the 22-day waiting period as this was the longest possible waiting period and only a potential problem in the context of the facial challenge.

[328] 505 U.S. 833 (1992).

[329] 432 U.S. 438 (1977).

physician. *Maher v. Roe*[330] upheld Connecticut's Medicaid Plan that, similar to the one in *Beal*, limited public assistance to medically necessary abortions despite its providing assistance for childbirth costs. *Poelker v. Doe*[331] upheld St. Louis' policy of providing publicly financed services for childbirth but refusing to provide corresponding services for non-therapeutic abortions in city-owned hospitals. According to these cases, constitutional protection was confined to noninterference by the government in the abortion area.

Harris v. McRae[332] made clear that government could refuse to provide public funding for even medically necessary abortions, despite funding all other medically necessary procedures, including childbirth services. The Court upheld the various versions of the Hyde Amendment that prohibited federal funding for abortions. The Court sustained the denial of federal funding for even abortions to protect the life of the mother or to end pregnancies that were the product of rape or incest. The *Harris* Court relied heavily on the philosophical distinction between positive and negative rights. The underlying rationale in *Harris* was that the right to choose an abortion did not amount to a government entitlement. The dissent argued that the *Harris* line of cases made the right established in *Roe* unavailable to poor persons.

As illustrated in *Planned Parenthood v. Danforth*, few direct restrictions on abortion procedures survived judicial scrutiny prior to *Webster v. Reproductive Health Services* and *Planned Parenthood v. Casey*.

In *City of Akron v. Akron Center for Reproductive Health, Inc.*,[333] the Court invalidated a statutory informed-consent requirement on the ground that it was designed to deter abortions. Among the requirements of the consent were informing the woman that the unborn child was a life at conception, describing the physiology of the fetus, and informing her of the particular risks of the abortion procedure to be employed. The *Akron* Court also invalidated a requirement that all second and third trimester abortions be performed in full-care hospitals. However, in *Simopoulos v. Virginia*,[334] a companion case to *Akron*, the Court upheld a requirement that second trimester abortions be performed in a full-care hospital or a licensed out-patient clinic.

Justice O'Connor's dissent in *Akron* was particularly important, as it articulated the "unduly burdensome" standard as an alternative approach to the trimester framework. This approach, which was controlling in *Casey*, was less rigid than the trimester scheme of *Roe* and provided state legislatures with greater latitude in regulating abortion. It applied strict scrutiny to abortion regulations only if they created an undue burden on the woman's right to choose an abortion. If a court did not find such a burden, it would review the regulation under a rationality standard. Additionally, the standard treated the state's interests in maternal health and potential life as substantial throughout the pregnancy, although, as *Casey* stated,

---

[330] 432 U.S. 464 (1977).

[331] 432 U.S. 519 (1977).

[332] 448 U.S. 297 (1980).

[333] 462 U.S. 416 (1983).

[334] 462 U.S. 506 (1983).

that interest could not justify "undue burdens" on the woman's right to terminate a pregnancy in the pre-viability stage.

In *Planned Parenthood Ass'n v. Ashcroft*,[335] a second companion case to *Akron*, the Court upheld a requirement that a second physician be present to care for the fetus at a post-viability abortion, unless a medical emergency precluded this, and that a pathology report be filed for every abortion. The protection afforded the post-viable fetus during abortion was limited, however, and could not entail a "trade-off" between the woman's health and the safety and survival of the fetus. *Thornburgh v. American College of Obstetricians & Gynecologists*[336] exemplified how stringently the right to choose abortion was protected prior to the Court's shift in *Webster* and *Casey*. The Court invalidated a number of provisions of a wide-ranging abortion regulation including the requirement of a report for each abortion performed.

In *Webster v. Reproductive Health Services*[337] the Court rejected the Solicitor General's argument for overruling *Roe*. The Court did uphold, against a facial challenge, various provisions of a Missouri statute restricting abortion. Chief Justice Rehnquist wrote for a plurality of four. Justice O'Connor provided the fifth vote for the plurality in upholding the various provisions of the statute, although her analysis differed considerably. The Court refused a facial challenge to the preamble of the Missouri statute which stated that life began at conception and afforded an interest in life to the unborn. Because the preamble could simply be read as a value judgment, the Court ruled that the facial challenge was not ripe.

Relying on the positive and negative rights distinction in *Harris*, the Court upheld the statute's prohibition of the use of public funds, facilities, or employees in abortions that were not necessary to save the life of the mother. A majority of five also upheld the statute's viability testing requirements but for different reasons.

The plurality and Justice O'Connor construed the viability testing provision to require viability testing for fetuses of 20 or more weeks only if the test was in the physician's reasonable professional judgment, relevant to determining viability and not dangerous to the fetus or the mother. So construed, the plurality stated that the provision "permissibly further[ed] the state's interest in protecting potential human life."[338] The plurality found that upholding this restriction was inconsistent with *Colautti v. Franklin*,[339] in which the Court basically had given physicians complete discretion over the viability decision so long as it was made in good faith.[340]

The *Webster* plurality departed from *Roe* in important ways. The plurality rejected both the trimester and viability concepts, reasoning that these theories had virtually no basis in the Constitution. The *Webster* plurality adopted the position of the dissents in *Akron* and *Thornburgh* by recognizing a state interest in potential

---

[335] 462 U.S. 476 (1983).

[336] 476 U.S. 747 (1986).

[337] 492 U.S. 490 (1989).

[338] *Id.* at 519–20.

[339] 439 U.S. 379 (1979).

[340] Justice O'Connor did not find this result in *Webster* inconsistent with *Colautti*.

human life beginning at the moment of conception and lasting throughout the pregnancy.[341]

Justice O'Connor's refusal to join the plurality indicated that while her "undue burden" standard might allow greater restrictions on abortions than would the trimester approach, she would not join the Justices who were prepared virtually to overrule *Roe*. She did rule, however, that the viability testing requirement did not unduly burden the right to have an abortion. She said that the decision was not inconsistent with "*Colautti* or any decision of this Court concerning a state's ability to give effect to its interest in potential human life."[342] Justice Scalia concurred with most of the plurality's decision except that he would have explicitly overruled *Roe*.

Justice Blackmun concurred in part and dissented in part, joined by Justices Brennan and Marshall. Most of Justice Blackmun's opinion criticized the plurality's abandonment of the trimester framework. Justice Blackmun also disagreed with the viability testing provisions as the tests would add needless cost to an abortion. In a footnote he criticized the Court for upholding the ban on abortion in public facilities, as the statute's definition of public facilities was tremendously broad and included abortions performed in private hospitals located on leased public property.

Justice Stevens concurred in that part of the decision upholding the state's prohibition on the use of public funds to perform abortions. He dissented from the portions of the Court's opinion that upheld the remainder of the law.

In *Planned Parenthood v. Casey*,[343] the majority formally adopted an "undue burden" standard, while reaffirming the essential meaning of *Roe*. In so doing, the majority rejected the heightened "strict scrutiny" standard to state regulation of abortion. The majority also rejected *Roe's* trimester framework, allowing the state to impose abortion regulations that would have been overruled under this framework, although prior decisions had clearly reached this point.

The statute at issue in *Casey* placed a number of restrictions on a woman's right to choose an abortion. Four of the statute's provisions were challenged: the requirement of informed consent, combined with a 24-hour waiting period; the condition of spousal notification; the parental consent requirement for minors under 18; and the requirement of record-keeping for abortion providers.

Justices O'Connor, Souter, and Kennedy together wrote the controlling plurality opinion in *Casey*. First, the plurality reaffirmed several principles of *Roe*. A woman has a right to choose abortion before viability without undue interference by the state. However, the state may restrict abortions after fetal viability so long as the regulations include exceptions for pregnancies endangering the woman's life or health. The plurality conceded that the state had legitimate interests not only in protecting the health of the woman but also the life of the fetus throughout the pregnancy.

---

[341] *See Webster*, 492 U.S. at 519–20.

[342] *Id.* at 530.

[343] 505 U.S. 833 (1992).

In reaffirming parts of *Roe*, the plurality relied heavily on the doctrine of *stare decisis*. First, although the rule in *Roe* had encountered opposition, it had not proven "unworkable." Second, reliance on *Roe* had shaped the reproductive attitudes of the populace for nearly 20 years; moreover, people have reasonably relied on *Roe's* continued force. Third, no evolution in constitutional law supported alteration of the rule. Fourth, although certain medical advances had called into question the trimester approach, viability was still a valid point of intervention. The plurality stated that reversing *Roe* in response to political pressure would undermine the Court's legitimacy. Consequently, even though the plurality stated that they might not decide *Roe* the same way had the case come before them as a new matter, they upheld viability as the point at which the state could regulate both from respect for precedent and from the ability of the fetus to survive independently outside the womb.

The plurality rejected *Roe's* trimester framework due to its unnecessarily rigid character and its diminishment of the importance of the substantial state interest in potential life that existed throughout the pregnancy. Instead, the Court adopted an "undue burden" standard posited by Justice O'Connor in earlier dissenting and concurring opinions. Under this approach, a regulation was unconstitutional if it unduly burdened a woman's right to choose an abortion. A regulation imposed an undue burden if "it has the purpose or effect of placing a substantial obstacle in the path of a woman seeking an abortion of a nonviable fetus."[344] The undue burden standard contrasted with the Court's previous strict scrutiny approach to this area. It allowed "structural mechanisms" through which the state, or a parent or guardian of a minor, could persuade a woman to choose childbirth over abortion.[345] It also allowed the state to advance its legitimate interest of furthering the woman's health; unlike *Roe*, it did not limit regulations furthering maternal health to the second trimester of the pregnancy. The Court would uphold measures that did not amount to undue burdens and were reasonably related to such goals as expressing respect for life. After viability, the *Casey* Court would allow regulation and even proscription of abortion unless the abortion was necessary to preserve the life or health of the mother.

In applying the undue burden standard to the *Casey* statute, the plurality upheld three of the four challenged provisions. They upheld the 24-hour waiting period and the requirement that a woman must certify in writing that her physician had informed her of the availability of state-published materials describing the fetus, medical assistance for childbirth, paternal child support, adoption agencies, and other abortion alternatives. The provision could be waived to avert severe adverse effects on the mental or physical health of the woman. Analogizing the provision of information to normal informed-consent requirements, the Court upheld it so long as the information provided was not misleading. Providing information failed to abridge the physician's right not to speak as such obligations lay within normal licensing requirements. While the waiting period could impose a burden on poor women, it did not impose a substantial obstacle based on the facts before the Court.

---

[344] *Id.* at 876.

[345] "What is at stake is the woman's right to make the ultimate decision, not a right to be insulated from all others in doing so." *Id.* at 877.

The plurality overruled both *Akron* and *Thornburgh* to the extent that they were inconsistent with its opinion.

A majority of Justices struck down the requirement that a woman certify in writing that she had notified her spouse of her abortion. Alternatively, a woman could certify that another man impregnated her, that her husband could not be found, that the pregnancy resulted from spousal sexual assault, or that such notification would subject her to the danger of physical assault. In light of the District Court's findings of spousal abuse surrounding pregnancy, the requirement was unconstitutional. The requirement posed a substantial obstacle due to its probable effect of deterring a significant number of women from exercising their right to choose abortion.

The *Casey* Court upheld the parental consent provision, requiring the informed consent of one parent. This provision included an exception for medical emergencies and allowed a "judicial bypass" if a determination could be made that the minor seeking an abortion had given informed consent, and that the abortion was in her best interests. The only portion of this requirement not supported by precedent was that of informed parental consent. The Court upheld this feature for the same reasons that it upheld informed consent generally.

With the exception of disclosure of spousal notification, the provision requiring abortion providers to keep records was upheld. While preserving the confidentiality of the woman's identity, the provision required identification of the treating and referring physicians; the women's age, prior pregnancies, and prior abortions; fetal weight and age; the date of the abortion and the procedure used; medical conditions that might complicate the abortion or medical complications from the abortion; when applicable, the basis for determining that the abortion was medically necessary; and the woman's marital status. Abortion facilities were required to report quarterly the number of abortions on their premises by trimester. The plurality found maintenance of such records advanced the state interest in health and posed no substantial obstacle to the right to abort.[346]

Justice Blackmun wrote an opinion concurring in the judgment in part, concurring in part, and dissenting in part. Justice Stevens wrote an opinion concurring in part and dissenting in part. Both Justices would have reaffirmed *Roe* in its entirety. Arguing that *Roe* protected the woman's rights to bodily integrity and family planning, Justice Blackmun would have struck down all of the regulations at issue. He opined that the plurality did not invalidate certain provisions because of an inadequate record. Justice Stevens would allow some regulation of abortion on the grounds of the state interest in protecting potential life, but thought that the "correct application" of the undue burden standard would still invalidate certain provisions upheld by the plurality. Specifically, Justice Stevens would also have invalidated the informed consent provision at issue, including parental informed consent and the 24-hour waiting period.

Chief Justice Rehnquist wrote an opinion concurring in the judgment in part and dissenting in part, joined by Justices White, Scalia, and Thomas. Chief Justice

---

[346] The Court had sustained a similar record-keeping provision in *Planned Parenthood v. Danforth*, 428 U.S. 52 (1976).

Rehnquist would have applied a rational relation test to uphold every challenged provision of the *Casey* statute. Chief Justice Rehnquist argued that, unlike other rights dealing with personal privacy or the family, the right to choose an abortion was not fundamental, because this right involved the destruction of life. Contesting the roots of *Roe* in tradition, Chief Justice Rehnquist noted that abortion after quickening[347] was prohibited at common law by a majority of states at the codification of the Fourteenth Amendment, and an overwhelming majority of states allowed abortion only to preserve the life or health of the mother at the time that *Roe* was decided.

Chief Justice Rehnquist criticized the plurality's *stare decisis* rationale, as the plurality itself did not follow *Roe* in many significant respects. The Chief Justice also criticized the plurality's refusal to reverse *Roe* on the theory that it was a politically divisive decision.

Justice Scalia, joined by Chief Justice Rehnquist and Justices White and Thomas, authored a separate dissent. He argued that the abortion right was the product of the personal predilections of judges and therefore such decisions should be left to the judgment of the legislative branches.

In *Leavitt v. Jane L.*,[348] the Court ruled that a Utah law prohibiting abortions after 20 weeks except when necessary to save the life of the pregnant women or to prevent grave health risks to the woman or grave defects to the child was severable from a provision invalidated by the District Court that had regulated abortions performed during the first 20 weeks. The Court held the provisions severable because of a clear severability or savings clause in the statute, and because the statutes were not sufficiently "interrelated"[349] as to prohibit the severing of one provision from the other. Justice Stevens' dissent said that the Court normally did not grant certiorari on state-law questions.

In *Mazurek v. Armstrong*,[350] the Court upheld a District Court's refusal to grant a preliminary injunction against a Montana statute that allowed only licensed physicians to perform abortions. Little evidence suggested that the law erected a "substantial obstacle" to obtaining an abortion.[351] Montana evidenced no tainted legislative motive in enacting the law. States have the power to decide who is qualified to perform professional activities within their borders. The Court rejected the claim that the statute was an unconstitutional bill of attainder directed at only one person. Indeed, the fact that the statute only affected one abortion provider demonstrated that the law's end was not to erect significant obstacles against abortion.

In *Ayotte v. Planned Parenthood of Northern New England*[352] the Court held that failure to provide a medical emergency exception was not sufficient to facially

---

[347] Quickening was the time that movement of the fetus could be felt in the womb.

[348] 518 U.S. 137 (1996).

[349] *Id.*

[350] 520 U.S. 968 (1997).

[351] *Id.* at 969.

[352] 546 U.S. 320 (2006).

invalidate an entire abortion statute. The 2003 New Hampshire Parental Notification Prior to an Abortion Act prevents physicians from performing abortions on pregnant minors until 48 hours after written notice was provided to a parent or guardian. Although the Act provided three exceptions to the parental notification requirement, it did not provide a medical emergency exception.

Writing for a unanimous Court, Justice O'Connor stressed that the Court was not revisiting abortion precedents. In this connection, she outlined established propositions, the first two legal and the third factual. First, states may require parental involvement in a minor's decision to terminate a pregnancy. Second, states may not restrict abortions that are necessary to preserve the life or health of the mother. Third, minors, like adults, may need immediate abortions to avoid serious health problems.

Because the statute was only invalid in a few applications, facial invalidation was unwarranted. Moreover, the statute contained a severability clause that would have allowed a court to merely remove the unconstitutional language. The Court remanded the case to determine whether the legislature would have intended total invalidation under the circumstances.

In *Madsen v. Women's Health Center*,[353] the Court upheld against a First Amendment challenge various provisions in an injunction that placed certain restrictions on protestors' activities outside abortion clinics.[354] In *National Organization for Women, Inc. v. Scheidler*,[355] the Court construed the Racketeer Influenced and Corrupt Organizations Act (RICO) to apply to abortion protestors not motivated by an economic purpose. The owners of two abortion clinics sued an anti-abortion group under RICO, alleging a nationwide conspiracy to close down abortion clinics through racketeering. While a unanimous Court agreed that RICO applied to abortion protestors, it declined to address whether application of RICO to these activities raised First Amendment concerns because defendants failed to present such issues to the Court.

In *Stenberg v. Carhart*,[356] the Court invalidated Nebraska's "partial birth abortion" statute because it placed an undue burden on a women's right to choose an abortion.[357] Writing for a majority, Justice Breyer stated that three points established by the joint opinion in *Planned Parenthood v. Casey*[358] set the standard in this case. First, a woman had a previability right to terminate her pregnancy.

---

[353] 512 U.S. 753 (1994).

[354] For further discussion of *Madsen*, see *infra* § 15.04[1].

[355] 510 U.S. 249 (1994).

[356] 530 U.S. 914 (2000).

[357] The statute at issue made it a felony carrying a prison term of up to 20 years and a fine of up to $25,000 for a doctor to perform a "partial birth abortion" defined as "an abortion procedure in which the person performing the abortion partially delivers vaginally a living unborn child before killing the unborn child and completing the delivery." The statute "further defines 'partially delivers vaginally a living unborn child before killing the unborn child' to mean 'deliberately and intentionally delivering into the vagina a living unborn child, or substantial portion thereof, for the purpose of performing a procedure that the person performing such procedure knows will kill the unborn child and does kill the unborn child.' "

[358] 505 U.S. 833 (1992).

Second, a statute was unconstitutional if it placed an undue burden on a woman seeking a previability abortion. An undue burden was a law that " 'has the purpose or effect of placing a substantial obstacle in the path of a woman seeking an abortion of a nonviable fetus.' "[359] Third, the State could regulate abortion postviability " 'except where it is necessary, in appropriate medical judgment, for the preservation of the life or health of the mother.' "[360]

The medical profession used two methods to perform second trimester abortions. "Dilation and evacuation" (D&E) was a form of "transcervical procedures performed at 13 weeks gestation or later."[361] Generally, D&E "involves (1) dilation of the cervix; (2) removal of at least some fetal tissue using nonvacuum instruments; and (3) (after the 15th week) the potential need for instrumental disarticulation or dismemberment of the fetus or the collapse of fetal parts to facilitate evacuation from the uterus."[362] After 16 weeks "vacuum aspiration becomes ineffective and the fetal skull becomes too large to pass through the cervix."[363] When the fetus was positioned "head first (a vertex presentation), the doctor collapses the skull; and the doctor then extracts the entire fetus through the cervix. If the fetus presents feet first (a breech presentation), the doctor pulls the fetal body through the cervix, collapses the skull, and extracts the fetus through the cervix."[364] This was called dilation and extraction, or D&X.

The Nebraska statute created a constitutional problem because it affected both pre- and postviability abortions and the state's regulatory interest was "considerably weaker" previability. Although the statute "regulates only a *method* of performing abortion," the State could not place women's health at risk due to complications in the "pregnancy *itself*" or by forcing them through regulation to choose "riskier" abortion procedures.

Casey protected procedures that were "necessary, in appropriate medical judgment." This should not be understood to give physicians "unfettered discretion" in choosing a procedure. However, under *Casey* a health exception was required if "substantial medical authority" showed that women's health would be endangered by banning a method of abortion. The procedure had to be available if " 'necessary, in appropriate medical judgment, for the preservation of the life or health of the mother.' "[365] Even if Nebraska primarily intended the statute to ban D&X, the Nebraska statute failed to distinguish between "D&E (where a foot or arm is drawn through the cervix) and D&X (where the body up to the head is drawn through the cervix)."[366]

---

[359] *Stenberg*, 530 U.S. at 921.

[360] *Id.*

[361] *Id.* at 924.

[362] *Id.* at 925.

[363] *Id.* at 927.

[364] *Id.* at 927.

[365] *Id.* at 930.

[366] *Id.* at 939.

Justice Stevens concurred, joined by Justice Ginsburg. Justice Stevens stated that a doctor should not have "to follow any procedure other than the one that he or she reasonably believes will best protect the woman in her exercise of this constitutional liberty."[367]

Justice O'Connor concurred, emphasizing that since even a postviability prohibition of abortion required a health exception, it followed that previability proscriptions also required such a health exception. This statute allowed for an exception to save the life of the mother but not her health.

Justice O'Connor also held the statute unconstitutional because it placed an undue burden on women's right to seek an abortion previability. The ban covered not just D&X but also D&E, which is the most common previability procedure in the second trimester. This created a substantial obstacle for women and imposed an "undue burden on a woman's right to terminate her pregnancy prior to viability."[368] Justice O'Connor would uphold a ban on D&X that contained an exception to protect the mother's health and life.

Justice Ginsburg concurred, joined by Justice Stevens. Justice Ginsburg noted that, "this law does not save any fetus from destruction, for it targets only 'a *method* of performing abortion.' "[369]

Chief Justice Rehnquist wrote a brief dissent expressing his disagreement with *Casey* but noting its precedential effect. He joined the dissents of Justices Kennedy and Thomas because he found they correctly apply *Casey's* principles.

Justice Scalia also dissented. He stated that *Casey's* undue burden standard was elusive and could not "be demonstrated true or false by factual inquiry or legal reasoning."[370]

Justice Kennedy wrote a dissenting opinion joined by Chief Justice Rehnquist. Justice Kennedy noted, "Nebraska seeks only to ban the D&X."[371] He found a problem with health exceptions that defer to an individual physician's judgment. As medical opinion was divided "on the propriety of the partial-birth abortion technique (both in terms of physical safety and ethical practice),"[372] the legislature should decide this matter.

Justice Thomas dissented, joined by the Chief Justice and Justice Scalia. He found that the "majority and Justice O'Connor twist *Roe* and *Casey*." While *Roe* and *Casey* protected abortion procedures "necessary" to protect the mother's health, the majority allowed any procedure that "has any comparative health benefits." Requiring a health exception "eviscerated *Casey's* undue burden standard and imposed unfettered abortion-on-demand."[373] The majority's actual standard was

---

[367] *Id.* at 946.

[368] *Id.* at 950.

[369] *Id.* at 951.

[370] *Id.* at 954.

[371] *Id.* at 960.

[372] *Id.* at 972.

[373] *Id.* at 1012.

"whether *any* doctor could reasonably believe"[374] that a particular abortion method would protect the woman.

In *Gonzales v. Carhart*,[375] the Court — against "a broad, facial" challenge — upheld the federal Partial Birth Abortion Act of 2003. Congress passed the Act in reaction to the Court's opinion in *Stenberg v. Carhart*.[376] Justice Kennedy wrote the opinion for the Court and was joined by Chief Justice Roberts, and Justices Scalia, Thomas and Alito. The Court said that the Act was more specific and precise than the one at issue in *Stenberg*.

In the United States, 85-90 % of abortions occurred during the first 3 months of gestation or the first trimester. Most of the remaining abortions have taken place during the second trimester and have been done using a surgical method referred to as "dilation and evacuation (D&E)." The general procedure was the same for all doctors. The doctor began by dilating the cervix. Then the doctor used forceps to remove the fetus. Because the friction involved in the procedure caused the fetus to tear apart, it may take the doctor 10-15 passes to evacuate the entire fetus. Some doctors chose to kill the fetus a day or two before the procedure, particularly in late second term abortions.

The Act — whose impetus was partial birth abortions — did not involve the standard D&E, but specifically dealt with a variation on the procedure referred to as an "intact D&E." This procedure involved fewer passes so that the fetus may be extracted largely intact. In an intact D&E, the fetus was killed just prior to birth. There were different methods for killing the fetus once it became lodged in the cervix. Some doctors forced scissors into the base of the skull. Others collapsed the skull using their forceps, killing the fetus just before it was born.

In passing the Act, Congress responded to the Court's holding in *Stenberg* in two ways. First, Congress made a series of factual findings in which they asserted that the *Stenberg* Court was required to accept the " 'very questionable findings issued by the district court judge.' "[377] Congress also found that a " 'moral, medical and ethical consensus exists and that the practice of performing a partial-birth abortion . . . . [was] a gruesome and inhumane procedure that [was] never medically necessary and should be prohibited.' "[378] Second, and more important, the Act's language was more specific than that in *Stenberg*.

Planned Parenthood v. Casey[379] "rejected both *Roe's* rigid trimester framework and the interpretation of *Roe* that considered all previability regulations of abortion unwarranted."[380] Moreover, *Casey* stated that: " 'regulations which do no more than create a structural mechanism by which the State, or the parent or guardian of a minor, may express profound respect for the life of the unborn are permitted, if they

---

[374] *Id.* at 1017.

[375] *Gonzales*, 550 U.S. 124 (2007).

[376] 530 U.S. 914 (2000).

[377] 550 U.S. at 141.

[378] *Id.*

[379] 505 U.S. 833 (1992).

[380] 550 U.S. at 146.

are not a substantial obstacle to the woman's exercise of the right to choose.' "[381]

In rejecting this facial challenge, the Court concluded that the Act was not void for vagueness and did not impose an undue burden from any overbreadth on the right to choose an abortion. Justice Kennedy first rejected the vagueness challenge as the Act explicitly defined the actions that comprised an illegal abortion. "First, the person performing the abortion must 'vaginally deliver a living fetus.' "[382] The Act did not restrict abortion procedures which delivered an expired fetus or any medical procedures which did not entail vaginal delivery, such as, hysterectomies. Second, the Act required that the fetus be "delivered, 'until, in the case of a head-first presentation, the entire fetal head is outside the body of the mother, or, in the case of breech presentation, any part of the fetal trunk past the navel is outside the body of the mother.' "[383] Third, the "doctor must perform an 'overt act, other than completion of the delivery, that kills the partially delivered living fetus.' "[384] The doctor had to perform this overt act following delivery to one of the anatomical landmarks defined in the Act.

Finally, the Act contained intent or knowledge requirements that pertained to each of the above-outlined acts involved in the performance of the prohibited abortion. For example, "the physician must have 'deliberately and intentionally' delivered the fetus to one of the Act's anatomical landmarks."[385] Additionally, the physician must have delivered the fetus " 'for the purpose of performing an overt act that [doctor] knows will kill [it].' "[386] Thus, the Act did not apply if a living fetus was delivered past a critical point by accident or there was no intent to kill the fetus.

In defining vagueness, *Kolender v Lawson*[387] required " 'that a penal statute define the criminal offense with sufficient definiteness that ordinary people could understand what conduct was prohibited and in a manner that did not encourage arbitrary and discriminatory enforcement.' "[388] The Congressional Act differed from the one at issue in *Stenberg* because it defined the line between potentially criminal conduct and a lawful abortion. *Stenberg* relied on vague language such as "delivery of a 'substantial portion' of the fetus."[389] A doctor might question what constituted a substantial portion. Moreover, past decisions also stated that "scienter requirements alleviate vagueness concerns."[390] Finally, in addressing the remaining part of the vagueness test, the Act did not encourage "arbitrary or discriminatory enforcement."[391] The Act's anatomical landmarks provided "objective standards"

---

[381] *Id.*

[382] *Id.* at 147.

[383] *Id.*

[384] *Id.* at 148.

[385] *Id.*

[386] *Id.*

[387] 461 U.S. 352 (1983).

[388] 550 U.S. at 149.

[389] *Id.*

[390] *Id.*

[391] *Id.* at 150.

that could be used to "establish minimal guidelines" for law enforcement.[392]

In the next major part of the opinion, the Court held that the Act did not impose an undue burden on second trimester abortions because it did not prohibit the standard D&E procedure that involved the piecemeal removal of the fetus. The Act specifically excluded most D&E procedures. Doctors intending to remove the fetus in parts from the start lack the scienter necessary for criminal liability. Moreover, the specific anatomical landmarks that were previously discussed differentiated the Act from *Stenberg's* "substantial portion"[393] which could be interpreted to mean delivery of even an arm or a leg. Finally, the doctrine of avoidance of constitutional issues reinforced the Court's conclusions that the Act did not cover a typical D&E procedure. " '[T]he elementary rule is that every reasonable construction must be resorted to, in order to save a statute from unconstitutionality.' "[394] In this case, the most reasonable interpretation was that the Act did not prohibit standard D&E procedures.

The Court also rejected the facial challenge that the Act imposed a substantial obstacle on a woman's right to choose to have an abortion. The Act proscribes a specific type of abortion in which a fetus was killed inches before the birth process is complete. In passing this Act, Congress stated: " 'Implicitly approving such a brutal and inhumane procedure by choosing not to prohibit it will further coarsen society to the humanity of not only newborns, but all vulnerable and innocent human life.' "[395] Congress also expressed concern for the effects that partial birth abortions had on the medical community. As reaffirmed, the government could use its regulatory power "to show its profound respect for the life within the woman."[396] If a regulation had a rational basis and did not impose an undue burden, it could "bar certain procedures and substitute others."[397] The Act's ban furthered "legitimate [governmental objectives] in regulating the medical profession . . . to promote respect for life, including life of the unborn."[398] While many may think that standard D&E can "devalue human life," Congress could still find that intact D&E "implicate[d] additional ethical and moral concerns." Congress "was concerned with 'drawing a bright line that clearly distinguishes abortion and infanticide.' "[399]

Even though it advanced legitimate state interests, the Act could still impose an unconstitutional burden on the right to an abortion if it barred a procedure " ' "necessary, in appropriate medical judgment for [the] preservation of the . . . health of the mother." ' "[400] While the Act would be unconstitutional had it subjected women to unnecessary health risks, there was "documented medical disagreement whether the Act's prohibition would ever impose significant health risks on women

---

[392] *Id.*

[393] 530 U.S. at 922.

[394] 550 U.S. at 153.

[395] *Id.* at 157.

[396] *Id.*

[397] *Id.*

[398] *Id.*

[399] *Id.* at 158.

[400] *Id.* at 161.

. . . [t]he law need not give abortion doctors unfettered choice in the course of their medical practice, nor should it elevate their status above other physicians in the medical community."[401] Medical uncertainty should not preclude regulation "in the abortion context any more than it does in other contexts." If an intact D&E was truly necessary, then the Act permits alternatives such as injection that kills the fetus prior to the delivery.

Whether a banned procedure is ever necessary to preserve a woman's health was not sufficient to make the law invalid on its face given the existence of safe alternatives. Balancing risks and marginal safety is within rational legislative competence. That one procedure is more convenient than another does not keep the State from imposing reasonable restrictions. As-applied challenges offer better opportunities to quantify and balance medical risk. As-applied challenges would not extend to threats of the woman's life as the Act already has a life exception. As plaintiffs failed to demonstrate "that the Act would be unconstitutional in a large fraction of relevant cases,"[402] the facial challenge failed.

Justice Thomas, joined by Justice Scalia, concurred. The Court's opinion accurately applied current jurisprudence, however, Justice Thomas reiterated his position that the general abortion jurisprudence including *Casey* and *Roe* had no basis in the Constitution. Moreover, the Court should not have addressed whether the Act was permissible under the Commerce Clause as the parties did not raise this issue.

Justice Ginsburg dissented, joined by Justices Stevens, Souter and Breyer. *Casey* clearly stated that any regulation of abortion, even post-viability abortions, must protect " 'the health of the woman.' "[403] The Court's decision also blurred the firmly drawn line between pre-viability and post-viability abortions. Moreover, the Court for the first time since *Roe* upholds an abortion regulation that lacks an exception safeguarding the women's health. In the past, the Act would not have survived the "close scrutiny" applied to state-decreed limitations on a woman's reproductive health. Previously, regulations could not force women to resort to "less safe methods of abortion."[404]

Many situations arise in which women may find themselves in need of late second-trimester abortions. For instance, minors might not be aware of their pregnancy until late or poor women may have financial difficulties that constrain their ability to seek proper medical care. Late abortions are also necessitated by conditions that do not arise or are not diagnosed until late in the second trimester. *Stenberg* required a health exception if " 'substantial medical authority' " demonstrated that banning a particular procedure " 'could endanger a woman's health.' "[405] A division of medical opinion indicated an uncertainly, not an absence, of risk. Consequently, the Act's ban on intact D&E required a health exception.

---

[401] *Id.* at 162.

[402] *Id.* at 167–68.

[403] *Id.* at 170 (Ginsburg, J., dissenting).

[404] *Id.* at 172.

[405] *Id.* at 174.

Justice Ginsburg's dissent also disputed the Congressional claim that the banned procedure was never necessary as "the evidence 'very clearly demonstrate[d] the opposite.' "[406] Compared to "dismemberment," intact D&E minimized the risk and trauma to the cervix as it entails fewer passes. Intact D&E also reduced the chances of fetal tissue being left in the uterus. Additionally, it diminished the chances of exposing the patient to sharp bony tissue and, because it takes less time, it would reduce the amount of bleeding and the risks of infection and anesthesia. Each District Court that considered the Congressional findings about the lack of necessity for an intact D&E viewed them as unreasonable and unsupported by the evidence.

The law did not even protect fetal life as it only targeted a method of abortion and did not save even one fetal life. The Court's use of the term "abortion doctor" and their use of the terms "baby" and "unborn child" for fetus evidences their "hostility to the right *Roe* and *Casey* secured."[407] Finally, a facial challenge to the Act was appropriate. A health exception does not apply in the large fraction of cases as it is intended "to protect women in *exceptional* cases."[408]

[2] The Family Relationship

The Court has also extended substantive due process protection to marriage and familial relationships. *Zablocki v. Redhail*[409] extended substantive due process, fundamental right status to the marital relationship. The Court invalidated an ordinance that enabled the state to prohibit marriage. The statute applied to parents who had a minor child not in their custody unless they could show present and future compliance with the support obligation. Justice Marshall applied heightened but not strict scrutiny because the Court recognized the state's need to enforce financial obligations and to advance the well-being of minors.

In *Turner v. Safley*,[410] the Court invalidated a regulation that allowed an inmate to marry only with the permission of the prison superintendent, and even then only for "compelling reasons." According to the record, only a pregnancy or the birth of an illegitimate child were considered "compelling reasons." Applying a "reasonable relationship" test, the Court concluded that "the marriage regulation does not withstand scrutiny."[411] Justice O'Connor's majority opinion rejected the government's claim that the regulation was reasonably related to prison security. Jealousy, or "love triangles," could arise in co-ed prisons apart from marriage and there were ready alternatives to address the security question short of the broad prohibition. Justice Stevens, joined by Justices Brennan, Marshall, and Blackmun, concurred in the judgment with regard to the marriage regulation, but objected to the majority's vague standard which would afford little protection for inmates.

---

[406] *Id.* at 176.

[407] *Id.* at 186.

[408] *Id.* at 189.

[409] 434 U.S. 374 (1978).

[410] 482 U.S. 78 (1987).

[411] *Id.* at 97.

The Court has been less willing to extend constitutional protection to extramarital relationships. Twice the Court has denied certiorari in cases involving extramarital relationships. In *Hollenbaugh v. Carnegie Free Library*,[412] the Court refused to review a decision sustaining the discharge of two public library employees living together in an adulterous relationship.

In addition to marriage, the Court has extended constitutional protection to the nuclear and extended family. In *Moore v. City of East Cleveland*,[413] the Court invalidated a highly restrictive zoning ordinance limiting single-dwelling housing occupancy to a narrowly defined number of family groupings, focused on the nuclear family. As written, the statute prohibited a grandmother from living with her son and two grandchildren because the grandchildren were cousins rather than brothers. Writing for the plurality, Justice Powell distinguished *Moore* from *Village of Belle Terre v. Boraas*,[414] which upheld an ordinance prohibiting unrelated individuals from sharing a single dwelling unit. In contrast, the ordinance in *Moore* infringed on the family relationship. As the extended family's status was a tradition deeply embedded in American society, it could not lightly be impaired by the state.

In a concurrence joined by Justice Marshall, Justice Brennan maintained that the ordinance displayed a cultural myopia that did not consider the important role of the extended family to ethnic and racial minority groups. Concurring only in the judgment, Justice Brennan considered the ordinance an unconstitutional taking, which arbitrarily and irrationally impaired property rights.

Justice Stewart's dissent, joined by Justice Rehnquist, and Justice White's separate dissent, criticized the majority's expansion of substantive due process rights beyond the marriage and childbearing decisions. In a separate opinion, Chief Justice Burger dissented on the grounds that the plaintiff failed to exhaust her administrative remedies before proceeding to court.[415]

Typically, the Court has critically scrutinized state laws that unduly interfere with the maintenance of the family unit or with individual rights exercised within the family context. Cases involving the family have posed such problems as parent-child relationships, the education of children, procreative rights, rights involved in divorce and child custody, and state regulation of marriage. In resolving conflicts among the interests of spouses, parents, children, and the state, the Court has relied on a number of constitutional sources. In *Wisconsin v. Yoder*,[416] the Court invoked the First Amendment's Free Exercise of Religion Clause to invalidate a state's application of its compulsory education law to Amish children when Amish parents objected to their children's continuing past the eighth grade. In *Caban v. Mohammed*,[417] the Court invalidated a state law based on gender discrimination under the Equal Protection Clause which denied a father the right to bar adoption of his illegitimate children, while permitting a mother to do so. State laws that

---

[412] 439 U.S. 1052 (1978).

[413] 431 U.S. 494 (1977).

[414] 416 U.S. 1 (1974).

[415] *See generally* C. Wright, Federal Courts 312–15 (5th ed. 1994).

[416] *See infra* § 17.05.

[417] 441 U.S. 380 (1979).

draw distinctions between legitimate and illegitimate children have also been invalidated on equal protection grounds.[418]

In the late 1970s, the Court turned increasingly to substantive due process analysis in its constitutional approach to family law issues. This approach sought to protect "fundamental values" found in the nation's history and tradition from "significant state interferences." Problems with, and criticisms of, this approach arose in providing definitional guidelines for what constituted a "fundamental value" or what state action rose to the level of "significant interference." The Court in *Zablocki* found that requiring judicial approval to marry significantly interfered with the fundamental right to marry. However, in *Califano v. Jobst*,[419] the Court sustained a Social Security Act provision that terminated the benefits of a disabled child upon the child's marriage to a non-beneficiary of the Act. In this instance the Court concluded that the governmental regulation did not substantially interfere with the right to marry, having at most an indirect impact.

In *Parham v. J.R.*,[420] the Court upheld Georgia's procedures for voluntary civil commitment of children by their parents. Chief Justice Burger concluded that the child's constitutional rights were adequately safeguarded by the informal pre-admission procedures and the traditional presumption that parents act in the best interests of their child. In balancing the interests of child, state, and parents, he gave greater weight to the parents' traditional interest in rearing their child and to the traditional concept of broad parental authority.

In *Santosky v. Kramer*,[421] the Court struck down, under the Due Process Clause, New York's procedure for depriving parents of the care and custody rights in their natural children. Under the New York law parental rights could be terminated by the Family Court upon a finding that the child had been "permanently neglected." If the State supported its allegations by "a fair preponderance of the evidence," the child could be declared permanently neglected and the natural parents' rights in the child could be permanently terminated. "The fundamental liberty interest of natural parents in the care, custody, and management of their child does not evaporate simply because they have not been model parents or have lost temporary custody of their child to the state."[422]

Applying the criteria from *Mathews v. Eldridge*,[423] Justice Brennan required a "clear and convincing evidence" standard of proof. The interest of the natural parent was strong, and the risk of error created by the state's procedure was substantial because of the comparative ease with which the state could marshal the

---

[418] *See* Trimble v. Gordon, 430 U.S. 762 (1977) (Illinois intestate succession law barring inheritance by illegitimate children from their fathers struck down, 5-4). *But see* Lalli v. Lalli, 439 U.S. 259 (1978) (New York law requiring particular form of paternity proof in order for illegitimate children to inherit by intestate succession upheld 5-4.). *See infra* § 12.01[2].

[419] 434 U.S. 47 (1977).

[420] 442 U.S. 584 (1979).

[421] 455 U.S. 745 (1982).

[422] *Id.* at 753.

[423] 424 U.S. 319 (1976); *see supra* § 8.05.

evidence. On the other hand, the government's interest in retaining its lower standard of proof was minimal.

While *Moore* exhibited some concern for the extended family, the Court's scrutiny has not gone far beyond the nuclear family. In *Lyng v. Castillo*,[424] the Court rejected a challenge to a Federal statute providing lower food stamp allotments to close relatives (spouses, children, parents and siblings) living together than to more distant relatives, or unrelated persons, living together. The former were treated as a single household for purposes of food stamp allotments, while the latter were considered separate households unless they customarily purchased food and prepared their meals together. The law was based on a recognition that there was an economy of scale in purchasing and preparing meals in common. Moreover, there was a larger potential for mistakes or fraud resulting from claims by close relatives of separate food purchase and preparation than from similar claims by distant relatives. Justice Stevens rejected the argument that the statute burdened the "fundamental right" of a person to decide family living relationships: "The 'household' definition does not order or prevent any group of persons from dining together . . . . It is exceedingly unlikely that close relatives would choose to live apart simply to increase their allotment of food stamps."[425]

The 1989 case of *Michael H. v. Gerald D.*[426] discussed "tradition," a central theme in modern substantive due process jurisprudence. The Court upheld against substantive and procedural due process challenges a California statute conclusively presuming that the father of the child was the man married to her mother. California had applied this statute to deny visitation rights to the child's natural father. Justice Scalia wrote for a plurality of four that only the Chief Justice joined in its entirely. Justice Scalia found no specific tradition protecting the rights of the natural father of a child conceived in an adulterous relationship.

In a concurrence joined by Justice Kennedy, Justice O'Connor refused to confine the Court to one specific historical method of deriving tradition. Concurring in the judgment, Justice Stevens noted that California law allowed California courts to grant visitation rights to anyone " 'having an interest in the welfare of the child.' "[427] In denying visitation to the alleged natural father under this provision, the California courts, in determining visitation rights, had taken paternity into account. In dissent, Justice Brennan basically abandoned the "tradition" analysis, and relied instead on the open-ended nature of the Constitution's text.

In *Troxel v. Granville*,[428] the Court invalidated a court order granting visitation rights to grandparents against a parent's will, when the parents never married. Writing for a plurality of four, Justice O'Connor noted that the "breathtakingly broad" statute allowed a court to "grant such visitation rights whenever 'visitation may serve the best interest of the child.' "[429] The lower court's decision broke from

---

[424]   477 U.S. 635 (1986).

[425]   *Id.* at 638. *See infra* § 12.02[1], for further discussion of this case.

[426]   491 U.S. 110 (1989).

[427]   *Id.* at 115.

[428]   530 U.S. 57 (2000).

[429]   *Id.* at 61.

the concept that "a fit parent will act in the best interest of his or her child."[430] Moreover, the parent never intended to completely deny visitation.

Concurring in the judgment, Justice Souter would affirm the decision of the Supreme Court of Washington that invalidated the non-parental visitation statute on its face, because it allowed courts to grant visitation rights to anyone at any time.

Concurring in the judgment, Justice Thomas invalidated the law under strict scrutiny because it violated the fundamental right of parents to rear their children articulated in *Pierce v. Society of Sisters*.[431]

Justice Stevens dissented, maintaining that the statute was neither invalid on its face nor as applied. He feared that the Court's decision threatened the best interests of the child standard, referred to 698 times in statutes and visitation laws around the nation. Justice Scalia dissented, giving little credence to a legal principle that elicited such diverse opinions among the majority. In dissent, Justice Kennedy noted that given the near universal adoption of the best interests standard, the Court would have difficulty invalidating this standard as violating " 'the concept of ordered liberty.' "[432]

[3] Homosexuality

In *Bowers v. Hardwick*,[433] police arrested a man in his bedroom for committing an act that violated the Georgia sodomy statute with another adult male. The statute defined sodomy as involving placement of sex organs into the mouth or anus of another. These acts were punishable by imprisonment for one to twenty years. Although the prosecutor dropped the charges, Hardwick sued for declaratory judgment to have the statute declared unconstitutional.

Although the statute's ban extended to heterosexual activities involving sex organs and the mouth or anus, including married individuals, the Court limited its decision to the homosexual activity at issue. Justice White's majority opinion rejected the claim that tradition supplied a fundamental right to engage in the behavior at issue as 32 of 37 states had sodomy laws when the Fourteenth Amendment was ratified. Until 1961, all 50 states outlawed sodomy, and 24 proscribed it at the time of this decision. Justice White said that law was "constantly based on notions of morality."[434] Recalling the repudiation of substantive due process in the 1930s, Justice White stated that institutional integrity would be compromised by continuing to expand its modern substantive due process jurisprudence. "The Court is most vulnerable and comes nearest to illegitimacy when it deals with judge-made constitutional law having little or no cognizable roots in the language or design of the Constitution."[435]

---

[430] *Id.* at 68.

[431] 268 U.S. 510 (1925).

[432] *Id.* at 101.

[433] 478 U.S. 186 (1986).

[434] *Id.* at 196.

[435] *Id.* at 194.

Justice White distinguished *Stanley v. Georgia*[436] in which the Court reversed a conviction for viewing obscene materials in one's home, as *Stanley* hinged on free speech interests. *Stanley* did not protect possessing drugs, firearms, or stolen goods in one's home. Nor would the Court protect all sexual conduct in the home by consenting adults; this could lead down a slippery slope toward protection of adultery, incest, and sex crimes.

Concurring, Chief Justice Burger amplified the lack of a tradition protecting sodomy. It had been proscribed throughout the history of Western Civilization. Among the examples he cited were Roman Law and Judeo-Christian morality. In an important concurring opinion supplying the crucial fifth vote, Justice Powell suggested that any prison sentence for homosexual sodomy, particularly one of long duration, could violate the Eighth Amendment.

The majority and dissent differed in characterizing what traditions were at stake in *Bowers*. Justice White characterized the constitutional right as the right to engage in sodomy. In contrast, Justice Blackmun's dissent found historical support for a "right to be left alone" or a right to privacy. He also criticized the Court's refusal to consider the statute's regulation of heterosexual behavior. Justice Blackmun noted that the *Bowers* Court left open challenges under the Eighth and Ninth Amendments, and the Equal Protection Clause of the Fourteenth Amendment. In a separate dissent joined by Justices Brennan and Marshall, Justice Stevens said that *Griswold v. Connecticut, Eisenstadt v. Baird*, and *Carey v. Population Services International*[437] stand for a right to engage in non-reproductive sexual conduct. Selectively restricting such behavior by homosexuals must be justified by something more than a dislike for homosexuals.

In *Lawrence v. Texas*,[438] the Court invalidated a Texas law that criminalized two persons of the same sex engaging in intimate sexual conduct. Constitutionally-protected liberty included not only the right to be free of government intrusion in private places, but also "freedom of thought, belief, expression, and certain intimate conduct."[439] *Lawrence* involved "liberty of the person both in its spatial and more transcendent dimensions."[440] Police officers entered an apartment where they observed two men engaging in a sexual act. After being arrested and held in custody overnight, petitioners were charged and convicted;[441] each was fined $200 and levied court costs of $141.25.

While this case had some similarities with *Bowers v. Hardwick*,[442] the statute in *Lawrence* only applied to same-sex sexuality. Also, unlike *Hardwick*, the petitioners in *Lawrence* were prosecuted. The laws at issue in both cases regulated

---

[436] *See infra* § 16.05[1].

[437] *See supra* § 8.05[1].

[438] 539 U.S. 558 (2003).

[439] *Id.* at 562.

[440] *Id.*

[441] The statute that petitioners violated "defines 'deviate sexual intercourse' as follows: (A) any contact between any part of the genitals of one person and the mouth or anus of another person; or (B) the penetration of the genitals or the anus of another person with an object."

[442] 478 U.S. 186 (1986).

sexual behavior in one's home, the most private human activity in the most private place. These personal relationships fell within the constitutionally-protected liberty of persons. Whether or not the law should recognize this personal relationship, a person should be allowed to pursue it without facing criminal punishment.

The Court disagreed with the assertion in *Bowers* that there was a long history of sodomy laws directed at homosexuals in Western civilization. Early American sodomy laws generally restricted sexual activity for purposes other than procreation. These laws were not enforced against consenting adults who engaged in sodomy in private. Instead, they were used to protect those who did not or were not able to consent. Laws aimed at proscribing same-sex relationships did not emerge until the last few decades of the 20th Century.

The British Parliament abolished laws punishing homosexual conduct in 1967. Five years prior to *Bowers*, the European Court of Human Rights invalidated laws that proscribed consensual homosexual conduct. Their decision was authoritative for all 45 member countries of the Council of Europe. While at the time *Bowers* was decided, there were 25 states with laws that proscribed the conduct referenced in *Bowers*, now only 13 states had such laws. Only 4 of these enforced their laws solely against homosexuals. The states that still had laws prohibiting sodomy, including Texas, tended to not enforce the regulation against consenting adults that engaged in this activity in private.

Petitioners also contended that the Texas statute was invalid under the Equal Protection Clause under *Romer v. Evans*.[443] The Court, however, focused on the continuing validity of *Bowers*. Had this statute been invalidated on equal protection grounds, the decision would not have addressed whether or not this conduct was substantively valid, and the stigma surrounding it might have remained. The offense was a class C misdemeanor, which would go on petitioners' criminal record, and would subject petitioners to resident registration laws in at least 4 States. They would also have to note the conviction on job applications.

Planned Parenthood v. Casey[444] stated that in order to overrule a precedent concerning a constitutional liberty interest, the Court must consider whether any individual or society has relied on the precedent. As there had been no such reliance on *Bowers*, the Court overruled it. *Bowers* caused confusion, as the precedents both before and after it were at odds with its central holding.

This case involved two consenting adults that engaged in an activity that is common to a homosexual way of life. There were no minors or persons who might be injured involved, and there was no public conduct or prostitution. The government was not giving formal recognition to homosexual relationships. The Court struck down the statute as it did not further a "legitimate state interest which can justify its intrusion into the personal and private life of the individual."[445]

Justice O'Connor concurred in the judgment, based on equal protection. Bowers did not allow moral disapproval of certain behavior to be a rational basis under the

---

[443] 517 U.S. 620 (1996).

[444] 505 U.S. 833 (1992).

[445] *Lawrence*, 539 U.S. at 578.

Equal Protection Clause to criminalize only homosexual sodomy. *Department of Agriculture v. Moreno*[446] and *Romer*[447] establish that moral disapproval did not satisfy rational basis review. The most obvious discrimination is one which makes criminal the conduct that defines the class. While the statute failed rational review under the Equal Protection Clause, other laws that distinguished between heterosexuals and homosexuals would not automatically fail such review. The state interest asserted in this case was the moral disapproval of same-sex relations. Other reasons might allow the state to promote the institution of marriage.

Justice Scalia dissented, joined by Chief Justice Rehnquist and Justice Thomas. The Court did not declare homosexual sodomy a "fundamental right" under the Due Process Clause. The majority also did not subject this statute to strict scrutiny, which would have been appropriate if homosexual sodomy were a fundamental right. The Court did not elucidate the reasons that *stare decisis* should prevail in *Casey* but not in *Lawrence*. Three members of the *Lawrence* majority co-authored an opinion in *Casey* that praised the doctrine of *stare decisis*.

Examples of permissible constraints on liberty include laws that proscribe prostitution, the use of heroin, and working over a prescribed number of hours. Until 1961, all 50 states prohibited sodomy. Today, 24 states and the District of Columbia imposed criminal penalties for sodomy even when performed between consenting adults in private. The right to engage in this behavior was not "deeply rooted in this Nation's history and tradition."

[4]   Right to Die

The right to die is one of the most complex liberty issues to face the Court. Highly controversial questions have developed with the advances in medical technology. Advocates of the right to die, who argue that technological advances threaten to reduce life to an undignified machine-like state, compete against a strong interest in preserving life and seeing that it is not terminated lightly.

In 1976, the New Jersey Supreme Court considered *In re Quinlan*,[448] a case brought by the parents of Karen Quinlan, an accident victim in a persistent vegetative state. Karen's parents sought to discontinue their daughter's respirator treatment. In granting the relief, the New Jersey Supreme Court decided the case on the basis of the daughter's right to privacy, despite the fact that the case was brought by her parents and the fact that evidence as to her own views on the right to die was insubstantial.

The United States Supreme Court first addressed a right to die issue in the 1990 case of *Cruzan v. Director, Missouri Department of Health*.[449] Nancy Cruzan sustained severe injuries in an automobile accident that left her in a persistent vegetative state. When it became apparent that Nancy's condition was irreversible, her parents sought a court order allowing them to remove their daughter's artificial

---

[446] 413 U.S. 528 (1973).

[447] 517 U.S. 620 (1996).

[448] 70 N.J. 10 (1976).

[449] 497 U.S. 261 (1990).

nutrition and hydration apparatus, an action that would cause Nancy's death. The Missouri Supreme Court denied the parents' request, finding that the life support systems could not be removed absent clear and convincing evidence that Nancy herself would have chosen death under these circumstances. The narrow issue before the Supreme Court was whether the Constitution prohibited Missouri's requirement of the clear and convincing evidence standard in the withdrawal of life-sustaining treatment.

Chief Justice Rehnquist's opinion began with an analysis of informed consent. Tort law in this area provided that a patient had the right to refuse treatment; moreover, the administration of medical treatment without consent constituted a battery. Chief Justice Rehnquist surveyed the diverse state court decisions dealing with the issue, which incorporated both constitutional and common law principles. While state courts had recognized a right of competent people to refuse medical treatment, the courts differed as to what happened when the patient was incompetent to make that decision. The Chief Justice indicated that Supreme Court precedent also suggested a constitutional right for a competent patient to terminate her own treatment, perhaps even to refuse food and water, and assumed *arguendo* that the Fourteenth Amendment afforded such a right. Cruzan's parents asserted a similar right for an incompetent patient. As that right must be asserted by a surrogate, the Chief Justice construed Missouri's evidentiary rule as helping to ensure that the surrogate's decision conformed to what the patient would have done.

Missouri asserted interests in protecting and preserving human life and in protecting the personal wishes of the incompetent. With regard to the latter, the Court noted that the state may choose not to second-guess decisions about the quality of life, and the state may recognize that even when family surrogates exist they may not always place the patient's interests first. The Court found Missouri's interests sufficient to justify the heightened clear and convincing evidence standard in right to die cases. This standard was a permissible means for the state to place an increased burden on those seeking to terminate an incompetent's life-sustaining equipment: the consequence of mistaking an incompetent person's desire for death was irreversible.

Chief Justice Rehnquist noted that virtually all states require written wills and refuse to honor oral evidence under the Statute of Frauds. The Court rejected Nancy's oral comments concerning her wish to die if faced with life as a "vegetable" because the comments did not provide evidence that Nancy would make that decision if consciously faced with the condition she suffered. In a footnote, the Court noted that it was not confronted with strong and probative evidence of the patient's expressed desire to appoint a surrogate to decide whether to terminate treatment.

In a concurrence necessary to form a majority, Justice O'Connor indicated that the right to terminate medical treatment, including food and water, implicated substantive due process rights. As not many persons leave written or oral instructions about what to do in these situations, Justice O'Connor suggested that there may be a constitutional duty for states to honor the decisions of certain surrogate decision-makers to terminate the treatment of an incompetent patient.

She specifically mentioned an agent with a durable power of attorney or a proxy honoring the intent expressed in a living will. Such means could safeguard the patient's interests.

In a separate concurrence, Justice Scalia flatly rejected any substantive due process right in such situations. He said that the Constitution did not guarantee a right to commit suicide; individual states should decide such matters. Justice Scalia analogized the right to die controversy to the historically controversial abortion issue, and argued that the Court should not become involved in another morass of that kind. The Equal Protection Clause sufficiently protected against irrational laws requiring the preservation of life.

In a dissent joined by Justices Marshall and Blackmun, Justice Brennan challenged Missouri's asserted interest in preserving Nancy Cruzan's life. Justice Brennan argued that the only legitimate state interest Missouri possessed was an interest in protecting the *accuracy* of a determination of the patient's wishes. He said that misreading the patient's intentions by continuing medical treatment was a decision just as irrevocable as permitting the patient to die. He objected to the rejection of informative evidence indicating the patient's wishes, particularly as few Americans formalize their preferences with written wills or health care directives. Based on separate conversations with Nancy, her mother, her sister, and a close friend all concluded that she would have wanted her life support systems terminated under the circumstances at issue. Her court-appointed guardian *ad litem* reached the same conclusion. States should ascertain the wishes of the patient without any bias for or against life. The appointment of a guardian *ad litem* was sufficient for that purpose. Justice Brennan also argued that in cases where it is impossible to determine the incompetent patient's wishes, the decision to terminate treatment should rest with the patient's family. In a separate dissent, Justice Stevens objected to state policy asserting an interest in preserving life that might conflict with the patient's best interests.

In *Washington v. Glucksberg*,[450] the Court held that Washington's prohibition against assisted suicide did not violate the Due Process Clause. Washington did afford criminal and civil immunity to a physician honoring a patient's request to withhold or withdraw medical treatment. Turning first to the country's history, legal traditions, and practices, the Court noted that assisted suicide is a crime in almost every state. For more than 700 years, the Anglo-American common law has discouraged or punished suicide and assisted suicide. All states except Oregon have rejected legislative proposals to legalize assisted suicide. Moreover, virtually every western democracy criminalized assisted suicide.

In addition to protecting against physical constraint, the Due Process Clause also protected the right to refuse medical treatment. However, to avoid reducing substantive due process to the policy preferences of individual justices, the Court exercised restraint before withdrawing another area from public debate. First, substantive due process "protects those fundamental rights and liberties which are, objectively, 'deeply rooted in this Nation's history and tradition.' "[451] Second, the

---

[450] 521 U.S. 702 (1997).

[451] *Id.*

fundamental liberty interest must be carefully described using the country's "history, legal traditions, and practices"[452] as guideposts. In *Cruzan v. Director, Missouri Department of Health*,[453] the Court recognized not a " 'right to die' "[454] but a constitutional right to " 'refuse life-saving hydration and nutrition.' "[455] A right to assisted suicide would reject legal doctrine handed down through the centuries and now adopted by almost every state. Plaintiffs asserted that *Cruzan* and *Planned Parenthood v. Casey*[456] construed the Due Process Clause as protecting all " 'basic and intimate exercises of personal autonomy.' "[457] The Court rejected the "sweeping conclusion"[458] that it protects "any and all important, intimate, and personal decisions."[459]

The state had an interest in protecting human life, particularly as those who contemplate suicide often suffer from depression or other mental disorders. It also had an interest in "protecting the integrity and ethics of the medical profession."[460] The state had an interest in protecting vulnerable groups, such as elderly, poor, and disabled persons, against coercion to end their lives and also from any "abuse, neglect, and mistakes"[461] that may result from "prejudice, negative and inaccurate stereotypes, and 'societal indifference.' "[462] Washington's ban also avoided the "erosion"[463] that assisted suicide could eventually lead to voluntary or involuntary euthanasia. As the ban on assisted suicide was "at least reasonably related"[464] to "important and legitimate"[465] state interests, the Court did not weigh the relative strengths and weaknesses of each, but concluded that the ban did not violate the Fourteenth Amendment, "either on its face or 'as applied to competent, terminally ill adults who wish to hasten their deaths by obtaining medication prescribed by their doctors.' "[466] The Court agreed with Justice Stevens that its decision did not preclude a future, more particularized claim. However, because due process did not extend heightened scrutiny to physician-assisted suicide, a successful claim would have to differ significantly from the one in *Glucksberg*. The Court's holding permitted serious, democratic debate on the issue of assisted suicide to continue.

Justice O'Connor concurred, joined by Justices Ginsburg and Breyer. She stated that the Court need not decide whether patients have a constitutional right to

---

[452] *Id.*

[453] 497 U.S. 261 (1990).

[454] *Glucksberg*, 521 U.S. at 722–23.

[455] *Id.*

[456] 505 U.S. 833 (1992).

[457] *Glucksberg*, 521 U.S. at 722–23.

[458] *Id.* at 727.

[459] *Id.*

[460] *Id.*

[461] *Id.* at 731.

[462] *Id.*

[463] *Id.* at 733.

[464] *Id.* at 735.

[465] *Id.*

[466] *Id.*

receive palliative care even if it would hasten death, as the law at issue permitted such care. The difficulties in defining terminal illness and the danger that assisted suicide may not be voluntary justify the ban at issue.

Justice Stevens concurred in the judgment, asserting that a person's life was too valuable to society to grant complete autonomy in deciding whether to die. However, just as the Court held some applications of capital punishment statutes unconstitutional, some specific situations could warrant invalidating prohibitions on assisted suicide. Terminally ill patients need not choose whether to die but how to die, thus alleviating the interest in "protecting the vulnerable from coercion and abuse, and preventing euthanasia."[467] Developing pain treatment was extremely important, yet palliative care could not relieve all of a patient's pain and suffering.

Concurring in the judgment, Justice Souter remarked that the "compelling interest test"[468] measured "the strength and the fitness"[469] of the State's interests. The substantiality of the individual liberty and the burden it bore determine how compelling the state interest had to be and how narrow the regulation had to be. The important interest at issue required careful scrutiny. Justice Souter did not decide whether the individual interests could in some circumstances be sufficiently "fundamental"[470] to invalidate the law. In this case, the law is not "arbitrary or purposeless;"[471] the legislature was better suited to deal with this issue at this time. Justice Breyer concurred, joining Justice O'Connor's opinion, except where Justice O'Connor joined the majority. Justice Breyer characterized the individual interest as the "right to die with dignity."[472] For him, a successful claim would have to seek avoiding severe physical pain related to death.

[5]   Other Autonomy Issues

Substantive due process issues have also arisen in areas other than marriage, family, procreation, and child rearing. In *Whalen v. Roe*,[473] the Court refused to extend constitutional protection to the accumulation and distribution of sensitive personal information. Specifically, the Court refused a challenge to New York's maintenance of computer records of the names and addresses of persons who had received a doctor's prescription for certain drugs for which lawful and unlawful markets existed. The State kept the information private, having used it only for two investigations. The *Whalen* Court recognized the potential harm to individual privacy that such storehouses of information present. Consequently, the Court did not foreclose future substantive due process challenges to unwarranted disclosures of sensitive information.

---

[467] *Id.* at 747.

[468] *Id.* at 782–83.

[469] *Id.*

[470] *Id.* at 782.

[471] *Id.* at 782.

[472] *Id.* at 790.

[473] 429 U.S. 589 (1977).

In *NASA v. Nelson*,[474] the Court upheld, as applied to NASA contract employees, a Homeland Security Presidential Directive requiring background checks. It assumed "without deciding, that the Constitution protects a privacy right." However, it held that the "Government's interests as employer and proprietor in managing its internal operations, combined with the protections against public dissemination provided by the Privacy Act of 1974, satisfy any 'interest in avoiding disclosure' that may 'arguably ha[ve] its roots in the Constitution.' "[475] The employees worked at the Jet Propulsion Laboratory (JPL), owned by NASA and operated by the California Institute of Technology under a government contract. The JPL "is the lead NASA center for deep-space robotics and communications."

For the background check, the JPL employees were first required to complete Standard Form 85 (SF-85), which primarily sought "basic biographical information."[476] However, the form's final question asked "whether the employee has 'used, possessed, supplied, or manufactured illegal drugs' in the last year."[477] The form did note that a truthful response "cannot be used as evidence against the employee in a criminal proceeding."[478] Once a completed SF-85 was on file, Form 42 was sent to the employee's former landlords and references. The two-page document asked "if the reference has 'any reason to question' the employee's 'honesty or trustworthiness.' "[479] It also asked "if the reference knows of any 'adverse information' concerning the employee's 'violations of the law,' 'financial integrity,' 'abuse of alcohol and/or drugs,' 'mental or emotional stability,' 'general behavior or conduct,' or 'other matters.' "[480] If the reference had checked " 'yes,' " the form asked for an "explanation in the space below" the form and also asked for any " 'additional information' ('derogatory' or 'favorable') that may bear on 'suitability for government employment or a security clearance.' "[481]

Writing for the Court (8-0), Justice Alito explained that *Whalen v. Roe*[482] considered a similar question concerning informational privacy. *Whalen* stated that the Court's decisions on privacy issues involve at least two different interests: "one, an 'interest in avoiding disclosure of personal matters'; the other, an interest in 'making certain kinds of important decisions' free from government interference."[483] Regarding the interest in avoiding disclosure, *Nixon v. Administrator of General Services*[484] rejected former President Nixon's challenge to the Presidential Recordings and Materials Preservation Act, which required the

---

[474] 131 S. Ct. 746 (2011).

[475] *Id.* at 751.

[476] *Id.* at 753.

[477] *Id.*

[478] *Id.*

[479] *Id.*

[480] *Id.*

[481] *Id.*

[482] 429 U.S. 589 (1977).

[483] *Nelson*, 131 S. Ct. at 755.

[484] 433 U.S. 425 (1977).

President to "turn over his presidential papers and tape recordings for archival review and screening."[485] *Whalen* and *Nixon* are the only two Supreme Court decisions squarely addressing a constitutional " 'right to informational privacy.' "[486] However, lower courts have interpreted *Whalen* and *Nixon* in a number of different ways. Many have held "that disclosure of at least some kinds of personal information should be subject to a test that balances the government's interests against the individual's interest in avoiding disclosure."[487]

As in *Whalen*, Justice Alito assumed that "the Government's challenged inquiries implicate a privacy interest of constitutional significance."[488] Nevertheless, "whatever the scope of this interest, it does not prevent the Government from asking reasonable questions of the sort included on SF-85 and Form 42 in an employment background investigation that is subject to the Privacy Act's safeguards against public disclosure."[489] The Government was not exercising "its sovereign power 'to regulate and license,' " but was instead conducting the "challenged background checks in its capacity 'as proprietor' and manager of its 'internal operation.' "[490] The Government's inquiry was "part of a standard employment background check of the sort used by millions of private employers."[491] Moreover, the Government has been doing employment investigations since the days of George Washington. Therefore, the questions at issue are "reasonable, employment related inquires that furthered the Government's" proprietary and managerial interests.[492]

The follow-up question in SF-85 regarding treatment for illegal-drug use was a "reasonable, employment-related inquiry."[493] The Government used the treatment inquiry as a "mitigating factor" for "illegal-drug users who are taking steps to address and overcome their problems."[494] Like the question in SF-85, the open-ended questions on Form 42 were "reasonably aimed at identifying capable employees who will faithfully conduct the Government's business."[495] Such questions were reasonable in light of "their pervasiveness in the public and private sectors."[496]

The Privacy Act protected the employees, by allowing the Government to "maintain records 'about an individual' only to the extent the records [we]re

---

[485] *Nelson*, 131 S. Ct. at 755.

[486] *Id.* at 756 n.9.

[487] *Id.*

[488] *Id.*

[489] *Id.* at 756–57.

[490] *Id.* at 757.

[491] *Id.* at 758.

[492] *Id.* at 759.

[493] *Id.* at 760.

[494] *Id.*

[495] *Id.* at 761.

[496] *Id.*

'relevant and necessary to accomplish' a purpose authorized by law."[497] Furthermore, the Privacy Act "require[d] written consent before the Government may disclose records pertaining to any individual" criminalizing willful violations.[498]

Justice Scalia, joined by Justice Thomas, concurred in the judgment. Justice Scalia commented that informational privacy was one of many "desirable things not included in the Constitution."[499] He criticized the Court's denying respondents' claim based on many factors: the respondents were "Government contractor employees" who were "working with highly expensive scientific equipment."[500] Also, the Government was seeking "only information . . . from third parties that is standard in background checks," and the Government would be liable for revealing such information.[501] Lastly, NASA's Privacy Act regulations were "very protective of private information."[502] As the Court cited "*all*" of these factors as the basis for its decision," the lack of one or more factors could result in a successful privacy challenge.[503] Justice Thomas agreed that "the Constitution does not protect a right to informational privacy."[504]

Kelley v. Johnson[505] Court rejected a police officer's challenge to a police department regulation specifying the style and length of a patrolman's hair. The officer claimed that the grooming regulations violated his freedom of expression under the First Amendment and his equal protection and due process rights under the Fourteenth Amendment. Justice Rehnquist deferred largely to the state's legislative decision: "Choice of organization, dress, and equipment for law enforcement personnel is a decision entitled to the same sort of presumption of legislative validity as are state choices designed to promote other aims within the cognizance of the state's police power."[506] In dissent, Justice Marshall argued that "the right in one's personal appearance is inextricably bound up with the historically recognized right of 'every individual to the possession and control of his own person.' "[507]

In *East Hartford Education Ass'n v. Board of Education*,[508] the Second Circuit sustained a school board's dress code for teachers. It concluded that a teacher's refusal to wear a tie did not " 'directly and sharply implicate constitutional

---

[497] *Id.* at 762.

[498] *Id.*

[499] *Id.* at 764 (Scalia, J., concurring).

[500] *Id.* at 769.

[501] *Id.*

[502] *Id.*

[503] *Id.*

[504] *Id.* (Thomas, J., concurring).

[505] 425 U.S. 238 (1976).

[506] *Id.* at 247.

[507] *Id.* at 253.

[508] 562 F.2d 838 (2d Cir. 1977).

values.' "[509] A public school teacher may properly be subjected to restrictions in his professional life that would be invalid if applied to the populace at large. Unless the dress code was so irrational as to be arbitrary, the courts would uphold it. While hair-length regulations for public employees have generally been upheld, hair-length regulations for students have sometimes been successful.[510]

Privacy claims have been made in connection with the purely personal use of marijuana in the home. While the Alaska Supreme Court upheld such a claim in *Ravin v. State*,[511] courts generally have rejected such claims. In *State v. Murphy*,[512] the Arizona Supreme Court concluded that the personal use of marijuana did not fall within the realm of "fundamental" personal rights or rights "implicit in the concept of ordered liberty." So long as the legislature had some rational or reasonable basis for proscribing the use of marijuana, the statute must stand. Cases involving state bans on the use of laetrile in treating cancer patients have also raised the personal autonomy issue. Again concluding that no fundamental privacy right was involved, the California Supreme Court in *People v. Privitera*,[513] applied the rational basis test and upheld the statute.[514]

Substantive due process challenges have also failed in the area of all-male clubs. In *Roberts v. United States Jaycees*,[515] the Jaycees, an all-male civic organization, raised two constitutional defenses against Minnesota's effort to enforce its Human Rights Act against the group's exclusionary membership policies. Both were rejected in a unanimous (7-0) opinion. One of the Jaycees' arguments was that the all-male policy was protected by a First Amendment claim of freedom of association.[516] The other aspect of freedom of association considered by the Court was based on an asserted due process claim of personal liberty. According to Justice Brennan, this claim derived from a line of cases in which "the Court has concluded that choices to enter into and maintain certain intimate human relationships must be secured against undue intrusion by the state because of the role of such relationships in safeguarding the individual freedom that is central to our constitutional scheme."[517]

In rejecting this argument, Justice Brennan wrote:

---

[509]   *Id.* at 847.

[510]   *See* Holsapple v. Woods, 500 F.2d 49 (7th Cir.), *(per curiam), cert. denied*, 419 U.S. 901 (1974) (invalidated regulation). *But see* Zeller v. Donegal Sch. Dist. Bd. of Educ., 517 F.2d 600 (3d Cir. 1975) (hair-length regulation upheld); Blau v. Fort Thomas Pub. Sch. Dist., 401 F.3d 381 (6th Cir. 2005) (upholding student dress code and reaffirming hair-length cases); Jacobs v. Clark County Sch. Dist., 526 F.3d 419 (9th Cir. 2008) (dress code upheld); Littlefield v. Forney Indep. Sch. Dist., 268 F.3d 275 (5th Cir. 2001) (dress code upheld).

[511]   537 P.2d 494 (Alaska 1975).

[512]   570 P.2d 1070 (Ariz. 1977).

[513]   591 P.2d 919 (Cal. 1979).

[514]   *See also* United States v. Fry, 787 F. 2d 903 (4th Cir. 1986).

[515]   468 U.S. 609 (1984).

[516]   For a discussion of this argument, *see infra* § 13.04.

[517]   468 U.S. at 617–18.

The personal affiliations that exemplify these considerations . . . are those that attend the creation and sustenance of a family . . . marriage . . . childbirth . . . the raising and education of children . . . and cohabitation with one's relatives. Family relationships . . . are distinguished by such attributes as relative smallness, a high degree of selectivity in decisions to begin and maintain the affiliation, and seclusion from others in critical aspects of the relationship . . . [S]everal features of the Jaycees clearly place the organization outside of the category of relationships worthy of this kind of constitutional protection.[518]

Specifically, the Court relied on the Jaycees' size, the routine recruiting of members with no regard for individual qualifications, and the participation by women in many activities of the Jaycees. This participation undermined the argument that the exclusion of women from membership was an essential part of the associational relationship. "Moreover, much of the activity central to the formation and maintenance of the association involves the participation of strangers to that relationship."[519]

A similar result was reached in *Board of Directors of Rotary International v. Rotary Club of Duarte*.[520] A unanimous Court (Justices O'Connor and Blackmun not participating) upheld a California civil rights law on grounds that Rotary Club membership did not involve "the kind of intimate or private relation that warrants constitutional protection."[521] A First Amendment "expressive conduct" challenge to the law was also rejected.[522]

In *New York State Club Ass'n v. City of New York*,[523] the Court unanimously upheld a New York ordinance that barred discrimination in certain private clubs that had over 400 members. The primary opposition to the law was by clubs that barred women from membership. In rejecting a facial challenge to the law, the Court held that it could be applied "at least to some of the large clubs."[524] Justice White's majority opinion recognized that some smaller clubs covered by the law might conceivably be able to assert claims of "intimate" or "expressive" association.[525]

§ 8.07　PERSONAL PROPERTY RIGHTS: NEW FORMS OF PROTECTION FOR NEW PROPERTY INTERESTS

As the Court expanded the scope of personal rights and generally continued its restrictive approach to protection for property rights, it also accorded protection to new rights that blurred the line between "personal" and "property" rights. These

---

[518] *Id.* at 619–20.

[519] *Id.* at 621.

[520] 481 U.S. 537 (1987).

[521] *Id.* at 546.

[522] *See infra* § 10.01 and § 13.04 for additional discussion of this case.

[523] 487 U.S. 1 (1988).

[524] *Id.* at 12.

[525] *See infra* § 10.01 and § 13.04 for additional discussion of this case.

cases, which might best be described as involving "personal property" rights, blend substantive and procedural due process analyses.

Many of the "personal property rights" cases involve the question of legislated government entitlements, where the government bestows some privilege on individuals, such as welfare or employment. Another class of cases involves governmental deprivation of constitutionally-based liberty or property interests in areas such as corporal punishment or non-renewal of government contracts. These two types of cases share a common thread in that they do not deprive the government of the power to engage in a certain action or deprive an individual of a particular entitlement. Instead, they demand procedural safeguards before the government can take action.

Goldberg v. Kelly[526] represents the "entitlement" strand of cases. In *Goldberg*, the Court addressed the deprivation of government entitlements in the form of welfare rights. The Court held unconstitutional New York's review of the termination by a post-termination, evidentiary hearing. The Court stated that due process required the government to provide a pre-termination evidentiary hearing before depriving a welfare recipient of benefits, in order to prevent the devastation that would occur from wrongful termination. While the pre-termination hearing did not have to conform to the procedural requirements of a formal adjudication, it had to provide the recipient with fair notice and the opportunity to be heard before the government could terminate an individual's benefits. The recipient also had to confront adverse witnesses, present evidence orally, employ counsel (although the state need not provide counsel), and have an impartial hearing officer who had not participated in the termination. The decision-maker had to articulate the reasons for the decision and indicate the evidence relied on.

Goldberg is important because government entitlements are so pervasive. Each time a government entitlement is denied, the possibility of a *Goldberg*-type challenge is presented. Moreover, *Goldberg* entitlement challenges enjoy greater success than similar challenges predicated on asserted constitutional interests, because the government is depriving someone of a right that the government itself has chosen to provide. In his dissent in *Goldberg*, Justice Black predicted that the imposition of these kinds of procedural requirements would make the government reluctant to extend such benefits in the first place. Courts do not grant such challenges routinely, however, and the Supreme Court has not extended *Goldberg*-style procedural rights to many new areas and those procedural rights accorded have not been robust.

In another line of cases, *Paul v. Davis*[527] involved an asserted governmental impairment of a constitutionally-based liberty interest in reputation rather than a statutory entitlement. In *Paul*, a man was mistakenly identified as a shoplifter on flyers that indicated names and pictures of alleged shoplifters. The man brought a § 1983 action claiming that the police deprived him of his "liberty" in violation of the Fourteenth Amendment. The Court held that the Constitution did not require procedural protection for an individual's interest in his reputation. To have a valid

---

[526] 397 U.S. 254 (1970).

[527] 424 U.S. 693 (1976).

due process claim,[528] the state must alter or extinguish a right or status recognized by state law and also damage the individual's reputation. *Paul* illustrates the Court's reluctance to extend procedural protection to constitutionally-based liberty or property interests.

Goldberg and *Paul* represent the two strands of cases the Court fashioned when confronted by a claim that the government deprived an individual of a property or liberty interest without adequate procedural protection. In cases like *Goldberg*, that involve the deprivation of a government entitlement, the relevant question is not whether the property interest involved was entitled to procedural protection, but how much protection to afford.

The *Paul v. Davis* line of cases imposed a threshold barrier to the consideration of the procedural issue. A court must first determine whether a "property" or "liberty" interest was infringed.[529] Despite *Paul v. Davis* and its progeny, the Court has recognized a substantial number of personal "liberty" or "property" interests. Although the person asserting the right has not always succeeded under this approach, the Court has reached the procedural issue.[530] For example, the Court has held that a "liberty" interest is involved where a school child is subjected to corporal punishment, although no hearing is required.[531]

Although *Goldberg* and *Paul* are reference points to establish whether a government entitlement or liberty interest exists, they do not determine the nature of the "process" that is due. In *Mathews v. Eldridge*,[532] the Court described the

---

[528] *See also* Siegert v. Gilley, 500 U.S. 226 (1991), where the Court relied on the "stigma plus" test of *Paul* in its holding that defamation in an employee recommendation letter was not an infringement of a "liberty interest" under the Due Process Clause. The employee resigned from his job and the allegedly defamatory reference letter was written by his former supervisor. The Court suggested that harm to reputation coupled with loss of present employment would present a valid due process claim but not when such harm is coupled with loss of future employment. *See id.* at 233–34.

[529] *See* Town of Castle Rock v. Gonzales, 545 U.S. 748 (2005) (finding no property interest in police enforcement of a restraining order); Collins v. City of Harker Heights, 503 U.S. 115 (1992) (no federally recognized "liberty" interest in safety training for one's workplace); Siegert v. Gilley, 500 U.S. 226 (1991) (defamation is not a protected "liberty" interest); Olim v. Wakinekona, 461 U.S. 238 (1983) (transfer of prisoner from one state prison to a prison in another state did not implicate protected "liberty" interests); Leis v. Flynt, 439 U.S. 438 (1979) (the right of an out-of-state attorney to appear *pro hac vice* held not protected by the Due Process Clause); Board of Regents v. Roth, 408 U.S. 564 (1972) *and* Perry v. Sindermann, 408 U.S. 593 (1972) (non-tenured teachers generally did not have "property" interests sufficient to require hearing on a decision not to renew contract).

[530] *See, e.g.*, Ingraham v. Wright, 430 U.S. 651 (1977) ("liberty" interest is involved when a school child was subjected to corporal punishment, although no hearing was required). *See also* Wilkinson v. Austin, 545 U.S. 209 (2005) (prisoner has liberty interest in not being transferred to maximum security prison); Gilbert v. Homar, 520 U.S. 924 (1997) (procedures available after employment suspension satisfied due process); Logan v. Zimmerman Brush Co., 455 U.S. 422 (1982) (the right to use a state-created adjudicatory procedure for the hearing of complaints under a state fair employment practices act was a protected "property" interest); Board of Curators v. Horowitz, 435 U.S. 78 (1978) (hearing required before suspension of a student but not where student was dismissed from medical school for academic reasons); Memphis Light, Gas & Water Div. v. Craft, 436 U.S. 1 (1978) (utility may not cut off services without giving customer opportunity to settle billing dispute through a meeting); Goss v. Lopez, 419 U.S. 565 (1975).

[531] *See* Ingraham v. Wright, 430 U.S. 651 (1977).

[532] 424 U.S. 319 (1976).

elements involved in its determination of the type of due process required:

> First, the private interest that will be affected by the official action; second, the risk of erroneous deprivation of such interest through the procedure used, and the probable value, if any, of additional or substitute procedural safeguards; and finally, the Government's interest, including . . . the fiscal and administrative burdens that the additional or substitute procedural requirements would entail.[533]

Generally, the Court has not required the pre-termination hearing specified in *Goldberg*. Another rare instance in which the Court demanded a determination prior to government action was *Zinermon v. Burch*.[534] In that case, the Court found a constitutional right to provide procedural safeguards to determine whether a person was competent to give voluntary consent before he could check himself into a mental institution.

Cleveland Board of Education v. Loudermill[535] illustrated the variance in procedural due process protection afforded different constitutional or legislative interests. *Loudermill* involved the termination of a tenured government employee. Such employment was recognized by state law as a property interest. Statutory procedure mandated an opportunity to respond in writing before termination and a post-termination administrative review.

Although the state had no responsibility to confer such a property interest in government employment, it was obligated to conform to the standards of procedural due process in order to terminate the right once it was given.[536] In *Loudermill*, a formal adjudication was not required, but due process compelled some form of pre-termination hearing providing notice and the opportunity to be heard. Based on the *Mathews* factors, the *Loudermill* Court held that the State's procedure were constitutionally adequate.

In *Gilbert v. Homar*,[537] a unanimous Court held that a tenured employee suspended after being arrested for a felony had no due process right to a pre-suspension hearing. A public university suspended a police officer without pay who had been arrested for a drug felony. Like a grand jury indictment, an arrest by an independent entity showed that the suspension was not arbitrary, and the charges were an objective factor that would usually arouse serious public concern. While the circumstances did not demand a pre-suspension hearing, the risk of erroneous deprivation did require a prompt hearing. The case was remanded to assess the sufficiency of a post-suspension hearing held 17 days after the charges against the employee were dropped.

In *Walters v. National Ass'n of Radiation Survivors*,[538] the Court applied the *Mathews v. Eldridge* analysis in rejecting a facial challenge to a law enacted during

---

[533] *Id.* at 335.

[534] 494 U.S. 113 (1990).

[535] 470 U.S. 532 (1985).

[536] *See* Arnett v. Kennedy, 416 U.S. 134, 167 (1974).

[537] 520 U.S. 924 (1997).

[538] 473 U.S. 305 (1985).

the Civil War. The law placed a $10 limit on fees that may be paid to lawyers representing veterans in claims for service-connected death or disability. Congress had apparently created this administrative system so there would be no need for lawyers who might take a large share of the veteran's benefits. Also, according to Justice Rehnquist's majority opinion, Congress wanted to simplify the procedure for processing large numbers of claims. Applying the *Mathews* approach, Justice Rehnquist concluded that the government interest was valid and was advanced by the fee limitation. Lawyers would complicate and increase the cost of the process. There was little evidence that errors occurred under the system or that the presence of lawyers would diminish the probability of error. As for the private interest that would be affected, the Court concluded that the benefits were "more akin to the Social Security benefits involved in *Mathews* than they are to the welfare payments upon which the recipients in *Goldberg* depended for their daily subsistence."[539] Justice Stevens, joined by Justices Brennan and Marshall, vigorously dissented, claiming that the $10 fee limitation was antiquated and irrational.

In *Sandin v. Conner*,[540] a prisoner alleged that he was deprived of procedural due process when he was prohibited from presenting a witness at a disciplinary hearing in which he was sentenced to 30 days of solitary confinement. The prisoner argued that a prison regulation that required that guilt be found only where there is " 'substantial evidence' " created a protected liberty interest. Chief Justice Rehnquist, writing for the 5-4 majority, said that the liberty interest inquiry should not focus on the language of the regulation, but on the nature of the deprivation. Unless the punishment exceeded the sentence in an unexpected way, a liberty interest may be created only for restraints that impose an "atypical and significant hardship on the inmate in relation to the ordinary incidents of prison life."[541] In this case, a sentence of 30 days in solitary confinement-with discipline was not very different from that experienced by other prisoners, and was not an unusual and serious burden on a prisoner serving a life sentence of 30 years.

In *Foucha v. Louisiana*,[542] the Court held that a Louisiana statute violated the Due Process Clause by allowing a defendant acquitted by reason of insanity to remain committed to a mental institution even though the individual no longer suffered from any mental illness. Petitioner, once a criminal defendant acquitted by reason of insanity and now recommended by a hospital review committee for release, was sent back to a psychiatric hospital because he could not establish that he was not dangerous to himself or others. Justice White, writing for the Court, found that because petitioner could no longer be held as an insanity acquittee, the state must follow certain constitutionally adequate procedures to establish the grounds for his confinement. Furthermore, even if the Constitution permitted his continued confinement in a mental institution against his will, the confinement was improper absent a civil commitment proceeding to determine his current mental health. At such an adversarial proceeding the state, not petitioner, had the burden of establishing dangerousness.

---

[539] *Id.* at 333.

[540] 515 U.S. 472 (1995).

[541] 515 U.S. at 484.

[542] 504 U.S. 71 (1992).

In *Turner v. Rogers*,[543] an indigent defendant who failed to pay child support was denied appointment of counsel at the civil contempt hearing. Writing for the Court, Justice Breyer held "that the Due Process Clause does not *automatically* require the state to provide counsel at civil contempt proceedings to an indigent non-custodial parent who is subject to a child support order, even if that individual faces incarceration [for up to a year]. In particular, that Clause does not require that counsel be provided where the opposing parent or other custodian [to whom support funds are owed] is not represented by counsel and the State provides alternative procedural safeguards."[544] These safeguards include or must be equivalent to: "(1) notice to the defendant that his 'ability to pay' is a critical issue in the contempt proceeding; (2) the use of a form (or the equivalent) to elicit relevant financial information from him; (3) an opportunity at the hearing for him to respond to statements and questions about his financial status, [e.g., those triggered by his responses on the form]; and (4) an express finding by the court that the defendant has the ability to pay."[545] The Court remanded the case because defendant "received neither counsel nor the benefit of alternative procedures like those the Court describes."[546] Justice Thomas dissented joined by Justice Scalia, and joined in part by Chief Justice Roberts and Justice Alito. Justice Thomas would affirm the decision below because the basis on which the Court vacated the judgment had not been raised by either party.

---

[543] 131 S. Ct. 2507 (2011).

[544] *Id.* at 2520.

[545] *Id.* at 2519.

[546] *Id.* at 2520.

Chapter 9

RACIAL EQUALITY

INTRODUCTION

Following America's Civil War, the Thirteenth, Fourteenth, and Fifteenth Amendments to the United States Constitution were passed to ensure that freedom meant equality for the newly freed slaves. While the Thirteenth and Fifteenth Amendments were concrete, directly addressing slavery and equal rights, the Fourteenth Amendment was more amorphous. Doubts about Congressional power to protect individuals against state civil rights violations, especially racial infringements, necessitated broad language and interpretation of the Fourteenth Amendment. Today, these amendments continue to be tested against the relentless specter of racial inequality.[1]

The notion of "equality" is a recurring theme in American constitutional law.[2] The Equal Protection Clause of the Fourteenth Amendment was designed to impose upon the states a duty to prohibit legislative classifications and administrative behavior that discriminated against particular groups in the distribution of certain fundamental rights.[3] Drawing on *United States v. Carolene Products*,[4] the suspect class strand of equal protection jurisprudence prohibits government discrimination against groups of people based on race, national origin, gender alienage, illegitimacy and certain other criteria. Chapters 9, 10, 11, and part of 12 discuss this dominant strand of equal protection jurisprudence. The fundamental rights strand of equal protection jurisprudence prohibits discrimination with respect to certain fundamental rights-primarily voting, travel, and access to the judicial process. This less extensive area of equal protection jurisprudence is discussed in Chapter 12. The impetus that shaped equal protection analysis was discrimination based on race, specifically the legacy of constitutionalized slavery.

As background for the interpretation of the Equal Protection Clause, it is appropriate to discuss the status of the race issue as it stood prior to the Civil War. In 1857, the United States Supreme Court handed down a case that virtually

---

[1] For discussion of the civil rights movement and the problems that continue to prevent the achievement of racial equality today, *see* D. Bell, *Foreword: The Civil Rights Chronicles*, 99 HARV. L. REV. 4 (1985).

[2] *See* K. KARST, BELONGING TO AMERICA 2 (1989) ("to define the scope of the ideal of equality in America is to define the boundaries of the national community").

[3] *See generally* J. Tussman & J. TenBroek, *The Equal Protection of Laws*, 37 CAL. L. REV. 341 (1949) (classic treatment of the principles underlying the Equal Protection clause).

[4] *See supra* § 8.05.

constitutionalized slavery.[5] *Dred Scott v. Sandford* involved the status of a slave living with his master in a "free" state. In 1834, the slave, Dred Scott, accompanied his master, Dr. John Emerson from Missouri, a State where slavery was legal, across the Mississippi River to Illinois, a State where slavery was illegal. Two years later they moved to the free territory of Wisconsin where both lived until 1838, when they returned to Missouri.

Wisconsin is north of the latitude line of 36/30E. The Missouri Compromise, a congressional act passed in 1820, mandated that slavery was illegal in any state or territory above this latitude. Any states or territories below that line could make slavery legal. When a territory decided to enter the Union as a state, it would choose whether it would be a slave state or a free state.

Upon Dr. Emerson's death, Scott sued for his freedom, contending that he was a free man because he had resided in the free state of Illinois, and the free territory of Wisconsin. After receiving an unfavorable decision in a Missouri Federal court,[6] Scott appealed to the United States Supreme Court. The Court addressed the threshold issue of whether a person who descended from African slaves could be a United States citizen. In an opinion by Chief Justice Taney, the Court held that the drafters of the Constitution had not intended blacks, whether free or not, to be citizens of the United States or of any state. Accordingly, the federal courts did not have diversity jurisdiction. It is not known if a majority of the Justices joined in this part of the opinion. If so, the decision the Court made on the merits is arguably dicta.

The discussion of the merits focused on whether Wisconsin or Illinois residency would dictate freedom. The Court said that freedom could not have been attained by residing in the free Wisconsin territory. Operating under the premise that slaves were property, the Court found that the Missouri Compromise unconstitutionally violated the Fifth Amendment Due Process Clause by depriving slave owners of their property if they moved above the 36/30E line. Accordingly, Scott did not become free by residing in the free Wisconsin territory.

The second issue was whether Scott was emancipated by residing in the free state of Illinois. The Court reasoned that because Scott was taken to Illinois as a slave, was held there as such, and was brought back to Missouri in that status, the law of Missouri applied and Scott remained a slave.

---

[5] Dred Scott v. Sandford, 60 U.S. (19 How.) 393 (1857). The spelling of the appellee's name in the U.S. Reports is inaccurate. The proper spelling is "Sanford." *See* J. Vishneski, *What the Court Decided in Dred Scott v. Sandford*, 32 AM. J. LEGAL HIST. 373 (1988). The Constitution itself had certain provisions regarding slavery. Article I, Section 2, Clause 3 provided that a slave counted as 3/5 of a person for purposes of legislative apportionment. Article 1, § 9, Clause 1 provided a constitutional right to import slaves. This latter provision was not amendable until 1808. *See* U.S. CONST. art. V.

[6] The agreed statement of facts in the case maintained that Dr. Emerson had sold Dred Scott to Sanford shortly before the federal suit. Scott sued Sanford in federal court based on diversity of citizenship claiming that Sanford was a citizen of New York and Scott was a citizen of Missouri. Sanford filed a plea in abatement stating that there was no federal jurisdiction because, as a descendant of African slaves, Scott could not be a citizen of Missouri. Scott filed a demurrer to the plea in abatement and it was sustained. However, at trial the Circuit Court ruled in favor of Sanford. *See* W. EHRLICH, THEY HAVE NO RIGHTS: DRED SCOTT'S STRUGGLE FOR FREEDOM 76–78 (1979).

Dred Scott remains one of the most tragic decisions in the history of the United States Supreme Court. The precedential impact of *Dred Scott* was vigorously contested in the Lincoln-Douglas debates of 1858, with Lincoln arguing for a narrow construction limited only to Dred Scott.

§ 9.01 SEGREGATION IN PUBLIC FACILITIES

[1] The Rise and Fall of "Separate but Equal"

Following the Civil War, the Thirteenth, Fourteenth, and Fifteenth Amendments were promulgated. The Thirteenth Amendment prohibited slavery and involuntary servitude. The Fifteenth Amendment prohibited denying the right to vote based on race, and the Fourteenth Amendment contained the Equal Protection Clause.[7]

In *Plessy v. Ferguson*,[8] the Court upheld the "separate but equal" doctrine against a challenge under the Equal Protection Clause. Plessy challenged the constitutionality of a Louisiana Act requiring, under criminal penalty, "equal but separate" railway carriages for members of different races.[9] Plaintiff had been arrested for violating the Act by purchasing a ticket for a first class seat and refusing to move from that seat to the separate section for "colored" people.

As a defense to his criminal prosecution, Plessy challenged the constitutionality of the Act on Thirteenth Amendment grounds as violating the ban on slavery and on Fourteenth Amendment grounds as depriving him of the reputation of belonging to the dominant race. The Court quickly disposed of the Thirteenth Amendment argument, saying that the *Slaughter-House Cases* did not construe the Thirteenth Amendment to extend beyond slavery or involuntary servitude. Further, the Court rejected the Equal Protection challenge by distinguishing between political and social equality. The Equal Protection Clause, the Court held, sought to enforce only political equality. Laws that prohibited interracial marriage, mandated separate but equal schools, and required separate but equal railway cars, involved social equality, which the Equal Protection Clause did not reach. As an example of political equality, the Court cited *Strauder v. West Virginia*[10] in which the Court held that a West Virginia law limiting juries to white males discriminated by implying legal inferiority. The majority opined, "If the civil and political rights of both races be equal, one cannot be inferior to the other civilly or politically. If one race be inferior to the other socially, the Constitution of the United States cannot put them on the same plane."[11]

In a famous dissent, Justice Harlan took a much broader view of the Fourteenth Amendment, arguing that it guaranteed civil as well as political rights. Justice Harlan's conception is summarized by his classic quote: "Our Constitution is color-

---

[7] *See* The Slaughter-House Cases, 83 U.S. 36 (1873).

[8] 163 U.S. 537 (1896).

[9] The plaintiff in the case was seven-eighths Caucasian and one-eighth African.

[10] 100 U.S. 303 (1880).

[11] *Plessy*, 163 U.S. at 551.

blind, and neither knows nor tolerates classes among citizens."[12] Unlike the majority's discussion of property rights, Justice Harlan focused on personal liberty, equal citizenship, and civil rights.

In the landmark case of *Brown v. Board of Education*,[13] the Court rejected the apartheid system that *Plessy* sanctioned by striking down the doctrine of "separate but equal." In each of the various state court appeals that made up *Brown*, black students sought the aid of the courts in obtaining admission to the white public schools of their community after having been denied admission under laws requiring or permitting segregation according to race.

The plaintiffs challenged the segregation as a deprivation of equal protection. They asserted that segregated public schools were not "equal" and could not be made "equal." Citing the "separate but equal" doctrine, all but one of the various state courts in which actions were brought denied relief. The doctrine was upheld in that case as well, but the plaintiffs were admitted to the white schools due to the blatant superiority of the white schools.

When the cases reached the Supreme Court, the "separate but equal" doctrine was becoming a judicially unenforceable standard. In a series of cases preceding *Brown*, the NAACP chose not to attack the "separate but equal" doctrine directly but rather sought equal opportunities, as well as facilities, for black children. Cases before *Brown* broadened the concept of equal opportunity and forced courts to make factual findings, particularly about the inadequacy of separate graduate school programs.

In *Brown*, Chief Justice Warren began by asking what effect the authors of the Fourteenth Amendment intended to have upon public education. His answer was inconclusive, however, because radical changes had taken place in the nature of the country's public school system since the time of the Amendment. Chief Justice Warren then examined the history of the "separate but equal" doctrine. He noted that the *Slaughter-House Cases* interpreted the Fourteenth Amendment to prohibit every kind of state-imposed discrimination against black persons. However, the doctrine of "separate but equal" did not arise until *Plessy*. Moreover, subsequent cases applying *Plessy* in the educational context did not challenge the doctrine,[14] but followed *Plessy* by mandating equality between black and white schools. The lower courts had found that the segregated schools at issue were equal or being made equal in all tangible aspects. Against this backdrop, the *Brown* Court considered the effects segregation had on public education.

The majority opinion emphasized the importance of public education to society and the individual. The Court stated that education was important because it ensured an informed electorate and enabled citizens to exercise their rights intelligently. The majority further stated that education fostered equal opportunity by aiding in the advancement of one's place in society. These reasons may help to explain the Court's strong action taken in the school desegregation area.

---

[12] *Id.* at 559.

[13] 347 U.S. 483 (1954).

[14] Sweatt v. Painter, 339 U.S. 629 (1950); McLaurin v. Oklahoma State Regents, 339 U.S. 637 (1950).

Additionally, the Justices may have envisioned an opportunity to begin changing attitudes in the impressionable and unadulterated minds of children.

In reaching its decision, the Court relied in part on *Sweatt v. Painter* and *McLaurin v. Oklahoma State Regents*, which allowed intangible factors to be considered in determining whether separate schools are in fact equal.[15] The Court found that segregation generated feelings of inferiority in black children that were detrimental to their education. Accordingly, the Court found that segregation in public education denied black children equal educational opportunities. In its famous "Footnote 11," the Court supported its findings by citing a number of sociological and psychological studies. Whether the use of these studies as grounds for the decision in *Brown* was proper has been debated.[16] It has also been suggested that this decision was based on moral considerations rather than sociological or legal ones.[17] Specifically, Chief Justice Warren opined that "separate educational facilities are inherently unequal."[18]

In *Bolling v. Sharpe*,[19] the companion case to *Brown*, the Court applied the *Brown* holding and the Equal Protection Clause generally to the federal government through the Due Process Clause of the Fifth Amendment. In that case, the Court held that the segregated schools of the District of Columbia violated the Fifth Amendment Due Process Clause. The Court has never wavered from applying equal protection principles to the federal government, even though the Fifth Amendment contains no Equal Protection Clause, and the Fourteenth Amendment applies only to the states. At times the Court's application of equal protection principles to the federal government through the Due Process Clause has been termed reverse incorporation.[20]

Brown marked the beginning of the gradual dismantling of the system of apartheid that was particularly common in many Southern states. In the first few years after *Brown*, the Court applied the principles of the *Brown* decision to public facilities, including buses, beaches, libraries, parks, and other recreational facilities, which indicates that *Brown* was not based primarily on the special circumstances of segregation in the education context. An issue that has arisen from this extension is whether a state can avoid the constitutional obligation to

---

[15] *See id.*

[16] *See, e.g.*, C. Black, *The Lawfulness of the Segregation Decisions*, 69 YALE L.J. 421, 428 (1960) (A rationale for the school segregation cases can be stated more simply, "The fourteenth amendment commands equality, and segregation as we know it is inequality."); L. Pollak, *Racial Discrimination and Judicial Integrity: A Reply to Professor Wechsler*, 108 U. PA. L. REV. 1, 33 (1959) ("judicial neutrality . . . does not preclude the disciplined exercise by a Supreme Court Justice of that Justice's individual and strongly held philosophy"); H. Wechsler, *Toward Neutral Principles of Constitution Law*, 73 HARV. L. REV. 1, 32–33 (1959) ("The Court did not declare, as many wish it had, that the fourteenth amendment forbids all racial lines in legislation . . . [The decision] must have rested on the view that racial segregation is, in principle, a denial of equality to the minority against whom it is directed . . . But this position also presents problems."). *See also* E. Cahn, *Jurisprudence*, 30 N.Y.U. L. REV. 150 (1955).

[17] *See* E. Cahn, *Jurisprudence*, 31 N.Y.U. L. REV. 182 (1956).

[18] *Brown*, 347 U.S. at 495.

[19] 347 U.S. 497 (1954).

[20] *See* B. Clark, *Judicial Review of Congressional Section Five Action: The Fallacy of Reverse Incorporation*, 84 COLUM. L. REV. 1969 (1984).

desegregate public facilities by discontinuing the facility entirely. The decisions on this issue have been inconclusive.[21]

[2] Enforcing Brown: The Fashioning of Judicial Relief

The prohibitory injunctions necessary to dismantle much of the discriminatory system still in effect after *Brown*, such as separate water fountains, bathrooms, and bus seating, were relatively straightforward remedies. However, the mandatory injunctions necessary to desegregate public schools are remedies that have remained more controversial and more difficult to effectuate. The *Brown* Court was sensitive to the magnitude of the remedy in school cases.[22] Therefore, in *Brown II*,[23] (the enforcement follow-up to *Brown I*), the Court invited the Attorney General of the United States and those of all the states requiring or permitting racial discrimination in public education to present their views on the question of relief. Based upon the evidence, the Court determined that the proper implementation of desegregation remedies rested with the good faith efforts of local school authorities. Accordingly, the cases were remanded to the lower courts with instructions to fashion remedies using equitable principles, taking into account speed and the effective functioning of the schools during this massive undertaking.

The Court stated that school authorities must make a prompt and reasonable start. Once such a start was made, the defendant school boards had the burden of establishing the necessity of additional time. Moreover, such a request must be made in the public interest and consistent with good faith compliance at the earliest practical date. Lower courts should take into account problems relating to administration, physical plant, transportation system, personnel, changing school districts and attendance areas, and revision of local laws and regulations. Because the lower courts were closer to the problems, the Court gave them supervisory jurisdiction with broad-ranging equitable powers to secure desegregation "with all deliberate speed."[24]

From the beginning, there was considerable resistance to *Brown*. In *Cooper v. Aaron*,[25] Arkansas amended its state constitution to command the state legislature to oppose school desegregation. Accordingly, Arkansas passed a law allowing students to choose not to attend integrated schools. However, the Little Rock School Board agreed to comply with *Brown* and implemented a desegregation plan for the local high school. The Governor dispatched the Arkansas National Guard to the School and placed it off limits to black students.

---

[21] *Compare* Griffin v. County Sch. Bd., 377 U.S. 218 (1964) (closing of public schools with County providing public funds to assist children to attend private schools held unconstitutional), *with* Palmer v. Thompson, 403 U.S. 217 (1971) (closing of municipal swimming pool upheld in absence of showing that city was continuing to operate segregated pools; motive of city officials held immaterial).

[22] *See Bolling*, 347 U.S. at 490 n.4.

[23] Brown v. Bd. of Educ., 349 U.S. 294 (1955).

[24] *Id.* at 301.

[25] 358 U.S. 1 (1958).

Eventually, a Federal District Court issued a preliminary injunction enjoining the Governor and the Guard from obstructing the integration plan. When the black students came to the School, however, large demonstrations began outside the building. As a result, President Eisenhower ordered federal troops to the School to protect the black students. Subsequently, the School Board sought a stay of the integration plan. The district court granted the stay and the court of appeals reversed the decision. In a Special Term the Court unanimously affirmed the decision of the court of appeals.[26]

The decision, in an extraordinary and unprecedented gesture, was signed by all nine Justices individually. The Court ruled that the Equal Protection Clause prohibited any agent of the state from denying a person within its jurisdiction the equal protection of the laws. In reply to claims by the Governor and the Legislature of Arkansas that the states were not bound by *Brown*, the Court invoked *Marbury v. Madison*[27] in emphasizing that the federal judiciary was supreme in expounding the Constitution.

In subsequent cases, the Court started to define the types of remedies that would satisfy *Brown*. In *Goss v. Board of Education*,[28] it rejected a voluntary transfer program as part of a formal desegregation plan. The transfer system perpetuated segregation by only allowing transfer from desegregated schools to segregated schools.[29] Justice Clark's majority opinion, indicated that the Court was becoming impatient with the pace of compliance with *Brown*.

In a major enforcement case, *Green v. County School Board*,[30] the Court rejected a "freedom of choice" plan.[31] Although such a scheme could be part of an overall desegregation plan, it alone was insufficient to comply with *Brown*. School boards that had operated state-compelled dual systems had "the affirmative duty to take whatever steps might be necessary to convert to a unitary system in which racial discrimination would be eliminated root and branch."[32]

In 1971, the Court handed down the watershed school desegregation remedy case of *Swann v. Charlotte-Mecklenburg Board of Education*.[33] The School District's desegregation plan, based upon geographic zoning with a free-transfer provision, was approved by the District Court in 1965. However, by 1969, 15 years after *Brown*, about half the black students in the school district were in formerly

---

[26] *See id.* at 14.

[27] 5 U.S. (1 Cranch) 137 (1803).

[28] 373 U.S. 683 (1963).

[29] The plan at issue permitted a student assigned to a desegregated school to transfer to a school where the majority of the students were of his or her own race.

[30] 391 U.S. 430 (1968).

[31] New Kent County, Virginia maintained one combined elementary and high school for whites and one combined school for blacks. The "freedom of choice" plan permitted students to choose which of the two schools in the county they wished to attend. After three years under the New Kent Board's "freedom of choice" plan, not one white child had opted to attend the previously all-black school and 85 percent of the black children still attended that school.

[32] *Id.* at 437–38.

[33] 402 U.S. 1 (1971).

all-white schools, while the others remained in virtually all-black schools.

The District Court's numerous hearings led to the conclusions that certain actions of the school board were discriminatory, and that the residential patterns in the city and county resulted in part from federal, state, and local government action beyond the reach of the board. Nevertheless, the District Court ordered the School Board to present a more effective plan. The District Court subsequently rejected the Board's modified plan and substituted one fashioned by its own experts.

Once a constitutional violation has been established, the district court is empowered to fashion a broad equitable remedy to correct past wrongs. Chief Justice Burger rejected the imposition of quotas requiring that each school's racial balance reflect that of the entire school system. However, awareness of the racial mix was a useful starting point. The Court did not automatically reject all one-race schools. Nevertheless, when one-race schools exist in a racially mixed school district, the school authorities have the burden of proving that the racial composition of these schools was not the result of their present or past discriminatory activities.

The Chief Justice suggested gerrymandering or clustering of attendance zones as one remedy for correcting past discrimination. Clustering attendance zones of primarily white areas and primarily black areas of the school district often necessitated busing. The Court acknowledged the desirability of neighborhood schools and viewed busing as an interim measure necessary to correct past discrimination. The Court also acknowledged the negative impact of the costs of busing on the educational process and sought to minimize those costs. In a highly mobile society, once a school system was unitary and had completely complied with *Brown*, the Court would no longer force the system to continue to bus.

Swann was the first case to reach the Court where population shifts had made the link between the original *de jure* segregation and the continuing segregation less clear than in cases like *Green* and *Goss*. Nevertheless, the Court made clear that once *de jure* segregation has infected a system, broad system-wide relief was justified.

For many years, school desegregation focused on the Southern states, where dual systems were often explicitly codified. However, in 1973, the Court focused its desegregation remedies on a Northern school district in *Keyes v. School District No. 1, Denver, Colorado*.[34] The School District in *Keyes* had never been operated under a constitutional or statutory provision that mandated or permitted school segregation. Instead, plaintiffs alleged that the School Board, by use of various techniques such as the manipulation of student attendance zones, school-site selection, and a neighborhood school policy had created or maintained racially or ethnically segregated schools throughout the School District.

The District Court found that there had been intentional segregation in one part of the School District and therefore ordered desegregation of that area. The Supreme Court said that desegregation remedies were generally limited to the

---

[34] 413 U.S. 189 (1973).

part of a School District where plaintiffs proved intentional discrimination. However, if plaintiffs proved that school authorities had carried out a systematic program of segregation affecting a "meaningful proportion" of students, schools, teachers, and facilities, a presumption arose of segregation throughout the school district. This presumption shifted the burden onto the defendant school board to demonstrate that the district was divided into clearly unrelated segments and that the segregative policies in one unit did not cause *de facto* segregation in other units. Thus the school board had to demonstrate independent subdivisions to rebut the presumption of district-wide segregation. If the school board could not make this showing, the district court could find a dual system and impose a duty to integrate schools throughout the district.

Writing for the majority, Justice Brennan stated that even if the school board proved that the district was divided into clearly unrelated segments, demonstrating intentional discrimination in one portion may be probative of intentional segregation in others.

Justice Powell's opinion, concurring in part and dissenting in part, criticized the *de jure/de facto* distinction in the school segregation context and suggested that a discriminatory impact test be used instead. In Southern schools where segregation was statutory, the plaintiff effectively only had to prove effect, but in the North, where the discrimination was more subtle, the plaintiff had to prove intent. Justice Powell also criticized the use of large-scale busing to remedy school segregation. Justice Powell expressed his belief that any child, white or black, who was compelled to leave his neighborhood and spend a significant portion of his day being transported to a distant school suffers an impairment of his liberty. He suggested drawing attendance zones and planning the construction of new schools in a way that increased integration.

Justice Rehnquist's dissent stated that the majority dramatically extended *Brown*. He criticized the use of presumptions to avoid difficult discriminatory intent findings.

Subsequent cases continued to alleviate, in the school desegregation area, the discriminatory intent requirement that normally applied in equal protection cases. In *Columbus Board of Education v. Penick*,[35] the Court found a constitutional violation when *Brown* was decided in 1954, based on official segregation by the school board in a part of the district. The Court stated that such a finding gave rise to a continuing affirmative obligation on the defendant school board to eliminate the segregation found in 1954, even though the District Court had not found official segregation after 1954. In *Dayton Board of Education v. Brinkman*,[36] the companion case to *Columbus*, the Court also upheld system-wide desegregation remedies based on a factual showing of purposeful segregative acts in a meaningful portion of the school district in 1954.

Justice Stewart's dissent noted that, unlike *Columbus*, the District Court in *Dayton* found that plaintiff had failed to establish a causal nexus between past

---

[35] 443 U.S. 449 (1979).

[36] 443 U.S. 526 (1979).

intentional discrimination prior to 1954 and current discriminatory effects. He argued that the Court ignored the considerable deference it had afforded to federal district court findings in desegregation cases. Justice Stewart also noted the difficulty of a school board establishing that acts prior to 1954 played no role in current segregation. The Supreme Court set aside these findings, emphasizing that the school board had a continuing duty to eradicate the dual system that existed at the time *Brown* was decided. The failure to fulfill that duty, along with some post-*Brown* actions indicating segregative intent, gave rise to a *prima facie* case of discrimination.

Keyes, Columbus, and *Dayton* facilitated establishing a *prima facie* case of intentional discrimination. The geographic presumption of *Keyes* allowed a finding of system-wide discrimination from a finding of intentional discrimination in a small segment of a school district. *Columbus* and *Dayton* imposed a temporal presumption upon school boards that generated the duty to eradicate the effects of any pre-*Brown* intentional discrimination that existed in 1954. Thus, a finding of intentional segregation in a small part of a school district at some time before *Brown* could establish a system-wide violation and justify a system-wide remedy.

Basically, these presumptions eroded the intentional discrimination requirement in school desegregation cases. However, the Court did not similarly relax this requirement in other areas, such as employment or housing. Schools have a special role in achieving equal opportunity and children are less encumbered with racial attitudes. There has been some alleviation of the discriminatory intent requirement in the voting area. This may have been because, as with education, the Court viewed voting as foundational to a democracy and to the opportunity to advance in society.

[3] Limiting the Remedies

In 1974, the Supreme Court first began to limit remedies for intentional segregation. In *Milliken v. Bradley*,[37] the Court refused to allow an interdistrict remedy when the lower court found only the city district of Detroit to have intentionally discriminated. The Court held this despite findings by the District Court that discrimination in the city district caused segregation in suburban districts and that remedies imposed upon the Detroit district would leave many of the district's schools 75–90 percent black, which would increase "white flight" into the suburbs.

Writing for the majority, Chief Justice Burger would allow interdistrict remedies where evidence existed of some conspiratorial action among the districts. Additionally, he would permit an interdistrict remedy upon a finding of *de jure* segregation in one district that substantially caused segregation in another adjacent district, or where school district lines had been drawn on the basis of race. For the most part, school districts were not merely political boundaries, but reflections of a tradition of local control over public education. An interdistrict remedy would interfere with this local control. Although federalism considerations were always present when fashioning school desegregation remedies, consolidation

---

[37] 418 U.S. 717 (1974).

in the absence of direct constitutional violations threatened to disrupt the structure of public education, causing severe logistical problems and governance issues among the districts. Thus, *Milliken* made interdistrict remedies difficult to obtain.[38]

Justice White's dissent in *Milliken* cited the unchallenged finding of the district court that an intracity desegregation plan was both more burdensome for many of Detroit's black children and more expensive than an interdistrict remedy. An interdistrict remedy could sometimes lower costs and shorten travel distances than an intracity remedy, as busing could occur across the district line to white suburban neighborhoods. Moreover, an intracity remedy would only aggravate the problems of white flight, which could actually increase segregation in Detroit. Finally, Justice White believed that the Court should defer to the district court and court of appeals which were in better positions to fashion an appropriate remedy for segregation in Michigan.

Justice Marshall's dissent argued that the school board was simply an agent of the state. Because the state was responsible, an interdistrict remedy should have been available. Justice Marshall predicted that under the majority opinion, metropolitan areas would be divided into separate cities, one for blacks and one for whites.

While *Milliken* placed a geographic limit on school desegregation remedies, *Pasadena City Board of Education v. Spangler*[39] imposed temporal limits on desegregation orders. *Spangler* held that once a court implemented a racially neutral attendance plan, it could not modify its order to accommodate changes in the school population that were caused by population shifts rather than the segregative actions of school officials. The District Court in this case had ordered annual readjustment of attendance zones even after the Board had adopted a racially neutral student assignment plan.

In *Board of Education of Oklahoma City v. Dowell*,[40] the Court ruled that a District Court could dissolve a desegregation order if it found that the School Board "had complied in good faith with the desegregation decree since it was entered, and whether, in light of every facet of school operations, the vestiges of past *de jure* segregation had been eliminated to the extent practicable."[41] In making this determination, the district court should look not only at student assignments, but " 'to every facet of school operations-faculty, staff, transportation, extra-curricular activities and facilities.' "[42]

---

[38] Interdistrict remedies have been ordered by lower courts since *Milliken*, and the Supreme Court has declined review, apparently satisfied that the criteria in *Milliken* were met. *See, e.g.*, Evans v. Buchanan, 416 F. Supp. 328 (D. Del. 1976), *aff'd*, 555 F.2d 373 (3d Cir.), *cert. denied*, 434 U.S. 880 (1977) (Wilmington, Del.); United States v. Missouri, 515 F.2d 1365 (8th Cir.), *cert. denied*, 423 U.S. 951 (1975) (St. Louis County, Mo.). Additionally, in *Hills v. Gautreaux*, 425 U.S. 284 (1976), the Court found that *Milliken* did not preclude the Court's approval of a remedy, in a housing discrimination case, which extended beyond the City of Chicago.

[39] 427 U.S. 424 (1976).

[40] 498 U.S. 237 (1991).

[41] *Id.* at 238.

[42] *Id.* at 250.

In *Freeman v. Pitts*,[43] the Court stated that the judiciary should return the supervision of school districts to local school boards as early as possible. The equitable powers of a federal district court ended once a dual system had become unitary. Only additional intentional discrimination justified an additional remedy. In determining partial withdrawal of judicial supervision, a court should consider whether the school district had fully complied with the part of the decree to be eliminated and whether not eliminating those provisions would help compliance with those parts of the decree that would remain in place. a school district also had to demonstrate to the public and the victims of discrimination its good faith commitment to comply with the entire decree and to obey those constitutional provisions that it had violated. Courts should afford particular weight to consistent good faith compliance.

In *Missouri v. Jenkins*,[44] the Court held that a District Court in Kansas City had abused its discretion in imposing a property tax increase to fund specific court-ordered desegregation remedies. The District Court could have ordered the school district to levy property taxes itself to raise the required monies; it also could have enjoined the operation of state laws prohibiting such increases.

In *Missouri v. Jenkins (Jenkins II)*,[45] the Court invalidated a lower court order commanding the State to fund salary increases and remedial "quality education" programs for the Kansas City, Missouri, School District (KCMSD). A Federal District Court found the State and the KCMSD liable for intradistrict violations for operating a segregated school system within KCMSD. In an effort to desegregate KCMSD, the District Court ordered a magnet school and capital improvements plan. This program included one-time costs of more than $640 million and annual costs of nearly $200 million. The State claimed that the district court exceeded its authority in adopting the KCMSD remedial plan.

Relying on *Board of Education of Oklahoma City v. Dowell*, Chief Justice Rehnquist stated that the appropriate inquiry into the district court's remedies must evaluate whether they helped to restore the victims of segregation to the position they would have occupied had such segregation not occurred. The Chief Justice found that magnet schools were a proper remedy when used in an intradistrict way. However, the District Court's plan used magnet schools in order to attract students from outside the KCMSD. Courts cannot use magnet schools to circumvent the constitutional requirement of an interdistrict violation for an interdistrict remedy. The tremendous white flight from KCMSD was caused by the court's remedy rather than any action by the school district.

Moreover, the District Court's remedy of increasing spending to bring whites into the KCMSD had no objective limitations in amount or duration. The goal of desegregation was to restore local autonomy to school districts that complied with the Constitution. Courts could not simply institute indefinite funding and withhold partial unitary status until student achievement test scores reached the national average, unless these low scores had resulted from *de jure* segregation.

---

[43] 503 U.S. 467 (1992).

[44] 495 U.S. 33 (1990).

[45] 515 U.S. 70 (1995).

Concurring in the judgment, Justice O'Connor maintained that interdistrict remedies were appropriate when redressing interdistrict violations or when intradistrict violations had interdistrict effects. In this case, the district court's plan redressed neither type of violation. Concurring in the judgment, Justice Thomas stated that the notion that black students necessarily suffer great harm from segregation assumes black inferiority.

Justice Souter dissented, joined by Justices Stevens, Ginsburg, and Breyer. Justice Souter argued that this decision departed from _Freeman v. Pitts_.[46] The state failed to show that continued judicial control was unnecessary to implement remaining orders, or good faith compliance to parents and children of the disfavored race. The state only showed compliance — not even compliance to the extent practicable.

Justice Souter argued that the _de jure_ violations in KCMSD produced the interdistrict effects of citizens crossing district borders which led to increased segregation inside both KCMSD and surrounding suburban districts. In a separate dissent, Justice Ginsburg objected to the swift curtailment of the desegregation remedy in a district that was 68.3 percent black.

In _Parents Involved in Community Schools v. Seattle School District_,[47] Chief Justice Roberts announced the judgment of the divided Court in Parts I, II, III-A, and III-C. His opinion was joined by Justices Scalia, Thomas, and Alito in Parts III-B and IV. _Parents_ combined cases involving two public school districts — Seattle and Jefferson County — that voluntarily adopted raced-based student classification programs. In Seattle, the District used white and non-white classifications to allocate spots in overpopulated schools. In Jefferson County, the District used black or "other" classifications to make elementary school assignment and transfer request decisions. Both districts used an individual student's race to assign her to a school. The district's goal for each assignment was to meet pre-established racial composition quotas for each school.

In Part I, Chief Justice Roberts, writing for the Court, identified the primary issue as "whether a public school that had not operated legally segregated schools or has been found to be unitary may . . . rely upon that classification in making school assignments."[48] The Seattle School District plan permitted students to select which district high school they would like to attend and rank their preferences. The District used a tiebreaking system to prevent oversubscription. First, the District gave a preference to students whose siblings attended the school. Second, the District considered the student's race and the racial balance of the school. In the District, "approximately 41 percent of enrolled students are white; the remaining 59 percent, comprising all other racial groups, are classified by Seattle for assignment purposes as nonwhite."[49] The District attempted to maintain schools whose racial compositions were "within 10 percentage points of

---

[46] _See id._

[47] 551 U.S. 701 (2007).

[48] _Id._ at 710.

[49] _Id._ at 712.

the district's overall white/nonwhite racial balance."[50] Oversubscribed schools that did not meet this criterion were " 'integration positive.' "[51] The District would select students who would help " 'bring the school into balance.' "[52] If necessary, the District would then consider the student's proximity to the school as a third tiebreaker.

For the 2000–2001 term, five schools were oversubscribed. Approximately 82 percent of all incoming ninth graders requested one of these schools. The District classified three of these schools as " 'integration positive' " because in the previous school year more than 51 percent of students in them were white. Seattle had never maintained segregated schools and was never under a court order to desegregate. However, most students in northern Seattle were white and most students in southern Seattle were nonwhite.

Turning to the Jefferson County School District, in 1975 a Federal court ordered desegregation of Jefferson County's schools after the court had determined in 1973 that the County operated a segregated school district. In 2000, the court determined that the District had reached unitary status and dissolved the desegregation decree. Subsequently, Jefferson County enacted the plan at issue. It required the percentage of black enrollment at all non-magnet schools to be at least 15 percent, but no more than 50 percent. In Jefferson County, about "34 percent of the district's 97,000 students are black; most of the remaining 66 percent are white."[53] Once assigned, students could request a transfer to other non-magnet schools for any reason. However, the District reserved the right to reject a request based on the school's available space or racial composition.

Again writing for a majority in Part III-A, Chief Justice Roberts noted that both school districts had to show that their individual race-based plans were " 'narrowly tailored' to achieve a 'compelling' government interest."[54] In prior cases, the Court acknowledged two interests that qualified as compelling. The first was a need to cure previous intentional discrimination. The harm must be traceable to segregation because " 'the Constitution is not violated by racial imbalance in the schools, without more.' "[55]

Second, *Grutter v. Bollinger*[56] recognized the compelling interest in maintaining diversity in higher education. This interest is not concerned solely with racial composition, but includes " 'all factors that may contribute to student body diversity.' "[57] The *Grutter* program did not focus solely on racial classification. Instead, racial classification was one of many individual factors in a " 'highly

---

[50] *Id.*

[51] *Id.*

[52] *Id.*

[53] *Id.* at 716.

[54] *Id.* at 720.

[55] *Id.* at 721.

[56] 539 U.S. 306 (2003).

[57] 551 U.S. at 722 (quoting *Grutter*, 539 U.S. at 337).

individualized, holistic review.' "[58]

In contrast, the Seattle and Jefferson County plans did not consider an individual's race to expose their students to " 'widely diverse people, cultures, ideas, and viewpoints.' "[59] Unlike the Grutter program, race was the only factor considered rather than one of many, which made these programs similar to the University of Michigan undergraduate plan struck down in *Gratz v. Bollinger*.[60] Moreover, the *Grutter* Court specifically narrowed its holding to higher education programs. Consequently, *Grutter* did not govern the plans at issue.

In Part III-B, joined by Justices Scalia, Thomas, and Alito, the Chief Justice explained that the Court has repeatedly struck down plans whose sole purpose was racial balance. In the cases at issue, the Districts' plans were based solely on racial demographics rather than on "any pedagogic concept of the level of diversity needed to obtain the asserted educational benefits."[61] Even the "undefined 'meaningful number' "[62] required by *Grutter* was permissible because its purpose was to achieve a genuinely diverse student population. The plurality stated that "racial balancing has 'no logical stopping point' "[63] as demographic shifts will necessitate continued recalibrations.

Again writing for the majority in Part III-C, the Chief Justice determined that the plans were not narrowly tailored. Their small effect on student assignments meant that other measures could well have been just as effective. Moreover, the school districts did not demonstrate that they considered alternatives to overt racial classification. "Narrow tailoring requires 'serious, good faith consideration of workable race-neutral alternatives.' "[64]

In Part IV, Chief Justice Roberts once again wrote for a plurality of Justices Scalia, Thomas, and Alito. The Chief Justice stated that Justice Breyer's dissent avoids the "distinction between *de jure* and *de facto* segregation."[65] *Brown v. Board of Education*[66] held that " 'separate but equal' " facilities deprived black students of educational opportunities because racial classifications and separation "denoted inferiority." Prior to *Brown*, districts denied students access to certain schools based on their race. The school districts here have failed to carry the heavy burden that would permit such practices "once again — even for very different reasons."[67]

In his concurrence, Justice Thomas compared the dissent's argument for allowing race-based considerations to that of the segregation advocates in *Brown*. Specifically, "racial imbalance without intentional state action to separate the races

---

[58] *Id.*

[59] *Id.* at 723.

[60] 539 U.S. 244 (2003).

[61] 551 U.S. at 726.

[62] *Id.* at 729.

[63] *Id.* at 731.

[64] *Id.* at 735.

[65] *Id.* at 736.

[66] 347 U.S. 483 (1954).

[67] 551 U.S. at 747.

does not amount to segregation."[68] The dissent's allusion to preserving "their 'hard-won gains' " conflated the concepts of segregation and racial balancing.[69] The Court has permitted "race-based measures for remedial purpose in two narrow situations."[70] First, such measures may be permissible when they were "constitutionally compelled" to remedy schools that were previously segregated by law. Second, the holding in *Richmond v. J.A. Croson Co.*[71] permitted a government unit to use race-based considerations when the government unit itself had caused the past segregation. However, the more time that passed from the era of state-mandated segregation, "the less likely it is that racial imbalance has a traceable connection to any prior segregation."[72]

Scholars disagreed as to whether racial balancing leads to any educational benefits. Evidence also existed that black students attending historically black colleges achieved better academic results than those attending predominantly white colleges. Resembling the arguments of the dissent, "segregationists repeatedly cautioned the Court to consider practicalities and not to embrace too theoretical a view of the Fourteenth Amendment."[73]

Justice Kennedy concurred in the judgment and joined Parts I, II, III-A, and III-C. He believed that the focus on race "may entrench the very prejudices we seek to overcome."[74] He did not join Parts III-B and IV because the plurality failed to recognize that diversity is a compelling state interest. "Diversity, depending on its meaning and definition, is a compelling educational goal a school district may pursue."[75]

Jefferson County failed to pass strict scrutiny because its explanation of "how and when" it uses racial classifications was "so broad and imprecise."[76] For instance, it did not clearly explain who made the school assignment decisions or if there was any oversight of the process. The District also failed to explain the precise circumstances which trigger a race-based assignment or how it decides "which of two similarly situated children will be subjected to a given race-based decision."[77] Seattle explained its process more clearly and extensively, but it failed to explain "how, in the context of a diverse student population, a blunt distinction between 'white' and 'non-white' "[78] encouraged diversity. For example, "a school with 50 percent Asian-American students and 50 percent white students but no African-American, Native-American, or Latino students would qualify as balanced, while a school with 30 percent Asian-American, 25 percent African-American, 25

---

[68] *Id.* at 750 (Thomas, J., concurring).

[69] *Id.*

[70] *Id.*

[71] 488 U.S. 469 (1989).

[72] 551 U.S. at 756.

[73] *Id.* at 777.

[74] *Id.* at 782 (Kennedy, J., concurring).

[75] *Id.* at 783.

[76] *Id.* at 785.

[77] *Id.*

[78] *Id.* at 787.

percent Latino, and 20 percent white students would not."[79] Not only did Seattle fail to narrowly tailor its plan, but it could be self-defeating. He suggested that other problems exist with the Seattle plan, but did not specifically discuss them.

Turning to his disagreements with the plurality opinion, Justice Kennedy disagreed with its conclusion that "the Constitution requires school districts to ignore the problem of de facto resegregation in schooling."[80] Unfortunately, Justice Harlan's famous assertion in his dissent in *Plessey v. Ferguson*[81] that " 'our Constitution is color-blind' " regrettably "cannot be a universal constitutional principle" in the "real world."[82] Schools are free to adopt general race-conscious measures if they do not systematically target individual students solely on the basis of race, and their goal is to further equal educational opportunities for their entire student body. Permissible measures include: selecting locations for new schools generally recognizing the demographics of the area; setting aside funds for special programs; "recruiting students and faculty in a targeted fashion;" hiring faculty in a targeted way; and collecting various enrollment, performance, and other statistics based on race. As these measures did not tell students that they are being typed, based on race, they did not likely require strict scrutiny. In contrast, defining each student based on "a crude system of individual racial classifications"[83] was permissible only as a last resort to accomplish a compelling interest.

Joining Part III-C of the Court's opinion, Justice Kennedy agreed that since the schools' measures affected only a small number of student assignments, the schools could have achieved their desired objectives by other means. Such means could have been the facially race-neutral means previously outlined or, "if necessary, a more nuanced, individual evaluation of school needs and student characteristics that might include race as a component."[84]

The dissent was trying to justify "the explicit, sweeping, classwide racial classifications at issue here" and misread the Court's precedents. *Freeman v. Pitts*[85] recognized a compelling interest in remedying past intentional discrimination. *Grutter* recognized a compelling state interest in fostering diversity in higher education. The dissent's permissive test, however, resembled rational-basis review, rather than strict scrutiny, which risked inviting widespread governmental use of racial classifications. A school district's objectives of avoiding racial isolation or of achieving a diverse student population both qualify as compelling state interests.

In dissent, Justice Stevens noted that in *Brown* only blacks suffered discrimination. In contrast, both races bear the burdens of the programs at issue in this case.

---

[79] *Id.*

[80] *Id.* at 788.

[81] 163 U.S. 537 (1896).

[82] 551 U.S. at 788.

[83] *Id.* at 789.

[84] *Id.* at 790.

[85] 503 U.S. 467 (1992).

Justice Breyer dissented, joined by Justices Stevens, Souter, and Ginsburg. The Court has previously approved "of 'narrowly tailored' plans that are no less race-conscious" than the ones currently before it, and "understood that the Constitution *permits* local communities to adopt desegregation plans even where it does not *require* them to do so."[86] The plurality's opinion threatened the local communities' objectives of integrated primary and secondary education, promised by *Brown*. Until recently, the racial integration was progressing considerably, but now it has "stalled." Now "more than one in six black children attend a school that is 99-100% minority."[87]

Under the Seattle plan, students could transfer, regardless of race, after spending one year at a high school not of their choice. Under a Louisville, Kentucky desegregation plan, transfer was also available to elementary and middle school students. However, the Louisville plan forbade transfer where it would lead to less than 15% or more than 50% black student population in a school. Both the Seattle and Louisville programs were remedial in nature. Louisville began to desegregate in response to a 1975 Federal court order. Seattle's plan began as the result of a Federal lawsuit settlement.

In Justice Breyer's view, applying a more lenient standard than strict scrutiny in this case "would not imply abandonment of judicial efforts carefully to determine the need for race-conscious criteria and the criteria's tailoring in light of the need."[88] Nonetheless, he would apply the version of strict scrutiny embodied in *Grutter*, and ask whether both plans were "narrowly tailored" to serve a "compelling governmental interest." Such interest consisted of three elements: (1) remedial: "in setting right the consequences of prior conditions of segregation;"[89] (2) educational: "in overcoming the adverse educational effects produced by and associated with highly segregated schools;"[90] and (3) democratic: "in producing an educational environment that reflects the 'pluralistic society.' "[91] Desegregation studies showed that black students' educational achievements improved in integrated schools and classes. They performed better when removed from racial isolation early, and were more likely to move into higher-paid occupations traditionally closed to African-Americans.

Justice Breyer disagreed with the plurality's distinction between *de jure* ("by state action") and *de facto* ("caused by other factors") segregation, because it deals with "what the Constitution *requires* school boards to do, not what it *permits* them to do."[92] The plans at issue passed even the strictest "narrow tailoring" test. They only defined the broad ranges, were less burdensome than other race-conscious measures the Court had previously approved, and tried to overcome the history of segregation, thus being narrowly tailored. The plans were the embodiment of

---

[86] 551 U.S. at 803 (Breyer, J., dissenting).

[87] *Id.* at 806.

[88] *Id.* at 836.

[89] *Id.* at 838.

[90] *Id.* at 839.

[91] *Id.* at 840.

[92] *Id.* at 844.

community experience; they sought to enhance student choice. Justice Breyer concluded that invalidating these plans "threaten[ed] the promise of *Brown*."[93]

The Court has extended principles of desegregation to race-based colleges. In *United States v. Fordice*,[94] the Court required Mississippi to eliminate its dual system of higher education. Three predominantly white universities enjoyed the greater resources and had both educational and research missions. One predominantly black university, Jackson State, had a more limited research and educational mission related to its urban setting. Two predominantly black and two predominantly white "regional" colleges had primarily undergraduate education missions. During the 1980s, 99 percent of Mississippi's white students were enrolled in the predominantly white schools, which averaged 80–91 percent white students. Of the black students, 71 percent attended the predominantly black schools, which enrolled 92–99 percent black students.

Rejecting the State policy of freedom of choice in educational institutions, Justice White's majority opinion required the State to eliminate its *de jure* system of segregated higher education. The State had the burden of eliminating all such policies "to the extent practicable and consistent with sound educational practices."[95] Moreover, the State was not relieved of its constitutional obligations until "it eradicates policies and practices traceable to its prior *de jure* dual system that continues to foster segregation."[96]

First, the Court found that the State's sole reliance on ACT scores for admissions cut-offs was not based on sound educational policies. The Court also found suspect the different ACT score requirements for predominantly white and black institutions with the same missions. It found inadequate justification for the different ACT score cut-offs for admission to institutions with different missions. In particular, the Court found that educational institutions in many other states used ACT scores in conjunction with grades, a formula which increased the eligibility of black students to attend the predominately white state universities. Second, the Court found unnecessary duplication of programs related to retaining the dual system of education. Third, it wanted the lower courts to inquire whether the different missions were justified by sound educational practice. Fourth, the Court found that State maintenance of eight educational institutions was related to maintaining a dual system.

The Court remanded the case to the District Court to ascertain whether any of these policies could "practicably be eliminated without eroding sound educational policies."[97] The Court did not want the State simply to increase funding for black colleges, as this would allow a "separate but 'more equal' "[98] system. Justice White did not rule out that greater funding for predominantly black institutions might be part of dismantling the dual system.

---

[93] *Id.* at 868.

[94] 505 U.S. 717 (1992).

[95] *Id.* at 729.

[96] *Id.* at 728.

[97] *Id.* at 743.

[98] *Id.*

§ 9.02 OTHER FORMS OF RACIAL DISCRIMINATION

[1] General Principles: Purposeful Discrimination and Suspect Classes

The school desegregation cases illustrate that an Equal Protection Clause violation requires a finding of discriminatory intent. Even though these cases lightened the burden of proving discriminatory intent, simply proving discriminatory effect or impact was not sufficient. The Court has imposed a much tougher discriminatory intent requirement to prove discrimination in such areas as employment, housing, zoning, and voting, when laws, neutral on their face, have a demonstrably uneven impact on different racial groups. The task for the judiciary is to define the nature of the governmental action and to tailor an appropriate corrective remedy.

This section addresses additional principles that have been developed by the Court in dealing with race and ethnicity discrimination claims. Many of these concepts are also applicable in cases involving sex discrimination, and discrimination against aliens and illegitimates. However, as discussed in subsequent chapters, some concepts such as standards of scrutiny vary with regard to certain classifications.

In the famous case of *Korematsu v. United States*,[99] the Court articulated the suspect class analysis that continues to comprise the principal strand of heightened equal protection scrutiny. During World War II, a military order directed that all persons of Japanese ancestry be excluded from designated "Military Areas." Petitioner, an American citizen of Japanese descent, was convicted in a Federal District Court for violating that order. No question was raised as to the petitioner's loyalty to the United States.

In upholding the conviction, Justice Black, writing for the majority, stated that legal restrictions that curtailed the civil rights of a single racial group were inherently suspect. Such restrictions based on race were suspect classifications that were subject to the most exacting scrutiny, and only the most pressing public necessity could justify them. As the Fourteenth Amendment did not apply to the Federal government, the Court construed the Due Process Clause of the Fifth Amendment as guaranteeing equal protection.[100]

The Court held that it was not beyond the war power of Congress and the Executive to exclude those of Japanese ancestry from the West Coast war area, as the exclusion had "a definite and close relationship to the prevention of espionage and sabotage."[101] The Court emphasized the military urgency of the situation, even

---

[99] 323 U.S. 214 (1944). For an interesting discussion of the wartime cases involving Japanese Americans, *see* E. Rostow, *The Japanese American Cases-A Disaster*, 54 YALE L.J. 489 (1945).

[100] The Court first used this analysis to invalidate a Congressional statute in *Bolling v. Sharpe*, 347 U.S. 497 (1954). This case is discussed *supra* § 9.01.

[101] *Korematsu*, 323 U.S. at 217. In *Ex Parte Endo*, 323 U.S. 283 (1944), the Court invalidated a detention order against an American citizen of Japanese ancestry on the theory that the Congressional statute on which the government relied permitted evacuation and exclusion, not detention.

though the exclusion order did not take effect until five months after the attack on Pearl Harbor. There was much concern at the time that Japan would attempt to invade the United States, and there was evidence that some Japanese-Americans were disloyal. The Court's decision to uphold the order illustrated the deference it afforded military decisions made under the pressures of national emergencies.

In his concurrence, Justice Frankfurter maintained that the Court's decision did not carry the Court's moral approval of the actions taken by the executive and legislative branches. The validity of actions taken under the war power must be judged wholly in the context of war.

In dissent, Justice Roberts maintained that the facts exhibited a clear violation of constitutional rights. Unlike curfew orders upheld in time of emergency, the exclusion order was not temporary, but "part of an over-all plan for forcible detention."[102] Justice Roberts characterized the general program as a concentration camp for Japanese-Americans based on race, not disloyalty. Justice Murphy, also dissenting, found that the order violated due process because Korematsu had not received a hearing. The order unreasonably assumed that all Japanese-Americans would commit sabotage and espionage. Justice Murphy succinctly labeled the act as the legalization of racism. Justice Jackson's dissent focused on the precedential effect of the Court's decision. He differentiated between an order sanctioned by the elected branches and one upon which the Court bestowed its constitutional imprimatur.

Although the Court had in the past struck down laws which discriminated on the basis of race,[103] it did so to achieve the immediate purpose intended by the post-Civil War Amendments, namely to protect the rights of African Americans.[104] *Korematsu* was the first case to articulate the concept of suspect classifications. Since *Korematsu*, the Court has invariably struck down laws that discriminate against racial minorities.[105]

The "suspect class" concept has become an integral part of the equal protection analysis and was a key component of the "two-tiered" standard of equal protection developed by the Warren Court. Under this standard, laws that affected "fundamental interests"[106] or "suspect classes" were upheld only if necessary to promote a compelling state interest. In contrast, other laws were sustained if they bore only a reasonable relationship to a legitimate state end. The Warren Court applied the suspect classification strand of two-tiered analysis to government

---

[102] *Korematsu*, 323 U.S. at 232. One year earlier the Court had upheld the curfew order against a citizen of Japanese ancestry on the grounds that the order was a reasonable exercise of the war power. *See* Hirabayashi v. United States, 320 U.S. 81 (1943).

[103] *See* Strauder v. West Virginia, 100 U.S. 303 (1880).

[104] *See* The Slaughter-House Cases, 83 U.S. (16 Wall.) 36 (1873).

[105] Congress has sought to make amends for the "evacuation, relocation, and internment" suffered by Japanese-Americans during the Second World War. In the Civil Liberties Act of 1988, it apologized to Japanese-American citizens and permanent residents. It also recognized the "fundamental injustice" of these events and promised to make restitution to "those individuals of Japanese ancestry who were interned." *See* 50 App. U.S.C. § 1989.

[106] For further discussion of the fundamental rights strand of equal protection jurisprudence, *see infra* §§ 12.02–12.04.

action that discriminated against racial and ethnic minorities. The Court's more recent affirmative action jurisprudence has extended strict scrutiny to all laws that discriminate based on race even if the disadvantaged group is white.[107] Moreover, the Court's two-tiered equal protection jurisprudence has evolved into a multi-tiered approach with, for example, middle-tiered scrutiny used for discrimination based on gender[108] and illegitimacy.[109] Indeed, even the middle-tier of equal protection is fraying, as the middle-tier standard in gender cases may be more strict than that in illegitimacy cases. A lower standard of heightened rationality is being used for laws that discriminate based on mental retardation.[110]

As a rationale for increased equal protection scrutiny in certain areas, the concept of suspect classes has remained influential. One way to justify a stricter standard of judicial review for suspect classifications stems from Justice Stone's famous *Carolene Products*[111] footnote four. In that footnote, Justice Stone spoke of statutes directed at certain religious groups, nationalities, and racial minorities that comprised "discrete and insular minorities." Laws necessarily involve line-drawing, but lines adversely affecting discrete and insular minorities required a more searching judicial scrutiny, since these are groups who have historically been unable to protect themselves using the political process. Justice Stone's formulation had considerable influence when the courts were faced with claims that aliens, women, and illegitimates, among others, were "suspect classes" entitled to the heightened review that the categorization requires. Discrimination based on race, national origin, and state laws involving alienage receive strict scrutiny, while discrimination based on gender and illegitimacy receive middle-tier scrutiny.

Demonstrating its hostility to racial classifications, the Court has invalidated laws that were racially neutral on their face but challenged as being discriminatory in their administration. In *Yick Wo v. Hopkins*,[112] the Court expressly made the point that facially neutral laws violated the Equal Protection Clause if they were administered in a racially discriminatory manner. *Yick Wo* struck down a law regulating laundries that was applied and administered to disadvantage only Chinese laundry owners. The challenged law prohibited the operation of laundries in wooden buildings without permission from the County Board of Supervisors. Although petitioners' laundries had passed safety and health inspections, they were denied operating licenses. In fact, the record disclosed that 200 Chinese applicants were not permitted to operate wooden laundries, while approximately 80 non-Chinese were allowed to operate such laundries. This overwhelmingly disproportionate impact alone was enough to convince the Court of discriminatory intent.

---

[107] *See infra* Chapter 11. The Court also has applied strict scrutiny to laws that discriminate based on alien status.

[108] *See infra* Chapter 10.

[109] *See infra* § 12.01[2].

[110] *See infra* § 12.01[4].

[111] 304 U.S. 144, 153 (1938). For more extensive discussion of *Carolene Products, see supra* § 8.03.

[112] 118 U.S. 356 (1886).

In *United States v. Armstrong*,[113] the Court denied discovery to substantiate charges of selective prosecution of black persons for crack cocaine distribution because defendants failed to show that similarly situated whites were not prosecuted.

The Court has also invalidated neutral statutes that were applied in an even-handed manner to all races, but which were based on racial classifications. *Loving v. Virginia*[114] struck down a Virginia law banning interracial marriages even though it applied equally to all races. The petitioners, a white man and a black woman, traveled to the District of Columbia to be legally married and then returned to reside in Virginia. Both were convicted of violating state law. The Supreme Court overturned the conviction. It held that the statute violated equal protection by using racial classifications to restrict the freedom to marry without an overriding purpose. Additionally, the statutes violated the Due Process Clause by restricting the freedom to marry.

Not only has the Supreme Court held that the Equal Protection Clause prohibits state-imposed racial discrimination, but it has also held that states cannot foster private acts of racial discrimination. In *Anderson v. Martin*,[115] the Court invalidated a Louisiana statute that required a candidate's race to appear on election ballots. Labelling the candidates by race at a crucial stage of the electoral process was a state-furnished vehicle by which racial prejudice could be aroused and used against one race to advantage white or black candidates depending upon the circumstances.

In *Hunter v. Underwood*,[116] the Court struck down a facially neutral law that was passed with a racially discriminatory intent. The law in *Hunter* was a part of the Alabama Constitution that denied voting rights to persons convicted of crimes involving felonies and moral turpitude misdemeanors. Although the section was racially neutral on it face, it had a racially disproportionate impact. The legislative intent as well as other evidence established a clear purpose to discriminate against blacks.

The Court has also struck down the use of racial classifications with ostensibly benign intent. In *Palmore v. Sidoti*,[117] a state court divested a natural mother of the custody of her infant child and granted custody to the natural father because of the mother's remarriage to a person of a different race. The trial court found that there was no issue as to either party's devotion to the child, adequacy of housing facilities, or respectability of the new spouse of either parent. Instead, the trial court based its holding in part on the social stigmatization that it believed the child would suffer because of her mother's remarriage to a black man. As such, the state court concluded that the best interests of the child would be served by awarding custody to the father.

---

[113] 517 U.S. 456 (1996). For additional discussion of this case, *see infra* § 9.02[5].

[114] 388 U.S. 1 (1967).

[115] 375 U.S. 399 (1964).

[116] 471 U.S. 222 (1985).

[117] 466 U.S. 429 (1984).

Although recognizing that the child's welfare must be the controlling factor in the decision, the Supreme Court held that the hypothetical effects of racial prejudice resulting from remarriage to a person of another race did not justify removing a child from the otherwise qualified mother. Although the classification affected both blacks and whites, it failed strict scrutiny. Any racial classification had to be necessary to accomplish a compelling governmental interest.[118] Constitutional rights must be protected despite hostility to their exercise.

Bob Jones University v. United States,[119] and *Goldsboro Christian Schools, Inc. v. United States*,[120] upheld Internal Revenue Service denials of tax exempt status to two educational institutions, because of their racially discriminatory practices. Goldsboro Christian School denied admission to blacks, and Bob Jones University admitted blacks but imposed a disciplinary code that forbade interracial dating. Both schools based their policies on religious beliefs. Nevertheless, the Court unanimously concluded that an educational institution engaged in racial discrimination was not charitable within the meaning of the IRS Code. The Court rejected the schools' claims that the Free Exercise Clause of the First Amendment justified their behavior. The decisions evidenced the strong policy of the Court against racial discrimination.

Not all racial classifications are invalid. The Court has upheld a few affirmative action programs involving racial classifications, particularly those enacted by Congress.[121] Additionally, the government may require the designation of individuals by race for certain statistical purposes, such as the national census, or gathering health data.[122]

In *Lee v. Washington*,[123] the Court left open the possibility that prison security and discipline might justify segregation. However, the Court in *Johnson v. California* significantly decreased that possibility by deciding to apply strict scrutiny to prison segregation plans.[124] *Johnson* (5-3) applied strict scrutiny to California's policy of racially segregating prisoners for up to their first 60 days. Justice O'Connor stated that separate facilities could not be equal, citing *Brown v. Board of Education*.[125] Neither the Federal government nor any states utilized racial segregation in managing their prisons. Justice Ginsburg concurred, joined by Justices Souter and Breyer. Justice Stevens dissented. Justice Thomas dissented, joined by Justice Scalia, noting that California gangs, which are largely race-based, endangered prisoners with race-based violence.

---

[118] *See* McLaughlin v. Florida, 379 U.S. 184, 196 (1964).

[119] 461 U.S. 574 (1983).

[120] 456 U.S. 922 (1982).

[121] *See infra* Chapter 11.

[122] *See* Tancil v. Woolls, 379 U.S. 19 (1964).

[123] 390 U.S. 333 (1968).

[124] 543 U.S. 499 (2005).

[125] 347 U.S. 483 (1954).

[2] Racial Discrimination in Employment

The Court's race discrimination jurisprudence largely focuses on the areas of schools, employment, housing, voting, and the criminal justice system. Establishing an equal protection violation in any of these areas requires a finding of discriminatory intent, not only discriminatory impact. For policy reasons, the Court has, however, made it easier to establish discriminatory intent in certain areas like school desegregation and the right to vote. In the school desegregation area, the *Columbus* and *Keyes* temporal and geographic presumptions effectively rendered discriminatory intent much easier to prove. The policy reasons for this relaxation may have included the importance of education in advancing democracy and equal opportunity.

Employment is not an area in which the Court has relaxed the discriminatory intent requirement. In fact, *Washington v. Davis*[126] was perhaps the key case enshrining this requirement in equal protection jurisprudence. In *Davis*, the Supreme Court upheld against an equal protection challenge a test for candidates for police officer. The test was used generally throughout the Federal service and was developed by the Civil Service Commission, not the Police Department. It excluded a disproportionately high number of black applicants. The Court held that discriminatory impact did not establish an equal protection violation. The plaintiffs must show evidence of discriminatory intent or purpose. Such an intent could be proved from the totality of relevant facts, including total exclusion of minorities or seriously disproportionate impact. Facts that could not be explained by non-racial considerations could also be used to show discriminatory intent. Additionally, the Court stated that if a statute was discriminatory on its face, it was invalid absent some compelling reason.

The written test in *Davis* was facially neutral in ascertaining whether police recruits possessed a particular level of verbal skill. Moreover, it served the legitimate governmental purpose of improving the communication skills of employees. Even if the plaintiffs could have established an inference of racial discrimination, it was negated by the fact that the force made affirmative efforts to recruit black police officers, that the racial composition of the recruitment classes and the force was changing, and that the test in question was *related* to the training program.

The Court noted several problems with basing an equal protection violation on discriminatory impact alone. Such an approach could have invalidated a whole range of tax, welfare, public service, regulatory, and licensing statutes: the disparity in average income between black persons and white persons meant that these laws benefitted, or burdened, one race more than the other, thus effecting a disproportionate impact.

The line between discriminatory intent and impact is not always clear. Justice Stevens' concurrence in *Davis* pointed out that the evidentiary standard for proving purposeful discrimination varied in different types of cases. For example, in the school segregation area, the standard has been diluted by *Keyes*, *Columbus*,

---

[126] 426 U.S. 229 (1976).

and *Dayton*. In *Yick Wo*, the discriminatory impact was so overwhelming that it alone established a *prima facie* case of intent. Justice Stevens maintained that often the most probative evidence of intent was objective evidence of what actually happened, rather than the subjective intention of the decision-maker.[127]

[3] Housing and Zoning

In *Arlington Heights v. Metropolitan Housing Development Corp.*,[128] plaintiffs were denied a rezoning request which would have allowed them to build multiple-family units for low and moderate income tenants. The Court refused to find an equal protection violation based on the lack of discriminatory intent. In doing so, the Court clarified the standard for proving discriminatory intent in equal protection cases. Under *Arlington Heights*, a plaintiff need only show that discrimination was a motivating factor in the decision, not the sole or even the primary factor. The reason for this standard was that a legislative or administrative body operating under a broad mandate rarely was motivated by a single concern. As plaintiffs had failed to demonstrate even some discriminatory motivation, the Court upheld the zoning denial.

The Court reiterated that impact was seldom sufficient, standing alone, to establish discriminatory intent. Sometimes a clear pattern could emerge in a facially neutral statute that was inexplicable on grounds other than race. Even then, only extremely stark patterns of discriminatory impact would alone be sufficient to prove discriminatory intent.[129] While disparate impact was by itself insufficient, it was an important starting point.

The *Arlington Heights* opinion listed a number of relevant factors in proving discriminatory intent in zoning cases. First, there could have been a series of official actions taken for invidious purposes. Second, a specific sequence of events that occurred before the challenged decision could indicate discriminatory intent. For example, an area that had been zoned for multi-family housing might suddenly have been changed to single-family zoning after the board learned of a plan to build integrated housing projects. Third, a zoning board's departure from normal procedures for decision-making could indicate an improper motive. Fourth, a zoning board's departure from factors that it usually considered important could indicate discriminatory intent, especially if the eliminated factors favored a decision different from the one taken. Fifth, legislative or administrative history of statements by members of the decision-making body during the decision-making process could indicate discriminatory intent.

Once the plaintiff established a *prima facie* case of intentional discrimination, the burden of persuasion shifted to the defendant to show that the decision would

---

[127] This treatise only covers the discriminatory intent requirement in equal protection jurisprudence. The requirements for statutory causes of action, for example, employment discrimination under Title VII of the Civil Rights Act of 1964, range beyond the scope of this treatise. *See* 42 U.S.C. § 2000 *et seq.*

[128] 429 U.S. 252 (1977).

[129] *See, e.g.*, Gomillion v. Lightfoot, 364 U.S. 339 (1960) (gerrymandered voting district with 28 sides). *See also* Yick Wo v. Hopkins, 118 U.S. 356 (1886).

have been the same even without the impermissible intent. This notion resembles the concept of causality in tort law.

Several housing cases demonstrate the broad principle that equal protection scrutiny also applies to referenda and state and local constitutional provisions.[130] In *Reitman v. Mulkey*,[131] the Court invalidated an amendment to the California Constitution that prohibited the State from limiting a private property owner's right to sell or rent her property as she saw fit. The amendment would have allowed private property owners to discriminate in the sale or lease of their property. The Court stated that the intent of the amendment was to allow, or even involve the State in, private racial discrimination. Four dissenters argued that the amendment was a neutral provision that merely had the effect of repealing earlier laws.

Hunter v. Erickson[132] invalidated a city charter amendment that conditioned the implementation of existing or future anti-housing discrimination statutes upon approval by a majority of voters in a general election. The amendment effectively nullified the City's recently enacted fair housing ordinance. A referendum requirement of a majority vote definitionally burdened minorities. The Court focused on the disparate treatment of anti-discrimination regulations evident on the face of the statute. That this disparate treatment resulted from a referendum did not insulate it from constitutional scrutiny.

A state could require local approval, by popular referendum, of low-rent public housing projects. In *James v. Valtierra*,[133] the majority found that such a provision did not make distinctions based on race because it required popular approval whether or not the housing project exclusively would be occupied by racial minorities.

Several other housing cases illustrate the severe penalties that court-ordered desegregation can attract. In *United States v. City of Yonkers*,[134] the Second Circuit reviewed a civil contempt fine imposed on the City of Yonkers and individual council members. The trial court had imposed the fine to obtain compliance with a consent decree intended to implement low-income housing legislation after the City had been found liable for intentional housing discrimination. The City's fine began at a mere $100 per day and doubled each day of non-compliance.[135] The Court of Appeals capped the penalty at $1,000,000 per day. The Supreme Court denied certiorari on the City's petition to review this fine. *Spallone v. United States*[136] reversed a fine imposed on the individual council members. In addition to the City's penalty, individual council members were fined $500 per day and threatened with subsequent imprisonment if the appropriate legislation was not enacted within

---

[130] *See* Washington v. Seattle Sch. Dist. No. 1, 458 U.S. 457 (1982), and Crawford v. Bd. of Educ., 458 U.S. 527 (1982), for application of this principle in the school desegregation area.

[131] 387 U.S. 369 (1967).

[132] 393 U.S. 385 (1969).

[133] 402 U.S. 137 (1971).

[134] 856 F.2d 444 (2d Cir. 1988).

[135] At this rate, the fine would reach $1,000,000 by day 14 and exceed $26 billion by day 28.

[136] 493 U.S. 265 (1990).

eight days. Imposition of individual fines in this case was an abuse of discretion. Such personal liability would encourage legislators not to vote for their constituencies but for their pocketbooks.

In *Cuyahoga Falls v. Buckeye Community Hope Foundation*,[137] plaintiffs brought an action against city officials claiming that a referendum repealing a city affordable housing ordinance violated equal protection. During a "citizen-driven petition drive,"[138] a private individual could make statements that may be relevant to an equal protection violation yet not comprise state action under the Fourteenth Amendment. In contrast, when a decision-maker or referendum sponsor made a statement during a referendum, this could qualify as evidence of discriminatory intent. In *Cuyahoga Falls*, the plaintiffs were unable to show that city officials exercised coercive power, either overt or covert, that affected voters' decision-making during the drive to transform the actions or statements of private voters into state action.

[4] Voting

Early voting rights cases attempted to eliminate racially gerrymandered districts that were drawn to dilute or eliminate the voting strength of black persons. Black neighborhoods were broken into strangely shaped districts to insure a white majority in each of the districts, effectively preventing the election of black candidates. In cases like *Gomillion v. Lightfoot*,[139] the Supreme Court eliminated these practices. *Gomillion*, for example, invalidated a highly irregular, twenty-eight sided voting district.

Shaw v. Reno[140] Court applied *Gomillion* to invalidate a racially-based gerrymander designed to foster the election of black candidates. The Court held that irrational reapportionment schemes, which were inexplicable on grounds other than race, had to be narrowly tailored to serve a compelling state interest. Although it remanded the case for further consideration, the *Shaw* Court did suggest certain race-based districting that may pass strict scrutiny. One example would be a narrowly tailored districting plan that was reasonably necessary to avoid retrogression of the voting strength of a racial minority in violation of Section 5 of the Voting Rights Act (VRA). Another example would be avoiding vote dilution of a racial minority in violation of Section 2 of the VRA. Even in this latter instance, the racially gerrymandered district had to satisfy several conditions. The minority group had to be large, compact, politically cohesive, and historically defeated by white bloc voting in the pre-existing district. At minimum, Justice O'Connor appeared to indicate that racial redistricting would be permitted only in response to racially polarized voting, only if the state uses sound districting practices, and only if the residential patterns of the adversely affected racial group enabled the creation of districts in which they would constitute a majority.

---

[137] 538 U.S. 188 (2003).

[138] *Id.* at 196.

[139] 364 U.S. 339 (1960).

[140] 509 U.S. 630 (1993).

In *Miller v. Johnson*,[141] the Court invalidated a voter district designed predominantly with racial motivations. A population increase entitled Georgia to an eleventh congressional seat. The Justice Department, under Section 5 of the VRA, finally accepted Georgia's third attempt at redistricting, a plan approximating the "max-black" proposal of the ACLU. The new eleventh district split 26 counties, connected some neighborhoods 260 miles apart and covered 6,784.2 miles sometimes being connected only by narrow land bridges.

Justice Kennedy, writing for the 5-4 majority, stated that *Shaw v. Reno* did not require the demonstration of a bizarrely drawn district to establish an equal protection violation. However, a bizarrely drawn district might provide powerful circumstantial evidence that race was the predominant legislative purpose. To establish an equal protection violation, plaintiff had to show through circumstantial evidence of the district's form and demographics, or more direct evidence of racially motivated legislative purpose, that race was the "predominant factor" behind the districting decision. Plaintiff had to establish that the legislature subordinated traditional race-neutral districting principles including "compactness; contiguity, respect for political subdivisions or communities defined by actual shared interests, to racial considerations."[142] In determining whether to allow cases to go to discovery or trial under this analysis, courts must consider the dominant role of state legislatures in apportionment decisions. In this case, the District Court's finding that race was the predominant factor was not clearly erroneous. Using narrow land bridges to include 80 percent of the district's black population patently showed that race was the predominant factor.

A redistricting plan that featured race as the predominant factor had to pass strict scrutiny. Georgia lacked the requisite compelling state interest. The Judiciary would effectively be surrendering its power to review race-based redistricting to the Executive Branch if the Justice Department's determination of compliance with Section 5 of the VRA had satisfied strict scrutiny. That Act allowed the Justice Department to stretch new districting plans to avoid retrogression in minority voting strength, not to carve the electorate into racial voting blocs. In a crucial concurrence, Justice O'Connor maintained that this case, like *Shaw*, would only affect extreme instances of racial gerrymandering, and not the vast majority of congressional districts fashioned according to "customary districting principles."[143] Even race can be a factor, just not the predominant factor. Justice Ginsburg dissented, joined by Justices Stevens, Souter, and Breyer. Justice Ginsburg disagreed with the Court as finding that the eleventh district was extremely irregular, compared with other, pre-existing districts in Georgia. *Shaw* involved extremely irregular, race-based lines. Instead, this case simply required that race was used as the predominant factor. State legislatures are better equipped than federal courts to consider the factors that determine the drawing of district lines.

---

[141] 515 U.S. 900 (1995).

[142] *Miller*, 515 U.S. at 916.

[143] *Id.* at 928.

In *Shaw v. Hunt*,[144] the Court invalidated same redistricting plan that it had remanded to the lower courts in *Shaw v. Reno*. The Federal Attorney General's office criticized North Carolina's initial plan creating one majority-black district, District 1, because it failed to " 'give effect to black and Native American voting strength' "[145] in certain portions of the State. As a result, the State created a second majority-black district, District 12. The "boundary lines" of the two new districts were considered "unconventional."[146] Chief Justice Rehnquist, writing for the majority (5-4), only addressed the constitutionality of District 12 because it was the only one where plaintiffs were residents and, consequently, had standing.

North Carolina's redistricting plan was subject to strict scrutiny because it was grounded primarily in racial considerations. The State proffered three separate interests to sustain District 12. The first asserted interest was "eradicat[ing] the effects of past and present discrimination."[147] Curing generalized, societal discrimination was not a compelling interest; the state must specifically identify past or present, public or private, discrimination before using a race-conscious remedy. Moreover, the State failed to establish before implementing the plan that creating District 12 was necessary to eradicate racial discrimination.

The State's second and third asserted compelling interests — complying with Sections 2 and 5 of the VRA — also failed to survive strict scrutiny. The Court found it unnecessary to consider a question left unanswered in *Miller, i.e.,* whether "compliance with the Voting Rights Act, on its own, could be a compelling interest."[148] Section 5 did not require the creation of District 12 because the *Miller* Court concluded that Section 5 does not authorize a maximization policy similar to that pursued in North Carolina in this case. Assuming that compliance with Section 2 comprised a compelling state interest, District 12 was not narrowly tailored to achieve such compliance. Section 2 liability requires that the impacted minority group be geographically compact. The State could not reasonably have shown that such a group existed in District 12.

Justice Stevens dissented, joined in part by Justices Ginsburg and Breyer. Justice Stevens maintained that District 12 was created with the "race-neutral, traditional districting criteria" of protecting incumbents and separating rural and urban voters. If strict scrutiny applied even when a majority-minority district is drawn using traditional districting principles, then a state cannot create one "to fulfill its obligation under the Voting Rights Act without inviting constitutional suspicion."[149]

Even if strict scrutiny was the correct standard, District 12 advanced the compelling interests of facilitating the participation of a previously disadvantaged minority in the legislative process and of avoiding burdensome and costly litigation under Sections 2 and 5 of the VRA. Moreover, District 12 was narrowly tailored to

---

[144] 517 U.S. 899 (1996).

[145] *Id.* at 902.

[146] *Id.*

[147] *Id.* at 908.

[148] *Id.* at 911.

[149] *Id.* at 908.

achieve the interest of avoiding liability because it would now be more difficult for a potential litigant to establish a cause of action by creating more majority-minority districts than the State did. Justice Stevens believed that the Court should not interfere with this cooperative process among state and federal actors. Justice Souter filed a separate dissenting opinion, joined by Justices Ginsburg and Breyer, in which he incorporated the reasoning of his dissent in *Bush v. Vera*.

In *Bush v. Vera*,[150] the Court (3-2-4) invalidated three Texas congressional districts as unconstitutional racial gerrymanders. After an increase in population gave Texas three new Congressional seats, the Texas Legislature created a new majority-African-American district, a new majority-Hispanic district, and reconfigured an existing district as a majority-African-American district. The Justice Department pre-cleared this districting plan under Section 5 of the VRA.

Justice O'Connor wrote a plurality opinion, joined by Chief Justice Rehnquist and Justice Kennedy, stating that strict scrutiny applies when racial considerations predominate in legislative districting decisions. The plurality sustained the finding of the three-judge district court that race predominated. One study ranked the three districts among the 28 most irregular districts in the country. The plurality also agreed with the district court that the districts had " 'no integrity in terms of traditional, neutral redistricting criteria.' "[151] The State admitted that it wanted to create three majority-minority districts. Texas also used a computer program that allowed it to draw the district lines on the basis of racial demographics.

While none of these factors was independently sufficient to attract strict scrutiny, their combination was. The plurality proceeded to look at each district individually to determine whether race was the predominant factor.

The first district was 50 percent African-American and 17.1 percent Hispanic. This bizarrely shaped district was precisely tailored to cross political subdivisions and reach into other minority neighborhoods. While the district lines had some correlation with transportation modes, common media sources, and consistent urban character, the legislature lacked this information " 'in any organized fashion.' "[152]

Turning to the other two districts, the plurality noted that, according to a leading study, they were two of the three most bizarrely shaped districts in the United States. The State again claimed that incumbency protection accounted for the bizarre shapes of the districts. The plurality, however, agreed with the district court that the legislature's goal to create majority-minority districts far outweighed its efforts to protect incumbents, as the lines of both districts correlated almost exactly with race while both districts were similarly Democratic.

In determining whether any of the racial distracting was "narrowly tailored to advance a compelling state interest," the plurality rejected the State's three asserted compelling state interests. Assuming without deciding that the results test of Section 2(b) of the VRA comprised a compelling state interest, the State had

---

[150] 517 U.S. 952 (1996).

[151] *Id.* at 960.

[152] *Id.* at 966.

to show that: (1) the minority group was large enough yet compact enough to comprise a majority, (2) that it was politically cohesive, and (3) that block voting by the white majority usually defeats the minority group's preferred candidate. None of the three districts satisfied the first requirement, as all were "bizarrely shaped and far from compact."[153] These characteristics suggested a predominant racial motivation. The plurality also rejected as compelling the State's interest in " 'ameliorating the effects of racially polarized voting attributable to' "[154] discrimination. Such a remedy must be necessary to cure " 'specific, identified discrimination.' "[155]

Race-based districting was justified only if the state used legitimate districting principles and the residential patterns of the minority group allow for the creation of majority-minority districts. Finally, the plurality rejected Texas' claim that complying with VRA Section 5 was a compelling state interest. Rather than maintain the same percentage of African-American population in one of the districts, Texas had increased that percentage and had not supported this increase by showing it was essential to avoid retrogression.

Justice O'Connor also wrote a separate concurring opinion. A state may avoid strict scrutiny, even when taking race into account, so long as it does not subordinate traditional districting criteria to the use of race for its own sake or as a proxy in order to create majority-minority districts. Moreover, states cannot reduce minority voting strength in racially polarized districts. However, a district that is bizarrely shaped, non-compact, created for predominantly racial reasons, and neglects race-neutral districting principles is unconstitutional.

Justice Kennedy joined the plurality opinion, but wrote a concurring opinion saying that strict scrutiny should apply to all districts, including all majority-minority districts, that are created using predominantly racial criteria, but not to those that may simply have bizarre shapes. He also disagreed with Justice O'Connor's use of the predominant motivation test a second time in determining whether a districting plan was narrowly tailored.

Justice Thomas, concurring in the judgment and joined by Justice Scalia, said that the intentional creation of majority-minority districts was "sufficient to show that race was a predominant, motivating factor."[156]

Justice Stevens dissented, joined by Justices Ginsburg and Breyer. In his view, all of Texas' new districts were political rather than racial gerrymanders. Incumbency was the controlling concern, noting that three majority-white districts in Texas also rank among the most oddly shaped in the nation. Justice Stevens also maintained that the legislature sometimes used race as a proxy for political affiliation.

Justice Souter also dissented, joined by Justices Ginsburg and Breyer. While blacks comprise 11.1 percent of Texas' population, they only have 4.9 percent of the

---

[153] *Id.* at 979.

[154] *Id.* at 981.

[155] *Id.* at 982.

[156] *Id.* at 1000 (Thomas, J, concurring).

seats in Congress. Not only do courts have difficulty isolating the predominant motive in a districting decision, but numerous traditional districting principles also take race into account. The plurality also did not indicate how much reliance on racial data it would allow. The Court has left the states on a "tightrope"[157] risking suits under the Equal Protection Clause if they draw majority-minority districts and under the VRA if they do not. Justice Souter would confine *Shaw I* to its facts or throw out its cause of action entirely.

In *Abrams v. Johnson*,[158] the Court upheld a redistricting plan for Georgia's congressional districts fashioned in response to the Court's remand in *Miller v. Johnson*. When the Georgia legislature could not agree on a new redistricting plan, the three-judge District Court crafted its own plan with only one majority-black district, under which the 1996 general elections occurred. The District Court's plan did not split any counties outside the Atlanta area. The District Court also attempted to protect incumbents from contests with each other. The District Court found that Georgia did not have a sufficiently concentrated black population to justify adding a second majority-black district. Unlike the Georgia legislature's 1991 redistricting plan, which was denied Justice Department preclearance, the District Court's plan did not contain two majority-black districts. Racial motives subsumed all other policies in the 1992 precleared plan and the other proposed redistricting plans which advocated two or three majority black districts. Consequently, "the trial court acted well within its discretion"[159] in determining that it could not develop a redistricting plan containing two majority-black districts without engaging in racial gerrymandering.

Second, the trial court's plan did not violate Section 2 of the VRA because the absence of a second majority-black district did not result in impermissible vote dilution. If race predominantly motivates drawing districts, the plan must serve a compelling state interest. The Court has assumed but not decided that compliance with Section 2 can be a compelling state interest. However, insufficient evidence existed to suggest that the district court's plan resulted in vote dilution violating Section 2. Nor did the district court's plan violate the retrogression principle of Section 5 of the VRA.

Justice Breyer dissented joined by Justices Stevens, Souter, and Ginsburg. Approximately 27 percent of Georgia's voting age population was African-Americans. The dissent criticized the Court for holding suspect the policy preferences of the Justice Department while allowing the policy preferences of other interested parties, such as farmers or consumers. "Until 1972, Georgia had not elected any African-American Members of Congress since Reconstruction,"[160] and since 1972, it has elected only four.

Under the record, the legislature could have reasonably believed that VRA Section 2 or 5 required the creation of a second majority black district. The reasonable belief of avoiding such a violation negates any inference that the

---

[157] *Id.* at 1006.

[158] 521 U.S. 74 (1997).

[159] *Id.*

[160] *Abrams*, 521 U.S. at 108.

legislation was transgressing the predominant racial motive test of *Miller*. Allowing the legislature to rely upon a reasonable interpretation of the evidence enables it to retain some discretionary redistricting authority. The dissent also faulted the Court for not defining or limiting the scope of the phrase " 'predominant racial motive.' "[161]

In *Lawyer v. Department of Justice*,[162] the Florida Supreme Court amended the redistricting plan to include an irregularly shaped Senate District 21, which contained a voting age population of 45.8 percent black and 9.4 percent Hispanic and encompassed parts of four counties in the Tampa Bay area. The settlement agreement at issue in this case decreased the black voting age population of District 21 from 45.0 percent to 36.2 percent and included portions of three counties instead of four.

Writing for a 5-4 majority, Justice Souter upheld the state attorney general's authority to propose a redistricting plan. In participating in the litigation, counsel for the Senate and the House affirmed the legislature's refusal to develop a new plan in formal session and endorsed the attorney general's authority to suggest a new plan on behalf of the State.[163]

Justice Souter did uphold as not clearly erroneous the district court's determination that District 21 did not "subordinate traditional districting principles to race."[164] A district spanning more than one county is common in Florida as it has 67 counties and 40 Senate seats. Moreover, the 36.2 percent black voting age population did not render the district " 'safe' "[165] for black-preferred candidates.

Justice Scalia dissented, joined by Justices O'Connor, Kennedy, and Thomas, stating that Florida's Constitution afforded the legislature the authority to reapportion, and the attorney general could not attain similar authority through his settling authority. The District Court erred by not providing the legislature with an opportunity to redistrict before imposing its own plan.

If the Court has broadly proscribed race-based gerrymandering except in narrowly tailored remedial cases, it has encountered greater difficulty ferreting out race-based discrimination in multi-member districts. In *Mobile v. Bolden*,[166] the Court upheld an at-large system of municipal elections in Mobile, Alabama. The system required that a candidate for City Commissioner run for election in the city at large and be elected by a majority of the total city-wide vote. Black citizens of Mobile filed a class action suit alleging that the at-large method of electing City Commissioners unfairly diluted the voting strength of black persons in violation of

---

[161] *Id.* at 116–17.

[162] 521 U.S. 567 (1997).

[163] Interpreting the record differently, the dissent stated that no resolution authorized counsel for the President of the Senate and the Speaker of the House to accept the settlement agreement on behalf of the legislature. The dissent also cited a letter written by a state senator, explicitly denying that the attorney general had redistricting authority.

[164] *Lawyer*, 521 U.S. at 568.

[165] *Id.* at 581.

[166] 446 U.S. 55 (1980).

the VRA, and the Fourteenth and Fifteenth Amendments. The District Court and the Court of Appeals found for the plaintiffs and ordered that the at-large voting system be replaced with election of members from single-member districts.

The Supreme Court reversed. Justice Stewart found that the system did not violate the Fifteenth Amendment, as that amendment prohibited interference with registration or voting because of race. Additionally, the plurality found no Fourteenth Amendment violation, as there was no evidence of discriminatory intent behind the voting system.[167] While at-large voting naturally disadvantaged minority parties, its mere existence did not establish purposeful discrimination. Concurring in the judgment, Justice Stevens upheld the at-large districting as valid reasons had prompted it, not invidious discrimination. Focusing on objective factors rather than intent, he would invalidate a plan that was extraordinary, a vestige of history, or with no greater justification than the figure in *Gomillion*. Justice Blackmun concurred only in the result. He agreed with the District Court's finding of discriminatory intent, but thought that the District Court should have considered other remedies than forcing the city to shift to a mayor-city council system. Justices Brennan, White, and Marshall filed dissenting opinions.

Rogers v. Lodge[168] involved the use of at-large elections to fill positions on the County Board of Commissioners of Burke County, Georgia.[169] No black person had ever been elected to the Board. In contrast to *Bolden*, the Court struck down the at-large voting system because of the district court's specific finding of discriminatory intent. The Supreme Court held that the discriminatory intent finding of the district court was not clearly erroneous.

The *Rogers* case indicated that the Supreme Court would grant substantial deference to district courts in determining discriminatory intent. The key distinction between *Mobile* and *Rogers* appears to be the explicit finding of discriminatory intent by the district court.

In *Hunt v. Cromartie*,[170] the Court overturned a district court's grant of summary judgment, which held that a congressional district was the product of racial gerrymandering. In response to *Shaw v. Hunt*,[171] the state developed an alternative plan for District 12, in which the district crossed only six counties rather than 12, the area decreased by more than half, and blacks constituted less than 50 percent of the voting population. However, the district retained "its basic 'snakelike' shape."

Writing for a unanimous Court, Justice Thomas complained that plaintiffs presented only circumstantial evidence of discriminatory intent, even though their evidence "tends to support an inference" of such intent. Moreover, after extensive analysis, the State's expert concluded that the political motive of creating a

---

[167] The District Court had found discriminatory intent. However, the plurality stated that the finding was based on disparate impact and purposeful discrimination that was irrelevant to the voting system or too distant in time.

[168] 458 U.S. 613 (1982).

[169] According to the 1980 census, 38 percent of the registered voters in the County were black.

[170] 526 U.S. 541 (1999).

[171] 517 U.S. 899 (1996).

Democratic district explained the district's boundaries "at least as well, and somewhat better than," racial motivation. In addition, "the sensitive nature of redistricting and the presumption of good faith that must be accorded legislative enactments" belied summary judgment in this case.

In *Easley v. Cromartie (Cromartie II)*,[172] the Court held clearly erroneous the finding of the three-judge District Court that race was a predominant factor in the districting plan for North Carolina's Congressional District 12. Writing for the majority, Justice Breyer noted that courts should use "extraordinary caution"[173] when examining claims alleging that a State has used race to draw a district's boundaries. Such caution is especially appropriate when the State's districting plan is justified by a "legitimate political explanation"[174] and the voting population is "one in which race and political affiliation are highly correlated."[175]

While the Court generally shows the utmost deference to factual findings of a lower court upheld by a court of appeals, no other court had reviewed the three-judge District Court in this case. Moreover, the trial was short, and "the key evidence consisted primarily of documents and expert testimony. Credibility evaluations played a minor role."[176] Because race and political affiliation were closely connected in North Carolina, a plaintiff must first show "that the legislature could have achieved its legitimate political objectives in alternative ways that are comparably consistent with traditional districting principles."[177] Second, a plaintiff must establish that those alternatives would have created "greater racial balance."[178]

Dissenting, Justice Thomas, joined by Chief Justice Rehnquist, and Justices Scalia and Kennedy, believed the Court's "incantations"[179] of the clearly erroneous standard masked its actual approach of " 'extensive review.' "[180]

[5] The Criminal Justice System

In *Batson v. Kentucky*,[181] a black defendant challenged the prosecutor's use of all of his peremptory challenges to strike every black person from the jury. The Court held that race-based peremptory challenges violated equal protection. They not only harmed the defendant, but also undermined public confidence in the criminal justice system. To establish a *prima facie* case of racially discriminatory use of peremptories: (1) "The defendant first must show that he is a member of a cognizable racial group . . . and that the prosecutor has exercised peremptory

---

[172] 532 U.S. 234 (2001).

[173] *Id.* at 242.

[174] *Id.*

[175] *Id.*

[176] *Id.* at 243.

[177] *Id.* at 258.

[178] *Id.*

[179] *Id.* at 259 (Thomas, J., dissenting).

[180] *Id.* at 260.

[181] 476 U.S. 79 (1986).

challenges to remove from the venire members of the defendant's race."[182] (2) The defendant can assume that peremptory challenges allow persons to discriminate who wish to discriminate. 3) Using these facts and any other relevant facts, the defendant must establish an inference of race-based exclusion from the jury.

Once the defendant makes a *prima facie* showing, the burden shifts to the state to give a racially neutral explanation for challenging black jurors. This showing need not rise to the level justifying a challenge for cause. The prosecutor, however, cannot satisfy her burden merely by stating that she struck jurors of the defendant's race based on the assumption that the jurors would be biased in favor of the defendant because of their shared race.

In his dissent, Chief Justice Burger argued that the holding created a middle ground between peremptories and challenges for cause that would spark considerable difficulty for trial judges in applying the Court's standard.

Griffith v. Kentucky[183] applied *Batson* retroactively to all cases, state and federal, pending on direct review or not yet final. The Court did not follow its prior rule of denying retroactivity in cases where the new rule constituted a "clear break" with past decisions.

Holland v. Illinois[184] afforded standing to a white criminal defendant to mount a Sixth Amendment challenge to the exclusion, through peremptories, of blacks from his jury. For Sixth Amendment standing, each defendant could challenge a venire as not representing a fair cross section of the community, even if the defendant did not belong to the systematically excluded group. However, after affording the defendant standing, the Court rejected his Sixth Amendment claim. An impartial jury requires a fair cross section at the venire stage, but not at the petit jury stage.

In *Powers v. Ohio*,[185] the Court held that criminal defendants could mount an equal protection attack for using peremptory challenges to exclude jurors not of defendant's race. Black jurors had been excluded in a criminal trial involving a white defendant. The Defendant had a right to be tried by a jury selected by nondiscriminatory criteria. Moreover, the Court afforded the defendant third-party standing to enforce the right of a juror not to be struck for reasons of race.[186] While a *Batson* challenge did not hinge on the juror and the defendant sharing the same race, shared race remains relevant to establishing bias in making race-based exclusions.

---

[182] *Id.* at 96.

[183] 479 U.S. 314 (1987).

[184] 493 U.S. 474 (1990).

[185] 499 U.S. 400 (1991).

[186] Third-party standing pertained first, because the third-party defendant had suffered injury in fact. Second, the defendant and excluded jurors had a common interest in eradicating racial discrimination in jury selection. Third, economic and other barriers rendered it unlikely that excluded jurors would bring such suits themselves.

Georgia v. McCollum[187] held that equal protection prohibited a criminal defendant from using peremptory challenges to exclude jurors based on their race. Race-based exclusions harmed jurors and the integrity of the courts. Defendant's use of peremptory challenges involved state action, as the source of authority for peremptory challenges was state law. Moreover, the criminal defendant was a state actor, as peremptory challenges were benefits and assistance received from the state.

Edmonson v. Leesville Concrete Co.[188] extended the *Batson* challenge to civil suits. Again, state action was present because state law provided the source of the right and the civil litigant made extensive use of state machinery. For reasons similar to those articulated in *Powers*, the challenging litigant had third-party standing to contest the use of race-based peremptory challenges on behalf of the excluded jurors.

The Court appears to give great deference to trial courts in evaluating *Batson* challenges. In *Hernandez v. New York*,[189] the prosecutor used peremptory challenges to exclude all jurors who would have difficulty accepting the translator's rendition of Spanish-language testimony. The trial judge found this explanation race neutral despite the fact that it may have resulted in the disproportionate removal of Latino jurors and despite the availability of a less drastic alternative than exclusion. Writing for a plurality of four, Justice Kennedy noted that the prosecutor based his claims on observations of the jurors rather than mere assumptions. Giving great deference to the trial court, the Court noted that a disproportionate impact on one ethnic group did not give rise to a Batson challenge. Two other Justices found the absence of discriminatory intent dispositive.

In *J.E.B. v. Alabama*,[190] the Court extended *Batson* to gender-based peremptory challenges. The State used all nine of its peremptory challenges to strike men during *voir dire* in a paternity suit. "African-Americans and women share a history of total exclusion"[191] from jury service. The other party can rebut the *prima facie* case by showing that the challenge was based on a juror characteristic other than gender. "This does not mean, of course, that every jury must contain representatives of all the economic, social, religious, racial, political and geographical groups of the community."[192] It does, however, prohibit "systematic and intentional exclusion of any of these groups."[193] This language may signal other permissible *Batson* challenges.

---

[187] 505 U.S. 42 (1992).

[188] 500 U.S. 614 (1991).

[189] 500 U.S. 352 (1991).

[190] 511 U.S. 127 (1994).

[191] *Id.* at 136.

[192] *Id.* at 145.

[193] *Id.*

Johnson v. California[194] (8-1) invalidated California's application of the "more likely than not" standard to establish a *Batson prima facie* case. A *Batson prima facie* case only required evidence sufficient to permit an inference of discrimination. While the party making the *Batson* challenge had the ultimate burden of persuasion, this burden only arose after the nonmoving party had offered a reason for excluding the specific veniremen. The prosecutor's refusal to offer a reason supported the inference of discrimination. The prosecutor in this case had used peremptory challenges to remove all three black prospective jurors. The inferences that discrimination may have occurred established the defendant's *prima facie* case. Justice Breyer concurred. Justice Thomas dissented.

In *Rice v. Collins*,[195] the Court, in a habeas challenge, rejected a *Batson* challenge to a prosecutor's use of a preemptory challenge to remove a young black woman from the jury venire where the prosecutor supported the challenge by stating that the juror had "rolled her eyes in response to a question from the court," and was young and lacked ties to the community, which might make the juror too tolerant of drug dealing. State court credibility determinations in *Batson* challenges are generally reviewed for clear error and state court factual findings and are presumed correct unless rebutted by clear and convincing evidence although "[r]easonable minds" may "disagree about the prosecutor's credibility, . . . on habeas review."

In *Snyder v. Louisiana*[196] the Court reversed a trial court's finding of lack of discriminatory intent as clearly erroneous. While thirty-six potential jurors survived challenges for cause, the prosecution used preemptory strikes to eliminate all five remaining black jurors. The prosecution's explanation striking one of the black jurors was that the potential juror looked nervous throughout the questioning. The trial judge did not question this challenge. The prosecution also argued that the same juror was a student-teacher who might be concerned about missing class; consequently, he might vote for a lesser sentence. These rationales were insufficient to meet the highly deferential clearly erroneous test. Moreover, the prosecutor declined to use a preemptory strike on a white juror with a more pressing time commitment. Justice Thomas dissented joined by Justice Scalia. Justice Thomas stated that the majority was merely "paying lip service" to the deferential clearly erroneous standard.

In *United States v. Armstrong*,[197] the Court rejected two black defendants' request for discovery on a selective prosecution claim because defendants failed to show governmental refusal to prosecute similarly situated whites. Defendants, indicted on charges of distributing crack cocaine produced affidavits stating that all of the 24 crack cocaine cases closed by the Office in 1991 involved black defendants; from defense counsel averring that Caucasian users and dealers were equal in number to their minority counterparts; and from a criminal defense attorney averring that many nonblacks are prosecuted in state courts for crack offenses.

---

[194] 545 U.S. 162 (2005).

[195] 546 U.S. 333 (2006).

[196] 552 U.S. 472 (2008).

[197] 517 U.S. 456 (1996).

Writing for the Court (8-1), Chief Justice Rehnquist noted that selective prosecution claims require courts to exert power over the prosecutorial function, an area of broad Executive discretion. To establish such an equal protection violation, defendant must show discriminatory purpose and effect. As discovery will also impose burdens on prosecutorial functions, obtaining it requires a similarly rigorous standard to that for a selective prosecution claim. Defendants in this case failed to "produce some evidence that similarly situated defendants of other races could have been prosecuted, but were not."[198] The affidavits recounted hearsay or "personal conclusions based on anecdotal evidence."[199]

Justice Stevens, dissenting, maintained that the District Court did not abuse its discretion in demanding some governmental response to defendant's showing in light of the extraordinarily high number of blacks being exposed to the stringent penalties imposed for crack cocaine.

In *McCleskey v. Kemp*[200] the Court rejected an equal protection claim that Georgia administered its capital sentencing process in a racially discriminatory manner. Defendant McCleskey supported his claim with an extensive statistical report. The study alleged that defendants who murdered whites were much more likely to receive the death sentence than those who murdered blacks. It also alleged that black defendants were more likely to receive the death penalty. Finally, the study claimed that black defendants, such as McCleskey, who killed whites were most likely to be sentenced to death.[201]

The Court stated that McCleskey's equal protection challenge[202] would succeed only if he proved that the decision-makers in *his* particular case acted with discriminatory purpose in sentencing. However, McCleskey presented no such evidence indicating such a discriminatory purpose. Instead, he contended that the study supported an inference from its general statistics to a specific conclusion that his sentence was racially biased.

McCleskey is a controversial decision. At one level, the case follows from the Court's discriminatory intent requirement. The state would have a difficult time rebutting a showing of discriminatory impact alone, were it forced to do so. Both prosecutors and particularly juries have traditionally not been required to explain their charging or sentencing decisions. Criticism of the *McCleskey* decision alleges

---

[198] *Id.* at 465.

[199] *Id.* at 470.

[200] 481 U.S. 279 (1987).

[201] The study examined over 2,000 murders that occurred in Georgia in the 1970s and accounted for 230 variables that could have given a non-racial explanation for the disparities. The raw numbers indicated that those charged with killing whites were sentenced to death in 11 percent of the cases. However, those charged with killing blacks were sentenced to death in 1 percent of the cases. In cases involving white victims, 22 percent of the black defendants and 8 percent of the white defendants received the death sentence. The study also found that prosecutors sought the death penalty in 70 percent of the black defendant/white victim cases; 32 percent of the white defendant/white victim cases; 15 percent of the black defendant/black victim cases; and 19 percent of the white defendant/black victim cases.

[202] Justice Powell also rejected defendant's Eighth Amendment challenge.

that the Court has chosen to ignore the equal protection problems that exist in capital punishment cases.[203]

Justice Blackmun's dissent argued that McCleskey had made as much of a *prima facie* case as had been made in *Batson* by those alleging racial bias in peremptory challenges. One commentator went so far as to compare the decision to *Dred Scott, Plessy v. Ferguson,* and *Korematsu.*[204]

---

[203] R. Kennedy, McCleskey v. Kemp: *Race, Capital Punishment, and the Supreme Court,* 101 Harv. L. Rev. 1388 (1988).

[204] *Id.* at 1389.

Chapter 10

EQUAL RIGHTS FOR THE SEXES

INTRODUCTION

After World War II, the Women's Movement compelled a re-evaluation of the role of women in American society and of the long-standing attitudes toward women. The law embodied these roles and attitudes, often in forms more subtle than with race. Many such laws, seemingly designed to protect women, actually perpetuated long-held stereotypical views about the characteristics of both men and women.[1]

Over time, the Court changed its approach to gender-based classifications. Using the Equal Protection Clause, it fashioned a middle-tier standard of scrutiny in the gender area. Section 10.01 traces the evolution of this middle-tier standard and the scope of its application in gender cases. Much of the Court's gender discrimination jurisprudence relates to employment, benefit programs, and pregnancy. These areas are treated in Sections 10.02, 10.03, and 10.04, respectively.

§ 10.01   CHANGING ATTITUDES TOWARD GENDER-BASED CLASSIFICATIONS

For much of our Constitutional history, the Supreme Court did not construe the Equal Protection Clause as prohibiting gender discrimination.[2] In *Goesaert v. Cleary*,[3] the Court upheld a Michigan statute prohibiting a woman from being a bartender unless she was the wife or daughter of the male owner of a licensed liquor establishment. Using a rationality standard, the Court stated that the Michigan legislature could have completely prohibited women from being bartenders. Consequently, it could also make exceptions when circumstances supposedly shielded women from the moral and social problems that the law was designed to address.

---

[1] Many laws were derived in part from reform-minded legislation intended to protect women and children from sweat shop working conditions. One such case, *Muller v. Oregon*, 208 U.S. 412 (1908), upheld an Oregon law setting maximum hours for women factory workers. For many years, the Court struggled with the continuing validity of laws that allegedly protected women as a class against, for example, burdensome conditions of employment. While *Muller* has been criticized for its paternalistic attitude toward women, the decision marked a departure from the Supreme Court's conservative *laissez faire* attitude toward state economic regulation.

[2] An early example of the court's failure to construe the Equal Protection Clause to prohibit gender discrimination occurred in *Bradwell v. State*, 83 U.S. (16 Wall.) 130 (1873). In *Bradwell* the Court upheld a state law barring women from practicing law. In a concurring opinion, Justice Bradley wrote that "[t]he paramount destiny and mission of woman are to fulfil the noble and benign offices of wife and mother." *Id.* at 141.

[3] 335 U.S. 464 (1948).

The Court applied heightened scrutiny to gender discrimination in *Reed v. Reed*.[4] Although the Court did not extend heightened scrutiny explicitly but used instead language that more nearly resembled a simple rationality test, *Reed* struck down a statute that preferred males to serve as estate administrators over equally qualified females. The state assumed that men possessed more business experience than women, thus better qualifying them as estate administrators. Rejecting these generalized assumptions, which the state defended on grounds of administrative convenience, the Court required the state to conduct hearings to ascertain the qualifications of men and women on an individualized basis. Making this determination based on assumptions, would only perpetuate a stereotypical view of women.

Two years later, the Court made its most serious attempt to extend strict scrutiny to gender discrimination. In *Frontiero v. Richardson*,[5] the federal statutes in question combined to allow a uniformed serviceman to claim his wife as a dependent regardless of whether she was actually dependent upon him. A servicewoman, however, could only claim her husband as a dependent if he was actually dependent upon her for over half of his support.

As the Equal Protection Clause of the Fourteenth Amendment only applies to the states,[6] the Court struck down the statutes as violating the equal protection standard interpreted to be part of the Due Process Clause of the Fifth Amendment. Justice Brennan's plurality opinion, joined by Justices Douglas, White, and Marshall, ruled that classifications based on gender "are inherently suspect and must therefore be subjected to close judicial scrutiny."[7] In support of heightened scrutiny, the plurality noted first the extensive history of discrimination against women. Second, sex, like race, was an immutable characteristic determined at birth that did not reflect the actual capabilities of the individual. Third, the plurality cited Title VII, the Equal Pay Act, and the Equal Rights Amendment in noting that Congress had concluded that gender classifications were "inherently invidious."[8]

The government argued that administrative convenience justified the statutes' gender classifications because women often were actually dependent upon their husbands but the converse was rarely true. It was rational, therefore, to require only female members to establish their husbands' dependency. The Court rejected this argument because the government offered no evidence that the differential classification was actually cheaper than an individual determination and because administrative convenience was insufficient to withstand strict scrutiny. Justice Powell, joined by Chief Justice Burger and Justice Blackmun, concurred in the judgment but objected to the characterization of gender as a suspect classification.

Since *Frontiero*, the Court has never again attempted to make sex a suspect class and instead has devised a middle-tier analysis[9] to invalidate a number of govern

---

[4]   404 U.S. 71 (1971).

[5]   411 U.S. 677 (1973).

[6]   *See* the discussion of reverse incorporation, *supra* § 9.01[1].

[7]   *Frontiero*, 411 U.S. at 682.

[8]   *Id.* at 687.

[9]   It is possible to argue that the refusal to extend suspect classification to gender is consistent with the *Carolene Products* footnote. *See supra* § 8.05[1]. The footnote provides a justification for extending

ment programs. In *Craig v. Boren*,[10] the Court struck down an Oklahoma statute that prohibited the sale of 3.2 percent beer to males under the age of 21 and to females under age 18. In *Craig*, the Court applied a middle-tier standard: a gender classification "must serve important governmental objectives and must be substantially related to achievement of those objectives."[11]

The state in *Craig* introduced a variety of statistical surveys designed to show that arrest and accident rates involving alcohol were far greater for males in the 18–21 age category who could not drink than for their female counterparts who could. Although the protection of public health and safety represented an important function of state and local governments, that objective did not justify the classification because it did not appear on the face of the statute or in the legislative history. In any event, the gender-based distinction at issue did not closely serve the state's professed objective of advancing public health and safety. Oklahoma offered a series of statistics purporting to connect this measure to asserted health and safety ends. Rather than consider the aggregate weight of this statistical showing, the Court broke down the data and discovered problems with each individual statistic. The Court found most relevant that Oklahoma arrested 0.18 percent of females between 18 and 21, and 2 percent of males in that age group for driving while under the influence. Although this disparity was statistically relevant, arresting 2 percent of males was an insufficient basis to regulate them. None of the statistics correlated the dangerousness of 3.2 percent beer to the age-sex differential drawn by the State. In addition, the State did not show that outlawing 3.2 percent beer reduced the number of males who drove while intoxicated.

The Court was obviously reluctant to allow statistics to justify gender discrimination. Arguably, the most effective way for the state to present statistics, such as those used here, was to assess their collective weight taken together. Had the state been permitted to aggregate the statistics in this way, it could have asserted that the strengths of some studies could have compensated for problems with the others. However, Justice Brennan scrutinized the studies individually because many of the studies were based on, and consequently reflected, stereotypes about men and women that the Equal Protection Clause prohibits. If the statistics had been accepted, a logical circle would have developed, because the law at issue nurtured the stereotype that the statistics validated, and then the statistics could have been used to justify the law.

Moreover, statistical analysis is difficult to apply to the normative considerations of equal protection. The Court noted that it would not use statistics indicating different drinking levels among different ethnic groups to uphold laws differentiating access to alcohol according to ethnicity. This reasoning followed the earlier reluctance of the Court to accept such statistical generalizations to justify other types of gender discrimination.[12]

---

strict scrutiny to discrete and insular minorities. Women, however, are not a minority but are, in fact, a numerical majority. But it is also possible to argue that the political process effectively treated women as a discrete and insular minority. Consequently, gender lines should receive strict scrutiny.

[10] 429 U.S. 190 (1976).

[11] *Id.* at 197.

[12] For instance, in the Title VII area, the Court has rejected the argument that women should be

Justice Rehnquist's dissent in *Craig* rejected heightened scrutiny for discrimination against men as men had not experienced to a history or pattern of past discrimination. Justice Rehnquist also criticized the Court's middle tier standard, finding the words "important" and "substantial" vague. Such vagueness allowed judges to predicate decisions on their personal beliefs and prejudices.

In *Rostker v. Goldberg*,[13] the Court upheld Congress' exclusion of women from registration for the draft. Justice Rehnquist's majority opinion reflected some of the criticisms he had raised in his *Craig* dissent, such as, his reluctance to extend heightened scrutiny to discrimination against men. Nevertheless, the majority appeared at times to rely on the *Craig* middle tier standard in upholding the statute. The majority stated, for example, that the government's interest in raising an army was important. Moreover, the Court stated that exempting women from draft registration was closely related to Congress' purpose of preparing a draft for combat troops. Justice Marshall noted in his dissent that the Court subjected the statute to a lesser degree of scrutiny than that used in *Craig*, often using the language commonly associated with a rationality test.

In deciding that the exemption of women was closely related to the stated purpose of a draft, the Court seemed to apply a "similarly situated" analysis. As women were not similarly situated to men in the draft context, Congress could differentiate in its registration requirement. The Court afforded great deference to Congress, particularly to Congress's determination that women could not serve in combat roles or be drafted specifically for non-combat roles.[14]

In fact, *Rostker* may reflect the deference that the Court has often extended to the military. The result, however, also appears to have relied in part on the Court's view that the gender classifications at issue were based on relevant and actual differences between the sexes. Whether these differences were sufficiently relevant to warrant the statutory classification may well have created the fault line that divided the Court.

Justice White's dissent emphasized that persons of either gender could perform non-combat missions. In a separate dissent, Justice Marshall argued that the Court was endorsing a stereotypical view of women. The Court had not decided the constitutionality of statutes restricting women from combat duty. Even assuming that this was an important government interest, Justice Marshall disagreed that Congress' program was substantially related to that goal.

Michael M. v. Superior Court[15] upheld a California statutory rape law that imposed criminal liability on a male who had sexual intercourse with a female under 18 but not on a female who had sex with an underaged male. The 17 1/2 year old

---

forced to contribute more to pension plans because they tended to outlive men. The Court found that Title VII prohibited discrimination against individuals because they were members of a particular sex. *See* City of Los Angeles, Dep't of Water & Power v. Manhart, 435 U.S. 702 (1978), *infra* § 10.03.

[13] 453 U.S. 57 (1981).

[14] Congress determined that during mobilization it wanted flexibility to commit any non-combat troops to combat duty at any time and therefore could not draft women for non-combat roles. The Court accepted this determination despite contrary opinions of the President and the military services.

[15] 450 U.S. 464 (1981).

male defendant challenged the law on equal protection grounds. The Court stated that gender-based classifications were not inherently suspect and were subject only to a rationality test applied with a " 'sharper focus' when gender-based classifications are challenged."[16] Justice Rehnquist's majority opinion concluded that the classification was "sufficiently related"[17] to the end sought by the state. Young men and women were not similarly situated as to the problems and risks of sex. By imposing criminal sanctions on men, the statute provided a deterrent for men, while the risk of pregnancy already provided a substantial deterrent for women. Given the nature of the harm sought to be prevented, the age of the man involved was irrelevant.

In both *Rostker* and *Michael M.*, the Court's view that men and women were not similarly situated resulted in substantially reduced scrutiny approaching a rationality test. Some wondered whether these decisions indicated a new, relaxed scrutiny in the gender discrimination area. In 1982, however, the Court arguably altered the *Craig* test to tighten the standard in gender discrimination cases. In *Mississippi University for Women v. Hogan*,[18] the Court struck down a state statute excluding males from a state-supported professional nursing school.

From the founding of the Mississippi University for Women (MUW) in 1884, state law limited enrollment to women. Mississippi had no other single-sex public college or university. Plaintiff, a male registered nurse, applied for admission to the MUW School of Nursing's four-year baccalaureate program. Although he was otherwise qualified, he was denied admission solely because of his sex.

To justify gender-based classifications, the government had the burden of establishing " 'an exceedingly persuasive justification.' "[19] To do so, the government must demonstrate a direct and substantial relationship between the classification and the legitimate and important government objective it purported to serve. This test must be applied free of preconceived or stereotypical notions concerning the roles and abilities of males and females. Consequently, if the stated purpose of the classification was to protect one gender because of inherent handicaps or inferiorities, then the objective itself was illegitimate.

Often, when the Court strikes down a program using heightened scrutiny, it summarily accepts the government's proffered objectives, but disapproves of the means used to reach those objectives. In *Hogan*, the Court rejected both the government's objectives and the means used to advance those objectives. Mississippi argued that the purpose of its admission policy was to compensate for past discrimination against women. Writing for the Court, Justice O'Connor stated that a compensatory purpose would not be accepted here because there was no evidence of past discrimination against women in this context or that women lacked opportunities to obtain training in nursing. Thus, the policy only perpetuated the stereotype that nursing was exclusively a women's profession. Mississippi also failed to prove that its policy was substantially and directly related to the stated objective.

---

[16] *Id.* at 468.

[17] *Id.* at 473.

[18] 458 U.S. 718 (1982).

[19] *Id.* at 724.

The fact that the school allowed men to audit classes undermined the State's argument that the presence of men in classrooms adversely affected women students.

Mississippi also argued that the School's policy was protected under Title IX, which exempted from its gender discrimination proscription schools that have traditionally and continually single-sex institutions. The majority emphasized that Congress could not pass laws under Section 5 of the Fourteenth Amendment to restrict constitutional rights declared by the Court. The Court has decided that Congress could use Section 5 to expand the rights guaranteed under Section 1 of the Fourteenth Amendment.[20] However, *Hogan* treated Section 5 as a one-way ratchet so that the Congress could not use it to contract constitutional rights that the Court had guaranteed.

Justices Powell and Blackmun dissented, making quasi-First Amendment arguments. Both argued that students should be free to choose between single-sex and co-educational schools in the interest of educational diversity. Chief Justice Burger's dissent argued that the holding was limited to professional nursing schools. In his dissent, Justice Blackmun argued that the decision jeopardized virtually all single-sex, educational institutions run by the government. His dissent also emphasized that publicly-supported nursing programs were available to men at other campuses in Mississippi.

One could read the *Hogan* and the *Craig* cases on the one hand with the *Michael M.* and *Rostker* cases on the other as inconsistent approaches to gender discrimination. Alternatively, one could attempt to reconcile these two lines of cases by arguing that *Michael M.* and *Rostker* relaxed scrutiny because the laws reflected real gender differences, while the discrimination in *Craig* and *Hogan* was based on stereotypes. Critics would argue that the distinctions in all of these cases rest on stereotypes. At times, the Court's gender discrimination approach has been confusing. The cases cover a wide scope of issues including alimony, age of majority, jury selection, all-male clubs, and illegitimacy.

In *Orr v. Orr*,[21] the Court invalidated an Alabama statute which provided that, upon divorce, a husband, but not a wife, could be required to pay alimony. Even assuming that the institution of marriage had discriminated against women and that gender was often a reliable indicator of need, the statute already provided for hearings to determine the financial condition of the parties. As the state's purpose could have been served by gender-neutral classifications, the Court would not permit a gender-based distinction.

In a case resembling the *Craig* age of majority issue, the Court struck down a law, which provided that males would attain majority at 21, while females would attain majority at 18. In *Stanton v. Stanton*,[22] a divorced wife sued to have her former husband's support payments for her daughter continue after age 18. The husband claimed that he was only obligated to pay until the girl turned 18, which

---

[20] *See* J. Attanasio, *The Constitutionality of Regulating Human Genetic Engineering: Where Procreative Liberty and Equal Opportunity Collide*, 53 U. CHI. L. REV. 1274, 1318–19 (1986).

[21] 440 U.S. 268 (1979).

[22] 421 U.S. 7 (1975).

was the age of majority for females under Utah law.

Several important cases have involved gender discrimination in jury selection. In *Taylor v. Louisiana*,[23] the Court reversed the conviction of a male defendant because of a jury selection system that excused women from service unless they signed a declaration of willingness to serve. The Court ruled that a system that operated to exclude women from the jury deprived the defendant of his Sixth Amendment right to a jury drawn from a fair cross-section of the community.

In *J.E.B. v. Alabama*,[24] the Court held that the systematic exclusion of a gender group by use of peremptory challenges violated the Equal Protection Clause. In a jury pool consisting of 12 males and 24 females, both J.E.B. and the state of Alabama utilized their respective peremptory challenges to excuse potential male jurors. The resulting jury was entirely female. Writing for the 6-3 majority, Justice Blackmun reaffirmed *Taylor*, which required the maintenance of the diverse and representative character of a jury under the Sixth Amendment. "Intentional discrimination on the basis of gender by state actors violates the Equal Protection Clause, particularly where, as here, the discrimination serves to ratify and perpetuate invidious, archaic, and overbroad stereotypes about the relative abilities of men and women."[25]

The Court rejected the argument that gender discrimination has never reached the level of racial discrimination. African-Americans and women "share a history of total exclusion"[26] in the context of the jury selection process, rendering the decision as to which class has suffered more from discrimination immaterial. Moreover, gender-based classifications in jury selection were only permissible when used as a means by which the state furthered its legitimate interest in attaining an impartial jury. Here, Alabama attempted to justify the all-female jury on the perception that women would be more responsive to a mother in a paternity suit. The Court rejected this perpetuation of gender stereotypes.

In *Virginia v. United States*,[27] the Court firmly signaled fairly high scrutiny for gender-based classifications. The case prohibited "Virginia from reserving exclusively to men the unique educational opportunities"[28] afforded by the Virginia Military Institute (VMI). VMI's success in producing numerous military and civil leaders resulted from its unique " 'adversarial method' "[29] of training. After losing its first appeal in this case, Virginia proposed a parallel program for women: Virginia Women's Institute for Leadership (VWIL).[30] VWIL differed from VMI in not adopting the adversarial method, and more generally in "academic offerings,

---

[23] 419 U.S. 522 (1975).

[24] 511 U.S. 127 (1994).

[25] *Id.* at 131.

[26] *Id.* at 136.

[27] 518 U.S. 515 (1996).

[28] *Id.* at 519.

[29] *Id.* at 520.

[30] *Id.* at 526.

methods of education, and financial resources."[31]

Writing for a 7-1 majority, Justice Ginsburg held that VMI's all-male policy violated equal protection because it denied to women who were " 'capable of all the individual activities required of VMI cadets' "[32] this extraordinary educational opportunity. "Focusing on the differential treatment or denial of opportunity for which relief is sought, the reviewing court must determine whether the proffered justification is 'exceedingly persuasive.' The burden of justification is demanding and it rests entirely on the State. The State must show 'at least that the [challenged] classification serves important governmental objectives and that the discriminatory means employed' are 'substantially related to the achievement of those objectives.' The justification must be genuine, not hypothesized or invented post hoc in response to litigation. And it must not rely on generalizations about the different talents, capacities, or preferences of males and females."[33]

Not all sex classifications are proscribed. Government cannot draw lines based on purported " 'inherent differences' "[34] of race or national origin. "Physical differences between men and women, however, are enduring."[35] However, inherent gender differences should be cause for celebration, but not for denigration of the members of either sex or for artificially constraining opportunity. Gender classifications may compensate women for economic disabilities or promote equal employment opportunity.

In response to arguments that single sex schools advance diversity and undercut "traditional gender classifications," the Court did "not question the State's prerogative evenhandedly to support diverse educational opportunities." Instead, it addressed the unique opportunity at VMI. Single-sex education could be advantageous to some students, and diverse educational approaches could provide societal benefits. Nevertheless, when VMI was established, higher educational opportunities for women were hardly contemplated. Moreover, VMI continued to follow the no women policy initiated but abandoned by the University of Virginia.

Justice Ginsburg also rejected Virginia's second argument that admitting women would alter VMI's adversative method. She acknowledged the finding below that coeducation would undoubtedly affect certain aspects of VMI's program — " 'physical training, the absence of privacy, and the adversative approach.' "[36] However, neither side disputed VMI's methods could be applied to women.

Mississippi University for Women v. Hogan prohibited excluding qualified men and women based on fixed ideas of gender roles and abilities. The assertion that coeducation would destroy VMI and its adversative system was the kind of "self-fulfilling prophecy"[37] once routinely used to deny opportunities to women.

---

[31] *Id.*

[32] *Id.* at 530.

[33] *Id.* at 532–33.

[34] *Id.* at 533.

[35] *Id.*

[36] *Id.* at 540.

[37] *Id.* at 543.

Moreover, women's success and participation in the nation's Federal military academies and armed forces belied fears about VMI.

The VWIL program for women was not comparable to VMI. An adequate remedy required that those denied opportunity or advantages receive the benefit they would have obtained absent discrimination. Analogizing VMI to the separate but equal program invalidated in *Sweatt v. Painter*,[38] the Court rejected Virginia's assertion that gender differences justified the different approaches of the two institutions. Although admitting women to VMI would result in some minor alterations, the U.S. code required the same academic and other standards for the Military, Naval, and Air Force Academies, except for a few adjustments required by physiological differences. The justifications offered by Virginia for denying admission to qualified women were not "exceedingly persuasive."[39]

Chief Justice Rehnquist concurred in the judgment. The " 'exceedingly persuasive justification' "[40] standard was vague, and should only be used to indicate the difficulty of meeting the already vague test of requiring a substantial relationship to an important governmental objective. Moreover, Virginia did not abridge equal protection solely by excluding women, but rather, by maintaining VMI without providing a comparable women's institution. While VMI could not have been replicated quickly, the legislature might have avoided liability had it at least made a genuine attempt to devote sustained comparable resources to an alternate institution.

Justice Scalia dissented. He asserted that the Court lacked authority to invalidate a practice that the Bill of Rights did not expressly prohibit and that has enjoyed "a long tradition of open, widespread, and unchallenged use"[41] from the beginning of the Republic. The Court also substituted the "exceedingly persuasive" test for the *Craig* standard. Virginia's program should have survived middle-tier scrutiny considering the long history of single-sex colleges in advancing the State's important objective of providing higher education. The Court's decision pointed toward the unconstitutionality of all single-sex educational programs. It also affected private educational institutions receiving public funds. Justice Thomas did not participate.

Disputes over single-sex institutions have extended beyond those cases, like *Hogan*, that involve institutions of higher learning. *Roberts v. United States Jaycees*[42] did not involve discrimination by the state, but rather the constitutionality of state laws seeking to proscribe gender discrimination. A unanimous Court rejected a freedom of association defense by the United States Jaycees, an all-male private organization, against the application of a Minnesota law that proscribed race and gender discrimination in admission practices. Justice Brennan concluded that the state's interest in the eradication of discrimination against women was sufficiently compelling to justify any incidental intrusion that may result on the

---

[38] 339 U.S. 629 (1950).

[39] *Virginia v. United States*, 518 U.S. at 556.

[40] *Id.* at 559 (Rehnquist, C.J., concurring).

[41] *Id.* at 568 (Scalia, J., dissenting).

[42] 468 U.S. 609 (1984).

freedom of association of male members.

Similarly, in *Board of Directors of Rotary International v. Rotary Club of Duarte*,[43] the Court rejected constitutional challenges to the application to a local Rotary Club of a California statute that barred gender discrimination in all business establishments. Whatever rights may have existed to First Amendment expressive association were overcome by the State's compelling interest in assuring equal access to women. In both cases, the Court held that membership in the Jaycees or Rotary Club did not involve the type of intimate association that was an element of "liberty" protected by the Due Process Clause of the Fourteenth Amendment.

In *New York State Club Ass'n v. City of New York*,[44] the Court unanimously rejected a facial challenge to a New York City law that prohibited discrimination in private all-male clubs that met certain criteria, including having more than 400 members. Since the law could be constitutionally applied to at least some large clubs, the Court relied on the *Rotary* and *Roberts* decisions in rejecting a facial challenge. Justice White's majority opinion, however, recognized that there might conceivably be some clubs with the characteristics specified in the law that might be able to assert claims of "intimate" or "expressive" association.

The Court has upheld several statutes that have afforded different treatment to fathers and mothers of illegitimate children. In *Parham v. Hughes*,[45] a 5-4 majority of the Court upheld a Georgia statute that permitted a suit for the wrongful death of an illegitimate child to be brought by the mother but not by the father unless he had legitimated the child. Justice Powell's decisive concurring opinion concluded that the statute was substantially related to the state's objective of avoiding difficult problems of proving paternity. Four dissenters argued that the problem of proving paternity in a wrongful death action was an insufficient justification for the gender-based classification.

Caban v. Mohammed[46] invalidated a section of the New York Domestic Relations Law that allowed an unwed mother to block the adoption of her child by withholding her consent, while the unwed father could not. The distinction between unmarried mothers and fathers did not bear a substantial relation to the important state interest in providing adoptive homes for illegitimate children.

In *Lehr v. Robertson*,[47] the Court upheld the alternative methods of notice New York provided to a mother and father of an illegitimate child in an adoption proceeding. The mother was entitled to notice, but the father only received notice if he had listed himself as the father, had developed a parental relationship with the child, or had married the mother before the child reached six months of age. The Court distinguished *Caban* by stating that the New York provision at issue in *Lehr* considered the quality of the relationship between the father and the child.

---

[43] 481 U.S. 537 (1987).

[44] 487 U.S. 1 (1988).

[45] 441 U.S. 347 (1979).

[46] 441 U.S. 380 (1979).

[47] 463 U.S. 248 (1983).

Moreover, the different notice practices actually reflected that the mother and father were not similarly situated.

In *Nguyen v. INS*,[48] the Court upheld a Federal statute requiring U.S. citizen fathers to follow more complex procedures than U.S. citizen mothers to establish the U.S. citizenship of a nonmarital child. Writing for the majority, Justice Kennedy explained that in conferring citizenship on a nonmarital child, the law required a U.S. citizen father before his child turned 18, to legitimize the child; declare paternity under oath; or receive a court order of paternity. In contrast, the child automatically received its mother's nationality.[49] Since Nguyen's father failed to take one of these three affirmative steps required by the statute, his son remained a citizen of Vietnam and could be deported as a result of his criminal history.

The Court found the statute served " 'important governmental objectives' "[50] and did not violate equal protection even though it required more of fathers than mothers. As the law passed heightened scrutiny, the Court did not decide whether a more deferential standard of review should apply to Congress' immigration and naturalization power. First, the statute served Congress' interest in ensuring that a biological relationship did exist between the father and child. Even though Nguyen's father had taken a DNA test, this was not one of the specified ways to establish paternity under the statute. Rather than require DNA tests, which may be costly, unreliable, and unavailable in some areas, Congress was "reasonable"[51] in imposing other methods to establish paternity. It would be a "hollow neutrality"[52] to require gender-neutral terms in ensuring the existence of a biological relationship.

Second, Congress sought to ensure that a true, meaningful relationship existed between the parent and child. Where a mother knew her child at the moment she gave birth, there was no guarantee that an unwed father even knew his child existed. This was fact, "not a stereotype."[53]

The Court also found that the fit between Congress' objectives and the statute was " 'exceedingly persuasive' "[54] since the additional requirements imposed on fathers were " 'substantially related' "[55] to the achievement those goals. Moreover, any imposition on fathers was slight, particularly since the statute gave them 18 years to complete one of three simple requirements. At bottom, the statute acknowledged "basic biological differences"[56] between men and women in the birth process.

---

[48] 533 U.S. 53 (2001).

[49] The only requirement was that the mother had previously lived in the United States for at least one year.

[50] 533 U.S. at 62.

[51] *Id.* at 63.

[52] *Id.* at 64.

[53] *Id.* at 68.

[54] 533 U.S. at 70.

[55] *Id.*

[56] *Id.* at 73.

Justice O'Connor dissented, joined by Justices Souter, Ginsburg, and Breyer. Justice O'Connor argued that Congress could have achieved the same objectives by imposing gender-neutral requirements, such as DNA testing of both mothers and fathers. It appeared that the majority subjected the statute to a rational basis test rather than heightened scrutiny. The decision validated the notion that sole parental responsibility should be placed on the unmarried mother while freeing the father.

§ 10.02 EMPLOYMENT DISCRIMINATION BASED ON GENDER

As with race discrimination, Title VII of the Civil Rights Act of 1964[57] proscribes gender discrimination by private and most public employers. Even with public employers, the existence of statutory claims under federal and state law often obviates the necessity of reaching constitutional claims. Discussion of Title VII and correlative state causes of action range beyond the scope of this volume. The discussion here is limited to claims of employment discrimination arising under the Equal Protection Clause.

In *Frontiero v. Richardson*,[58] the Court invalidated federal statutes that allowed men in the service to claim their wives as dependents, but required women in the service to make a showing that their husbands were dependents. *Schlesinger v. Ballard*[59] upheld the Navy's mandatory discharge provision that required male Navy lieutenants with more than nine years of service to be discharged when they were twice passed over for promotion. Women lieutenants, on the other hand, could complete 13 years of commissioned service before being subject to mandatory discharge for want of promotion. Plaintiff, a male lieutenant, was twice passed over for promotion and thus subject to the mandatory discharge provision before he had served 13 years.

Writing for the majority, Justice Stewart distinguished *Frontiero* on two grounds. First, the gender classification in *Frontiero* was based upon dated and overbroad generalizations about men and women. In this case, however, the gender classifications were based on clear evidence that male and female Naval officers were not similarly situated with regard to career opportunities, primarily due to the lack of combat-related responsibilities for women.

Second, in contrast to the administrative convenience justification offered in *Frontiero*, the government in *Schlesinger* insisted that operation of the mandatory discharge provisions resulted in promotions that matched the needs of the Navy and served to motivate qualified officers to conduct themselves so that they might realistically look forward to advancement. In validating this purpose, Justice Stewart deferred to Congress' broad authority over the armed forces. Justice Brennan's dissenting opinion, joined by Justices Douglas and Marshall, contended that gender classifications were suspect and that the classification in this case should not have been upheld because it served no compelling governmental

---

[57] 42 U.S.C.A. § 200e (1994).

[58] 411 U.S. 677 (1973).

[59] 419 U.S. 498 (1975).

purpose. In a separate dissenting opinion, Justice White agreed, in large part, with Justice Brennan's assertions.

Schlesinger also concerned the recurrent issue in gender discrimination cases of differentiating between benign discrimination and stereotyping. Although benign discrimination can be an effective method of redressing past discrimination, it can also perpetuate stereotypical views of the roles of men and women.

Personnel Administrator v. Feeney[60] upheld the Massachusetts Veterans Preference Statute requiring that all veterans who qualified for state civil service positions had to be considered for appointment ahead of qualifying non-veterans. Women applicants for civil service jobs alleged that the statute favored men because they historically had served in the military in far greater numbers than women.

The Court held that the plaintiff failed to demonstrate that the law reflected any purpose to discriminate based on sex. The Court posited a two-step inquiry to scrutinize a facially gender-neutral statute challenged on the ground that it adversely affected members of one sex in a disproportionate way. First, was the statutory classification really gender-neutral? If it was gender-neutral, a court must then determine whether the adverse effect on women was based on purposeful gender-based discrimination or some alternative explanation. The Court found the statute was not gender-based because it distinguished between veterans and non-veterans, not men and women. Moreover, the preference advantaged women who were veterans, and disadvantaged many men who were not veterans.

Having found the law gender neutral, the *Feeney* Court next turned to determine whether the plaintiff had shown that the law had at least a partially gender-based discriminatory purpose. Although the legislature had intentionally granted a preference to veterans and was likely aware of the disproportionate impact, "discriminatory purpose" required more than awareness of the natural and feasible consequences of a particular action.[61] It required a showing that the legislature acted affirmatively to enact legislation " 'because of' not merely 'in spite of' "[62] adverse consequences for a particular group. Although the foreseeability of adverse consequences was evidence of a discriminatory purpose, it did not prove such purpose since the legislative history and all other evidence pointed to a legitimate, nondiscriminatory purpose. The District Court found that the legislature had not designed or re-enacted the preference because it would accomplish the collateral goal of keeping women in a stereotypical and predefined place in the Massachusetts Civil Service.

The Court also refused to impute to Massachusetts any alleged discriminatory intent by the Federal government against women in the military. Justice Stewart's majority opinion concluded that the alleged Federal discrimination involved a different decision made by a different set of decision-makers than the defendants in this case.

---

[60] 442 U.S. 256 (1979).

[61] The Court said that discriminatory intent must be proved by objective evidence and cited *Village of Arlington Heights v. Metropolitan Housing Authority, supra* § 9.02[3].

[62] *Feeney*, 442 U.S. at 279.

Justice Marshall dissented. "Where the foreseeable impact of a facially neutral policy is so disproportionate, the burden should rest on the State to establish that sex-based considerations played no part in the choice of the particular legislative scheme."[63] Massachusetts failed to prove that gender considerations played no part in the classification. Having found the requisite discriminatory intent, Justice Marshall concluded that the government program was not substantially related to the proffered governmental objectives. Massachusetts could have achieved its goal by such gender-neutral methods as point preference systems, educational subsidies, or other special programs designed to assist veterans.

Feeney illustrates the effect of the intentional discrimination requirement on gender cases in limiting equal protection challenges to deliberately biased laws. In *Washington v. Davis*[64] the plaintiff had also relied heavily on the extremely disparate impact of employment policies on blacks to infer discriminatory purpose. The *Davis* Court, however, had concluded that something more was necessary, despite the fact that the discriminatory impact of the policies was quite extensive. *Davis* stated that much legislation has discriminatory impact, and it would not be desirable to have all such legislation subject to heightened equal protection scrutiny.[65]

§ 10.03   GENDER DISCRIMINATION IN GOVERNMENT BENEFIT PROGRAMS

Some government benefit programs are designed to discriminate in favor of women. The Court both has upheld some of these programs and invalidated others. As in other areas of gender discrimination, cases involving government benefit programs have attempted to define the elusive line between the legitimate need to remedy past discrimination and the maintenance of stereotypical views of women.[66]

In *Kahn v. Shevin*,[67] the Court upheld a Florida statute that afforded widows an annual $500 property tax exemption, but did not extend an analogous benefit to widowers. The Florida Supreme Court had upheld the classification because it advanced the goal of alleviating the heavier financial burden suffered by female survivors. The Supreme Court agreed. Justice Douglas stated that due to overt discrimination and a male-dominated culture, the job market was inhospitable to women. Past and present discrimination against women often resulted in the husband being the principal wage earner. The purpose of the statute was to alleviate the disproportionately heavy burden that the loss of a spouse placed on widows.

---

[63] *Feeney*, 442 U.S. at 284.

[64] 426 U.S. 229 (1976). The *Davis* case held that a neutral law did not violate the Equal Protection Clause solely because it resulted in a racially disproportionate impact; instead, the disproportionate impact had to be traced to an intention to discriminate on the basis of race in order for the law to be invalid. For further discussion of *Davis, see supra* § 9.02[2].

[65] *See supra* § 9.02[2].

[66] *See* Baker, *Neutrality, Process, and Rationality: Flawed Interpretations of Equal Protection*, 58 Tex. L. Rev. 1029 (1980).

[67] 416 U.S. 351 (1974).

Relying on *Reed v. Reed*,[68] the *Kahn* Court found that the classification had a fair and substantial relation to this purpose of the statute.

Justice Brennan, joined by Justice Marshall, dissented. He once again advocated subjecting gender classifications to strict scrutiny. Although the purpose in this case was compelling, the statute was necessary to achieve that purpose. Justice Brennan thought the statute should only apply to needy widows rather than benefitting all widows, some of whom might be wealthy or be the family's principal wage earner. Justice White also dissented, contending that gender classifications required more justification than Florida offered.

Weinberger v. Wiesenfeld[69] set aside a Social Security provision that paid benefits to a widow and children when the husband died, but paid only the minor children and not the widower when the wife died. The Court concluded that the gender-based classification in this case was indistinguishable from the program invalidated in *Frontiero v. Richardson*[70] as embodying archaic notions of the role of women and men in a family structure. The majority opinion stated that the generalization underlying the statute in Weinberger impliedly asserted that male workers' earnings were vital to support their families, while those of female workers were not. Under this regime, payments made into the Social Security system by female wage earners did not count as much as those made by men. The provision also discriminated against men by failing to acknowledge their equal constitutional right to companionship, care, custody, and management of their children.

The government contended that the purpose of the law was to help women offset the economic disadvantage peculiar to women, in a manner similar to the statute at issue in *Kahn v. Shevin*. The *Weinberger* Court rejected this position, concluding that the assertion of a benign, compensatory purpose did not prevent an inquiry into the actual purpose of the statute. The legislative history demonstrated that the actual purpose of the statute was to allow women to choose whether to work, or to stay home and raise children. Thus, the actual purpose was not to compensate women, but to perpetuate the stereotypical role of the woman as the principal caretakers of children. Based on this actual purpose, the Court invalidated the statute.

In *Califano v. Westcott*,[71] the Court held unconstitutional an Aid to Families with Dependent Children (AFDC) provision. The provision extended benefits to families whose dependent children were deprived of parental support if the father became unemployed, but did not provide such support if the mother became unemployed. The government argued that the challenged provision was designed to deal with the problem of unemployed fathers who deserted their families so they could qualify for the program. The *Westcott* Court relied on *Frontiero* and *Weinberger* in holding that benefits accruing to a family could not be dependent on whether the wage earner was the mother or the father.

---

[68] 404 U.S. 71 (1971). For additional discussion of *Reed, see supra* § 10.01.

[69] 420 U.S. 636 (1975).

[70] 411 U.S. 677 (1973). For additional discussion of *Frontiero, see supra* § 10.01.

[71] 443 U.S. 76 (1979).

In *Califano v. Goldfarb*,[72] the Court relied on *Weinberger* and *Frontiero* to invalidate a provision of the Social Security Act that paid benefits based on the earnings of a deceased husband to his widow. However, similar benefits based on the earnings of a deceased wife would be payable to her surviving husband only if she had been providing at least half of her husband's support. Justice Brennan's opinion concluded that the provision discriminated against female workers because their earnings resulted in less protection for their surviving spouses than the earnings of men. Congress had defined its purpose not in terms of the needs of survivors but rather in terms of "dependency." Thus, surviving wives who were not needy, but had been dependents, would receive benefits, whereas surviving husbands who had not been dependents would receive no benefits regardless of need. This benefits structure tended to refute the claim that the statute was designed to compensate women for the disadvantages of sex discrimination.

After *Califano v. Goldfarb*, a large number of non-dependent males became eligible for spousal benefits. To minimize the fiscal drain, Congress enacted a pension-offset provision requiring Social Security recipients to offset federal and state pensions against the spousal benefits received under Social Security. To compensate female and dependent male recipients who had planned for retirement under the old law, Congress enacted a five-year exception to the pension offset provision. This effectively recreated the same gender-based classification operating against non-dependent men that was held invalid in *Goldfarb*. In *Heckler v. Mathews*,[73] the Court unanimously rejected the challenge of a retired postal worker who was the non-dependent spouse of his retired wife.[74] The Court held that the temporary revival of the gender-based classification, which had denied him the benefit for the five-year exemption, was "directly and substantially related to the important governmental interest of protecting individuals who planned their retirements in reasonable reliance on the law in effect prior to that decision."[75]

In *Califano v. Webster*,[76] the Court upheld a section of the Social Security Act (eliminated in 1972) that distinguished between men and women in calculating the number of years used to determine the level of earnings for purposes of old-age insurance benefits. In computing average earnings, women could exclude three additional lower earning years than similarly situated men.

The Court concluded that the statutory scheme at issue more closely resembled those upheld in *Kahn* and *Schlesinger* than those struck down in *Wiesenfeld* and *Goldfarb*. The *Webster* Court found in the legislative history a deliberate intention to compensate women for prior discrimination rather than to sustain stereotypical views about the proper role of women. What appears to distinguish these cases, then, is whether the legislative purpose of Congress was compensatory rather than indicative of a stereotypical view of women.

---

[72] 430 U.S. 199 (1977).

[73] 465 U.S. 728 (1984).

[74] Because of the pension offset provision discussed above, his benefit were reduced by the amount of his postal service pension, which he would not have suffered for five years had he been a woman.

[75] *Heckler*, 465 U.S. at 751.

[76] 430 U.S. 313 (1977).

Finally, one problem that continues is whether or how to count as a constitutional violation discrimination against men that results from benign legislation. The Court is more likely to uphold benign discrimination when the statutory purpose was an attempt to rectify past disparate treatment of women and not the product of overbroad generalizations that women are the weaker sex, child rearers, or dependents.

Related to avoiding stereotyping is the limited weight that the Court has afforded statistics in gender discrimination.[77] In cases involving Title VII, which statutorily prohibits gender, race, and certain other forms of discrimination in public and private employment, the Court has emphasized that employment-related decisions must be made on an individual rather than a statistical gender-related basis. In *City of Los Angeles, Department of Water & Power v. Manhart*,[78] the Court sustained a Title VII challenge to a city department's requirement that female employees contribute more to the pension fund than male employees. The department justified this practice by showing that women tended to live longer than men.

Writing for the majority, Justice Stevens concluded that the express language of Title VII effected a per se prohibition against treating individuals differently based on their sex. The policy behind the statute required that courts focus on fairness to individuals rather than on fairness to classes. Although actuarial tables may correctly predict outcomes with respect to a general class, that did not guarantee that any individual woman would outlive the average man. Chief Justice Burger, joined by Justice Rehnquist, concurred in part and dissented in part. He contended that the department's practice treated women as individually as possible in light of the impossibility of knowing an individual's lifespan.

In *Arizona Governing Committee for Tax Deferred Annuity & Deferred Compensation Plans v. Norris*,[79] a 5-4 majority relied on *Manhart* in holding that Title VII was violated when an employer offered lower retirement benefits to a woman than to a man making equal contributions. The Court concluded that all benefits derived from future contributions should be calculated without regard to the beneficiaries' sex. However, this "gender neutral" requirement was to be applied only to prospective applications. Thus, benefits derived from contributions made prior to the decision could continue to be based on existing plans.

§ 10.04   DISCRIMINATION INVOLVING PREGNANCY

A final area that implicates gender discrimination involves pregnancy. Since the early constitutional decisions reported here, statutes have dominated this area of the law. Title VII prohibits discrimination in employment because of pregnancy and the Family and Medical Leave Act[80] provides minimum federal leave periods for

---

[77] *See* Craig v. Boren, 429 U.S. 190 (1976). *See supra* § 10.01.

[78] 435 U.S. 702 (1978).

[79] 463 U.S. 1073 (1983).

[80] 5 U.S.C. § 6382 (1994).

pregnancy that state law can exceed. Discussion of these statutory schemes range beyond the scope of this volume.[81]

In *Cleveland Board of Education v. LaFleur*,[82] the Court struck down various school board regulations that required pregnant school teachers to take maternity leave without pay, sometimes as early as five months before the due date. A teacher could return to her duties some months after the birth of the child if a doctor attested to her health. Some school boards did not guarantee that they would rehire a teacher after this obligatory maternity leave.

The school boards argued that the regulations were necessary for two reasons. First, a strict cutoff date advanced continuity of classroom instruction because the school would know exactly when a pregnant teacher was leaving and thus could prepare accordingly. Second, some teachers would be physically unable to perform some of their duties during the latter stages of pregnancy.

Writing for the Court, Justice Stewart held that such maternity regulations violated the freedom of choice with regard to marriage and family life guaranteed by the Due Process Clause. As the regulations forced a pregnant teacher to leave work, they placed a heavy burden on a teacher's decision to have a child. The Court held that the rules had no rational relationship to the valid state interests set forth by the school boards. The Court also used an "irrebuttable presumption" analysis. By asserting that all pregnant women would be unable to fulfill their duties and therefore must take leave, the rules contained an irrebuttable presumption, even with medical evidence to the contrary. As they failed to provide for individualized determinations, these rules were invalid.[83]

Justice Powell concurred in the result but opposed the use of an irrebuttable presumption analysis. He stated that this analysis was really equal protection masquerading as due process. Justice Rehnquist, joined by Chief Justice Burger, dissented. The invalidation of the regulations should have rested on equal protection Clause, not due process. He also argued that the "irrebuttable presumption" analysis could be used to strike down virtually any underinclusive statute.

The Court has since largely abandoned the irrebuttable presumption analysis in due process cases. Instead, it uses equal protection categories analyzing whether the government's action is overinclusive or underinclusive.[84]

---

[81] For discussion of constitutional and statutory protections against discrimination involving pregnancy, *see* P. Wright-Carozza, *Organic Goods: Legal Understandings of Work, Parenthood, and Gender Equality in Comparative Perspective*, 81 CAL. L. REV. 531 (1993).

[82] 414 U.S. 632 (1974).

[83] In a footnote, Justice Stewart refused to foreclose the possibility that alternatives other than individualized determinations might be constitutional. He suggested that a uniform termination during the last few weeks of pregnancy might be constitutional if the state could present a strong showing of the need for such a plan.

[84] This "irrebuttable presumption" analysis was widely criticized. For examples, *see* Note, *Irrebuttable Presumptions: An Illusory Analysis*, 27 STAN. L. REV. 449 (1975). *See also* Note, *The Irrebuttable Presumption Doctrine in the Supreme Court*, 87 HARV. L. REV. 1534 (1974).

Geduldig v. Aiello[85] upheld a California disability insurance system that paid benefits to persons in private employment temporarily unable to work because of disability not covered by worker's compensation. Plaintiffs challenged the program's exclusion from coverage of disabilities resulting from normal pregnancy.[86]

California contended that paying benefits for normal pregnancy and delivery would be so extraordinarily expensive as to render maintenance of the program impossible.[87] The Supreme Court, in an opinion by Justice Stewart, held that the exclusion from coverage of disabilities resulting from pregnancy did not violate the Equal Protection Clause. The State chose to insure some but not all risks. If the line drawn by the state was rationally supportable, the Court would not judge where it should be drawn. The Court recognized the State's legitimate interest in maintaining the program's self-supporting nature and in providing adequate coverage for those disabilities covered. California also had an interest in keeping the employee contribution level sufficiently low so as not to unduly burden participants.

In a footnote, the Court stated that the exclusions from coverage were made not because of gender but only because of the physical condition of pregnancy. The program distinguished between pregnant women and non-pregnant persons, rather than between men and women. There was no risk from which men were protected and women were not. Because only women could become pregnant, the Court recognized that every legislative classification concerning pregnancy was a sex-based classification. However, absent a showing that distinctions involving pregnancy were pretexts to effect discrimination against one sex or another, legislatures were free to include or exclude pregnancy from a disability program, just as they could exclude any other physical condition.

Justice Brennan dissented, joined by Justices Douglas and Marshall. Justice Brennan noted that less favorable treatment was given to a gender-linked disability peculiar to women but not to disabilities that affected only or primarily males, such as prostatectomies and circumcision.

Geduldig addressed the question of how to define gender discrimination. The *Geduldig* Court defined the issue as discrimination between pregnant persons and non-pregnant persons rather than discrimination between the sexes, and was criticized for drawing the distinction in those terms. Whatever one thinks of the Court's analysis, the case illustrates dramatically the importance of how gender discrimination is defined.

---

[85] 417 U.S. 484 (1974).

[86] The provision did not bar the payment of benefits for disability from medical complications during delivery. Therefore, at issue was whether the California disability insurance program invidiously discriminated against women by not paying insurance benefits for disabilities that accompanied normal pregnancy and childbirth.

[87] The State maintained that the cost would increase between $120.2 million and $131 million annually, or between a 33 percent and 36 percent increase in the present payments under the program. Plaintiffs, on the other hand, contended that the increased cost would be $48.9 million annually, or a 12 percent increase over present expenditures.

In *General Electric Co. v. Gilbert*,[88] the Court held that a disability plan that excluded pregnancy coverage did not violate Title VII. Justice Rehnquist's majority opinion reaffirmed *Geduldig's* conclusion that the pregnancy exclusion was not discrimination based on sex under Title VII. A finding of discriminatory effect alone could create a *prima facie* case of discrimination under Title VII. Justice Rehnquist argued, however, that there was no such finding in *Gilbert* because there was no evidence that the package of benefits in this case was worth more to men than to women.

Justice Brennan's dissent, joined by Justice Marshall, argued that the exclusion of pregnancy was not a sex-neutral classification but was one aspect of a sex-conscious process that relegated women to a secondary status in the labor force. Justice Stevens dissented on the grounds that apart from the question of motive, a disability plan that excluded pregnancy discriminated on the basis of sex because only women could get pregnant. Although *Geduldig's* interpretation of the Constitution remains good law,[89] Title VII has been amended expressly to prohibit discrimination on the basis of pregnancy.[90]

In *Bray v. Alexandria Women's Health Clinic*,[91] the Court addressed gender issues arising in the context of abortion protests. Writing for the Court, Justice Scalia determined that anti-abortion protestors' attempts to block access to health clinics did not give rise to an action under 42 U.S.C. § 1985(3), which prohibited conspiracies to deprive or hinder persons from enjoying equal protection under the laws. Regardless of whether the statute should be construed to extend to gender, the protestors did not intend to affect women in general because of their gender as required by the statute. The Court found that the protestors did not plan their demonstrations with reference to women in a class, but instead with reference to "physical intervention 'between abortionists and the innocent victims.' "[92]

---

[88] 429 U.S. 125 (1976).

[89] *See* Strimling, *The Constitutionality of State Laws Providing Employment Leave for Pregnancy: Rethinking* Geduldig *After* Cal. Fed., 77 CAL. L. REV. 171 (1989).

[90] *See* The Pregnancy Discrimination Act of 1978.

[91] 506 U.S. 263 (1993).

[92] *Id.* at 270. For a discussion of successful RICO and injunctive measures against abortion protestors, *see supra* § 8.06[1] and *infra* § 15.04[1].

Chapter 11

AFFIRMATIVE ACTION

INTRODUCTION

One of the critical problems of justice in any society is the allocation of goods and resources. Certainly, in a free enterprise system, two of the most important such resources are education and employment. A society may determine who receives these goods based purely on merit, however defined. In American society, concepts of merit are often largely underpinned by the related criteria of utility and efficiency. The stated focus is on the particular candidate's aptitude for the job or educational program at issue. Criteria other than merit also influence selection processes. For many jobs, connections might compete with merit as a criterion for allocation.[1] The affirmative action cases discussed in this chapter examine the legitimacy of using race, ethnicity, or gender as criteria for preferring one candidate for a job or school over another. The Chapter includes both constitutional and statutory analyses as the Court's analysis of constitutional and statutory affirmative action issues tends to overlap.

Two quotes encapsule the two competing paradigms or approaches that the Court has used in the affirmative action area. The first quote comes from the famous dissent of Justice Harlan in *Plessy v. Ferguson*.[2] Justice Harlan stated:

> But in view of the constitution, in the eye of the law, there is in this country no superior, dominant, ruling class of citizens. There is no caste here. Our constitution is color-blind, and neither knows nor tolerates classes among citizens.[3]

One might call this the color-blind paradigm, for it basically maintains that the Constitution will not permit racial lines of any sort. However, because affirmative action programs include the gender area, one might call this the non-discrimination paradigm.

The second quote comes from Justice Marshall's opinion in *Regents of University of California v. Bakke*.[4] Justice Marshall presents a far different approach for trying to achieve equality:

---

[1] Some employers might argue, for example, that irrespective of whether connections reflect the candidate's aptitude to perform a particular job, the good will that they generate advances the economic interests of the company.

[2] 163 U.S. 537 (1896).

[3] *Id.* at 559.

[4] 438 U.S. 265 (1978).

It is because of a legacy of unequal treatment that we now must permit the institutions of this society to give consideration to race in making decisions about who will hold positions of influence, affluence and prestige in America. For too long, the doors to those positions have been shut to Negroes. If we are ever to become a fully integrated society, one in which the color of a person's skin will not determine the opportunities available to him or her, we must be willing to take steps to open those doors. I do not believe that anyone can truly look into America's past and still find that a remedy for the effects of that past is impermissible.[5]

Justice Marshall stated that the Constitution itself disadvantaged black persons for a long time. Consequently, he argued that some redress must be made to create a level playing field for achieving equality of opportunity. This might be called the affirmative action paradigm, or the race and gender conscious paradigm.

Critics argue that this method recognizes and utilizes racial, ethnic, and gender lines in a manner that the law has proscribed in other contexts. Proponents argue that these lines are justified, and indeed necessary, to redress past societal discrimination against minorities and women. Each viewpoint has impacted the shape and outcome of the Court's decisions in this area. This Chapter is split in two parts. Due to the importance of education, the first section examines affirmative action in education. The second section reviews affirmative action in employment, first in general terms and then in the specific area of minority set-aside programs.

§ 11.01   EDUCATION

Regents of California v. Bakke[6] upheld a challenge to the special admissions program of the Medical School of the University of California at Davis. The program was designed to ensure the admission of a specified number of students from certain "disadvantaged" minority groups. The plaintiff was an unsuccessful white applicant to the medical school. There were essentially two admissions programs. The regular admissions process had a cut-off of a 2.5 GPA to select some of the pool of about 3,000 applicants for further consideration in an entering class of 100. The special admissions program was designed to admit 16 minority students into the class.

The two admissions processes had different admissions committees. The special committee, most of whom were minorities, reviewed applicants who identified themselves as minorities (defined as Blacks, Chicanos, Asians, and American Indians). The special committee recommended minority candidates until the prescribed number of spaces were filled. Minority candidates could also compete for admissions through the regular process. Bakke, a white applicant, was rejected twice, when minority applicants with significantly lower grade point averages, MCAT scores, and bench-mark scores were admitted.[7]

---

[5] *Id.* at 401–02.

[6] 438 U.S. 265 (1978).

[7] Bench-mark scores were the ratings by the admissions committee that served as the basis to select candidates for a personal interview.

Justice Powell announced the judgment of the Court. While a number of other opinions concurred in part and dissented in part, Powell's "majority of one" controlled. Concurring in the judgment, Justices Brennan, White, Marshall, and Blackmun joined in Justice Powell's approval of some affirmative action, but they would have upheld the specific program at issue in *Bakke*. Concurring in the judgment, Justice Stevens, Chief Justice Burger, Justice Stewart, and Justice Rehnquist joined Justice Powell in striking down the specific affirmative action program at issue. Construing Title VI of the Civil Rights Act of 1964 to require the anti-discrimination paradigm in federally funded programs, Justice Stevens would have broadly invalidated affirmative action in education. Thus, Justice Powell, and those joining Justice Stevens' opinion, created a majority to invalidate the program at issue based on Title VI.

Justice Powell's analysis began with Title VI, which prohibited discrimination in education and other activities receiving federal assistance. The Court refused to hold the state's admission scheme illegal under a color-blind interpretation of Title VI. Justice Powell construed Title VI only to proscribe federal funding of entities that used racial classifications that violated the equal protection. Title VI did not require that all federal funding be withheld from programs that were not absolutely color blind. This construction of Title VI essentially transformed the case into an equal protection case.

The University characterized the special admissions program as a goal, asserting that there was no definite ceiling or floor on the number of minority students admitted. In contrast, Bakke characterized the special admissions program as a quota, requiring that all positions be filled. The courts below agreed with Bakke in this respect because white applicants could not compete for the 16 places reserved for the special admissions program. Justice Powell stated that the label attached to the program was irrelevant given the express distinction drawn based on race and ethnic status.

Even though race was an acknowledged factor, the University maintained that the Court should not place the program under strict scrutiny. The University argued that white males were not a group that *United States v. Carolene Products*[8] described as a discrete and insular minority requiring protection from the majoritarian process. Justice Powell responded, however, that racial and ethnic distinctions were inherently suspect. He noted that we are a nation of minorities, and that it is difficult to single out one group as meriting special Fourteenth Amendment protection over others. Each minority group has had to struggle to overcome prejudices, not of a monolithic majority but of different majorities composed of various minorities. While one might argue that the underlying purpose of the Fourteenth Amendment was to eradicate a society divided along racial lines, the *Slaughter-House Cases*[9] established that the Fourteenth Amendment was framed in universal terms to protect all persons.

The fact that the discrimination against white persons served the otherwise favorable purpose of helping minorities did not save it from being suspect. Despite

---

[8] 304 U.S. 144 (1938). This case is discussed *supra* § 8.05[1].

[9] 83 U.S. 36 (1873). This case is discussed *supra* § 8.01.

the recitation of a benign purpose, equal protection did not favor one group over another but protected all persons. In a footnote, Justice Powell quoted Professor Alexander Bickel's comments on the issue, stating that the immorality and illegality of discrimination based on race was well-established.[10] That understanding must apply across the board and cannot hinge on whether the particular racial discrimination was harmful or helpful to black persons.

Even if benign discrimination was permissible, there would be no principled basis for courts to decide which groups should receive heightened scrutiny.[11] Courts would have to evaluate the prejudice and harm minority groups have suffered in order to decide which groups should benefit from preferential programs without exacting scrutiny. As these programs would evolve, courts would be required, of necessity, to reevaluate each group's judicial ranking to determine which group still required preferential treatment. The constitutional principle of equal protection would become mutable and based on shifting social and political judgments, thereby undermining consistent construction of the Constitution over time.[12]

Justice Powell enumerated several reasons for rejecting racial preferences. First, he questioned the notion that racial preferences were always benign, as such preferences could impose burdens on individual members of an ethnic group to advance the interests of the group. Second, racial preferences could force minorities to labor under the stereotype that they could not succeed without the preference. Third, racial preferences could impose the burden of redress on innocent persons who did not create the harm.

Justice Powell distinguished prior acceptance of preferential classifications. For example, busing and other remedies for school segregation were intended to redress a specific constitutional violation and did not exceed the scope of that violation. Similarly, employment discrimination remedies also focused on a particular defendant's discrimination against a class of workers, not societal discrimination. The courts in these areas based their remedies on findings of constitutional or statutory violations. In *Bakke*, there was no finding of a specific constitutional violation requiring a race-conscious remedy.

The analysis of preferential programs in the gender discrimination area involved a materially different context. There were fewer analytical and practical problems with preferential programs premised upon sex because there were only two possible classifications. Moreover, racial classifications were perceived as inherently odious because of a long, tragic history not shared by gender classifications.

For the minority admissions program to be upheld, Justice Powell required a state to " 'show that its purpose or interest is both constitutionally permissible and substantial, and that its use of a classification is necessary . . . to the accomplishment of its purpose or the safeguarding of its interest.' "[13] Justice Powell applied

---

[10] *Bakke*, 438 U.S. at 295 n.35 (quoting A. BICKEL, THE MORALITY OF CONSENT 133 (1975)).

[11] *Id.* at 296.

[12] Justice Powell also noted that the political and sociological analysis required by such a scheme "simply does not lie within judicial competence." *Id.* at 297.

[13] *Id.* at 305 (quoting *In re Griffiths*, 413 U.S. 717, 721 (1973) (internal quotations omitted)).

strict scrutiny normally used to analyze racial classifications.

The University posited four interests to justify its special admissions program. First, it sought to reduce " 'the historic deficit of traditionally disfavored minorities in medical schools and the medical profession.' "[14] Justice Powell stated that if the purpose of the special admissions program was to guarantee a certain percentage of a particular minority within the student body, the purpose was facially invalid. Such an objective amounted to preferring one group for the sake of race, which the Constitution prohibited.

Justice Powell also rejected the second asserted interest of curing societal discrimination suffered by particular minorities. He stated that the Court has never approved a classification that aided members of victimized groups at the expense of innocent people absent judicial, legislative, or administrative findings of specific discrimination. The third asserted purpose of promoting health care services to communities currently underserved was rejected as the record contained no evidence that the special admissions program would effectuate that goal.

Justice Powell did accept as compelling the fourth proffered interest that a diverse student body encouraged a robust exchange of ideas. This argument engaged the First Amendment interest in freedom of speech. The argument allowed the Court to invoke a justification of constitutional magnitude rather than choosing the interests of one race over another. Moreover, this approach was flexible in not asserting an absolute preference of one group but an assortment of preferences to achieve diversity. Outside of the educational context, however, where the First Amendment interests were not so clearly at stake, this argument would likely not apply.

Although diversity was a compelling state interest, the University's separate admissions program was not a necessary means of achieving that end. The special admissions program focused solely on ethnic diversity. Justice Powell stated that true diversity encompassed a wide range of characteristics of which racial background was a single, albeit important, feature. Justice Powell suggested the Harvard College admissions program as a likely acceptable method of achieving diversity. This program considered factors such as economic disadvantage, race, and ethnicity along with geographical location and special talents in assessing potential contributions to the diversity of the university. The Harvard program emphasized that it did not impose a quota in connection with race, just as it did not impose a quota for football players. In addition, the weight attributed to a particular quality could vary from year to year, depending on the mix of students and the applicants for the incoming class.

In a footnote, Justice Powell stated that a presumption of legality existed for admission decisions that took race into account but were made on an individualized, case-by-case basis. This presumption could be rebutted by showing that the university did not follow a policy of individual comparisons, or that the policy systematically excluded certain groups. Such a showing would shift the burden to the university to establish a legitimate educational purpose for the policy.

---

[14] *Id.* at 306.

Having held the University's special admissions program unconstitutional, the question remained whether the program had caused plaintiff Bakke harm. The University conceded that it could not meet its burden of proving that but for the unlawful discrimination, Bakke still would not have been admitted. Thus, the Court upheld the injunction ordering Bakke's admittance.

Justices Brennan, White, Marshall, and Blackmun wrote a separate opinion concurring in the judgment in part and dissenting in part. The four Justices concurred with Justice Powell that the Title VI standard mirrored that of the Equal Protection Clause. They also agreed with Justice Powell that race could be used as a factor in the University's admissions process, but they disagreed with Justice Powell about the constitutionality of the Davis program and about the color-blind paradigm of the Constitution. The term "color-blind" could not be used to mask the use of race to disadvantage minority groups for over 200 years, a reality that had contemporary effects.

For the Brennan group, the classification in *Bakke* differed from traditional racial classifications because no fundamental rights were involved. Moreover, white persons did not exhibit any of the traditional indicia of suspect classes discussed in *Carolene Products*. Nevertheless, racial classifications, like those based on gender, had too often been used to stigmatize politically powerless segments of the society. Both classifications were also immutable.

The Brennan group fashioned a two-part test to scrutinize affirmative action plans. The first prong applied the middle-tier scrutiny afforded to gender-based classifications: affirmative action programs must serve an important government interest and utilize means substantially related to achieving those interests. This formula would allow affirmative action programs to remove disparate racial impact that was the product of specific past discrimination or of more general societal discrimination. The second prong of the Brennan group's test would require that affirmative action programs not stigmatize a group or single out those least represented in the political process to bear the burden of the program. In this way, paternalistic stereotyping or the painting of one particular group with a badge of inferiority would be avoided.

Applying the two-part test, the Davis program could be sustained. It advanced the important government interest of addressing substantial and chronic societal discrimination and did not stigmatize any discrete group or individual. It created no ceiling on the number of minority admittees, and it used race in a reasonable manner considering the percentage of the beneficiaries of the Davis program relative to their representation in the population as a whole.

While Justice White alone found that Title VI did not create a private cause of action, he was one of the concurring Justices in the Brennan group. Justice Marshall's dissent focused on the history of discrimination against black persons in America and the constitutional and legal underpinnings of that discrimination. In his view, the Constitution should not be used as a barrier to undo the discrimination that it originally helped to effectuate. Analogizing affirmative action to desegregation, Justice Blackmun characterized this remedy as an interim measure toward an integrated society.

Justice Stevens, joined by Chief Justice Burger, Justice Stewart, and Justice Rehnquist, concurred in the judgment in part and dissented in part. Justice Stevens did not reach the constitutional issue. He interpreted Title VI to require evaluations to be color-blind, thereby prohibiting Bakke from being denied admission based on race. The Stevens' group provided the majority that, together with Justice Powell's opinion, invalidated the Davis program under Title VI. Although Justice Powell and the four Justices in the Brennan group applied Title VI, they adopted a constitutional standard in interpreting it.

Because Title VI applies to all federally funded programs, *Bakke* applies to private schools that receive such funding as well. Were it not for Title VI, the Court would have to make a preliminary finding of state action to apply equal protection or other constitutional standards for non-governmental institutions.

Bakke did not resolve what constitutional standard to apply to affirmative action in education. Justice Powell applied one standard; the Brennan group applied another; and Justice Stevens' opinion did not reach the constitutional question. The practical impact of Justice Powell's opinion on affirmative action in education may be that colleges and universities could achieve a result similar to the Davis program, but be virtually immune from challenge if they approximate the Harvard plan.

In *Grutter v. Bollinger*,[15] the Court held that the use of race in admissions decisions by the University of Michigan Law School did not violate equal protection. The Law School, in assessing each applicant and determining his likely "contributions to the intellectual and social life of the institution,"[16] considered such variables as the applicant's recommendations, essays, undergraduate institution, and course selections. The Law School's expert testified that if race had not been factored into the admissions decision, only 10 percent of those under represented minorities that were admitted in 2000 would have been accepted, causing the percentage of under-represented minorities in the entering class to drop from 14.5 percent to 4 percent.

Justice Powell's opinion in *Regents of California v. Bakke*[17] required that government-imposed racial classifications must be "narrowly tailored to further compelling governmental interests."[18] In *Bakke*, Justice Powell rejected three governmental interests as not compelling. The first was the need to reduce the historic imbalance of races in medical schools and in the medical profession, which Justice Powell rejected as unlawful "racial balancing." The second was "remedying societal discrimination,"[19] which Justice Powell rejected due to the "unnecessary burdens on innocent third parties"[20] who had played no role in causing the harm. Third, Justice Powell rejected the interest in increasing the number of physicians in underserved communities. Even if this interest was compelling, the program did not advance it. However, Justice Powell did find compelling the interest in attaining

---

[15]   539 U.S. 306 (2003).

[16]   *Id.* at 315.

[17]   438 U.S. 265 (1978).

[18]   539 U.S. at 326.

[19]   *Id.* at 323.

[20]   *Id.* at 324.

"a diverse student body."[21] The First Amendment has long been concerned with academic freedom. Quoting *Keyishian v. Board of Regents of University of State of New York*,[22] Justice Powell emphasized that the nation's future depended on training leaders who had been exposed to the customs and ideas of its diverse peoples.

Marks v. United States[23] established that "when a fragmented Court decides a case and no single rationale explaining the result enjoys the assent of five Justices, the holding of the Court may be viewed as that position taken by those Members who concurred in the judgments on the narrowest grounds."[24] The *Grutter* Court did not determine whether *Marks* required that Justice Powell's opinion be binding. Instead, it used reasons endorsing Justice Powell's view that having a diverse student body was a compelling governmental interest that justified race-based admissions.

"The Fourteenth Amendment 'protects *persons*, not *groups*.'"[25] Government group classifications based on race were usually prohibited. *Adarand Constructors, Inc. v. Pena*[26] required that race-based classifications be narrowly tailored "to further compelling governmental interests."[27] *Gomillion v. Lightfoot*[28] determined that context mattered in such cases. A judicial remedy for past discrimination was not the only governmental interest concerning race that would survive strict scrutiny. *Grutter* recognized a compelling state interest in using race to attain "a diverse student body."[29] The complex education judgments concerning the benefits of diversity in the school are within the expertise of the university. The Court has historically given deference to a university's academic decisions if they fell within constitutional boundaries. For the university to fulfill its mission of finding students who would contribute to the "robust exchange of ideas,"[30] the Court would presume "good faith" absent a contrary showing. The Law School was not aiming to obtain a "specified percentage of a particular" ethnic group,[31] which would be unconstitutional racial balancing. Rather, it was trying to capture a "critical mass" sufficient to generate the educational benefits that arose from diversity. The admissions policy used by the Law School advanced " 'cross-racial understanding,' helps to break down racial stereotypes,"[32] and advanced understanding among persons of different races. Consequently, classroom discussions were more " 'enlightening and interest

---

[21] *Id.*

[22] 385 U.S. 589 (1967).

[23] 430 U.S. 188 (1977).

[24] 539 U.S. at 325.

[25] *Id.* at 326.

[26] 515 U.S. 200 (1995).

[27] *Id.* at 227.

[28] 364 U.S. 339 (1960).

[29] 539 U.S. at 324.

[30] *Id.*

[31] *Id.* at 329.

[32] *Id.* at 330.

ing.' "[33]

A diverse student body was better prepared for " 'an increasingly diverse workforce and society.' "[34] American businesses and professions were involved in an increasingly diverse global marketplace. Many leaders would have attended both a university and a law school. For our citizens to consider this leadership legitimate, talented persons of all races and ethnicities must have access to legal education. Minority students would not bring some standard viewpoint, but rather increasing diversity would break down such stereotypical beliefs.

The means chosen had to be "specifically and narrowly framed to accomplish"[35] the Law School's interest in a diverse student body. Establishing a quota or a separate admission track for minorities would fail this test. Universities could, however, consider race a "plus" in the individualized consideration of each applicant. From 1993 to 2000, African-Americans, Latinos, and Native-Americans composed 13.5 percent–20.1 percent of the Law School's classes. The difference between under-represented minority students who applied and ultimately enrolled in the Law School was substantial. This difference varied from year to year within each group. Most important, each applicant in Michigan's race-conscious admissions program received individualized consideration. No student was automatically accepted or rejected based on any one "soft" variable. The Law School based its idea of diversity on a wide variety of factors. Students who had "lived or traveled widely abroad, are fluent in several languages, have overcome personal adversity and family hardship,"[36] participated extensively in community service, and succeeded in other careers were considered capable of making notable contributions to the class.

Public undergraduate institutions in Texas, Florida, and California have adopted a percentage plan, advocated by the United States, that automatically admitted students who graduated in a certain class rank from any high school in the state. Such programs may not work for graduate and professional schools. The race-neutral alternatives considered by the Law School did not allow it to maintain its academic selectivity yet attain a student body that was diverse in ways other than race.

Race-conscious admissions programs must be continually scrutinized to ensure they do not " 'unduly burden individuals who are not members of the favored racial and ethnic groups.' "[37] They must be limited in time. Sunset provisions or period reviews could determine if the program was still necessary. Universities in states where racial preferences in admissions were prohibited were experimenting with alternative, race-neutral approaches. Twenty-five years from now, these programs "will no longer be necessary."[38]

---

[33] *Id.*

[34] *Id.*

[35] *Id.* at 333.

[36] *Id.* at 338.

[37] *Id.* at 341.

[38] *Id.* at 343.

Justice Ginsburg filed a concurring opinion joined by Justice Breyer. That race-conscious programs must eventually end was consistent with the "international understanding of the office of affirmative action."[39] Over 70 percent of both African-American and Hispanic children attended majority-minority schools. It was possible, though not certain, that affirmative action would not be necessary in the next generation.

Chief Justice Rehnquist filed a dissenting opinion in which Justices Scalia, Kennedy, and Thomas joined. Chief Justice Rehnquist described the Law School's race-conscious program as blatant racial balancing. While the Court discussed strict scrutiny, "its application of that review is unprecedented in its deference."[40] Of the 12 Hispanics and 12 African-Americans with LSAT and GPA qualifications in the same range that applied for admission in 2000, only 2 of the Hispanics were admitted while all 12 of the African-Americans were. "[T]he Law School's disparate admissions practices with respect to these minority groups demonstrate that its alleged goal of 'critical mass' is simply a sham."[41] From 1995 to 2000, the percentage of minority students who applied for admission closely tracked the percentage of minority students who were offered admission. Moreover, unlike other race-preference programs, this one lacked any time limits.

Dissenting, Justice Kennedy supported Justice Powell's opinion in *Bakke*. Race could be considered as "one, nonpredominant factor"[42] in an admissions program. Eighty to eighty-five percent of available seats in an entering law school class were given to students based on LSAT scores and GPAs. Race was likely "outcome determinative"[43] for minorities for the remaining 15 to 20 percent of seats. From 1995 to 1998, there was little fluctuation among admitted minority students. The percentage of enrolled minorities remained between 13.5 to 13.8 percent. From 1995 to 1998, offers extended varied between 13.4 percent and 15.6 percent. Moreover, by the end of admission season, decisions were based strictly on race. A constitutionally valid race-conscious admissions program had to maintain individual assessment throughout the entire process. "Deference is antithetical to strict scrutiny."[44]

Justice Scalia concurred in part and dissented in part, joined by Justice Thomas. Justice Scalia said that the differing results in this case and *Gratz v. Bollinger*[45] would prolong the controversy and litigation resulting in future lawsuits. Future challenges would likely consider whether the scheme in question sufficiently evaluated each applicant " 'as an individual' and whether it sufficiently avoids 'separate admissions tracks' to fall under *Grutter* rather than *Gratz*."[46] Other future litigation would consider whether a university, in quest of its "critical mass," had

---

[39] *Id.* at 344 (Ginsburg, J., concurring).

[40] *Id.* at 380 (Rehnquist, C.J., dissenting).

[41] *Id.* at 383.

[42] *Id.* at 387 (Kennedy, J., dissenting).

[43] *Id.* at 389.

[44] *Id.* at 394.

[45] 539 U.S. 244 (2003).

[46] *Grutter*, 539 U.S. at 348 (Scalia, J., concurring in part).

pursued a quota rather than "a permissible goal."[47] Still other suits would challenge whether racial diversity offered any educational benefits in a particular setting. Certain litigation could challenge the university's genuine interest in "the educational benefits of diversity."[48] For example, a university that preached multiculturalism could promote racial segregation on its campus through "minority-only student organizations, separate minority housing opportunities, separate minority student centers, even separate minority-only graduation ceremonies."[49] Finally, some suits could claim that a university's racial preferences have exceeded or fallen short of the " 'critical mass' "[50] approved here. Some of the suits in this category could be filed by minority students who felt short-changed by the institution's "generic minority 'critical mass.' "[51]

Justice Thomas, joined by Justice Scalia, concurred in part and dissented in part. Justice Thomas stated that the problems of Michigan Law School's "elitist admissions policy"[52] were self-inflicted and could not be solved through racial discrimination. The Law School sought diversity for "aesthetic" reasons that did not help the poor or uneducated. Michigan did not have a compelling interest in having a law school, let alone an elite one. As fewer than 16 percent of the Law School's graduates remained in Michigan and only 27 percent were from Michigan, having an elite school "does little to advance the welfare of the people of Michigan."[53] Justice Thomas stated that "the Law School should be forced to choose between its classroom aesthetic and its exclusionary admissions system."[54] The Law School could achieve its interest in diversity without the use of racial discrimination if they would simply accept all students who met their minimum qualifications. Growing evidence indicates that black students do not thrive in racially heterogeneous environments. University administrators have undertaken racial, ethnic, and religious experimentation through selective admissions tests.

In general, black students have experienced lower performance on the LSAT than other groups. Although law schools realized this, they continued to use the test as a measure for admission. They attempted to adjust for this discrepancy by using racial discrimination to obtain their racial aesthetics. The Court should not defer to the Law School's practice of adhering to measures that they know produce racially skewed results. In admitting students who were less prepared, the Law School unfairly placed these students in competition with more prepared students, and the unprepared found that they were not able to succeed. Affirmative action programs also cheapened the accomplishments of blacks whose achievements are based on their ability rather than the color of their skin.

---

[47] *Id.*

[48] *Id.* at 349.

[49] *Id.*

[50] *Id.*

[51] *Id.*

[52] *Id.* at 350 (Thomas, J., concurring in part).

[53] *Id.* at 360.

[54] *Id.* at 361.

He interpreted the majority opinion to prohibit a school from deciding between different minority groups and agreed with this. Racial discrimination that did not aid a university in obtaining a " 'critical mass' " of under-represented minorities remained unconstitutional. Therefore, the Law School could not allow race to play a part in deciding between similarly situated blacks and Hispanics, or between whites and Asians. Justice Thomas also concurred, with strong caveats, that affirmative action should end in 25 years.

In *Gratz v. Bollinger*,[55] the Court struck down the University of Michigan's undergraduate admissions program. First, Chief Justice Rehnquist rejected a standing argument based on the plaintiffs' never having applied for admittance as a transfer student. The Chief Justice held that not only had he been denied admissions as an undergraduate but he stood ready to transfer.

Turning to the merits, the Court subjected all racial classifications to strict scrutiny, regardless of " 'the race of those burdened or benefited by a particular classification.' "[56] An applicant must receive 100 points to be guaranteed admission to the undergraduate program. An applicant that fell into the category of an " 'underrepresented minority' " automatically received 20 points based solely on his/her race. A policy that granted one-fifth of the points needed to be guaranteed admission to an applicant based entirely on the applicant's race was "not narrowly tailored to achieve the interest in educational diversity."[57] Justice Powell's opinion in *Bakke* stressed that a university should consider "each particular applicant as an individual, assessing all of the qualities that individual possesses, and in turn, evaluating that individual's ability to contribute to the unique setting of higher education."[58]

By distributing 20 points to an applicant based on his race, Michigan has made race a decisive factor "for virtually every minimally qualified, underrepresented minority applicant."[59] In contrast, an applicant would receive, at most, five points, for artistic talent. The undergraduate admissions program allowed an applicant's file to be flagged for individualized consideration. This exception in the University's policy only applied to minimally qualified under-represented minority applicants; an admissions counselor attached a "plus" for an applicant's race, making this factor determinative.

The University maintained that using its Law School's admission policy that the Court upheld in *Grutter v. Bollinger*, was impractical due to " 'the volume of applications and the presentation of applicant information.' "[60]

Violations of equal protection also constituted a Title VI violation when committed by an institution that received federal funding. Likewise, with respect to § 1981, it would now " 'proscribe discrimination in the making or enforcement of contracts

---

[55] 539 U.S. 244 (2003).

[56] *Id.* at 270.

[57] *Id.*

[58] *Id.* at 271.

[59] *Id.* at 272.

[60] *Id.* at 275.

against, or in favor of, any race.' "[61] Moreover, purposeful discrimination equal protection also violated § 1981.

Justice O'Connor's concurring opinion distinguished Grutter's "individualized review of applicants." In the Michigan undergraduate program, 100 points on a 150 point scale effected automatic admission. 95–99 points qualified an applicant as "admit or postpone," while 90–94 points put an applicant into the "postponed or admitted" category. From 75 to 89 points was "delayed or postponed." A total of 110 points could be assigned for academic performance, and up to 40 points could be earned for the other, nonacademic factors. An applicant received 10 points for being a Michigan resident. If an applicant was the child of alumni, she received an additional 4 points. An outstanding essay could be granted up to 3 points. A total of 5 points could be added for an applicant's personal achievement, leadership, or public service. Twenty bonus points were automatically assigned if an applicant was a member of an under represented minority group, attended a predominantly minority or disadvantaged high school, or had been recruited for athletics. The counselor could flag an application if he/she "is academically prepared, has a selection index score of at least 75 (for non-Michigan residents) or 80 (for Michigan residents), and possesses one of several qualities valued by the University. These qualities included 'high class rank, unique life experiences, challenges, circumstances, interests or talents, socioeconomic disadvantage, and underrepresented race, ethnicity, or geography.' "[62] Although the program did assign 20 points to other "soft" variables, such as leadership and service, personal achievement, and geographic diversity, these bonuses were limited to much lower levels. The most bonus points an impressive high school leader could receive was five points. The University's undergraduate admissions program was a "nonindividualized, mechanical one."[63]

Concurring, Justice Thomas said that the Equal Protection Clause prohibited a state from using racial discrimination in higher education admissions. Justice Breyer concurred in the judgment. He joined Justice O'Connor's concurring opinion except the part that joined the Court's opinion. Justice Breyer also joined Part I of Justice Ginsburg's dissent. Policies of inclusion were more likely to comport "with the basic constitutional obligation that the law respect each individual equally."[64]

Justice Stevens filed a dissenting opinion, which Justice Souter joined. Because neither petitioner was reapplying to the University at the time the suit was filed nor had done so since, neither had standing. Justice Souter would not require the University to adopt a percentage system similar to those used at public universities in California, Florida, and Texas that would guarantee admission to a "fixed percentage of the top students from each high school in Michigan."[65] This approach was just as race conscious as Michigan's, but in a less open way.

---

[61] *Id.* at 276.

[62] *Id.* at 278 (O'Connor, J., concurring).

[63] *Id.* at 280.

[64] *Id.* at 282 (Breyer, J., concurring).

[65] *Id.* at 297 (Stevens, J., dissenting).

Justice Ginsburg dissented, joined by Justice Souter and by Justice Breyer in Part I. "Unemployment, poverty, and access to health care vary disproportionately by race. African-American and Hispanic children are too often educated in poverty-stricken and underperforming schools. Adult African-Americans and Hispanics generally earn less than whites with equivalent levels of education."[66] Agreeing with the "contemporary human rights documents,"[67] she distinguished between race-conscious laws that aim to increase inequality and those that aim to eliminate it. As non-minority applicants greatly outnumbered minority applicants, even substantial race-based preferences would not significantly diminish admissions opportunities for applicants who did not receive them.[68]

§ 11.02 EMPLOYMENT

[1] Title VII and the Equal Protection Clause

Title VII of the Civil Rights Act of 1964 is the principal federal statute dealing with employment discrimination based on race, gender, and certain other impermissible criteria. The following section treats the legality of affirmative action in employment for both public and private employees under the Equal Protection Clause. It also discusses some of the Court's affirmative action jurisprudence in the Title VII area, as there is considerable overlap between the Court's jurisprudence under Title VII and equal protection in this area.

From the beginning, several factors have generally strongly influenced the result in affirmative action cases. For example, *Wygant v. Jackson Board of Education*[69] demonstrates that affirmative action in the layoff context is more difficult than in, for example, hiring or promotion. *Wygant* involved a layoff scheme designed to protect minorities by laying off some non-minority teachers with greater seniority before laying off minority teachers with less seniority. The provision required that layoffs not reduce the existing percentage of minority teachers in the workforce. Writing for a plurality of four, Justice Powell concluded that the layoff provision was not narrowly tailored to serve a compelling state interest. The plurality rejected the rationale of providing minority teachers as role models for minority students. With no logical stopping point, the idea that black students were better off with black teachers could lead to the system rejected in *Brown v. Board of Education*. The plurality also refused to uphold a plan that was predicated on curing societal discrimination. Instead, it required some discrimination by the governmental unit involved that was based on statistical evidence.

---

[66] *Id.* at 299–300 (Ginsburg, J., dissenting).

[67] United Nations-initiated Conventions have sought to eliminate racial and gender discrimination.

[68] Admitting the top high school students based on high school grades would yield "significant minority enrollment in universities only if the majority-minority high school population [was] large enough to guarantee that, in many schools, most of the students in the top 10 or 20% [were] minorities." However, these plans created "perverse incentives" for parents to enroll their children in "low-performing segregated schools."

[69] 476 U.S. 267 (1986).

In her concurrence, Justice O'Connor joined that part of the plurality opinion that discussed specific findings of racial discrimination. Still, requiring government to admit illegal discrimination as a precondition for affirmative action would diminish its incentives to engage in proactive affirmative action. Justice White hinted that the layoff policy at issue was discriminatory, but he concurred only in the judgment.

Justice Powell, Chief Justice Burger, and Justice Rehnquist also invalidated the plan based on its layoff context. These Justices were more reluctant to accept affirmative action in the layoff context because the expectations of those who already have the job were greater than those seeking employment. This plurality of three reasoned that layoffs directly impacted individuals while hiring programs could more appropriately diffuse the burden among a large and anonymous pool of applicants. Some have criticized this distinction: whether one fails to be hired or is laid off because of affirmative action, one still has no job. Justice White was a fourth Justice who expressed broad disagreement about affirmative action in the layoff context.

Justice Marshall's dissent in *Wygant*, joined by Justices Brennan and Blackmun, emphasized that the affirmative action plan at issue had been the product of collective bargaining. He also maintained that nothing was sacred about a seniority system, noting that *United Steelworkers v. Weber*[70] had approved a collective bargaining agreement altering a seniority system for promotion. Resembling Justice Powell's analysis in *Bakke*, Justice Stevens' dissent emphasized the important public purpose of maintaining an ethnically diverse faculty that can better convey the diversity of the nation as a whole.

As the next three cases demonstrate, another factor that strongly influences these cases is whether the Court perceives the program at issue as a goal or quota. Other influential factors include how flexible the remedy is, how long it will last, and how much weight is placed on race or gender in the employment decision. In *Local 28 of the Sheet Metal Workers' International Ass'n v. EEOC*,[71] a Title VII case, the District Court had ordered the union to reach a goal of 29 percent non-white membership within six years; this goal was extended and modified several times. Writing for a plurality of four, Justice Brennan stated that the order would pass even the demanding compelling state interest test. In his crucial concurring opinion, Justice Powell characterized the remedial order as a temporary, flexible goal rather than a quota.

In dissent, Chief Justice Burger maintained that Title VII did not permit racial preferences benefitting minority employees who were not actual victims of identifiable past discrimination. In separate opinions, Justices White and O'Connor characterized the relief as a strict racial quota.

In *United States v. Paradise*[72] the Court validated a hiring scheme requiring that Alabama hire one black state trooper for every white state trooper hired until

---

[70] 443 U.S. 193 (1979).

[71] 478 U.S. 421 (1986).

[72] 480 U.S. 149 (1987).

25 percent of the force was black. This remedy followed a finding that the Alabama Department of Public Safety had systematically excluded blacks from employment as state troopers. Writing for a plurality of four, Justice Brennan found that the program would meet even the compelling state interest test. He emphasized that the remedy was imposed only after a consistent history of failure by the Department to comply with the District Court's prior remedial orders. Justice Brennan also noted that the program fell far short of the remedy actually needed to eliminate the effects of past discrimination, for it only applied if there were qualified blacks in the market. Moreover, the remedy was temporary, focused on the corporal level, and did not involve layoffs. Justice Brennan stated that appellate courts should afford deference to district courts in fashioning relief.

Justice Powell concurred, characterizing the relief as narrow, fair, and flexible. Justice Stevens concurred in the judgment, emphasizing that this program was fashioned after the District Court had repeatedly found past violations. Justice O'Connor dissented, characterizing the remedy as a quota. Justice White's dissent argued that the District Court had exceeded its equitable powers.

Johnson v. Transportation Agency[73] upheld an affirmative action plan intended to remedy under-representation not only of minorities but also of women in certain positions. Although 76 percent of the office and clerical workers at the Agency were women, they held less than 10 percent of administrator, professional, and technical positions. Moreover, there were no women in any of the 238 skill craft worker positions at issue in this case. The Agency's plan set aside no specific positions for minorities or women but instead authorized consideration of ethnicity or gender as a factor when evaluating qualified candidates. Writing for the Court, Justice Brennan noted that this feature supported the legality of the plan because, as in *Bakke*, these criteria were not the sole factors in choosing an applicant. Moreover, the disparities between the scores of the woman and the rejected male applicant were small.

In a footnote, the Court stated that it was not measuring the action of this public employer against an equal protection standard because that issue had not been briefed below. Because the case was decided under Title VII, its result was applicable to private employers. Its public employment context also renders the case important for constitutional jurisprudence. After all, as the case involved a public employee, the Court would not have construed Title VII as permitting a practice that would violate equal protection.

Justice Brennan first considered whether a manifest imbalance existed reflecting an under-representation of women or minorities in traditionally segregated job categories. Such an imbalance would provide the basis of a voluntary affirmative action plan that considered the gender of those applying for skilled craft jobs. In assessing manifest imbalance, Justice Brennan distinguished between skilled and unskilled jobs. To determine manifest imbalance for jobs that require no special qualifications, he simply compared the percentage of women and minorities in the area labor market with the percentages in the particular job category. For jobs requiring specific qualifications, he compared the percentages of

---

[73] 480 U.S. 616 (1987).

women or minorities in the area labor market possessing such qualifications with the percentages in the particular job category.

Concurring in the judgment, Justice O'Connor would require an employer to show a manifest imbalance that would be large enough to establish a Title VII pattern and practice case. The majority specifically rejected this position on the ground that employers would have significant disincentives against compiling evidence of a possible Title VII claim against themselves in order to institute an affirmative action plan.

Beyond establishing that the purpose was to cure a manifest imbalance, the Court scrutinized the effects of the plan. Justice Brennan said that the plan at issue did not authorize blind hiring of female applicants, but only that gender be taken into account as one of many factors. Moreover, the plan did not specify that positions be set aside for women or minorities. In contrast to the layoffs in *Wygant*, the Court found that the affirmative action in this case did not deprive the plaintiff of a particular job he already had. The male employee had no legitimate expectation of the promotion at issue; he was one of seven qualified candidates whom the Agency director was authorized to promote. The plaintiff still had his job and would remain eligible for other promotions. Also, unlike *Wygant*, the program was designed to *attain* a balanced workforce, not *maintain* one. Finally, the temporary plan was applied on a flexible, case-by-case basis to gradually change the workforce without any specific deadline.

In his concurrence, Justice Stevens candidly stated that the construction of Title VII offered by the Court in *Johnson* and *Weber* was at odds with the original, color-blind and gender neutral intent of the drafters of Title VII. Nevertheless, he claimed that the Court's gloss on Title VII had become part of the fabric of the law to which he felt compelled to adhere. Justice Brennan replied that Congress had a chance to amend Title VII after the Court's construction in *Weber* and had not done so.

Justice Scalia's dissent stated that one could not discern the intent of the Congress that enacted Title VII on the failure of the present Congress to enact legislation disagreeing with a Court decision.[74] Justice Scalia maintained that the affirmative action plan essentially commanded managers to promote women and minorities, not just consider minority or female status as one factor among many. The plan told managers to identify people who were minimally qualified and to promote any women or minorities among those who were so qualified. The fear of a pattern and practice of discrimination by simply showing statistical disparities gave employers strong incentives to promote or hire women and minorities. On the other hand, Justice Scalia argued that *Johnson* effectively shielded employers from liability to white males for allegations of reverse discrimination.

In *Martin v. Wilks*,[75] the Court allowed non-minority employees to reopen affirmative action decrees involving minority employees. Although under Federal Rule of Civil Procedure 24 the non-minority employees would have been allowed to

---

[74] To support this point, Justice Brennan cited G. Calabresi: *A Common Law for the Age of Statutes* (1982).

[75] 490 U.S. 755 (1989).

intervene in the first suit as a matter of right, the rule imposed no duty on them to intervene. Therefore, the non-minority parties retained the right to bring a subsequent action challenging the court-approved plan.

In *Ricci v. DeStefano*,[76] the Court held that discarding promotional examinations taken by New Haven firefighters, on the basis of racially disparate results, violated Title VII by discriminating against those "who had performed well."[77] Following its contract with the union, New Haven implemented a merit-based promotion examination designed by an outside consultant. Based on the examinations, 10 white candidates were eligible for promotion to 8 lieutenant positions, and 7 whites and 2 Hispanics were eligible for promotion to 7 captain positions. However, the City disregarded the examinations to avoid a disparate impact lawsuit by minority groups. Subsequently, 17 white firefighters and 1 Hispanic firefighter, who were denied a chance at promotion, brought suit.

Although Title VII differs from the Constitution, constitutional principles provided guidance in the statutory context. Writing for a majority of five, Justice Kennedy stated that Title VII prohibited "race-based action" like this one "unless the employer can demonstrate a strong basis in evidence that, had it not taken the action, it would have been liable under the disparate-impact statute."[78] Employers only had discretion when they have a strong basis in evidence of disparate-impact liability; they need not, however, have "a provable, actual violation."[79] The Court did not decide whether the Constitution permitted discrimination for a "legitimate fear of disparate impact"[80] litigation.

Title VII afforded employers significant discretion to develop an inclusive promotion process, but once established, employers could not then invalidate the test results and thus upset "an employee's legitimate expectation not to be judged on the basis of race. Doing so, absent a strong basis in evidence of an impermissible disparate impact,"[81] comprised a prohibited racial preference under Title VII. Before it was administered, Title VII allowed an employer to consider how to construct a "test or practice in order to provide a fair opportunity for all individuals, regardless of their race."[82]

Even if the City had been motivated by a desire to avoid disparate-impact liability, there was not "an objective, strong basis in evidence" that the tests were "inadequate."[83] The Court concluded that no genuine issue of material fact existed, and that the law entitled the firefighters to summary judgment.

The minorities' pass rate on the exam was approximately one-half the pass rates for white candidates, which fell well "below the 80-percent standard set by the

---

[76] 129 S. Ct. 2658 (2009).

[77] *Id.* at 2664.

[78] *Id.*

[79] *Id.* at 2676.

[80] *Id.*

[81] *Id.* at 2677.

[82] *Id.*

[83] *Id.*

EEOC to implement the disparate-impact provision of Title VII."[84] Had the City certified the examinations, not one black candidate for any of the then-vacant positions would have been considered. Nevertheless, the significant statistical disparity was "far from a strong basis in evidence."[85] Title VII required disparate-impact liability "only if the examinations were not job related and consistent with business necessity, or if there existed an equally valid, less-discriminatory alternative that served the City's needs but that the City refused to adopt."[86] No genuine dispute existed that the exams were job-related, and the City "lacked a strong basis in evidence of an equally valid, less-discriminatory testing alternative."[87] A few statements made by an individual who had little knowledge of the test did not create the requisite genuine issue of fact. The individual was a "direct competitor" of the consultant company that designed the examination, and became employed by the City.

Concurring, Justice Scalia stated that the Court's decision was merely postponing the day the Court must confront whether Title VII's disparate-impact provisions were consistent with the Equal Protection Clause. Disparate-impact theory could be justified as an "evidentiary tool" to establish a *prima facie* showing of discriminatory intent.

Justice Alito's concurred, joined by Justices Scalia and Thomas. A reasonable jury could find that upon the City's disclosure of the racial makeup of those firefighters scoring highest on the exam, an influential community leader lobbied the City to disregard the test results.

Dissenting, Justice Ginsburg, joined by Justices Stevens, Souter and Breyer, noted that the population of New Haven was 40% African-American and 20% Hispanic. For entry level jobs, minorities were slightly underrepresented, but in officer ranks of captain or higher, there was major underrepresentation as only 9% were African-American and 9% were Hispanic. Furthermore, only 1 of 21 fire captains was African-American. The promotion process should be judged against this context of "entrenched inequality."[88]

The passage rate on the lieutenant exam for African-American candidates was about half the rate for Caucasian candidates and even lower for Hispanic candidates. On the captain exam, African-American and Hispanic candidates passed at about half the rate of Caucasian test takers. Moreover, while nearly half of the lieutenant candidates were African-American or Hispanic, the test left none eligible for the eight open lieutenant positions. The majority failed to show "why the evidence of the tests' multiple deficiencies does not create at least a triable issue under a strong-basis-in-evidence standard."[89]

---

[84] *Id.* at 2678.

[85] *Id.*

[86] *Id.*

[87] *Id.* at 2679.

[88] *Id.* at 2691 (Ginsburg, J., dissenting).

[89] *Id.* at 2707.

[2] Government Set Asides

In *Fullilove v. Klutznick*[90] the Court rejected a facial challenge to provisions of the Public Works Employment Act requiring state or local recipients of federal public works funds to spend at least 10 percent of the funds on minority business enterprises (MBEs). The division of the Court, and the amorphous language that characterized some of the opinions, makes the legal rules emerging from the decision difficult to ascertain. Nevertheless, the Court's more recent decision in *Adarand Constructors, Inc. v. Pena*[91] severely limited minority set-aside programs.

Writing for a plurality of three in *Fullilove*, Chief Justice Burger upheld that set-aside program using the Commerce Power, the Spending Power, and Section 5 of the Fourteenth Amendment. The Chief Justice appeared to use a rationality standard in upholding the Congressional purpose of eliminating barriers to minority access to public contracting funds. While he stated that the Congressional means should be narrowly tailored, he exhibited considerable deference to Congress. Justices White and Powell joined Chief Justice Burgers' opinion.

Consistent with his opinion in *Bakke*, Justice Powell's concurrence upheld the challenged affirmative action program using strict scrutiny. In his concurring opinion, joined by Justices Brennan and Blackmun, Justice Marshall found that the racial classifications at issue served important governmental objectives, and were substantially related to achieving those objectives. This standard was very similar to that in the Brennan group's opinion in *Bakke*. Three Justices dissented. In his dissent, Justice Stewart cited Justice Harlan's dissent in *Plessy v. Ferguson* as authority for a color-blind Constitution.

In *City of Richmond v. J. A. Croson Co.*,[92] the Court invalidated a Richmond requirement that prime contractors working for it award 30 percent of their subcontracts to minority contractors. A plurality of three distinguished *Fullilove* primarily on the basis that Congress had enacted the statute in *Fullilove* using its special powers under Section 5 of the Fourteenth Amendment. Section 5 specifically empowered Congress to enforce the Equal Protection Clause against the states, whereas the Equal Protection Clause constricted state power in matters involving race. This difference required that a specific finding of past discrimination support a state program even though *Fullilove* did not require Congress to make such a finding. Moreover, in *Fullilove*, Congress allowed a waiver of its 10 percent affirmative action requirement if minority contractors were unavailable or were using the set-aside to charge unreasonable prices.

For the first time, a majority of the Court applied a compelling state interest test to affirmative action cases. Justice O'Connor relied heavily on Justice Powell's opinion in *Bakke*, in which he wrote only for himself on this point. According to *Croson*, the state had to demonstrate a compelling interest that the program served remedial purposes rather than "illegitimate notions of racial inferiority or

---

[90] 448 U.S. 448 (1980).

[91] 515 U.S. 200 (1995).

[92] 488 U.S. 469 (1989).

simple racial politics."[93] The means had to be so closely tailored to advancing this goal as to eliminate any inference of such an illegitimate purpose. A majority of five also noted that minority groups controlled the government of Richmond. Under a *Carolene Products* analysis, this reinforced the necessity for strict scrutiny, because white persons disadvantaged by the program were a political minority in the city government.

Four Justices found that the factual findings of the Richmond City Council did not establish a compelling remedial purpose. Neither conclusory recitations of past discrimination nor of a remedial purpose justified a 30 percent quota. While the City did find that minorities comprised 50 percent of its population yet received only .67 percent of its prime contracts, the key basis for comparison was not the minority population in a given geographic area, but the minority population qualified to do the work in that geographic area. The lack of findings of past discrimination undercut the argument for establishing a compelling remedial purpose.

Any remedial purpose was further undercut by the gross over-inclusiveness of the program. First, a plurality of four noted that the program extended beyond black persons to Aleuts, Orientals, Indians, Eskimos and Spanish-speaking people for whom the City had not even attempted to make findings of past discrimination. Indeed, there was no evidence that members of some of these groups had ever resided in Richmond. Second, a majority noted that the City did not consider racially neutral means to accomplish this goal. Third, a majority noted that 30 percent comprised a rigid numerical quota based on assumptions that minorities would choose certain jobs in proportion to their representation in the population. Moreover, a majority pointed out that the plan lacked a waiver in the event higher prices charged by a minority contractor were not attributable to past discrimination.

A plurality of four also afforded guidance regarding what steps state and local governments had to follow in formulating appropriate plans. Findings necessary to underpin an affirmative action plan included:

1) direct evidence that nonminority contractors had systematically excluded minority contractors;

2) significant statistical differences between the number of qualified minority contractors available and interested in performing a particular service and the number actually doing work; or

3) individual instances of discrimination supported by statistical proof. Individual instances standing alone support individual remedies rather than an affirmative action plan.[94]

Even when appropriate findings existed, an affirmative action plan should be proposed only "in extreme cases."[95] The state or local government should first try

---

[93] *Id.* at 493.

[94] *Id.* at 509.

[95] *Id.*

anti-discrimination legislation or race-neutral measures such as helping to finance small businesses-which could include many minority businesses. Finally, any plan should be a temporary measure tailored in duration and scope to the injury described by the findings.

Justice Stevens filed a separate opinion concurring in part and concurring in the judgment, in which he disagreed that findings of past discrimination were always necessary to institute an affirmative action plan. Instead, he focused on the eccentricities of the Richmond plan.

Concurring in the judgment, Justice Scalia broadly condemned all benign discrimination plans. He adhered to a color-blind construction of the Equal Protection Clause.

In his dissent, Justice Marshall, joined by Justices Brennan and Blackmun, criticized the majority for disaggregating the City's factual findings rather than considering them together. He also noted that the City had modeled its 30 percent figure on *Fullilove*. The figure fell roughly halfway between the percentage of minority contractors and the percentage of minorities in Richmond's population.

Justice Marshall was troubled by Justice O'Connor's emphasizing that minority groups controlled Richmond. He found it "insulting" to apply strict scrutiny on the basis that minorities control the government. Moreover, overall, on the state and national levels, white persons still controlled government.

Justices Scalia's and Kennedy's concurring opinions were far less tolerant of affirmative action than those parts of Justice O'Connor's opinion that were supported by a plurality of only three or four. Thus, her majority position in *Croson* would seem to have defined the broadest affirmative action program that a majority of the Court would allow for minority set-asides by state or local government. Moreover, her opinion was written in language that was sufficiently broad so that it might extend beyond the minority set aside context to other affirmative action.

In *Metro Broadcasting, Inc. v. FCC*,[96] a majority of the Court afforded Congress considerable authority to mandate affirmative action. That case upheld two affirmative action rules of the FCC. The first enhanced the positions of groups with some active minority ownership in the competition for broadcast licenses. This policy deemed minority ownership a plus among six other race-neutral factors, including proposed program service, in allocating broadcast licenses. The second policy allowed "distress sale" stations to be assigned only to FCC approved enterprises with over 50 percent minority ownership before any competitive process took place.

Writing for a 5-4 majority, Justice Brennan relied on the plurality's test in *Fullilove* to apply middle-tier scrutiny to race-conscious rules fashioned by Congress: the program must be substantially related to achieving an important governmental objective. In *Metro Broadcasting*, the important government objective was promoting diversity in programming. This interest had First Amendment content.

---

[96] 497 U.S. 547 (1990).

The specific policies at issue were substantially related to achieving this important objective. Congress found severe under-representation of minorities in the broadcast media. Both Congress and the FCC found a relationship between minority ownership and programming diversity. While the Court did not simply defer to this judgment, it gave " 'great weight' " in reviewing such empirical questions to Congress' decisions and the FCC's experience.[97] The policies at issue did not stereotype, for example, in assuming that a discrete category of programming appealed to minority audiences. Congress limited the plans' duration by appropriating money for limited periods and holding annual hearings to reevaluate it. Finally, the burdens on non-minorities were slight. One policy merely allocated a plus in the selection process; the other gave an absolute preference only in the area of distress sales that had accounted for .4 percent of all broadcast sales since 1979.

Concurring, Justice Stevens emphasized the relationship to the legitimate objective of broadcast diversity. Pursuing this objective did not stigmatize favored or disfavored ethnic groups.

In a dissent joined by three other Justices, Justice O'Connor relied on *Croson* to apply strict scrutiny. She distinguished *Fullilove* on the grounds that *Metro Broadcasting* did not involve an exercise of Congress' power under Section 5 of the Fourteenth Amendment.[98] Moreover, Congress did not fashion these measures to remedy specific discrimination.

The measures taken failed strict scrutiny. The validity of broadcast diversity was, at best, unsettled in First Amendment jurisprudence, as it held out the danger of censorship. Moreover, the law was not narrowly tailored to advance this objective because the policies assumed a strong nexus between race and particular viewpoints in programming. Thus, it was essentially stereotyping. Finally, the measures imposed a considerable burden on non-minority groups. The burden was particularly strong in distress sales, as the plan created an exclusive market available only to minorities. Even the licensing enhancement was a strong factor that could be pivotal in a competitive market. Justice Kennedy filed a separate dissent, broadly criticizing benign classifications as stigmatizing their beneficiaries and fostering intolerance among disfavored classes.

The Supreme Court partially overruled *Metro Broadcasting, Inc. v. FCC* in *Adarand Constructors, Inc. v. Pena*.[99] Writing for a 5-4 majority, Justice O'Connor extended strict scrutiny to a race-based affirmative action program established by the Federal government. The Federal program sought to award at least 5 percent of Federal prime and sub-contracts to businesses that were at least 51 percent owned by " 'socially and economically disadvantaged' "[100] individuals. Under the Act, Black, Hispanic, Asian Pacific, Subcontinent Asian, Native Americans, and other groups designated by the Small Business Administration enjoyed a presumption of disadvantage which others had to establish by clear and convincing evidence.

---

[97] *Id.* at 569.

[98] *Id.* at 607.

[99] 515 U.S. 200 (1995).

[100] *Id.* at 205.

As this was a Federal program and the Equal Protection Clause only applied to the states, the Court scrutinized the program under the Due Process Clause of the Fifth Amendment. Justice O'Connor noted that while the language of the Fifth Amendment was not as explicit as the Equal Protection Clause, all racial classifications mandated by any government actor must be reviewed under strict scrutiny.

The Court's adoption of an intermediate scrutiny for federal racial classifications in *Metro Broadcasting* was inconsistent with prior precedent, such as *Richmond v. J.A. Croson Co. Metro Broadcasting's* middle-tier standard undermined the congruence of the Court's jurisprudence in applying similar standards of review to Federal and state racial classifications. In so doing, *Metro Broadcasting* undercut both the skepticism associated with all racial classifications and the consistency of treatment towards groups regardless of race. These concepts — congruence, skepticism, and consistency — stemmed from the basic idea that the Fifth and Fourteenth Amendments protect persons rather than groups.

Justice O'Connor applied strict scrutiny notwithstanding Congress's special power to enforce the Equal Protection Clause using Section 5 of the Fourteenth Amendment. The Justices would not address, however, previously articulated differing views of the authority that Section 5 granted Congress to handle racial discrimination and the extent to which courts should defer to that authority.[101]

In a part of her opinion joined only by Justice Kennedy, Justice O'Connor distinguished overruling *Metro Broadcasting* from her refusal to overrule *Roe v. Wade* in *Planned Parenthood v. Casey*. First, *Metro Broadcasting* was inconsistent with prior, " 'intrinsically sounder' " precedent. Second, *Metro Broadcasting* was not "a long-established precedent that has become integrated into the fabric of the law."[102] Writing again for the majority, Justice O'Connor also overruled *Fullilove v. Klutznick* insofar as *Fullilove* subjected federal racial classifications to less rigorous standards than strict scrutiny. The Court did not decide, however, whether the *Fullilove* program would have survived strict scrutiny. The Court was confident that the strict scrutiny standard would not invalidate all governmental affirmative action. To survive, a program had to be narrowly tailored to advance a compelling state interest. The Court remanded the case for review of whether the program at issue satisfied that test.

Justice Stevens dissented, joined by Justice Ginsburg. He believed that a lesser level of scrutiny should apply to programs that benefit historically oppressed groups than to programs that perpetuate such oppression. Justice Stevens would also afford greater deference to congressional programs designed to promote equality than he would afford to state programs.

Justice Souter also dissented, joined by Justices Ginsburg and Breyer. Justice Souter doubted that the Court's strict scrutiny standard would have produced a different result in *Fullilove*. Moreover, the majority did not resolve what impact Section 5 should have in satisfying strict scrutiny.

---

[101] *Id.* at 227.

[102] *Id.* at 233.

Justice Ginsburg wrote a separate dissent, joined by Justice Breyer. She would have left improving the program at issue to the political branches.

Chapter 12

EQUAL PROTECTION FOR OTHER GROUPS AND INTERESTS

INTRODUCTION

As the previous chapters indicate, the Equal Protection Clause of the Fourteenth Amendment, in conjunction with the equal protection aspects of the Fifth Amendment Due Process Clause, has been essential to remedying race and gender discrimination by the local, state, and federal governments. However, these are not the only identifiable classes of persons to which the Equal Protection Clause pertains. Section 12.01 discusses the extent to which the Court has treated other identifiable groups, such as illegitimate children, aliens, the aged, or the mentally retarded, as discrete and insular minorities. This Section also discusses the different levels of scrutiny afforded laws affecting each of these groups.

Another less definable group that has sought protection under the Equal Protection Clause is the poor. Although the Court has not recognized the poor as a discrete and insular minority, it has given heightened scrutiny to laws that deny fundamental rights based on wealth. These fundamental rights include access to courts, voting, and perhaps to some small degree, education. The jurisprudential methodology of this fundamental rights strand of equal protection jurisprudence is different from the methodology of the discrete and insular minority strand of equal protection jurisprudence. Section 12.02 discusses the fundamental rights strand of equal protection jurisprudence as it pertains to rights to necessities and court access for the poor. The fundamental rights strand of equal protection jurisprudence extends beyond wealth-based distinctions, however. In this connection, Section 12.03 discusses interference with the right to vote based on wealth, apportionment, political affiliation, and other characteristics. Section 12.04 discusses protection of the rights to domestic and international travel.

Laws that neither distinguish between discrete and insular minorities nor affect fundamental rights fall into the generic category of economic and social legislation. As discussed in Section 12.05, the Court has generally left such policy-making judgments to the legislative and executive branches. Accordingly, economic and social legislation and other policy judgments that do not make distinctions based on certain identifiable classes or fundamental rights receive virtually no constitutional scrutiny under the Equal Protection Clause, the Due Process Clause, or otherwise. Thus, the vast majority of governmental taxing, spending, and regulatory decisions receive virtually no constitutional scrutiny. Equal protection jurisprudence seeks to ensure that all participate in the democratic process of making these various governmental decisions and that the Court carefully scrutinizes governmental decisions involving groups that the democratic processes historically have victim ized.

§ 12.01   DISCRETE AND INSULAR MINORITIES

[1]   Aliens

[a]   Resident Aliens

Scrutiny for classifications based on alienage varies with several factors. First, as the title of this sub-section indicates, the Court generally only scrutinizes discrimination against resident aliens but not discrimination against illegal aliens.[1] Second, the Court subjects discrimination against aliens by state or local governmental bodies to far more rigorous scrutiny than it applies to discrimination against aliens by the Federal government.

In *Graham v. Richardson*,[2] a case involving eligibility for state welfare benefits, the Court declared that classifications based on alienage, like those based on nationality or race, were inherently suspect and subject to close judicial scrutiny. "Aliens as a class are a prime example of a 'discrete and insular' minority for whom such heightened judicial solicitude is appropriate."[3] The standard for protecting aliens, "though variously formulated, requires the State to meet certain standards of proof. In order to justify the use of a suspect classification, a state must show that its purpose or interest is both constitutionally permissible and substantial, and that its use of the classification is 'necessary . . . to the accomplishment' of its purpose or the safeguarding of its interest."[4]

The Court has used strict scrutiny to invalidate state laws that excluded resident aliens from the legal profession,[5] denied them welfare benefits,[6] prevented aliens from becoming notaries public,[7] barred them from all classes of state competitive civil service jobs,[8] and restricted their access to financial aid.[9] As discussed *infra*, the Court has extended far less scrutiny to federal provisions that discriminate on the basis of alienage.

Even in the context of state and local governments, an important limitation on the application of strict scrutiny to classifications based on alienage is the

---

[1] *Cf. infra* § 12.01[1][b].

[2] 403 U.S. 365 (1971).

[3] *Id.* at 372 (citations omitted).

[4] *In re* Griffiths, 413 U.S. 717, 721–22 (1973). The *Griffiths* Court attributed no significance to the different terms used to describe the state's interest, *i.e.*, "substantial," "important," "overriding," or "compelling." *Id.* at 722 n.9.

[5] *Id.*

[6] Graham v. Richardson, 403 U.S. 365 (1971). The *Graham* Court invalidated a state law requiring aliens to reside in the United States for a specified number of years as a condition of receiving welfare benefits.

[7] Bernal v. Fainter, 467 U.S. 216 (1984).

[8] Sugarman v. Dougall, 413 U.S. 634 (1973).

[9] Nyquist v. Mauclet, 432 U.S. 1 (1977).

"political-function" exception. This exception "applies to laws that exclude aliens from positions intimately related to the process of democratic self-government."[10] A classification based on alienage must satisfy a two-part test in order to fall within the political-function exception. "First, the specificity of the classification will be examined: a classification that is substantially overinclusive or underinclusive tends to undercut the governmental claim that the classification serves legitimate political ends."[11] Second, the classification may be applied "only to 'persons holding state elective or important nonelective executive, legislative, and judicial positions,' those officers who 'participate directly in the formulation, execution, or review of broad public policy' and hence 'perform functions that go to the heart of representative government.' "[12] A classification that falls within this political function exception is valid if it "bears a rational relationship to this [legitimate state] interest."[13] The Court has upheld, under the political-function exception, laws that exclude aliens from becoming police[14] and probation officers,[15] as well as a law that denied aliens the chance to teach in public schools unless they declared their intent to become citizens.[16]

State laws discriminating against aliens may also be invalid on preemption grounds. The Court used preemption as an alternative basis for its holding in *Graham,* and relied on it to strike down a University of Maryland rule denying lower in-state tuition to resident aliens.[17]

The Court generally has declined to subject to strict scrutiny Federal laws that treat resident aliens differently from citizens. For example, while the Court has strictly scrutinized state civil service provisions that discriminate against aliens,[18] it has declined to extend that analysis to the federal government because of the "paramount federal power over immigration and naturalization."[19] The Federal Civil Service Commission regulation at issue in *Hampton v. Mow Sun Wong* barred all aliens from Federal competitive Civil Service jobs. Nevertheless, the Federal government may not "arbitrarily subject all resident aliens to different substantive

---

[10] *Bernal,* 467 U.S. at 220. The Court stated:

> The rationale behind the political-function exception is that within broad boundaries a State may establish its own form of government and limit the right to govern to those who are full-fledged members of the political community. Some public positions are so closely bound up with the formulation and implementation of self-government that the State is permitted to exclude from those positions persons outside the political community, hence persons who have not become part of the process of democratic self-determination. *Id.* at 221.

[11] Cabell v. Chavez-Salido, 454 U.S. 432, 440 (1982).

[12] *Id.* (quoting *Sugarman v. Dougall,* 413 U.S. 634, 647 (1973)).

[13] Ambach v. Norwick, 441 U.S. 68, 80 (1979).

[14] Foley v. Connelie, 435 U.S. 291 (1978).

[15] Cabell v. Chavez-Salido, 454 U.S. 432 (1982).

[16] Ambach v. Norwick, 441 U.S. 68 (1979).

[17] Toll v. Moreno, 458 U.S. 1, 17 (1982). The Court found that denying lower tuition to nonimmigrant, domiciled aliens conflicted with federal policy of offering tax breaks and other benefits to international organizations as an incentive for them to locate in the United States.

[18] *See* Sugarman v. Dougall, 413 U.S. 634 (1973).

[19] Hampton v. Mow Sun Wong, 426 U.S. 88, 100 (1976).

rules from those applied to citizens."[20] The Court found that the exclusion from consideration for Federal employment of all resident aliens amounted to the deprivation of a liberty interest that must comply with due process.

In invalidating the Civil Service restriction, the Court found that due process required that the decision be made by the President, Congress, or any agency directly regulating immigration, or that the regulation be "justified by reasons which are properly the concern"[21] of the Civil Service Commission. The Court did not decide whether the regulation would have been struck down on equal protection grounds had it been imposed by Congress or the President.

[b] Illegal Aliens

The issue in *Plyler v. Doe*[22] was whether or not a Texas law denying free public education to undocumented, school-age children violated equal protection. Writing for the majority, Justice Brennan held that the Equal Protection Clause applied to these children.[23] While undocumented aliens were not a suspect class, the law discriminated against their innocent children. Moreover, while education was not a fundamental right,[24] it had higher value than a social welfare benefit in keeping together the fabric of our society. As complete deprivation of basic education would place these innocent children at a lifelong disadvantage, the State had the burden of showing that the classification was rationally related to a substantial state interest.[25] The *Plyler* Court used this test to reject all three of the interests asserted by the State: (1) that the restriction would deter the flow of illegal aliens into the state; (2) that the restriction would improve the education of other children in the state; and (3) that the children of illegal aliens were singled out because they would be less likely to remain in the state. Accordingly, the law violated equal protection.[26] Justices Marshall, Blackmun, and Powell each wrote concurring opinions. In dissent, Chief Justice Burger argued that in allocating its finite resources, "it simply is not 'irrational' for a state to conclude that it does not have the same responsibility to provide benefits for persons whose very presence in the state and this country is illegal as it does to provide for persons lawfully present."[27]

---

[20] *Id.* at 101.

[21] *Id.* at 116.

[22] 457 U.S. 202 (1982). This case can be usefully compared with *San Antonio Independent School District v. Rodriguez*, 411 U.S. 1 (1973), *infra* § 12.02[1].

[23] *Plyler*, 457 U.S. at 210–16.

[24] *Rodriguez*, 411 U.S. at 35. In his concurring opinion in *Plyler*, Justice Marshall reiterated his view that education is a fundamental right protected by the Equal Protection Clause. *Plyler*, 457 U.S. at 230–31.

[25] *Plyler*, 457 U.S. at 223–24.

[26] In *Martinez v. Bynum*, 461 U.S. 321, 328–29 (1983), the Court upheld, a valid residency requirement, a section of the same law at issue in *Plyler*. This portion of the law denied free tuition to minors living apart from their parents or guardians if the child's presence in the school district was primarily to receive free tuition.

[27] *Plyler*, 457 U.S. at 250. Chief Justice Burger also noted a number of federal programs from which illegal aliens were excluded.

[2]   Illegitimate Children

Unlike the treatment of distinctions based on alienage, laws that treat illegitimate children differently from legitimate children are not subject to strict scrutiny.[28] However, such distinctions must be "substantially related to permissible state interests."[29]

Laws discriminating based on legitimacy often deal with inheritance and probate matters. In *Trimble v. Gordon*,[30] the Court addressed an Illinois law that allowed illegitimate children to inherit by intestate succession from their mothers, but not their fathers. To legitimate the child, the law required that the putative father not only acknowledge the child but marry the mother. After a court had decided that Gordon was Trimble's father, Gordon acknowledged paternity and paid child support but did not wed Trimble's mother. Accordingly, when Gordon died intestate, Trimble was barred from inheriting the estate.

The State asserted two interests in support of the statute. First, it claimed that the law promoted legitimate family relationships. While the Supreme Court recognized the importance of this interest, it found virtually no relationship between this purpose and the statute. Second, the State claimed an interest in establishing an accurate and efficient method of property distribution upon death of the intestate. While this interest was valid, the statute was not " 'carefully tuned to alternative considerations,' "[31] such as proof of paternity sufficient to establish a claim to the decedent's estate. Therefore, the statute violated the equal protection.

In *Lalli v. Lalli*,[32] the Court upheld a New York statute that required an illegitimate child to obtain an order of filiation declaring paternity to succeed by intestate succession. The order had to be issued in a proceeding commenced while the child's mother was pregnant or within two years of birth. The child in *Lalli* acknowledged that he could not produce the required order, but presented other evidence that the decedent was his father. The Court upheld the statute as rationally related to the State's interest in the orderly distribution of the intestate's estate. The Court distinguished the statute from the one in *Trimble* because it did not require the parents to marry; it merely stated an evidentiary requirement.

However, in *Clark v. Jeter*,[33] the Court unanimously invalidated a Pennsylvania statute imposing a six-year limitation on the time in which a suit can be brought proving paternity of an illegitimate child. There was, however, no limitation on the period in which a legitimate child could seek support through a paternity determination. Applying an intermediate level of scrutiny, the law was not substantially related to the state's interest in avoiding litigation of fraudulent claims in light of the existence of longer periods of limitations for similar actions.

---

[28]   Lalli v. Lalli, 439 U.S. 259, 265 (1978); Mathews v. Lucas, 427 U.S. 495, 506 (1976).

[29]   *Lalli*, 439 U.S. at 265.

[30]   430 U.S. 762 (1977).

[31]   *Id.* at 772 (quoting *Mathews*, 427 U.S. at 513).

[32]   439 U.S. 259 (1978).

[33]   486 U.S. 456 (1988).

[3] The Aged

Classifications based on age are subject to *de minimis* constitutional scrutiny. The Court established a rational basis standard in *Massachusetts Board of Retirement v. Murgia*.[34] *Murgia* upheld a law requiring mandatory retirement of all uniformed state police officers at age 50. In a *per curiam* opinion, the Court determined that the rationality standard was proper by reference to its traditional two-tier equal protection analysis of protected and unprotected classifications.[35]

A legislative classification was subject to strict scrutiny only when the classification interfered with a fundamental right or disadvantaged a suspect class. After determining that the right to government employment was not per se fundamental, the Court considered whether or not the aged was a suspect class. The Court defined a suspect class as one " 'saddled with such disabilities, or subjected to such a history of purposeful unequal treatment, or relegated to such a position of political powerlessness as to command extraordinary protection from the majoritarian political process.' "[36] The aged "have not experienced a 'history of purposeful unequal treatment' or been subjected to unique disabilities on the basis of stereotyped characteristics not truly indicative of their abilities."[37] Nor were the aged a discrete and insular group needing protection from the majority, as everyone will be a member of that group if he or she lives a normal life expectancy.

The Court upheld the challenged statute as rationally related to a legitimate state interest.[38] The Court has also upheld against equal protection challenges a Federal law requiring foreign service personnel to retire at age 60,[39] and a provision of the Missouri Constitution requiring all state judges to retire at age 70.[40]

[4] The Mentally Retarded

In *City of Cleburne, Texas v. Cleburne Living Center*,[41] a Texas city denied a special use permit to a group home for the mentally retarded. The Fifth Circuit Court of Appeals held that the mentally retarded were a "quasi-suspect" class entitled to more than a rationality standard of review. Because the ordinance requiring the special use permit did not substantially further an important governmental interest, the appellate court reasoned, it violated equal protection.

---

[34] 427 U.S. 307, 312–13 (1976).

[35] The decision came at around the time when the middle tier was emerging in gender cases. *See supra* § 10.01.

[36] *Id.* at 313 (quoting *San Antonio School Dist. v. Rodriguez*, 411 U.S. 1, 28 (1973)).

[37] *Id.*

[38] In dissent, Justice Marshall attacked both the result reached by the majority and the two-tiered equal protection analysis. Justice Marshall's dissent is discussed in the next subsection.

[39] Vance v. Bradley, 440 U.S. 93 (1979).

[40] Gregory v. Ashcroft, 501 U.S. 452 (1991).

[41] 473 U.S. 432 (1985).

The Supreme Court reviewed its equal protection jurisprudence.[42] Justice White concluded that the Court subjected to strict scrutiny the suspect classifications of race, alienage, and national origin, and infringements of fundamental rights such as the right to vote. It subjected to middle-tier scrutiny the quasi-suspect classifications of gender and illegitimacy.

The Court gave four reasons why the mentally retarded were not a quasi-suspect class entitled to heightened scrutiny. First, the disabilities of the mentally retarded were both real and diverse, requiring carefully tailored legislative assistance informed by professional advice. Second, the legislative response to the needs of the mentally retarded "belies a continuing antipathy or prejudice and a corresponding need for more intrusive oversight by the judiciary."[43] Subjecting these laws to heightened judicial scrutiny could deter legislation benefitting the mentally retarded. Third, this legislative response demonstrated that the mentally retarded were not politically powerless. Finally,

> [i]f the large and amorphous class of the mentally retarded were deemed quasi- suspect . . . it would be difficult to find a principled way to distinguish a variety of other groups who have perhaps immutable disabilities setting them off from others, who cannot themselves mandate the desired legislative responses, and who can claim some degree of prejudice from at least part of the public at large.[44]

Despite holding that mentally retarded individuals were not a quasi-suspect class, the Court struck down the challenged law because it did not pass the rationality test. First, the City allowed other multiple occupancy dwellings, such as nursing homes and fraternity houses, without requiring a special use permit. Consequently, prohibiting a group home for the retarded would have to "threaten legitimate interests of the City in a way that other permitted uses such as boarding homes and hospitals would not."[45] The City offered no rational basis for believing that the group home for the mentally retarded at issue posed a special threat. The City offered five reasons for requiring a special use permit for the home. First, owners of the surrounding property would react negatively to having a group home for the retarded nearby. The Court held that "mere negative attitudes, or fear, unsubstantiated by factors which are properly cognizable in a zoning proceeding"[46] constituted an insufficient basis for treating homes for the retarded differently from other group homes.

Second, the City claimed that students of a nearby junior high school might harass the residents. In rejecting this rationale, the Court noted that the school itself was attended by approximately 30 mentally retarded students. Third, the City argued that the home should not be located where proposed because it was in a flood

---

[42] *Id.* at 439–42. Justice White helpfully reviewed the analytical framework of the Court's equal protection jurisprudence.

[43] *Id.* at 443.

[44] *Id.* at 445–46. The Court listed the aging, disabled, infirm, and mentally ill as examples of other groups which might also deserve quasi-suspect class protection if the mentally retarded received it.

[45] *Id.* at 448.

[46] *Id.* at 448.

plain. The Court noted that this factor should also apply to nursing homes in the location, but they did not need special use permits.

Fourth, the City was concerned about the legal responsibility for actions of the residents. However, the City was not similarly concerned about its liability for permitted uses, such as a fraternity house, that would present similar hazards. Fifth, the City voiced concern over the number of people who would occupy the home. However, they did not show why it was rational to impose a density regulation on homes for the mentally retarded but not on other group homes. Moreover, the proposed home met all Federal and state standards for group housing.

Denying the special use permit at issue rested "on an irrational prejudice against the mentally retarded."[47] Accordingly, the Court invalidated the ordinance as applied to the proposed home.[48]

Concurring, Justice Stevens attacked the Court's analytical framework for equal protection cases. He maintained that the various cases "reflect a continuum of judgmental responses to differing classifications."[49] He argued for a rational basis test that examined three questions: "What class is harmed by the legislation, and has it been subjected to a 'tradition of disfavor' by our laws? What is the public purpose that is being served by the law? What is the characteristic of the disadvantaged class that justifies the disparate treatment?"[50] Justice Stevens claimed that the answers to these questions would determine whether or not the legislation had a rational basis. He argued that this test would result in the "virtually automatic invalidation of racial classifications,"[51] while leaving most economic legislation intact. Cases involving classifications based on gender and alienage would have varying results. These differing results would not be the product of a middle-tier standard of review, but rather of the fact that the characteristics of these groups were sometimes relevant to legislative choices.

Like Justice Stevens' concurrence in *Cleburne*, Justice Marshall's dissent in *Murgia*[52] also charged that two-tiered equal protection analysis was simplistic.[53] He claimed that the Court really engaged in a more sophisticated analysis, focusing on "the character of the classification in question, the relative importance to individuals in the class discriminated against of the governmental benefits that they

---

[47] *Id.* at 450.

[48] In *Heller v. Doe*, 509 U.S. 312 (1993), the Court upheld, against an equal protection challenge, Kentucky's system of applying a lesser standard for the involuntary commitment of mentally retarded people than that required for the mentally ill.

[49] *Cleburne*, 473 U.S. at 451.

[50] *Id.* at 453.

[51] *Id.*

[52] Mass. Bd. of Retirement v. Murgia, 427 U.S. 307 (1976). *See supra* § 12.01[3]. Justice Stevens did not participate in *Murgia*.

[53] Justice Marshall's *Murgia* dissent focused on the two-tiered equal protection analysis that was still dominant at that time. He had expressed similar dissatisfaction with the Court's "rigidified approach to equal protection analysis" in *San Antonio School District v. Rodriguez*, 411 U.S. 1 (1973) (Marshall, J., dissenting).

do not receive, and the state interests asserted in support of the classification."[54] Justice Marshall viewed the Court's reluctance to find new suspect classes and fundamental rights as a natural result of its verbal adherence to the rigid tiered analysis. Classifications receiving strict scrutiny were virtually always invalidated. Accordingly, the Court was reluctant to expand strict scrutiny to new categories because such an expansion "involves the invalidation of virtually every classification bearing upon a newly covered category."[55]

Justice Marshall also disagreed with the majority's analysis in *Cleburne*.[56] Although he agreed that the ordinance was invalid, Justice Marshall would have declared it facially so. Additionally, Justice Marshall attacked the majority for refusing to admit that a higher level of scrutiny had been given to this ordinance. He claimed that the ordinance surely would have survived traditional rational basis review; therefore, the majority must have applied a new form of the rationality test. Justice Marshall referred to this as " 'second order' rational basis review."[57] Justice Marshall saw two dangers in the majority's failure to admit its new approach. First, it invited lower courts to apply the same "searching inquiry" of economic legislation, a "regrettable step back toward the days of *Lochner v. New York*."[58] Second, the Court failed to give guidance to the lower courts as to when and how second order rational basis review should be applied, leaving lower courts rudderless.

[5] Sexual Orientation

In *Romer v. Evans*,[59] the Court struck down Colorado constitutional Amendment 2 that precluded all laws prohibiting "discrimination on the basis of 'homosexual, lesbian or bisexual orientation, conduct, practices or relationships.' "[60] Writing for a 6-3 majority, Justice Kennedy stated that the Constitution demands neutrality in the law and bans " 'classes among citizens.' "[61]

Amendment 2 not only repealed existing local ordinances prohibiting discrimination against homosexual persons but also prohibited all future "legislative, executive or judicial action at any level of state or local government designed to protect"[62] these individuals. Rejecting Colorado's argument that Amendment 2 simply put homosexuals in the same position as all other persons, the Court stated that Amendment 2 placed homosexuals in a class by themselves, depriving only them of protection against discrimination.

---

[54] *Murgia*, 427 U.S. at 318.

[55] *Id.* at 319 (footnote omitted).

[56] *See Cleburne*, 473 U.S. at 455 (Marshall, J., concurring in part and dissenting in part). Justices Brennan and Blackmun joined his opinion.

[57] *Id.* at 458.

[58] *Id.* at 460. *See supra* § 8.05[1] for a discussion of *Lochner*.

[59] 517 U.S. 620 (1996).

[60] *Id.* at 624.

[61] Plessy v. Ferguson, 163 U.S. 537, 559 (1896).

[62] *Romer*, 517 U.S. at 624.

Moreover, the broad language of Amendment 2 suggested that it may not be limited to laws passed specifically to protect gays and lesbians, but it could also extend to broader laws, generally arbitrary decisions or discrimination in, for example, insurance or government employment.

As "most legislation classifies for one purpose or another,"[63] a law will pass equal protection scrutiny if it bears a rational relationship to a legitimate state end, and it "neither burdens a fundamental right nor targets a suspect class."[64] However, "Amendment 2 fails, indeed defies, even this conventional inquiry."[65] First, it imposes "a broad and undifferentiated disability on a single group."[66] Second, the reasons given for the amendment are so removed from its overall reach that it seems based only on animosity toward homosexuals and therefore has no "rational relationship to legitimate state interests."[67] A law such as Amendment 2 that declared "that in general it shall be more difficult for one group of citizens than for all others to seek aid from the government is itself a denial of equal protection of the laws in the most literal sense."[68] Citing *Department of Agriculture v. Moreno*,[69] equal protection had to mean " 'that a bare . . . desire to harm a politically unpopular group cannot constitute a legitimate governmental interest.' "[70]

The majority rejected the state's rationale that Amendment 2 protects the right of freedom of association of other Colorado citizens, particularly landlords and employers. The State's interest in conserving its legal resources to fight discrimination against other groups also did not justify Amendment 2. The illegitimate end underlying this "status-based enactment" was to make homosexuals "unequal to everyone else."[71] Colorado could not "so deem a class of persons a stranger to its laws."[72]

In his dissent, Justice Scalia, joined by Chief Justice Rehnquist and Justice Thomas, characterized Amendment 2 as a "rather modest attempt by seemingly tolerant Coloradans to preserve traditional sexual mores against the efforts of a politically powerful minority to revise those mores through use of the laws."[73] He maintained that the majority's holding contradicted *Bowers v. Hardwick*[74] and equated opposition to homosexuality to racial or religious bias. The Constitution does not address this issue, leaving its resolution to the democratic process. As *Bowers* allowed states to criminalize homosexual conduct, states can also enact

---

[63] *Id.* at 631.

[64] *Id.*

[65] *Id.* at 632.

[66] *Id.*

[67] *Id.*

[68] *Id.* at 633.

[69] 413 U.S. 528, 534 (1973).

[70] *Romer*, 517 U.S. at 634.

[71] *Id.* at 635.

[72] *Id.*

[73] *Id.*

[74] *See supra* § 8.04.

laws "merely disfavoring homosexual conduct."[75]

Amendment 2 only prohibited special treatment of gays and lesbians. Homosexual employees still enjoyed the same benefits received by other nonhomosexual employees, such as pensions required by state law to be paid to all state employees. Amendment 2 "would prevent the State or any municipality from making death-benefit payments to the 'life partner' of a homosexual when it does not make such payments to the long-time roommate of a nonhomosexual employee."[76] Moreover, the majority reasoned that a particular group was denied equal protection when, to obtain advantage or to avoid disadvantage, "it must have recourse to a more general and hence more difficult level of political decision-making than others."[77]

Even if the "homosexual 'orientation' "[78] provision of Amendment 2 were invalid, a facial challenge to Amendment 2 would still fail. While a facial challenge had to establish that the Act was invalid under all circumstances, *Bowers* allowed Amendment 2 to be constitutionally "applied to those who engage in homosexual conduct."[79] Eminently reasonable, Amendment 2 "is designed to prevent piecemeal deterioration of the sexual morality favored by a majority of Coloradans."[80] Invalidating it "is an act, not of judicial judgment, but of political will."[81]

Since *Romer*, the Court has decided *Texas v. Lawrence*,[82] which offered greater protection for homosexual relationships under the Due Process Clause.[83]

§ 12.02   EQUAL PROTECTION FOR THE POOR

[1]   Wealth as a Suspect Classification; Fundamental Rights to Necessities

As the introductory note to this Chapter indicated, the Court has not regarded the poor as a discrete and insular minority. Accordingly, laws differentiating based on wealth are not subject to heightened scrutiny. Affording heightened scrutiny to laws that distinguish on the basis of wealth would call into question a wide range of social programs.[84] However, regulations affecting the poor sometimes also involve the fundamental rights strand of equal protection. This section examines the Court's response to the discrete and insular minority arguments and fundamental rights arguments raised by the poor.

---

[75] *Romer*, 517 U.S. at 641.

[76] *Id.* at 638.

[77] *Id.* at 639.

[78] *Id.* at 642.

[79] *Id.* at 643.

[80] *Id.* at 653.

[81] *Id.*

[82] 539 U.S. 558 (2003).

[83] For further discussion of *Lawrence, see supra* § 8.06[3].

[84] *See infra* § 12.05.

One of the most important areas in which the Court has examined the equal protection rights of the poor is public education. In *San Antonio Independent School District v. Rodriguez*,[85] the Court examined the method of funding public schools in Texas. Texas used a complex system of funding in which school districts paid into a state fund based primarily on assessed property values. The districts then received allotments from the fund that they were free to supplement with additional local property taxes and federal aid. The Court examined the funding of the Edgewood Independent School District and the Alamo Heights Independent School District, the poorest and richest districts respectively. Edgewood received $222 per pupil from the state fund, $108 per pupil in federal funds, and contributed an additional $26 per pupil from local taxes, for a total of $356 per pupil. The same numbers for the Alamo Heights district were $225, $36, and $333, respectively, for a total of $594 per pupil.

The lower court had subjected the funding system to strict scrutiny, finding that wealth was a suspect classification and that education was a fundamental right. The Supreme Court rejected both conclusions. The Court identified three ways in which the funding system could be thought to discriminate. First, it could discriminate against " 'poor' persons whose incomes fell below some identifiable level."[86] Second, the system could discriminate against "those who are relatively poorer than others."[87] Finally, it could discriminate against people who lived in relatively poor school districts, regardless of income.

Justice Powell's majority opinion determined that the people discriminated against in the Court's precedents shared two characteristics: "because of their impecunity they were completely unable to pay for some desired benefit, and as a consequence, they sustained an absolute deprivation of a meaningful opportunity to enjoy that benefit."[88] The Court found that none of the possible theories of discrimination contained the two elements. First, there was no showing that the funding system discriminated against a definable class of "poor" people.[89] Second, even if such a class could be defined, its members were not completely deprived of educational opportunities.[90] The Court refused "to extend its most exacting scrutiny to review a system that allegedly discriminates against a large, diverse, and amorphous class, unified only by the common factor of residence in districts that happen to have less taxable wealth than other districts."[91]

---

[85] 411 U.S. 1 (1973).

[86] *Id.* at 19.

[87] *Id.*

[88] *Id.* at 20. *Cf.* Plyler v. Doe, 457 U.S. 202 (1982), which later invalidated a Texas statute that completely denied free public education to children who were illegal aliens.

[89] There was "no basis on the record in this case for assuming that the poorest people — defined by reference to any level of absolute impecunity — are concentrated in the poorest districts." *Rodriguez*, 411 U.S. at 23.

[90] The absolute deprivation case could be presented if, for example, the state deprived poor people of an education if they did not pay tuition. In contrast, in this case, the state actually made a financial contribution to provide the poor with a minimal level of education.

[91] *Rodriguez*, 411 U.S. at 28. "The system of alleged discrimination and the class it defines have none of the traditional indicia of suspectness: the class is not saddled with such disabilities, or subjected to such a history of purposeful unequal treatment, or relegated to such a position of political powerlessness

Having rejected the suspect class argument, Justice Powell turned to the issue of fundamental rights. The Court stated that it was not the importance of the service performed by the state that determined whether or not it was fundamental. The Court did not sit as a super-legislature creating fundamental rights. To determine which rights were fundamental, the Court asked whether it was "explicitly or implicitly guaranteed by the Constitution."[92] the Constitution did not explicitly protect education. The Court refused to hold education implicitly protected as essential to exercising other constitutional rights, such as speaking and voting. First, although a fully informed citizenry would be better equipped to exercise free speech and voting rights, it was not the Court's job to implement such values by "intrusion into otherwise legitimate state activities."[93] Second, even if some level of education was protected as necessary to meaningfully exercise other constitutional rights, there was no showing that the Texas system failed to provide that level of education. Because the Texas funding system did not affect a suspect class or involve a fundamental right, the Court did not apply strict scrutiny. the system satisfied the required rational basis test.

Justice White, joined by Justices Douglas and Brennan, dissented. Justice White claimed that the funding system was not rationally related to its purpose of increasing local initiative and choice by allowing school districts with low tax bases to fund education using property taxes. Moreover, the appellees constituted a sufficiently identifiable class.

Justice Marshall, joined by Justice Douglas, also dissented. Justice Marshall reiterated his dislike of the tiered approach to equal protection scrutiny. Instead, he adopted appellee's nexus standard: The more essential an activity was to exercising specific constitutional rights, the more protection it should receive. This approach offered education considerable protection because of its nexus to free speech. Moreover, while the Court had not treated the poor as a suspect class, the invidiousness of wealth as a classification varied with the good being distributed. Distributing the fundamental right of education based on wealth was invidious and did not survive strict scrutiny.[94]

The *Rodriguez* Court saw many difficulties with applying strict scrutiny to educational funding. Equality in education could not be precisely determined, and therefore could only be implemented in the most relative sense. The Court also feared that accepting appellee's fundamental rights argument would require it to find many additional fundamental rights. For example, those who lack adequate food and clothing may be the least effective at utilizing their free speech and voting rights, requiring food and clothing to be recognized as fundamental. The *Rodriguez* case also required expertise in taxing, spending, and educational policy, areas of legislative prerogative that defy judicially manageable standards.

---

as to command extraordinary protection from the majoritarian political process." *Id.*

[92] *Id.* at 33–34.

[93] *Id.* at 36.

[94] In his dissent, Justice Marshall described a number of financing schemes that he maintained would help to equalize education without impairing local control of education and educational funding.

Finally, in the federal system, educational policy was traditionally left to the states. Some states have held that their systems of public school financing violate provisions of their state constitutions. Some states have specific constitutional protections of education. Several commentators have remarked that judicial remedies in these state court cases have proven difficult to fashion.[95]

As previously noted, some language in *Rodriguez* and *Plyler v. Doe*[96] indicates that complete deprivation of education for lack of wealth or other reasons violates the Constitution. In *Kadrmas v. Dickinson Public Schools*,[97] the Court upheld a North Dakota program charging a busing fee as applied to parents of school children at or near the poverty level. The state authorized school boards to waive the transportation fee and did not allow students to be deprived of grades or a diploma for failure to pay.

The Court has addressed policies affecting the poor in areas other than education. In *Dandridge v. Williams*,[98] it refused to extend strict scrutiny to a Maryland law that set a maximum amount of Federal Aid to Families with Dependent Children (AFDC), regardless of family size. While the Constitution imposed certain procedural restrictions on welfare administration,[99] it did not restrict difficult determinations of how to allocate limited welfare funds. These economic and social policy determinations were scrutinized under a rationality standard.[100]

In the area of housing, the Court has upheld laws that required voter approval for low-rent public housing projects,[101] and that give lower welfare benefits to people receiving AFDC than to participants in other Federal programs.[102]

Although it is unusual, the Court occasionally has invalidated statutes on the grounds that they discriminate against the poor without a rational basis. *Department of Agriculture v. Moreno*[103] struck down a law that denied food stamps to households that included unrelated persons. The Court found that the true purpose of the statute was to prevent "hippie communes" from participating in the food stamp program. This purpose was not a legitimate government interest. Similarly, in *Department of Agriculture v. Murry*,[104] the Court invalidated a statute that denied food stamps to households that included a person under 18 who was a dependent for tax purposes, when the dependent was not living in the

---

[95] *See, e.g.*, J.W. GUTHRIE, SCHOOL FINANCE POLICIES AND PRACTICES (1980); Note, *Strategies for School Finance Reform Litigation in the Post-Rodriguez Era*, 21 NEW ENG. L. REV. 817 (1986).

[96] *See supra* § 12.01[1][b].

[97] 487 U.S. 450 (1988).

[98] 397 U.S. 471 (1970).

[99] *See supra* § 8.06.

[100] *See infra* § 12.05.

[101] James v. Valtierra, 402 U.S. 137 (1971).

[102] Jefferson v. Hackney, 406 U.S. 535 (1972).

[103] 413 U.S. 528 (1973).

[104] 413 U.S. 508 (1973).

household that claimed the deduction. However, in *Lyng v. Castillo*,[105] the Court upheld a statute that treated close relatives who lived together as a household for food stamp purposes, but treated more distant relatives living together as separate households, unless they purchased their food and prepared meals together. The Court held that close relatives were not a suspect class, and that the restriction did not substantially interfere with family arrangements, thereby burdening a fundamental right. In *Shapiro v. Thompson*,[106] the Court invalidated several state and District of Columbia statutes requiring that AFDC recipients reside in the jurisdiction for at least one year to receive benefits. The holding was not premised on poverty, however. The state failed to pass the compelling state interest test required to justify the law's infringement on the right of domestic travel.[107]

[2]   Access to the Justice System

Access to the courts, both criminal and civil, has become very expensive. On several occasions, the Court has addressed constitutional challenges to barriers erected by cost. In *Griffin v. Illinois*,[108] the Court ruled that equal protection required that indigent defendants be provided a trial transcript if necessary to perfect an appeal. In the landmark decision of *Gideon v. Wainwright*,[109] the Court held that the Sixth Amendment, applicable to the states through the Fourteenth Amendment, required states to provide trial counsel to indigent criminal defendants.

The Court extended *Griffin* and *Gideon* in *Douglas v. California*,[110] holding that the Fourteenth Amendment required states to provide counsel to indigent criminal defendants on their first appeal as a matter of right. The procedure at issue in *Douglas* allowed the appellate court to independently review the record when an indigent defendant requested counsel. The California court could deny the request only if the appointment of counsel would not assist the court or the defendant. In invalidating this program, Justice Douglas stated that defendant's right to counsel in an appeal as a matter of right should not hinge on defendant's wealth.[111]

Justice Harlan, joined by Justice Stewart, dissented in *Douglas*. Justice Harlan noted that the Court's holding appeared to rely on both the Equal Protection and Due Process Clauses. Because California did not deny the poor a right to appeal, the procedure did not violate the Equal Protection Clause. Because the procedure was fair, it did not violate the Due Process Clause.

In *Ross v. Moffitt*,[112] the Court refused to extend *Douglas* to discretionary appeals to the North Carolina Supreme Court or to applications for review by the

---

[105] 477 U.S. 635 (1986).

[106] 394 U.S. 618 (1969).

[107] For further discussion of *Shapiro, see infra* § 12.04[1].

[108] 351 U.S. 12 (1956).

[109] 372 U.S. 335 (1963).

[110] 372 U.S. 353 (1963).

[111] *Id.* at 355.

[112] 417 U.S. 600 (1974).

United States Supreme Court. Writing for the majority, Justice Rehnquist found that neither equal protection nor due process required a state to provide counsel to indigent criminal defendants on discretionary appeal. Trial counsel was a "shield" against the state; appellate counsel was a "sword" used to overturn a prior determination of guilt.[113] Moreover, it was not unfair for the state to refuse to provide counsel when it was not obligated to provide an appeal in the first place. As required by *Douglas*, North Carolina furnished counsel to indigent criminal defendants before the state Court of Appeals. The North Carolina and United States Supreme Courts granted review based on the public policy significance of the questions presented, not on whether the decision below was incorrect. Both courts had sufficient information without counsel to make the review determination, including the trial record, the brief prepared by counsel for the first appeal, and the opinion of the first appellate court.

In *Evitts v. Lucey*,[114] the Court held that the Fourteenth Amendment required "effective assistance of counsel"[115] on the first appeal as a matter of right. This meant that counsel "must play the role of an active advocate, rather than a mere friend of the court."[116] As *Douglas* rested on due process and equal protection grounds, it pertained to indigent and non-indigent defendants. Similarly, the right to effective counsel on appeal applied whether counsel was appointed or retained.

Pennsylvania v. Finley[117] held that indigent criminal defendants were not entitled to appointed counsel in a post-conviction proceeding. *Finley* involved a challenge to a state law that allowed court-appointed counsel in post-conviction proceedings to move to withdraw from a frivolous case, at which time the court would investigate the request and rule on the motion. Since *Ross* did not require counsel in a discretionary appeal, *a fortiori* the Constitution did not require appointment of counsel after exhaustion of the appellate process. Moreover, *Evitts* did not pertain if a state created a right to counsel when the Federal Constitution did not require one; such counsel was not governed by Federal constitutional standards.

Indigent criminal defendants have rights beyond free legal counsel. In *Ake v. Oklahoma*,[118] the Court held that a defendant had a right to an examination by and the assistance of a psychiatrist in some situations. Ake had been charged with murdering a couple and wounding their two children. His behavior at arraignment prompted the judge *sua sponte* to order a psychiatric evaluation. The psychiatrist recommended a long period of observation to determine whether or not Ake was competent to stand trial. The mental hospital first determined that he was not competent to stand trial, but later, the chief psychiatrist determined that he was.[119]

---

[113] *Id.* at 610–11.

[114] 469 U.S. 387 (1985).

[115] *Id.* at 389.

[116] *Id.* at 394.

[117] 481 U.S. 551 (1987).

[118] 470 U.S. 68 (1985).

[119] At this time, Ake was taking an anti-psychotic drug three times a day.

Ake's attorney asserted a constitutional right to a court-appointed psychiatrist to determine Ake's mental state at the time of the crime. Ake could not afford to retain a psychiatrist to testify on his behalf. The trial court rejected the request. On the insanity defense, the trial court instructed the jury that Ake was to be presumed sane and that he had the burden of producing evidence that raised a reasonable doubt as to his sanity at the time of the crime. Ake was convicted on all counts.

The Court emphasized that the consistent theme of the counsel cases discussed above was that indigent defendants must have " 'an adequate opportunity to present their claims fairly' "[120] which required the provision of certain "basic tools."[121] Three factors were relevant in determining whether a particular safeguard was a basic tool: (1) the private interest affected; (2) the governmental interest affected; and (3) the probable value of the additional safeguards and "the risk of the erroneous deprivation of the affected interest if those safeguards are not provided."[122]

In applying these factors, the Court found that the private interest in the accuracy of the proceedings with defendant's life or liberty at stake was "uniquely compelling."[123] The government's asserted interest in saving money was unsubstantiated in light of the government's and defendant's interest in accurate disposition. The Federal government and over 40 states provided psychiatrists for indigent criminal defendants, recognizing that a psychiatrist was crucial to preparing testimony and cross examination to establish the insanity defense. Reversing the decision below, the Court held "that when a defendant demonstrates to the trial judge that his sanity at the time of the offense is to be a significant factor at trial, the State must, at a minimum, assure the defendant access to a competent psychiatrist who will conduct an appropriate examination and assist in evaluation, preparation, and presentation of the defense."[124] The right was only to a "competent Psychiatrist" and not to one whom defendant personally chose or hired. The Court's holding also applied to the sentencing phase of a capital crime when the state introduced evidence of future dangerous propensities of the convicted criminal.

Chief Justice Burger concurred, noting his view that *Ake* applied only to capital cases. Dissenting, Justice Rehnquist would require a higher showing than the majority to have a court-appointed psychiatrist. In any event, a right to a psychiatrist, should not extend to assistance in the preparation and presentation of the defense as required by the majority but only to a competent opinion "from a psychiatrist who acts independently of the prosecutor's office."[125] In his view, a psychiatrist was not an advocate.

---

[120] *Ake*, 470 U.S. at 77 (quoting *Ross v. Moffitt*, 417 U.S. 600, 612 (1974)).

[121] *Id.* (quoting *Britt v. North Carolina*, 404 U.S. 226, 227 (1971)).

[122] *Id.*

[123] *Id.*

[124] *Id.* at 83.

[125] *Id.*

The Court has also examined the relationship between wealth and sentencing. In *Bearden v. Georgia*,[126] a unanimous Court struck down a Georgia procedure that revoked petitioner's probation and imprisoned him for the remainder of the probationary period when he was unable to pay a fine in restitution for a theft. Relying on the Due Process and Equal Protection Clause, Justice O'Connor avoided tiered analysis. She considered the defendant's interests, the extent to which the state's actions affected those interests, the "rationality of the connection between legislative means and purposes,"[127] and the existence of alternative means for achieving the state's purposes. The *Bearden* Court found that imprisonment did not further the state's interest in restitution and rehabilitation when the person had made a good faith effort to find a job and pay the fine. The Court also rejected the State's claim that imprisonment was an effective form of punishment for failure to pay the fine. Other methods of punishment and deterrence existed, such as fines with more time to pay or community service requirements. The majority held that imprisonment was permissible only if "the Georgia courts determine that petitioner did not make sufficient bona fide efforts to pay his fine, or determine that alternate punishment is not adequate to meet the State's interest in punishment and deterrence."[128]

Justice White wrote a concurring opinion that was joined by three other Justices. These Justices would allow the court to revoke probation and impose a jail sentence "that in terms of the state's sentencing objectives will be roughly equivalent to the fine and restitution that the defendant failed to pay."[129] Because the lower courts did not make such a determination, the four Justices concurred in the result reached by the majority.

The Court had reached results similar to *Bearden* in *Williams v. Illinois*[130] and *Tate v. Short*.[131] *Williams* struck an Illinois law that required an indigent person sentenced to both a fine and imprisonment to "work off" the fine he was unable to pay by spending an extra 101 days in jail. *Tate* struck down a Texas law that converted a fine into a prison sentence for inability to pay. The constitutional infirmity in these cases, as in *Bearden*, was that the state could not impose a prison sentence because of inability, rather than unwillingness, to pay.

The Court also has addressed claims by the poor of denial of judicial access in civil cases. *Boddie v. Connecticut*[132] held that a state could not condition access to the courts, for the purpose of obtaining a divorce decree, on a person's ability to pay costs and fees. In *United States v. Kras*,[133] the Court refused to extend its holding in *Boddie* to bankruptcy court. Justice Blackmun's 5-4 majority opinion distinguished *Boddie* on the grounds that the state had a monopoly on the means

---

[126] 461 U.S. 660 (1983).

[127] *Id.* at 667.

[128] *Id.* at 674.

[129] *Id.* at 675.

[130] 399 U.S. 235 (1970).

[131] 401 U.S. 395 (1971).

[132] 401 U.S. 371 (1971).

[133] 409 U.S. 434 (1973).

for obtaining a legal divorce, and that failure to obtain a divorce interfered with the ability to pursue other fundamental associational rights. In contrast, failure to achieve a discharge in bankruptcy did not interfere with fundamental rights.

Additionally, other means, such as negotiation, were available to resolve the conflict. Because court fees in bankruptcy cases involved neither a suspect classification nor a fundamental right, the fee imposed in this case only had to meet a rational basis test. The Court found that the fee was rationally related to the goal of making the bankruptcy system self-sustaining. In *Ortwein v. Schwab*,[134] a 5-4 majority upheld a $25 filing fee imposed by Oregon as a condition for judicial review of a denial of welfare benefits.

In *Little v. Streater*,[135] the Court struck down a Connecticut statute that required a party in a paternity suit requesting blood grouping tests to bear the costs of the test. Under Connecticut law, the mother's testimony made out a *prima facie* case against the putative father, requiring him to produce evidence beyond his own testimony. The statute violated due process because state law created a heavy evidentiary imbalance and then effectively foreclosed an indigent from obtaining potential conclusive proof of non-paternity. The Court noted in a footnote that the State provided the only forum for resolving the dispute, and that the interests of the alleged father and child were both constitutionally significant. Accordingly, the case was more like *Boddie*, than *Kras* or *Ortwein*.

In *M.L.B. v. S.L.J.*,[136] the Court held that inability to pay an appeals fee may not prevent appellate review of a parental termination decree. The mother was unable to pay record preparation fees approximating $2,352.36. The state denied her leave to appeal *in forma pauperis*. The Court (6-3) stated that equal protection required waiving court fees in civil cases only when the case involved a fundamental right. For example, the Court had upheld fees required for a discharge in bankruptcy and an appeal of the denial of welfare benefits. However, as choices about marriage, family life, and the upbringing of children comprised fundamental rights involving due process and equal protection concerns, an appeal of a parental termination should be treated like an appeal of a petty criminal offense. Since parental status termination severed the parent-child bond and irrevocably destroyed the family relationship, a parent should have the opportunity to appeal to avoid its devastating effects. This adverse action contrasted sharply with cases where litigants sought state aid "to subsidize their privately initiated action"[137] as in bankruptcy, or "to alleviate the consequences of differences in economic circumstances that existed apart from state action"[138] as in denial of welfare benefits.

---

[134] 410 U.S. 656 (1973).

[135] 452 U.S. 1, 6–7 (1981).

[136] 519 U.S. 102 (1996).

[137] *Id.* at 124.

[138] *Id.*

§ 12.03   EQUALITY IN THE POLITICAL PROCESS

[1]   Distinctions Based on Wealth

The centrality of voting rights in a democracy makes it essential that arbitrary restrictions not be allowed. Accordingly, the Court has given strict scrutiny to laws that make it difficult to exercise voting rights or dilute the value of a vote. The Court has also reviewed laws that restrict minority party access to the ballot.

In *Harper v. Virginia State Board of Elections*,[139] the Court invoked equal protection to invalidate a law requiring voters to pay a $1.50 poll tax as a prerequisite for voting in state elections. Justice Douglas' majority opinion found that voting was a fundamental right because it preserved other basic civil and political rights. Rather than addressing the source of the right to vote, Justice Douglas stated that "once the franchise is granted to the electorate, lines may not be drawn which are inconsistent with the Equal Protection Clause of the Fourteenth Amendment."[140] Applying strict scrutiny, the Court found that the poll tax did not further the state's asserted interest in encouraging citizens to vote intelligently. "To introduce wealth or payment of a fee as a measure of a voter's qualifications is to introduce a capricious or irrelevant factor. The degree of discrimination is irrelevant."[141]

Justice Black dissented, arguing that the poll tax should be abolished by an act of Congress under Section 5 of the Fourteenth Amendment or by a constitutional amendment. The Twenty-Fourth Amendment only enforced a person's right to vote without paying a poll tax in federal elections. Also dissenting, Justice Harlan claimed that a rational basis test should be used, because the classification in question did not involve race.

The Court has also invalidated restrictions on the right to vote based on property ownership. In *Kramer v. Union Free School District*,[142] the Court invalidated a New York statute that restricted voting rights in school district elections to those who were otherwise qualified to vote and were: (1) owners or lessors of real taxable property in the district; (2) spouses of qualified property owners; or (3) parents or guardians of a child enrolled in the school district during the previous year. New York maintained that the statute limited the right to vote to those who were primarily interested in school affairs. The Court noted that the state was "denying some citizens any effective voice in the governmental affairs which substantially affect their lives."[143] Statutes that grant the right to vote to some citizens of requisite age and deny it to others must be justified by a compelling state interest. Chief Justice Warren rejected the claim that strict scrutiny was inappropriate because the school board did not have general legislative powers.

---

[139] 383 U.S. 663 (1966).

[140] *Id.* at 665.

[141] *Id.* at 668.

[142] 395 U.S. 621 (1969).

[143] *Id.* at 627.

In applying this standard, the Court did not decide whether the state had a legitimate interest in limiting the vote to those primarily interested in or affected by a particular governmental unit. However, the New York requirement was not narrowly tailored because it gave the right to vote to people with little interest in the outcome (*i.e.*, an unemployed, uninterested lessee who paid taxes) and denied it to some with a strong interest in the results (*i.e.*, an interested, employed person who paid taxes but lived with his parents).

Justice Stewart dissented, joined by Justices Black and Harlan. He would have applied a rational basis test. Justice Stewart argued that states had broad powers to regulate voting unless the regulation disadvantaged a suspect class or violated a fundamental right.

Although personal wealth could not be a factor in granting the right to vote for governments that exercised general governmental powers, it could be considered for some local governments that did not. *Salyer Land Co. v. Tulare Lake Basin Water Storage District*[144] upheld a statute that apportioned votes based on the value of the voter's property. The statute allowed only landowners to vote for the directors of the Tulare Water Storage District. The water district made and executed projects that addressed local water problems associated with farming; the costs for each property owner were based on the benefit to his respective piece of land. Each property owner had one vote for each $100 of assessed property value. As a result, some owners did not have any votes, and one corporate owner had 37,825 votes.

Justice Rehnquist's majority opinion held that the law did not violate the principle of one-person-one-vote, established for legislative bodies in *Reynolds v. Sims*[145] and extended to school board elections in *Kramer*. Justice Rehnquist distinguished these cases on the grounds that legislatures and school boards provided general public services and benefits, whereas the decisions of the water district affected only the landowners. The district existed "to provide for the acquisition, storage, and distribution of water for farming in the Tulare Lake Basin. It provides no other general public services such as schools, housing, transportation, utilities, roads, or anything else of the type ordinarily financed by a municipal body . . . There are no towns, shops, hospitals, or other facilities designed to improve the quality of life within the district boundaries, and it does not have a fire department, police, buses or trains."[146] The district did not exercise "what might be thought of as 'normal governmental authority' "[147] and it assessed costs in proportion to benefits received. That the costs were assessed only against landowners provided a rational basis for excluding non-landowners from the vote. Moreover, because the activities of the water district disproportionately affected landowners, the distribution of votes according to land value was also rationally based. For example, the landowner with 37,825 votes also had to pay $817,685 of a

---

[144] 410 U.S. 719 (1973).

[145] 377 U.S. 533 (1964).

[146] *Id.* at 728–29.

[147] *Id.* at 729.

$2,500,000 project.[148]

Justice Douglas dissented, joined by Justices Brennan and Marshall. Justice Douglas would have applied strict scrutiny. The district's actions in such areas as irrigation, water storage, and flood control affected all residents including non-landowners. The water district exercises general governmental power in such areas as irrigation, water storage, and flood control that affected all residents including non-landowners. He also argued that various characteristics of the water districts (*i.e.*, eminent domain and governmental immunity) indicated that the districts possessed general governmental powers that would require application of the one-person-one-vote rule. Finally, Justice Douglas objected to allowing corporations to vote.

However, in *Quinn v. Millsap*,[149] the Court held equal protection violated by a state-created board that predicated membership on ownership of real property, even though the board possessed only limited recommendatory powers.

[2]   Other Barriers to Political Participation: Apportionment, Ballot Access for Minority Parties, Gerrymandering

One of the landmark cases of the Warren Court was *Reynolds v. Sims*,[150] which established the rule of one-person-one-vote. In *Reynolds*, the plaintiffs challenged Alabama's apportionment of the state legislature. Alabama had not reapportioned its legislature since 1900, despite the fact that the state constitution required reapportionment every ten years. As a result, 25.1 percent of the population could elect a majority of the state senate, and 25.7 percent of the population could elect a majority of the state house. Population varied up to 41 to 1 in Senate districts and up to 16 to 1 in House districts.

The state legislature adopted two plans to correct this imbalance. The first, known as the "67-Senator Amendment," gave each of the 67 counties one representative and one senator. Additionally, another 39 representatives would be allotted according to population. This proposed constitutional amendment was to be submitted to Alabama voters in the 1962 general election and would be in effect until a new apportionment could be made using the 1970 census.

The second plan, known as the "Crawford-Webb Act," was enacted as an alternative to the 67-Senator Amendment, if the voters or federal courts rejected the latter Amendment. Under this statutory alternative, the Senate would consist of 35 senators, apportioned along county lines. The House would have 106 members. Each county would have one member, and the remaining 39 members would be distributed on a rough population basis, using a formula that required increasingly more population for a county to receive additional member seats.

---

[148] *Id.* at 733–34.

[149] 491 U.S. 95 (1989).

[150] 377 U.S. 533 (1964).

The Supreme Court invalidated the existing apportionment of the Alabama legislature and both of the proposed alternatives. Tracing a long history of cases in the voting rights area, the Court stated that "the Constitution of the United States protects the right of all qualified citizens to vote, in state as well as federal elections."[151] The Court had previously held that a state could not establish districts that diluted a person's vote for members of the United States House of Representatives[152] or in state-wide primary elections.[153] The Court now extended the one-person-one-vote standard to state legislatures.

The right to vote was fundamental and restrictions on it had to be "meticulously scrutinized."[154] Vote dilution based on residence was just as invidious as discrimination based on race. Chief Justice Warren held that "seats in both houses of a bicameral state legislature must be apportioned on a population basis."[155] Because neither the current system nor the two alternatives were apportioned on the basis of population, the Court invalidated all three. It rejected the "federal model" of giving a set number of senators per county, finding this model uniquely justified by our system of federalism. the model was the result of "compromise and concession indispensable to the establishment of our federal republic"[156] from a group of formerly independent states. While the Constitution did not require "mathematical nicety," the best of the three alternatives, the 67-Senator plan, had population variance ratios of nearly 5 to 1.

The Court recognized the "practical impossibility" in attaining exact equality in population across districts. It found that states could attempt to take into account historical voting lines and political subdivisions, so as to prevent widespread partisan gerrymandering. Some states may prefer single-member districts while others may prefer multi-member districts. It also recognized that there may be a rational basis for some deviation from strict populational representation in one or both houses of a bicameral legislature. History alone, geography alone, or economic or other group interests were not permissible factors. Modern transportation and communications rendered improbable most claims that geographic considerations justify "deviations from population-based representation."[157] More important was "insuring some voice to political subdivisions, as political subdivisions."[158] The paramount "objective must be substantial equality of population among the various districts, so that the vote of any citizen is approximately equal in weight to that of any other citizen in the State."[159]

---

[151] *Id.* at 554.

[152] Wesberry v. Sanders, 376 U.S. 1 (1964).

[153] Gray v. Sanders, 372 U.S. 368 (1963).

[154] *Reynolds*, 377 U.S. at 562.

[155] *Id.* at 568.

[156] *Id.* at 574.

[157] *Id.* at 580.

[158] *Id.* at 580.

[159] *Id.* at 579. In fashioning remedies in other cases, the Court recognized that district courts may find it necessary to allow imminent, impending elections to take place under an unconstitutional apportionment plan. In making this determination, it "should consider the proximity of a forthcoming

In his dissent, Justice Harlan argued that the Court completely ignored Section 2 of the Fourteenth Amendment, which reduced a state's representation in the United States House of Representatives if the state denied or abridged a qualified citizen's right to vote. Justice Harlan examined the history of the amendment and concluded that it was not intended to limit "the power of the States to apportion their legislatures as they saw fit."[160] Justice Harlan also criticized the Court's standards for implementing the decision as being unworkable and not rooted in any constitutional principle. The decision undermined our system of federalism.

Since *Reynolds*, the Court has elaborated on what constitutes a permissible deviation from the one-person-one-vote standard. It has required strict adherence to the principle in Congressional districting, but has been somewhat more lenient with state and local governments. The Court has upheld systems under which a district was over-represented by 9.6 percent[161] and a system with an 11.9 percent deviation for representation on a county governing board.[162] In *Brown v. Thomson*,[163] the Court upheld a plan under which each county received one representative in the Wyoming House of Representatives, even though the average deviation from equal apportionment was 16 percent and the maximum deviation was 89 percent. However, the decision was limited to the narrow question of whether the dilution of the plaintiff's right to vote resulting from the allotment of one representative to the State's least populous county violated equal protection. The system as a whole was not before the Court, and two members of the 5-4 majority expressed the "gravest doubts that a statewide legislative plan with an 89 percent maximum deviation could survive constitutional scrutiny."[164]

In *Abrams v. Johnson*,[165] the Court upheld a District Court's redistricting plan that appellants contended should have contained two and possibly three majority-black districts.[166] One of the reasons for this contention was that the redistricting plan violated the congressional one-person-one-vote guarantee of Article I, § 2. Court-ordered redistricting plans must attain higher levels of population equality than legislative plans. They may exhibit only a *de minimis* variation among the populations of congressional districts. The overall population deviation is the

---

election and the mechanics and complexities of state election laws, and should act and rely on general equitable principles." *Id.* at 585. In companion cases to *Reynolds*, the Court invalidated apportionment systems in five other states: *WMCA, Inc. v. Lomenzo*, 377 U.S. 633 (1964) (New York); *Lucas v. Forty-Fourth Gen. Assembly*, 377 U.S. 713 (1964) (Colorado); *Maryland Comm. for Fair Representation v. Tawes*, 377 U.S. 656 (1964) (Maryland); *Davis v. Mann*, 377 U.S. 678 (1964) (Virginia); and *Roman v. Sincock*, 377 U.S. 695 (1964) (Delaware).

[160] *Reynolds*, 377 U.S. at 595.

[161] Mahan v. Howell, 410 U.S. 315 (1973).

[162] Abate v. Mundt, 403 U.S. 182 (1971).

[163] 462 U.S. 835 (1983).

[164] *Id.* at 850. *See, e.g.*, Karcher v. Daggett, 462 U.S. 725 (1983) (invalidating plan in which the largest deviation between state legislature districts was 0.6984 percent of the average district because apportionment could have easily been made more even, and the State's justification of preserving the voting strength of racial minorities was based on "general assertions").

[165] 521 U.S. 74 (1997).

[166] For additional discussion of the aspects of the case involving alleged racial discrimination in districting, *see supra* § 9.02[4].

difference in population between the two districts with the largest disparity, and the average population deviation is the average of all districts' deviation from the one-person-one-vote rule. Terming the objections "futile,"[167] the Court noted that the District Court's plan had an overall population deviation of 0.35 percent and an average deviation of 0.11 percent.

Moreover, with the exception of Texas, Georgia had the largest number of counties, 159, in the country. Each of these small counties represented a community of interest to an unusually great degree. These myriad counties provided useful "building blocks"[168] for voting districts and needed not be divided in half. In any event, any violation of the one-person-one-vote rule should require readjusting district boundary lines rather than creating a second black-majority district. Finally, Georgia was one of the fastest growing states in the country. Consequently, equitable considerations cautioned against drawing another redistricting plan.

Board of Estimate v. Morris[169] invalidated a provision of New York City's charter, that allowed a 78 percent deviation from the one-person-one-vote requirement for electing members of the city's Board of Estimate. The Court held that the one-person-one-vote principle applied to the Board of Estimate, a governmental body with general powers impacting the entire city.[170]

In addition to the one-person-one-vote cases, the Court has examined challenges to various other restrictions on participation in the political process. The Court has invalidated statutes that require one year of state residency as a prerequisite to voting,[171] but has upheld 50-day requirements.[172] Conflicting results were obtained in two cases involving state laws that established cut-off dates requiring a certain period of party affiliation as a condition for voting in the primaries.[173] The Court has upheld disenfranchisement of convicted felons who had served their sentences.[174]

The Court has examined various state restrictions on parties seeking to be placed on the ballot. In *Williams v. Rhodes*,[175] the Court invalidated an Ohio system that required new parties to obtain more signatures than established parties in order to be included on the ballot. The system also placed different requirements on the structure of the new party and its primary system. In *Anderson v. Celebrezze*,[176] the Court struck down an Ohio statute that required early filing deadlines for presidential candidates, which particularly hurt

---

[167] *Abrams*, 521 U.S. at 100.

[168] *Id.*

[169] 489 U.S. 688 (1989).

[170] Shortly thereafter, the electorate approved a new city charter abolishing the Board of Estimate.

[171] Dunn v. Blumstein, 405 U.S. 330 (1972).

[172] Marston v. Lewis, 410 U.S. 679 (1973); Burns v. Fortson, 410 U.S. 686 (1973).

[173] *Compare* Rosario v. Rockefeller, 410 U.S. 752 (1973), *with* Kusper v. Pontikes, 414 U.S. 51 (1973).

[174] Richardson v. Ramirez, 418 U.S. 24 (1974).

[175] 393 U.S. 23 (1968).

[176] 460 U.S. 780 (1983).

candidates from third parties. The requirement violated the voters' freedom of association under the First Amendment.

In *Tashjian v. Republican Party of Connecticut*,[177] the Court (5-4) struck down a state statute that required voters in a party primary to be registered members of the party. Justice Marshall's majority opinion found the law to be an unconstitutional infringement on the First Amendment associational rights of the Republican party. The law interfered with the party's internal process for choosing its own candidates.

In *Jenness v. Fortson*,[178] the Court upheld less stringent requirements than those invalidated in prior cases for placing independent candidates on the ballot. Key differences there involved a much lower petition requirement and no necessity of formal party endorsement. The Court has also upheld a system requiring a minority party candidate to procure 1 percent of all votes cast in the primary in order to be placed on the ballot for the general election.[179] The Court, however, invalidated excessive filing fees for candidates.[180]

Restrictions on an officeholder's ability to run for another office may be enacted consistent with the Fourteenth Amendment. In *Clements v. Fashing*,[181] the Court upheld a provision of the Texas Constitution that treated the announcement of candidacy as an automatic resignation from the public office currently occupied by the candidate. The Court also upheld another Texas constitutional provision that barred certain officeholders from running for other offices until their present term expired. The 5-4 majority found that candidacy was not a fundamental right and therefore, strict scrutiny did not apply. Unless the restrictions were based on wealth or constituted undue burdens on new or small parties, a rationality standard applied.

The right to vote could also effectively be impaired by political gerrymandering. This practice involves political parties arranging political districts to their own advantage. The practice resembles the racial gerrymandering struck down in such cases as *Gomillion v. Lightfoot*,[182] but politically gerrymandered lines are designed to advantage certain political parties rather than certain racial groups. *Davis v. Bandemer*[183] addressed a challenge to an Indiana plan in which districts were of approximately equal population, but were irregularly shaped. Additionally, there were both single member and multi-member districts. The results of the first election under the new plan were that the Democrats received a much smaller percentage of seats compared to the percentage of the popular vote that they won.

---

[177] 479 U.S. 208 (1986).

[178] 403 U.S. 431 (1971). *See also* Storer v. Brown, 415 U.S. 724 (1974) *and* American Party of Texas v. White, 415 U.S. 767 (1974), both of which upheld multiple requirements on access to the ballot.

[179] Munro v. Socialist Workers Party, 479 U.S. 189 (1986).

[180] Lubin v. Panish, 415 U.S. 709 (1974) (fee of $700 based on percentage of salary in public job); Bullock v. Carter, 405 U.S. 134 (1972) (fees based on various formulae including percentage of prospective salary in public job ranged as high as $8,900).

[181] 457 U.S. 957 (1982).

[182] *See supra* § 9.02[4].

[183] 478 U.S. 109 (1986).

Writing for a majority of six, Justice White held that the Democrats' challenge to the apportionment plan was not a political question and was thus justiciable. In light of *Baker v. Carr*,[184] the majority thought that there were judicially discernible and manageable standards by which to decide political gerrymander cases. Moreover, the Constitution did not allocate such questions to a co-equal branch of government and deciding this question did not present a risk of foreign or domestic disturbance.

Only a plurality of four reached the merits. Writing for this plurality, Justice White concluded that those challenging the law had to prove both intentional discrimination against an identifiable group and discriminatory effect. Although the plurality did not take issue with the District Court's finding of discriminatory intent, showing that the percentage of Democratic winners was less than the percentage of Democratic votes did not establish discriminatory effect. The plurality noted that such outcomes were "inherent in the winner-take-all, district-based elections,"[185] and the Constitution did not require proportional representation. In an individual district, the inquiry focused on the challenger's ability to participate in party slating and nominating of candidates, and in voting. In statewide challenges, the focus was on the voters' direct influence on the election of the entire legislature. In either case, "an equal protection violation may be found only where the electoral system substantially disadvantages certain voters in their opportunity to influence that political process effectively. In this context, such a finding of unconstitutionality must be supported by evidence of continued frustration of the will of a majority of the voters or effective denial to a minority of voters of a fair chance to influence the political process."[186]

Historically, Indiana voters sometimes preferred Democrats and sometimes preferred Republicans. Moreover, there was no finding that the 1981 reapportionment had relegated the Democrats to a minority party or that they had no hope of improving their position in the 1990 census. Consequently, the District Court's findings did not sustain a cause of action.

In offering guidance on what constituted a statewide political gerrymander, the plurality also drew on multi-district racial gerrymander cases.[187] These have relied on a history of disproportionate results together with "strong indicia of lack of political power and the denial of fair representation."[188]

Chief Justice Burger concurred in the judgment, arguing that the Framers intended to leave political gerrymandering cases to correction by the political process. Justice O'Connor, joined by the Chief Justice and Justice Rehnquist, concurred in the judgment. Justice O'Connor claimed that the Equal Protection Clause guaranteed everyone an equal vote. It failed to guarantee that a group's voting strength would not be diluted. The special circumstance of racial minorities being suspect classes and having been excluded from the political process made

---

[184] *See supra* § 2.12[7].

[185] *Davis*, 478 U.S. at 130.

[186] *Id.* at 133.

[187] *See supra* § 9.02[4].

[188] *Davis*, 478 U.S. at 139.

racial gerrymandering claims justiciable. Justice O'Connor warned that claims of political gerrymandering could entangle the Court in deciding "the competing claims of political, religious, ethnic, racial, occupational, and socio-economic groups."[189]

Justice Powell, joined by Justice Stevens, concurred in the finding of justiciability but dissented from the remainder of the opinion. Justice Powell complained that the plurality failed to give lower courts and legislatures any guidance regarding how to establish a case of political gerrymandering. He listed a number of factors to establish a *prima facie* case, the most important of which was how voting districts were shaped and whether they adhered to normal political boundaries. Other factors included the legislative procedures and the history surrounding the adoption of the apportionment plan. Beyond proof concerning these facts, a *prima facie* case should present evidence of population disparities and statistical evidence of vote dilution. Justice Powell thought that the District Court's findings met these criteria.

In *Crawford v. Marion County Election Board*,[190] Justice Stevens writing for a plurality held that Indiana may require its citizens to present government-issued photo identification in order to vote in person. The statute at issue did not require such identification for voting by absentee ballot or from a resident of a "state-licensed facility such as a nursing home." Moreover, an acceptable form of identification was available to state citizens free of charge upon verification of their residence and identity. The plurality concluded that these facts did not support a facial attack on the statute.

Harper v. Virginia Board of Elections[191] had held that a state could not require its citizens to pay a poll tax of $1.50 to vote. Imposing even a nominal tax on the right to vote violated equal protection because a voter's wealth or payment of a fee became a requirement for electoral participation. In *Anderson v. Celebrezze*,[192] the Court refused to identify any one factor that would determine whether a burden was too severe. Even a seemingly minor burden, such as the tax in *Harper*, could not stand without "relevant and legitimate state interests 'sufficiently weighty to justify the limitation.' "

The plurality next analyzed four interests presented by the State to justify the burdens of the new law: modernizing state elections, discovering and preventing voter fraud, correcting voter registration lists, and promoting voter confidence. Using government-issued photo identification to modernize elections was consistent with two recent federal statutes requiring reevaluation of state electoral procedures and the National Commission on Federal Election Reform (Carter-Baker Report). The prevention of in-person voter fraud was also a valid interest, despite a lack of evidence that it had ever occurred in Indiana.

---

[189] *Id.* at 147 (O'Connor, J., concurring).

[190] 553 U.S. 181 (2008).

[191] 383 U.S. 663 (1966).

[192] 460 U.S. 780 (1983).

Under *Harper*, the statute would be invalid if voters had to pay any fee to obtain the required identification. However, most voters already had an acceptable form of identification and if not, the State provided identification free of charge. Moreover, traveling to the nearest Bureau of Motor Vehicles (BMV) did not substantially burden the right to vote.

This statute did place a heavier burden on a limited group of people. Obtaining a birth certificate, which was needed to receive a free identification, was slightly more difficult for elderly citizens born outside the state and citizens facing economic hardship. Problems also existed for the homeless and voters whose religion prohibited being photographed. These challenges were somewhat decreased by the availability of provisional ballots, which were counted but required a trip to the circuit court clerk's office to sign an affidavit. Still, the statute was not "wholly unjustified," and the plurality found that no class of voters faced "excessively burdensome requirements." As the right to vote was not unduly burdened, the State's interests were enough to defeat a facial challenge. Moreover, even if the burden was unjustified, invalidating the entire statute was inappropriate. Finally, the plurality noted that the statute was not invalid simply because the legislative vote which enacted it was totally divided along party lines: each party was unanimous in its approval or opposition.

Justice Scalia, joined by Justices Thomas and Alito, concurred in the judgment, stating that petitioners' burden was slight and justified. Citing *Burdick v. Takushi*,[193] Justice Scalia called for a deferential standard for "nonsevere, nondiscriminatory restrictions." Common burdens spread widely through the populace are not severe, including burdens "requiring 'nominal effort' of everyone." A burden became severe when it went beyond a mere inconvenience. A generally applicable statute was not unconstitutional if it had a disparate impact but lacked discriminatory intent. Finally, resolving this case on the facts, without accepting or rejecting precedent, promoted uncertainty of the law and encouraged more litigation.

Dissenting, Justice Souter, joined by Justice Ginsburg, did not find the burdens imposed by the statute minor or acceptable under *Burdick*, which required that the interests advanced by a statute outweighed the burden it created. The mere availability of absentee ballots to the elderly and disabled could not justify the denial of their right to vote in person. Indigents who wished to vote in person had either to pay $3 to $12 for a birth certificate; or cast a provisional ballot, an option also available to voters with religious objections to being photographed. Casting a provisional ballot, however, still required voters to bear the cost of traveling to the circuit court clerk within ten days of the election. This statute was passed without any proof of prior in-person voting fraud within the State, and it adversely affected nearly 43,000 eligible voters who did not already have the required identification.

Justice Breyer, also dissenting, did not agree with the plurality that the burden was too uncertain to allow a facial challenge or with Justice Scalia that the burden was slight or justified. Instead, Justice Breyer found that the travel and expense required to obtain the necessary identification posed a significant challenge to non-

---

[193] 504 U.S. 428 (1992).

drivers who are more likely to be poor, elderly, or disabled.

In *Vieth v. Jubelirer*,[194] a plurality of four stated that political gerrymandering was non-justiciable due to a lack of any discoverable or manageable standard of review. Article I, § 4 of the Constitution gave states the power to create election districts, and gave Congress the power to change those districts. Congress has used this power to regulate elections and particularly to restrain political gerrymandering. After reviewing the subsequent failure to provide a "judicially discernible" standard for adjudicating claims of political gerrymandering, the plurality determined that *Davis v. Bandemer*[195] had been incorrectly decided.

The Constitution distinguished political and race-based gerrymandering, anticipating the former, but making the latter unlawful. Gerrymandering commonly gave rise to partisan electoral advantage, but not all gerrymandering generated race-based claims. While "courts might be justified in accepting a modest degree of unmanageability to enforce a constitutional command," the same obligation does not exist to enforce a command that is "both dubious and severely unmanageable."[196] The standard set forth under *Bandemer* is based on the idea the groups have the "right to proportional representation."[197] *Reynolds v. Sims*[198] established the principle of one person, one vote. This standard requires that each individual, not each group, have equal say in electing representatives. It is easy to administer by simply making the number of representatives proportional to the population.

The three standards proposed in the dissenting opinions confirmed that a "constitutionally discernable standard" did not exist. Justice Scalia stated that the issue was not "whether severe partisan gerrymanders violate the Constitution," but whether courts can discern violations, and fashion remedies.[199]

Justice Kennedy concurred in the judgment, agreeing with the plurality's position that there are currently no judicially manageable standards for political gerrymandering cases. However, he left open the possibility of future challenges, due to technological developments that may "make more evident the precise nature of the burdens gerrymanders impose on the representational rights of voters and parties."[200] When a gerrymander has the "purpose and effect of imposing burdens on a disfavored party," the First Amendment may supply a better basis than the Equal Protection Clause for intervention.[201]

In his dissent, Justice Stevens agreed with the Court's refusal to create rules to review all political gerrymandering on a statewide basis, but was disturbed by the District Court's failure to follow precedent in dismissing plaintiff's claim of district-

---

[194] 541 U.S. 267 (2004).

[195] 478 U.S. 109 (1986).

[196] *Vieth*, 541 U.S. at 286.

[197] *Id.* at 288.

[198] 377 U.S. 533 (1964).

[199] *Vieth*, 541 U.S. at 292 (Scalia, J., concurring).

[200] *Id.* at 313 (Kennedy, J., concurring).

[201] *Id.* at 315.

based, political gerrymandering. Relying on the racial gerrymandering cases, he would "ask whether the legislature allowed partisan considerations to dominate and control the lines drawn, forsaking all neutral principles."[202] In his dissent joined by Justice Ginsburg, Justice Souter would adopt a test similar to a summary judgment standard. Specifically, he would require a plaintiff to "satisfy elements of a *prima facie* cause of action, at which point the state would have the opportunity not only rebut the evidence supporting the plaintiff's case, but to offer an affirmative justification for the districting choices."[203] In his dissent, Justice Breyer urged the Court to focus on "extreme cases." Specifically, he would remedy "the unjustified entrenching in power of a political party that voters have rejected."[204]

In *League of United Latin American Citizens v. Perry*,[205] a divided Court partially upheld most of a redistricting plan against political gerrymandering claims under equal protection; however, the Court invalidated one district and upheld another against racial voter dilution claims. In the 2002 elections, the nonpartisan Texas plan created out of the Balderas litigation resulted in a victory for a majority of Democrats for Congress but Republican victories in a majority of state offices. Subsequently, the Texas legislature created a new congressional district map which led to Republicans winning the majority of the congressional seats in the 2004 elections.

Justice Kennedy, joined by Justices Stevens, Souter, Ginsburg, and Breyer, declined to resolve the question of whether an equal protection claim may be raised for political gerrymandering.[206] Instead, the majority turned to the merits. While the Constitution called for state legislatures to apportion their congressional districts, and legislatively drawn plans were more desirable than judicially drawn plans, a legislature could not rely on "improper criteria"[207] to redistrict. The majority concluded that the legislature's plan did not violate the Constitution by replacing the court-drawn plan or by redistricting mid-decade. To hold otherwise would have left the 1991 Democrat-biased plan in place, while striking down the similarly Republican-biased 2003 plan.

Nevertheless, the third part of Justice Kennedy's majority opinion, in which Justices Stevens, Souter, Ginsburg, and Breyer joined, held that District 23 of the redistricting plan violated § 2 of the Voting Rights Act by diluting the Latino vote.[208] Texas had a long history of minority-voter discrimination against African-Americans and Hispanics. Rearranging District 23 turned back the progress of a

---

[202] *Id.* at 339 (Stevens, J., dissenting).

[203] *Id.* at 346.

[204] *Id.* at 365 (Breyer, J., dissenting).

[205] 548 U.S. 399 (2006).

[206] *See* Davis v. Bandemer, 478 U.S. 109 (1986) *and* Vieth v. Jubelirer, 541 U.S. 267 (2004).

[207] *LULAC*, 548 U.S. at 416.

[208] Although the plan created a replacement majority-minority district, this attempt did not relieve the violation since this recourse was only available if the minority groups in both areas could not otherwise have been accommodated. Moreover, a compact district may not be dismantled and replaced by a noncompact district. In equal protection challenges, compactness focused on district line-drawing to determine discriminatory intent. In contrast, § 2 of the Voting Rights Act assessed compactness of the minority population, not of the district.

minority group that was becoming more "politically active and cohesive."[209] The Texas Legislature intentionally redrew district lines to protect an incumbent whose status was threatened by the increased political influence of a cohesive Latino community. While Texas' behavior may have indicated an equal protection violation, the Court did not decide the equal protection or First Amendment issues as District 23 violated § 2 of the Voting Rights Act.

The fourth part of Justice Kennedy's opinion was only joined by Chief Justice Roberts and Justice Alito. Justices Scalia and Thomas concurred in the judgment. Justice Kennedy rejected the claim that District 24 diluted African-American votes. African-Americans in the district only held a majority in Democratic primaries. Extending § 2 voter dilution claims to this scenario "would unnecessarily infuse race into virtually every redistricting."[210]

Justice Stevens concurred in part and dissented in part. Joined by Justice Breyer concurring in part and dissenting in part, Justice Stevens concluded that the plan was completely invalid and would therefore replace it with the prior court-drawn nonpartisan plan. Replacing the court-drawn neutral plan only served partisan purposes. For Justice Stevens, equal protection would not allow redistricting solely " 'to minimize or cancel out the voting strength of racial *or political* elements of the voting population.' "[211] In his opinion, Justice Breyer stated that the entire plan violated equal protection as it was purely motivated by partisan concerns.

Chief Justice Roberts' separate opinion, joined by Justice Alito, agreed with the majority that the claims did not provide " 'a reliable standard for identifying unconstitutional political gerrymanders.' "[212] Chief Justice Roberts dissented from the majority's invalidation of District 25 as a § 2 violation.[213] Justice Scalia, joined by Justice Thomas, concurred in the judgment in part and dissented in part. He maintained that the constitutionality of partisan gerrymandering is nonjusticiable. Chief Justice Roberts and Justices Stevens, Souter, Thomas, Ginsburg, Breyer, and Alito all agreed with Justice Scalia's conclusion that compliance with § 5 of the Voting Rights Act in creating a majority-minority voting district may comprise a compelling state interest.

In *Bush v. Palm Beach County Canvassing Board*,[214] the Court vacated the Florida Supreme Court's decision giving four counties a 12-day extension to file amended election returns for the 2000 Presidential election. Under the Florida Election Code, the standard filing deadline was seven days after the election. Arguing they needed more time to complete the manual recount requested by then Vice-President Al Gore, the involved counties asked the Florida Secretary of State for a filing extension. The Secretary found an extension unjustified. Nevertheless,

---

[209] *LULAC*, 548 U.S. at 439.

[210] *Id.* at 446.

[211] *Id.* at 461 (quoting *Fortson v. Dorsey*, 379 U.S. 433, 439 (1965) (emphasis added)).

[212] *Id.* at 492.

[213] Chief Justice Roberts maintained that the Court had never compared the compactness of minority populations in one area versus another when evaluating a § 2 violation.

[214] 531 U.S. 70 (2000).

the Florida Supreme Court extended the deadline by 12 days.

In a unanimous *per curiam* decision, the Court stated that the basis for Florida Supreme Court's decision was unclear. First, the Court was uncertain what role Article II, § 1, cl. 2 played in the Florida Court's decision. Second, the Court questioned whether the Florida Supreme Court considered 3 U.S.C. § 5 in its decision. Under Art. II, § 1, cl. 2, state legislatures determine how to appoint their electors. Moreover, 3 U.S.C. § 5 "creates a 'safe harbor' for a State."[215] When a state legislature has allowed for "final determination of contests or controversies"[216] pursuant to a state law enacted prior to election day, that determination is "conclusive if made at least six days prior to said time of meeting of the electors."[217]

The Florida Supreme Court may have interpreted the Florida Election Code without considering "the extent to which the Florida Constitution could, consistent with Art. II, § 1, cl. 2, 'circumscribe the legislative power.' "[218] As the Court could not determine how Art. II, § 1, cl. 2 and 3 U.S.C. § 5 fit into the Florida Supreme Court's ruling, it vacated the decision and remanded the case.

In *Bush v. Gore*,[219] the Court reversed the Florida Supreme Court's decision which had allowed several Florida counties to recount ballots for the 2000 Presidential election, holding that a lack of uniform standards for determining voter intent violated equal protection. On November 26, 2000, the State of Florida certified its election results, declaring Governor George Bush the winner. Vice-President Albert Gore filed a complaint challenging the certification in Governor Bush's favor. Denying relief, the Leon County Circuit Court held that Vice-President Gore "failed to meet his burden of proof."[220]

On December 8, the Supreme Court of Florida ordered the Circuit Court to count by hand some 9,000 ballots in Miami-Dade County. The Florida Supreme Court also ordered the State to include in its certification 215 votes in Palm Beach County and 168 votes in Miami-Dade County for Vice-President Gore. Governor Bush asserted that Vice-President Gore only gained 176 votes in Palm Beach County; so the Circuit Court was asked to resolve this dispute on remand. Additionally, the Florida Court ordered manual recounts to begin immediately in counties where "undervotes"[221] had not been manually tabulated. The U.S. Supreme Court granted Governor Bush's application to stay the proceedings on December 9, 2000.

In a *per curiam* opinion, the Court noted that national statistics show approximately 2 percent of ballots cast in Presidential elections fail to register a vote. In some instances, these failures have resulted from voters intentionally not

---

[215] *Id.* at 77.

[216] *Id.*

[217] *Id.* at 77–78.

[218] *Id.* at 77.

[219] 531 U.S. 98 (2000).

[220] *Id.* at 101.

[221] *Id.* at 100.

choosing a candidate or from voter error, like voting for more than one candidate or incorrectly marking the ballot. Only those votes satisfying the established legal requirements were "eligible for inclusion in the certification."[222]

Article II of the Constitution gave state legislatures plenary power to select the manner of appointing electors, including selecting the electors themselves. When the power to elect the President was vested in a state's citizens, "the right to vote as the legislature has prescribed is fundamental; and one source of its fundamental nature lies in the equal weight accorded to each vote and the equal dignity owed to each voter."[223] Consistent with equal protection, a state could not, once it vested this power in its people, value one individual's vote over another's.[224] This included denying a person's right to vote "by a debasement or a dilution. *Reynolds v. Sims*."[225]

Ballots used in several Florida counties became a source of controversy among voters and parties to this suit. Designed to be perforated by a stylus, some ballots were not fully punched, leaving "a piece of the card — a chad"[226] dangling by one or two corners. In other instances, the ballots were indented, but not perforated, so the voting machine failed to count them. As a result, the Florida Supreme Court ordered that "the intent of the voter be discerned from such ballots."[227]

In reversing the Florida Supreme Court, the Court said that discerning the " 'intent of the voter' "[228] was "unobjectionable as an abstract proposition,"[229] but the use of a uniform standard to determine voter intent is necessary. Many areas of the law search for the actor's intent by questioning witnesses, unlike here: "The fact finder confronts a thing, not a person."[230] Also problematic was applying a state-wide standard evenly across the different counties, as well as within a single county where variances could occur depending on the particular recount team. For example, in Miami-Dade, "three members of the county canvassing board applied different standards in defining a legal vote."[231] In addition, Palm Beach County altered its counting standards in the middle of its recount process.

The Florida Supreme Court required the inclusion of the recounts in Miami-Dade and Palm Beach counties. Moreover, that Court appeared to mandate *sub silento* the inclusion of the recount totals from Broward County, which were not completed until after the original November 14 certification by the Secretary of State. Each county used a different standard in deciding what constituted a legal vote. The Broward County recount, for example, "uncovered almost three times as

---

[222] *Id.* at 103.

[223] *Id.* at 104.

[224] *See, e.g.*, Harper v. Virginia Bd. of Elections, 383 U.S. 663 (1996).

[225] *Bush*, 531 U.S. at 105.

[226] *Id.*

[227] *Id.*

[228] *Id.* at 106–07.

[229] *Id.* at 106.

[230] *Id.*

[231] *Id.*

many new votes,"[232] a result quite inconsistent with their respective populations. Furthermore, the recounts in these three counties not only included "so-called undervotes, but [also] extended to . . . so-called overvotes,"[233] where the voter cast more than one vote. However, the Florida Supreme Court did not order inclusion of overvotes in other counties even if they revealed voter intent. An estimated "110,000 overvotes"[234] existed statewide.

Another equal protection problem was that the Florida Supreme Court included a partial recount from Miami-Dade County. Moreover, the Florida Supreme Court's decision broadly allowed partial recounts, including votes that had been counted by the certification deadline, while excluding votes that the recount teams did not have time to count.

The Florida Supreme Court's decision also did not say who would recount the ballots. Counties organized ad hoc teams of judges with no previous training.

The Court noted that its "consideration is limited to the present circumstances."[235] The issue was "not whether local entities, in the exercise of their expertise, may develop different systems for implementing elections."[236] Rather, when a court imposed "a statewide remedy, there must at least be some assurance that the rudimentary requirements of equal treatment and fundamental fairness are satisfied."[237]

To comply with equal protection and due process would require "the adoption (after opportunity for argument) of adequate statewide standards for determining what is a legal vote, and practical procedures to implement them, [as well as] orderly judicial review of any disputed matters."[238] Moreover, inclusion of overvotes could necessitate "a second screening,"[239] and the Secretary of State, as required by Florida law, would have to evaluate the accuracy of any equipment used in this process.

Seven Justices agreed that the recount raised constitutional problems "that demand a remedy."[240] The only disagreement among these Justices concerned the specific nature of the remedy. For example, Justice Breyer proposed remanding the case and extending the certification deadline until December 18, so that the Florida Supreme Court could order recount procedures consistent with this opinion. "Because the Florida Supreme Court has said that the Florida legislature intended to obtain the safe-harbor benefits of 3 U.S.C. § 5,"[241] requiring that states choose their electors by December 12, this proposed remedy "could not be a part of

---

[232] *Id.* at 107.

[233] *Id.*

[234] *Id.* at 108.

[235] *Id.* at 109.

[236] *Id.*

[237] *Id.* at 109.

[238] *Id.* at 110.

[239] *Id.*

[240] *Id.* at 111.

[241] *Id.*

an 'appropriate' order authorized"[242] by Florida law.

Chief Justice Rehnquist, joined by Justices Scalia and Thomas, concurred. Respecting the legislature's power to appoint electors under Art. II, "we must ensure that postelection state-court actions do not frustrate the legislative desire to attain the 'safe harbor' provided by § 5."[243]

In Florida, the Secretary of State was the "chief election officer"[244] in charge of " 'maintain[ing] uniformity in the application, operation, and interpretation of the election laws.' "[245] On November 21, 2000, the Florida Supreme Court, in *Palm Beach County Canvassing Board v. Harris*,[246] "extended the 7-day statutory certification deadline established by the legislature."[247] Though this Court vacated that decision and remanded the case, the Florida Supreme Court reached the same conclusion on December 11, 2000. By extending the protest period, the Florida Supreme Court altered the State's election code. The Florida Court's decision signaled that certification mattered: "The certified winner would enjoy presumptive validity."[248] However, the Florida Supreme Court's most recent opinion "empties certification of virtually all legal consequence,"[249] departing from Florida law. For example, the Florida Supreme Court determined that courts should review de novo decisions concerning whether to recount votes after the mandatory certification deadline. This determination disregarded the State's election code, which gave the canvassing boards discretion whether to recount ballots and "sets strict deadlines subject to the Secretary's rejection of late tallies and monetary fines for tardiness."[250]

In addition, Florida statutory law certainly could not be read to "*require* the counting of improperly marked ballots."[251] It was no excuse that some voters found the ballots used in some counties confusing, as each precinct provided voters with detailed instructions. For example, in areas using punch-card ballots, voters were directed "to punch out the ballot cleanly."[252] The approach "scheme that the Florida Supreme Court's opinion attributes to the legislature is one in which machines are *required* to be 'capable of correctly counting votes,' § 101.5606(4), but which nonetheless regularly produces elections in which legal votes are predictably *not* tabulated."[253] The Secretary of State had the power to interpret Florida's

---

[242] *Id.*

[243] *Id.* at 113.

[244] *Id.* at 116.

[245] *Id.* at 116.

[246] 772 So. 2d 1220 (Fla. 2000).

[247] *Bush*, 531 U.S. at 117–18.

[248] *Id.*

[249] *Id.*

[250] *Id.* at 118.

[251] *Id.* at 118–19.

[252] *Id.* at 119. The instructions for punch-card ballots read: "AFTER VOTING, CHECK YOUR BALLOT CARD TO BE SURE YOUR VOTING SELECTIONS ARE CLEARLY AND CLEANLY PUNCHED AND THERE ARE NO CHIPS LEFT HANGING ON THE BACK OF THE CARD."

[253] *Id.* at 119.

election code, the Florida Court ignored her interpretation: "there is no basis for reading the Florida statutes as requiring the counting of improperly marked ballots."[254] Before this election, no recount had ever sought to include such votes.

The Florida Court's decision also conflicted with 3 U.S.C. § 5 and its safe harbor provision. Four days prior to that statute's deadline for a final determination of Florida's electors, the Florida Supreme Court, on December 8, 2000, "ordered recounts of tens of thousands of so-called 'undervotes' spread through 64 of the State's 67 counties."[255] With additional review by the Florida Supreme Court and the U.S. Supreme Court, the recount process could not have been completed by the statutory deadline.

Dissenting, Justice Stevens, joined by Justices Ginsburg and Breyer, argued that it was not the Court's job to second-guess the Florida Supreme Court's interpretation of Florida law. Under Art. II, § 1, cl. 2, each state determined the manner in which it selected Presidential electors. The highest court of a state interpreted the state's laws, including its election laws. Moreover, § 5, like Art. II, expected the participation of state courts in construing state election laws and in settling disputes under those laws.

Even if the recount procedure did violate the Equal Protection Clause, the majority's holding could not be justified. Under Florida law, "all ballots that reveal the intent of the voter constitute valid votes."[256] The Court should have remanded requiring more specific procedures to implement this standard.

Justice Souter also dissented, joined by Justice Breyer and by Justices Stevens and Ginsburg in part. Justices Souter and Breyer agreed that the varying rules used by the counties for determining a voter's intent did raise equal protection problems. The evidence showed that different rules were applied to "to identical types of ballots used in identical brands of machines and exhibiting identical physical characteristics (such as 'hanging' or 'dimpled' chads)."[257] No conceivable "legitimate state interest [could be] served by these differing treatments of the expressions of voters' fundamental rights. The differences appear wholly arbitrary."[258]

Unlike the majority, however, Justice Souter would have remanded the case, so that the Florida courts could establish uniform standards. He disagreed with the Court that a legal recount could not have beeen conducted by the December 18 deadline, despite one Florida Justice's estimate that "disparate standards potentially affected 170,000 votes."[259] Additionally, "no showing has been made of legal overvotes uncounted, and counsel for Gore made an uncontradicted representation to the Court that the statewide total of undervotes is about

---

[254] *Id.* at 120.

[255] *Id.* at 121.

[256] *Id.* at 126.

[257] *Id.* at 134.

[258] *Id.*

[259] *Id.* at 135.

60,000."[260] While this effort would have been arduous, the Court stayed Florida's efforts.

Justice Ginsburg also dissented, joined in part by Justice Stevens, and by Justices Souter and Breyer. It was one thing to disagree with the Florida Court's interpretation of Florida's laws, but it is another to impose the Court's own interpretation of those laws.

Also dissenting, Justice Breyer, joined in part by Justices Stevens, Ginsburg, and Souter, agreed that the use of different standards to determine voter intent could result in favoring one candidate over another, and the time "was, and is too short to permit the lower courts to iron out significant differences through ordinary judicial review."[261] As such, "in these very special circumstances, basic principles of fairness may well have counseled the adoption of a uniform standard to address the problem."[262] Whether "the Constitution would place limits upon the content of a uniform standard"[263] did not have to be decided, in light of the majority's holding.

Justice Breyer would have remanded the case "with instructions that, even at this late date, would permit the Florida Supreme Court to require recounting all undercounted votes in Florida."[264] The shortage of time did not justify the Court's actions, even if, as the majority asserted, there was no time for the Secretary to examine and approve the necessary equipment. "The majority reaches this conclusion in the absence of any record evidence."[265] As neither party alleged "electoral fraud, dishonesty, or the like,"[266] state courts should have decided whether a recount could have been conducted prior to the scheduled meeting of the electors.

§ 12.04 THE RIGHT TO TRAVEL

[1] Domestic Travel

In *Shapiro v. Thompson*,[267] the Court held unconstitutional three laws that limited welfare assistance to persons who had lived in the state for at least one year. The states involved gave several justifications for the laws. First, by denying them benefits, people who would likely be lifetime burdens on state public assistance programs were deterred from entering the state. This step preserved the fiscal integrity of the welfare system and conserved more resources for long term residents of the state. The Court did not doubt that the restriction would prevent the poor from entering the state; however, this purpose imposed an

---

[260] *Id.*

[261] *Id.* at 145–46.

[262] *Id.* at 146.

[263] *Id.*

[264] *Id.*

[265] *Id.* at 146.

[266] *Id.* at 153.

[267] 394 U.S. 618 (1969).

"unreasonable burden" on the right to travel. Although no specific constitutional provision guaranteed the right to travel from state to state, the Court had long recognized this right as " 'fundamental to the concept of our Federal Union.' "[268]

The states also claimed that even if it was impermissible to deter all indigents from entering their territory, the regulation could be justified as an attempt to deter those who would enter solely for the purpose of obtaining higher welfare benefits. The Court denied this justification as too broad in lumping together all new residents who applied for welfare.[269] Moreover, to the extent that it favored long-term residents for having paid taxes, this rationale could be invoked to deprive new residents of all state services — even police and fire protection — brought to its logical conclusions.

Finally, the States and the District of Columbia offered four administrative and related justifications for the restrictions: (1) they made it easier to plan the welfare budget; (2) they established an objective test for residency; (3) they deterred fraudulently collecting benefits from multiple jurisdictions; and (4) they encouraged prompt entry into the work force. None of these justifications were necessary to advance a compelling state interest.[270] For example, many of these rationales also applied to long-term residents.

The Court also rejected a claim that Congress had authorized one-year residency requirements. The majority found that the statute was not an approval of one-year requirements; and even if it were, it would be unconstitutional as Congress could not authorize an equal protection violation. In dissent, Chief Justice Warren, joined by Justice Black, argued that Congress could have used its commerce power to regulate the right of interstate travel so long as it did not abridge other constitutional rights. They thought that the decision would lead to the invalidation of residency requirements for voting, college tuition, and admittance to certain professions.[271]

Justice Harlan filed a lengthy dissent. Initially, he lamented the expansion of the "suspect class" branch of equal protection. In light of the purposes of the Fourteenth Amendment, he believed that equal protection should only be applied to racial classifications. He also attacked the "fundamental rights" prong of equal protection jurisprudence, arguing that virtually all statutes affected some important right. Justice Harlan felt that this branch of equal protection

---

[268] *Id.* at 630. The right had previously been justified by the Privileges and Immunities Clause of Article IV and the Fourteenth Amendment. *See, e.g.,* Twining v. New Jersey, 211 U.S. 78 (1908); Paul v. Virginia, 75 U.S. 168 (1869). For additional discussion of the right to travel, *see* Justice Stewart's concurring opinion in *Shapiro*, 394 U.S. at 642.

[269] Actually, the Court described this position as a "non-rebuttable presumption" assuming all new residents who are welfare recipients came to the state solely for this purpose. For a short time, the Court used this irrebuttable presumption analysis to strike down laws as violating a right to an individual determination. This technique was generally employed in equal protection cases, and created some doctrinal confusion in terms of what constitutional provision had been violated. Thus, the Court has abandoned it. *See supra* § 10.04.

[270] *See Shapiro*, 394 U.S. at 634.

[271] For state restrictions on admittance to the legal profession, *see supra* § 6.11. For restrictions on the right to vote and lower college tuition, *see infra* text accompanying note 276.

jurisprudence was unnecessary because restrictions on rights secured by the Constitution should be subject to scrutiny under substantive due process analysis.

Justice Harlan then made a four-part analysis of whether the one-year residency requirement placed an undue burden on the right to interstate travel. First, he concluded that the right to interstate travel asserted here could not be justified by the Commerce Clause because Congress approved the restrictions at issue. Second, the Privileges and Immunities Clause of Article IV was of no help since it only forbade states from distinguishing between its own citizens and citizens of other states. When they brought this suit, those challenging the law were residents, and therefore citizens, of the states that denied them benefits. Third, the Privileges and Immunities Clause of the Fourteenth Amendment prevented states from interfering with the relationship between citizens and the national government. As Congress had approved these restrictions, the Clause was not violated. Finally, Justice Harlan concluded that the right to travel was one of the liberty interests secured by the Due Process Clause of the Fifth Amendment. He then argued that the burden on travel was outweighed by various state interests including maintaining the fiscal integrity of the welfare system and preventing fraud.

Since *Shapiro*, the Court has reviewed durational residency requirements in a number of other contexts. The Court has not formalistically applied the compelling state interest test to invalidate all restrictions on the right to travel. Instead, it appears to examine the importance of the state interest, the need for it in accomplishing the state's objections, and the actual burden or deterrent effect of the requirement on interstate travel. While the Court has rejected a one-year residency requirement for eligibility to vote,[272] it has upheld 50-day residency requirements for eligibility to vote.[273] The Court invalidated a law that imposed a one-year residency requirement on indigents seeking non-emergency medical care in a public hospital.[274] It has upheld a one-year requirement as a condition of instituting a divorce action against a non-resident.[275] Finally, the Court has recognized the power of states to impose durational requirements as a condition of qualifying for lower, in-state tuition for colleges.[276]

The Court upheld a Georgia law making child abandonment a misdemeanor and child abandonment accompanied by leaving the state a felony. While the state could not impose a penalty for leaving its boundaries, the greater penalty imposed here reflected the more serious nature of abandoning a child and leaving the state.[277] The Court invalidated a one-time civil service preference to honorably discharged

---

[272] Dunn v. Blumstein, 405 U.S. 330 (1972).

[273] Marston v. Lewis, 410 U.S. 679 (1973); Burns v. Fortson, 410 U.S. 686 (1973).

[274] Memorial Hosp. v. Maricopa County, 415 U.S. 250 (1974).

[275] Sosna v. Iowa, 419 U.S. 393 (1975).

[276] Starns v. Malkerson, 326 F. Supp. 234 (D. Minn. 1970), aff'd, 401 U.S. 985 (1971). *But cf.* Vlandis v. Kline, 412 U.S. 441 (1973), which struck down Connecticut's in-state tuition preference on the ground that it created an "irrebuttable presumption" preventing individuals in certain categories from ever establishing bona fide residency. The Court's virtual abandonment of the irrebuttable presumption doctrine makes the continuing validity of *Vlandis* doubtful.

[277] Jones v. Helms, 452 U.S. 412 (1981).

veterans who were New York residents at the time they entered the service as a violation of the right to migrate and equal protection of the laws.[278]

In *Saenz v. Roe*,[279] the Supreme Court struck down, as against the right to travel, a California statute that denied new residents the same level of welfare benefits available to those who had been California citizens for more than 12 months. The Court's precedents have established that the right to travel contains at least three components: "[The] right of a citizen of one State to enter and leave another State, the right to be treated as a welcome visitor rather than an unfriendly alien temporarily present in the second State, and, for those travelers who elect to become permanent residents, the right to be treated like other citizens of that State." The California statute provided that, during the first 12 months of California residency, the State would limit new residents to the amount of welfare benefits that they would have received in their previous home state. This limitation violated the third aspect of the right to travel.

Writing for a majority of seven, Justice Stevens stated that the right to enter and leave a state was expressly mentioned in the Articles of Confederation, and may have been " 'conceived from the beginning to be a necessary concomitant of the stronger Union the Constitution created.' "[280]

The second component of the right to travel was protected by the express language of the Privileges and Immunities Clause of Article IV, § 2: "The Citizens of each State shall be entitled to all Privileges and Immunities of Citizens in the several States." The clause freed U.S. citizens from most forms of discrimination when visiting other states. The Court had validated some discrimination favoring residents, for example, "requiring the nonresident to pay more than a resident for a hunting license, or to enroll in the state university."

Justice Stevens focused on the third aspect of the right to travel prohibiting discrimination against nonresidents. The Privileges and Immunities Clause of the Fourteenth Amendment protected this third component. Justice Miller's opinion in the *Slaughter-House Cases* stated that one of the privileges conferred by the clause "is that a citizen of the United States can, of his own volition, become a citizen of any State of the Union by a *bona fide* residence therein with the same rights as other citizens of that State." The majority said that discrimination among citizens who received welfare benefits was not an acceptable means for accomplishing California's asserted fiscal purpose of reducing its welfare spending.[281] The Citizenship Clause of the Fourteenth Amendment "does not provide for, and does not allow for, degrees of citizenship based on length of residence."

Finally, congressional approval of durational residence requirements did not render them constitutional. The Court had "consistently held that Congress may

---

[278] Attorney General of New York v. Soto-Lopez, 476 U.S. 898 (1986).

[279] 526 U.S. 489 (1999).

[280] United States v. Guest, 383 U.S. 745, 758 (1966).

[281] The courts below found "that the 'apparent purpose of [the statute] was to deter migration of poor people to California.' " Roe v. Anderson, 134 F.3d 1400, 1404 (9th Cir. 1998).

not authorize the States to violate the Fourteenth Amendment." The Citizenship Clause of the Fourteenth Amendment limited "the powers of the National Government as well as the States."

Chief Justice Rehnquist and Justice Thomas joined each other in separate dissents. Chief Justice Rehnquist objected to the majority's use of "any provision of the Constitution — and surely not a provision relied upon for only the second time since its enactment 130 years ago" to strike down a "good-faith residency requirement." He found no difference between California's one-year limitation on the amount of welfare benefits, and one-year residence requirements previously upheld by the Court for in-state tuition benefits, divorce, and voting in primary elections.

Justice Thomas said that the Privileges and Immunities Clause did not establish "the right of the newly arrived citizen to the same privileges and immunities enjoyed by other citizens of the same state." In an appropriate case, the Court might reevaluate whether the Privileges and Immunities Clause "should displace, rather than augment, portions of our equal protection and substantive due process jurisprudence."

[2]   International Travel

In *Regan v. Wald*,[282] the Court reviewed restrictions issued by the executive branch that prohibited business transactions with Cuba. These restrictions effectively barred almost all tourist and business travel to Cuba. The majority and dissent differed primarily over the question of statutory interpretation. The dissenters claimed that Congress had intended to prevent the President from issuing the restrictions. The majority disagreed and addressed the right to travel issue. It concluded that the President's power over foreign policy was sufficient to justify travel restrictions as a means of deterring the flow of money into Cuba.[283]

Although restrictions on the right to travel internationally have had more success in the courts than restrictions on interstate travel, they do not always pass constitutional muster. In *Kent v. Dulles*,[284] the Court recognized that the right to travel was part of the "liberty" protected by the Fifth Amendment's Due Process Clause, and then rejected the governments' argument that the Passport Act authorized the Secretary of State to deny passports to people believed to be Communists. In light of the constitutional right that was implicated, the statute had to be narrowly construed.

In *Aptheker v. Secretary of State*,[285] the Court invalidated a law that denied passports to members of Communist organizations. While the decision primarily rested on the First Amendment, the Fifth Amendment right to travel was being

---

[282]   468 U.S. 222 (1984).

[283]   In *Zemel v. Rusk*, 381 U.S. 1 (1965), the Court upheld a denial of travel to Cuba during the Cuban missile crisis.

[284]   357 U.S. 116 (1958).

[285]   378 U.S. 500 (1964).

restricted in a way inconsistent with the First Amendment. In *Haig v. Agee*,[286] the Court upheld the Secretary of State's revocation of a former CIA agent's passport. The former agent had traveled around the world for five years exposing CIA operatives. Chief Justice Burger's majority opinion noted that, unlike the right to interstate travel which was virtually unlimited, the right to international travel was a liberty interest protected by the Due Process Clause and could be regulated in accordance with that clause.[287]

§ 12.05　"ECONOMIC AND SOCIAL LEGISLATION"

The foregoing sections of this Chapter demonstrate that the Court has afforded considerable scrutiny to government regulations that discriminate against suspect classifications or that discriminatorily distribute certain fundamental rights. In contrast, economic and social legislation has received *"de minimis"* scrutiny by the Court. For example, in *Railway Express Agency v. New York*,[288] the Court upheld, against due process and equal protection challenges, a New York City traffic regulation that prohibited advertising on commercial vehicles unless the ads were for the business of the vehicle's owner. Addressing the due process claim, Justice Douglas found the regulation unnecessary and refused to pass judgment on the City's finding that the law reduced traffic hazards caused by distracting advertisements. On equal protection, Justice Douglas concluded that even if the City's opinion that the classification reduced traffic hazards was incorrect, it "does not contain the kind of discrimination against which the Equal Protection Clause affords protection."[289] The Court also was not troubled that the City prohibited certain signs but allowed others. Equal protection did not require the eradication of all evils of the same sort.[290]

Justice Jackson filed a lengthy concurring opinion. He argued that the Court should be slow to invalidate laws on due process grounds, because such a ruling foreclosed all regulation in the particular area. By contrast, invalidating laws on equal protection grounds merely required broader applicability of the regulation.

Other major cases employing lower scrutiny for economic and social regulation include *McGowan v. Maryland*,[291] in which the Court upheld Sunday Closing or Blue Laws, despite a wide variety of exceptions for certain vendors; and *New Orleans v. Dukes*,[292] which upheld a law barring pushcart vendors from the French Quarter unless they had operated there for at least eight years — even though the

---

[286] 453 U.S. 280 (1981).

[287] Even assuming arguendo that "First Amendment protections reach beyond our national boundaries," disclosures obstructing our national security services were not protected. *Id.* at 308.

[288] 336 U.S. 106 (1949).

[289] *Id.* at 110.

[290] Today, the Supreme Court would afford greater scrutiny to the advertising regulation at issues in *Railway Express* under the doctrine of commercial speech. For a discussion of commercial speech, *see infra* § 16.04.

[291] 366 U.S. 420 (1961).

[292] 427 U.S. 297 (1976).

exception applied only to two vendors.[293]

In *Dukes*, the Court overruled an earlier decision, *Morey v. Doud*,[294] which had invalidated a statute exempting one company from its regulation of money order forms. The Court has, however, made exceptions to the general rule of "*de minimis*" scrutiny of economic and social regulation.[295] This tendency is particularly pronounced in cases involving laws that discriminate against non-resident individuals and citizens.[296] Often these cases would also attract scrutiny under the Commerce Clause or the Privileges and Immunities Clause of Article IV.

In *General Motors Corp. v. Tracy*,[297] the Court upheld against an equal protection challenge a sales tax exemption which applied to regulated public utilities, but not to other sellers of natural gas. The Court stated that the exemption turned not on where the companies operated, but on what kind of services they provided. Both in-state and out-of-state companies could qualify for the exemption, depending on what services they provided. The State had a rational basis for favoring regulated gas utilities over unregulated sellers of natural gas.

In *Vacco v. Quill*,[298] the Court held that a New York ban on assisted suicide did not violate equal protection. Although New York's prohibition on assisted suicide significantly affected all citizens, it did not intrude on fundamental rights or concern suspect classifications. Thus, the court presumed that this ban was valid. The statutes banning assisted suicide and allowing patients to decline life-saving treatment did not differentiate between persons: any competent person could

---

[293] Other cases in which the Court did not find an equal protection violation include *Northeast Bancorp, Inc. v. Board of Governors*, 472 U.S. 159 (1985) (Massachusetts and Connecticut laws that give preference to companies that want to buy banks in those states if they own banks in New England); *Schweiker v. Wilson*, 450 U.S. 221 (1981) (inmates of public institutions who receive Medicaid benefits excluded from Supplemental Security Income benefits); *U.S. R.R. Ret. Bd. v. Fritz*, 449 U.S. 166 (1980) (distribution of "windfall" retirement benefits based on years of employment); *New York City Transit Auth. v. Beazer*, 440 U.S. 568 (1979) (refusal to hire anyone taking methadone, even as part of a drug rehabilitation program); *Idaho Dep't of Employment v. Smith*, 434 U.S. 100 (1977) (allowing night school students to collect unemployment benefits, but not day students); and *City of Charlotte v. Int'l Ass'n of Firefighters*, 426 U.S. 283 (1976) (refusing to withhold union dues owing from employees' paychecks).

[294] 354 U.S. 457 (1957).

[295] *See, e.g.*, Allegheny Pittsburgh Coal Co. v. County Comm'n, 488 U.S. 336 (1989) (invalidating a property tax system which re-valued property when sold but made only minor reassessments of other property, resulting in taxes up to 35 times higher for petitioner's property than similarly situated property). *But cf.* Nordlinger v. Hahn, 505 U.S. 1 (1992) (upholding acquisition value scheme — as against property value scheme — that reassessed a recently acquired house at five times the value of comparable houses).

[296] Metropolitan Life Ins. Co. v. Ward, 470 U.S. 869 (1985) (invalidating Alabama law that imposed lower tax on domestic insurance companies); Williams v. Vermont, 472 U.S. 14 (1985) (statute allowing only Vermont residents who purchase a car out of state and register it in Vermont to deduct sales tax paid from Vermont use tax violated Equal Protection Clause); Hooper v. Bernalillo County Assessor, 472 U.S. 612 (1985) (New Mexico constitutional provision exempting honorably discharged Vietnam veterans who served for at least 90 days and who were residents of the state before May 8, 1976, from real property tax violated Equal Protection Clause). *But cf.* Northeast Bancorp, Inc. v. Board of Governors, 472 U.S. 159 (1985) (denying equal protection challenge to Connecticut and Massachusetts statutes preferring New England regional ownership of state banks to owners from other states).

[297] 519 U.S. 278 (1997).

[298] 521 U.S. 793 (1997).

refuse medical treatment, but no one could participate in an assisted suicide. This basic difference comported with the law's treatment of causation and intent. For instance, when a patient declined life-saving treatment, the underlying disease caused death. However, when a patient took a lethal medication prescribed by a physician, the medication caused death, and the assisting physician intended that death would occur. The American Medical Association also recognized this difference. Moreover, the majority of state legislatures, including New York, have distinguished refusing life-saving treatment from suicide. In *Cruzan v. Director, Missouri Department of Health*,[299] the Court noted that most states impose criminal penalties on those who assisted suicides. A state may allow palliative care that may carry the expected but "unintended 'double effect' of hastening the patient's death."[300]

Substantial public concerns, including "prohibiting intentional killing and preserving life; preventing suicide; maintaining physicians' role as their patients' healers; protecting vulnerable people from indifference, prejudice, and psychological and financial pressure to end their lives; and avoiding a possible slide towards euthanasia,"[301] rendered these statutes rationally related to a legitimate interest.

Justice O'Connor concurred, stating that patients may receive palliative care even if it will hasten death. Justice Stevens concurred in the judgment. As the three terminally ill patients died before this case reached the Court, it could not consider the statute's application to these individuals. Concurring in the judgment, Justice Souter stated that his analysis was predicated exclusively on the Due Process Clause. Also concurring in the judgment, Justice Breyer emphasized the need to protect "personal control over the manner of death, professional medical assistance, and the avoidance of unnecessary and severe physical suffering-combined."[302]

In *Engquist v. Oregon Department of Agriculture*,[303] the Court refused to apply the "class-of-one" theory of equal protection to public employment matters. Plaintiff's "class-of-one" equal protection claim alleged that she was fired for "arbitrary, vindictive, and malicious reasons," not because of her belonging to any particular identified class. Chief Justice Roberts stated that the primary concern of the Equal Protection Clause is to protect against arbitrary classifications, and that the considerations applicable were different when the government was acting as an employer than when it is acting in its capacity as sovereign. The "class-of-one" theory did not apply in the public employment context. The Court frequently acknowledged that the government had more latitude in its dealings with citizen employees when acting as an employer than it did in its dealings with the general population when acting as a sovereign authority. The Court's precedent in the public employment area established two main principles. First, while government employees retain their constitutional rights, those rights must be balanced by the employment context. Second, the Court must assess whether the claim implicated

---

[299] *See supra* § 8.06[4].

[300] *Vacco*, 521 U.S. at 806–08.

[301] *Id.*

[302] *Id.* at 790. For additional discussion, *see* Washington v. Glucksberg, *supra* § 8.06[4].

[303] 553 U.S. 591 (2008).

the basic concerns of the asserted constitutional right, or whether the asserted right more easily gave way to the government's needs as an employer.

The Court previously had upheld a "class-of-one" claim involving government regulation of private property in *Village of Willowbrook v. Olech*.[304] *Olech*, however, relied on precedent regarding tax schemes and assessments of the property. Quoting from the judicial oath, the Chief Justice stated that "such legislative or regulatory classifications" should apply "without respect to persons." When government treats differently persons who seem to be similarly situated, equal protection demands at least a rational explanation. The government in Olech departed from its own clear, consistent standard in only one case. Specifically, the board required a 33-foot easement for *Olech*, rather than the standard 15-foot easement. This differential treatment raised a concern that the classification was arbitrary, and the Court required a rational basis for the distinctions.

In contrast, some state actions are inherently discretionary. Discretionary state actions plainly include employment decisions, which are generally subjective and rest on many factors that are difficult to express and quantify. In the public employment context, a "class-of-one" theory of equal protection runs counter to the employment-at-will doctrine which allowed an employee to be terminated for any reason or no reason at all. Congress and the states have statutorily limited much of their discretion under the employment-at-will doctrine with various statutory schemes protecting public employees from discharge for impermissible reasons. However, government could comply but not function if every employment decision came under constitutional scrutiny.

Justice Stevens dissented, joined by Justices Souter and Ginsburg. While government employers must have discretionary authority, that discretion requires choosing among rational alternatives. While equal protection did not prohibit unwise decisions, it did proscribe arbitrary ones without any rational justification. Moreover, today, new statutes and constitutional decisions have almost rendered the employment-at-will doctrine insignificant.

---

[304] 528 U.S. 562 (2000).

Chapter 13

POLITICAL SPEECH AND ASSOCIATION

INTRODUCTION

This chapter introduces the fundamental rationales for protecting political speech and association by tracing generally the historical and doctrinal evolution of freedom of expression. The 45 words contained in the First Amendment underwrite several important guarantees. Some commentators have suggested that the First Amendment has primacy over other constitutional provisions. Justices Douglas and Black even maintained that the First Amendment was an *absolute*.

The restrictions that the First Amendment imposes on Congress are clear. "Congress shall make no law respecting an establishment of religion, or prohibiting the free exercise thereof; or abridging the freedom of speech, or of the press; or the right of the people peaceably to assemble, and to petition the Government for a redress of grievances."[1] While the Amendment only explicitly restricts Congress, there has never been any serious challenge to its applicability to all branches of the federal government.

First Amendment restrictions on the states were first recognized in *Gitlow v. New York*,[2] when the Court "assumed" that freedoms of speech and of the press were among the "liberties" protected from state infringement by the Due Process Clause of the Fourteenth Amendment.

Much of the development of free speech jurisprudence has been spurred by foreign and domestic pressures during this century. The fear of internal subversion during World War I, the threat of the Soviet Union, the repressive internal response to this threat culminating in the McCarthy era, and our government's efforts to stifle criticism from such varied groups as the Ku Klux Klan, the Nazis, civil rights advocates, and anti-Vietnam War protesters, are just a few examples of the pressures that have influenced First Amendment jurisprudence.

The development of free speech jurisprudence, in the context of the varied standards of protection that the Court has afforded to subversive speech, is outlined in Section 13.01. This Section also introduces the ideas of two of the most influential free speech commentators, Alexander Meiklejohn and Thomas Emerson. Examining questions of political association, Section 13.02 identifies the limits on the government's authority to sanction persons for their membership in political groups. Section 13.03 considers the extent to which associational rights can be infringed by governmental investigations of organizations. Associational rights in

---

[1] U.S. Const. amend. I.

[2] 268 U.S. 652 (1925).

other contexts are explained in Section 13.04. Looking again at free speech concerns, Section 13.05 focuses on the rights of government employees, including their freedom to criticize the government, their ability to participate in political campaigns, and their protection from patronage dismissals.

§ 13.01 THE BASIC MODEL FOR PROTECTING FREE SPEECH

This section deals with many older cases that are no longer good law. However, these cases contribute to an understanding of the development of the principles that have provided strong protection for freedom of speech. Many of these principles were developed in the classic concurring and dissenting opinions of Justices Oliver Wendell Holmes and Louis Brandeis.

[1] Advocacy of Unlawful Objectives

During World War I, Congress passed two statutes to quell opposition to the War. The Espionage Act of 1917 proscribed the publication or utterance of statements intended to obstruct the armed forces. The Sedition Act of 1918 made it a felony to publish or utter mere criticism of the government. These laws produced almost two thousand prosecutions and approximately one thousand convictions.[3] In 1919 and 1920, after World War I, the Supreme Court reviewed five major cases that challenged these laws as violations of the First Amendment's protection of free speech.[4]

In *Schenck v. United States*,[5] Justice Holmes first articulated his famous "clear and present danger" test. In a unanimous opinion, the Court affirmed the conviction of Socialist Party officials under the Espionage Act. Schenck, the party's general secretary, circulated 15,000 pamphlets to conscripts of World War I. Printed on one side of the pamphlet was the Thirteenth Amendment, which forbids slavery and involuntary servitude. The other side told conscripts to resist the draft. While the pamphlet charged that the Conscription Act violated the Thirteenth Amendment, it advocated only peaceful measures in opposition to the draft. Moreover, there was no evidence that Schenck or his pamphlets actually did obstruct the draft.

The conviction was upheld because defendants only had to intend to obstruct the draft. Justice Holmes essentially assumed intent on the part of the defendants by pointing out that defendants "intended to have some effect, and we do not see what effect [the pamphlet] could be expected to have upon persons subject to the draft except to influence them to obstruct the carrying of it out."[6] Consequently, the publication and dissemination of the pamphlet alone established the intent

---

[3] 1919 Att'y Gen. Ann. Rep. 22.

[4] *See* Gilbert v. Minnesota, 254 U.S. 325 (1920); Abrams v. United States, 250 U.S. 616 (1919); Schenck v. United States, 249 U.S. 47 (1919); Frohwerk v. United States, 249 U.S. 204 (1919); Debs v. United States, 249 U.S. 211 (1919).

[5] 249 U.S. 47 (1919).

[6] *Id.* at 51.

required for a conviction under the Espionage Act.

In interpreting the First Amendment, Justice Holmes maintained that at the very least it prohibited prior restraints. Thus, the government was restricted from enjoining speech before it was uttered or published. Once spoken or written, however, government could proscribe it.

In a classic illustration that free speech is not absolute, Justice Holmes wrote: "The most stringent protection of free speech would not protect a man in falsely shouting fire in a theater and causing a panic."[7] The much lower standard for protecting the subversive speech at issue in this case was the famous "clear and present danger" test: "The question in every case is whether the words used are used in such circumstances and are of such a nature as to create a clear and present danger that they will bring about the substantive evils that Congress has a right to prevent." Justice Holmes, as a prominent torts scholar and in the best traditions of tort law, made protection of speech under the "clear and present danger" test contingent "upon the circumstances in which it is done." The constitutional inquiry therefore was one of the "proximity and degree" of danger. Again reflecting the influence of tort law, Justice Holmes' test resembled a proximate cause inquiry. It focused on the closeness of the causal relationship between the speech and the harm to be avoided. The "shouting fire in a crowded theater" example illustrated how some speech could have such a close nexus to actual physical harm that it must be circumscribed.

Justice Holmes was also very deeply influenced by his service in the Civil War.[8] His "clear and present danger" standard helped to protect the nation's ability to carry on the War. Justice Holmes admitted that if the nation had not been at war, the message in the pamphlets would have received constitutional protection.

Should our nation's involvement in armed conflict be subject to continuing criticism by the people? The tension between war and free speech is part of democracy itself. How much discussion is necessary to arrive at a decision to go to war, and when does further discussion compromise the original majoritarian decision to fight? How can the rights of those who oppose the war, or those who just want to keep discussing the issue, be protected?

One week after *Schenck* was decided, Justice Holmes again wrote for a unanimous Court in *Debs v. United States*.[9] *Debs*, even more than *Schenck*, illustrated the lack of protection that the clear and present danger test afforded speech. Eugene Debs, a Socialist Party leader and five-time presidential candidate,[10] was convicted under the Espionage Act for remarks in a speech delivered to his supporters. The trial court sentenced Debs to ten years in prison for obstructing the recruitment of servicemen and for inciting a mutiny.

---

[7] *Id.* at 52.

[8] *See* Missouri v. Holland, 252 U.S. 416, 433 (1920) (Justice Holmes stating "it was enough for . . . [The Framers] to realize or to hope that they had created an organism; it has taken a century and has cost their successors much sweat and blood to prove that they had created a nation.").

[9] 249 U.S. 211 (1919).

[10] Debs won nearly a million votes in 1920, running his campaign from his jail cell. Yassky, *Eras of the First Amendment I*, 91 COLUM. L. REV. 1699, 1718 (1991).

Before the speech, Debs signed the "Anti-war Proclamation and Program," which served as the Socialist Party's platform. The platform charged that capitalism was the cause of the War and recommended "continuous, active, and public opposition to the War through demonstrations, mass petitions, and any other means within [the people's] power." Although Debs was not prosecuted for signing the proclamation, the Court relied in part on Debs' signature to "infer" his intent to obstruct the War.

The Court was not concerned with the part of the speech that pertained to the growth and success of socialism. Instead, Justice Holmes focused on the part of Debs' speech in which he told his audience that he had just returned from a visit to the workhouse where his loyal comrades were paying for their devotion to the working class. His comrades had been convicted of aiding and abetting one another in failing to register for the draft. After praising several of them for their efforts, Debs said that he had to be "prudent" and might not be able to say all that he thought, intimating to the listeners that they could infer that he meant more. Justice Holmes considered this innuendo incriminating.

This part of the decision may have exerted the greatest chilling effect on speech. Since language often is ambiguous, most people would be reluctant to discuss controversial political issues if they feared that their words might be construed in a way that violates a statute. Rather than finding specific intent to oppose the War, Justice Holmes allowed the jury to find that the "natural and intended effect" of Debs' speech was to obstruct the war. Does the analysis in *Debs* allow government to prosecute someone for making a speech during wartime urging people to resist the draft?

Eight months after *Schenck* and *Debs*, the Court adopted a standard even less protective of speech than the clear and present danger test. In *Abrams v. United States*,[11] the Court upheld the convictions of five Bolshevik sympathizers under the Espionage Act as amended in 1918. The defendants were opposed to President Wilson's intervention in the Russian Revolution. They published two anti-war pamphlets that called on munitions factory workers to stop producing bullets that would be used to kill Russians. The pamphlets also called for a general strike to halt the production and shipment of arms.

Although the Court relied on *Schenck* summarily to dispose of the defendants' First Amendment challenges, the majority paid little attention to the "clear and present danger" test. Focusing on the "probable effect" that a general strike would have on the War, the Court found that the only question for review was whether the jury had sufficient evidence to establish guilt. Responding to defendants' argument that their only intent was to promote the Bolshevik cause and not to undermine the war effort, the Court noted that the general strike they advocated necessarily impeded the war effort with Germany.

Justice Holmes, joined by Justice Brandeis, dissented. He construed the Espionage Act to require "imminent" danger *or* the "specific intent" to cause immediate harm. "In this case sentences of twenty years imprisonment have been imposed for the publishing of two leaflets that I believe the defendants had as much

---

[11] 250 U.S. 616 (1919).

right to publish as the Government has to publish the Constitution of the United States now vainly invoked by them."[12] The jury in *Abrams* made a content-based determination as to the value of the speech when deciding guilt. Criticizing content discrimination, Justice Holmes said that the First Amendment guaranteed the free trade of ideas in the marketplace: "the best test of truth is the power of the thought to get itself accepted in the competition of the market."[13]

To counter ignorant or silly ideas, Justice Holmes favored more speech, not less. If time or more speech could correct false speech, then the danger would not be sufficiently immediate to justify governmental suppression of speech. He would require the kind of threat to the law "that an immediate check is required to save the country."[14] By bolstering it with such important notions as specific intent and immediacy, Justice Holmes began to tighten up the clear and present danger test that he had originally fashioned in *Schenck*.

Justice Holmes used his marketplace of ideas metaphor to justify strong protection for free speech. While he was a skeptic, he thought that the clash of ideas provided the best opportunity for truth to emerge. Consistent with this metaphor, Justice Holmes would also protect false speech. Sometimes false speech was valuable in attracting responses that help to clarify the truth. Ultimately, Justice Holmes acknowledged that belief in the marketplace of ideas was essentially an act of faith that truth would prevail. Some commentators have criticized the market approach to free speech as greatly advantaging established groups who already had greater access to the marketplace of ideas.

Many have speculated whether Justice Holmes had changed the position he had taken in *Schenck* and *Debs* and, if so, why. One might argue that Justice Holmes' position in *Abrams* was consistent with his position in those earlier cases since they had directly involved the war effort with Germany. On the other hand, Professor Gerald Gunther has maintained that Justice Holmes' chance encounter and subsequent correspondence with a young Judge Learned Hand deeply influenced his ideas about protection for speech.[15]

In *Gitlow v. New York*,[16] the Court for the first time applied the First Amendment against the states by incorporating it under the Fourteenth Amendment. Nevertheless, the Court still upheld Benjamin Gitlow's conviction against the constitutional challenge. Gitlow, a member of an extremist faction of the Socialist Party, was convicted for publishing "The Left Wing Manifesto,"[17] a document that called for a "proletariat revolution and the Communist reconstruction of society." New York's Criminal Anarchy statute punished, as felons, individuals who advertised or taught the overthrow of government by force.

---

[12] *Id.* at 629.

[13] *Id.* at 630.

[14] *Id.*

[15] *See* G. Gunther, *Learned Hand and the Origins of Modern First Amendment Doctrine: Some Fragments of History*, 27 STAN. L. REV. 719 (1975).

[16] 268 U.S. 652 (1925).

[17] *Id.* at 655.

Justice Sanford held the statute to be valid as an exercise of New York's police power that advanced the state's fundamental right to self-preservation. Justice Sanford found the clear and present danger test inapplicable in this case because the New York statute only punished language and did not require the Court to look into the nexus between the speech and the harm. "A single revolutionary spark may kindle a fire that, smoldering for a time, may burst into a sweeping and destructive conflagration."[18] New York did not have to wait for actual disturbances before acting. In essence, the Court was satisfied if the legislature acted rationally in determining that the state had an interest in prohibiting the advocacy of violent overthrow of the government.

Justice Holmes dissented, joined by Justice Brandeis. Addressing the majority's position that the manifesto was not merely a theory but an incitement, Justice Holmes responded: "Every idea is an incitement. It offers itself for belief and if believed it is acted on unless some other belief outweighs it or some failure of energy stifles the movement at its birth."[19] He added that "[e]loquence may set fire to reason."[20] At some level, Justice Holmes continued his enterprise of tightening the clear and present danger test. This continual tightening of the test, however, illustrated one of its great weaknesses: the words "clear," "present," and "danger" inherently involved questions of degree. Consequently, the test could easily be manipulated to afford greater or lesser protection for speech.

In *Whitney v. California*,[21] the Court upheld the conviction of Anita Whitney for conspiring to overthrow the government under California's Criminal Syndicalism Act. The Court inferred her "specific intent" to overthrow the government from her membership in the Communist Labor Party. The California statute prohibited the "advocacy" of crimes or unlawful violent acts as a means to bring about political change. It also forbade the assembly or formation of groups teaching criminal syndication. Part of the evidence used to convict Whitney was based on her association with the Communist Labor Party. At the Party's convention, Whitney had supported a resolution seeking to move the Party away from its militant stance and toward participation in the electoral process. Nevertheless, the Court upheld her conviction because she remained a member after the resolution was defeated.

Justice Brandeis' concurrence in *Whitney* actually was written as a dissent in another case involving a more violent-leaning member of the Communist Party. The case became moot, however, when the defendant died before the Court had finished its review.[22] Joined by Justice Holmes, Justice Brandeis concurred with the result in *Whitney* because the petitioner had failed to raise the proper constitutional objection below.[23]

---

[18] *Id.* at 669.

[19] *Id.* at 673.

[20] *Id.*

[21] 274 U.S. 357 (1927).

[22] *See* R. Cover, *The Left, The Right and The First Amendment: 1918–1928*, 40 Md. L. Rev. 349 (1981).

[23] Instead of alleging lack of the requisite clear and present danger, Whitney contended that she lacked the intent to accomplish the unlawful objectives of the Communist Labor Party.

Justice Brandeis criticized the Court's application of the clear and present danger test as ambiguous. He said that a danger was "clear" when it was "serious." While he recognized government's interest in self-preservation, he argued that speech may not be suppressed simply because it may lead to violence or the destruction of property. The danger feared must be substantial. He defined "present" danger as "imminent" danger. The evil to society must be so immediate that it may transpire before the opportunity for full discussion. According to Justice Brandeis' definition of the clear and present danger test, government could only suppress speech in times of emergency when the danger of harm was *both* serious and imminent. While government may proscribe incitement, attempts to incite, or conspiracy to incite, government could not prohibit advocacy, preparation, or assembly.

Justice Brandeis' opinion contained most of the rationales for the modern Court's strong protection for freedom of political speech. The key rationale was that of allowing people to develop their own personalities, and to enable decisions to be made by a democratic deliberative process rather than by the arbitrary exercise of authority. Free speech was the key to liberty that the Founders valued as both an end and as a means. Freedom of speech advanced the pursuit of truth. It also provided an avenue for dissent, which preserved societal stability. Permitting freedom of speech actually was conservative. By fostering gradual societal change and by allowing everyone to have their say, it actually helped to prevent revolution.

Justice Brandeis' rationales for protecting free speech, particularly the promotion of democracy and self-fulfillment, were embraced and elaborated on by noted First Amendment scholars Alexander Meiklejohn and Thomas Emerson. According to Alexander Meiklejohn, the essential reason for protecting speech was that the free exchange of different ideas was necessary for a democratic society.[24] If the people were truly to be the ultimate decision-makers, they had to be informed enough to exercise effective choice in voting and influencing government. To be informed decision-makers, the public required not only speech about political ideas but also literary, scientific and educational speech. All were necessary in shaping political discourse. Meiklejohn predicated broad protection of free speech on the public's right to know and the audience's right to receive information. Thomas Emerson, on the other hand, focused on the speaker's right to speak.

In contrast to Meiklejohn, Thomas Emerson offered four rationales for protecting free speech: (1) individual self-fulfillment; (2) the pursuit of knowledge and truth; (3) participation in democracy and in other aspects of our culture; and (4) political dissent to effect social change.[25] In addition to these important rationales for protecting free speech, Emerson elaborated the speech-action continuum.

---

[24] *See* A. MEIKLEJOHN, FREEDOM OF SPEECH AND ITS RELATION TO SELF-GOVERNMENT (1948); Meiklejohn, *The First Amendment is an Absolute*, 1961 SUP. CT. REV. 245. *See also* W. Brennan, *The Supreme Court and the Meiklejohn Interpretation of the First Amendment*, 79 HARV. L. REV. 1 (1965).

[25] T. EMERSON, THE SYSTEM OF FREEDOM OF EXPRESSION 6–7 (1970).

Emerson's speech-action continuum had pure speech on one end and pure conduct on the other. Most forms of expression that people engaged in fell somewhere in-between the two extremes. Emerson interpreted the First Amendment to afford greater protection for behavior that more closely resembled speech and less protection for behavior that more closely resembled conduct. Again, indicating the importance of Justice Brandeis' opinion in *Whitney*, the speech-action continuum has important similarities with the distinction that Justice Brandeis made between advocacy and incitement.

Following a series of dissents and concurrences by Justices Holmes and Brandeis during the 1920s, the Court dramatically increased protection for speech during the 1930s and 1940s. In 1951, the Court reversed this trend in *Dennis v. United States.*[26]

In *Dennis*, the Court reviewed the convictions of 11 of the national leaders of the American Communist Party for violations of the Smith Act, which was America's first peacetime sedition act since 1798. The Smith Act outlawed organized advocacy that called for changing the government by force or violence. Tailored with the American Communist Party in mind and passed in 1940, the Smith Act came to life during the Cold War when the fear of the Communist threat, both at home and abroad, reached almost hysterical proportions. *Dennis* helped pave the way for the abuses that characterized the McCarthy era.

In a plurality opinion, Chief Justice Vinson found that even the clear and present danger test, developed by Justices Holmes and Brandeis, bore little relationship to the Communist threat, because it would prevent the government from meeting the slow and secretive danger of Communist infiltration. Instead, the plurality of four abandoned the clear and present danger test in favor of a loose balancing approach heavily skewed toward the government's interest in self-preservation. Potential subversion should be stopped before it became a clear and present danger.

Justice Frankfurter's concurrence recognized that Chief Justice Vinson's virtually open balancing approach needed to be confined. He offered three rules, based on historical analysis, to accomplish this. His first and most important principle required that the judiciary give substantial deference to the legislature when balancing competing interests. Because the legislature had access to more information concerning national security, it was better able to assess the risks involved with the Communist threat. This principle allowed Congress considerable freedom to set the balance by granting it discretion to determine what constituted a threat to national security. Justice Frankfurter's second rule allowed the balancing of interests to adapt to the demands of the current situation. This made free speech protection situation-specific. His third principle asserted that the Court could determine that certain types of speech were protected and other types were not. In *Dennis*, he distinguished between speech as an interchange of ideas, which was protected, and "advocacy," which was not.

In his concurring opinion, Justice Jackson distanced himself from the clear and present danger test saying that it was fashioned for the hot head on the street

---

[26] 341 U.S. 494 (1951).

corner. He characterized the Communist Party as a continuing conspiracy seeking government overthrow.

Justices Black and Douglas wrote separate dissenting opinions. Justice Douglas described the case as involving a charge for "conspiracy to advocate and teach."[27] Rather than suppressing the teachings of Stalin, Marx, and Engels, the government should allow them to be exposed to the light of criticism, to show the ugliness of Communism. For Justice Douglas, the only way that the Communist Party could hurt our nation was if we were to let them do so by giving up our freedom of speech.

Justice Black characterized the conviction as a prior restraint. The First Amendment's phrasing, "Congress shall pass no law," should be interpreted literally. Justice Black's absolutist approach to free speech, also embraced by Justice Douglas, was criticized by Justice Frankfurter as being simplistic and naive. "Absolute rules," Justice Frankfurter said, "breed absolute exceptions."[28] While the Court never adopted the absolutist approach to freedom of speech, Justices Black's and Douglas' position powerfully influenced the modern Court's stringent protection for free speech.

Six years after *Dennis*, the Court overturned the convictions of 14 lower level leaders of the American Communist Party under the Smith Act in *Yates v. United States*.[29] In contrast to *Dennis*, the *Yates* Court construed the Smith Act to require incitement of action forcibly to overthrow the government. While the case was decided on statutory interpretation grounds, the interpretation was motivated by constitutional concerns. Moving away from a balancing approach toward a bright lines approach, the *Yates* test maintained that certain speech was presumptively protected unless it met certain criteria.[30]

Brandenburg v. Ohio[31] is emblematic of the bright lines approach that characterized the free speech jurisprudence of the Warren Court and continues to exert considerable influence on free speech doctrine. In the historically sensitive area of subversive speech, the *Brandenburg* test exemplifies the depth of the modern Court's commitment to the First Amendment's guarantee of free speech. In *Brandenburg*, the Court reviewed the conviction of a Ku Klux Klan leader under Ohio's Criminal Syndicalism statute,[32] a statute similar to the one the Court sustained in *Whitney*.

Brandenburg invited a Cincinnati television reporter and his cameraman to film a Klan "rally," where Brandenburg made speeches to fellow Klansmen. Although most of the content of the speeches was inaudible, Brandenburg clearly made

---

[27] *Id.* at 582.

[28] *Id.* at 523.

[29] 354 U.S. 298 (1957).

[30] Essentially, the Court demanded advocacy to move people violently to overthrow the government.

[31] 395 U.S. 444 (1969).

[32] Ohio's Criminal Syndicalism statute prohibited "advocat[ing] . . . the duty, necessity, or propriety of crime, sabotage, violence, or unlawful methods of terrorism as means of accomplishing industrial or political reform." *Id.* at 444.

several derogatory remarks about African-Americans and Jews.[33] Boasting that the Klan had the largest membership of any organization in the state, Brandenburg proclaimed that 400,000 of its members were planning a march in Washington, D.C. and then in Florida and Mississippi. He continued: "We're not a revengent [sic] organization, but if our President, our Congress, our Supreme Court continues to suppress the white, Caucasian race, it's possible that there might have to be some revengance [sic] taken."[34] Although Brandenburg himself was not armed, several people in one film carried weapons.

In overturning the conviction, the Court declared that the First Amendment did "not permit a State to forbid or proscribe advocacy . . . except where such advocacy is directed to inciting or producing imminent lawless action and is likely to incite or produce such action."[35] This was a "bright lines" or categorical approach to free speech issues, at least in the political context. To meet the *Brandenburg* test, the speech must fit within certain categories. First, the speech must be an incitement. The *Brandenburg* Court also required that the speech be objectively likely to produce imminent lawless action, and that the speaker subjectively intended to produce such imminent lawless action. The speech must meet all three of these criteria before government can proscribe it. To illustrate the test, the Court contrasted teaching the moral necessity of using force, with preparing or steeling a group for violent action. The Court held the Ohio Criminal Syndicalism statute unconstitutional on its face. As the Ohio statute was similar to the one upheld in *Whitney*, the Court overruled *Whitney*.

Justice Douglas' concurring opinion rejected the clear and present danger test outright. The test's flexibility allowed it to be easily manipulated by judges, who represented the status quo, to squash small threats.

Hess v. Indiana[36] applied the *Brandenburg* test to overturn the conviction of an Indiana University student for disorderly conduct during an anti-war demonstration. After Hess and his fellow demonstrators were curbside off the street, Hess was arrested when a sheriff overheard him say something that was later stipulated to be, "We'll take the fucking street later" or "We'll take the fucking street again." In a *per curiam* opinion, the Court characterized Hess' speech as "[at] best . . . counsel for present moderation; at worst, it amounted to nothing more than advocacy of illegal action at some indefinite future time."[37] As Hess involved a situation with greater danger of "imminent lawless action" than the small group of Klansmen on film in *Brandenburg*, it demonstrated the stringency with which the Court applied the *Brandenburg* test.

In *NAACP v. Claiborne Hardware Co.*,[38] the Court held that *Brandenburg* did not permit a civil action for a speech made by the leader of an economic boycott

---

[33] Some of the language he used was " 'Bury the Niggers' " and " 'The Nigger will have to fight for every inch he gets from now on.' " *Id.* at 446.

[34] *Id.*

[35] *Id.* at 447.

[36] 414 U.S. 105 (1973).

[37] *Id.* at 108.

[38] 458 U.S. 886 (1982).

that called for violence against boycott violators. The Court did say that if acts of violence had followed the speech, a "substantial question" would have been presented regarding liability. This *dicta*, suggesting that actionability hinges on what happened after the speech, contrasted with the apparent thrust of *Brandenburg*, *i.e.*, that the objective assessment of imminent lawless action focus on the time that the speech was uttered.

[2]   Other Basic Ideas in Protecting Free Speech

In *Meese v. Keene*,[39] the Court upheld a provision of the Foreign Agents Registration Act that required certain material defined as "political propaganda" to be labeled as having been "prepared, edited, issued or circulated" by an agent of a foreign government. The Court did not consider the label pejorative, saying that it simply provided information.

In *Illinois ex rel. Madigan v. Telemarketing Associates*,[40] the Court held that the First Amendment does not protect for-profit organizations from fraudulent misrepresentations that they make concerning the percentage of proceeds that will go to charity. VietNow, a nonprofit organization, contracted with Telemarketers, a professional fund-raising company. Under the contract, Telemarketers would retain 85 percent of the proceeds, with 15 percent going to VietNow.

The First Amendment leaves room for fraud claims. In soliciting donations, the fundraisers told one affiant that 90 percent or more of the contributions would go to the veterans. Intentional lies, like this one, are unprotected speech. *Schaumburg v. Citizens for a Better Environment*[41] invalidated on overbreadth grounds an ordinance requiring charitable organizations to use at least 75 percent of their contributions directly for the " 'charitable purpose of the organization.' "[42] This " 'unduly burdensome' prophylactic rule,"[43] incorrectly assumed that charities derived no benefit from the information disseminated through the solicitation process itself. To prove fraud, Illinois required plaintiffs to show by clear and convincing evidence that the defendant knowingly "made a false representation of a material fact."[44] This assertion must have been made "with the intent to mislead the listener,"[45] and the defendant must have succeeded in doing so. An appellate court is able independently to review the findings made by the trial court. Justice Scalia, joined by Justice Thomas, filed a concurring opinion.

---

[39]   481 U.S. 465 (1987).

[40]   538 U.S. 600 (2003).

[41]   444 U.S. 620 (1980).

[42]   *Secretary of State v. Joseph H. Munson Co.*, 467 U.S. 947 (1984), did not allow a similar law that provided an exception from the 75 percent cap if it prevents the organization from fund-raising. *Riley v. National Federation of Blind of N.C., Inc.*, 487 U.S. 781 (1988), struck down a law establishing a rebuttable presumption of unreasonableness if charities paid fund-raising fees greater than 35 percent of the donation.

[43]   *Telemarketing Assocs.*, 538 U.S. at 616.

[44]   *Id.* at 620.

[45]   *Id.*

In *Minnesota State for Community Colleges v. Knight*,[46] the Court sustained a state statute limiting public employees' right to "meet and confer" on employment-related matters. The Court held that if professional employees have selected an exclusive bargaining agent, the employer may not meet and confer with any member of the bargaining unit except through the exclusive representative.

In *University of Pennsylvania v. EEOC*,[47] the Court held that the First Amendment provided universities with no special privileges against disclosing relevant "peer review materials" used in tenure decisions when charges of race or gender discrimination were pending. While the Court acknowledged the importance of legitimate academic decision-making, it found the connection to academic freedom "speculative."[48] In contrast to *Keyishian v. Board of Regents, infra*, the government was not attempting to regulate content of the university speech through selection of faculty. Instead, the government was merely attempting to prevent the selection of faculty by the University on grounds prohibited by Title VII.

§ 13.02   MEMBERSHIP IN POLITICAL ORGANIZATIONS AS A BASIS FOR GOVERNMENT SANCTIONS

The right of association is not explicitly mentioned in the First Amendment but has been derived from the right to free speech. Alexis de Tocqueville characterized freedom of association as "endemic" to the right of free speech.[49] He observed that the "most natural privilege of man, next to the right of acting for himself, is that of combining his exertions with those of his fellow creatures and interacting in common with them."[50] The right to speak lacks meaning without the right to associate with others to exchange ideas.

Much like the subversive speech cases, the early association cases upheld the convictions of Communist Party leaders under the Smith Act. In *Scales v. United States*,[51] for example, the Court upheld a jury verdict under the Smith Act that convicted Scales, the Chairman of the North and South Carolina Districts of the Communist Party. The Court found that the jury had properly determined that the Communist Party advocated the violent overthrow of the government, and that Scales was an active party member. The key inquiry was whether Scales had the specific intent to bring about the violent overthrow of the government.

The Court held that it was reasonable for the jury to infer that Scales' specific purpose was to effectuate the illegal, revolutionary activities he advocated. Justices Douglas and Black, in separate dissents, reiterated their dissatisfaction with the balancing approach used by the majority. Justice Douglas continued his attempts to

---

[46] 465 U.S. 271 (1984).

[47] 493 U.S. 182 (1990).

[48] *Id.* at 200.

[49] 1 ALEXIS DE TOCQUEVILLE, DEMOCRACY IN AMERICA 203 (P. Bradely ed., 1954).

[50] *Id.*

[51] 367 U.S. 203 (1961).

draw a line between speech and action, arguing that Scales was convicted for his beliefs and not his conduct.[52]

In *Noto v. United States*,[53] the Court set aside a Smith Act conviction because the evidence of illegal party advocacy was insufficient to support this conviction. The Court merely required evidence of a "call to violence" that could be imputed to the Communist party as a whole.

In *Keyishian v. Board of Regents*,[54] the Court upheld, on overbreadth and vagueness grounds, a challenge by faculty members of the State University of New York at Buffalo to portions of New York's Feinberg law. They attacked a statutory requirement that they sign a statement saying that they were not Communists, and that they had never been Communists. If the teachers refused to sign, they were dismissed.

Writing for the majority, Justice Brennan focused on certain terms in the statutes, such as the term "seditious," that he found to be unconstitutionally vague. A teacher could not possibly know what constituted "seditious" and "non-seditious" speech or conduct. The case also recognized academic freedom as having "transcendent value."[55] The First Amendment did not "tolerate laws that cast a pall of orthodoxy over the classroom."[56]

The Court also found unconstitutionally overbroad statutory sections that disqualified members of listed organizations from employment. Membership with knowledge of the illegal aims of the organization was not enough to justify exclusion from their teaching positions. In addition, the government had to establish membership with the specific intent to advance the illegal aims of the organization.[57]

Since *Keyishian*, and particularly in the 1970s, many cases involving membership laws were struck down using the overbreadth doctrine. Overbreadth is a doctrine peculiar to the First Amendment. When a law reaches both protected and unprotected speech, the Court is concerned about the potential chilling effect the law might have on those who wish to engage in protected speech. When a law is overbroad, the Court strikes down the entire law, even though the person challenging the law may have engaged in speech that is constitutionally unprotected.[58]

Some overbroad laws, like the one in *Keyishian*, are also vague. Laws are vague when individuals are unable to tell whether their conduct is legal or illegal. While

---

[52] *Id.* at 263.

[53] 367 U.S. 290 (1961).

[54] 385 U.S. 589 (1967).

[55] *Id.* at 603.

[56] *Id.*

[57] While government cannot compel public employees to swear that they will not become members of the Communist Party, *see* Elfbrandt v. Russell, 384 U.S. 11 (1966), lower courts have allowed oaths upholding the Constitution of the United States or opposing the violent overthrow of the government. *See* Cole v. Richardson, 405 U.S. 676 (1972); Knight v. Board of Regents, 269 F. Supp. 339 (S.D.N.Y. 1967), *aff'd per curiam*, 390 U.S. 36 (1968).

[58] The overbreadth doctrine frequently provides standing to those who lack it. *See infra* § 13.05[2].

overbreadth is a uniquely First Amendment challenge, vagueness involves due process concerns of the Fifth and Fourteenth Amendments. Only a law that involves free speech concerns can be overbroad, while any law can be vague. For example, an environmental regulation can be vague. The Court's use of "void for vagueness" to strike down a statute reflects the idea of fundamental fairness in American jurisprudence: in order for the law to be constitutional, a person must know from a statute whether her conduct violates the statute. Overbreadth and vagueness are discussed in greater detail in § 13.07[1].

The Court has adhered to the basic distinction between mere membership and advancing the illegal aims of the group involved. In *Dawson v. Delaware*,[59] the Court vacated a capital sentence imposed after a Delaware trial court improperly admitted, at the sentencing hearing, a stipulation noting defendant's membership in the Aryan Brotherhood prison gang and describing the nature of that gang. As the prosecution never established that Dawson's membership indicated anything more than abstract beliefs, it was not relevant evidence, and consequently it violated defendant's right of association. However, in *Wisconsin v. Mitchell*,[60] the Court upheld a sentence enhancement provision for hate crimes. Unlike Dawson, the defendant was not being punished for membership in a group, but instead for assaulting the victim because of his race.[61]

§ 13.03 DISCLOSURE OF POLITICAL AFFILIATIONS

In *Communist Party v. Subversive Activities Control Board (SACB)*,[62] the Court narrowly upheld an SACB order that required the Communist Party to register as an organization controlled by a foreign government "controlling the world Communist movement." At the time of registration, the organization was also ordered to submit to the SACB a list of its members. Once the organization registered, its members were subject to a variety of restrictions. For example, they could not work in defense plants, become officers or employees of unions, hold nonelective public office, or apply for passports.

Justice Frankfurter's majority opinion upheld the registration requirement. He refused to consider the penalties resulting from the registration because they were not ripe for adjudication. Much like his *Dennis* concurrence, Justice Frankfurter emphasized the importance of deference to the legislature. He said that the decision did not allow the imposition of similar requirements on any politically unpopular group, but only on foreign dominated organizations that existed "primarily to advance the objectives of a world movement controlled by the government of a *foreign* country."[63]

Justice Black's dissent criticized Justice Frankfurter's ripeness determination. Justice Black argued that the burdens imposed by the Act would scare people away

---

[59] 503 U.S. 159 (1992).

[60] 508 U.S. 476 (1993).

[61] For additional discussion of *Mitchell, see infra.*

[62] 367 U.S. 1 (1961).

[63] *Id.* at 104 (emphasis in original).

from the Communist Party and from challenging the order itself. Therefore, the penalty provisions might never come before the Court again. Chief Justice Warren, Justice Douglas, and Justice Brennan also wrote dissenting opinions, but only Justice Black concluded that the act violated the First Amendment.

Four years later, the Supreme Court held that an SACB order directing two Communist Party members to register violated their Fifth Amendment privilege.[64] Moreover, the Court invalidated another provision of the law preventing a Communist Party member from using a passport in *Aptheker v. Secretary of State*.[65] Justice Goldberg's majority opinion concluded that the prohibition was overbroad because it applied to any Communist Party member, regardless of the individual's status as active or non-active, knowledge of the party's objectives, or intent to bring about those objectives.

In *United States v. Robel*,[66] the Court upheld an overbreadth challenge to the provision of the statute that prohibited members of the Communist Party from being employed in defense plants. Chief Justice Warren's majority opinion emphasized that the Court was not denying Congress the power to keep Communists out of sensitive defense positions. In a footnote, Chief Justice Warren explicitly declined to use an approach that balanced the Congressional and First Amendment interests. Instead, he required Congress to tailor legislation narrowly to avoid the conflict. Justice Brennan's concurrence stated that Congress could exclude Communist Party members from sensitive defense facilities.

The Court also upheld legislative inquiries into membership in the Communist Party. In *Barenblatt v. United States*,[67] the Court upheld a contempt of Congress conviction of a university professor who refused to answer questions asked by a subcommittee of the House Committee on Un-American Activities.[68] Barenblatt expressly declined to base his refusal to answer the committee's questions on the Fifth Amendment's self-incrimination clause. Instead, he justified his refusal based on the importance of the First Amendment's protection of freedom of association, particularly in an academic environment. In upholding Barenblatt's contempt citation, the Court used a balancing test that placed significantly greater emphasis on Congress' right to engage in legislative inquiry.

Once the door was opened for legislative investigations of the Communist Party, legislatures could try to investigate other groups by characterizing them as Communist-infiltrated. In *Gibson v. Florida Legislative Investigation Committee*,[69] the Legislative Investigation Committee of Florida ordered the President of the Miami branch of the NAACP to appear before it, answer questions, and bring membership records. The inquiry purportedly sought to examine Communist infiltration of the organization. While Gibson appeared before the Committee and

---

[64] *See* Albertson v. Subversive Activities Control Bd., 382 U.S. 70 (1965). *See also* Communist Party v. United States, 331 F.2d 807 (D.C. Cir. 1963), *cert. denied*, 377 U.S. 968 (1964).

[65] 378 U.S. 500 (1964).

[66] 389 U.S. 258 (1967).

[67] 360 U.S. 109 (1959).

[68] The Committee was formally known as the Dies Committee.

[69] 372 U.S. 539 (1963).

answered questions, he refused to bring membership records.

Acknowledging the legislature's inherent power to conduct investigations, the Court emphasized that the inquiry at issue infringed on the right of association. Consequently, to obtain the information sought, the state must show that the inquiry bore a substantial relationship to a compelling state interest. The Court stated that in the past a showing that the Communist Party was involved had been enough to establish a compelling state interest. However, the record did not establish any links between the Communist Party and the NAACP sufficient to overcome the infringement on associational rights.

Justice Harlan's dissent criticized the Court's reasoning as circular because the entire purpose of the legislative inquiry at issue was to establish the nexus required by the Court. This circularity, which stymied investigations, was indicative of the majority's intent to protect associational rights.

The Court has allowed some inquiries into Communist Party membership, however. In *Konigsberg v. California*[70] and *In re Anastaplo*,[71] the Court sustained state refusals to admit bar applicants who refused to answer questions concerning membership in the Communist Party.

Protection for free speech extends beyond nondisclosure of political party to safeguarding the anonymity of speakers who have other political affiliations or take certain political positions. In *McIntyre v. Ohio Elections Commission*,[72] the Court held that a statute prohibiting the distribution of anonymous campaign literature violates the First Amendment. McIntyre had anonymously distributed some leaflets in which she expressed her opposition to a proposed school tax. This behavior violated an Ohio law requiring the name and address of the distributor to be printed on the leaflet.

Justice Stevens stated that the public interest in having anonymous expression far outweighs any benefit that would be obtained by compelling disclosure. As the statute attempted to regulate "pure speech," the Court subjected the law to "exacting scrutiny." The state argued that its interests in preventing fraudulent and libelous statements and in providing the electorate with relevant information were sufficiently compelling to justify the prohibition of anonymous handbills. In rejecting these arguments, the Court stated that while the identity of the author was a helpful factor in evaluating a message, its absence did not outweigh the value of the expression itself. The Court did accept the state's asserted interest in preventing election fraud due to electoral misrepresentations. However, the Court ultimately found this interest insufficient to justify the statute's broad proscription as more specific sections of the Ohio Code prohibited making false statements during political campaigns.

The Court distinguished *Buckley v. Valeo*.[73] In contrast to the Ohio statute at issue, the disclosure requirement upheld in *Buckley* required that those expending

---

[70] 366 U.S. 36 (1961).

[71] 366 U.S. 82 (1961).

[72] 514 U.S. 334 (1995).

[73] *See infra* § 16.02.

money in support of a political campaign report the amount and use of such funds. *Buckley* permitted a narrowly drawn disclosure requirement because of the important state interest in avoiding corruption.

Concurring, Justice Ginsburg noted that the Ohio statute even applied to the individual leafletter, and that the majority opinion did not prohibit disclosure "in other, larger circumstances."[74] Concurring in the judgment, Justice Thomas argued that the Framers must have intended that anonymous political speech be permitted because of the anonymity in The Federalist Papers and in the first federal elections.

Justice Scalia dissented, joined by Chief Justice Rehnquist. He argued that traditional and longstanding practices such as the prohibition of anonymous political speech bear a strong presumption of constitutionality. These longstanding traditions far outweigh any speculation on the unclear intent of the Framers towards anonymous political speech. Even without historical practice, safeguarding the electoral process outweighs any right to anonymity in political speech.

Justice Scalia predicted that this new right to anonymity would spawn considerable litigation. For example, can groups anonymously seek parade permits or book space in government owned theaters? Can letters to the editor in government periodicals be anonymous?

In *Buckley v. American Constitutional Law Foundation*,[75] the Court invalidated Colorado requirements for ballot initiatives that petition circulators be registered voters, that they wear identification nametags, and that their compensation be disclosed. In rejecting the registered voters requirement, the majority found that Colorado's asserted purpose of maintaining jurisdiction over petition circulators who are lawbreakers was satisfied by the separate requirement that circulators submit affidavits averring their current addresses.

The residency affidavit also rendered the badge requirement superfluous, while avoiding the risk that circulators would experience harassment. Colorado's badge requirement failed "exacting scrutiny." The Court did not decide on the constitutionality of badges revealing whether the circulator was a volunteer or paid and the identity of the payor.

Justice Ginsburg's majority opinion also invalidated the requirement of revealing the identities of and amounts earned by paid circulators. In contrast, the majority upheld, under *Buckley v. Valeo*, disclosing the identities of and amounts paid by those who compensate circulators. Justice Ginsburg also noted that Colorado required proponents of initiatives to submit "valid signatures representing five percent of the total votes cast for all candidates for Secretary of State at the previous general election" enacted for the purpose of "ensur[ing] grass roots support." She also described a list of uncontested "process measures" prescribed by Colorado "in aid of efficiency, veracity, or clarity."[76]

---

[74] *Buckley*, 514 U.S. at 358.

[75] 525 U.S. 182 (1999).

[76] These measures included "a signature verification method, a large, plain-English notice alerting potential signers of petitions to the proposed law's requirements, and the text of the affidavit to which all circulators must subscribe." *Id.* at 205.

Justice Thomas concurred in the judgment, arguing that the Court should have applied "strict scrutiny" as the law "directly regulates core political speech."

Chief Justice Rehnquist dissented. For the majority, "any ballot initiative regulation is unconstitutional if it either diminishes the pool of people who can circulate petitions or makes it more difficult for a given issue to ultimately appear on the ballot." Justice O'Connor, joined by Justice Breyer, concurred in the judgment in part and dissented in part. Justice O'Connor would have upheld the registered voter requirement.

In *Doe v. Reed*,[77] the Court held that disclosure of referendum petitions authorized by the Washington Public Records Act (PRA) did not violate the First Amendment. The PRA was used to obtain the names and addresses of those who signed a petition for a referendum on a law which expanded certain benefits of state-registered domestic partners, including same-sex partnerships. Plaintiffs must meet the standards for a facial challenge. Buckley requires those opposing disclosure to demonstrate a " 'reasonable probability that the compelled disclosure [of personal information] will subject them to threats, harassment, or reprisals from either Government officials or private parties.' "[78] The Court rejected the facial challenge as only modest burdens attend disclosure of most state referenda in areas like tax or budget.

Concurring, Justice Breyer largely joined Justice Stevens' opinion. Justice Alito also concurred. He would require prompt judicial remedies well before the relevant speech occurred with a low burden of proof.

Justice Sotomayor concurred, joined by Justices Stevens and Ginsburg. Justice Sotomayor urged skepticism on as-applied challenges to disclosure of the identities of participants in the referendum process as the Constitution advances transparency.

Concurring in part and concurring in the judgment, Justice Stevens stated that a significant threat of harassment would have to exist for a successful as-applied challenge. Concurring, Justice Scalia warned about expanding the mistake of *McIntyre v. Ohio Elections Comm'n*. Prohibiting disclosure of petition signatures undercuts the centuries-old practice of legislating and voting publically. Dissenting, Justice Thomas viewed compelled disclosure as a harsh burden on First Amendment rights.

§ 13.04 ASSOCIATIONAL RIGHTS TO ASSIST TERRORIST ORGANIZATION

Holder v. Humanitarian Law Project upheld a federal law prohibiting "the provision of 'material support or resources' " to foreign terrorist organizations.[79] The statute did not violate freedom of speech or association and was not impermissibly vague.

---

[77] 130 S. Ct. 2811 (2010).

[78] *Id.* at 2820.

[79] 130 S. Ct. 2705 (2010).

The prohibition on material support was premised on a congressional finding that designated foreign terrorist organizations " 'are so tainted by their criminal conduct that any contribution to such an organization facilitates that conduct.' "[80] The Secretary of State designates a " 'foreign terrorist organization,' " which can be appealed within 30 days. Plaintiffs seek to support two foreign terrorist organizations, the Partiya Karkeran Kurdistan (PKK) and the Liberation Tigers of Tamil Eelam (LTTE). The PKK aims to establish an independent Kurdish state in southeastern Turkey, and the LTTE seeks an independent Tamil state in Sri Lanka. The Government presented evidence that both groups have committed numerous terrorist attacks, some of which harmed American citizens. The LTTE appealed its designation as a foreign terrorist organization, but the D.C. Circuit upheld it. Two U.S. citizens and six domestic organizations filed suit in 1998 claiming "they wished to provide support for the humanitarian and political activities of the PKK and the LTTE in the form of monetary contributions, other tangible aid, legal training, and political advocacy, but that they could not do so for fear of prosecution under § 2339B."[81]

Congress decided to make the mental state for a violation of § 2339B "knowledge about the organization's connection to terrorism, not specific intent to further the organization's terrorist activities."[82] *Scales v. United States*[83] was distinguishable, for § 2339B criminalizes providing " 'material support' " and not "mere membership."[84]

Chief Justice Roberts wrote for Court. The material-support statute was not unconstitutionally vague under the Due Process Clause of the Fifth Amendment. The Court does subject to a stringent vagueness test statutes that impact the right of free speech or association, but " ' "perfect clarity and precise guidance have never been required even of regulations that restrict expressive activity." ' "[85] If a statute clearly proscribes one's speech, he cannot succeed in a vagueness claim "for lack of notice. And he certainly cannot do so based on the speech of others."[86] He may, however, have a valid First Amendment overbreadth claim. The statutory terms " 'training,' 'expert advice or assistance,' 'service,' and 'personnel' " are not vague, as they do not require "untethered, subjective judgments."[87] Moreover, the statute's knowledge requirement "further reduces any potential for vagueness."[88] Although the statute's scope "may not be clear in every application," the terms clearly apply to the conduct at issue.[89] A "person of ordinary intelligence" would understand that most of the plaintiffs' proposed activities "readily fall within the scope of the terms

---

[80] *Id.* at 2724.

[81] *Id.* at 2714.

[82] *Id.* at 2717.

[83] 361 U.S. 952 (1960).

[84] *Holder*, 130 S. Ct. at 2718.

[85] *Id.* at 2719.

[86] *Id.*

[87] *Id.* at 2720.

[88] *Id.*

[89] *Id.*

'training' and 'expert advice or assistance.' "[90] Moreover, the preenforcement timing of the challenge renders scope of application questions "entirely hypothetical."[91]

The material-support statute, as applied to the plaintiffs, did not abridge freedom of speech. Congress has not banned " 'pure political speech.' "[92] The "plaintiffs may say anything they wish on any topic," including the PKK and LTTE.[93] Congress banned " 'material support,' " which generally is not speech. The Government presses this point too far, claiming that only conduct is at issue, not speech. However, "the statute is carefully drawn to cover only a narrow category of speech to, under the direction of, or in coordination with foreign groups that the speaker knows to be terrorist organizations."[94] The regulations are content-based as they prohibit plaintiffs from speaking to the PKK and LTTE. Consequently, *United States v. O'Brien* is inapplicable.

In enacting the statute, Congress "considered and rejected the view that ostensibly peaceful aid would have no harmful effects."[95] Specific findings on the serious threat of international terrorism showed that foreign terrorist organizations " 'are so tainted by their criminal conduct that *any contribution to such an organization* facilitates that conduct.' "[96] The PKK has killed more than 22,000 people, and the LTTE "has engaged in extensive suicide bombings and political assassinations, including killings of the Sri Lankan President, Security Minister, and Deputy Defense Minister."[97] The LTTE also killed 100 people with a truck bomb. Material support "frees up other resources within the organization that may be put to violent ends. It also importantly helps lend legitimacy to foreign terrorist groups — legitimacy that makes it easier for those groups to persist, to recruit members, and to raise funds — all of which facilitate more terrorist attacks."[98] Money is fungible, and although terrorist organizations that also pursue civilian and humanitarian activities emphasize those activities, evidence exists that the PKK and the LTTE "have not 'respected the line between humanitarian and violent activities.' "[99]

The dissent argues that there is " 'no natural stopping place' " for the argument that support is fungible, but Congress has specified such a point: "The statute reaches only material support coordinated with or under the direction of a designated foreign terrorist organization. Independent advocacy that might be viewed as promoting the group's legitimacy is not covered."[100] Allowing American citizens to provide material support to terrorist organizations may also strain

---

[90] *Id.*

[91] *Id.* at 2722.

[92] *Id.* at 2723.

[93] *Id.* at 2722–23.

[94] *Id.* at 2723.

[95] *Id.* at 2725.

[96] *Id.* at 2724.

[97] *Id.* at 2725.

[98] *Id.*

[99] *Id.* at 2726.

[100] *Id.*

relations with our allies. Moreover, the Court saw "no reason to question Congress's finding that 'international cooperation is required for an effective response to terrorism.' "[101] Congress and the Executive's factual evaluations deserve deference. The Court does "not defer to the Government's reading of the *First Amendment*," but respect is appropriate in collecting evidence and drawing factual inferences.[102] Information on national security, foreign policy, and evolving terrorist threats is difficult to obtain and assess, yet the dissent "slights these real constraints in demanding hard proof" with " 'detail' " and " 'specific facts.' "[103] The "Government, when seeking to prevent imminent harms in the context of international affairs and national security, is not required to conclusively link all the pieces in the puzzle before we grant weight to its empirical conclusions."[104]

The Court also credited Congress with being conscious of its constitutional limits. The statute only applies to the limited number of foreign terrorist organizations, who may seek judicial review of their designation. Moreover, Congress responded to adverse lower court holdings in this litigation by clarifying the statute with narrower definitions. Also, some exceptions exist to the ban on material support, including medicine and religious materials. Most important, Congress did not restrict independent advocacy.

The dissent ignores some real dangers. For example, the United Nations had to close a Kurdish refugee camp in Iraq controlled by the PKK, who did not respect the camp's " 'neutral and humanitarian nature.' "[105] Had the PKK been trained on how to work with the United Nations, then the U.N. "could readily have helped the PKK in its efforts to use the United Nations camp as a base for terrorist activities."[106]

Not all future applications of the material-support statute to speech will survive First Amendment scrutiny. Regulation of independent speech may not be constitutional, even if the speech benefitted foreign terrorist organizations. The Court also did not suggest that such regulations could extend to domestic organizations.

Lastly, the statute did not violate plaintiffs' freedom of association because it only prohibited material support, not being a member of the group or promoting and supporting its political goals. The Preamble to the Constitution and Madison in The Federalist Papers proclaim security against foreign danger an essential object of the Government.

Justice Breyer dissented, joined by Justices Ginsburg and Sotomayor. The dissent agreed that the statute was not unconstitutionally vague. However, Justice Breyer objected to the Court concluding that the Constitution permits criminal prosecution for coordinated teaching and advocacy with designated organizations that furthers their lawful political objectives. The "Government has not met its

---

[101] *Id.*

[102] *Id.* at 2727.

[103] *Id.*

[104] *Id.* at 2728.

[105] *Id.* at 2730.

[106] *Id.*

burden of showing that an interpretation of the statute that would prohibit this speech- and association-related activity serves the Government's compelling interest in combating terrorism."[107] Consequently, the statute should be interpreted to exclude this kind of activity.

The plaintiffs, all United States citizens or associations, seek an injunction and declaration allowing them to "(1) 'train members of [the] PKK on how to use humanitarian and international law to peacefully resolve disputes'; (2) 'engage in political advocacy on behalf of Kurds who live in Turkey'; (3) 'teach PKK members how to petition various representative bodies such as the United Nations for relief'; and (4) 'engage in political advocacy on behalf of Tamils who live in Sri Lanka.' "[108] *Brandenburg v. Ohio*[109] held that "the *First Amendment* protects advocacy even of *unlawful* action so long as that advocacy is not 'directed to inciting or producing *imminent lawless action* and . . . *likely to incite or produce* such action.' Here the plaintiffs seek to advocate peaceful, *lawful* action to secure *political* ends; and they seek to teach others how to do the same."[110] Under *Scales*, a person does not lose First Amendment protection for freedom of association by associating with a group that uses unlawful means to achieve its ends. The statute here imposes criminal penalties at least arguably with content-based distinctions, and should be strictly scrutinized for a " 'compelling' need that cannot be 'less restrictively' accommodated."[111] Even assuming *arguendo* that strict scrutiny is inapplicable, the Court should "at the very least 'measure the validity of the means adopted by Congress against both the goal it has sought to achieve and the specific prohibitions of the *First Amendment*.' "[112] The Government's "compelling countervailing interest" was national security.[113]

There is no *"obvious"* way that advocacy for peaceful political change or teaching the PKK or LTTE to petition the United Nations for political change is fungible with "more sinister ends in the way that donations of money, food, or computer training are fungible."[114] Moreover, speech, association, and related activities will often, perhaps always, help legitimize an organization. This argument has "no natural stopping place."[115] The Communist Party was part of a world movement that (1) "sought to employ 'espionage, sabotage, terrorism, and any other means deemed necessary, to establish a Communist totalitarian dictatorship,' and (2) 'endeavor[ed]' to bring about "the overthrow of existing governments by . . . force if necessary."[116] Nevertheless, the Court protected the "right to belong to that party — despite whatever 'legitimating' effect membership might have had — as long as

---

[107] *Id.* at 2731 (Breyer, J., dissenting).

[108] *Id.* at 2731–32.

[109] 395 U.S. 444 (1969).

[110] *Holder*, 130 S. Ct. at 2733 (Breyer, J., dissenting).

[111] *Id.* at 2734.

[112] *Id.*

[113] *Id.*

[114] *Id.* at 2735.

[115] *Id.* at 2736.

[116] *Id.* at 2737.

the person did not share the party's unlawful purposes."[117]

When free speech is threatened, *Whitney v. California*[118] requires the judiciary to determine "whether there actually did exist at the time a clear danger; whether the danger, if any, was imminent; and whether the evil apprehended was one so substantial as to justify the stringent restriction interposed by the legislature."[119] The Government's foreign affairs expertise frequently warrants deference, but the Court must decide whether the Government has shown an interest that justifies criminalizing speech activity that is otherwise protected by the First Amendment, regardless of the effect on other nations.

When, like here, "there is 'a serious doubt' as to the statute's constitutionality," it should be construed constitutionally. Criminal penalties should be limited to speech and associational activities which the defendant knows or intends "will assist the organization's unlawful terrorist actions."[120] Congress primarily sought to end assistance with fungible money or goods, and the statute itself states it shall not be construed or applied to abridge First Amendment rights.

§ 13.05 ASSOCIATION, POLITICAL PARTIES, AND THE ELECTORAL PROCESS

[1] Regulation of Parties and Ballots

In *Eu v. San Francisco County Democratic Central Committee*,[121] a unanimous Court invalidated, on freedom of association grounds, sections of the California Election Code that regulated the internal organization of political parties in the state. Regulations on, for example, the size and composition of party central committees were not necessary to serve a compelling state interest. Parties had broad discretion in fashioning their own internal structures. Regulations to ensure fair and honest elections could, for example, impose voter eligibility requirements.

The *Eu* Court also invalidated restrictions governing a party's ability to endorse or oppose candidates in primary elections. These would hamper a party's ability to spread its message and voters' ability to receive information. The restrictions were not necessary to advance the compelling interests in stable government and in protecting voters from confusion and undue influence.

In *Norman v. Reed*,[122] the Court struck down an Illinois requirement that a new political party collect 25,000 signatures from *each* district in the county in order to run candidates for county office from any district. Such a requirement made party access to the ballot far more onerous for local elections than for statewide

---

[117] *Id.*

[118] 274 U.S. 357 (1927) (Brandeis, J., concurring).

[119] *Holder*, 130 S. Ct. at 2739 (Breyer, J., dissenting).

[120] *Id.* at 2740.

[121] 489 U.S. 214 (1989).

[122] 502 U.S. 279 (1992).

elections.[123] The Court acknowledged the legitimate state interest in restricting the ballot to parties with demonstrated public support, but noted that "any severe restriction" must be "narrowly drawn to advance a state interest of compelling importance."[124]

In *Timmons v. Twin Cities Area New Party*,[125] the Court upheld a Minnesota law that prohibited candidates from appearing on the ballot as the candidate of more than one party. The Party could endorse candidates not appearing under its name on the ballot, or try to convince candidates to run under its banner. However, the Party had no First Amendment right to use the ballot to express candidate support. The State's interest was " 'sufficiently weighty to justify the limitation' "[126] imposed on the Party's rights. This weightiness need not be established by elaborate empirical evidence. Here, Minnesota had an interest in ensuring that minor party candidates are actually supported on their own merits. Minnesota also had an interest in a stable political system that may result in favoring the two-party system and may limit "the destabilizing effects of party-splintering and factionalism."[127]

In *California Democratic Party v. Jones*,[128] the Court found that blanket primaries infringe on association rights. Proposition 198 allowed voters in California primaries to choose candidates regardless of the party affiliation of the voter or the candidate.

Writing for the majority, Justice Scalia stressed that along with the right to associate comes "the right not to associate." Proposition 198 failed the compelling state interest test. Neither were the state interests compelling, nor was a blanket primary necessary to serve the state interests. The Court did not decide the constitutionality of the open primary where a voter may only vote on one party's ballot. Justice Kennedy concurred in the opinion.

Justice Stevens dissented, joined by Justice Ginsburg only in his analysis. Justice Stevens emphasized that the power of a state to control the election process is "a quintessential attribute of sovereignty."[129]

In *Burdick v. Takushi*,[130] the Court held that an Hawaiian election statute that prohibited write-in voting did not unreasonably infringe upon a citizen's rights of freedom of expression and association. The plaintiff wanted to cast a write-in vote for a congressional candidate in a race in which only one candidate appeared on the ballot.

---

[123] *See* Ill. State Bd. of Elections v. Socialist Workers Party, 440 U.S. 173 (1979).

[124] *Norman*, 502 U.S. at 288.

[125] 520 U.S. 351 (1997).

[126] *Id.* at 364.

[127] *Id.* at 367.

[128] 530 U.S. 567 (2000).

[129] *Id.* at 590.

[130] 504 U.S. 428 (1992).

A 6-3 majority of the Court refused to subject the statute to strict scrutiny and, instead, embraced a more a flexible standard. The Court weighed "the character and magnitude" of the voter's asserted injury "against the precise interests put forward by the State as justifications for the burden imposed by its rule," taking into consideration "'the extent to which those interests make it necessary to burden the plaintiff's rights.'"[131] In so doing, the Court found that even though Hawaii made no provision for write-in voting in its primary or general elections, the three methods which it did provide allowed for easy access to the ballot.[132]

In *Clingman v. Beaver*,[133] the Court upheld an Oklahoma semi-closed primary election system that allows voters registered to a particular political party to vote only in that party's primary election. Independents could vote in any primary that a party opened to them. Justice Thomas noted the states' broad constitutional authority over elections for senators and representatives. Moreover, voters easily could switch their party registration. However, plaintiffs have not even tried to register or formally associate with the Libertarian Party. "When a state electoral provision places no heavy burden on associational rights, 'a State's important regulatory interests will usually be enough to justify reasonable, nondiscriminatory restrictions.'" Here, Oklahoma's primary system ensures that primary elections reflect the views of party members; helps parties' "electioneering and party-building efforts;" and prevents individuals and other parties from manipulating the outcome of the parties' primaries by, for example, switching blocs of voters in an organized way.

Justice O'Connor, joined in part by Justice Breyer, concurred in part and concurred in the judgment. Justice Stevens dissented, joined by Justice Ginsburg and in part by Justice Souter. The case implicates not only the right of voters to associate, but also their right to vote in very important primary elections.

In *Washington State Grange v. Washington Republican Party*,[134] the Court rejected a facial challenge to statute I-872. The statute provided that candidates would be identified on the ballot by the political party they designated; and the top two vote winners would advance to the general election, regardless of party preference. On its face, the statute did not severely burden the associational rights of political parties. Moreover, the contention that this process would confuse voters could "be evaluated only in the context of an as-applied challenge."

In *California Democratic Party v. Jones*,[135] the Court struck down blanket primaries, where voters could vote for a party's nominees even if they were not a

---

[131] *Id.* at 434 (quoting *Anderson v. Celebrezze*, 460 U.S. 780, 789 (1983)).

[132] The three methods referred to by the Court are: (1) via a party petition filed within certain specified time parameters; (2) via the exception for "established parties that have qualified by petition for three consecutive elections and received a specified percentage of the vote in the preceding election"; or (3) via a designed nonpartisan ballot which required a nomination ballot with a certain amount of voter support in the primary.

[133] 544 U.S. 581 (2005).

[134] 552 U.S. 442 (2008).

[135] 530 U.S. 567 (2000).

part of that party. I-872, however, required a candidate to declare his party preference or independent status.

The Court disfavors the speculative nature of facial challenges because this can lead to interpreting statutes prematurely. Moreover, they undermined judicial restraint. Justice Thomas noted that the Constitution granted states broad powers to conduct congressional elections; states enjoyed similar powers over state elections.

Unlike the California primary, I-872 did not purport to select a party's nominees, which a party could do in any way it wanted, but only to reduce the number of candidates to two for the general election. The parties argued that voters will mistakenly assume that these final candidates are the parties' nominees, or at least that the party approves of them. The Court refused to strike down the statute on the "mere possibility of voter confusion." Presumably, the state could design a ballot that eliminates voter confusion. The Court explained that ballots could include a disclaimer that party preference is not an endorsement by a party, but is only a designation provided by the candidate. As I-872 did not severely burden political parties, Washington did not need a compelling interest for structuring its primaries in this manner. Its interest in giving voters information about candidates was enough to uphold the statute.

Chief Justice Roberts concurred, joined by Justice Alito. The record failed to suggest that Washington could not design ballots that prevented voters from assuming that the party listed by the candidates was an indication of an endorsement of that party.

Justice Scalia dissented, joined by Justice Kennedy. Justice Scalia argued that nominating candidates for political office is the fundamental purpose of a political party. Washington's process severely burdened the parties' associational rights without a compelling interest. The statute allowed the state to exercise its exclusive power over ballots "to undermine the expressive activities of political parties."

[2] Judicial Elections

In *Republican Party of Minnesota v. White*,[136] the Court invalidated a Minnesota law stating that a candidate for judicial office cannot "announce his or her views on disputed legal and political issues." The "announce clause" foreclosed position statements on issues likely to come before the candidate as a judge. The clause did allow "general discussions of case law and judicial philosophy," and even discussion of past decisions, if the candidate stated that *stare decisis* did not bind her. The candidate could also discuss " 'character,' 'education,' 'work habits,' " and administrative approaches. The clause also permitted the candidate to discuss questions preapproved by the Judicial Board relating to cameras in court, reducing caseload, judicial administration, and fairer treatment for women and minorities. These limiting constructions did not narrow the scope of the announce clause to the ABA's 1990 canon, which "prohibits a judicial candidate from making 'statements that commit or appear to commit the candidate with respect to cases, controversies

---

[136] 536 U.S. 765 (2002).

or issues that are likely to come before the court.' " Minnesota's " 'pledges or promises' clause," which was not at issue, prohibits judicial candidates from making such pledges or promises as impairing impartiality.

Justice Scalia subjected the announce clause to strict scrutiny, and rejected Minnesota's asserted interests in judicial impartiality and the appearance of impartiality. A court requires impartiality regarding the parties, but not the issues before it, as judges always have biases about legal views.

Even if impartiality means being open-minded, a judge's campaign announcement would certainly be less likely to influence him than his decision in a previous case. The electioneering context does not justify "an *abridgement* of the right to speak" with voters, which lies at the core of both the First Amendment and the electoral process. The Court neither asserted nor implied that the First Amendment requires judicial campaigns to be the same as legislative campaigns. However, "the announce clause still fails strict scrutiny because it is woefully underinclusive, prohibiting announcements by judges (and would-be judges) only at certain times and in certain forms."

Justice Scalia thought that Justice Ginsburg's dissent "greatly exaggerates the difference between judicial and legislative elections," as state judges make common law and shape state constitutions. A long, universal tradition of prohibiting this conduct would have required a strong presumption of constitutionality; however, "the movement toward nonpartisan judicial elections" only emerged in the 1870s.

Concurring, Justice O'Connor noted that Minnesota had chosen to elect judges in contested popular elections, which may infringe on judicial impartiality in various ways including campaign donations. Instead, Minnesota could have adopted the Missouri Plan in which judges are appointed by a high elected official from a list submitted by a nonpartisan nominating committee. They subsequently face recall or retention elections in which they are unopposed.

Concurring, Justice Kennedy would have invalidated the law regardless of compelling state interests as the regulated speech does not fall within any of the recognized exceptions to content-based restrictions.

Justice Stevens dissented, joined by Justices Souter, Ginsburg, and Breyer. Unlike executives and legislators who are supposed to respond to the popular will, judges are supposed to decide issues of law and fact. Moreover, judges announcing their views misleads voters into thinking that judges decide cases based on their "personal views rather than precedent." The Court's decision "put States to an all or nothing choice of abandoning judicial elections or having elections in which anything goes."

Justice Ginsburg dissented, joined by Justices Stevens, Souter, and Breyer: " 'judge[s] represen[t] the Law,' " not voters. The announce clause advances the interest in judicial integrity. It also advances the due process interest in impartiality. A judge lacks impartiality when she "has a 'direct, personal, substantial, and pecuniary' interest in ruling against" a litigant, which could entail the maintenance of judicial office. The announce clause also protects against judicial candidates circumventing the pledges and promises clause.

In *New York State Board of Elections v. López Torres*,[137] the Court upheld a state statute prescribing the nomination process for the New York Supreme Court, New York's trial court of general jurisdiction. Under the statute, party nominees are automatically listed on the general-election ballot, while non-party candidates must follow an alternate procedure. To be considered a party nominee, a candidate must be nominated by a political party "at a convention of delegates chosen by party members in a primary election." Party nominees are automatically listed on the general election ballot. Otherwise, independent candidates and candidates of political organizations (groups that have not received the 50,000 votes required to be a recognized party) must submit a nomination petition and collect signatures of voters in their district.

Writing for the Court, Justice Scalia stated that political parties have a First Amendment right to create membership restrictions and a nomination process that will yield a judicial candidate whom the party feels "best represents its political platform." Answering respondent's challenge that the specific process used by her party was unfair, Justice Scalia noted that the Constitution does not mandate a "fair shot" or even playing field for individuals seeking a party nomination. The Court also rejected respondent's argument that the First Amendment required a more competitive nomination process that would decrease the "one-party rule" present in parts of the state. Such trends may simply demonstrate the voters' approval of that party's chosen candidates.

Concurring, Justice Stevens, joined by Justice Souter, added that the Court was not endorsing this particular electoral system or nomination process. Justice Kennedy's concurrence stated that the law may have been invalid without an alternate means of appearing on the ballot. Specifically, a candidate not nominated by any political party could submit a petition signed by 4,000 voters or fewer, depending on the district. Justice Kennedy also commented that the campaigning and fundraising required of elective office may impair real and perceived "judicial independence and judicial excellence."

§ 13.06 ASSOCIATIONAL RIGHTS IN OTHER CONTEXTS

[1] Political Boycotts

The Court has protected associational rights in contexts other than legislative inquiries or government sanctions for membership. In *NAACP v. Claiborne Hardware Co.*,[138] several merchants sought in state court to enjoin protesters from continuing an economic boycott, and also to recover losses caused by the boycott. The boycott of white merchants began after black leaders failed to receive an adequate response to the NAACP's demands for racial equality and integration.[139]

---

[137] 552 U.S. 196 (2008).

[138] 458 U.S. 886 (1982).

[139] The second petition called for the desegregation of all public schools and public facilities, the hiring of black policemen, public improvements in black residential areas, selection of blacks for jury duty, integration of the bus stations so that blacks could use all facilities, and an end to verbal abuse by law enforcement officers.

The Mississippi court returned a judgment against the NAACP and awarded $1,250,699 plus interest.[140]

Writing for a unanimous Court, Justice Stevens focused not on the random peripheral acts of violence that allegedly attended the boycott, but on the boycott itself. Admitting that the boycott "took many forms," the Court characterized it as protected speech and non-violent picketing. While the defendants sought to persuade others to join the boycott through social pressure and the "threat" of social ostracism, the boycott did not lose its protected character simply because it embarrassed or coerced others. While states may legitimately impose damages for consequences of violent conduct, they may not award compensation for the consequences of non-violent, protected activity. The evidence did not establish that the business losses had been proximately caused by unlawful conduct. Consequently, the record did not contain sufficient evidence to sustain common-law tort liability.

The Court also rejected imposing liability on several of the named defendants solely because of their association with the NAACP. Civil liability may not be imposed merely because an individual belonged to a group whose members committed acts of violence. For liability to be imposed by reason of association alone, a plaintiff must show that the group itself possessed unlawful goals, and that the individual had the specific intent to further those illegal aims.

The Court made clear that the decision did not affect government's ability to regulate economic associations that suppress competition, secondary boycotts, or picketing by labor unions. The Court emphasized that government had broad power to regulate economic activity which contrasted with the peaceful political picketing in Claiborne.

[2] Private Clubs and Other Associations

In *Roberts v. United States Jaycees*,[141] the Court upheld the use of Minnesota's Human Rights Act to compel the all-male Jaycees to admit women. "While freedom of association . . . plainly supposes a freedom not to associate," Minnesota had a compelling state interest, "unrelated to the suppression of ideas, that cannot be achieved through means significantly less restrictive of associational freedoms."[142] Nothing in the record indicated why the admission of women would impede the Jaycee's ability to engage in protected association activities.

Roberts was followed by *Board of Directors v. Rotary Club of Duarte*,[143] in which a unanimous Court again upheld a statute compelling the admission of women into an all-male club. Even if a burden on association rights could be shown, the state had a compelling interest in assuring to women equal access to business contacts and the acquisition of leadership skills.

---

[140] The theory for recovery was the common law tort of malicious interference with a business relationship.

[141] 468 U.S. 609 (1984).

[142] *Id.* at 622.

[143] 481 U.S. 537 (1987).

In *New York State Club Ass'n v. City of New York*,[144] the Court unanimously rejected a facial challenge to a New York City law that prohibited discrimination against women and minorities by certain private clubs with more than 400 members. The principal opposition to the law came from clubs that barred women from membership. Justice White's majority opinion recognized that some clubs may be able to claim that the law abridged their "intimate or expressive" rights of association, but many of the large clubs covered by the law could not. Consequently, the Court rejected appellant's overbreadth facial challenge. There was no evidence that a substantial number of clubs existed to which the law could not be constitutionally applied and whose associational rights would be impaired.

In *Dallas v. Stanglin*,[145] the Court unanimously upheld a city ordinance that created an age-restrictive licensing system for dance halls. Writing for the Court, Chief Justice Rehnquist noted that "[d]ance hall patrons . . . are not engaged in the sort of 'intimate human relationships' referred to in *Roberts v. United States Jaycees*."[146] The type of associational activity taking place in such places did not comprise "expressive association" protected by the First Amendment. Moreover, the Court rejected the assertion that the Constitution safeguards "a generalized right of 'social association' that includes chance encounters in dance halls."

In *Boy Scouts of America and Monmouth Council v. Dale*,[147] the Court held that a New Jersey public accommodations laws violated the Boy Scouts' First Amendment right of expressive association. James Dale, a former Eagle Scout, sued the Boy Scouts for revoking his adult membership based on his being an "avowed homosexual and gay rights activist."[148] The New Jersey Supreme Court had held that the State's public accommodations law prohibited the Boy Scouts from discriminating based on Dale's sexual orientation.

Chief Justice Rehnquist's majority opinion focused on the right of expressive association, which applies to groups engaged in public and private speech. The Boy Scouts claimed to teach, "that homosexual conduct is not morally straight."[149] Moreover, "it does 'not want to promote homosexual conduct as a legitimate form of behavior.' "[150] The Court accepted the written evidence in the record of these positions as establishing the authenticity of the statements.

The Chief Justice compared the case to *Hurley v. Irish-American Gay, Lesbian and Bisexual Group of Boston, Inc.*[151] Dale's presence as an assistant scoutmaster would infringe on "the Boy Scout's choice not to propound a point of view contrary to its beliefs."[152]

---

[144] 487 U.S. 1 (1988).

[145] 490 U.S. 19 (1989).

[146] *See supra* § 8.06[5].

[147] 530 U.S. 640 (2000).

[148] *Id.* at 643.

[149] *Id.* at 651.

[150] *Id.*

[151] 515 U.S. 557 (1995).

[152] 530 U.S. at 654.

Justice Stevens dissented, joined by Justices Souter, Ginsburg, and Breyer. Justice Stevens found that neither the words "morally straight" nor "clean" refer to homosexuality. Instead, these terms failed to convey any position on sexuality.

While an organization may decide what message it expresses, the Court must decide whether the organization is actually conveying that message. The Court must use *"independent* analysis, rather than deference to a group's litigating posture."[153] This case is distinguishable from *Hurley* because Dale's membership in the Boy Scouts did not convey a deliberate message merely by presence. He did not "carry a banner or a sign; he did not distribute any fact sheet; and he expressed no intent to send any message."[154] A person's mere involvement in particular organizations does not communicate "on behalf of those organizations any more than does the inclusion of women, African-Americans, religious minorities, or any other discrete group."[155]

Justice Souter also wrote a dissent joined by Justices Ginsburg and Breyer. Justice Souter stressed that for a group to assert a right of expressive association, it must identify "a clear position to be advocated over time in an unequivocal way."[156]

§ 13.07   FREE SPEECH PROBLEMS OF GOVERNMENT EMPLOYEES

[1]   Restraints on Political Activity

Most government employees cannot suffer adverse employment consequences for their political affiliations. While the government cannot restrict the political affiliation of its employees, it can prohibit them from engaging in political activities.

Broadrick v. Oklahoma[157] upheld against an overbreadth challenge a state statute proscribing certain partisan campaign activities. The Oklahoma statute was similar to the Hatch Act, a federal statute that essentially prohibited federal employees from participating in certain political activity.[158] The Oklahoma statute specifically forbade state employees from soliciting contributions, working in any campaign, or holding any party office. In short, the statute restricted most of the political activity of a government worker beyond the voicing of individual points of view or the casting of votes.

---

[153] *Id.* at 686.

[154] *Id.* at 695.

[155] *Id.* at 697–98.

[156] 530 U.S. at 701.

[157] 413 U.S. 601 (1973).

[158] In *United States Civil Service Commission v. Letter Carriers*, 413 U.S. 548 (1973), the Court applied the *Broadrick* reasoning to federal employees. Affirming the provisions of the Hatch Act that prohibited federal employees from actively participating in political campaigns, the Court noted that the limitations of such prohibition were specifically and narrowly defined so as to preclude a successful challenge on either overbreadth or vagueness grounds.

The statute served a legitimate objective. It helped ensure that government would attract qualified people by removing any concerns about campaigning, and it eliminated the risk that elected bosses would exercise political extortion against their subordinates. The Court had already upheld government's ability to enact statutes with such objectives.[159] Consequently, the government employees limited their challenges to the alleged overbreadth and vagueness of the particular statutes at issue.

As previously discussed,[160] vagueness is a Fifth or Fourteenth Amendment due process challenge, essentially maintaining that a statute does not afford sufficient notice of what behavior violates it. In rejecting the vagueness challenge, the Court conceded that certain phrases like "take part in" or "partisan" were not entirely clear. The Court recognized, however, that the English language had limits. Moreover, even if the outermost boundaries of the Act were imprecise, the activities in which appellants engaged fell well within its prohibitions.

In free speech cases, overbreadth and vagueness challenges are often asserted together even though overbreadth is a First Amendment challenge and vagueness is a Fifth or Fourteenth Amendment due process challenge, not confined to speech cases. A vagueness challenge simply asserts that the law fails to give adequate notice. Overbreadth is another facial challenge to a law, asserting that the law regulates protected speech as well as unprotected conduct. The doctrine requires that an entire statute be invalidated because of its chilling effect on protected speech. Unlike vagueness, overbreadth will invalidate an entire statute even though, for the relevant conduct in the case at issue, the statute may affect only unprotected conduct.

Consequently, the overbreadth doctrine has standing *and* substantive components. In *Broadrick*, appellants admitted that their conduct could be proscribed by a properly drafted law, but argued that the statute at issue also restricted protected speech such as wearing campaign buttons or displaying bumper stickers. As their conduct was not constitutionally protected, according to a previous Supreme Court decision, appellants lacked standing, as the statute did not personally harm them. However, overbreadth challenges could be made by litigants whether or not they had standing, that is, whether or not their behavior was protected by the First Amendment.

The substantive component of the overbreadth doctrine enables a court to overturn an entire statute, even if a criminal defendant before the Court engaged in unprotected conduct and goes free. The *Broadrick* Court had narrowed the use of this far-reaching doctrine. As a threshold requirement, the Court would not hold a statute overbroad if the statute has been or could have been subjected to a limiting construction.

When conduct rather than pure speech was at issue, the Court also imposed a requirement of substantial overbreadth for the statute to be invalidated. While the term "substantial overbreadth" is vague, the facts of the case indicated that this

---

[159] *See* United Pub. Workers of Am. v. Mitchell, 330 U.S. 75 (1947).

[160] *See supra* § 13.02.

standard was difficult to meet. The *Broadrick* Court noted that certain activities restricted by the statute may be constitutionally protected (like wearing campaign buttons), but nevertheless refused to hold the statute substantially overbroad. Moreover, the Court indicated that the substantial overbreadth requirement was widely applicable. Substantial overbreadth was not required, however, to invalidate censorial statutes like the one at issue in *Keyishian* that regulated a particular group or viewpoint.

The Court has relaxed the traditional standing requirements in this area to permit attacks on overly broad statutes, and thus avoid the chilling effect such statutes can have on freedom of speech.

In *Osborne v. Ohio*,[161] the Court distanced itself from earlier suggestions that overbreadth challenges may only be brought by those who lack standing. The Court upheld a conviction under an Ohio statute that prohibited the possession and viewing of child pornography against an overbreadth challenge. Defendant argued that the statute banned all "nude" pictures of children and that it lacked a scienter requirement. The Court rejected both arguments because narrowing constructions by the Ohio Supreme Court obviated overbreadth problems.[162] Nonetheless, the Court stated, "In the First Amendment context, we permit defendants to challenge statutes on overbreadth grounds, regardless of whether the individual defendant's conduct is constitutionally protected."[163]

Nevertheless, in *Madsen v. Women's Health Center*,[164] the Court refused to supply standing to third parties seeking to mount an overbreadth challenge. In that case, protestors of an abortion clinic challenged the application of an injunction restricting such protests to persons acting in connection with the protestors. A 6-3 majority refused to entertain the challenge on the grounds that the protestors lacked standing to mount it. The Court denied standing even though certain portions of the injunction did apply to them, and the protestors successfully challenged certain parts of the injunction.[165]

In *Schenck v. Pro-Choice Network*,[166] the Court upheld provisions of a District Court injunction that imposed "fixed buffer zone" restrictions on demonstrations outside abortion clinics. However, the Court struck down the injunction's "floating buffer zone" restrictions as violating the First Amendment. The fixed buffer zone prohibited demonstrating within 15 feet around any doorway, driveway, or other entrance of an abortion clinic. The floating buffer zone prohibited demonstrating "within fifteen feet of any person or vehicle seeking access to or leaving" an

---

[161]   495 U.S. 103 (1990).

[162]   The Ohio Supreme Court construed Ohio law to require a scienter requirement of at least recklessness and only to ban nude pictures that "constitute[] a lewd exhibition or involve[] a graphic focus on the genitals, and where the person being depicted is neither the child nor the ward of the person charged." *Id.* at 113.

[163]   *Id.* at 112 n.8.

[164]   512 U.S. 753 (1994).

[165]   For further discussion of *Madsen, see infra* § 15.04[2].

[166]   519 U.S. 357 (1997).

abortion clinic.[167] Two sidewalk counselors could stay in the buffer zones to talk with those entering or leaving the clinic. Once an individual indicated that she did not want counseling, the counselors had to stop counseling, retreat 15 feet from the people having been counseled, and remain outside the buffer zones.

The Court applied the test from *Madsen* to ascertain whether these provisions "burdened more speech than necessary" to advance the government's interests.[168] The government's interests in ensuring public order and safety, protecting property, facilitating street and sidewalk traffic, and "protecting a woman's freedom to seek pregnancy-related services" were sufficient to underpin "an appropriately tailored injunction to allow unimpeded access to the clinics."[169]

Applying these standards, the floating buffer zones burdened speech more than was necessary to serve the government's interest. Excepting the two sidewalk counselors, the floating buffer zones completely prevented defendants from conversing at a normal distance with or handing leaflets to persons on public sidewalks entering or leaving clinics. Using a traditional public forum to distribute leaflets and express views on a controversial issue lies at the heart of the First Amendment. The 17 foot sidewalk at one of the plaintiff's clinics illustrates the onerous nature of floating buffer zones. Unless an individual entering or leaving the clinic walked along one edge of the sidewalk, protesters would have to walk in the street. The uncertainties accompanying floating buffer zones risked a chilling effect on much more speech than the injunction prohibited. Similarly, the floating buffer zone around vehicles unconstitutionally burdened the ability of sidewalk picketers to "chant, shout, or hold signs peacefully."[170]

However, the Court did uphold the fixed buffer zones around doorways, driveways, and other entrances as the record showed that the protesters were impeding access to the clinics. Following *Madsen*, the Court afforded deference to the District Court's "reasonable assessment" that 15 feet were required to keep the entrances clear.[171] The Court also refused to invalidate the fixed buffer zones because the District Court failed to issue an injunction that did not restrict speech before issuing the speech-restrictive injunction. Such non-issuance was only one factor in considering the validity of the speech-restrictive injunction.

The Court also upheld the cease and desist provisions aimed at sidewalk counselors, as helping to ensure physical access to the building. The Court also refused to characterize the cease and desist order as content-based. While the order only applied to protesters, they were the only ones who had performed the acts being enjoined.

Justice Scalia, joined by Justices Kennedy and Thomas, concurred in part and dissented in part. Justice Scalia agreed with the majority that there is no right to be free of unsolicited speech in public while entering or exiting an abortion clinic.

---

[167] *Id.* at 366.

[168] *Id.* at 371.

[169] *Id.* at 372.

[170] *Id.* at 380.

[171] *Id.* at 381.

However, the District Court founded its injunction on the rights to be left alone and to be free of unwanted speech, rather than a right to unimpeded access. Justice Scalia criticized the majority for predicating its decision on postulated rationales rather than those actually used by the District Court.

In *United States v. National Treasury Employees Union*,[172] the Court again declined use of overbreadth to extend the standing of a third party. In that case, government employees rated GS-16 and below challenged an honoraria ban. These employees asked that the statute be held facially unconstitutional even as it applied to government employees rated above GS-16. The Court did enjoin the statute as applied to government employees at or below the GS-16 level, because of its chilling effect on speech. Nevertheless, the Court refused to use the overbreadth doctrine to afford plaintiffs standing to challenge the ban's application to government employees above GS-16. The Court only provided a remedy to redress the harm suffered by the litigants before it.[173]

Moreover, in the earlier case of *Brockett v. Spokane Arcades*,[174] the Court rejected an overbreadth challenge to a Washington law that defined "prurient" as "that which incites lasciviousness or lust." As the party asserting overbreadth had standing, Justice White found that the court of appeals should not have found the statute facially overbroad. Instead, the lower court should have invalidated the law "only insofar as the word 'lust' is to be understood as referring to protected materials."[175]

In *Massachusetts v. Oakes*,[176] a divided Court ruled that a legislative amendment of a statute, enacted after the Court had granted certiorari, did not moot an overbreadth challenge. The Massachusetts Supreme Court had reversed the conviction of Oakes under a statute that prohibited adults from posing or exhibiting minors in a "state of nudity" on overbreadth grounds. After the United States Supreme Court granted *certiorari*, the Massachusetts legislature amended the statute in an attempt to cure the overbreadth problem. Justice O'Connor, joined by Chief Justice Rehnquist, Justices White and Kennedy, found that the subsequent amendment of the statute mooted the overbreadth challenge. Justice Scalia, writing for Justices Blackmun, Brennan, Marshall, and Stevens, held that the amendment did *not* moot the overbreadth challenge.[177] Nevertheless, six Justices ultimately rejected the overbreadth challenge and upheld defendant's conviction for taking partially nude pictures that exhibited the breasts of his 14 year-old stepdaughter. Justice Scalia, joined by Justice Blackmun, concluded that while the overbreadth challenge was not moot, the original statute was not substantially overbroad "judged in relation to [its] plainly legitimate sweep."[178]

---

[172] 513 U.S. 454 (1995).

[173] *See also* Board of Trustees v. Fox, *infra* § 16.04[1].

[174] 472 U.S. 491 (1985).

[175] *Id.* at 504.

[176] 491 U.S. 576 (1989).

[177] *Id.* at 586.

[178] *Id.* at 588 (quoting *Broadrick v. Oklahoma*, 413 U.S. 601, 615 (1973)).

In *Board of Airport Commissioners v. Jews for Jesus*,[179] the Court invalidated a complete ban on free speech activities in airports. This regulation failed the substantial overbreadth test. Also, in *City of Houston v. Hill*,[180] the Court invalidated a Houston, Texas ordinance providing that it "shall be unlawful for any person to assault, strike or in any manner oppose, molest, abuse or interrupt any policeman in the execution of his duty, or any person summoned to aid in making an arrest." The Court struck down the law as substantially overbroad because it "criminalizes a substantial amount of constitutionally protected speech, and accords the police unconstitutional discretion in enforcement."[181]

In *Secretary of State v. J.H. Munson, Co.*,[182] the Court (5-4) allowed an apparent overbreadth challenge to a statute which prohibited solicitation by a charitable organization that spends more than 25 percent of its gross fund-raising income "in connection with any fund-raising activity." It was not simply that the statute applies to both protected and unprotected activity, but that "in all its applications it operates on a fundamentally mistaken premise that high solicitation costs are an accurate measure of fraud."[183]

In *Virginia v. Hicks*,[184] a unanimous Court rejected an overbreadth challenge to the trespass policy of the Richmond Redevelopment and Housing Authority (RRHA). The city of Richmond conveyed public streets to RRHA, which were " 'closed to public use and travel.' "[185] RRHA's trespass policy prohibited anyone other than a resident or employee from entering the streets without " 'a legitimate business or social purpose for being on the premises.' "[186] To be overbroad, a law must apply a substantial amount of protected speech "not only in an absolute sense, but also relative to the scope of the law's plainly legitimate applications."[187] The rules at issue extend to all persons seeking to enter these private streets for any purpose, expressive or otherwise.

[2] Patronage Dismissals

As the overbreadth analysis in cases such as *Keyishian* and *Robel* demonstrate, the First Amendment restricts government's ability to sanction public employees because of their views. Those cases involved dismissal for membership in the Communist Party on the theory that the organization is devoted to subverting the government. The following cases examine the free speech rights of government employees in other contexts.

---

[179] 482 U.S. 569 (1987).

[180] 482 U.S. 451 (1987).

[181] *Id.*

[182] 467 U.S. 947 (1984).

[183] *Id.* at 966.

[184] 539 U.S. 113 (2003).

[185] *Id.* at 115–16.

[186] *Id.* at 116.

[187] *Id.* at 120.

Branti v. Finkel[188] restricted patronage dismissals of government employees. In *Branti*, two assistant public defenders were awarded a permanent injunction restricting their newly appointed boss from firing them simply because they were Republicans and their boss was a Democrat. The Court concluded that, while public employment was not a right, once the government provided certain benefits like public employment, it must allocate this legislated entitlement according to constitutional criteria, not strictly by political affiliation.

In *Elrod v. Burns*,[189] the Court had limited dismissals for political affiliation to government employees occupying policy-making positions. In *Elrod*, the patronage dismissals involved clerks, deputies, and janitors. In *Branti*, the newly appointed public defender tried to distinguish *Elrod* by characterizing the role of his assistants as being significantly different than that of clerks, deputies, and janitors. Rejecting this argument, the Court stated that, ultimately, the inquiry was not whether the person dismissed occupied a policy-making or confidential position which had been the test propounded in *Elrod*. Ultimately, government must demonstrate that party affiliation was an appropriate requirement for the effective performance of the public office involved-although the *Elrod* inquiry must surely be relevant in making this determination.

The dissent argued that this new standard was amorphous. Moreover, as the patronage system was essential to the strength of political parties, curtailing it would eliminate those who worked for candidates in hopes of gaining patronage appointments. The dissent was convinced that curtailing patronage would advantage wealthier candidates with greater access to the media, as opposed to less wealthy candidates who relied more heavily on grassroots support.

The majority focused instead on the issue of fairness to the individuals who, but for their political affiliation, would still have been employed. In the case of public defenders, their positions only required allegiance to their indigent clients and the justice system. In a footnote, the Court cited cases reversing the dismissal from government of members of the Communist Party. The Court might have had difficulty reconciling its protection of Communist Party members against dismissal for political affiliation, if it failed to protect Democrats and Republicans. It might have justified such a distinction on the basis that members of majority parties could be restrained through the political process.

In *Rutan v. Republican Party*,[190] the Court extended *Branti* to hold that party patronage practices may not affect "promotion, transfer, recall and hiring decisions involving low-level public employees."[191] The governor of Illinois had issued an executive order requiring his permission to hire or to create new government positions. Although there was "no legal entitlement" to government employment, the Court held that the government cannot condition such employment on persons foregoing their constitutional rights — such as freedom of speech. To pass constitutional muster, such patronage must be "narrowly tailored to further vital

---

[188] 445 U.S. 507 (1980).

[189] 427 U.S. 347 (1976).

[190] 497 U.S. 62 (1990).

[191] *Id.* at 64.

government interests."[192] The Court stated that *high-level* employees may be chosen or dismissed based on their political views, but that *low-level* employees may not.

Justice Scalia's dissent in *Rutan* differentiated between the government's roles as "lawmaker" and as "employer." He argued that the latter required fewer constitutional restrictions, particularly when the government practice was not expressly prohibited by the Bill of Rights and had a long tradition dating back to the founding of our nation. He also argued that lack of patronage contributed to the decline of political parties and the concomitant ascent of the power of money in political campaigns.

In *O'Hare Truck Service v. City of Northlake*,[193] the Court held that a claim by independent contractors for government retaliation for political association or allegiance stated a good cause of action. Plaintiff, O'Hare Truck Service (O'Hare), was removed from the defendant's list of available towing companies shortly after its owner had refused to contribute to the Mayor's reelection campaign and instead openly supported the Mayor's opponent.

Writing for the majority (7-2), Justice Kennedy said that this case did not involve government sanctions against its employee or contractor for the exercise of freedom of speech that would have engaged the balancing test articulated in *Pickering v. Board of Education*.[194] Instead, *Elrod v. Burns*[195] and *Branti v. Finkel* said that the appropriate inquiry is whether the political affiliation requirement at issue is reasonable for the employment in question. This is the appropriate "inquiry where political affiliation alone is concerned, for one's beliefs and allegiances ought not to be subject to probing or testing by the government."[196] In applying this test, some case-by-case adjudication will necessarily be required. The Court would also use *Branti's* "reasonableness analysis"[197] when adverse government action is based on both speech and political affiliation.

In extending the *Elrod* and *Branti* inquiry to government contractors, the Court noted that if plaintiff had provided his towing services as a government employee, the government could not have fired him for refusing to give political and financial support to the mayor's campaign. The threat of losing a government contract had considerable coercive effects. Indeed, had the Mayor tied continuing the towing contract to a contribution, criminal bribery would be at issue.

Nevertheless, the Constitution allowed government much discretion in awarding contracts for goods and services. For example, economic factors may lead government to keep certain contractors or to exchange others for new ones without

---

[192] *Id.* at 73.

[193] 518 U.S. 712 (1996).

[194] *See infra* § 13.07[3].

[195] 427 U.S. 347 (1976).

[196] *O'Hare,* 518 U.S. at 719.

[197] *Id.*

undertaking "the costs and complexities of competitive bidding."[198] So long as the rationale is not pretextual, government might continue with a contractor to "maintain stability, reward good performance, deal with known and reliable persons, or ensure the uninterrupted supply of goods and services."[199] Alternatively, government might switch contractors "to stimulate competition, encourage experimentation with new contractors, or avoid the appearance of favoritism."[200] Governments can terminate a contractor for reasons other than political affiliation — such as unreliability — or when "political 'affiliation is an appropriate requirement for the effective performance' of the task in question."[201]

Justice Scalia dissented, joined by Justice Thomas, and filed the same dissenting opinion in this case as in *Board of Commissioners v. Umbehr*.[202] Justice Scalia maintained that using patronage to award government contracts was a practice not specifically prohibited by the Bill of Rights and an "open, widespread and unchallenged"[203] tradition dating back to the beginning of the Nation. As such, it should be upheld. Justice Scalia also argued that the majority's decision not to apply the *Pickering* balancing test in *O'Hare* contradicted the Court's approach in *Umbehr*.

[3] Employee's Rights to Criticize Government

[a] Free Speech

Generally, the Court protects a government employee's criticism of government when it is a matter of "public concern," and allows it to be regulated in order to promote the efficient performance of public services. For example, *Pickering v. Board of Education*[204] held unconstitutional the dismissal of a public school teacher for criticizing the school board in a letter to the editor. The letter criticized the division of funds between education and athletics. The Court held that this was protected speech.

Protection of government employees can extend to private as well as public criticism. In *Givhan v. Western Line Consolidated School District*,[205] the Court set aside the dismissal of a government employee for criticizing — in strong language, inside the principal's office — the allegedly discriminatory policies of the school. The private nature of the conversation did not impair constitutional protection.

Connick v. Myers,[206] however, indicated that while the private or public nature of the conversation did not undercut constitutional protection, the content of the

---

[198] *Id.* at 725.

[199] *Id.*

[200] *Id.*

[201] *Id.*

[202] *See infra* 39 U.S. 563 (1968).

[203] *O'Hare*, 518 U.S. at 726.

[204] 391 U.S. 563 (1968).

[205] 439 U.S. 410 (1979).

[206] 461 U.S. 138 (1983).

conversation may be highly relevant. Specifically, a public employee's criticism of the government lacked constitutional protection if it did not involve a matter of public concern.

In *Connick*, Sheila Myers was fired from her position as an Assistant District Attorney after she circulated an intra-office questionnaire. The questionnaire solicited views from her fellow staff members on matters of office policy and morale, their level of confidence in their supervisors, and whether they felt pressured to work in political campaigns. Admittedly, what sparked the creation and circulation of the questionnaire was Myers' transfer to a different division of the criminal court. After distributing the questionnaire, District Attorney Connick confronted her and terminated her employment on the grounds of insubordination.

The Court upheld the discharge because most of the questions in Myers' questionnaire were attempts to build up ammunition to combat her transfer, not matters of public concern. She did not convey the information to the public; and even if she had, it would only have indicated dissatisfaction by one employee. Justice White held that the only question involving a matter of public concern inquired whether public employees were compelled to work on political campaigns, a question that involved coercion of beliefs. The Court did not consider other questions involving grievance procedures and office morale matters of public concern.

The dissent would have construed matters of public concern broadly as involving all subjects in which the public could be reasonably interested in formulating its opinions of the local district attorney. Underlying the majority's differentiation involving matters of public concern appears to have been the concept of efficiency in the provision of government services. The Court seems to have differentiated between government in its role as formulator of policy and its role as provider of services, concluding that the latter responsibility broadens government's discretion.

Speech that met this threshold inquiry of being a matter of public concern still had to be balanced against the state's justification for the adverse employment action. In this balancing inquiry, the state bore the burden of clearly demonstrating that the speech " 'substantially interfered' with official responsibilities."[207] The government's burden varied with the nature of the employee's expression.

Courts should carefully weigh the government's interests in the fulfillment of its public responsibilities, including effectiveness, efficiency, and integrity. In this case, the Court gave the employer broad discretion because the questionnaire impaired the close working relationships necessary to perform government services. The government might have to make a stronger showing if the speech more directly involved a matter of public concern. The Court also considered the time, place, and manner in which the questionnaire was distributed. For example, the questionnaire was distributed at the offices to cause trouble, not for the purpose of gathering and distributing information to the public. Framing the criticisms in questionnaire form was irrelevant because the statements could be made in question form just as easily as they could in declarative sentences. Finally, the Court noted that the questionnaire was distributed during an employment dispute.

---

[207] *Id.* at 150.

In *Board of Commissioners v. Umbehr*,[208] the Court extended First Amendment protection to independent contractors for "termination of at-will government contracts in retaliation for their exercise of the freedom of speech."[209] Plaintiff, an independent contractor, alleged that the Board of County Commissioners terminated his contract with the county for open and extensive criticism of the board.

Writing for a 7-2 majority, Justice O'Connor noted that government employees and independent contractors were similarly situated in receiving financial benefits. Moreover, fear of losing these benefits might prevent them from speaking, even when they have intimate knowledge about "matters of public concern."[210]

Rather than entirely reject a cause of action for independent contractors, the Court found that the balancing test of *Pickering v. Board of Education* can be applied to "accommodate the differences between employees and independent contractors."[211] Applying the unconstitutional conditions doctrine, independent contractors are somewhere between employees and persons having less close relationships with the government, such as, claimants of tax exemptions or small government subsidies. These latter categories of people resemble ordinary citizens whose views cannot be repressed. On remand, "Umbehr must show that the termination of his contract was motivated by his speech on a matter of public concern."[212] The Board must "show, by a preponderance of the evidence that, in light of their knowledge, perception and policies at the time of the termination, the Board members would have terminated the contract regardless of his speech,"[213] or that "the County's legitimate interests as contractor, deferentially viewed, outweigh the free speech interests at stake."[214] The Court did not address the possibility of suits by bidders or applicants for new government contracts, who lack the relationship with government that existing contractors have.

Justice Scalia's dissenting opinion, in which Justice Thomas joined, was identical to his dissent in *O'Hare Truck Service v. City of Northlake*.[215] Justice Scalia disagreed with the majority's extension of *Elrod v. Burns*[216] and *Branti v. Finkel*[217] to the termination of a government contract with an independent contractor. *Elrod* and *Branti* conflict with the long-standing American political tradition of "rewarding one's allies,"[218] but not one's opponents. Even if one agrees with these decisions, their principles should not be extended to an independent contractor whose business would not be destroyed by the loss of one contract. Public employees, on the other hand, are individuals who would lose their entire livelihood if fired.

---

[208] 518 U.S. 668 (1996).

[209] *Id.*

[210] *Id.* at 676.

[211] *Umbehr*, 518 U.S. at 678.

[212] *Id.* at 685.

[213] *Id.*

[214] *Id.*

[215] See *supra* § 13.07[2].

[216] See *supra* § 13.07[2].

[217] See *supra* § 13.07[2].

[218] *Umbehr*, 518 U.S. at 688.

Justice Scalia also argued that extending speech and political affiliation protection to independent contractors will greatly increase the volume of litigation involving government contracting. For example, it may afford a cause of action to a white supremacist contractor submitting the lowest bid on a private security job in a public housing system.

At least when retaliation for speech rather than party affiliation is alleged, the *Umbehr* majority followed the *Pickering* approach, requiring "a case-by-case assessment of the government's and the contractor's interests."[219] Justice Scalia believed that to reconcile *O'Hare* with *Umbehr*, the Court divided speech rights into two different categories: "(l) the 'right of free speech,' where 'we apply the balancing test from *Pickering*,' and, (since 'this right of free speech' presumably does not exhaust the Free Speech Clause) (2) 'political affiliation,' where we apply the rigid rule of *Elrod* and *Branti*."[220] When both rights pertain, *Pickering* balancing, rather than "categorical liability,"[221] applied. Justice Scalia criticized the Court for causing confusion and for "not setting forth any comprehensible rule."[222] He also predicted that the Court would extend the protections afforded in these cases to contract bidders.

Rankin v. McPherson[223] reinstated an employee who remarked after President Reagan was shot: " 'If they go for him again, I hope they get him.' " After finding the speech a matter of public concern, the Court emphasized that the employee did not discredit or interfere with efficient functioning of the office. She made a private remark in a private conversation with her boyfriend that another employee overheard. Also significant was the fact that she did not have a policy-making or confidential role that could have impaired the agency's functioning. Although the employee was a deputy constable, she did not carry a gun or wear a uniform but performed only clerical duties. Employees must be more cautious about their speech to the extent of their authority and public accountability.

Reinstatement is a permissible remedy when the government has discharged an employee in violation of her speech rights. The employee must first demonstrate that the employer's unconstitutional conduct played a substantial part in a decision to take adverse employment action. Then the burden shifts to the governmental employer to establish by a preponderance of the evidence that it would have taken the same adverse employment action irrespective of the protected conduct. This is basically a tort inquiry, establishing the causal nexus between the unconstitutional behavior and the harm.[224]

In *City of San Diego, California v. Roe*,[225] the Court, in a unanimous *per curiam* opinion, held that a police officer's sexually explicit videos, masturbating in uniform, was not a matter of public concern. Consequently, the police department could

---

[219] *Id.* at 702.

[220] *Id.* at 704.

[221] *Id.* at 706.

[222] *Id.*

[223] 483 U.S. 378 (1987).

[224] *See* Givhan v. Western Line Consol. Sch. Dist., 439 U.S. 410 (1979).

[225] 543 U.S. 77 (2004).

terminate the officer for selling the videos on eBay. To determine whether speech involves a matter of public concern, courts should look at the entire record. This standard is the same as that for an invasion of privacy action at common law. Matters of public concern include subjects "of legitimate news interest." They can also include "certain private remarks, such as negative comments about the President." However, "this is not a close case," as the police officer's activities neither involved political news nor public information about the police department's functioning. Instead, the officer's speech purposefully exploited the police department, harming its "mission and functions."

In *United States v. National Treasury Employees Union*,[226] the Court invalidated the application to government employees at, or below GS-16, of a congressional statute prohibiting federal employees from accepting any honoraria derived from making speeches or writing articles. The prohibition applied even when neither the subject of the speech or article nor the group paying for it had any connection with the government employee's official duties.

Writing for the 5-1-3 majority, Justice Stevens first noted that, because the statute in question chilled speech before it occurred, the Government's burden was greatly increased. The Court quoted *Pickering v. Board of Education* stating that government employees do not relinquish "the First Amendment rights they would otherwise enjoy as citizens to comment on matters of public interest."[227] In this case, the plaintiffs' speech remained protected because it was citizen comment on matters of public concern, rather than employee comment related to personal status in the workplace. To restrict such speech, the Government must show that the interests of both potential audiences and present and future employees in a broad range of present and future expression are outweighed by that expression's necessary impact on the actual operation of the government. Even though the honorarium ban did not proscribe any speech, it levied a "significant burden" on government employee's right to speak and consequently on the Public's right to receive such information by banning any payment. In dicta, Justice Stevens implied that the ban might have been appropriate if Congress had demanded a nexus between the speaker's employment and either the subject matter of the expression or the identity of the payor. Because government employees at or below GS-16 challenged the ban, the Court only invalidated its application to these employees.

Justice O'Connor concurred in part and dissented in part. She agreed that the remedy was properly limited to employees at or below the GS-16 level. Dissenting, she would only have enjoined the honorarium ban for speech that did not have a nexus between the expressive activity and the speaker's government employment. This was the only relief that the plaintiffs had requested.

Chief Justice Rehnquist dissented, joined by Justices Scalia and Thomas. The Chief Justice stated that, when determining the free speech rights of government employees, the Court must balance the interests of the government employee as a citizen to comment on matters of public concern, against the interest of the government employer in effectively delivering public services. In this case, Con

---

[226] 513 U.S. 454 (1995).

[227] 391 U.S. 563, 568 (1968).

gress's interest in avoiding possible improprieties by its employees was reasonable. Moreover, the ban did not prohibit anyone's speech; it just prohibited the government employees from receiving honoraria.

For government employees in the military, a different standard pertains. In *Brown v. Glines*,[228] the Court upheld the discharge of an army captain for circulating a petition without complying with the Air Force regulations requiring pre-publication review. The regulations only allowed denial of permission for "a clear danger to the loyalty, discipline, or morale of members of the Air Force, or material interference with the accomplishment of a military mission."[229] The Court emphasized the importance of the military context.

In *Garcetti v. Ceballos*,[230] the Court held that when a public employee's speech is restricted by his job responsibilities, the First Amendment does not protect it. In *Garcetti*, a public employee discovered what he believed to be inaccuracies in an affidavit while performing his job responsibilities. He claimed that after notifying various personnel about his discovery he suffered retaliation.

First, the Court noted that government entities may restrict a public employee's speech as their employer so long as the restriction prevents speech that "has some potential to affect the entity's operations."[231] The government, like any employer, must ensure that services are rendered efficiently. In contrast, when a public employee's speech involves a matter of public concern, government may only impose "those speech restrictions that are necessary for their employers to operate efficiently and effectively."[232] As *Connick v. Myers*[233] stated, however, this constitutional protection does not extend to employee grievances.

In *Ceballos*, the employee's speech was directly related to his job responsibilities. Consistent with federalism and the separation of powers, established precedents forbid "judicial supervision" overriding "managerial discretion" in supervision of government employees.[234] Public employees maintain some protection for public speech unrelated to their employment responsibilities as this activity resembles that of a private citizen. However, the Court cautioned that "the listing of a given task in an employee's written job description is neither necessary nor sufficient to demonstrate that conducting the task is within the scope of the employee's professional duties for First Amendment purposes."[235] The Court declined to consider the applicability of its analysis to speech involving scholarship or teaching: the employer-employee relationship does not fully encompass the constitutional interests in academic freedom. Finally, various whistleblower and labor laws protect public employees when exposing issues within the government.

---

[228] 444 U.S. 348 (1980).

[229] *Id.* at 350 (quoting Air Force Reg. 35-15(3)(a)(2) (1970)).

[230] 547 U.S. 410 (2006).

[231] *Id.* at 418.

[232] *Id.* at 419.

[233] 461 U.S. 138 (1983).

[234] *Ceballos*, 547 U.S. at 423.

[235] *Id.* at 425.

Dissenting, Justice Stevens rejected the dichotomy between a public employee speaking as a private citizen or pursuant to her job responsibilities. Also dissenting, Justice Souter argued that a public employee's speech arising out of her job responsibilities might be more valuable to the public due to the employee's superior knowledge. Moreover, the majority's rule encourages government to draft expansive job descriptions thereby reducing First Amendment protections. Whistle-blower statutes vary too dramatically to reduce the need for First Amendment protection. Finally, in a separate dissent, Justice Breyer agreed that the majority ruling is "too absolute"[236] but argued that Justice Souter's standard does not adequately consider the management concerns of government entities.

In *Waters v. Churchill*,[237] an employee sued her employer, claiming that she had been discharged for speech that involved a matter of public concern under the analysis set forth in *Connick v. Myers*. The employee denied that she had actually uttered the remarks that prompted her discharge, and she argued that the finder of fact should determine whether she had done so. While the Court rejected this position, it noted that no general test existed for resolving when the First Amendment requires particular procedural safeguards. Such procedural issues must be decided on a case-by-case basis. Justice O'Connor noted that the Court has afforded the government greater latitude in its role as employer than in its role as sovereign. When a public employer intends to discharge an employee for alleged insubordinate remarks, the employer must, at a minimum, conduct a reasonable investigation of the incident and believe the results of such inquiry to be true. The employer's action cannot be taken without evidence of what was said or based upon "extremely weak evidence when strong evidence is clearly available."[238] While the care need not reach the level necessitated by trial procedure, it should rise to the level of care that a reasonable manager would take to make the particular employment decision at issue. Justice O'Connor stated that a wide variety of factual investigations might satisfy this test. In the case at issue, the employee based his decision on the word of two trusted employees whose credibility was endorsed by three hospital managers, and a face-to-face meeting with the employee.

Concurring with the plurality, Justice Souter emphasized that the employer must not only make a reasonable inquiry but must also actually believe the results of that inquiry. Concurring in the judgment, Justice Scalia, joined by Justices Kennedy and Thomas, argued that the First Amendment did not require any particular factual investigation. It only required the finder of fact to inquire into the employer's actual intent in making the employment decision at issue.

Dissenting, Justice Stevens, joined by Justice Blackmun, would have required the trier of fact to ascertain what the employee actually said. As these two Justices would have required a more exacting factual inquiry and three Justices would have imposed a lighter one, the principles announced by the plurality would appear to be generally able to control a majority.

---

[236] *Id.* at 446 (Breyer, J., dissenting).

[237] 511 U.S. 661 (1994).

[238] *Id.* at 677.

[b] Petition Clause

In *Borough of Duryea v. Guarnieri*,[239] Charles Guarnieri filed a successful union grievance reversing the City Council's decision to terminate him as chief of police. Upon his return, "the council issued 11 directives instructing Guarnieri in the performance of his duties," including prohibiting overtime, restricting use of his police car to " 'official business,' " and requiring the police department to work in a " 'smoke free building.' "[240] Guarnieri filed a lawsuit claiming "that his first union grievance was a petition protected by the Petition Clause," and that the 11 directives issued "were retaliation for that protected activity."[241] After being denied overtime, Guarnieri further "alleged that his § 1983 lawsuit was a petition and that the denial of overtime constituted retaliation for his having filed the lawsuit."[242] The Supreme Court declined to decide Guarnieri's claim, remanding the case for determination of whether Guarnieri's grievance was a petition of "public concern."

Justice Kennedy wrote for the Court. "This Court's precedents confirm that the Petition Clause protects the right of individuals to appeal to courts and other forums established by the government for resolution of legal disputes."[243] Guarnieri's claim could also have invoked protection under freedom of speech. While the Court did not find the Speech and Petition Clause "identical," they do "share substantial common ground" and "are 'cognate rights.' "[244] Still, there is a difference between the two rights. "The right to petition allows citizens to express their ideas, hopes, and concerns to their government and their elected representatives, whereas the right to speak fosters the public exchange of ideas that is integral to deliberative democracy as well as to the whole realm of ideas and human affairs."[245] Thus, while "both speech and petition advance personal expression," the right to petition is "generally concerned with expression directed to the government."[246]

Justice Kennedy recognized government's "significant interest in disciplining public employees who abuse the judicial process." Broad-ranging invocation of the Petition Clause by government employees "would subject a wide range of government operations to invasive judicial superintendence" thereby raising "serious federalism and separation-of-powers concerns."[247] Moreover, "the Petition Clause is not an instrument for public employees to circumvent these legislative enactments when pursuing claims based on ordinary workplace grievances."[248]

Even beyond limiting the speech of government employees, " 'government has significantly greater leeway in its dealings with its citizen-employees than it does

---

[239] 131 S. Ct. 2488 (2011).

[240] *Id.* at 2492.

[241] *Id.*

[242] *Id.*

[243] *Id.* at 2494.

[244] *Id.*

[245] *Id.* at 2495.

[246] *Id.*

[247] *Id.* at 2496.

[248] *Id.* at 2497.

when it brings its sovereign power to bear on citizens at large.' "[249] The government has a substantial interest in "managing its internal" operations. "The public concern test" protects this interest. "Petitions to the colonial legislatures concerned topics as diverse as debt actions, estate distributions, divorce proceedings,"[250] and pleas to modify criminal sentences. "The proper scope and application of the Petition Clause . . . cannot be determined merely by tallying up petitions to the colonial legislatures."[251] Instead, courts must "identify the historic and fundamental principles that led to the enumeration of the right to petition."[252] This right originated in the "Magna Carta, which confirmed the right of barons to petition the King."[253]

When "a public employee petitions as an employee on a matter of purely private concern, the employee's First Amendment interest must give way,"[254] as it does in speech issues. "When a public employee petitions as a citizen on a matter of public concern, the employee's First Amendment interest must be balanced against the countervailing interest of the government in the effective and efficient management of its internal affairs."[255]

As with free speech claims, "whether an employee's petition relates to a matter of public concern will depend on 'the content, form, and context of [the petition], as revealed by the whole record.' "[256] Moreover, the place where "a petition is lodged will be relevant to the determination of whether the petition relates to a matter of public concern."[257] For example, one "filed with an employer using an internal grievance procedure in many cases will not seek to communicate to the public or to advance a political or social point of view beyond the employment context."[258] The Court remanded the case to apply its public concern analysis.

Justice Thomas concurred in the judgment. "For the reasons set forth by Justice Scalia, I seriously doubt that lawsuits are 'petitions' within the original meaning of the Petition Clause of the First Amendment."[259]

Justice Scalia concurred in part and dissented in part. "The Court has never actually *held* that a lawsuit is a constitutionally protected 'Petition,' nor does today's opinion" so hold.[260] "There is abundant historical evidence that 'Petitions' were directed to the executive and legislative branches of government, not to the courts."[261] Justice Scalia also disagreed "with the Court's decision to apply the

---

[249] *Id.*

[250] *Id.* at 2498.

[251] *Id.*

[252] *Id.*

[253] *Id.* at 2499.

[254] *Id.* at 2500.

[255] *Id.*

[256] *Id.*

[257] *Id.*

[258] *Id.*

[259] *Id.* at 2501 (Thomas, J., concurring).

[260] *Id.* at 2503 (Scalia, J., concurring in part and dissenting in part).

[261] *Id.*

'public concern' framework of *Connick v. Myers*."[262] He noted that "petitions to redress *private* grievances were such a high proportion of petitions at the founding."[263] Moreover, the language "of the Petition Clause does not distinguish petitions of public concern from petitions of private concern."[264]

[4] Special Protection for Legislators and Other Government Employees

Article I, Section 6, Clause 1 of the Constitution is the Speech and Debate Clause. It exempts members of Congress from legal action for what they have said in speeches or debates. "For any speech and debate in either House, they shall not be questioned." Such protection is necessary to the integrity of a deliberative body.

In *Hutchinson v. Proxmire*,[265] the Court found that the heart of the Clause was speech or debate in either House. The Clause only reached other speech that was integral to the processes of deliberations and communications of committee hearings or congressional proceedings. The protection extended to aides as well as members.

In *Proxmire*, the Court refused to extend the protection of the Speech and Debate Clause to Congressional newsletters and press releases, which Senator Proxmire argued were essential to the functioning of a legislator. The Court permitted a libel action by a recipient of Senator Proxmire's "*Golden Fleece Award*," given for wasteful government spending. Many state constitutions also contain Speech and Debate Clauses protecting state legislators. Government officials in the executive branch enjoy similar immunities from defamation actions, particularly if their speech is within the scope of their official duties.[266]

---

[262] *Id.* at 2504.

[263] *Id.* at 2505.

[264] *Id.*

[265] 443 U.S. 111 (1979).

[266] *See* Barr v. Matteo, 360 U.S. 564 (1959), extending an absolute privilege against defamation actions. *Harlow v. Fitzgerald*, 457 U.S. 800 (1982), may qualify *Barr* by extending only qualified, good faith immunity to federal executive officials, but a reference to *Barr* in a later case would indicate that its absolute privilege against defamation actions remains.

Chapter 14

GOVERNMENT AND THE MEDIA: PRINT AND ELECTRONIC

INTRODUCTION

While freedom of speech and of the press are each explicitly specified in the First Amendment, the cases in this Chapter indicate that the Court treats both of these freedoms in the same way. Still, certain doctrines in First Amendment jurisprudence have particular applicability to the press. Section 14.01 begins with one such doctrine, the prohibition against prior restraints. Over time, the Court has taken a particularly dim view of any attempt by the government to suppress speech before it even has the chance to be introduced into the marketplace of ideas. Section 14.02 treats the related subject of the ability of the government to restrict the press from publishing information that it has somehow acquired about active governmental investigations. For example, the First Amendment restricts a judge's ability to issue a gag order in a pending case. Section 14.03 moves one step back in information development to deal with a right of access to government information. If government cannot suppress information that the press or others already know about, perhaps it can control the information flow about government affairs by denying a right of access to that information.

Section 14.04 begins with a different kind of access issue, public access to the electronic and print media. As the section concerns government regulation of the media, it also discusses taxation of the media and special problems relating to the regulation of the electronic media. Continuing with access issues, Section 14.05 discusses government access to information possessed by the press, such as compelling by subpoena the disclosure of confidential sources. This section thus focuses on regulation of yet another point in the information flow. Finally, Section 14.06 discusses various kinds of sanctions that can be imposed once the information is out. The limited options dictate that this section focus on civil actions for defamation and infringement on various privacy rights.

§ 14.01   THE DOCTRINE AGAINST PRIOR RESTRAINTS

Understanding the power of information, particularly when widely distributed, governments have long sought to impose restrictions on the press.[1] Well before the United States existed, Sir William Blackstone suggested that the common law looked with considerable disdain on governments imposing prior restraints on

---

[1] For some history of the relationship between government and the press, see Murphy, Near v. Minnesota *in the Context of Historical Developments*, 66 U. MINN. L. REV. 95, 98–108 (1981).

publication: "The Liberty of the press is indeed essential to the nature of a free state; but this consists in laying no *previous* restraint upon publication, and not in freedom from censure for criminal matter when published."[2]

The Supreme Court afforded strong protection against prior restraints in the classic case of *Near v. Minnesota*.[3] The Minnesota statute at issue permitted state authorities to seek an injunction against the owner or publisher of a "newspaper, magazine or other periodical" for "engag[ing] in the business of regularly publishing . . . malicious, scandalous and defamatory material."[4] The statute afforded a defense if the owner could prove not only that the publication was true, but also that the material was published with good motives and for justifiable ends. If the publisher failed to meet this burden, a judge suppressed that publication and would punish any further publication by contempt sanctions. To escape this injunction against future publication, the owner had to satisfy the court that any subsequent publication of his was truly new and different.

Minnesota sought to use this statute to close *The Saturday Press* for publishing a series of articles accusing high officials of corruption and dereliction of duties. The Supreme Court struck down this statute. Writing for a 5-4 majority, Chief Justice Hughes characterized the Minnesota law as "the essence of censorship."[5] He treated the ban on future publication as a prior restraint even though it had been imposed by a court as a penalty for previous behavior. The majority distinguished prior restraints from imposing criminal or civil penalties on speech after it had occurred. One might wonder why the Court drew this distinction. After all, if the Constitution permits government to exact penalties on speech after it occurs, simple deterrence theory would predict that those penalties would discourage future speech. Whether it compelled silence directly by injunction or indirectly by subsequent penalty, the government has in both cases suppressed ideas.

While free speech jurisprudence protects against prior restraints, it also severely limits penalties for speech after the speech has occurred.[6] Nevertheless, the protection against prior restraints is more stringent. This strong protection may stem in part from the importance of prior restraints to repressive regimes. If a speaker is penalized for speech that has been uttered, at least the ideas have reached the public and germinated so that they may effect social change. Moreover, after exposure to the ideas, members of the society may agree with the speaker which may reduce or eliminate his penalty. In contrast, the secretive process by which prior restraints are imposed may result not only in the suppression of the speaker's ideas, but also in his never reaching an audience again.

The Court struck down the statute at issue in *Near*. Chief Justice Hughes did, however, list several possible instances in which the Court might permit a prior restraint, a list which has been considerably modified by subsequent case law. The

---

[2] W. BLACKSTONE, COMMENTARIES 151–52 (emphasis in original), *quoted in* Near v. Minnesota, 283 U.S. 697, 713 (1931).

[3] 283 U.S. 697 (1931).

[4] *Id.* at 701–02.

[5] *Id.* at 713.

[6] *See, e.g.*, the discussion of *Brandenburg v. Ohio*, *supra* § 13.01.

Court discussed examples of permitting prior restraints including obscenity and revealing the sailing dates of troop carriers already at sea. Obscene materials remain among the most likely instances in which a prior restraint will apply, although even for these materials prior restraints are quite difficult to obtain.[7] The other example involving troop military maneuvers was quoted approvingly in Justice Brennan's opinion in *New York Times Co. v. United States*.[8]

New York Times Co. v. United States — often referred to as the *Pentagon Papers* case — illustrates the stringency of the modern Court's protection against prior restraints. Shortly after the *New York Times* and *Washington Post* published the first in a series of classified government documents on the Vietnam War (the Pentagon Papers), the United States sued to enjoin publication. The Southern District of New York refused to enjoin the *New York Times*. On appeal, the Second Circuit, *en banc*, remanded the case to the District Court to determine whether the disclosure of certain items would irreparably endanger the security of the United States. The District of Columbia District Court refused to enjoin the *Washington Post* and the Court of Appeals for the District of Columbia affirmed. Temporary restraining orders in both Circuits prevented publication pending the decision by the Supreme Court. Thus, no permanent injunctions on publication were at issue in this case.

The Supreme Court, in a *per curiam* opinion, stated that any prior restraint bore " 'a heavy presumption against its constitutional validity,' " and the Government carried a " 'heavy burden' " of showing justification for the imposition of such restraint.[9] As the government failed to meet its burden, the Court refused to impose any prior restraints in this case. Beyond the general and vague *per curiam* opinion, each of the six Justices in the majority penned separate, and analytically different, concurring opinions.

Justices Black and Douglas each concurred in the other's opinion. Taking an absolutist position, Justice Black stated "that the press must be left free to publish news, whatever the source, without censorship, injunctions, or prior restraints."[10] Justice Black summarily rejected the Solicitor General's attempt to justify a prior restraint on national security grounds.

Justice Douglas appeared to indicate that under the proper circumstances Congress may use its "war power" to authorize the Executive to apply for a prior restraint. As Congress had not declared war on Vietnam, and the Executive had no power to make war, Justice Douglas did not decide the extent to which Congress could have invoked its war power to authorize prior restraints.[11]

Writing separately, Justice Brennan criticized even the interim restraints issued in these cases as the government based its position on its "surmise or conjecture"

---

[7] Beyond the substantive considerations, restraints on obscene materials, like all prior restraints, must also be fashioned with certain procedural safeguards, including prompt judicial review. For further discussion of these procedural safeguards, *see infra* § 16.05.

[8] 403 U.S. 713 (1971).

[9] *Id.* at 714.

[10] *Id.* at 717.

[11] *Id.* at 722.

that publication might impair national security.[12] He stated that precedent limited prior restraints to wartime. Quoting *Near*, he would have permitted a prior restraint to " 'prevent actual obstruction to its recruiting service or the publication of the sailing dates of transports or the number of troops.' "[13] He also suggested that a prior restraint might be issued to prevent setting a nuclear holocaust in motion. For even a temporary restraint to issue, Justice Brennan would require government proof "that publication must inevitably, directly, and immediately cause the occurrence of an event kindred to imperiling the safety of a transport already at sea."

Justice Stewart, joined by Justice White, cautioned that an informed citizenry was needed to restrain the tremendous powers of the Executive over national defense and international relations. Nevertheless, to exercise these awesome powers effectively, the Executive requires "confidentiality and secrecy." Unlike the opinions previously discussed, Justice Stewart afforded the President inherent authority to seek prior restraints to protect sensitive information relating to defense and international relations. While Justice Stewart was convinced that some of the documents at issue should remain secret, the government had not established that disclosing "any of them will surely result in direct, immediate, and irreparable damage to our nation or its people."[14] In light of this opinion, government lawyers should be careful in selecting which documents they attempt to restrain.

Justice Stewart allowed greater possibilities for prior restraints than did Justices Black, Douglas, or Brennan. Moreover, because Justice White joined Justice Stewart's position and three Justices dissented, Justice Stewart's opinion represented the most protection that a majority of the Court afforded against prior restraints.

Justice White, joined by Justice Stewart, emphasized that Congress had not passed legislation permitting a prior restraint under the circumstances of this case, and that the Executive failed to comply with congressional legislation authorizing criminal sanctions for publishing specified intelligence or military information. Consequently, the Executive relied on inherent authority to restrain these materials under its proffered " 'grave and irreparable consequences test.' "[15] In contrast to specific congressional legislation, this test offered little guidance for lower courts considering prior restraints — particularly as the opinion did not disclose the contents of the materials at issue, which remained under seal.[16] Justice White did not rule out the possibility that the government could enjoin these materials pursuant to a congressional statute. Congress had addressed sanctions for the behavior at issue and had chosen to rely on criminal sanctions rather than injunctive relief. Without deciding the issue of criminality, he "would have no difficulty in sustaining convictions under these sections," when circumstances did not warrant a

---

[12] *Id.* at 726–27.

[13] *Id.* at 727 (quoting *Near*, 283 U.S. at 716).

[14] *Id.* at 730.

[15] *Id.* at 732.

[16] *Id.* at 732–33.

prior restraint.[17]

Justice Marshall's concurrence characterized the issue as whether "this Court or the Congress has the power to make law."[18] Congress had specifically declined to enact legislation giving the President the injunctive powers that he was seeking. A court issuing a judicial prior restraint against this legislative backdrop would violate separation of powers.

Chief Justice Burger wrote a dissenting opinion and Justice Harlan penned a separate dissent joined by Chief Justice Burger and Justice Blackmun. Both opinions criticized the speed with which the Court acted.[19] The pace did not allow adequate time to adjudicate the many complex questions in this case.

Turning to the merits, Justice Harlan limited judicial scrutiny to two inquiries: first, the judiciary must determine that the dispute properly lay in the President's foreign relations authority. Second, the judiciary should require that the head of the relevant department — for example, the Secretary of State or of Defense — make the determination that disclosure would irreparably harm national security. Because Justice Harlan construed the decision of the majority as an improper redetermination of the probable impact of the *Times* and *Post* disclosures on national security, he dissented.

The Court has addressed the doctrine against prior restraints in other contexts. Specific instances include demonstration permits,[20] obscene materials,[21] and classified CIA information. In *Snepp v. United States*,[22] the Court, in a *per curiam* summary decision, rejected the Court of Appeals' remedy of punitive damages and imposed a "constructive trust" on an author's profits based on the author's failure to submit the material in advance of publication as required by the CIA employment agreement.

In *Madsen v. Women's Health Center*,[23] the Court declined to apply prior restraint analysis to a broad-ranging injunction issued by a Florida court against abortion protestors and instead inquired whether the injunction burdened no more speech than necessary to serve a significant government interest. Using this test, the Court upheld the part of the injunction that restricted noise during certain times of the day as well as a 36-foot buffer zone around an abortion clinic's entrances and driveway. It also used the test to invalidate other parts of the injunction, including a 36-foot buffer zone that applied to the private property adjacent to the

---

[17] *Id.* at 737.

[18] *Id.* at 741.

[19] Chief Justice Burger noted that unlike the *Times*, which had kept these 7,000 pages of materials for months, the government and the various courts that had considered these materials had not had sufficient time to review them. Three days separated the application to review the decisions of the two courts of appeals and oral argument before the Supreme Court.

[20] *See* Cox v. New Hampshire, 312 U.S. 569 (1941), *infra* § 15.02.

[21] *See infra* § 16.05[2].

[22] 444 U.S. 507 (1980).

[23] 512 U.S. 753 (1994).

clinic, a proscription on "images observable"[24] from the clinic, a prohibition on physically approaching potential patients within 300 feet of the clinic, and a prohibition on picketing within 300 feet of the residence of a clinic employee.

Chief Justice Rehnquist wrote for the majority. "Prior restraints do often take the form of injunctions. Not all injunctions which may incidentally affect expression, however, are 'prior restraints' in the sense that the term was used in *New York Times Co.*"[25] The protestors would not be "prevented from expressing their message in any one of several different ways; they are simply prohibited from expressing it within the 36-foot buffer zone."[26] Moreover, the injunction at issue in *Madsen* "was not issued because of the content of petitioners' expression, as was the case in *New York Times Co.*, but because of their prior unlawful conduct."[27]

In *Tory v. Cochran*,[28] the Court invalidated a permanent injunction as a remedy in a defamation action. Based on a finding of a continuous pattern of defamatory activity, the injunction prohibited the defendant "from 'picketing,' from 'displaying signs, placards, or other written or printed material,' and from 'orally uttering statements' " about plaintiff or his law firm " 'in any public forum.' " Justice Breyer held (7-2) that plaintiff Johnnie Cochran's death did not moot the injunction, but the underlying reason for it was considerably reduced or destroyed. The Court held that the injunction was "an overly broad prior restraint upon speech," without "plausible justification." Justice Thomas dissented, joined by Justice Scalia.

In *Eldred v. Ashcroft*,[29] the Court held that Congress did not violate either the Copyright Clause of the Constitution, or the First Amendment when it extended the length of protection for a copyright in the Copyright Term Extension Act (CTEA). In 1998, Congress increased copyright protection from 50 to 70 years, following the death of the author whose works were at issue in this case. This protection applies to all material copyrighted after January 1, 1978. In 1993, the European Union (EU) established a copyright term of life plus 70 years. The EU denied this longer protection to the works of any non-member nation that did not afford the same protection. The CTEA, considered "rational" by the Court, extended the protection for both existing and future copyrights. This follows "unbroken congressional practice."[30]

In rejecting heightened scrutiny under the First Amendment, the Court noted that copyright laws "*promote* the creation and publication of free expression."[31] They only protect the method of expressing ideas. The ideas, theories, and facts themselves are not protected. Even the expression of the facts and ideas in a

---

[24] *Id.* at 772.

[25] *Id.* at 764 (citations omitted).

[26] *Id.*

[27] *Id.*

[28] 544 U.S. 734 (2005).

[29] 537 U.S. 186 (2003).

[30] *Id.* at 200.

[31] *Id.* at 219.

copyrighted work were available for "fair use."[32]

Dissenting, Justice Stevens maintained that persons intending to use an invention or copyrighted work when it enters the public domain should be protected against "retroactive modification." Dissenting, Justice Breyer contended that a statute exceeding the proper bounds of the Copyright Clause may promote a purpose which conflicts with the First Amendment and undercuts the "speech-related benefits" provided by both clauses.[33]

§ 14.02 THE RIGHT TO REPORT JUDICIAL AND GOVERNMENTAL AFFAIRS

Related to the doctrine of prior restraints is the ability to disseminate information acquired in ongoing trials or other government investigations. The specific issue is whether a judge or other official conducting an inquiry can suppress, or at least delay, the dissemination of information about it. The issue arises most prominently in the context of a gag order stopping the press from reporting on a specific case. In *Nebraska Press Ass'n v. Stuart*,[34] a state trial judge entered an order restraining several press and broadcast associations, publishers, and individual reporters from disseminating accounts of confessions or admissions made by the accused or facts "strongly implicative" of the accused in a widely reported murder of six persons.[35] The crime immediately attracted widespread news coverage by local, regional and national newspapers, radio and television stations. Three days after the crime, the prosecution and defense counsel joined in asking the county court to enter an order restricting news coverage or public disclosure because widespread coverage and "the reasonable likelihood of prejudicial news would make difficult, if not impossible, the impaneling of an impartial jury and tend to prevent a fair trial."[36] As modified by the Nebraska Supreme Court, the order prohibited reporting "(a) the existence and nature of any confessions or admissions made by the defendant to law enforcement officers, (b) any confessions or admissions made to any third parties, except members of the press, and (c) other facts 'strongly implicative' of the accused."[37]

---

[32] The CTEA itself incorporated certain First Amendment safeguards. It allowed "libraries, archives, and similar institutions to 'reproduce' and 'distribute, display, or perform in facsimile or digital form' copies of certain published works 'during the last 20 years of any term of copyright' for purposes of 'preservation, scholarship, or research' if the work is not already being exploited commercially and further copies are unavailable at a reasonable price." *Id.* at 220. The CTEA also allowed "small businesses, restaurants, and like entities" to play music from a "licensed radio, television, and similar facilities" without having to pay performance royalties. *Id.*

[33] Justice Breyer would find that this copyright statute "lacks the constitutionally necessary rational support (1) if the significant benefits that it bestows are private, not public; (2) if it threatens seriously to undermine the expressive values that the Copyright Clause embodies; and (3) if it cannot find justification in any significant Clause-related objective." *Id.* at 245 (Breyer, J., dissenting).

[34] 427 U.S. 539 (1976).

[35] *Id.*

[36] *Id.* at 542.

[37] *Id.* at 545.

Chief Justice Burger noted that in these rare sensational cases, a tension arises between the strong protection against prior restraints and the Sixth Amendment's guarantee of trial by an impartial jury that has been applied to the states through the Fourteenth Amendment. As the Framers did not "assign priorities between First Amendment and Sixth Amendment rights" neither would the Court. These two rights seldom conflicted, however. Jury impartiality was not unmanageably threatened in typical criminal cases that received little or no publicity, but only in those rare cases that did. Even when pretrial publicity presented a reasonable likelihood of prejudicing the jury, the judge could not exclude the press from the trial.[38] The Sixth Amendment required "strong measures" to ensure a fair trial. For example, the judge could issue a continuance, transfer the case, or sequester the jury. If publicity during the trial prejudiced the proceedings, the judge could order a new trial.[39]

Turning to the First Amendment concerns, Chief Justice Burger characterized the order at issue as a prior restraint. Prior restraints posed the gravest danger to free expression because they instantly sanctioned the speaker and suppressed information — albeit only temporarily in this case.

In a rare invocation of the oft-criticized plurality opinion in *Dennis v. United States*,[40] the Court opined that " 'the gravity of the "evil" discounted by its improbability, justifies such invasion of free speech as is necessary to avoid the danger.' "[41] Taken from the basic torts test for negligence,[42] this straight balancing test was not very protective of speech. Rendering this loose balancing test more stringent, the Court took into account the following factors in applying it: "(a) the nature and extent of pretrial news coverage; (b) whether other measures would be likely to mitigate the effects of unrestrained pretrial publicity; and (c) how effectively a restraining order would operate to prevent the threatened danger. The precise terms of the restraining order are also important."[43]

The Court's application of this guidance demonstrated the difficulty of actually obtaining a pretrial gag order. The trial judge only found that pretrial publicity " 'could impinge' " on a fair trial.[44] Moreover, the record contained little evidence that the lower courts considered the availability of adequate alternative measures. Questioning the efficacy of the trial court's order, Chief Justice Burger also noted that it lacked personal jurisdiction to restrain publication in another state. At bottom, the record did not clearly establish that additional publicity would render impossible finding 12 jurors who would follow instructions to decide the case based on the evidence presented in court. The speculative findings made by the trial court did not rise to the level of certainty required to issue a prior restraint.

---

[38] *See* Richmond Newspapers Inc. v. Virginia, *infra* § 14.03.

[39] The judge should, however, try to avert such problems with appropriate pretrial measures.

[40] *Dennis* is discussed *supra* § 13.01.

[41] *Nebraska Press*, 427 U.S. at 562.

[42] *See* United States v. Carroll Towing Co., 159 F.2d 169 (2d Cir. 1947).

[43] *Nebraska Press*, 427 U.S. at 562.

[44] *Id.* at 562. Indeed, the Chief Justice noted that rumors flying around the town of 850 could have prejudiced the trial more than the press reports.

While there were no dissenters to the Chief Justice's opinion, six Justices concurred in four separate opinions. Justice White expressed considerable doubt that a gag order would ever be constitutional.[45] Justice Powell would allow a pretrial gag order to issue only if it was necessary to prevent the dissemination of prejudicial publicity that otherwise poses a high likelihood of preventing, directly and irreparably, the impaneling of a jury meeting the Sixth Amendment requirement of impartiality. This requires a showing that (i) there is a clear threat to the fairness of trial, (ii) such a threat is posed by the actual publicity to be restrained, and (iii) no less restrictive alternatives are available.[46]

Justice Powell's standard is quite important as the remaining four Justices did not join the majority opinion but only concurred in the judgment. Specifically, Justices Brennan, Stewart, Marshall, and Stevens all expressed substantial doubt that such a gag order would ever pass constitutional muster. Consequently, Justice Powell's standard — which appears to be more stringent than the Chief Justice's majority opinion — may represent the minimum test that must be met for a gag order to issue. Arguably, not even this standard will support a gag order as five Justices — including Justice White — expressed varying degrees of doubt that they would ever allow a pretrial gag order.

In *Smith v. Daily Mail Publishing Co.*,[47] the Court invalidated a West Virginia statute that prohibited the publication in a newspaper of the name of a person charged as a juvenile offender, without the written approval of the juvenile court. The Court further determined that the statute's specific focus on newspapers, instead of a general ban on publication by all forms of communication, was unconstitutional.

In *Cox Communications Corp. v. Cohn*,[48] the Court held unconstitutional a common law privacy action against a television station for broadcasting the name of a rape victim who had been murdered in the attack.[49] The Court relied on the fact that the victim's name had been released in official court records. *Florida Star v. B. J. F.*[50] reinforces this point. That case disallowed a privacy cause of action for the publication of the name of a rape victim legally obtained by police error.

Unlike *Nebraska Press Ass'n v. Stuart*, *Landmark Communications, Inc. v. Virginia*[51] did not involve a prior restraint but a post hoc sanction. In *Landmark*, a newspaper accurately reported a pending confidential inquiry, alleging judicial misconduct. The Virginia courts had imposed criminal sanctions on the newspaper for breaching the confidentiality of proceedings before the commission. A unanimous Court reversed the imposition of criminal sanctions. The Court found that the state's interests in confidentiality did not outweigh the First Amendment right to publish truthful information about confidential proceedings. The commission could

---

[45] *Id.* at 570 (White, J., concurring).

[46] *Id.* at 571 (Powell, J., concurring).

[47] 443 U.S. 97 (1979).

[48] 420 U.S. 469 (1975).

[49] *Id.* at 496–97.

[50] 491 U.S. 524 (1989).

[51] 435 U.S. 829 (1978).

have protected confidentiality by applying careful internal procedures; for example, by sanctioning the speech of its staff and witnesses before it. This approach would force prosecutors to trace all leaks back to a commission employee or witness. Tracing the information back to its source is often made more difficult by constitutional decisions and statutes protecting the confidential sources of reporters.[52]

In *Seattle Times v. Rhinehart*,[53] a unanimous court upheld a protective order under Federal Rules of Civil Procedure Rule 26(c) prohibiting defendant newspaper from publishing information acquired through pretrial discovery. A religious group sued defendant newspaper for defamation. The newspaper sought discovery of information about the group, and the religious group sought a protective order prohibiting the newspaper from publishing information obtained through discovery. A unanimous Supreme Court upheld the order, rejecting the newspaper's characterization of it as a prior restraint. With little discussion of First Amendment issues, Justice Stevens said that the order stopped the media from abusing judicial process.

In *Cable News Network v. Noriega*,[54] a Federal District Court order temporarily enjoined the Cable News Network (CNN) from broadcasting a taped communication between criminal defendant Manuel Noriega and his attorney. CNN had refused to make the tapes available to the judge. Without finding the tapes necessary to guarantee a fair trial, the trial court enjoined their broadcast until the judge could review them. Citing *Nebraska Press Ass'n v. Stuart* and *New York Times Co. v. United States*, Justice Marshall joined by Justice O'Connor, dissented from the denial of certiorari.

In *Gentile v. State Bar*,[55] a majority of the Court upheld a state's authority to restrict attorneys' comments in the press about pending criminal proceedings. Specifically, the Court allowed a state to prohibit an attorney from making extrajudicial statements that he knew or reasonably should have known would have a "substantial likelihood of materially prejudicing" an adjudicative proceeding. Writing for the majority, Chief Justice Rehnquist emphasized that the "substantial likelihood test" was aimed at comments likely to prejudice the trial's outcome and "comments that are likely to prejudice the jury venire, even if an untainted panel can ultimately be found."[56] The substantial likelihood test was narrowly tailored to advance the state's important objectives. It appropriately balanced the state's interests in fair trials with the lawyer's interest in free speech. The Chief Justice indicated that courts could exercise control over lawyers, witnesses, parties, court personnel, and law enforcement personnel coming under their jurisdiction to protect the court's processes.

A different majority, however, set aside the sanction issued under this disciplinary rule as its safe harbor provision was void for vagueness. Despite its general prohibition against making these kinds of comments in the press, the rule contained

---

[52] *See infra* § 14.05.

[53] 467 U.S. 20 (1984).

[54] 498 U.S. 976 (1990).

[55] 501 U.S. 1030 (1991).

[56] *Id.* at 1075.

a safe harbor provision that allowed a lawyer to state " 'without elaboration . . . the general nature of the . . . defense.' "[57] Writing for this majority, Justice Kennedy[58] found the words "elaboration" and "general" unconstitutionally vague as they were terms of degree. Without any settled usage, these words rendered this safe harbor unconstitutionally vague so that it could trap unwary attorneys.

§ 14.03   ACCESS BY THE MEDIA TO GOVERNMENT ACTIVITY

Affording a right to publish news about governmental and judicial proceedings is different from affording access to those proceedings. To be published, information must first be acquired. The issues of access focus on a point in the information stream that is prior to publication. While government can rarely impose a prior restraint to stop the dissemination of information already known, government can block the flow of information at an earlier stage by denying public access to its activities.

In *Houchins v. KQED, Inc.*,[59] government officials refused KQED permission to inspect and take pictures in a prison facility. KQED filed suit. Although no formal policy regarding public access to the jail was in place at the time of the suit, Sheriff Houchins reported that a program for access was being implemented at the time suit was filed; this program was announced approximately one month after suit was filed. Tours were limited to 25 persons and did not allow cameras, tape recorders, or inmate interviews. KQED argued that such restrictions did not permit it to do its work.

A majority of the Court upheld the government's order denying the station's requested access to the prison. Writing for a plurality of four, Chief Justice Burger said that access to the prison was a legislative rather than a judicial question. The Constitution did not require government to grant access to government information within its control. Moreover, once the government did afford access, it did not have to grant any greater right of access to the press than to the general public.

Concurring in the judgment, Justice Stewart agreed that the Constitution did not guarantee a right of access to the government. Although he agreed that the press had no greater right of access than the general public, Justice Stewart thought that a truly equal right for the press required that they be able to bring equipment necessary for effective reporting, including television cameras and sound equipment.

Justice Stewart based his position in part on the Press Clause of the First Amendment. The Court generally predicates its free press decisions on the broad jurisprudence of the Speech Clause, and Justice Stewart's opinion was a rare attempt to infuse the Press Clause with independent content to address special needs of the media.

---

[57] *Id.* at 1048.

[58] Justice O'Connor provided the crucial swing vote for each of the different majorities.

[59] 438 U.S. 1 (1978).

Justice Stewart's view that the media should be able to bring in their equipment carries additional weight as three dissenting Justices would have required a far broader right of general media and public access.[60] While the dissenters recognized the necessity of keeping some governmental affairs secret, they construed the First Amendment to afford a broad right of access to governmental information.

Richmond Newspapers, Inc. v. Virginia[61] established a right of access to judicial proceedings. Defendant's second-degree murder trial had ended in a mistrial three times. At least one mistrial was caused by pretrial publicity. Defendant moved to close his fourth trial to the public. The prosecutor had no objection and the judge ordered the closure. Members of the press sought to vacate the order. As defendant wanted the trial closed, the case did not implicate defendant's Sixth Amendment right to a public trial. Instead, the case pitted defendant's Sixth Amendment right to a fair trial against a First Amendment right of access asserted by the press. The state noted that the Constitution did not explicitly guarantee to the public any right of access to criminal trials. While the state was correct in its textual argument, a unanimous Court held that a right of access is necessary if the explicit guarantees of speech and publication had any meaning. Access was supported by the long tradition of openness of criminal trials.

Demonstrating the seriousness with which it viewed the access to trials, the Court dismissed the fact that the closure order involved defendant's fourth trial. As the trial judge had rejected a constitutional right for the press or the public to attend trials, he made no findings that would support closure and did not examine whether alternatives would have ensured a fair trial. In contrast to the pretrial phase, fairness was easier to protect at trial: witnesses or jurors could be sequestered. The Court required "an overriding interest articulated in findings" to close a criminal trial.

Analogizing to the reasonable time, place, and manner restrictions permitted in public forums,[62] the Court allowed "reasonable limitations on access" that would ensure "quiet and orderly" trials. In this connection, access could be limited by the seating capacity of the courtroom and could provide preferential seating for the press.

In addition to the Chief Justice's opinion for the Court, there were five concurrences and one dissent. In his concurrence, Justice Stewart suggested other considerations, such as preservation of trade secrets, that may justify limitations upon the public's right of access.

In dissent, Justice Rehnquist refused to read a prohibition against closure orders into the First or Sixth Amendments, once both sides had consented to the order.

How can *Richmond Newspapers* be reconciled with *Houchins*? The answer may rest in the tradition of public trials which contrasts sharply with the history of closed prisons. The language of the cases would point toward opening court

---

[60] The dissent would have upheld the lower court's injunction which specifically allowed photographic and sound equipment.

[61] 448 U.S. 555 (1980).

[62] *See infra* § 15.02.

proceedings while allowing legislative and executive proceedings to remain closed. The Court's sharply contrasting treatment of the different branches may rest on separation of powers reasons. The decisions may express greater latitude for the judiciary to grant a constitutional right of access over its own branch than over the executive or legislative branches.[63]

Since *Richmond Newspapers*, the Court has extended the right of access in trial and many pretrial proceedings. In *Chandler v. Florida*,[64] the Court found that the Sixth Amendment was not violated by a Florida rule that allowed the televising of criminal trials over defendant's objection. In *Globe Newspapers Co. v. Superior Court*,[65] the Court struck down a Massachusetts statute that made closure of a trial mandatory during the testimony of a rape victim under 18 years old.

In *Press-Enterprise Co. v. Superior Court (Press Enterprise I)*,[66] the Court unanimously extended the holding in *Richmond Newspapers* to voir dire. As in *Richmond Newspapers*, the Court closely examined the history of voir dire and determined that jury selection has been a public process since at least the Sixteenth Century. The Court found that an order excluding the press from a voir dire in a rape-murder case was not narrowly tailored to serve an overriding interest. In *Gannett v. DePasquale*,[67] the Court had upheld closure of a pretrial suppression moved by defendant against a Sixth Amendment challenge on the grounds that Sixth Amendment rights ran solely to defendants. Decided before *Richmond Newspapers*, the Court made short shrift of the First Amendment claim.

In *Waller v. Georgia*,[68] the defendant sought to open his suppression hearing which the trial Court had closed over defendant's objection. As the defendant requested the open hearing, the Court ordered the open hearing and rested its decision on the Sixth Amendment. The Court did not address defendant's First Amendment claim.

In *Press-Enterprise Co. v. Superior Court (Press Enterprise II)*,[69] the Court required access to California's preliminary hearing unless "closure is essential to preserve higher values and is narrowly tailored to serve that interest."[70] The trial judge had ordered the trial closed to protect defendant's right to a fair trial. California's preliminary hearing involved a full blown proceeding with counsel, including direct and cross examination in which a neutral magistrate determined probable cause.[71] Emphasizing that these hearings traditionally had been open in California, the Court required access despite the absence of a jury. While the

---

[63] Congress has afforded considerable access to information possessed by federal agencies in the Freedom of Information Act, 5 U.S.C. § 552 (1982).

[64] 449 U.S. 560 (1981).

[65] 457 U.S. 596 (1982).

[66] 464 U.S. 501 (1984).

[67] 443 U.S. 368 (1979).

[68] 467 U.S. 39 (1984).

[69] 478 U.S. 1 (1986).

[70] *Id.* at 9.

[71] The prosecutor could bring a preliminary hearing in lieu of seeking an indictment from a grand jury. Even after an indictment, the accused could seek such a preliminary hearing as a matter of right.

preliminary hearing could not lead to a conviction, findings of probable cause at California preliminary hearings generally led to conviction at trial.

Presley v. Georgia[72] held that exclusion of the public from voir dire violated defendant's Sixth Amendment rights. The right to a public trial rests on both the First and Sixth Amendments. The Court determined in *Press-Enterprise I*[73] that the First Amendment requires voir dire to be open to the public. Later, the Court held in *Waller v. Georgia*[74] that under the Sixth Amendment the right to a public trial exists in a pretrial hearing to suppress evidence. These precedents clearly provide defendant a Sixth Amendment right to a voir dire open to the public. Whether the First and Sixth Amendment rights to a public trial are "coextensive," remains "an open question."[75]

An open trial may sometimes be closed to the public, for example, when it would compromise a fair trial, jeopardize sensitive information protected by the government, involve concrete threats of inappropriate communications with jurors, or endanger safety. To determine if closure is proper, there must be " 'an overriding interest that is likely to be prejudiced,' "[76] and " 'closure must be no broader than necessary to protect that interest.' "[77] Finally, trial courts must consider alternatives to closure, even if the parties themselves do not offer alternatives, and make findings specific enough for appellate review. If courtroom space is limited, courts may reserve rows for the public, divide the jury venire panel, or warn prospective jurors not to speak or interact with the audience. As the trial court in this case failed to consider all reasonable alternatives to closure, its closure order was unwarranted.

Justice Thomas, joined by Justice Scalia, dissented. Justice Thomas would reject summary disposition as neither *Waller* nor *Press Enterprise I* is directly on point.

In *Nixon v. Warner Communications*,[78] the Court held that because the general public had no right of access to the Nixon Tapes, the press could claim no greater right. The majority noted that Congress had provided for eventual public access to the tapes. Four Justices dissented on statutory grounds.

§ 14.04   PROTECTING THE NEWSGATHERING PROCESS

While § 14.03 focuses on access to governmental activities, § 14.04 focuses on the news- gathering process. Instead of access to information, this section treats the protection of information already gathered. Along an information continuum, then, this section focuses on protecting the sources of information that have already been obtained. Of course, the protection of sources has important implications for

---

[72] 130 S. Ct. 721 (2010).

[73] Press-Enterprise Co. v. Super. Ct. of Cal., Riverside Cty., 464 U.S. 501 (1984).

[74] 467 U.S. 39 (1984).

[75] *Presley*, 130 S. Ct. at 724.

[76] *Id.* (quoting *Waller*, 467 U.S. at 48).

[77] *Id.* (quoting *Waller*, 467 U.S. at 48).

[78] 435 U.S. 589 (1978).

obtaining the information in the first place. Without anonymity, many sources simply will not "talk." This issue was squarely presented in *Branzburg v. Hayes*[79] where the Court was asked to afford reporters a First Amendment privilege against revealing their sources to a grand jury. The Court had before it four separate cases. Three involved state grand jury proceedings while the other, *Caldwell v. United States*,[80] involved a reporter refusing to testify before a federal grand jury. In each case a reporter, who had personal knowledge of activities being investigated by a grand jury, was subpoenaed to testify about his knowledge. In each the reporter asserted a First Amendment privilege to withhold the information.

The Court framed the issue narrowly, noting that the government was not seeking a prior restraint or commanding the press to publish certain information or to alter its content. The *Branzburg* case did not seek to prohibit confidential sources or require their indiscriminate disclosure. The case only involved whether reporters were, like other citizens, obliged to comply with grand jury subpoenas and respond to questions relevant to a criminal investigation.

Writing for the majority, Justice White noted that the First Amendment did not exempt the press from every incidental burden imposed by a generally applicable civil or criminal statute. For example, the press could be excluded from grand jury proceedings, Supreme Court conferences, and meetings of officials from the Executive branch and of private organizations. Moreover, the historical evidence demonstrated that the media had never enjoyed a privilege to keep confidential information from a grand jury.[81]

The Court found that the important workings of the grand jury outweighed any uncertain burden resulting on the news-gathering process. While fear of identification in a grand jury investigation could deter some sources, the Court noted that the press had flourished for many years without such a constitutional privilege.

Justice White also listed several difficulties that impeded fashioning any such privilege. First, the Court noted the difficulty of defining who was a newsperson qualifying for the privilege. Second, every grand jury subpoena of a privileged newsperson would require courts to make preliminary determinations regarding the justifiability of an exception to the privilege.

The Court enumerated several protections for the press against the grand jury. First, the press could try to persuade Congress, state legislators, or state courts (under state law) to grant a reporter's privilege. Second, the press could write about any unfairness it perceived in the government's subpoena. Third, if the press could prove bad faith or harassment by the prosecutors or the grand jury, the judiciary could issue protective orders. Fourth, individual reporters could assert their Fifth Amendment protection against self-incrimination.

Concurring in both the judgment and in Justice White's opinion, Justice Powell stressed that although no express privilege was granted, a reporter could not be required to give information that was only remotely or tenuously relevant to the

---

[79] 408 U.S. 665 (1972).

[80] 434 F.2d 1081 (9th Cir. 1970).

[81] *Branzburg*, 408 U.S. at 665.

grand jury investigation or that revealed confidential sources without a legitimate law enforcement need. Justice Powell's opinion would appear to be somewhat more protective than Justice White's, although he concurred in Justice White's opinion.

In dissent, Justice Douglas contended that a newsperson had an absolute right not to respond to a grand jury subpoena. Alternatively, the newsperson could attend the grand jury proceedings and assert a First Amendment privilege refusing to answer certain questions. Justice Douglas predicted that the Court's opinion would deter potential sources from communicating with reporters. The opinion would also chill the information being conveyed by the media.

Justice Stewart wrote a separate dissent joined by Justices Brennan and Marshall. Justice Stewart maintained that a right to publish necessitated a right to gather news, which in turn necessitated a right to protect the confidentiality of sources. Justice Stewart proposed the adoption of a reporter's privilege: To compel a reporter to reveal confidential information before a grand jury, "the government must (1) show that there is probable cause to believe that the newsman has information that is clearly relevant to a specific probable violation of law; (2) demonstrate that the information sought cannot be obtained by alternative means less destructive of First Amendment rights; and (3) demonstrate a compelling and overriding interest in the information."[82]

Justice Stewart pointed out that law enforcement officials were not the only ones who needed the information at issue before the Court. If sources of such information dried up for fear of exposure, members of society would lack the information to make decisions on these important issues. A number of lower courts have actually followed Justice Stewart's opinion, suggesting a qualified privilege.[83] In addition, many states have afforded statutory privileges to newspersons. These, of course, would not apply before a federal grand jury.

While *Branzburg* does not afford a constitutional privilege to protect confidential sources, the Court has upheld, against a First Amendment challenge, a state law promissory estoppel action by confidential sources against the press for breaching the promise of confidentiality. In *Cohen v. Cowles Media Co.*,[84] an advisor to a gubernatorial campaign provided information about the other party's candidate for lieutenant governor. The newspapers identified him in their articles. Writing for the Court, Justice White said that the press must comply with generally applicable laws that have an incidental effect on news-gathering and reporting. For example, the press must comply with trespass laws in acquiring information. They must also comply with copyright, tax, antitrust, and labor law. The Minnesota Supreme Court had set aside awards of $200,000 of compensatory damage and $500,000 of punitive damages. The United States Supreme Court allowed the promissory estoppel action but left it to the Minnesota Supreme Court to decide whether to reinstate the damage awards.

---

[82] *Id.* at 743 (Stewart, J., dissenting).

[83] *See* Note, *Disclosure of Confidential Sources in International Reporting*, 61 S. Cal. L. Rev. 1631 (1988).

[84] 501 U.S. 663 (1991).

In dissent, Justice Blackmun said that the burden on free speech was not incidental because the publication of important political speech was involved. Justice Souter also dissented, stressing the public's interest in the information and suggesting that he might permit a promissory estoppel action by a private individual.

Also relating to the news-gathering process, *Zurcher v. Stanford Daily*[85] sustained a warrant to search newspaper offices. The police obtained a warrant to search the *Stanford Daily* offices after demonstrating probable cause to believe that the office contained photographs taken by the newspaper that could identify demonstrators who had assaulted police. The police searched the newspaper's darkrooms, filing cabinets, computer disks, and waste baskets, but not locked drawers or rooms. The search afforded the opportunity to read notes and correspondence.

Justice White held that the press was afforded no special treatment under the Fourth Amendment concerning warrants to search property. He did, however, require that the Fourth Amendment be applied with "scrupulous exactitude" when the third party not accused of a crime was a newspaper, as First Amendment interests were at stake. When presumptively protected materials were sought, the warrant should be exact in scope leaving little discretion to the officer conducting the search. The Court also predicted that prosecutors generally would opt for subpoenas unless there was a likelihood that the evidence would be destroyed.

The Privacy Protection Act of 1980[86] afforded by statute much of the protection that the *Zurcher* decision refused to extend under the Constitution. The statute severely limited the use of search warrants to obtain material in the possession of the media, requiring law enforcement officials to rely primarily on subpoenas.

In *Wilson v. Layne*,[87] the Court invalidated a " 'media ride along' " under the Fourth Amendment. A photographer and a reporter from the *Washington Post* had entered the home of a fugitive's parents with police officers who attempted to execute an arrest warrant and mistakenly restrained the fugitive's father. Chief Justice Rehnquist held that the presence of the media inside the home "was not related to the objectives of the authorized intrusion." Because this Fourth Amendment violation was not established at the time of the incident and the officers had no way to know that inviting the media along would be illegal, the officers enjoyed qualified immunity from a suit for damages.[88]

In *Simon & Schuster v. Members of New York State Crime Victims Board*,[89] the Court struck down a New York statute requiring that profits of persons convicted of a crime or who acknowledged the crime in writing be deposited in an escrow account for their victims and creditors. Writing for the majority, Justice O'Connor said that the statute discriminated against speech based on its content. Accepting victim

---

[85]　436 U.S. 547 (1978).

[86]　Pub. L. No. 96-440, 94 Stat. 1979.

[87]　526 U.S. 603 (1999).

[88]　*Accord* Hanlon v. Berger, 526 U.S. 808 (1999) (companion case).

[89]　502 U.S. 105 (1991).

compensation as a compelling state interest, the statute was overinclusive in extending to all works in which the author mentioned the commission of a crime.

Consequently, it would cover the *Confessions of St. Augustine* and *The Autobiography of Malcolm X.* Unlike prior restraints, punishments imposed after publication do not directly stop the dissemination of ideas. Still, such punishments exerted a chilling effect on speech. Even civil damage awards could have such an impact.

§ 14.05   ACCESS TO THE MEDIA

The cases in this section deal with public access to communicate in the media rather than media and public access to governmental affairs. *Red Lion Broadcasting Co. v. FCC*[90] stands as one of the few cases in which the Court has promoted the egalitarian view of freedom of speech. The Court focused on the importance of public access to the marketplace of ideas. Specifically, the case upheld the Federal Communications Commission's (FCC) Fairness Doctrine.[91] The doctrine afforded a free opportunity to reply to persons who have been personally attacked on a particular radio or television station in political editorials or in discussions of controversial public issues. While the FCC has since abrogated the administrative Fairness Doctrine,[92] the constitutional doctrine enunciated in the *Red Lion* case remains good law.

Resisting the application of the Fairness Doctrine, defendant radio broadcasters contended that the First Amendment afforded them the right not to broadcast what they did not want to broadcast. Writing for a unanimous Court, Justice White rejected the characterization of the station as a private entity upon which such conditions could not be imposed. Instead, the Court characterized the broadcast media as a scarce forum in which Congress could stop one voice from drowning out all others. This characterization was underpinned by the fact that the broadcast media must use scarce publicly owned airwaves. In an earlier case, the Court had established the power of the government to regulate and license this scarce medium.[93] While technological advances had created more access, uses for the media had developed apace. Moreover, even if technological scarcity disappeared, broadcasters that the government had licensed earlier had been given an economic advantage that others would find difficult to overcome. The Court found the broadcast media both a technologically and economically scarce resource. Consequently, the Court viewed broadcasting as a privilege rather than a right. With a government-granted privilege, the government could impose certain duties, such as the Fairness Doctrine.

Countering the argument that regulations fostered diverse views in this scarce marketplace, the broadcasters argued that if controversial programming obliged them to allot time at no cost to speakers whose views they found unpalatable, then

---

[90] 395 U.S. 367 (1969).

[91] *Id.* at 375.

[92] *See* Fairness Doctrine Alternatives Report, 2 FCC Record 5272 (1987).

[93] Nat'l Broad. Co. v. United States, 319 U.S. 190 (1943).

self-censorship would severely curtail coverage of controversial public issues. Based on past industry practice, the Court found this argument speculative. If self-censorship occurred, the FCC could require broadcasters to cover controversial issues even though such coverage would attract a right of reply. The Court noted that different and more serious First Amendment problems would be presented if government stopped or censored a particular program on the broadcaster's own views or other views that had been denied access to the broadcast media. Moreover, the case did not involve government views dominating the airwaves.

On August 4, 1987, the Federal Communications Commission abolished the Fairness Doctrine.[94] Since this time, there have been Congressional efforts and litigation to revive the doctrine. The First Amendment analysis propounded in *Red Lion* of course, is not affected by the FCC's decision. Specifically, the Court has upheld the diversity of viewpoint interests articulated in *Red Lion* in its affirmative action decision of *Metro Broadcasting, Inc. v. FCC*.[95]

The Court displayed a less generous approach to access to the broadcast media in *Columbia Broadcasting System, Inc. v. Democratic National Committee*.[96] That decision upheld an FCC policy that allowed broadcasters to refuse the purchase of advertising. Supporting the Commission's ruling, the Court concluded that the First Amendment did not mandate a private right of access to the broadcast media. Citing *Red Lion*, Chief Justice Burger argued that a private right of paid access to the media would favor those with the wealth to purchase such access. The Chief Justice was also concerned that a broad right of private access would embroil the FCC into determining which advertisers would enjoy access.

Concurring, Justice Stewart argued that compelling broadcasters to accept advertising with which they disagreed violated their First Amendment rights. Also concurring, Justice Douglas said that radio and television have the same First Amendment rights as newspapers. Accordingly, he would set aside even the Fairness Doctrine. Justice Douglas had not participated in *Red Lion*.

Justice Brennan dissented, joined by Justice Marshall. Justice Brennan construed *Red Lion* as guaranteeing listeners a wide-ranging spectrum of views in the broadcast media. He found the Fairness Doctrine inadequate to ensure the debate on diverse views to which the public was constitutionally entitled. The Court permitted broadcasters virtually absolute control over who and what would be covered, how material would be presented, and who would speak.

In *CBS v. FCC*,[97] the Court (6-3) upheld Section 317(a)(7) of the Federal Communications Act that allowed legally qualified candidates for office the right to purchase air time on a reasonable basis. The Court made clear that its holding only affected the broadcast media and that it was not approving any general right of

---

[94] *See* Fairness Doctrine Alternatives Report, 2 FCC Record 5272 (1987).

[95] 497 U.S. 547 (1990). For additional discussion of *Metro Broadcasting, see supra* § 11.02[2].

[96] 412 U.S. 94 (1973).

[97] 453 U.S. 367 (1981).

access to the media.[98] The Court has also held that the FCC lacked statutory authority to enforce any right of access to cable television.[99]

Miami Herald Publishing Co. v. Tornillo[100] rejected a right of access to the print media. The Court, in a unanimous decision, struck down Florida's "right of reply" statute. Similar to the FCC regulations upheld in *Red Lion*, the Florida law required newspapers printing editorials critical of political candidates to publish the candidates' replies at no cost.

The candidate seeking a right to reply made arguments similar to the ones that the Court had embraced in *Red Lion*. Arguing economic rather than technological scarcity, he focused on the concentration of ownership of newspapers nationally, the fact that many cities had but one newspaper, and the frequent common ownership of newspapers and television and radio stations. While the Court was sympathetic to these concerns, Chief Justice Burger held the statute unconstitutional because it forced the newspaper to print material that it had refused to print. Consequently, the right exacted economic costs which could deter the publisher from printing what it wished. The statute also intruded into the editors' decision-making process. Concurring, Justice Brennan noted that the Court did not address the constitutionality of right of retraction statutes. Also concurring, Justice White — author of *Red Lion* — stated that defamation was the appropriate remedy in this case.[101]

Even though *Tornillo* and *Red Lion* are difficult to distinguish, it is noteworthy that Red Lion was not mentioned in any of the *Tornillo* opinions. The cases may reaffirm that the Court sometimes treats the broadcast media and print media differently, without always explaining the reasons for this different treatment.

§ 14.06 TAXATION

The First Amendment also imposes certain constraints on taxing the media. In *Minneapolis Star & Tribune v. Minnesota Commissioner of Revenue*,[102] the Court held that Minnesota's imposition of a special tax on newspapers violated the First Amendment. While Minnesota exempted newspapers and other periodicals from its general sales and use taxes, it imposed a use tax on the cost of paper and ink. The tax, however, exempted the first $100,000 spent for paper and ink. As the *Star & Tribune* had the largest circulation of all Minnesota papers, it paid nearly two-thirds of the total amount collected under this tax.

The tax would have been unconstitutional if the Minnesota legislature had enacted it for the purpose of curbing newspaper circulation. Writing for the majority, Justice O'Connor found no such legislative intent in this case like that which had existed in *Grosjean v. American Press Co.*[103] While the government could

---

[98] In this connection, the Court specifically reaffirmed its holding in *Miami Herald Publishing Co. v. Tornillo*.

[99] *See* FCC v. Midwest Video Corp., 440 U.S. 689 (1979).

[100] 418 U.S. 241 (1974).

[101] He lamented that the Court had severely curtailed this cause of action.

[102] 460 U.S. 575 (1983).

[103] 297 U.S. 233 (1936). *Grosjean* invalidated a tax on the gross receipts from advertising in large

impose generally applicable taxes on newspapers, a tax singling out the press for special treatment had to be "necessary to achieve an overriding government interest."[104] Moreover, the Minnesota tax singled out those newspapers that used more than $100,000 worth of paper and ink per year — a very small percentage of Minnesota newspapers. The Court viewed such a narrowly focused tax as having great potential for abuse. No interest that Minnesota proposed justified such a risk.

In his dissenting opinion, Justice Rehnquist noted that the newspaper would have paid three times more taxes had it been subject to Minnesota's general sales tax. Both he and Justice White would have upheld special taxes on the press that did not impose a greater burden on the press.[105]

In *Arkansas Writers' Project v. Ragland*,[106] the Court invalidated an Arkansas sales tax that taxed "general interest" magazines but exempted newspapers and religious, professional, trade, and sports journals. In addition to discriminating among publishers, the Arkansas tax discriminated based on the content of the publications.

In *Leathers v. Medlock*,[107] the Court upheld the application of the state sales tax to cable television, even though the tax exempted certain newspaper and magazine sales.[108] The statute as originally written extended the sales tax to cable but exempted satellite broadcast service in addition to certain newspapers and magazine sales. The Arkansas legislature modified the statute to extend the tax to all radio, video, and television service including satellite broadcasting. The Arkansas Supreme Court held unconstitutional the original version of the tax, which extended to cable but exempted satellite broadcast services. The United States Supreme Court upheld both versions.

Justice O'Connor framed the constitutional question as "whether the First Amendment prevents a State from imposing its sales tax on only selected segments of the media." Because the challengers were cable operators, subscribers, and trade organizations, the analysis focused on the discrimination against cable television, which the Court treated as part of the press.

Distinguishing *Grosjean, Minneapolis Star,* and *Arkansas Writers'*, the Court emphasized that this is a generally applicable tax not confined to a narrow group. Moreover, this generally applicable sales tax was broad-based and content neutral, including a large number of diverse cable operators. The First Amendment permitted differential taxation of speakers including press sources only if the tax was "directed at, or presents the danger of suppressing particular ideas."[109]

---

newspapers. Imposed in addition to the general sales tax, the court found that this second tax was specifically designed to limit circulation.

[104] *Minneapolis Star*, 460 U.S. at 582.

[105] Only Justice Rehnquist would have upheld the $100,000 exclusion that discriminated among Minnesota press sources.

[106] 481 U.S. 221 (1987).

[107] 499 U.S. 439 (1991).

[108] The tax exempted receipts from magazine and newspaper subscription sales and over-the-counter sales of newspapers.

[109] 499 U.S. at 440.

Justice Marshall dissented, joined by Justice Brennan. Justice Marshall thought that this case was indistinguishable from *Minneapolis Star*. He noted that the case involved discrimination between different sources of the same media, whereas this case involved differential taxation of different media. He also noted that the only reason the state offered for discriminating among media was raising revenue, a rationale that usually did not allow discrimination in the free speech area. Discriminating against cable had an impact on the types of ideas disseminated because this medium often includes ideas that do not appear elsewhere.

§ 14.07 ELECTRONIC MEDIA

[1] Broadcast Media

In *FCC v. League of Women Voters*,[110] the Court struck down (5-4) that part of the Public Broadcasting Act which forbade any public broadcasting stations that received a government grant from engaging in editorializing.[111] The case announced a general middle tier standard to scrutinize restrictions on the broadcast media. Restrictions on the broadcast media would be upheld if they were "narrowly tailored to further a substantial governmental interest, such as ensuring adequate and balanced coverage of public issues."[112] In applying this test, the Court would balance the interests of the public and broadcasters under the facts of the particular case. Justice Brennan justified the middle tier standard on two grounds. First, it supported the *Red Lion* view of technological scarcity which allowed the government to regulate the airwaves. Second, the standard allowed leeway to ensure that the public received a balanced presentation of views.

Applying the middle tier test to the editorializing ban at issue, the Court noted that the ban was based on the content of speech and that editorializing was a form of speech central to the First Amendment. The Court rejected the interest in preventing government from propagandizing, saying that Congress had provided other protections against this including a bipartisan board for the private Public Broadcasting Corporation. The Court also rejected the contention that the ban was a legitimate exercise of Congress' spending power. Not only did federal funds pay for only a small fraction of the station's activities, but Congress did not allow the station to confine federal money to non-editorial activities.[113] The Court emphasized the narrowness of its decision; it did not forbid congressional regulation of the "content, timing, or character" of speech by public broadcasting stations.

In dissent, Justice Rehnquist, joined by Chief Justice Burger and Justice White, argued that Congress rationally determined, in the proper exercise of its spending power, that the taxpayers who funded public broadcasting would not like to see

---

[110] 468 U.S. 364 (1984).

[111] *Id.* at 395.

[112] *Id.* at 365.

[113] Funding only a fraction of the station's activities distinguished this case from *Reagan v. Taxation with Representation in Washington, infra* § 16.03, in which the Court held that Congress' refusal to permit a tax deduction for lobbying was a legitimate exercise of its spending power.

their money used to editorialize or endorse political candidates.

Justice Stevens also dissented. Recalling the harsh voice of Adolph Hitler's propaganda, he agreed with Congress' decision to limit the potential impact of government funds on pervasive and powerful organs of mass communication.

In *Arkansas Educational Television Commission v. Forbes,*[114] the Court upheld the Arkansas Educational Television Commission's (AETC) exclusion of a candidate from a candidate's debate because he had not attracted substantial public interest and was not considered a serious candidate by the news media covering the election. At trial, the jury found the decision was not based on the broadcaster's opposition to the candidate's views.

Writing for the Court, Justice Kennedy explained that public and private broadcasters typically exercise editorial discretion to meet programming obligations. Because a public broadcaster operates as a state run agency, it must — unlike a private broadcaster — adhere to constitutional restrictions. Generally, public broadcasting is not a public forum; however, candidate debates present a narrow exception to this rule. Debates differ from general broadcasting because the candidates express their own views and not those of the broadcaster. Candidate debates also present a unique occasion during which the nation's constituents concentrate on the electoral process.

While the debate was a forum, it was a nonpublic forum. This classification only required AETC's decision to exclude plaintiff to be reasonable and viewpoint neutral. The decision to exclude plaintiff met these criteria as it was based on his general lack of support. Justice Stevens dissented, joined by Justices Souter and Ginsburg.[115]

[2] Cable Television

In *City of Los Angeles v. Preferred Communications, Inc.,*[116] one cable television company asserted that a municipality's grant of an exclusive franchise to another cable company violated its First Amendment rights. The excluded cable company alleged that the excess capacity on the city's utility lines could also accommodate its service. Without deciding the case, a unanimous Court held that cable television enjoys First Amendment rights. The Court remanded the case to develop the factual allegations.

One could analogize cable television to the print media on the ground that cable need not use the airwaves. On the other hand, one could also analogize the media to broadcasting because of the similar video and audio characteristics. In *Turner Broadcasting System, Inc. v. FCC,*[117] the Court provided guidance about the standards for scrutinizing regulations of cable television. In *Turner,* the Court upheld the constitutionality of the must-carry provisions of the Cable Television

---

[114] 523 U.S. 666 (1998).

[115] For additional discussion of *Forbes, see infra* § 15.04[1].

[116] 476 U.S. 488 (1986).

[117] 512 U.S. 622 (1994).

Consumer Protection and Competition Act of 1992. These must-carry provisions required cable television systems to carry local broadcast stations. Much of the Court's analysis was devoted to determining the appropriate level of scrutiny for the provisions at issue.

Writing for the Court, Justice Kennedy rejected any broad-based application of *FCC v. League of Women Voters* to cable television. The middle tier standard in that case stemmed from the frequency scarcity of the broadcast media, a technological limitation that did not burden cable television. Nor would any structural dysfunction in the cable market justify a broad-based middle tier standard.

In the free speech area, the Court imposed strict scrutiny for content-based regulations and middle tier scrutiny for non-content-related restrictions, such as the one at issue. The must carry rules were simply designed to protect cable access for local broadcasters and their viewers against the economic power of cable operators.

The cable operators maintained that the regulations should receive strict scrutiny because the regulations forced speech on cable that the operators would not have chosen to carry. This problem did not demand strict scrutiny as ideas were not being forced on the operators based on their content as they had been in *Miami Herald Co. v. Tornillo*. Nor did Congress favor one class of speakers (broadcasters) over another (cable operators). Congress merely wished to protect access for local broadcasters and their audiences.

Applying the middle tier standard in *United States v. O'Brien*,[118] the regulations had to advance a substantial governmental interest which was unrelated to the suppression of speech, and not burden substantially more speech than required to advance that interest. The government's proffered interests of preserving free local broadcast television, furthering program diversity, and advancing competition, were both substantial and unrelated to the suppression of speech.

In analyzing whether the must-carry rules were narrowly tailored to advance those interests, a plurality of four afforded Congress substantial deference. The Court wanted to ascertain whether Congress' conclusions were reasonable and based on substantial evidence. The two conclusions were that many cable operators would not carry local broadcasters absent the must-carry provisions and that many local broadcasters would deteriorate or fail absent the must-carry provisions. The plurality thought that the lower court had insufficient evidence to grant summary judgment on these propositions. Accordingly, the plurality reversed, requiring the government to build the record on remand. Justice Stevens added a fifth vote to provide a majority in favor of remand. He would have preferred simply to affirm the summary judgment dismissing the challenge to the must carry rules.

Justice O'Connor dissented, joined by Justices Scalia, Ginsburg, and in substantial part, by Justice Thomas. Justice O'Connor said that the must-carry provisions expressed content-based preferences for local programming, for

---

[118] 391 U.S. 367 (1968).

educational programming, for news and public affairs programming, and even for diversity of viewpoint. These restraints on the editorial discretion of cable operators had to be justified by means necessary to advance a compelling state interest. The interest in localism could not satisfy this test.

In *Turner Broadcasting System, Inc. v. FCC (Turner II)*,[119] the Court reviewed the lower court's determination of the genuine issues of material fact that existed after *Turner I*: whether the must-carry provisions furthered important governmental interests and did not burden more speech than was necessary.

Writing for a majority in all but one small portion of the opinion, Justice Kennedy again applied *United States v. O'Brien*. Congressional action was necessary to avoid a decline in the amount of media accessible to consumers. As television is "an essential part of the national discourse,"[120] Congress had a substantial interest in maintaining a large number of broadcasters to ensure that all consumers may receive information and entertainment equal to that received by cable subscribers. To the extent that Justice Kennedy relied on an anti-competitive rationale, he wrote for a plurality of four. As horizontal concentration and vertical integration rose, so did the incentives and ability of cable operators to drop local broadcasters.

Substantial evidence validated Congress' judgment that the must-carry provisions directly and effectively promoted the government's interests. The provisions allowed many local broadcasters to continue being carried over cable with accompanying audience access and advertising revenues.

Nor did the must-carry provisions burden substantially more speech than necessary to further the governmental interests. Since the content-neutral regulations did not inherently threaten free speech like content-based regulations, the Court applied intermediate scrutiny. Justice Kennedy noted that "94.5 percent of the 11,628 cable systems nationwide have not had to drop any programming in order to fulfill their must-carry obligations; the remaining 5.5 percent have had to drop an average of only 1.22 services from their programming; and cable operators nationwide carry 99.8 percent of the programming they carried before enactment of must-carry."[121] Moreover, as cable capacity increases, the current burden of must-carry will only diminish. The actual burden of the regulatory system consisted of the 5,880 local broadcast channels carried by cable operators. Absent must-carry, cable operators would drop most of those stations. However, this burden was "congruent"[122] with the benefits it afforded; it was "narrowly tailored to preserve a multiplicity of broadcast stations for the 40 percent of American households without cable."[123] Congress should continue to reconcile competing economic interests in the rapidly changing field of television, and the courts should not invalidate a Congressional judgment supported by substantial evidence grounded in reasonable factual findings.

---

[119] 520 U.S. 180 (1997).

[120] *Id.* at 194.

[121] *Id.* at 214.

[122] *Id.* at 215.

[123] *Id.* at 216.

Justice Stevens concurred, stating that the issue would have been different had the statute regulated the content of speech rather than the structure of the market.

Justice Breyer concurred in all of the majority opinion, except insofar as it relied on an anti-competitive rationale. He maintained that the statute prevented a serious reduction in the quality and quantity of available programming for those not subscribing to cable, and that must-carry advanced the long-standing national communications policy of requiring the greatest dissemination of information from a multitude of sources. Through must-carry, Congress struck a reasonable balance between results that restrict and enhance speech.

Justice O'Connor, joined by Justices Scalia, Thomas, and Ginsburg, dissented. Justice O'Connor contended that the FCC's depiction of must-carry as a way to protect the stations and the Court's regard for self-expression and the local origin of broadcasting demonstrated a content-based preference for local programming. More generally, Justice O'Connor criticized the majority's extreme deference toward Congress, as the Court did not even weigh less restrictive alternatives.

In *Denver Area Educational Telecommunications Consortium, Inc. v. FCC*,[124] a sharply divided Court invalidated Section 10(b) of the Television Consumer Protection and Competition Act of 1992 (Act) that required cable operators to restrict the availability of patently offensive programming on leased access commercial channels and Section 10(c) of the Act that empowered cable operators to regulate similar programming on public access channels. These provisions were "not appropriately tailored to achieve the basic, legitimate objective of protecting children from exposure to 'patently offensive' material."[125] A different majority upheld Section 10(a) of the Act that afforded operators discretion to prohibit or restrict patently offensive programming on leased access channels. Justice Breyer delivered a plurality opinion joined in its entirety only by Justices Stevens and Souter.

In Part I of his opinion, Justice Breyer, joined by Justices Stevens, O'Connor, and Souter, discussed the history and specifics of the three provisions of the Act at issue.

Justices Stevens, O'Connor, and Souter joined Part II of Justice Breyer's opinion, which upheld the constitutionality of Section 10(a). Justice Breyer believed it premature to analogize to "categorical standards" that the Court has applied to broadcasting, common carriers, or bookstores. These categorical approaches "import law developed in very different contexts into a new and changing environment and they lack the flexibility necessary to allow government to respond to very serious practical problems without sacrificing the free exchange of ideas the First Amendment is designed to protect."[126] Instead, Justice Breyer adopted a more narrow approach "by closely scrutinizing Section 10(a)."[127] Specifically, the

---

[124] 518 U.S. 727 (1996).

[125] *Id.* at 733.

[126] *Id.* at 740.

[127] *Id.* at 743.

plurality concluded that Section 10(a) was "a sufficiently tailored response to an extraordinarily important problem."[128]

First, Section 10(a) has "an extremely important justification" that the "Court has often found compelling — the need to protect children from patently offensive sex-related material."[129] Second, leased channels had access to cable only through the 1984 Act of Congress. Section 10(c) balances access for leased channels with "restoring to cable operators a degree of the editorial control that Congress removed in 1984."[130] Third, analogizing to the ban upheld in *FCC v. Pacifica Foundation*, the plurality noted that cable, like broadcasting, was uniquely accessible to children and pervasively present in the lives of Americans, including in the homes. Fourth, by allowing a cable operator to rearrange broadcast times instead of having to impose outright bans, Section 10(a) "likely restricts speech less than, not more than, the ban at issue in *Pacifica*."[131]

Justice Breyer distinguished the ban in *Sable Communications of California, Inc. v. FCC*[132] on the ground that the obscene telephone service at issue in *Sable* "was significantly less likely to expose children to the banned material, was less intrusive, and allowed for significantly more control over what comes into the home than either broadcasting or the cable transmission system."[133] The plurality also distinguished *Turner Broadcasting System, Inc. v. FCC*, which relied on cable's lack of spectrum scarcity, not its effects on children.

The plurality also refused to decide whether the "public forum doctrine applied to leased access channels."[134] Justice Breyer remained reluctant to allow a doctrine developed in another area to control "such a new and changing area."[135] Moreover, while government may create a limited public forum, the Court has not decided that dedicating a public forum to a particular content requires strict scrutiny.

Rejecting the argument that Section 10(a) is vague, the plurality said that the language in *Miller v. California* identifies what materials a state may regulate as obscene. Moreover, *FCC v. Pacifica Foundation*,[136] noted that "what is 'patently offensive' depends on context, degree, and time of broadcast."[137]

In Part III, writing for a majority comprised of Justices Stevens, O'Connor, Kennedy, Souter, and Ginsburg, Justice Breyer invalidated Section 10(b) which required cable operators to block leased channels displaying " 'patently offensive' sex-related material." Section 10(b) was not a " 'least restrictive alternative or

---

[128] *Id.*

[129] *Id.*

[130] *Id.* at 747.

[131] *Id.* at 745.

[132] 492 U.S. 115 (1989). *See infra* § 15.01.

[133] *Denver Area Educ. Telecomms. Consortium, Inc.*, 518 U.S. at 748.

[134] *Id.* at 749.

[135] *Id.*

[136] 438 U.S. 726 (1978). *See infra* § 15.01.

[137] *Denver Area Educ. Telecomms. Consortium, Inc.*, 518 U.S. at 752.

narrowly tailored,' " and was "considerably more 'extensive than necessary.' "[138] The Court acknowledged a compelling state interest in protecting children. The provision restricts viewer discretion, as a cable operator has 30 days to respond to a subscriber's written request to unblock or reblock a restricted channel. Moreover, requiring written notice to unblock such channels may deter subscribers who fear advertent or inadvertent disclosure of their desire to view such materials. These "added costs and burdens"[139] may prompt a cable system operator to ban such programming entirely. Less restrictive alternatives to protect children included blocking upon telephone request and a lockbox.

In Part IV of his opinion, joined only by Justices Stevens and Souter, Justice Breyer invalidated Section 10(c), even though it afforded cable operators with the same power to regulate public access channels that Section 10(a) afforded with leased access channels. Four important differences distinguished the two provisions. First, unlike leased access channels, "cable operators have not historically exercised editorial control"[140] over public access channels. Consequently, "Section 10(c) does not restore to cable operators editorial rights that they once had."[141] Second, unlike leased access channels, public access channels are partly financed with public funds and supervised by local supervisory boards which can address child exposure to offensive programming. Third, local supervision designed to secure programs valued by the community tends to obviate the need for a " 'cable operator's veto' "[142] for public access channels. Finally, "the public/nonprofit programming control systems now in place would normally avoid, minimize, or eliminate"[143] programming that could adversely impact children.

In Part V, Justice Breyer, joined by Justices Stevens, O'Connor, and Souter, found Section 10(a) to be severable from the invalidated Sections 10(b) and (c). Congress intended severability and Section 10(a) could still advance the Act's basic objective independent of the two other provisions.

In separate concurring opinions, Justices Stevens and Souter emphasized their unwillingness to adhere to categorical standards in such a dynamic industry. Rejecting the public forum categorization of cable television, Justice Stevens would even allow government impartially to restrict access to classical music — or perhaps even political speech — if the government concluded that enough such speech was already broadcast.

Concurring in part and dissenting in part, Justice O'Connor believed Section 10(c) should be upheld because like Section 10(a), Section 10(c) furthered the compelling interest of protecting children from indecent programming.

Concurring in part and dissenting in part, Justice Kennedy, joined by Justice Ginsburg, would have invalidated the entire Act. Justice Kennedy criticized the

---

[138] *Id.* at 755.

[139] *Id.* at 754.

[140] *Id.* at 761.

[141] *Id.*

[142] *Id.* at 763.

[143] *Id.* at 763–64.

plurality for failing to apply clear legal standards. He also criticized the plurality's suggestion that more deference be given to restrict speech conveyed over emerging technologies because they are not certain what standard should apply. With regard to Section 10(c), the manner in which public access channels are created and the purpose they serve indicate they are public forums by designation. State and local governments require this access. As the cable operator stood in the shoes of government, strict scrutiny applied to the content-based restrictions permitted by Section 10(c). As Section 10(a) involved restricting speech on a common carrier (the cable system), *Sable Communications of California, Inc. v. FCC*[144] required that strict scrutiny apply. All three provisions failed strict scrutiny because the government could protect children by simply allowing subscribers to elect to block access.

Concurring in part and dissenting, Justice Thomas, joined by Chief Justice Rehnquist and Justice Scalia, would uphold all three provisions. Justice Thomas maintained that government's mandatory access for leased and public channels was forced speech. He also criticized the plurality for ignoring *Turner*: its analogizing cable to the print media entailed "some form of heightened scrutiny."[145] Public access programmers had no right to challenge Section 10(c) as a violation of freedom of speech as they "have no constitutional right to speak through the cable medium."[146] Public access channels cannot be scrutinized under public forum analysis because they are not public property.

Section 10(b) passed strict scrutiny as it was narrowly tailored to achieve the compelling interest of protecting children. The less restrictive alternatives proffered by the Court were inadequate because they could not provide constant assurance that children would not be exposed to indecent programming.

In *United States v. Playboy Entertainment Group, Inc.*,[147] the Court struck down Section 505 of the Telecommunications Act of 1996, because the government failed to prove that it was the least restrictive means of preventing "signal bleed" over cable television. Section 505 required cable providers to completely scramble all channels which primarily feature sexual programming. As this option was currently infeasible economically, the Act allowed cable providers the alternative of transmitting such programming from 10 p.m. to 6 a.m.

Scrambling channels is commonly used to restrict access to certain customers. Signal bleed occurs when audio or visual segments of a program can be heard or seen despite the cable operator's scrambling. Congress enacted Section 505 to prevent children from viewing or hearing adult programming.

Writing for the majority, Justice Kennedy stated that as households view 30 to 50 percent of all adult programming before 10 p.m., the time restriction alternative significantly limited communication. In addition to restricting Section 505's

---

[144] *See infra* § 15.01[3].

[145] *Denver Area Educ. Telecomms. Consortium, Inc.*, 518 U.S. at 820–21 (Thomas, J., concurring in part and dissenting in part).

[146] *Id.* at 822.

[147] 529 U.S. 803 (2000).

transmission times, Section 505 of the Telecommunication Act afforded the subscribers the right to request cable operators to fully block channels free of charge.

A content-based regulation "must be narrowly tailored to promote a compelling Government interest."[148] Section 505 did regulate content, whereas the alternative Section 504 provided a less restrictive alternative through targeted voluntary blocking of adult channels. Unlike the broadcast media, cable operators can block a particular unwanted channel in a particular household. The District Court had found that with sufficient notice, Section 504's voluntary blocking requests could adequately protect consumers.

Justices Stevens and Thomas filled separate concurring opinions. Justice Thomas argued that under *Miller v. California*,[149] some communities may be able to restrict some of the programming at issue in this case as obscene.

Justices Scalia and Breyer filed separate dissenting opinions. Justice Breyer was joined by Chief Justice Rehnquist and Justices O'Connor and Scalia in his dissent. Justice Breyer maintained that the government proved that signal bleed is a serious problem. The parties admit that basic scrambling does not block the audio portions of a program. Moreover, Playboy's own study showed that 75 percent of cable operators did not comply with Section 505. If signal bleed was not a significant problem, why did "*so many cable operators switch to night time hours?*"[150]

Speech-related statutes must meet a high standard, but the standards do "permit Congress to enact a law that increases the cost associated with certain speech, where doing so serves a compelling interest that cannot be served through the adoption of a less restrictive, similarly effective alternative."[151] When government seeks to protect children, "the First Amendment poses a barrier that properly is high, but not insurmountable."[152]

[3] The Internet

In *Reno v. ACLU*,[153] the Court struck down the Communications Decency Act of 1996 (CDA), which was designed to safeguard minors from "indecent" and "patently offensive" transmissions on the Internet.

Writing for the Court, Justice Stevens first distinguished the CDA from the statute upheld in *Ginsberg v. New York*,[154] which posited a more protective standard for selling obscenity to minors than to adults. Unlike the statute in *Ginsberg*, the CDA has no exemption for parental consent or participation.

---

[148] *Id.* at 813.

[149] 413 U.S. 15 (1973).

[150] *Playboy Entm't Group, Inc.*, 529 U.S. at 840 (Breyer, J., dissenting).

[151] *Id.* at 846.

[152] *Id.* at 847.

[153] 521 U.S. 844 (1997).

[154] *See infra* § 16.05[1].

Moreover, the law in *Ginsberg* was applicable only to commercial dealings, while the CDA applied to all transmissions on the Internet. Also in contrast to *Ginsberg*, the CDA failed to define terms like "indecent" with the precision required by the Court's test for obscenity.[155]

Justice Stevens then distinguished *FCC v. Pacifica Foundation*,[156] which upheld FCC restrictions on when indecent material could be broadcast over radio. Unlike *Pacifica*, the "CDA's broad categorical prohibitions are not limited to particular times."[157] Moreover, these restrictions were not overseen by an agency like the FCC that was "familiar with the unique characteristics of the Internet."[158] Additionally, the CDA provided for criminal penalties, unlike the order at issue in *Pacifica*. Historically, the broadcast media has "received limited First Amendment protection," in significant part because warnings could not prevent listeners from unintentionally tuning into offensive programming.[159] In contrast, little risk exists of unintentionally accessing offensive material on the Internet.

Other important differences with broadcasting include the absence of a history of government regulation and scarcity of access. The Internet allows for broad-based, cost-effective communication of all kinds, including print, audio, video, and "interactive real-time dialogue."[160] By using "Web pages, mail exploders, and newsgroups, the same individual can become a pamphleteer."[161]

The Court next found the terms "indecent" and "patently offensive" vague, as they involve "material that 'in context, depicts or describes, in terms patently offensive as measured by contemporary community standards, sexual or excretory activities or organs.' "[162] Such an indeterminate regulation may have a "chilling effect on free speech."[163] Indeed, the CDA's severe criminal penalties may cause speakers not to communicate even arguably unlawful speech.

Far from being narrowly tailored, the CDA would burden communication among adults because it would criminalize sending an indecent message across the Internet, if the sender knew or should have known that a minor could view it. Effective technology did not exist at the time of the case to exclude minors from the materials without denying them to adults. Even if the Act was construed to require knowledge that a minor was involved in the communication, it would still afford a heckler's veto to people who made it known that they had, for example, placed a minor in a chat group.

---

[155] For a discussion of the constitutional standard for obscenity, *see infra* § 16.05[1].

[156] 438 U.S. 726 (1978). *See infra* § 15.01.

[157] *Reno*, 521 U.S. at 867.

[158] *Id.*

[159] *Id.*

[160] *Id.* at 870.

[161] *Id.*

[162] *Id.* at 871.

[163] *Id.* at 872. For additional discussion of the problems of this standard under obscenity principles, *see infra* § 16.05[1].

The CDA's reach may make it a felony to speak frankly on topics of safe sex, rape, or art featuring nude subjects. A parent might be incarcerated for sending her 17-year-old child a message on birth control. Less restrictive alternatives included restricting the CDA to commercial sites or allowing parents to select what materials their children may view. While the CDA provided the use of a credit card or age verification device was an affirmative defense, most non-commercial sites would find such methods economically infeasible.

Justice O'Connor, joined by the Chief Justice, concurred in the judgment in part and dissented in part. In Justice O'Connor's view, the CDA attempted to create "adult zones" on the Internet where adults could access indecent or offensive material, but minors could not. Its "zoning" attempt fails insofar as it substantially burdens the rights of adults to access such material. However, Justice O'Connor would uphold the CDA insofar as it prohibits transmitting a communication knowing that all of its recipients are minors.

In *Ashcroft v. ACLU*,[164] the Court in a 6-3 decision upheld an injunction against enforcement of the Child Online Protection Act (COPA). The Government bears the burden of proof to establish the constitutionality of COPA. Consequently, the respondents "must be deemed likely to prevail unless the Government has shown that respondents' proposed less restrictive alternatives are less effective than COPA."[165] The record revealed a "number of plausible, less restrictive alternatives" to COPA, allowing a majority of five to conclude that the injunction was not an abuse of discretion.[166] "Filters may well be more effective than COPA."[167] As "40% of harmful-to-minors content comes from overseas" and verifications systems may be evaded by minors using credit cards, the Court questioned the ability of COPA to effectively combat offensive materials.[168] Filters may be used for email and internet content. The injunction would only remain in effect until a trial on the merits took place. In his concurring opinion, Justice Stevens, joined by Justice Ginsburg, noted that each COPA violation carried a potential fine up to $50,000 and six months in jail, with intentional violators potentially subject to an additional fine of $60,000 per day.

In his dissent, Justice Scalia noted that Court precedents do not protect " 'pandering' by 'deliberately emphasizing the sexually provocative aspects of [their nonobscene products] in order to catch the salaciously disposed.' "[169] In his dissent, Justice Breyer, joined by Chief Justice Rehnquist and Justice O'Connor, emphasized that "the parties agreed that a Web site could store card numbers or passwords at between 15 and 20 cents per number," a nominal financial burden.[170] Disputing the majority's emphasis on filters, Justice Breyer pointed out that, due

---

[164] 542 U.S. 656 (2004).

[165] *Id.* at 666.

[166] *Id.*

[167] *Id.*

[168] *Id.* at 667.

[169] *Id.* at 676 (Scalia, J., dissenting) (quoting *United States v. Playboy Entertainment Group, Inc.*, 529 U.S. 803, 831 (2000)).

[170] *Id.* at 682 (Breyer, J., dissenting).

to their reliance on key words or phrases, which are used to block sites containing undesirable substance, filters do not have the ability to block out a specific category of images. Without words, a filter "cannot distinguish between the most obscene pictorial images and the Venus de Milo" and therefore blocks a lot of valuable material.[171]

In *United States v. American Library Ass'n*,[172] the Court upheld the Children's Internet Protection Act (CIPA) which required libraries to install Internet filtering software in order to receive federal funding. Adults could request the librarian to disable the filter or unblock a specific site.

§ 14.08　DEFAMATION AND PRIVACY

[1]　Public Figures versus Private Individuals

In *New York Times v. Sullivan*,[173] the Court held that the First Amendment constrained common law defamation actions. The Commissioner of the City of Montgomery, Alabama, who supervised the Fire and Police Departments, brought a libel action against four Alabama clergymen and the New York Times Company for publishing an allegedly defamatory advertisement about him. For example, the advertisement stated that the police had arrested Dr. Martin Luther King seven times; in fact, they had arrested him four times.[174] A jury awarded the Commissioner damages of $500,000.

Under Alabama defamation law, which was typical at the time, the statements at issue were libelous per se because they damaged the Commissioner's reputation in his trade or business. Consequently, there was strict liability just for publishing the material, unless defendant could prove truth in all its particulars. Moreover, actual damages were presumed.

It was necessary for the Court to clear two preliminary hurdles presented by the Alabama law before it could consider the First Amendment issues. The State first argued that a common law libel action between two private parties involved no state action. Consequently, there was no constitutional issue. Justice Brennan responded that the State had exercised power; its form did not matter for purposes of establishing state action.[175]

The Court also dismissed the State's contention that the First Amendment does not protect statements placed in a commercial advertisement. The State relied on *Valentine v. Chrestensen*,[176] which refused to extend First Amendment protection to commercial advertising. The Court held that this was not a commercial

---

[171]　*Id.* at 685.

[172]　539 U.S. 194 (2003).

[173]　376 U.S. 254 (1964).

[174]　Although, neither advertisement mentioned the Commissioner by name, the jury could read it as referring to him under the colloquy doctrine of tort law.

[175]　*New York Times*, 376 U.S. at 265.

[176]　316 U.S. 52 (1942).

advertisement, but rather a political advertisement entitled to full First Amendment Protection. Any other result would deter the media from accepting editorial advertising, an important outlet of ideas. As described in § 16.04, *infra*, the Court has extended considerable protection to pure commercial advertisements since its decision in *New York Times v. Sullivan*.[177]

In resisting defendant's claim that its advertisement was protected speech, plaintiff cited Supreme Court precedent refusing to protect libel. The Court refused to predicate its decision on "mere labels" of state law. In so doing, the Court refused to apply the existing two-tiered theory of speech categorizing some speech as presumptively protected and some speech as not protected:[178]

> In deciding the question now, we are compelled by neither precedent nor policy to give any more weight to the epithet "libel" than we are to any other "mere labels" of state law. Like insurrection, contempt, advocacy of unlawful acts, breach of the peace, obscenity, solicitation of legal business, and the various other formulae for the repression of expression that have been challenged in this Court, libel can claim no talismanic immunity from constitutional limitations. It must be measured by standards that satisfy the First Amendment.[179]

The Court said that falsity and reputational harm did not strip speech of constitutional protection. In this connection, Justice Brennan cited the Sedition Act of 1798, which had imposed a criminal punishment of a $5,000 fine and five years in prison for defamatory material about the President, Congress, or the national government. Congress and the President subsequently rejected the Act, repealing it and making amends to those punished. Now for the first time, a majority of the Court stated that such criminal penalties for defamatory speech were unconstitutional. Justice Brennan stated that large civil damage awards could chill government criticism even more dramatically than the Sedition Act.

The Court held that a public official plaintiff in a defamation action relating to his official conduct must prove that the defendant published the defamatory falsehood with actual knowledge of its falsity or with reckless disregard as to its truth or falsity. Under this standard, the plaintiff must prove falsity, altering the common law doctrine that truth was a defense.[180] Moreover, the Court required plaintiff to prove this standard with "convincing clarity," or as later decisions have indicated, with clear and convincing evidence.[181] The standard applied to media and non-media defendants, which were both involved in this case.

---

[177] See *infra* § 16.04.

[178] See Kalven, *The New York Times Case: A note on the Central Meaning of the First Amendment*, 1964 SUP. CT. REV. 191. The Court articulated the two-tiered theory of speech in *Chaplinsky v. New Hampshire, infra* § 15.01[1].

[179] *New York Times*, 376 U.S. at 268–69.

[180] Justice Brennan noted that federal officials enjoy absolute immunity for their speech made within the outer boundaries of their duties. See *Barr v. Matteo*, 360 U.S. 564 (1959). Many states afforded the speech of their officials similar protection. Viewed in this context, the result in *New York Times* could be viewed as an effort to provide a roughly equivalent right for the public to criticize government officials.

[181] See *Gertz v. Robert Welch, Inc.*, 418 U.S. 323 (1974).

The Court did not define who was a public official in this case. However, in *Rosenblatt v. Baer*,[182] the Court went so far as to hold that a county recreation area supervisor was a public official for *New York Times* purposes. The test for determining whether a particular plaintiff was a public official was whether "the position in government has such apparent importance that the public has an independent interest in the qualifications and performance of the person who holds it, beyond the general public interest in the qualifications and performance of all governmental employees." The Court also ruled that such an official should "appear to [have] substantial responsibility for or control over the conduct of governmental affairs."[183]

The Court has articulated a similarly broad definition of official conduct. In *Monitor Patriot Co. v. Roy*,[184] the Court applied the *New York Times* standard to a charge that a 1960 candidate for the United States Senate had been a "small-time bootlegger during the Depression." At least for candidates running for public office, the Court found it difficult to determine what statements about private or public life would be irrelevant. The Court did leave open some possibilities for public officials who were not candidates.

The *New York Times* Court also left undefined the reckless disregard standard itself. Unfortunately, the Court referred to this as an actual malice test. In common law tort doctrine, actual malice generally indicates spite or ill will, and is required by the tort law doctrine of some states to award punitive damages. The term has no such meaning in *New York Times*. In fact, meeting the common law actual malice standard is neither necessary nor sufficient to meeting the *New York Times* standard.

To meet the reckless disregard standard, plaintiff must establish that defendant in fact entertained serious doubts about the truth of the statement. This is a subjective standard.[185] To determine lack of good faith, plaintiff could prove, for example, that the story was the product of the reporter's imagination or of an unverified telephone call, or that "there are obvious reasons to doubt the veracity of the informant or the accuracy of his reports."[186] In *New York Times* itself, some of the allegations made in the advertisement were contradicted by facts contained elsewhere in the newspaper's files. In *Curtis Publishing Co. v. Butts*,[187] the Court found reckless disregard based on deficiencies in investigatory procedures that resulted in serious published charges made in a context that did not involve "hot news." The defendant had almost exclusively relied on the affidavit of one source who was on probation for bad check charges, and defendant had not attempted to corroborate this story.

---

[182] 383 U.S. 75 (1966).

[183] *Id.* at 85.

[184] 401 U.S. 265 (1971).

[185] St. Amant v. Thompson, 390 U.S. 727 (1968).

[186] *Id.* at 732.

[187] 388 U.S. 130 (1967).

McDonald v. Smith[188] applied the *New York Times* standard to a letter of recommendation. The case refused to afford absolute immunity to a defendant who expressed libelous falsehoods in a letter to the President about a person being considered for public office. The Court held that the *New York Times* standard was the appropriate level of protection on the facts of this case.

In *Hustler Magazine v. Falwell*,[189] the Court extended the reckless disregard standard to a tort action for intentional infliction of emotional distress brought by Jerry Falwell, a nationally known minister. *Hustler* magazine provided an advertisement for Campari Liqueur in which celebrities talked about their "first times." By the end of the Campari ads, it was clear that this meant the first time the celebrity drank Campari. In the *Hustler* parody, Falwell stated that his " 'first time' was a drunken, incestuous rendezvous with his mother in an outhouse." At the bottom of the page, the ad contained a small print disclaimer "ad-parody — not to be taken seriously." The table of contents described the ad as "Fiction; Ad and Personality Parody."

The trial court denied a claim for libel because the parody was not intended to be understood as depicting facts and, therefore, was not false. A unanimous Supreme Court reversed the trial court's allowance of a claim for intentional infliction of emotional distress. Chief Justice Rehnquist required a public figure or public official to meet the reckless disregard standard to recover for this tort.

After *New York Times*, the Court handed down several decisions extending its reckless disregard reach to more kinds of defamatory speech. In *Curtis Publishing Co. v. Butts*,[190] the Court applied the standard to the libel complaint of the University of Georgia football coach. In *Associated Press v. Walker*,[191] the Court applied the *New York Times* test to a retired army general. Although neither was a public official, both were held to be public figures who had ready access to the media and played influential roles in society.

In *Gertz v. Robert Welch, Inc.*,[192] a lawyer was defamed by a newspaper in a number of ways, one among them being the imputation that he was a Communist. Writing for the Court, Justice Powell provided a rationale for affording less protection for defamation of public officials or figures than of private individuals. The former have greater access to the media to respond to charges made against them and by thrusting themselves into the limelight, they assume the risk of public scrutiny. Furthermore, those who have great influence in societal affairs should be exposed to greater risk of public scrutiny.[193] When defamation of private plaintiffs by media defendants is at issue, however, Justice Powell permitted the states to

---

[188]   472 U.S. 479 (1985).

[189]   485 U.S. 46 (1988).

[190]   388 U.S. 130 (1967).

[191]   *Id.* (reported as same case).

[192]   418 U.S. 323 (1974).

[193] Justice Powell also criticized the extension of the *New York Times* standard to defamation of private individuals when the information involved a matter of public concern. Not only was this public concern concept vague, but such a determination should not be committed to judges. *See* Rosenbloom v. Metromedia, Inc., 403 U.S. 29 (1971).

define the standard, as long as that standard was not strict liability. Consequently, the standard would have to be either negligence or intentional tort.

Gertz limited the applicability of this standard to media defendants. The appropriate standard for private plaintiffs against non-media defendants remains an open question. Justice Powell also limited the damages that private individuals could recover from media defendants to actual injury. Actual injury included not only out-of-pocket loss but also "impairment of reputation and standing in the community, personal humiliation, and mental anguish and suffering."[194] While juries had to base their awards on actual evidence, they did not have to assign actual dollar amounts to the injury. This definition arguably still permitted much in the way of speculative damages. Private individuals could only recover presumed or punitive damages against the media if they met the *New York Times* standard by showing reckless disregard for the truth. In *Curtis Publishing Co. v. Butts*, the Court upheld a punitive damage award won by a public figure plaintiff who had successfully met the reckless disregard standard. Of course, to recover punitive damages, plaintiffs might also have to meet whatever spite or ill will standards that may exist under state law.

The *Gertz* Court also more precisely defined the concept of a public figure. There could be voluntary general public figures who have "such pervasive fame or notoriety"[195] or who "occupy positions of such pervasive power and influence"[196] that they always have public figure status in all defamation actions. More common would be limited public figures who, having voluntarily thrust themselves into a particular controversy, are public figures only for those issues involved in that controversy. In "extremely rare" cases there could be involuntary public figures, who are drawn into controversies without any action on their ends.

Increasingly, the key to defining a public figure seemed to be that the individual thrust himself into the public eye or into a position of prominence.[197] The Court seemed to imply that involuntary public figures would almost always be limited public figures. It may be reluctant to categorize individuals as general public figures because they could then be criticized generally, without neither general access to the media nor access to a libel action to counter a defamation against them.

In dissent, Justice Douglas said that the amorphous negligence standard would exert a chilling effect on speech. In a separate dissent, Justice Brennan stated a negligence standard that would also allow juries to impose their own personal prejudices. Justice White, also dissenting, stated that the Framers of the Constitution had demonstrated no intention to change the common law of libel as the Court was doing in the *Gertz* case. He viewed this case as different from *New York Times*, which involved public officials.

Since *Gertz*, the Court has further narrowed the public figure concept by focusing on plaintiff's thrusting herself into a public controversy. In *Time, Inc. v.*

---

[194] *Gertz*, 418 U.S. at 350.

[195] *Id.* at 351.

[196] *Id.* at 345.

[197] *See* Time, Inc. v. Firestone, 424 U.S. 448 (1976).

Firestone,[198] the Court refused to hold the wife of one of the wealthiest industrial families a public figure — even after a well-publicized divorce proceeding. She "did not assume any role of especial prominence in the affairs of society . . . and she did not thrust herself to the forefront of any particular public controversy in order to influence the resolution of the issues involved in it."[199] Her involvement in a divorce that was a "cause célèbre" was not enough to transform her into a public figure, nor was holding a few press conferences to satisfy inquisitive reporters. The Court remanded the case, however, because the trial court failed to make any findings of fault with regard to the newspaper's reporting of the trial proceedings. The negligence had to be in the reporting of the proceedings, even if some of the facts that came out in the proceedings were false. Ordinarily, a person can be liable for repeating defamatory remarks, but one has a privilege for neutral reportage of official proceedings.

In *Hutchinson v. Proxmire*,[200] plaintiff was a scientist who had been awarded the "Golden Fleece" award by Senator Proxmire for government waste. Neither the award nor the small number of writings that plaintiff had published in professional journals transformed him into a public figure. Finally, in *Wolston v. Reader's Digest, Inc.*,[201] the Court refused to extend public figure status to a plaintiff who had been convicted in 1958 for failing to appear before a grand jury investigating Soviet espionage. The 1958 conviction did not transform him into a public figure in a 1974 libel action for being called a "Soviet agent" in a book. Plaintiff had not thrust himself into any controversy, and the fact that he had been convicted of a crime during an earlier period was not enough to render him a public figure. The dissent complained that the case would have a chilling effect on history writers.

[2] Opinions

Defamation actions apply to false statements of fact that damage reputation. *Milkovich v. Lorain Journal Co.*[202] held that a statement of opinion was subject to a defamation action if it implied underlying factors which were defamatory. Prefacing a factual statement with words like "I think" or "[i]n my opinion" did not insulate it from a defamation action. Even if the speaker stated the facts underlying the opinion, the statement could still be actionable if those facts were incomplete or in error, or if the speaker assessed them incorrectly; the facts themselves could be actionable if false and defamatory. Thus, in *Milkovich* the Court held actionable a statement implying that plaintiff perjured himself. The Court said that the language was not "loose, figurative, or hyperbolic,"[203] but instead was capable of being proven true or false.

In dissent, Justice Brennan feared that the Court's opinion would chill conjecture; one example of this could concern press speculation over the role of

---

[198] *Id.*

[199] *Id.* at 453.

[200] 443 U.S. 111 (1979).

[201] 443 U.S. 157 (1979).

[202] 497 U.S. 1 (1990).

[203] *Id.* at 21.

NASA officials in the Challenger Space Shuttle disaster.

[3] Quoted Material

In *Masson v. New Yorker Magazine*,[204] the Court held the alteration of quotations actionable for defamation unless the quotation conveyed to the reader that it was used as a literary device rather than a factual statement. Actionability required a material change in meaning as opposed to a minor inaccuracy. If the quotation was attributable to a public figure, its alteration must have been reckless or deliberate to meet the *New York Times* standard.

[4] Jurisdictional and Other Procedural Rules

A number of cases in the defamation area deal with whether regular or unusual procedural rules will apply to defamation cases; for the most part, the Court has applied normal procedural rules. For example, in *Herbert v. Lando*,[205] the Court held that the plaintiff in a defamation case had the right during pretrial discovery to probe the media's editorial decision-making process. The discovery at issue included depositions of narrators, editors, and producers of a television show. The media objected to the intrusiveness of the decision, but without it, plaintiffs might have found it almost impossible to meet the subjective *New York Times* standard. In his concurring opinion in *New York Times*, Justice Black, joined by Justice Douglas, would have extended an absolute right to publish the advertisement.

Bose Corp. v. Consumers Union[206] imposed a more specialized procedure rule specific to defamation actions. *Bose* required appellate courts to make an independent review of the record to determine whether the facts of a particular case indicated that the reckless disregard standard had been met. The District Court's finding of the *New York Times* reckless disregard standard was not subject to the clearly erroneous standard typically applied to District Court findings under Rule 52(a) of the Federal Rules of Civil Procedure. Instead, the appellate court must subject this finding to *de novo* review. The *Bose* Court recalled that *New York Times* itself had obliged appellate courts to make an independent review of the record below in the context of a state jury verdict.

Several procedural defamation issues have involved personal jurisdiction. *Keeton v. Hustler Magazine, Inc.*,[207] held that the sale of 10,000-15,000 magazines in a state provided "minimum contacts" to establish personal jurisdiction over it in that state. *Calder v. Jones*[208] held that the distribution of an allegedly defamatory article by the National Enquirer in California was enough to establish personal jurisdiction over its editor and writer, who were Florida residents.

---

[204] 501 U.S. 496 (1991).

[205] 441 U.S. 153 (1979).

[206] 466 U.S. 485 (1984).

[207] 465 U.S. 770 (1984).

[208] 465 U.S. 783 (1984).

In the summary judgment area, *Anderson v. Liberty Lobby*[209] held that in deciding summary judgment in a case under the *New York Times* standard, the judge must take the reckless disregard and the summary judgment standards into account. A defendant's motion for summary judgment should be denied if a rational trier of fact could find reckless disregard by clear and convincing evidence.

[5] Matters of Public Concern

In determining constitutional protection for defamatory speech, *Dun & Bradstreet v. Greenmoss Builders, Inc.*,[210] suggested a classification different from the old categories of determining whether the plaintiff was a public figure to also inquiring about whether the speech pertained to a matter of public concern. The Court held that the Constitution did not restrict the ability of a state to allow presumed or punitive damages rules for statements that did not involve matters of public concern. Dun & Bradstreet's credit report told five of its clients that the plaintiff was bankrupt; however, only one of the plaintiff's employees was bankrupt. The mistake was made by a 17-year-old high school intern. The information obtained by the student was not verified or checked by any other Dun & Bradstreet employee, as was required by the company's own procedures.

In this factual context, the Court allowed state law to control the award of presumed and punitive damages without meeting the reckless disregard standard that had been required by *Gertz* for the award of punitive or presumed damages.

Writing for a plurality of three, Justice Powell distinguished this case from *Gertz* on grounds that the speech in *Gertz* involved a matter of public concern — *i.e.*, magazine statements about a lawyer concerning events in a highly publicized trial. The *Dun & Bradstreet* plurality predicated its denial of constitutional scrutiny on the lesser value of speech that did not involve a matter of public concern. In determining what was a matter of public concern, Justice Powell considered the "content, form, and context . . . as revealed by the entire record."[211] Applying this amorphous standard to the facts, Justice Powell noted the report in this case did not involve public issues; the speech interested only Dun & Bradstreet and its five business clients who could not circulate it. It was both false and damaging, but unlike advertising, did not involve the free flow or exchange of information. The speech was more objectively verifiable than certain other forms of speech deserving greater protection. Finally, it was solely motivated by a desire for profit.[212]

In determining whether allegedly defamatory speech involved a matter of public concern, the plurality listed a number of relatively amorphous factors. Exactly how far its holding extends is difficult to predict. Justice Powell's plurality opinion was joined only by Justices Rehnquist and O'Connor. In separate concurring opinions, however, Chief Justice Burger and Justice White recommended far less protection

---

[209] 477 U.S. 242 (1986).

[210] 472 U.S. 749 (1985).

[211] Justice Powell also used this test in *Connick v. Myers. See supra* § 13.05[3].

[212] 472 U.S. at 762.

for defamation than even the plurality was willing to afford. Both argued that *Gertz* should be overruled. Moreover, both also wanted to reexamine *New York Times* itself. Justice White suggested the possibility of adopting a negligence standard to protect the press against libel suits by public figures.

When it was first decided, *Dun & Bradstreet* had potentially large implications. Bankruptcy is arguably a matter of public concern. Newspapers and other news media are profit-seeking entities; much of their information is objectively verifiable and newspaper reporters are not easily deterred. Arguably, the Court was changing its defamation jurisprudence to focus on whether the speech was a matter of public concern, rather than whether the defamation plaintiff was a public or private figure.

Subsequent cases would seem to undercut the larger implications of the decision. Notably, in *Hustler Magazine v. Falwell*, a unanimous Court reaffirmed *New York Times v. Sullivan*. The Court simply applied the reckless disregard standard without discussing whether the underlying speech involved a matter of public concern.

With regard to private defamation plaintiffs, the law remains somewhat uncertain. The narrow holding of *Dun & Bradstreet* is that with a non-media defendant, state law controls the imposition of presumed and punitive damages if the speech does involve a matter of public concern. Arguably, a state could also impose liability without fault under such circumstances, but no subsequent decisions since *Dun & Bradstreet* have altered *Gertz's* requirement that the plaintiff at least show negligence.

Philadelphia Newspapers v. Hepps[213] focused on both the identity of the parties and whether the speech involved a matter of public concern. It required a private plaintiff to bear the burden of proving the falsity of an alleged defamatory statement when there was a media defendant and the speech involved a matter of public concern.

[6] Invasions of Privacy

Separate from protection against damage to reputation, is protection against public revelation of private facts. These private facts need not even be damaging to reputation. In a famous article written around the turn of the century, Warren and Brandeis described several different sorts of privacy actions.[214] As with defamation, the Constitution has imposed certain limitations on these privacy actions. In *Zacchini v. Scripps-Howard Broadcasting Co.*,[215] a television station broadcast the entire performance of Mr. Zacchini being launched as a human cannonball. The case upheld against a constitutional challenge a right of publicity, which implicated a commercial, proprietary interest. The majority focused on the economic incentives for a performer to produce such an event. If others were

---

[213] 475 U.S. 767 (1986).

[214] Samuel Warren & Louis Brandeis, *The Right to Privacy*, 4 HARV. L. REV. 193 (1890).

[215] 433 U.S. 562 (1977).

allowed to display the event without compensating the performer, the performer would lose that incentive.

Important to the plaintiff's case was the fact that the news broadcast the entire act. Moreover, the plaintiff had specifically asked the reporter not to film the act. With regard to damages, the majority stated that if the publicity caused more people to attend so that he made more money, Mr. Zacchini could recover nothing.

Time, Inc. v. Hill[216] involved another sort of privacy action. False light privacy involves discussing private facts about an individual and casting them into a false and objectionable (although not necessarily defamatory) light. An example of this could be using someone's picture in a bawdy advertisement. *Time* required that the *New York Times* standard be met in all false light privacy actions, but *Time* was decided before *Gertz. Gertz* may not require a private plaintiff in a false light privacy action to meet the reckless disregard standard as a constitutional matter. However, noted torts theorists William Prosser and Page Keeton have suggested that the reckless disregard test was inherent to a false light privacy cause of action, as the culpable conduct must have involved deliberately falsifying or sensationalizing information.[217]

Florida Star v. B. J. F.[218] involved a true privacy action. In this case, a reporter trainee published the name of a rape victim, violating both police policy and the newspaper's own policy. The police had inadvertently released the victim's name. While the Court denied the action, it did not rule out the possibility of a true privacy action. True privacy actions generally involve private figures, since public figures lose their privacy. *Florida Star* left open the possibility of a true privacy action when private facts were revealed that had not been inadvertently disclosed to the public. It is questionable, however, whether a "true" privacy action can survive a publisher's decision that a matter is newsworthy.

In *Bartnicki v. Vopper*,[219] the Court invalidated a federal and state wiretapping statute that imposed liability on persons who knowingly disclosed unlawfully obtained electronic communications. An unidentified person illegally intercepted and taped a cell phone conversation between Plaintiffs Bartnicki and Kane, who were involved in heated negotiations between a teacher's union and a school board. Eventually, the tape fell into the hands of Defendant Vopper, who broadcast the conversation on his radio talk show. Under the statute, Vopper could be punished for disclosing the conversation even though he was not the one who illegally taped it.

In striking down the statutes, the Court noted that the laws were content-neutral; however, their "naked prohibition against disclosures"[220] was "a regulation of pure speech."[221] Rarely will a law that punishes the publication of truthful

---

[216] 385 U.S. 374 (1967).

[217] PROSSER & KEETON ON THE LAW OF TORTS, § 113, at 804–5 (W. Page Keeton ed., 5th ed.).

[218] 491 U.S. 524 (1989).

[219] 532 U.S. 514 (2001).

[220] *Id.* at 526.

[221] *Id.*

information pass constitutional muster. The holding did not apply to punishing individuals who illegally obtain information.

Though the Court found the State's interest in protecting privacy interests more persuasive, this case did not involve "disclosures of trade secrets or domestic gossip or other information of purely private concern."[222] Therefore, the majority concluded the privacy concerns at stake in this case were outweighed by the interest in disclosing matters of public importance. The First Amendment continues to protect speech about a public matter despite an unidentified person's unlawful conduct.

Concurring, Justice Breyer, joined by Justice O'Connor, believed the plaintiffs "had little or no *legitimate* interest"[223] in keeping private phone discussions about " 'blowing off . . . [school board members'] front porches.' "[224] Furthermore, the plaintiffs were "limited public figures"[225] acting on behalf of the teacher's union. The Constitution allows legislatures "to respond flexibly"[226] to the potential technological threats to individual privacy. Eavesdropping on a cellular telephone conversation conducted in public differs from "eavesdropping on encrypted cellular phone conversations or those carried on in the bedroom."[227] In particular, legislatures should be encouraged to implement "more effective privacy-protecting technologies."[228] Chief Justice Rehnquist dissented, joined by Justices Scalia and Thomas. Today's technologies have compromised individual privacy; we risk invasion into "our personal and business e-mails, our medical and financial records, or our cordless and cellular telephone conversations."[229] As a result, almost every state has enacted laws to deter these invasions. By invalidating these statutes, the Court has chilled the speech of those who rely on these electronic devices.

The dissent also criticized the majority for its reliance on the *Daily Mail*[230] cases. In those cases, the reporters received their information legally through "consensual interviews,"[231] and the relevant information "was already 'publicly available.' "[232] In contrast, the statutes at issue were content neutral laws that only restricted unlawfully obtained communications. For the dissent, this case should have been decided like *New York v. Ferber*,[233] where the Court "upheld against First Amendment challenge a law prohibiting the distribution of child

---

[222] *Id.* at 533.

[223] *Id.* at 539 (Breyer, J., concurring).

[224] *Id.*

[225] *Id.*

[226] *Id.* at 541.

[227] *Id.*

[228] *Id.*

[229] *Id.* (Rehnquist, C.J., dissenting).

[230] *See, e.g.*, Smith v. Daily Mail Publishing Co., 443 U.S. 97 (1979).

[231] *Bartnicki*, 532 U.S. at 548.

[232] *Id.* at 546.

[233] 458 U.S. 747 (1982).

pornography."[234]

---

[234] *Bartnicki*, 532 U.S. at 551.

Chapter 15

SPEECH IN PUBLIC PLACES

INTRODUCTION

First Amendment jurisprudence has long extended a right to speak on certain government property that qualifies as a public forum. This right to speak in the public forum permits everyone to introduce their views for free. The public forum is particularly important for those who would otherwise lack adequate resources to access the marketplace of ideas. Without such free access, the right to free speech for many would be illusory.

This right of access is not absolute, however. An unlimited right of access to the public forum would jeopardize the First Amendment rights of everyone. If everyone spoke at the same time in the same public forum, the resulting chaos would prevent all speakers from communicating their respective messages. The Constitution permits the government to place limited time, place, and manner restrictions on the right to speak in a public forum to ensure that those who wish to speak can be heard. These restrictions must be content neutral because by arbitrarily dictating where, when, or under what circumstances people can speak, the government could effectively suppress speech. For example, government could advise a speaker whom it disfavored that she could speak only at 4 a.m. in a deserted area. On the other hand, it could allow a preferred speaker access to the town square at noon. Such abuses of time, place, and manner restrictions could result in the suppression of speech just as effectively as more direct methods of censorship.

This chapter focuses on the permissible scope of restrictions the government can impose on speech in a public forum. The first section focuses on offensive speech in public places. This section considers *what* can be said in public places (*i.e.*, the permissible scope of content-based restrictions that the government can impose). The remaining sections focus on *where* one can speak, that is, on which property constitutes a public forum.

§ 15.01 OFFENSIVE SPEECH IN PUBLIC PLACES

[1] General Principles

The Court has a long tradition of allowing government to place certain restrictions on offensive speech in the public forum. In *Chaplinsky v. New Hampshire*,[1] for example, the Court rejected constitutional protection for what it referred to as "fighting words." This case rejected protection for calling a law

---

[1] 315 U.S. 568 (1942).

enforcement officer "a God damned racketeer" and "a damned Fascist."[2] The Court defined "fighting words" as "those which by their very utterance inflict injury or tend to incite an immediate breach of the peace."[3] Several cases since *Chaplinsky* appear to have narrowed the fighting words doctrine.[4] For example, fighting words must be directed at a particular person. The exception is, however, still valid as a content-based restriction on speech.

The modern Court has steered away from restricting speech because it is offensive. In *Cohen v. California*,[5] the Court reversed a conviction for wearing a jacket with the message "Fuck the Draft" in a courthouse. As Justice Harlan noted, the line between offensive and inoffensive speech is vague, for "one man's vulgarity is another's lyric."[6] Generally, if the offended viewer can simply avert his eyes, the modern Court will protect the speech from restrictions based on content.[7] Another reason the Court has been more reluctant to allow restrictions based on the offensiveness of speech is because the modern Court has granted significant constitutional protection to the emotive function of speech. The Court has recognized that speech conveys not only ideas but emotions. "In fact, words are often chosen as much for their emotive as their cognitive force."[8]

The Court has indicated that speech intended to provoke a hostile audience to violence fell outside the ambit of constitutional protection. Generally, this "hostile audience" doctrine provided that provocative speech could be subject to the state's police power only if the speaker provoked violence by his or her words. A speaker who did not provoke such violence could not be arrested for breach of the peace merely because of the reaction of the hostile crowd.[9] If anything, the state must protect the speaker from the hostile crowd.[10] Still, there have been signs from the Court that, under narrowly drawn statutes, the state may have the power to put an end to a speech if the best efforts of the police cannot maintain order due to the divergent views of those exercising their free speech and assembly rights in public places.[11] Query how much of this doctrine remains after *National Socialist Party*

---

[2] *Id.* at 568.

[3] *Id.* at 572.

[4] Several cases may indicate a narrowing of the fighting words doctrine by overturning convictions on overbreadth grounds. *See, e.g.*, Lewis v. City of New Orleans, 415 U.S. 130 (1974) (mother said to policeman "damn m. f. police" and threatened to complain to superintendent); Gooding v. Wilson, 405 U.S. 518 (1972) (antiwar protestor said to policeman during scuffle: "White son of a bitch I'll kill you! You son of a bitch, I'll choke you to death").

[5] 403 U.S. 15 (1971).

[6] The Court also found that the message could not be restricted as obscene. The words were not "erotic" or likely to "conjure up such psychic stimulation in anyone likely to be confronted with" the jacket. *Id.* at 25.

[7] Erznoznik v. City of Jacksonville, 422 U.S. 205 (1975) (allowing facial challenge of an ordinance prohibiting exhibition of non-obscene films visible from public streets).

[8] *Cohen*, 403 U.S. at 26.

[9] *See* Feiner v. New York, 340 U.S. 315 (1951); Terminiello v. Chicago, 337 U.S. 1 (1949).

[10] *See* Collin v. Smith, 578 F.2d 1197 (7th Cir.), *cert. denied*, 439 U.S. 916 (1978).

[11] *See* the concurring opinion of Justice Black, joined by Justice Douglas, in *Gregory v. Chicago*, 394 U.S. 111 (1969).

of America v. Skokie?[12]

[2] Hate Speech

In the *Skokie* cases of the 1970s, the Supreme Court had the opportunity to establish the extent to which a state could restrict hate speech on the basis of its content, but declined to do so when it denied certiorari to hear *Collin v. Smith*.[13] This case would have determined the extent to which a Nazi party had the right to demonstrate in a city — Skokie, Illinois — predominantly populated by Jewish citizens, a large number of whom were Holocaust survivors.

Collin began with the related case of *National Socialist Party of America v. Skokie*.[14] Both cases involved a proposed march through Skokie by The National Socialist Party of America (NSPA). When the NSPA applied for a permit, they were informed that they would be required to post a bond of $350,000 or provide insurance coverage in that amount before demonstrating. In response, the NSPA decided to congregate at the Skokie village hall, which Skokie permitted. However, as resistance to the pending demonstration grew, particularly among Jewish Holocaust survivors, Skokie obtained an injunction stopping NSPA from demonstrating. The injunction prohibited NSPA from marching in the uniform of the party, and from displaying the swastika or distributing pamphlets that incited or promoted hatred against persons of the Jewish faith or of any other faith. NSPA applied for a stay of the injunction pending an appeal. The stay was denied by the Illinois trial and appellate courts, and by the Illinois Supreme Court. The letter also determined that NSPA had no right to an immediate appeal of the injunction.

The United States Supreme Court reversed. In a 5-4 decision, the Court found that before any prior restraint on the march could issue, NSPA's rights must be protected by procedural safeguards, through either a stay of the injunction pending appeal or the right to an immediate appeal. Otherwise, the Court held, NSPA would be deprived of its First Amendment rights during a period of appellate review that would likely take more than one year to complete.

On remand, the state appellate and supreme courts ultimately reversed the injunction.[15] Even the swastika portion of the injunction was removed because the swastika was not considered within the fighting words exception to the First Amendment. Moreover, the anticipation of a hostile audience did not justify a prior restraint.

Before the litigation surrounding the injunction was resolved, Skokie passed three ordinances. One ordinance prohibited the dissemination of any materials within the Village of Skokie that "incite or promote hatred against . . . persons of any faith or ancestry, race or religion."[16] Another ordinance prohibited the wearing

---

[12] 432 U.S. 43 (1977).

[13] 578 F.2d 1197 (7th Cir. 1978).

[14] 432 U.S. 43 (1977).

[15] *See* Village of Skokie v. National Socialist Party of America, 373 N.E.2d 21 (Ill. 1978); Village of Skokie v. National Socialist Party of America, 366 N.E.2d 347 (Ill. 1977).

[16] *Skokie*, 366 N.E.2d at 352.

of "military-style uniforms" in demonstrations or marches. A third ordinance required that groups of 50 or more demonstrators post a $350,000 insurance bond before a permit could be granted.

NSPA eventually applied for and was denied a permit under these new ordinances. As a result, NSPA filed suit in Federal District Court asking that the ordinances be declared void. The District Court found the ordinances unconstitutional.[17] It struck down each ordinance under several constitutional doctrines including the prior restraint, vagueness, overbreadth, and symbolic speech doctrines. Like the Illinois state courts, the Federal District Court found that the demonstration by the Party did not meet the fighting words exception to constitutional protection.

The District Court found it "better to allow those who preach racial hatred to expend their venom in rhetoric rather than to be panicked into embarking on the dangerous course of permitting the government to decide what its citizens may say and hear."[18] The Court also questioned the constitutional validity of restricting speech on the basis of its tendency to induce violence. The Seventh Circuit affirmed.[19]

This time, the Supreme Court denied certiorari, with Justices White and Blackmun dissenting. Justice Blackmun noted that the facts of the *Skokie* case created an opportunity to examine whether there is any constitutional limitation on this kind of offensive speech.

> There indeed may be no such limit, but when citizens assert, not casually but with deep conviction, that the proposed demonstration is scheduled at a place and in a manner that is taunting and overwhelmingly offensive to the citizens of that place, that assertion, uncomfortable though it may be for judges, deserves to be examined. It just might fall into the same category as one's "right" to cry "fire" in a crowded theater, for "the character of every act depends upon the circumstances in which it is done."[20]

Skokie also raised the issue of libel against a particular racial or ethnic group. Could the racist hate speech contemplated in *Skokie* be banned under a group defamation theory? In *Beauharnais v. Illinois*,[21] the Court upheld a conviction under a criminal statute for distribution of a leaflet that maligned black persons. On concluding that the statute was sufficiently narrow, the Court relied in part on the fact that certain types of speech, such as fighting words and libel, did not receive constitutional protection at the time. Although never explicitly overruled by the Supreme Court, *Beauharnais* has probably not survived *New York Times v. Sullivan*.[22]

---

[17] *See* Collin v. Smith, 447 F. Supp. 676 (N.D. Ill. 1978).

[18] *Id.* at 702.

[19] *See* Collin v. Smith, 578 F.2d 1197 (7th Cir.), *cert. denied*, 439 U.S. 916 (1978).

[20] *Id.* at 919 (Blackmun, J. dissenting), citing *Schenck v. United States*, 249 U.S. 47, 52 (1919).

[21] 343 U.S. 250 (1952).

[22] 376 U.S. 254 (1964). Also discussed *supra* § 14.08[1].

In *R. A. V. v. St. Paul*,[23] the Court began to answer some of the questions that it had avoided in *Skokie*. Several teenagers were convicted under an ordinance that prohibited placing symbols on public or private property so as to arouse anger based on race, religion, or gender.[24]

The *R. A. V.* Court found the ordinance invalid on its face because it prohibited speech solely on the basis of content. Writing for a majority of five, Justice Scalia noted that the First Amendment did allow restrictions based on content in certain categories of speech like libel, obscenity, or fighting words. Quoting from *Chaplinsky*, Justice Scalia stated that such words were "of such slight social value as a step to truth that any societal benefit that may be derived from them is clearly outweighed by the social interest in order and morality."[25]

While the government may proscribe such categories of speech, it could not do so based on the ideas or viewpoints of the speaker. For example, while the government could proscribe libel per se, it could not do so solely because the speech was critical of the government. Moreover, the government need not either proscribe all speech or none. For example, the government did not have to proscribe all obscenity to regulate it validly, but could choose to prohibit only obscene speech over the telephone. Even content-based restrictions could be made within a given category of proscribable speech so long as they were not related to a particular viewpoint. For example, the government could choose to proscribe only the most prurient obscene speech. It could also choose to proscribe only violent threats against the President's life, not only violent threats against his life that included criticism of his policies.[26] The Court also stated that the government could proscribe a sub-category of speech based on some statutory provision unrelated to the content distinction. For example, the government could proscribe sexually derogatory fighting words because they violate the anti-discrimination policy of Title VII.

Although the Minnesota Supreme Court construed the ordinance at issue to prohibit only fighting words, the ordinance only applied to fighting words that insulted or provoked violence based on race, religion, or gender. It did not proscribe fighting words based on, for example, political affiliation or homosexuality. Beyond discriminating based on the content or ideas within the category of fighting words, the ordinance impermissibly discriminated based on viewpoint. For example, it permitted the use of the fighting words to hold a sign referring to "anti-Catholic bigots" but not "papists," because the ordinance proscribed words that would provoke violence on the basis of religion. The *R.A.V.* Court also rejected a hostile ordinance justification for the statute.

---

[23] 505 U.S. 377 (1992).

[24] The St. Paul Bias-Motivated Crime Ordinance provided:

Whoever places on public or private property a symbol, object, appellation, characterization or graffiti, including, but not limited to, a burning cross or Nazi swastika, which one knows or has reasonable grounds to know arouses anger, alarm or resentment in others on the basis of race, color, creed, religion, or gender commits disorderly conduct and shall be guilty of a misdemeanor. *Id.* at 379.

[25] *R. A. V.*, 505 U.S. at 383 (quoting *Chaplinsky v. New Hampshire*, 315 U.S. at 572 (1942)).

[26] 18 U.S.C. § 871; *see also* Watts v. United States, 394 U.S. 705 (1969).

Justice Scalia said that content and viewpoint distinctions made by the statute were not necessary to advance a compelling state interest. While the interest in protecting historically disfavored groups was compelling, the means of content and viewpoint discrimination were not reasonably necessary to achieve those interests.

Justice White, joined by Justices Blackmun, O'Connor, and Stevens concurred in the judgment. Justice White characterized the majority as offering an under inclusiveness approach, forcing the government to regulate more speech. He would simply have held the ordinance overbroad because it extended beyond fighting words to punish speech that conveyed anger or resentment.

In *Virginia v. Black*,[27] the Court invalidated a statute that defined cross burning as prima facie evidence of intent to intimidate. A state may ban "cross burning carried out with the intent to intimidate;"[28] however, Virginia violated the First Amendment by passing a statute that allowed the act of cross burning itself to be evidence of the intent to intimidate. The First Amendment allows a State to restrict a " 'true threat,' " which entails the speaker's conveying "a serious expression of an intent to commit an act of unlawful violence to a particular individual or group of individuals."[29] The speaker need not intend to carry out the threat as the prohibition protected against the fear of violence. Historically, cross burning in the United States made the victim fear that he was the target of future violence.

The prima facie evidence provision of the statute conflated situations in which an intent to intimidate existed with situations in which it did not. The burning of a cross at a political rally would likely be protected expression. *"An inference merely applies to the rational potency or probative value of an evidentiary fact to which the fact finder may attach whatever force or weight it deems best."*[30]

Justice Stevens filed a concurring opinion. Dissenting, Justice Thomas noted that our cultural understanding of cross burning was one of "lawlessness." Understandably, a victim of such act would fear physical violence. The statute at issue did not seek to quash expression; merely prohibit conduct.

Justice Scalia filed an opinion concurring in part, concurring in the judgment in part, and dissenting in part. Justice Thomas joined all parts of Justice Scalia's opinion discussed here. Responding to the Court's implication that the provision was overbroad, Justice Scalia maintained that the small class of persons who could impermissibly be convicted under this provision included individuals who: "(1) burn a cross in public view, (2) do not intend to intimidate, (3) are nonetheless charged and prosecuted, and (4) refuse to present a defense."[31] This small set of cases did render the statute substantially overbroad. Justice Souter, joined by Justices Kennedy and Ginsburg, concurred in the judgment in part and dissented in part. The same objective could be achieved through a content-neutral statute that bans

---

[27] 538 U.S. 343 (2003).

[28] *Id.* at 347.

[29] *Id.* at 359.

[30] *Id.* at 395.

[31] *Id.* at 374 (Scalia, J., dissenting).

intimidation. This statute would not single out particular content, and so would pass scrutiny.

The Court distinguished *R.A.V.* in *Wisconsin v. Mitchell.*[32] In *Mitchell*, the Court rejected a First Amendment challenge to a Wisconsin law authorizing sentence enhancement for hate crimes. The defendant's sentence for an aggravated battery conviction was increased from a maximum of two years to four years because he intentionally selected his victim because of the victim's race. The Wisconsin statute also authorized sentence enhancement if the victim was selected based on religion, disability, sexual orientation, ethnicity, or gender.

The *Mitchell* Court reasoned that the sentence enhancement was based on the defendant's racial motive in committing a crime, rather than on his abstract beliefs. The statute at issue differed from the ordinance in *R.A.V.*, which impermissibly prohibited expression based on *content*, whereas the Wisconsin statute focused on *conduct, i.e.,* a racially-based assault.

[3]   Sexually Offensive Speech

Sexually obscene speech is not protected by the First Amendment.[33] What about speech that does not meet the Court's definition of obscenity but is arguably still offensive? The Court has been less protective of sexually offensive speech than it has of other expression:

> [E]ven though we recognize that the First Amendment will not tolerate the total suppression of erotic materials that have some arguably artistic value, it is manifest that society's interest in protecting this type of expression is of wholly different, and lesser, magnitude than the interest in untrammeled political debate.[34]

To a greater or lesser extent, members of the Court have openly acknowledged the validity of certain content-based restrictions on sexually offensive expression. They have tended to respect the state's interest in preventing the secondary effects of adult entertainment — *e.g.*, prostitution and other criminal activity, or decline in property values.

In *Young v. American Mini Theatres, Inc.*,[35] the Court upheld a Detroit zoning ordinance that forbade adult motion picture theaters from locating within 1,000 feet of any two other regulated uses or within 500 feet of residential areas. Regulated uses referred to 10 different kinds of establishments in addition to adult theaters.[36] Justice Powell joined the first two portions of the opinion (dealing with vagueness and prior restraint) to make a majority of five.

---

[32] 508 U.S. 476 (1993).

[33] *See Miller v. California, infra* § 16.05[1].

[34] Young v. American Mini Theatres, Inc., 427 U.S. 50, 70 (1976).

[35] *Id.*

[36] The specified regulated uses included adult bookstores, shoeshine parlors, second-hand stores, and pool halls.

Writing for the Court, Justice Stevens rejected a vagueness attack, finding the challenged ordinances readily susceptible of a narrowing construction. Because Justice Stevens found speech at issue "on the borderline between pornography and artistic expression,"[37] the majority limited the availability of the vagueness doctrine to protect such expression. Justice Stevens also spoke for a majority in rejecting the prior restraint contention. All theaters were subject to some zoning laws because of the legitimate interest in planning and regulating the use of property for commercial purposes. The restriction required dispersion of adult theaters. No claim was made that the restriction at issue limited the total number of theaters allowed in the city or denied access to the market to those who wished to view the films.

Only a plurality of four joined the third section of Justice Stevens' opinion rejecting an equal protection claim. Although the plurality acknowledged an equal protection interest against regulating the content of speech, it treated this argument as a First Amendment issue. Justice Stevens stated that the Court routinely decides the amount of protection that speech receives based on its content. Examples of this approach included the fighting words doctrine,[38] commercial speech,[39] and defamation that concerns public figures.[40]

Although the restrictions were based on the content of the films, the plurality found the distinction permissible because of the offensive character of the sexually-oriented materials that Detroit wished to restrict. The plurality stated that it would be an impermissible content-based regulation if the government was motivated by hostility for the particular point of view being expressed. The City's purpose, however, was not to suppress offensive speech.[41] The regulations were unaffected by whatever social, political, or philosophical message the adult films intended to communicate. Rather, the City's purpose was to limit the deterioration and crime that resulted from the concentration of adult theaters in certain areas.

Justice Powell, concurring in part of the opinion and concurring in the judgment, provided the vote necessary to form a majority. He generally disagreed with the basic thrust of the plurality's analysis which predicated protection for different kinds of speech on its underlying value. Instead, Justice Powell characterized the regulation as a permissible exercise of zoning power. He focused on the rights of the speaker and the listener. First, he asked whether the ordinance imposed any content limitations on creators of adult movies or on their ability to make the movies available to whomever they desired. He then considered whether the ordinance significantly restricted the access to the movies by those who wished to see them. Finding neither to be the case, Justice Powell characterized the ordinance as a location, "anti-skid-row" regulation with an incidental effect on free speech inter

---

[37] *Young,* 427 U.S. at 61.

[38] *See supra* § 15.01[1].

[39] *See infra* § 16.04.

[40] *See* New York Times Co. v. Sullivan, 376 U.S. 254 (1964).

[41] The plurality distinguished *Erznoznik v. City of Jacksonville,* 422 U.S. 205 (1975), in which the City's main, impermissible purpose was to protect its citizens from exposure to such "offensive" expression. The City outlawed displays of nudity on drive-in movie screens.

ests. Applying the four-part test of *United States v. O'Brien*,[42] the incidental burden on freedom of expression was justified by the anti-skid row purpose of the ordinance.

In *City of Los Angeles v. Alameda Books, Inc.*,[43] the Court upheld a Los Angeles ordinance that prohibited "more than one adult entertainment business" occupying the same building. The ordinance defines adult establishments as "an adult arcade, bookstore, cabaret, motel, theater, or massage parlor or a place for sexual encounters." Writing for a plurality of four, Justice O'Connor concluded that "it is rational for the city to infer that reducing the concentration of adult operations in a neighborhood, whether within separate establishments or in one large establishment," will advance the City's interest in reducing crime. Justice O'Connor left the question of the content neutrality of the ordinance to the lower courts.

Justice Scalia filed a concurring opinion. Justice Kennedy concurred in the judgment. He required that the purpose of the ordinance must be splitting adult businesses, rather than forcing their closure in a way that would not substantially diminish the amount of speech. Justice Souter dissented, joined by Justices Stevens, Ginsburg, and Breyer. By forcing adult businesses to divide into two or more separate units, the regulations will double their overheads.

Although not limiting the number of theaters seemed to be significant to the Court in *Young*, the ordinance in *City of Renton v. Playtime Theatres, Inc.*[44] required all adult theaters to be within a 520 acre area. The *Renton* Court upheld the ordinance despite a conclusion of the Court of Appeals that limiting adult theatres to these 520 acres would impose a substantial restriction on speech, as most of the land in the area was already developed. Chief Justice Rehnquist opined that the First Amendment did not guarantee these theatres or other speech-related businesses the right to obtain sites cheaply. Unlike *Young*, which upheld an ordinance dispersing the theaters, *Renton* upheld a regulation that forced them to stay in one area of the city. The Court partly based its decision on the "secondary effects" that such theatres have on property values, and the quality of urban life.[45] The "secondary effects doctrine" built on some of the reasoning in *Young*. In subsequent cases, however, the Court has appeared to limit the doctrine to sexually offensive speech and that the secondary effect to be avoided must be content neutral, such as urban blight.

In *FCC v. Pacifica Foundation*,[46] the FCC attempted to sanction a radio station for broadcasting, in the middle of the day, a George Carlin monologue full of sexually explicit epithets entitled "seven dirty words." The Court found the FCC sanctions constitutional.

Writing for a plurality of three, Justice Stevens rejected the station's overbreadth challenge to the FCC's regulation barring indecent speech. Although the

---

[42] 391 U.S. 367, 377 (1968). *See* the discussion regarding symbolic speech, *infra* § 16.01.

[43] 535 U.S. 425 (2002).

[44] 475 U.S. 41 (1986).

[45] *Id.* at 47.

[46] 438 U.S. 726 (1978).

FCC's definition of "indecent" might allow the agency to restrict certain patently offensive references to genitals or sexual activity that were not obscene, such references "surely lie at the periphery of First Amendment concern."[47] Justice Stevens applied a sliding-scale test based on the speech's capacity to offend and on its "social value," which varied with the context in which the speech was made. Although entitled to some protection, the words sanctioned "ordinarily lack literary, political, or scientific value" and are " 'vulgar,' 'offensive,' and 'shocking.' " The plurality again acknowledged that it would be more protective of the monologue if its content was in some degree political.

In a part of the opinion joined by Justices Powell and Blackmun, a majority of the Court upheld the specific order of the FCC placing a record of the event in the station's file. The majority noted that the Court has treated the broadcast media differently from other avenues for speech.[48] Different treatment was attributable to the broadcast media's ability to come into the home and its ready access to children. Justice Stevens took into account that the message was broadcast rather than transmitted closed circuit, that it was transmitted in the afternoon, and that the conversation contained more than a few expletives.

Justice Powell concurred in the judgment joined by Justice Blackmun. He emphasized that the messages over the broadcast media could reach children and private homes. He also noted that the order did not prohibit broadcasting the monologue during late night hours when children would not be listening. The monologue could also be performed at a club with an adult audience or recorded for purchase by adults.

In his dissent, Justice Brennan said that the majority had suppressed the emotive function of speech. The majority allowed government to discriminate among speakers, forcing some to speak in ways in which they are neither capable nor comfortable.

In *Denver Area Educational Telecommunications Consortium, Inc. v. FCC*,[49] the Court struck down parts of the Television Consumer Protections and Competition of 1992 that required cable companies to restrict the availability of "patently offensive" programming on leased access channels. Noting the similarity of cable and radio, and relying on their *Pacifica* decision, the Court did uphold a part of the statute that empowered cable companies to change schedules to make adult materials available at times when children generally do not have access to the medium. However, the Court struck down a similar provision allowing cable companies discretion to restrict the times that these materials are available on public access channels. The local boards that supervise public access channels could minimize or eliminate programming that could be deemed offensive to the children of the community.

---

[47] *Id.* at 743.

[48] *See, e.g.*, Red Lion Broad. v. FCC, 395 U.S. 367 (1969).

[49] 518 U.S. 727 (1996). The case is more fully discussed in § 14.07[2].

In *Reno v. ACLU*,[50] the Court struck down the Communications Decency Act of 1996 (CDA), pointing out that the CDA's obscenity standard fell short of the test for obscenity established in *Miller v. California*.[51] While the CDA banned " 'patently offensive' " material, it lacked the additional qualification of the *Miller* test's second prong that required the material to be defined as obscene by applicable state law.[52] The CDA also lacked the other two prongs of the *Miller* test, that the work must " 'appeal to the "prurient" interest,' "[53] and that, under a national standard, the work lack " 'serious literary, artistic, political, or scientific value.' "[54] In contrast, the CDA bans " 'patently offensive' " material according to community standards. As the Internet is a worldwide network, the community standard definition of obscenity would necessarily be that standard of the community most easily offended on the Internet.

The Court also relied on the principle of protecting children from offensive speech in *Bethel School District No. 403 v. Fraser*,[55] which upheld discipline for sexually suggestive speech at a school assembly. The school setting was integral to the Court's reasoning. As suggested in *Pacifica*, however, the presence of children will not permit government to suppress offensive speech if ready alternatives are available.

In *Erznoznik v. City of Jacksonville*,[56] the Court invalidated an ordinance that prohibited the display of nudity where it was visible on the public streets. The ordinance was focused on drive-in theaters. Although the city relied on protecting children, the Court noted that the ordinance was not solely limited to nudity that was obscene for youths and, therefore, the Court struck it down as facially overbroad.

Similarly, in *Sable Communications v. FCC*,[57] Justice White, writing for a 6-3 majority, upheld part of a statute banning obscene commercial phone messages. The Court, however, unanimously held unconstitutional the statute's prohibition of *all* dial-a-porn messages that were offensive, but not obscene. The *Sable* Court recognized the government's compelling interest in protecting children from access to indecent dial-a-porn messages. Nevertheless, the outright ban was not as narrowly drawn as FCC credit card, access codes, and scrambling codes that were sufficient to prevent access to children. The Court distinguished the outright ban in this case from the sanctions in *Pacifica*, which merely "sought to channel it [the offensive expression] to times of day when children most likely would not be exposed to it."[58] Moreover, unlike *Pacifica*, this case did not involve a captive audience.

---

[50]　521 U.S. 844 (1997).

[51]　*See infra* § 16.05[1].

[52]　*Reno v. ACLU*, 521 U.S. at 872–73.

[53]　*Id.*

[54]　*Id.*

[55]　478 U.S. 675 (1986).

[56]　422 U.S. 205 (1975).

[57]　492 U.S. 115 (1989).

[58]　*Id.* at 127.

The Court has also upheld some restrictions on nude dancing as another form of speech that is sexually offensive, but not obscene. In *Schad v. Borough of Mount Ephraim*,[59] the Court stated that "nude dancing is not without its First Amendment protection from official regulation."[60] It struck down a zoning ordinance barring coin-operated machines that permitted the viewing of live nude dancers. The Court rejected the argument that the ordinance was a reasonable time, place, and manner restriction. There was no justification for excluding such a broad category of protected expression, and the interests purportedly served by the ordinance could be served by less restrictive means than an outright ban.

In a more recent decision, *Barnes v. Glen Theatre, Inc.*,[61] the Court found that nude dancing was "within the outer perimeters of the First Amendment, although only marginally so."[62] *Barnes* involved an Indiana public indecency statute that required dancers to wear "pasties" and "G-strings." Writing for a plurality of three, Chief Justice Rehnquist allowed the state to prohibit *completely* nude dancing, holding that the Indiana statutory requirement that the dancers must wear "pasties and G-strings does not violate the First Amendment."[63] As nude dancing was expressive conduct, the plurality applied the test for protection of expressive conduct in *United States v. O'Brien*.[64]

The plurality noted that public indecency statutes reflect a long tradition of state laws prohibiting public nudity. Thus, the statute at issue furthered a substantial governmental interest in protecting societal order and morality. This governmental interest was unrelated to the suppression of free expression because the state wished to prohibit public nudity irrespective of whether it was part of expressive conduct. For example, the statute also banned public nudity on beaches. Moreover, the statute did not seek to suppress erotic speech as it continued to permit much erotic expression. Finally, the plurality concluded that the G-string and pasties requirements were the minimum means necessary to advance the state's interest.

Concurring in the judgment, Justice Scalia would have applied a rationality test. The statute represented a general regulation of conduct not directed at expression. Concurring in the judgment, Justice Souter agreed with the plurality's use of the *O'Brien* test. However, he would not have used the State's interest in morality. Instead, he found the State's interests in protecting against the "secondary effects" caused by these establishments, such as prostitution, to be substantial.

Erie v. Pap's A.M.[65] upheld a city ordinance banning public nudity and requiring dancers to wear, at a minimum, "pasties and a G-string." Writing for a plurality of four in the free speech portion of the opinion, Justice O'Connor relied on *United*

---

[59] 452 U.S. 61 (1981).

[60] *Id.* at 65.

[61] 501 U.S. 560 (1991).

[62] *Id.* at 565.

[63] *Id.*

[64] 391 U.S. 367 (1968). For additional discussion of *O'Brien, see infra* § 16.01.

[65] 529 U.S. 277 (2000).

States v. O'Brien,[66] as the ban on public nudity was unrelated to the suppression of expression. *Barnes v. Glen Theatres*[67] had upheld a nearly identical statute.

The terms of the Erie ordinance regulated conduct alone. The ordinance banned all types of public nudity whether or not it was accompanied by expression. The "ordinance does not attempt to regulate the primary effects of the expression, *i.e.*, the effect on the audience of watching nude erotic dancing, but rather the secondary effects, such as the impacts on public health, safety and welfare."[68]

Again relying on *O'Brien*, the plurality said that it would not invalidate a statute based on an improper legislative purpose. Any effect that pasties and G-strings may have on the erotic message is "*de minimis*." *Young v. American Mini Theatres, Inc.*,[69] stated that "'society's interest in protecting this type of expression is of a wholly different, and lesser, magnitude than the interest in untrammeled political debate.'"[70]

Justice O'Connor discussed "incidental burdens" and "secondary effects" as theories that are not identical, but closely related in this case. Justice O'Connor applied the four-part *O'Brien* test. Taking the first part of the test, the legislation lay clearly within the city's police powers. Second, "regulating conduct through a public nudity ban and . . . combating the harmful secondary effects associated with nude dancing are undeniably important"[71] government interests.

Regulation furthers the government interest of protecting against crime and other health and safety problems. As previously stated, requiring the dancers to wear pasties and G-strings has only a minimal negative effect, if any, in furthering the government interest of protecting against secondary effects. Third, as previously discussed, "the government interest is unrelated to the suppression of free expression." Fourth, "the restriction is no greater than is essential" to advance the government interest. "The ordinance regulates conduct, and any incidental impact on the expressive element of nude dancing is *de minimis*."[72]

Justice Scalia, joined by Justice Thomas, concurred in the judgment. Both the Erie ordinance and the Indiana statute at issue in *Barnes* restrict, "not merely nude dancing, but the act — irrespective of whether it is engaged in for expressive purposes — of going nude in public."[73]

Justice Souter concurred in part and dissented in part. Relying on *O'Brien*, he agreed with the plurality that the City's "interest in combating the secondary effects associated with nude dancing establishments is an interest unrelated to the

---

[66]   391 U.S. 367 (1968).

[67]   501 U.S. 560 (1991).

[68]   *Pap's A.M.*, 529 U.S. at 291.

[69]   427 U.S. 50 (1976).

[70]   *Pap's A.M.*, 529 U.S. at 294.

[71]   *Id.* at 296.

[72]   *Id.* at 301.

[73]   *Id.* at 308 (Scalia, J., concurring in the judgment).

suppression of expression."[74] However, Erie did not provide a sufficient evidentiary showing to uphold the ordinance.

Justice Stevens, joined by Justice Ginsburg, dissented. Until now, the *O'Brien* test was only used in reference to zoning regulations. In contrast, "the Court has now held that such effects may justify the total suppression of protected speech."[75] Unlike the statute in *Barnes* that was not aimed at a particular form of speech, the Erie ordinance was aimed at nude dancing establishments in its scope and its enforcement. For example, the City did not enforce the ordinance to ban the nude play *Equus*.

§ 15.02 SPEECH IN TRADITIONAL PUBLIC FORUMS: STREETS, SIDEWALKS, PARKS

The cases in the previous section discussed the limited scope of permissible content-based restrictions in the public forum. Recall that *Young* involved zoning regulations based on the impact of private theaters on public streets and sidewalks. *Pacifica* involved the broadcast media which the Court has long treated as a quasi public forum. As the first section concerned questions of what can be said, the remainder of this Chapter concerns questions of what constitutes a public forum or where one can speak for free as a matter of right.

Certain public property — streets, sidewalks, and parks — are so historically associated with the exercise of free speech rights that denial of access to anyone is constitutionally forbidden.[76] However, unlimited access to such public forums would likely lead to chaos and thereby decrease First Amendment protection. Consequently, the Constitution permits the state to place reasonable time, place, and manner restrictions on access to public forums. Therefore, in addition to questions of what constitutes a public forum, the remainder of the Chapter will be concerned with content-neutral restrictions on when, where, and how one can speak in the public forum.

The Court has long struggled with the permissible scope of restrictions that are appropriate to the public forum. This struggle has always involved balancing the need for order in society with the need to preserve the effective exercise of liberty. Two of the early cases that laid the foundation for the Court's public forum theory were *Cantwell v. Connecticut*[77] and *Cox v. New Hampshire*.[78]

In *Cantwell v. Connecticut*, three Jehovah Witnesses played phonographic records critical of certain religions, particularly Catholicism, in a 90 percent-Catholic neighborhood. They played the record to any passerby who would listen and would then request a donation. The State convicted the Cantwells for not applying for a solicitation permit and for violating a breach of the peace statute. The

---

[74] *Id.* at 310 (Souter, J., concurring in part and dissenting in part).

[75] *Id.* at 317 (Stevens, J., dissenting).

[76] *See* Hague v. CIO, 307 U.S. 496 (1939).

[77] 310 U.S. 296 (1940).

[78] 312 U.S. 569 (1941).

city's anti-solicitation statute required that anyone soliciting funds for religious, charitable, or philanthropic purposes obtain approval from the secretary of the public welfare council. The statute gave broad discretion to the secretary to revoke permits, including the discretion to determine whether the cause was in fact religious and whether the manner of solicitation would conform to certain standards.

The Court held that the anti-solicitation statute unconstitutionally restricted the defendant's First Amendment right to solicit support for his views. Some regulation of charitable solicitation was permissible — for example, protection against fraud. However, because the statute at issue provided an administrative official with "unfettered discretion" to suppress expression, it effectively amounted to an impermissible prior restraint. The extent of the authority granted to the secretary gave him the power to make decisions on the basis of content and to censor those whose views he disapproved. The fact that the acts of the licensing officer were subject to judicial review did not save the statute because the discretion granted still amounted to a prior restraint pending the review.

The *Cantwell* Court also set aside the breach of the peace conviction which was not based on a specific statute, but on common law breach of the peace. The common law offense was overbroad: the amorphous scope of the common law offense allowed the judiciary and executive to restrict a wide variety of protected conduct.[79] While Cantwell's record playing aroused animosity, his behavior did not create an immediate threat to public safety or order.

Cox v. New Hampshire[80] upheld a New Hampshire statute requiring that groups who wished to parade on public streets obtain a license in advance. In this case, small groups of 15 to 20 Jehovah's Witnesses silently marched single file on the city streets distributing leaflets and carrying signs critical of organized religion. The Jehovah's Witnesses did not have a license, nor did they try to obtain one. The Court upheld the statute's authority to restrict the time, place, and manner of free speech in a public forum.

Unlike the restrictions in *Cantwell*, the board that issued the license was not provided with arbitrary or unfettered discretion to determine whether to grant the license. The statute limited the board's inquiry only to considering the impact on the public's convenience in using the highways.

Moreover, the Court noted the necessity of public order to promote free speech liberties. Without order, chaos would ensue and quickly restrain freedom just as much as organized suppression. Content-neutral time, place, and manner restrictions on the use of highways and public streets promoted the public convenience and public safety. For example, the state could force a protestor to obey a traffic light even though he would like to run through the red light to make a statement or because of some religious duty. Likewise, the interest the state asserted in *Cox* was

---

[79] In the guideline overbreadth opinion of *Broadrick v. Oklahoma, supra* § 13.07[1], the Court in dicta suggested that an ordinary breach of the peace statute could pass overbreadth scrutiny. Such statutes contrast sharply with the amorphous commonlaw breach of the peace conviction at issue in *Cantwell*.

[80] 312 U.S. 569 (1941).

for public convenience and safety on the highway.[81]

The Court found that the permit in *Cox* served the public safety and convenience by: 1) affording the opportunity for proper policing; 2) preventing confusion from overlapping parades; 3) securing the convenient use of streets by other travelers; and 4) minimizing the risk of disorder. The license requirement, both in the long run and in the aggregate, advanced liberty and order by furthering the right to speak and by making sure the speaker could be effective.

The *Cox* Court also upheld the licensing fee of not more than $300 because it was not a revenue tax, but rather was designed to meet the expenses incident to the administration of the law.

Some of *Cox's* guidance on licensing fees has been qualified by *Forsyth County v. Nationalist Movement*.[82] In that case, the Court struck down a $100 fee imposed for processing a parade license. The challenged statute allowed the county administrator to impose a licensing fee of up to $1000 per day for administrative expenses and enforcing public order. The Court objected that the scheme left the amount charged to the unreviewable discretion of the inspector and required that statutes guide this discretion with "narrow, objective, and definite standards."[83]

The Court has invalidated a number of speech restrictions in the public forum because they afforded government officials standardless discretion to restrict speech. In *Lovell v. City of Griffin*,[84] the Court applied the prior restraint doctrine to strike down an overly-broad ordinance that prohibited the distribution of all pamphlets or other literature without a permit. Similarly, the Court has struck down a statute giving unbridled discretion to the chief of police to prohibit sound amplification devices like sound trucks.[85] On the other hand, it upheld an ordinance allowing city officials to ban such devices if they emitted "loud and raucous noises."[86]

In *Thomas v. Chicago Park District*,[87] the Court unanimously decided that a permit system to use public parks did not have to incorporate the procedural safeguards of *Freedman v. Maryland*.[88] The Chicago ordinance required a permit "to 'conduct a public assembly, parade, picnic, or other event involving more than fifty individuals,' or engage in any activity such as 'creating or emitting any Amplified Sound.' " Applications must be decided within 14 days, and can only be denied in writing based on 13 grounds, which limit administrative discretion. Applicants may appeal denials to the General Superintendent of Parks, and then to a court.

---

[81] Note, also, that the traffic light example is much closer to action than to speech. The First Amendment offers less protection to action.

[82] 505 U.S. 123 (1992).

[83] *Id.* at 131.

[84] 303 U.S. 444 (1938).

[85] *See* Saia v. New York, 334 U.S. 558 (1948).

[86] Kovacs v. Cooper, 336 U.S. 77 (1949).

[87] 534 U.S. 316 (2002).

[88] 380 U.S. 51 (1965).

Finding *Freedman* inapplicable, Justice Scalia neither required the Park District to "initiate litigation every time it denies a permit," nor specify a deadline for prompt judicial review of challenges. Unlike the censorship of films at issue in *Freedman*, the ordinance in this case is a content-neutral time, place, and manner restriction. Moreover, its standards adequately constrain administrative discretion and preserve effective judicial review. Grounds for denial of a permit include the filing of an incomplete or materially false application, unpaid damage to a park, a prior applicant for the same time and place, unreasonable health or safety dangers, and violation of a prior permit.

In *Watchtower Bible & Tract Society of New York, Inc. v. Village of Stratton*,[89] the Court invalidated a municipal ordinance requiring a permit to go on private property to explain or promote any cause. The Village has never denied an application for a permit, nor has it ever revoked a permit. Even those with a permit cannot canvass residents who have filed a no solicitation form that lists a series of 19 exceptions, including Scouting Organizations, Camp Fire Girls, Jehovah's Witnesses, and Christmas Carolers.

The ordinance's broad sweep applied to visiting neighbors attempting to gain support for a political candidate or for replacing a garbage collector. A different result might have been obtained had the ordinance focused on commercial activities and soliciting funds, as such an ordinance arguably would have been tailored to the Village's interests in protecting residential privacy and preventing fraud.

In addition to its sweeping effect, Justice Stevens identified three other concerns resulting from a permit requirement. First, the permit requirement undermines anonymous speech. While prohibiting anonymity may sometimes be justified — for example, to protect "the integrity of a ballot-initiative process," or to prevent fraudulent transactions, the Village ordinance goes well beyond such interests. Second, obtaining a permit may rail against a person's political or religious views. Third, the permit requirement curtails spontaneous speech. The "breadth and unprecedented nature" of the ordinance rendered it invalid, as did its not being tailored to the Village's stated interests. Justice Breyer concurred, joined by Justices Souter and Ginsburg. Justice Scalia, joined by Justice Thomas, concurred in the judgment. Chief Justice Rehnquist dissented.

In *City of Lakewood v. Plain Dealer Publishing Co.*,[90] the Court struck down an ordinance affording city officials standardless discretion in placing news racks on public property. The Court ruled that the discretion of government officials to impose such restrictions must be limited in the text of the statute, by binding judicial or administrative construction, or by well-established practice. Without any specified limits placed on the officials, the ordinance amounted to a prior restraint.

While the Court severely constricts broad administrative discretion to permit or prohibit speech in the public forum, it affords greater latitude in administrative discretion to decide time, place, and manner restrictions. In *Ward v. Rock Against*

---

[89] 536 U.S. 150 (2002).

[90] 486 U.S. 750 (1988).

Racism,[91] the Court upheld New York City's "Use Guidelines" that required performers in Central Park's band shell to use the City's sound equipment and sound technician. The technician, in consultation with the event's sponsors, would control volume.

Justice Kennedy, writing for the Court, noted that musical performances deserved First Amendment protection. However, the Court upheld the "Use Guidelines" as valid time, place, and manner restrictions in a public forum. Although the guidelines provided for flexibility and discretion, the Court did not find that the discretion was so great as to constitute a prior restraint. It was the City's practice to defer to the sponsor's wishes regarding the sound quality, and to confer with the performing groups before making restrictions on sound quality. With respect to sound volume, the goal of the City's guidelines was to ensure that the sound was sufficient to reach all the listeners. Thus, the City's own limiting construction was relevant in making the determination that the guidelines did not grant administrative officials too much discretion.

Once a state allows a private organization to use public property, the state may not then control the speech of the organization. In *Hurley v. Irish-American Gay, Lesbian, & Bisexual Group*,[92] the Supreme Court held that requiring a private organization to include the Irish-American Gay, Lesbian, and Bisexual Group (GLIB) in its annual St. Patrick's Day parade violated the First Amendment. In 1992, the South Boston Allied War Veterans Council denied GLIB's application to march in the parade. The state court ordered that the Council allow GLIB to participate under the state's public accommodations law. The state court held that the parade, traveling up and down the streets of South Boston, was a place of public accommodation, and the state law prohibited discrimination based on sexual orientation.

Writing for a unanimous Court, Justice Souter found that parades, like protest marches, constituted expression protected by the First Amendment. While the public accommodations law did not regulate speech facially, the state court's application of the law regulated the parade organizer's speech. This application violated the "principle of speaker's autonomy"[93] by requiring a private organization to express a message that it did not wish to communicate. Justice Souter stressed that a speaker's " 'right to tailor the speech, applies not only to expressions of value, opinion, or endorsement, but equally to statements of fact the speaker would rather avoid.' "[94]

The Court rejected GLIB's assertion that its decision in *Turner Broadcasting System, Inc. v. FCC*[95] required GLIB's participation. Unlike cable viewers who understand that cable operators act as passive receptacles for expression, the Court found it doubtful that spectators of the parade would understand it to be presented without any endorsement from the private organization. Moreover, because GLIB

---

[91] 491 U.S. 781 (1989).

[92] 515 U.S. 557 (1995).

[93] *Id.* at 575.

[94] *Id.*

[95] *See supra* § 14.07[2].

could have conducted its own parade, there was no danger of preventing access as there had been in *Turner Broadcasting*.

In *Snyder v. Phelps*,[96] the Court set aside a jury verdict and held that the First Amendment barred tort claims against protestors at a military funeral.[97] The jury found liability and imposed millions of dollars in damages on Westboro Baptist Church for picketing near a soldier's funeral service. "The [Westboro] church's congregation believes that God hates and punishes the United States for its tolerance of homosexuality, particularly in America's military," and over the last twenty years has picketed nearly 600 funerals.[98]

The picketing of Matthew Snyder's funeral took place "approximately 1,000 feet from where the funeral was held." Those picketing "displayed their signs for about 30 minutes before the funeral began and sang hymns and recited bible verses. None of the picketers entered church property or went to the cemetery. They did not yell, or use profanity, and there was no violence associated with the"[99] protest. "The funeral procession passed within 200 to 300 feet of the picket site," and although Snyder's father ("Snyder") "could see the tops of the picket signs as he drove to the funeral, he did not see what was written on the signs until later that night, while watching a news broadcast covering the event."[100]

Snyder brought suit against Westboro, and "a jury found for Snyder on the intentional infliction of emotional distress, intrusion upon seclusion, and civil conspiracy claims, and held Westboro liable for $2.9 million in compensatory damages and $8 million in punitive damages."[101] The trial court "remitted the punitive damages award to $2.1 million."[102]

Chief Justice Roberts delivered the opinion of the Court. "Whether the First Amendment prohibits holding Westboro liable for its speech in this case turns largely on whether that speech is of public or private concern, as determined by all the circumstances of the case. '[S]peech on "matters of public concern" . . . is "at the heart of the First Amendment." ' "[103] Specifically, "speech deals with matters of public concern" when the speech relates to "any matter of political, social, or other concern to the community, or when it 'is a subject of legitimate news interest; that is, a subject of general interest and of value and concern to the public.' "[104]

---

[96] 131 S. Ct. 1207 (2011).

[97] A few weeks after the funeral, one of the picketers posted a message on Westboro's web site discussing the picketing which contained religiously oriented denunciations of the Snyders. However, that posting was not properly before the Court as "Snyder never mentioned it in his petition for certiorari."

[98] *Id.* at 1213.

[99] *Id.*

[100] *Id.* at 1213–14.

[101] *Id.* at 1214.

[102] *Id.*

[103] *Id.*

[104] *Id.* at 1216.

The Court distinguished *Dun & Bradstreet*,[105] which had held that an "individual's credit report 'concerns no public issue.' "[106] In deciding whether speech is public or private, the Court must "examine the " 'content, form, and context' " of that speech, " 'as revealed by the whole record.' " "[107] When considering "content, form, and context, no factor is dispositive, and it is necessary to evaluate all the circumstances of the speech."[108] In First Amendment cases, "the Court is obligated 'to "make an independent examination of the whole record" in order to make sure that "the judgment does not constitute a forbidden intrusion on the field of free expression." ' "[109]

The content of the congregation's signs plainly highlighted a public concern, as issues such as "political and moral conduct of the United States and its citizens, the fate of our Nation, homosexuality in the military, and scandals involving the Catholic clergy are all matters of public import."[110] And "even if a few of the signs — such as 'You're Going to Hell' and 'God Hates You' — were viewed as containing messages related to Mathew Snyder or the Snyders specifically, that would not change the fact that the overall thrust and dominant theme of Westboro's demonstration spoke to broader public issues."[111] The Court was not concerned that "Westboro's speech on public matters was in any way contrived to insulate speech on a private matter from liability," since "Westboro had been actively engaged in speaking on the subjects" long before this funeral.[112]

" 'Even protected speech is not equally permissible in all places and at all times.' "[113] For example, "Westboro's choice of where and when to conduct its picketing is not beyond the Government's regulatory reach — it is 'subject to reasonable time, place, or manner restrictions' that are consistent with the standards announced in this Court's precedents."[114] Also, "Maryland now has a law imposing restrictions on funeral picketing, as do 43 other states, and the Federal Government."[115] If "these laws are content neutral, they raise very different questions from the tort verdict at issue in this case."[116] Regardless, Maryland's law "was not in effect at the time of the events at issue." Consequently, the Court had "no occasion to consider how it might apply" to the facts here, or "whether it or other similar regulations are constitutional."[117]

---

[105] 472 U.S. 749 (1985).

[106] *Snyder*, 131 S. Ct. at 1216.

[107] *Id.*

[108] *Id.*

[109] *Id.*

[110] *Id.* at 1217.

[111] *Id.*

[112] *Id.*

[113] *Id.* at 1218.

[114] *Id.*

[115] *Id.*

[116] *Id.*

[117] *Id.*

In the past the Court has "identified a few limited situations where the location of targeted picketing can be regulated under provisions that the Court has determined to be content neutral."[118] For example, in *Frisby v. Schultz*,[119] the Court "upheld a ban on picketing 'before or about' a particular residence."[120] In *Madsen v. Women's Health Center, Inc.*,[121] the Court approved an "injunction requiring a buffer zone between protestors and an abortion clinic entrance."[122] In contrast, "the facts here are obviously quite different, both with respect to the activity being regulated and the means of restricting those activities."[123] The major difference is that the church members had "the right to be where they were."[124] The congregation "complied with police guidance on where the picketing could be staged," and "the picketing was conducted under police supervision some 1,000 feet from the church, out of sight of those at the church."[125] Moreover, the picketing "was not unruly; there was no shouting, profanity, or violence."[126]

The record demonstrated that Snyder's distress "turned on the content and viewpoint of the message conveyed, rather than any interference with the funeral itself."[127] Under *Texas v. Johnson*,[128] "a bedrock principle underlying the First Amendment" forbids government prohibition "of an idea simply because society finds the idea itself offensive or disagreeable."[129]

In *Snyder*, the trial court instructed the jury "that it could hold Westboro liable for intentional infliction of emotional distress based on a finding that Westboro's picketing was 'outrageous.' " However, this standard "would allow a jury to impose liability on the basis of the jurors' tastes or views, or perhaps on the basis of their dislike of a particular expression."[130]

Turning to the intrusion upon seclusion claim, "the burden normally falls upon the viewer to avoid further bombardment of [his] sensibilities simply by averting [his] eyes."[131] As a general matter, the Court has "applied the captive audience doctrine only sparingly to protect unwilling listeners from protected speech," and the Court declined to expand the doctrine.[132] Here, "Snyder could see no more than the tops of the signs when driving to the funeral," and "there is no indication that

[118] *Id.*

[119] 487 U.S. 474 (1988).

[120] *Snyder*, 131 S. Ct. at 1218.

[121] 512 U.S. 753 (1994).

[122] *Snyder*, 131 S. Ct. at 1218.

[123] *Id.*

[124] *Id.*

[125] *Id.*

[126] *Id.* at 1218–19.

[127] *Id.* at 1219.

[128] 491 U.S. 397 (1989).

[129] *Snyder*, 131 S. Ct. at 1219.

[130] *Id.*

[131] *Id.* at 1220.

[132] *Id.*

the picketing in any way interfered with the funeral service itself."[133] Therefore, the First Amendment barred recovery for both intention infliction of emotional distress and intrusion upon seclusion. Without those torts as a basis, Snyder's claim of civil conspiracy was also barred.

Justice Breyer concurred in the opinion, but recognized that the Court did "not examine in depth the effect of television broadcasting" or address an internet posting about the protesters that was introduced at trial.[134] Moreover, "suppose that A were physically to assault B, knowing that the assault (being newsworthy) would provide A with an opportunity to transmit to the public his views on a matter of public concern. The constitutionally protected nature of the end would not shield A's use of unlawful, unprotected means. And in some circumstances the use of certain words as means would be similarly unprotected."[135] However, such hypothetical did not apply to Westboro, for it communicated its views through lawful picketing and could not be heard or seen from the funeral. "To uphold the application of state law in these circumstances would punish Westboro for seeking to communicate its views on matters of public concern without proportionately advancing the state's interest in protecting its citizens against severe emotional harm."[136]

Justice Alito dissented. "Our profound national commitment to free and open debate is not a license for the vicious, verbal assault that occurred in this case."[137]

§ 15.03   THE CIVIL RIGHTS MOVEMENT, MASS DEMONSTRATIONS, AND NEW RULES FOR NEW PUBLIC FORUMS

Cases involving mass demonstrations[138] brought new pressures on public forum analysis, more severe than the single-speaker or small-group forms of expression cases like in *Cantwell*.[139] The pressures on public forum analysis became even greater when the demonstrators took their messages to public facilities other than streets and parks. For example, in *Brown v. Louisiana*,[140] the Court protected a right to conduct a peaceful, quiet sit-in a public library. In *Adderley v. Florida*,[141] the Court upheld convictions for trespassing with "malicious and mischievous" intent for demonstrations on the grounds of a county jailhouse.

---

[133] *Id.*

[134] *Id.* at 1221 (Breyer, J., concurring).

[135] *Id.*

[136] *Id.* at 1222.

[137] *Id.* (Alito, J., dissenting).

[138] *See* Cox v. Louisiana, 379 U.S. 536 (1965) (*Cox I*) and Cox v. Louisiana, 379 U.S. 559 (1965) (*Cox II*).

[139] *See supra* § 15.02.

[140] 383 U.S. 131 (1966).

[141] 385 U.S. 39 (1966).

Cox v. Louisiana (Cox I)[142] involved a peaceful civil rights demonstration at the state courthouse. The demonstrators were convicted of breaching the peace and obstructing public passages. The state attempted to uphold the convictions of the demonstrators on the basis that violence may have erupted as a result of the peaceful demonstration.[143] However, the Court found that the demonstrators had not advocated violence, and no violence was threatened by the crowd. Moreover, the record indicated that there were an adequate number of police in the area to protect the demonstrators and handle the crowd.

The Court set aside the breach of the peace conviction because Cox's activity was protected expression and because the breach of the peace statute under which he was convicted was vague and overbroad:[144] it would have allowed punishment for activities — like "interrupting" or "hindering" — that were protected under the First Amendment. The Court struck down the statute against obstructing public passages because of the unfettered discretion it gave to officials to determine who could demonstrate in public areas and effectively to control what messages were heard in the public forum. The statute was, therefore, overbroad and amounted to a prior restraint by the police.

Cox v. Louisiana (Cox II),[145] a companion case, involved the same demonstration but challenged a statute that prohibited picketing within a certain area of a courthouse. The Court upheld this statute because it was narrowly drawn. The Court found that the state interest in protecting the judicial system from the pressures of a picketing crowd was a "legitimate interest." The conviction, however, was reversed on narrow due process grounds, because the police originally told Cox that he could demonstrate near the courthouse. Cox had been prosecuted for picketing in a place where police specifically had given him permission to be.

In contrast, the Court protected picketing on state house grounds in *Edwards v. South Carolina*.[146] In *Edwards*, the Court did not, however, make clear whether the breach of the peace statute on which the conviction was based was unconstitutionally vague or overbroad, or whether the statute was unconstitutional as applied to state house protests. Whatever difference in treatment these cases exhibit may have been attributable to the difference between the legislative and judicial branches of government. The former is designed to be responsive to public influences, while the latter is designed to uphold the law and not succumb to the pressures of mob rule.

Cox II has been narrowed in *United States v. Grace*.[147] In *Grace*, the Court held a Congressional provision prohibiting the display of any banner or notice on the grounds or in the building of the Supreme Court unconstitutional as it applied to the demonstration of a single person on the public sidewalks around the Supreme Court

---

[142] 379 U.S. 536 (1965) (*Cox I*).

[143] One of the leaders of the demonstration appealed to the demonstrators to sit at segregated lunch counters. The sheriff deemed this inflammatory.

[144] For discussion of vagueness and overbreadth, *see* § 13.05[2].

[145] 379 U.S. 559 (1965).

[146] 372 U.S. 229 (1963).

[147] 461 U.S. 171 (1983).

itself. Defendant held a placard on the sidewalk on the perimeter of the Court's grounds.

While *Grace* may narrow the impact of *Cox II*, its precise impact is difficult to gauge. Not only did the Court fail to distinguish *Cox II*, but the large demonstration adjacent to the courthouse in *Cox II* contrasted sharply with the demonstration at issue in *Grace*.

§ 15.04 THE MODERN APPROACH: LIMITING SPEECH ACCORDING TO THE CHARACTER OF THE PROPERTY

[1] Classifying Public Property into Various Types of Public Forums

The modern Court's public forum analysis is confined to public or government property. Even within the category of government property, there are public forums and non-public forums. Among public forums, there are different types affording different speech rights.

Perry Education Ass'n v. Perry Local Educators' Ass'n[148] is the guideline opinion for modern public forum analysis. In *Perry*, the Court separated public property into various categories of public fora. The Court also determined what regulations the government may impose upon speech in the various categories of public forums. *Perry* developed a rigid "cubby-hole" approach that continues to dominate public forum analysis today.

Perry involved a rival teachers' union, Perry Local Educators' Association (PLEA), that sought to regain access to teachers' mailboxes in the schools. At one time, both the PLEA and the Perry Education Association (PEA) had access to the mailboxes. However, the school board denied the PLEA access after the teachers voted for exclusive representation by the PEA. PLEA contended that the denial of access to the mailboxes was an impermissible restriction based on content. In upholding the school's authority to restrict access, the Court found that rights of access to public property differed depending on the character of the property at issue.

Writing for a 5-4 majority, Justice White categorized public property into three different types of public forums: (1) traditional public forums; (2) public forums by designation; and (3) non-public forums. Traditional public forums included streets, sidewalks, and parks. These areas have immemorially been used to discuss public questions. Permissible restrictions on speech in the traditional public forum were limited. The government could not close these forums off to the public, thereby prohibiting all communicative activity. Content-based exclusions based on the speaker's viewpoint or based on the subject matter of the speech must be "necessary to serve a compelling state interest and narrowly drawn to achieve that

---

[148] 460 U.S. 37 (1983).

end."[149] Lastly, "regulations of the time, place, and manner must be content-neutral and narrowly tailored to serve a significant government interest, and leave open ample alternative channels of communication."[150]

A second category of public forums was the public forum by designation. Public forums by designation consisted of public property that the state had opened up for expressive activity. There were two categories of public forums by designation, general and limited. General public forums by designation were those that the state had opened up for all types of expressive activity. The state could close off public forums by designation at any time. However, as long as it kept them open, the same constitutional restriction on regulations of speech that pertained to traditional public forums also pertained to public forums by designation.

Limited public forums by designation were places that government had opened for speech by certain groups or for certain subjects. The limitations placed on the forum must be related to the character or use of the property. The Court offered examples in *Widmar v. Vincent*,[151] in which a University opened up classrooms to student groups, and in *City of Madison Joint School District v. Wisconsin Employment Relations Commission*,[152] which limited school board access to the subjects of school board business. Otherwise, the same constitutional standards for general public forums by designation also prevailed in limited public forums by designation.

A non-public forum was public property that was neither by tradition nor designation a forum for public communication. In this type of property, the state could impose all restrictions on speech that were reasonable and not an effort to suppress expression based merely on the speaker's viewpoint. Content restrictions based only on viewpoint of the speaker were not allowed, but content restrictions based on subject matter were.

This non-public forum categorization was driven by the Court's concern with the government's role as a provider of services. The First Amendment did not guarantee the exchange of ideas on property simply because it was owned or controlled by the government. When the government acted in its business capacity to serve the public, it needed leeway to operate efficiently.

In *Perry*, the Court found that teachers' mailboxes did not constitute a public forum, partly because no policy of general access was ever granted to the unions. Moreover, allowing certain groups such as the YMCA and the Girl Scouts to place mail in the boxes was not enough to constitute a limited public forum by designation. If the mailboxes were a limited public forum, the *Perry* majority contended that the extent of the forum was limited to entities similar to the groups that had gained access, such as, the YMCA and Girl Scouts. The schools' principals had not opened the mailboxes to groups that dealt with the terms and conditions of employment. The Court found the regulations reasonable because their purpose

---

[149] *Id.* at 45.

[150] *Id.*

[151] 454 U.S. 263 (1981). The case is discussed *infra* § 15.06.

[152] 429 U.S. 167 (1976).

was to prevent the schools from becoming battlefields for inter-union fights. In assessing the reasonableness of the scheme, the Court also noted that PLEA had available ample alternative channels of communication including bulletin boards, meeting facilities, and the United States Mail.

Justice White also held that the distinction in allowing the PEA but excluding the PLEA was not viewpoint discrimination, impermissible even in the non-public forum. Although the PEA had access and it dealt with the terms and conditions of employment, the Court distinguished PEA's access because of its status as official bargainer. Moreover, there was no indication that the school board had intended to discriminate against the PLEA.

The Court treated the mailboxes as a non-public forum in which regulations on speech must be reasonable and not mere viewpoint discrimination. One could argue that allowing the PEA to present its views on terms and conditions of employment while not allowing the PLEA to do so was impermissible viewpoint discrimination. The dissent criticized the majority for differentiating based on the viewpoint of the speaker. Justice Brennan inferred intent to discriminate from the exclusive access policy. He also argued that the reason for the policy was to deny rivals effective communication. The majority reasoned, however, that the School District was not engaging in viewpoint discrimination but, rather, was making distinctions based on the status of the speaker and the character of the property. Arguably, *Perry* protects the speech of political groups which are in power (PEA), while not protecting those that are not in power (PLEA).

In his dissenting opinion in *Greer v. Spock*,[153] decided a few years before *Perry*, Justice Brennan proposed an alternative approach to that of *Perry*. In *Greer*, the Court upheld the denial of access to Socialist Party candidates to give speeches and distribute political literature on a military base. The majority in *Greer* and the majority in *Adderley v. Florida*,[154] which denied protests outside jails, hinted at the *Perry* approach of classifying a particular piece of government property as a public forum or non-public forum.

In contrast to this categorization approach, Justice Brennan's dissent in *Greer* would have taken a more flexible, sliding-scale approach to public forum analysis. According to Justice Brennan, the right to speak never hinged on whether a particular area comprised a public forum. A better, more traditional approach would have been for the Court to examine whether the type of speech at issue was compatible with the activities at the given locale. This dissent encapsulated the sliding scale approach which dominated public forum jurisprudence until several years prior to the *Perry* classification or "cubby-hole" approach.

Cornelius v. NAACP Legal Defense & Educational Fund, Inc.[155] gave further guidance on the *Perry* classification scheme. In particular, *Cornelius* further explained how to determine whether a public forum by designation existed. *Cornelius* involved a government employees' charity drive, the Combined Federal

---

[153]   424 U.S. 828 (1976).

[154]   385 U.S. 39 (1966).

[155]   473 U.S. 788 (1985).

Campaign (CFC). The drive included charities that provided direct health or welfare services to the needy, but excluded the NAACP and other organizations that engaged in advocacy, lobbying, and litigation. Writing for a 4-3 majority, Justice O'Connor held this charitable solicitation to be speech, despite the fact that the CFC conveyed little information beyond the names of the charitable organizations involved. The Court characterized the brochure that solicited the funds for the drive as speech, even though it did not describe the charities but only mentioned them by name. Prior cases treating charitable solicitation as speech generally involved asking for money with additional communication about the particular cause involved.[156] Although the *Cornelius* Court held that charitable solicitation was speech, the Court ultimately found that the government had not created a public forum with this charity drive.

The *Cornelius* Court stated that the government created a public forum by designation only by intentionally opening government property to public discourse. It "does not create a public forum by inaction or by permitting limited discourse, but only by intentionally opening a non-traditional forum for public discourse."[157] The Court would not find a public forum in the face of clear evidence of a contrary intent by the government, nor would it infer such governmental intent or create a public forum when the nature of the property was inconsistent with the expression at issue. In determining the government's intent to designate a public forum, the Court relied on government policies and practices, the nature of the property, and its compatibility with the expressive activity. The government had not evidenced any intent to create an open forum for expression about charitable solicitation. The context of the federal workplace buttressed this conclusion.

In *Cornelius*, the Federal government did not open the forum to all tax-exempt organizations. Allowing access to the CFC was not a ministerial decision. Consistent with *Perry* and other free speech decisions outside the public forum area, the Court emphasized the importance of not interfering with the operations of the government workplace.

Because the CFC was a non-public forum, the government's restrictions needed only to be viewpoint neutral and reasonable in light of the forum's purpose and all of the surrounding circumstances. The President reasonably could conclude that spending money on food and shelter for the needy was more beneficial than litigation. Moreover, evidence existed that some government employees had failed to contribute to the CFC when it had included political and advocacy organizations that were not traditional charities. While avoidance of controversy was not a permissible reason to restrict speech in a public forum, it was a permissible reason to restrict speech in a non-public forum. In a non-public forum, reasonableness must be assessed in light of the circumstances, including the nature of the property. The Court remanded the case to determine whether the government had engaged in viewpoint discrimination, as the government had allowed into the CFC certain groups that did not provide direct health or welfare services, such as the World Wildlife Fund.

---

[156] *See, e.g.,* Village of Schaumburg v. Citizens for a Better Env't, 444 U.S. 620 (1980).

[157] *Cornelius*, 473 U.S. at 802.

The dissent argued that the Court effectively eliminated the category of the limited public forum. Here the government had opened a limited public forum on charitable speech to certain kinds of expressive activities but excluded others, based on the group's viewpoint of how best to serve those in need. Specifically, the government allowed groups to speak who thought that the best way to serve the disadvantaged was to provide services directly, while it prohibited groups from speaking who thought that the best way to serve the disadvantaged was to advance social and political change.

Several cases decided before *Perry* began the trend of limiting access to speak on government property. In *Lehman v. City of Shaker Heights*,[158] the Court found that the regulations restricting political advertisements on buses were permissible even though the City had allowed commercial messages to be exhibited on the buses. Decided before *Perry*, the plurality said that the space for signs on the bus was not a public forum, but instead a commercial activity. In a concurring opinion that provided the crucial fifth vote, Justice Douglas emphasized protecting the captive audience of bus riders. In dissent, Justice Brennan argued that the City preferred certain commercial messages over political debate.

In *Heffron v. International Society for Krishna Consciousness*,[159] the Court upheld a Minnesota state-fair policy restricting to designated booths the solicitation of funds and sale or distribution of literature. Justice White described the restriction as a reasonable time, place, and manner restriction that served the significant government interest of crowd control. The fair was a limited public forum in which many exhibitors temporarily could present their products or views. The booth arrangement was an adequate means to sell or distribute literature or to solicit, leaving other available channels for protected speech that did not involve the solicitation of funds, or the sale or distribution of materials on fairgrounds.

In *U.S. Postal Service v. Council of Greenburgh Civic Ass'ns*,[160] the Court upheld a federal regulation prohibiting the insertion of unstamped mail into mailboxes used to receive mail at private residences. The Court held that mailboxes could not be regarded as public forums.

Perry solidified the process begun in these cases of classifying public forums into several categories. *Perry*, and particularly *Cornelius*, made clear that the government can make the public forum by designation a very small category. In other cases decided after *Perry*, the Court also narrowed access to traditional public forums like parks, streets, and sidewalks.

In *City Council v. Taxpayers for Vincent*,[161] a candidate for mayor challenged a Los Angeles ordinance that prohibited posting posters or placards — even small ones — on utility poles, street lamp posts, etc.[162] The Court examined whether the

---

[158] 418 U.S. 298 (1974).

[159] 452 U.S. 640 (1981).

[160] 453 U.S. 114 (1981).

[161] 466 U.S. 789 (1984).

[162] As quoted by the Court, the Los Angeles ordinance read as follows: Sec. 28.04. Hand-bill, signs-public places and objects:

poles constituted public forums and refused to treat the poles as part of the city streets and sidewalks that were traditional public forums. Treating the poles as non-public forums, the Court upheld the regulations. The regulations were not an effort to suppress expression only because of opposition to the speaker's views. Moreover, they reasonably advanced the City's interest in aesthetics.

Several public forum cases concern zoning requirements involving signs of various sorts that affect the public forum. *Metromedia, Inc. v. San Diego*[163] invalidated a ban on signs except on-site commercial signs used to advertise the occupant's business and except certain on-site and off-site signs displaying noncommercial messages, such as, temporary political campaign signs, signs carrying news items or displaying religious symbols. A plurality objected to the content discrimination that the ordinance made between commercial and noncommercial speech, and between various forms of noncommercial speech.

Several concurring Justices necessary to form a majority treated this as a total ban on outdoor advertising. They said that the City's proffered interests in aesthetics and traffic safety were not sufficient to justify the broad ban on First Amendment rights. The plurality also hinted that it might also have invalidated the law on this ground.[164]

In *City of Ladue v. Gilleo*,[165] the Court held that a city ordinance which banned all residential signs, with narrowly-tailored exemptions, violated a homeowner's right to free speech. Addressing the two analytical strands from *Metromedia Inc. v. San Diego*,[166] Justice Stevens stated that the Court must first ask whether Ladue could prohibit all signs, and secondly, only if necessary, consider whether it was improper for Ladue to permit exemptions for certain residential signs such as religious and commercial signs.

Taking the total ban first, the Court did note the significant government interest in minimizing "visual clutter." However, the comprehensive nature of the city of Ladue's virtually complete ban on residential signs intensified its detrimental impact on the free communication of political, religious, and personal messages by residents. Moreover, Justice Stevens found the restriction at issue to have "foreclosed a venerable means of communication that is both unique and important" and for which there was no viable alternative.[167]

The decision did not leave the City powerless to regulate residential signs. Other considerations might apply in a case, for example, where residents displayed

---

(a) No person shall paint, mark or write on, or post or otherwise affix, any hand-bill or sign to or upon any sidewalk, crosswalk, curb, curbstone, street lamp post, hydrant, tree shrub, tree stake or guard, railroad trestle, electric light or power or telephone or telegraph or trolley wire pole, or wire appurtenance thereof or upon any fixture of the fire alarm or police telegraph system or upon any lighting system, public bridge, drinking fountain, life buoy, life preserver, life boat or other life saving equipment, street sign or traffic sign.

[163] 453 U.S. 490 (1981).

[164] For additional discussion of this case, *see infra* § 16.04[1].

[165] 512 U.S. 43 (1994).

[166] 453 U.S. 490 (1981).

[167] *Gilleo*, 512 U.S. at 54.

political or other signs for a fee or residential signs advertising off-site commercial enterprises. Off-site signs afford less incentive to protect against visual clutter. Even for residential signs, government could regulate to eliminate obstruction or other harms.

In *Burson v. Freeman*,[168] the Court upheld a Tennessee statute that prohibited the solicitation of votes and the display or distribution of campaign materials within 100 feet of the entrance to a polling place. Justice Blackmun, writing for a plurality of four with only eight Justices participating, acknowledged that the Tennessee statute at issue barred speech in a "quintessential public forum."[169] However, he also noted that, even in a quintessential public forum, government could impose time, place, and manner restrictions on expressive activity, provided such restrictions "are *content-neutral*, are narrowly tailored to serve a significant government interest, and leave open ample alternatives for communication."[170]

The statute at issue in *Burson*, however, was *not* a facially content-neutral time, place, or manner restriction and, therefore, it was subjected to strict scrutiny: "The State must show that the 'regulation is necessary to serve a compelling state interest and that it is narrowly drawn to achieve that end.' "[171]

Attempting to weigh Tennessee's asserted interest in protecting the rights of its citizens to vote freely, with the individual right to engage in political discourse, Justice Blackmun held that Tennessee's regulation was a "rare case in which we have held that a law survives strict scrutiny."[172] Justice Blackmun's historical analysis revealed "a persistent battle against two evils: voter intimidation and election fraud," both of which justified the regulation.[173]

In his concurring opinion, Justice Kennedy stated that First Amendment interests occasionally had to yield to protect a narrow range of competing constitutional rights. The free speech interests at issue had to yield to accommodate the fundamental right to vote.

Concurring in the judgment, Justice Scalia would have upheld the statute on the grounds that "streets and sidewalks around polling places have traditionally not been devoted to assembly and debate."[174] Consequently, the areas around polling places did not constitute traditional public forums. Justice Stevens dissented, joined by Justices O'Connor and Souter. Justice Stevens argued that the statute failed to withstand strict scrutiny. Campaigning outside the polls was a "minor nuisance" that was important for a "vibrant democracy."[175]

---

[168] 504 U.S. 191 (1992).

[169] Public forums included places " 'which by long tradition or by government fiat have been devoted to assembly and debate,' such as parks, streets and sidewalks." *Id.* at 196 (citing *Perry Educ. Ass'n v. Perry Local Educators' Ass'n*, 460 U.S. 37 (1983)).

[170] *Id.* at 197 (emphasis added). *See* Ward v. Rock Against Racism, 491 U.S. 781 (1989).

[171] *Id.* at 198 (quoting *Perry Educ. Ass'n v. Perry Local Educators' Ass'n*, 460 U.S. 37, 45 (1983)).

[172] *Id.* at 211.

[173] *Id.* at 206.

[174] *Id.* at 215 (Scalia, J., concurring in the judgment) (emphasis added).

[175] *Id.* at 228 (Stevens, J., dissenting).

In *Arkansas Educational Television Commission v. Forbes*,[176] the Court determined that a state-owned public television station was a non-public forum and that the station's decision to exclude a congressional candidate from a televised debate was a "reasonable, viewpoint neutral exercise of journalistic discretion."[177] Public broadcasters are typically immune from viewpoint discrimination claims because they must utilize a significant amount of editorial discretion. Were they not insulated from such claims, even "principled" programming decisions could be characterized as "viewpoint based."[178]

A candidate debate comprises a "narrow exception" to the public broadcasters' immunity because it differs from general broadcasting in affording candidates an opportunity to express their own views without modification by the broadcaster. Debates also differ significantly from other broadcasting because they are the only occasions when the nation focuses on an election. While the candidate debate at issue was a forum, it was a nonpublic forum. The debate was not a designated public forum as government did not intend "to make the property 'generally available.' "[179] The Arkansas Educational Television Commission made the same kind of candidate-by-candidate determinations comparable to the charity-by-charity determinations made in *Cornelius* after charitable organizations in general had been allowed to participate.

Had candidate debates been classified public forums, the broadcaster would have had to accept the participation of any eligible candidate, and some recent Presidential and Congressional elections have had as many as 11 to 22 eligible candidates on a ballot. The Court concluded that plaintiff was excluded not because of his viewpoint, but because he had generated no appreciable public interest. Moreover, the public station's decision to exclude plaintiff was reasonable, in part because neither the voters nor the news media considered him a serious candidate.

Justice Stevens dissented, joined by Justices Souter and Ginsburg. He argued that AETC's decision to exclude Forbes was standardless, as access to state-sponsored debates had not been based upon preset criteria. Justice Stevens also maintained that Forbes, while not previously elected, had enjoyed substantial public support in earlier elections. As AETC invited all " 'viable' " or " 'newsworthy' " candidates as AETC itself maintained, AETC created a limited public forum by designation.[180]

In *United States v. Kokinda*,[181] the Court held that the U.S. Postal Service could prohibit solicitation on sidewalks located entirely on postal property. The sidewalk at issue ran from the Post Office building to the Post Office parking lot, thereby distinguishing it from the sidewalk adjacent to a city street. A plurality of four emphasized the government's role as a proprietor managing its internal operations. Even though the government had allowed limited discourse on the

---

[176] 523 U.S. 666 (1998).

[177] *Id.* at 669.

[178] *Id.* at 674.

[179] *Id.* at 679.

[180] For additional discussion of *Forbes, see supra* § 14.07[1].

[181] 497 U.S. 720 (1990).

sidewalk in the past, it had not created even a limited public forum because it had not intentionally opened a nontraditional forum for public discourse. Compelling government to treat all categories of speech equally in a non-public forum would "create, in the name of the First Amendment, a disincentive for the government to dedicate its property to any speech activities at all."[182] Concurring in the judgment, Justice Kennedy construed the regulation as a narrow restriction on the solicitation of the immediate payment of money. As such, he upheld it as a reasonable time, place, and manner restriction irrespective of whether the sidewalk was a public or a non-public forum.

In *International Society for Krishna Consciousness, Inc. v. Lee*,[183] the Court upheld a ban on solicitation in airports, finding that airports were not traditional public forums. Airports have not been used from time immemorial as avenues for expressive activity. The Court also distinguished other transportation facilities like railway stations and bus terminals on the ground that they were traditionally privately owned. Moreover, airports were a comparatively new mode of transportation. The terminals were not public forums by designation, as the government only intended that they facilitate patron transportation to terminals. The anti-solicitation statutes were not merely aimed at viewpoint and were reasonable, as the ban protected airport patrons against the disruption of the in-person solicitation.[184]

A different majority struck down a ban on leafletting in airports. Four dissenters would have held airports public forums. Supplying the crucial fifth vote to invalidate the leafletting ban, Justice O'Connor found the ban unreasonable even in a nonpublic forum.

In *Pleasant Grove City, Utah v. Summum*,[185] the Court held that public forum analysis does not apply to the display of a permanent monument in a public park which "is a traditional public forum for speeches and other transitory acts."[186] A permanent monument placed in a public park is a form of government speech which is, consequently, not protected speech.

Summum, a religious organization, sought to display a stone monument of "the Seven Aphorisms of SUMMUM" that was similar in size and nature to a Ten Commandments monument in the park that had been previously donated by another private group. The city denied authorization.

Justice Alito explained that the Constitution "restricts government regulation of private speech"[187] not of government speech. Restraints do exist on government speech; for example, it cannot violate the Establishment Clause. Moreover, public

---

[182] *Id.* at 733.

[183] 502 U.S. 1022 (1992).

[184] While airports were not public forums, the Court has held that a regulation banning all First Amendment activity in the airport was facially overbroad. *See* Board of Airport Comm'rs v. Jews for Jesus, 482 U.S. 569 (1987).

[185] 129 S. Ct. 1125 (2009).

[186] *Id.*

[187] *Id.* at 1131.

officials involved "in advocacy may be limited by law, regulation, or practice."[188] Ultimately, the electorate oversees all government speech.

"Permanent monuments displayed on public property typically represent government speech."[189] Both government-financed and privately financed or donated monuments displayed on public property are government speech.

By selecting certain monuments that contain "such content-based factors as esthetics, history, and local culture" government conveys "a government message."[190]

The City maintained approval authority over all permanent monuments in the Park and, also owns most of them, including the Ten Commandments. While a public park is a traditional public forum, this doctrine applies when government property or government programs are "capable of accommodating a large number of public speakers without defeating the essential function of the land or the program. For example, a park can accommodate many speakers and, over time, many parades and demonstrations."[191] Applying the viewpoint neutrality requirement in traditional public forums to monuments would require government to display either all or no donated monuments. Consequently, most parks would effectively have to refuse all such donations.

Concurring, Justice Stevens, joined by Justice Ginsburg, stated that the decision does not give government broad discretion to communicate "offensive or partisan messages."[192] Even if the Constitution "neither restricts nor protects government speech, government speakers,"[193] government remains bound by its other restrictions including the Establishment and Equal Protection Clauses.

Concurring, Justice Scalia, joined by Justice Thomas, noted that *Van Orden v. Perry*[194] rejected an Establishment Clause challenge to a "virtually identical Ten Commandments monument"[195] with all the Justices agreeing that "government speech was at issue."[196]

Concurring, Justice Breyer maintained that the government speech doctrine had limits. For example, government may not be able to select monuments based on reasons "unrelated to the display's theme, say solely on political grounds."[197]

Concurring in the judgment, Justice Souter agreed that the monument at issue was government speech, but rejected "the position that public monuments are

---

[188] *Id.* at 1132.

[189] *Id.*

[190] *Id.* at 1134.

[191] *Id.* at 1137.

[192] *Id.* at 1139 (Stevens, J., concurring).

[193] *Id.*

[194] 545 U.S. 677 (2005).

[195] *Summum*, 129 S. Ct. at 1139 (Scalia, J., concurring).

[196] *Id.* at 1139.

[197] *Id.* at 1140 (Breyer, J., concurring).

government speech categorically."[198] He would "try to keep the inevitable issues open"[199] at the intersection between the government speech doctrine and the Establishment Clause.

[2] Reasonable Time Place and Manner Restrictions

Once one does have a public forum, *Perry* defined what restrictions government could impose on speech in that public forum. Among the most important were reasonable time, place, and manner restrictions. *Perry* set forth the standard for these restrictions. As previously noted, *Perry* required that they be content neutral, narrowly tailored to serve a significant government interest, and leave open ample alternative channels of communication. Other decisions have afforded additional guidance on the scope of permissible time, place, and manner restrictions.

Once the Court finds that a place is a traditional public forum, it is very protective. Recall that in *United States v. Grace*,[200] the Court held unconstitutional a congressional ban on expression on sidewalks bordering the streets surrounding the Supreme Court building. The Court found a total ban to be an unreasonable time, place, and manner restriction.

Similarly, in *Boos v. Barry*,[201] the Court struck down an absolute ban on demonstrations within 500 feet of a foreign embassy. The Court held that this was an overbroad regulation in a traditional public forum. The Court also rejected a "secondary effects" justification for the ban noting that the secondary effects doctrine was confined generally to offensive speech. Moreover, the secondary effects test was content neutral. However, in *Boos*, the government justified its ban on embassy demonstrations on the basis that the speech criticized a foreign government.

In *Clark v. Community for Creative Non-Violence*,[202] the Court upheld a National Park Service ban on sleeping in the parks as a content-neutral time, place, and manner restriction. The Court upheld this restriction against a challenge by homeless persons who wanted to sleep in the park to demonstrate their plights. The homeless argued that possible injury to the parks could have been averted by restricting the duration, size, or frequency of the demonstration. The Court retorted that the judiciary would not second guess park officials as to the appropriate level of protection or how best to achieve it. Moreover, the protestors could have communicated their messages in other ways.

In *Ward v. Rock Against Racism*,[203] the Court upheld sound amplification restrictions as reasonable time, place, and manner restrictions. The Court explicated the "narrowly-tailored" language in *Perry* as not requiring "the least

---

[198] *Id.* at 1141 (Souter, J., concurring in the judgment).

[199] *Id.* at 1142.

[200] 461 U.S. 171 (1983).

[201] 485 U.S. 312 (1988).

[202] 468 U.S. 288 (1984).

[203] 491 U.S. 781 (1989).

restrictive means" available to government or even the most appropriate means available. In this connection, the Court specifically indicated that means would pass the narrowly tailored analysis even if other means would better serve the government's interests. Government's interests must have been better served with the regulation than without it, and the regulation must not have been substantially broader than necessary to achieve the governmental objective. The band criticized both the volume control itself and the discretion the City's guidelines afforded government in determining the appropriate volume.

On the narrowly tailored prong, the Court reiterated that the City's interests were better served with the Guidelines than without them. The Court also explicated the requirement that alternative means of communication be left open. Restrictions on the volume of speech did not violate this requirement as they did not alter the quantity or content of speech. Such restrictions could even diminish the audience, so long as a showing was made that alternative channels of communication were inadequate. Both *Ward* and *Clark* represent relatively rare examples of permissible manner restrictions. Particularly as the Court protects the emotive quality of speech, restrictions on the manner of speaking can easily shade into content-based restrictions.

In *Frisby v. Schultz*,[204] the Court addressed the issue of whether a content-neutral ban "before or about" a residence was constitutional. The Court construed the law as prohibiting "only focused picketing taking place solely in front of a particular residence."[205] Thus, the Court held that it was constitutional to prohibit the picketing by abortion opponents outside the home of a physician who performed abortions. The Court viewed the law as a content-neutral time, place, and manner restriction that was "narrowly tailored to serve a significant government interest, and leave open ample alternative channels of communication." However, in *Madsen v. Women's Health Center, Inc.*,[206] the Court clearly indicated that laws or injunctions that prohibit picketing within 300 feet of certain residences were unconstitutional as they burdened more speech than necessary and lacked sufficient justification.

In *Madsen*, the Court upheld an injunction placing certain restrictions on protests around abortion clinics. The Court distinguished between injunctions and "generally applicable statutes." Chief Justice Rehnquist stated that "there are obvious differences . . . between an injunction and a generally applicable ordinance" and that "these differences require a somewhat more stringent application of general First Amendment principles in this context."[207] The Court did not deem standard time, place, and manner analysis to be "sufficiently rigorous." Instead, the Court inquired "whether the challenged provisions of the injunction burden no more speech than necessary to serve a significant government interest."[208]

---

[204] 487 U.S. 474 (1988).

[205] *Id.* at 483.

[206] 512 U.S. 753 (1994).

[207] *Id.* at 765.

[208] *Id.* at 765.

Accordingly, the Court upheld part of a Florida court injunction which, among other things, prohibited "singing, chanting, whistling, shouting, yelling, use of bullhorns, auto horns, sound amplification equipment or other sounds or images observable to or within earshot of the patients inside" an abortion clinic "from 7:30 until noon, on Monday through Saturdays, during surgical procedures and recovery periods."[209] Chief Justice Rehnquist held that the noise restrictions burdened no more speech than necessary to protect patient well-being.

However, the Court did invalidate applying the 36-foot buffer zone to the back and side of the clinic as not advancing the State's interest in vehicular traffic. The Court also struck down as unconstitutional the part of the injunction that prohibited picketing, demonstrating, or using sound amplification equipment within 300 feet of the residences of any abortion clinic's employees, staff, owners, or agents. The Court struck down the injunction not because it was content-based, but rather because it lacked sufficient justification. Instead, "a limitation of the time, duration of picketing, and number of pickets outside a smaller zone could have accomplished the desired the result."[210]

Justice Scalia, joined by Justices Kennedy and Thomas, concurred and dissented in part. Referring to the injunction against demonstrators at the clinic, Justice Scalia stated that, "the judicial creation of a 36-foot zone in which only a particular group, which had broken no law, cannot exercise its rights of speech, assembly and association, and the judicial enactment of a noise prohibition, applicable to that group and that group alone, are profoundly at odds with our First Amendment precedents and traditions."[211] Justice Scalia stated that the injunction in *Madsen* amounted to a content-based prior restraint.

He took issue with the standard that the majority had implemented, believing that the injunction at issue deserved, at the very least, "strict scrutiny." This was so for three reasons. First, this "injunction was sought against a single-issue advocacy group by persons and organizations with a business or social interest in suppressing that group's point of view." Second, injunctions were products of "individual judges rather than of legislatures." Freedom of expression "should not lightly be placed within the control of a single man or woman." Third, "the injunction is a much more powerful weapon than a statute, and so should be subjected to greater safeguards."[212]

The injunction was unconstitutional even under the standard the majority had implemented,. The "significant interest" that the majority had purportedly attempted to protect was, in Justice Scalia's view, not in need of protection as there was no evidence of prior violations. In addition, the second part of the majority's test, that the injunction "burden no more speech than necessary," was not met. In support of his opinion, Justice Scalia presented several options that the Court could have implemented, but did not: "the Court could have (for the first time) ordered the demonstrators to stay out of the street (the original injunction did not

---

[209] *Id.* at 772.

[210] *Id.* at 775.

[211] *Id.* at 785 (Scalia, J., concurring in part and dissenting in part).

[212] *Id.* at 793.

remotely require that). It could have limited the number of demonstrators permitted on the clinic side of" the street. "And it could have forbidden the pickets to walk on the driveway."[213]

In conclusion, Justice Scalia stated that "the notion that injunction against speech need not be closely tied to any violation of law, but may simply implement sound social policy; and the practice of accepting trial-court conclusions permitting injunctions without considering whether those conclusions are supported by any findings of fact — these latest by-products of our abortion jurisprudence ought to give friends of liberty great concern."[214]

In *Schenck v. Pro-Choice Network*,[215] the Court upheld provisions of a District Court injunction that imposed "fixed buffer zone" restrictions on demonstrations outside abortion clinics. However, the Court struck down the injunction's "floating buffer zone" restrictions as violating the First Amendment. The fixed buffer zone prohibited demonstrating within 15 feet around any doorway, driveway, or other entrance of an abortion clinic. The floating buffer zone prohibited demonstrating " 'within fifteen feet of any person or vehicle seeking access to or leaving' " an abortion clinic.[216] Two sidewalk counselors could stay in the buffer zones to talk with those entering or leaving the clinic. Once an individual indicated that she did not want counseling, the counselors had to stop counseling, retreat 15 feet from the people having been counseled, and remain outside the buffer zones.

The Court applied the test from *Madsen* to ascertain whether these provisions "burdened more speech than necessary" to advance the government's interests.[217] The government's interests in ensuring public order and safety, protecting property, facilitating street and sidewalk traffic, and "protecting a woman's freedom to seek pregnancy-related services" were sufficient to underpin "an appropriately tailored injunction to allow unimpeded access to the clinics."[218]

Applying these standards, the floating buffer zones burdened speech more than was necessary to serve the government's interests. With the exception of the two sidewalk counselors, the floating buffer zones completely prevented defendants from conversing at a normal distance with or handing leaflets to persons on public sidewalks entering or leaving clinics. Using a traditional public forum to distribute leaflets and express views on a controversial issue lies at the heart of the First Amendment. The 17-foot sidewalk at one of the plaintiff's clinics illustrates the onerous nature of floating buffer zones. Unless an individual entering or leaving the clinic walked along one edge of the sidewalk, protesters would have to walk in the street. Moreover, the uncertainties accompanying floating buffer zones risked a chilling effect on much more speech than the injunction prohibited. Similarly, the floating buffer zone around vehicles unconstitutionally burdened the ability of

---

[213] *Id.* at 813.

[214] *Id.* at 815.

[215] 519 U.S. 357 (1997).

[216] *Id.* at 367.

[217] *Id.* at 373.

[218] *Id.* at 375–76.

sidewalk picketers to "chant, shout, or hold signs peacefully."[219]

However, the Court did uphold the fixed buffer zones around doorways, driveways, and other entrances as the record showed that the protesters were impeding access to the clinics. Following *Madsen*, the Court afforded deference to the District Court's "reasonable assessment" that a distance of 15 feet was needed to keep the entrances clear.[220] The Court also refused to invalidate the fixed buffer zones because the District Court had failed to issue an injunction that did not restrict speech before issuing the speech-restrictive injunction. Such non-issuance was only one factor in considering the validity of the speech-restrictive injunction.

The Court also upheld the cease and desist provisions aimed at sidewalk counselors as helping to ensure physical access to the building. In addition, the Court refused to characterize the cease and desist order as content-based. While the order only applied to protesters, they were the only ones who had performed the acts being enjoined.

Justice Scalia, joined by Justices Kennedy and Thomas, concurred in part and dissented in part. Justice Scalia agreed with the majority, that there is no right to be free of unsolicited speech in public while entering or exiting an abortion clinic. However, the District Court predicated its injunction on the rights to be left alone and to be free of unwanted speech, rather than a right to unimpeded access. Consequently, Justice Scalia criticized the majority for basing its decision on postulated rationales rather than those actually used by the District Court.

In *Hill v. Colorado*,[221] the Court upheld a Colorado statute "that regulates speech-related conduct within 100 feet of the entrance to any health care facility."[222] The statute made "it unlawful within the regulated areas for any person to 'knowingly approach' within eight feet of another person, without that person's consent, 'for the purpose of passing a leaflet or handbill to, displaying a sign to, or engaging in oral protest, education, or counseling with such other person.' "[223] However, a stationary protester need not reposition herself if someone passes within the eight feet.

Supporters and opponents of the clinics testified that protests often result in blocked entrances and "confrontational" situations outside abortion clinics. However, no evidence existed that petitioner in this case had exhibited such behavior.

Writing for a majority of six, Justice Stevens said that the government cannot restrict free speech merely because the expression may offend the audience. However, the "recognizable privacy interest in avoiding unwanted communication varies widely in different settings."[224] The Court here was not deciding whether an

---

[219] *Id.* at 380.

[220] *Id.* at 381.

[221] 530 U.S. 703 (2000).

[222] *Id.* at 707.

[223] *Id.*

[224] *Id.* at 716.

individual has the " 'right' to avoid unwanted expression."[225] Instead, the statute's purpose is to guard persons from possible injury, physical or emotional, that an individual might encounter when entering a health facility.

Courts often look for the speaker's purpose by studying the content of the speech, which can show whether the speech is "a threat, blackmail, an agreement to fix prices, a copyright violation, a public offering of securities, or an offer to sell goods."[226] The Colorado statute is "content neutral." It seeks to protect "those who enter a health care facility from the harassment, the nuisance, the persistent importuning, the following, the dogging, and the implied threat of physical touching that can accompany an unwelcome approach within eight feet of a patient."[227]

The statute was a content neutral time, place, and manner restriction, which was narrowly tailored. The 8-foot buffer did not interfere with an effective use of signs. Turning to oral communication, the law did not prohibit amplification equipment. Nor did it restrict the number of protesters or their noise level even though prior cases such as *Madsen v. Women's Health Center*[228] had upheld such restrictions.

In contrast to the 15-foot buffer zone invalidated in *Schenck v. United States*,[229] an 8-foot zone provides "a 'normal conversational distance.' "[230] Moreover, no violation occurred if an individual passed within 8 feet of a stationary protestor. The knowledge requirement protected the speaker who mistakenly did not keep the requisite distance. While the 8-foot buffer did hinder the ability to distribute handbills, a protester could stand "near the path of oncoming pedestrians"[231] to distribute leaflets. Moreover, these restrictions applied "only within 100 feet of a healthcare facility."[232]

Justice Stevens rejected plaintiff's overbreadth argument, stating that "the comprehensiveness of the statute is a virtue, not a vice, because it is evidence against there being a discriminatory governmental motive."[233] In addition, when regulating both speech and conduct, overbreadth must be substantial.

The statute was not "impermissibly vague" because it had a scienter requirement. It only applied to a person who "knowingly" advances within the buffer zone, without consent, for the purpose of engaging in oral protest, education, or counseling. Even more importantly, "speculation about possible vagueness in hypothetical situations" did not "support a facial attack."[234] The prior restraint issue was weaker here than "in *Schenck* and *Madsen* where particular speakers

---

[225] 530 U.S. at 718 n.25.

[226] *Id.* at 721.

[227] *Id.* at 724.

[228] 512 U.S. 1277 (1994).

[229] 249 U.S. 47 (1919).

[230] *Hill*, 530 U.S. at 726–27.

[231] *Id.* at 727.

[232] *Id.* at 730.

[233] *Id.* at 731.

[234] *Id.* at 733.

were at times completely banned within certain zones."[235] The Colorado statute at issue would only affect unwanted contact.

Justice Souter concurred, joined by Justices O'Connor, Ginsburg, and Breyer. Although a person may have the right to communicate unpopular opinions, an individual was not completely free from responsibility for objectionable conduct intended "to shock members of the speaker's audience."[236] Justice Souter found that a reasonable time, place, or manner restriction was justifiable unless it "results in removing a subject or a viewpoint from effective discourse"[237] or the statute was not narrowly tailored. Justice Souter said that a content-based restriction must be enacted "because of the content of the speech"[238] or because the government did not approve of the message expressed. In contrast, the statute at issue protected persons around the facility who did not want to be approached.

Justice Scalia dissented, joined by Justice Thomas. Justice Scalia stated that the Court upheld the content-based law because it advanced abortion rights. The State had particularly targeted "protest, counseling, and education." In addition, for the first time the Court focused on a governmental interest positively repudiated by the State to uphold the statute. The Court claimed the "unwilling listener's interest in avoiding unwanted communication" derived from the " 'right to be let alone.' "[239] However, the State does not have the power to determine what expressions " 'are sufficiently offensive to require protection for the *unwilling listener or viewer*.' "[240]

Justice Scalia also maintained the decision could adversely affect organized labor: Modern free speech jurisprudence did not allow the " 'right to be free' from 'persistent importunity, following and dogging.' "[241]

Justice Scalia maintained that the "real state interest" actually asserted by Colorado was "unimpeded access to health care facilities."[242] In contrast to subsection (3) of the statute which was at issue, subsection (2) was "narrowly tailored" to advance the State's interest: it imposed criminal and civil liability on any person who " 'knowingly obstructs, detains, hinders, impedes, or blocks another person's entry to or exit from a health care facility' " thus rendering subsection (3) unnecessary. The Court "abandoned any pretense at compliance with [the overbreadth] doctrine, and acknowledged — indeed, boasted — that the statute it approves 'takes a prophylactic approach.' "[243]

Justice Kennedy dissented. The statute was a "textbook example" of a content-based law. If faced with a statute "regulating 'oral protest, education, or counseling' within 100 feet of the entrance to any lunch counter, our predecessors

---

[235] *Id.*

[236] *See* United States v. O'Brien, 391 U.S. 367 (1968).

[237] *Hill*, 530 U.S. at 736.

[238] *Id.*

[239] *Id.* at 751 (Scalia, J., dissenting).

[240] *Id.*

[241] *Id.* at 754.

[242] *Id.*

[243] *Id.* at 762.

would not have hesitated to hold it was content based or viewpoint based."[244]

Moreover, the law was "more vague and overly broad than any criminal statute the Court had sustained." For example, " 'protest,' " " 'counseling,' " and " 'education' " are all "imprecise" words.[245]

Justice Kennedy said the majority flips precedent "on its head, stating the statute's overbreadth is 'a virtue, not a vice.' "[246] He termed "whimsical" the operation of the statue. "The happenstance of a dental office being located in a building brings the restricted-speech zone into play,"[247] which would bar an unrelated protest against an environmental group based in the same building. A narrowly tailored statute would have focused on "pinching or shoving or hitting"[248] which could carry criminal and tort liability.

In *Scheidler v. National Organization For Women, Inc.*,[249] the Court held that shutting down an abortion clinic was not considered extortion as protestors had not obtained the property as required by the Hobbs Act. If the protestors' actions constituted extortion, the Court would replace the requirement "that property must be obtained from another"[250] with the idea that extortion could be established by "interfering with or depriving someone of property."[251] Because all of the predicate acts that are necessary to find a RICO violation were reversed, Chief Justice Rehnquist reversed the RICO conviction.

Justice Ginsburg filed a concurring opinion which Justice Breyer joined. She thought that RICO " 'would have been applicable to the civil rights sit-ins' "[252] had " 'illegal force or threats' "[253] stopped business operations. Justice Ginsburg said that RICO had departed from " 'the original conception of its enactors.' "[254] Justice Stevens filed a dissent.

Finally, there are certain procedural steps that protestors may have to undertake to resist even unconstitutional statutory requirements or court orders. Persons generally cannot ignore a permit requirement unless it is invalid on its face.[255] In situations where the claim is that there has been an invalid application of a valid permit requirement, the cases impose limitations on the right of a speaker to ignore the requirement's procedures or judicial restraints on the ability to assemble. Speakers must comply with a valid permit requirement before filing suit. However, a valid permit requirement must provide the opportunity for prompt

---

[244] *Id.* at 767 (Kennedy, J., dissenting).

[245] *Id.* at 773.

[246] *Id.* at 775.

[247] *Id.* at 776.

[248] *Id.* at 777.

[249] 537 U.S. 393 (2003).

[250] *Id.* at 405.

[251] *Id.*

[252] *Id.* at 411 (Ginsburg, J., concurring).

[253] *Id.*

[254] *Id.*

[255] *See* City of Lakewood v. Plain Dealer Publ'g Co. This is discussed *supra* § 15.02.

judicial review of the denial of the permit, and prompt consideration of the merits of the First Amendment claim if a temporary injunction has been issued.[256] A scheme that does not comport with these requirements is invalid on its face. Similarly speakers may not simply ignore a judicial restraint on speech unless it is transparently invalid or frivolous, but must petition to have the restraint set aside on appeal.[257]

[3]　Private Property: Shopping Centers and Company Towns

The question has arisen whether privately-owned property open to the public, such as shopping centers and company towns, should be considered public forums for First Amendment purposes. For private property to be considered a public forum, state action must be present.

Using the public function doctrine, *Marsh v. Alabama*[258] held that First Amendment guarantees applied to a company town. Under this public function doctrine, state action was present when the privately-owned property performs a public function by being an arm of the state. The company, with the permission of the state, had opened up the town property to the public in general and had functioned just like any other town. Thus, the company essentially exercised a public function rendering constitutional prohibitions including the First Amendment, applicable to the company town.

The Court rejected arguments that the company's right to control the inhabitants of its town were coextensive with the right of a homeowner to regulate the conduct of his guests. Ownership did not mean absolute dominion. The more the owner, for his own benefit, opened his property to the public, the more the owner's rights became circumscribed by the statutory and constitutional rights of those who used the property.

Initially, the Court applied the public function doctrine to shopping centers. In *Amalgamated Food Employees Union Local 590 v. Logan Valley*[259] the Court applied the public function doctrine of *Marsh* to find that a shopping center was a public forum. In *Logan Valley*, the state court enjoined union members from picketing in front of an employer's store inside a shopping center. The Supreme Court invalidated the state court injunction that had limited the picketing to public areas outside the center. The majority gave little weight to the property rights of the mall owner. Instead, it analogized the inside of the shopping mall to the downtown shopping district in *Marsh*. The Court also differentiated the shopping center from a private home in that the mall owner lacked a realistic claim of privacy in his mall.

---

[256] *See* Shuttlesworth v. Birmingham, 394 U.S. 147 (1969); Carroll v. President & Comm'rs of Princess Anne, 393 U.S. 175 (1968); Freedman v. Maryland, 380 U.S. 51 (1965); Poulos v. New Hampshire, 345 U.S. 395 (1953).

[257] *See* Walker v. City of Birmingham, 388 U.S. 307 (1967).

[258] 326 U.S. 501 (1946).

[259] 391 U.S. 308 (1968).

After *Logan Valley*, the Court subsequently has refused to use public function doctrine to find state action by shopping malls. In *Lloyd Corp. v. Tanner*,[260] the Court allowed the shopping center to ban five anti-war demonstrators from the mall. The Court distinguished *Logan Valley* as involving labor picketing directed at one store in the shopping center; the picketers had no other way to reach their intended audience. In contrast, the anti-war demonstrators' message had no relation to any purpose for which the shopping center was built and being used.

Subsequently, in *Hudgens v. NLRB*,[261] the Court stated that *Lloyd's* attempt to distinguish *Logan Valley* was based on whether the speech related to labor picketing amounted to content discrimination. The *Hudgens* Court stated that *Lloyd* had in fact overruled *Logan Valley*.[262] The *Hudgens* Court concluded that shopping centers were not public forums because no state action existed. Because shopping centers were private property, the Constitution did not interfere with the mall owners' power to suppress speech, regardless of its relationship to the mall.

Justice Marshall dissented and would apply the public function analysis to shopping centers. He wrote:

> In *Logan Valley* we recognized what the Court today refuses to recognize — that the owner of the modern shopping center complex, by dedicating his property to public use as a business district, to some extent displaces the "State" from control of historical First Amendment forums, and may acquire a virtual monopoly of places suitable for effective communication. The roadways, parking lots, and walkways of the modern shopping center may be as essential for effective speech as the streets and sidewalks in the municipal or company-owned town.[263]

A number of commentators have criticized the Court's decision in *Hudgens* as exalting the property rights of the mall owner over competing rights to freedom of speech.[264]

A state may under state law treat a shopping centers as public forums. The state's ability to do this has been upheld in the face of challenges by mall owners that treating the malls as public forums deprived the owners of property rights under the Fifth Amendment, and privacy or free expression rights under the First Amendment. In *PruneYard Shopping Center v. Robins*,[265] a unanimous Court held that although a speaker had no First Amendment right to use a shopping center as a public forum, states could still recognize such a right under their own constitutions (or presumably other state laws).

---

[260] 407 U.S. 551 (1972).

[261] 424 U.S. 507 (1976).

[262] *Hudgens*, like *Logan Valley*, involved labor picketing.

[263] *Hudgens*, 424 U.S. at 539 (Marshall, J., dissenting).

[264] *See, e.g.*, Dorsen & Gora, *Free Speech, Property, and the Burger Court: Old Values, New Balances*, 1982 Sup. Ct. Rev. 195.

[265] 447 U.S. 74 (1980).

§ 15.05   SPEECH IN PUBLIC SCHOOLS

The extent of protection granted to speech in the public school setting varies. Greater protection has been extended to student expression that is *not* related to curricular or extracurricular activities. Thus, students may express their own opinions as long as they do not "materially and substantially interfere with" the operation or requirements of the school or impinge on the rights of others.[266] Less protection has been granted to student expression that relates to curricular or extracurricular activities.[267]

Tinker v. Des Moines Independent Community School District involved students who were suspended from school for wearing black armbands to protest the Vietnam War. The Court held that the suspensions were an impermissible restriction on the students' free speech rights. The decision was largely driven by the majority's view of schools as a place to exchange ideas. "It can hardly be argued that either students or teachers shed their constitutional rights to freedom of speech or expression at the schoolhouse gate."[268] In dissent, Justice Black emphasized that the purpose of school was to learn and that to advance that purpose, discipline had to be maintained.

The majority found the wearing of armbands to be "closely akin to 'pure speech' " and, therefore, entitled to full protection under the First Amendment. The Court distinguished this case from *United States v. O'Brien*,[269] which provided less protection for the burning of draft cards. The regulation in *O'Brien* focused on the *action* of burning the draft card, while the prohibition at issue in *Tinker* focused on the communicative content of the armbands. Moreover, school officials did not prohibit students from wearing any other symbols, which would make the restriction on the armbands based on its message and content. The Court held that wearing armbands did not materially and substantially interfere with school discipline or school activities.

Tinker was subsequently narrowed by *Hazelwood School District v. Kuhlmeier*.[270] In *Hazelwood*, the Court held that the school newspaper was not a public forum and, therefore, school authorities could censor the student paper as long as their actions were reasonable. The student newspaper was not a public forum as school officials had not demonstrated the intent to transform the newspaper into a forum for public discourse. Although students were given some control over the newspaper's content, the control was just a part of the teaching process. School policies clearly indicated the intent of school officials to retain control.

The Court distinguished *Tinker*, holding that the *Tinker* standard applied to students' own expression on school premises but not to expression by students using the school's resources. The Court viewed public schools as places where teachers

---

[266] Tinker v. Des Moines Indep. Community Sch. Dist., 393 U.S. 503 (1969).

[267] Hazelwood Sch. Dist. v. Kuhlmeier, 484 U.S. 260 (1988).

[268] *Tinker*, 393 U.S. at 506.

[269] 391 U.S. 367 (1968).

[270] 484 U.S. 260 (1988).

imparted knowledge and skills. Consequently, the First Amendment allowed schools to determine the style and content "of student speech in school sponsored expressive activities so long as their actions are reasonably related to legitimate pedagogical concerns."[271] The Court was concerned with the teaching mission of schools and with not placing a school's imprimatur on activities that it disapproved.

Hazelwood substantially narrowed *Tinker*. If *Tinker* applied, the prohibition on expression would likely be invalidated unless discipline or the rights of the other students was materially and substantially affected. If *Hazelwood* applied, the Court would look to see if the official action was reasonable. Because *Hazelwood* extended to all school-sponsored activity, its rule would apply in far more instances than the *Tinker* rule. The differing results in the two cases largely reflected the dual role of schools. They also reflected the decline in protection the Court is willing to extend. Like *Perry*, which was driven by the desire to force government to function as an effective provider of services, *Hazelwood* was driven by the desire to provide school officials efficient authority to convey knowledge.

Board of Education v. Pico[272] invalidated state removal of certain books from libraries of junior and senior high schools. A plurality of three found it significant that none of the books removed were required reading. The plurality found it improper for local school boards to remove books from school libraries simply because they disliked the message, or for political or partisan reasons. However, the plurality would allow school board officials to remove books that were "pervasively vulgar" or not suitable for educational purposes. Justice Blackmun concurred in most of the decision. He would require the school board to demonstrate that it had not removed the books because it disagreed with their viewpoint. Completing the majority of five, Justice White concurred on procedural grounds that the case had come before the Court on summary judgment.

In *Bethel School District No. 403 v. Fraser*,[273] the Court allowed a school to impose penalties on a student who gave a speech nominating a classmate for student government. The speech contained suggestive language and was given before an audience that included 14-year-old students. The Court found the penalties imposed unrelated to any viewpoint discrimination and upheld the disciplinary action of the school. Emphasizing the *in loco parentis* role of the schools, the Court determined that the First Amendment did not prevent schools from determining when lewd and vulgar speech undermined the school's basic educational mission.

In *Morse v. Frederick*,[274] the Court held that schools can restrict student speech that encouraged illegal drug use. In *Morse*, a student was suspended for holding up a sign that read "BONG HiTS 4 JESUS" at the Olympic torch event which students were released from school to attend.[275]

---

[271] *Id.* at 273.

[272] 457 U.S. 853 (1982).

[273] 478 U.S. 675 (1986).

[274] 551 U.S. 393 (2007).

[275] *Id.* at 397.

Chief Justice Roberts wrote the majority opinion, joined by Justices Scalia, Kennedy, Thomas, and Alito. The Court found the banner could be reasonably interpreted to encourage illegal drug use and was not political speech regarding the legalization of marijuana. Further, the student himself did not contend that the banner had any political or religious meaning.

Concurring, Justice Thomas emphasized that *Tinker's* analysis has no basis in the Constitution because it interferes with traditional *in loco parentis* powers that have been held by school officials since the framing period. Also concurring, Justice Alito, joined by Justice Kennedy, noted that restrictions on student speech advocating drug use are "at the far reaches of what the First Amendment permits."[276]

Dissenting, Justice Stevens, joined by Justices Souter and Ginsburg, maintained that the banner did not encourage illegal drug use. The banner's message was motivated by a desire to appear on television and had no meaning. Moreover, the majority's broad holding would restrict students' legitimate First Amendment rights to debate political issues regarding the legalization of drugs. Concurring in part and dissenting in part, Justice Breyer opined that the case should have been decided on grounds other than the First Amendment.

§ 15.06 RELIGIOUS SPEECH IN PUBLIC PLACES

The additional concerns and issues raised by the Establishment Clause make religious speech in public places more complicated than other speech.[277] The fear is that allowing religious speech on public property could be considered an establishment of religion. However, if religious speech is prohibited from public property purely because it is religious, then the government has arguably partaken in content-based distinctions prohibited by the First Amendment.

In two school cases that involved providing student religious groups access to school facilities, the Court had to reconcile the Free Speech and Establishment Clauses. In both cases, the Court reasoned that allowing religious speech on public property did not violate the Establishment Clause.

First, in *Widmar v. Vincent*,[278] the Court held that a public university could not exclude student religious groups from access to university facilities once it had opened its doors to other student groups. In this pre-*Perry* case, the Court found that the university had created a public forum once it had accommodated public meetings for its students. Public universities possessed many of the characteristics of a public forum, at least for its students.[279] The state contended, however, that its content-based ban on religious speech did not violate freedom of speech because the state had a compelling interest in avoiding an Establishment Clause violation.

---

[276] *Id.* at 425 (Alito, J., concurring).

[277] *See* discussion *infra* in Chapter 17.

[278] 454 U.S. 263 (1981).

[279] *Perry* later said that the university in *Widmar* had created a limited public forum for students.

Applying the test of *Lemon v. Kurtzman*,[280] the Court held that accommodating the student religious groups did not violate the Establishment Clause. Allowing religious groups on campus had a secular purpose and did not entangle the state in religious affairs. Moreover, the primary effect of the law did not advance religion. Providing student religious groups access did not convey state approval of any religion. The state would only be admitting religious groups as part of a policy to allow all groups. Because there was no Establishment Clause problem, the state could not justify its exclusionary policy based on the religious content of the student groups.

The Equal Access Act extended *Widmar* to public high schools. Under the Act, once a high school granted access to one non-curricular student organization, school authorities could not exclude any student group because of the content of its speech, including religious student groups. In *Board of Education v. Mergens*,[281] the Court held that a public school's recognition of certain student organizations but not a religious club violated the Act, even though the school had allowed the club to meet on campus.[282] The Court also found that the Equal Access Act did not violate the Establishment Clause. The Court's analysis paralleled that of *Widmar*. The Act served the secular purpose of prohibiting discrimination among various types of speech. Its primary effect did not advance religion in high school. High school students were old enough to appreciate that the Act neutrally required equal access and did not enforce religion.[283] The Court's decision was based only on statutory grounds. The Court declined to address whether the First Amendment required the same result.

In *Lamb's Chapel v. Center Moriches Union Free School District*,[284] a religious group was forbidden from displaying films about child rearing and family values from the Christian perspective on school premises. The school opened its grounds after hours to social and political organizations but not for religious purposes. In striking down this ban, the Court viewed as "a close question" the issue of whether the school premises were a limited public forum. Even as a non-public forum, excluding family films with Christian perspectives comprised unconstitutional viewpoint discrimination as the school allowed subjects like child rearing to be discussed from a secular perspective.

In *Rosenberger v. University of Virginia*,[285] the Court (5-4) held that the University of Virginia violated the Freedom of Speech Clause when it refused to fund a student-run newspaper published with a religious viewpoint. The University allowed recognized student organizations to have their printing costs defrayed by

---

[280] 403 U.S. 602 (1971).

[281] 496 U.S. 226 (1990).

[282] The Court construed non-curricular activity broadly to include organizations like the chess club. The Act said that the recognition of even one non-curricular organization transformed the school into a limited open forum. This statutory definition of a limited open forum was broader than the constitutional definition of a limited public forum specified in *Widmar* which required the government to open a forum for communicative purposes. This would appear to require participation by more than one group.

[283] Nor did the Act foster excessive entanglement between government and religion.

[284] 508 U.S. 384 (1993).

[285] 515 U.S. 819 (1995).

the Student Activities Fund. Having established a public forum in which it encouraged diversity of student views, the University's denial of funding amounted to unconstitutional viewpoint discrimination. This discrimination was not necessary to avoid establishing religion. The University itself did not treat the newspaper as a religious organization. Relying on *Widmar v. Vincent*, the Court found that providing funds to print a student newspaper was no different than providing the funds necessary for providing the meeting space in *Widmar*. Moreover, the funds were paid directly to the printer, not to the student group.[286]

In *Capitol Square Review Board v. Pinette*,[287] the Supreme Court held that a private display of a cross on Capitol Square, a traditional public forum, did not violate the Establishment Clause. While the Board allowed the display of a Christmas tree and menorah, it rejected the Ku Klux Klan's application to display an unattended cross on the grounds during the Christmas season.

Writing for the Court, Justice Scalia relied on *Lamb's Chapel v. Center Moriches Union Free School District* and *Widmar v. Vincent* in rejecting the State's Establishment Clause defense. The Square was open to the public, the display was not state sponsored, and all groups seeking to use the grounds were held to the same application process and terms. Consequently, the State could not invoke an Establishment Clause defense to deny the Klan's application.

The majority, however, could not agree on whether to apply the endorsement test. Writing only for a plurality, Justice Scalia, rejected the application of the "so-called 'endorsement test.' "[288] He stressed the difference " 'between government speech endorsing religion, which the Establishment Clause forbids, and private speech endorsing religion, which the Free Speech and Free Exercise Clauses protect.' "[289] Justice Scalia explained that the State would have violated the Establishment and Speech Clauses if it had given preferential treatment to religious over non-religious displays or favored only certain religious groups. Restricting religious expression because of its proximity to a government body would result in what Justice Scalia called a " 'transferred endorsement test' "[290] — relying on the misperceptions of a hypothetical, reasonable observer. The plurality would permit government to require private disclaimers indicating that government did not endorse the expression.

Concurring in part and in the judgment, Justice O'Connor — joined by Justices Souter and Breyer — asserted that this case was not an exception to the endorsement test as Justice Scalia suggested. Instead, Justice O'Connor insisted that the endorsement test requires the Court to determine whether a reasonable, informed observer would understand the expression as State endorsement of religion. The Court should deem this observer "aware of the history and context of the community and forum in which the religious display appears."[291] In this case,

---

[286] For additional discussion of *Rosenberger, see infra* § 16.03.

[287] 515 U.S. 753 (1995).

[288] *Id.* at 763.

[289] *Id.* at 765.

[290] *Id.* at 767.

[291] *Id.* at 780 (O'Connor, J., concurring).

such an observer would understand that Capitol Square was a traditional public forum. Justice O'Connor would require government itself to include a disclaimer near the private display denying any state sponsorship or endorsement.

Dissenting, Justice Stevens construed the Establishment Clause as creating a strong presumption against religious displays on public property. He was particularly critical of the perception of official endorsement of religion created by a cross placed on public property in front of a Statehouse. In a footnote, he criticized Justice O'Connor's reasonable observer test as simply assuming too much knowledge.

In *Good News Club v. Milford Central School*,[292] the Court reversed a grant for summary judgment that would have allowed a public school to exclude a religious club from using the school's premises for afterschool activities involving Bible lessons. Both parties conceded that "Milford created a limited public forum"[293] by opening up the school's facilities.

Writing for the Court, Justice Thomas said the school's exclusion of the Club constituted "impermissible viewpoint discrimination,"[294] and the restriction was not necessary to avoid an Establishment Clause violation. In reaching its decision, the Court analogized Good News' activities to those at issue in *Lamb's Chapel v. Center Moriches Union Free School District:*[295] the meetings were held after school, the school did not sponsor the activities, and any student could attend the meetings with a parent's permission. Moreover, the school allowed other organizations to use its facilities, as in *Widmar v. Vincent*.[296] The school sought to distinguish these cases based on the presence of elementary school children.

Rejecting the school's Establishment Clause argument, the Court explained that "allowing the Club to speak on school grounds would ensure neutrality, not threaten it."[297] Moreover, the parents who must give consent would not feel "coercive pressure"[298] to participate in Good News' activities. The school argued that impressionable elementary school children would automatically believe that it was endorsing religion since the activities were on school grounds. The Court rejected such a categorical approach and further held that the facts did not support endorsement for the purposes of summary judgment.

First, the Club met after school hours in a special room used by the high school and the middle school, not by elementary school students. Second, the Club's instructors were not schoolteachers. Third, the children who engaged in Good News' activities ranged from ages 6 to 12.[299] The Court concluded that the children would no more likely misperceive the Club's inclusion as endorsement than they

---

[292] 533 U.S. 98 (2001).

[293] *Id.* at 106.

[294] *Id.* at 110–11.

[295] 508 U.S. 384 (1993).

[296] 454 U.S. 263 (1981).

[297] *Good News Club*, 533 U.S. at 119.

[298] *Id.* at 115.

[299] The Equal Access Act did not apply here as it only applies to public secondary schools.

would perceive its exclusion as hostility toward religion. An endorsement inquiry does not involve individual perceptions; instead, it concerns whether the reasonable observer is " 'deemed aware of the history and context of the community and forum.' "[300]

Justice Scalia concurred. Comparing Good News' activities to those engaged in by the Boy Scouts of America, he noted that while the Boy Scouts may advocate " 'morally straight [and] clean' "[301] living, the Club may talk about morality but "may not defend the premise"[302] on which it exists.

Concurring in part, Justice Breyer asserted three points. First, neutrality is only one factor used to examine an Establishment Clause claim. Second, religious endorsement may be the crucial issue in this case. Whether endorsement is perceived depends on such circumstances as the time and nature of the meetings, as well as the children's ages. Third, the majority's holding simply meant the school was not entitled to summary judgment on either its Free Speech or Establishment Clause claim.

Justice Stevens dissented. He categorized religious speech into three parts: religious speech on a particular subject from a particular religious perspective; worship; and "proselytizing or inculcating belief in a particular religious faith."[303] In a limited public forum like the one at issue, the first type of religious speech can exist while excluding the other two types, so long as this is done consistently.

Justice Souter also dissented, joined by Justice Ginsburg. The Club wants to use the school's premises *"for an evangelical service of worship."*[304] The activities in *Widmar* are distinguishable as "the nature of the university campus and the sheer number of activities offered precluded the reasonable college observer from seeing government endorsement."[305] Similarly, *Lamb's Chapel* did not support an endorsement claim because of the time and the diversity of community use. In contrast, Good News is only one of four groups using the school's premises. Moreover, the Club appears to be the only one meeting immediately after school hours.

Christian Legal Society v. Martinez[306] upheld a law school's requirement that a religious student organization accept "all-comers," including students who did not share the group's core religious beliefs.[307] The Court said that the Hastings College of the Law (Hastings) may "condition its official recognition of a student group — and the attendant use of school funds and facilities — on the" group's making membership and leadership available to all students.[308] The Christian Legal Society (CLS) contended that Hastings violated its freedom of speech, freedom of

---

[300] *Good News Club*, 533 U.S. at 119.

[301] *Id.* at 124 (Scalia, J., concurring).

[302] *Id.*

[303] *Id.* at 130 (Stevens, J., dissenting).

[304] *Id.* at 138 (Souter, J., dissenting).

[305] *Id.* at 143.

[306] 130 S. Ct. 2971 (2010).

[307] *Id.* at 2978.

[308] *Id.*

association, and free exercise of religion by refusing CLS " 'Registered Student Organization' " (RSO) status.[309]

The Court treated the RSO as a limited public forum. First, a less restrictive scrutiny applies to both speech and association claims in limited public forums. Second, applying strict scrutiny, which has been applied where laws burden expressive association, would negate the ability of the state to reserve limited public forums for certain groups. Third, precedent has distinguished between government regulations that compel certain actions and those that simply deny government benefits. "Hastings, through its RSO program, is dangling the carrot of subsidy, not wielding the stick of prohibition."[310] The Court distinguished *Hurley v. Irish-American Gay, Lesbian and Bisexual Group of Boston, Inc.*,[311] which invalidated a state law requirement that gay individuals be permitted to march in a St. Patrick's Day parade. *Hurley*, however, involved a traditional public forum, the street.

The Hastings policy was reasonable in light of the RSO forum's function and all of the surrounding circumstances. As "judges lack the on-the-ground expertise and experience of school administrators," courts should "resist 'substitut[ing] their own notions of sound educational policy for those of the school authorities which they review.' "[312] Hastings' "all-comers requirement" ensures that a student is not forced to fund a group that would reject her as a member.[313] Moreover, the all-comers policy " 'encourages tolerance, cooperation, and learning among students.' "[314] It also develops conflict-resolution skills. CLS retains alternative channels to communicate including school facilities, chalkboards, and bulletin boards. Moreover, CLS could also communicate using electronic media or social-networking sites. In fact, the year after CLS lost RSO status, CLS doubled the number of students at its meetings and events.

At bottom, "the *advisability* of Hastings' policy does not control its *permissibility*."[315] In a limited public forum, access restrictions " 'need not be the most reasonable or the only reasonable limitation.' "[316] CLS could not substantiate its concern that the all-comers policy would lead to "hostile takeovers" and "saboteurs."[317] Should such actions occur, "Hastings presumably would revisit and revise its policy."[318]

---

[309] *Id.* at 2979.

[310] *Id.* at 2986 (quoting *Norwood v. Harrison*, 413 U.S. 455, 463 (1973)).

[311] 515 U.S. 557 (1995).

[312] 130 S. Ct. at 2988 (quoting *Bd. of Ed. of Hendrick Hudson Cent. Sch. Dist., Westchester Cty. v. Rowley*, 458 U.S. 176, 206 (1982)).

[313] *Id.* at 2989–90.

[314] *Id.* at 2990 (quoting App. 349).

[315] *Id.* at 2992.

[316] *Id.* (quoting *Cornelius v. NAACP Legal Defense & Ed. Fund, Inc.*, 473 U.S. 788, 808 (1985)).

[317] *Id.*

[318] *Id.* at 2993.

A policy requiring acceptance of all comers was "viewpoint-neutral."[319] While RSOs must drop "access barriers, they may express any viewpoint they wish — including a discriminatory one."[320] CLS's contention that " 'peculiarity, incoherence, and suspect history of the all-comers policy all point to pretext' " may be considered on remand "if, and to the extent, it is preserved."[321]

Concurring, Justice Stevens rejected the dissent's view that Hastings' refusal to exempt CLS from its Nondiscrimination Policy was religious discrimination. While "the *First Amendment* may protect CLS's discriminatory practices off campus, it does not require a public university to validate or support them."[322] A free society must "tolerate" groups who "mistreat Jews, blacks, and women," or in this case, homosexuals. "It need not subsidize them, give them its official imprimatur, or grant them equal access to law school facilities."[323]

Concurring, Justice Kennedy noted that broad diversity in RSOs advanced by the all-comers policy promotes professional, "vibrant dialogue" in a law school.[324] However, CLS would have a substantial claim if it could show that Hastings "adopted or enforced its policy with the intent or purpose of discriminating or disadvantaging a group on account of its views" or "that the all-comers policy was either designed or used to infiltrate the group or challenge its leadership in order to stifle its views."[325]

Justice Alito dissented, joined by Chief Justice Roberts and Justices Scalia and Thomas. "The proudest boast of our free speech jurisprudence is that we protect the freedom to express 'the thought that we hate.' "[326] However, today's decision denies protection for speech "that offends prevailing standards of political correctness in our country's institutions of higher learning."[327] Currently, Hastings recognizes over 60 RSOs; CLS is the only organization that Hastings has ever been denied RSO status. Contrary to the majority's suggestion, the all-comers policy is not viewpoint neutral; instead, it is "a pretext to justify viewpoint discrimination."[328] Overwhelming evidence establishes that CLS was denied RSO status under the school's Nondiscrimination Policy, not the accept-all-comers policy, which first surfaced when a former dean discussed it in a deposition in this case.[329] Before the

---

[319] *Id.*

[320] *Id.* at 2993 n.26.

[321] *Id.* at 2995 (quoting Reply Brief 23).

[322] *Id.* at 2996 (Stevens, J., concurring).

[323] *Id.* at 2998.

[324] *Id.* at 3000 (Kennedy, J., concurring).

[325] *Id.*

[326] *Id.* (Alito, J., dissenting) (quoting *United States v. Schwimmer*, 279 U.S. 644, 654–55 (1929)).

[327] *Id.*

[328] *Id.* at 3001.

[329] The majority refused to focus on the Nondiscrimination Policy as both sides have stipulated to the existence of the all-comers policy. However, CLS did not stipulate that its application had been denied under the accept-all-comers policy or that it even existed in Fall of 2004. The majority did not recognize the binding effect of the answer which admitted that the all-comers policy did not exist when CLS was denied recognition.

accept-all-comers policy was unveiled in July 2005, Hastings routinely registered student organizations whose bylaws limited "membership and leadership positions to those who agreed with the groups' viewpoints."[330]

Although the majority stated that CLS had access to school facilities, CLS was given access only if registered organizations were not using them and was occasionally required to pay, treatment common among other community groups. Moreover, CLS did not flourish after losing RSO status; in the fall of 2005, CLS had seven members.

Refusing registration because CLS's "bylaws impermissibly discriminated on the basis of religion and sexual orientation" constituted viewpoint discrimination on both grounds.[331] Animal rights groups could deny membership to students who advocated animal testing for cosmetics, but CLS is "required to admit avowed atheists."[332]

To encourage diversity, Hastings could permit groups of students, no matter how small, to form the groups they want. "In sum, Hastings' accept-all-comers policy is not reasonable in light of the stipulated purpose of the RSO forum: to promote a diversity of viewpoints 'among' — not within — 'registered student organizations.' "[333]

Since the "argument that Hastings selectively enforces its all-comer policy" was not addressed in the lower courts, the Court could sidestep this issue by remanding it to the Ninth Circuit.[334] Denigrating free speech, the Court's holding "permits small unpopular groups to be taken over by students who wish to change the views that the group expresses."[335]

---

[330] *Id.* at 3004. The Association of Trial Lawyers of America at Hastings required each member to " 'adhere to the objectives of the Student Chapter as well as the mission of ATLA.' " *Id.* (quoting App. to Pet. for Cert. at 110a). Also, student voting membership of Silenced Right was limited to those who " 'are committed' to the group's 'mission' of 'spread[ing] the pro-life message.' " *Id.* (quoting App. to Pet. for Cert. at 142a–143a).

[331] *Id.* at 3010.

[332] *Id.*

[333] *Id.* at 3016 (quoting App. at 216).

[334] *Id.* at 3018.

[335] *Id.* at 3019.

Chapter 16

SPECIAL DOCTRINES IN THE SYSTEM OF FREEDOM OF EXPRESSION

INTRODUCTION

In *Chaplinsky v. New Hampshire*,[1] the Court sketched a two-tiered approach to protection for freedom of expression, dividing speech into two categories: that which received constitutional protection and that which did not. *New York Times v. Sullivan*[2] invited a transition from a comparatively narrow scope of First Amendment protection to a more diffuse and creative application of guarantees for freedom of expression. Citizens sought constitutional protection for such diverse areas as symbolic expression, funding of political campaigns, unconstitutional conditions on government funding, commercial advertising, and obscenity. The Supreme Court has addressed these issues using the paradigm fashioned in *New York Times v. Sullivan*. Rather than classify these areas as protected or unprotected speech, the Court has fashioned tests, tailored to each of these areas, that have protected a tremendous amount of expressive behavior.

Section 16.01 considers constitutional protection for what commentators have called expressive conduct or symbolic speech. The doctrinal foundations were laid in cases arising out of the anti-war, civil rights, and other movements of the 1960s. Section 16.02 examines constitutional protection for contributions and expenditures by political campaigns. Extending constitutional protection to some of these activities has helped to bolster political action committees and has otherwise deeply influenced the political process. Section 16.03 examines what content-and viewpoint-based distinctions government can make in doling out its largess. The abortion counseling case illustrates one early example of this dilemma. Section 16.04 turns to the question of constitutional protection for commercial advertising — including lawyer advertising — an area that traditionally had not received institutional protection. Finally, section 16.05 explores the Court's struggle with the degree of protection appropriate for sexually explicit materials. While the Court rhetorically has steadfastly refused to extend constitutional protection to materials that are actually obscene, it has wavered on the extent of protection for sexually explicit materials — for some time in effect affording nearly absolute protection — and more recently affording somewhat less.

---

[1] *See supra* § 15.01.

[2] *See supra* § 14.08.

§ 16.01 EXPRESSIVE CONDUCT

In simple terms, "expressive conduct," often used interchangeably with the term "symbolic speech," refers to the communication of ideas through one's conduct. Expressive conduct raises some interesting constitutional questions because it combines expression, which typically receives First Amendment protection, and conduct, which typically does not. Legislatures may resort to regulation of conduct as a pretext for suppressing ideas. Alternatively, even well-intentioned legislatures may find it impossible to restrict unacceptable conduct without also infringing on the free exchange of ideas incidental to that conduct. This reality imposes difficult choices on courts. Theoretically, courts could extend to expressive conduct approximately the same level of protection as they afford pure speech, or give expressive conduct no protection whatsoever. Predictably, the Supreme Court has rejected both of these rather extreme courses, as each fails to recognize that symbolic speech combines expression and conduct. This dualistic nature may account for the Court's posture of affording expressive conduct some constitutional protection but substantially less protection than pure speech.

Allowing legislatures some latitude to restrict conduct that expresses an idea makes sense. For example, one would certainly allow government to punish a motorist who ran a red light even if she did so to protest the existence of traffic signals. On the other hand, one would not allow government to single out for punishment only those motorists who run stoplights as a form of protest. This latter position would essentially punish people for their expression rather than their action. While these two propositions would generate broad agreement, many others would generate more controversy. The Supreme Court faced such problems in *United States v. O'Brien.*[3] Although it subsequently struggled with these issues and for a time wavered in its jurisprudential approach, the *O'Brien* analysis now has considerable influence.

In *O'Brien*, the defendant was arrested for burning his draft card in front of a crowd on the steps of the Boston Courthouse as a form of protesting the draft. He was prosecuted under a federal statute that made it illegal knowingly to destroy or mutilate a draft card. O'Brien claimed that the burning of draft cards should receive constitutional protection as expressive conduct.

The Court held that O'Brien's actions were not constitutionally protected. Chief Justice Warren opined that "when 'speech' and 'non-speech' elements are combined in the same course of conduct, a sufficiently important governmental interest in regulating the non-speech element can justify incidental limitations on First Amendment freedoms."[4] Chief Justice Warren fashioned the following four-part test which attempted to balance these competing concerns. A government regulation is sufficiently justified:

(1) if it is within the constitutional power of the Government;

(2) if it furthers an important or substantial governmental interest;

---

[3] 391 U.S. 367 (1968).

[4] *Id.* at 376.

(3) if the governmental interest is unrelated to the suppression of free expression;

(4) and if the incidental restriction on alleged First Amendment freedoms is no greater than is essential to the furtherance of that interest.[5]

This has become the basic test for analyzing constitutional protection for expressive conduct. In applying this test, Chief Justice Warren determined that Congress possessed the authority to enact this law under its Article I, § 8 power to raise and support armies. Because the Court consistently has afforded Congress broad regulatory power under Article I, few congressional statutes would fail this part of the test. However, some exercises of legislative power by the President,[6] or certain regulations of interstate commerce by state governments,[7] would be more vulnerable under this first part of the test.

Turning to the second prong of the test, the Court found that prohibiting the destruction and mutilation of draft cards implicated important governmental interests. First, the cards advanced the just and efficient administration of the draft in helping to determine whether a person had registered for it. The cards could be particularly useful in times of crisis in our mobile society. Second, the cards facilitated communication with local draft boards. Third, the cards reminded their holders of their obligations to notify their draft boards of changes of address and status. Fourth, prohibiting alteration or other mutilation helped to prevent the draft cards from being forged or otherwise used deceptively.

In its analysis, the Court did not discuss in detail the last two requirements of the test. It rejected the defendant's contention that Congress passed the regulation at issue for the impermissible purpose of suppressing free speech. Moreover, although the Court found the legislative purpose to be fundamentally indeterminate, it did believe that the regulation was aimed at the maintenance of an effective draft and that the regulation was "narrowly tailored" to effectuate that government interest. Chief Justice Warren indicated that, even were the Court able to discern the legislature's motives, it would not strike down a facially constitutional law based on an improper Congressional purpose.[8]

The test in *O'Brien* was an attempt by the Court to provide some degree of protection for behavior that combined elements of speech and conduct. Thomas Emerson described this gray area as the middle region of his speech/conduct continuum. He found that there was "a fundamental distinction between belief, opinion and communication of ideas on the one hand, and different forms of conduct on the other."[9] According to Emerson, expression should be protected and freely allowed, whereas action could be controlled subject to constitutional requirements. In order to determine whether a particular behavior more closely approximated

---

[5] *Id.* at 377.

[6] *See, e.g., Youngstown*, 343 U.S. 579 (1952).

[7] *See* Chapter 5.

[8] In other contexts, the Court has since been more willing to examine legislative purpose in enacting legislation. *See, e.g.,* Wallace v. Jaffree, 472 U.S. 38 (1985) (Establishment Clause), and Kassel v. Consolidated Freightways Corp., 450 U.S. 662 (1981) (state regulation of interstate commerce).

[9] T. EMERSON, THE SYSTEM OF FREEDOM OF EXPRESSION 8 (1970).

speech or action, Emerson analyzed several factors. He looked to see the context in which the words were spoken; whether the behavior had a tendency to cause violence; whether the behavior was intended as speech or action by the speaker; and how it was perceived by the audience. Finally, he looked to see if the government regulation focused on the speech or the action element.[10]

In *Spence v. Washington*,[11] the Court set aside a conviction for using tape to form a peace symbol on the American flag in violation of a state law forbidding the exhibition of an American flag to which figures, symbols, and other extraneous materials were attached. This case did not raise the issue of the government's property right in the flag because the case involved the display of a privately owned flag on private property.

The Court in *Spence* found that the defendant's actions were a form of protected expression. The Court did not apply the *O'Brien* test because the state's interest was in preserving the flag as a national symbol, and this interest directly focused on regulating expression. Since the government did not assert another governmental interest unrelated to expression, the Court stated that the *O'Brien* test was inapplicable.[12]

In *Tinker v. Des Moines Independent Community School District*,[13] three students were suspended after they wore black armbands at school in protest of the Vietnam War. Justice Fortas, writing for the majority, found that the students' behavior was "akin to 'pure speech.' "[14] As a result, the Court did not use the *O'Brien* analysis because *O'Brien* involved speech plus conduct. The Court could not find any evidence that the wearing of the armbands interfered with the operation of the school or the rights of other students.

Some commentators construed *Spence* and *Tinker* as a shift away from the *O'Brien* test and towards the application of a balancing approach used in cases prior to *O'Brien*. To the extent that these cases may have signaled a move away from the *O'Brien* test,[15] *Clark v. Community for Creative Non-Violence*[16] and other more recent cases illustrate that the four-prong *O'Brien* test is ascendant once again.

In *Clark*, a group of homeless people sought to protest in Washington, D.C. by sleeping in tent cities set up in the National Park across from the White House and in the Mall. The Court assumed for purposes of this decision that sleeping in the park was expressive conduct entitled to some First Amendment protection.[17] The Court used both expressive conduct and public forum analysis to uphold the

---

[10] *See id.* at 7–8, 17–18, 80–81.

[11] 418 U.S. 405 (1974).

[12] *See id.* at 414 n.8.

[13] 393 U.S. 503 (1969). For additional discussion of *Tinker, see supra* § 15.05.

[14] *Id.* at 507.

[15] *See* Texas v. Johnson, 491 U.S. 397 (1989).

[16] 468 U.S. 288 (1984).

[17] The majority specifically stated that it did not differ with the conclusion of the Court of Appeals that sleeping in the park constituted expressive conduct.

government's regulation prohibiting camping in non-designated National Parks as a reasonable manner restriction.

Applying the test for time, place, and manner restrictions established in *Perry Education Ass'n v. Perry Local Educators' Ass'n*,[18] the Court found the content neutral regulation narrowly tailored to advance the government's substantial interest in conserving the parks.[19] For similar reasons, the Court also upheld the regulation under the *O'Brien* test. Justice White rejected the position of the Court of Appeals that the regulation must be the least restrictive means of protecting the government's interest under the fourth prong of the *O'Brien* test. Instead, he afforded the Park Service considerable discretion in its selection of means. Interestingly, Justice White described the four-prong test of *O'Brien* as similar to the analysis used for time, place, and manner restrictions.[20]

The issue of what constitutional protection expressive conduct merits has most recently been debated in the flag burning cases. The Court had previously addressed the issue of flag desecration in *Spence v. Washington*. In an earlier case, *Street v. New York*,[21] the Court reversed a conviction for burning a flag while shouting " 'we don't need no damn flag.' "[22] The 5-4 majority said that the record was unclear as to whether defendant had been convicted for the act of burning the flag or for uttering the words while burning the flag.

In *Texas v. Johnson*,[23] the defendant burned an American flag at a political demonstration outside of the Republican National Convention in Dallas. He was convicted under a State law that prohibited the desecration of the flag.[24] Texas conceded that the defendant's flag burning involved expressive conduct as it was done in connection with a political protest. To justify its prohibition, Texas proffered two government interests: the first involved preventing breaches of peace by people observing the desecration; second, the State was interested in preserving the flag as a symbol of nationhood and national unity.

With regard to the State's first declared interest, the Court found that no actual breach of peace had occurred. As for the second interest, the Court found that the government's interest in preserving the flag's symbolic value was directly related to the suppression of free expression. For the *O'Brien* standard and its diminished scrutiny to apply, the state's regulation of expressive conduct must have been unrelated to the suppression of speech. As the regulation in this case was related to

---

[18] 460 U.S. 37 (1983); *supra* § 15.04[2].

[19] For additional discussion of the *Clark* Court's public forum analysis, *see supra* § 15.04[1].

[20] The Court also has suggested this similarity in other cases.

[21] 394 U.S. 576 (1969).

[22] *Id.* at 578.

[23] 491 U.S. 397 (1989).

[24] Tex. Penal Code Ann. § 42.09 (1989) stated:

(a) A person commits an offense if he intentionally or knowingly desecrates: . . .

(3) a state or national flag.

(b) For purposes of this section, "desecrate" means deface, damage, or otherwise physically mistreat in a way that the actor knows will seriously offend one or more persons likely to observe or discover his action.

the suppression of speech, it had to pass the most exacting scrutiny.

In its analysis, the Court found that the State did permit the burning of a flag in order to properly dispose of a flag. As a result, the Court invalidated the statute as a content-based restriction regulating how the symbol of the flag could be used.

In dissent, Chief Justice Rehnquist argued that Congress and the states could recognize a limited property interest in the flag. In addition, Chief Justice Rehnquist contended that the defendant's actions amounted to "fighting words"[25] and that the defendant had other modes of expression available for expressing his political beliefs.

In *United States v. Eichman*,[26] the Supreme Court struck down a federal law prohibiting flag desecration. Justice Brennan, writing for a 5-4 majority, found *Texas v. Johnson* controlling. The federal government argued that the law did not make any distinctions based on the content of the individual's intended message. Justice Brennan rejected this argument, finding that the government's interest in protecting the flag as a symbol of the nation was directed at suppressing a particular type of communication, *i.e.*, disrespect for the flag. As a result, the *O'Brien* test and its lower level of scrutiny did not apply. Instead, the statute failed under the "most exacting scrutiny" because the government could not prohibit "expressive conduct because of its likely communicative impact."[27]

In *Nevada Commission on Ethics v. Carrigan*,[28] the Court upheld against an overbreadth challenge a recusal provision that prohibited a public official from voting upon or " 'advocat[ing] the passage or failure' "[29] of a proposal in which he has a conflict of interest. Writing for the Court, Justice Scalia referenced a tradition of similarly "applicable conflict-of-interest recusal rules" which " 'creates a strong presumption' "[30] of constitutionality. For example, recusal rules applicable to federal judges have been in place since the establishment of the courts. State common-law rules also "have long required recusal of public officials with a conflict."[31] Moreover, "virtually every State has enacted some type of recusal law, many of which, not unlike Nevada's, require public officials to abstain from voting on all matters presenting a conflict of interest."[32] Legislators' votes were non-expressive conduct "engaged in for an independent governmental purpose,"[33] because the voting power "is not personal to the legislator but belongs to the people."[34] Therefore, voting by legislators does not warrant First Amendment

---

[25] *See* Chaplinsky v. New Hampshire, 315 U.S. 568 (1942) (words that have a direct tendency to incite listeners to violence are not constitutionally protected).

[26] 496 U.S. 310 (1990).

[27] *Id.* at 318.

[28] 131 S. Ct. 2343 (2011).

[29] *Id.* at 2346.

[30] *Id.* at 2347–48.

[31] *Id.* at 2349.

[32] *Id.*

[33] *Id.* at 2350–51.

[34] *Id.* at 2350.

protection.

Justice Kennedy concurred. "The constitutionality of a law prohibiting a legislative or executive official from voting on matters advanced by or associated with a political supporter is therefore a most serious matter from the standpoint of the logical and inevitable burden on speech and association that preceded the vote."[35]

Justice Alito concurred, stating that conflict-of-interest recusal rules were permissible restrictions since the time of the founders. He maintained that a legislator's vote is speech. The majority was correct in saying that "the vote may express, not the legislator's sincere personal view, but simply the view that is favored by the legislator's constituents. But the same is sometimes true of legislators' speeches."[36]

§ 16.02   EXPENDITURES OF MONEY IN THE POLITICAL ARENA

In *Buckley v. Valeo*,[37] the Supreme Court decided the constitutionality of certain provisions of the Federal Election Campaign Act of 1971, amended in 1974 in the wake of the Watergate scandal. Several senators and representatives challenged the Act.

The Court upheld the Act's limitations on contributions to political campaigns. However, the Court struck down the Act's provisions limiting a candidate's total campaign expenditures, and limiting the candidate's personal contribution to her own campaign. The Court also invalidated the limits on expenditures by others that advanced a particular candidate but were not made directly to the campaign.

The *per curiam* opinion analogized speaking and the spending of money to advance an idea as similar for constitutional purposes. Because the Act limited the quantity and diversity of political speech, it implicated political expression and association.

In determining the applicable standard of review, the Court refused to analogize the Act's contribution and expenditure limitations to the limitations on conduct allowed in *United States v. O'Brien*. Spending money for political campaigns had a more direct relationship to expression than the conduct of burning a draft card in *O'Brien*. Even if the limitations had been scrutinized under the *O'Brien* standard, the Court stated that they would still have failed the *O'Brien* requirement of being unrelated to suppressing communication, as the government had intended to restrict communication. The Court also rejected the characterization of the contribution and expenditure limitations as time, place, and manner restrictions, because they directly restricted the quantity of political communication.

The Court contrasted the expenditure and contribution limitations at issue. Expenditure limitations imposed substantial restraints on the quantity and diver

---

[35] *Id.* at 2353.

[36] *Id.* at 2354.

[37] 424 U.S. 1 (1976).

sity of political speech. A contribution, however, was only a symbolic expression of support for a candidate and her views. Accordingly, the limitations on contributions imposed little direct restraint on the contributor's political expression. Moreover, the Court found no indication that contribution limitations would adversely affect the funding of campaigns and political associations.

In upholding the contribution limitations, the Court indicated that it would do so only where the state demonstrated "a sufficiently important interest and employs means closely drawn to avoid unnecessary abridgment of associational freedoms."[38] The Court found that the contribution limitations did advance Congress's primary purpose of eliminating corruption, or the appearance of corruption, in the political process. Further, the contribution limitations focused narrowly on avoiding the purchase of particular political results while allowing persons to speak, volunteer services, and even make limited contributions. The Constitution did not limit Congressional regulation only to instances of actual corruption.[39]

With regard to the limitations on expenditures advocating the election or defeat of a clearly identified candidate, the Court found that the provision's vagueness would allow it to be easily circumvented. In addition, this limitation did not avoid political corruption, as it concerned expenditures made independent of the candidate and his campaign. Consequently, this limitation did not "satisfy the exacting scrutiny applicable to limitations on core First Amendment rights of political expression."[40]

The Court also invalidated the limitations on expenditures from a candidate's personal resources, as they infringed the candidate's right to speak on behalf of her own candidacy. Preventing actual or apparent corruption did not sustain these provisions, particularly because the contribution limitations, that the Court had upheld, already advanced this goal. The Court discounted the government's interest in equalizing the financial resources of candidates, maintaining that candidates could out-spend their rivals by being better fund-raisers. For reasons similar to those used to strike down *personal* campaign expenditures, the Court also struck down the limitations on *overall* campaign expenditures.

The Court next examined the disclosure provisions, which required campaigns to keep records for the Federal Election Commission (FEC) of names and addresses of each person making a contribution above $10.[41] The provisions also mandated disclosure of non-candidate campaign expenditures exceeding $100. Because compelled disclosure infringed on privacy and associational interests, it required "exacting scrutiny." Nevertheless, the Court upheld the compelled disclosure provisions as generally being "the least restrictive means" of curbing "campaign

---

[38] *Id.* at 25.

[39] For discussions of the corrupting force of money in politics, *see* E. DREW, POLITICS AND MONEY: THE NEW ROAD TO CORRUPTION (1983); J. NOONAN JR., BRIBES (1984); and J. Blum, *The Divisible First Amendment: A Critical Functionalist approach to Freedom of Speech and Electoral Campaign Spending*, 58 N.Y.U. L. REV. 1273 (1983).

[40] *Buckley*, 424 U.S. at 44.

[41] If the contribution exceeded $100, the contributor's occupation and place of business also had to be recorded.

ignorance and corruption." First, the disclosure provisions would inform voters about the sources of campaign funds and how these funds were spent, which would alert voters to the influences on the candidate. Second, the requirements would deter corruption by exposing large contributions and expenditures. Third, the information would help the FEC to police the Act.

The Court recognized that the disclosure provisions could adversely affect minority parties. Consequently, the Court stated that minority parties could obtain an exemption from the disclosure provisions if they showed a probability that compelled disclosure would subject contributors to "threats, harassment or reprisals from Government officials or private parties."[42] The Court indicated that proof could include specific examples of past harassment against the party or its members. New parties could prove a similar pattern of threats or specific manifestations of hostility against established minority parties with similar views.[43]

The Court also rejected the argument that it should strike down the disclosure provisions because of their low thresholds. The Court found these thresholds rational, as the Act only required the party to keep records of contributions of $10 or more, and did not require public disclosure.[44]

Finally, the Court addressed Subtitle H, limiting the total expenditures for a presidential campaign to $20,000,000 when the candidate accepted public funding. The provision also stated that a candidate from a new or minor party could spend no more money than a major party candidate, and would only get Federal funding (under a special formula for minor party candidates) if her party received more than five percent of the vote in the preceding election. Major party candidates also received some funding for their campaigns in the primaries.

The Court upheld Subtitle H because it furthered the electoral process by providing more money for that process. In addition, the strength of minority candidates was no less with government funding than without it. Moreover, Subtitle H fell short of imposing speech limitations because the candidates voluntarily accepted the expenditure ceilings in exchange for federal funds.

In his partial concurrence and partial dissent, Chief Justice Burger expressed concern that the Court's piecemeal analysis of the Act destroyed the intent of Congress, and rendered the Act unworkable. He also criticized the disclosure provisions by saying that they might deter young executives and others from contributing to minority parties. In addition, he criticized as artificial the Court's distinction between campaign contributions and other political expenditures, arguing that all such limitations were invalid.

In his partial concurrence and partial dissent, Justice White stated that the majority endorsed the simple proposition that "money talks." While restricting

---

[42] *Buckley*, 424 U.S. at 74.

[43] In *Brown v. Socialist Workers '74 Campaign Comm.*, 459 U.S. 87 (1982), the Court used its *Buckley* analysis to invalidate an Ohio campaign disclosure statute as applied to the Socialist Workers Party. The law required disclosure of recipients of campaign contributions and of campaign expenditures.

[44] In a separate section of the opinion, the Court upheld a requirement that individuals personally file with the FEC if they have made expenditures in a given calendar year that were not campaign contributions but supported clearly identifiable candidates.

expenditures of money involved speech interests, spending money was not the same as speaking. Nothing in the record before the Court indicated that the expenditure or contribution limitations at issue would cripple campaigns. Congress could have determined that "reasonably effective" campaigns could have been conducted within these established limits.

In his partial concurrence and partial dissent, Justice Marshall argued that this decision would diminish confidence in the political system because the wealthy would be perceived as having a distinct advantage in the electoral process. He would have upheld the provision limiting how much a candidate could contribute to his own campaign.

Justice Rehnquist, in his partial concurrence and dissent, argued that the public funding provisions indefinitely enshrined the Democratic and Republican parties in a preferred position.

Several campaign financing decisions following *Buckley* have involved Political Action Committees (PACs). In *Federal Election Commission v. National Conservative Political Action Committee*,[45] the Court invalidated provisions of the Federal Election Campaign Act that made it a crime for PACs to spend more than $1,000 on the election of a presidential candidate who had accepted public financing. Writing for the majority, Justice Rehnquist found that PAC speech was fully protected political speech despite the fact that contributors to PACs could not control a PAC's use of the funds. PACs provided a means for the less wealthy to pool their political clout.

In *California Medical Ass'n v. Federal Election Commission*,[46] the Court upheld a section of the Federal Election Campaign Act limiting the amount that individuals could contribute to a particular PAC. The Court relied on *Buckley* in finding that such contributions received less constitutional protection than other expenditures. In contrast, in *Citizens Against Rent Control v. City of Berkeley*,[47] the Court found unconstitutional a municipal ordinance that established a contribution limit for groups formed to support or oppose a measure placed on the ballot for popular vote. The Court stressed that this case did not involve the narrow exception to First Amendment protection identified in *Buckley*, regarding large contributions to individual candidates.

In *Colorado Republican Federal Campaign Committee v. Federal Election Commission*,[48] the Court invalidated the application of the Federal Election Campaign Act of 1971 (FECA) to an independent expenditure made by a political party. The Colorado Republican Federal Campaign Commission (Colorado Party) challenged an FEC ruling that the amount spent on ads attacking a likely Democratic senatorial candidate exceeded the limits imposed upon party "expenditures in connection with the general election campaign of candidates for Federal

---

[45] 470 U.S. 480 (1985).

[46] 453 U.S. 182 (1981).

[47] 454 U.S. 290 (1981).

[48] 518 U.S. 604 (1996).

office."[49]

The FECA limited party expenditures in coordination with a candidate which were considered indirect contributions and could exceed $5,000 a year. However, expenditures made by political parties had much higher limits.[50]

Justice Breyer, joined by Justices O'Connor and Souter, concluded that the Colorado Party's expenditures for radio advertisements were a constitutionally-protected " 'independent' expenditure,"[51] rather than a " 'coordinated' expenditure."[52] The Colorado Party presented direct evidence that the Party developed the advertisements itself and not in agreement with any candidate. The plurality deferred considering a facial challenge that any limit on coordinated expenditures by political parties also violates the First Amendment until it could ascertain whether Congress intended the coordinated expenditure limits to be severable and to remain even if the independent expenditure limits were invalidated.

In his dissent, Justice Stevens maintained that all senatorial campaign expenditures made by a political party are contributions and, thus, may be limited by Congress. Such limits prevented actual or perceived corruption, leveled the political playing field, and prevented the circumvention of the Act's limits on contributions to individual candidates.

Justice Kennedy, joined by Chief Justice Rehnquist and Justice Scalia, concurred in the judgment and dissented in part. Justice Kennedy would hold unconstitutional any limitation on expenditures made by political parties, including coordinated expenditures, as a party's expenditures on a candidate's campaign are indistinguishable from a candidate's expenditures on her own campaign, which are constitutionally protected.

Justice Thomas concurred in the judgment and dissented in part, joined by the Chief Justice and Justice Kennedy. Justice Thomas believed that the Court should overrule its entire campaign financing jurisprudence. As "one of the main purposes of a political party is to support its candidate in elections,"[53] constitutional protection should extend to coordinated expenditures. Justice Thomas also rejected *Buckley's* distinction between campaign contributions and expenditures as constitutionally insignificant, believing that the First Amendment prohibits limits on both contributions and independent expenditures.

Another cluster of cases after *Buckley* involves political expenditures by corporations. In *First National Bank v. Bellotti*,[54] the Court held that a state could not prohibit corporations from spending money to express their views, even on issues that were not directly related to their property, business, or assets.

---

[49] 2 U.S.C. § 441a(d)(1).

[50] Independent expenditures could not exceed "the greater of $20,000 or '2 cents multiplied by the voting age population of the State.' " 518 U.S. at 611.

[51] *Id.* at 613.

[52] *Id.*

[53] *Id.* at 634.

[54] 435 U.S. 765 (1978).

In *Bellotti*, a Massachusetts law restricting corporate expenditures to matters relating to business interests prohibited several Massachusetts companies from publicizing their views on a proposed referendum concerning a graduated personal income tax. Writing for the majority, Justice Powell stated that corporations enjoyed free speech rights, although he did not address whether they enjoyed the same speech rights as natural persons. Justice Powell found no compelling state interest in suppressing their speech based on its content.

Massachusetts claimed that the statute protected citizens' participation in the electoral process and their confidence in government. The Court responded that there was no showing that corporate political speech had "been overwhelming or even significant in influencing referenda in Massachusetts, or that there has been any threat to the confidence of the citizenry in the government."[55] The Court conceded that these arguments would merit consideration had there been such a showing. At any rate, the First Amendment did not permit government to equalize the relative voices of speakers in society.

The State also asserted that the statute protected the interests of individual shareholders who might disagree with the corporation's expressed views. The Court rejected this argument, pointing out that the statute was underinclusive, because it did not cover other corporate activities, such as lobbying, which might also offend minority shareholders. The statute was also underinclusive in its failure to mention such groups as labor unions, trusts, and other associations which might also have minorities with differing views. The statute was overinclusive in that it prohibited corporate speech even if all the members of the corporation agreed with the speech.

In dissent, Justice White conceded that corporate speech was protected by the First Amendment. However, he argued that corporate speech was not entitled to full First Amendment protection because it did not further self-actualization, one of the primary interests proffered for protecting free speech. For Justice White, the State's interest in preventing the economic skewing of the political process was sufficiently important to restrict a corporation's expression when the speech was unrelated to its business. Justice White also emphasized that incorporation in a state was a privilege which gave a corporation power to amass wealth. This privilege, Justice White argued, should not aid a corporation in dominating the political affairs of the state: "The state need not permit its own creation to consume it."[56]

In *Brown v. Hartlage*,[57] the Court invalidated the Kentucky Corrupt Practices Act, which made it unlawful for a candidate to promise money, or other resources, in return for a commitment to support the candidate. Justice Brennan's majority opinion recognized that some types of promises may be prohibited even though made in the form of words. But the First Amendment does not permit the state to limit a candidate's promise that constituents may financially profit from the candidate's election.

---

[55] *Id.* at 789.

[56] *Id.* at 809.

[57] 456 U.S. 45 (1982).

In *Federal Election Commission v. Massachusetts Citizens for Life, Inc.* ("*MCFL*"),[58] the Court struck down limitations on expenditures by a nonprofit corporation to influence the election of particular candidates. MCFL published a newsletter disseminating the voting records of particular candidates, in violation of a Massachusetts law prohibiting corporations from spending money to influence elections. The Court found that, since its goal was not to amass capital, the nonprofit corporation did not present the same threat of corruption as a typical for-profit corporation. The Court penned a narrow decision holding the law unconstitutional as applied to MCFL. First, MCFL was a nonprofit corporation formed to disseminate ideas rather than earn profits. Second, MCFL had no shareholders who might disagree with its ideas. Third, MCFL was not a conduit established by a labor union or a for-profit corporation to circumvent restrictions on electioneering.

In *Federal Election Commission v. Beaumont*,[59] Justice Souter upheld (7-2) a 1907 federal law that prohibited nonprofit advocacy corporations from "contributing directly to candidates for federal office."[60] The statute allowed corporations to form and control PACs which could solicit contributions from corporate employees and shareholders. These PACs could in turn contribute to candidates for federal office. Justice Kennedy concurred in the judgment. Justice Thomas, joined by Justice Scalia, dissented.

The Court again addressed the issue of a for-profit corporation's political speech in *Austin v. Michigan Chamber of Commerce*.[61] In *Austin*, the Court upheld a Michigan statute that prohibited corporations from using general treasury funds for contributions or independent expenditures to support or oppose candidates for state office. The statute did permit corporations to make political expenditures from segregated political funds to which persons could contribute. Relying on *Buckley v. Valeo*, the Court stated that contributions to political campaigns constituted speech, and the statute's limitation on a corporation's campaign spending did burden its political speech. However, the Court found the state's expressed interest in preventing corruption sufficiently compelling to uphold the statute.

Writing for the majority, Justice Marshall found that the statute was aimed at "the corrosive and distorting effects of immense aggregations of wealth that are accumulated with the help of the corporate form and that have little or no correlation to the public's support for the corporation's political ideas."[62] In addition, Justice Marshall found the statute to be narrowly tailored to prevent this corruption because the statute did not ban all political expenditures by a corporation but only required that the money be spent through segregated funds. As a result, the corporation's political expenditures could accurately reflect the views of those contributing to the separate fund while allowing those not contributing to remain associated with the corporation for economic and other nonpolitical reasons.

---

[58] 479 U.S. 238 (1986).

[59] 539 U.S. 146 (2003).

[60] *Id.* at 149.

[61] 494 U.S. 652 (1990).

[62] *Id.* at 660.

The Chamber of Commerce asserted that the law was unconstitutional as applied to nonprofit corporations. In rejecting this contention, the Court distinguished *Massachusetts Citizens for Life* on several grounds. Most importantly, three quarters of the members of the Chamber of Commerce were for-profit corporations. Justice Marshall also rejected the argument that the statute was underinclusive because it did not cover entities like labor unions. Whatever capital such unincorporated associations may amass was done without the special state help of the corporate structure.

Justice Kennedy's dissent argued that this was the first time that the Court allowed restrictions on political expenditures. The decision also permitted some nonprofit corporations to speak but not others. Finally, Justice Kennedy pointed out that the statute's distinctions were based on the content of the speech (political campaigns) and the identity of the speaker. Justice Kennedy's views eventually triumphed. *Citizens United v. Federal Election Commission*[63] overturned *Austin v. Michigan Chamber of Commerce* and struck down a federal ban on corporations using their general treasury funds to pay for electioneering communications.

In *Nixon v. Shrink Missouri Government PAC,*[64] the Court upheld a Missouri statute limiting campaign contributions for candidates running for state office.[65] Under this system, Fredman, a candidate for Missouri State Auditor, had an inflation adjusted contribution cap of $1,075. *Buckley v. Valeo*[66] found danger of corruption in large campaign contributions. However, the $1,000 contribution limit upheld in *Buckley* was not a minimum constitutional threshold for legislation.

The District Court found that contribution limits did not impair state-wide campaigns. Contribution limits were too low if they impeded candidates' raising " 'the resources necessary for effective advocacy.' "[67] They were also invalid if they "render political association ineffective, drive the sound of a candidate's voice below the level of notice, and render contributions pointless."[68] A candidate must be able to build an effective campaign with the money the regulation allows. The majority refused to re-examine *Buckley* itself because the parties did not request this.

Concurring, Justice Stevens would have decided the case under a substantive due process analysis involving the liberty and property rights of the candidates and contributors, arguing that "money is property; it is not speech."[69]

Justice Breyer, joined by Justice Ginsburg, concurred. Too low a limit on contributions could unfairly favor incumbents by amplifying their existing media and reputational advantages. While the $1,075 limit was questionable, "the type of

---

[63] 130 S. Ct. 876 (2010).

[64] 528 U.S. 377 (2000).

[65] The statute placed limits ranging from $250 for offices involving populations fewer than 100,000; and $1000 for offices involving populations of more than 250,000. The state adjusted these amounts for inflation.

[66] 424 U.S. 1 (1976).

[67] 528 U.S. at 397.

[68] *Id.*

[69] *Id.* at 398.

election at issue; the record of adequate candidate financing post-reform; and the fact that the statute indexes the amount for inflation"[70] showed that the statute did not severely disadvantage Fredman.

Justice Breyer also commented that the expenditures of independently wealthy candidates "might be considered contributions to their own campaigns."[71] If *Buckley* denies the government the ability to resolve such campaign finance problems, then the Court should re-examine *Buckley*.

Dissenting, Justice Kennedy would also re-evaluate *Buckley*. He substantially agreed with Justice Thomas's dissent that government may not be able to limit campaign contributions or expenditures. However, he would not dismiss the possibility that some limits on both expenditures and contributions might allow public officials to focus on their governmental responsibilities instead of fundraising.

Justice Thomas, joined by Justice Scalia, dissented, arguing that *Buckley* should be overruled. He would place campaign contributions under strict scrutiny and hold the Missouri statute unconstitutional. He pointed out that after the regulation, spending on state-wide elections fell by well over 50% and contested primaries for state-wide office fell from 10 to 1.

In *Randall v. Sorrell*,[72] the Court invalidated both the expenditure and contribution limits of Vermont's campaign finance statute. Established precedent invalidated the expenditure limits. The contribution limits were invalid because their low maximum levels and other restriction were not carefully tailored.

The statute limited spending of incumbent candidates running for statewide office to 85% and those incumbents running for the State Senate or House to 90% of approximately the following amounts: governor, $300,000; lieutenant governor, $100,000; other statewide offices, $45,000. The limitations also applied to expenditures by a political party that are coordinated with candidate campaigns.[73] Contributions for statewide offices including governor and lieutenant governor were limited to $400; contributions for state senator to $300; and contributions for state representative to $200. These limits applied to both political committees and political parties. Finally, the statute limited the amount an individual can contribute to a political party to $2,000 per "2-year general election cycle."[74]

First, Justice Breyer relied on *Buckley v. Valeo*[75] in analyzing the constitutionality of the Act's expenditure limits. He emphasized that only in extremely rare and specific circumstances may the Court abandon established precedent. This principle is particularly important when the Court has repeatedly interpreted the law in the

---

[70] *Id.* at 404.

[71] 528 U.S. at 405.

[72] 548 U.S. 230 (2006).

[73] Moreover, "any party expenditure that 'primarily benefits six or fewer candidates who are associated with the political party' is 'presumed' to be coordinated with the campaign and therefore to count against the campaign's expenditures limit." *Id.* at 239.

[74] *Id.*

[75] 424 U.S. 1 (1976).

same way over time. Based on this interpretation of *stare decisis*, Justice Breyer, joined only by Chief Justice Roberts, found no reason to overrule *Buckley*.

Writing for the plurality, Justice Breyer explained that the Court typically relied on the legislature's specific expertise to determine appropriate limits for campaign costs unless the limits were so obviously low that they would have inhibited challengers from competing with incumbents. The plurality believed that the Vermont statute fell in this latter category since the limits were significantly lower than those of other states. For example, a person could only contribute a total of $200 for both the primary and general elections. In the year that *Buckley* was decided, this total would have amounted to approximately $57 per election rather than the $1,000 per election limit considered in *Buckley*.

Moreover, Vermont's limits were the lowest among all 50 states. The plurality found that the contribution limits unconstitutionally restricted speech based on a combination of five factors. The plurality found particularly disturbing the adverse impact of these low contribution limits on candidates challenging incumbents as challengers frequently incurred higher costs. Second, the plurality agreed with the District Court's assessment that such low limits would significantly reduce political opposition. Third, the statute did not provide an exception for volunteer costs despite these "very low"[76] contribution limits. Fourth, the contribution limits were not indexed for inflation. Fifth, no "special justification"[77] legitimated these low contribution limits. Therefore, the plurality found that the statute was not "narrowly" tailored and "disproportionately burden[ed] numerous First Amendment interests."[78] The plurality concluded that severing some of the limits from the statute was not possible.[79]

Four Justices concurred in the judgment but disagreed with various parts of the plurality's analysis. Justice Alito found the plurality's discussion of whether to revisit *Buckley* unnecessary since those challenging the Vermont statute did not make a case for re-examining *Buckley*. Justice Kennedy questioned the Court's overall approach to determine which limits are too low. Justice Thomas, joined by Justice Scalia, reiterated his view that the *Buckley* Court should have invalidated both the contribution and expenditure limits in *Buckley*.

Dissenting, Justice Stevens would overrule those parts of *Buckley* that struck down expenditure limits; as Justice White's dissent in *Buckley* recognized, "it is quite wrong to equate money and speech."[80] Justice Stevens maintained that expenditure limits were more analogous to time, place, and manner restrictions than to content-based restrictions. Finally, Justice Souter filed a dissenting opinion, joined by Justice Ginsburg and in part by Justice Stevens. Justice Souter would defer to the Vermont legislature's determinations of both appropriate expenditure

---

[76] *Randall*, 548 U.S. at 260.

[77] *Id.* at 261.

[78] *Id.* at 262.

[79] This "would require us to write words into the statute (inflation indexing), or leave gaping loopholes (no limits on party contributions), or to foresee which of many different possible ways the legislature might respond to the constitutional objections we have found." *Id.*

[80] *Id.* at 276 (Stevens, J., dissenting).

and contribution limits although the deference was not absolute.

In *Federal Election Commission v. Colorado Republican Federal Campaign Committee*,[81] the Court upheld a restriction in the Federal Campaign Act of 1971 limiting a political party's coordinated expenditures with a candidate. The Court first examined this case in *Colorado Republican Federal Campaign Committee v. Federal Election Commission (Colorado I)*.[82] That decision invalidated the Act's restriction on independent party spending. However, in this second appeal, the Court agreed with the Act's treatment of coordinated expenditures as direct contributions to a candidate, which the Act capped at $2,000 per election cycle. Otherwise, donors could give up to the $20,000 annual limit to political parties, which the parties could then pass along to candidates as coordinated expenditures.

The evidence "shows that even under present law substantial donations turn parties into matchmakers whose special meetings and receptions give the donors the chance to get their points across to candidates."[83] The Party, however, argued that more effective safeguards, like the earmarking rule, were already in place to prevent circumvention.[84] The Court countered that the earmarking provision "would reach only the most clumsy attempts to pass contributions through to candidates."[85] Rejecting the alternative that circumvention could be avoided by capping contributions to parties at less than $20,000 as opposed to limiting coordinated spending, the majority said that "Congress was entitled to its choice."[86]

Justice Thomas dissented, joined by Justices Scalia and Kennedy, and by Chief Justice Rehnquist as to Part II. He continued to argue that *Buckley v. Valeo*[87] should be overruled. However, even if *Buckley* was not overruled, coordinated expenditures were not the same as contributions; and political parties were not the same as political committees. A political candidate's actions and a party's public image were intertwined. Moreover, the restriction did not serve the important interest of curbing corruption, as the "aim of a political party is to influence its candidate's stance."[88] Finally, government could avoid circumvention problems with more narrowly tailored alternatives, such as enforcing the earmarking provision or simply lowering the $20,000 cap on annual contributions to political parties.

In *McConnell v. Federal Election Commission*,[89] the Supreme Court largely denied a facial challenge to the Bipartisan Campaign Reform Act of 2002 (BCRA) which amended the Federal Election Campaign Act of 1971 (FECA). BCRA particularly limited use of "soft money" by political parties and issue ads. Soft money represented contributions given to political parties rather than to specific

---

[81] 533 U.S. 431 (2001).

[82] *Cf. Colorado I*, 454 U.S. 290 (1981).

[83] 533 U.S. at 461.

[84] The earmarking rule treated contributions that were directed to a particular candidate as direct contributions.

[85] 533 U.S. at 462.

[86] *Id.* at 465.

[87] 424 U.S. 1 (1976).

[88] 533 U.S. at 476.

[89] 540 U.S. 93 (2003).

candidates. In 1984 soft money accounted for only 5% of the two main political parties' spending, but by 2000, that number jumped to 42%. Moreover, of the total amount of soft money raised, 60% came from just 800 donors.

FECA § 323 restricted soft money contributions. The Court recognized again, as in *Buckley*[90] and *Shrink Missouri*,[91] that limits on campaign contributions affected freedom of association more than the freedom of speech, because contributions were used " 'to affiliate a person with a candidate' and 'enabl[e] like-minded persons to pool their resources.' "[92] Even if contribution limits significantly interfered with freedom of association, they needed only be "closely drawn" to serve a "sufficiently important interest."[93] *Buckley* had used this same lower standard of review.

Limits on soft money contributions protected the important governmental interests in preventing the actual corruption that may be related to large contributions, and the lost public confidence spurred by the appearance of such corruption. This standard "shows proper deference to Congress' ability to weigh competing constitutional interests in an area in which it enjoys particular expertise."[94] It also allowed Congress latitude to anticipate and avert attempts to circumvent regulations.

Basically, FECA § 323 limited wealthy individuals, corporations, and unions from making large contributions to federal elections, officeholders, and candidates. Limiting the dollar amounts or forcing unions and corporations to contribute them through PACs did not alter the political message bound up with the solicitation. Instead, the restriction promoted wider "dissemination of information by forcing parties, candidates, and officeholders to solicit from a wider array of potential donors."[95] Moreover, FECA § 323 did not regulate activities by regulating the internal process of the political parties, but instead imposed amount limitations on a greater number of contributions to parties and candidates.

The possibility of corruption or the appearance of corruption existed when large contributions were made to a national party. The amount of soft money a candidate raised often affected the degree to which the party assisted her campaign. Donors often requested parties to use hard and soft money contributions for specific candidates. National party committees and candidate committees often organized joint fundraising committees. National parties could manipulate the legislative calendar, could create access to candidates or officeholders in exchange for large donations, or could influence decision-making based on the desires of donors rather than on the merits of a particular issue. Even if such abuses occurred infrequently, "the potential for such undue influence was manifest."[96] Thus, such concerns over corruption clearly fell within the realm of sufficiently important governmental interests.

---

[90] Buckley v. Valeo, 424 U.S. 1 (1976).

[91] Nixon v. Shrink Mo. Gov't PAC, 528 U.S. 377 (2000).

[92] *McConnell*, 540 U.S. at 135 (quoting *Buckley*, 424 U.S. at 22).

[93] *Id.* (quoting *Shrink Mo.*, 528 U.S. at 387–88).

[94] *Id.* at 137.

[95] *Id.* at 140.

[96] *Id.* at 153.

FECA § 323(a) subjected hard money to source and amount limits. The plaintiffs attempted to argue that § 323(a) was substantially overbroad because it included all money raised by the national parties even when the money was ultimately used for state or local elections. Federal officeholders and candidates primarily populated and ran the national committees of the two major political parties. Regardless of the ultimate use of the money, the close connections between the federal officeholders and the national parties were "likely to create actual or apparent indebtedness on the part of federal officeholders."[97] The plaintiffs also claimed substantial over-breadth because § 323(a) comprehended minor parties which received very few large soft-money contributions. *Buckley* rejected similar arguments. In order to ensure the integrity of the electoral process, it was reasonable that all parties and candidates abided by the same rules regardless of the size of their political party. Moreover, § 323(a) applied only when an organization had official status. A "minor party may bring an as-applied challenge if § 323(a) prevents it from 'amassing the resources necessary for effective advocacy.' "[98]

Plaintiffs asserted that FECA § 323(a) "impermissibly interferes with the ability of the national committees to associate with state and local committees," but the Court found nothing on the face of the provision that prevented collaboration in raising and spending soft money.[99] Moreover, national party officials could collabo-rate in their official capacities with their state and local counterparts in raising and spending hard money and may do the same for soft money in their unofficial capacities.

FECA § 323(b) prevented state and local committees from using soft money donations or becoming conduits for such donations. However, the Levin Amendment in FECA § 323(b)(2) allowed state and local parties to use annual Levin donations of up to $10,000 per person to fund "Voter registration activity, voter identification drives, [Get Out the Vote] drives, and generic campaign activities" that promoted a party rather than a specific candidate.[100] In upholding § 323(b), the Court afforded Congress substantial deference in the matter to prevent funds donated to state and local parties from being used to circumvent the national limits on soft money. Section 323(b) was "narrowly focused on regulating contributions that pose the greatest risk" of corruption and was "a closely-drawn means of countering both corruption and the appearance of corruption."[101]

Similarly, FECA § 323(b)'s prohibition on transferring Levin funds among state parties was necessary to prevent circumvention of the $10,000 limit. This ban prevented donors from making "multiple $10,000 donations to various committees that could then transfer the donations to the committee of choice."[102] Rejecting a facial challenge that FECA § 323(b) overly restricts the amount of funds available, the Court said that the standard was not whether it reduced the amounts available

---

[97] *Id.* at 155.

[98] *Id.* at 159 (quoting *Buckley*, 424 U.S. at 21).

[99] *Id.*

[100] *Id.* at 163.

[101] *Id.* at 167.

[102] *Id.* at 171.

in previous elections but whether it drove the party's "voice below the level of notice."[103] The Court left open the possibility of as-applied challenges. Section 323(b) was "closely drawn to match the important governmental interest of preventing corruption and the appearance of corruption."[104]

FECA § 323(d) "prohibits national, state, and local party committees from making or directing 'any donatio[n]' to qualifying" tax-exempt organizations or from soliciting tax-exempt organizations that are engaged in political activities.[105] Once again, the Court upheld this ban as a reasonable "anticircumvention measure."[106] To avoid overbreadth concerns, the Court construed the statute as allowing parties to donate to tax-exempt organizations funds the parties raised which met FECA source, amount and disclosure limitations.

FECA § 323(e) forbade federal candidates and officeholders soliciting, receiving, directing, transferring, or spending soft money in federal elections. It also limited their ability to do so in state or local elections. Following *Buckley*, the Court upheld such restrictions as contribution limitations "subject to less rigorous scrutiny."[107]

Section 323(f) limited the source and the amount of soft money contributions that state and local candidates or officeholders could raise or spend to support or "a clearly identified candidate for federal office."[108] Section 323(b) did not limit the total amount a state or local candidate or officeholder could spend on such "public communications." Instead, it limited the source and the amount of contributions that could be used to directly influence federal elections.

The Court rejected an equal protection argument that Title I of the Bipartisan Campaign Reform Act of 2002 (BCRA) discriminated in favor of special interest groups and against political parties. Special interest groups did not have nearly the same influence over legislation that political parties had.

BCRA Title II restricted "electioneering communication," which included any "broadcast, cable or satellite communication" that "refers to a clearly identified candidate for federal office."[109] The Court rejected plaintiffs' argument that *Buckley* protected all such so-called "issue advocacy," which avoided using such "magic words" as "vote for" or "defeat."[110]

BCRA § 201 required disclosure of the names of people contributing $1,000 or more to a person or group that spent more than $10,000 per year on electioneering communications. *Buckley* rejected facial attacks against such requirements absent "reasonable probability" of harm. Similarly, the Court allowed disclosure of executory contracts for electioneering communications. Such disclosures would not

---

[103] *Id.* at 173 (quoting *Shrink Mo.*, 528 U.S. at 397).

[104] *Id.*

[105] *Id.* at 178.

[106] *Id.*

[107] *Id.* at 182.

[108] *Id.* at 184 (quoting 2 U.S.C. § 441i(f)(1)).

[109] *Id.* at 189.

[110] *Id.* at 191.

have to reveal in advance the content of future advertisements, but would afford pre-election disclosure of who supported a candidate.

BCRA § 202 treated all payments for "electioneering communications" coordinated with a candidate or party as contributions to and payments by that candidate or party. Such coordinated disbursements could be treated in the same way as other coordinated disbursements. Section 203 included electioneering communications in the prohibition against corporations and unions using funds to expressly advocate for or against a federal candidate. Corporations or unions could still fund such electioneering communications using segregated funds or PACs. Issue ads broadcast shortly before federal elections were the "functional equivalent of express advocacy."[111] Even though the restriction did not apply to print media or the internet, reform could occur one step at a time. The Court also rejected the argument that the restriction on electioneering communications discriminated in favor of media companies, as media companies were different. BCRA § 204 extended to nonprofit organizations the prohibition against using general treasury funds to pay for electioneering communications, but the Court previously had determined that such a restriction did not apply to *MCFL* organizations.[112] However, this exemption did not invalidate this provision as Congress was aware of the *MCFL* exemption.

BCRA § 315(d)(4) required that if a party wanted to spend more than $5,000 for its candidate, it had to forego ads that used the "magic words" of "elect" or "defeat." Having political parties avoid these words failed to qualify as a meaningful governmental interest as candidates could easily evade the "magic words" requirement.

The Court also rejected the argument that BCRA § 214 was overbroad and unconstitutionally vague because it required no agreement for a coordinated expenditure that attracted the BCRA's source and amount restrictions. Unspoken agreements could exist that would benefit the candidate in the same way as a cash donation. The joint opinion of Justices Stevens and O'Connor concluded that the government had the power of self-protection against the ill effects of aggregated wealth in our political system. In another portion of the Court's opinion, Chief Justice Rehnquist invalidated BCRA § 318's prohibition on donations by minors to candidates or to political parties as an anti-circumvention matter. As minors were protected by the First Amendment, the provision "sweeps too broadly."[113] There were more tailored ways to prevent this problem, such as establishing a total allotted family donation or prohibiting contributions by very young children.

Another part of the Court's opinion written by Justice Breyer rejected a facial challenge to BCRA § 504, which required broadcasters to keep a record of all "election message requests" made by the public about a candidate or a federal election. The FCC already required that a record be kept of all "candidate requests" (requests made by or on the behalf of a candidate), showing the "classes

---

[111] *Id.* at 206.

[112] *See* Fed. Election Comm'n v. Mass. Citizens for Life, 479 U.S. 238 (1986).

[113] *McConnell*, 540 at 232.

of time," "rates charged," and "when the spot aired."[114] This data would make the public aware of how much money candidates had been spending to publicize their messages, and would facilitate compliance with the disclosure and source requirements. Chief Justice Rehnquist agreed with the plaintiffs that such a requirement could reveal sensitive campaign strategy.

Broadcasters were also required to keep a record of all "issue requests" made by the public about legislation or any "political matter of national importance."[115] The Court determined that this requirement allowed for a determination of whether the "broadcasters are too heavily favoring entertainment" and were offering opportunities to discuss different views on public issues.[116] The Court left open the possibility of as-applied challenges.

Justice Scalia's dissent noted that incumbents received much larger hard-money contributions than challengers.[117] Criticizing the majority, he stated that Court precedent required that "exacting scrutiny" be applied in this case. The right to free speech "would be largely ineffective if it did not include the right to engage in financial transactions that are the incidents of its exercise."[118] Of course, "the government may apply general commercial regulations to those who use money for speech if it applies them even handedly to those who use money for other purposes."[119]

Freedom of speech included the right to pool money to disseminate ideas. Given the premise of democracy, there was no such thing as too much speech. It was also the nature of democracy that supporters enjoyed greater access. The $3.9 billion spent on the 2000 election was about half as much as Americans spent on movie tickets and a fifth as much as they spent on cosmetics and perfume.

Justice Thomas dissented in part and concurred in the judgment in part.[120] These constrictions on core political speech amounted to the "most significant abridgement of the freedoms of speech and association since the Civil War."[121] Broad bribery prohibitions would better deter corruption and would eliminate the appearance of corruption. The restrictions at issue were not simply contribution limits, but rather "limitations on independent expenditures."[122]

Justice Thomas also criticized the forced disclosure requirements of BCRA § 201, stating that they were in violation of the right to anonymous speech that has been upheld since the founding of the country. *Buckley* was incorrectly decided; however, even under the *Buckley* framework, the electioneering communications

---

[114] *Id.* at 235.

[115] *Id.* at 240.

[116] *Id.*

[117] Justice Scalia dissented from the majority opinion on Titles I and IV, and dissented in part on Title II.

[118] *McConnell*, 540 U.S. at 252 (Scalia, J., dissenting).

[119] *Id.*

[120] Justice Thomas concurred in the judgment on Title II, and dissented on Titles I, V, and § 311.

[121] *McConnell*, 540 U.S. at 264 (Thomas, J., dissenting).

[122] *Id.* at 272.

restrictions of Title II were found unconstitutional.

Justice Kennedy also dissented from the majority's opinion regarding Titles I and II. The "generic favoritism" rationale adopted by the majority sharply contrasted with *Buckley's* concerns with corruption or the appearance of corruption. "Democracy is premised on responsiveness."[123] The majority incorrectly assumed that the regulations at issue were contribution limits rather than expenditure limits and thus entitled to the lesser scrutiny. Actually, the regulations were "neither contribution nor expenditure limits, or are perhaps both at once."[124] The restrictions created "significant burdens on speech itself" and also "markedly greater associational burdens than the significant burden created by contribution limitations."[125] *Austin v. Michigan Chamber of Commerce*[126] was the only other time the Court had allowed the censorship of political speech "based on the speaker's corporate identity."[127] Even under that ruling, BCRA § 203's prohibition on using corporate or union funds for electioneering communications was unconstitutional. Historically, the Court had recognized that corporations faced difficulties when forced to communicate through PACs. "The majority can articulate no compelling justification for its scheme of compulsory ventriloquism."[128] The temporal and geographic proxies of § 203 created a "severe and unprecedented ban on protected speech."[129]

Chief Justice Rehnquist joined Justice Kennedy's opinion regarding Title I, but added that the provision did not simply regulate donations that influenced an election, but all donations to political committees regardless of the eventual use of the money. This overinclusive restriction prevented state parties from using non-federal funds for other party activities such as voter registration and voter identification unconnected to federal candidates.

In *Federal Election Commission v. Wisconsin Right To Life, Inc. (WRTL)*,[130] the Court declared § 203 of the Bipartisan Campaign Reform Act of 2002 (BCRA) unconstitutional as applied to the corporate advertisements at issue because they were "not the 'functional equivalent' of express campaign speech." BCRA § 203 restricted corporate broadcasts shortly before an election that named a federal candidate for elected office and targeted the electorate. During this time, it was a federal crime for any labor union or incorporated entity to "pay for any 'electioneering communication'" from general treasury funds.[131] As part of a lobbying campaign, WRTL aired three commercials prior to the 2004 federal primary election that referred to Washington Senators by name. The commercials encouraged citizens to contact these Senators to request that they oppose a federal judicial

---

[123] *Id.* at 297 (Kennedy, J., dissenting).

[124] *Id.* at 309.

[125] *Id.* at 313.

[126] 494 U.S. 652 (1990).

[127] *McConnell*, 540 U.S. at 326.

[128] *Id.* at 333.

[129] *Id.* at 334.

[130] 551 U.S. 449 (2007).

[131] *Id.* at 457.

nominee filibuster. BCRA § 203 prevented WRTL from broadcasting these commercials less than 30 days prior to the primary election.

Chief Justice Roberts delivered the judgment of the Court and the opinion of the Court with respect to Parts I and II. In *McConnell v. Federal Election Commission*,[132] the Court had rejected a facial challenge to BCRA § 203. The Court distinguished issue advocacy from campaign speech or express advocacy of a particular candidate. Chief Justice Roberts first held that the speech at issue was "not the 'functional equivalent' of express campaign speech."[133] Second, the Court found that the interests justifying campaign speech regulation did not justify issue advocacy restrictions. Consequently, the Court held § 203 "unconstitutional as applied to the advertisements at issue."[134]

Only Justice Alito joined Parts III and IV of the Chief Justice's opinion. In Part III, the Chief Justice said that regulating WRTL's ads was not narrowly tailored to achieve a compelling state interest. Under *McConnell*, only regulation of express campaign speech "survives strict scrutiny."[135]

An ad comprised express campaign speech or its functional equivalent "only if the ad is susceptible of no reasonable interpretation other than as an appeal to vote for or against a specific candidate."[136] The ads focused on issue promotion and advocated contacting public officials to take a position on the particular legislative issue. Second, the ads "do not mention an election, candidacy, political party, or challenger; and they do not take a position on a candidates' character, qualifications, or fitness for office."[137]

Chief Justice Roberts also rejected Justice Scalia's criticism that his "*no reasonable interpretation*" test is vague. He said that "in a debatable case, the tie is resolved in favor of protecting speech."[138]

The government argued "that an expansive definition of 'functional equivalent' " was necessary to prevent issue advocacy from circumventing "the rule against express advocacy."[139] Rejecting this argument in Part IV of his opinion, Chief Justice Roberts rejected the "desire for a bright-line rule" as a compelling state interest. The plurality acknowledged that the state had a compelling interest in addressing " 'the corrosive and distorting effects of immense aggregations of wealth that are accumulated with the help of the corporate form.' "[140] However, "the interest recognized in *Austin*[141] as justifying regulation of corporate campaign

---

[132] 540 U.S. 93 (2003).

[133] 551 U.S. at 461.

[134] *Id.*

[135] *Id.* at 465.

[136] *Id.* at 470.

[137] *Id.*

[138] *Id.* at n.7.

[139] *Id.* at 479.

[140] *Id.*

[141] Austin v. Michigan Chamber of Commerce, 494 U.S. 652 (1990).

speech" did not apply "to issue advocacy."[142]

In conclusion, Chief Justice Roberts distinguished the Court's holding from *McConnell* and confirmed that its precedent was undisturbed. *"McConnell* held that express advocacy of a candidate or his opponent by a corporation shortly before an election may be prohibited, along with the functional equivalent of such express advocacy."[143] However, when the issue was "what speech qualifies as the functional equivalent of express advocacy subject to such a ban" the Court would "give the benefit of the doubt to speech, not censorship."[144]

Justice Alito's concurrence predicted that if the Court's test "impermissibly chills political speech," then the Court might reconsider *McConnell*.[145]

Justice Scalia, joined by Justices Kennedy and Thomas, concurred in part and in the judgment. Justice Scalia explained that no test for distinguishing between express and issue advocacy "can both (1) comport with the requirement of clarity that unchilled freedom of political speech demands, and (2) be compatible with the facial validity of § 203 (as pronounced in *McConnell*)."[146] He would reconsider *McConnell* as it forced the Court to differentiate "issue-speech from election-speech with no clear criterion."[147]

Justice Souter dissented, joined by Justices Stevens, Ginsburg, and Breyer. "Devoting concentrations of money in self-interested hands to the support of political campaigning . . . threatens the capacity of this democracy to represent its constituents and the confidence of its citizens in their capacity to govern themselves."[148] The no other reasonable interpretation test flatly contradicted *McConnell*. This decision permitted companies and unions to easily circumvent the ban on their making campaign contributions "simply by running 'issue ads' without express advocacy, or by funneling the money through an independent corporation like WRTL."[149]

In *Citizens United v. Federal Election Commission*, the Supreme Court struck down a federal law that prohibited corporations and unions from using general treasury funds to make independent expenditures for " 'electioneering communication' " or for speech expressly advocating the election or defeat of a candidate.[150] The Court also overturned *Austin v. Michigan Chamber of Commerce* and the portion of *McConnell v. Federal Election Commission* that upheld limits on corporate electioneering communications. However, the Court upheld disclaimer and disclosure requirements on corporate political speech.

---

[142] 551 U.S. at 481.

[143] *Id.* at 482.

[144] *Id.*

[145] *Id.* (Alito, J., concurring).

[146] *Id.* at 483–84 (Scalia, concurring in part and in the judgment).

[147] *Id.* at 484.

[148] *Id.* at 507 (Souter, J., dissenting).

[149] *Id.* at 536.

[150] 130 S. Ct. 876, 886 (2010).

Citizens United released a film in 2008 that criticized Senator Hillary Clinton, entitled *Hillary: The Movie*. The organization received most of its funds from individuals, but in addition accepted a small portion from for-profit corporations. Citizens United sought to pay to make its film available through video-on-demand within 30 days of the 2008 primary election, which would have violated the restrictions on corporate expenditures. The Court requested reargument to determine whether to overturn *Austin* and that portion of *McConnell* upholding a facial challenge on § 441b, the prohibition on corporate expenditures. The Court allowed a facial challenge because the distinction between facial and as-applied challenges was "not so well defined."[151] Only addressing an as-applied challenge would prolong the chilling effect of § 441b on corporate expenditures. Corporations fearing the possibility of civil and criminal penalties would either refrain from speaking or request an advisory opinion from the FEC. This was an "unprecedented governmental intervention into the realm of speech."[152]

Section 441b punished by felony any corporation, even nonprofit advocacy corporations, that broadcasted electioneering communications or expressly advocated for or against a candidate within 30 days of a primary election and 60 days of a general election. The statute's exception for a corporation's PAC did "not alleviate the *First Amendment* problems," for "PACs are burdensome alternatives; they are expensive to administer and subject to extensive regulations."[153] As an indication of this, "fewer than 2,000 of the millions of corporations in this country have PACs."[154]

Writing for the majority, Justice Kennedy said that laws that burden political speech must pass strict scrutiny. Government must prove that the restriction " 'furthers a compelling interest and is narrowly tailored to achieve that interest.' "[155] *Bellotti* recognized that the First Amendment protected corporations. *Bellotti* struck down a ban of independent corporate expenditures on referenda, but did not address state bans on independent expenditures to support or oppose candidates. *Austin* upheld such a ban, finding a compelling governmental interest in preventing " 'the corrosive and distorting effects of immense aggregations of wealth that are accumulated with the help of the corporate form and that have little or no correlation to the public's support for the corporation's political ideas.' "[156]

Austin and its progeny collided with pre-*Austin* precedent that prohibited speech restrictions based on the speaker's corporate identity. *Austin's* reasoning would allow the government to prohibit a corporation from printing books expressing political views. Justice Kennedy noted that the Government's arguments did little to defend *Austin's* antidistortion of wealth rationale. *Buckley* explicitly denied the antidistortion rationale by rejecting that the government had an interest in

---

[151] *Citizens United*, 130 S. Ct. at 893.

[152] *Id.* at 896.

[153] *Id.* at 897. Every PAC had to file an organizational statement and detailed monthly reports with the FEC. Also, each PAC had to have a treasurer who received donations, kept detailed records of the donations and the identity of donors, and preserved receipts for three years.

[154] *Id.*

[155] Fed. Election Comm'n v. Wis. Right to Life (WRTL), 551 U.S. 449, 464 (2007).

[156] *Citizens United*, 130 S. Ct. at 903.

equalizing the ability to influence elections. The *Austin* majority distinguished corporations from wealthy individuals on the ground that state law afforded the corporate structure special financial advantages. However, " 'the State cannot exact as the price of those special advantages the forfeiture of *First Amendment* rights.' "[157] Also, it was irrelevant for First Amendment purposes that corporate funds were amassed without regard to public support for the corporation's political ideas.

While some media corporations had " 'immense aggregations of wealth,' " they were all exempt from § 441b.[158] This exemption also applied to corporations consisting of both a media business and an unrelated business. Greater influence over government officials did not necessarily entail corruption. " 'Favoritism and influence are not . . . avoidable in representative politics.' "[159] Moreover, the Government's other asserted interest in protecting dissenting shareholders from funding political speech could even ban the political speech of media corporations. The statute was underinclusive in protecting dissenting shareholders because it only prohibits speech within 30 or 60 days of an election. The statute was overinclusive by covering all corporations, including nonprofit and single-shareholder corporations. The Court did not address whether the Government had a compelling interest in preventing foreign individuals or entities from influencing domestic politics.

The Court determined whether to adhere to *stare decisis* based on the precedent's workability, antiquity, " 'the reliance interests at stake, and of course whether the decision was well reasoned.' "[160] As neither party defended *Austin's* rationale, the pull of *stare decisis* diminished. Apparently, § 441b would prohibit a corporate blog post. "The *First Amendment* does not permit Congress to make these categorical distinctions based on the corporate identity of the speaker and the content of the political speech."[161] Moreover, no serious reliance interest was at stake.

The Court overruled *Austin* and returned to the principle of *Buckley* and *Bellotti* that the Government could suppress political speech because of the speaker's corporate identity. Section 441b's ban on independent corporate expenditures was invalid and could not be applied to the film *Hillary*. The Court thus overruled that part of *McConnell*.

Citizens United also challenged the FEC's disclaimer and disclosure require-ments. BCRA § 311 required independent electioneering communications to include a statement disclaiming candidate authorization and also the name and address or website address of the person or group funding the communication. Under BCRA § 201 organizations must also file FEC statements disclosing the person making the expenditure, the amount, the election to which it is directed, and the names of certain contributors. *Buckley* subjects disclosure and disclaimer "requirements to

---

[157] *Id.* at 905.

[158] *Id.*

[159] *Id.* at 910.

[160] *Id.* at 912

[161] *Id.*

'exacting scrutiny,' which require[s] a 'substantial relation' between the disclosure requirement and a 'sufficiently important' governmental interest."[162] Disclosures were justified based on a governmental interest in " 'provid[ing] the electorate with information' about the sources of election-related spending."[163] *McConnell* used this interest to reject facial challenges to BCRA §§ 201 and 311. Disclosure helped to identify groups running advertisements using " ' "dubious and misleading names." ' "[164]

As-applied challenges to disclosure requirements would succeed if a group showed a " ' "reasonable probability" ' that disclosure of its contributors' names ' "will subject them to threats, harassment, or reprisals from either Government officials or private parties." ' "[165] Justice Kennedy also rejected Citizens United's argument that § 311 was underinclusive because its required disclaimer, that the advertisement was not produced by a party or candidate, did not apply to print or Internet advertising. Disclosures in the era of modern technology and the Internet can provide rapid information that shareholders and citizens needed to hold corporations and elected officials accountable. The Court upheld BCRA §§ 201 and 311, and affirmed their application to *Hillary*.

Chief Justice Roberts concurred, joined by Justice Alito. Regardless of whether the Court labeled Citizens United's challenge " 'facial' or 'as-applied,' " the consequences were the same.[166] Chief Justice Roberts termed *stare decisis* a " 'principle of policy.' "[167] The Court should be more willing to depart from a precedent that did more damage than good to the orderly development of the law. First, *Austin* was inconsistent with *Buckley's* "explicit repudiation" of a governmental interest in equalizing the ability to influence elections.[168] It was also inconsistent with *Bellotti*. Second, *Austin* had been consistently disputed within this Court, which undermined "the precedent's ability to contribute to the stable and orderly development of the law."[169] Moreover, *Austin* is "uniquely destabilizing" by threatening to subvert decisions outside corporate speech. Its logic would authorize broad prohibition of political speech in the name of equality.[170] The Government's arguments to reaffirm *Austin* were "radically reconceptualizing its reasoning," and thus these new arguments were not entitled to the special deference given to precedent.[171]

Justice Scalia filed a concurrence, in which Justice Alito joined and Justice Thomas joined in part. The dissent argued that the original understanding of the First Amendment did not support this decision. However, even if the Founders

---

[162] *Id.* at 914.

[163] *Id.* at 914.

[164] *Id.*

[165] *Id.*

[166] *Id.* at 919.

[167] *Id.* at 920.

[168] *Id.* at 921.

[169] *Id.* at 922.

[170] *Id.* at 922.

[171] *Id.* at 924.

disliked founding-era corporations and it was proper to exclude from First Amendment coverage what the Founders disliked, modern corporations might not be excluded. Most of the Founders' resentment applied to corporations with state-granted monopolies.

Justice Stevens dissented in part, joined by Justices Ginsburg, Breyer, and Sotomayor. Justice Stevens concurred with the Court's decision to uphold BCRA's disclosure provisions. The real issue was not if, but how, Citizens United may finance its electioneering. Citizens United, a wealthy nonprofit with millions of dollars in assets, could have spent unrestricted sums to broadcast *Hillary* at any time other than 30 days before the primary election. This ruling "threatens to undermine the integrity of elected institutions across the Nation."[172]

Justice Stevens disagreed with treating this case as a facial challenge. The Court had "repeatedly emphasized in recent years that '[f]acial challenges are disfavored.' "[173] The Court here negated Congress' efforts to combat corruption where previous legislation had failed, and overruled a "virtual mountain of research" without any evidence except how the law affected Citizens United. The Court taking free reign to construe litigants' claims would upend not only the distinction between as-applied and facial challenges, but the basic relationship between litigants and courts. There were narrower grounds to decide this case. As one alternative, "the Court could have ruled, on statutory grounds, that a feature-length film distributed through video-on-demand does not qualify as an 'electioneering communication' " under § 441b.[174] Moreover, "the Court could have expanded the *MCFL* exemption to cover § 501(c)(4) nonprofits that accept only a *de minimis* amount of money from for-profit corporations."[175]

The Court's central argument for trumping *stare decisis* "is that it does not like *Austin*."[176] The majority's arguments against *stare decisis* say almost nothing about the Court's standard considerations of the precedent's antiquity, workability, and the reliance interests at stake. "*Austin* has been on the books for two decades, and many of the statutes called into question by today's opinion have been on the books for a half-century or more."[177] The Court also offers no argument that *Austin* and *McConnell* are unworkable. Moreover, more than half of the States, along with leading groups in business, organized labor, and nonprofit organizations seek to preserve *Austin*, including the United States Chamber of Commerce and the AFL-CIO. This ruling "strikes at the vitals of *stare decisis*," for the "majority opinion is essentially an amalgamation of resuscitated dissents," and the "only relevant thing that has changed since *Austin* and *McConnell* is the composition of this Court."[178]

---

[172] *Id.* at 931 (Stevens, J., dissenting).

[173] *Id.* at 932.

[174] *Id.* at 937.

[175] *Id.*

[176] *Id.* at 938.

[177] *Id.* at 941.

[178] *Id.* at 942.

Under § 441b there are many options for corporate political speech. Corporate and union PACs in the last election cycle raised nearly a billion dollars. Corporations with a common ideology can make unlimited expenditures through an *MCFL* organization which ensures that it remains free from business or union interests. Corporations can spend unlimited sums to communicate to executives and shareholders, "fund additional PAC activity through trade associations, to distribute voting guides and voting records, to underwrite voter registration and voter turnout activities, to host fundraising events for candidates within certain limits, and to publicly endorse candidates through a press release and press conference."[179] Existing law only prohibits speech by a labor union or a non-MCFL, nonmedia corporation if it was a broadcast, cable, or satellite communication that could reach 50,000 persons in the relevant electorate, was made within 30 days of a primary or 60 days of a general federal election, was paid for with general treasury funds, and was " 'susceptible of no reasonable interpretation other than as an appeal to vote for or against a specific candidate.' "[180]

It had long been recognized that corporations have the "distinctive potential" to corrupt the electoral process.[181] Moreover, within campaign finance, corporate spending was " 'furthest from the core of political expression, since corporations' *First Amendment* speech and association interests are derived largely from those of their members and of the public in receiving information.' "[182]

Justice Scalia's concurrence did not dispatch the argument that the founding generation cautiously viewed corporate power, narrowly viewed corporate rights, and "conceptualized speech in individualistic terms."[183] Justice Scalia "emphasizes the unqualified nature of the *First Amendment* text," but to be able to claim that views on newspapers must track those on corporations, he seemingly read out the Free Press Clause.[184]

In 1907, Congress made an express distinction between corporate and individual spending on elections, banning all corporate contributions to federal candidates by the Tillman Act. In *McConnell*, we found corporate spending restrictions "faithful to the compelling governmental interests in ' "preserving the integrity of the electoral process, preventing corruption," ' " and sustaining confidence in government and the individual citizen's active, alert responsibility that is necessary to secure wise conduct in a democratic government.[185] Corporations' option to form PACs made the answer even easier.

Bellotti dealt with dramatically different facts than *Austin*. The statute challenged in *Bellotti* barred a business corporation " 'from making contributions or expenditures "for the purpose of . . . influencing or affecting the vote on any question submitted to the voters, other than one materially affecting any of the

---

[179] *Id.* at 944.

[180] *Id.*

[181] *Id.* at 947.

[182] *Id.*

[183] *Id.* at 951.

[184] *Id.*

[185] *Id.* at 957.

property, business or assets of the corporation." ' "[186] The statute even labeled income taxation as not materially affecting the assets of the corporation, for the legislature had enacted the statute to limit corporate speech on a proposed state constitutional amendment that authorized a graduated income tax. The statute also did not allow corporations to spend through PACs. All six Members of the *Austin* majority were on the Court for *Bellotti*, and none even hinted at a tension between the decisions.

Corruption could take many forms, as the congressional record for the BCRA showed. The BCRA legislative and judicial " 'record powerfully demonstrates that electioneering communications paid for with the general treasury funds of labor unions and corporations endears those entities to elected officials in a way that could be perceived by the public as corrupting.' "[187] There is no such record here because "the Government had no reason to develop a record at trial for a facial challenge the plaintiff had abandoned."[188] Members of the Court suggested in *McConnell* that the BCRA "may be little more than 'an incumbency protection plan,' " however there is an absence of evidence in the record of " 'invidious discrimination against challengers.' "[189]

Who is speaking when a corporation publishes an advertisement? The officers or directors hold the best claim; it is certainly not the customers or employees, nor the shareholders who are removed from day-to-day decisions. Recognizing the weakness of arguing for the corporation's "right to electioneer," the majority emphasized the listener interests.[190] If the audience's interest was overriding, then "the public's perception of the value of corporate speech should be given important weight."[191]

The majority "raised some interesting and difficult questions about Congress' authority to regulate electioneering by the press."[192] However, *"that is not the case before us."*[193] The holding did not protect shareholders from coerced speech, which the existence of PACs did by assuring that those who pay for an electioneering communication actually support its content.

Justice Thomas concurred in part and dissented in part. He would invalidate the disclosure, disclaimer, and reporting requirements in BCRA §§ 201 and 311. "Congress may not abridge the 'right to anonymous speech' based on the " 'simple interest in providing voters with additional relevant information.' " "[194] He also

---

[186] *Id.* at 959.

[187] *Id.* at 966. In *Caperton* the Court accepted that "at least in some circumstances, independent expenditures on candidate elections will raise an intolerable specter of *quid pro quo* corruption." *Id.* at 967.

[188] *Id.* at 966–67.

[189] *Id.* at 968.

[190] *Id.* at 973.

[191] *Id.*

[192] *Id.* at 976.

[193] *Id.*

[194] *Id.* at 980 (Thomas, J., concurring in part and dissenting in part). Some opponents of California's Proposition 8 on banning same-sex marriage "compiled contributors' information and created Web sites with maps showing the locations of homes or businesses of Proposition 8 supporters. Many supporters

noted "the threat of retaliation from *elected officials.*"[195]

In a series of cases relating to unions, the Court made clear that unions could not charge fees to non-member dissenting employees to support political activities, such as lobbying, not related to their collective bargaining activity.[196]

In *Davenport v. Washington Education Ass'n,*[197] the Court held that state governments may require unions to obtain affirmative consent from a nonmember before the nonmember's dues paid for collective bargaining purposes may be used for unrelated ideological purposes. This requirement is constitutional even though it exceeds the constitutional minimum established in *Abood v. Detroit Board of Education*[198] *Abood* merely required unions to give nonmembers the opportunity to object to their dues being used for ideological purposes.

Ysursa v. Pocatello Education Ass'n[199] upheld a law allowing a public employee to direct his employer to deduct funds from his wages for remittance as union dues, but prohibiting deductions for the union's political action committee. The state law also prohibited "payroll deductions for political activities."[200] Chief Justice Roberts found the law did not limit political speech, but simply declined to promote it with "public employee checkoffs for political activities."[201]

Justice Ginsburg concurred in part and concurred in the judgment. Justice Breyer dissented, noting that stopping one avenue of funding at least indirectly affected speech. Justice Souter also dissented, citing a "reasonable suspicion of viewpoint discrimination"[202] against union speech. Justice Stevens dissented on statutory grounds.

In *Keller v. State Bar,*[203] the Court held that the California Bar could not use mandatory dues to finance political activities that dissenting members did not support. Analogizing to the union cases, the Court stated that the standard was whether the disputed expenditure involved "regulating the legal profession and improving the quality of legal services."[204] While this standard would be difficult to apply, activities like endorsing gun control or nuclear freeze initiatives were not permissible while compulsory dues could be spent in proposing new ethical values. California could help to resolve the difficult questions in between these instances with "an adequate explanation of the basis for its fee, a reasonably prompt opportunity to challenge the amount of the fee before an impartial decision maker,

---

(or their customers) suffered property damage, or threats of physical violence or death, as a result." *Id.*

[195] *Id.* at 981.

[196] *See, e.g.,* Lehnert v. Ferris Faculty Ass'n., 500 U.S. 507 (1991); Abood v. Detroit Bd. of Educ., 431 U.S. 209 (1977).

[197] 551 U.S. 177 (2007).

[198] 431 U.S. 209 (1977).

[199] 129 S. Ct. 1093 (2009).

[200] *Id.* at 1096.

[201] *Id.* at 1906.

[202] *Id.* at 1109.

[203] 496 U.S. 1 (1990).

[204] *Id.* at 13.

and an escrow for the amounts reasonably in dispute."[205]

In *Davis v. Federal Election Commission*,[206] the Court invalidated two provisions of the federal Bipartisan Campaign Reform Act of 2002 (BCRA) known as the " 'Millionaire's Amendment.' " Under the BCRA, a candidate was considered self-financing if she personally spent more than $350,000 on her own campaign. When a self-financing candidate ran against a non-self-financing candidate, asymmetrical campaign contribution limits and reporting requirements were imposed on each. Specifically, the non-self-financing candidate could accept three times the normal limit of individual contributions and unlimited coordinated party expenditures until such contributions were equal to the personal expenditures of their self-financing opponent; at that point, the normal limits were reimposed. In contrast, the self-financing candidate did not have any of the above fund-raising advantages. Moreover, the self-financing candidate was required to report: a " 'declaration of intent' " to spend more than $350,000 within 15 days of entering a race, an " 'initial notification' " within 24 hours of crossing the $350,000 mark, and an " 'additional notification' " within 24 hours of each additional expenditure from personal funds of $10,000 or more. The non-self-financing candidate faced less demanding disclosure requirements. These candidates were required to report only when: based on notification by a self-financing opponent, they believed $350,000 in personal funds had been spent; their additional contributions became equal to that opponent's personal expenditures; or they had to return "excess funds."

A uniform change in contribution limits was facially constitutional under *Buckley v. Valeo*.[207] Even those limits, however, must be " 'closely drawn' to serve a 'sufficiently important interest.' " While campaign contribution limits could be impermissibly low, there was no constitutionally unacceptable upper limit. The Court has never upheld the imposition of disparate campaign contribution limits on candidates competing in the same election.

The BCRA effectively penalized self-financing candidates for exercising their First Amendment right to personally finance their own campaign speech. Candidates were forced to choose between limiting their personal expenditures and consequently their speech, or campaigning under the burden imposed by the BCRA's "discriminatory" contribution limits.

The Court found no "compelling state interest" in eliminating real or perceived corruption and noted that *Buckley* rejected leveling candidates' financial resources as such an interest. This sort of equalization would allow Congress to infringe on the voters' right to independently evaluate candidates based on all their strengths — which could include fame, personal wealth, or wealthy supporters. If the permissible interests of preventing corruption or the perception that congressional seats may be bought were not served by the current contribution limits, those limits should be uniformly raised or eliminated altogether.

---

[205] *Id.* at 16.

[206] 554 U.S. 724 (2008).

[207] 424 U.S. 1 (1976).

Justice Alito subjected BCRA's reporting requirements to "exacting scrutiny," under which a court must find a "relevant correlation" or "substantial relation" between the claimed governmental interest and the disclosed information. As the seriousness of the burden on First Amendment rights increases, so also must the strength of the government's interest. The BCRA requirements did not meet this standard, as the government could not justify the severity of the burden these symmetrical contribution limits imposed on First Amendment rights.

Justice Stevens dissented, joined by Justices Souter, Ginsburg, and Breyer. The BCRA simply reduced the inequality between non-self-financing candidates and their self-financing opponents. In his *Buckley* dissent, Justice White explained that such limitations are comparable to "time, place, and manner regulations," rather than direct limitations on speech. Justice Stevens noted that quantity limitations are common in other situations involving "high-value speech," such as Supreme Court oral arguments and briefs. Quantity limitations are often beneficial to speakers as well as their audiences. Without such restrictions, candidates could overwhelm voters and cloud important issues. Consequently, limiting the quantity of speech is not the same as limiting its content, which would violate the First Amendment. The BCRA was also consistent with *Buckley's* rejecting of expenditure limitations as it did not restrict any speech at all, but allowed the non-self-financing candidate a voice equal to that of his opponent.

Finally, Justice Stevens rejected the conclusion that preventing real and perceived corruption are the only governmental interests weighty enough to justify campaign finance regulations. The government has legitimate, long-standing interests in minimizing the effect of a candidate's wealth on an election and the perception that wealth is the sole determinant in a political race. These concerns have typically arisen in past decisions involving corporations, but the same reasoning should also apply to individual wealth. Moreover, the self-financing candidate's opponent received no unfair advantage as he could only take advantage of the increased limits until he was financially equal to his opponent.

Justice Ginsburg, joined by Justice Breyer, wrote a separate dissent. She agreed with Justice Stevens that the challenged provisions did not violate *Buckley's* holding, but thought that the issues presented in this case did not require reconsideration of the *Buckley* decision.

In *Arizona Free Enterprise Club's Freedom Club PAC v. Bennett*, the Court held that "Arizona's matching funds scheme substantially burdens protected political speech without serving a compelling state interest."[208] Arizona granted publicly funded candidates "additional 'equalizing' or matching funds" in both primary and general elections.[209] "During the general election, matching funds were triggered when the amount of money a privately financed candidate receives in contributions, combined with the expenditures of independent groups made in support of the privately financed candidate," are more than "the general election allotment of state funds to the publicly financed candidate."[210] Once that occurred, "every dollar that

---

[208] 131 S. Ct. 2806, 2813 (2011).

[209] *Id.* at 2814.

[210] *Id.*

a candidate receives in contributions — which includes any money of his own that a candidate spends on his campaign" triggered "an almost one dollar increase in public funding to each of the publicly financed candidates."[211] Moreover, additional expenditures by independent groups can result in dollar-for-dollar matching funds as well."[212] That matching provision "is not activated, however, when independent expenditures are made in opposition to a privately financed candidate."[213] Such funds would "top out at two times the initial authorized grant of public funding to the publicly financed candidate."[214]

Chief Justice Roberts delivered the opinion of the Court (5-4). In the similar case of *Davis v. Federal Election Commission*,[215] the law at issue provided that "if a candidate for the United States House of Representatives spent more than $350,000 of his personal funds," limits on contributions to opponents' campaigns trebled from $2300 to $6900.[216] "If the law at issue in *Davis* imposed a burden on candidate speech, the Arizona law unquestionably does so as well."[217] If anything, the differences between the laws made "the Arizona law *more* constitutionally problematic, not less."[218]

The first difference was that while "the penalty in *Davis* consisted of raising the contribution limits for one of the candidates," the benefited candidate "still had to go out and raise" that money.[219] "Second, depending on the specifics of the election at issue, the matching funds provision can create a multiplier effect" as each dollar spent could fund multiple publicly funded candidates.[220] Third, all spending by independent groups, "whether such support was welcome or helpful — could trigger matching funds."[221] This "disparity in control — giving money directly to a publicly financed candidate in response to independent expenditures that cannot be coordinated with the privately funded candidate — is a substantial advantage for the publicly funded candidate."[222]

Consequently, "the burdens that this regime places on independent expenditure groups are akin to those imposed on the privately financed candidates themselves."[223] Like the privately financed candidate, "spending one dollar can result in the flow of dollars to multiple candidates the group disproves of."[224] However, in

---

[211] *Id.*

[212] *Id.*

[213] *Id.*

[214] *Id.* at 2815–16.

[215] Davis v. Fed. Election Comm'n, 554 U.S. 724 (2008).

[216] *Bennett*, 131 S. Ct. at 2817; *See* Davis, 554 U.S. at 729.

[217] *Id.* at 2818.

[218] *Id.*

[219] *Id.*

[220] *Id.* at 2819.

[221] *Id.*

[222] *Id.*

[223] *Id.*

[224] *Id.*

some respects, "the burden the Arizona law imposes on independent expenditure groups is 'worse than the burden it imposes on privately financed candidates.' "[225] A candidate "at least has the option of taking public financing" unlike independent expenditure groups.[226]

The Court rejected the State's argument that "the matching funds provision actually" increases the amount of speech.[227] "Any increase in speech resulting from the Arizona law is of one kind and one kind only — that of publicly financed candidates."[228] This increase came at the expense of "privately financed candidates and independent expenditure groups" as the law decreased their speech.[229] The Court has "rejected government efforts to increase the speech of some at the expense of others."[230] Chief Justice Roberts continued: "It is not the amount of funding that the State provides to publicly financed candidates that is constitutionally problematic," but the trigger for that funding "in direct response to the political speech of privately financed candidates and independent expenditure groups."[231]

As the law "imposes a substantial burden on the speech," it must be " 'justified by a compelling state interest.' "[232] Arizona argued that the law was designed to " 'level the playing field.' "[233] However, *Buckley* declared that "limits on overall campaign expenditures could not be justified by a purported government 'interest in equalizing the financial resources of candidates.' "[234] Moreover, "even if the ultimate objective of the matching funds provision is to combat corruption — and not 'level the playing field' — the burdens that the matching funds provision imposes on protected political speech are not justified."[235]

Lastly, the Court made clear that it was not calling "into question the wisdom of public financing."[236] However, the way government "chooses to encourage participation in its public funding system matters."[237]

Justice Kagan dissented, joined by Justices Ginsberg, Breyer, and Sotomayor. "Campaign finance reform over the last century has focused on one key question: how to prevent massive pools of private money from corrupting our political system. If an officeholder owes his election to wealthy contributors, he may act for their benefit alone, rather than on behalf of all" constituents.[238]

---

[225] *Id.*

[226] *Id.*

[227] *Id.* at 2820.

[228] *Id.*

[229] *Id.* at 2821.

[230] *Id.*

[231] *Id.* at 2824.

[232] *Id.*

[233] *Id.* at 2825.

[234] *Id.* at 2826 (quoting *Buckley v. Valeo*, 424 U.S. 1, 56 (1976)).

[235] *Bennett*, 131 S. Ct. at 2826.

[236] *Id.* at 2828.

[237] *Id.*

[238] *Id.* at 2830 (Kagan, J., dissenting).

That is why nearly "one-third of the States have adopted some form of public financing."[239] Congress viewed public financing for presidential elections as the only way to eliminate the "danger of corruption, while still ensuring that a wide range of candidates had access to the ballot."[240] The presidential public financing system involves a "lump-sum grant at the beginning of the election cycle," and *Buckley* declared that scheme constitutional.[241] Justice Kagan noted that "the dynamic nature of our electoral system makes *ex ante* predictions about campaign expenditures almost impossible. And that creates a chronic problem for lump-sum public financing programs."[242] Thus, the Arizona "program's designers found the Goldilocks solution, which produces the 'just right' grant to ensure that a participant in the system has the funds needed to run a competitive race."[243] Moreover, in response to the majority opinion that the Act inhibits expenditure groups, Justice Kagan noted that "expenditures by these groups have risen by 253%" since the Arizona law has existed.[244]

Once the publicly financed candidate has received three times the amount of the initial disbursement, he gets no further public funding, and remains "barred from receiving private contributions, no matter how much more his privately funded opponent spends."[245] Essentially, the Arizona statute "subsidizes and so produces *more* political speech."[246] Thus, "what petitioners demand is essentially a right to quash others' speech through the prohibition of a (universally available) subsidy program."[247]

In upholding "the presidential public financing system," *Buckley* rejected the principal challenge to that system which "came from minor-party candidates not eligible for benefits."[248] The Court "rejected that attack in part because we understood the federal program as supporting, rather than interfering with, expression."[249] The "very notion that additional speech constitutes a 'burden' is odd and unsettling."[250] The Court has "never, not once, understood a viewpoint-neutral subsidy given to one speaker to constitute a First Amendment burden."[251]

The District Court had found that "petitioners had presented only 'vague' and 'scattered' evidence of the law's deterrent impact."[252] Even the lump-sum system

---

[239] *Id.*

[240] *Id.* at 2831.

[241] *Id.*

[242] *Id.* at 2832.

[243] *Id.*

[244] *Id.* at 2834 n.5.

[245] *Id.* at 2832–33.

[246] *Id.* at 2833.

[247] *Id.* at 2835.

[248] *Id.* at 2836.

[249] *Id.*

[250] *Id.*

[251] *Id.* at 2837.

[252] *Id.* at 2837 n.6.

upheld in *Buckley* "may deter speech."[253] Moreover, this Court has repeatedly upheld "disclosure and disclaimer requirements" despite their deterrent effects on campaign speech.[254] "Any burden that the Arizona law imposes does not exceed the burden associated with contribution limits, which we have also repeatedly upheld."[255] Thus, "the Court errs in holding that the government action in this case substantially burdens speech." Moreover, the deterring "corruption or the appearance of corruption is a compelling government interest."[256]

§ 16.03   GOVERNMENT SPENDING ON SPEECH RELATED ACTIVITIES

Another series of questions involves whether the First Amendment might restrict government spending to advance particular ideas or viewpoints. To this point, the Court has taken a relatively hands off approach. In *Regan v. Taxation With Representation*,[257] the Court upheld Congress' refusal to afford a tax deduction for lobbying. The Court held that the government was not obliged to subsidize any speech activities. The Court also rejected an equal protection challenge based on the fact that the government did allow veterans' organizations deductions for lobbying. No basis for the equal protection challenge existed as the government was not obliged to subsidize the exercise of a fundamental right.

In *Rust v. Sullivan*,[258] the Court rejected a facial challenge against that part of the Public Health Service Act (Title X) which authorized expenditures to advance family planning methods but excepted abortion. Entities receiving federal funds could neither engage in abortion counseling nor refer a woman to abortion services, even upon her specific request. The regulations also prohibited funded projects from engaging in activities that "encourage, promote, or advocate abortion as a method of family planning," including lobbying or sponsoring speakers. Finally, the regulations required physical and financial separation of the Title X project from prohibited abortion activities, including separate accounting and personnel. The Court rejected the argument that Title X allowed unconstitutional viewpoint discrimination by permitting counseling which favored bringing the pregnancy to term, while prohibiting counseling for abortion.

Relying on *Maher v. Roe*[259] and *Harris v. McRae*,[260] which upheld government funding of childbirth but not abortion, the Court noted that government may make a value judgment favoring childbirth over abortion. The Court stated that there is a difference between interfering with an activity and subsidizing it. Relying on

---

[253] *Id.* at 2838.

[254] *Id.*

[255] *Id.*

[256] *Id.* at 2841.

[257] 461 U.S. 540 (1983).

[258] 500 U.S. 173 (1991).

[259] 432 U.S. 464 (1977); *supra* § 8.06[1].

[260] 448 U.S. 297 (1980); *supra* § 8.06[1].

Regan v. Taxation With Representation,[261] the Court stated that the government was not required to fund competing lines of political philosophy, or speech that embodied all competing points of view. Nor did the law in question impose an unconstitutional condition on the recipients of federal funds. While members of the grantee's staff could not counsel abortion at work, they retained their speech rights as private individuals outside the workplace.

The Court emphasized, however, that the ability of recipients of government funds to speak outside their work would not always justify government control of the content of speech. In this connection, the Court stated that imposing such conditions on universities could implicate vagueness or overbreadth concerns. The Court also emphasized the limited scope of the doctor-patient relationship at issue, and the fact that the doctor could note to the patient that abortion advice was not within the scope of the program.

Justice Blackmun dissented, joined by Justices Marshall and O'Connor. Justice Blackmun maintained that neither the language nor legislative history of Title X supported the construction that the Secretary had imposed on the regulations. The statute could be construed to prohibit using federal funds only in performing abortions. As the Secretary's interpretation raised serious constitutional questions, he would have construed the statute differently under the canon that a statute should be construed to avoid serious constitutional questions.

Joined by Justices Marshall and Stevens, Justice Blackmun also objected to the government's actions on constitutional grounds. The government could not condition federal funds and employment based on acceptance of a particular viewpoint. Moreover, the dissenters argued that the government was suppressing true information about an activity that was constitutionally protected. Not only did this suppression violate the First Amendment, but it also unconstitutionally constricted a woman's right freely to decide whether to choose an abortion.

In *Rosenberger v. University of Virginia,*[262] the Court (5-4) invalidated denying a student-run newspaper funding because of its religious viewpoint. The University of Virginia allowed student organizations to receive funding from the Student Activities Fund (SAF) for various outside contractors, including printers. Full-time students at the University were required to pay a mandatory fee of $14 to support the SAF. One student organization, Wide Awake Productions (WAP), published a newspaper with a Christian viewpoint. The University did not consider WAP a religious organization that would have vitiated the opportunity for funding. Instead, the University classified WAP as a source of student news which qualified WAP for funding from the SAF. However, SAF denied WAP's request to pay for its printing costs maintaining that funding would have violated the Establishment Clause.

Justice Kennedy held that the denial of funding was unconstitutional viewpoint discrimination. Having established a public forum in which it encouraged diverse student views, the University could not single out the religious perspective on issues for denial of funding. Justice Kennedy analogized this case to *Lamb's Chapel v.*

---

[261] 461 U.S. 540, *supra* note 257.

[262] 515 U.S. 819 (1995).

Center Moriches Union Free School District[263] in which the Court invalidated the government's predicating access to government property based on viewpoint discrimination.

Nevertheless, the University asserted that it should enjoy substantial discretion in allocating University funds. In *Rust v. Sullivan*,[264] the government did not allocate funding to encourage diverse private speech but instead engaged private actors to convey a government message about family planning. The State may allocate funds in the way that it wishes to convey its own message. Here, the University required the student organizations to sign agreements of disassociation disclaiming any support or endorsement of the newspaper's expression by the University. Consistent with *Regan v. Taxation With Representation*,[265] government can single out certain organizations — such as veterans groups — for more favorable treatment in its funding decisions but not based on the viewpoint of the group's message.

The Court rejected the argument that providing funding would violate the Establishment Clause. Funding would exhibit neutrality towards religion and not endorsement. The Court distinguished the student fee used to support diverse student activities from a tax used to support a church.[266] Moreover, the University explicitly disassociated itself from whatever speech it funds.

Finally, the Court distinguished this case from the government unconstitutionally giving money to a religious institution. The newspaper was not a religious institution; payments were made directly "to third-party contractors"; and the funding was no different than the access to the University's facilities permitted to religious organizations in *Widmar v. Vincent*.[267]

Justices O'Connor and Thomas filed concurring opinions. Justice Souter dissented, joined by Justices Stevens, Ginsburg, and Breyer. Justice Souter believed that the Establishment Clause mandated the University's denial of funds. He criticized the majority as allowing, for the first time, a public institution directly to fund a core religious activity.

In *Board of Regents of the University of Wisconsin System v. Southworth*,[268] the Court upheld a viewpoint neutral student activity fee. Writing for the majority, Justice Kennedy stated that students allocated the fee, not university officials. The majority required that the University be viewpoint neutral in allocating funds to student organizations. As the parties had stipulated that two of the three methods of fee allocation at issue in this case were viewpoint neutral, the Court upheld these methods. Justice Kennedy remanded for further findings on the third method requiring a student referendum.

---

[263] *See supra* § 15.06.

[264] 500 U.S. 173, *supra* note 258.

[265] 461 U.S. 540, *supra* note 257.

[266] The issue was not presented as to whether a student could demand a *pro rata* portion of her fee returned if it is spent on speech to which she does not subscribe.

[267] *See supra* § 15.06.

[268] 529 U.S. 217 (2000).

Justice Souter concurred in the opinion. He asserted that the allocation of activities fees was integral to the University's educational mission and therefore was protected by academic freedom.

In *United States v. American Library Ass'n*,[269] the Court upheld (6-3) a statute that withheld funding from public libraries unless they installed computer software that prevented viewing pornography. Congress worried that federal programs that assisted libraries in obtaining Internet access "were facilitating access to illegal and harmful pornography."[270] To protect minors, the Children's Internet Protection Act (CIPA) required libraries to install software that blocked obscene images and child pornography in order to continue receiving government funding for Internet access.

Internet access did not establish a public forum, either traditional or designated. Unlike an open forum, the staffs at public libraries enjoyed broad discretion in making decisions concerning the content of their collections. If the software used blocked constitutionally protected speech, adult users could simply ask the librarian to disable the filter or unblock a specific site. *Rust v. Sullivan*[271] afforded the government broad discretion to limit the use of public funds. Traditionally, libraries have not included pornographic material in their collections.

Justice Kennedy concurred in the judgment. Also concurring in the judgment, Justice Breyer maintained that any speech-related harm was a small burden that was not disproportionate to the Act's legitimate objectives.

Dissenting, Justice Stevens argued that filtering software will under-block some harmful sites while over-blocking many legitimate sites. Justice Souter also filed a dissenting opinion, joined by Justice Ginsburg. He contended that libraries have evolved toward a rule allowing any adult "access to any of its holdings."[272]

In *Legal Services Corp. v. Velazquez*,[273] the Court struck down a Congressional restriction on using Legal Services Corporation (LSC) funds to challenge existing welfare laws. Congress established LSC to distribute funds to local organizations which provided indigent persons with legal assistance. Since the program's inception, Congress has limited the use of LSC funds. For example, recipient organizations could not use grants towards political parties or political campaigns.[274] Congress also barred recipients from using LSC grants " 'in litigation, lobbying, or rulemaking, involving an effort to reform a Federal or State welfare system.' "[275] The restriction at issue in this case prohibited LSC attorneys from challenging existing welfare laws.

---

[269] 539 U.S. 194 (2003).

[270] *Id.* at 200.

[271] 500 U.S. 173 (1991).

[272] 539 U.S. at 238.

[273] 531 U.S. 533 (2001).

[274] *Id.* at 537. Congress also prohibited the use of funds in most criminal matters, in suits concerning "nontherapeutic abortions, secondary school desegregation, military desertion, or violations of the Selective Service statute," and for class-action suits unless LSC approved.

[275] *Id.* at 538.

Citing to *Board of Regents of the University of Wisconsin System v. South-worth*,[276] *Rust v. Sullivan*,[277] and *Rosenberger v. University of Virginia*,[278] Justice Kennedy explained that funding decisions based on viewpoint can be upheld in situations where the government, itself, is the speaker or where the government uses private speakers to communicate information about a governmental program. In contrast, the Court found LSC "was designed to facilitate private speech,"[279] and the attorneys funded by LSC represented individuals against the government. Attorneys spoke on behalf of their clients, not the government.

The restriction in this case resembled the prohibition of editorializing by public broadcasting in *FCC v. League of Women Voters of California*.[280] By dictating what claims attorneys could litigate, Congress sought to control "an existing medium of expression,"[281] to thereby "distort its usual functioning."[282] The restriction interfered with an attorney's ability to fully represent his client and altered "the traditional role of attorneys in much the same way broadcast systems or student publication networks were changed"[283] in the above-mentioned public forum cases. For example, when even a potential question of statutory validity arises, the attorney must withdraw. If a judge were to ask whether the case posed any constitutional issues, the LSC-funded attorney, in accordance with the restriction, could not respond. At base, this restriction interfered with the courts' duty to interpret the law articulated in *Marbury v. Madison*,[284] as it prohibited "expression upon which courts must depend for the proper exercise of judicial power."[285] Under separation-of-powers principles, the government could not quell constitutional challenges and insulate its own laws from judicial scrutiny.

According to the Court, the Act only funded claims that Congress deemed acceptable. Even more unsettling, the Court believed that indigent clients denied representation by LSC-funded attorneys would probably not seek other legal counsel. Unlike the program at issue in *Rust* where a patient could participate in Government-funded family planning counseling and also could receive abortion counseling from another organization, the LSC program required an attorney to withdraw if a question involving the validity of a welfare statute arose, thus leaving the client without the opportunity for joint representation. Further distinguishing *Rust*, the Court said the LSC restriction conveyed "no programmatic message."[286]

---

[276] 529 U.S. 217 (2000).

[277] 500 U.S. 173 (1991).

[278] 515 U.S. 819 (1995).

[279] *Velazquez*, 531 U.S. at 542.

[280] 468 U.S. 364 (1984).

[281] *Velazquez*, 531 U.S. at 543.

[282] *Id.*

[283] *Id.* at 544. As this case concerned a subsidy, the Court said that limited forum cases, such as *Perry Education Ass'n v. Perry Local Educators' Ass'n*, 460 U.S. 37 (1983), *Lamb's Chapel v. Center of Moriches Union Free School District*, 508 U.S. 384 (1993), and *Rosenberger*, may be instructive though not controlling.

[284] 5 U.S. (1 Cranch) 137 (1803).

[285] *Velazquez*, 531 U.S. at 545.

[286] *Id.* at 548.

Indeed, Congress could limit what types of legal relationships and representation it would support, but it could not isolate its laws from judicial scrutiny. Where private speech was at issue, Congress could not use funding to suppress ideas it disliked.

Justice Scalia dissented, joined by Chief Justice Rehnquist and Justices O'Connor and Thomas. First, attorneys have a duty to explain why they cannot pursue a claim. They may also refer the client to another lawyer. Second, under *National Endowment for Arts v. Finley*,[287] subsidies, like the LSC program, "may *indirectly* abridge speech," so long as the funding scheme is not "manipulated" to have a "coercive effect."[288] Only in *Rosenberger*, where the government created a public forum and based funding on viewpoint, has the Court found "such selective spending unconstitutionally coercive."[289] As the LSC program does not create a public forum, establishing coercion is practically impossible.

Justice Scalia considered the case directly analogous to *Rust*. The LSC Act did not create a public forum, had always restricted the use of funds, and had never pretended to endorse all viewpoints. Moreover, it did not "discriminate on the basis of viewpoint, since it funds neither challenges to nor defenses of existing welfare law."[290] The Court could point to no precedent limiting government funding that " 'distorts an existing medium of expression.' "[291] Additionally, a client without an LSC attorney stood in "no *worse* condition than he would have been in had the program never been enacted."[292] In Justice Scalia's view, the only plausible way to distinguish this case from *Rust* was on the inability of attorneys to engage in joint representation with a non-government funded attorney challenging welfare laws. "This difference, of course, is required by the same ethical canons that the Court elsewhere does not wish to distort."[293]

The dissent also took issue with the Court's refusal to address the severability issue. Justice Scalia believed that Congress would not have agreed to fund welfare litigation absent the restriction invalidated by the majority. The Court did not discuss severability or the Second Circuit's decision to only invalidate a portion of the statute, as neither party raised the issue before the Court.

In *Rumsfeld v. Forum for Academic & Institutional Rights*,[294] a unanimous Court held that the Solomon Amendment, 10 U.S.C. § 983, did not violate the First Amendment rights of law schools. Law schools claimed that the military's policies towards homosexuals violated their nondiscrimination policies. Thus, many law schools restricted military recruiters' access to their students. In reaction, the Solomon Amendment provided "that if any part of an institution of higher education denies military recruiters access equal to that provided other recruiters, the entire

---

[287] 524 U.S. 569 (1998).

[288] *Velazquez*, 531 U.S. at 552 (Scalia, J., dissenting).

[289] *Id.*

[290] *Id.* at 553.

[291] *Id.* at 557. "Judicial decisions do not stand as binding 'precedent' for points that were not raised, not argued and hence not analyzed."

[292] *Id.* at 557.

[293] *Id.*

[294] 547 U.S. 47 (2006).

institution"[295] lost certain funds. Rather, "it looks to the result achieved by the policy" by comparing the recruiting access that a law school provided military versus non-military recruiters.

Turning to the question of whether the Solomon Amendment constituted an unconstitutional condition on the receipt of federal funds, Chief Justice Roberts noted that "judicial deference . . . is at its apogee when Congress legislates under its authority to raise and support armies."[296] Congress could have required schools to allow equal access to military recruiters under its authority to raise and support armies. Congress' choice to promote its goal through funding conditions deserved at least the same deferential treatment as a mandate imposed on universities.

The First Amendment prohibited the government from telling people what to say. The Solomon Amendment, however, regulated law schools' conduct, not speech. Law schools remained free to express their views on the military's employment policy. While recruiting assistance provided by the law schools could contain elements of speech such as sending emails or posting notices on bulletin boards on an employer's behalf, such services were dramatically different from requiring children to recite the Pledge of Allegiance in public school, or requiring motorists "to display the state motto 'Live Free or Die' on their license plates."[297] Rather, the alleged compelled speech was "incidental to the Solomon Amendment's regulation of conduct." The Court further noted that requiring access to military recruiters does not constitute compelled speech.

Prior decisions have extended First Amendment protections to conduct that was inherently expressive, such as flag burning. The Court, however, refused to extend this protection to the conduct regulated by the Solomon Amendment finding that it was not inherently expressive. "If combining speech and conduct were enough to create expressive conduct, a regulated party could always transform conduct into 'speech' simply by talking about it."[298] *United States v. O'Brien*[299] permitted content-neutral regulations that promoted a substantial government interest if that interest could not have been achieved more effectively absent the regulation. "Military recruiting promotes the substantial government interest in raising and supporting the armed forces — an objective that would be achieved less effectively if the military were forced to recruit on less favorable terms than other employers."

The Court also rejected the law schools' claim that the Solomon Amendment violated their expressive association. In *Boy Scouts of America v. Dale*,[300] the Court held that a New Jersey law requiring Boy Scouts "to accept a homosexual as a scoutmaster" violated this freedom. In contrast, military recruiters did not become part of the law schools they visit, and the Solomon Amendment did not force law schools to accept any particular members.

---

[295] *Id.* at 51.

[296] *Id.* at 58.

[297] *Id.* at 61 (quoting *Wooley v. Maynard*, 430 U.S. 705 (1977)).

[298] *Id.* at 66.

[299] 391 U.S. 367 (1968).

[300] 530 U.S. 640 (2000).

§ 16.04   COMMERCIAL SPEECH

[1]   Protection for Commercial Speech: General Principles

In *Virginia State Board of Pharmacy v. Virginia Citizens Consumers Council, Inc.*,[301] the Court extended constitutional protection to commercial speech, or commercial advertising. Before *Virginia Pharmacy*, the Court specifically declined, in several decisions, to afford commercial speech constitutional protection.[302] In two decisions immediately prior to *Virginia Pharmacy* the Court began moving toward constitutional protection of commercial speech.[303]

Virginia Pharmacy involved a Virginia law preventing licensed pharmacists from advertising the prices of drugs. A group of private consumers of pharmaceutical products challenged this law. The Court held that this group had standing to bring the suit because where there was a right to speak, there was also a correlative right to receive information.

Writing for the majority, Justice Blackmun concluded that commercial speech simply proposed a commercial transaction. The pharmacist did not wish to express an opinion, relate some newsworthy fact, or even make general comments about commercial matters. He simply wished to communicate the idea that, " 'I will sell you the X prescription drug at the Y price.' " Justice Blackmun elaborated on this definition, stating that commercial speech was speech that did no more than propose a commercial transaction and was removed from any exposition of ideas and from truth, science, morality and the arts in general.[304]

Justice Blackmun stated that this communication should not be wholly outside the protection of the First Amendment. First, he found that the public's interest, on a day-to-day basis, in the information the pharmacies had to offer could be greater than its interest in political debate. Second, Justice Blackmun stated that our free market economy required that individuals' economic decisions be intelligent and well-informed. In addition, commercial speech was indispensable to the free flow of information, and thus to the formation of intelligent opinions about how the free market system should be regulated.

The State argued that allowing pharmacists to advertise competitive prices would encourage them to cut corners, ultimately damaging the health of their customers. Moreover, advertising would undermine the professional relationship

---

[301]   425 U.S. 748 (1976).

[302]   *See, e.g.*, Breard v. Alexandria, 341 U.S. 622 (1951) (upheld the constitutionality of an ordinance that prohibited unsolicited sales of magazine subscriptions from door to door) *and* Valentine v. Chrestensen, 316 U.S. 52, 54 (1942) ("We are equally clear that the Constitution imposes no such restraint on government as respects purely commercial advertising.").

[303]   *See also* Bigelow v. Virginia, 421 U.S. 809 (1975) (reversing a conviction under a Virginia statute prohibiting advertising the availability of abortion); Pittsburgh Press Co. v. Pittsburgh Comm'n on Human Relations, 413 U.S. 376 (1973) (holding that a municipal human relations ordinance that prohibited a newspaper from carrying sex designated advertising columns for nonexempt job opportunities did not violate newspaper publisher's First Amendment Rights).

[304]   The Court later refined its definition of commercial speech in *Bolger v. Youngs Drug Prods. Corp.*, 463 U.S. 60 (1983). *See infra* text accompanying note 307.

that existed between pharmacists and patients, and affect the status of pharmacists as professionals.

Justice Blackmun responded that pharmacists were constrained by the disciplinary rules of their profession. Furthermore, different kinds of pharmacists would occupy the market. Some pharmacists would practice in the traditional manner and charge higher prices for their increased service, while others would offer lower prices because of higher volume and lower service. The market should accommodate different types of pharmacists. Justice Blackmun also argued that the State's asserted interests were predicated on enforcing ignorance, and a particular view of the pharmaceutical profession, rather than letting the people make an informed decision as to what was best for them. Whatever problems might be caused by advertising could be averted by regulating the underlying market, rather than the advertising.

Justice Blackmun argued that a state could regulate commercial speech through time, place and manner restrictions, restrictions on false commercial speech, and restrictions on commercial speech that was deceptive or misleading. Government also could prohibit advertising illegal transactions. Moreover, because advertising was not as easily chilled by regulations as traditionally protected speech, the doctrines of overbreadth, vagueness, and prior restraints — that protect political and other traditionally protected speech — may not apply to commercial speech. To avoid misleading advertising, government may also be able to regulate the form of commercial speech or require additional information, warnings or disclaimers.[305]

Virginia Pharmacy attempted to define commercial speech. This definition is quite important as the Court indicated that it would not afford commercial speech a number of protections afforded to traditionally protected speech. The Court gave further guidance on defining commercial speech in *Bolger v. Youngs Drug Products Corp.*[306] In *Bolger*, the Court invalidated a federal law that prohibited the mailing of unsolicited advertisements of contraceptives. At issue were a flier and two pamphlets mailed to private homes. The pamphlets were entitled "Condoms in Human Sexuality," and "Plain Talk About Venereal Disease." One pamphlet repeatedly described the drug company's product by name, while the other pamphlet referred to condoms generally.

Writing for the majority, Justice Marshall held that this material was commercial speech. Unlike the advertisements at issue in *Virginia Pharmacy*, the pamphlets were more than mere proposals to engage in commercial transactions. The fact that the pamphlets were advertisements did not by itself suffice to characterize them as commercial speech. The material could not be classified as commercial speech simply because the material referred to a specific product. Finally, the fact that the sender of the material had an economic motivation for the mailing did not by itself turn the material into commercial speech. Nonetheless, the combination of all these characteristics supported the lower court's determination that these mailings amounted to commercial speech.

---

[305] *See Virginia Pharmacy*, 425 U.S. at 771 n.24.

[306] 463 U.S. 60 (1983).

Justice Marshall noted that the defendant still had full constitutional protection to discuss public issues not made in the context of commercial transactions. Advertising, however, should not receive full constitutional protection just because it referred to public issues. While the contraception mailings were commercial speech, they were constitutionally protected because they supplied important information, and unwilling recipients could remove their names from company mailing lists.

The standard for constitutional protection of commercial speech was delineated in *Central Hudson Gas & Electric Corp. v. Public Service Commission*.[307] This case invalidated the Public Service Commission's regulation prohibiting advertising by a public utility. Apprehensive that affording commercial speech full constitutional protection could dilute protection for traditionally protected speech, the Court established a four-part, middle-tier test. First, to invoke First Amendment protection, the speech must concern lawful activity and not be misleading. Second, the regulation must serve a substantial government interest. Third, the regulation must directly advance the state's asserted interest. Fourth, the regulation must not be more extensive than necessary to serve that interest.[308]

In this case, the State's interest in conserving energy was substantial and the regulation directly advanced that interest. However, the complete suppression of the utility's commercial speech was broader than necessary to protect that interest. Dissenting, Justice Rehnquist said that the decision was reminiscent of *Lochner v. New York*[309] in striking down an economic regulation.

In *Pacific Gas & Electric Co. v. Public Utilities Commission*,[310] the Court invalidated a California Commission order requiring public utilities to insert in their billing envelopes information presented by an organization representing rate payers. The plurality relied on cases like *Miami Herald v. Tornillo*[311] to extend to business corporations the right not to be compelled to provide public forums.[312]

In *Linmark Associates, Inc. v. Township of Willingboro*,[313] the Court invalidated as a content-based regulation an ordinance banning the use of real estate "for sale" and "sold" signs by property owners. The Court found a lack of evidence to support the City's assertion that the ban prevented "white flight" and maintained integrated neighborhoods. The legislature acted to prevent residents from obtaining information about sales activity which was important in making critical life choices about where to live.

---

[307] 447 U.S. 557 (1980).

[308] *Id.* at 566.

[309] *See supra* § 8.05[1].

[310] 475 U.S. 1 (1986).

[311] *See supra* § 14.05.

[312] In *Consolidated Edison Co. v. Public Serv. Comm'n*, 447 U.S. 530 (1980), the Court invalidated a New York Public Service Commission order prohibiting utilities from discussing political matters like nuclear power in billing inserts. This was really a political speech case.

[313] 431 U.S. 85 (1977).

The Court addressed the constitutionality of a city ordinance banning most billboards in *Metromedia, Inc. v. City of San Diego*.[314] The ordinance allowed some on-site commercial signs designating the name of the owner or occupant of the premises, or identifying the goods produced or services rendered on the premises. The City claimed that this regulation preserved the City's aesthetic appearance and improved traffic safety.

Demonstrating considerable legislative deference, the Court upheld the ordinance's restriction of commercial speech. The Court found that the City met the first, second, and fourth prongs of the *Central Hudson* test. With respect to the third requirement that the ordinance directly advance the government's interest, the Court was hesitant "to disagree with the accumulated, commonsense judgments of local lawmakers and of the many reviewing courts that billboards were real and substantial hazards to traffic safety."[315] The Court found the ordinance's ban on noncommercial speech unconstitutional. Allowing on-site commercial messages while disallowing noncommercial messages favored commercial speech over noncommercial speech. The Court also found that the ordinance's exceptions for certain types of off-site, noncommercial signs discriminated on the basis of a sign's content. As the ordinance unconstitutionally regulated noncommercial speech, the Court held the entire ordinance invalid on its face.[316]

In *City of Ladue v. Gilleo*,[317] the Court invalidated a city ordinance that prohibited the display of all signs on residential property, except real estate signs. The Court relied on both *Linmark* and *Metromedia* to invalidate the ordinance. Although conceding that the City of Ladue could regulate the physical characteristics of signs to avoid obstruction or other harms, this particular ordinance "foreclosed a venerable means of communication that is both unique and important."[318] Justice Stevens also suggested that other considerations might apply in a case, for example, where residents displayed political or other signs for a fee or residential signs advertising off-site commercial enterprises.

In *Posadas de Puerto Rico Associates v. Tourism Co.*,[319] the Court upheld, against a facial challenge, a Puerto Rican statute that restricted advertisements for gambling directed at residents of Puerto Rico, while allowing gambling ads directed at tourists.

Writing for the majority, Justice Rehnquist found that the state's interest in reducing gambling by residents was substantial. The Court also found the legislature's belief that the regulation directly advanced its interest was

---

[314] 453 U.S. 490 (1981).

[315] *Id.* at 509.

[316] The ordinance contained a severability provision which stated that if certain parts of the ordinance were held unconstitutional, the constitutional parts should remain in force. Therefore, the Court remanded to the state courts to ascertain whether the commercial speech regulations could stand alone.

[317] 512 U.S. 43 (1994). For further discussions of this case, *see supra* § 15.04[1].

[318] *Id.* at 54.

[319] 478 U.S. 328 (1986).

"reasonable." Lastly, the regulations were no broader than necessary to advance the government's interest. The plaintiff argued that to satisfy the government's interest, the government could require more speech designed to discourage gambling. Choosing between this alternative and suppression was within the legislature's discretion and noted that the government could prohibit gambling altogether if it so chose. While a majority of the Court has not explicitly overruled this case, *Posadas* is probably no longer good law.

In *Board of Trustees v. Fox*,[320] the Court also relaxed the middle-tier scrutiny afforded commercial speech. This case involved a commercial speech challenge to a university regulation that prohibited Tupperware parties and other commercial activities on school property, including dormitory rooms.

The plaintiffs contended that noncommercial speech was also involved because other subjects, such as how to be financially responsible and how to run an efficient home, were discussed at the Tupperware parties. They argued that the commercial speech was "inextricably intertwined" with the traditionally protected speech. Consequently, the plaintiffs asserted that the entire Tupperware party must be classified as noncommercial. The Court rejected this argument because nothing in the nature of these noncommercial messages required that they be combined with the commercial messages. Moreover, the purpose of Tupperware parties was to propose a commercial transaction. Therefore, the Court treated the case as involving only commercial speech.

The Court's analysis focused on the fourth part of the *Central Hudson* test, which required a regulation to be no more extensive than necessary to serve the State's asserted interest. Writing for the Court, Justice Kennedy stated that "necessary" was less onerous than the least-restrictive-means standard. The Court required "the government goal to be substantial, and the cost to be carefully calculated. Moreover, since the State bears the burden of justifying its restrictions . . . it must affirmatively establish the reasonable fit we require."[321] The State cleared this hurdle. In addition, the Court acknowledged the discretion of legislatures to regulate a field that was traditionally subject to governmental regulation.

The Court also rejected overbreadth challenges to the commercial speech applications of the ordinance saying that the overbreadth doctrine did not apply to commercial speech. As to the applications of the ordinance to noncommercial speech, the Court stated that those who had standing to challenge a statute's various applications could mount overbreadth challenges. Confining the doctrine to those who lacked standing would be incongruous. Nevertheless, the Court refused to use overbreadth challenges that were not necessary as the determination of substantial overbreadth was difficult. Consequently, they would wait for as-applied challenges on the noncommercial speech parts of the ordinance.[322]

---

[320] 492 U.S. 469 (1989).

[321] *Id.* at 480.

[322] For discussion of the overbreadth doctrine, *see supra* § 13.05[2].

In *City of Cincinnati v. Discovery Network, Inc.*,[323] the Court applied the "reasonable fit" standard articulated in *Fox*[324] to strike down a city ordinance prohibiting the distribution of promotional materials through newsracks placed on public property. Cincinnati had authorized two companies to place over 100 newsracks, which did not contain newspapers, on public property. The City had already afforded broader prerogatives to newspapers. One company used its newsracks to dispense free magazines promoting the company's educational, recreational, and social programs. Portions of these magazines described "current events of general interest." The other company distributed magazines that contained real estate advertising, but also provided information about such matters as interest rates and market trends. The City subsequently revoked authority for these 100 newsracks, citing a preexisting ordinance which prohibited the distribution of commercial materials, while continuing to allow between 1,500 and 2,000 newsracks dispensing newspapers.

Writing for the Court, Justice Stevens noted that the blurry distinction between commercial and noncommercial speech was a matter of degree. Newspapers contained much commercial advertising, while the publications at issue contained much material that was not " 'core' commercial speech." Assuming that the speech at issue was commercial speech, Justice Stevens concluded that the distinction between commercial and noncommercial speech did not support banning all commercial newsracks. Moreover, because the City continued to allow many newspaper newsracks, the ban had "no relationship whatsoever" to the City's professed interests in aesthetics.

United States v. Edge Broadcasting Co.[325] upheld, against an as-applied challenge, a Federal statute prohibiting the broadcasting of lottery advertisements, except those for state-run lotteries aired by stations licensed in states that conducted lotteries. Although the plaintiff broadcaster was licensed by North Carolina, a non-lottery state, over 90 percent of its listeners and advertisers resided across the border in Virginia, a lottery state.

Justice White's majority opinion focused on the third and fourth factors of the *Central Hudson* test. The Court evaluated whether the general ban directly advanced the substantial state interest of respecting the state lottery policy in light of its general applicability to all North Carolina broadcasters and not only the plaintiff in this case. Relying on *Fox*, Justice White noted that the fit required by the fourth *Central Hudson* factor need not be "necessarily perfect, but reasonable." Applying the ban to Edge was reasonable to prevent Virginia from controlling what advertisements North Carolina stations could broadcast. Moreover, the fact that North Carolina residents could hear the lottery advertisements of Virginia stations did not undercut the fit between the ban as applied to Edge and the government's interest. To further the government's purpose of reducing the demand for lotteries, the ban only had to reduce lottery advertising, not eradicate it.

---

[323] 507 U.S. 410 (1993).

[324] 492 U.S. 469, *supra* note 320.

[325] 509 U.S. 418 (1993).

Justice Stevens filed a dissenting opinion in which Justice Blackmun joined. Banning truthful speech about the legal lottery in Virginia was "patently unconstitutional."

In *Rubin v. Coors Brewing Co.*,[326] a unanimous Court invalidated a provision of the Federal Alcohol Administration Act that prohibited disclosing on labels the alcohol content of beer. The Court also invalidated the provision's prohibition of descriptive words implying high alcohol content, such as "strong" or "extra strength."

The parties agreed that the prohibited information was commercial speech. The Court relied on the *Central Hudson* test. The parties agreed that the prohibited information was not misleading. As strength wars could lead to alcoholism, Justice Thomas found that the ban secured a substantial government interest. However, the "overall irrationality" of the Act prevented the ban from "directly and materially" advancing the government's interest.[327] For example, the regulations permit labeling the alcohol content of wines and other spirits and advertising the alcohol content of beer. Moreover, the provision's regulation of speech was not "sufficiently tailored to its goal."[328] The regulation was "more extensive than necessary"[329] because the government could advance its interest without infringing on First Amendment rights. For example, it could have directly limited the alcohol content of beer, or it could have limited the labeling ban to the malt liquor market where the fear of a strength war was most prevalent. Concurring in the judgment, Justice Stevens would have afforded the speech at issue full First Amendment protection.

In *44 Liquormart, Inc. v. Rhode Island*,[330] a unanimous Court invalidated two Rhode Island statutes prohibiting the advertisement of retail prices of alcoholic beverages. The first statute prohibited in-state vendors and out-of-state manufacturers, wholesalers, and shippers from advertising the price of any alcoholic beverage sold in the state, except price tags and small display signs. The second statute prohibited publication or broadcast of advertisements referring to the price of alcoholic beverages. The 44 Liquormart, Inc., ran an ad in a Rhode Island newspaper which the State charged implied bargain liquor prices.

Justice Stevens wrote for a majority of six in some parts of his opinion, and for only three or four Justices in other parts. Joined by Justices Kennedy, Souter, and Ginsburg, Justice Stevens construed key commercial speech precedents as prohibiting blanket bans on commercial speech that was neither deceptive nor related to unlawful activity. Joined only by Justices Kennedy and Ginsburg, Justice Stevens maintained that neither "greater objectivity" nor "greater hardiness"[331] justify any deferential review of complete bans on truthful, non-misleading commercial speech. While the typical reason for allowing greater regulation of

---

[326] 514 U.S. 476 (1995).

[327] *Rubin*, 514 U.S. at 488.

[328] *Id.* at 490.

[329] *Id.* at 491.

[330] 517 U.S. 484 (1996).

[331] *Id.* at 502.

commercial speech than noncommercial speech is protecting consumers from "commercial harms,"[332] bans on truthful, non-misleading commercial speech rarely serve this purpose. Therefore, the plurality reviewed the Rhode Island ban with "special care."[333]

Joined by Justices Kennedy, Souter and Ginsburg, Justice Stevens found that Rhode Island's price advertising prohibition failed the *Central Hudson* test.[334] *Edenfield v. Fane*[335] required the State to show "not merely that its regulation will advance its interest, but also that it will do so 'to a material degree.' "[336] The record contained neither factual findings nor evidentiary support that the speech prohibition would significantly advance the State's interest in promoting temperance.

Moreover, less restrictive alternatives were "more likely to achieve the State's goal of promoting temperance."[337] Such alternatives included increasing price by added regulation or taxation, limiting per capita purchases as with prescription drugs, or educating people about problems drinking causes.

Justice Stevens, joined by Justices Kennedy, Thomas, and Ginsburg, explicitly rejected much of the reasoning of *Posadas de Puerto Rico Associates v. Tourism Co.* Contradicting *Posadas*, the plurality of four stated that the legislatures lacked discretion to reduce alcohol consumption by suppressing advertising rather than by a less speech-restrictive alternative. The plurality opined that the State lacked discretion to ban truthful, non-misleading information for the "paternalistic purposes"[338] allowed in *Posadas*. The plurality also contradicted *Posadas'* "greater-includes-the lesser"[339] argument, maintaining that it cannot be assumed "that the State's power to regulate commercial activity is 'greater' than its power to ban truthful, non-misleading commercial speech."[340] Government cannot treat speech regulations simply as another means used to achieve its objectives. The plurality also refused to uphold the regulations as valid because they were related to a " 'vice' activity,"[341] a contention that the Court had already rejected in *Rubin v. Coors Brewing Co.*

Finally, in Part VII of the opinion, a majority of six held that the Twenty-first Amendment, which repealed prohibition and delegated to the states "the power to prohibit commerce in, or the use of, alcoholic beverages,"[342] did not shield the

---

[332] *Id.*

[333] *Id.* at 504.

[334] Central Hudson Gas & Elec. Corp. v. Public Serv. Comm'n, 447 U.S. 557 (1980).

[335] *See infra* § 16.04[2].

[336] *44 Liquormart*, 517 U.S. at 505.

[337] *Id.* at 507.

[338] *Id.* at 510.

[339] *Id.* at 511.

[340] *Id.*

[341] *Id.* at 513.

[342] *Id.* at 514.

regulation at issue from First Amendment scrutiny, as it does not limit other constitutional provisions.

Justice Scalia concurred in the judgment. While he shared Justice Thomas' discomfort with the *Central Hudson* test, he did not believe that the Court could reject the test on the record before it. As the language of the First Amendment was indeterminate and its basic protection of political speech was not at issue, Justice Scalia determined constitutional protection based on what traditions of regulating commercial speech existed when the First and Fourteenth Amendments were framed.

In his concurrence, Justice Thomas said that the balancing test of *Central Hudson* did not apply when government sought "to keep legal users of a product or service ignorant in order to manipulate their choices in the marketplace."[343] In this case, he would simply strike down the regulations under the reasoning and holding of *Virginia Board of Pharmacy v. Virginia Citizens Consumer Council, Inc.* Justice O'Connor concurred in the judgment in a separate opinion joined by Chief Justice Rehnquist and Justices Souter and Breyer. Even assuming the regulation satisfied the first three prongs of the *Central Hudson* test, it would fail the fourth since the fit between the State's means and ends was not "narrowly tailored."[344] In this connection, alternative channels of communicating the restricted speech exist. As the State failed to show a "reasonable fit" between its ban on price advertising and its goal of temperance, Justice O'Connor found that the Court need go no further than to apply the established *Central Hudson* test.

In *Greater New Orleans Broadcasting Ass'n, Inc. v. United States*,[345] the Court invalidated application of a prohibition on "broadcast advertising of lotteries and casino gambling" in Louisiana where the advertised gambling was legal. The Court applied the four-prong test established in *Central Hudson*, and noted that each prong of the test is interconnected: The answer to one of the questions in the test may affect the answer to one of the other three questions.

Under the second prong, the Court found that the government had a "substantial" interest in reducing the social costs related to gambling and aiding states that prohibit gambling. The Court questioned these interests in light of the many exceptions in the statute, such as, gambling run by American Indian tribes and state-sponsored gambling.

To meet the third prong of the *Central Hudson* test, the government cannot speculate that "the speech restriction directly and materially advances the asserted governmental interest," but instead " 'must demonstrate that the harms it recites are real and that its restriction will in fact alleviate them to a material degree.' " The fourth prong does not require the government to utilize the "least restrictive means conceivable," but the "costs and benefits" imposed on free speech must be "carefully calculated," and the solution chosen must be "one whose scope is in proportion to the interest served."

---

[343] *Id.* at 518.

[344] *Id.* at 529.

[345] 527 U.S. 173 (1999).

The Louisiana statute fell based on its own inconsistencies, for example, distinguishing tribal and state-sponsored gambling enterprises from privately owned ones. The statute bans accurate product information based on the identity of the speaker. Rather than restricting advertising, the government could directly limit abuses by imposing betting limits or admissions restrictions. The statute's many exceptions also undercut the government's second proffered interest in aiding states with anti-gambling policies. The statute allows a "variety of speech that poses the same risks the Government purports to fear, while banning messages unlikely to cause any harm at all."

In *United States v. United Foods, Inc.*,[346] the Court invalidated a mandatory assessment imposed on fresh mushroom producers used to fund generic advertising promoting mushroom sales. Distinguishing *Glickman v. Wileman Brothers & Elliot, Inc.*,[347] the majority said the mandatory assessments in that case comprised "nothing more than an additional economic regulation"[348] which was "ancillary to a more comprehensive program restricting marketing autonomy."[349] By contrast, the mushroom program at issue in *United Foods* only involved advertising without a larger regulatory scheme. As such, it resembled the compelled speech subsidies in *Keller v. State Bar*,[350] which the Court previously rejected.

Concurring, Justice Stevens noted that other governmental interests, such as "health or artistic concerns,"[351] may justify a compelled subsidy in some instances. Concurring in the judgment, Justice Thomas would have subjected any mandatory advertising assessment to strict scrutiny.

Dissenting, Justice Breyer, joined by Justices Ginsburg and O'Connor, argued that the mushroom program was indistinguishable from the program in *Glickman*, which neither restrained any producer "to communicate any message to any audience,"[352] nor compelled any producer to participate in any form of speech.

In *Johanns v. Livestock Marketing Association*,[353] the Court rejected a facial challenge to a generic beef advertising campaign, funded by a $1 government assessment per head of cattle (called a "checkoff"), as the checkoff funded the government's own speech. Those subject to the checkoff sued because they disagreed with the messages of the advertisements they were funding. Plaintiffs relied on *United States v. United Foods, Inc.*[354]

Justice Scalia noted that compelled speech challenges fell into two categories. First, the Court has invalidated cases of "true 'compelled speech'" in which

---

[346] 533 U.S. 405 (2001).

[347] 521 U.S. 457 (1997).

[348] 533 U.S. at 415.

[349] *Id.* at 411.

[350] 496 U.S. 1 (1990).

[351] 533 U.S. at 418 (Stevens, J., concurring).

[352] *Id.* at 404 (Breyer, J., dissenting).

[353] 544 U.S. 550 (2005).

[354] 531 U.S. 1009 (2000).

government compelled an individual to express a message with which he disagreed.[355] Second, in "compelled subsidy" cases such as *United Foods*, the Court has stopped government from imposing fees on an individual to subsidize a message with which he disagreed. However, such mandatory fees are permissible if they are part of a " 'broader regulatory scheme.' " Moreover, a compelled subsidy of government's own speech does not necessarily violate the First Amendment, as compelled support of the government is constitutional and it is inevitable that some funds raised by the government will be spent on speech to advocate its own positions.

The advertisements are government speech despite the prominent role of the Beef Board, which is not a government entity, in the advertising campaign: Government had set the overall message and approved every word. Further, the advertisements are government speech despite their being funded by a targeted assessment rather than general tax revenues. There is "no *First Amendment* right not to fund government speech." Finally, the Court rejected a facial challenge on the basis that crediting the advertisements to " 'America's Beef Producers' " impermissibly implies that plaintiffs endorse a message with which they do not agree. This theory may support an as-applied challenge if the producers establish that beef advertisements were actually attributed to them.

Justices Thomas and Breyer each wrote concurring opinions. Justice Thomas stated that an as-applied challenge would exist if the advertisements "associated" their generic message with the plaintiffs. Justice Ginsburg concurred in the judgment.

Justice Souter dissented, joined by Justices Stevens and Kennedy. He argued that this case was indistinguishable from *United Foods*, as the speech regulation was not "incidental" to a "comprehensive regulatory scheme." Moreover, the advertisements were not government speech because government was not required to signal that it was providing the advertisements.

In *Lorillard Tobacco Co. v. Reilly*,[356] the Court invalidated several restrictions focused on signs advertising tobacco products. The goal of the restrictions was to prevent minors from using tobacco products. The first set of regulations banned outdoor advertising of tobacco products "within 1,000 foot radius of any public playground, playground area in a public park, elementary school or secondary school."[357] These outdoor restrictions did pass the third prong of *Central Hudson*,[358] as the "harms" recited by the State were "real" and the restriction would "in fact alleviate them to a material degree."[359] To satisfy this standard, the State could use "studies and anecdotes pertaining to different locales altogether,"[360] as well as "history, consensus, and 'simple common sense,' "[361] but it

---

[355] *See* West Virginia Board of Education v. Barnette, 319 U.S. 624 (1943) (invalidating a law compelling school children to recite the Pledge of Allegiance).

[356] 533 U.S. 525 (2001).

[357] *Id.* at 534–35.

[358] 447 U.S. 557 (1980).

[359] 533 U.S. at 555.

[360] *Id.*

could not base its decision on "mere 'speculation [and] conjecture.' "[362]

However, the restrictions failed the fourth part of *Central Hudson*, which examined the "reasonable 'fit' "[363] between the government's means and the ends it sought to accomplish. The outdoor regulations were too broad and did not carefully consider the " 'costs and benefits associated with the burden on speech.' "[364] For example, the impact of the regulations on speech would vary depending on whether the area was rural, suburban, or urban. Thus, the restrictions failed to " 'demonstrate a careful calculation of the speech interests involved.' "[365]

The range of communications restricted was also too broad. For example, a retailer could not answer questions about its tobacco products if asked outdoors. Moreover, the outdoor restrictions did not distinguish between small signs and large billboards. They also prohibited indoor advertising of tobacco products visible from the outside of a store.

Also invalidated was an indoor, point-of-sale regulation requiring retailers located within 1,000 feet of a school or playground to place smokeless tobacco products and cigar advertisements at least five-feet above the floor. This restriction failed both the third and fourth prongs of *Central Hudson*. The regulation may prove ineffective as some children are taller than five-feet, and even those who are not can still simply look up to see the advertisements. The Court distinguished between "tobacco advertisements and displays that entice children, much like the floor-level candy displays," and this "blanket height restriction."[366]

The Court did uphold prohibition of self-service displays and a requirement that retailers keep tobacco products in areas only accessible to employees. Consistent with the test from *United States v. O'Brien*,[367] this restriction concerned the placement of products, not the "communication of ideas."[368] It was "narrowly tailored to prevent access to tobacco products by minors, [was] unrelated to expression, and [left] open alternative avenues for vendors to convey information about products."[369]

Justice Kennedy, joined by Justice Scalia, concurred in part and concurred in the judgment. Justice Thomas, also concurring in part and in the judgment, would have subjected the regulations to strict scrutiny.

Although Justice Souter agreed with the Court on most points, he would have remanded the outdoor restrictions for a trial. Justice Stevens, joined by Justices Ginsburg and Breyer, dissented. First, Justice Stevens would have remanded the

---

[361] *Id.* at 555.

[362] *Id.* at 561.

[363] *Id.* at 556.

[364] *Id.* at 561.

[365] *Id.* at 562.

[366] *Id.* at 567.

[367] 391 U.S. 367 (1968).

[368] 533 U.S. at 569.

[369] *Id.* at 570.

1,000-foot outdoor restriction for trial, as tailoring such restrictions to areas like playgrounds was necessary. Second, he would uphold the restrictions on indoor sales practices regulations — including the requirement that advertisements be placed at least five feet above the floor — as they regulated "conduct, not speech."[370]

In *Thompson v. Western States Medical Center*,[371] the Court invalidated an advertising ban on "compounded drugs" which exempted them from the normal testing required to approve new drugs so long as pharmacists did not promote or advertise them. Writing for the majority, Justice O'Connor applied the *Central Hudson* test. The Government has important interests both in wanting to subject new drugs to FDA approval, and in permitting compounded drugs that can tailor medications to meet the special needs of particular patients. Consequently, government should be able to differentiate "between small-scale compounding and large-scale drug manufacturing." Nonetheless, the government failed to demonstrate that its advertising restrictions are " 'not more extensive than is necessary to serve' " these interests as it could have differentiated between compounding and manufacturing with lines unrelated to speech. For example, the government could have limited compounding to "prescriptions already received," or it could have capped "the amount of any particular compounded drug, either by drug volume, number of prescriptions, gross revenue, or profit that a pharmacist or pharmacy could make or sell in a given period of time." The government's ban may also prevent useful advertising, such as, information about compounds that made it easier for children to swallow pills.

Justice Thomas concurred, but reaffirmed his position that the *Central Hudson* test should not apply to commercial speech restrictions, "at least when, as here, the asserted interest is one that is to be achieved through keeping would-be recipients of the speech in the dark."

Justice Breyer dissented, joined by Chief Justice Rehnquist and Justices Stevens and Ginsburg. Recalling the history of the Due Process Clause, Justice Breyer feared that "an overly rigid 'commercial speech' doctrine" will constitutionalize what should be legislative or regulatory decisions about health and safety.

In *Sorrell v. IMS Health, Inc.*,[372] the Court invalidated a Vermont statute that "restricts the sale, disclosure, and use of pharmacy records that reveal the prescribing practices of individual doctors."[373] Absent the prescriber's consent, this "prescriber-identifying information" could "not be sold, disclosed by pharmacies for marketing purposes, or used for marketing by pharmaceutical manufacturers."[374]

---

[370] *Id.* at 604 (Stevens, J, dissenting).

[371] 535 U.S. 357 (2002).

[372] 131 S. Ct. 2653 (2011).

[373] *Id.* at 2659.

[374] *Id.*

Writing for the majority, Justice Kennedy found that a clear purpose behind the statute was to combat the marketing practice of "detailing." Detailing entails the sale of prescriber-identifying information, which pharmaceutical manufacturers use for marketing their brand-name drugs. The statute possessed an evident "counter-detailing" intent, which sought "to promote the use of generic pharmaceuticals."[375] The legislative findings "confirm that the law's express purpose and practical effect are to diminish the effectiveness of marketing by manufacturers of brand-name drugs" because "detailers, in particular those who promote brand-name drugs, convey messages that 'are often in conflict with the goals of the state.' "[376]

Vermont's statute "disfavors marketing, that is, speech with a particular content. More than that, the statute disfavors specific speakers, namely pharmaceutical manufacturers."[377] Consequently, the statute " 'goes even beyond mere content discrimination, to actual viewpoint discrimination.' "[378]

The State's justifications for the law failed both a heightened judicial scrutiny and a less restrictive commercial speech test. Under the more lenient commercial speech standard, "the State must show at least that the statute directly advances a substantial governmental interest and that the measure is drawn to achieve that interest."[379] The purpose behind "these standards ensure not only that the State's interests are proportional to the resulting burdens placed on speech but also that the law does not seek to suppress a disfavored message."[380]

The State tried to justify the statute based on "medical privacy" and "improved public health and reduced healthcare costs."[381] Although it could be understood that "physicians have an interest in keeping their prescription decisions confidential," Vermont's law failed "to serve that interest."[382] The statute "permits insurers, researchers, journalists, the State itself, and others" to use prescriber-identifying information for any purpose besides marketing.[383] Moreover, the State did not argue "that detailing is false or misleading."[384]

Technology's ability to "find and publish personal information" inevitably created "serious and unresolved" privacy and dignity issues.[385] The State may have had a better argument if the "statute provided that prescriber-identifying information could not be sold or disclosed except in narrow circumstances."[386]

---

[375] *Id.* at 2660–61.

[376] *Id.* at 2661.

[377] *Id.* at 2663.

[378] *Id.* (quoting *R. A. V. v. St. Paul*, 505 U.S. 377, 391 (1992)).

[379] *Id.* at 2667–68.

[380] *Id.* at 2668.

[381] *Id.*

[382] *Id.*

[383] *Id.*

[384] *Id.* at 2672.

[385] *Id.*

[386] *Id.*

Vermont "has burdened a form of protected expression that it found too persuasive."[387]

Justice Breyer dissented, joined by Justices Ginsburg and Kagan. Justice Breyer would have upheld the statute because its "effect on expression is inextricably related to a lawful governmental effort to regulate a commercial enterprise."[388] Heightened scrutiny was not warranted because free speech precedent "offers considerably less protection to the maintenance of a free marketplace for goods and services."[389] Consequently, Justice Breyer would "defer significantly to legislative judgment — as the Court has done in cases involving the Commerce Clause or the Due Process Clause."[390] Failure to do so risked, as Justice Rehnquist once said, a " 'retur[n] to the bygone era of *Lochner v. New York.*' "[391]

Justice Breyer also expressed concern that the majority would extend the same heightened standard to other government regulators, such as the Food and Drug Administration (FDA). Prescriber-identifying information only exists because Vermont's regulations required it. Before this decision, the Court had "*never* found that the *First Amendment* prohibits the government from restricting the use of information gathered pursuant to a regulatory mandate."[392]

Many regulatory lines are based on content. Never before had the Court "justified greater scrutiny" on commercial regulations for " 'content-based' " or " 'speaker-based' " restrictions.[393] "The Federal Reserve Board regulates the content of statements, advertising, loan proposals, and interest rate disclosures, but only when made by financial institutions."[394] Likewise, "the FDA oversees the form and content of labeling, advertising, and sales proposals of drugs, but not of furniture."[395]

Vermont's statute would withstand scrutiny under both "*Central Hudson*'s 'intermediate' commercial speech standard as well as any more limited 'economic regulation' " standard.[396] Applying the *Central Hudson* test, Justice Breyer found that the interests of " 'protecting the public health' " and " 'the privacy of prescribers' " as well as ensuring " 'unbiased information' " and low cost, are both " 'substantial' " and content neutral. Regulating public health lay within the state's traditional "police powers."[397] Detailing involved "diverting attention from scientific

---

[387] *Id.*

[388] *Id.* at 2673 (Breyer, J., dissenting).

[389] *Id.* at 2674.

[390] *Id.* at 2674–75.

[391] *Id.* at 2675.

[392] *Id.* at 2677.

[393] *Id.*

[394] *Id.*

[395] *Id.*

[396] *Id.* at 2679.

[397] *Id.* at 2682.

research about a drug's safety and effectiveness, as well as its cost."[398] Consequently, "Vermont's attempts to ensure a 'fair balance' of information was no different from the FDA's similar requirement."[399]

Vermont's law "works no more than modest First Amendment harm; the prohibition is justified by the need to ensure unbiased sales presentations, prevent unnecessarily high drug costs, and protect the privacy of prescribing physicians."[400] The "regulatory context" here is very important. "At best the Court opens a Pandora's Box of First Amendment" claims.[401] "At worst, it reawakens *Lochner's* pre-New Deal threat of substituting judicial for democratic decisionmaking" in regards to "ordinary economic regulation."[402]

[2]   Lawyer and Other Professional Advertising

The Court extended First Amendment protection under the commercial speech doctrine to advertising by lawyers in *Bates v. State Bar*.[403] Relying heavily on *Virginia Pharmacy*,[404] *Bates* struck down a state disciplinary rule prohibiting lawyer advertising. The advertisement in question appeared in a newspaper and offered routine legal services such as uncontested divorces, uncontested personal bankruptcies, and adoption proceedings at "very reasonable rates."

Writing for the majority, Justice Blackmun held that lawyers had a First Amendment right to advertise the prices at which they would perform routine services. The state bar offered several justifications for its ban on "price advertising," such as adversely affecting lawyer professionalism, diminishing the quality of legal services, and inherently misleading the public because legal services were by nature individualized.

Justice Blackmun rejected all of the state bar's contentions. He would allow regulation of false or misleading advertising because of the public's lack of sophistication in legal services. For example, statements concerning the quality of legal services could be deceptive or misleading so as to warrant restriction. These reasons may also justify restriction of in-person solicitation or require warnings or disclaimers in advertisements. None of these considerations, however, permitted suppression of the advertisement in question. Despite extending First Amendment protection to lawyer advertising, the Court refused to hold the state bar prohibitions on advertising overbroad. The Court, following its decision in *Virginia*

---

[398] *Id.*

[399] *Id.* at 2682–83.

[400] *Id.* at 2685.

[401] *Id.*

[402] *Id.*

[403] 433 U.S. 350 (1977).

[404] In a footnote in *Virginia Pharmacy*, Justice Blackmun had suggested that the Court's holding applied specifically to pharmacists, and that other factors might be involved in considering the commercial speech of lawyers and doctors. Chief Justice Burger, in his concurrence, also stressed that the decision was strictly limited to pharmacists. Despite this language limiting the holding, Justice Rehnquist, the only dissenter to the opinion, correctly predicted that the decision would pave the way for lawyer and doctor advertising.

Pharmacy, declined to use the overbreadth doctrine in the commercial speech area.

Some of the cases following *Bates* have focused on whether the advertising sought was misleading. In *Friedman v. Rogers*,[405] the Court upheld a broad ban on trade names being used by optometrists. The Court feared various forms of deception including different individuals practicing under the same trade name over time, different trade names creating the illusion of competition among different offices of the same firm, and trade names giving a false impression of standardized care.

In *In re R. M. J.*,[406] the Court invalidated a Missouri rule that set forth precise language by which a lawyer could describe her areas of practice but required a disclaimer of certification of expertise, limited the distribution of announcement cards, and prevented the listing of jurisdictions in which she was licensed to practice. Such information was not inherently misleading and any possible deception could have been cured by measures short of a total ban.

In *Peel v. Attorney Registration & Disciplinary Commission*,[407] the Court invalidated a state prohibition on lawyers' claims of certification and specialization. Writing for a plurality, Justice Stevens declared that the states could not absolutely prohibit entire categories of speech, such as practice areas, if the information could be presented non-deceptively. In this case, the lawyer had made these specialization claims on his letterhead.

Similarly, in *Ibanez v. Florida Department of Business & Professional Regulation*,[408] the Court invalidated the prohibition by a state board of accountancy of using the designations "CPA" and "CFA" in juxtaposition with each other. The state board thought that this juxtaposition might mislead the consumer into thinking that both certifications were performed by the state. Justice Ginsburg rejected bans on commercial speech that were "potentially misleading"[409] and instead required the Board to demonstrate that its ban would alleviate real injuries "to a material degree."[410] Absent actual harm, the Court would not even require a disclaimer that the term "specialist" conveyed neither governmental approval of the claim nor the educational, testing, or other basis for it. While the Court did not reject tailored disclaimers preventing "deception or confusion,"[411] the one at issue eliminated using "specialist" on business cards, letterhead, and in the Yellow Pages. Justice O'Connor dissented, joined by Chief Justice Rehnquist.

The Court has permitted a wide variety of targeted solicitation by newspaper, by mail, and in person. In *Zauderer v. Office of Disciplinary Counsel*,[412] the Court

---

[405] 440 U.S. 1 (1979).

[406] 455 U.S. 191 (1982).

[407] 496 U.S. 91 (1990).

[408] 512 U.S. 136 (1994).

[409] *Id.* at 146.

[410] *Id.* at 143.

[411] *Id.* at 146.

[412] 471 U.S. 626 (1985).

extended constitutional protection to targeted newspaper advertisements in which an attorney offered to represent women who had suffered injuries from using the Dalkon Shield Intra-uterine Device. The Court held that the First Amendment protected advertisements that were not misleading and did not propose an illegal transaction. The Court found that the prohibition did not directly advance state interests, such as preventing overreaching and "stirring up litigation." However, the Court did find misleading the ad's promise that no legal fees would be owed if there was no recovery.

The Court again addressed the problem of direct mail advertising in *Shapero v. Kentucky Bar Ass'n*.[413] In *Shapero*, the Court invalidated a bar association's prohibition of direct mail solicitation. The lawyer in this case had sent mailings to potential clients against whom foreclosures were pending. In his majority opinion, Justice Brennan stated that these mailings did not present a danger of coercion, and any possible false or misleading information could be minimized by requiring that the letters be reviewed.

In *Florida Bar v. Went For It, Inc.*,[414] however, the Court limited constitutional protection for direct mail solicitation by lawyers. Writing for a 5-4 majority, Justice O'Connor upheld a Florida regulation prohibiting lawyers from soliciting accident victims until 30 days after the date of the disaster. The regulation passed the *Central Hudson* test.[415] It "directly and materially" advanced even a "compelling" state interest in protecting the privacy of citizens and upholding the integrity of the legal profession. The Court distinguished *Shapero*[416] saying that it involved a broad-based ban on all direct-mail advertising, whereas the Florida regulation only mandated a 30-day blackout period of soliciting accident victims. The "fit" between the interest and the regulation must only be "reasonable," not "perfect."[417] During the period that the ban lasted, accident victims could still obtain important information about lawyers through myriad other avenues including legal directories, advertisements in the media, signs, and written communications that did not solicit.

In *Ohralik v. Ohio State Bar Ass'n*,[418] the Court held that a state can discipline lawyers for soliciting clients in person, because the potential for overreaching is great when a lawyer personally solicits an unsophisticated, injured, or distressed lay person. Broad prophylactic measures could be enacted as a deterrent. In contrast, *In re Primus*[419] held that solicitation of prospective litigants by a civil liberties organization was permissible. The state may not punish a lawyer, "who, seeking to further political and ideological goals through an associational activity, including litigation, advises a lay person of her legal rights and discloses in a subsequent letter that free legal assistance is available from a nonprofit

---

[413] 486 U.S. 466 (1988).

[414] 515 U.S. 618 (1995).

[415] *See supra* § 16.04[1].

[416] *See supra* note 413.

[417] *Florida Bar*, 515 U.S. at 632.

[418] 436 U.S. 447 (1978).

[419] 436 U.S. 412 (1978).

organization."[420] The Court did not find the same concerns that were present in *Ohralik*, such as overreaching, misrepresentation, invasion of privacy, or pressuring a potential client.

In *Edenfield v. Fane*,[421] the Court invalidated a ban on in-person solicitation by CPAs. Writing for the Court, Justice Kennedy noted that in-person solicitation enabled the seller to direct proposals to those most interested, allowed a potential buyer to evaluate the seller personally, and provided the opportunity for direct and detailed communication regarding the service offered. For "nonstandard products like the professional services offered by CPAs, these benefits are significant."[422]

Justice Kennedy cautioned that *Ohralik* only allowed such a prophylactic rule against in-person solicitation when the situation inherently posed dangers of misconduct. Unlike lawyers, CPAs were trained to be independent and objective, and were not "trained in the art of persuasion." The prospective business clients in this case were far more sophisticated than the young accident victim in *Ohralik*. To justify a prophylactic rule, the state had to establish that the rule prevented harms that were likely to occur. In dissent, Justice O'Connor saw little difference between the dangers of overreaching by accountants and lawyers.

In *Tennessee Secondary School Athletic Ass'n v. Brentwood Academy*,[423] the Court held that the Athletic Association's rule, which prohibited high school coaches from using "'undue influence'" in recruiting middle school students, did not violate the First Amendment. The Tennessee Secondary School Athletic Association (TSSAA) sanctioned one of its member schools, Brentwood Academy, for violating the rule. Brentwood's football coach had sent eighth-grade students a letter soliciting them to join the Academy's athletic program.

First, the Court noted that TSSAA's rule struck "nowhere near the heart of the First Amendment."[424] There was a "difference of constitutional dimension" between general advertising to the public and in-person solicitation "in a coercive setting."[425] The Court relied on *Ohralik v. Ohio State Bar Ass'n*,[426] which held that in-person solicitation by the lawyer was not protected by the First Amendment because it posed the risk of overreaching. Similarly, in this case the high school coach's in-person solicitation of impressionable eighth-graders presented the risk of undue influence.

The athletic association's interest in enforcing rules can sometimes justify restricting the speech of its "voluntary participants."[427] Moreover, because the government's interest in efficiency can sometimes warrant curtailing employee speech, the athletic league's interest in enforcing the rules can in some

---

[420] *Id.* at 414.

[421] 507 U.S. 761 (1993).

[422] *Id.* at 766.

[423] 551 U.S. 291 (2007).

[424] *Id.* at 296.

[425] *Id.*

[426] 436 U.S. 447 (1978).

[427] 551 U.S. at 299.

circumstances outweigh the speech rights of its voluntary participants. While TSSAA did not have an "unbounded authority to condition membership on the relinquishment of any and all constitutional rights,"[428] it could impose such conditions that were necessary to ensure its effective and efficient management. TSSAA member schools remained free to advertise their athletic programs to the public at large through brochures and billboards.

Justice Kennedy concurred in part and concurred in the judgment, and Justice Thomas concurred in the judgment.

§ 16.05   OBSCENITY

[1]   The Constitutional Standard

Chief Justice Earl Warren, a former prosecutor, characterized obscenity as the most difficult problem faced by his Court "[because] we have to balance two constitutional rights with each other." The "state and national government [have] a right to have a decent society," but "[o]n the other hand, we have the First Amendment." According to Chief Justice Warren, obscenity cases raised the question of "how far people can go under the First Amendment . . . without offending the right of the government to maintain a decent society."[429]

In *Chaplinsky v. State of New Hampshire*,[430] the Court, in dicta, took the position that obscenity did not receive constitutional protection. In the 1957 case of *Roth v. United States*,[431] the Court first established that the First Amendment did not protect obscenity. Balancing the state's interest in preserving morality and order with an individual's right to freedom of expression, the Court posited the following test for determining what material was obscene: "material which deals with sex in a manner appealing to prurient interest."[432]

In its 1966 decision in *Memoirs v. Massachusetts*,[433] a plurality of the Court formulated a new three-part test for obscenity. "It must be established that (a) the dominant theme of the material taken as a whole appeals to a prurient interest in sex; (b) the material is patently offensive because it affronts contemporary community standards relating to the description or representation of sexual matters; and (c) the material is utterly without redeeming social value."[434] The *Roth* Court had used the language "utterly without redeeming social value" to explain why the Constitution did not protect obscenity. The *Memoirs* Court transformed that reasoning into a required part of the test for defining obscenity

---

[428] *Id.* at 300.

[429] M. LANDSBERG, A CONVERSATION WITH CHIEF JUSTICE EARL WARREN 6 (1969), *quoted in* G. E. WHITE, EARL WARREN: A PUBLIC LIFE 250 (1982).

[430] 315 U.S. 568 (1942).

[431] 354 U.S. 476 (1957).

[432] *Id.* at 489.

[433] 383 U.S. 413 (1966).

[434] *Id.* at 418. While a plurality of four supported the *Memoirs* test, two other Justices, Black and Douglas, would have afforded absolute protection.

that would receive no constitutional protection. Tremendous protection for sexually explicit speech ensued.

In the years after the *Memoirs* decision, the Court began a process of summarily reversing obscenity convictions. This process, which became known as "Redrupping," began with *Redrup v. New York*.[435] It allowed the Court to avoid making content-based value judgments of various controverted materials.

The current test for obscenity was delineated in *Miller v. California*,[436] which presented attractive facts for the Court to somewhat reduce constitutional protection for obscenity. In *Miller*, the defendant mailed very explicit materials to people who had in no way solicited them and were deeply offended by them. Chief Justice Burger, writing for the majority, characterized the mailing as being an aggressive sales action thrust upon unwilling recipients and juveniles. The Court set out the following test:

> (a) whether 'the average person, applying contemporary community standards' would find that the work, taken as a whole, appeals to the prurient interest;

> (b) whether the work depicts or describes, in a patently offensive way, sexual conduct specifically defined by the applicable state law; and

> (c) whether the work, taken as a whole, lacks serious literary, artistic, political or scientific value.[437]

The critical difference between the *Memoirs* and *Miller* tests was that *Miller* did not require that the work was "utterly without redeeming social value," a criterion that was virtually impossible to meet. Instead, the third element simply required that the work lack "serious literary, artistic, political, or scientific value."

Perhaps to escape the charge that the test permitted courts to engage in censorship or content discrimination, the Court substituted the jury as the key decision-maker in obscenity cases. The Court clarified this requirement in *Jenkins v. Georgia*[438] when it held that the jury did not have unchecked discretion to determine what was obscene. The *Jenkins* Court restricted the material that could be regulated under the *Miller* test to "hardcore pornography," and required judges to supervise juries to enforce this limitation.

Another question raised by the *Miller* test involved its introduction of community standards to accommodate regional attitudes toward these materials. In *Smith v. United States*,[439] the Court held that juries should apply contemporary community standards to the first two elements of the *Miller* test.[440] In addition, state

---

[435] 386 U.S. 767 (1967).

[436] 413 U.S. 15 (1973).

[437] *Miller*, 413 U.S. at 24.

[438] 418 U.S. 153 (1974).

[439] 431 U.S. 291 (1977).

[440] *See also* Hamling v. United States, 418 U.S. 87, 104 (1974) ("[a] juror is entitled to draw on his own knowledge of the views of the average persons in the community or vicinage from which he comes for making the required determination").

legislatures could not prescribe community standards for juries. However, a state could "impose a geographic limit on the determination of community standards by defining the area from which the jury could be selected in an obscenity case, or by legislating with respect to the instructions that must be given to the jurors in such cases."[441] The third element of the *Miller* test, whether the work "lacks serious literary, artistic, political or scientific value," was to be determined by a reasonable person standard.[442] Unlike the first two parts of the *Miller* test, this was a national standard.[443]

With regard to the second element of the *Miller* test, Chief Justice Burger offered some examples of what a state could define as patently offensive conduct:

(a) Patently offensive representations or descriptions of ultimate sexual acts, normal or perverted, actual or simulated.

(b) Patently offensive representation or descriptions of masturbation, excretory functions, and lewd exhibitions of the genitals.[444]

The second element did not require a state to state all specific conduct that was obscene, as the second element of *Miller* might be read to require.[445]

Several pre-*Miller* cases shed further light on other factors involved in determining whether material was obscene. *Smith v. California*[446] established that obscenity convictions carry a scienter requirement. The Court found that imposing strict liability on the bookseller would cause him "to restrict the books he sells to those he has inspected."[447]

The manner in which dealers sold sexually explicit material could determine whether it would be afforded constitutional protection. In *Ginzburg v. United States*,[448] the Court, in a 5-4 decision, held that juries could consider the way in which particular materials were marketed in determining whether the materials were obscene. The Court stated that "pandering" tactics demonstrated the seller's intent to appeal "solely" to prurient interests.

While *Miller* set the current standard for obscenity protection, *Paris Adult Theatre I v. Slaton*[449] rendered it broadly applicable by extending the standard to willing recipients of sexually explicit material. The *Paris Adult* Court distinguished *Stanley v. Georgia*,[450] which held that one cannot be convicted for having obscene materials in one's home. The Court refused to extend the protection afforded the private exhibition of obscene materials in one's home to public displays of obscenity.

---

[441] *Smith*, 431 U.S. at 303.

[442] *See* Pope v. Illinois, 481 U.S. 497 (1987).

[443] *Id.*

[444] *Smith*, 413 U.S. at 25.

[445] *See* Ward v. Illinois, 431 U.S. 767 (1977).

[446] 361 U.S. 147 (1959).

[447] *Id.* at 153.

[448] 383 U.S. 463 (1966).

[449] 413 U.S. 49 (1973).

[450] 394 U.S. 557 (1969).

Stanley itself has been narrowed in *Osborne v. Ohio*,[451] which upheld a conviction for possessing child pornography in one's home.

Justice Brennan's dissent in *Paris Adult Theater* criticized the majority for allowing content discrimination. Justice Brennan did concede the need for a different standard for minors and non-consenting adults. In a separate dissent, Justice Douglas argued that obscenity should be fully protected. He expressed concern that suppression limited the exchange of ideas within society and that the Court was engaging in censorship.

In *American Booksellers v. Hudnut*,[452] the Court summarily affirmed a decision of the Seventh Circuit Court of Appeals invalidating an Indianapolis ordinance[453] that imposed civil penalties for "pornography."[454] The Seventh Circuit Court of Appeals had held the definition defective because it was not viewpoint neutral.

The Court has allowed government to regulate the undesirable effects accompanying pornography. In *Arcara v. Cloud Books, Inc.*,[455] the Court upheld an order, based on a New York statute, closing a bookstore for one year because it had been used for prostitution. The fact that the business being closed was a bookstore had no First Amendment implications. The *Arcara* Court refused to apply the test from *United States v. O'Brien*[456] requiring constitutional protection for symbolic expression, because the statute on which the order was based regulated non-expressive activity. The Court has also allowed a variety of zoning restrictions to control the undesirable effects of pornographic theatres, even if the exhibited material is not obscene.[457]

Technology has led the Court to rule on more modern forms of the marketing of sexually explicit materials. In *Sable Communications v. FCC*,[458] the Court upheld,

---

[451]   495 U.S. 103 (1990).

[452]   771 F.2d 323 (1985), *aff'd*, 475 U.S. 1001 (1986).

[453]   "Pornography" under the ordinance is "the graphic sexually explicit subordination of women, whether in pictures or in words, that also includes one or more of the following:

    (1) Women are presented as sexual objects who enjoy pain or humiliation; or

    (2) Women are presented as sexual objects who experience sexual pleasure in being raped: or

    (3) Women are presented as sexual objects tied up or cut up or mutilated or bruised or physically hurt, or as dismembered or truncated or fragmented or severed into body parts; or

    (4) Women are presented as being penetrated by objects or animals; or

    (5) Women are presented in scenarios of degradation, injury, abasement, torture, shown as filthy or inferior, bleeding, bruised, or hurt in a context that makes these conditions sexual; or

    (6) Women are presented as sexual objects for domination, conquest, violation, exploitation, possession, or use, or through postures or positions of servility or submission or display."

[454]   For a critical appraisal of the statute at issue in *Hudnut*, see E. Carr, *Feminism, Pornography, and the First Amendment: An Obscenity-Based Analysis of Proposed Anti-Pornography Laws*, 34 UCLA L. Rev. 1265 (1987).

[455]   478 U.S. 697 (1986).

[456]   391 U.S. 367 (1968).

[457]   *See, e.g.*, Young v. Am. Mini Theatres, Inc., *supra* § 15.01[3] and City of Renton v. Playtime Theatres, Inc., *supra* § 15.01[3].

[458]   492 U.S. 115 (1989).

against a facial challenge, a Federal statute's ban on obscene commercial telephone messages. At the same time, the Court unanimously struck down that part of the statute banning messages that were merely indecent. As First Amendment protection does not extend to obscene speech, the Court found no constitutional impediments to a ban on obscene "dial-a-porn." In contrast, the outright ban on indecent messages was not narrowly tailored to serve the "compelling interest of protecting the physical and psychological well-being of minors."[459] Access to indecent messages could be restricted using FCC access codes, credit cards, and scrambling rules.

In *Ginsberg v. New York*,[460] the Court applied a different standard for obscenity of materials sold to minors. This lesser standard was geared to the *Memoirs* test as *Ginsberg* was decided before *Miller*. However, the *Ginsberg* Court upheld the conviction for selling to a 16-year-old a magazine depicting female "nudity" as defined by this New York Penal Law, that is, showing the " 'female buttocks with less than a full opaque covering, or the showing of the female breast with less than a fully opaque covering to the top of the nipple.' " Decided before *Miller*, the *Ginsberg* Court refashioned the old *Memoirs* test specifically to treat minors by withholding protection for material which "(i) predominantly appeals to the prurient, shameful or morbid interest of minors, and (ii) is patently offensive to prevailing standards in the adult community as a whole with respect to what is suitable material for minors, and (iii) is utterly without redeeming social importance for minors."[461] Whether the *Miller* test should be modified to accommodate minors is an open question.

Continuing its line of cases protecting minors from pornography, the Court unanimously held that child pornography was not protected by the First Amendment in *New York v. Ferber*.[462] In *Ferber*, the State sought not only to regulate the use of children in obscene sexual acts, but to extend its regulations to non-obscene uses of children as well. Because the statute in question suppressed speech on the basis of content, the Court scrutinized it under the compelling state interest standard. Writing for the majority, Justice White provided several reasons for allowing much broader regulation of sexual activity involving children. Among these were safeguarding the physical and psychological well-being of children.

Moreover, there was little value in obscene representations of children because adults could be used to simulate children. Justice White stated that child pornography was a category of speech outside First Amendment protection. Moreover, the Court stated that it has refused First Amendment protection to a broad category of speech based on its content, when, as in this case, the harm overwhelmingly exceeded any interest that might have existed in the expression. To scrutinize child pornography, the Court readjusted the *Miller* formula in the following respects: "A trier of fact need not find that the material appeals to the prurient interest of the average person; it is not required that sexual conduct portrayed be done so in a

---

[459] *Id.* at 126.

[460] 390 U.S. 629 (1968).

[461] *Id.* at 633.

[462] 458 U.S. 747 (1982).

patently offensive manner; and the material at issue need not be considered as a whole."[463]

Finally, the Court rejected an overbreadth challenge to the statute in question, finding that its potential regulation of pictures in medical textbooks and magazines such as National Geographic would likely represent an exceedingly small number of the statute's applications.

The Court relied heavily on *Ferber* in *Osborne v. Ohio*,[464] in upholding a conviction for possessing child pornography in one's home. The Court narrowed *Stanley v. Georgia*,[465] which protected a right to view obscene materials in the privacy of one's home. The statute in *Osborne* destroyed "a market for the exploitive use of children," while the one in *Stanley* served a "paternalistic interest in regulating [the defendant's] mind."

In *Ashcroft v. The Free Speech Coalition*, the Court invalidated as substantially overbroad parts of the Child Pornography Prevention Act of 1996 (CPPA) that prohibited "sexually explicit images that appeared to depict minors but were produced without using any real children." The CPPA proscribed materials that did not meet the test for obscenity set forth in *Miller v. California*. First, the materials "need not appeal to the prurient interest," as the CPPA banned all depictions "of sexually explicit activity, no matter how it is presented." Second, the CPPA banned more than patently offensive images. "Pictures of what appear to be 17-year-olds engaging in sexually explicit activity do not in every case contravene community standards." Third, the CPPA prohibited speech that had "serious literary, artistic, political, or scientific value." Teenage sexuality "is a fact of modern society and has been a theme in art and literature throughout the ages." Moreover, age eighteen was "higher than the legal age for marriage in many States, as well as the age at which persons may consent to sexual relations." Finally, *Miller* required that the whole work be considered; "a single explicit scene" does not determine a work's "artistic merit." In contrast, the CPPA punishes the possessor of a film containing "a single graphic depiction of sexual activity" regardless of the redeeming value of the work.

In contrast to child pornography at issue in *New York v. Ferber*, "the CPPA prohibited speech that recorded no crime and created no victims by its production. Virtual child pornography is not 'intrinsically related' to the sexual abuse of children." *Ferber* focused on how child pornography was made rather than the context of "what it communicated." Recognizing that some child pornography "might have significant value," *Ferber* permitted using a young looking person over the statutory age or a simulation, both prohibited under § 2256(8)(B).

Justice Kennedy rejected the governmental interests in preventing pedophiles from seducing children, as cartoons and candy could be used for this purpose as well. Nor could legal speech be banned because it encouraged people being pedophiles. Justice Kennedy also rejected the government's argument that simu

---

[463] *Id.* at 764.

[464] 495 U.S. 103 (1990); *supra* § 13.05[2].

[465] 394 U.S. 557 (1969).

lated child pornography would make it difficult to prosecute actual child pornography as the images would be too difficult to distinguish. "Government may not suppress lawful speech as the means to suppress unlawful speech."

Justice Kennedy also invalidated as substantially overbroad the CPPA's separate pandering ban which prohibited promoting images as sexually explicit depictions of minors. While "pandering may be relevant, as an evidentiary matter, to the question whether particular materials are obscene," the CPPA punished "possession of material described, or pandered, as child pornography by someone earlier in the distribution chain."

Concurring in the judgment, Justice Thomas noted that technology eventually may render impossible the enforcement of child pornography laws because simulated images could not be distinguished from images of real children. At that time, "the Government may well have a compelling interest in barring or otherwise regulating some narrow category of 'lawful speech' in order to enforce effectively laws against pornography made through the abuse of real children."

Justice O'Connor concurred in part, and dissented in part. In Part I of her opinion, Justice O'Connor agreed with the majority that the pandering ban of § 2256(8)(D) "fails strict scrutiny." In Part I, Justice O'Connor also would hold overbroad the prohibition on child pornography "only insofar as it is applied to the class of youthful-adult pornography."

In Part II of her opinion, Justice O'Connor, joined by Chief Justice Rehnquist and Justice Scalia, disagreed that the ban on virtual-child pornography was overbroad. Justice O'Connor read the statute "only to bar images that are virtually indistinguishable from actual children." Government had a "compelling interest in protecting our Nation's children." Virtual child pornography whet "the appetites of child molesters who may use the images to seduce young children." Moreover, "rapid" advances in computer technology rendered "reasonable," the government's concern that computer-generated images may enable actual child pornography to evade liability.

Chief Justice Rehnquist, with whom Justice Scalia joined in part, dissented. The Chief Justice agreed with Justice O'Connor that "Congress has a compelling interest in ensuring the ability to enforce prohibitions of actual child pornography, and we should defer to its findings that rapidly advancing technology soon will make it all but impossible to do so." Moreover, the CPPA could have been construed to limit only unprotected speech. Its definition of "sexually explicit conduct" only extended to " 'visual depictions' of: '[a]ctual or simulated . . . sexual intercourse, including genital-genital, oral-genital, anal-genital, or oral-anal, whether between persons of the same or opposite sex; . . . bestiality; . . . masturbation; . . . sadistic or masochistic abuse; . . . or lascivious exhibition of the genitals or pubic area of any person.' " Chief Justice Rehnquist would also uphold the pandering prohibition, but limit its reach to the panderer.

In *United States v. X-Citement Video, Inc.*,[466] the Court (7-2) upheld the constitutionality of the Protection of Children Against Sexual Exploitation Act of

---

[466] 513 U.S. 64 (1994).

1977,[467] against a challenge that it lacked the necessary scienter requirement. Writing for the Court, Justice Stevens read the term "knowingly" to modify the phrase "use of a minor" even though this was not the "most grammatical reading."[468] Justice Stevens noted that the Court previously had supplied scienter requirements in criminal statutes that do not explicitly contain them. He also noted that the Court tried to interpret a statute constitutionally so long as the construction does not explicitly contradict Congress's intent.

In *Ashcroft v. American Civil Liberties Union*,[469] the Court rejected a facial challenge against the Child Online Protection Act's (COPA) reliance on "community standards" to identify " 'material that is harmful to minors.' " Writing for a plurality of four, Justice Thomas noted that unlike the Communications Decency Act of 1996 (CDA), invalidated in *Reno v. American Civil Liberties Union*,[470] the Child Online Protection Act (COPA) not only criminalized works that " 'depic[t], describ[e], or represen[t], in a manner patently offensive with respect to minors,' particular sexual acts or parts of the anatomy," but "they must also be designed to appeal to the prurient interests of minors, and 'taken as a whole, lack[ ] serious literary, artistic, political, or scientific value for minors.' " Moreover, following *Miller v. California*, COPA adopts a national standard to assess serious value.

Writing for a plurality of three, Justice Thomas concluded that publication over the Internet is necessarily national. When a publisher sends material to a community, it must "abide by that community's standards," even if the publisher "decides to distribute its material to every community in the Nation." If the application of community standards to the Web rendered COPA unconstitutional, *Miller* also could not apply to the Web; however, *Reno* has held that "the application of the CDA to obscene speech was constitutional."

Writing for a majority, Justice Thomas held that COPA's reliance on community standards did not "*by itself* render the statute substantially overbroad." The Court did not express "any view as to whether COPA suffers from substantial overbreadth for other reasons, whether the statute is unconstitutionally vague, or whether the District Court correctly concluded that the statute likely will not survive strict scrutiny."

Concurring in part and concurring in the judgment, Justice O'Connor would adopt "a national standard for defining obscenity on the Internet." Concurring in part and concurring in the judgment, Justice Breyer also would adopt a "nationally uniform adult-based standard." Application of this standard by different local juries does not violate the First Amendment.

Justice Kennedy concurred in the judgment, joined by Justices Souter and Ginsburg. To assess substantial overbreadth, it was "necessary to know what speech COPA regulates and what community standards it invokes." Justice Stevens dissented.

---

[467] 18 U.S.C. § 2252 (1994).

[468] *X-Citement Video*, 513 U.S. at 70.

[469] 535 U.S. 564 (2002).

[470] 521 U.S. 844 (1997); this case is discussed in § 14.07[2].

In *United States v. Williams*,[471] the Court upheld a federal statute that criminalized the "pandering or solicitation of child pornography." In addressing Williams' overbreadth challenge, Justice Scalia construed the statute at issue. First, *New York v. Ferber*[472] had held that the government may ban child pornography. Distinguishing *Free Speech Coalition*, Justice Scalia noted that the statute at issue did not restrict the underlying material. Instead, it criminalized "the collateral speech" of pandering or soliciting such material, that is, the offers and requests for the material.

Justice Scalia noted five characteristics of the statute important in upholding it against an overbreadth challenge. First, the statute at issue included a scienter requirement. Second, the majority concluded that the statute's verbs — "advertises, promotes, presents, distributes, or solicits" — implied an intent to regulate both commercial and noncommercial transactions. Although less obvious than "advertises" or "solicits," the verb "promotes" was equivalent to recommending in the provision's context. Third, the statute required that the defendant subjectively have believed that the material at issue was actual child pornography and objectively must have manifested that belief. Fourth, the defendant must have subjectively intended to make the recipient believe the material was actual child pornography. Fifth, unlike in *Free Speech Coalition*, the statute's prohibition required the material to depict actual minors even if the sexual conduct was simulated, unless the depiction was actually obscene.

"Offers to engage in illegal transactions" are not protected by the First Amendment because they have no "social value." Instead, such offers are akin to speech criminalized for its inducement of commercial or noncommercial illegal activities such as conspiracy, incitement, and solicitation. Nevertheless, "there remains an important distinction between a proposal to engage in illegal activity and the abstract advocacy of illegality."

Finally, Justice Scalia addressed the dissent's concern that the majority's holding essentially overrules *Free Speech Coalition*. He explained that First Amendment protections of *virtual* child pornography remained intact. Rather, the statute at issue prohibited transactions of material believed or intended to induce others to believe involved *actual* minors.

Concurring, Justice Stevens emphasized that the statute's reach was constrained by its lascivious intent requirement. Dissenting, Justice Souter, joined by Justice Ginsburg, concluded that upholding the statute's pandering prohibition undermined the rationales in *Ferber* and *Free Speech Coalition*. Justice Souter argued that transactions involving a mistaken belief that fake pornography is real was not a crime but rather "an incomplete attempt to commit a crime."

In *United States v. Stevens* the Court invalidated a law prohibiting depictions of animal cruelty as "substantially overbroad."[473] The statute was aimed at prohibiting " 'crush videos,' " which depict the "intentional torture and killing of helpless

---

[471] 553 U.S. 285 (2008).

[472] 458 U.S. 747 (1982).

[473] 130 S. Ct. 1577, 1592 (2010).

animals."[474] The Government urged that "depictions of animal cruelty" be a new category of unprotected speech, but the Court declined to "carve out" such depictions from First Amendment protection.[475]

Writing for the Court, Chief Justice Roberts addressed a facial challenge to the statute. Typical analysis would require " 'no set of circumstances' " under which an act would be constitutional.[476] However, in free speech cases a facial challenge can invalidate a statute "as overbroad if 'a substantial number of its applications are unconstitutional, judged in relation to the statute's plainly legitimate sweep.' "[477] The statute was alarmingly overbroad. For example, depiction of conduct not considered illegal in one state would become criminal if it was later found in a state where the conduct is illegal.

The statute's "exceptions clause" did not save it.[478] The clause exempted " 'any depiction that has serious religious, political, scientific, educational, journalistic, historical, or artistic value,' "[479] following *Miller v. California*. "*Most* of what we say to one another" does not fit within any of these categories and is nevertheless protected speech.[480] The market for constitutionally permissible depictions, like hunting magazines and videos, which are prohibited by the statute, dwarfs the market for impermissible depictions. The Court did not "decide whether a statute limited to crush videos or other depictions of extreme animal cruelty would be constitutional."[481]

Justice Alito dissented, arguing that invalidation based on overbreadth should be " 'a last resort.' "[482]

In *Brown v. Entertainment Merchants Association*,[483] the Court invalidated a California law which prohibited "the sale or rental of 'violent video games' to minors, and require[d] their packaging to be labeled '18.' "[484] The law included games which involve " 'killing, maiming, dismembering, or sexually assaulting an image of a human being, if those acts are depicted' in a manner that '[a] reasonable person, considering the game as a whole, would find appeals to a deviant or morbid interest of minors,' that is 'patently offensive to prevailing standards in the community as to what is suitable for minors,' and that 'causes the game, as a whole, to lack serious literary, artistic, political, or scientific value for minors.' "[485] Violators could receive civil fines of up to $1,000.

---

[474] *Id.* at 1583.

[475] *Id.* at 1585–86.

[476] *Id.* at 1587.

[477] *Id.*

[478] *Id.* at 1590.

[479] *Id.*

[480] *Id.* at 1591.

[481] *Id.* at 1592.

[482] *Id.* at 1593 (Alito, J., dissenting).

[483] 131 S. Ct. 2729 (2011).

[484] *Id.* at 2732.

[485] *Id.* at 2732–33.

Justice Scalia wrote for the Court. Resembling "the protected books, plays, and movies that preceded them, video games communicate ideas — and even social messages — through many familiar literary devices (such as characters, dialogue, plot, and music) and through features distinctive to the medium (such as the player's interaction with the virtual world)."[486] Historically, " 'esthetic and moral judgments about art and literature . . . are for the individual to make, not for the Government' to decree."[487] Even with today's "ever-advancing technology, 'the basic principles of freedom of speech and the press, like the First Amendment's command, do not vary' when a new and different medium for communication appears."[488] Most fundamentally, " 'government has no power to restrict expression because of its message, its ideas, its subject matter, or its content' " with the exception of a " 'few limited areas,' " such as, obscenity, incitement, and fighting words.[489]

In *United States v. Stevens*[490] the Court had invalidated the statute at issue as an "impermissible content-based restriction on speech" as there was "no American tradition of forbidding the *depiction* of animal cruelty — though States have long had laws against *committing* it."[491] Moreover, as "speech about violence is not obscene," it was "of no consequence that California's statute mimics the New York statute regulating obscenity-for-minors that we upheld in *Ginsberg v. New York*."[492] However, unlike the law at issue in *Ginsberg*, the California Act sought "to create a wholly new category of content-based regulation that is permissible only for speech directed at children."[493] Minors have "a significant measure of First Amendment protection, and only in relatively narrow and well-defined circumstances may government bar" material from being disseminated to them.[494] Perhaps the law "would fare better if there were a longstanding tradition in this country of specially restricting children's access to depictions of violence," but no such tradition exists.[495]

California asserted that "video games present special problems because they are 'interactive,' in that the player participates in the violent action on screen and determines its outcome."[496] However, Justice Scalia noted that this "is nothing new" as "readers of choose-your-own-adventure stories have been able to make decisions that determine the plot by following instructions about which page to turn to."[497]

---

[486] *Id.* at 2733.

[487] *Id.*

[488] *Id.*

[489] *Id.*

[490] 130 S. Ct. 1577 (2010).

[491] *Brown*, 131 S. Ct. at 2734.

[492] *Id.* at 2735 (quoting *Ginsberg v. New York*, 390 U.S. 629 (1968)).

[493] *Id.*

[494] *Id.*

[495] *Id.* at 2736.

[496] *Id.* at 2737–38.

[497] *Id.* at 2738.

While the "degree" of video game violence may be disgusting, "disgust is not a valid basis for restricting expression."[498]

As the Act restricted "the content of protected speech, it [was] invalid unless California [could] demonstrate" that the Act was "justified by a compelling government interest" and "narrowly drawn to serve that interest."[499] However, California could not "show a direct causal link between violent video games and harm to minors."[500] The State's research was " 'based on correlation, not evidence of causation.' "[501] Moreover, the State's expert admitted that the effects of "violent video games are 'about the same' " as the effects of "exposure to violence on television."[502] Therefore, the Court held that California's "regulation is wildly underinclusive when judged against its asserted justification, which in our view is alone enough to defeat it."[503]

The Act was also "underinclusive in another respect."[504] The State was "perfectly willing to leave this dangerous, mind-altering material in the hands of children so long as one parent (or even an aunt or uncle) says it's OK."[505] Moreover, the Court doubted "that punishing third parties for conveying protected speech to children *just in case* their parents disapprove of that speech is a proper governmental means of aiding parental authority."[506] That would "largely vitiate the rule that 'only in relatively narrow and well-defined circumstances may government bar public dissemination of protected materials to [minors].' "[507]

The "video-game industry has in place a voluntary rating system," which encourages retailers "to rent or sell 'M' rated games to minors only with parental consent."[508] Consequently, "filling the remaining modest gap in concerned-parents' control can hardly be a compelling state interest."[509] Also, the Act was "vastly overinclusive" since not all of the childrens' parents "*care* whether they purchase violent video games."[510]

Justice Alito, joined by Chief Justice Roberts, concurred in the judgment. Because of today's "new and rapidly evolving technology, this Court should proceed with caution."[511] Also, there is an important distinction between devoting many hours to "controlling the actions of a character who guns down scores of innocent

---

[498] *Id.*

[499] *Id.*

[500] *Id.*

[501] *Id.* at 2739.

[502] *Id.*

[503] *Id.* at 2740.

[504] *Id.*

[505] *Id.*

[506] *Id.*

[507] *Id.*

[508] *Id.*

[509] *Id.* at 2741.

[510] *Id.*

[511] *Id.* at 2742 (Alito, J., concurring).

victims" and "reading a description of violence in a work of literature."[512]

Justice Alito considered the Act "impermissibly vague," and thus did not "reach the broader First Amendment issues addressed by the Court."[513] For California to comply with *Miller v. California*,[514] it would need to target "a narrower class of graphic depictions."[515] For example, "the California Legislature could have made its own judgment regarding the kind and degree of violence that is acceptable in games played by minors (or by minors in particular age groups). Instead, the legislature relied on undefined societal or community standards,"[516] and included the "terms 'deviant' and 'morbid' [which] are not defined in the statute."[517] At the time of *Miller*, "obscenity had long been prohibited, and this experience had helped to shape certain generally accepted norms concerning expression related to sex."[518] No such history exists "regarding expression related to violence."[519] And, the "California law draws no distinction between young children and adolescents."[520]

On the broader free speech issues, Justice Alito did not consider *Stevens* controlling. First, unlike the law in *Stevens*, the California law at issue "does not regulate the sale or rental of violent games by adults," or regulate adults renting or purchasing such games for children.[521] Second, *Stevens* did not apply strict scrutiny but instead merely "rejected the Government's contention that depictions of animal cruelty were categorically outside the range of *any* First Amendment protection."[522] After "today's decision, a State may prohibit the sale to minors of what *Ginsberg* described as 'girlie magazines,' but a State must surmount a formidable (and perhaps insurmountable) obstacle if it wishes to prevent children from purchasing the most violent and depraved video games imaginable."[523] In addition, "*Stevens* expressly left open the possibility that a more narrowly drawn statute" might be constitutional.[524]

Importantly, "the California law reinforces parental decisionmaking in exactly the same way as the New York statute upheld in *Ginsberg*."[525] The "video-game industry's voluntary rating system" was adopted "in response to the threat of federal regulation, a threat that the Court's opinion may now be seen as largely

---

[512] *Id.*

[513] *Id.* at 2743–43.

[514] 413 U.S. 15 (1973).

[515] 131 S. Ct. at 2745.

[516] *Id.*

[517] *Id.*

[518] *Id.* at 2746.

[519] *Id.*

[520] *Id.*

[521] *Id.* at 2747.

[522] *Id.*

[523] *Id.*

[524] *Id.*

[525] *Id.*

eliminating."[526] Moreover, compliance with the voluntary rating system left "much to be desired."[527] For example, "[a] 2004 Federal Trade Commission Report showed that 69 percent of unaccompanied children ages 13 to 16 were able to buy M- rated games."[528]

The majority also failed to grasp the realism of the video games that the regulation impacts. Victims are "dismembered, decapitated, disemboweled, set on fire, and chopped into little pieces. They cry out in agony and beg for mercy."[529] Some games allow players to reenact the "murders at Columbine High School and Virginia Tech. The objective of one game is to rape a mother and her daughters."[530]

Justice Thomas dissented. "The practices and beliefs of the founding generation establish that 'the freedom of speech,' as originally understood, does not include a right to speak to minors (or a right of minors to access speech) without going through the minors' parents or guardians."[531] While "the original public under-standing" of the Constitution does not always match "modern sensibilities," the idea "that parents have authority over their children and that the law can support that authority persists today."[532] As the law allows a minor to obtain "a violent video game with his parent's or guardian's help," it principally regulates "speech that bypasses a minor's parent."[533]

Justice Breyer also dissented. "A facial challenge to this statute based on the First Amendment can succeed only if 'a substantial number of its applications are unconstitutional, judged in relation to the statute's plainly legitimate sweep.' "[534] Also, "it is more difficult to mount a facial First Amendment attack on a statute that seeks to regulate activity that involves action as well as speech."[535]

Upholding the statute would not "create a 'new categor[y] of unprotected speech,' " as the majority suggested.[536] "No one here argues that depictions of violence, even extreme violence, *automatically* fall outside the First Amend-ment."[537] As in *Ginsberg*, California advanced the "compelling" interest of "(1) the 'basic' parental claim 'to authority in their own household to direct the rearing of their children,' " and "(2) the State's 'independent interest in the well-being of its youth.' "[538] Nowadays, "5.3 million grade-school-age children of working parents

---

[526] *Id.* at 2747–48 (citations omitted).

[527] *Id.* at 2748.

[528] *Id.* at n.6.

[529] *Id.*

[530] *Id.*

[531] *Id.* at 2751 (Thomas, J., dissenting).

[532] *Id.* at 2769.

[533] *Id.* at 2761.

[534] *Id.* at 2762 (Breyer, J., dissenting).

[535] *Id.*

[536] *Id.*

[537] *Id.*

[538] *Id.* at 2767.

are routinely home alone."[539] Some video games are used to help soldiers train. Predictably, " 'meta-analyses,' *i.e.*, studies of all the studies, have concluded that exposure to violent video games 'was positively associated with aggressive behavior, aggressive cognition, and aggressive affect,' and that 'playing violent video games is a *causal* risk factor for long-term harmful outcomes.' "[540]

This evidence is sufficient "for this Court to defer to an elected legislature's conclusion that the video games in question are particularly likely to harm children."[541] Moreover, there is "no 'less restrictive' alternative to California's law that would be 'at least as effective.' "[542] The evidence supports the argument that extreme violence "can prove at least as, if not more, harmful to children as photographs of nudity."[543]

[2]   Procedural Issues in Obscenity Cases: "Prior Restraints" and Seizure of Materials

Prior restraints on expressive conduct are serious intrusions on First Amendment rights, but they have sometimes been sustained in the case of obscene materials, provided there is an opportunity for prompt judicial determination of the obscenity allegations.[544] In *Freedman v. Maryland*,[545] the Supreme Court established that prior restraints must comply with the following requirements:

(1) the burden of instituting judicial proceedings, and of proving that the material is unprotected, must rest on the censor;

(2) any restraint prior to judicial review can be imposed only for a specified brief period and only for the purpose of preserving the status quo;

(3) a prompt final judicial determination on the merits must be assured.[546]

The Supreme Court found that the *Freedman* test was not met in *Southeastern Promotions Ltd. v. Conrad*,[547] in which a company wanted to perform the play *Hair* in a municipal theater. The board of directors of the theater prohibited the production. The Court held that the board order prohibiting the play was an unlawful prior restraint as the board did not seek prompt judicial review and judicial review on the merits did not occur until five months after the order took effect.

---

[539] *Id.*

[540] *Id.* at 2768.

[541] *Id.* at 2770.

[542] *Id.*

[543] *Id.* at 2771.

[544] For additional discussion of prior restraints, *see* § 14.01.

[545] 380 U.S. 51 (1965).

[546] *Id.* at 58–59.

[547] 420 U.S. 546 (1975).

The *Freedman* test was somewhat relaxed by *FW/PBS, Inc. v. City of Dallas*,[548] in which the Court held unconstitutional an ordinance's licensing requirements — primarily targeting businesses engaged in sexually explicit speech — because they failed to provide adequate procedural safeguards. The Court found that the ordinance lacked sufficient time limits on the official charged with license issuance. This violated *Freedman's* requirement that any restraint prior to judicial review be imposed only for a specified brief period. Moreover, the ordinance did not provide license applicants with an opportunity for prompt judicial review as required by *Freedman*.

The Court in *Dallas* invalidated the licensing requirements on these grounds alone. It concluded that the complete procedural protections established in *Freedman* were not required as "the licensing scheme at issue in these cases does not present the grave 'dangers of a censorship system.' "[549] Accordingly, the Court did not demand that the City bear the burden of going to court to suppress the contested speech and bear the burden of proof once in court.[550]

Freedman also did not apply in other contexts. The *Freedman* test need not be met when a copy of the material was seized under a warrant for evidence, rather than to stop its viewing pending suit. Of course, if other copies of the seized materials existed, these could still be sold or viewed, which could not occur under a prior restraint. The standard for probable cause in such cases was the same as for other warrants.[551] Moreover, a warrant was not necessary when allegedly obscene materials were purchased by an undercover agent.[552]

In *Littleton v. Z. J. Gifts*,[553] the Court upheld a city ordinance requiring a license for adult businesses. The Court said that *Freedman v. Maryland* and *FW/PBS, Inc. v. City of Dallas* required not only prompt access to judicial review, but also "prompt judicial determination."[554] However, Z.J. Gifts did not suffer any judicial delay, but merely brought a facial challenge to the regulation. Because the "regulation simply conditions the operation of an adult business on compliance with neutral and nondiscretionary criteria, and does not seek to censor content, an adult business is not entitled to an unusually speedy judicial decision of the *Freedman* type."[555] The laws of Colorado already provided for a system of review flexible enough to usually permit prompt decisions but protect First Amendment interests. The Court did leave open the door to as-applied challenges for "undue delay."[556]

---

[548] 493 U.S. 215 (1990).

[549] *Id.* at 228.

[550] The Court also allowed rentals of motel rooms for less than 10 hours to be regulated by the licensing scheme. It rejected the motel owners' claim that the licensing scheme violated privacy rights. The Court stated that "personal bonds" formed in motel rooms in less than 10 hours did not merit the requested constitutional protection.

[551] *See* New York v. P. J. Video, 475 U.S. 868 (1986); Heller v. New York, 413 U.S. 483 (1973).

[552] *See* Maryland v. Macon, 472 U.S. 463 (1985).

[553] 541 U.S. 774 (2004).

[554] *Id.* at 778.

[555] *Id.* at 784.

[556] *Id.*

In *Jacobson v. United States*,[557] the Court reversed the defendant's conviction for violating the Child Protection Act on the grounds that he was entrapped. The government sent him questionnaires, catalogs, and correspondence in which it pressured defendant to purchase the materials at issue to advance the fight against censorship.

The Court examined the constitutionality of using in obscenity prosecutions the Racketeering Influenced and Corrupt Organization Act (RICO) in *Fort Wayne Books, Inc. v. Indiana* and *Sappenfield v. Indiana*.[558] The two cases involved the prosecution of two adult bookstores using various aspects of Indiana's RICO law. A RICO violation consisted of a "pattern of racketeering activity" evidenced by at least two predicate offenses. The types of crimes constituting predicate offenses were described by the particular RICO statute. A RICO violation was a crime distinct from its predicate offenses, carrying separate civil and criminal sanctions.

The Court in *Sappenfield* held that the use of obscenity as a predicate offense was not unconstitutionally vague. Accepting such an argument would have entailed overruling *Miller*, and the Court said that the *Miller* standard was not vague. The *Sappenfield* Court also rejected the claim that the harsh prison sentences and fines imposed by RICO were unconstitutional when applied in the First Amendment context. The Court rejected a claim that RICO penalties, which were harsher than those imposed for obscenity violations, created "an improper chilling effect on First Amendment freedoms."[559] The Court did not find the difference between RICO punishment and that for obscenity violations to be significant. Although the penalties for a RICO violation were more severe, the Court likened the severe RICO punishment to enhanced sentencing for multiple obscenity violations.

In *Fort Wayne Books*, a unanimous Court held unconstitutional a pretrial seizure in a civil RICO action of the contents of three adult bookstores. Although a single copy of a book or film could be seized as evidence of a crime, a finding of probable cause could not provide the basis for a prior restraint on all expressive materials in a bookstore, even if these materials could eventually be subject to disgorgement as a RICO penalty.

In *Alexander v. United States*,[560] the Court held that requiring the convicted seller of obscene materials to forfeit his entire wholesale and retail businesses under the Racketeer Influenced and Corrupt Organizations Act (RICO) did not constitute a prior restraint. The case was remanded to determine whether the forfeiture, considered in addition to the owner's prison term and fine, constituted an excessive fine under the Eighth Amendment.

The defendant, Alexander, was convicted on 17 counts of obscenity and three counts of violating RICO. The RICO counts were predicated on the obscenity counts. Each conviction was based on the jury's determination that the defendant had distributed, throughout his "adult entertainment empire," multiple copies of

---

[557] 503 U.S. 540 (1992).

[558] 489 U.S. 46 (1989).

[559] *Id.* at 59.

[560] 509 U.S. 544 (1993).

three obscene videotapes and four obscene magazines. Defendant was sentenced to six years in prison and fined $100,000. At a subsequent forfeiture proceeding, the same jury found that defendant had used ten tracts of real estate and 31 businesses to further his racketeering activities. The District Court ordered the defendant to forfeit his business property under RICO forfeiture provisions.

Alexander argued that the effect of the RICO forfeiture was indistinguishable from the prior restraint in *Near v. Minnesota*.[561] Writing for the majority, Chief Justice Rehnquist said that *Near* involved an injunction that permanently restrained future speech. The RICO forfeiture, however, merely deprived Alexander "of specific assets that were found to be related to his previous racketeering violations."[562] Under the forfeiture order, Alexander would still be "perfectly free to open an adult book store or otherwise engage in the production and distribution of erotic materials; he just cannot finance these enterprises with assets derived from his prior racketeering offenses."[563] Moreover, in contrast to prior restraint precedents involving obscenity, the assets in this case were not forfeited because they were believed to be obscene, but "because they were directly related to petitioner's past racketeering violations."[564] Also unlike prior restraint cases, Alexander was afforded the procedural safeguard of a full criminal trial which connected the forfeited assets to racketeering offenses. Finding a prior restraint in the case at bar would severely "blur the line separating prior restraints from subsequent punishments."[565]

Chief Justice Rehnquist also rejected Alexander's overbreadth argument, noting that RICO did not impose criminal sanctions for constitutionally protected speech. Defendant's "real complaint" was not overbreadth, but that the statute could serve to chill and deter future protected expression. Relying on *Fort Wayne Books*, the Court said that "the threat of forfeiture has no more of a 'chilling effect' on free expression than threats of a prison term or a large fine."[566] As the First Amendment permitted both "stiff criminal penalties for obscenity offenses" and "forfeiture of expressive materials for criminal conduct," the combination of the two would not be impermissible either.

Finally, the Court remanded to determine whether the forfeiture, combined with defendant's six-year prison term and $100,000 fine, was an excessive fine under the Eighth Amendment. The forfeiture did not differ from a monetary fine for Eighth Amendment purposes. Whether the forfeiture was excessive had to be evaluated against defendant's extensive racketeering activities which had continued for a substantial time period.

Justice Souter, concurring in the judgment in part and dissenting in part, agreed that the case did not involve a prior restraint and that it should be remanded on the Eighth Amendment issue. However, he agreed with the dissent that the First

---

[561] 283 U.S. 697 (1931). *See supra* § 14.01.

[562] *Alexander*, 509 U.S. at 551.

[563] *Id.*

[564] *Id.* at 544.

[565] *Id.* at 554.

[566] *Alexander*, 509 U.S. at 545.

Amendment forbade the forfeiture of that portion of the materials that were not first judged obscene.

Justice Kennedy, joined by Justices Blackmun and Stevens in dissent, criticized the majority for allowing government to destroy "a book and film business and its entire inventory of legitimate expression as punishment for a single past speech offense."[567] Permissible fines and jail terms differed from destroying protected publications together with the facilities to publish and distribute them. The forfeiture raised the same policy concerns of state censorship and chilling protected speech. In *Near*, for example, the nuisance statute struck down by the Court was aimed at suppressing the offending publication. Similarly, the purpose of RICO was to destroy a speech business for its owner's past speech rather than for its own content. In addition to calling the forfeiture a prior restraint, the dissent criticized the destruction of books not adjudicated obscene as being without precedent. Three Justices joined the entire dissent, and four Justices at least part of it.

---

[567] *Id.* at 560.

Chapter 17

GOVERNMENT AND RELIGIOUS FREEDOM

INTRODUCTION

The Bill of Rights begins with the command that "Congress shall make no laws respecting an establishment of religion, or prohibiting the free exercise thereof."[1] The textual position of the religion clauses serves as a commentary on the central role religious freedom plays in our society and democracy generally. James Madison, author of the Bill of Rights, viewed the free exercise of religion as a right "precedent both in order of time and degree of obligation to the claims of Civil Society."[2] Indeed, the institution of democracy itself relies on the existence of a public free to choose "according to the dictates of conscience."[3] The religion clauses work in tandem to preserve a single ideal, religious freedom. The Establishment Clause mandates a kind of mutual noninterference by church and state in each other's affairs. This mutual noninterference helps to foster the freedom of religious belief and practice mandated by the Free Exercise Clause. The application of this singular ideal has proven to be a complex matter, however. While the clauses may be mutually sustaining, there exists a certain tension between them as well. In our modern welfare state, stringent separation of government and religion may at times deprive religion of an otherwise generally available benefit; thus, free exercise is inhibited. Conversely, the Supreme Court has recently held that free exemptions of religious practitioners from otherwise generally applicable laws favor religion in a manner inconsistent with strict separation. Over time, the ebbs and flows in the Supreme Court's religion clause jurisprudence reflects this tension between the clauses.

This chapter describes the Court's highly complex religion jurisprudence. Section 17.01 discusses the Court's early religion clause decisions and the competing jurisprudential approaches that have emerged. These approaches, separation of church and state and accommodation of religion, still inform the Court's decisions in this area today.

Ensuing sections discuss the Court's decisions according to the general factual categories in which claims arise. Section 17.02 focuses on the Court's application of the Establishment Clause to cases involving aid to religious institutions. Most of the

---

[1] U.S. Const. amend. I.

[2] James Madison, Memorial and Remonstrance, *reprinted in* Everson v. Board of Education, 330 U.S. 1 (1947).

[3] *See id.* Thomas Jefferson, too, held religious freedom preeminent. A man of many accomplishments, Jefferson asked that in his epitaph he be remembered for only three: authoring the Declaration of Independence, founding the University of Virginia, and authoring the Virginia Statute for Religious Freedom. K. Hall et al., American Legal History 74 (1991).

decisions concern aid to religious schools. Section 17.03 considers decisions in which the government has supported some form of religious practice, such as prayer in public schools. Section 17.04 concerns cases where religious institutions have become involved in governmental decisions.

Finally, the Court's decisions can be divided into claims relying primarily on the Establishment Clause and those resting on the Free Exercise Clause. Thus, Section 17.05 considers cases whose analysis focuses on free exercise. The Court has applied varying levels of scrutiny to laws affecting free exercise, with the trend toward more lax scrutiny in recent years. Section 17.05 concludes with a brief discussion of the recently enacted Religious Freedom Restoration Act and the effect this legislation will have on religion clause jurisprudence.

§ 17.01   COMPETING APPROACHES: WALL OF SEPARATION VERSUS ACCOMMODATION

The Supreme Court heard relatively few religion cases during the first century and one-half after ratification of the First Amendment.[4] These early cases, focusing primarily on the Establishment Clause, lacked any unifying principle other than a marked deference for the legislature.[5] In the 1940s and 1950s, the Court handed down a series of decisions developing two competing approaches to interpretation of the religion clauses. These approaches — the wall of separation between church and state, and the accommodation of religion — continue to dominate the Court's decisions today.

Everson v. Board of Education[6] construed the Establishment Clause to require a complete separation of church and state. A New Jersey school board adopted a program for reimbursing parents for the cost of sending their children to Catholic schools by public transportation.[7] Writing for the Court, Justice Black looked to the historical backdrop against which the religion clauses were promulgated, particularly the colonists' efforts to escape religious persecution. Justice Black concluded that the Establishment Clause "was intended to erect 'a wall of separation between Church and State,' "[8] and "[t]hat wall must be kept high and impregnable. We could

---

[4] It was not until 1899 — over 100 years after ratification of the Bill of Rights — that the Court first reviewed an establishment claim in *Bradfield v. Roberts*, 175 U.S. 291 (1899). However, several earlier Supreme Court decisions dealt implicitly with constitutional protection of religious liberty. *See* Davis v. Beason, 133 U.S. 333 (1890); Reynolds v. United States, 98 U.S. 145 (1879); Vidal v. Philadelphia, 43 U.S. (2 How.) 127 (1844); Terrett v. Taylor, 13 U.S. (9 Cranch) 43 (1815).

[5] *Bradfield v. Roberts* exemplifies this deference. The dispute in *Bradfield* involved a Congressional appropriation to the Commissioners of the District of Columbia for a hospital to be built and operated by the Roman Catholic Church. The Court upheld the appropriation, reasoning that because the Commissioners acted within the scope of their authority and the Church did not actually hold title to the property, there was "nothing sectarian" in the undertaking. *Bradfield*, 175 U.S. at 299–300.

[6] 330 U.S. 1 (1947).

[7] *Everson*, 330 U.S. at 29–30. The prohibition of the Establishment Clause applies to state governments as well as the federal government. The Clause was first incorporated into the Fourteenth Amendment's due process guarantee in *Cantwell v. Connecticut*, 310 U.S. 296 (1940).

[8] *Id.* at 16 (quoting *Reynolds v. United States*, 98 U.S. 145, 164 (1879)). The "wall" metaphor was first

not approve the slightest breach."[9] For Justice Black, however, the school board resolution did not breach the wall of separation because providing transportation was a public function and not a religious function.

Although the *Everson* decision did not rest explicitly on the Free Exercise Clause, the Court cited *Pierce v. Society of Sisters*[10] to illustrate the free exercise interests at work in the case. *Pierce* afforded parents a constitutional right to send their children to parochial schools. The *Everson* majority did not hold that a failure to reimburse transportation would violate the free exercise right to attend a parochial school. However, the majority did suggest that providing such reimbursement was consistent with the neutrality mandated by the tension between the religion clauses: "State power is no more to be used so as to handicap religions, than it is to favor them."[11]

Justice Black likened the transportation reimbursement to other public functions such as fire and police services provided to religious schools on a neutral basis. On the other hand, the state could not advance the religious functions of religious institutions by, for example, supporting a church school that taught religion. State support over public functions such as transportation did not favor religion over other beneficiaries of the kind of public welfare services at issue. Justice Black suggested that depriving religion of public services like police and fire protection would handicap religious institutions in violation of the Free Exercise Clause. Taken together, free exercise and establishment guaranteed state neutrality toward religion. Citing *Pierce v. Society of Sisters*,[12] Justice Black noted that the First Amendment guaranteed a right to send one's children to religious schools.

Everson exhibited a deep tension. On the limited facts in *Everson*, it was not clear how far Justice Black's distinction between public functions and religious functions extended. It could have been used to assist religions in ways far beyond bus service. In the context of the modern welfare state, one could argue that education itself was a public function. If so, aid to parochial schools in the form of providing textbooks or salaries for teachers who did not teach religion would arguably escape the prohibition of the Establishment Clause because such aid would not benefit religion, but further a proper public function. Perhaps Justice Black specifically prohibited such aid to avoid any misunderstanding on this score. On the other hand, separation — at least in the absolute terms articulated by Justice Black — would have seemed to bar the government from aiding even a public function such as transportation if it collaterally benefitted religion.

Dissenting, Justice Jackson argued that Catholic education was central to the church's religious function. Subsidizing the transportation of parochial school children supported this essentially religious function in violation of the Establishment Clause.

---

coined by Thomas Jefferson in a letter to the Danbury Baptist Association in 1802. *See* Lynch v. Donnelly, 465 U.S. 668, 673 (1984).

[9] *Everson*, 330 U.S. at 18.

[10] 268 U.S. 510 (1925).

[11] *Everson*, 330 U.S. at 18.

[12] 268 U.S. 510 (1925).

Justice Rutledge's dissent argued that parochial school parents could benefit from their education tax expenditure simply by sending their children to public schools. Thus, by choosing to send their children to parochial schools, parents were simply choosing not to avail themselves of the generally available benefits provided by their tax dollars. Justice Rutledge also argued that their payment of taxes for public schools was no different than payments by childless couples.

Establishment decisions subsequent to *Everson* more clearly have turned on whether the Court favored protecting freedom of religion by accommodating free exercise or by maintaining a strict wall of separation. In *Illinois ex rel. McCollum v. Board of Education*,[13] the Court invoked the wall metaphor to strike down a program releasing public school students from their secular instruction for a short time to receive optional religious instruction on school premises. Again writing for the majority, Justice Black ruled that the program violated the Establishment Clause because the state's tax-supported public school buildings and compulsory attendance laws were being used to disseminate religious doctrines. Allowing parochial school teachers access to public classrooms involved government aid to a religious function rather than a public function. This program raised the specter of significant entanglement between church and state because religious school instructors would have been subjected to the approval and supervision of the school superintendent. In Justice Black's view, such entanglement could not be reconciled with the separation required by the Establishment Clause.

Justice Reed's dissent took a decidedly accommodationist tone. He observed that the Founders, such as Jefferson and Madison, had approved of the University of Virginia's requirement that students attend worship services. In Justice Reed's view, the Establishment Clause only barred aid to religion that supported some ecclesiastical function, such as aid directly to the church itself. In contrast, education was a public function so that the support of religion in education did not support the church itself. According to Justice Reed, the majority's rigid interpretation of the Establishment Clause was out of step with the nation's long history of permitting incidental benefits to religion.

Just four years later in *Zorach v. Clauson*,[14] a 5-4 majority upheld a released time program similar to the one struck down in *McCollum*. The pivotal difference was that the religious instruction in *Zorach* was not conducted on public school grounds.[15] A centerpiece for the accommodationist approach, Justice Douglas' majority opinion noted that complete separation would disrupt many religious traditions embedded in the fabric of our society. As examples, he noted legislative chaplains, courtroom oaths, giving religious students days off for holy days, and the

---

[13] 333 U.S. 203 (1948).

[14] 343 U.S. 306 (1952).

[15] *Id.* at 312–15. The Court also distinguished the case before it from *McCollum* on the grounds that the *Zorach* release time program did not expend public funds. *Id.* at 308–09. In his concurrence in *McCollum*, however, Justice Jackson had pointed out that any expense in the program at issue in that case was "incalculable and negligible." *McCollum*, 333 U.S. at 234 (Jackson, J., concurring). The dispositive factual distinction between the two cases thus appears to have been the location at which the religious instruction took place. *See* William P. Marshall, *"We Know It When We See It"; The Supreme Court and Establishment*, 59 S. CAL. L. REV. 495, 524–25 n.175 (1986).

prayer " 'God save the United States and this Honorable Court.' "[16] Justice Douglas reasoned that the First Amendment did not prohibit public schools' efforts to "accommodate their schedules to a program of outside religious instruction."[17] Striking down the program would have undermined government neutrality. Such an infringement on "the religious needs of the people" would have constituted "hostility to religion."[18] Justice Douglas distinguished the *McCollum* program because it was conducted inside the school building where the force of the state could be invoked to promote religion. The majority did not consider any coercive effects that the program may have caused by singling out those who did not attend the religion classes as non-religious persons. Peer pressure could spur non-religious children to exercise some form of religion.[19]

In dissent, Justice Jackson focused on the use of state power to compel students to choose between attending secular or religious instruction during school hours. He viewed the off-campus location of the religion classes as too subtle a distinction to be dispositive, particularly in view of the fact that in both *McCollum* and the case before him the state used its compulsory attendance laws to enforce such a choice.

Adhering to a strict wall of separation paradigm, Justice Black in dissent also saw no difference between the programs in *McCollum* and *Zorach*. For Justice Black, the only release time program that could be constitutionally upheld would be one that involved religious instruction entirely apart from normal school hours. Jurisprudentially, he characterized the majority's approach as a balancing analysis where the focus was on whether the state has entered too far into the area of religion. Justice Black instead favored a categorical approach denying the state any entry into the realm of religion.

Almost 40 years later, the Court explained the *McCollum/Zorach* distinction this way: "The difference in symbolic impact helps to explain the difference between the cases. The symbolic connection of church and state in the *McCollum* program presented the students with a graphic symbol of the 'concert or union of dependency' of church and state . . . . This very symbolic union was conspicuously absent in the *Zorach* program."[20]

McCollum and *Zorach* respectively reflect the separation and accommodation approaches. Virtually all of the Establishment Clause decisions of the modern Court represent one or the other of these approaches. Most have favored a separationist approach, but a number of recent decisions have placed greater emphasis on accommodation. Often, both concerns occur in the same opinion.

---

[16] *Zorach*, 343 U.S. at 313.

[17] *Id.* at 315.

[18] *Id.*

[19] *Cf.* Lee v. Weisman, 505 U.S. 577, 593 (1992) (the Court was concerned that a school district's supervision and control of a middle school graduation ceremony would place "subtle and indirect public and peer pressure" on students to stand during a prayer).

[20] School Dist. v. Ball, 473 U.S. 373, 391 (1985) (quoting *Zorach*, 343 U.S. at 312). One constitutional scholar argues that the program in *Zorach* was actually more suspect in terms of its symbolic impact because greater benefits accrued to the religious institutions in question in that they did not incur the expense of transporting their teachers to public schools and could instruct students in the more religiously "inculcating" atmosphere of their own buildings. Marshall, *supra* note 15, at 525.

§ 17.02   THE ESTABLISHMENT CLAUSE AND AID TO RELIGIOUS INSTITUTIONS

[1]   Tension Between Burdening Free Exercise and Promoting Establishment

Many of the Court's attempts to reconcile the values embodied in free exercise and establishment have been in circumstances where the government has provided some form of aid to religious institutions. Often, such cases require the Court to choose, in some measure, between burdening free exercise or promoting establishment. *Walz v. Tax Commission*[21] is a classic example of such a conundrum.

At issue in *Walz* was the constitutionality of a New York property tax exemption for charitable organizations, including religious organizations. If the Court upheld the exemption, religion would have been benefitted; if the Court struck down the exemption, the exercise of religion would have been burdened by taxation. Moreover, either course would have necessitated some involvement in religious affairs, whether to determine a particular institution's eligibility for tax exemption or to determine its tax liability. Chief Justice Burger reflected at length about the competing values in the religion clauses:

> The Court has struggled to find a neutral course between the two Religion Clauses, both of which are cast in absolute terms, and either of which, if expanded to a logical extreme, would tend to clash with the other . . . . The general principle deducible from the First Amendment and all that has been said by the Court is this: that we will not tolerate either governmentally established religion or governmental interference with religion.

> Short of those expressly prescribed governmental acts there is room for play in the joints productive of a benevolent neutrality which will permit religious exercise to exist without sponsorship and without interference . . . . Adherence to the policy of neutrality that derives from an accommodation of the Establishment and Free Exercise Clauses has prevented the kind of involvement that would tip the balance toward government control of churches or governmental restraint on religious practice . . . . No perfect or absolute separation is really possible; the very existence of the Religion Clauses is an involvement of sorts — one that seeks to mark boundaries to avoid excessive entanglement.[22]

Against the background of these general observations, Chief Justice Burger turned to the "purpose" and "effect" test set out by the Court seven years earlier in *Abington School District v. Schempp*.[23] The Chief Justice found that the general purpose of the legislation was to grant a tax exemption to charitable organizations which the state considered beneficial to the public interest, irrespective of whether

---

[21]   397 U.S. 664 (1970).

[22]   *Id.* at 668–70.

[23]   374 U.S. 203 (1963). *See supra* § 17.03.

the organizations were religious in nature. The purpose of the particular exemption for the religious organizations at issue was neither to advance nor inhibit religion, but to spare the exercise of religion the burden of property taxation imposed on profit-making institutions. The Chief Justice opined that the "limits of permissible state accommodation to religion are by no means co-extensive with the non-interference mandated by the Free Exercise Clause."[24] Reflecting an accommodationist position, this stance afforded the legislature a range of discretion in which the legislature could regulate without violating the dictates of either Clause.

Chief Justice Burger then explored whether the exemption brought about the impermissible effect of an excessive government entanglement with religion. Application of the excessive entanglement standard required choosing between the lesser of two entanglements:

[G]ranting tax exemptions to churches necessarily operates to afford an indirect economic benefit and also gives rise to some, but yet a lesser, involvement than taxing them. In analyzing either alternative the questions are whether the involvement is excessive, and whether it is continuing one calling for official and continuing surveillance leading to an impermissible degree of entanglement.[25]

Applying this test of degree, Chief Justice Burger concluded that exemption created less entanglement than taxation and tended to "reinforce the desired separation insulating" church and state from one another.[26]

In the context of complex modern life, the absolute separation decreed in *Everson* was impossible to achieve. Again reflecting an accommodationist position, the Chief Justice said that government must exercise "benevolent neutrality toward churches and religious exercise generally so long as none was favored over others and none suffered interference."[27]

Dissenting, Justice Douglas asserted that the tax exemption amounted to a subsidy which established religion.[28] As to the Chief Justice's "benevolent neutrality," it could not be squared with the First Amendment's demand that the government not only be neutral as between religious sects, but also that it be neutral as between believers and non-believers. Justice Douglas observed that *Everson* prohibited aid to all religions, not just aid to one at the expense of others.

In addition to accommodationist and separationist positions, another important distinction between the opinions of Chief Justice Burger and Justice Douglas appears to have been their differing characterizations of the effects of the statute. The Chief Justice took it at face value as an exemption. Although he did not expressly rely on free exercise grounds, his opinion contained many references to unburdening religion. In contrast, Justice Douglas viewed the statute as authorizing a subsidy. From that perspective, free exercise concerns were not implicated,

---

[24] *Walz*, 397 U.S. at 673.

[25] *Id.* at 674–75.

[26] *Id.* at 676.

[27] *Id.* at 676–77.

[28] *Id.* at 693 (Douglas, J., dissenting).

and the benefit derived was more clearly in violation of the mandated separation and neutrality. The importance of how a benefit is characterized is a recurring theme in religion clause decisions. Its importance would become clear the next year in *Lemon v. Kurtzman*,[29] a case involving government aid to religious schools, where Chief Justice Burger would apply essentially the same standards with opposite results.

[2]   Aid to Religious Schools

Cases involving government aid to religious schools have proved particularly fractious for the Court. The outcome in particular cases has often depended upon whether a majority of the Court leans toward the separation or accommodation paradigm. *Lemon v. Kurtzman*[30] involved establishment challenges to Rhode Island and Pennsylvania statutes. Both statutes provided for subsidizing teachers' salaries in non-public schools. Chief Justice Burger advanced a textual argument in striking down the subsidies. For the Chief Justice, the word "respecting" in the Establishment Clause evidenced the Framers' intent to prohibit not only laws that actually established a religion, but also laws that moved toward such establishment.

To determine which laws fell within the proscribed category, Chief Justice Burger articulated the test that would dominate establishment jurisprudence and consolidate the preeminence of the separationist approach until the early 1990s. The Chief Justice "gleaned" the test from "the cumulative criteria developed by the Court over many years."[31] In *Walz*, Chief Justice Burger had considered excessive entanglement as one type of effect forbidden under the *Schempp* purpose/effect test. In *Lemon*, the Chief Justice set out the excessive entanglement standard as a separate inquiry added to the two-part *Schempp* test: "First, the statute must have a secular legislative purpose; second, its principal or primary effect must be one that neither advances nor inhibits religion; finally, the statute must not foster an excessive government entanglement with religion."[32]

In applying the test, the Chief Justice indicated that the statutes' permissible legislative purposes were to promote quality secular education in all schools subject to compulsory attendance laws. Turning to the primary effect prong, the state legislators had recognized that church-related schools were governed by a religious mission. This recognition was evidenced by legislative efforts designed to insure that state support furthered only secular purposes without furthering the religious mission. For example, the Rhode Island statute limited aid to the subjects of mathematics, languages, physical science, and physical education. These courses posed less danger for the inculcation of religious values than might arise in courses such as history or literature. Moreover, the Rhode Island statute required that the state subsidy to non-public school teachers not increase their salary to the point where it would be greater than the salary of public school teachers. Without this limitation, the subsidy would have provided an economic incentive for the best

---

[29] 403 U.S. 602 (1971).

[30] *Id.*

[31] *Id.* at 612.

[32] *Id.* at 622.

teachers to go to non-public schools, thereby arguably establishing religion. The Chief Justice did not decide whether these limitations were sufficient to save the statutes under the effect prong, but relied instead on the excessive entanglement prong to strike down the statutes.

In doing so, he examined the character and purposes of the religious institutions, the nature of the aid provided by the state, and the resulting relationship between the government and the institutions. First, the Chief Justice summarized the integral role that parochial schools play in the church's mission of inculcating religious faith. Teachers, in particular, play an important part in providing a religious atmosphere. Next, he observed that earlier decisions had ruled that state aid in the form of bus transportation, such as that in *Everson*, as well as funding for school lunches, public health services, and even secular textbooks did not offend the Establishment Clause. The secular content of textbooks, for example, could be ascertained in advance. Conversely, the content of the teachers' speech could not be determined in advance. He did not, however, predicate his opinion on a finding of bad faith that teachers would insidiously inject religion into the classroom. Rather, the Chief Justice assumed that religious content in the classroom would be inevitable. He concluded that the State would need to conduct a "comprehensive, discriminating, and continuing surveillance" of teachers in order to ensure a wholly secular curriculum.[33] Such "prophylactic contacts will involve excessive and enduring entanglement between state and church."[34]

Chief Justice Burger's addition of the entanglement inquiry to the *Schempp* purpose/effect test arguably placed legislators in a difficult position. If they were insensitive to establishment concerns, they violated the primary effect test. However, if legislators were sensitive to these same concerns and scrutinized programs accordingly, that scrutiny could generate an entanglement issue.

The Chief Justice also discussed entanglement of a different character: the potential for political divisiveness in religious issues. The Rhode Island and Pennsylvania programs would require continuing annual appropriations in amounts that would have to keep pace with increases in costs and population. Chief Justice Burger predicted that under such circumstances, candidates and voters might tend to align according to their faith, creating "political divisions along religious lines [which] was one of the principal evils" the Establishment Clause was meant to prohibit.[35]

Comparing Chief Justice Burger's *Lemon* opinion to his opinion in *Walz*, it becomes apparent that the accommodative tone of the *Walz* opinion was absent in *Lemon*. One might differentiate the cases on the ground that *Walz* involved exemptions and *Lemon* involved more of a subsidy.

An additional distinction between the two cases may be that the Court was less apt to accommodate state involvement in religious affairs when impressionable

---

[33] 403 U.S. at 619.

[34] *Lemon*, 403 U.S. at 619.

[35] *Id.* at 622.

young minds were involved. Whether or not such a concern was at work in *Lemon* was not immediately discernible from the opinion.[36] It would more clearly become a critical factor in later cases.[37]

In *Committee for Public Education & Religious Liberty (P.E.A.R.L.) v. Nyquist*,[38] the Court applied the *Lemon* test to a program involving three forms of aid: a provision of funds for maintaining and repairing facilities; a provision reimbursing low-income parents directly for tuition costs; and a provision for tax relief for those parents not qualifying for the tuition reimbursement. Applying the first prong of the *Lemon* test, Justice Powell refused to make "metaphysical judgments"[39] between the religious and secular objectives of the New York program. The legislative purposes behind the various parts of the program included the State's responsibility to provide for the health, welfare, and safety of children in non-public and public systems. The legislature also passed the law out of equity and economic self-interest, in that the State realized a benefit from the existence of the non-public institutions. Despite the careful drafting of the New York law, the Court maintained that legislative objectives were difficult to prove. The Court was unwilling to accuse legislators of bad faith; nor would it make value judgments as to the legitimacy of their objectives.

Instead, the Court applied the primary effect prong of *Lemon* to strike down the programs. Justice Powell modified the primary effect test in stating that in order for a program to be constitutional, any promotion of religion must be only remote and incidental. While later decisions required that "the" primary effect advance religion, the *Nyquist* Court stated that a law was unconstitutional if it had "a" primary effect advancing religion.

For Justice Powell, advancing the secular educational role of parochial schools would be a permissible effect. However, the advancement of the religious role would be an impermissible effect. Justice Powell distinguished *Everson* and *Walz* on the basis that the programs in those cases did not involve direct aid to sectarian interests.

Here, Justice Powell found that the funds for maintenance and repair could be used to maintain and repair a chapel or provide heat and light to classrooms where religion was taught. The repair and maintenance of a school chapel involved entanglement problems. The tuition reimbursement, although it went to parents rather than directly to the schools, did not qualify as indirect either, because "the effect of the aid [was] unmistakably to provide desired financial support for non-

---

[36] In his analysis of the character and nature of the religious institutions receiving aid, the Chief Justice merely noted that the "process of inculcating religious doctrine is, of course, enhanced by the impressionable age of the pupils." *Id.* at 616.

[37] *See, e.g.*, Lee v. Weisman, 505 U.S. 577 (1992). In an opinion striking down the practice of offering state-sponsored prayers at public school graduation ceremonies, Justice Kennedy observed that "there are heightened concerns with protecting freedom of conscience from subtle coercive pressure in the elementary and secondary public schools." *Id.* at 593.

[38] 413 U.S. 756 (1973).

[39] *Id.* at 783.

public, sectarian institutions."[40]

With respect to the tax relief provisions, Justice Powell opined that it was difficult to characterize the state's actions in this part of the program. The district court found the tax relief to be in the form of a credit, but to the extent that the subtraction was made from adjusted gross income before taxes were paid, it more closely resembled a deduction. The Court left the characterization question open in *Nyquist*, but this distinction eventually became a critical one in the later case of *Mueller v. Allen*.[41] Despite its unclear classification, the *Nyquist* Court concluded that the tax relief was basically a subsidy and was unconstitutional under the primary effect test. Justice Powell observed that unlike the property tax exemption in *Walz*, the tax relief at issue in this case lacked historical precedent.

Finally, Justice Powell was concerned about political pressure that might be applied to enlarge sectarian programs. While such divisiveness alone was not sufficient to invalidate a program, it was "a 'warning signal' not to be ignored."[42]

In dissent, Justice Rehnquist, joined by Chief Justice Burger and Justice White, found that any distinctions between *Walz* and the New York programs actually favored upholding the programs. In *Walz*, the benefit was a complete forgiveness of taxes that had been made directly available to churches themselves; in *Nyquist*, the benefit was a reduction in taxes available directly to the parents of school children. The benefit only indirectly helped parochial schools. For Justice Rehnquist, the programs were consistent with government neutrality toward religion. Justice Rehnquist rejected the majority's characterization of the programs as an "incentive to parents to send their children to sectarian schools."[43] Instead, he characterized the programs as neutral in helping to redress the extra burden of parents of parochial school children who paid for public services not used by them.

Following *Nyquist*, a number of cases in this area involved various kinds of material aid to religious schools. The Court has construed the Establishment Clause to prohibit much of this aid. In *Levitt v. P.E.A.R.L.*,[44] (handed down the same day as *P.E.A.R.L. v. Nyquist*) the Court invalidated a New York law that reimbursed non-public schools for the cost of administering state-mandated tests. Some of the examinations were state-prepared; others were traditional teacher-prepared tests. Because latter tests involved the discretion of teachers supervised by religious institutions, they presented "the substantial risk that these examinations . . . will be drafted with an eye, unconsciously or otherwise, to inculcate students in the religious precepts of the sponsoring church."[45] The statute failed to provide any means to assure that these internally prepared tests were free of religious instruction. Moreover, the lump-sum, per-pupil payments did not represent actual costs of performing reimbursable secular services but covered

---

[40] *Id.* at 783.

[41] 463 U.S. 388 (1983).

[42] *Nyquist*, 413 U.S. at 798.

[43] *Id.* at 808 (Rehnquist, J., dissenting).

[44] 413 U.S. 472 (1973).

[45] *Id.* at 480.

all testing services, some of which were potentially religious. The overall effect of the statute, concluded the Court, would to be advance religious education.

In *Meek v. Pittenger,*[46] the Court invalidated all but the textbook loan provisions of two Pennsylvania statutes providing auxiliary services, instructional material, and equipment to non-public elementary and secondary schools. The scheme supplied extensive educational aid in the form of auxiliary services such as counseling, psychological services, speech and hearing therapy, testing, and related services for exceptional or educationally disadvantaged students, and educational equipment such as maps, charts, films, records, periodicals, projectors, recorders, and laboratory paraphernalia. Of the non-public schools eligible for the assistance, 75 percent were church-affiliated. Writing for the Court, Justice Stewart found that it would be unrealistic to attempt to separate the secular educational functions and the religious functions of church-related schools. "Even though earmarked for secular purposes, 'when it flows to an institution in which religion is so pervasive that a substantial portion of its functions are subsumed in the religious mission,' state aid has the impermissible primary effect of advancing religion."[47] Moreover, the extent of state supervision necessary "to ensure that a strictly nonideological posture is maintained"[48] in the delivery of such services would constitute an excessive entanglement of church and state.

The Ohio statute at issue in *Wolman v. Walter*[49] responded to the Court's decision in *Meek v. Pittenger.* A deeply divided Court sustained the provisions authorizing funding for textbooks, testing and scoring, diagnostic services, and therapeutic and remedial services. Other portions providing instructional materials and equipment and field trip services were found unconstitutional. The textbook provision was upheld on the precedential strength of *Board of Education v. Allen.*[50] Because the State supplied the tests, conducted the scoring, and gave no direct financial aid for testing, both the risk that the tests would be used as part of religious teaching and the need for State supervision triggering excessive entanglement were eliminated.

The therapeutic and remedial services provisions also passed the purpose and entanglement tests. They would be administered by public employees and conducted only on sites not identified with sectarian schools. The Court found that the limited contact of a diagnostician with a child, unlike the teacher-student relationship, provided no opportunity for inculcating sectarian views. In contrast, the Court struck down the provisions of the Act that provided for the lending of instructional materials and equipment, and the funding of field trips. Because it was impossible to separate the secular educational function from the sectarian, such funding constituted impermissible direct aid to sectarian education. Moreover, it would necessitate excessive entanglement to ensure the purely secular use of the

---

[46] 421 U.S. 349 (1975).

[47] *Id.* at 365.

[48] *Id.* at 369.

[49] 433 U.S. 229 (1977).

[50] 392 U.S. 236 (1968).

funds. *Meek* and *Wolman* have been substantially overruled by *Mitchell v. Helms.*[51]

P.E.A.R.L. v. Regan[52] upheld a New York statute that attempted to cure the constitutional deficiencies of the testing reimbursement statute invalidated in *Levitt*. The new scheme provided reimbursement to non-public schools for the actual costs of administering mandatory state-prepared examinations and keeping certain required records. The new statute did not reimburse the costs of teacher-prepared tests, a provision held invalid in *Levitt*. Moreover, the new statute, unlike the earlier version, provided for audits of school records to ensure that only actual costs incurred in providing the secular services were reimbursed. Despite differences between the New York statute and the testing provisions approved in *Wolman*, the Court found that decision controlling.[53] Non-public schools lacked control over the content of the test and over the sectarian personnel used to grade it. This negated the risk that the test would impart religious views. The Court concluded that the mere fact of direct cash reimbursement did not change either the primary purpose or effect of the funding. Moreover, the audit procedures assured reimbursement only for permissible secular functions in a straightforward and routine method that did not raise the problem of excessive entanglement.

Justice Blackmun dissented, joined by Justices Brennan and Marshall. Justice Blackmun argued that the direct financial assistance had the impermissible effect of advancing religion. In a separate dissent, Justice Stevens deplored the "largely ad hoc decisions" that attempted to distinguish between impermissible and constitutionally valid aid to non-public schools. He urged the reinstitution of the stringent wall of separation between church and state.

In *Mueller v. Allen*,[54] the Court applied the *Lemon* test to uphold a state statute allowing a tax deduction for educational expenses. Justice Powell, who wrote the *Nyquist* opinion, joined the *Mueller* majority. Writing for the Court, Justice Rehnquist stated that few laws would be struck down for failure to pass the secular purpose prong of the *Lemon* test. Consistent with earlier decisions, the Court was reluctant to attribute unconstitutional motives to state legislatures. It is difficult to determine how the Court discerned the legislative objectives of the statute at issue in *Mueller* as they were neither expressed nor implied in its text or legislative history. The Court characterized the objectives as advancing an educated populace, alleviating the fiscal strain of schooling, furthering competition between public and non-public systems, and facilitating the highest quality education for its children. The Court apparently divined these purposes, stating that they were constitutionally permissible secular purposes that the legislature could have had.

The Court focused much of its analysis on the primary effect prong of the *Lemon* test. The Minnesota statute met this part of the test first because the

---

[51] 530 U.S. 793 (2000).

[52] 444 U.S. 646 (1980).

[53] Even though the New York law, unlike the Ohio statute, provided for grading by the sectarian school personnel with state reimbursement for the administration and grading costs, the Court concluded that these differences were "not of constitutional dimension." *Id.* at 654.

[54] 463 U.S. 388 (1983).

deduction was only one among many deductions in the tax code, including medical expenses and charitable contributions. Recognizing the legislature's knowledge of local conditions and of tax burdens, the Court deferred to the legislature in this area. Second, the statute allowed deductions to all parents and benefitted all children, not just those whose children attended non-public schools. The nondiscriminatory language of the statute satisfied the primary effect test. In his dissent, Justice Marshall controverted this point: although in theory the deduction was available to all parents, in practice approximately 96 percent of parents eligible for the deduction sent their children to parochial schools. Most parents who sent their children to public schools could avail themselves of the full $700 deduction only if they purchased at least $700 in pencils, notebooks, and bus rides. Justice Marshall found that the effect of the statute was no different than that struck down in *Nyquist,* i.e., the advancement of religion. In response, Justice Rehnquist refused to predicate constitutional findings on statistical evidence. For him, a facially neutral statute passed the primary effect test.

As a third reason for upholding the statute under the primary effect test, the Court stated that the benefits were channeled directly to parents rather than to schools. The Court cited *Widmar v. Vincent,*[55] stating that this type of system removed any state imprimatur on a particular religion or religion generally, thus mitigating any entanglement problems. The finding of direct aid to parents seemed to be critical to the Court's decision. Interestingly, the Court did not distinguish *Nyquist,* in which the Court had invalidated aid channeled directly to parents. Justice Rehnquist stated that *Nyquist* represented an exception to the rule and classified the *Mueller* decision in the mainstream.

The Court also noted that the program was intended in part to buttress the fiscal integrity of parochial schools. Serious difficulties might have arisen if parochial schools closed, because they had become an integral part of the state's education system. Writing for four dissenters, Justice Marshall found the true tax deduction at issue in this case indistinguishable from the hybrid deduction/credit struck down in *Nyquist.* Both programs afforded parents financial incentives to send their children to sectarian schools.

Two cases decided shortly after *Mueller* demonstrate the importance of the *Mueller* distinction that the aid be distributed to parents rather than to sectarian institutions. In *Grand Rapids School District v. Ball,*[56] the Court struck down separate "Shared Time" and "Community Education" schemes which respectively took place during and after school hours on parochial school premises.

The Shared Time program entailed public school teachers offering various "remedial" and "enrichment" classes to non-public school students on the premises of non-public schools during the regular school day. Forty of the forty-one schools involved were sectarian, and the record did not indicate that any public school students attended any of these programs. In addition to teachers, the State provided supplies and materials necessary for instruction.

---

[55] 454 U.S. 263 (1981).

[56] 473 U.S. 373 (1985).

The Community Education program offered pupils at non-public schools a variety of academic and non-academic courses. In contrast to the Shared Time program, the Community Education program entailed courses taught at the end of the regular school day. Generally, these Community Education courses were taught by private school teachers employed part-time by the school district for the purposes of the program.

For both the Shared Time and Community Education programs, the State leased classrooms for $6 per classroom per week. During Shared Time instruction, a sign was posted denominating the particular room a "public school classroom." The State inspected such classrooms to ensure that they were free of religious symbols; it also adjusted the teaching schedule to accommodate religious holidays.

The Court held that both programs violated the *Lemon* primary effect test in three ways. First, relying on *Meek v. Pittenger*, the majority feared that public school teachers teaching in such pervasively sectarian environments could subtly or overtly convey religious messages. Second, having public school teachers teach at religious schools presented a dangerous symbolic union between church and state which involved concerns similar to those voiced in *McCollum v. Board of Education*.[57] Third, the programs subsidized the sectarian education by providing some of the school's secular education.

Dissenting, Justice O'Connor and Chief Justice Burger would have upheld the Shared Time Program but not the Community Education Program. In separate dissenting opinions, Justices White and Rehnquist would have upheld both programs. Justice Rehnquist noted that the record failed to demonstrate even one instance of inculcating religion.

Aguilar v. Felton[58] was decided the same day as *Grand Rapids* and involved a shared time program similar to the one invalidated in *Grand Rapids*. In another 5-4 decision, the Court also struck down this scheme. Specifically, New York City used federal funds to pay public school teachers and other personnel who provided "remedial reading, reading skills, remedial mathematics, English as a second language, and guidance services" to educationally-deprived children. The teachers and other personnel instructed students enrolled in both public and parochial schools. With respect to parochial school students, teachers from the public schools presented classes on the premises of the parochial schools. City officials told the teachers involved to avoid religious matters and to minimize contact with parochial school officials. Moreover, classrooms used for the lessons were to be cleared of religious symbols. To monitor compliance with these directives, City officials periodically made unannounced visits to the schools during periods of instruction.

The close supervision of the program prompted the Court to strike down the program on the entanglement part of the *Lemon* test. Concurring, Justice Powell argued that the program also violated the primary effect prong of *Lemon* as it relieved religious schools of their own duty to provide supplemental and remedial education. In dissent, Justice O'Connor criticized the entanglements part of the

---

[57] *See supra* § 17.01.

[58] 473 U.S. 402 (1985).

Lemon test. She argued that the Court exaggerated the amount of supervision necessary to avert religious indoctrination as no evidence of such indoctrination by public school teachers existed. Echoing these objections in his dissent, Chief Justice Burger said that the majority's concerns bordered on paranoia. In his dissent, Justice Rehnquist said that the Court placed the state in a Catch-22 in which no supervision violated the primary effect prong of *Lemon* and supervision violated the entanglement prong. In the case of *Board of Education of Kiryas Joel Village School District v. Grumet*,[59] Justices O'Connor and Kennedy explicitly called for reconsideration of *Aguilar* and *Grand Rapids*.

Recent decisions have cast serious doubt on the continued vitality of the *Lemon* standard in Establishment Clause cases. In *Zobrest v. Catalina Foothills School District*,[60] for example, the Court did not even mention the *Lemon* test.[61] Invoking the Individuals with Disabilities Education Act (IDEA), a deaf pupil requested that a public school district provide him with an interpreter at his sectarian school. The school district refused, arguing that the Establishment Clause barred Zobrest's request. The Court, however, held that the provision of an interpreter did not violate the Establishment Clause.

Writing for the majority, Chief Justice Rehnquist categorized IDEA as a neutral "social welfare program" providing benefits "to a broad class of citizens defined without reference to religion."[62] According to the Chief Justice, the Establishment Clause did not bar such programs merely because religious institutions may receive an incidental benefit. In upholding the program, the Court relied heavily on *Mueller v. Allen* and *Witters v. Washington Department of Services for the Blind*.[63] In *Mueller*, incidental aid to the sectarian schools occurred " 'only as a result of numerous private choices of individual parents of school-age children.' "[64] In *Witters*, the Court upheld the extension of a general state program of vocational assistance to a blind seminary student. Neither of the cases involved direct assistance to religious institutions; nor did the programs in those cases create financial incentives for parents to seek a sectarian education for their children, as both programs provided benefits notwithstanding religion.

Chief Justice Rehnquist found the assistance at issue in *Zobrest* to have been "part of a general government program that distributes benefits neutrally to any child qualifying as 'handicapped' under the IDEA," regardless of the religious or nonreligious nature of the school attended.[65] As in *Witters*, parents had no financial incentives to choose a sectarian school. "When the government offers a neutral

---

[59] 512 U.S. 687 (1994).

[60] 509 U.S. 1 (1993).

[61] *See also* Lee v. Weisman, 505 U.S. 577 (1992). In *Lee*, a school graduation prayer case, the majority did not predicate its decision on the *Lemon* test. Justice Kennedy, writing for the Court, struck down the prayer because of its subtle coercive effects and divisive potential. Justice Scalia, joined in his dissent by Chief Justice Rehnquist and Justices White and Thomas, articulated a test of direct or legal coercion grounded in a historical practice.

[62] *Zobrest*, 509 U.S. at 8.

[63] 474 U.S. 481 (1986).

[64] *Zobrest*, 509 U.S. at 1 (quoting *Mueller*, 463 U.S. at 399).

[65] *Id.* at 10.

service on the premises of a sectarian school as part of a general program that 'is in no way skewed towards religion,' it follows under our prior decisions that provision of that service does not offend the Establishment Clause."[66] In fact, unlike *Mueller* or *Witters*, none of the funds supplied by the state "ever find their way into the sectarian school's coffers." Even indirect economic benefit would only accrue if the sectarian school was making a profit on a handicapped student who would not have attended without a state-supplied interpreter and whose tuition would not have been replaced by that of another student.

The Court rejected the argument that this case was distinguishable from *Mueller* and *Witters* because the interpreter was a public employee. In offering this argument, the school district relied on two cases involving direct governmental aid to sectarian schools. In *Meek v. Pittenger*,[67] the Court invalidated a statute providing "massive aid" to sectarian schools through the direct loan of educational materials and services, including tape recorders, on-site instruction and counseling by public employees. In *Grand Rapids School District v. Ball*,[68] the Court struck down a statute allowing public school employees and instructional materials to be used in sectarian schools. Chief Justice Rehnquist found that the programs in *Meek* and *Ball* differed from the IDEA. Those programs involved direct grants of government assistance that relieved sectarian schools of educational expenses they would otherwise have borne. The IDEA afforded its primary benefits to handicapped students, providing sectarian schools with only incidental benefits to the extent that they benefitted at all. Moreover, the services provided by a sign-language interpreter varied greatly from those supplied by a teacher or counselor. The Court stated that "the Establishment Clause lays down no absolute bar to the placing of a public employee in a sectarian school."[69] The requested interpreter would simply " 'transmit everything that is said in exactly the same way it was intended.' "[70]

Justice Blackmun wrote a dissenting opinion. In the first part of the dissent, which Justices Stevens, O'Connor, and Souter joined, Justice Blackmun maintained that the Court should remand the case to ascertain whether it could have been decided on statutory grounds.[71] Although the argument was not raised below, the United States and several lower courts had maintained that IDEA did not require government to provide interpreters in private schools when the service was available at public schools.[72]

Part II of Justice Blackmun's dissent, joined only by Justice Souter, reached the constitutional issues. Justice Blackmun noted that public employees would be

---

[66] *Id.*

[67] 421 U.S. 349 (1975).

[68] 473 U.S. 373 (1985).

[69] *Zobrest*, 509 U.S. at 13. In *Wolman v. Walter*, 433 U.S. 229 (1977), the Court allowed public employees to provide health services to children on the premises of sectarian schools.

[70] *Zobrest*, 509 U.S. at 13.

[71] Justice O'Connor filed a separate dissent, joined by Justice Stevens, also arguing that the statutory and regulatory questions could have determined the result and thus should have been resolved first.

[72] Moreover, at least one lower court had construed the federal regulation to prohibit providing interpreters in sectarian schools.

interpreting religious instruction, Catholic Mass, and communication of secular subjects from a religious perspective. Objecting to the majority's characterization of the IDEA as a "general welfare program," Justice Blackmun noted that *Meek* and *Ball* struck down general welfare programs providing remedial aid to public and private school students.[73] Moreover, *Board of Education v. Allen*[74] invalidated the provision of tape recorders and slide projectors to sectarian schools. Like sign-language interpreters, such provisions could impermissibly supply "the medium" for transmission of a religious message. Justice Blackmun distinguished *Mueller* and *Witters*, saying that government involvement with sectarian schools in those cases only entailed tax relief or monetary payment. He also cautioned that requiring public employees to perform services in sectarian schools could restrict their individual liberty by requiring them to obey religious rules. For example, Hindu schools often required staff to dress modestly.

Zobrest was also notable for the absence of the *Lemon* test. In *Board of Education of Kiryas Joel Village School District v. Grumet*,[75] the Court further distanced itself from *Lemon*. In the concurring opinion, Justice O'Connor noted that the *Zobrest* majority and other recent cases did not focus on *Lemon*. Instead, the Court has fashioned a number of tests, each covering a narrow, more homogeneous group of issues. One broader test that has gained considerable influence on the Court is Justice O'Connor's endorsement test that is discussed in § 17.03.

In *Agostini v. Felton*,[76] the Court overruled *Aguilar v. Felton* and parts of *Grand Rapids School District v. Ball*. *Aguilar* had construed the Establishment Clause to bar New York City from sending public school teachers into parochial school classrooms to offer federally mandated remedial education. On remand, the District Court entered a permanent injunction. *Agostini* held that *Aguilar* was no longer consistent with the Court's understanding of the Establishment Clause and that the petitioners deserved relief from the injunction under Federal Rule of Civil Procedure 60(b)(5).

In the 1960s, Congress sought to target funding to local education agencies (LEAs). The Board of Education of the City of New York received federal funds to provide remedial and support services to at-risk students. Ten percent of the eligible students attended private schools, which were overwhelmingly sectarian. The Board's attempt to bus private school students into public schools for after-school classes failed. After sending public school teachers into private schools after hours also achieved " 'mixed results,' " the Board instituted the program in *Aguilar* where the Board sent public school teachers to private schools during school hours.[77]

In training sessions, the City reminded teachers that: (i) they were public school employees, accountable only to public school supervisors; (ii) they could only select

---

[73] *Zobrest*, 509 U.S. at 20 (Blackmun, J., dissenting).

[74] 392 U.S. 236 (1968).

[75] 512 U.S. 687 (1994). This case is discussed in § 17.04.

[76] 521 U.S. 203 (1997).

[77] *Agostini*, 521 U.S. at 210–11.

and teach students from a population eligible for the program; (iii) materials and equipment used were only to be used for the program; (iv) they could not engage in cooperative instruction with private school teachers; (v) they were not to involve themselves in any way with religious instruction in the school. Moreover, religious symbols were removed from the classrooms used; the teachers could only consult with private school teachers to assess student needs; and a publicly employed supervisor would make at least one unannounced visit to each classroom every month to make sure that no religious instruction occurred in the program.

Writing for the Court, Justice O'Connor first abandoned the presumption that the mere presence of a public employee in a parochial setting has the "impermissible effect of state-sponsored indoctrination or constitutes a symbolic union between government and religion."[78] The Court had moved away from this presumption in *Zobrest v. Catalina Foothills School District*, which upheld a publicly-employed sign language interpreter assisting a student in a private school. In *Witters v. Washington Department of Services for the Blind*, which allowed a blind person to use a federal tuition grant for religious ministry training, the Court moved away from the principle in *Ball* that all government funds that directly benefit a religious institution's education programs were invalid.

No evidence in *Agostini* indicated that any public school teacher had ever tried to broach the topic of religion. Absent such evidence, it was unreasonable to assume a " 'symbolic union' between church and state" because of the presence of public school teachers in parochial school.[79]

The Court rejected the dissent's concern that the funding relieved sectarian schools of services that they would otherwise have had to provide. No evidence existed that the program supplanted the services otherwise provided by the parochial schools. Instead, it provided supplementary assistance for children in need. The Court refused to consider the program a government subsidy to religion based on the number of sectarian students it helped. The program did not have the impermissible effect of promoting religion. Instead, it allotted funds on criteria that neither favored nor disfavored religion and were available to all eligible children.

The Court also rejected *Aguilar's* conclusion that the program led to excessive entanglement of church and state. The Court considered entanglement as a part of its inquiry into the law's effect. The Court assessed effect by looking at the nature of the government aid and the nature of the organization benefitted. *Aguilar's* conclusion of excessive entanglement rested on the fear that the program would require " 'pervasive monitoring.' "[80] The system of unannounced visits in this case was not excessive.

" 'Administrative cooperation' " with parochial schools or the danger of " 'political divisiveness' " alone did not merit a finding of excessive entanglement.[81]

---

[78] *Id.* at 223.

[79] *Agostini*, 521 U.S. at 227.

[80] *Id.* at 230.

[81] *Id.*

In summary, the Court found that the program "does not run afoul of any of three primary criteria we currently use to evaluate whether government aid has the effect of advancing religion: it does not result in governmental indoctrination; define its recipients by reference to religion; or create an excessive entanglement."[82] Nor did the program endorse religion in any way.

Justice Souter dissented, joined by Justices Stevens and Ginsburg. Justice Souter argued that the program relieved private schools of the responsibilities of teaching remedial skills, thus subsidizing the private schools by allowing them to concentrate their funds on other subjects, including sectarian instruction. Off-site programs did not relieve the schools of their responsibilities nearly as much as on-campus instruction. Justice Souter disputed the Court's reading of *Zobrest*, arguing that the signer was more of an instrumentality than an instructor. He further distinguished *Zobrest* and *Witters* as cases in which aid went to isolated students who chose to put the aid to use in a religious environment.

Justice Ginsburg also dissented, joined by Justices Stevens, Souter, and Breyer. Justice Ginsburg argued that Federal Rule of Civil Procedure 60(b)(5) had been misapplied in the case. She first noted that the case could not have been reheard under the Supreme Court's rules. Moreover, the District Court was correct in holding that *Aguilar* had not been overruled, and the Court should only review that determination.

In *Mitchell v. Helms*,[83] the Court upheld a longstanding school aid program which lent " 'library services and materials' " including " 'assessments, reference materials, computer software and hardware for instructional use, and other curricular materials.' "[84] Under the federal statute, materials had to be " 'secular, neutral, and nonideological.' "

Writing for a plurality of four, Justice Thomas applied the test in *Agostini v. Felton*.[85] First, plaintiffs did not challenge that the law at issue had a secular purpose. Second, in applying the *Agostini* effects test, plaintiffs failed to challenge the holding below that the program did not involve excessive entanglement. Accordingly, Justice Thomas narrowed his analysis to the other two parts of the *Agostini* effects test.

First, the plurality found no religious indoctrination occurred in religious schools that could be attributed to government action. To avoid government indoctrination, the Court has consistently relied on the doctrine of neutrality, which upholds broad-based government aid provided without regard to religion. One way of ensuring neutrality is that government aid reaches religious institutions only through the private, independent choices of individuals.

The third criterion in the *Agostini* secular effects test evaluates whether an aid program defines its recipients with reference to religion. Importantly, aid cannot create incentives to choose a religious school. While private choice is clearer when

---

[82] *Id.* at 234–35.

[83] 530 U.S. 793 (2000).

[84] *Id.* at 802.

[85] 521 U.S. 203 (1997).

aid goes directly to an individual who applies it to religious schools, the Establishment Clause does not require this approach.

The plurality accepted plaintiffs' contention that aid cannot be religious in nature but rejected their " 'no divertibility' rule."[86] If a religious school received aid that was non-religious in content and that could be used in a public school, the aid could also be applied to any use in a private school.

The plurality criticized the dissent's position that courts should consider any aid to "pervasively sectarian" schools, particularly primary and secondary schools, constitutionally suspect. This analysis, while once embraced by the Court, was hostile to those who take religion seriously.

Applying these two *Agostini* factors to this case, the federal law did not define aid recipients by reference to religion. Aid was allocated on a per capita basis, by the number of students enrolled in the school, with some additional funds for the poor. Aid did not result in government indoctrination as it was made available to public and private schools regardless of religious affiliation. The aid followed a private decision to attend a particular school. The aid did not result in religious indoctrination because it could not have religious content. While the program improperly loaned 191 books over three years, these "scattered *de minimis*"[87] violations were remedied prior to litigation.[88] The plurality overruled *Meek v. Pittenger* and *Wolman v. Walter* to the extent that they conflict with this decision.

Justice O'Connor concurred in the judgment joined by Justice Breyer. She joined the plurality in holding that *Meek* and *Wolman* were overruled to the extent that they are inconsistent with the Court's judgment. Justice O'Connor thought that the plurality announced an exceptionally broad rule allowing aid to religious institutions so long as it flowed on a neutral basis and was secular in nature. She also criticized the plurality's permitting direct aid and actual diversion of aid to promote a non-secular mission. While she thought neutrality important, it could not be the sole criterion. She also emphasized the importance of private choice arguing that an emphasis on per capita aid could result in direct monetary payments to religious organizations.

Justice O'Connor said that the Court still focuses on the impermissible purpose and effect of advancing religion even though the way the Court evaluates these matters has changed to emphasize the following three points: "(1) whether the aid resulted in governmental indoctrination, (2) whether the aid program defines its recipients by reference to religion, and (3) whether the aid creates an excessive entanglement between the government and religion."[89]

With regard to government indoctrination, the program did not define persons by religion as it embraced private, including religious, and public school students. Funds could only supplement and not supplant non-government funds available to religious schools. Further, no funds went directly to religious schools but materials

---

[86] 530 U.S. at 820.

[87] *Id.* at 835.

[88] *Id.*

[89] *Id.* at 845 (O'Connor, J., concurring).

were merely lent to the schools. Moreover, all equipment had to be used for secular purposes.

Justice O'Connor disagreed with previous cases that distinguished between lending texts and lending materials noting that either could be diverted for religious purposes. She would not presume that any such aid would be diverted but instead required evidence of actual diversion. Here federal, state, and local laws required that materials not be used for religious purposes. Further, state and local government monitored that the materials were not used for religious purposes. While one second grade class and another theology class may have diverted materials, this was "*de minimis*," as was buying 191 books over a three year period.

Justice Souter dissented, joined by Justices Stevens and Ginsburg. Justice Souter criticized the majority's emphasis on the law's neutrality. Under *Everson v. Board of Education of Ewing*, government cannot give aid to any institution for support of its religious mission. If the Court solely uses neutrality, much government aid will flow to religious institutions.

Three areas of analysis complement neutrality. First, aid to schools that are "pervasively religious," particularly primary and secondary religious schools, must be given heightened constitutional scrutiny. Second, the Court must look to the directness or indirectness with which aid is distributed, or if it is given by independent choices. Third, there are different characteristics of aid: "its religious content; its cash form; its divertibility or actual diversion to religious support; its supplantation of traditional items of religious expense; and its substantiality."[90]

The dissent criticized the Court for admitting there was actual diversion of the aid in this case, but effectively stating that the diversion did not matter.

In *Zelman v. Simmons-Harris*,[91] the Court upheld a voucher program which included religious schools against an Establishment Clause challenge. The Cleveland public schools faced an educational " 'crisis' " as "[o]nly 1 in 10 ninth graders could pass a basic proficiency examination"; "students at all levels performed at a dismal rate compared with students in other Ohio public schools"; and "[m]ore than two-thirds of high school students either dropped or failed out before graduation." In response, Ohio enacted the Pilot Project Scholarship program. The program "provides financial assistance to families in any Ohio school district that is or has been 'under federal court order requiring supervision and operational management of the district by the state superintendent.' " Only the Cleveland School District fell into this category. "Families with incomes below 200% of the poverty line are given priority and are eligible to receive 90% of private school tuition up to $2,250. For these lowest-income families, participating private schools may not charge a parental co-payment greater than $250. For all other families, the program pays 75% of tuition costs, up to $1,875, with no co-payment cap." Second, the program provided tutorial aid. "Students from low-income families receive 90% of the amount charged for such assistance up to $360. All

---

[90] *Id.* at 885 (Souter, J., dissenting).

[91] 536 U.S. 639 (2002).

other students receive 75% of that amount."

The Pilot Project Scholarship Program was "part of a broader undertaking by the State to enhance the educational options of Cleveland's schoolchildren . . . . That undertaking included programs governing community and magnet schools." Community schools enjoyed "academic independence," and received $4,518 in state funding. Magnet schools generally "emphasize a particular subject area, teaching method, or service to students," and received $7,746, including $4,167 of state funding.

Writing for the majority, Chief Justice Rehnquist noted that the Court's decisions consistently have distinguished between government programs that directly funded religious schools, with programs in which government funds only reached the schools through "the genuine and independent choices of private individuals." The Court stated, "[w]here a government aid program is neutral with respect to religion, and provides assistance directly to a broad class of citizens who, in turn, direct government aid to religious schools wholly as a result of their own genuine and independent private choice, the program is not readily subject to challenge under the Establishment Clause." The Ohio program is neutral toward religion. "It is part of a general and multifaceted undertaking" to help the children of a failed school district, conferring its benefits "to a broad class of individuals defined without reference to religion." All schools in the district may participate as may public schools in adjoining districts.

Moreover, the program at issue "creates financial *dis*incentives for religious schools, with private schools receiving only half the government assistance given to community schools and one-third the assistance given to magnet schools." Adjacent public schools receive two to three times the state funding of a private religious school. Moreover, families enrolling in private religious or nonreligious schools must copay tuition, whereas those choosing community, magnet, or traditional public schools pay nothing. "Although such features of the program are not necessary to its constitutionality, they clearly dispel the claim that the program 'creates . . . financial incentives for parents to choose a sectarian school.' "

Nor does the scholarship program endorse religious practices and beliefs. Specifically, "no reasonable observer would think a neutral program of private choice, where state aid reaches religious schools solely as a result of the numerous independent decisions of private individuals, carries with it the *imprimatur* of government endorsement." Instead, such an observer would regard the program as "a broader undertaking to assist poor children in failed schools, not as an endorsement of religious schooling in general."

Nor did Chief Justice Rehnquist attach constitutional significance to "the fact that 96% of the scholarship recipients have enrolled in religious schools." In *Mueller v. Allen,* the Court "found irrelevant that 96% of parents taking deductions for tuition expenses paid tuition at religious schools." Moreover, the 96% figure does not consider enrollments in community schools, magnet schools, or traditional public schools with tutorial assistance. Including some or all of these children "drops the percentage enrolled in religious schools from 96% to under 20%." Moreover, 96% represents only one school year. "In the 1997-1998 school year, by contrast only 78% of scholarship recipients attended religious schools."

Finally, the Court distinguished *P.E.A.R.L. v. Nyquist*, in which the program's " 'function' was '*unmistakably* to provide desired financial support for nonpublic, sectarian institutions' " as spurred by the " 'increasingly grave fiscal problems' " faced by religious schools. *Nyquist* simply "does not govern neutral educational assistance programs that, like the program here, offer aid directly to a broad class of individual recipients defined without regard to religion."

Justice O'Connor concurred. Justice Thomas' concurrence emphasized the disparate educational opportunities for urban children. Despite *Brown v. Board of Education*, urban children, including those in Cleveland, "have been forced into a system that continually fails them." For example "[o]f Cleveland eighth graders taking the 1999 Ohio proficiency test, 95 percent in Catholic schools passed the reading test, whereas only 57 percent in public schools passed. And 75 percent of Catholic school students passed the math proficiency test, compared to only 22 percent of public school students." Nevertheless, the relative success of religious and private schools does not control the result "because the State has a constitutional right to experiment with a variety of different programs to promote educational opportunity."

Dissenting, Justice Stevens noted that the educational crisis afflicting Cleveland schools should not affect the voucher program's constitutionality.

Justice Souter dissented, joined by Justices Stevens, Ginsburg, and Breyer. Ohio's Pilot Project Scholarship Program will pay for "instruction not only in secular subjects but in religious as well, in schools that can fairly be characterized as founded to teach religious doctrine." Justice Souter found illogical the majority's application of the neutrality test, in which it looks "to every educational option," including public school. "The scale of the aid to religious schools approved today is unprecedented." More aid increases the likelihood that "public money was supporting religious as well as secular instruction."

Justice Breyer, with whom Justices Stevens and Souter joined, also dissented. Voucher programs differ "in both *kind* and *degree* from aid programs upheld in the past." They differ in kind because they help to finance teaching religion to children, "a core function of the church." Moreover, "[v]ouchers also differ in *degree*. The aid programs recently upheld by the Court involved limited amounts of aid to religion. But the majority's analysis here appears to permit a considerable shift of taxpayer dollars from public secular schools to private religious schools."

Financial aid to church-related colleges has fared better in the face of establishment challenges than has aid to elementary and secondary schools. The same three-part test used in the pre-college cases — "purpose," "primary effect" and "excessive entanglements" — has been more easily satisfied in the higher education cases. *Tilton v. Richardson*[92] involved federal construction grants to church-colleges for facilities devoted exclusively to secular educational purposes. In upholding the grants, Chief Justice Burger's plurality opinion noted that religious indoctrination was not a substantial purpose of these colleges and that college students were not as susceptible to religious teachings. Moreover, the very nature of a college curriculum would tend to curb sectarian influence and reduce the risk

---

[92] 403 U.S. 672 (1971).

that the primary effect of these grants would be to encourage or support religious activities. Because the inspection necessary to determine that the facilities were devoted to secular education would be minimal, the Court found that the entanglement of church and state was not excessive.

Two years after *Tilton*, the Court upheld a construction aid program that permitted all colleges, regardless of religious affiliation, to borrow funds at low interest rates by using state-issued revenue bonds. In *Hunt v. McNair*,[93] Justice Powell, writing for the majority (6-3), reiterated the rationale of *Tilton*.

In *Roemer v. Maryland*,[94] the Court considered a program of annual, non-categorical grants to private colleges — irrespective of church affiliation — as long as the funds were not used for sectarian purposes. Ensuring that government grants were used only for secular purposes raised a more serious entanglement problem than the single, one-time aid presented. Although Justice Blackmun's plurality opinion recognized that greater supervision would be required to police such grants, the Court upheld the program. Chief Justice Burger and Justice Powell joined Justice Blackmun's opinion. Justice White wrote a separate concurrence joined by Justice Rehnquist. Justices Brennan, Marshall, and Stevens dissented.

[3] Government Support to Religious Institutions in Contexts Other Than Religious Schools

A number of cases involve government support for religious institutions other than religious schools. In this context, the Court has not been quite as rigid in enforcing stringent separation.

In *Bowen v. Kendrick*,[95] the Court upheld the Adolescent Family Life Act, which allowed the government directly to fund educational programs undertaken by a broad range of organizations, including religious institutions. The Act specifically provided federal funds for educational programs addressing problems relating to family life and adolescent sexual relations.

Writing for a 5-4 majority, Chief Justice Rehnquist first turned to the facial challenge. Applying the *Lemon* test, he had no difficulty finding a secular purpose of reducing teenage pregnancy. Turning to the more difficult primary effect prong, the Court refused to constitutionally bar religious institutions from "participating in publicly sponsored social welfare programs."[96] Chief Justice Rehnquist observed that while religious organizations did receive money administered through the statute, there was no requirement that the group receiving money had to be a religious organization. Consequently, the Court found that the Act displayed neutrality toward religious institutions, and any effect of advancing religion was incidental and remote. The Court concluded that even if a significant amount of the funds appropriated under the *Bowen* statute would go to religious groups, the Act

---

[93] 413 U.S. 734 (1973).

[94] 426 U.S. 736 (1976).

[95] 487 U.S. 589 (1988).

[96] *Id.* at 608 (citing *Bradfield v. Roberts*, 175 U.S. 291 (1899)).

was facially neutral with respect to religion because a wide spectrum of public and private organizations beyond those with religious affiliations could meet the Act's requirements.

Chief Justice Rehnquist took particular exception to the District Court's finding that the Act created a "crucial symbolic link" between government and religion.[97] Citing the example of religiously affiliated hospitals receiving government aid, Chief Justice Rehnquist argued that the mere intersection of an organization's "religious mission" and the government's "secular purposes" was not sufficient to make the statute facially unconstitutional.[98] The relevant inquiry was whether the statute provided aid to "pervasively sectarian" institutions.[99] The Court distinguished *Bowen* from cases involving aid to parochial schools by emphasizing that in those cases the state funds did flow to pervasively sectarian institutions. The Court further found the religious institution at issue in *Bowen* less like parochial elementary and secondary schools, than religiously-affiliated colleges and universities which the Court had allowed government to fund.[100]

Finally, the Court found no violation of the entanglement test. Chief Justice Rehnquist described a "Catch 22" when government supervision intended to maintain separation itself became an entanglement. The visits of government personnel to religious institutions to insure compliance with the Act did not entail the level of supervision that would give rise to the danger of establishing religion or infringing on freedom of religion. Again, the finding that the institutions were not pervasively sectarian distinguished the case from decisions involving parochial schools.

The as-applied challenge to the statute focused on whether the institutions involved were using the funds for religious indoctrination. Chief Justice Rehnquist required the challengers to show on remand that the institutions were pervasively sectarian, which would involve more than demonstrating that the counseling was religiously inspired.

Concurring, Justice O'Connor elaborated on the majority's "pervasively sectarian" standard. With regard to the as applied challenge, she stated: "First, *any* use of public funds to promote religious doctrines violates the Establishment Clause. Second, extensive violations — if they can be proved in this case — will be highly relevant in shaping an appropriate remedy that ends such abuses."[101]

Writing for the four dissenters, Justice Blackmun criticized the majority's narrowing the *Lemon* test to focus on the facial neutrality of the law, and its focus on whether the aid flowed to pervasively sectarian institutions. Relying on the District Court's findings, Justice Blackmun viewed the institutions in question as more analogous to parochial schools, with their predominantly religious mission,

---

[97] *Id.* at 613.

[98] *Id.*

[99] *Id.*

[100] *See, e.g.*, Tilton v. Richardson, 403 U.S. 672 (1971).

[101] *Bowen*, 487 U.S. at 623 (O'Connor, J., concurring).

than to colleges and universities, with their primary mission of providing a secular education.

The "pervasively sectarian" inquiry used in *Bowen* has not been used in cases where a law benefits only religious institutions. In *Texas Monthly, Inc. v. Bullock*,[102] a general interest magazine brought an Establishment Clause challenge against a Texas sales tax exemption applicable only to religious periodicals that consisted wholly of writings promulgating the teaching of religious faiths. In a 6-3 decision, the Court struck down the exemption. Writing for a plurality of three, Justice Brennan said that government policies could have secular benefits that incidentally helped religion. Relying on *Walz* and *Mueller*, Justice Brennan said that the benefits provided to religious organizations could be characterized as incidental when those benefits were shared by many nonreligious organizations. By exempting only periodicals published or distributed by religious institutions, the law at issue in *Texas Monthly* forced taxpayers to become "indirect and vicarious 'donors.' "[103]

Justice Brennan rejected the State's proffered compelling interests of avoiding both a Free Exercise violation or excessive entanglement. Payment of a sales tax neither violated religious belief nor inhibited religious activity. Actually, greater entanglement would be prompted in granting the exemption than simply enforcing a generally applicable tax. Moreover, the exemption conveyed a " 'message of endorsement' to slighted members of the community. This is particularly true where, as here, the subsidy is targeted at writings that promulgate the teaching of religious faiths."[104] Justice Brennan opined that to pass muster under the Establishment Clause, the exemption would have to be broad enough to include "all groups that contribute to the community's cultural, intellectual, and moral betterment," or at the very least, include publications addressing nonreligious issues or criticizing religious belief or activity.[105]

The plurality admitted that its decision stood in some tension with two of the Court's free exercise decisions, *Murdock v. Pennsylvania*[106] and *Follett v. McCormick*.[107] In both of those cases, the Court had struck down license and occupation taxes imposed on Jehovah's Witnesses who conducted door-to-door proselytizing and selling of religious reading materials. Justice Brennan attempted to distinguish *Murdock* and *Follett* by noting that the majority in both cases characterized the door-to-door distribution of reading materials as a form of "preaching." The State could not tax a preacher " 'for the privilege of delivering a sermon.' "[108] The Texas sales tax, however, was not a license or occupation tax levied against religious missionaries. Moreover, the sales tax represented such a

---

[102] 489 U.S. 1 (1989).

[103] *Texas Monthly*, 489 U.S. at 14 (quoting *Bob Jones Univ. v. United States*, 461 U.S. 574, 591 (1983)).

[104] *Id.* at 15 (quoting *Corporation of Presiding Bishop v. Amos*, 483 U.S. 327, 348 (1987)).

[105] *Id.*

[106] 319 U.S. 105 (1943).

[107] 321 U.S. 573 (1944).

[108] *Texas Monthly*, 489 U.S. at 22 (quoting *Murdock*, 319 U.S. at 112).

small fraction of the total value of each sale, that it would "pose little danger of stamping out missionary work involving the sale of religious publications."[109] For Justice Brennan, the burden on free exercise imposed by the sales tax was too insubstantial to overcome the establishment concerns in the case.

Concurring in the judgment, Justice White said that the Press Clause of the First Amendment forbade predicating a tax exemption on the content of the publication. Justice Blackmun, joined by Justice O'Connor, also concurred in judgment. Disagreeing with Justice White, Justice Blackmun, like the dissent, said that a free exercise interest would be enough to overcome any compelling state interest necessary to allow discrimination based on the content of speech. Justice Blackmun described Justice Brennan's resolution of the conflict between establishment and free exercise values as "subordinating the Free Exercise value, even . . . at the expense of longstanding precedents" like *Murdock* and *Follett*.[110] On the other hand, Justice Scalia's dissent "would subordinate the Establishment Clause value."[111] Justice Blackmun suggested that a carefully drawn law, exempting not only religious publications but also those devoted to philosophical matters from a non-religious perspective, could obviate the need for either value to dominate. However, a tax exemption limited to only religious publications can only indicate "a statutory preference for the dissemination of religious ideas."[112] In such cases the free exercise issues need not even be reached.

In dissent, Justice Scalia, joined by Chief Justice Rehnquist and Justice Kennedy, considered the exemption of exclusively religious literature to be not only permissible, but possibly even "constitutionally compelled in order to avoid interference with the dissemination of religious ideas."[113] To Justice Scalia, Justice Brennan's opinion seemed to say that the exemption was not required by the Free Exercise Clause and was forbidden by the Establishment Clause. But whether or not free exercise required the exemption, Justice Scalia perceived a broad middle ground where government accommodation of religion need not implicate either clause.

In *Jimmy Swaggart Ministries v. Board of Equalization*,[114] the Court upheld, against both free exercise and establishment challenges, a State's imposition of general use and sales taxes on a religious organization for distributing religious materials. The State of California imposed on its residents both a sales tax and a use tax for goods purchased out-of-state. Aside from the serving of meals, religious organizations were not exempt from either of these taxes. Jimmy Swaggart Ministries (JSM) offered many items for sale during evangelical crusades, including religious books, records, tapes, and a monthly magazine.

Writing for a unanimous Court, Justice O'Connor rejected free exercise objections made by JSM. The California tax was a generally applicable measure

---

[109] *Id.* at 24.

[110] *Id.* at 27 (Blackmun, J., concurring).

[111] *Id.*

[112] *Id.* at 28.

[113] *Id.* at 41 (Scalia, J., dissenting).

[114] 493 U.S. 378 (1990).

that religious organizations must obey along with everyone else. She distinguished a flat license tax on religious literature or other religious activities which would amount to a prior restraint "on the exercise of religious liberty." The Court left open the question of whether a more onerous generally applicable tax might violate free exercise. Justice O'Connor also held that the tax did not violate the Establishment Clause by fostering excessive entanglement.

Lemon and other tests discussed in this section have been applied to scrutinize nondiscriminatory government aid to religion. When that aid discriminates among religious groups, the Court has used the compelling state interest test. In *Larson v. Valente*,[115] the statute imposed registration and reporting requirements on charitable institutions, but exempted those religions that received less than half their support from nonmembers. The Unification Church successfully argued that the law at issue established a government preference among religions that was not based on any compelling state interest. By politicizing religious affiliation, this discrimination among religious groups also violated the excessive entanglement prong of the *Lemon* test. Application of the *Lemon* test assumed uniformity of benefits among religious groups.

§ 17.03   GOVERNMENT SUPPORT OF RELIGIOUS PRACTICES

The modern Court has generally not permitted much government support for religious practices or displays. As in other areas of the Court's religion jurisprudence, however, many cases exhibit the same tension between separationist and accommodationist positions.

The watershed modern case is *Engel v. Vitale*,[116] in which the Court struck down state-mandated prayer in public school classrooms. The New York Board of Regents required teachers at the beginning of each school day to lead the class in the following recitation: " 'Almighty God, we acknowledge our dependence upon Thee, and we beg Thy blessings upon us, our parents, our teachers and our Country.' "[117] The Court flatly stated that "each separate government in this country should stay out of the business of writing or sanctioning official prayers and leave that purely religious function to the people themselves and to those the people choose to look to for religious guidance."[118]

In finding that the prayer violated the Establishment Clause, Justice Black discussed two concerns. First, state involvement in a religious practice poses the danger of religious persecution. Evidence that recitation of the prayer resulted in religious persecution was not readily apparent in *Engel*. Nevertheless, the Court noted that the pressure exerted on students to say the prayer and the exclusion of students if they refused to participate might raise the specter of persecution. "When the power, prestige and financial support of government is placed behind a

---

[115] 456 U.S. 228 (1982).

[116] 370 U.S. 421 (1962).

[117] *Id.* at 422.

[118] *Id.* at 435.

particular religious belief, the indirect coercive pressure upon religious minorities to conform to the prevailing officially approved religion is plain."[119] Because the gravity of harm from persecution was so great, the Court sought to avoid any hint of governmental action that might lead to religious strife.

Justice Black was also concerned that state involvement in a religious practice might be demeaning to religion. The State composed the prayer and civil officials appeared to be assuming religious duties, thereby impairing the sanctity of religious authorities and transforming the private nature of religious practice into a public issue. The State might have allowed ministers, rabbis, and priests to compose the prayers; however, that could have posed entanglement problems. Moreover, free exercise problems might have arisen as only those individuals who were members of the particular sect composing the prayer might have felt comfortable reciting it.

In *Abington School District v. Schempp*,[120] a State law required teachers to read, without comment, at least ten verses from the Bible before the school day began. The law also required teachers to lead their classes in a voluntary recitation of the Lord's Prayer. The State claimed that the law furthered such secular purposes as the promotion of moral values, the contradiction of the trend toward materialism, the perpetuation of our institutions, and the teaching of literature. In an analysis that helped lead to the *Lemon* test, the Court stated that the Bible was clearly a sectarian instrument and that Bible reading had the primary effect of advancing religion. The Court rejected the argument that the refusal to allow Bible reading or any religious practice worked to establish a religion of secular humanism.

The *Abington* majority also stated that religious practices in public schools violated the free exercise rights of minorities who might feel that their beliefs were impugned by these practices. Echoing *Engel*, the Court noted that the Establishment Clause did not require a showing that a law directly coerced non-observing individuals. Consequently, the fact that the statute permitted students to be excused from the exercises on a written request from a parent did not save the statute from invalidation. The Court did, however, allow study of the Bible or religion when presented objectively as part of a secular program of education, in contrast to being presented as a religious practice.

In his dissent, Justice Stewart elaborated on points that he had raised earlier in *Engel*. Justice Stewart argued that there was a substantial free exercise claim on the part of those who affirmatively desired to have their children's school day open with Bible readings, and such a claim could not be overcome without a showing of direct governmental coercion. He noted past decisions in which the discriminatory barring of religious groups from public property violated the First Amendment.

In *Stone v. Graham*,[121] the Court invalidated a Kentucky statute that required public school superintendents to post a copy of the Ten Commandments — purchased with private contributions — in every public classroom. Each plaque

---

[119] *Id.* at 431.

[120] 374 U.S. 203 (1963).

[121] 449 U.S. 39 (1980).

bore a notation explaining the purpose of the display as demonstrating secular application of the Ten Commandments " 'in its adoption as the fundamental legal code of Western Civilization and the Common Law of the United States.' "[122] The Court's *per curiam* opinion rejected the government's argument that the statute served no secular legislative purpose, since the Ten Commandments was a sacred text. Therefore, the statute was unconstitutional under the *Lemon* test. The Court distinguished the objective study of the Bible in the school curriculum from the mere posting of Biblical texts which did not serve an educational function. Justice Rehnquist, in dissent, objected to the majority's summary rejection of the secular purpose expressly articulated by the Kentucky legislature. Chief Justice Burger, Justice Blackmun, and Justice Stewart also dissented from the Court's summary disposition.

In *Wallace v. Jaffree*,[123] the Court used the secular purpose prong of the *Lemon* test to strike down a state law allowing a moment of silence for "voluntary prayer" in public school classrooms. Writing for the Court, Justice Stevens stated that "one of the questions we must ask is 'whether the government intends to convey a message of endorsement or disapproval of religion.' "[124] After reviewing the legislative history of the statute, particularly comments by the bill's sponsor,[125] Justice Stevens concluded that the statute was enacted for the "sole purpose of expressing the State's endorsement of prayer."[126] This conclusion was buttressed by the fact that the statute was an amendment to an earlier statute which merely provided that a one minute period of silence be " 'observed for meditation.' "[127] The amended version was almost identical to the original except the addition of the words "or voluntary prayer" after the word "meditation."[128] Thus, the purpose of the amendment was clearly to promote prayer in the classroom. The Court echoed *Engel* in its concern that the promotion of prayer in the classroom would intrude on the "individual freedom of conscience protected by the First Amendment [which] embraces the right to select any religious faith or none at all."[129] Maintaining a meditative silence could arguably be squared with non-theistic beliefs; prayer could not.

The time at which the Court decided to take up *Wallace* was significant. When the lower court issued its decision, several other cases existed involving simple moments of silence. The Court chose to review *Wallace*, however, and it is not clear what the Court would permit states to do after this decision. Justice Stevens' opinion suggested, and Justices Powell and O'Connor strongly stated, that each would uphold some kind of moment of silence statute. Obviously, the three dissenters would also uphold a true moment of silence statute as they would have

---

[122]   *Id.* at 40.

[123]   472 U.S. 38 (1985).

[124]   *Id.* at 60.

[125]   The bill's sponsor, Senator Donald Holmes, stated that the bill had no other purpose than that of returning voluntary prayer to the classroom. *See id.* at 65.

[126]   *Id.* at 60.

[127]   *Id.* at 40.

[128]   *Id.*

[129]   472 U.S. at 53.

upheld the prayer and moment of silence statute at issue.

Justice Powell concurred with the Court's ruling that the statute at issue violated the purpose prong of the *Lemon* test because it was solely religious in character. He emphasized, however, that the *Lemon* test did not require that the legislature have an exclusively secular motive. Thus, had the statute also had a secular purpose, Justice Powell might have voted to uphold it. He also believed that a "straightforward moment-of-silence statute" — apparently one that did not expressly encourage prayer — would be upheld under the primary effect and entanglement prongs of *Lemon*.[130]

Justice O'Connor's concurrence focused primarily on the endorsement test that she fashioned in her *Lynch v. Donnelly* concurrence. "The relevant issue is whether an objective observer . . . would perceive [the statute] as a state endorsement of prayer in public schools."[131] For Justice O'Connor, a true moment-of-silence statute would not involve excessive entanglement, nor would it be an intentional endorsement if a plausible secular purpose existed. Justice O'Connor expressly adopted an accommodationist tone in discussing the free exercise issues present in the case. "The endorsement test does not preclude government from acknowledging religion or from taking religion into account in making law and policy." Free exercise sometimes compels accommodation of religion. However, allowing all legislation that advances free exercise would nullify the Establishment Clause. "The solution to the conflict between the Religion Clauses lies not in 'neutrality,' but rather in identifying workable limits to the government's license to promote free exercise of religion."[132]

For Justice O'Connor, these "workable limits" were at least partially defined by the reach of the Free Exercise Clause. When the government enacted a law lifting a burden on free exercise, the purpose of the legislation was clearly to accommodate religion. Thus, it was "disingenuous" to require such a law to have a secular purpose when it was compelled by the Free Exercise Clause. Justice O'Connor emphasized, however, that the burden lifted by such a law must be state-imposed. She noted that in the case before her, no law prevented students from praying voluntarily in public school classrooms. Indeed, before the amendment at issue, Alabama law had already provided for a moment of silence during which students might have prayed.

In dissent, Chief Justice Burger maintained that the Court exhibited hostility toward religion in suggesting that it would uphold a pure moment of silence but not one that "includes the word prayer." The Chief Justice also distanced himself from his own *Lemon* test that he construed as calling for a series of "signposts."

In separate dissents, Justices White and Rehnquist called for a broad-ranging reconsideration of the Court's establishment jurisprudence. Justice Rehnquist in particular penned an extensive critique of the wall of separation metaphor and the *Lemon* test which he viewed as enforcing it. He also interpreted the primary thrust of the Establishment Clause as being to prevent discrimination among different

---

[130] *Id.* at 66 (Powell, J., concurring).

[131] 472 U.S. at 76 (O'Connor, J., concurring).

[132] *Id.* at 70, 81–83.

religions rather than through strict neutrality between "religion and irreligion."

The Court again returned to the issue of prayer in public schools in *Lee v. Weisman*.[133] In *Lee*, a 5-4 majority ruled that non-sectarian prayers offered under the direction and guidance of school officials at public high school graduation ceremonies violated the Establishment Clause. Every year, school officials permitted the principal of a Providence, Rhode Island junior high school to invite clergy to deliver an invocation and benediction at the school's graduation ceremony. Participating clergy were provided with a copy of a pamphlet titled " 'Guidelines for Civic Occasions,' " and were asked that the prayers be nonsectarian.[134] The Court upheld the District Court's order permanently enjoining the Providence School District from including prayers in graduation ceremonies.

The majority was divided over what establishment test to use. Writing for the Court, Justice Kennedy declined to reconsider the Court's decision in *Lemon v. Kurtzman*, although invited to do so by the school district and amicus curiae for the United States.[135] Instead, he applied his coercion analysis, previously set out in his concurring opinions in *County of Allegheny v. ACLU*[136] and *Board of Education v. Mergens*[137] and by other Justices in other cases. Justice Kennedy relied heavily on two facts which established coercion. First, the fact that "State officials direct[ed] the performance of a formal religious exercise" at the graduation "may appear to the nonbeliever or dissenter to be an attempt to employ the machinery of the State to enforce a religious orthodoxy."[138] Justice Kennedy explained that

> the school districts supervision and control of a high school graduation ceremony places public pressure, as well as peer pressure, on attending students to stand as a group or, at least, maintain respectful silence during the Invocation and Benediction. This pressure, though subtle and indirect, can be as real as any overt compulsion.[139]

Second, "attendance and participation" was effectively required.[140] Although the parties had stipulated to the fact that attendance at graduation was voluntary, Justice Kennedy rejected the argument as formalistic. Government could not force citizens to forego their rights and benefits in order to avoid a "state-sponsored religious practice."[141] By obliging attendance and directing the prayers, "the State, in a school setting, in effect required participation in a religious exercise."[142] Justice

---

[133] 505 U.S. 577 (1992).

[134] The pamphlet was prepared by the National Conference of Christians and Jews, and offered guidelines for composing " 'public prayer in a pluralistic society.' " Weisman v. Lee, 728 F. Supp. 68, 69 (D.R.I. 1990).

[135] "We can decide the case without reconsidering the general constitutional framework by which public schools' efforts to accommodate religion are measured." *Lee*, 505 U.S. at 587.

[136] 492 U.S. 573, 659 (1989).

[137] 496 U.S. 226, 261–61 (1990).

[138] 505 U.S. at 586–92.

[139] *Id.* at 593.

[140] *Id.* at 586.

[141] *Id.* at 596.

[142] *Id.* at 594.

Kennedy expressed "heightened concerns with protecting freedom of conscience from subtle coercive pressure in the elementary and secondary public schools."[143]

Justice Blackmun concurred, joined by Justices Stevens and O'Connor. He stated that the prayers at issue violated the primary effect prong of the *Lemon* test. As to Justice Kennedy's coercion test, Justice Blackmun found that this was a sufficient but not a necessary cause for an establishment violation. Such government pressure indicated an endorsement or promotion of religion.

Justice Souter's concurrence was also joined by Justices Stevens and O'Connor. Like Justice Blackmun, Justice Souter believed that adopting the coercion test exclusively might leave some rights protected by the Establishment Clause unvindicated. In the past, the Court has invalidated many state laws and practices which were not coercive but suggested endorsement of religion.

Justice Souter also disputed what he termed the "non-preferentialist" view of the dissenters, a view that the Clause only prohibited government from preferring one religion over another, rather than requiring government neutrality between religion and irreligion. However, government neutrality in religious matters "does not foreclose it from ever taking religion into account. The State may 'accommodate' the free exercise of religion by relieving people from generally applicable rules that interfere with their religious callings."[144]

In dissent, Justice Scalia, joined by Chief Justice Rehnquist and Justices Thomas and White, took issue with Justice Kennedy's "psycho-coercion" test.[145] In *County of Allegheny v. ACLU*, that test had been applied with reference to "historical practice and understandings." Justice Scalia noted several examples of public ceremonies where prayer had traditionally been offered, including inaugural addresses, the opening of congressional sessions, and the opening invocation of the Supreme Court. Prayers at graduation ceremonies were not sufficiently different to be treated differently. Students at graduation ceremonies, no more than at any other public function where prayer was offered, were not psychologically coerced to pray or even to bow their heads. The Court "claims only that students are psychologically coerced 'to stand . . . or, at least, maintain a respectful silence.' "[146]

Justice Scalia claimed that the Court's use of a psychological coercion standard went "beyond the realm where judges know what they are doing."[147] Only coercion backed by *"threat of penalty"* could invalidate such "characteristically American" prayers as those offered at Deborah Weisman's graduation ceremony.[148] Finally, Justice Scalia noted that all of the opinions essentially ignored the *Lemon* test.

---

[143] *Id.* at 592.

[144] 505 U.S. at 627.

[145] *Id.* at 641 (Scalia, J., dissenting).

[146] *Id.* at 637.

[147] *Id.* at 636.

[148] *Id.* at 642 (stating that the prayers "could have come from the pen of George Washington or Abraham Lincoln himself").

In *Santa Fe Independent School District v. Doe*,[149] the Court held that a school district policy allowing prayer at varsity football games violated the Establishment Clause. The policy stated that the student council would conduct a student body election by secret ballot to determine whether students wanted a " 'brief invocation,' " which " 'must be nonsectarian and nonproselytizing,' " at home varsity football games " 'to solemnize the event.' "[150] A student elected from a list of volunteers would present the invocation.

Following *Lee v. Weisman*,[151] Justice Stevens found that a student election would not protect individuals with minority views. As a football game is a "school-sponsored function conducted on school property,"[152] a spectator who understood the policy would perceive it as endorsing prayer. Even if attendance at the game was totally voluntary, the pre-game invocation would effectively coerce everyone in attendance to be involved in a religious activity.

Justice Stevens allowed a facial challenge to the policy as it lacked " 'a secular legislative purpose' " as required by the first prong of the test in *Lemon v. Kurtzman*.[153] The plain language of the policy expressed a clear preference for a "traditional religious 'invocation.' " Further evidencing its religious purpose, the district promulgated its football game invocation policy in the context of having enacted other prayer-related policies "that unquestionably violated the Establishment Clause."[154]

Chief Justice Rehnquist's dissent, joined by Justices Scalia and Thomas, emphasized that this challenge came before the district's policy went into effect. Consequently, the Court lacked a record of offensive action to review. The dissent disagreed with the majority's rigid use of the "oft-criticized test of *Lemon*."[155] The Chief Justice distinguished *Lee* because there a "graduation prayer given by a rabbi was 'directed and controlled' by a school official."[156]

In *Edwards v. Aguillard*,[157] the Court faced the issue of instruction in religiously connected ideas rather than prayer. The Court struck down a Louisiana statute which required that "creation science" be taught in public schools whenever evolution was taught. Writing for a plurality of four, Justice Brennan struck down the law under the secular purpose prong of the *Lemon* test, concluding that the law lacked a "clear secular purpose."[158] The Court's usually deferential inquiry into legislative purpose must give way to greater vigilance when the Court was dealing with elementary and secondary schools. "Students in such institutions are impres

---

[149]   530 U.S. 290 (2000).

[150]   *Id.* at 298.

[151]   505 U.S. 577 (1992).

[152]   530 U.S. at 307.

[153]   403 U.S. 602 (1971).

[154]   530 U.S. at 315.

[155]   *Id.* at 319 (Rehnquist, C.J., dissenting).

[156]   *Id.* at 324.

[157]   482 U.S. 578 (1987).

[158]   *Id.* at 585.

sionable and their attendance is involuntary."[159]

Justice Powell, joined by Justice O'Connor, concurred. He believed that a school's curriculum did not violate the Establishment Clause merely because it coincided with religious beliefs. "In fact, since religion permeates our history, a familiarity with the nature of religious beliefs is necessary to understand many historical as well as contemporary events."[160] The determining factor for Justice Powell was whether the introduction of material regarding religious belief was intended to advance a particular religious belief, regardless of whether that belief was supported by scientific evidence.

Dissenting, Justice Scalia stated that he had understood the secular purpose prong of the *Lemon* test as being satisfied unless there was no secular purpose at all. Given the procedural posture of the case having come up on summary judgment, Justice Scalia believed that more deference should have been given to the Louisiana legislature's explicitly stated secular purpose of protecting academic freedom. More fundamentally, Justice Scalia believed the purpose prong should be abandoned altogether because "determining the subjective intent of legislators is a perilous enterprise," not supported by the text of the Establishment Clause.[161] While the Court has been very circumspect about allowing school-sponsored prayer or instruction in public school classrooms, it has allowed student groups to engage in these activities.

Widmar v. Vincent[162] invalidated a regulation that prevented student religious groups from using university facilities. Justice Powell predicated the holding on the Free Speech Clause and avoided using the Free Exercise Clause. The majority rejected the State's argument that its exclusion of religious groups was necessitated by a compelling state interest of avoiding an establishment violation. Evaluating the regulation under the *Lemon* test, the Court found that an open forum policy, which included nondiscrimination against religious speech, constituted a secular purpose and would avoid entanglement with religion. With respect to the primary effect prong of *Lemon*, Justice Powell conceded that religious groups would likely benefit from access to university facilities; however, he stated that merely " 'incidental' benefits [do] not violate the prohibition against the 'primary advancement' of religion."[163] For Justice Powell, the benefits to religion in this case were clearly incidental because the university did not confer its imprimatur on particular religious sects or practices. Moreover, the forum was open to over 100 other university student groups. In a footnote, the Court added that because university students were young adults and were less impressionable that younger students, religious influences need not be as strongly guarded against.

Board of Education v. Mergens[164] upheld the Equal Access Act against an establishment challenge. The Act afforded a right for student high school groups to

---

[159] *Id.* at 584.

[160] *Id.* at 607 (Powell, J., concurring).

[161] *Id.* at 638 (Scalia, J., dissenting).

[162] 454 U.S. 263 (1981).

[163] *Id.* at 273.

[164] 496 U.S. 226 (1990). This case is discussed *supra* § 15.06.

meet at public schools during non-instructional time if the school created a limited public forum. Once it allowed any student groups to meet, the Act forbade discrimination based on the content of the group's ideas.

Westside High denied students' request to form a Christian Club which would be open to all students. The purpose of the club was to discuss the Bible and share fellowship and prayer. The school predicated its denial of access to the club on establishment grounds. Rejecting the establishment rationale, Justice O'Connor, writing for a plurality of four, applied *Lemon*. The Act had a secular purpose of preventing content discrimination against speech. The Act did not have the primary effect of advancing religion as secondary school students were mature enough to understand that the school was not endorsing religion.

Avoiding any misperception of official endorsement, the Act limited the participation of school officials in meetings and required that meetings be held during non-instructional time. The school had many diverse student groups, not just religious ones. Finally, custodial oversight by school employees did not amount to excessive entanglement.

Concurring in the judgment, Justice Kennedy, joined by Justice Scalia, agreed that the Act did not violate the Establishment Clause. Relying on his test in *County of Allegheny v. ACLU*, Justice Kennedy said that the government neither gave direct benefits in such a degree as to establish religion, nor did it coerce students to participate in these groups. Justices Brennan and Marshall also concurred in the judgment. They were concerned about any message of school endorsement that might be inferred, as Westside currently used its clubs to transmit values. Justice Stevens dissented.

In *Lamb's Chapel v. Center Moriches Union Free School District*,[165] the Court held that allowing a religious group to display Christian films on public school property, after-hours, would not constitute an establishment of religion. The majority used the *Lemon* test in its analysis. Writing for the majority, Justice White also concluded that this practice would not offend Justice O'Connor's endorsement test.[166]

In other decisions outside of the public school context, the Court has been somewhat more receptive to state involvement with religious practices. In *Marsh v. Chambers*,[167] the Court upheld state-sponsored prayers in state legislatures rather than public schools. Observing that the complaining party was an adult, the Court ruled that Nebraska's payment of chaplains and the opening of each legislative session with a prayer did not violate the Establishment Clause. Chief Justice Burger's majority opinion stressed history and the Framers' intent to justify the decision. He noted that the Congress that drafted the First Amendment also opened its sessions with a prayer.

Justice Brennan's dissent, joined by two other Justices, traced the Court's Establishment Clause decisions and concluded that the majority opinion could not

---

[165] 508 U.S. 384 (1993).

[166] 463 U.S. 783 (1983).

[167] 463 U.S. 783 (1983).

be squared with the cumulative criteria the Court had developed since *Everson*. Justice Brennan viewed the Constitution as an evolving document. Thus, the diversity of religious thinking — particularly regarding the entry of large non-Christian populations into the country and the rise of secular humanism, agnosticism, and atheism — might mandate a different set of rules than those existing when the First Amendment was drafted. For Justice Brennan, the issue was whether a particular act of state sponsorship of religious practice would offend the sensibilities of contemporary Americans, in all their diversity.

In *Good News Club v. Milford Central School*,[168] the Court reversed a grant for summary judgment that would have allowed a public school to exclude a religious club from using the school's premises for afterschool activities involving Bible lessons. Both parties conceded that "Milford created a limited public forum" by opening up the school's facilities.

Writing for the Court, Justice Thomas said the school's exclusion of the Club constituted "impermissible viewpoint discrimination," and the restriction was not necessary to avoid an Establishment Clause violation. In reaching its decision, the Court analogized Good News' activities to those at issue in *Lamb's Chapel v. Center Moriches Union Free School District*: the meetings were held after school, the school did not sponsor the activities, and any student could attend the meetings with a parent's permission. Moreover, the school allowed other organizations to use its facilities, as in *Widmar v. Vincent*. The school sought to distinguish these cases based on the presence of elementary school children.

Rejecting the school's Establishment Clause argument, the Court explained that "allowing the Club to speak on school grounds would ensure neutrality, not threaten it." Moreover, the parents who must give consent would not feel "coercive pressure" to participate in Good News' activities. The school argued that impressionable elementary school children would automatically believe that it was endorsing religion since the activities were on school grounds. The Court rejected such a categorical approach and further held that the facts did not support endorsement for the purposes of summary judgment.

First, the Club met after school hours in a special room used by the high school and the middle school, not by elementary school students. Second, the Club's instructors were not schoolteachers. Third, the children who engaged in Good News' activities ranged from ages 6 to 12. The Court concluded that the children would no more likely misperceive the Club's inclusion as endorsement than they would perceive its exclusion as hostility toward religion. An endorsement inquiry does not involve individual perceptions; instead, it concerns whether the reasonable observer is " 'deemed aware of the history and context of the community and forum.' " Justice Scalia concurred. Comparing Good News' activities to those engaged in by the Boy Scouts of America, Justice Scalia noted that while the Boy Scouts may advocate " 'morally straight [and] clean' " living, the Club may talk about morality but "may not defend the premise" on which it exists.

Concurring in part, Justice Breyer asserted three points. First, neutrality is only one factor used to examine an Establishment Clause claim. Second, religious

---

[168] 533 U.S. 98 (2001).

endorsement may be the crucial issue in this case. Whether endorsement is perceived depends on such circumstances as the time and nature of the meetings, as well as the children's ages. Third, the majority's holding simply meant the school was not entitled to summary judgment on either its Free Speech or Establishment Clause claim.

Justice Stevens dissented. He categorized religious speech into three parts: religious speech on a particular subject from a particular religious perspective; worship; and "proselytizing or inculcating belief in a particular religious faith." In a limited public forum like the one at issue, the first type of religious speech can exist while excluding the other two types, so long as this is done consistently.

Justice Souter also dissented, joined by Justice Ginsburg. The Club wants to use the school's premises "for an evangelical service of worship." The activities in *Widmar* are distinguishable as "the nature of the university campus and the sheer number of activities offered precluded the reasonable college observer from seeing government endorsement." Similarly, *Lamb's Chapel* did not support an endorsement claim because of the time and the diversity of community use. In contrast, Good News is only one of four groups using the school's premises. Moreover, the Club appears to be the only one meeting immediately after school hours.

Another important series of cases concerns the involvement in the display of religious symbols. In *Lynch v. Donnelly*,[169] Chief Justice Burger allowed a municipality to display in a private park a Christmas nativity scene that it owned. At the outset of the opinion, the Chief Justice adopted an accommodationist tone in observing that " 'total separation' of church and state 'is not possible in an absolute sense.' "[170] The Chief Justice also criticized the wall metaphor as "not a wholly accurate description of the practical aspects of the relationship that in fact exists between church and state."[171] He also noted the inescapable tension between establishment and free exercise values. In upholding the display, Chief Justice Burger applied the *Lemon* test. The Chief Justice effectively loosened the secular purpose prong by stating that this prong would be satisfied unless there was no question that the statute or activity was motivated wholly by religious considerations. For the Chief Justice, the creche at issue was displayed to celebrate the national holiday of Christmas and to depict the origins of that holiday. These amounted to legitimate secular purposes under the highly deferential standard used by the Court.

Turning to the primary effect prong, the Chief Justice stated that comparisons of the relative benefits to religion of different forms of governmental support were difficult to make. Faced with the task of making such elusive distinctions in the abstract, the Chief Justice devised analogies, finding that the use of the creche was no more beneficial to religion than was the supplying of books in *Board of Education v. Allen*[172] or transportation for non-public schools in *Everson*.[173] Chief

---

[169] 465 U.S. 668 (1984).

[170] *Id.* at 672.

[171] *Id.* at 673.

[172] 392 U.S. 236 (1968).

[173] Chief Justice Burger also compared the display of the crèche to practices upheld in several other

Justice Burger also compared the creche to practices not ruled upon by the Court, such as the display of religious paintings in public museums. He argued that just as paintings had artistic value apart from their religious symbolism, the creche had independent worth in that it represented an historical event. For Chief Justice Burger, the benefit to religion in *Lynch* was incidental, indirect, and remote and certainly no greater than any benefit conferred by endorsing a holiday called "Christ's Mass" or displaying religious paintings in governmental museums.

Finally, the creche display passed the entanglement prong of *Lemon*. The Court focused on administrative entanglement, finding that the city had not specifically designed the creche, nor had it spent a great deal on its upkeep. Moreover, the Court refused to hold that political divisiveness alone could comprise excessive entanglement. In any event, beyond the lawsuit itself, no evidence of divisiveness existed over the entire history of the display of the creche.

Several times the Chief Justice referred to the creche in the context of the overall display. Some have wondered whether the outcome was conditioned in part on the creche's having been part of an overall holiday display which included reindeer, a Santa Claus house, and other secular symbols of Christmas. In his dissent, Justice Brennan criticized the majority for focusing only on the general holiday context in which the creche appeared, rather than the "clear religious import of the crèche" itself.[174]

In her concurring opinion, Justice O'Connor first proposed her endorsement approach to establishment cases, which became quite influential on the Court. The Establishment Clause was not violated when there was neither excessive entanglement nor government endorsement or disapproval of religion. For Justice O'Connor, entanglement became excessive, and thereby unconstitutional, when it threatened to interfere with the independence of religious institutions or to give the institutions access to government or government powers not fully shared by non-adherents of the religion.

Justice O'Connor de-emphasized the secular purpose test, calling it merely the subjective component of the objective inquiry into the effect of a law or government practice. Instead, Justice O'Connor reformulated the first two prongs of the *Lemon* test as being concerned with whether a government practice was intended to or had the effect of conveying a message of government endorsement or disapproval of religion. This endorsement test required that the governmental practice must have the purpose or unintentional effect of making religion relevant, in reality or in public perception, to status in the political community. The government's legitimate secular purposes of "solemnizing public occasions, expressing confidence in the future, and encouraging the recognition of what is worthy of appreciation in society"[175] did not constitute endorsement of religion.

---

establishment decisions, including *Marsh v. Chambers*, 463 U.S. 783 (1983) (legislative prayer); *Roemer v. Board of Pub. Works*, 426 U.S. 736 (1976) (federal grants to church-supported colleges); *Tilton v. Richardson*, 403 U.S. 672 (1971) (federal grants for buildings of church-sponsored colleges); *Walz v. Tax Comm'n*, 397 U.S. 664 (1970) (tax exemption for church property); *McGowan v. Maryland*, 366 U.S. 420 (1961) (Sunday closing laws); and *Zorach v. Clauson*, 343 U.S. 306 (1952) (release time program).

[174] *Lynch*, 465 U.S. at 705 (Brennan, J., dissenting).

[175] *Id.* at 693 (O'Connor, J., concurring).

In *County of Allegheny v. ACLU*,[176] the Court struck down a creche display but upheld another display of a Hanukkah menorah next to a Christmas tree. In a part of the opinion supported by a majority of five, Justice Blackmun applied Justice O'Connor's endorsement test. Drawing on the definition of endorsement proposed in Justice O'Connor's concurrence in *Lynch*, Justice Blackmun concluded that endorsement could comprise taking "a position on questions of a religious belief or from 'making a adherence to a religion relevant in any way to a person's standing in the political community.' "[177]

In ascertaining whether the display of the creche would be perceived as an impermissible endorsement of religion, Justice Blackmun cited *Lynch* for the proposition that "the effect of the government's use of religious symbolism depends upon its context."[178] Accordingly, he conducted an extensive analysis of the various surrounding elements which contributed to the total effect of the display, including the proximity of other decorations to the creche, the floral frame surrounding it, the performance of Christmas carols in front of the creche, the general physical setting, and a sign displaying ownership of the creche by a religious organization.

The Court noted that the creche in *Lynch* was displayed among a variety of other figures including Santa's house and reindeer. In contrast, the creche in this case was displayed alone on the Grand Staircase, the main part of the building housing the county seat. A sign noting that the creche display was owned by the Roman Catholic Holy Name Society, not the City, did not render the display constitutional.

A different majority of six upheld the display of a Christmas tree and a Hanukkah menorah. Justice Blackmun, writing only for himself, said that the context of the menorah display with a Christmas tree and a sign saying that the city was saluting liberty during the holiday season sufficiently reduced any danger of endorsement. Justice Blackmun would, however, have remanded the case to determine whether the display had a secular purpose and did not entail excessive entanglement under the *Lemon* test.

In her concurring opinion, Justice O'Connor sustained the display of the religious menorah next to the secular Christmas tree. With the sign saluting liberty, this combination of religious and secular symbols conveyed a message of pluralism.

In an opinion joined by Justices Marshall and Stevens, Justice Brennan would have struck down both displays as establishing religion. He said that both the menorah and the Christmas tree were religious symbols. Moreover, the Establishment Clause did not permit religious displays for the purpose of conveying pluralism. In a separate opinion joined by Justices Brennan and Marshall, Justice Stevens said that governmental displays of any religious symbols could cause societal foment.

In a dissent joined by Chief Justice Rehnquist, Justice White and Justice Scalia, Justice Kennedy would have upheld both the display involving the creche and that involving the menorah. Justice Kennedy claimed that the result in this case rests on

---

[176]   492 U.S. 573 (1989).

[177]   *Id.* at 594.

[178]   *Id.* at 597.

"minutiae."[179] He also criticized the endorsement test as difficult to apply. In its stead, he proposed the following test: "Non-coercive government action within the realm of flexible accommodation or passive acknowledgment of existing symbols does not violate the Establishment Clause unless it benefits religion in a way more direct and more substantial than practices that are accepted in our national heritage."[180] The displays at issue neither coerced nor proselytized; they were representations of holidays that had religious and secular aspects. They were merely "celebrat[ing] the season" and acknowledging the history of these holidays.

In *Capitol Square Review Board v. Pinette*,[181] the Court (7-2) held that allowing the Ku Klux Klan to display an unattended cross on Capitol Square near the Statehouse in Columbus, Ohio would not violate the Establishment Clause. Because Capitol Square was a public forum equally accessible to all groups in the community, a state could only impose restrictions on protected expression that were "necessary, and narrowly drawn, to serve a compelling state interest."[182] While avoiding an establishment of religion would comprise such an interest, the Court relied on *Widmar v. Vincent* and *Lamb's Chapel v. Center Moriches Union Free School District* to reject an establishment violation in this case. The Court also rejected application of *County of Allegheny v. ACLU* as the creche in that case was not displayed in a public forum open to all.

None of the five separate opinions in the seven Justice majority applied the *Lemon* test. Writing for only a plurality of four in part of his opinion, Justice Scalia refused to apply the "endorsement test" because the government had not expressed any support or approval of the display.

Concurring in part and concurring in the judgment, Justice O'Connor — joined by Justices Souter and Breyer — disagreed with Justice Scalia. For Justice O'Connor, the endorsement test required the Court to ask whether an "informed observer" — aware of the forum's history — would view the cross as an endorsement of religion by the state. To satisfy this test, Justice O'Connor would have required the display of a government disclaimer of any endorsement. In the context of a forum that had traditionally been public, such a disclaimer would have been sufficient to avoid perceptions of endorsement. Justices Stevens and Ginsburg wrote separate dissenting opinions.

Van Orden v. Perry[183] held that a monument displaying the Ten Commandments on the grounds of the Texas State Capitol did not violate the Establishment Clause. The "monolith" was donated to the State and funded by the Fraternal Order of the Eagles of Texas, "a national social, civic, and patriotic organization." Located on the grounds surrounding the Capitol, the monument was one of "17 monuments and 21 historical markers commemorating the 'people, ideals, and events that compose Texan identity.'" The text of the Ten Commandments was surrounded by religious and patriotic symbols. Forty years passed before anyone brought a First Amend

---

[179] *Id.* at 674 (Kennedy, J., dissenting).

[180] *Id.* at 662–63.

[181] 515 U.S. 753 (1995).

[182] *Id.* at 761.

[183] 545 U.S. 677 (2005).

ment claim against the monument; the plaintiff had passed it frequently for six years before filing this lawsuit.

Writing for the majority, Chief Justice Rehnquist noted that "our institutions presuppose a Supreme Being, yet these institutions must not press religious observances upon their citizens." The Court faces a tension between maintaining the division of church and state and averting "a hostility to religion by disabling the government from in some ways recognizing our religious heritage." As the Court stated, two years after the case was decided, the *Lemon* test provides " 'helpful signposts.' " Consequently, Chief Justice Rehnquist did not use it in this case. Regardless of the "fate" of *Lemon*, this decision was "driven both by the nature of the monument and by our Nation's history."

There are many representations of the Ten Commandments and other religious symbols on government property, including Moses carrying them in the Supreme Court courtroom. However, Moses was not only a religious leader but also a lawgiver, and the Commandments also have "an undeniable historical meaning" as the many displays in Washington demonstrate. "Simply having religious content or promoting a message consistent with a religious doctrine does not run afoul of the Establishment Clause." *Stone v. Graham* had invalidated a statute requiring the Ten Commandments to be placed in every classroom; however, the Court has " 'been particularly vigilant' " in enforcing the Establishment Clause in elementary and secondary schools. *Stone* does not extend to displays of the Ten Commandments like the one here "that lacks a 'plainly religious,' 'pre-eminent purpose.' " The Texas monument has "dual significance, partaking of both religion and government."

Justice Scalia concurred, maintaining that the Constitution permits "a State's favoring religion generally, honoring God through public prayer and acknowledgment, or, in a nonproselytizing manner, venerating the Ten Commandments." Justice Thomas concurred. The text and history of the Establishment Clause do not support its incorporation against the states. Moreover, the Framers limited the Clause to " 'actual legal coercion,' " such as mandatory observances or taxes for a religious purpose. This case does not require any action by the plaintiff.

Justice Breyer concurred in the judgment. This is a "borderline case" which requires "the exercise of legal judgment" about the monument's context rather than a legal test. The monolith conveys both religious and secular messages, including "the Commandments' role in shaping civic morality." The Eagles wanted to emphasize this message to curb juvenile delinquency. While a new monument "is certainly likely to prove divisive," 40 years elapsed before anyone challenged the Texas monument, suggesting that "as a practical matter of degree this display is unlikely to prove divisive." Finding that this monument violates the Establishment Clause would show "a hostility toward religion" and "encourage disputes concerning the removal of longstanding depictions of the Ten Commandments." The Establishment Clause tries to avoid "religiously based divisiveness."

Justice Stevens dissented, joined by Justice Ginsburg. Many people believe that the Ten Commandments are God's own words to Moses which represent the code of the Judeo-Christian God. If endorsement of "a particular deity's command to 'have no other gods before me' " is acceptable, textual displays that do violate the

Establishment Clause are difficult to imagine. Justice Souter also dissented, joined by Justices Stevens and Ginsburg. While government need not remain absolutely neutral toward religion, the Establishment Clause does generally require neutrality. Moreover, the Court has never limited *Stone* to the classroom setting. As a state capitol building is the "civic home" of each of the state's citizens, it should not support a specific religious position. Justice O'Connor's dissent largely agreed with Justice Souter's.

McCreary County v. American Civil Liberties Union of Kentucky[184] invalidated a display of the Ten Commandments in certain courthouses, holding that the "manifest objective may be dispositive of the constitutional enquiry." The first displays consisted of framed copies of an abridged version of the Commandments. After being sued the counties authorized a second display, stating that "the Ten Commandments are the 'precedent legal code upon which the civil and criminal codes of . . . Kentucky are founded.'" The second version included "eight other documents in smaller frames, each either having a religious theme or excerpted to highlight a religious element." The third display contained "nine framed documents of equal size" with the Ten Commandments quoted at greater length than previous documents, and the statement: "'The Ten Commandments provide the moral background of the Declaration of Independence and the foundation of our legal tradition.'"

The 5-4 majority focused on governmental neutrality. Relying on the *Lemon* test, which requires a "'secular purpose,'" the Court stated that purpose is judged by an "'objective observer'" who considers the "'text, legislative history, and implementation of the statute.'" The secular purpose must be "genuine, not a sham, and not merely secondary to a religious objective," as determined by a reasonable observer who has a reasonable memory and takes "historical context" into consideration. The Court took this case on appeal from a preliminary injunction against the display, and therefore reviewed the legal rulings of the District Court de novo and the final conclusion for abuse of discretion.

The second display juxtaposed "the Commandments to other documents with highlighted references to God." The "reasonable observer could not forget" these references, and they had never been repealed in any event. The third display quoted the religious language of the Commandments more extensively than the first two.

While history does not "forever taint" attempts "to deal with the subject matter," purpose must be "understood in light of context." Moreover, sacred texts can be integrated into governmental displays, as evidenced by the courtroom of the Supreme Court depicting Moses with part of the "secularly phrased Commandments" alongside "17 other lawgivers." However, the display violates neutrality which protects "the integrity of individual conscience" and guards "against . . . civic divisiveness." The original understanding of the Constitution does not consistently reject the neutrality principle. Justice Souter criticized the dissent's assertion that the Framers embraced monotheism.

Justice O'Connor concurred. Our "constitutional boundaries" have enabled "private religious exercise to flourish." Current world events evidence "the violent

---

[184] 545 U.S. 844 (2005).

consequences of the assumption of religious authority by government." The history of the display at issue conveys an "unmistakable message of endorsement to the reasonable observer."

Justice Scalia dissented, joined by the Chief Justice and Justices Kennedy and Thomas. He stated that governmental neutrality was only supported by "the Court's own say-so." This decision "modifies *Lemon* to ratchet up the Court's hostility to religion." The " 'objective observer' " analysis inherently "focuses not on the actual purpose of government action, but the 'purpose apparent from government action.' " Moreover, while *Lemon* only requires " 'a secular . . . purpose,' " the majority requires that the secular purpose " 'predominate.' " The frequency with which the Commandments are displayed evidences that they found the rule of law, and symbolize the role of religion. The majority advances "a revisionist agenda of secularization." Indeed, a reasonable observer would not likely "even have been aware of the resolutions."

In *Salazar v. Buono*,[185] the Court overturned an injunction that barred a congressional statute that transferred federal land displaying a Latin cross war memorial to a private party. Congress had enacted the statute following an initial injunction under the Establishment Clause against the government's permitting the display of the privately-erected cross on federal land.

The original district court injunction "permanently forbade the Government 'from permitting the display of the Latin cross in the area of Sunrise Rock in the Mojave National Preserve.' " While the appeal of the injunction was pending, Congress enacted a law "directing the Secretary of the Interior to transfer to the VFW (Veterans of Foreign Wars) the Government's interest in the land that had been designated a national memorial. In exchange, the Government was to receive land elsewhere in the preserve" from two private citizens. The District Court "permanently enjoined the Government from implementing" the land-transfer statute.

Writing for a plurality, Justice Kennedy set aside the injunction against the land-transfer statute because the land-transfer represented a change in circumstances from the original injunction. Justice Kennedy also stated that placement of the cross on federal land "was not an attempt to set the imprimatur of the state on a particular creed. Rather, those who erected the cross intended simply to honor our Nation's fallen soldiers." Moreover, the cross had grown "entwined in the public consciousness," having "stood on Sunrise Rock for nearly seven decades before the statute was enacted." It is the only World War I national memorial.

Justice Kennedy noted that the original injunction was assumed proper for purposes of the opinion, and cautioned that the opinion should not be read to suggest agreement with the original injunction. "The goal of avoiding governmental endorsement does not require eradication of all religious symbols in the public realm. A cross by the side of a public highway marking, for instance, the place where a state trooper perished need not be taken as a statement of governmental support for sectarian beliefs. The Constitution does not oblige government to avoid

---

[185] 130 S. Ct. 1803 (2010).

any public acknowledgment of religion's role in society. Rather, it leaves room to accommodate divergent values."

The " 'reasonable observer' " test is generally not applied to displays on private land. Even if this standard were proper, the cross satisfied it by evoking the image of "thousands of small crosses in foreign fields marking the graves of Americans who fell in battles," which has far more than a religious meaning.

The District Court should have considered "less drastic relief than complete invalidation of the land-transfer statute," such as, requiring signs indicating that the VFW owned the land. The case was remanded, as the District Court was best able to analyze the "highly-fact specific" nature of this issue.

Chief Justice Roberts concurred. Justice Alito concurred in part and concurred in the judgment. He disagreed with remanding the case because the "facts are sufficiently clear to allow the statute to be implemented." Also, demolishing the monument would be interpreted as government hostility to religion, not neutrality. Justice Scalia, joined by Justice Thomas, concurred in the judgment. Justice Scalia found that Buono lacked standing as the District Court's order expanded the original injunction.

Justice Stevens dissented, joined by Justices Ginsburg and Sotomayor. To any reasonable observer, the appearance of government endorsement of the cross will continue after the land transfer, regardless of the changed name on the title to the "small patch of underlying land. This is particularly true because the Government has designated the cross . . . as a national memorial." Moreover, the purpose of the land transfer is to preserve the display. The "reasonable observer would still think that government is endorsing a sectarian message."

Justice Breyer filed a separate dissent, arguing that the law of injunctions offers a district court "considerable leeway to interpret the meaning and application of its own injunctive order." The District Court did not abuse its discretion here.

Several cases involving government support for religious practices treat exemptions from governmental regulations. In *Estate of Thornton v. Caldor*,[186] for example, the Court held that the Establishment Clause prevented the State from compelling a private employer to give its employee the absolute right not to work on the employee's chosen weekly day of worship. An 8-1 majority opinion, authored by Chief Justice Burger, stressed that the Connecticut law made no allowance for the convenience or interests — religious or otherwise — of the employer or other employees. Justice O'Connor's concurrence stressed that the majority opinion did not cast doubt on the validity of the provisions of Title VII of the 1964 Civil Rights Act which required employers to make "reasonable" accommodations for an employee's religious practices, unless such accommodation would cause undue hardship to the employer's business.

The balance was struck in favor of greater accommodation in *Corporation of the Presiding Bishop v. Amos*.[187] The Court unanimously upheld an exemption for

---

[186] 472 U.S. 703 (1985).

[187] 483 U.S. 327 (1987).

religious organizations from Title VII's prohibition against religious discrimination in employment. The Mormon Church was thereby permitted to discriminate in its hiring based on adherence to certain religious tenets, at least as applied to nonprofit activities such as the operation of a gymnasium. Justice White's majority opinion concluded that the purpose prong of *Lemon* was satisfied because of the permissible purpose of "alleviat[ing] significant governmental interference with the ability of religious organizations to define and carry out their religious missions."[188] As to the effect prong, Justice White said it prohibited the state from advancing religion but did not prohibit the state from allowing a religion to advance its own tenets: "A law is not unconstitutional simply because it allows churches to advance religion, which is their very purpose."[189] Nor did the exemption impermissibly entangle church and state. On the contrary, "the statute effectuates a more complete separation of the two and avoids the kind of intrusive inquiry into religious belief that the District Court engaged in in this case."[190] In separate concurring opinions, Justices Brennan and O'Connor noted that the exemption would not apply to secular activity carried on by a church, but favored a presumption that the non-profit activities of a church were part of its religious mission.[191]

§ 17.04   ESTABLISHMENT OF RELIGION THROUGH RELIGIOUS INSTITUTIONS BECOMING INVOLVED IN GOVERNMENTAL DECISIONS

To some extent, the Court's many discussions of the secular purpose prong of *Lemon* reveal that religious motivation may help to shape public policy. As indicated in the various opinions in *Wallace v. Jaffree*, for example, religious values may properly inform public policy, provided that such laws were not enacted solely for the purpose of advancing religion.[192] This view takes account of the reality that, as long as legislators hold religiously-founded values and as long as legislators' values are reflected in public policy, religion will indirectly impact the content of our laws. However, the Court has invalidated more direct links where religious organizations themselves have control over public policy.

In *Larkin v. Grendel's Den, Inc.*,[193] an 8-1 majority struck down a law that allowed religious institutions the power to veto government decisions. A Massachusetts General Law provided that premises within five hundred feet of a church or school could not receive a liquor license if the governing body of the church or school filed a written objection to the granting of such a license. Writing for the Court, Chief Justice Burger noted that deference was normally due to legislative zoning

---

[188] *Id.* at 335.

[189] *Id.* at 337 (emphasis added).

[190] *Id.* at 339.

[191] *See also* St. Martin Evangelical Lutheran Church v. South Dakota, 451 U.S. 772 (1981) (exempting church-affiliated academy from the Federal Unemployment Tax Act, as a matter of statutory construction).

[192] See particularly Justice O'Connor's discussion of religiously-motivated legislative purpose in *Wallace*, 472 U.S. at 70, 82–83.

[193] 459 U.S. 116 (1982).

judgments. Nevertheless, where, as in this case, a veto power had been delegated to a religious body, such deference was not warranted. Applying the *Lemon* test, the Chief Justice readily found that the law served the valid secular purpose of protecting churches and schools from the "hurly-burly" associated with liquor outlets. This objective, however, could be achieved through other means, such as an outright ban on liquor outlets within a certain distance from churches and schools, or by requiring licensing hearings in which the views of such institutions could be voiced and considered.

Chief Justice Burger noted that there was no guarantee that the veto power would be wielded in a religiously neutral manner. Nothing prevented churches from using this power, for example, to ensure that only members of a particular congregation received licenses. Chief Justice Burger was also concerned about the symbolic union of church and state that accompanied such sharing of legislative power. Consequently, he found that the statute had the primary effect of advancing religion. The statute also violated the entanglement prong of *Lemon* because it "enmeshes churches in the processes of government and creates the danger of '[p]olitical fragmentation and divisiveness along religious lines.' "[194] Chief Justice Burger concluded that "few entanglements could be more offensive to the spirit of the Constitution."[195]

More recently, in *Board of Education of Kiryas Joel Village School District v. Grumet*,[196] the Court invalidated a New York law that created a separate school district according to the boundaries of an exclusively religious community. The Satmar Hasidic Sect moved from Eastern Europe to Brooklyn after World War II and later to an approved but undeveloped subdivision in the town of Monroe, New York. There they formed the village of Kiryas Joel which encompassed just 320 acres, owned and inhabited entirely by Satmars. The members of the sect strictly adhere to Jewish custom law, avoiding assimilation into the modern world.

After *Aguilar v. Felton*[197] and *School District of Grand Rapids v. Ball*[198] prohibited states from providing publicly-funded classes on religious school premises, the handicapped children of Kiryas Joel were forced to attend programs in the public school system outside the village. This arrangement subjected the children to severe trauma by exposing them to alien customs in an unfamiliar world. As a result, all handicapped children from the village except one were transferred to private schools or went without any education at all.

The New York legislature, or the school district in which the Village of Kiryas Joel was located, could have adopted programs on neutral sites for the education of handicapped children from Kiryas Joel. Instead, the New York legislature responded by enacting Chapter 748, creating the separate school district for Kiryas Joel. The village school district used its plenary power to create a school with only a special education program for disabled children from inside and outside the

---

[194] *Id.* at 127.

[195] *Id.*

[196] 512 U.S. 687 (1994); *see supra* § 17.02[2].

[197] 473 U.S. 402 (1985); *see supra* § 17.02.

[198] 473 U.S. 373 (1985).

village. If any child in the village sought a public school education, the district would pay for a program in a nearby district.

Writing for plurality, Justice Souter began by stating, " 'A proper respect for both the Free Exercise and the Establishment Clauses compels the State to pursue a course of "neutrality" toward religion,' favoring neither one religion over others nor religious adherents collectively over non-adherents."[199] The statute deviated from this maxim by relinquishing the State's discretionary power over public education "to a group defined by its character as a religious community," while offering "no assurance that governmental power has been or will be exercised neutrally."[200]

Although the New York law granted civic power to a group of qualified voters of a religious community rather than to a religious institution, this distinction was without constitutional significance. The State could not deliberately delegate civic powers to an individual or group on the grounds of religious identity. Where, as here, "fusion" was at issue, the relevant inquiry should distinguish "between a government's purposeful delegation on the basis of religion and a delegation on principles neutral to religion, to individuals whose religious identities are incidental to their receipt of civic authority."[201] The New York legislature was fully aware that the carved out district contained only members of the Satmar sect. Moreover, this action was counter to the longstanding trend in New York of consolidating school districts.

The plurality also took exception to the fact that a special privilege was conferred on the Satmar sect that would not be available to other religious and nonreligious groups. This treatment violated the tenet that government should not prefer one religion over another, or religion to irreligion. Finally, while government may accommodate religion, accommodation would not save actions, such as that of the New York legislature, which threatened neutrality among religions by establishing the beliefs of a particular sect — even a small sect.

Concurring, Justice Blackmun emphasized that the majority opinion did not depart from *Lemon v. Kurtzman*.[202] Justice Stevens, joined by Justices Blackmun and Ginsburg, also concurred. Public schools could have taken other steps to meet the concerns of the Satmar parents, such as greater promotion and understanding of cultural diversity. Moreover, it was revealing that a large number of the full-time students at the school were Hasidic handicapped children from outside the village. The school thus served a population defined by religion rather than geography. Justice O'Connor, concurring in part and concurring in the judgment, emphasized equal treatment irrespective of religious or nonreligious beliefs. The "Religion Clauses — the Free Exercise Clause, the Establishment Clause, the Religious Test Clause,[203] and the Equal Protection Clause as applied to religion — all speak with one voice on this point: Absent the most unusual circumstances, one's religion ought

---

[199] *Grumet*, 512 U.S. at 696.

[200] *Id.*

[201] *Id.* at 699.

[202] For further discussion of this case, *see supra* § 17.02[2].

[203] U.S. Const. art. VI, cl. 3.

not affect one's legal rights or duties or benefits."[204] Once government establishes religious affiliation as a relevant criterion of political standing, the Establishment Clause was violated.

In the instant case, New York could have enacted a general law allowing all villages to operate their own school districts. Alternatively, the Court could have allowed the State to revive the kind of publicly-funded programs on parochial school grounds, taught by public school teachers, that were invalidated in *School District v. Ball* and *Aguilar v. Felton.* "The Court should, in a proper case, be prepared to reconsider *Aguilar,* in order to bring our Establishment Clause jurisprudence back to what I think is the proper track — government impartiality, not animosity, towards religion."[205] In Justice O'Connor's view, the movement away from the rigid *Lemon* test was well under way, indicating the Court's willingness to substitute a number of tests, each covering a narrower, more homogeneous range of issues.

Justice Kennedy, concurring in the judgment, rejected the implication of the Court's decision that accommodation of a particular religious group was invalid because the legislature might not confer the same accommodation on a like group. The New York law alleviated a unique burden on the Satmar's religious practice without burdening non-Satmars. Moreover, creating the school district did not display favoritism toward Satmars as there was no evidence of similar requests having been rejected. However, laws come into question when the accommodation has induced the government to draw political boundaries: "the Establishment Clause forbids the government to use religion as a line-drawing criterion."[206]

Justice Scalia, joined by Chief Justice Rehnquist and Justice Thomas, dissented. Justice Scalia charged that the majority treated tolerance of a religious group's special needs as an impermissible establishment of religion. Indeed, "the Founding Fathers would be astonished to find that the Establishment Clause — which they designed 'to insure that no one powerful sect or combination of sects could use political or governmental power to punish dissenters,' — has been employed to prohibit characteristically and admirably American accommodation of the religious practices (or more precisely, cultural peculiarities) of a tiny minority sect."[207]

The Kiryas Joel school for handicapped students included all of the notable characteristics of any public school. "The only thing distinctive about the school is that all the students share the same religion."[208] Moreover, civic authority was transferred to citizens who happened to share the same religion rather than to a religious institution or church leader. Justice Scalia said that the law was not motivated by religion but extended similar educational benefits to a group of children who were impeded by differences in dress, culture, and language. In fact, even if the legislature had been religiously motivated, the law advanced the best traditions of accommodation. Finally, Justice Scalia advocated that the *Lemon* test

---

[204]　512 U.S. at 715 (O'Connor, J., concurring).

[205]　*Id.* at 717–18.

[206]　*Id.* at 728 (Kennedy, J., concurring).

[207]　*Id.* at 732 (Scalia, J., dissenting) (citations omitted).

[208]　*Id.* at 733.

should be abandoned and replaced by reliance on the longstanding traditions of the American people.

In *Rosenberger v. University of Virginia*,[209] the Court (5-4) held that funding the printing costs for a student-run newspaper with a religious viewpoint did not violate the Establishment Clause. Because the University classified the newspaper as an informative news source and not a religious activity, the newspaper was qualified to apply for University funding. However, the University denied the funding to avoid violating the Establishment Clause.

Writing for the Court, Justice Kennedy found that the University singled out the religious viewpoint in denying funding, which violated the newspaper's free speech rights by engaging in viewpoint discrimination. The Court found that the funding would exhibit neutrality toward religion, not state endorsement of religion. Even though students at the University were required to pay a mandatory fee of $14 to support the funding of student activities, this fee was not a tax to support a church because student groups had access to the funding. Moreover, the University required student groups to include a disclaimer of the University's involvement in their activities. Nor was the government unconstitutionally giving money to a religious institution. First, the newspaper was not a religious institution. Second, the University directly paid the third-party contractors, not the student groups.

Finally, the Court found no difference between disbursing funds for a service and providing the service, such as printing, on the campus. In this connection, providing such services was no different from the access to University facilities permitted in *Widmar v. Vincent*.[210] The Court concluded that any benefit received by the student group was merely incidental.[211]

§ 17.05 FREE EXERCISE OF RELIGION

Establishment and free exercise jurisprudence developed somewhat concurrently. Like the Establishment Clause, the Free Exercise Clause was seldom the subject of litigation prior to the mid-twentieth century. Early Supreme Court cases where the Free Exercise Clause was implicated invariably resulted in a rejection of the free exercise claim. The nature of a typical free exercise claim may help to explain this result. Laws that are typically the objects of a free exercise challenge do not directly prohibit religious beliefs or practices. Instead, such laws are usually facially neutral, generally applicable laws that burden the free exercise of a particular sect. The challenger, in effect, is put in the position of seeking an exemption on religious grounds from an otherwise proper expression of the popular will. The Court's willingness to recognize such exemptions has vacillated through the years.[212]

---

[209] 515 U.S. 819 (1995).

[210] *See supra* § 17.03.

[211] For further discussion of this case, *see supra* § 15.06.

[212] For an historical perspective on the history of free exercise exemptions from generally applicable laws, *see* M. McConnell, *The Origins and Historical Understanding of Free Exercise of Religion*, 103 HARV. L. REV. 1409 (1990).

In the Court's early free exercise jurisprudence, this balance between religious liberty and the general welfare was struck in favor of the latter. *Reynolds v. United States*[213] is typical of the Court's early hostility toward recognizing free exercise-based exemptions from generally-applicable laws. In *Reynolds*, a Mormon claimed that his conviction under an anti-polygamy law violated the Free Exercise Clause because polygamy was mandated by church doctrine. The Court upheld the conviction by constructing a belief/practice dichotomy defining the scope of protection afforded by the Clause. Religious beliefs, according to the *Reynolds* Court, received absolute protection. Religious practices, however, where they are "in violation of social duties or subversive of good order,"[214] received no protection. The Court found that the practice of polygamy, being morally reprehensible, was appropriately characterized as the latter, and thus was not a religious practice falling within the scope of the Free Exercise Clause's protection.

In *Cantwell v. Connecticut*,[215] the Court appeared more sympathetic to free exercise concerns than it had been in *Reynolds*. A Jehovah's Witness was convicted under a statute forbidding solicitation without a license. The Court was particularly troubled by the unfettered discretion given public officials under the licensing scheme, and concluded that the statute imposed an unconstitutional prior restraint on both free speech and on the free exercise of religion. In its analysis, the *Cantwell* Court maintained the *Reynolds* belief/practice distinction, albeit without the heavy overtones of majoritarian morality suggested in *Reynolds*. According to the *Cantwell* Court, religious belief was afforded "absolute" protection, while religious practice may be regulated "for the protection of society."[216] The power to regulate religious practice must not be exercised so as to "unduly . . . infringe" on freedom of religion.[217] This "undue infringement" standard, while an improvement from the almost nonexistent level of scrutiny for laws burdening religion in *Reynolds*, still favored state power over individual religious liberty. *Cantwell* might have been different had the case not also involved a violation of freedom of expression. *Cantwell* is also important for having incorporated the Free Exercise Clause into the Fourteenth Amendment as a restriction on state action.

In *Braunfeld v. Brown*,[218] Jewish merchants challenged a Sunday closing law as violating their free exercise rights. *Braunfeld* was a companion case to *McGowan v. Maryland*,[219] in which the Court upheld Sunday closing laws against an Establishment Clause challenge. The *McGowan* Court reasoned that although Sunday closing laws were originally motivated by religious beliefs, their contemporary purpose and effect was to ensure a uniform day of rest for citizens. This secular purpose and effect insulated the law from claims that it impermissibly established Christianity by placing other religions at an economic disadvantage.

---

[213] 98 U.S. 145 (1878).

[214] *Id.* at 164.

[215] 310 U.S. 296 (1940).

[216] *Id.* at 303–04.

[217] *Id.* at 304.

[218] 366 U.S. 599 (1961).

[219] 366 U.S. 420 (1961).

In *Braunfeld*, the merchants claimed that because their religion already required them to close on Saturdays, the Sunday closing law had the effect of allowing them to conduct business only five days per week. This placed them at a competitive disadvantage with respect to merchants who could remain open six days a week. The Court upheld the Sunday closing law, distinguishing between laws that directly prohibited a particular religious practice and laws that indirectly burdened a religious practice as an unintended consequence. The Sunday closing law fell in the latter category, for it was not directed at forcing Jewish merchants to close an additional day, but merely required that all merchants close on Sunday. The Court also suggested that the State could enact a law exempting from the Sunday closing laws those merchants whose religious beliefs required them to close on another day, thus also suggesting that such a law would not be an invalid establishment.

While upholding the law against a free exercise challenge, the Court added that the law would have been invalid if the State could have accomplished its purpose in a manner that did not burden religious practice. This final caveat would play a part two years later in the Court's watershed decision in *Sherbert v. Verner*.[220] *Sherbert* marked the beginning of the modern Court's application of heightened scrutiny to laws burdening free exercise. In *Sherbert*, a Seventh-Day Adventist was denied unemployment compensation because she refused to work on Saturday, as required by her faith. Writing for the majority, Justice Brennan stated that in order to invalidate a statute under the Free Exercise Clause, the challenger must demonstrate that the law had the effect of substantially infringing on her religious practices. The Court explained that the infringement need only be incidental. Justice Brennan found that the denial of unemployment benefits because of religious beliefs constituted a "substantial infringement,"[221] or "coercive effect,"[222] on the free exercise of religion.

Once the challenger demonstrated a substantial burden on her free exercise of religion, the government must then justify that the substantial infringement on religion was justified by a compelling state interest. In *Sherbert*, the government claimed that the law was intended to prevent the filing of spurious claims by "claimants feigning religious objections to Saturday work."[223] The Court found no evidence that such a concern was well-founded. The government had not presented this interest to the state court; nor had it shown that spurious claims actually had diluted the unemployment fund. Moreover, even if the interest had been compelling, Justice Brennan declared that the government program must have been the least restrictive means to effectuate that interest. In *Sherbert*, the program discriminated in favor of Sunday worshipers. The government also failed to demonstrate that less restrictive means would not have combatted the alleged abuses of spurious claims. Justice Brennan did concede in the majority opinion that if one's religion dictated that one not work at all, a different result might have ensued.

---

[220] 374 U.S. 398 (1963).

[221] *Id.* at 406.

[222] *Id.* at 404.

[223] *Id.* at 407.

Justice Brennan distinguished *Sherbert* from *Braunfeld*. *Braunfeld* recognized that the Sunday closing law would make the practice of religious beliefs by Jewish merchants more expensive. Nevertheless, this burden on their religious beliefs was subsumed by the compelling state interest in having a uniform day of rest. The Sabbatarians could have been exempted from the law, but the *Braunfeld* Court found that the administrative burdens in allowing such exemptions were strong enough to overcome challenges to the law. Justice Brennan also found that in *Braunfeld*, the State maintained neutrality toward religion.

Justices Harlan and White dissented, arguing that there should be sufficient play in establishment and free exercise doctrine to permit deference to a range of legislative decisions. When viewed in light of *Estate of Thornton v. Caldor*,[224] it is clear that *Braunfeld* and *Sherbert* did not resolve the inherent tension between free exercise and establishment that arises in legislative attempts to draft constitutional Sunday closing laws. In *Estate of Thornton*, the Court struck down as an establishment of religion the state's attempt to eliminate the *Braunfeld* problem by providing an exemption for Sabbatarians. The 8-1 majority stressed that the absolute exemption made no allowances for the interests, religious or otherwise, of the employer or other employees.

One issue not addressed by the Court in *Braunfeld* or *Sherbert* was whether the conduct at issue was truly religiously-motivated. This question was fundamental to the Court's inquiry because if the challenger's basis for her objection to a law was not a religious belief, but some secular value instead, the Free Exercise Clause did not apply. In both *Braunfeld* and *Sherbert*, the Court assumed that the objection was religiously motivated because the Sabbatarian practices of Orthodox Jews and Seventh Day Adventists were well-established.

In *Wisconsin v. Yoder*,[225] the claimant's religious motivation was not as obvious. The parents of Amish children challenged the state's compulsory education laws, claiming that their children should be exempted from attending public school because of their religious beliefs. The Court concluded that the parents' objection was based on their religious beliefs, rather than merely their distinctive cultural values. Accordingly, it ruled that Amish children need not attend public school after the eighth grade. The Court considered a number of factors in determining whether the burdened conduct was a religious practice protected by the Free Exercise Clause, or whether it was merely a traditional way of life falling outside of the Clause's protection. Among the factors the Court considered were whether the practice was a shared belief by an organized group rather than a personal experience; whether the belief related to certain theocratic principles and the interpretation of religious literature; whether the system of beliefs pervaded and regulated the daily lives of the Amish; and whether the system of belief and the resultant lifestyle had existed for a substantial period of time.

After considering these factors, the Court concluded that the parents' objections to the compulsory education laws were religiously motivated. The Court then used a means/ends analysis to reject the State's asserted interests in compulsory

---

[224] 472 U.S. 703 (1985).

[225] 406 U.S. 205 (1972).

education and an informed citizenry. The Amish's own vocational training and the children's attendance in school through the eighth grade were sufficient to satisfy these interests. *Yoder* provided guidance in establishing what was a religious, as opposed to a secular, practice in the context of a group that was admittedly religious.

The detailed analysis performed by the Court in *Yoder* contrasted sharply with that of *Thomas v. Review Board*.[226] In *Thomas*, the Court ignored the *Yoder* factors and relied instead on a person's own convictions that a practice or belief was religiously motivated. *Thomas* afforded a Free Exercise Clause right to unemployment compensation for a Jehovah's Witness who quit his job because his religious beliefs prevented him from participating in the production of war materials.

Writing for the majority in *Thomas*, Chief Justice Burger set out a fair amount of the record revealing that another Jehovah's Witness did not object to producing war materials and that Thomas himself had wavered on his own convictions. The Court, however, eschewed any detailed analysis of the record and merely ruled that there was sufficient evidence to indicate that Thomas quit his job because of an "honest conviction" that his faith forbade producing war materials.[227] The Chief Justice explained that "it is not for us to say that the line [Thomas] drew was an unreasonable one . . . . Courts are not arbiters of scriptural interpretation."[228] No mention was made of the multiple factors set out in *Yoder* for determining whether an objection to a generally applicable law was truly religiously motivated or merely a matter of philosophical choice. After *Thomas*, the factors delineated by the Court in *Yoder* appear somewhat limited in influence as an analytical tool.

After assuming that a free exercise interest was at stake, the *Thomas* Court turned to the compelling state interest analysis articulated in *Sherbert* and *Yoder*. If a particular regulation, or a condition of a government benefit "unduly burdens" religion, it was generally invalid unless the burden on religion was no greater than necessary to promote an overriding secular interest. In *Thomas*, the state's asserted interest in preventing widespread unemployment was not supported by the record, and thus did not justify the burden placed on Thomas' religious beliefs.

Thomas illustrates the Court's reluctance to decide whether a particular belief or practice is "religious," and thus falls within the scope of protection of the Free Exercise Clause. In most cases, if there is any support in the record, the Court seems content to assume that a belief or practice is religiously motivated, preferring instead to weed out free exercise claims that lack merit by balancing interests under the compelling interest analysis. The Court's reluctance to decide this question is understandable as it would seem to require the Court to speculate on matters of theology. The question is an important one, however, because it considers the threshold issue of whether the Free Exercise Clause should apply at all to the conduct in question.

---

[226] 450 U.S. 707 (1981).

[227] *Id.* at 716.

[228] *Id.* at 715–16.

In *Locke v. Davey*,[229] the Court denied a challenge to a state college scholarship program that denied funds to students majoring in devotional theology. The scholarship program did not violate the Free Exercise Clause. High school graduates were given grants of $1,000 to $1,500 from the state's general fund to assist with college expenses. In 2000, the grant totaled $1,542 for students who met the academic and economic criteria required for eligibility. Consistent with the Washington Constitution, the grant could be used for any degree program except devotional theology. Despite receiving a scholarship, Davey was prohibited from using the funds to "pursue a double major in pastoral ministries and business management/administration" at Northwest College, a private, Christian college.[230]

Chief Justice Rehnquist noted that "the Establishment Clause and the Free Exercise Clause are frequently in tension," and to alleviate this tension there is " 'room for play in the joints' between them" so that "some state actions permitted by the Establishment Clause [are] not required by the Free Exercise Clause."[231] *Witters* held there was no violation of the Establishment Clause when funding a student's voluntary pursuit of a devotional theology degree, but the Free Exercise Clause did not require state funding of the program.[232] Such a program "imposes neither criminal nor civil sanctions on any type of religious service or rite," and "does not require students to choose between their religious beliefs and receiving a government benefit," because the government has not chosen "to fund a distinct category of instruction."[233]

Under the scholarship program, students may use the funds to "attend pervasively religious schools" or to attend schools that include devotional theology in their required classes.[234] Neither the operation of the scholarship program nor the Washington Constitution indicate any "animus towards religion," and such "denial of funding for vocational religious instruction alone is [not] inherently constitutionally suspect."[235] Washington has a substantial interest in excluding such funding, while the restriction places a minor burden on scholarship recipients.

In his dissent, Justice Scalia, joined by Justice Thomas, argued that the restriction was unconstitutional on its face because it withheld on the basis of religion a generally available benefit. In his own dissent, Justice Thomas noted that the program denied funding to pursue any degree in theology, while acknowledging that the parties agreed that "theology" was limited to degrees in "devotional theology."

Closely related to the issue of what constitutes a religious practice is the question of what constitutes a "religion" under the religion clauses. The Court had occasion to provide some guidance on this issue in its Establishment Clause decision in

---

[229] 540 U.S. 712 (2004).

[230] *Id.* at 717.

[231] *Id.* at 719 (citing *Walz v. Tax Comm'n of the City of New York*, 397 U.S. 664, 669 (1970)).

[232] Witters v. Wash. Dep't of Servs. for the Blind, 474 U.S. 481 (1986).

[233] *Locke*, 540 U.S. at 721.

[234] *Id.* at 724.

[235] *Id.* at 725.

Torcaso v. Watkins.[236] In *Torcaso,* the Court struck down a religious test for public office that required the candidate to profess a belief in God. In invalidating the test, Justice Black explained that the State could not "aid those religions based on a belief in the existence of God as against those religions founded on different beliefs."[237] In a footnote, Justice Black expanded on this passage: "Among religions in this country which do not teach what would generally be considered a belief in the existence of God are Buddhism, Taoism, Ethical Culture, Secular Humanism and others."[238] Thus, the Court's concept of what is "religious" is broad enough to include practices motivated by non-theistic ideologies. The difficulty with this approach is that there is no bright line for distinguishing between "religious" beliefs and beliefs premised on what are merely philosophical viewpoints. Because of this difficulty, the Court seems satisfied if the belief in question appears to be sincerely held by its proponent.

The Court has shed some light on the issue in its conscientious objector cases.[239] While those cases ostensibly involved questions of statutory construction rather than constitutional issues, many commentators think that the statutory construction has free exercise dimensions. In *United States v. Seeger,* for example, the Court stated that conscientious objector status might be conferred on those who held a "sincere and meaningful belief which occupies in the life of its possessor a place parallel to that filled by the God of those admittedly qualifying for the exemption."[240]

The Court affirmed its broad approach to this threshold issue in a recent free exercise case involving unemployment compensation. In *Frazee v. Illinois Department of Employment Security,*[241] the Court unanimously held unconstitutional Illinois' denial of unemployment benefits to William Frazee, who refused to work on Sundays because it was "the Lord's day." Frazee claimed to be a Christian, but not a member of a particular sect.

Justice White, writing the majority opinion, characterized *Sherbert, Thomas,* and *Hobbie v. Unemployment Appeals Commission*[242] as follows: "[N]one of those decisions turned on that consideration or on any tenet of the sect involved that forbade the work the claimant refused to perform. Our judgments in those cases rested on the fact that each of the claimants had a sincere belief that religion required him or her to refrain from the work in question."[243] Justice White continued: "There is no doubt that '[o]nly beliefs rooted in religion are protected by

---

[236] 367 U.S. 488 (1961).

[237] *Id.* at 495.

[238] *Id.* at n.11.

[239] *See* Gillette v. United States, 401 U.S. 437 (1971); Welsh v. United States, 398 U.S. 333 (1970); United States v. Seeger, 380 U.S. 163 (1965).

[240] 380 U.S. at 176.

[241] 489 U.S. 829 (1989).

[242] 480 U.S. 136 (1987). *Hobbie* followed in the tradition of *Sherbert* and *Yoder,* declaring unconstitutional a denial of unemployment benefits where the employee was fired for refusing to work on Saturdays after she had converted to the Seventh Day Adventist Church.

[243] *Frazee,* 489 U.S. at 832–33.

the Free Exercise Clause.' Purely secular views do not suffice. Nor do we underestimate the difficulty of distinguishing between religious and secular convictions and in determining whether a professed belief is sincerely held."[244] Because of that difficulty, the Court was willing to accept the claim that a belief is religiously motivated at face value. Perhaps because of this definitional problem, in cases where a "religious" belief or practice can also be characterized as expression, the Court has sometimes been more eager to decide the claim on free speech grounds. In *Wooley v. Maynard*,[245] for example, the Court ruled that two Jehovah's Witnesses could not be constitutionally subjected to criminal sanctions for covering over a license plate motto that they found repugnant to their religious beliefs. Skirting the specifically religious nature of appellee's objection, the Court based its decision on broad freedom of expression grounds.[246]

Sherbert, Yoder, Thomas, and *Hobbie* represent the apex of the Court's protection of free exercise of religion. In recent years, the Court has appeared less willing to recognize free exercise exceptions to generally-applicable laws. In some cases, the Court has rejected the free exercise claim because the balance tips in favor of the interest asserted by the state. In *Goldsboro Christian Schools v. United States*,[247] a school that went from kindergarten through high school denied admission to blacks based on the Biblically-premised religious beliefs of the sect running the school. In *Bob Jones University v. United States*,[248] a religious university claimed that its denomination did not allow interracial marriage or dating. The Court held that these claims were "sincerely-held religious beliefs" protected by the Free Exercise Clause. Nevertheless, the government's interest in preventing racial discrimination in education constituted a compelling state interest under *Sherbert*. The Court relied on the belief/conduct distinction articulated in earlier decisions and stated that the First Amendment created an absolute prohibition against regulation of religious beliefs. However, the "Court has found certain governmental interests so compelling as to allow even regulations prohibiting religiously based conduct."[249] In this case, the government only denied tax exempt status.

In certain special contexts, such as cases involving the military or the administration of the Social Security program, the Court also has permitted governmental interests to override free exercise concerns even though those interests might not be considered "compelling." *Goldman v. Weinberger*[250] evidences the fairly lax scrutiny with which the Court analyzes military regulations that allegedly interfere with free exercise rights. Justice Rehnquist, writing for the majority, emphasized

---

[244] *Id.* at 833. For further discussion of this issue, *see* L. TRIBE, AMERICAN CONSTITUTIONAL LAW 1179–88 (2d ed. 1988); J. Choper, *Defining "Religion" in the First Amendment*, 1982 U. ILL. L. REV. 579; S. Ingber, *Religion or Ideology: A Needed Clarification of the Religion Clauses*, 41 STAN. L. REV. 233 (1989).

[245] 430 U.S. 705 (1977).

[246] *See also* Board of Educ. v. Barnette, 319 U.S. 624 (1943) (striking down a statute requiring public school students, even those who objected on religious grounds, to salute the flag).

[247] 454 U.S. 1121 (1981).

[248] 461 U.S. 574 (1983).

[249] *Id.* at 603.

[250] 475 U.S. 503 (1986).

that military regulations are entitled to considerable deference. Accordingly, the Court upheld a regulation forbidding an Orthodox Jew from wearing his yarmulke while on duty. Similarly, in *Bowen v. Roy*,[251] the Court refused to recognize a religiously-motivated challenge to the use of Social Security numbers for welfare programs. The Native American claimant believed that the use of a Social Security number would spiritually prejudice his daughter. The "legitimate and important public interest" of preventing welfare fraud, however, overrode the claimant's free exercise concerns.[252]

Even outside of such special contexts, the Court in recent years has often allowed government programs to prevail over free exercise concerns. In *Lyng v. Northwest Indian Cemetery*,[253] the result turned on resurrecting the direct/indirect burden distinction made in *Braunfeld*. In *Lyng*, a 5-3 majority permitted the United States Forest Service to construct a road through Native American burial grounds in a national forest that were used by three tribes for sacramental purposes. Justice O'Connor's majority opinion distinguished the free exercise burden in this case from those in *Sherbert, Thomas, Yoder,* and *Hobbie*. Instead, she analogized the burden to that in *Roy*: "In neither [*Roy* nor *Lyng*] would the affected individuals be coerced by the Government's action into violating their religious beliefs; nor would either governmental action penalize religious activity by denying any person an equal share of the rights, benefits, and privileges enjoyed by other citizens."[254] For Justice O'Connor, the compelling state interest test did not even come into play. Although the Court had consistently held that even indirect burdens on free exercise were subject to strict scrutiny, Justice O'Connor reasoned:

> This does not and cannot imply that incidental effects of government programs, which may make it more difficult to practice certain religions but which have no tendency to coerce individuals into acting contrary to their religious beliefs, require government to bring forward a compelling justi-fication for its otherwise lawful actions. The crucial word in the constitu-tional text is "prohibit."[255]

Justice Brennan's sharp dissent challenged the notion that the Free Exercise Clause prohibited only government actions that coerced conduct inconsistent with religious belief. The constitutional guarantee " 'is directed against any form of government action that frustrates or inhibits religious practice.' "[256]

In *Hernandez v. Commissioner*,[257] the Court also rejected a free exercise claim without applying the *Sherbert* compelling interest test. This time, the Court rejected the claim on the threshold issue of whether the government action had

---

[251] 476 U.S. 693 (1986).

[252] *Id.* at 709; *see also* United States v. Lee, 455 U.S. 252 (1982) (rejecting a free exercise challenge to paying Social Security tax because of the government's "very high" interest in assuring comprehensive participation in the Social Security program).

[253] 485 U.S. 439 (1988).

[254] *Id.* at 449.

[255] *Id.* at 450–51.

[256] *Id.* at 456 (Brennan, J., dissenting).

[257] 490 U.S. 680 (1989).

imposed a substantial burden on free exercise of religion. Petitioners were members of the Church of Scientology, a sect supported primarily by payments made by members in return for one-on-one "auditing," or counseling. The Internal Revenue Service disallowed the deductibility of these payments on the ground that they were a "*quid pro quo* exchange," rather than a "contribution or gift" under 26 U.S.C. § 170(c).[258]

Justice Marshall first distinguished this case from *United States v. Lee.*[259] In *Lee*, the Court found that a religious objection to paying social security tax was outweighed by the government's interest in assuring comprehensive participation in the Social Security program. In contrast, the Church of Scientology did not forbid the payment of taxes. Thus, petitioners were not placed in the position of either violating their faith or facing criminal sanctions. Moreover, the burden of having less money to spend on "auditing" because of the denial of the deductibility of payments "would seem to pale by comparison to the overall federal income tax burden."[260] Justice Marshall rejected the argument that "an incrementally larger tax burden interferes with their religious activities."[261] Such an argument "knows no limitation."[262]

A recent low point for the scope of protection afforded by the Free Exercise Clause came with the 1990 decision of *Department of Human Resources v. Smith*.[263] Justice Scalia's majority opinion severely constricted the use of the *Sherbert* compelling interest test. The dispute in *Smith* began when respondents, who were members of the Native American Church, were fired from their jobs at a private drug rehabilitation center for ingesting peyote as part of a sacramental ritual. The State of Oregon determined that they were ineligible for unemployment benefits because they had been fired for work-related misconduct. The Oregon Supreme Court interpreted the state's controlled substance laws to prohibit the ingestion of peyote, even for sacramental purposes.

Justice Scalia first asserted that the only governmental action ever invalidated by the Court under the *Sherbert* test was the denial of unemployment benefits in *Sherbert, Thomas,* and *Hobbie.* He noted that such decisions did not involve the violation of a criminal statute as in the present case. Justice Scalia further distinguished the unemployment cases as involving exemption systems that entailed "individualized government assessment" of the reasons for the relevant conduct.[264] Only in such circumstances did the *Sherbert* test require the government to show a compelling reason for creating a burden on the exercise of religion. Moreover, Justice Scalia noted, although the Court's decisions in *Yoder* and *Cantwell* did

---

[258] The Internal Revenue Code qualities certain organizations for tax exempt status, entitling them to receive charitable contributions.

[259] 455 U.S. 252 (1982).

[260] *Hernandez*, 490 U.S. at 699.

[261] *Id.* at 700.

[262] *Id.*

[263] 494 U.S. 872 (1990).

[264] *Id.* at 884.

invalidate generally applicable statutes, those decisions were "hybrid situation[s]," also involving free speech claims.[265]

Smith, however, was a non-hybrid case involving a neutral, generally applicable statute. According to Justice Scalia, the use of the *Sherbert* test to require government to show a compelling interest under such circumstances would be tantamount to making a religious objector, "by virtue of his beliefs, 'to become a law unto himself.' "[266] Applying the *Sherbert* compelling state interest test to all cases involving a religiously-grounded objection to a neutral, generally-applicable law "would open the prospect of constitutionally required religious exemptions from civic obligations of almost every conceivable kind."[267] Oregon's prohibition of peyote use was a generally applicable law that easily passed muster.

Justice O'Connor concurred in the judgment, joined in part by Justices Brennan, Marshall, and Blackmun. Justice O'Connor strenuously objected to the majority's interpretation of precedent and its rejection of the *Sherbert* test. Neither the Court's prior decisions, nor "[t]he First Amendment . . . distinguish[es] between laws that are generally applicable and laws that target particular religious practices."[268] Justice O'Connor countered Justice Scalia's slippery slope argument by observing that courts using the *Sherbert* test have been successful in "strik[ing] sensible balances between religious liberty and competing state interests."[269] For Justice O'Connor, that balance was struck when the government could demonstrate a compelling state interest. In a portion of her opinion in which Justices Brennan, Marshall, and Blackmun did not join, she concluded that the state of Oregon had a sufficiently compelling interest in controlling illicit drug use to overcome respondents' free exercise claim.

Justice Blackmun dissented, joined by Justices Brennan and Marshall. Because the sacramental use of peyote was "integral" to respondents' worship, and because the state's justification for refusing to exempt such use from its criminal laws was "entirely speculative," Justice Blackmun would balance the interests at issue in favor of respondents.[270]

Smith's constriction of the *Sherbert* compelling interest test was left untouched in *Church of the Lukumi Babalu Aye, Inc. v. City of Hialeah*.[271] In *Lukumi*, the Court invalidated under the Free Exercise Clause an ordinance enacted to prevent members of the Santeria faith from performing animal sacrifices, a principal tenet of their religion. In response to the imminent founding of a Santeria church in Hialeah, Florida, the city council passed various ordinances prohibiting religious ritual animal sacrifice with certain exceptions. Consistent with *Smith*, the *Lukumi* Court premised its decision on the fact that the ordinances, though ostensibly of general applicability, were not neutral, but directed at the Santerias specifically.

---

[265] *Id.* at 882.

[266] *Id.* at 885 (quoting *Reynolds*, 98 U.S. at 167).

[267] *Id.* at 888.

[268] *Id.* at 894 (O'Connor, J., concurring).

[269] *Id.* at 902.

[270] *Id.* at 911 (Blackmun, J., dissenting).

[271] 508 U.S. 520 (1993).

Justice Kennedy wrote for the majority in all but one section of the opinion. Relying on *Smith*, the Court scrutinized the neutrality and general applicability of the ordinances at issue. An ordinance's language or context could indicate lack of facial neutrality. Although the ordinances at issue mentioned "sacrifice" and "ritual," these terms did not conclusively impair facial neutrality as they had secular as well as religious meanings. Nonetheless, the ordinances represented masked hostility against the Santeria religion because their object was to suppress that religion.

While adverse impact will not always establish "an impermissible targeting," Santeria rituals were nearly the only conduct affected by the ordinances. The ordinances had many exceptions, including Kosher slaughter, hunting, and fishing. In fact, the ordinances allowed ritualistic animal killing, so long as the animal was raised and killed for food purposes and the slaughter occurred on properly zoned and licensed property. Providing such individualized exceptions without making an exception for religious practices demonstrated a lack of neutrality that government must justify with compelling reasons.

The fact that the ordinances were not narrowly tailored also suggested that the City sought to suppress Santeria sacrifices. Undercutting its purported interest in public health, the City conceded that the ordinances would prohibit Santeria sacrifices even if performed in properly zoned and licensed slaughterhouses. The interest in preventing animal cruelty could have been achieved by narrower restrictions directed to those ends.

In addition to lacking neutrality, the ordinances were not generally applicable. The ordinances were substantially underinclusive with regard to achieving the asserted government interests. Rather than generally promoting the City's purported interest in preventing cruelty to animals, they prohibited few slaughters other than those performed during Santeria worship. Undercutting the City's asserted public health concerns, the ordinances failed to address improper disposal after nonreligious animal killings.

Regulations that were not neutral or not generally applicable had to be narrowly tailored to advance a compelling state interest. Justice Kennedy concluded that the City's asserted interests were not compelling. The fact that the ordinances impermissibly restricted only protected religious conduct and failed to restrict secular conduct resulting in similar harm impaired the compelling nature of the city's asserted interests. In separate opinions, Justice Souter and Justice Blackmun, joined by Justice O'Connor, concurred in judgment but called for a reexamination of *Smith*.

Although the *Lukumi* decision appears more friendly to free exercise claims, it is a decision of limited applicability. Most free exercise claims do not involve laws that so obviously discriminate against religious exercise. Instead, most free exercise claims involve laws in the *Smith* genre; that is, laws which are facially neutral, generally applicable, and only burden religion incidentally. Thus, as a practical matter, the *Lukumi* decision's limited reach leaves *Smith's* general rejection of strict scrutiny in free exercise cases essentially intact.

Smith faces attack from another camp, however. In 1993, Congress passed the Religious Freedom Restoration Act,[272] expressly aimed at restoring the *Sherbert* compelling interest test to free exercise jurisprudence.[273] Congress expressly found that in *Employment Division v. Smith,* the Supreme Court virtually eliminated the requirement that the government justify burdens on religious exercise imposed by laws neutral toward religion . . . [T]he compelling interest test as set forth in prior Federal court rulings is a workable test for striking sensible balances between religious liberty and competing prior governmental interests.[274] Section 2000bb-1 essentially codifies the *Sherbert* compelling interest test, providing that government may only substantially burden a person's exercise of religion if it demonstrates that its interest is compelling and that the means chosen is the least restrictive of alternatives.[275]

In *City of Boerne v. Flores,*[276] the Court struck down the Religious Freedom Restoration Act of 1993 (RFRA) because it exceeded Congress' remedial authority under Section 5 of the Fourteenth Amendment. In this case, a religious group challenged under RFRA the denial of permission to enlarge a church under an historic landmark preservation ordinance.

Congress passed RFRA in reaction to the Court's decision in *Department of Human Resources v. Smith.* RFRA was enacted to prevent all levels of government from interfering with the free exercise of religion through laws of general application unless the government could show that the law furthered compelling government interest and was the least restrictive alternative available. Writing for the Court, Justice Kennedy found that RFRA altered the meaning of the Free Exercise Clause, "changing what the right is," and not simply enforcing the Clause.[277] The Court also noted that it had not construed the Free Exercise Clause to require a least restrictive alternative test even before the *Smith* decision.

Comparing RFRA with the Voting Rights Act, the Court noted that the legislative history of the RFRA was bereft of examples demonstrating instances of laws of general application being motivated by religious bigotry. Instead of responding or preventing unconstitutional behavior, RFRA unconstitutionally altered substantive constitutional rights.

---

[272] Religious Freedom Restoration Act of 1993, Pub. L. No. 103-141, 107 Stat. 1488 (codified at 42 U.S.C. § 2000bb).

[273] Congress made its intentions quite clear in this respect:

The purposes of this chapter are—

(1) to restore the compelling interest test as set forth in *Sherbert v. Verner,* 374 U.S. 398 (1963) and *Wisconsin v. Yoder,* 406 U.S. 205 (1972) and to guarantee its application in all cases where free exercise of religion is substantially burdened; and

(2) to provide a claim or defense to persons whose religious exercise is substantially burdened by government.

42 U.S.C. § 2000bb(b) (1988).

[274] 42 U.S.C. §§ 2000bb(a)(4), 2000bb(a)(5). Note the similarity in language with Justice O'Connor's concurrence in *Smith.*

[275] 42 U.S.C. § 2000bb-1(b).

[276] 521 U.S. 507 (1997).

[277] 521 U.S. at 508.

Concurring, Justice Stevens maintained that RFRA violated the Establishment Clause, as it gave to religious institutions and believers a tool not available to atheists or agnostics.

Defending his decision in *Smith* against Justice O'Connor's dissent, Justice Scalia concluded that legislatures, not courts, ought to fashion exemptions to laws of general applicability to advance religious freedom.

Justice O'Connor dissented, joined by Justice Breyer. Justice O'Connor agreed that RFRA was not a proper exercise of Congress' enforcement power under Section 5 of the Fourteenth Amendment (although Justice Breyer did not think it necessary to reach this conclusion). Justice O'Connor argued that *Smith* was wrongly decided. By the time the Bill of Rights was adopted, government accommodation of religion was commonly accepted. Disputing Justice Scalia's claim that only legislatures made religious accommodations, she noted that early in our history, the principle of judicial review had not yet developed.

In a separate dissent, Justice Souter also seriously questioned the validity of *Smith* by also involving Justice O'Connor's historical arguments.

In *Cutter v. Wilkinson*,[278] the Court rejected a facial challenge asserting that the Religious Land Use and Institutionalized Persons Act of 2000 (RLUIPA) violates the Establishment Clause. The plaintiffs alleged a violation of their right to practice " 'nonmainstream' religions" such as "Satanist, Wicca, and Asatru" and "the Church of Jesus Christ Christian," as protected by the RLUIPA.

In *Locke v. Davey*, the Court had discussed the " 'play in the joints between' the Free Exercise and Establishment Clauses." After the Court struck down the Religious Freedom Restoration Act in *City of Boerne v. Flores*, Congress passed the RLUIPA under their Spending and Commerce powers. The Act applies to institutions receiving federal funds, or interstate or international commerce. One section deals with "land-use regulation;" and the other, with "religious exercise by institutionalized persons." The section at issue prohibited substantial burdens on religious exercise unless "the burden furthers 'a compelling governmental interest' and does so by 'the least restrictive means.' " The Court declared that this Act fell within the space between the two religion clauses, and was a "permissible legislative accommodation of religion."

The Act "alleviates exceptional government-created burdens on private religious exercise," for it applied to institutions such as mental hospitals and prisons, where government control was unparalleled. In applying the RLUIPA, "courts must take adequate account of the burdens a requested accommodation may impose on nonbeneficiaries," and ensure that it is "administered neutrally among different faiths." In this case, the state already provided for "religious services for mainstream faiths." RLUIPA did not "elevate accommodation of religious observances over an institution's need to maintain order and safety." It simply must be "applied in an appropriately balanced way, with particular sensitivity to security concerns." Justice Thomas wrote a concurring opinion.

---

[278] 544 U.S. 709 (2005).

In *Gonzales v. O Centro Espirita Beneficente Uniao do Vegetal* (UDV),[279] the Court upheld a preliminary injunction prohibiting the government from enforcing the Controlled Substances Act ban on the defendant's use of a sacramental tea, *hoasca*. Defendant used the tea as part of communion.

The Religious Freedom Restoration Act of 1993 (RFRA) required the government to satisfy the compelling interest test when the "sincere exercise of religion is being substantially burdened." Additionally, the Controlled Substances Act allowed for such exemptions. Congress allowed courts to find exemptions to the Act, and made an exemption for Indian Tribes with respect to peyote, another Schedule 1 substance. This specific exemption undermined the government's argument that the uniform application of the Controlled Substances Act was a compelling interest. The government failed to show a compelling interest in prohibiting "UDV's sacramental use of *hoasca*."

---

[279] 546 U.S. 418 (2006).

CONSTITUTION OF THE UNITED STATES

WE THE PEOPLE of the United States, in Order to form a more perfect Union, establish Justice, insure domestic Tranquility, provide for the common defence, promote the general Welfare, and secure the Blessings of Liberty to ourselves and our Posterity, do ordain and establish this Constitution for the United States of America.

ARTICLE I

SECTION 1.

All legislative Powers herein granted shall be vested in a Congress of the United States, which shall consist of a Senate and House of Representatives.

SECTION 2.

1* The House of Representatives shall be composed of Members chosen every second Year by the People of the several States, and the Electors in each State shall have the Qualifications requisite for Electors of the most numerous Branch of the State Legislature.

2 No Person shall be a Representative who shall not have attained to the Age of twenty-five Years, and been seven Years a Citizen of the United States, and who shall not, when elected, be an Inhabitant of that State in which he shall be chosen.

3 [Representatives and direct Taxes shall be apportioned among the several States which may be included within this Union, according to their respective Numbers, which shall be determined by adding to the whole Number of free Persons, including those bound to Service for a Term of Years, and excluding Indians not taxed, three fifths of all other Persons.]** The actual Enumeration shall be made within three Years after the first Meeting of the Congress of the United States, and within every subsequent Term of ten years, in such Manner as they shall by Law direct. The Number of Representatives shall not exceed one for every thirty Thousand, but each State shall have at Least one Representative; and until such enumeration shall be made, the State of New Hampshire shall be entitled to chuse three, Massachusetts eight, Rhode-Island and Providence Plantations one, Connecticut five, New-York six, New Jersey four, Pennsylvania eight, Delaware one, Maryland six, Virginia ten, North Carolina five, South Carolina five, and Georgia three.

4 When vacancies happen in the Representation from any State, the Executive Authority thereof shall issue Writs of Election to fill such vacancies.

---

* Note: The superior number preceding the paragraphs designates the number of the clause.

** Note: The part included in brackets was changed by amendments XIII, XIV, and XV.

5 The House of Representatives shall chuse their Speaker and other Officers; and shall have the sole Power of Impeachment.

SECTION 3.

1 The Senate of the United States shall be composed of two Senators from each State, [chosen by the Legislature]* thereof, for six Years; and each Senator shall have one Vote.

2 Immediately after they shall be assembled in Consequence of the first Election, they shall be divided as equally as may be into three Classes. The Seats of the Senators of the first Class shall be vacated at the Expiration of the Second Year, of the second Class at the Expiration of the fourth Year, and the third Class at the Expiration of the sixth Year, so that one-third may be chosen every second Year; [and if Vacancies happen by Resignation, or otherwise, during the Recess of the Legislature of any State, the Executive thereof may make temporary Appointments until the next Meeting of the Legislature, which shall then fill such Vacancies].**

3 No Person shall be a Senator who shall not have attained to the Age of thirty Years, and been nine Years a Citizen of the United States, and who shall not, when elected, be an inhabitant of that State for which he shall be chosen.

4 The Vice President of the United States shall be President of the Senate, but shall have no Vote, unless they be equally divided.

5 The Senate shall chuse their other Officers, and also a President pro tempore, in the absence of the Vice President, or when he shall exercise the Office of President of the United States.

6 The Senate shall have the sole Power to try all Impeachments. When sitting for that Purpose, they shall be on Oath or Affirmation. When the President of the United States is tried, the Chief Justice shall preside: And no Person shall be convicted without the Concurrence of two-thirds of the Members present.

7 Judgment in Cases of Impeachment shall not extend further than to removal from Office, and disqualification to hold and enjoy any Office of honor, Trust, or Profit under the United States: but the Party convicted shall nevertheless be liable and subject to Indictment, Trial, Judgment, and Punishment, according to Law.

SECTION 4.

1 The Times, Places and Manner of holding Elections for Senators and Representatives, shall be prescribed in each State by the Legislature thereof; but the Congress may at any time by Law make or alter such Regulations, except as to the Places of chusing Senators.

2 The Congress shall assemble at least once in every Year, and such Meeting shall [be on the first Monday in December,] unless they shall by Law appoint a different

---

* The part included in brackets was repealed by clause 1 of amendment XVII.

** The part included in brackets was changed by clause 2 of amendment XVII.

Day.*

SECTION 5.

1 Each House shall be the Judge of the Elections, Returns, and Qualifications of its own Members, and a Majority of each shall constitute a Quorum to do Business; but a smaller Number may adjourn from day to day, and may be authorized to compel the Attendance of absent Members, in such Manner, and under such Penalties as each House may provide.

2 Each House may determine the Rules of its Proceedings, punish its Members for disorderly Behavior, and, with the Concurrence of two thirds expel a Member.

3 Each House shall keep a Journal of its Proceedings, and from time to time publish the same, excepting such Parts as may in their Judgment require Secrecy; and the Yeas and Nays of the Members of either House on any question shall, at the Desire of one fifth of those Present, be entered on the Journal.

4 Neither House, during the Session of Congress, shall, without the Consent of the other, adjourn for more than three days, nor to any other Place than that in which the two Houses shall be sitting.

SECTION 6.

1 The Senators and Representatives shall receive a Compensation for their Services, to be ascertained by Law, and paid out of the Treasury of the United States. They shall in all Cases, except Treason, Felony and Breach of the Peace, be privileged from Arrest during their Attendance at the Session of their respective Houses, and in going to and returning from the same; and for any Speech or Debate in either House, they shall not be questioned in any other Place.

2 No Senator or Representative shall, during the Time for which he was elected, be appointed to any civil Office under the Authority of the United States, which shall have been created, or the Emoluments whereof shall have been encreased during such time; and no Person holding any Office under the United States, shall be a Member of either House during his Continuance in Office.

SECTION 7.

1 All Bills for raising Revenue shall originate in the House of Representatives; but the Senate may propose or concur with Amendments as on other Bills.

2 Every Bill which shall have passed the House of Representatives and the Senate, shall, before it become a Law, be presented to the President of the United States; if he approve he shall sign it, but if not he shall return it, with his Objections to that House in which it shall have originated, who shall enter the Objections at large on their Journal, and proceed to reconsider it. If after such Reconsideration two thirds of that House shall agree to pass the Bill, it shall be sent, together with the Objections, to the other House, by which it shall likewise be reconsidered, and if approved by two thirds of that House, it shall become a Law. But in all such Cases

---

* The part included in brackets was changed by section 2 of amendment XX.

the Votes of both Houses shall be determined by Yeas and Nays, and the Names of the Persons voting for and against the Bill shall be entered on the Journal of each House respectively. If any Bill shall not be returned by the President within ten Days (Sundays excepted) after it shall have been presented to him, the Same shall be a Law, in like Manner as if he had signed it, unless the Congress by their Adjournment prevent its Return, in which Case it shall not be a Law.

3 Every Order, Resolution, or Vote to which the Concurrence of the Senate and House of Representatives may be necessary (except on a question of Adjournment) shall be presented to the President of the United States; and before the Same shall take Effect, shall be approved by him, or being disapproved by him, shall be repassed by two thirds of the Senate and House of Representatives, according to the Rules and Limitations prescribed in the Case of a Bill.

SECTION 8.

1 The Congress shall have Power To lay and collect Taxes, Duties, Imposts and Excises, to pay the Debts and provide for the common Defence and general Welfare of the United States; but all Duties, Imposts and Excises shall be uniform throughout the United States;

2 To borrow money on the credit of the United States;

3 To regulate Commerce with foreign Nations, and among the several States, and with the Indian Tribes;

4 To establish an uniform Rule of Naturalization, and uniform Laws on the subject of Bankruptcies throughout the United States;

5 To coin Money, regulate the Value thereof, and of foreign Coin, and fix the Standard of Weights and Measures;

6 To provide for the Punishment of counterfeiting the Securities and current Coin of the United States;

7 To Establish Post Offices and post Roads;

8 To promote the Progress of Science and useful Arts, by securing for limited Times to Authors and Inventors the exclusive Right to their respective Writings and Discoveries;

9 To constitute Tribunals inferior to the supreme Court;

10 To define and punish Piracies and Felonies committed on the high Seas, and Offenses against the Law of Nations;

11 To declare War, grant Letters of Marque and Reprisal, and make Rules concerning Captures on Land and Water;

12 To raise and support Armies, but no Appropriation of Money to that Use shall be for a longer Term than two Years;

13 To provide and maintain a Navy;

14 To make Rules for the Government and Regulation of the land and naval Forces;

15 To provide for calling forth the Militia to execute the Laws of the Union, suppress insurrections and repel Invasions;

16 To provide for organizing, arming, and disciplining the Militia, and for governing such Part of them as may be employed in the Service of the United States, reserving to the States respectively, the Appointment of the Officers, and the Authority of training the Militia according to the discipline prescribed by Congress;

17 To exercise exclusive Legislation in all Cases whatsoever, over such District (not exceeding ten Miles square) as may, by Cession of particular States, and the acceptance of Congress, become the Seat of the Government of the United States, and to exercise like Authority over all Places purchased by the Consent of the Legislature of the State in which the Same shall be, for the Erection of Forts, Magazines, Arsenals, dock-Yards, and other needful Buildings; And

18 To make all Laws which shall be necessary and proper for carrying into Execution the foregoing Powers, and all other Powers vested by this Constitution in the Government of the United States, or in any Department or Officer thereof.

SECTION 9.

1 The Migration or Importation of Such Persons as any of the States now existing shall think proper to admit, shall not be prohibited by the Congress prior to the Year one thousand eight hundred and eight, but a tax or duty may be imposed on such Importation, not exceeding ten dollars for each Person.

2 The privilege of the Writ of Habeas Corpus shall not be suspended, unless when in Cases of Rebellion or Invasion the public Safety may require it.

3 No Bill of Attainder or ex post facto Law shall be passed.

4* No capitation, or other direct, Tax shall be laid, unless in Proportion to the Census or Enumeration herein before directed to be taken.

5 No Tax or Duty shall be laid on Articles exported from any State.

6 No preference shall be given by any Regulation of Commerce or Revenue to the Ports of one State over those of another: nor shall Vessels bound to, or from, one State be obliged to enter, clear, or pay Duties in another.

7 No money shall be drawn from the Treasury, but in Consequence of Appropriations made by Law; and a regular Statement and Account of the Receipts and Expenditures of all public Money shall be published from time to time.

8 No title of Nobility shall be granted by the United States: And no Person holding any Office of Profit or Trust under them, shall, without the Consent of the Congress, accept of any present, Emolument, Office, or Title, of any kind whatever, from any King, Prince, or foreign State.

---

* *See also* amendment XVI.

SECTION 10.

1 No State shall enter into any Treaty, Alliance, or Confederation; grant Letters of Marque and Reprisal; coin Money; emit Bills of Credit; make any Thing but gold and silver Coin a Tender in Payment of Debts; pass any Bill of Attainder, ex post facto Law, or Law impairing the Obligation of Contracts, or grant any Title of Nobility.

2 No State shall, without the Consent of the Congress, lay any Imposts or Duties on Imports or Exports, except what may be absolutely necessary for executing its inspection Laws; and the net Produce of all Duties and Imposts, laid by any State on Imports or Exports, shall be for the Use of the Treasury of the United States; and all such Laws shall be subject to the Revision and Control of the Congress.

3 No State shall, without the Consent of Congress, lay any duty of Tonnage, keep Troops, or Ships of War in time of Peace, enter into any Agreement or Compact with another State, or with a foreign Power, or engage in War, unless actually invaded, or in such imminent Danger as will not admit of delay.

ARTICLE II

SECTION 1.

1 The executive Power shall be vested in a President of the United States of America. He shall hold his Office during the Term of four Years, and, together with the Vice-President, chosen for the same Term, be elected, as follows:

2 Each State shall appoint, in such Manner as the Legislature thereof may direct, a Number of Electors, equal to the whole Number of Senators and Representatives to which the State may be entitled in the Congress: but no Senator or Representative, or Person holding an Office of Trust or Profit under the United States, shall be appointed an Elector.

[The Electors shall meet in their respective States, and vote by Ballot for two persons of whom one at least shall not be an Inhabitant of the same State with themselves. And they shall make a list of all the Persons voted for, and of the Number of Votes for each; which List they shall sign and certify, and transmit sealed to the Seat of the Government of the United States, directed to the President of the Senate. The President of the Senate shall, in the Presence of the Senate and House of Representatives, open all the Certificates, and the Votes shall then be counted. The Person having the greatest Number of Votes shall be the President, if such Number by a Majority of the whole Number of Electors appointed; and if there be more than one who have such Majority, and have an equal number of Votes, then the House of Representatives shall immediately chuse by Ballot one of them for President; and if no Person have a Majority, then from the five highest on the List the said House shall in like Manner chuse the President. But in chusing the President, the Votes shall be taken by States, the Representation from each State having one Vote; A quorum for this Purpose shall consist of a Member or Members from two-thirds of the States, and a Majority of all the States shall be necessary to a Choice. In every Case, after the Choice of the President the Person having the greatest Number of Votes of the Electors shall be the Vice President. But if there should remain two or more who have equal Votes, the Senate shall chuse from them by Ballot the Vice President.]*

3 The Congress may determine the Time of chusing the Electors and the Day on which they shall give their Votes; which Day shall be the same throughout the United States.

4 No person except a natural born Citizen, or a Citizen of the United States, at the time of the Adoption of this Constitution, shall be eligible to the Office of President; neither shall any Person be eligible to that Office who shall not have attained to the Age of thirty-five Years, and been fourteen Years a Resident within the United States.

5 In case of the removal of the President from Office, or of his Death, Resignation or Inability to discharge the Powers and Duties of the said Office, the same shall devolve on the Vice President, and the Congress may by Law provide for the Case of Removal, Death, Resignation or Inability, both of the President, and Vice President, declaring what Officer shall then act as President, and such Officer shall act accordingly, until the Disability be removed, or a President shall be elected.

6 The President shall, at stated Times, receive for his Services, a Compensation, which shall neither be encreased nor diminished during the Period for which he shall have been elected, and he shall not receive within that Period any other Emolument from the United States, or any of them.

7 Before he enter on the Execution of His Office, he shall take the following Oath or Affirmation: "I do solemnly swear (or affirm) that I will faithfully execute the Office of President of the United States, and will to the best of my Ability, preserve, protect and defend the Constitution of the United States."

SECTION 2.

1 The President shall be Commander in Chief of the Army and Navy of the United States, and of the Militia of the several States, when called into the actual Service of the United States; he may require the Opinion, in writing, of the principal Officer in each of the executive Departments, upon any subject relating to the Duties of their respective Offices, and he shall have Power to grant Reprieves and Pardons for Offences against the United States, except in Cases of Impeachment.

2 He shall have Power, by and with the Advice and Consent of the Senate, to make Treaties, provided two-thirds of the Senators present concur; and he shall nominate, and by and with the Advice and Consent of the Senate, shall appoint Ambassadors, other public Ministers and Consuls, Judges of the supreme Court, and all other Officers of the United States, whose Appointments are not herein otherwise provided for, and which shall be established by Law; but the Congress may by Law vest the Appointment of such inferior Officers, as they think proper, in the President alone, in the Courts of Law, or in the Heads of Departments.

3 The President shall have Power to fill up all Vacancies that may happen during the Recess of the Senate, by granting Commissions which shall expire at the End

---

* The part included in brackets has been superseded by section 3 of amendment XII.

of their next Session.

SECTION 3.

He shall from time to time give to the Congress Information of the State of the Union, and recommend to their Consideration such Measures as he shall judge necessary and expedient; he may, on extraordinary Occasions, convene both Houses, or either of them, and in Case of Disagreement between them, with Respect to the Time of Adjournment, he may adjourn them to such Time as he shall think proper; he shall receive Ambassadors and other public Ministers; he shall take Care that the Laws be faithfully executed, and shall Commission all the Officers of the United States.

SECTION 4.

The President, Vice President and all civil Officers of the United States, shall be removed from Office on Impeachment for, and Conviction of, Treason, Bribery, or other high Crimes and Misdemeanors.

ARTICLE III

SECTION 1.

The judicial Power of the United States, shall be vested in one supreme Court, and in such inferior Courts as the Congress may from time to time ordain and establish. The Judges, both of the supreme and inferior Courts, shall hold their Offices during good Behavior, and shall, at stated Times, receive for their Services a Compensation which shall not be diminished during their Continuance in Office.

SECTION 2.

1 The judicial Power shall extend to all Cases, in Law and Equity, arising under this Constitution, the Laws of the United States, and Treaties made, or which shall be made, under their Authority; to all Cases affecting Ambassadors, other public Ministers and Consuls; to all Cases of admiralty and maritime Jurisdiction; to Controversies to which the United States shall be a Party; to Controversies between two or more States; between a State and Citizens of another State;* between Citizens of different States; between Citizens of the same State claiming Lands under Grants of different States, and between a State, or the Citizens thereof, and foreign States, Citizens or Subjects.

2 In all Cases affecting Ambassadors, other public Ministers and Consuls, and those in which a State shall be Party, the supreme Court shall have original Jurisdiction. In all the other Cases before mentioned, the supreme Court shall have appellate Jurisidiction, both as to Law and Fact, with such Exceptions, and under such Regulations as the Congress shall make.

3 The trial of all Crimes except in Cases of Impeachment shall be by Jury; and such Trial shall be held in the State where the said Crimes shall have been

---

* This clause has been affected by amendment XI.

committed; but when not committed within any State, the Trial shall be at such Place or Places as the Congress may by Law have directed.

SECTION 3.

1 Treason against the United States shall consist only in levying War against them, or, in adhering to their Enemies, giving them Aid and Comfort. No Person shall be convicted of Treason unless on the Testimony of two Witnesses to the same overt Act, or on Confession in open Court.

2 The Congress shall have power to declare the Punishment of Treason, but no Attainder of Treason shall work Corruption of Blood, or Forfeiture except during the Life of the Person attainted.

ARTICLE IV

SECTION 1.

Full Faith and Credit shall be given in each State to the public Acts, Records, and judicial Proceedings of every other State. And the Congress may by general Laws prescribe the Manner in which such Acts, Records and Proceedings shall be proved, and the Effect thereof.

SECTION 2.

1 The Citizens of each State shall be entitled to all Privileges and Immunities of Citizens in the several States.

2 A Person charged in any State with Treason, Felony, or other Crime, who shall flee from Justice, and be found in another State, shall on demand of the executive Authority of the State from which he fled, be delivered up, to be removed to the State having Jurisdiction of the Crime.

3* [No person held to Service or Labour in one State, under the Laws thereof, escaping into another, shall, in Consequence of any Law or Regulation therein, be discharged from such Service or Labour, but shall be delivered up on Claim of the Party to whom such Service or Labour may be due.].

SECTION 3.

1 New States may be admitted by the Congress into this Union; but no new State shall be formed or erected within the Jurisdiction of any other State; nor any State be formed by the Junction of two or more States, or parts of States, without the Consent of the Legislatures of the States concerned as well as of the Congress.

2 The Congress shall have Power to dispose of and make all needful Rules and Regulations respecting the Territory or other Property belonging to the United States; and nothing in this Constitution shall be so construed as to Prejudice any Claims of the United States, or of any particular State.

---

* This clause has been affected by amendment XIII.

SECTION 4.

The United States shall guarantee to every State in this Union a Republican Form of Government, and shall protect each of them against Invasion; and on Application of the Legislature, or of the Executive (when the Legislature cannot be convened) against domestic Violence.

ARTICLE V

The Congress, whenever two-thirds of both Houses shall deem it necessary, shall propose Amendments to this Constiution, or, on the Application of the Legislatures of two-thirds of the several States, shall call a Convention for proposing Amendments, which, in either Case, shall be valid to all Intents and Purposes, as part of this Constitution when ratified by the Legislatures of three-fourths of the several States, or by Conventions in three-fourths thereof, as the one or the other Mode of Ratification may be proposed by the Congress; Provided that no Amendment which may be made prior to the Year One thousand eight hundred and eight shall in any Manner affect the first and fourth Clauses in the Ninth Section of the first Article; and that no State, without its Consent, shall be deprived of its equal Suffrage in the Senate.

ARTICLE VI

1 All Debts contracted and Engagements entered into, before the Adoption of this Constitution shall be as valid against the United States under this Constitution, as under the Confederation.

2 This Constitution, and the Laws of the United States which shall be made in Pursuance thereof; and all Treaties made, or which shall be made, under the Authority of the United States, shall be the supreme Law of the Land; and the Judges in every State shall be bound thereby, any Thing in the Constitution or Laws of any State to the Contrary notwithstanding.

3 The Senators and Representatives before mentioned, and the Members of the several State Legislatures, and all executive and judicial Officers, both of the United States and of the several States, shall be bound by Oath or Affirmation, to support this Constitution; but no religious Test shall ever be required as a Qualification to any Office or public Trust under the United States.

ARTICLE VII

The Ratification of the Conventions of nine States, shall be sufficient for the Establishment of this Constitution between the States so ratifying the Same.

Done in Convention by the Unanimous Consent of the States present the Seventeenth Day of September in the Year of our Lord one thousand seven hundred and Eighty seven and of the Independence of the United States of Americal the Twelfth. IN WITNESS wherof We have herunto subscribed our Names.

G. WASHINGTON — Presidt. and Deputy from Virginia

Attest. — WILLIAM JACKSON, Secretary.

New Hampshire. — John Langdon, Nicholas Gilman.

Massachusetts. — Nathaniel Gorham, Rufus King.

Connecticut. — Wm. Saml. Johnson, Roger Sherman.

New York. — Alexander Hamilton.

New Jersey. — Wil: Livingston, David Brearley, Wm. Paterson, Jona: Dayton.

Pennsylvania. — B. Franklin, Thomas Mifflin, Robt. Morris, Geo. Clymer, Thos. FitzSimons, Jared Ingersoll, James Wilson, Gouv Morris.

Delaware. — Geo: Read, Gunning Bedford Jun, John Dickinson, Richard Bassett, Jaco: Broom.

Maryland. — James McHenry Dan of St. Thos. Jennifer, Danl. Carroll.

Virginia. — John Blair — James Madison, Jr.

North Carolina. — Wm. Blount, Richd. Dobbs Spaight, Hu Williamson.

South Carolina. — J. Rutledge, Charles Cotesworth Pinckney, Charles Pinckney, Pierce Butler.

Georgia. — William Few, Abr. Baldwin.

AMENDMENT I

Congress shall make no law respecting an establishment of religion, or prohibiting the free exercise thereof; or abridging the freedom of speech, or of the press; or the right of the people peaceably to assemble and to petition the Government for a redress of grievances.

AMENDMENT II

A well regulated Militia, being necessary to the security of a free State, the right of the people to keep and bear Arms, shall not be infringed.

AMENDMENT III

No Soldier shall, in time of peace be quartered in any house, without the consent of the Owner, nor in time of war, but in a manner to be prescribed by law.

AMENDMENT IV

The right of the people to be secure in their persons, houses, papers, and effects, against unreasonable searches and seizures, shall not be violated, and no Warrants shall issue, but upon probable cause, supported by Oath or affirmation and particularly describing the Place to be searched, and the persons or things to be seized.

AMENDMENT V

No person shall be held to answer for a capital, or otherwise infamous crime, unless on a presentment or indictment of a Grand Jury, except in cases arising in the land or naval forces, or in the Militia, when in actual service in time of War or public danger; nor shall any person be subject for the same offence to be twice put in jeopardy of life or limb; nor shall be compelled in any criminal case to be a witness against himself, nor be deprived of life, liberty, or property, without due process of law; nor shall private property be taken for public use, without just compensation.

AMENDMENT VI

In all criminal prosecutions, the accused shall enjoy the right to a speedy and public trial, by an impartial jury of the State and district wherein the crime shall have been committed, which district shall have been previously ascertained by law, and to be informed of the nature and cause of the accusation: to be confronted with the witnesses against him; to have compulsory process for obtaining witnesses in his favor, and to have the Assistance of Counsel for his defence.

AMENDMENT VII

In suits at common law, where the value in controversy shall exceed twenty dollars, the right of trial by jury shall be preserved, and no fact tried by jury, shall be otherwise reexamined in any Court of the United States, than according to the rules of the common law.

AMENDMENT VIII

Excessive bail shall not be required, nor excessive fines imposed, nor cruel and unusual punishments inflicted.

AMENDMENT IX

The enumeration in the Constitution, of certain rights, shall not be construed to deny or disparage others retained by the people.

AMENDMENT X

The powers not delegated to the United States by the Constitution, nor prohibited by it to the States, are reserved to the States respectively, or to the people.

(Ratification of the first ten amendments was completed December 15, 1791.)

AMENDMENT XI

The Judicial power of the United States shall not be construed to extend to any suit in law or equity, commenced or prosecuted against one of the United States by Citizens of another State, or by Citizens or Subjects of any Foreign State.

(Declared ratified January 8, 1798.)

AMENDMENT XII

The electors shall meet in their respective states and vote by ballot for President and Vice-President, one of whom, at least, shall not be an inhabitant of the same state with themselves; they shall name in their ballots the person voted for as President, and in distinct ballots the person voted for as Vice-President, and they shall make distinct lists of all persons voted for as President, and of all persons voted for as Vice-President, and of the number of votes for each, which lists they shall sign and certify, and transmit sealed to the seat of the government of the United States, directed to the President of the Senate; The President of the Senate shall, in presence of the Senate and House of Representatives, open all the certificates and the votes shall then be counted; The person having the greatest number of votes for President, shall be the President, if such number be a majority of the whole number of Electors appointed; and if no person have such majority, then from the persons having the highest numbers not exceeding three on the list of those voted for as President, the House of Representatives shall choose immediately, by ballot, the President. But in choosing the President, the votes shall be taken by states, the representation from each state having one vote; a quorum for this purpose shall consist of a member or members from two-thirds of the states, and a majority of all the states shall be necessary to a choice. [And if the House of Representatives shall not choose a President whenever the right of choice shall devolve upon them, before the fourth day of March next following, then the Vice-President shall act as President, as in the case of the death or other constitutional disability of the President.]* The person having the greatest number of votes as Vice-President, shall be the Vice-President, if such number be a majority of the whole number of Electors appointed, and if no person have a majority, then from the two highest numbers on the list, the Senate shall choose the Vice-President; a quorum for the purpose shall consist of two-thirds of the whole number of Senators, and a majority of the whole number shall be necessary to a choice. But no person constitutionally ineligible to the office of President shall be eligible to that of Vice-President of the United States.

(Declared ratified September 25, 1804.)

AMENDMENT XIII

SECTION 1.

Neither slavery nor involuntary servitude, except as a punishment for crime whereof the party shall have been duly convicted, shall exist within the United States, or any place subject to their jurisdiction.

SECTION 2.

Congress shall have power to enforce this article by appropriate legislation.

(Declared ratified December 18, 1865.)

AMENDMENT XIV

SECTION 1.

All persons born or naturalized in the United States, and subject to the jurisdiction thereof, are citizens of the United States and of the State wherein they reside. No State shall make or enforce any law which shall abridge the privileges or

---

* The part included in the brackets has been superseded by section 3 of amendment XX.

immunities of citizens of the United States; nor shall any State deprive any person of life, liberty, or property, without due process of law; nor deny to any person within its jurisdiction the equal protection of the laws.

SECTION 2.

Representatives shall be apportioned among the several States according to their respective numbers, counting the whole number of persons in each State, excluding Indians not taxed. But when the right to vote at any election for the choice of electors for President and Vice-President of the United States, Representatives in Congress, the Executive and Judicial officers of a State, or the members of the Legislature thereof, is denied to any of the male inhabitants of such State, being twenty-one years of age, and citizens of the United States, or in any way abridged, except for participation in rebellion, or other crime, the basis of representation therein shall be reduced in the proportion which the number of such male citizens shall bear to the whole number of male citizens twenty-one years of age in such State.

SECTION 3.

No person shall be a Senator or Representative in Congress, or elector of President and Vice-President, or hold any office, civil or military, under the United States, or under any State, who, having previously taken an oath, as a member of Congress, or as an officer of the United States, or as a member of any State legislature, or as an executive or judicial officer of any State, to support the Constitution of the United States, shall have engaged in insurrection or rebellion against the same, or given aid or comfort to the enemies thereof. But Congress may by a vote of two-thirds of each House, remove such disability.

SECTION 4.

The validity of the public debt of the United States, authorized by law, including debts incurred for payment of pensions and bounties for services in suppressing insurrection or rebellion, shall not be questioned. But neither the United States nor any State shall assume or pay any debt or obligation incurred in aid of insurrection or rebellion against the United States, or any claim for the loss or emancipation of any slave; but all such debts, obligations and claims shall be held illegal and void.

SECTION 5.

The Congress shall have power to enforce, by appropriate legislation, the provisions of this article.

(Declared ratified July 28, 1868.)

AMENDMENT XV

SECTION 1.

The right of citizens of the United States to vote shall not be denied or abridged by the United States or by any State on account of race, color, or previous condition of servitude

SECTION 2.

The Congress shall have power to enforce this article by appropriate legislation.

(Declared ratified March 30, 1870.)

AMENDMENT XVI

The Congress shall have power to lay and collect taxes on incomes, from whatever source derived, without apportionment among the several States, and without regard to any census or enumeration.

(Declared ratified February 25, 1913.)

AMENDMENT XVII

The Senate of the United States shall be composed of two Senators from each State, elected by the people thereof, for six years; and each Senator shall have one vote. The electors in each State shall have the qualifications requisite for electors of the most numerous branch of the State legislatures.

When vacancies happen in the representation of any State in the Senate, the executive authority of such State shall issue writs of election to fill such vacancies: *Provided,* That the legislature of any State may empower the executive thereof to make temporary appointments until the people fill the vacancies by election as the legislature may direct.

This amendment shall not be so construed as to affect the election or term of any Senator chosen before it becomes valid as part of the Constitution.

(Declared ratified May 31, 1913.)

AMENDMENT XVIII

[SECTION 1.]

After one year from the ratification of this article the manufacture, sale, or transportation of intoxicating liquors within, the importation thereof into, or the exportation thereof from the United States and all territory subject to the jurisdiction thereof for beverage purposes is hereby prohibited.

[SECTION 2.]

The Congress and the several States shall have concurrent power to enforce this article by appropriate legislation.

[SECTION 3.]

This article shall be inoperative unless it shall have been ratified as an amendment to the Constitution by the legislatures of the several States, as provided in the Constitution, within seven years from the date of the submission hereof to the

States by the Congress.]*

AMENDMENT XIX

The right of citizens of the United States to vote shall not be denied or abridged by the United States or by any State on account of sex.

Congress shall have power to enforce this article by appropriate legislation.

(Declared ratified August 26, 1920.)

AMENDMENT XX

SECTION 1.

The terms of the President and Vice-President shall end at noon on the 20th day of January, and the terms of Senators and Representatives at noon on the 3d day of January, of the years in which such terms would have ended if this article had not been ratified; and the terms of their successors shall then begin.

SECTION 2.

The Congress shall assemble at least once in every year, and such meeting shall begin at noon on the 3d day of January, unless they shall by law appoint a different day.

SECTION 3.

If, at the time for the beginning of the term of the President, the President elect shall have died, the Vice-President elect shall become President. If a President shall not have been chosen before the time fixed for the beginning of his term, or if the President elect shall have failed to qualify, then the Vice-President elect shall act as President until a President shall have qualified; and the Congress may by law provide for the case wherein neither a President elect nor a Vice-President elect shall have qualified, declaring who shall then act as President, or the manner in which one who is to act shall be selected, and such person shall act accordingly until a President or Vice-President shall have qualified.

SECTION 4.

The Congress may by law provide for the case of the death of any of the persons from whom the House of Representatives may choose a President whenever the right of choice shall have devolved upon them and for the case of the death of any of the persons from whom the Senate may choose a Vice-President whenever the right of choice shall have devolved upon them.

---

* Amendment XVIII was repealed by section 1 of amendment XXI. (Declared ratified January 29, 1919.)

SECTION 5.

Sections 1 and 2 shall take effect on the 15th day of October following the ratification of this article.

SECTION 6.

This article shall be inoperative unless it shall have been ratified as an amendment to the Constitution by the legislatures of three-fourths of the several States within seven years from the date of its submission.

(Declared ratified February 6, 1933.)

AMENDMENT XXI

SECTION 1.

The eighteenth article of amendment to the Constitution of the United States is hereby repealed.

SECTION 2.

The transportation or importation into any State, Territory, or possession of the United States for delivery or use therein of intoxicating liquors, in violation of the laws thereof, is hereby prohibited.

SECTION 3.

This article shall be inoperative unless it shall have been ratified as an amendment to the Constitution by conventions in the several States, as provided in the Constitution, within seven years from the date of the submission hereof to the States by the Congress.

(Declared ratified December 5, 1933.)

AMENDMENT XXII

SECTION 1.

No person shall be elected to the office of the President more than twice, and no person who has held the office of President, or acted as President, for more than two years of a term to which some other person was elected President shall be elected to the office of the President more than once. But this article shall not apply to any person holding the office of President when this Article was proposed by the Congress, and shall not prevent any person who may be holding the office of President, or acting as President, during the term within which this Article becomes operative from holding the office of President or acting as President during the remainder of such term.

SECTION 2.

This article shall be inoperative unless it shall have been ratified as an amendment to the Constitution by the legislatures of three-fourths of the several

States within seven years from the date of its submission to the States by the Congress.

(Declared ratified March 1, 1951.)

AMENDMENT XXIII

SECTION 1.

The District constituting the seat of Government of the United States shall appoint in such manner as the Congress may direct:

A number of electors of President and Vice President equal to the whole number of Senators and Representatives in Congress to which the District would be entitled if it were a State, but in no event more than the least populous State; they shall be in addition to those appointed by the States, but they shall be considered, for the purposes of the election of President and Vice President, to be electors appointed by a State; and they shall meet in the District and perform such duties as provided by the twelfth article of amendment.

SECTION 2.

The Congress shall have power to enforce this article by appropriate legislation.

(Declared ratified April 3, 1961.)

AMENDMENT XXIV

SECTION 1.

The right of citizens of the United States to vote in any primary or other election for President or Vice President, for electors for President or Vice President, or for Senator or Representative in Congress, shall not be denied or abridged by the United States or any State by reason of failure to pay any poll tax or other tax.

SECTION 2.

The Congress shall have power to enforce this article by appropriate legislation.

(Declared ratified February 4, 1962.)

AMENDMENT XXV

SECTION 1.

In case of the removal of the President from office or of his death or resignation, the Vice President shall become President.

SECTION 2.

Whenever there is a vacancy in the office of the Vice President, the President shall nominate a Vice President who shall take office upon confirmation by a majority vote of both Houses of Congress.

SECTION 3.

Whenever the President transmits to the President pro tempore of the Senate and the Speaker of the House of Representatives his written declaration that he is unable to discharge the powers and duties of his office, and until he transmits to them a written declaration to the contrary, such powers and duties shall be discharged by the Vice President as Acting President.

SECTION 4.

Whenever the Vice President and a majority of either the principal officers of the executive departments or of such other body as Congress may by law provide, transmit to the President pro tempore of the Senate and the Speaker of the House of Representatives their written declaration that the President is unable to discharge the powers and duties of his office, the Vice President shall immediately assume the powers and the duties of the office as Acting President.

Thereafter, when the President transmits to the President pro tempore of the Senate and the Speaker of the House of Representatives his written declaration that no inability exists, he shall resume the powers and duties of this office unless the Vice President and a majority of either the principal officers of the executive department or of such other body as Congress may by law provide, transmit within four days to the President pro tempore of the Senate and the Speaker of the House of Representatives their written declaration that the President is unable to discharge the powers and duties of his office. Thereupon Congress shall decide the issue, assembling within forty-eight hours for that purpose if not in session. If the Congress, within twenty-one days after receipt of the latter written declaration, or, if Congress is not in session, within twenty-one days after Congress is required to assemble, determines by two-thirds vote of both Houses that the President is unable to discharge the powers and duties of his office, the Vice President shall continue to discharge the same as Acting President; otherwise, the President shall resume the powers and duties of his office.

(Declared ratified February 10, 1967.)

AMENDMENT XXVI

SECTION 1.

The right of citizens of the United States, who are eighteen years of age or older, to vote shall not be denied or abridged by the United States or by any State on account of age.

SECTION 2.

The Congress shall have power to enforce this article by appropriate legislation.

(Declared ratified July 1, 1971.)

AMENDMENT XXVII

No law varying the compensation for the services of the Senators and Representatives shall take effect, until an election of Representatives shall have intervened.

(Declared ratified May 7, 1992.)

TABLE OF CASES

[References are to pages]

TABLE OF CASES

[References are to pages]

[References are to pages]

[References are to pages]

D

[References are to pages]

[References are to pages]

[References are to pages]

[References are to pages]

M

[References are to pages]

O

P

[References are to pages]

[References are to pages]

[References are to pages]

U

V

W

[References are to pages]

INDEX

[References are to sections.]

[References are to sections.]

[References are to sections.]

[References are to sections.]

[References are to sections.]

[References are to sections.]

[References are to sections.]